SIPRI Yearbook 1990
World Armaments and Disarmament

D1395382

sipri

Stockholm International Peace Research Institute

SIPRI is an independent international institute for research into problems of peace and conflict, especially those of arms control and disarmament. It was established in 1966 to commemorate Sweden's 150 years of unbroken peace.

The Institute is financed mainly by the Swedish Parliament. The staff, the Governing Board and the Scientific Council are international.

The Governing Board and the Scientific Council are not responsible for the views expressed in the publications of the Institute.

Governing Board

Ambassador Dr Inga Thorsson, Chairman (Sweden)
Egon Bahr (Federal Republic of Germany)
Professor Francesco Calogero (Italy)
Dr Max Jakobson (Finland)
Professor Dr Karlheinz Lohs (German Democratic Republic)
Professor Emma Rothschild (United Kingdom)
Sir Brian Urquhart (United Kingdom)
The Director

Director

Dr Walther Stützle (Federal Republic of Germany)

sipri

Stockholm International Peace Research Institute
Pipers väg 28, S-171 73 Solna, Sweden
Cable: PEACERESEARCH STOCKHOLM
Telephone: 46 8/55 97 00

SIPRI Yearbook 1990

World Armaments and Disarmament

sipri

Stockholm International Peace Research Institute

OXFORD UNIVERSITY PRESS
1990

Oxford University Press, Walton Street, Oxford OX2 6DP

Oxford New York Toronto
Delhi Bombay Calcutta Madras Karachi
Petaling Jaya Singapore Hong Kong Tokyo
Nairobi Dar es Salaam Cape Town
Melbourne Auckland
and associated companies in
Berlin Ibadan

Oxford is a trade mark of Oxford University Press

Published in the United States
by Oxford University Press, New York

British Library Cataloguing in Publication Data
SIPRI yearbook of world armaments and
disarmament.—1990–
1. Arms control—Periodicals   2. Disarmament—Periodicals
3. Arms and armour—
I. Stockholm International Peace Research Institute II. World armaments
and disarmament.
ISSN 0953–0282
327.1'74'05   JX1974
ISBN 0–19–827862–4

Library of Congress Cataloging in Publication Data
LC card number
83-443843

Typeset and originated by
Stockholm International Peace Research Institute
Printed and bound in Great Britain by
Biddles Ltd., Guildford and King's Lynn

Contents

Part I. Weapons and technology

Part II. Military expenditure, the arms trade and armed conflicts

Part III. Developments in arms control

Part IV. Special features

Annexes

Acknowledgements

We are proud to have secured the co-operation of two distinguished international researchers and experts outside the SIPRI staff and aside from the regular contributors to the *Yearbook*: Dr Catherine M. Kelleher and Dr Harald Müller. We are also grateful to those who provided us with valuable suggestions as to how to improve the *Yearbook* to the benefit of a globally dispersed readership.

A dedicated staff produced the *Yearbook*, under Connie Wall's experienced editorial leadership.

This year, in the midst of changing world developments which necessitated a last-minute reappraisal of 1989, special thanks are due in particular to the editors—Billie Bielckus, Paul Claesson, Jetta Gilligan Borg, Donald Odom and Gillian Stanbridge—who also set the book in final camera-ready format.

We also extend thanks to the secretaries—Cynthia Loo, Marianne Lyons and Ricardo Vargas-Fuentes—and to Gerd Hagmeyer-Gaverus for programming and other computer assistance.

Dr Walther Stützle
Director of SIPRI

GLOSSARY AND CONVENTIONS

Acronyms

ABM	Anti-ballistic missile
ACE	Allied Command Europe (NATO)
ACM	Advanced cruise missile
ADM	Atomic demolition munition
AFAP	Artillery-fired atomic projectile
AFB	Air Force Base
ALCM	Air-launched cruise missile
ASAT	Anti-satellite
ASEAN	Association of South-East Asian Nations
ASLCM	Advanced sea-launched cruise missile
ASM	Air-to-surface missile
ASUW	Anti-surface warfare
ASW	Anti-submarine warfare
ATBM	Anti-tactical ballistic missile
ATC	Armoured troop carrier
ATTU	Atlantic-to-the-Urals (zone)
AWACS	Airborne warning and control system
BMD	Ballistic missile defence
BW	Biological warfare/weapons
BWC	Biological Weapons Convention
CBM	Confidence-building measure
CBW	Chemical and biological warfare/weapons
CD	Conference on Disarmament
CEP	Circular error probable
CFE	Conventional Armed Forces in Europe (Negotiation)
CMEA	Council for Mutual Economic Assistance (as COMECON)
COCOM	Coordinating Committee
COMECON	Council for Mutual Economic Assistance (as CMEA)
CORRTEX	Continuous reflectometry for radius versus time experiments
CSBM	Confidence- and security-building measure
CSCE	Conference on Security and Co-operation in Europe
CTB(T)	Comprehensive test ban (treaty)
CTOL	Conventional take-off and landing
CW	Chemical warfare/weapons
CWC	Chemical Weapons Convention
CWFZ	Chemical weapon-free zone
DEW	Directed-energy weapon
DST	Defence and Space Talks
EC	European Community
ECU	European Currency Unit
EFA	European Fighter Aircraft
ELINT	Electronic intelligence
ELV	Expendable launch vehicle
EMP	Electromagnetic pulse
Enmod	Environmental modification
ERW	Enhanced radiation (neutron) weapon
EUCLID	European Cooperative Long-term Initiative on Defence
FBS	Forward-based system
FEL	Free electron laser
FOC	Full operational capability
FOFA	Follow-on forces attack
FOST	Force Océanique Stratégique
FOTL	Follow-on to Lance
FROD	Functionally related observable difference
FROG	Free-rocket-over-ground
GBR	Ground-based radar
GLCM	Ground-launched cruise missile
HLTF	High Level Task Force
IAEA	International Atomic Energy Agency
ICBM	Intercontinental ballistic missile
ICJ	International Court of Justice
IEPG	Independent European Programme Group
INF	Intermediate-range nuclear forces

IOC	Initial operational capability	PNE(T)	Peaceful Nuclear Explosions (Treaty)
IRBM	Intermediate-range ballistic missile	PTB(T)	Partial Test Ban (Treaty)
JVE	Joint verification experiment	R&D	Research and development
KEW	Kinetic-energy weapon	RMA	Restricted Military Area
Laser	Light amplification by simulated emission of radiation	RPV	Remotely piloted vehicle
		RV	Re-entry vehicle
LDDI	Less developed defence industry	SACEUR	Supreme Allied Commander, Europe
MAD	Mutual assured destruction	SALT	Strategic Arms Limitation Talks
MARV	Manoeuvrable re-entry vehicle	SAM	Surface-to-air missile
M(B)FR	Mutual (and Balanced) Force Reduction (Talks)	SCC	Standing Consultative Commission
MD	Military District	SDI	Strategic Defense Initiative
MIRACL	Mid-Infrared Advanced Chemical Laser	SDIO	SDI Organization
		SICBM	Small ICBM
MIRV	Multiple independently targetable re-entry vehicle	SLBM	Submarine-launched ballistic missile
MLRS	Multiple launcher rocket system	SLCM	Sea-launched cruise missile
		SLV	Space launch vehicle
MOU	Memorandum of Understanding	SNF	Short-range nuclear forces
		SSD	Special Session on Disarmament (UN)
MRV	Multiple re-entry vehicle		
MSOW	Modular stand-off weapon	SS(M)	Surface-to-surface (missile)
MTCR	Missile Technology Control Regime	SRAM	Short-range attack missile
		SRBM	Short-range ballistic missile
NATO	North Atlantic Treaty Organization	SSBN	Nuclear-powered, ballistic-missile submarine
NNA	Neutral and non-aligned (states)	SSGN	Guided-missile submarine, nuclear-powered
NPG	Nuclear Planning Group	SSN	Nuclear-powered attack submarine
NPT	Non-Proliferation Treaty		
NRRC	Nuclear Risk Reduction Centre	START	Strategic Arms Reduction Talks
NST	Nuclear and Space Talks	SVC	Special Verification Commission
NSWTO	Non-Soviet WTO		
NTI	National trial inspection	SWS	Strategic weapon system
NTM	National technical means (of verification)	TASM	Tactical air-to-surface missile
		TEL	Transporter–erector–launcher
NTS	Nevada test site	TLI	Treaty-limited item
NWFZ	Nuclear weapon-free zone	TNF	Theatre nuclear forces
OECD	Organization for Economic Co-operation and Development	TTB(T)	Threshold Test Ban (Treaty)
		V/STOL	Vertical/short take-off and landing
OMG	Operational Manoeuvre Group	WEU	Western European Union
		WTO	Warsaw Treaty Organization (Warsaw Pact)
O&M	Operation and maintenance		
OSI	On-site inspection		
OSIA	On-Site Inspection Agency		

Glossary

Anti-ballistic missile (ABM) system	Weapon system for intercepting and destroying ballistic missiles and their warheads in flight.
Anti-Ballistic Missile (ABM) Treaty	Treaty signed by the Soviet Union and the United States in 1972 in the SALT I process which prohibits the development, testing and deployment of sea-, air-, space- or mobile land-based ABM systems.
Ballistic missile	A missile which follows a ballistic trajectory (part of which may be outside the earth's atmosphere) when thrust is terminated.
Binary chemical weapon	A shell or other device filled with two chemicals of relatively low toxicity which mix and react while the device is being delivered to the target, the reaction product being a supertoxic chemical warfare agent, such as nerve gas.
Biological weapon (BW)	Living organisms or infective material derived from them, which are intended for use in warfare to cause disease or death in man, animals or plants, and the means of their delivery.
Chemical weapon (CW)	Chemical substances—whether gaseous, liquid or solid— which might be employed as weapons in combat because of their direct toxic effects on man, animals or plants, and the means of their delivery.
Circular error probable (CEP)	A measure of missile accuracy: the radius of a circle, centred on the target, within which 50 per cent of the weapons aimed at the target are expected to fall.
Conference on Disarmament (CD)	Multilateral arms control negotiating body, based in Geneva, which is composed of 40 states, including all the nuclear weapon powers. The CD reports to the UN General Assembly.
Conference on Confidence- and Security-Building Measures and Disarmament in Europe	The Stockholm Conference, part of the 35-nation CSCE process, was held in 1984–86. The Stockholm Document was signed on 19 September 1986. *See also*: Confidence- and Security-Building Measures (CSBM) Negotiations.
Conference on Security and Co-operation in Europe (CSCE)	Conference of 33 states plus the USA and Canada (35 states), which began in 1973 and in 1975 adopted a Final Act (also called the Helsinki Declaration), containing, among others, a Document on confidence-building measures and disarmament. Follow-up meetings were held in Belgrade (1977–78), Madrid (1980–83) and Vienna (1986–89).
Confidence- and Security-Building Measures (CSBM) Negotiations	The CSBM Negotiations, part of the 35-nation CSCE process, build upon the results of the Stockholm Conference and have been held in Vienna since March 1989.
Conventional Armed Forces in Europe (CFE) Negotiation	Negotiation between the 23 states members of NATO and the Warsaw Treaty Organization on conventional force reductions in Europe, held in Vienna since March 1989. Part of the CSCE process.

Conventional weapon

Weapon not having mass destruction effects. *See also:* Weapon of mass destruction.

Cruise missile

Unmanned, self-propelled, guided weapon-delivery vehicle which sustains flight through aerodynamic lift, generally flying at very low altitudes to avoid radar detection, sometimes following the contours of the terrain. It can be air-, ground- or sea-launched and deliver a conventional or nuclear warhead.

Defence and Space Talks

Talks between the USA and the USSR, conducted since 1985 parallel to START under the Geneva Nuclear and Space Talks (NST), on ballistic missile defences and on means of preventing an arms race in space. *See also:* Nuclear and Space Talks.

First-strike capability

Theoretical capability to launch a single attack on an adversary's strategic nuclear forces that nearly eliminates the second-strike capability of the adversary.

Flexible response

The NATO doctrine for reaction to an attack with a full range of military options, including the use of nuclear weapons.

Helsinki Declaration

See: Conference on Security and Co-operation in Europe.

Initial operational capability (IOC)

Date by which a weapon system is first operationally deployed, ready for use in the field.

Intercontinental ballistic missile (ICBM)

Ground-launched ballistic missile with a range in excess of 5500 km.

Intermediate-range nuclear forces (INF)

Theatre nuclear forces with a range of from 1000 up to and including 5500 km. *See also*: Theatre nuclear forces.

Kiloton (kt)

Measure of the explosive yield of a nuclear weapon equivalent to 1000 tons of trinitrotoluene (TNT) high explosive. (The bomb detonated at Hiroshima in World War II had a yield of about 12–15 kilotons.)

Launcher

Equipment which launches a missile. ICBM launchers are land-based launchers which can be either fixed or mobile. SLBM launchers are missile tubes on submarines.

Launch-weight

Weight of a fully loaded ballistic missile at the time of launch.

Megaton (Mt)

Measure of the explosive yield of a nuclear weapon equivalent to 1 million tons of trinitrotoluene (TNT) high explosive.

Multiple independently targetable re-entry vehicle (MIRV)

Re-entry vehicles, carried by a missile, which can be directed to separate targets along separate trajectories (as distinct from MRVs).

Multiple re-entry vehicle (MRV)

Re-entry vehicle, carried by a missile, directed to the same target as the missile's other RVs.

Mutual assured destruction (MAD)

Concept of reciprocal deterrence which rests on the ability of the nuclear weapon powers to inflect intolerable damage on one another after receiving a nuclear attack. *See also:* Second-strike capability.

National technical means of verification (NTM)	The means used to monitor compliance with treaty provisions which are under the national control of individual signatories to an arms control agreement.
Neutral and non-aligned (NNA) states	The group of 12 European states (Austria, Cyprus, Finland, Holy See [Vatican City], Ireland, Liechtenstein, Malta, Monaco, San Marino, Sweden, Switzerland and Yugoslavia) which work together in the CSCE.
Nuclear and Space Talks (NST)	Negotiations between the USA and the USSR on strategic nuclear weapons (START) and space weapons and defence issues (the Defence and Space Talks), held in Geneva since March 1985. The INF negotiations of 1985–87 were also included in NST. *See also:* Nuclear and Space Talks.
Nuclear Risk Reduction Centres (NRRC)	Established by the 1987 US–Soviet NRRC Agreement. The two centres, which opened in Washington and Moscow in 1988, exchange information by direct satellite link in order to minimize misunderstandings which might carry a risk of nuclear war.
Peaceful nuclear explosion (PNE)	Application of a nuclear explosion for non-military purposes such as digging canals or harbours or creating underground cavities.
Re-entry vehicle (RV)	That part of a ballistic missile which carries a nuclear warhead and penetration aids to the target and re-enters the earth's atmosphere and is destroyed in the terminal phase of the missile's trajectory.
Second-strike capability	Ability to receive a nuclear attack and launch a retaliatory blow large enough to inflict intolerable damage on the opponent. *See also:* Mutual assured destruction.
Short-range nuclear forces (SNF)	Nuclear weapons with ranges up to 500 km; not limited by the INF Treaty. *See also*: Theatre nuclear forces.
Special Verification Commission (SVC)	US–Soviet consultative body established in accordance with the INF Treaty, to promote the objectives and implementation of the Treaty.
Standing Consultative Commission (SCC)	US–Soviet consultative body established in accordance with the SALT agreements, to promote the objectives and implementation of the agreements.
Stockholm Conference	*See*: Conference on Confidence- and Security-Building Measures and Disarmament in Europe.
Strategic Arms Limitation Talks (SALT)	Negotiations between the Soviet Union and the United States which opened in 1969 and sought to limit the strategic nuclear forces, both offensive and defensive, of both sides. The SALT I Interim Agreement and the ABM Treaty were signed in 1972. The negotiations were terminated in 1979, when the SALT II Treaty was signed. *See also:* START.
Strategic Arms Reduction Talks (START)	Negotiations between the Soviet Union and the United States, initiated in 1982, which seek to reduce the strategic nuclear forces of both sides. Suspended in December 1983 but resumed under the Nuclear and Space Talks that opened in Geneva in March 1985. *See also*: Nuclear and Space Talks.

Strategic Defense Initiative (SDI)	The programme announced by President Reagan in his 1983 'Star Wars' speech for research and development of systems capable of intercepting and destroying nuclear weapons in flight and rendering the USA safe from the threat of a nuclear strike by another state.
Strategic nuclear weapons	ICBMs, SLBMs and bomber aircraft carrying nuclear weapons of intercontinental range (over 5500 km) which allows them to reach the territories of the other strategic nuclear weapon powers.
Terminal guidance	Guidance provided in the final, near-target phase of the flight of a missile.
Theatre nuclear forces (TNF)	Nuclear weapons with ranges of up to and including 5500 km. In the 1987 INF Treaty, nuclear missiles are divided into intermediate-range (over 1000 km) and shorter-range (500–1000 km). Also called non-strategic nuclear forces. Nuclear weapons with ranges up to 500 km are called short-range nuclear forces. Those with ranges of 150–200 km are often called battlefield nuclear forces. *See also*: Short-range nuclear forces.
Throw-weight	The sum of the weight of a ballistic missile's re-entry vehicle(s), dispensing mechanisms, penetration aids, and targeting and separation devices.
Toxins	Poisonous substances which are products of organisms but are inanimate and incapable of reproducing themselves. Some toxins may also be produced by chemical synthesis.
Warhead	That part of a weapon which contains the explosive or other material intended to inflict damage.
Weapon of mass destruction	Nuclear weapon and any other weapon which may produce comparable effects, such as chemical and biological weapons.
Yield	Released nuclear explosive energy expressed as the equivalent of the energy produced by a given number of tons of trinitrotoluene (TNT) high explosive. *See also:* Kiloton and Megaton.

Conventions

..	Data not available or not applicable
—	Nil or a negligible figure
( )	Uncertain data
m.	million
b.	billion (thousand million)
$	US $, unless otherwise indicated

Introduction: More questions than answers— how to manage the change

WALTHER STÜTZLE

The year 1989 marked the dramatic end of an important and crisis-laden chapter in post-war East–West history. It also marked the start of new developments, the course of which we obviously cannot predict. We do, however, know some of the questions that will have to be addressed.

Since 1989 was more than an ordinary calendar year, it presented difficulties to the authors of a calendar year-oriented *Yearbook*, and the surprising speed with which the revolution erupted in Eastern and Central Europe did not slow down as 1990 began. Following the coming into power in August 1989 of the first non-communist government in Poland, the genuinely free elections to be held in Hungary, the German Democratic Republic and Czechoslovakia are clearly further milestones in that development. The same is true for President Gorbachev's foreign policy and the consequences of domestic developments in the Soviet Union: that is, a revived and armed nationalism and a worsening economy. Neither can the manifold roots of this new chapter in European history be uncovered at a moment so close to the events, nor can the political consequences be fully assessed within the traditional framework of the *SIPRI Yearbook*. What is very clear, however, is that political developments substantially determine the prospects for arms control and not vice versa.

I. Europe

If ever there was a Year of Europe,[1] 1989 clearly was such a year. It was in Europe that the cold war broke out some 40 years ago and has flourished ever since. Thus it was in Europe that the end of this 'war' eventually had to occur. In 1989 this goal was reached. It is for the end of the cold war more than any other important development that 1989 will be remembered.

No doubt the end of the cold war is not a single-cause event. However, it is equally clear that the fundamental change which Mikhail Gorbachev has brought to Soviet policy since assuming responsibility in the Kremlin in March 1985 is the most crucial single factor of and contribution to the change. Without him the two superpowers might have failed to begin to learn the positive lesson of the 1980s, that is, that the political dividend of expensive military instruments is on the decline and that demilitarization of East–West relations holds much greater political promise. It was in this context that problems of so different a nature as the Soviet occupation of Afghanistan or the Reagan dream of seeking security behind an anti-missile

---

[1] Henry Kissinger in 1973 declared the year 1973 as the 'Year of Europe'. Few felt that it was appropriate at the time.

curtain (the Strategic Defense Initiative, or SDI) were addressed. The Soviet Union decided to withdraw its forces from Afghanistan, and the USA retreated from its most ambitious SDI goals. The enormous bills incurred by such policies, both financial and political, helped to change the priorities from a primarily militarily to mainly politically founded security.

In view of the legacy of his predecessors, Gorbachev saw no other way to pull the Soviet Union back from the brink of economic bankruptcy but to fundamentally change priorities. In a landmark speech to the United Nations in December 1988 he admitted the failure of the communist system, proclaimed the entry of the Soviet economy into the world economic system as the Soviet Union's foremost strategic objective, and announced substantial unilateral troop reductions (equal to the size of the Federal German *Bundeswehr*) to reduce the military burden on the economy.[2]

Gorbachev encouraged his allies to reform and went out of his way to assure the West that he meant what he said. He used appearances before Western audiences to withdraw explicitly the old Brezhnev doctrine[3] and to confirm the right of each country to adopt its own political system.[4] In 1989 this encouragement of reform reached a degree that could rightly be called 'a Brezhnev doctrine in reverse'. The result clearly was a collapse of the communist system, underlined by the deletion of respective constitutional provisions that decreed the leading role of the Communist Party in the European Warsaw Treaty Organization countries.

He did not shy away from applying his reform pressure on the Soviet Union's most important strategic ally in Europe, the German Democratic Republic, and from denying the then ruling Socialist Unity Party of Germany (SED) élite the help of Soviet forces in order to suppress the opposition.[5] His visit to Berlin (East) on the 40th anniversary of the GDR (on 7 October 1989) made the special Gorbachev approach tangibly clear: he appeals to the people through publicly reminding the leadership of what its new duty is. The brotherly kiss for SED chief Erich Honecker did not prevent Gorbachev from publicly coining the phrase: 'Those who delay are punished by life itself'.[6] After the Gorbachev visit, events in the GDR proceeded speedily. For Honecker, serious trouble began only 11 days later, on 18 October 1989. On 9 November 1989 the Berlin Wall was opened up.

[2] See 'Speech by Mikhail Gorbachev at the 43rd Session of the UN General Assembly, December 7, 1988', in *Soviet Diplomacy Today* (Soviet Ministry of Foreign Affairs), 1989. On the state of the Soviet economy, see Anders Åslund, *Gorbachev's Struggle For Economic Reform: The Soviet Reform Process, 1985–1988* (Pinter Publishers: London, 1989).

[3] 'The philosophy of the "common European home" concept rules out the probability of an armed clash and the threat of force, the military force above all—alliance against alliance, inside the alliances, wherever'; Mikhail Gorbachev's Address to the Parliamentary Assembly of the Council of Europe on 6 July 1989, in *Daily Review*, vol. 35, no. 16 (7 July 1989).

[4] Joint Soviet–FRG Declaration (Gemeinsame Erklärung von Bundeskanzler Kohl und Generalsekretär der KPdSU Gorbatschow) of 13 June 1989, in *Bulletin der Bundesregierung*, no. 61 (15 June 1989), p. 542.

[5] Willy Brandt went so far as to say that 9 Oct. 1989 might well be remembered as a special day of German–Soviet friendship, because it was the Soviet Army officers who prevented demonstrations in Leipzig developing into bloodshed; see 'Interview mit Willy Brandt: Warten bis irgendwann nach dem Jahr 2000?', in *Süddeutsche Zeitung*, 14 Dec. 1989, p. 14.

[6] As quoted in *The Independent*, 18 Oct. 1989; or 'Gefahren warten nur auf jene, die nicht auf das Leben reagieren', quoted in *Frankfurter Allgemeine Zeitung*, 7 Oct. 1989, p. 2.

Since 23 January, pieces of this ugly concrete construction have been on sale by a GDR import–export company, although only to owners of hard currency.

By the end of 1989 all the Soviet allies in Eastern and Central Europe, with the unfortunate exception of Romania,[7] had gone through a markedly peaceful revolution with striking results: a non-communist government in Poland (19 August), the election of former opposition thinker and writer Vaclav Havel to the Czechoslovak presidency (29 December), a free vote in Hungary on the future election procedure for the Hungarian President and a formal declaration from the five WTO countries which had intervened in Czechoslovakia in 1968, saying that their action had been 'unlawful'.[8] When 1989 began, Europe was still a divided continent; as the year drew to an end, Albania was left as the only communist stronghold in Eastern Europe—not yet visibly affected by reform, and sealed off from the rest of Europe.

In doing what he did, the Soviet leader answered a number of important questions as well as produced new ones. He made it clear that the Soviet Union was ready to seek more than a sheer reduction of the military burden in Europe: the search for a new political structure within the Conference on Security and Co-operation in Europe (CSCE) framework was accepted as a principal political goal, with all its ensuing consequences.

Next to the breakdown of communist regimes throughout Eastern and Central Europe, the re-emergence of the German question was the single most important consequence of Gorbachev's policy. As early as June 1987, when talking to Federal German President Richard von Weizsäcker, the Soviet leader observed that history will answer the German question.[9] What seemed to be stating the obvious was, in reality, a break with the respective policies of his predecessors, who relentlessly maintained that history had already and definitely dealt with the German question. In 1989 it became clear how right Gorbachev was, although his own attitude most likely was instrumental in unleashing the rapidly accelerating new developments. However, to accept, even to encourage, the dynamic forces of history does not necessarily mean to let them develop without control. Thus, President Gorbachev, although accepting the right of the German people to unity,[10] made it quite clear that, for some time, Soviet interest would require the continued existence of two German states. And Foreign Minister Eduard Shevardnadze, speaking in Brussels, publicly addressed seven questions to the FRG. Among them was: 'If the German states were to express in some

---

[7] Because Ceausescu's Securitate police used force against the population, bloodshed was not avoided; eventually Ceausescu and his wife Elena, who fled the capital, were arrested by the regular army and executed on 25 Dec. 1989.

[8] See 'Statement by the leaders of Bulgaria, the GDR, Hungary, Poland and Soviet Union', *Pravda*, 5 Dec. 1989.

[9] Gorbachev, M., 'What will be in one hundred years will be decided by history'; 'Erklärung der TASS nach dem Gespräch von Weizsäcker–Gorbatschow am 7.7.1987', in *Pravda*, 8 July 1987.

[10] On 5 Dec. 1989, the day FRG Foreign Minister Genscher was visiting Moscow, TASS reported that the Soviet leadership was ready to discuss unification as long as the FRG was ready to take the interests of all countries concerned into account; GDR Prime Minister Modrow, after his visit to Moscow on 30 Jan. 1990, enunciated a plan on how to reach unification of the two German states; see *Neues Deutschland*, 31 Jan. 1990, p. 1.

form their desire to take action toward uniting the Germans, would they be ready to take into consideration the interests of other European states and to seek on a collective basis mutually acceptable answers to all questions and problems that might arise in that regard, including the conclusion of a European peace settlement?'.[11]

However, neither Gorbachev nor Shevardnadze spelled out what would be acceptable to the Soviet Union. Gorbachev did, however, clearly signal that he preferred to preserve proven elements of stability; this he did by explicitly asking the United States to stay in Europe,[12] and by reversing the previous Soviet view on alliances. Still, he did not offer a view on how the ultimate political structure in Europe should look. In that regard the Soviet Union showed the same reactions as did the FRG's allies: concern, but no concept.

On the level of political rhetoric, allies of the FRG had always proclaimed as a desirable development what they now find difficult to come to terms with. France, the UK and the USA had in 1952 even committed themselves to bring about 'German reunification'.[13] In 1989, however, a continued undertone of suspicion determined the allies' attitude more than anything else. French President François Mitterrand convened a hastily arranged European Community (EC) summit meeting in Paris (on 18 November), and in December heads of state and government of the EC (on 8–9 December) and NATO Foreign Ministers (on 15 December) coined a formula that reflected more concern about the prospect of a united Germany than respect for the right of self-determination.[14]

It is evident that the Soviet Union has not accepted a united Germany that is also a member of NATO, as US Secretary of State James A. Baker has suggested.[15] Nor can the Western countries be expected to let the FRG seek a united Germany that would have security relations with the Soviet Union but none with the West. It was no surprise, therefore, that the EC and NATO countries, at the end of 1989, resorted to a very broad formula—that the

---

[11] See Eduard Shevardnadze, Address to the Political Commission of the European Parliament, Brussels, 19 Dec. 1989, in *Pravda*, 20 Dec. 1990, documented in *Daily Review*, vol. 30, no. 24 (1990).

[12] Mikhail Gorbachev's Address to the Parliamentary Assembly of the Council of Europe on 6 July 1989 (see note 3, p. 4); also in the joint communiqué with FRG Chancellor Kohl (see note 4).

[13] 'Pending the peace settlement, the Signatory States will cooperate to achieve, by peaceful means, their common aim of a reunified Germany enjoying a liberal-democratic constitution, like that of the Federal Republic, and integrated within the European community'; Art. 7, sec. 2 of 'Convention on Relations Between the Three Powers and the Federal Republic of Germany, May 26, 1952, As Amended by Schedule I of the Protocol on Termination of the Occupation Regime in Germany, Signed at Paris, October 23, 1954', *Documents on Germany 1944–1985* (US Department of State: Washington, DC, 1985), p. 428.

[14] See EC Strasbourg Declaration, Heads of State and Government, 8/9 Dec. 1989, sec. 'European Political Cooperation': 'We seek the strengthening of the state of peace in Europe in which the German people will regain its unity through free self-determination'; see *Bulletin Quotidien Europe*, no. 5150 (10 Dec. 1989), special edn, p. 9. NATO Foreign Ministers used the same formula; see Communiqué of 15 Dec. 1989 meeting in Brussels, in *Nato Review*, Dec. 1989.

[15] See 'Baker sets out U.S. view on one Germany', *International Herald Tribune*, 1 Dec. 1989, p. 8. Early in 1990 President Bush confirmed the Baker position.

process leading to unity 'has to be placed in the perspective of the European integration'.[16]

But what kind of 'European integration' is envisaged: a European Community (EC), with a united Germany as a member? An EC with the GDR as the second German state becoming party to the treaty or with the GDR as an associated member of the EC? What solution would be acceptable to the Soviet Union? Might not either solution have a deterring effect on France and Britain, in view of the economic potential of the two German states?[17] Even today, the combined gross national products (GNPs) of the GDR and the FRG come close to the combined GNPs of the UK and France; hence, the economic balance within the EC would further tilt to the disadvantage of these two nuclear weapon powers if the GDR and the FRG established closer economic and political ties, let alone established unification. And what about the consequences of a policy under which the EC would accept all the reformed East and Central European countries as members? What interest could the Soviet Union have to make this an attractive model for the USSR as well? How can the two German states reassure their neighbours, most notably with respect to Poland's western border and to the military status of a future Germany?

Paris and London should now regret not having used the opportunity to achieve the proclaimed goal of fully integrating the European Community before the East–West relationship was dramatically changed. By comparison, full integration would have been an easy task before 9 November 1989. Now, with the German question back in the number one place on the European agenda and German unity again a realistic goal, West European integration is a far more difficult objective, involving a complex constellation of forces and interests with a much longer list of unanswered questions. However, whatever political model might eventually emerge, the relationship between politico-economic integration on the one hand and the wider security interests of all 35 CSCE countries on the other hand has to be fully appreciated. Is a 'West European political union' in that context still a plausible goal? And if so, would it not be attractive for Paris and London, exactly for the reasons that could make it unappealing to Bonn and Berlin (East)? Could it be that Europe is now heading for a situation in which the EC rules on economic and cultural co-operation will gradually be accepted throughout Europe, while foreign, security and defence policy will remain a national responsibility in a newly created framework of a co-operative security system? In such a new system, what would then be the role of the two superpowers?

---

[16] See note 14.

[17] Among the numerous examples of concern about this prospect, see Arthur Schlesinger, Jr, 'Germany's fate will determine Europe's', *Wall Street Journal*, 21 Dec. 1989; 'A unified Germany would be the dominating economic power in Europe, and political influence would not lag far behind. . . . Overwhelming military power would be bound to reinforce both the will and the ability to dominate Europe by diplomatic, political and economic means. Who can be absolutely sure? By the turn of the century, a unified Germany, the most powerful and dynamic state in Europe, may be demanding Lebensraum—a revision of its eastern borders, a new Anschluss with Austria, a new outreach to German speaking minorities in neighboring countries.'

Only a year ago, it would have been interesting, although not immediately relevant, to research these and related questions. With the German question again the most burning one, it is not only timely but also urgent to think the options through.

For more than 40 years US troops have been kept in Europe for three main reasons: fear of the Soviet threat, the need to make German rearmament palatable to France, and the hope that Western Europe would eventually emerge as a unified, self-supporting political entity. A major change occurred in 1989. In May, President George Bush put the gradual reduction of US troops in Europe on to Washington's official political agenda. The move resulted from the need to strike a compromise; it did not emerge as an element of a grand US strategy. The compromise was needed (a) to satisfy increasing congressional pressure for cuts in the defence budget, (b) to overcome Bonn's reluctance simply to subscribe to US modernization plans for short-range nuclear forces (SNF), and (c) to regain the arms control initiative from Gorbachev. Without consulting his allies, Bush surprised the Brussels NATO summit meeting in May by announcing that, within the CFE (Negotiation on Conventional Armed Forces in Europe) framework, the United States would not only reduce its troops in Europe to 275 000 'ground and air forces stationed outside of national territory' but also include its Air Force in CFE reductions.[18] From the circumstances under which Bush made his move it is clear that his strategic objective was but to buy time and to prevent, in what was only his fifth month in office, a major Alliance crisis that otherwise seemed unavoidable.[19]

Bush's move was announced 'long' before 9 November 1989; but the revolution in Eastern Europe turned it into a move of far-reaching strategic importance. It turned an issue that the Atlantic Alliance had for years considered to be taboo into not only a measure which was hailed by all heads of state and government but also one with the effect of lending further urgency to the arms control process in Europe. Nowhere did the effect become clearer than in the CFE Negotiation.

In 1989 the willingness of political leaders to reduce conventional troops in Europe outpaced the capability of the CFE negotiators to produce commensurate results.[20] This was reflected by the fact that, although shortly before Christmas 1989 (less than nine months after the CFE Negotiation had commenced) the two alliances managed to table a draft treaty, it contained more blanks than mutually acceptable language. This development of 1989 confirms that it is the overall political climate more than any specific arms control plan that determines the arms control perspective, but this CFE development in 1989 also raises the question of how far the CFE process can go without first having conceptually addressed some of the key

---

[18] See 'Bush calls for new cuts in conventional arms', *USIS, NATO Summit, special file,* EURO 502, 29 May 1989.

[19] See Catherine M. Kelleher, 'The debate over the modernization of NATO's short-range nuclear missiles', chapter 18.

[20] For the development of the CFE and CSBM Negotiations in 1989, see Jane M. O. Sharp, 'Conventional arms control in Europe', chapter 13.

questions: What is the ultimate objective of CFE? Is it armed parity on a considerably lower and cheaper level? Or is it to make war impossible through changes in the political and military structure in Europe? If the latter, as now seems more likely than it did three years ago when the negotiations for the currently valid CFE mandate opened, what will the future role of the two military alliances be, if any? Given the disappearance of the threat perception and the vigorous effort to cut the instruments of threat, what then actually is the long-term function of alliances, which rested so much on the perception of threat? Will the alliances eventually be replaced by a co-operative security system, as already publicly referred to by FRG Foreign Minister Hans-Dietrich Genscher?[21]

How should a negotiating agenda be formulated that not only addresses all forces, including nuclear and naval forces, but also allows for a step-by-step process in order not to obstruct the process? What role do the two superpowers envisage for themselves in the newly emerging European structure? How will the USA organize a link to Europe that would allow for reinforcements in time of crisis and conflict but would permit a very low-profile presence in peacetime? How can the Soviet Union adjust to the mounting demand of the East Europeans for the withdrawal of Soviet forces without reviving traumatic security concerns *vis-à-vis* Germany? And how can conversion of the armaments industry, redirection of resources, transparency of military budgets and control of arms exports be made an integral part of both a new economic policy and a confidence-building security regime in Europe?[22]

As the CSCE states move closer to the exploration of these and other questions—once a first CFE agreement is concluded—it should become obvious that confidence- and security-building measures (CSBMs) will have to play a far more critical role than that provided in the 1986 Stockholm Document and than is generally appreciated, in order to ease the transition process. In fact, if agreement on a considerably higher degree of transparency in military capabilities and activities in Europe through refined confidence-building measures and constraints is reached first, it may then be easier to agree, in the second round of the CFE talks, on more substantial reductions of troops and armament. Rather than trying to make the armed forces slowly disappear, the history- and psychology-loaded, sensitive political system in Europe may find it easier to eliminate war forever through measures that make it visibly impossible for the political leadership to use armed forces for offensive political goals. After all, arms control is a continuing process, sensitive to concomitant positive political circumstances as much as to negative ones. Arms control is not a finished product.

---

[21] See 'Rede des Bundesministers des Auswärtigen Hans-Dietrich Genscher aus Anlaß des "Dreikönigstreffens" der FDP', 6 Jan. 1990, Stuttgart, p. 22 of distributed manuscript. Genscher describes this as the second stage of a process that will first see the development of co-operative structures between the two alliances.

[22] See Saadet Deger, 'World military expenditure,' chapter 5; and Ian Anthony, Agnès Courades Allebeck, Espen Gullikstad, Gerd Hagmeyer-Gaverus and Herbert Wulf, 'Arms production', chapter 8, for important observations relevant for future research work in the field.

One of the most positive results of 1989 is the profound improvement in the political climate, which renders new concepts realistic, relevant and timely. However, this will not make it easier to develop them, although it will be much more attractive to do so. Not only were political leaders ahead of experts in the field of conventional arms control in 1989, but people in most of the East European countries were also ahead of their respective governments; and NATO became much more responsive to changes in the East. Although it is too early to speculate about possible answers to all these questions, it is time to recognize that, for some time to come, change will remain the most constant feature of what used to be called East–West relations. As new opportunities and new risks arise, the crucial task will be this: to manage the change, not to seek continuity, in order to assure security.

II. Force reductions, weapon proliferation and debt: global security issues

Although 1989 certainly was the Year of Europe, other extremely important developments also occurred and/or gained further weight.

Washington and Moscow have met their commitments under the INF Treaty of 8 December 1987 ahead of schedule. Thus, at the end of 1989 all the land-based 'shorter-range' (500- to 1000-kilometre range) missile systems were removed and destroyed. But here the nuclear arms reduction success story ends.[23] Beyond this, 1989 rounded off a lost decade in terms of strategic nuclear arms and chemical weapon reductions.

As has been the case since 1972, there was no new agreement on the reduction of strategic nuclear weapons in 1989. In the Strategic Arms Reduction Talks (START), the Soviet Union proved flexible and ready to compromise in many ways: on the link between SDI and START, and on limiting sea-launched cruise missiles, that is, outside START. The Soviet Union also publicly admitted that the building of the Krasnoyarsk radar station was a violation of the 1972 Anti-Ballistic Missile (ABM) Treaty.[24] The USA, however, regarded none of the Soviet moves as sufficiently satisfactory to pave the way to a START agreement.[25] With Gorbachev approaching his sixth year in office, and in view of the many fundamental changes he has brought to some of the inconsiderate security policies of his predecessors, the question now is this: How long can the Soviet Union offer one concession after the other without getting the proper answer from Washington? Ever since the Kremlin accepted the Western definition of 'verification', one has wondered whether the West in general and the USA

[23] See Stephen Iwan Griffiths, 'The implementation of the INF Treaty', chapter 12.

[24] See *International Herald Tribune*, 24 Oct. 1989, p. 1. The way in which Shevardnadze phrased his statement, it was not without risk for the future relationship between the political leadership and the military. Implicitly the public avowal was a severe criticism of the military leadership for not telling the truth about Krasnoyarsk, which thus damaged the Soviet Union's international reputation. Reactions from the military are not known.

[25] See Regina Cowen Karp, 'US–Soviet nuclear arms control', chapter 11.

in particular confuse verification with unlimited access to Soviet data, but not vice versa.[26]

US hesitation in START raises the question of whether and when President Bush intends to resolve a fundamental conflict in his approach to US–Soviet relations: on the one hand, his publicly proclaimed support for Gorbachev's effort to pull the Soviet Union around, and on the other hand, his lack of political will in an area that for psychological more than other reasons is of central importance to Gorbachev's success—that is, strategic nuclear arms reductions, where considerable cuts could be executed without impairing national security.[27] Given the protracted debate on some of the START issues, such as the deterrence value of mobile intercontinental ballistic missiles (ICBMs), one wonders how long it will take to resolve the far more important issues which the concept of minimal nuclear deterrence entails, let alone a security regime that would aim at totally eliminating nuclear weapons.

The recurrent issue of a world-wide ban on the development, acquisition and production of chemical weapons also came no closer to solution in 1989. Although this is a far more complex problem than START, since it involves literally all states, Washington and Moscow still have room to push the issue decisively if they so wish.

Monitoring compliance with a total ban has been one of the most troublesome questions. Unlike his predecessors, Gorbachev accepted the Bush formula of 1984, that is, the right to demand an 'anytime, anywhere' challenge inspection. During the US elections Bush stated: 'And if I'm elected President, if I'm remembered for anything, it would be this: a complete and total ban on chemical weapons'.[28] In view of new obstacles to a global chemical weapon (CW) convention, created by Arab countries that claim to need the CW option to guard against an Israeli nuclear capability, much is to be said for a US–Soviet agreement that would, as a major first step, verifiably eliminate the CW capability of the two biggest CW powers. Although Moscow and Washington seemed to move closer to this bilateral solution, President Bush finally shied away from cashing in on the respective Soviet readiness enunciated at the United Nations in September 1989 and reportedly repeated at the Malta summit meeting in December.[29] Not only would such a bilateral step increase the political pressure on those who are still reluctant to accede to the concept of a global CW convention, but it would also effectively kill the untenable argument that a CW capability is needed to deter the use of chemical weapons. In the relationship

---

[26] A study might well be in order that would systematically compare US and NATO language on the verification issue of the pre-Gorbachev time with actual negotiating behaviour towards Gorbachev.

[27] Even if the two states agreed to cut 50 per cent of the currently held nuclear strategic warheads, more would remain at either side's disposal than was the case in 1972. On the hotly debated issue of SLCMs, see the excellent pro and con contributions in *International Security,* winter 1988/89. Better than from any other publication, it becomes very evident that a political decision is called for, since either decision can rightly claim support from experts.

[28] Quoted in Dunn, L. A., 'Chemical weapons arms control', *Survival,* May/June 1989, pp. 209–24.

[29] See S. J. Lundin, 'Multilateral and bilateral talks on chemical and biological weapons', chapter 14.

between nuclear powers or states that come under the nuclear umbrella of others, deterrence is certainly based on the nuclear element and not on chemical weapons. As for deterring a CW threat from Third World countries, in case of doubt advanced conventional weapons combined with protective anti-CW measures should surely be sufficient.

The time has come to appreciate that different weapon categories warrant different arms control approaches: while conventional arms reductions in Europe could not function without the participation of all the NATO and WTO member countries, the concept of banning chemical weapons completely could greatly profit if the USA and the USSR would start to rid themselves of the chemical weaponry which in any case is not needed to protect national or international security.

In 1989 it was also shown that the proliferation of advanced-technology weapons is still a mounting rather than a receding issue. One example is the spread of ballistic missile technology: by late 1989, 26 Third World countries were known to have ballistic missile and related projects. The major industrial countries have not yet been able to agree on an efficient control regime; Moscow and Beijing have not even joined the modest existing control arrangements, known as the Missile Technology Control Regime (MTCR).[30] The question to be asked is: When will the major technology powers jointly recognize that either they must act together or they will lose together? This is not to say that politically explosive regional conflicts, such as that in the Middle East, can be defused through a technology control regime. It is obvious that they cannot. However, it is equally obvious that political solutions are not helped by continuous transfers of military technology to the region. The opposite is true, as the Iraq–Iran War has clearly shown. Thus a new and major initiative is required to turn the loose MTCR arrangements into a more efficient control regime.

The fourth Non-Proliferation Treaty (NPT) Review Conference will be held in 1990. The agenda of this meeting is long and challenging. From what we know today, it must not be taken for granted that the most important anti-proliferation treaty will easily survive the Extension Conference in 1995. Not only is new technology emerging that facilitates the production of weapon-grade nuclear material,[31] but there are also serious shortcomings in the existing system of safeguards. However, new questions are also emerging, such as how to best deal in a verifiable procedure with the nuclear material that will be set free through the hoped-for massive cuts in nuclear warheads under a START agreement. The Swedish proposal to extend the NPT safeguards system for nuclear weapon states to all their nuclear facilities might be one way of effectively controlling the nuclear fuel cycle.[32]

The 1980s were also concluded as a lost decade with regard to debt, financial flows and international security. While the industrialized nations of

---

[30] See Aaron Karp, 'Ballistic missile proliferation', chapter 9.
[31] See Richard Kokoski, 'Laser isotope separation: technological developments and political implications', chapter 17.

the North seem to have discovered the attractions of *détente* dividends, the same positive change does not apply to their handling of the economic situation of the world's poor. At the end of 1989 the result was this: the debt burden of the Third World has increased dramatically. The cost of interest payments in the 1980s has been over five times that in the 1970s. In 1988, all the developing countries combined paid back $50 billion more than they actually got in new money. One can hardly think of a more striking proof of the underdeveloped understanding on the part of the industrialized countries for the long-term security effects of the mounting debt crisis.[33]

III. Conclusion

The decade of the 1990s may tell us whether the North is heading for both a new political and security structure in Europe and a considerably improved understanding of its responsibility to attend to the non-military dimensions of security, as they trouble the Third World. For obvious reasons, Europe's future and the need of the Soviet Union and the East and Central European countries to be helped in the reconstruction of their economies will tend to receive more immediate attention on the part of the Europeans than will the Third World. However, political stability in the 1990s will greatly depend on whether the North manages both to reconstruct economies in Europe and rescue Third World economies from bankruptcy. It is no small agenda that is ahead of us.

---

[32] See Harald Müller, 'Prospects for the fourth review of the Non-Proliferation Treaty', chapter 16.

[33] See Somnath Sen, 'Debt, financial flows and international security', chapter 6.

Part I. Weapons and technology

1. Nuclear weapons

Prepared by the *Nuclear Weapons Databook* staff, Washington, DC*

I. Introduction

It is difficult to characterize 1989. It was a year during which the entire foundation of the cold war seemed to crumble and the most fundamental assumptions about East–West relations and military strategy required a complete reappraisal. Even a narrow assessment of the nuclear weapon developments of 1989 must take into account the extraordinary political changes in Eastern Europe, the overwhelming economic and political pressures to reduce military expenditure and forces, and the unprecedented level of co-operation between the USA and the USSR. It appears that these developments may permit a fundamental change in the nuclear postures and practices of the nuclear weapon states. Against this backdrop, future historians may see 1989 as the year in which the post-World War II era ended and a new era began.

Even without this new situation the defence budgets of the five nuclear weapon nations in general and the budgets for nuclear weapons in particular are becoming severely constrained. For the fifth year in a row the US military budget declined, as measured in constant dollars. The Soviet Government stated, and the US Government apparently agrees, that Soviet military spending was less in 1989 than it was in 1988. France is now feel-ing the effect of its economic constraints, especially visible in the nuclear weapon programme. Nevertheless, nuclear weapon modernization continued in all five of the acknowledged nuclear weapon states: the USA, the USSR, the UK, France and China.

In the USA there was a decrease in the strategic arsenal because of bomb and submarine retirements. Further decreases are likely in coming years, irrespective of the prospective US–Soviet Strategic Arms Reduction Talks (START) agreement. US strategic nuclear capabilities, however, are not declining. The first B-2 'stealth' bomber was unveiled for its test-flights, and decisions were taken concerning the MX missile. Despite much NATO debate on nuclear weapon modernization, by the end of 1989 it appeared that the chances of introducing new types of US nuclear weapon into the Federal Republic of Germany were almost nil. Mounting domestic pressures to cut the military budget and the prospect of a conventional arms reduction agreement in Europe promise to reduce US military forces considerably in the 1990s. The nuclear weapons complex run by the Department of Energy

*Robert S. Norris, Thomas B. Cochran, Richard W. Fieldhouse, and Andrew S. Burrows, Natural Resources Defense Council, Inc., Washington, DC; William M. Arkin, Greenpeace USA, Washington, DC.

(DOE) faced new problems throughout 1989 and may have been unable to produce any nuclear weapons at the end of the year.

The events of 1989 make it clear that *perestroika* is making a difference to Soviet military and nuclear forces. Although the USSR is producing several models of new strategic missiles, as well as new bombers, the overall rate of production has declined. The nuclear stockpile appears to have reached a peak and is now headed gradually downward. Non-strategic nuclear forces are being reduced, unilaterally as well as in accordance with the INF Treaty (the 1987 US–Soviet Treaty on the Elimination of Intermediate-Range and Shorter-Range Missiles), apparently as part of a de-emphasis on nuclear capabilities. In the midst of declining defence spending and production, the Soviet military was busy during 1989 removing forces from Europe and elsewhere, including nuclear weapons, and restructuring or re-integrating remaining forces.

During 1989 the UK continued towards modernization of its submarine force, amid doubts about the Trident II missile to be purchased from the USA and about the ability of the British nuclear weapons complex to make warheads in time for the missiles. Although the UK has not yet decided whether to build a nuclear air-to-surface missile, it appears that warheads cannot be produced simultaneously for such a missile and the Trident II.

Economic constraints in France are forcing reduced military spending and thus the delay of several nuclear weapon programmes. The strategic submarine modernization programme is on schedule, but the next-generation intermediate-range ballistic missile (IRBM) is now expected four years later than planned. President François Mitterrand indicated that 300–400 strategic nuclear warheads were considered sufficient for France, although the French arsenal is planned to grow well above this level by 1993.

The dominant events in China in 1989 were the first Sino-Soviet summit meeting in 30 years and the harsh military and political reaction to popular demonstrations for political reform. China reportedly agreed in May to sell short-range ballistic missiles (SRBMs) to Syria, suggesting that these missiles may have been added to China's nuclear arsenal. Although little information was available on Chinese nuclear developments during 1989, China is continuing with its gradual modernization of its nuclear forces.

The tables showing the nuclear forces of all five nations as of January 1990 (tables 1.1–1.7) appear on pages 14–22 of this chapter. Table 1.8 (page 23) provides historical figures for the strategic forces of the five nations.

II. US nuclear weapon programmes

Because of fiscal constraints, changing operational requirements, tritium shortages and an impending START agreement, it is evident that the size of US strategic forces will not grow beyond the peak years of 1987 and 1988. It it also clear that the stockpile of non-strategic nuclear weapons will decrease as well. Budgetary pressures at the end of 1989 indicated that large cuts will be made in future military budgets, a prospect which will have some effect on both nuclear and conventional forces.

The year 1989 witnessed the first significant decline in numbers of strategic weapons, from about 13 000 to about 12 100. This was mainly due to the retirement of old gravity bombs from the Strategic Air Command (SAC) arsenal and the withdrawal of one strategic submarine. The bombs removed were for the 69 B-52Gs allocated in late 1988 for exclusively conventional missions. Numerous B28 bombs in the SAC stockpile were also removed, ahead of schedule, to help ease a potential tritium shortage. As the B-52Gs fully complete the transition to a stand-off role, fewer gravity bombs are needed for targets inside the Soviet Union. Irrespective of the pending START treaty, decreases are likely to continue in the number (although not the capability) of US strategic weapons for the next few years.

ICBMs

During 1989 the US operational intercontinental ballistic missile (ICBM) force remained at 1000 missiles with 2450 warheads, unchanged from 1988. Attention was focused on how to proceed with the rail-based MX missiles (officially designated MGM-118A)[1] and the Small ICBM. Decisions had been postponed because of the 1988 presidential election, the delay in confirming a new Secretary of Defense and the lengthy policy review by the Bush Administration. Finally, in late April President Bush decided to pursue both missile programmes, with initial deployment of the MX rail garrison in June 1992 followed by the Small ICBM in FY 1997. An important change, however, from the Reagan Administration was to stop MX deployment at 50 missiles and drop the request for an additional 50. The current plan is to re-base the silo-based MXs on railcars. On 29 November the Air Force announced its selection of six Air Force Bases (AFBs) as sites for MX rail garrison: Barksdale AFB, Bossier City, Louisiana; Dyess AFB, Abilene, Texas; Fairchild AFB, near Spokane, Washington; Grand Forks AFB, Grand Forks, North Dakota; Little Rock AFB, Little Rock, Arkansas; and Wurtsmith AFB, Oscoda, Michigan.

An accident that occurred at MX silo Q-10, at F. E. Warren AFB, Wyoming, on 12 June 1988 was disclosed early in the year.[2] Because of a weak epoxy bond, the 90-ton missile fell 6–8 inches (15–20 cm) from its support in its canister, pulling electrical cords from their housing. As a safety precaution the 10 warheads were removed on 19 June, as were those from five other missiles.

In the first test-flight in two years, an MX missile with seven re-entry vehicles was launched from Vandenberg AFB on 19 March by a SAC air-

---

[1] General Accounting Office, *ICBM Modernization: Status of the Peacekeeper Rail Garrison Missile System*, GAO/NSIAD-89-64, Jan. 1989.

[2] Smith, R. J., 'MX warheads are removed after mishap', *Washington Post*, 25 Jan. 1989, p. A1; 'Probe blames MX failure on fault in stage 1 joint', *Aviation Week & Space Technology*, 20 Feb. 1989, p. 22; Whipple, D., 'MX missile silo collapse examined in air force investigation report', *Caspar Star-Tribune*, 21 May 1989, p. A1.

crew aboard a modified EC-135 aircraft. The aircraft and crew from Ellsworth AFB, South Dakota, used the Airborne Launch Control System to launch the MX for the first time. During a second flight on 14 September, the first in the operational programme, the missile was destroyed three minutes after launch from Vandenberg AFB, California.

The MX operational test and evaluation programme was to have been conducted in two phases over a 15-year period. Phase I was supposed to begin shortly after initial operational capability (IOC) date of December 1986 and was to have consisted of 24 missile tests over three years (eight per year). The new plan is to conduct only three Phase I tests per year until the MX is fully deployed in rail garrison basing in fiscal year (FY) 1994 (assuming congressional approval). Phase I testing would not be completed until about mid-1995, six years later than originally planned. Phase II will consist of 84 test-flights over 12 years (seven per year).[3]

The first Small ICBM (now officially designated MGM-134A and dubbed 'Midgetman') test-flight was made on 11 May from Vandenberg AFB. The cold-launch from an above-ground silo appeared normal through first-stage separation. After about 70 seconds, however, the missile began to tumble end-over-end and was destroyed by the range safety officer. The test failure further jeopardized the future of the costly missile, which has never been popular with the Air Force or the Reagan or Bush Administrations. Secretary of Defense Richard Cheney told the House Armed Services Committee that the SICBM 'provides greater targeting flexibility and efficiency than highly MIRVed [equipped with multiple independently targetable re-entry vehicles] systems. It may be preferred over highly MIRVed systems for striking targets or newly emergent targets that require retargeting'.[4]

Strategic submarine programmes

The US Navy continues to retire older SSBNs either because they have been ordered to by Congress or to save money. During 1989 one submarine which carried Poseidon missiles was withdrawn from service. The *USS James Monroe* (SSBN-622) was decommissioned on 14 October. Two other submarines are scheduled for withdrawal early in 1990. The *USS Henry Clay* (SSBN-625) will begin deactivation in February 1990, and the *USS Daniel Webster* (SSBN-626) will be converted to a training vessel beginning in April 1990. Over the period from September 1985 to the spring of 1990 seven submarines with 112 SLBMs and approximately 1280 warheads will have been retired.

The commissioning of the *USS Pennsylvania* (SSBN-735) took place on 9 September. It will be the second submarine to carry Trident II SLBMs when it is deployed, scheduled for 1990. The third submarine to carry the

[3] General Accounting Office, *ICBM Modernization: Availability Problems and Flight Test Delays in Peacekeeper Program,* GAO/NSIAD-89-105, Mar. 1989.

[4] Statement of Secretary of Defense Richard B. Cheney before the House Armed Services Committee, 13 July 1989, p. 3.

new missiles, the *USS West Virginia* (SSBN-736), was launched on 14 October.

The FY 1990 defence budget requested funds for the seventeenth Trident submarine, and the five-year plan projects one submarine per year for the next four fiscal years. The Navy continues to evade the question of how many submarines it plans to have. The question will have to be resolved soon to decide the composition of US strategic forces under a START treaty. One proposal is to fill 6 of the 24 launchers on each submarine with concrete. This would permit 21 Trident submarines under the ballistic missile warhead counting rules agreed in the START negotiations (see also chapter 11).

The FY 1990 budget also requested funds for the purchase of 63 Trident II missiles, at a cost of $1.8 billion, bringing the number purchased so far to 216. The latest cost estimate of the Trident II submarine-launched ballistic missile (SLBM) programme is $35.5 billion for 899 missiles,[5] or almost $40 million apiece.

The final two (of 19) flat-pad test-flights were conducted on 9 and 26 January. The first of a scheduled nine Performance Evaluation Missile launches took place on 21 March, fired from the submerged *USS Tennessee*, off Cape Canaveral, Florida. The test was a failure.[6] Four seconds after the missile broke the surface of the water, it began to pinwheel uncontrollably and was destroyed. According to one account, the missile then entered the water and almost hit the launching submarine, which was at a depth of 90 feet (27 m). 'Chunks of live . . . solid propellent were found on the deck of the submarine when it docked after the test'.[7] This and several component delivery problems[8] caused the initial deployment date of the Trident SLBM to slip from December 1989 to the end of March 1990.

Although the Navy described the test on 2 August as a success, missile performance was erratic, with the missile leaning over after it surfaced, before stabilizing and heading down range. Safety officers were seconds away from destroying the missile.

The third test, on 15 August, also ended with the missile exploding soon after surfacing. The failures may be caused by a fundamental design flaw.[9] Apparently when the 130 000-lb (59 000-kg) missile pushes through the water after launch, it creates more turbulence than originally thought. As it travels through the water it creates a vacuum or bubble. Water rushes into

---

[5] DOD, *Selected Acquisition Report*, 31 Dec. 1988.

[6] Halloran, R., 'Navy Trident 2 missile explodes in its first underwater test firing', *New York Times*, 22 Mar. 1989, p. A1; Kolcum, E. H., 'Navy assesses failure of first Trident 2 underwater launch', *Aviation Week & Space Technology*, 27 Mar. 1989, pp. 18–19

[7] Kolcum, E. H., 'US Navy conducts successful underwater launch of Lockheed Trident 2 missile off Florida coast', *Aviation Week & Space Technology*, 7 Aug. 1989, p. 19.

[8] Propellant casting for the second-stage motors was halted after an explosion on 29 Mar. at the Hercules Magna, Utah, plant. A strike at the Kaiser plant in San Leandro, California, has halted delivery of nozzles for the second- and third-stage motors.

[9] Rosenthal, A., 'Trident failures in tests are tied to flawed design', *New York Times*, 17 Aug. 1989, p. A1; Rosenthal, A., 'Trident 2 failures laid to early success', *New York Times*, 18 Aug. 1989, p. A10; Morrocco, J. D., 'Second Trident 2 test failure points to missile design flaw', *Aviation Week & Space Technology*, 21 Aug. 1989, p. 26.

the bubble, and as the missile surfaces it creates a plume or column of water which continues to follow the missile.

The fourth test, on 4 December, was considered a success, although five design changes had been made to the missile since the previous test to compensate for earlier problems.[10] A fifth test was held on 13 December and a sixth test on 15 December, both of which were considered successful.

The Defense Nuclear Agency and the Department of Energy conducted a weapons effect test, code-named Disko Elm, at the Nevada test site on 14 September. It was the fourth and final Trident II missile system proof test. It demonstrated systems survivability while operating in a simulated boost-phase flight profile.

Strategic bomber programmes

After years of almost total secrecy about the B-2 'stealth' bomber an enormous amount of data became available during the year.[11] This occurred because the bomber made its maiden flight and because its high cost came under close scrutiny by Congress.[12] Almost everything about the aircraft is highly controversial. Charges and counter-charges abounded over its cost, mission, capabilities, history of secrecy, lack of oversight and likely role under a START treaty.

In an effort to win congressional support for the bat-winged aircraft Northrop Corporation, the prime contractor, released a list of 156 subcontractors in 46 states where tens of thousands of employees work on the aircraft. Approximately 14 000 Northrop employees work on the B-2.[13] Northrop also released data on how the $70.2 billion cost will be spent in 46 states and 383 (of 435) congressional districts. This makes it difficult for members of Congress to threaten cuts in the programme, as it would affect their constituents.[14] Approximately $23 billion has already been spent.

Eight test-flights took place during 1989. On 17 July a B-2 made a successful two-hour maiden flight from Palmdale, California, to Edwards AFB.[15] After takeoff the aircraft climbed to 10 000 feet (3000 m). The second test-flight, on 16 August, was cut short after 69 minutes (of a

[10] Schmalz, J., 'After skirmish with protesters, Navy tests missile', *New York Times*, 5 Dec. 1989, p. A1.

[11] Atkinson, R., 'Project Senior C. J. the story behind the B-2 bomber', *Washington Post*, 8 Oct. 1989, and 'Stealth: from 18-inch model to $70 billion muddle', p. A1; 'Unraveling stealth's "black world"', *Washington Post*, 9 Oct. 1989, p. A1; 'How stealth's consensus crumbled', *Washington Post*, 10 Oct. 1989, p. A1.

[12] Vartabedian, R., 'Why did AF end stealth on stealth?', *Los Angeles Times*, 2 Aug. 1989, p. 1.

[13] Northrop Corporation, *1988 Annual Report*, p. 21; Northrop Press Release, 'The B-2 nationwide industrial team', July 1989.

[14] The figures show that the money is not spread very evenly. Four states, California ($32.1 billion), Washington ($11.1 billion), Texas ($5.3 billion) and New York ($1.1 billion), account for over $50 billion of the total. Northrop would receive $16.2 billion. At the other end nine states get under $1 million apiece with West Virginia getting only $200 000, and four states, Alaska, Hawaii, North Dakota and Wyoming, getting nothing at all.

[15] Scott, W. B. and Dornheim, M. A., 'Post-flight review indicates airworthiness of B-2 design', *Aviation Week & Space Technology*, 24 July 1989, pp. 22–25.

planned 3- to 4-hour flight) becaue of a low oil pressure reading.[16] A third test-flight, of 4 hours and 36 minutes, was conducted on 26 August. The fourth and fifth flights occurred on 21 September (2 hours and 53 minutes), and 23 September (1 hour and 17 minutes).[17] The sixth flight, on 9 November, featured the first aerial refuelling of the aircraft. The seventh flight occurred on 18 November and lasted seven hours and 17 minutes, the longest to date. An eighth test-flight, of five hours and 48 minutes, was made on 22 November.

Official estimates of the cost keep rising. The most recent is $70.2 billion (in FY 1999 dollars) for 132 aircraft or $532 million per aeroplane,[18] making it the most expensive aeroplane ever built. Some Department of Defense (DOD) officials say $750 million per unit is a possibility. Cost estimates often overlook the cost of the nuclear weapons it will carry. According to Air Force Chief of Staff General Larry Welch, the 'stealth' fleet will be able to carry a total of 2000 nuclear warheads, or 16–18 per plane on average. These will include modern B83 and B61 bombs and SRAM IIs (short-range attack missiles). At a minimum this will add another $4 billion to the bill. Military construction costs and operating expenses must also be counted in the total life cycle costs.[19]

Specific details about yearly budget requests have been divulged. The proposed funding is $4.7 billion for FY 1990, $5.3 billion for FY 1991, $7.8 billion for FY 1992, $8.4 billion for FY 1993, $7.7 for FY 1994, and $13.6 billion to the conclusion of the programme. Prior year funding through FY 1989 totals $22.7 billion. Ten B-2 aircraft are in various stages of production. The second B-2 production aircraft (there are no prototypes) is scheduled to make its maiden flight in the spring of 1990.

By the end of the year Congress put a tight rein on the programme in the Defense Authorization bill. It authorized funds for two aircraft in the FY 1990 budget (instead of three), cutting the overall sum to $4.3 billion. The bill demanded various reports, certifications, notifications and assessments from the Air Force so as to keep better track of the aircraft's cost and test performance. Air Force generals put heavy pressure on Congress by claiming that they would oppose a future START treaty if the B-2 were cancelled or scaled back.

Controversy emerged over the range of the aircraft. The *Washington Post* reported that a leaked budget document revealed that the B-2 had an unrefuelled range of 6000 miles (9650 km), while the B-1B range is 6400

---

[16] 'B-2 flies with gear retracted on shortened second flight', *Aviation Week & Space Technology*, 21 Aug. 1989, p. 27.

[17] 'No. 1 B-2 completes first phase of flight envelope expansion tests', *Aviation Week & Space Technology*, 2 Oct. 1989, pp. 30–31. The fourth test-flight was scheduled for five hours but was cut short due to a crack in an engine gearbox which caused an oil pressure problem. High winds cut short the fifth flight.

[18] Smith, B. A. 'B-2 peak production delays drive up program costs', *Aviation Week & Space Technology*, 24 July 1989, pp. 26–27; Greve, F., 'How B-2 cost soared and soared in secret', *Miami Herald*, 20 Mar. 1989, p. 1.

[19] Cohen, Senator W. S., 'The B-2 bomber: mission questionable, cost impossible', *Arms Control Today*, Oct. 1989, pp. 3–8.

miles (10 300 km).[20] To counter the embarrassing leak, at a crucial time of congressional budget deliberations, the Air Force quickly declassified fresh details about the B-2's range and weapon loads, and urged that 'apples versus apples' be compared.[21] It stated that the lighter B-2 could fly 6600 nautical miles (nm) (12 223 km) on a high-altitude unrefuelled mission with a 24 000-lb (10 886-kg) weapon load (eight 2250-lb [1020-kg] SRAMs and eight 750-lb [340-kg] B61 bombs), compared with 5600 nm (10 371 km) for the B-1B similarly loaded. Increasing the load to 37 300 lb (16 783 kg) by substituting eight 2400-lb (1095-kg) B83 bombs for the B61s limits the range on a high–low–high-altitude mission to 4400 nm (8149 km) versus 4000 nm (7408 km) for the B-1B. If the extra 18 000 lb (8165 kg) of fuel is not carried by the B-1B, the ranges cited above decrease by another 400 nm. The 'low' portion assumes descending to a few hundred feet for a gas-consuming 1000 nm (1852 km) when penetrating the Soviet Union and dropping its weapons. Overall, says the Air Force, the B-2's fuel efficiency is nearly 50 per cent higher than the B-1B's and needs less than half the aerial refuelling support for its nuclear strike missions.

The Air Force declared the B-1B operational in September 1986 and received the 100th aircraft in April 1988. The force has been reduced to 97 aircraft due to crashes. There were no crashes during 1989. Although the fleet did achieve a higher utilization rate and experienced fewer problems, certain deficiencies in performance remain. According to the General Accounting Office (GAO) an additional $9.1 billion might have to be spent on 'potential enhancements and modifications' beyond the $31 billion already incurred.[22] The Air Force expects the B-1B to reach system maturity in 1994 after completing 200 000 cumulative flying hours.[23]

In an important development the Air Force decided in early 1989 not to make the B-1B a cruise missile launcher for the foreseeable future. The previous plan had been to use the B-1B in a mixed role as penetrating bomber and stand-off cruise missile carrier as the B-2 entered the inventory.

The hour of truth is fast approaching for the trouble-plagued AGM-129A Advanced Cruise Missile (ACM). A picture of the missile was released, and the first test-flight to occur in Canada took place on 2 March 1989, carried by a B-52 on a four-hour flight. Early in the year, the ACM test-flight failure rate hovered around 50 per cent, not a low enough level for congressional approval. Beginning with the FY 1987 Authorization Act, and subsequent acts, obligation of procurement funds were linked to the satisfactory completion of a set of developmental testing milestones. The Senate Armed Services Committee report on the Authorization Act, dated

[20] Wilson, G. C. 'B-2 "stealth" bomber has shorter cruising range than older, cheaper B-1', *Washington Post*, 6 Oct. 1989, p. A14; Biddle, W., 'B-2 comes up short', *Science*, 20 Oct. 1989, p. 322. A LTV Aircraft Products Group brochure, dated Sep. 1989, on the B-2 claims it can fly '6,000 nautical miles at high altitude unrefueled and 10,000 nautical miles with one air refueling'.

[21] Bond, D. F., 'USAF says B-2's range exceeds B-1B's with varied payloads, flight profiles', *Aviation Week & Space Technology*, 23 Oct. 1989, pp. 30–31.

[22] General Accounting Office, *Strategic Bombers: B-1B Cost and Performance Remain Uncertain*, GAO/NSIAD-89-55.

[23] General Accounting Office, *Strategic Bombers: Logistics Decisions Impede B-1B Readiness and Supportability*, GAO/NSIAD-89-129, p. 8.

19 July 1989, noted that: 'Those testing milestones have still not yet been successfully accomplished' and that 'its patience with this programme, the Air Force, and the two contractors is exhausted'.[24] New criteria were set, with programme termination threatened for early 1990 if the goals were not met. Soon after the harsh report, Defense Secretary Cheney told Congress that the ACM had 'recently completed three consecutive successful test flights and has now met the test-flight criteria previously put forth' and thus full-rate production funding should be granted.[25] The final Authorization language provides that FY 1990 funds may not be used to buy ACMs until there have been at least 10 successful developmental test-flights. Two more successful tests were conducted by the end of the year, with four more planned for early 1990.[26] The future of the missile, however, remains uncertain because of budgetary and arms control considerations.

Strategic defence

The importance and prominence of the Strategic Defense Initiative (SDI) waned during 1989 owing to a combination of factors.[27] The Bush Administration is less enthusiastic about SDI than was the Reagan Administration. The multi-billion dollar requests are an attractive target for a Congress under heavy pressure to cut the military budget. It seems possible that the five-year budget projected for SDI will be cut in half. Any bargaining leverage in the START negotiations was undermined by the Bush Administration when it agreed with the USSR in June to defer the issue until after a START treaty. It is reported that at the US–Soviet summit meeting in Malta on 2–3 December the previously contentious issue of SDI was barely discussed and that President Mikhail Gorbachev did not even mention it.[28]

Non-strategic nuclear forces

The US non-strategic stockpile is also decreasing. The process of with-drawal and destruction of missiles under provisions of the INF Treaty continued throughout the year, with little fanfare or problem (see also chapter 12). By the end of the year, with slightly over half of the time period expired, about half of the US missiles had been destroyed: 220 of 443 ground-launched cruise missiles (GLCMs) and 62 of 234 Pershing II

[24] US Congress, Senate Armed Services Committee (SASC), *National Defense Authorization Act for Fiscal Years 1990 and 1991*, Report 101-81, p. 71.

[25] Scarborough, R., 'Stealth deserves funding, Cheney says, citing tests', *Washington Times*, 25 Aug. 1989, p. 6.

[26] 'Advanced cruise missile flight tests successful; production to resume', *Aviation Week & Space Technology*, 1 Jan. 1990, p. 34.

[27] Gordon, M. R., '"Star Wars" fading as major element of US strategy', *New York Times*, 28 Sep. 1989, p. A1.

[28] Oberdorfer, D. and Hoffman, D., 'SDI given low priority at summit, aides say', *Washington Post*, 6 Dec. 1989, p. A25.

missiles had been destroyed. It is estimated that 70 Pershing II missiles and 212 GLCMs remained deployed at that time (see table 1.2). The last of 169 US Pershing 1A missiles were destroyed on 6 July at the Longhorn Army Ammunition Plant in Texas.

The question of whether or not to replace the Lance missile with a longer-range missile (known as Follow-on to Lance, or FOTL) generated a great deal of discussion during the first part of the year (see also chapter 18). The USA and the UK favoured a new missile while Belgium, the Netherlands and especially the Federal Republic of Germany opposed it. Also contentious was the issue of whether to enter into negotiations about reductions of short-range nuclear forces, the so-called 'third zero'. An elaborate compromise was reached at the NATO Brussels summit meeting at the end of May, whereby the USA agreed that it was 'prepared to enter into negotiations to achieve a partial reduction of American and Soviet land-based nuclear missile forces of shorter range to equal and verifiable levels' once implementation of the conventional arms treaty was 'underway'.[29] With regard to Lance, the joint summit communiqué stated that the 'question of the introduction and deployment of a follow-on system for the Lance will be dealt with in 1992, in the light of overall security develop-ments'. After the extraordinary political developments in Eastern Europe the issue took on a different character, especially as seen by the West Germans. One FRG official said in late November, 'The question of nuclear modernization makes us laugh. I don't think there is any possibility of it being implemented'.[30]

Naval nuclear forces

In April it was revealed that the Navy was quietly phasing out three types of short-range nuclear missile: the SUBROC, ASROC and Terrier.[31] The num-ber of nuclear warheads for the three systems is estimated to be 1100. In December it was learned that the schedule of warhead retirements was fur-ther ahead than anticipated.[32] All W45 Terrier warheads were retired by the Department of Energy by September 1988. The W44 ASROC warheads had been completely retired in September 1989. All W55 warheads for the nuclear-only SUBROC system are scheduled to be completely retired in FY 1990, no later than September 1990. Consequently, all these warheads were already removed from Navy vessels and returned to the DOE for final disassembly and disposal before 1990.

[29] Text is from the NATO 'Comprehensive concept of arms control and disarmament' report attached to the joint communiqué of NATO leaders, Brussels, 30 May 1989, excerpted in 'Excerpts from joint communique by leaders at NATO summit meeting', New York Times, 31 May 1989, p. A15.

[30] Freidman, T. L., 'Bonn aides, in Washington, say modernizing missile is dead issue', New York Times, 21 Nov. 1989, p. A8.

[31] Gordon, M. R., 'Navy phasing out nuclear rockets for close combat', New York Times, 30 Apr. 1989, p. A1.

[32] Warhead retirement dates are from Department of Energy, Albuquerque Operations Office, letter to the authors, 30 Nov. 1989.

According to Navy officials the move reflects changed Navy thinking about nuclear combat at sea, as well as difficulties in replacing the warheads. Furthermore, non-nuclear weapons perform better than they did when these nuclear weapons were first introduced. Additionally, nuclear weapons require special logistic, security and maintenance procedures that consume extensive personnel and resources.[33] The decision was not made public nor was it used to gain an arms control advantage. In January 1990, Admiral William J. Crowe, Jr, recently retired Chairman of the Joint Chiefs of Staff, publicly suggested that the United States should consider negotiating the elimination of all US and Soviet tactical nuclear weapons at sea.[34]

As a result of this partial denuclearization the US Navy will have a predominantly land-attack orientation and capability with its non-strategic nuclear weapons: Tomahawk sea-launched cruise missiles (SLCMs) aboard surface ships and submarines, and gravity bombs aboard aircraft-carriers. The only other remaining nuclear weapon will be the B57 nuclear depth bomb for anti-submarine warfare (ASW). It is carried aboard aircraft-carriers and stored at land bases for ASW aircraft. The FY 1990 budget requested $572 million for 400 conventional and nuclear Tomahawk SLCMs.

It is clear that the Navy will not reach its goal of 600 ships, and it may be that the figure of 568 ships at the end of 1989 will be the modern peak. In FY 1988 Congress appropriated full funding for two Nimitz Class aircraft-carriers, CVN 74 and CVN 75. Two other carriers approved in the FY 1983 budget are being built at the Newport News Shipbuilding and Drydock Company. The first of these, the *USS Abraham Lincoln* (CVN-72), was commissioned on 11 November. The *USS Coral Sea* (CV-43) will be decommissioned on 30 April 1990.

The lead ship of the Arleigh Burke Class guided missile destroyer (DDG 51) was commissioned on 16 September. It was funded in the FY 1985 budget. The Navy eventually wants to have 33 DDG 51 ships. It will carry the nuclear Tomahawk SLCM. The FY 1990 budget requested $3.6 billion for five DDG 51s in addition to the eight funded in prior years.

The first improved Los Angeles Class attack submarine was the *USS San Juan* (SSN-751) which was commissioned in June 1988. The improved versions, of which 21 are under construction, are 'Arctic-capable' and have the new AN/BSY-1 combat system. One submarine was removed from the FY 1990 budget and two in the FY 1991 budget. Funds for the 63rd and final Los Angeles Class submarine were requested in the FY 1990 budget. The Navy hopes to purchase two of its new SSN 21 Seawolf Class submarines in the FY 1991 budget.

---

[33] For a discussion of these procedures, see Fieldhouse, R. (ed.), SIPRI, *Security at Sea: Naval Forces and Arms Control* (Oxford University Press: Oxford, 1990), pp. 106–107, 165–67.

[34] Smith, R. J., 'Crowe suggests new approach on naval nuclear arms cuts', *Washington Post*, 8 Jan. 1990, p. A1.

Table 1.1. US strategic nuclear forces, January 1990

Weapon system				Warheads		
Type	No. deployed	Year deployed	Range (km)	Warhead x yield	Type	No. deployed
ICBMs						
Minuteman II	450	1966	12 500	1 x 1.2 Mt	W56	450
Minuteman III (Mk 12)	200	1970	13 000	3 x 170 kt	W62	600
Minuteman III (Mk 12A)	300	1979	13 000	3 x 335 kt	W78	900
MX	50	1986	11 000+	10 x 300 kt	W87	500
Total	**1 000**					**2 450**
SLBMs						
Poseidon (13 SSBNs)	208	1971	4 600	10 x 50 kt	W68	2 080
Trident I (20 SSBNs)	384	1979	7 400	8 x 100 kt	W76	3 072
Total	**592**					**5 152**
Bombers[a]						
B-1B	90	1986	9 800	ALCM ⎱	W80-1	1 600
B-52G/H	173	1958/61	16 000	SRAM ⎰	W69	1 100
FB-111A	48	1969	4 700	Bombs ⎰	[b]	1 800
Total	**311**					**4 500**
Refuelling aircraft						
KC-135 A/R/E	615	1957	..	..	..	..
KC-10A	60	1981	..	..	..	..

[a] Numbers reflect Primary Authorized Aircraft. An additional 7 B-1Bs, 21 B-52s and 10 FB-111s are in the total inventory. B-52Gs at Andersen, AFB, Guam; Loring AFB, Maine; and Barksdale AFB, Louisiana, some 47 aircraft, have exclusively conventional missions. Bombers are loaded in a variety of ways, depending on mission. B-1Bs normally carry up to 16 weapons (SRAMs and either B83 or B61 bombs). B-52s can carry a mix of 8–24 weapons. FB-111s can carry up to 6 weapons (SRAMs or B61 or B43 bombs).

[b] Bomber weapons include four different nuclear bomb designs (B83, B61-0, -1, -7, B53, B43) with yields from low-kt to 9 Mt, ALCMs with selectable yields from 5 to 150 kt, and SRAMs with a yield of 170 kt.

Sources: Cochran, T. B., Arkin, W. M. and Norris, R. S., *Nuclear Weapons Databook, Volume I: US Forces and Capabilities,* 2nd edn (Harper & Row: New York, forthcoming); authors' estimates.

The Navy and Marine Corps continue to buy various attack and ASW aircraft, although it is likely that the number of carrier air wings will be reduced because of future budget cuts. A new ASW plane, called the P-7A (formally known as Long-Range Air ASW Capability Aircraft or LRAACA), is a planned replacement for the older P-3A/Bs. Procurement would begin in FY 1992. In an effort to save money the Navy will retire 73 older P-3A/Bs early and temporarily reduce Primary Aircraft Authorization in active and reserve P-3 squadrons.

Table 1.2. US theatre nuclear forces, January 1990

Weapon system				Warheads		
Type	No. deployed	Year deployed	Range (km)	Warhead x yield	Type	No. in stockpile
Land-based systems						
Aircraft[a]	2 250	. .	1 060–2 400	1–3 x bombs	Bombs[a]	1 800
Missiles						
Pershing II	70	1983	1 790	1 x 0.3–80 kt	W85	125[b]
GLCM	212	1983	2 500	1 x 0.2–150 kt	W84	325[b]
Pershing 1A	72	1962	740	1 x 60–400 kt	W50	100[c]
Lance	100	1972	125	1 x 1–100 kt	W70	1 282
Nike Hercules	0	1958	160	1 x 1–20 kt	W31	0[d]
Other systems						
Artillery[e]	4 700	1956	30	1 x 0.1–12 kt	[e]	1 540
ADM (special)	150	1964	. .	1 x 0.01–1 kt	W54	150
Naval systems						
Carrier aircraft[f]	1 100	. .	550–1 800	1–2 x bombs	Bombs[f]	1 350
Tomahawk SLCM	300	1984	2 500	1 x 5–150 kt	W80-0	300
ASW aircraft[g]	710	. .	1 160–3 800	1 x <20 kt	B57	850

[a] Aircraft include the US Air Force F-4D/E, F-15E, F-l6A/B/C/D and F-111A/D/E/F. Bombs include three types (B43, B57 and B61) with yields from sub-kt to 1.45 Mt.

[b] Warheads will likely be placed in inactive reserve in the US stockpile.

[c] Missiles are deployed with FRG forces. Warheads are in US custody.

[d] The few remaining missiles deployed with the FRG will be retired in 1990.

[e] Total inventory of US Army and Marine Corps nuclear-capable artillery. There are two types of nuclear artillery (155-mm and 203-mm) with four different warheads: a 0.1-kt W48, 155-mm shell; a 1- to 12-kt W33, 203-mm shell; a 0.8-kt W79-1, enhanced-radiation, 203-mm shell; and a variable-yield (up to 1.1 kt) W79-0 fission warhead. The enhanced-radiation warheads will be converted to standard fission weapons.

[f] Aircraft include the US Navy A-6E, A-7E, F/A-l8A/B and Marine Corps A-6E and AV-8B. Bombs include three types with yields from 20 kt to 1 Mt.

[g] Aircraft include US Navy P-3A/B/C, S-3A/B and SH-3D/H helicopters. Some US B57 nuclear depth bombs are allocated for British Nimrod, Italian Atlantic and Netherlands P-3 aircraft.

Sources: Cochran, T. B., Arkin, W. M. and Norris, R. S., *Nuclear Weapons Databook, Volume 1: US Forces and Capabilities*, 2nd edn (Harper & Row: New York, forthcoming); Collins, J. M. and Rennack, D. E., *US/Soviet Military Balance*, Library of Congress/Congressional Research Service, Report no. 89-4665, 8 Aug. 1989; International Institute for Strategic Studies, *The Military Balance 1989–1990* (IISS: London, 1989); authors' estimates.

Table 1.3. Soviet strategic nuclear forces, January 1990

Weapon system					Warheads	
Type	NATO code-name	No. deployed	Year deployed	Range (km)	Warhead x yield	No. deployed
ICBMs						
SS-11 Mod. 2		150	1973	13 000	1 x 1.1 Mt	150
Mod. 3	Sego	210	1973	10 600	3 x 350 kt (MRV)	210[a]
SS-13 Mod. 2	Savage	60	1973	9 400	1 x 750 kt	60
SS-17 Mod. 2	Spanker	100	1979	10 000	4 x 750 kt (MIRV)	400
SS-18 Mod. 4/5	Satan	296/12	1979	11 000	10 x 550/750 kt (MIRV)	3 080
SS-19 Mod. 3	Stiletto	300	1979	10 000	6 x 550 kt (MIRV)	1 800
SS-24 Mod. 1/2	Scalpel	18/40	1987	10 000	10 x 550 kt (MIRV)	580
SS-25	Sickle	170	1985	10 500	1 x 550 kt	170
Total		**1 356**				**6 450**
SLBMs						
SS-N-6 Mod. 3	Serb	192	1973	3 000	2 x 1 Mt (MRV)	192[a]
SS-N-8 Mod. 1/2	Sawfly	286	1973	7 800	1 x 1.5 Mt	286
SS-N-17	Snipe	12	1980	3 900	1 x 1 Mt	12
SS-N-18 Mod. 1/3	Stingray	224	1978	6 500	7 x 500 kt	1 568
Mod. 2			1978	8 000	1 x 1 Mt	
SS-N-20	Sturgeon	120	1983	8 300	10 x 200 kt	1 200
SS-N-23	Skiff	96	1986	8 300	4 x 100 kt	384
Total		**930**				**3 642**
Bombers						
Tu-95	Bear B/C	20	1962	12 800	4 bombs or 1 AS-3	80
Tu-95	Bear G	45	1984	12 800	4 bombs and 2 AS-4	270
Tu-95	Bear H	80	1984	12 800	8 AS-15 ALCMs or bombs	640
Tu-160	Blackjack	17	1988	14 600	6 AS-15 ALCMs, 4 AS-16 SRAMs and 4 bombs	238
Total		**162**				**1 228**
Refuelling aircraft ..		140–170	..	..	..	..
ABMs						
ABM-1B	Galosh Mod.	32	1986	320	1 x unknown	32
ABM-3	Gazelle	68	1985	70	1 x low yield	68
Total		**100**				**100**

[a] SS-11 and SS-N-6 MRV warheads are counted as one.

Sources: Authors' estimates derived from: Cochran, T. B., Arkin, W. M., Norris, R. S. and Sands, J. I., *Nuclear Weapons Databook, Volume IV, Soviet Nuclear Weapons* (Harper & Row: New York, 1989); US Department of Defense, *Soviet Military Power*, 1st–8th edns; DIA, *Force Structure Summary–USSR, Eastern Europe, Mongolia, and Afghanistan*, DDB-2680-170-89, Feb. 1989; Berman, R. P. and Baker, J. C., *Soviet Strategic Forces:*

Requirements and Responses (Brookings Institution: Washington, DC, 1982); Congressional Budget Office, *Trident II Missiles: Capability, Costs, and Alternatives*, July 1986; Collins, J. M. and Rennack, D. E., *U.S./Soviet Military Balance*, Library of Congress/Congressional Research Service, Report no. 88-466S, 8 Aug. 1989; Background briefing on *SMP, 1986*, 24 Mar. 1986; SASC/SAC, *Soviet Strategic Force Developments, Senate Hearing 99-335*, June 1985; Polmar, N., *Guide to the Soviet Navy*, 4th edn (US Naval Institute, Annapolis, Md., 1986); TASS news agency report, 15 Dec. 1989.

The Navy plans to replace its A-6 attack aircraft with a new aircraft, designated the A-12, to serve as an all-weather carrier-based attack aircraft. The A-12 will incorporate stealth characteristics and will be nuclear-capable. For its part, the Marine Corps will have an attack aircraft force consisting entirely of AV-8B vertical/short take-off and landing (V/STOL) aircraft by early 1992, following the conversion of the VMA-214, the last active A-4M aircraft squadron. The planned number of AV-8Bs is 282 aircraft, organized in eight active squadrons of 20 plus those for training, spares and maintenance.

Department of Energy problems

The extensive safety and pollution problems with the Department of Energy nuclear weapons complex revealed in 1988 (see *SIPRI Yearbook 1989*, chapter 1) continued without relief in 1989. Seven plants were either shut down or encountered new difficulties in the second half of the year.[35] President Bush chose Admiral James D. Watkins, a former Chief of Naval Operations, to be the Secretary of Energy. Secretary Watkins ordered a full review of the problems and has taken some steps to begin the long and expensive process of cleaning up. The Rocky Flats plant in Colorado, where critical plutonium components are manufactured, was temporarily closed, beginning in November 1989.[36] This closure makes it likely that the USA could not produce any nuclear weapons at the end of the year. Plans to build a new plutonium production plant in Idaho were put on hold by Secretary Watkins because the DOE now expects to build only half as many nuclear weapons as had been assumed previously.[37]

III. Soviet nuclear weapon programmes

The year 1989 ended with a growing recognition and acceptance in the West that Soviet President Gorbachev's *perestroika* was having a major impact on Soviet nuclear forces. Modernization and growth of Soviet strategic offensive forces began to show signs of stabilization and slowing down, both in

[35] Wald, M., 'Promise of change in bomb program not yet fulfilled', *New York Times*, 7 Dec. 1989, p. A1.

[36] Schneider, K., 'A-plant is closing for safety review', *New York Times*, 30 Nov. 1989, p. B20.

[37] Smith, J., 'DOE may not build plutonium plant', *Washington Post*, 28 Nov. 1989, p. A6.

Table 1.4. Soviet theatre nuclear forces, January 1990

Weapon system					Warheads	
Type	NATO code-name	No. deployed[a]	Year first deployed	Range[b] (km)	Warhead x yield	No. deployed[a]
Land-based systems						
Aircraft						
Tu-26	Backfire A/B/C	190	1974	4 000	1–3 x bombs or ASMs	380
Tu-16	Badger A/G	200	1954	3 100	1–2 x bombs or ASMs	200
Tu-22	Blinder A/B	75	1962	2 400	1–2 x bombs or 1 ASM	75
Tactical aircraft[c]		2 485	..	700–1 300	1–2 x bombs	2 500
Missiles						
SS-20	Saber	190	1977	5 000	3 x 250 kt	570
SS-1c	Scud B	661	1965	300	1 x 1–10 kt	1 370
..	FROG 3/5/7	370	1965	70	1 x 1–25 kt	1 450
SS-21[d]	Scarab	289	1978	70	1 x 10–100 kt	310
SSC-1b	Sepal	50	1962	450	1 x 50–200 kt	50
SAMs[e]	..	5 900	1958–80	50–300	1 x low kt	2 400
Other systems						
Artillery[f]	..	6 760	1973–80	10–30	1 x low kt	2 000
ADMs	..	?	?	?	?	?
Naval systems						
Ballistic missiles						
SS-N-5	Sark	18	1963	1 400	1 x 1 Mt	18
Aircraft						
Tu-26	Backfire A/B/C	160	1974	4 000	1–3 x bombs or ASMs	320
Tu-16	Badger A/C/G	135	1955	3 100	4 x bombs or ASMs	540
Tu-22	Blinder A	20	1962	2 400	4 x bombs	80
ASW aircraft[g]	..	365	1966–82	..	1 x depth bombs	400
Anti-ship cruise missiles[h]						
SS-N-3 b/a,c	Shaddock/Sepal	228	1960	450	1 x 350 kt	120
SS-N-7	Starbright	64	1968	65	1 x 200 kt	32
SS-N-9	Siren	230	1969	280	1 x 200 kt	86
SS-N-12	Sandbox	216	1976	550	1 x 350 kt	80
SS-N-19	Shipwreck	160	1980	550	1 x 500 kt	72
SS-N-22	Sunburn	120	1981	100	1 x 200 kt	40
Land-attack cruise missiles						
SS-N-21	Sampson	15	1987	3 000	1 x 200 kt	90
ASW missiles and torpedoes						
SS-N-15	Starfish		1973	37	1 x 10 kt	
SS-N-16	Stallion	375	1979	120	1 x 10 kt	375
FRAS-1	..	25	1967	30	1 x 5 kt	25

Table 1.4 *cont.*

Type	NATO code-name	No. deployed[a]	Year first deployed	Range[b] (km)	Warheads Warhead x yield	No. deployed[a]
Torpedoes[i]	Type 65	475	1965	16	1 x low kt	475
	ET-80		1980	>16	1 x low kt	
Naval SAMs						
SA-N-1	Goa	65	1961	22	1 x 10 kt	220
SA-N-3	Goblet	43	1967	37	1 x 10 kt	

[a] For missile systems, the number is for operational or deployed missiles on launchers (see the Memorandum of Understanding of the INF Treaty, in *SIPRI Yearbook 1988*, appendix 13B).

[b] Range for aircraft indicates combat radius, without refuelling.

[c] Nuclear-capable tactical aircraft models include 130 MiG-21 bis Fishbed L, 855 MiG-27 Flogger D/J, 750 Su-17 Fitter C/D/H, and 750 Su-24 Fencer A/B/C/D/E. New estimate reflects distinction between ground attack and counter-air; see DIA, *Force Structure*, p. 18.

[d] Includes SS-21s in GDR and Czechoslovak units.

[e] Nuclear-capable land-based surface-to-air missiles probably include SA-2 Guideline, SA-5 Gammon and SA-10 Grumble.

[f] Nuclear-capable artillery include systems of the three calibres: 152-mm (D-20, M-1976, 2S3 and 2S5), 203-mm (M55, 2S7 and M-1980) and 240-mm (2S4 and M-240). Some older systems may also be nuclear-capable.

[g] Includes 90 Be-12 Mail, 45 Il-38 May and 60 Tu-142 Bear F patrol aircraft. Land- and sea-based helicopters include 95 Ka-25 Hormone and 75 Ka-27 Helix models.

[h] Number deployed is total launchers on nuclear-capable ships and submarines. Warheads based on an average of 2 nuclear-armed cruise missiles per nuclear-capable surface ship, except for 4 per Kiev and Kirov Class ships, and 4 per nuclear-capable cruise missile submarine, except for 12 on the Oscar Class.

[i] The two types of torpedo are the older and newer models, respectively, with the ET-80 probably replacing the Type 65.

Sources: Cochran, T. B., Arkin, W. M., Norris, R. S. and Sands, J. I., *Nuclear Weapons Databook, Volume IV, Soviet Nuclear Weapons* (Harper & Row: New York, 1989); Polmar, N., *Guide to the Soviet Navy*, 4th edn (US Naval Institute: Annapolis, Md., 1986); Department of Defense, *Soviet Military Power*, 1st–8th edns; DIA, *Force Structure Summary–USSR, Eastern Europe, Mongolia, and Afghanistan*, DDB-2680-170-89, Feb. 1989; Collins, J. M. and Rennack, D. E., *US/Soviet Military Balance*, Library of Congress/Congressional Research Service, Report No. 89-4665, 8 Aug. 1989; IISS, *The Military Balance 1989–1990* (Brassey's: London, 1989); NATO, *Conventional Forces in Europe: The Facts*, 25 Nov. 1988; interviews with US DOD officials, Apr. and Oct. 1986; Handler, J. and Arkin, W. M., *Nuclear Warships and Naval Nuclear Weapons: A Complete Inventory*, Neptune Paper no. 2 (Greenpeace/Institute for Policy Studies: Washington, DC, 1988).

preparation for the completion of the START treaty and in response to a generally lower level of defence spending. Non-strategic nuclear forces also showed major signs of reduction, particularly in those weapons with nuclear-only capabilities such as long-range sea-launched cruise missiles

Table 1.5. British nuclear forces, January 1990[a]

Weapon system				Warheads		
Type	No. deployed	Year deployed	Range (km)[b]	Warhead x yield	Type	No. in stockpile
Aircraft						
Tornado GR-1	220	1982	1 300	1–2 x 400/200 kt bombs[c]	WE-177A/B	155–175[d]
Buccaneer S2B	25	1962	1 700	1 x 400/200 kt bomb	WE-177A/B	
SLBMs						
Polaris A3-TK	64	1982[e]	4 700	2 x 40 kt	MRV	96[f]
Carrier aircraft Sea Harrier						
FRS.1[g]	42	1980	450	1 x 10 kt bomb	WE-177C	
ASW helicopters						
Sea King HAS 5	56	1976	–	1 x 10 kt depth bomb	WE-177C	25[h]
Lynx HAS 2/3	78	1976	–	1 x 10 kt depth bomb	WE-177C	

[a] British systems certified to use US nuclear weapons include 31 Nimrod ASW aircraft based in the UK, and 20 Lance launchers (1 regiment of 12 launchers, plus spares) and 135 artillery guns in 5 regiments (120 M109 and 15 M110 howitzers) based in FR Germany.

[b] Range for aircraft indicates combat radius, without refuelling.

[c] The US Defense Intelligence Agency (DIA) has confirmed that the RAF Tornados 'use two types of nuclear weapons, however, exact types are unknown'. The DIA further concludes that each RAF Tornado is capable of carrying 2 nuclear bombs, on the 2 outboard fuselage stations.

[d] The total stockpile of WE-177 tactical nuclear gravity bombs is about 180–200, of which 155–75 are versions A and B. All three weapons use the same basic 'physics package', and the yield is varied by using different amounts of tritium.

[e] The two-warhead Polaris A3-TK (Chevaline) was first deployed in 1982 and has now completely replaced the original three-warhead Polaris A-3 missile (first deployed in 1968).

[f] In previous *SIPRI Yearbooks* the British strategic stockpile was estimated at 128 warheads: 64 two-warhead Polaris A3-TK SLBMs on four SSBNs. It is now thought that Britain produced only enough warheads for three full boat-loads of missiles, or 48 missiles, with a total of 96 warheads. In Mar. 1987 French President Mitterrand confirmed that Britain had '90 to 100 [strategic] warheads'.

[g] The US DIA has concluded that the Sea Harrier is not nuclear-capable, even though every British Defence White Paper since 1981 states that it is.

[h] The C version of the WE-177 bomb is believed to be assigned to selected Royal Navy (RN) Sea Harrier FRS.1 aircraft and ASW helicopters. The WE-177C exists in both a free-fall and depth bomb modification, by varying the fuzing and casing options. There are an estimated 25 WE-177Cs, each with a yield of approximately 10 kt (possible variable yield).

Sources: British Ministry of Defence, *Statement on the Defence Estimates*, 1980–89 (Her Majesty's Stationery Office: London, annual); Campbell, D., 'Too few bombs to go round', *New Statesman*, 29 Nov. 1985, pp. 10–12; Nott, J., 'Decisions to modernise UK's nuclear contribution to NATO strengthen deterrence', *NATO Review*, vol. 29, no. 2 (Apr. 1981); US Defense Intelligence Agency, various reports released under the Freedom of Information Act; Urban, M., *The Independent*: including Urban, M., 'Outdated nuclear bomb's credibility in question', *The Independent*, 16 May 1988, p. 5; Urban, M., 'Clarification', *The Independent*, 17 May 1988. Additional sources: François Mitterrand, French President, an interview translated by the Service de Presse et d'Information of the French Embassy, London, 29 Mar. 1987, p. 6.

Table 1.6. French nuclear forces, January 1990

Weapon system				Warheads		
Type	No. deployed	Year deployed	Range (km)[a]	Warhead x yield	Type	No. in stockpile
Aircraft						
Mirage IVP/ASMP	18	1986	1 500	1 x 300 kt	TN 80	18
Mirage 2000N/ASMP[b]	42	1988	1 570	1 x 300 kt	TN-81	24
Jaguar A	45	1974[c]	750	1 x 6–8/25 kt bomb[d]	AN-52[e]	45
Refuelling aircraft						
C-135/FR	11	1965	..	..	..	..
Land-based missiles						
S3D	18	1980	3 500	1 x 1 Mt	TN-61	18
Pluton	44	1974	120	1 x 10/25 kt	AN-51[e]	70
Submarine-based missiles						
M-20	48	1977	3 000	1 x 1 Mt	TN-61	48
M-4A	16	1985	4 000–5 000	6 x 150 kt (MIRV)	TN-70[f]	96
M-4B	32	1987	6 000	6 x 150 kt (MIRV)	TN-71	192
Carrier-based aircraft						
Super Etendard/ASMP[g]	36	1978[c]	650	1 x 6–8/25 kt bomb or 1 x 300 kt ASMP	AN-52[e]	24

[a] Range for aircraft indicates combat radius, without refuelling, and does not include the 90- to 350-km range of the ASMP air-to-surface missile (where applicable).

[b] The Mirage 2000/ASMP has completely replaced the Mirage IIIE in the tactical nuclear role and will replace one Jaguar A squadron (15 aircraft) in July 1990. 75 Mirage 2000N aircraft are planned.

[c] The Jaguar A and Super Etendard aircraft were first deployed in 1973 and 1978, respectively, although they did not carry nuclear weapons (the AN-52) until 1974 and 1981, respectively.

[d] Two-thirds of the AN-52 stockpile reportedly consists of the low-yield variant, and one-third the high-yield variant. The AN-52 has an estimated weight of 455 kg, length of 4.2 m, diameter of 0.6 m and span of 0.8 m.

[e] The same nuclear device is used for both the AN-52 warhead (gravity bomb) and the AN-51 warhead (Pluton). Both warheads have the same higher yield of 25 kt (thus said to have the MR-50 charge in common), yet have lower yields of 6–8 kt and 10 kt, respectively.

[f] The *Inflexible* was the only SSBN to receive the TN-70. All subsequent refits of the M-4 into Redoutable Class SSBNs will incorporate the improved TN-71 warhead.

[g] The Super Etendard can carry either 1 AN-52 bomb or 1 ASMP missile. At full strength the AN-52 equipped 2 squadrons (24 aircraft) of Super Etendard: Flottilles 11F and 17F, based at Landivisiau and Hyères, respectively. From mid-1989 these two squadrons began receiving the ASMP missile. By mid-1990, all 20 aircraft (to be configured to carry the ASMP) will be operational. Although originally about 50–55 Super Etendard aircraft were to receive the ASMP, because of budgetary contraints the number of aircraft so configured dropped to 20.

Sources: Commissariat à l'Energie Atomique (CEA), 'Informations non classifiées sur l'armement nucléaire français', 26 June 1986; US Defense Intelligence Agency (DIA), *A Guide to Foreign Tactical Nuclear Weapon Systems under the Control of Ground Force Commanders*, DST-1040S-541-83, 9 Sep. 1983, with CHG 1 and 2 (secret, partially declassified), 17 Aug. 1984 and 9 Aug. 1985; Boucheron, J. M., *L'Equipement Militaire pour les Années 1990–1993* (Assemblée Nationale: Paris, 1989); Prime Minister, *L'Organisation de la Défense de la France*, no. 15 (Nov. 1985), p. 32.

Table 1.7. Chinese nuclear forces, January 1990

Weapon system				Warheads	
Type	No. deployed	Year deployed	Range (km)	Warhead x yield	No. in stockpile
Aircraft[a]					
H-5 (Il-28 Beagle)	20	1974	1 850	1 x bomb[b]	20
H-6 (Tu-16 Badger)	120	1965	5 900	1–3 x bombs	130
Land-based missiles					
DF-2 (CSS-1)	20–30	1966	1 450	1 x 20 kt	20–30
DF-3 (CSS-2)	60–80	1970	2 600	1 x 1–3 Mt	60–80
DF-4 (CSS-3)	~10	1971	4 800–7 000	1 x 1–3 Mt	10
DF-5 (CSS-4)	~10	1979	13 000	1 x 4–5 Mt	10
M9/SST 600	..	1989	600	1 x low kt	..
Submarine-based missiles[c]					
JL-1 (CSS-N-3)	24	1986	3 300	1 x 200 kt–1 Mt	26–38

[a] All figures for these bomber aircraft refer to nuclear-configured versions only. Hundreds of these aircraft are also deployed in non-nuclear versions.

[b] Yields of bombs are estimated to range from below 20 kt to 3 Mt.

[c] Two missiles are presumed to be available for rapid deployment on the Golf Class submarine (SSB). Additional missiles are being built for new Xia Class submarines.

Sources: *SIPRI Yearbook 1989*; Defense Intelligence Agency, *Handbook of the Chinese People's Liberation Army*, DDB-2680-32-84, Nov. 1984; Defence Intelligence Agency, 'A guide to foreign tactical nuclear weapon systems under the control of ground force commanders', DST-1040S-541, 4 Sep. 1987; Lewis, J. W. and Xue, L., *China Builds the Bomb* (Stanford University Press: Stanford, Calif., 1988); Jencks, H. W., 'PRC nuclear and space programs', in ed. R. Yang, *SCPS Yearbook on PLA Affairs, 1987* (Sun Yat-sen Center for Policy Studies: Kaohsiung, Taiwan, 1988), chapter 8; author's estimates.

---

and the INF (intermediate-range nuclear force) missiles. The fate of certain dual-capable nuclear delivery systems, particularly modern tactical fighter aircraft and self-propelled artillery, was uncertain, although their continued introduction did not necessarily denote additional nuclearization of conventional forces. The Soviet nuclear arsenal seems to have reached a peak in 1988 at some 33 000 nuclear warheads[38] and is beginning to undergo a gradual numerical decline. Soviet nuclear forces appear to be following a pattern similar to that of the USA for the past 10–20 years: certain military missions that once prominently relied on nuclear weapons are being phased out and replaced with conventional weapons. This has meant the retirement of many nuclear weapons which are the original first-generation warheads produced in the 1960s and 1970s.

The retirement of nuclear systems is thus beginning to play a role in the overall production and retirement capacity of the military industry and the

---

[38] See Norris, R. S. and Arkin, W. A., 'Nuclear Notebook: estimated Soviet nuclear stockpile, July 1989', *Bulletin of the Atomic Scientists*, July/Aug. 1989, p. 56.

Table 1.8. Strategic nuclear weapon arsenals of the USA, the USSR, the UK, France and China, 1946–89

Year[a]	USA		USSR		UK		France		China	
	L	W	L	W	L	W	L	W	L	W
1946	125	9	–	–	–	–	–	–	–	–
1947	270	13	–	–	–	–	–	–	–	–
1948	473	50	–	–	–	–	–	–	–	–
1949	447	200	–	–	–	–	–	–	–	–
1950	462	400	–	–	–	–	–	–	–	–
1951	569	569	–	–	–	–	–	–	–	–
1952	660	660	–	–	–	–	–	–	–	–
1953	720	878	–	–	–	–	–	–	–	–
1954	1 035	1 418	–	–	–	–	–	–	–	–
1955	1 260	1 755	–	–	8	–	–	–	–	–
1956	1 470	2 123	22	84	48	–	–	–	–	–
1957	1 605	2 460	28	102	73	–	–	–	–	–
1958	1 620	2 610	56	186	88	40	–	–	–	–
1959	1 551	2 496	108	283	96	70	–	–	–	–
1960	1 559	3 127	138	354	120	105	–	–	–	–
1961	1 532	3 110	187	423	120	163	–	–	–	–
1962	1 653	3 267	235	481	144	180	–	–	–	–
1963	1 812	3 612	302	589	144	207	–	–	–	–
1964	2 012	4 180	425	771	128	204	4	4	1	–
1965	1 888	4 251	463	829	88	199	32	32	2	2
1966	2 139	4 607	570	954	88	194	36	36	20	10
1967	2 268	4 892	947	1 349	88	189	36	36	25	20
1968	2 191	4 839	1 206	1 605	80	232	36	36	33	30
1969	2 109	4 736	1 431	1 815	48	144	36	36	48	45
1970	2 100	4 960	1 835	2 216	64	144	36	36	73	75
1971	2 087	6 064	2 075	2 441	64	144	45	45	97	102
1972	2 167	7 601	2 207	2 573	64	144	70	70	113	118
1973	2 133	8 885	2 339	2 711	64	144	86	86	130	125
1974	2 106	9 324	2 423	2 795	64	144	86	86	150	140
1975	2 106	9 828	2 515	3 217	64	144	102	102	165	155
1976	2 092	10 436	2 545	3 477	64	144	98	98	176	170
1977	2 092	10 580	2 562	4 242	64	144	114	114	186	176
1978	2 086	10 832	2 557	5 516	64	144	114	114	211	201
1979	2 086	10 800	2 548	6 571	64	144	114	114	238	230
1980	2 022	10 608	2 545	7 480	64	144	130	130	255	250
1981	1 966	10 688	2 593	8 296	64	144	130	130	262	262
1982	1 921	10 515	2 545	8 904	64	128	130	130	267	272
1983	1 905	10 802	2 543	9 300	64	112	126	126	279	284
1984	1 943	11 500	2 540	9 626	64	112	126	126	286	296
1985	1 965	11 974	2 538	10 012	64	96	142	222	298	308
1986	1 957	12 386	2 506	10 108	64	96	138	218	295	300
1987	2 001	13 002	2 535	10 442	64	96	138	298	280	290
1988	1 926	13 000	2 553	10 834	64	96	132	292	282	292
1989	1 903	12 100	2 448	11 320	64	96	132	372	274	284

L: Launchers; W: Warheads

[a] Figures are given as at the end of each year.

Sources: Cochran, T. B., Arkin, W. M. and Norris, R. S., *Nuclear Weapons Databook, Volume I,* forthcoming (for the USA), *Volume IV,* 1989 (for the USSR) and *Volume V,* forthcoming (for the UK, France and China).

nuclear weapons complex, and the production of nuclear systems and warheads also seems to have slowed generally. Series production of fourth-generation ICBMs (the SS-17, SS-18 and SS-19) was previously reported as having been concluded,[39] although in 1989, with the production of SS-24, SS-25 and SS-18 Mod. 5 ICBMs, there was again an increase in ICBM production ('after a dip in 1984–86').[40] The US intelligence community has reported 'production phase-out of older [submarine-launched ballistic] missiles and . . . slower production of two new missiles [the SS-N-20 and SS-N-23]'.[41] Fighter aircraft production has also declined significantly,[42] as has the production of long-range SLCMs, ships and submarines.[43] In addition, the USSR has closed three plutonium production reactors, the third on 12 August 1989.[44]

The status of Soviet R&D for future nuclear weapon systems remains unclear. In contrast to earlier practice, the Pentagon's most recent edition of *Soviet Military Power*, released in late September 1989, neglected to report on the status of Soviet 'stealth' technology developments,[45] an SS-18 follow-on (called the SS-X-26 in the press), an SS-24 follow-on, a MIRVed version of the SS-25,[46] a new class of SSBNs beyond the Typhoon and Delta IV, a new SLBM which previously had been reported under development, a missile to replace the Scud in ground forces,[47] the SA-X-12B Giant surface-to-air missile with anti-cruise and anti-tactical ballistic missile capabilities, a next-generation air-superiority fighter or counter-air fighter to follow the Su-27 and MiG-29, the supersonic SS-NX-24 SLCM, the Utka Class wing-in-ground effect vehicle, or a nuclear tactical air-to-surface missile (TASM). All of these weapons were featured in previous editions of the Pentagon's assessment of the Soviet threat.

Strategic offensive forces

At the end of 1989, Soviet strategic forces comprised 1356 ICBMs with 6450 warheads, 930 SLBMs with 3642 warheads, and 142 bombers with 1228 warheads. The trend seen in the past two years—equal deployments

---

[39] US Department of Defense (DOD), *Soviet Military Power 1989* (hereafter cited as DOD, *SMP 1989*), p. 39.

[40] DOD, *SMP 1989*, p. 32. The yearly average level of ICBM production remained constant in the 1982–84 and 1986–88 periods; DOD, *SMP 1989*, p. 34. According to DOD, *SMP 1989*, 'Total ICBM output was very low in 1984–1986, but production now has returned to the levels of the early 1980s', p. 35.

[41] DOD, *SMP 1988*, p. 40.

[42] DOD, *SMP 1989*, p. 34.

[43] DOD, *SMP 1989*, p. 34.

[44] TASS, 11 Aug. 1989.

[45] 'The Soviets are developing reduced-signature technologies and may be testing these technologies in aircraft and other military weapon systems. They may soon begin limited operational deployment of some "stealth" technologies. The Soviets are believed to have built several test facilities to support their research and development activities'; DOD, *SMP 1988*, p. 149.

[46] DOD, FY 1988 Annual Report, p. 25; DOD, FY 1988 Air Force Report, p. 15.

[47] According to the 1989 Joint Military Net Assessment, 'The Soviets will probably develop a new system to replace the aging [300-km range] SCUDs [missiles] for use at front and army level'; DOD, 1989 Joint Military Net Assessment, p. 4-3. DOD, *SMP 1989* makes no mention of such a missile.

and retirements of systems—continued, and the number of delivery vehicles and warheads remained about the same but with modest growth because of SLBM MIRVing. Between the end of 1987 and the end of 1988, the Soviet strategic nuclear forces grew from 10 442 to 10 834 warheads, and by the end of 1989 to 11 320 warheads (see table 1.8).[48]

The USSR deployed a new modification of the SS-18 heavy ICBM (the SS-18 Mod. 5) during 1989, as well as a new missile, the bomber-delivered AS-16 Kickback short-range attack missile (SRAM). Full-scale production of the AS-15 Kent air-launched cruise missile (ALCM) and the SS-24 Scalpel and SS-25 Sickle mobile ICBMs continued, although at a slower rate than anticipated. There are also indications that the SS-19 ICBM may be in the process of being retired *in toto*.

Continued deployment of new fifth-generation mobile ICBMs, and the appearance of a new heavy ICBM modification of the SS-18, were tempered by reports of the end of serial production of the Typhoon Class ballistic missile submarine (with the sixth and final submarine) and technical problems being experienced with the Blackjack bomber and the SS-N-23 Skiff SLBM. A general decrease in defence spending was also being reported at the end of the year.[49] One report also tabulated a 47 000-man reduction in strategic offensive forces manpower from 1980 to 1 January 1989, with much of the reduction occurring in the years of the Gorbachev Administration.[50]

ICBMs

The Soviet ICBM force stabilized at 6450 warheads in 1989, while new, and presumably more accurate, missiles replaced older ICBMs. The number of launchers declined by 22, to 1356, owing to retirement of older ICBMs. During 1989 the USSR deployed approximately 20 new road-mobile single-warhead SS-25s (adding to about 150 deployed the previous year) and some 50 additional 10-warhead SS-24s, for a total force of 18 in rail-garrison basing and some 40 in silos.[51] The deployment of SS-24s and SS-25s was offset by the retirement of 10 SS-11, 20 SS-17 and 50 SS-19 missiles.[52] The

[48] See Norris, R. S. and Arkin, W. M., 'Nuclear Notebook', *Bulletin of the Atomic Scientists*, Jan./Feb. 1988, p. 56 and Mar. 1989, p. 52. There may be some confusion over the number depending on whether one counts the warheads on the SS-11 Mod. 3 ICBMs and SS-N-6 SLBMs as single warheads or as three and two multiple re-entry vehicles (MRVs), respectively. The SS-11 Mod. 1 has been deactivated, according to the US Defense Intelligence Agency; DIA, *Force Structure Summary—USSR, Eastern Europe, Mongolia, and Afghanistan*, DDB-2680-170-89, Feb. 1989, p. 1.

[49] According to the US DOD, in 1988 the Soviet Union spent about $20 billion on strategic offensive forces; DOD, *SMP 1988*, p. 44.

[50] Collins, J. M. and Rennack, D. E., *U.S./Soviet Military Balance*, Library of Congress/Congressional Research Service, Report No. 89-466 S, 8 Aug. 1989, p. 5.

[51] The improved SS-24 Mod. 2, reported under development in 1988, turned out to be the silo-based version of the missile; DOD, *SMP 1988*, p. 101. New SS-25 bases have been identified at Irkutsk and Teykovo, in addition to the bases which already existed at Verkhnyaya Salda, Yoshkar Ola and Yurya. The SS-24 is being deployed at Kostroma and Pervomaysk; DIA, *Force Structure Summary* (note 48), p. 1.

[52] DOD, *SMP 1989*, p. 15; Cochran, T. B., Arkin, W. M., Norris, R. S. and Sands, J. I., *Nuclear Weapons Databook, Volume IV, Soviet Nuclear Weapons* (Harper & Row: New York, 1989), p. 99.

SS-19 Stiletto ICBM will be removed from the operational inventory as silo-based SS-24 missiles are deployed;[53] and since SS-19 silo conversion continues to accommodate the SS-24, the number of SS-19s which are actually out of the active inventory may be higher than reported.

By far the most significant nuclear news of the year appeared in *Soviet Military Power 1989*, which reported the deployment of the new SS-18 Mod. 5 missile, with greater accuracy, higher warhead yield and more throw-weight than the SS-18 Mod. 4.[54]

Strategic submarine programmes

The Soviet SLBM force stabilized in 1989 as well, despite the launching of the sixth units of the Typhoon and Delta IV Class submarines.[55] According to the US Department of Defense, the submarines 'are expected to join the operational force later in the year'.[56] Although five Delta IVs are assessed as being operational at the end of the year, the sixth is counted as having its missiles.

It is unclear whether the Soviet Union continues to have problems with the Delta IV and the SS-N-23 missile. As of mid-1988, none of the submarines had gone on patrol,[57] and no mention was made of Delta IV patrols in the Pentagon's *Soviet Military Power 1989* report. In addition, the report claimed that the Soviet Union deployed a modified version of the SS-N-23 missile in 1988.[58] It is assumed that this modified version corrected the problems encountered in the earlier missile.

The Soviet Navy continues to retire older Yankee Class submarines at an average rate of one each year. Thirty-four Yankee Class submarines were built in 1967–74; 12 remained at the end of the year.[59] Regular Yankee submarine patrols off the US coasts ceased in late 1987, and by mid-1989 all patrols outside of European and home waters had ended. The US Navy stated in June 1988 that deployment patterns changed as units of that class, and their older missile systems, reach the end of their active operational lives.

---

[53] DOD, *SMP 1989*, p. 45.

[54] DOD, *SMP 1989*, preface, p. 45.

[55] The fifth Typhoon Class submarine was launched in 1986, and the fifth Delta IV Class submarine was launched in early 1988; Statement of Rear Admiral William O. Studeman, Director of Naval Intelligence, US Congress, House Armed Services Committee, *Hearing FY 1989, Department of Defense Authorization*, hearing no. 100-70, p. 27.

[56] DOD, *SMP 1989*, p. 47.

[57] In Mar. 1988, the Director of Naval Intelligence testified before Congress that, 'Four DELTA IVs are assessed to be operational, although none has gone on patrol. SS-N-23, a highly sophisticated missile that probably pushes Soviet state of the art, apparently has suffered reliability problems. The missile is assessed to be operational, however, and work to improve its reliability continues'; see note 55, pp. 27–28.

[58] DOD, *SMP 1989*, p. 44.

[59] See also Cochran *et al.* (note 52), p. 138.

Strategic bomber programmes

Earlier reports that the Soviet intercontinental bomber force may take on a more central role in the future strategic force structures appears to be premature. The bomber force grew modestly in 1989, and there was an estimated 110-weapon increase in bomber-delivered weapons, but the rate of growth and projections in the future do not augur a massive shift in Soviet priorities. Three bomber types continued in production in 1989: the Bear G (a modification of older Bear B/C aircraft), the Bear H and the Blackjack— but two of the three had a diminished strategic nuclear capability.

The Blackjack A supersonic bomber programme was experiencing developmental and testing problems at the end of the year. Although declared operational in mid-1988, years behind schedule at that time, only about 15 had been deployed at the end of 1989.[60] One significant development was the deployment of a short-range attack missile, the AS-16 Kickback, similar to the US SRAM, on Blackjack bombers in 1989.[61] Virtually all of the increase in nuclear weapons within the bomber force in 1989 was accounted for by the addition of ALCMs and SRAMs on the Blackjack force. Sluggish deployment of the Blackjack will significantly limit the bomb-carrying capacity of the bomber force. On 20 August, at Tushino, north-west of Moscow, a Blackjack bomber was flown in public for the first time.

Bear G bombers, while accountable under START, have been reassigned to theatre and maritime roles, rather than continuing their intercontinental bomber roles, in a move similar to the US reassignment of B-52Gs to conventional missions.[62] Bear H bomber production appears to have ended (80 were deployed at the end of 1988); the USSR announced that about 90 Bear Hs will be produced.

Intercontinental training missions and long-range anti-shipping operations by Bear G and Bear H bombers, long an irritant in US–Soviet relations, also experienced a significant drop in 1989. An Icelandic report detailed a steep drop in interceptions by US F-15 fighters stationed on Iceland, and a drop has been experienced by Alaska-based interceptors.[63]

Strategic defence developments

One of the main components of the Soviet nuclear arsenal, the large force of strategic defence surface-to-air missiles (SAMs) deployed in the Soviet Union, is undergoing a gradual process of denuclearization as older nuclear-armed missiles are replaced by dual-capable or conventional-only missiles. The ongoing retirements of surface-to-air missiles follow a move made by the United States in the 1960s and 1970s, when thousands of nuclear-armed

---

[60] DOD, *SMP 1989*, p. 46.

[61] DOD, *SMP 1989*, p. 46. It is assumed that Blackjack bombers carry four AS-16 Kickback SRAMs per bomber.

[62] DOD, *SMP 1989*, p. 46; DOD, *SMP 1988*, pp. 51, 79.

[63] Diehl, D., 'Soviet intrusions into Iceland airspace dropping dramatically, expert says', *European Stars & Stripes*, 15 Oct. 1989, p. 2.

Nike Hercules SAMs, and Genie and Falcon air-to-air missiles, were also retired.

It is estimated that during 1989 the number of nuclear-armed SAMs in the Soviet strategic defence forces declined from 7000 to 5900 and that the number of nuclear warheads declined from 4000 to 2400.[64] The SA-10 continued in production and was deployed both around Moscow and in the Far East, replacing older SA-1, SA-2 and SA-3 missiles. Older nuclear-armed SA-1 SAMs, deployed around Moscow, appear to have been completely retired and replaced by the SA-10 during the past year.[65] TASS reported on 2 August 1989 that 60 'units' of the Air Defence Forces will be disbanded in 1989 and 1990, although it is unclear whether this includes nuclear-capable SAM units.[66]

The Pentagon also reported during 1989 that the upgrading of the antiballistic missile system around Moscow is still not completed, despite earlier reports of completion years ago.[67] The SA-X-12B Giant mobile SAM, which had been reported earlier as having some capability against cruise and ballistic missiles, was also not deployed in 1989.[68]

Long-range cruise missile programmes

During 1988, there was a significant slow-down in Soviet long-range cruise missile programmes, a trend which appeared to continue in 1989.[69] While some 690 AS-15 Kent air-launched cruise missiles have been deployed on Bear H and Blackjack bombers (660 AS-15s were estimated to be deployed at the end of 1988), the level will probably remain fairly stable, as the Bear H is completing production and the Blackjack is slow in introduction.[70]

The other cruise missile programmes seem to be progressing at much slower rates.[71] According to *Soviet Military Power 1989*: 'Since Gorbachev came to power, production of long-range (3,000 kilometres) cruise missiles, designed to be launched from bombers and submarines, rose by a factor of three'.[72] From a production rate of fewer than 50 missiles per year, this increase seems to be primarily ALCMs.

---

[64] DOD, *SMP 1989* shows a reduction of over 1000 surface-to-air missile launchers in strategic defence forces since 1988; p. 15.

[65] DOD, *SMP 1989*, pp. 50–51.

[66] Vladimir Chernyshev, TASS, 2 Aug. 1989, as quoted in Karber, P. A. and Amer, W. G., *The Gorbachev Unilateral Reductions and the Restructuring of Soviet/Warsaw Pact Forces*, Testimony before the House Armed Services Committee, 13 Sep. 1989, p. 2.

[67] DOD, 1989 Joint Military Net Assessment, p. 3-3; DOD, *SMP 1988*, pp. 44, 55–56.

[68] The SA-12A 'Gladiator' variant, intended for deployment in non-strategic forces, is already being fielded.

[69] DOD, *SMP 1988* did not even mention cruise missiles until page 40 of the report.

[70] According to *SMP 1989*, 'the majority of the current strategic air-delivered weapons inventory comprises AS-15s . . .'; DOD, *SMP 1989*, p. 46.

[71] According to the 1989 Joint Military Net Assessment, 'the Soviets *are expected* to deploy a number of sophisticated cruise missiles in the near future [emphasis added]'; DOD, 1989 Joint Military Net Assessment, p. 4-3.

[72] DOD, *SMP 1989*, p. 35.

Soviet Military Power 1989 reports that an annual average of 200 long-range SLCMs were produced in 1986–88.[73] However, the SS-N-21 Sampson SLCM is still not widely deployed. It continues to undergo flight-testing from Yankee Notch Class submarines[74] and '*can probably* be launched from any modern nuclear-powered class submarine. Specific *candidates* for employment are Yankee-Notch, Akula and Victor Class SSNs'.[75]

Referring to a new supersonic air-launched missile, designated AS-X-19 Koala, *Soviet Military Power 1989* states that such a missile is 'under development and when operational in the early 1990s could be deployed on the Bear H aircraft'.[76] The *1989 Joint Military Net Assessment* issued in June 1989 is even more cautious in predicting the deployment of this missile. It states that 'estimates are that work has *probably begun* on a new bomber-launched cruise missile'.[77]

The new supersonic SS-NX-24 SLCM is just beginning to be tested, and its development has been slowed. After years of declaring the missile imminently operational, *Soviet Military Power 1989* states that, 'Test activity for a sea-launched version [of the AS-X-19 air-launched cruise missile], the SS-NX-24, is continuing at a slow pace'.[78]

Non-strategic nuclear forces

The rapid elimination of four Soviet missiles under the INF Treaty—SS-20 Saber, SS-4 Sandal, SS-12M Scaleboard B and SS-23 Spider missiles—will have a significant impact on the size of the Soviet nuclear stockpile, with as many as 2000 warheads retired. As of 16 September 1989, according to Defence Minister Dmitri Yazov, the Soviet Union had eliminated 1259 INF missiles and 469 launchers, representing 68 and 57 per cent respectively of the totals to be eliminated (see also chapter 12).[79] The Minister also said that the Strategic Rocket Forces (SRF) would be reduced by 68 000 troops. These are assumed to be mostly personnel associated with the SS-4 and SS-20 missile systems (both assigned to the SRF).[80] As of the end of the year, 1498 of 1846 Soviet missiles had been eliminated (81 per cent), including all 80 SSC-X-4, all 6 SS-5, all 239 SS-23, all 718 SS-12, 116 of 149 SS-4 and 339 of 654 SS-20 missiles.[81] As of January 1990 it is estimated that 190 SS-20 missiles and no SS-4 missiles are deployed (see table 1.4).

---

[73] DOD, *SMP 1989*, p. 34.

[74] DOD, 1989 Joint Military Net Assessment, p. 3-5.

[75] DOD, *SMP 1989*, p. 47 [emphasis added]. Later in the report, it says that 'The SS-N-21, which is launched from torpedo tubes, *may be carried* by specific classes of properly equipped current-generation or reconfigured submarines [emphasis added]'; DOD, *SMP 1989,* p. 76.

[76] DOD, *SMP 1989*, p. 47.

[77] DOD, 1989 Joint Military Net Assessment, p. 3-2; emphasis added.

[78] DOD, *SMP 1989*, p. 47.

[79] *Izvestia,* 16 Sep. 1989.

[80] Collins and Rennack (note 50) report that 110 000 personnel are associated with INF weapons as of 1 Jan. 1989, a reduction of 40 000 personnel since 1988, and 68 000 since 1981, when manpower associated with IRBM/MRBM/GLCM forces peaked at 184 000.

[81] Data from US On-Site Inspection Agency, communication with the authors, 4 Jan. 1990.

The INF Treaty also means that follow-on missiles to the eliminated weapons—an SS-20 follow-on reported to be under development in 1987, and a long-range follow-on to the ageing SS-1c Scud missile—will now be impossible. The 24-year-old SS-1c Scud missile, currently assigned to Army formations, was reported in 1988 as taking on 'the ground force's primary nuclear fire support means',[82] as shorter-range FROG missiles reached the end of their useful life and began to be retired. However, the use of the Scud for primary nuclear duties might also reflect a shift in emphasis in artillery and rockets at the Army level and below, a trend which mirrors US moves of 20 years ago, when short-range Honest John rockets were removed from the division and replaced by modern 155-mm and 203-mm artillery guns (US divisions today have no nuclear missile systems assigned). The Lance missile, when deployed in the mid-1970s, was assigned to the Corps (equivalent to the Soviet Army), and the Pershing was assigned to the primary nuclear fire-support unit at the Army and Theater level.

The Soviet SS-21 Scarab missiles are being consolidated at Army level for general conventional fire-support roles. With the organizational change, the signs of decreases in short-range missiles in Soviet Ground Forces begins to make more sense to foreign observers. Over the long term, both the FROG and the Scud will probably be retired (they are reaching obsolescence and will be 25 years old in 1990) and will make way for the SS-21 and artillery.[83] The Soviet Union has been downplaying the capabilities of the SS-21. Maj.-General Yuri Lebedev, Deputy Department head in the Soviet General Staff, told *Novosti* in May 1989 that the range of the SS-21 and the FROG-7 it is replacing 'practically coincide'.[84]

Shifts in short-range missiles may help to explain the continued deployment of large numbers of heavy, longer-range, self-propelled artillery, replacing towed artillery and mortar systems. Production of nuclear-capable self-propelled artillery was reported by the US Department of Defense in 1988 as being at 'an all-time high',[85] and a new 152-mm towed howitzer may now be in production.[86] *Soviet Military Power 1989* reports that, 'Newer 122mm howitzers may have a nuclear capability . . . '[87]

The unilateral Soviet cuts announced by President Gorbachev at the United Nations on 7 December 1988 included reduction of 8500 artillery guns, some of which are thought to be nuclear-capable.[88] The only nuclear-capable artillery of the six tank divisions being eliminated in Eastern Europe includes 152-mm self-propelled artillery guns assigned to the division level artillery regiment. The disposition of the guns is unclear, and some concern has been raised as to whether the artillery will be totally withdrawn from

[82] DOD, *SMP 1988*, p. 55.

[83] According to *SMP 1989*, 'The inaccurate FROG artillery, with a range of about 70 kilometers, is being replaced by SS-21 systems, with vastly improved reliability, accuracy, and range'; DOD, *SMP 1989*, p. 67.

[84] 'SS-21 "no improvement" over Frog-7', *Jane's Defence Weekly*, 20 May 1989, p. 951.

[85] DOD, *SMP 1988*, p. 38.

[86] DOD, *SMP 1989*, p. 34.

[87] DOD, *SMP 1989*, p. 67.

[88] Karber and Amer (note 66), p. 15.

Eastern Europe with the six divisions, or whether they will be redistributed to the 24 'restructured' divisions remaining behind.[89]

Artillery withdrawals are, however, taking place. Defence Minister Yazov told *Izvestia* on 16 September 1989 that 1070 artillery systems 'have been reduced' over the past six months.[90] *Pravda* reported on 20 August 1989 that 169 guns had been withdrawn from the German Democratic Republic.[91] As of 1 July, 20 artillery pieces had also been withdrawn from Czechoslovakia, and artillery was reported withdrawn from Hungary in April 1989 with the 13th Tank Division.[92] General V. N. Lobov, First Deputy Chief of the Soviet General Staff and Chief of Staff of the Combined Forces of the Warsaw Pact, told a US congressional delegation in the GDR in August 1989 that the 'Soviet Union does not plan to increase the artillery strength of the Soviet forces deployed in Eastern Europe'.[93] Chief of the General Staff, General Mikhail A. Moiseyev, stated in *Krasnaya Zvezda* on 23 February 1989 that division restructuring will result in a '30 to 35 per cent reduction in the number of tanks, artillery systems and assault crossing means', suggesting additional artillery reductions.[94]

In May 1989, President Gorbachev announced that the USSR would unilaterally withdraw 500 'tactical nuclear weapons' from Eastern Europe, including 284 missile warheads, 166 nuclear bombs and 50 nuclear artillery shells. The bombs are assumed to be associated with the Su-24 Fencer aircraft that were withdrawn in 1989 (see below). The nuclear artillery shells are thought to be part of the pledge that the artillery associated with withdrawing divisions will be withdrawn.

The 284 missile warheads are assumed to be associated with the SS-12M Scaleboard B and SS-23 Spider missiles which have already been eliminated under the INF Treaty. They are also thought to be associated with the 24 SS-21 Scarab short-range missile launchers which will be withdrawn from Eastern Europe by the end of 1989.[95] In October, while visiting Helsinki, Gorbachev also stated that the Soviet Union had withdrawn all of its short-range nuclear missiles to sites beyond range of northern Europe.[96]

Tactical aircraft

The unilateral cuts announced by President Gorbachev at the UN in December 1988 included reduction of 800 combat aircraft, many of which

[89] Note 88.

[90] Note 79.

[91] On 1 June 1989, Col. General Omelichev, First Deputy Chief of Staff of the Soviet General Staff, was quoted by TASS as stating that 120 artillery pieces had been withdrawn from the GDR as of 1 June; quoted in Karber and Arner (note 66), p. 6.

[92] *Rude Pravo*, 1 July 1989; quoted in Karber and Arner (note 66), p. 11. See also *Jane's Defence Weekly*, 6 May 1989.

[93] Statement of Edward L. Warner III, Rand Corporation, 13 Sep. 1989, House Armed Services Committee, pp. 4–5.

[94] Goure, L., 'The Soviet strategic view', *Strategic Review*, spring 1989, p. 85.

[95] Interview with Defence Minister Yazov, *Izvestia*, 16 Sep. 1989.

[96] Keller, B., 'Gorbachev plans to destroy his A-armed subs in Baltic', *New York Times*, 27 Oct. 1989, p. A10.

are thought to be nuclear-capable.[97] Air Force reorganizations already under way may also be dissolving nuclear-capable units. TASS reported on 2 August 1989 that two air units, four air divisions and 19 air wings will be demobilized in 1989 and 1990.[98] On 16 September 1989, Defence Minister Yazov told *Izvestia* that 591 combat aircraft had been reduced in the past six months.[99] Moscow World Service reported on 26 August 1989 that one Air Force regiment had been disbanded in Poland and that one fighter unit was scheduled to be withdrawn from Hungary by 1 December 1989.[100]

Although the number of nuclear-capable fighter-bombers in the Soviet Air Forces increased by 800 aircraft in the 1980s (mostly Su-24 Fencers), many older aircraft and medium bombers are being retired, and the emphasis in aircraft production has shifted to non-nuclear fighter interceptors.[101] According to *Soviet Military Power 1989*, production of fighter aircraft in the Gorbachev years is now averaging 680 annually, compared with 950 in the pre-Gorbachev years.[102] Production of the nuclear-capable Flogger ended in the mid-1980s, and production of the nuclear-capable Fitter was 'cut drastically over the past several years'.[103] The number of nuclear-capable fighters is estimated to have declined from 3230 to 2500 in the past year, mostly as a result of the reassessment of the roles of 875 MiG-23 Floggers.[104]

The Soviet Union continues to build Backfire medium-range bombers, assigning them to the Strategic Air Armies and Soviet Naval Aviation (SNA) in place of Badger and Blinder bombers, which are being retired. Some 350 Backfires were in service in 1989 (190 in theatre forces and 160 assigned to naval aviation). None the less, the number of theatre bombers and SNA bombers in 1989 is at the lowest level of the 1980s.[105] The number of Badger and Blinder bombers retired in 1989 was approximately 145 aircraft.[106]

The Su-24 Fencer continues in production, replacing older Badger bombers and fighters.[107] Two regiments of Su-24 Fencer fighter-bombers were withdrawn from the GDR in 1989, and nuclear-capable MiG-23/27 fighters have also been withdrawn from Eastern Europe.[108]

[97] Defence Minister Yazov stated in *Izvestia* on 28 Feb. 1989 that reductions in Europe among the 'Warsaw Pact' countries include 930 warplanes; Goure, L., 'The Soviet strategic view', *Strategic Review*, spring 1989, p. 88.

[98] Vladimir Chernyshev, TASS, 2 Aug. 1989, quoted in Karber and Arner (note 66), p. 2. Defence Minister Yazov stated in *Izvestia* on 28 Feb. 1989 that 'our entire air grouping will be withdrawn from the Mongolian People's Republic'; Goure (note 94), p. 88.

[99] *Izvestia*, 16 Sep. 1989.

[100] Karber and Arner (note 66), p. 9. See also *Jane's Defence Weekly*, 6 May 1989.

[101] DOD, *SMP 1988*, p. 80.

[102] DOD, *SMP 1989*, p. 34.

[103] DOD, *SMP 1988*, p. 39.

[104] DIA, *Force Structure Summary* (note 48), p. 18.

[105] Collins and Rennack (note 50), pp. 39, 88.

[106] DOD, *SMP 1989*, p. 15; DOD, *SMP 1988*, p. 15.

[107] TASS reported on 17 July 1989 that one Bomber regiment had been replaced with Su-24 fighters, and that another was replaced with MiG-27 fighters; as quoted in Karber and Arner (note 66), p. 6.

[108] Karber and Arner (note 66), p. 15.

There were numerous reports in 1988 of a new nuclear-capable short-range tactical air-to-surface missile assigned to fighter aircraft, particularly the Su-24 Fencer. Although little information is available, the weapon referred to was possibly the AS-9 Kyle, the AS-11 Kilter anti-radiation missile or the AS-14 Kedge.[109] However, little was heard about the supposed development in 1989.

Naval nuclear forces

The Soviet Navy has become an increasingly important part of Gorbachev's public disarmament initiatives, and by the end of 1989 it was clear that a general and visible denuclearization process had begun. During a trip to Helsinki in the end of October, Gorbachev announced the planned elimination of the remaining four Golf II Class ballistic missile submarines from the Baltic Fleet by the end of 1990, and more important, stated that the USSR would remove certain types of sea-launched nuclear weapons from the Baltic Fleet.[110] In November, TASS reported the first test-flights aboard the Soviet Navy's new aircraft-carrier, and made a point of stating that: 'The Tblisi will not carry nuclear weapons'.[111] This followed the removal of nuclear-capable anti-submarine rockets and surface-to-air missiles from the fourth aviation ship of the Kiev Class, which was commissioned in 1988.

The growing pressure from the Soviet Union for the United States to meet it at the naval arms control negotiating table was constant, and with completion of START and CFE (Conventional Armed Forces in Europe) agreements looming, the likelihood of such talks in the future appeared more likely. At the 2–3 December US–Soviet summit meeting in Malta, President Gorbachev proposed eliminating non-strategic nuclear weapons from the US and Soviet Navies after the CFE treaty is reached.[112] Details of the proposal were not clear from US sources, who interpreted it differently, but President Bush did not agree to the proposal.[113]

The size of the Soviet naval force continued to decline in 1989 as the ageing and obsolescent fleet was being retired. Soviet naval activities out of home waters remained at their new low rate, and construction of new platforms (ships and submarines that would have been started under Gorbachev, as opposed to before him) showed signs of slowing.

During 1988, according to the US Navy, 'the Soviets scrapped or otherwise took out of active service more ships than any year in recent history'.[114] This development followed the retirement of a significant number of diesel-

[109] DOD, *SMP 1988*, p. 79; Collins and Rennack (note 50), p. 28, credit the AS-9 with a nuclear capability, but not the AS-11.

[110] Note 96; Associated Press Report, 'USSR nixing Baltic aimed arms', 26 Oct. 1989.

[111] TASS, Moscow, 'Aircraft take off from new Soviet Tblisi carrier', 22 Nov. 1989.

[112] Gordon, M. R., 'Gorbachev said to seek end of naval nuclear weapons', *New York Times*, 6 Dec. 1989, p. A16.

[113] Smith, R. J., ' Soviets urged ban on some nuclear arms at sea', *Washington Post*, 6 Dec. 1989, p. A25.

[114] Statement of Rear Admiral Thomas A. Brooks, Director of Naval Intelligence, before HASC, 22 Feb. 1989, p. 8.

powered submarines in the 1980s[115] and the retirement of at least 20 major surface combatants (4 cruisers and 16 destroyers) since 1987.[116] In 1989 and 1990, according to TASS, 24 more submarines and 45 naval surface ships will be 'scrapped'.[117] Defence Minister Yazov stated on 16 September 1989 that 40 warships had been reduced in the previous six months alone.[118] The Soviet Pacific Fleet was reported reduced by about 50 ships during the period 1984–88.[119]

Soviet shipbuilding levels have also declined. Submarine production levels have diminished since the mid-1980s.[120] In 1987 and 1988 the Soviet Navy launched eight attack submarines for its own use (excluding three Kilo Class submarines each year intended for export).[121] While *Soviet Military Power 1989* reports that a second production line for the Akula Class submarine was opened,[122] the Victor III and Akula, and possibly the Sierra attack submarine classes, remain in production.[123] A new Oscar Class cruise missile submarine, designated Oscar II, was observed in March in the Norwegian Sea.

Ship production levels are also showing signs of reduction, a sign that new orders have declined under Gorbachev. Four types of major surface combatant continued in production in 1989: the fourth Kirov Class cruiser and destroyers of the Udaloi and Sovremennii Classes. A new cruiser to follow the Kirov may also be in the early stages of construction.[124] Major warships being retired or decommissioned included Sverdlov Class cruisers, and Kashin, Kildin, Kotlin and Skoryy Class destroyers. The last Kanin Class destroyers were reported decommissioned in 1988.[125]

[115] DOD, *SMP 1988*, p. 129. Collins and Rennack (note 50), p. 109, report the retirement of 2 Echo II SSGN, 20 Foxtrot SS, 3 Golf SS, 8 Romeo SS, 16 Whiskey (four SSG and 12 SS), and 15 Zulu SS submarines in the 1980s.

[116] These ships have been either scrapped or stripped of weapons and electronics while awaiting scrapping . . .'; DOD, *SMP 1989*, p. 75.

[117] Vladimir Chernyshev, TASS, 2 Aug. 1989; as quoted in Karber and Arner (note 66), p. 2. The US Defense Intelligence Agency (DIA) reported that seven submarines had been scrapped by the USSR between Nov. 1987 and Feb. 1989; DIA, *Force Structure Summary* (note 48).

[118] *Izvestia*, 16 Sep. 1989.

[119] These ships include older Romeo diesel-powered submarines and Skorii, Kotlin and Kanin Class destroyers; Statement of Rear Admiral Thomas A. Brooks (note 114), p. 9.

[120] Brooks (note 114), p. 9.

[121] Brooks (note 114), p. 10; Studeman (note 55), pp. 32, 34; *SMP 1989*, p. 35. In 1988, the Soviet Navy launched one Akula (the fourth), one Victor III (the 23rd), one Oscar II (the fourth Oscar and the first Oscar II), one Delta IV (the fifth), and four Kilo class submarines (three of which were for export). In 1987, the Soviet Navy launched one Victor III (the 22nd), one Akula (the third), one Oscar (the third), one Beluga experimental submarine and four Kilo Class submarines (three of which were also for export).

[122] DOD, *SMP 1989*, preface.

[123] An Akula Class submarine was spotted by Norwegian intelligence in the Barents Sea in Oct., indicating that the submarines may be assigned to the Northern Fleet as well as the Pacific Fleet, where the first four submarines are home-ported. Admiral Thomas A. Brooks, Director of Naval Intelligence, stated in US Naval Institute *Proceedings* in Nov. 1989, p. 139, that there were 'apparently more nuclear submarines launched in 1989 than in any other year this decade.'

[124] DOD, *SMP 1989*, p. 35; Starr, B., 'Soviets building new cruiser', *Jane's Defence Weekly*, 15 July 1989, p. 57.

[125] Collins and Rennack (note 50), p. 101.

Soviet production of shorter-range cruise and anti-ship missiles to arm these new ships, according to the US DOD, has also declined slightly in the Gorbachev years.[126]

At the end of 1989, the first of the new Tbilisi Class of aircraft-carriers was conducting initial at-sea trials, while the second was being fitted out at the Nikolayev shipyard in the Black Sea. A follow-on carrier is in the early stage of construction at the same shipyard.[127] Because of problems of integrating and perfecting the catapult and arresting-gear system for use by conventional take-off and landing aircraft, the carrier is now accepted as being 'designed for ramp-assisted aircraft launch'.[128] In November TASS reported that aircraft trials had begun on the *Tbilisi*.[129]

There have been continuing significant reductions in naval operations, including drawing back on naval deployments outside of home waters. In 1988, Soviet ships 'spent more time in port and at anchor and less time at sea than in previous years'.[130] According to the US Navy: 'Most Soviet Navy exercises in 1988 continued to be relatively short, were conducted in ocean areas contiguous to the Soviet landmass and emphasized defense of the homeland and submarine bastions'.[131] In 1989 it was reported that all submarine patrols off the UK and western Africa had ceased, that patrols had been cut back in the Indian Ocean and that naval operations in the North Sea had continued to decline.[132]

Badger bombers assigned to Soviet Naval Aviation continue to be retired and replaced by Backfire bombers on a less than one-for-one basis.[133] In 1988, other than deployment of Backfire C bombers with the SNA, 'little SNA deployment activity occurred during the year. No new aircraft types were introduced'.[134]

Perestroika and the Soviet military

Among other things, 1989 will be remembered as the year that demonstrated that Mikhail Gorbachev could deliver on his promises of *perestroika* and unilateral changes in military forces. The role of Marshal Sergey Akhromeyev in an important advisory post and Defence Minister Yazov's leading role in speaking out in favour of military reforms were important achievements for the Soviet leader and exemplified the successful balancing act Gorbachev was able to maintain during the year with the opponents and critics of his bold programme.

---

[126] DOD, *SMP 1989*, p. 34.
[127] DOD, *SMP 1989*, p. 35.
[128] DOD, *SMP 1988*, preface.
[129] TASS, Moscow, 'Aircraft take off from new Soviet Tblisi carrier', 22 Nov. 1989.
[130] Brooks (note 114), p. 13.
[131] Brooks (note 114), p. 15.
[132] Starr, B., 'Soviets building new cruiser', *Jane's Defence Weekly*, 15 July 1989, p. 57; 'Soviet North Sea sightings continue to fall', *Jane's Defence Weekly*, 7 Oct. 1989, p. 730.
[133] Brooks (note 114), p. 15.
[134] DOD, *SMP 1989*, p. 77.

The effects of *perestroika* on the military establishment, however, continued to be a problem for the Soviet President. The Soviet specialist press published numerous articles detailing the military's internal difficulties, particularly deficiencies in training, efficiency and morale. Dissatisfaction continued to be voiced about the reduction in military spending, but these complaints were not so much disagreement with the disarmament process *per se* or with military reductions. They were largely concerns about the conditions of the military profession, and the treatment of demobilized officers, particularly the availability of jobs and housing.[135]

Although the generals and admirals continued to debate what *perestroika* meant for the armed forces, the military was occupied with real and immediate demands, most notably the monumental effort of withdrawing troops and equipment from Eastern Europe, reincorporating forces withdrawn from Afghanistan and other reorganization efforts.[136] Between April, when the first troops and equipment were withdrawn from Hungary, and August, three divisions, 2700 tanks, 380 artillery guns, 120 combat aircraft and 24 500 personnel were removed from Eastern Europe.[137] This is a major logistical achievement even by Western standards, and such changes clearly have a major impact on short-term combat readiness. By the end of 1989, the Soviet military found themselves observing the many rapid changes going on in Eastern Europe as well as the accelerated arms negotiations that would soon spell even further reductions, in the process of implementing the INF Treaty—with declining defence spending and production.

IV. British nuclear weapon programmes

The British Trident strategic submarine programme is still on schedule, yet uncertainties remain over the performance of the US Trident D5 missile to arm these boats, and the ability of the UK to produce the warheads in time for the missile. Britain continues to be plagued by indecision over its choice of a nuclear-armed stand-off missile to replace its ageing stock of WE-177 gravity bombs.

According to the latest defence White Paper, Britain proposed to spend $33.84 billion for the 1989–90 defence budget. Of this amount, the strategic

---

[135] When concerns relating to the effects of *perestroika* and turmoil in Soviet society on combat readiness of the armed forces were raised, criticism was largely reserved for lower-ranking officers, for the lack of integration of new technolgy for training and administration, and for the inefficiency of Soviet society, all problems being addressed in civil *perestroika* as well. See, e.g., Royal United Service Institute, *The RUSI Soviet Warsaw Pact Yearbook 1989* (Jane's Defence Data: Coulsdon, 1989), pp. 22–55.

[136] These other reorganization efforts, presumably intended to save money, reduce administrative headquarters and streamline command relationship, included the announcement in Sep. that two military districts were being eliminated. Commentary about both reorganizations included references to the fact that thousands of former officers and their families has no place to live; see Meyer, S. M., 'Soviets eliminate two military districts', *Soviet Defense Notes*, Oct. 1989.

[137] US Congress, House Armed Services Committee, *Status of the Soviet Union's Unilateral Force Reductions and Restructuring of its Forces, Report of the Committee Delegation to West Berlin, East Germany and the Soviet Union, 6–18 Aug. 1989*, 16 Oct. 1989, p. 4.

nuclear force will require 5.7 per cent, but only 0.6 per cent of service man-power and 1.3 per cent of civilian manpower.[138]

Continuing problems at Aldermaston

Problems at the Atomic Weapons Establishment (AWE) at Aldermaston, the hub of all British nuclear weapon research and production, are causing serious concern about the ability of the UK to develop and produce the war-heads for the Trident D5 missile and the tactical air-to-surface missile.

The British Ministry of Defence (MOD) has given a qualified assurance that sufficient warheads would be ready to meet the in-service date of all four Vanguard Class SSBNs, '*provided that* the new capital facilities come into operation as planned and that the difficulties caused by the current staffing shortfall can be overcome'.[139]

However, both staff shortages and construction problems at AWE Aldermaston are continuing to threaten to delay the deployment of *HMS Vanguard*, the first Trident SSBN. To help resolve these problems, the MOD appointed Rolls Royce Chairman Sir Francis Tombs to review the Trident programme. Tombs will focus on staff shortages in key areas[140] and on concern over the A90 warhead production facility at AWE Aldermaston.[141]

These problems could also threaten the development of the warhead for the TASM, thus possibly delaying the replacement of the RAF's WE-177 nuclear bomb (expected to be replaced about the turn of the century). Sir Michael Quinlan, Permanent Under Secretary of State for Defence, stated that the MOD 'might have to face awkward priorities' when allocating AWE staff between the production of Trident D5 warheads and a TASM warhead.[142]

Trident

Construction is in progress at the Vickers Shipyard at Barrow-in-Furness on the first two Vanguard Class SSBNs, *HMS Vanguard* and *HMS Victorious*. *HMS Vanguard* is due to be operational in 1994 and to enter service in the mid-1990s.

During 1989 the MOD negotiated with Vickers Shipbuilding and Engineering Ltd (VSEL) the contract for the third SSBN (SSBN 07). The contract for the final Trident submarine, SSBN 08, is not expected to be

[138] Fishlock, D., 'Britain plans defense spending increase; new financial moves', *Defense Week*, 8 May 1989, p. 9.

[139] 'UK Trident faces delay', *Jane's Defence Weekly*, 20 May 1989, p. 910; emphasis added.

[140] As of 1 Mar. 1989, AWE Aldermaston had a shortfall of 359 employees, compared to a shortfall of 216 on 1 Mar. 1988; 'UK Trident faces delay', *Jane's Defence Weekly*, 20 May 1989, p. 910.

[141] 'Rolls-Royce head to review UK's Trident', *Jane's Defence Weekly*, 9 Sep. 1989, p. 425.

[142] Quinlan was testifying before the UK House of Commons Defence Committee on the 1989–90 defence budget; 'Staff shortages threaten to delay UK nuclear bomb replacement', *Jane's Defence Weekly*, 27 May 1989, p. 985.

signed for a few years, as it will not need to be operational until SSBN 05 is withdrawn from service for its first refit.[143]

The latest official estimate of the cost of the Trident programme is £9.089 billion ($15.451 billion).[144]According to MOD estimates, 32 per cent (£2.923 billion, or $4.969 billion) of the Trident expenditure will be in the USA, compared to a November 1981 estimate of 44 per cent spent in the USA.[145] As of October 1989, Britain has spent $20 million on 'Trident missile production and advance procurement', with a further $42 million authorized for FY 1990.[146] Peak expenditure is expected in 1990–95.

The serious design flaws of the US Trident D5 missile, discovered during two failed test-flights from a submerged US Navy SSBN (see section II), have been of great concern to the UK. The British Ambassador in Washington, Sir Antony Acland, lobbied the US Senate to restore funding for the Trident D5 SLBM in the FY 1990 budget.[147] Acland was concerned that withholding of production funding could delay the arrival of the first missiles for the Royal Navy and would 'continue to impose time and cost penalties on the British Trident programme'.[148] Uncertainty over the future of the Trident missile is now so high that the UK regularly contributes money to a US Navy trust fund entitled 'Termination Liability', first introduced in FY 1989. Although Britain has so far committed only $2.755 million to this account, a further $9.925 million is authorized for FY 1990.[149]

Tactical air-to-surface missile

Pursuant to Staff Requirement (Air) 1244, the UK is seeking to acquire a nuclear-armed TASM with a range of approximately 500 km to replace its ageing WE-177 A/B free-fall nuclear bombs.[150] The new weapon is to be installed on RAF Tornado and Buccaneer strike aircraft, and RN Sea Harrier aircraft, by the turn of the century. The British decision on this nuclear

---

[143] Note 139.

[144] The figure is from the British Information Service, New York, Jan. 1990.

[145] Note 143. Most of this money is spent through the US Navy's Strategic Systems Program Office (SSPO). Since the inception of the Polaris Sales Agreement (1963) and through FY 1989, the UK has spent $2638 billion through the SSPO on Polaris, Chevaline and Trident weapon systems. The authors estimate that, as of Oct. 1989, roughly 74 per cent of this amount has been spent on Polaris and Chevaline, and 26 per cent on Trident.

[146] According to documents from the US Navy SSPO pertaining to the Polaris Sales Agreement.

[147] The Senate Appropriations Committee terminated funding for production of the missile in the FY 1990 budget following the two dramatic test failures. The House Appropriations Committee voted for $1791.5 million in Trident production funds; Starr, B., 'UK Ambassador joins Trident funding fight', *Jane's Defence Weekly*, 14 Oct. 1989, p. 754.

[148] Starr, B., 'UK Ambassador joins Trident funding fight', *Jane's Defence Weekly*, 14 Oct. 1989, p. 754.

[149] According to documents from the US Navy SSPO pertaining to the Polaris Sales Agreement.

[150] The MOD is expected to decide 'within a year' on the replacement of the RN's nuclear depth charges. Sir Michael Quinlan, Permanent Under Secretary of State for Defence, stated that the development of 'smart' homing torpedoes might eliminate the need for nuclear depth charges. Quinlan was testifying before the British House of Commons Defence Committee on the 1989–90 defence budget; 'Staff shortages threaten to delay UK nuclear bomb replacement', *Jane's Defence Weekly*, 27 May 1989, p. 985.

stand-off missile was initially expected in 1989, although it is now not expected until the end of 1990. A full-scale development decision would follow in late 1992.

Since the UK does not wish (and cannot afford) to develop the TASM unilaterally, the delays to date have centred around the decision of which foreign country to co-operate with, and also which foreign company.

Britain has three choices at present; all are based on existing or planned foreign weapon systems. Two US companies are competing for this contract. Boeing Aerospace is proposing the tactical Short Range Attack Missile, or SRAM-T. The SRAM-T is a tactical variant of the SRAM II now in development for introduction on US strategic bombers in 1993–94. Boeing is already under contract with the US Air Force to perform design concept studies on the SRAM-T for possible application to NATO aircraft. An off-the-shelf purchase of the SRAM-T is possible on cost grounds, although Britain would manufacture its own nuclear warhead, and possibly the engine or guidance system.[151] Martin Marietta is proposing a TASM based on the company's Supersonic Low-Altitude Target (SLAT).[152]

The French manufacturer Aérospatiale is also competing for this contract, offering joint development of the ASLP (Air-Sol Longue Portée) missile. France is already studying the ASLP, a successor to its 90- to 350-km range ASMP (Air-Sol Moyenne Portée) missile.[153] To co-operate with Britain, and to meet its timetable, France would have to accelerate the development of the 500- to 700-km range ASLP long-range air-to-ground missile. It is expected that a joint ASLP missile would feature an enlarged fuel cell and new guidance suite.[154]

In early 1989 the possibility of an Anglo-French TASM appeared to wane after Britain signed a Memorandum of Understanding (MOU) with the USA sanctioning US contractors to help Britain develop a TASM missile.[155] A British Aerospace/Hunting Engineering evaluation team conducted feasibility studies into the SRAM-T and SLAT options.[156] These included the signing of an agreement for a 'concept formulation phase' with Martin Marietta, to look at the feasibility of developing Martin Marietta's SLAT into a missile for deployment on RAF aircraft.[157]

This agreement seemed to spell an end to hopes of any Anglo-French co-operation on this missile. Furthermore, the MOD still seemed dissatisfied with the ASMP performance (range and accuracy) and timetable, and in May 1989 former British Defence Secretary George Younger stated that it

[151] Cook, N., 'USA, UK sign nuclear missile deal', *Jane's Defence Weekly*, 24 June 1989, p. 1285.

[152] Cook, N. and Isnard, J., 'UK stand-off missile choice delay', *Jane's Defence Weekly*, 4 Nov. 1989, p. 949.

[153] As the ASMP has an estimated life of 20 years, France is seeking a replacement (ASLP) for introduction around 2005–2006, on the Mirage 2000N and ACT Rafale aircraft; Boucheron, J. M., *L'Equipement Militaire pour les Années 1990–1993* (Assemblée Nationale: Paris, 2 Oct. 1989), report no. 897, p. 428.

[154] Note 152.

[155] The MOU authorized the USA to release SLAT and SRAM-T data to the UK; Barrie, D., 'UK/France revive nuclear dialogue', *Jane's Defence Weekly*, 23 Sep. 1989, p. 541.

[156] Note 152.

[157] Cook, N., 'USA, UK sign nuclear missile deal', *Jane's Defence Weekly*, 24 June 1989, p. 1285.

seemed unlikely that Britain would co-operate with France.[158] Nevertheless, in May 1989 the MOD was still discussing with France the possibility of development of a joint missile.[159]

By September Britain had renewed interest in France's offer of joint development of a nuclear-armed TASM. During a meeting in London that month, British Secretary of State for Defence Tom King and French Defence Minister Jean-Pierre Chevènement made it clear that, from a political standpoint, an Anglo-French nuclear weapon is still very much under consideration. King described this a 'serious option'.[160] The British MOD is now expected to award Aérospatiale a FFr 10 million ($1.6 million) pre-feasibility study for the ASLP, which should be completed in early 1990.[161]

Comparative analysis of the three options will continue through September 1990, leading to a British decision towards the end of 1990. The whole programme could cost less than £1 billion ($1.7 billion).[162]

Britain and arms control

Although the USA has reversed its objections to Soviet demands that combat aircraft be included in conventional arms reduction talks, Britain and France both voiced reservations over the inclusion of all aircraft types; French President Mitterrand ruled out the inclusion of its strategic Mirage IVP bombers (along with associated Boeing C-135FR tanker aircraft), while Prime Minister Margaret Thatcher ruled out inclusion of British dual-role aircraft such as the Tornado strike aircraft, which can carry both nuclear and conventional weapons. Among the older aircraft that can be expected to be scrapped are French and British Jaguars.[163]

Secretary of State for Defence King reiterated in September 1989 that the UK's strategic nuclear stockpile is 'not negotiable'.[164] This stockpile at present totals some 96 warheads (see table 1.3), enough for three full boat-loads of Chevaline SLBMs.[165]

[158] 'Britain backs away from joining France in producing air-launched nuclear missile', *Aviation Week & Space Technology*, 8 May 1989, p. 25.
[159] According to Quinlan (note 150).
[160] Barrie, D., 'UK/France revive nuclear dialogue', *Jane's Defence Weekly*, 23 Sep. 1989, p. 541.
[161] Note 152.
[162] Note 152.
[163] 'Britain, France raise concerns about cuts in combat aircraft', *Aviation Week & Space Technology*, 5 June 1989, p. 20.
[164] Dodds, H., 'UK's nuclear deterrent is "not negotiable", says King', *Jane's Defence Weekly*, 16 Sep. 1989, p. 479.
[165] In Mar. 1987 French President Mitterrand confirmed that Britain had enough warheads for only three SSBNs (out of four) with the statement that the UK has '90 to 100 [strategic] warheads'; President Mitterrand, an interview translated by the Service de Presse et d'Information of the French Embassy, London, 29 Mar. 1987, p. 6.

V. French nuclear weapon programmes

Substantial cost overruns have plagued most of the nuclear weapon programmes covered by France's 1987–91 defence budget. Long-anticipated defence budget cuts are finally being implemented, as reflected in the revised 1990–93 defence budget. Although no major nuclear programmes have been cancelled, the net result is yet further delays in the introduction of these systems.

Defence budget

France's defence budget for 1990 totals FFr 189.44 billion ($30.3 billion), a 3.88 per cent growth over the previous year. FFr 102.1 billion ($16.3 billion) is devoted to the equipment budget, approximately one-third of which covers strategic and 'pre-strategic' nuclear armaments (this figure is a reduction in the original estimates).[166] The Parliament accepted the defence procurement programme for 1990–93, totalling FFr 437.8 billion ($70.1 billion).

Several major nuclear weapon programmes are to be delayed: the *Charles de Gaulle* aircraft-carrier will enter service in 1998, two years later than originally planned; the Rafale carrier-borne aircraft could be delayed until the year 2002; and the S4 IRBM will enter service at the end of the century, four years later than planned.

Force Océanique Stratégique

The programme to update the existing SSBN force continued in 1989 with the delivery of the second SSBN refitted to carry the M-4 missile system (to replace the M-20 missile), the *L'Indomptable*.

After completion of its refit at the DCAN Naval dockyard at Brest in December 1988,[167] the SSBN *L'Indomptable* launched an M-4B missile on the Centre d'Essais des Landes (CEL) range on 11 April 1989, and then entered active service on 15 June 1989.[168]

With the *L'Inflexible* and *Le Tonnant*, the Force Océanique Stratégique (FOST) now has three SSBNs carrying the M-4, each with 96 warheads apiece. These refits will bring the SSBNs up to the standard of *L'Inflexible*, enabling them to remain operational until 2005–2010.[169]

Two further SSBNs will exchange their M20 missiles for the M-4B missile system, *Le Terrible* and *Le Foudroyant*. The defence budget allocated FFr 2.8 billion ($0.45 billion) for these refits between 1990 and

---

[166] Isnard, J., 'France details $29.6b FY90 defence budget', *Jane's Defence Weekly*, 28 Oct. 1989, p. 894.

[167] The refit began in Oct. 1986; 'DCN', *DGA Info*, no. 20 (Mar. 1989), p. 7.

[168] *DGA Info*, no. 22 (June 1989), p. 8. The SSBN was submerged in the Gulf of Gascogne at the time of the launch (23:16 local time); 'Missiles', *Air et Cosmos*, 26 Aug. 1989, p. 9.

[169] Boucheron (note 153), p. 220.

1993.[170] The SSBN *Le Terrible* began its refit at Cherbourg on 1 February 1988 after completing 49 patrols since entering service in 1973.[171] The boat will be readmitted into active service in June 1990 armed with M-4B missiles. The SSBN *Le Foudroyant* will finish its refit at Brest in 1993, thus completing the M4 refit programme.[172]

The SSBN *Le Redoutable* will not undergo refit to receive the M-4, as it is due for retirement in 1991.[173] At that time, all of the three submarines that France keeps on patrol at any one time will be equipped with the M-4 missile, ensuring a total of 288 warheads at sea, all targeted on 'the Capital and the principal cities of the Soviet Union'.[174]

France plans to acquire six 'new generation' SSBNs of the Triomphant Class to replace the six ageing Redoutable Class boats.[175] Two new SSBNs have been ordered to date; funding for their construction was provided in the 1987–91 defence programme law.

A special shipyard was built at Cherbourg for the construction of the Triomphant Class SSBNs. On 9 June 1989 construction began on the first boat in the series, *Le Triomphant*. The construction programme for the six 14 335-tonne boats is due to continue through 2008.[176] *Le Triomphant* is due to undergo sea trials in 1993 before entering service at the end of 1994. The second boat, to be called *Le Téméraire*, will enter service at the beginning of 1997.[177] The sixth and final submarine is planned to enter service in 2008.

Development costs of the new Triomphant Class SSBN are 42 per cent higher than the original estimate, while production costs are expected to be 12.1 per cent higher.[178] The 1990–93 defence budget allocated FFr 26 billion ($4.2 billion) for this programme during the period and anticipates the ordering of the third boat in the series.[179]

The first three Triomphant Class boats will initially carry an intermediate type of missile known as the M-45, since the M-5 (the successor to the M-4) will not be ready in time. Although the missile will still have six warheads, the M45 will have improved penetration aids and a new warhead, the TN 75.[180]

Under the 1987–91 defence programme the 12-warhead M-5 missile was forecast to enter service in 1999. Under the new law, the date has been pushed back to 'the beginning of the next century'.[181] The 1990–93 budget

---

[170] Boucheron (note 153), p. 220.

[171] Moirand, R., 'Réarmement du SNLE *Le Terrible* un an avant ses essais à la mer,' *Cols Bleus*, 18 Mar. 1989, p. 21.

[172] Boucheron (note 153), p. 220.

[173] Boucheron (note 153), pp. 220, 737.

[174] Boucheron (note 153), p. 418. This target set is to remain unchanged for the M45 SLBM system.

[175] The fact that the boats would be replaced on a one-for-one basis was first disclosed by the official French Navy periodical *Cols Bleus* in mid-Feb. 1989.

[176] Boucheron (note 153), p. 415.

[177] 'Missiles', *Air et Cosmos*, 13 May 1989, p. 7.

[178] As of July 1989; Boucheron (note 153), p. 173.

[179] Boucheron (note 153), p. 221.

[180] Boucheron (note 153), p. 223. The Commissariat à l'Énergie Atomique (CEA) is still defining the parameters of the TN-75 warhead; CEA, *Rapport Annuel 1988* (CEA: Paris, 1989), p. 61. These three SSBNs will be equipped to carry the M5 SLBM after 2005.

[181] Boucheron (note 153), p. 222.

thus delays the introduction of the M-5 SLBM to 2005, on the fourth boat in the series (previously planned for the third boat).[182]

S3D/S4 IRBM

In 1989 France celebrated the 20th anniversary of the completion of the silo construction programme of the Plateau d'Albion. These silos currently house 18 S3D IRBMs. Each year one operational S3D is withdrawn from alert and launched (without warhead) from an experimental silo at the CEL test range. The most recent launch on 21 March 1989 marked the 50th launch of a French IRBM.[183]

The S3D is to be operational up until the year 2000, according to General Maurice Schmitt, French Army Chief of Staff.[184] According to Aérospatiale, the prime contractor for all French IRBMs, the Plateau d'Albion is due to undergo a modernization process in the late 1990s, with the upgraded weapon system making 'maximum use of the existing facilities and ensure continuity of the land-based leg of the French nuclear triad'.[185]

Although the 1990 defence budget allocates approximately FFr 800 million ($128 million) for continued research and development work on the S4 missile, the IOC continues to be delayed, this time by as many as four years, to the 'turn of the century'.[186]

The two-stage S4 missile is envisioned to carry one TN-35 warhead of about 300-kt yield. However, several other options are also being considered for the missile to replace the S3D, including: new warheads for the S3D missiles; installing M-45 SLBM missiles (and later the M5) in the underground silos; and the development of an S45 missile, which would be both mobile and fixed-based, like the S4, but carrying improved penetration aids.[187]

Hadès missile

The Hadès is a semi-ballistic missile (i.e., manoeuvrable after the boost phase) with a range which will approach 500 km.[188] The CEA is developing several different nuclear warheads for the single-warhead Hadès missile, including a neutron warhead.[189] One of these warheads is called the TN-90, with a yield reportedly no higher than 80 kt.[190]

[182] 'Loi de programmation 1990–1993: adoptée', *Air et Cosmos*, 14 Oct. 1989, p. 7.

[183] '"Operation NAJA" une reussite', *Air Actualités*, no. 421 (May 1989), p. 34. This figure includes those missiles used for developmental purposes.

[184] Boucheron (note 153), p. 737.

[185] Aérospatiale, 'Twenty candles for the Plateau d'Albion', *Revue Aérospatiale*, Oct. 1989, p. 45.

[186] Note 182; 'France to delay S-4 missile program', *Aviation Week & Space Technology*, 23 Oct. 1989, p. 25; note 166, p. 895.

[187] 'Defense: budget 1990 et Loi de Programme', *Air et Cosmos*, 30 Sep. 1989, p. 9; Boucheron (note 153), p. 232.

[188] Boucheron (note 153), p. 242.

[189] CEA (note 180), p. 95.

[190] Boucheron (note 153), pp. 242, 246; Isnard, J., 'French missile's yield revealed', *Jane's Defence Weekly*, 23 Dec. 1989, p. 1359.

Although the fate of the Hadès missile remained uncertain for most of 1989, the adoption of the revised military programme act of 1990–93 ensured continued funding for the programme and confirms the planned 1992 deployment date with the French Army.

The French Army announced that the Hadès nuclear missile division is to comprise three artillery regiments (all of which currently operate the Pluton missile). The 15th Artillery Regiment at Suippes (Marne) will be the first unit to be equipped with the Hadès, at the end of 1992. The second Hadès unit will be located at the 3rd Artillery Regiment at Mailly (Aube).[191] The final regiment is thought to be the 74th, stationed at Belfort.

To date three experimental firings of Hadès have been undertaken at the CEL range, the most recent on 20 July 1989.[192] In the near future the 15th Artillery Regiment will conduct a tactical evaluation at CEL.

General Schmitt stated that, although the Hadès missiles are to be stationed in France in peacetime, there would be no prohibition against their transfer to FR Germany in time of crisis (as is presently the case with the Pluton missiles).[193]

French President François Mitterrand stated that since 'Hadès can be weapons only of final warning, they cannot be theatre or battle weapons',[194] and: 'On that premise there's no need to have masses of them'.[195] The programme of 90 missiles (mounted in pairs on mobile firing platforms) is estimated to cost FFr 15 billion ($2.4 billion), of which about half has already been spent on production development.[196]

Mirage 2000N

The Tactical Air Force (FATAC) now commands two Mirage 2000N/ASMP nuclear strike squadrons at the Luxeuil air base. Following the arrival of the aircraft at EC 1/4 'Dauphiné' in July 1988, the Mirage 2000N/ASMP became operational with the 2/4 'La Fayette' squadron on 1 July 1989.[197] Each squadron was provided with an initial allocation of 12 ASMP missiles, each with one TN-81 warhead.[198]

---

[191] 'Missiles', *Air et Cosmos*, 9 Sep. 1989, p. 5.

[192] The launches were conducted on 22 Nov. 1988, 8 Mar. 1989 and 20 July 1989; Boucheron (note 153), p. 242.

[193] 'Missiles', *Air et Cosmos*, 24 June 1989, p. 5.

[194] President Mitterrand, press conference, translated by the Service de Presse et d'Information of the French Embassy, London, document no. Sp.St/LON/61/89, 18 May 1989, p. 16.

[195] President Mitterrand, press conference in Brussels, translated by the Service de Presse et d'Information of the French Embassy, London, document no. Sp.St/LON/69/89, 30 May 1989, p. 3.

[196] Isnard, J., 'Rocard casts doubt over Hades, despite second test success', *Jane's Defence Weekly*, 25 Mar. 1989, pp. 496–97. As of July 1989, the development cost of Hadès was 6 per cent higher than the original forecast, while the development costs of the computerized command and control elements of the Hadès missile programme rose by 16 per cent; Boucheron (note 153), p. 173.

[197] A ceremony on 10 Nov. 1988 at Luxeuil marked the departure of the Mirage IIIE from EC 4. As of July 1989 the Mirage 2000N had completely taken over the nuclear role of the Mirage IIIE/AN-52 aircraft at the Fourth Fighter Wing (EC 4); 'Novembre en bref', *Air Actualités*, no. 416 (Dec. 1988), p. 8.

[198] CEA (note 180), p. 94.

The Mirage 2000N/ASMP aircraft has overrun its original costing by 23 per cent.[199] French defence budget cuts have reduced the number of Mirage 2000N/ASMP squadrons from five to three. The French Air Force Chief of Staff, Jean Fleury, said that he accepts the reduction in the number of Mirage 2000N/ASMP squadrons because such a decision will not affect the pre-strategic nuclear strike capabilities of the French Air Force.[200]

Nevertheless the FATAC still plans to acquire 75 Mirage 2000N aircraft.[201] As of October 1989, all 75 had been ordered, 24 had been delivered, with 18 more to follow before the end of 1989. All the aircraft are to be delivered by the end of 1992.[202]

According to retired Air Force General Roger Pessidous, the third and final fighter squadron to receive the Mirage 2000N/ASMP will be EC 4/7 at Istres (Bouches-du-Rhône) on 1 July 1990, replacing the Jaguar A in the pre-strategic nuclear role.[203] After that time, two Jaguar A squadrons will still remain in the nuclear role with the AN-52 gravity bomb.

Naval aviation

Following the last *'technico-operationnelle'* launch of the ASMP missile from a Super Etendard aircraft at the CEL range on 10 October 1988,[204] the ASMP became operational in 1989 on the Super Etendards embarked on the aircraft-carrier *Foch*.[205] The total development cost of updating the 20 Super Etendard aircraft to carry the ASMP missile is 56 per cent higher than the original estimate.[206]

The French Navy plans for two nuclear-powered aircraft-carriers to replace the Clemenceau Class carriers. Construction of the first ship, the *Charles de Gaulle*, began at the Brest Naval Dockyard (DCAN) on 14 April 1989.[207] The *Charles de Gaulle* is scheduled for sea trials in mid-1997 and to enter service in late 1998.[208]

According to the official French Navy periodical *Cols Bleus*, the *Charles de Gaulle*'s power will total 82 000 hp, compared to the 126 000 hp produced by the six oil-fired boilers of France's conventional Clemenceau Class carriers. This will translate to a maximum speed of 27 knots with both

---

[199] As of July 1989; Boucheron (note 153), p. 177.

[200] 'Perspectives pour l'Armée de l'Air', *Air et Cosmos*, 28 Oct. 1989, p. 32.

[201] Up until May 1989, the Air Force had planned to acquire 112 Mirage 2000Ns for five squadrons. France decided to equip two of those squadrons with the Mirage 2000N variant, leaving only three FATAC squadrons in the nuclear role. Although it originally seemed clear that this change would entail the reduction in the number of Mirage 2000N/ASMP aircraft from 75 to 45, this is not now the case; 'French cut ASMP Mirages to 45', *Jane's Defence Weekly*, 17 June 1989, p. 1209; 'Armeé de l'Air: programmes d'armement', *Air et Cosmos*, 7 Oct. 1989, p. 31.

[202] Note 200; Boucheron (note 153), p. 427.

[203] 'La guerre electronique en vedette', *Air et Cosmos*, 29 Apr. 1989, p. 32; Boucheron (note 153), p. 240.

[204] 'Missiles', *Air Actualités*, Dec. 1988, p. 43.

[205] Aérospatiale, *Tactical Missiles* (Aérospatiale: Paris, 1989), brochure DIC/P no. 093/89, p. 15.

[206] As of July 1989; Boucheron (note 153), pp. 175, 429.

[207] 'DCN', *DGA Info*, no. 22 (June 1989), p. 9.

[208] Captain Feuilloy, 'Le porte-avions *Charles de Gaulle*', *Cols Bleus*, 9 Sep. 1989, pp. 4–5; *Air et Cosmos* (note 185).

shafts and 20 knots using a single shaft. The *Charles de Gaulle* will be powered by two compact pressurized water reactors (PWRs), derived from the propulsion unit of France's new Triomphant Class SSBN.[209] Initially (from 1998 to 2004) it will carry the nuclear-capable Super Etendard/ASMP aircraft. In the long term (after 2004), it will embark Avion de Combat Marine (ACM) aircraft, or Rafale, in nuclear strike, interception and reconnaissance roles.[210] The French Navy plans to acquire 86 Rafale ACMs.

France and arms control

In May 1989 President Mitterrand provided an indication of the current French definition of 'sufficient [strategic nuclear] weaponry for our French defence'; he placed it at 'between 300 and 400 nuclear warheads'.[211] He further stated that as of May 1989, France had 'fewer than four hundred [strategic nuclear warheads]'.[212] Although France currently has approximately 372 strategic nuclear warheads,[213] this total will jump to 452 in mid-1990, and to 516 in 1993 (upon completion of the M4 refit programme).

In April 1989 Defence Minister Jean-Pierre Chevènement rejected the suggestion by Soviet arms control official Viktor Karpov that the 44 Pluton missiles be included in any arms control negotiations concerning SRBMs.[214] In May 1989, Mitterrand ruled out the inclusion of the Hadès missile (which will replace the Pluton in 1992) in arms control negotiations, since the range of Hadès is 'still less than the 500 km that might put them, in the view of our partners even if not in ours, within the ambit of the negotiations that have just concluded on medium-range nuclear weapons'.[215] Despite this unwillingness to include French nuclear weapons in arms control talks, France and the USSR did sign an agreement in July 1989 which will 'lead to exchanges of personnel both from operational formations and at staff officer and lower levels'.[216] On 4 July the two nations also signed an agreement designed to prevent incidents at sea between their navies. The French–Soviet Incidents at Sea Agreement is similar to those signed by the USSR with the USA, the UK and the FRG.

VI. Chinese nuclear weapon programmes

Two important political events dominated 1989 in China: the Sino-Soviet summit meeting between President Gorbachev and Chinese leaders on 15–18 May, and the popular 'pro-democracy' demonstrations that led to a brutal

---

[209] Feuilloy (note 208), pp. 4–6.
[210] Feuilloy (note 208), p. 5.
[211] Note 191.
[212] Note 192, p. 5.
[213] 336 warheads on M20 and M4 missiles, 18 on the S3D missiles and 18 on the Mirage IVP/ASMP aircraft.
[214] 'Missiles', *Air et Cosmos*, 22 Apr. 1989, p. 8.
[215] Note 191.
[216] Isnard, J., 'Chevènement visit paves way for Soviet treaty', *Jane's Defence Weekly*, 22 Apr. 1989, p. 689.

military reaction against demonstrators in Beijing and in other cities in China. As a consequence of these developments, little information about Chinese nuclear weapon developments during 1989 was available. It was reported during the year that China agreed to sell nuclear- and chemical-capable SRBMs to Syria, although no missiles were delivered in 1989. If this is true, non-export versions of the missiles may be in service with the nuclear forces of the Chinese People's Liberation Army (PLA). This could possibly be the only hardware addition to China's nuclear arsenal in 1989. The final noteworthy development of the year was the announcement on 9 November that Deng Xiaoping had resigned from his post as Chairman of the Central Military Commission (CMC) of the Chinese Communist Party and appointed Jiang Zemin as his successor (see below).[217]

The Sino-Soviet summit meeting

On 15 May President Gorbachev arrived in Beijing for an historic summit meeting with China's senior leaders, the first such meeting in 30 years. The two sides stated that the meetings 'normalized' relations between them and between their Communist Parties. The meetings produced several significant results. In a speech of 17 May to the Chinese public, President Gorbachev outlined changes to Soviet military forces in the Soviet Far East, stating that 436 intermediate- and shorter-range missiles based in the eastern USSR would be eliminated under the terms of the US–Soviet INF Treaty.[218] He announced the reduction in 1989–90 of 200 000 troops in Soviet Asia, including the reduction of 12 ground force divisions, 11 air force regiments and 16 warships from the Pacific Fleet. Gorbachev also announced the reduction of 75 per cent of Soviet forces in Mongolia, including three ground divisions and 'all air units'.

Moreover, President Gorbachev stated that the USSR is restructuring its military forces deployed along the Sino-Soviet border, but is also 'prepared to work for the withdrawal, on terms to be agreed with China, of military units and armaments from the border areas, leaving only personnel required for performing routine border duties'.[219] As stated in their joint communiqué of 18 May, 'both sides agreed to take measures to reduce armed forces in the area of the Sino-Soviet border to a minimum level in line with normal and good neighbourly relations between the two countries'.[220] This proposed demilitarization of the Sino-Soviet border would represent a radical change from the military situation that has existed for nearly 30 years and could lead to possibilities for other measures of military restraint or arms control involving China. If Sino-Soviet relations continue to improve and the military competition between them diminishes further, it would offer China

---

[217] Southerland, D., 'Deng resigns his last Party post', *Washington Post,* 10 Nov. 1989, p. A-1.

[218] For the text of Gorbachev's speech, see 'Mikhail Gorbachev's Address to Representatives of the Chinese Public', in *Visit of Mikhail Gorbachev to China, May 15–18, 1989: Documents and Materials* (Novosti Press Agency Publishing House: Moscow, 1989), pp. 10–26.

[219] Note 218, p. 13.

[220] Note 218, p. 62.

an opportunity to reduce its military and nuclear weapon programmes correspondingly.

Tiananmen Square

Ironically, Gorbachev's visit served as a source of inspiration for the students in Tiananmen Square who were advocating political reform and increased democracy in China. After a long confrontation and a growing mass of demonstrators, the Chinese leadership decided to quash the demonstrations with brutal force on 4 June. Hundreds of unarmed demonstrators were killed by soldiers of the PLA, an act that shook the faith of many Chinese people. The consequent upheaval and crackdown, including the imposition of martial law in Beijing, occupied the Chinese leaders and the PLA for much of the year and thus delayed some previously scheduled military activities, such as the testing of conventional weapons.[221] It is not known whether the nuclear weapon programme was affected by the military and political response to the demonstrations.

Missile sales

During 1989 there were continuing reports that Syria was trying to acquire Chinese M-Type SRBMs known in the West as the M-9.[222] In 1988, after the sale of Chinese DF-3A ballistic missiles to Saudi Arabia was revealed, several US officials expressed concern about Chinese missile sales to Chinese leaders in Beijing and believed they had an understanding from the Chinese Government that it would not sell ballistic missiles to other Middle Eastern nations.[223] It is reported that Syrian officials reached an agreement with China in Beijing in May and, according to an official of the Israeli Defence Ministry, deliveries of the first missiles are expected to begin in mid-1990.[224]

China has offered the M-9 for sale at arms exhibitions and advertised its capabilities (see table 1.7).[225] Its 600-km range puts it in the class of shorter-range missiles eliminated under the US–Soviet INF Treaty.[226] The missile is 9.1 metres long, 1 metre wide, is carried and launched by a truck and has a

---

[220] Note 218, p. 62.

[221] For example, a Beijing TV broadcast of 2 Aug. reported that the Bacheng weapon testing centre had accelerated its test schedule to make up for time lost during the military reaction to the demonstrations. See 'Conventional weapons tested after delay', in US Department of Commerce, Foreign Broadcast Information Service (FBIS), *China Daily* (hereafter referred to as FBIS-CHI-89-), 3 Aug. 1989, p. 36.

[222] See Senator Helms's speech 'Red China's ballistic missile sales to Syria', with related articles in *Congressional Record*, vol. 135, no. 164 (20 Nov. 1989), pp. S16261–62.

[223] See SIPRI, *SIPRI Yearbook 1989: World Armaments and Disarmament* (Oxford University Press: Oxford, 1989), pp. 36–37.

[224] Reported on the NBC Nightly News, with Tom Brokaw, 21 Nov. 1989.

[225] US Defense Intelligence Agency, *A Guide to Foreign Tactical Nuclear Weapon Systems Under the Control of Ground Force Commanders*, DST-1040S-541-87, 4 Sep. 1987, p. 79, shows a photo of the missile, labelled 'M-9/SST-600', on display and presents a table of its advertised characteristics.

[226] Syria is said to have taken an interest in the M-9 when the USSR refused to sell Syria its SS-23 missiles, all of which have been destroyed under the INF Treaty.

lift-off weight of 6.2 tons. It is the first Chinese land-based ballistic missile to use solid fuel.[227] Using an inertial guidance system, its accuracy is advertised to be less than 0.1 per cent of the range used, or about 600 m at maximum range. Thus it is well suited to carry a nuclear warhead, as it may be designed to do for Chinese use, or a chemical warhead. It is possible that the missile is already or will be in service with the PLA before being sold to foreign nations, as has been previous Chinese practice. China is not involved in the Missile Technology Control Regime effort to stem the proliferation of ballistic missile capabilities (see also chapter 9). It is reported that Libya is also interested in acquiring M-9 missiles.

On 8 December President Bush sent two high-level aides to Beijing on a secretive and controversial trip to improve US–Chinese relations. The US officials raised the subject of Chinese missile sales with Chinese leaders and reportedly received non-proliferation assurances from the Chinese.[228] Following the one-day visit, the Chinese Foreign Ministry issued a statement saying that, except for the sale of DF-3A missiles to Saudi Arabia, 'China has never sold, nor is planning to sell missiles to any Middle East country'.[229] It was later revealed that the same two aides had already visited China in July on a secret mission, about which little was acknowledged.

Other developments

Besides the possible addition of M-9 SRBMs to China's nuclear forces, no other significant Chinese nuclear weapon developments are known to have taken place in 1989, although it appears that gradual modernization of the nuclear forces continued.

Some previously unreported facts were revealed during 1989 about China's nuclear submarine force. In a series of newspaper articles, China's ballistic missile submarine unit was identified as 'Unit 09', commanded by Rear Admiral Yang.[230] The articles reported that from late 1985 to early 1986 a Chinese SSBN navigated more than 20 000 nautical miles (37 000 km) and 'broke the 84-day record of continuous underwater navigation set by an American submarine'. In the spring of 1988 a Chinese nuclear submarine reportedly navigated the Taiwan Strait into the South China Sea and conducted a 'successful test voyage at extreme depths'.

In April it was reported that a new degaussing ship had become operational in the Chinese Navy.[231] The large ship, named *Dongqin No. 863,* is designed to reduce or remove the magnetic signature of submarines and ships before they go on patrol, thus making them more difficult to detect by

---

[227] See SIPRI, *SIPRI Yearbook 1988: World Armaments and Disarmament* (Oxford University Press: Oxford, 1988), p. 53.

[228] Sciolino, E., 'President defends aides' China visit', *New York Times,* 12 Dec. 1989, p. A9.

[229] Oberdorfter, D. and Hoffman, D., 'Scowcroft warned China of new Hill sanctions', *Washington Post,* 15 Dec. 1989, pp. A1, A39.

[230] 'Ta Kung Pao on nuclear submarine base', FBIS-CHI-89-091, 12 May 1989, pp. 32–33. Two articles appeared in *Ta Kung Pao,* by Chung Ti, 'Visit to China's nuclear submarine unit', 7 May 1989, p. 1, and 8 May 1989, p. 2.

[231] 'Large degaussing ship operational in PLA Navy', FBIS-CHI-89-070, 13 Apr. 1989, pp. 22–23.

magnetic means and less susceptible to magnetically fuzed mines. This would be especially important for China's SSBN force because it has a relatively small number of submarines.

It was reported in a Chinese newspaper that the Institute of Engineering of the Second Artillery Corps—China's nuclear weapon command—had completed a 'large, integrated guided missile training simulator' for training missile launch techniques.[232] Given the high costs of missiles and missile testing, the simulator is intended to permit training military personnel in missile launch operations without firing actual missiles. This would give nuclear missile launch officers an affordable training option.

Deng's resignation

Despite resigning from his last official Communist Party position as Chairman of the CMC, it is widely believed that Deng will maintain his predominant influence in making Chinese policy for the foreseeable future and may thus continue to be regarded as China's paramount leader. Nevertheless, his resignation opens the question of who has political control of China's nuclear forces. Traditionally, the Chairman of the Communist Party Central Military Commission has been the only individual who could authorize the use of nuclear weapons. Without his personal approval, no nuclear weapons are to be launched. Since the founding of the People's Republic of China in 1949 there have been only four Chairmen of the CMC: Mao Zedong, Hua Guofeng, Deng Xiaoping and now Jiang Zemin. Deng might manage to retain his personal authority regarding the military and nuclear weapons—a *de facto* nuclear command authority—which would mean that the CMC could not act without his approval, even though he is no longer its Chairman. In any event, it should prove interesting to observe the evolution of political control over Chinese nuclear forces within the CMC, absent Deng.

---

[232] 'Scientists complete missile training simulator', FBIS-CHI-89-079, 26 Apr. 1989, p. 30.

2. Nuclear explosions

RAGNHILD FERM

I. Introduction

The United States, the Soviet Union, the United Kingdom and France continued nuclear testing in 1989. A total of 27 tests were conducted during the year, a number which is considerably lower than the yearly average for the past 28 years (excluding 1986 when the Soviet test moratorium was in effect). This was because the USA and the USSR conducted fewer tests than usual (eleven and seven respectively). However, France carried out eight explosions—the same number as in the six preceding years—and the UK one (in co-operation with the USA). China did not conduct any tests at all in 1989. All nuclear tests in 1989 were below the 150-kiloton limit stipulated in the 1974 US–Soviet Threshold Test Ban Treaty (TTBT). For the first time in almost three decades no so-called peaceful nuclear explosion (PNE) was conducted.

The progress made in 1989 towards a limitation of nuclear testing is documented in chapter 15.

II. Nuclear explosions in 1989

US explosions

According to available records the number of US tests in 1989 was the lowest since 1961. No unannounced tests were detected. The seismic array operated by the California Institute of Technology (Caltech) now has about 200 stations and can detect all but the smallest US tests. Yields can generally be estimated within a factor of 30 per cent or less once the proper site calibration has been included. It is maintained that with the Caltech equipment and other monitors it is possible to detect events at the Nevada test site down to 0.1 kiloton.[1]

In October 1989 the US congressional Office of Technology Assessment (OTA) issued a report on the possible health risks connected with nuclear testing at the Nevada test site. It generally discounts allegations by activists living near the test site that US authorities have played down testing risks and not provided adequate warning of potential radiation leaks. The OTA report states that the 126 underground nuclear tests conducted since 1970 have released only a tiny fraction of the radioactive material released by tests conducted before 1970, not to mention that emitted by the early atmospheric tests at the Nevada test site. Nevertheless the report criticizes the secrecy surrounding the US testing programme, suggests that all tests could

---

[1] Geary, R. R., 'Nevada test site's dirty little secrets', *Bulletin of the Atomic Scientists*, Apr. 1989.

be announced and recommends that more information be made available to local residents to mitigate their concern over the testing programme.[2]

Soviet explosions

The Soviet Union conducted 10 fewer nuclear explosions in 1989 than in the previous year. The body-wave magnitudes of the Soviet explosions registered by the Hagfors Observatory of the Swedish National Defence Research Institute (FOA) suggest that the explosions were slightly smaller than those conducted in 1988. All Soviet nuclear tests during the year took place at the Semipalatinsk test site in East Kazakhstan (the second test site, in use since the 1950s, is on the island of Novaya Zemlya in the Arctic Ocean). The fact that no explosions occurred outside the known weapon testing sites may indicate that the Soviet programme of explosions for non-military purposes is being phased out. The USSR probably started conducting PNEs in the late 1960s for various purposes, for example, the creation of underground storage areas for gas, and stimulation of gas and oil production. In 1982, 1983 and 1984 more than 45 per cent of the Soviet nuclear explosions were conducted outside the official test sites, probably for the above-mentioned and other purposes. PNEs were resumed after the Soviet test moratorium (August 1985–February 1987) but not to the same extent as in the years before the moratorium. The USA conducted its last PNE in 1973 and formally terminated its PNE programme in 1977. Public concern over environmental issues and diminished interest in PNE uses on the part of industry were among the reasons for bringing it to an end—reasons which may also be valid in the Soviet Union today.

Public concern in the USSR about nuclear testing increased in 1989. An interdepartmental commission, appointed to investigate the state of the environment and the health of the population in the Semipalatinsk area where most Soviet tests have been conducted, presented its results in July 1989. The local population expressed distrust of the commission's conclusion that the level of radiation near the test site did not exceed background levels.[3] However, in order to take account of the concerns of local residents, the commission recommended a reduction in the number of tests and their yield. The commission also investigated the leak of radioactive gas from the Soviet nuclear test carried out on 12 February 1989 and concluded that a partial leak of inert radioactive gases in Semipalatinsk presented no danger to local residents.

A public movement, 'Nevada–Semipalatinsk', was founded after the 12 February incident. Its programme includes a test ban, and in the autumn of 1989 a series of demonstrations against tests, organized by the movement and members of several international organizations, including the International Physicians for the Prevention of Nuclear War, were held near

---

[2] US Congress, Office of Technology Assessment, *The Containment of Underground Nuclear Explosions* (OTA–ISC–414) (US Government Printing Office: Washington, DC, May 1988), pp. 3–7, 76–78.

[3] *FBIS-SOV-89-154*, 11 Aug. 1989, pp. 87–89, citing an article in *Krasnaya Zvezda*, 21 July 1989.

the Semipalatinsk test site. There have also been protests concerning environmental pollution in the area around the Semipalatinsk test site. Soviet mass media have reported on unacceptable environmental conditions in the region, where it is claimed that the death rate from leukaemia and other forms of cancer is increasing.[4] In addition a spokesman for the opponents of the testing activities claimed that the 19 October 1989 test caused an earthquake.[5] As a consequence of the protests and an increased awareness of the effects of nuclear testing the Supreme Soviet of Kazakhstan requested that the authorities close the test site.[6] Probably as a result of the protests, the Soviet Prime Minister announced in November 1989 that no more tests would be carried out in 1989.[7] According to available records, no Soviet tests were conducted from January to mid-March 1990.

On 27 November 1989 the Supreme Soviet adopted a resolution on 'urgent measures to overhaul the country's ecology'.[8] In one section of the resolution the Soviet Defence Ministry and the Ministry of Nuclear Energy, Engineering and Industry were urged to consider ceasing nuclear tests at the Semipalatinsk test site and to submit proposals at the beginning of 1990 for measures to be taken. In addition, the Soviet Council of Ministers is requested to study the environmental effects of the nuclear tests that have been carried out at the Novaya Zemlya test site. The mass media assumed that the Soviet Government intends to move all future tests to this test site.[9] This has raised concerns in Norway and caused the Government to ask Soviet authorities for clarification.[10] However, by late March 1990, no decision had been taken by the Supreme Soviet.[11]

In his speech before the UN General Assembly in September 1989[12] the Soviet Foreign Minister stated that the USSR had revised its nuclear testing programme both in terms of the number and yield of explosions. He also reiterated the Soviet proposal for a US–Soviet moratorium on nuclear explosions.

French explosions

Despite vigorous international protests, France continued its nuclear weapon tests in the Tuamotu archipelago of French Polynesia. France has refused to sign the protocols to the South Pacific Nuclear Weapon Free Zone Treaty (the Treaty of Rarotonga), which include a prohibition on nuclear tests in the South Pacific region.

[4] *FBIS-SOV-89-198*, 16 Oct. 1989, pp. 101–103.
[5] *Dagens Nyheter*, 24 Oct. 1989.
[6] *Moscow News*, 17 Dec. 1989.
[7] *FBIS-SOV-89-222*, 20 Nov. 1989, p. 66.
[8] 'Resolution of the USSR Supreme Soviet on urgent measures to overhaul the country's ecology', published in *Pravda*, 3 Dec. 1989.
[9] See, for example, 'Soviets to close major site of underground atomic tests', *Washington Post*, 10 Mar. 1990.
[10] *International Herald Tribune*, 3–4 Mar. 1990.
[11] *Izvestia*, 10 Mar. 1990.
[12] UN document A/44/PV.6, 27 Sep. 1989.

On 27 November 1989 a test was conducted at the Fangataufa atoll, where the most powerful French tests are carried out. Estimated by the New Zealand observatory in the Cook islands at 90 kt this was the largest French test in 10 years.

The French Government announced in June 1989 that the number of nuclear tests would be reduced, mainly to cut defence costs.[13] The French Prime Minister visited the South Pacific region in August–September and paid a three-day visit to French Polynesia. He then confirmed that the tests would be reduced from eight to six per year but stressed that this cut-back would keep testing at a strictly adapted level sufficient to ensure the efficacy of French weapons.[14] He has also stated that France should not yield to pressure from Pacific governments to end the tests, and ruled out the possibility of a referendum, requested by local politicians opposing the tests, on the tests conducted in French Polynesia.

Whenever criticism is voiced concerning testing in French Polynesia, French authorities refer to earlier investigations that supposedly demonstrate that the tests pose no health risk to the residents nor any harm to the environment.[15] Although there has been no investigation by medical experts of the relation of health problems to nuclear testing, it has been claimed that leukaemia, thyroid cancer and brain tumours have increased among the population. In addition Australian scientific experts argue that nuclear testing in the Pacific could be partly responsible for the dramatic rise in *ciguatera* food poisoning among the islanders over the past 30 years.[16] Between 1970 and 1984 *ciguatera* poisoning increased tenfold in French Polynesia. The damage caused by the nuclear explosions to the coral reefs and the subsequent disruption of the ecology of the atolls seem to be the only explanations for this increase.[17]

[13] *Le Monde*, 9 June 1989.

[14] *Le Monde*, 29 Aug. 1989.

[15] For details of investigations conducted in 1982, 1983 and 1987, see *SIPRI Yearbooks 1984, 1985* and *1989*.

[16] *Ciguatera* is a disease that results from eating certain species of tropical fish containing toxins produced by coral reef dinoflagellate plankton species. The toxins have no observable effect on fish.

[17] Ruff, T. A., '*Ciguatera* in the Pacific: a link with military activities', *The Lancet*, vol. 1 (28 Jan. 1989), pp. 201–204.

Appendix 2A. Nuclear explosions, 1945–89

Table 2A.1. Registered nuclear explosions in 1989

Date	Origin time (GMT)	Latitude (deg)	Longitude (deg)	Region	Body wave magnitude[a]
USA					
10 Feb.	200600.0	37.077 N	116.001 W	Nevada	5.4
24 Feb.	161500.0	37.128 N	116.122 W	Nevada	
9 Mar.	140500.0	37.143 N	116.067 W	Nevada	5.1
15 May	131000.0	37.108 N	116.121 W	Nevada	4.6
26 May	180700.0	37.086 N	116.055 W	Nevada	
22 June	211500.8	37.283 N	116.412 W	Nevada	5.4
27 June	153102	37. N	116. W	Nevada	5.3
14 Sep.	150000.1	37.236 N	116.163 W	Nevada	
31 Oct.	153000.0	37. N	116. W	Nevada	5.6
15 Nov.	202000.1	37.107	116.013W	Nevada	
20 Dec.				Nevada	
USSR					
22 Jan.	035706.6	49.924 N	78.831 E	E. Kazakhstan	
12 Feb.	041506.8	49.925 N	78.740 E	E. Kazakhstan	7.0
17 Feb.	040106.9	49.868 N	78.079 E	E. Kazakhstan	5.1
8 July	034657.6	49.873 N	78.815 E	E. Kazakhstan	6.8
2 Sep.	041702.0	50.023 N	79.045 E	E. Kazakhstan	5.8
4 Oct.	113006.0	50. N	78. E	E. Kazakhstan	5.2
19 Oct.	094957.0	49.928 N	79.016 E	E. Kazakhstan	6.8
UK					
8 Dec.	150002.0			Nevada	5.7
France					
11 May	164458.1	21.881 S	138.978 W	Mururoa	5.6
20 May	175900	21. S	139. W	Mururoa	4.5
3 June	172958.4	21.832 S	139.010 W	Mururoa	5.0
10 June	172958.1	22.252 S	138.740 W	Fangataufa	5.5
24 Oct.	162957	21. S	139. W	Mururoa	5.4
31 Oct.	165700	21. S	139. W	Mururoa	5.2
20 Nov.	172900			Mururoa	5.3
27 Nov.	170000			Fangataufa	5.6

[a] Body wave magnitude (m_b) indicates the size of the event. m_b data for the US, Soviet and British tests were provided by the Hagfors Observatory of the Swedish National Defence Research Institute (FOA) and data for the French tests by the Australian Seismological Centre, Bureau of Mineral Resources, Canberra.

Table 2A.2. Estimated number of nuclear explosions 16 July 1945–5 August 1963 (the signing of the Partial Test Ban Treaty)

a = atmospheric
u = underground

Year	USA a	USA u	USSR a	USSR u	UK a	UK u	France a	France u	Total
1945	3	0							3
1946	2[a]	0							2
1947	0	0							0
1948	3	0							3
1949	0	0	1	0					1
1950	0	0	0	0					0
1951	15	1	2	0					18
1952	10	0	0	0	1	0			11
1953	11	0	4	0	2	0			17
1954	6	0	7	0	0	0			13
1955	17[a]	1	5[a]	0	0	0			23
1956	18	0	9	0	6	0			33
1957	27	5	15[a]	0	7	0			54
1958	62[b]	15	29	0	5	0			111
1949–58, exact years unknown			18						18
1959	0	0	0	0	0	0			0
1960	0	0	0	0	0	0	3	0	3
1961	0	10	50[a]	1	0	0	1	1	63
1962	39[a]	57	43	1	0	2	0	1	143
1 Jan.–5 Aug. 1963	4	25	0	0	0	0	0	2	31
Total	**217**	**114**	**183[c]**	**2**	**21**	**2**	**4**	**4**	**547**

[a] One of these tests was carried out under water.

[b] Two of these tests were carried out under water.

[c] The total figure for Soviet atmospheric tests includes the 18 additional tests conducted in the period 1949–58, for which exact years are not available.

Table 2A.3. Estimated number of nuclear explosions 6 August 1963–31 December 1989

a = atmospheric
u = underground

Year	USA[a] a	USA[a] u	USSR a	USSR u	UK[a] a	UK[a] u	France a	France u	China a	China u	India a	India u	Total
6 Aug.–31 Dec. 1963	0	15	0	0	0	0	0	1					16
1964	0	38	0	6	0	1	0	3	1	0			49
1965	0	36	0	9	0	1	0	4	1	0			51
1966	0	43	0	15	0	0	5[b]	1	3	0			67
1967	0	34	0	17	0	0	3	0	2	0			56
1968	0	45[c]	0	13	0	0	5	0	1	0			64

Table 2A.3. *cont.*

Year	USA[a] a	USA[a] u	USSR a	USSR u	UK[a] a	UK[a] u	France a	France u	China a	China u	India a	India u	Total
1969	0	38	0	16	0	0	0	0	1	1			**56**
1970	0	35	0	17	0	0	8	0	1	0			**61**
1971	0	17	0	19	0	0	5[b]	0	1	0			**42**
1972	0	18	0	22	0	0	3	0	2	0			**45**
1973	0	16[d]	0	14	0	0	5	0	1	0			**36**
1974	0	14	0	18	0	1	7[b]	0	1	0	0	1	**42**
1975	0	20	0	15	0	0	0	2	0	1	0	0	**38**
1976	0	18	0	17	0	1	0	4	3	1	0	0	**44**
1977	0	19	0	18	0	0	0	8[e]	1	0	0	0	**46**
1978	0	17	0	27	0	2	0	8	2	1	0	0	**57**
1979	0	15	0	29	0	1	0	9	1[f]	0	0	0	**55**
1980	0	14	0	21	0	3	0	13	1	0	0	0	**52**
1981	0	16	0	22	0	1	0	12	0	0	0	0	**51**
1982	0	18	0	31	0	1	0	6	0	1	0	0	**57**
1983	0	17	0	27	0	1	0	9	0	2	0	0	**56**
1984	0	17	0	29	0	2	0	8	0	2	0	0	**58**
1985	0	17	0	9	0	1	0	8	0	0	0	0	**35**
1986	0	14	0	0	0	1	0	8	0	0	0	0	**23**
1987	0	14	0	23	0	1	0	8	0	1	0	0	**47**
1988	0	14	0	17	0	0	0	8	0	1	0	0	**40**
1989	0	11	0	7	0	1	0	8	0	0	0	0	**27**
Total	**0**	**590**	**0**	**458**	**0**	**19**	**41**	**128**	**23**	**11**	**0**	**1**	**1271**

[a] See note *a* below.
[b] One more test was conducted this year, but it did not cause any detonation.
[c] Five devices used simultaneously in the same test are counted here as one explosion.
[d] Three devices used simultaneously in the same test are counted here as one explosion.
[e] Two of these tests may have been conducted in 1975 or 1976.
[f] This explosion may have been conducted underground.

Table 2A.4. Estimated number of nuclear explosions 16 July 1945–31 Dec. 1989

USA[a]	USSR	UK[a]	France	China	India	Total
921	643	42	177	34	1	1818

[a] All British tests from 1962 have been conducted jointly with the United States at the Nevada Test Site. Therefore, the number of US tests is actually higher than indicated here.

Sources for tables 2A.1–2A.4

Swedish National Defence Research Institute (FOA), various estimates; Norris, R. S., Cochran, T. B. and Arkin, W. M., 'Known US nuclear tests July 1945 to 31 December 1988', *Nuclear Weapons Databook*, Working Paper no. 86–2 (Rev. 2C) (Natural Resources Defense Council: Washington, DC, Jan. 1989); Australian Seismological Centre, Bureau of Mineral Resources, Geology and Geophysics, Canberra; Cochran, T. B., Arkin, W. M., Norris, R. S. and Sands, J. I., *Nuclear Weapons Databook, Vol. IV, Soviet Nuclear Weapons* (Harper & Row: New York, 1989), chapter 10; Burrows, A. S., Norris, R. S., Arkin, W. M. and Cochran, T. B., 'French nuclear testing, 1960–88', *Nuclear Weapons Databook*, Working Paper no. 89–1 (NRDC: Washington, DC, Feb. 1989); 'Known Chinese nuclear tests, 1964–1988', *Bulletin of the Atomic Scientists* (Oct. 1989), p. 48 (see also Nov., p. 52); and various estimates.

3. Military use of outer space

JOHN PIKE

I. Introduction

The dramatic changes in the Soviet Union and Eastern Europe during 1989 have had opposite effects on Soviet and US military space programmes.[1] While *perestroika* in the Soviet Union has led to the lowest number of space launches in almost two decades[2] and an extensive public debate over the level of spending on space,[3] the US military space effort has largely ignored international developments.

II. Soviet strategic defence programmes

The most notable development in the Soviet anti-missile programme[4] during 1989 was the completion of upgrades of the Moscow anti-missile installations.[5] Since the early 1980s the Soviet Union has gradually upgraded the elements of the anti-missile system around Moscow that is permitted under the Anti-Ballistic Missile (ABM) Treaty.[6] Despite these improvements, the Moscow system is not judged to pose a significant threat to the capability of US strategic missiles to reach their targets.[7]

The SH-11 long-range exo-atmospheric interceptor missile (smaller than the massive Galosh) is a three-stage rocket with a range of 300 km and a multi-megaton warhead. The SH-08 short-range endo-atmospheric interceptor probably has two stages, solid fuel, a range of about 100 km and a low-yield nuclear warhead. It is similar in design and mission to the US Sprint missile, although its maximum acceleration is reportedly significantly lower. The Pill Box phased-array battle management radar (which replaced the Try Add radars at Moscow ABM sites) is similar in function to US Missile Site

---

[1] Many aspects of the discussion of Soviet military space activities are based on discussions with Nicholas Johnson, as well as Michael Cassut, Geoffrey Perry and Saunders Kramer. Over the years their works have provided the essential core of insight into the Soviet space effort. Although their individual contributions are not adequately recognized in the following footnotes, many of the sources are based on their careful monitoring of Soviet flight activity. Their assistance in the preparation of this work is greatly appreciated, although the responsibility for the interpretations in this chapter is the author's alone.

[2] 'Soviet ends year with lowest launch total since 1972', *Soviet Aerospace*, 15 Jan. 1990, p. 4.

[3] 'Roundtable discussion on Soviet space exploration', *JPRS-USP*, 89-010, 22 Nov. 1989, pp. 56–60.

[4] Zaloga, S., *Soviet Air Defence Missiles* (Jane's Information Group: Coulsdon, Surrey, 1989), pp. 11848, is the source for the discussion below. This book provides unprecedented detail in describing Soviet strategic defence systems, and must rank as one of the more significant books of 1989.

[5] Statement of the Director of Central Intelligence Before the Senate Armed Services Committee, 23 Jan. 1990, p. 6.

[6] Department of Defense, *Soviet Military Power 1987* (US Government Printing Office: Washington, DC, Mar. 1987), pp. 46–50.

[7] *Department of Defense Appropriations for Fiscal Year 1990*, US Senate Appropriations Committee, Defense Subcommittee, 101st Congress, 1st Session, part 6, pp. 300–301.

Radar of the Sentinel and Safeguard systems. This radar, located in the Moscow suburb of Pushkino, provides 360° coverage, supplementing the coverage provided by the older Dog House and Cat House radars.[8] The Pechora-type bistatic phased-array early-warning radar will supplement the older Hen House radars. Deployment began in the late 1970s, and a total of 11 are currently operational or under construction.[9]

Soviet attitudes towards the future roles of strategic defences in general, and towards the US Strategic Defense Initiative (SDI) in particular, appear to be in a state of flux. For instance, Alexei Arbatov, long noted for his criticism of the SDI programme, has written favourably about the prospects of deploying a thin nationwide system 'for defense from a strike by terrorists or other possible nuclear powers, from unsanctioned and accidental launchings',[10] such as has been suggested by Senator Sam Nunn and others in the United States. But Arbatov was strongly criticized by Major General I. Liubimov of the Main Political Administration of the Soviet armed forces. Liubimov notes that, 'As is known, the USSR has taken most important unilateral solutions [including] renunciation of anti-satellite weapons testing', while Defense Secretary Richard Cheney is 'holding out for the continuation of works on the SDI programme'. He concludes that Arbatov's suggestion for a thin nationwide anti-missile system 'would practically signify a withdrawal from the ABM Pact. The Soviet Union takes a decisive stand against such a position'.[11]

III. US strategic defence programmes

Although many observers expected President Bush to moderate Ronald Reagan's enthusiasm for SDI, the Bush Administration has expressed strong support for the programme. Defense Secretary Cheney noted that, 'I have been a strong advocate of SDI. I remain a strong advocate of SDI. I prefer the broad interpretation of the [ABM] Treaty. I think it is the correct interpretation of the Treaty'.[12] Although 1989 was the first year in which the Congress actually reduced the budget of the Strategic Defense Initiative Organization (SDIO) below the previous year's level, these reductions are expected to have little impact on the course of the programme (see also chapter 5).

The only significant test under the SDI programme was the 24 March 1989 launch of the Delta Star sensor satellite,[13] which continued operations

[8] Goure, D., 'Soviet radars: the eyes of Soviet defenses', *Military Technology*, no. 5 (1988), pp. 36–38.

[9] Gertz, B., 'CIA warns of verification woes in future treaty', *Washington Times*, 21 Dec. 1988, p. A3.

[10] Arbatov, A., 'How much defense is sufficient?', *International Affairs* (Moscow), Mar. 1989.

[11] Liubimov, I., 'On the sufficiency of defense and the insufficiency of competence', *The Communist of the Armed Forces*, no. 16 (Aug. 1989). This polemical exchange was analysed in Bishop, L., *The Soviet Defense Debate: A Review Essay* (American Committee on US–Soviet Relations: Washington, DC, Sep. 1989) from which the English translation of these passages is taken.

[12] US Senate Appropriations Committee (note 7), p. 27.

[13] Kolcum, E., 'SDIO begins measuring booster plumes with Delta Star sensors', *Aviation Week & Space Technology*, 3 Apr. 1989, pp. 26–27.

throughout the year.[14] The primary mission of Delta Star was to improve capabilities for tracking Soviet missiles during the boost phase of their flight.[15] The second SPEAR (Space Power Experiment Aboard Rocket) flight, originally planned for August, was delayed until early 1990.[16]

The Phase One SDI system

The initial plans for actually deploying SDI systems were established in August 1987, when the Defense Acquisition Board authorized plans for the demonstration and validation of the weapons and sensors needed for a system that could be deployed in the mid- to late 1990s.[17] Despite a number of changes since then, the overall plan remains largely the same.[18] The primary mission defined for the system was the protection of US land-based missile silos from a Soviet counterforce attack. The system was required to demonstrate the ability to intercept 50 per cent of the Soviet force of 308 SS-18 ICBMs (which currently constitute the core of the Soviet counter-silo capability) as well as 30 per cent of all Soviet missile warheads. (START would lessen the demands upon the defence system.)

This initial phase of deployment of a strategic defence system would consist of both space-based and ground-based weapon and sensor systems.[19] The SDIO estimates that deployment of this initial phase of the strategic defence system could be accomplished for slightly less than $70 billion. Following a go-ahead for deployment of the system in 1993, the system would achieve an initial operational capability around 1998, with a full operational capability early in the 21st century.

Space-based interceptors and 'Brilliant Pebbles'

The initial boost-phase layer of the strategic defence system would consist of Space-Based Interceptors (SBI) that would home in on the hot exhaust plume of Soviet missiles during the first few minutes of their flight. Each SBI platform would carry 5–10 interceptor rockets, each weighing about 100 kg, as well as target-tracking sensors. The interceptors would also be used to attack Soviet post-boost vehicles as they dispensed their multiple warheads.

The initial tests of the SBI are planned for 1990. In addition, the first of two tests of the Air Force LEAP (Lightweight Exoatmospheric Advanced Projectile) system built by Boeing is anticipated in 1990, with a second test in 1991 and a test of a more sophisticated Army version to follow.[20]

[14] 'Delta Star cruises through first five months', *SDI Monitor*, 4 Sep. 1989.
[15] 'Delta Star mission includes laser detection system', *SDI Monitor*, 3 Apr. 1989, pp. 91–93.
[16] 'Milspace testing', *Military Space*, 28 Aug. 1989, p. 8.
[17] Gilmartin, T., 'Pentagon advisory panel chairman urges gradual evolutionary approach to SDI', *Defense News*, 25 July 1988, p. 30.
[18] Norman, C., 'Cut price plan offered for SDI deployment', *Science*, 7 Oct. 1988, pp. 24–25.
[19] See Pike, J., 'Military use of outer space', SIPRI, *SIPRI Yearbook 1989: World Armaments and Disarmament* (Oxford University Press: Oxford, 1989), note 9, p. 85.
[20] 'Air Force gets ready for first LEAP test flight', *SDI Monitor*, 5 Jan. 1990, pp. 3–4.

Over time the contribution of SBI to the architecture for the initial deployment of the strategic defence system has declined. The original 1987 plan called for approximately 3000 interceptors to be carried on approximately 300 carrier vehicle satellites. By 1988 plans called for about 1500 interceptors deployed on about 150 carrier vehicle satellites.[21]

The most significant change in SBI plans came in early 1989 with intense examination of the so-called Brilliant Pebbles concept (the name implying improved capabilities compared with the SBI 'smart rocks').[22] Proposed by Lawrence Livermore National Laboratory scientist Lowell Wood (who had previously championed the nuclear-bomb pumped X-ray laser), the Brilliant Pebble concept differed from the more traditional SBI concept in several respects.[23] Instead of grouping interceptors together in carrier vehicle satellites, each Brilliant Pebble would orbit separately, improving the survivability of the system by presenting a less attractive target for Soviet attack. This dispersal, as well as the use of advanced construction techniques, would also permit each Brilliant Pebble to weigh about 40 kg, compared to the 100 kg of the traditional SBI. The overall cost of the system would be reduced by building each Brilliant Pebble using commercially available sensor and computer hardware. Each Brilliant Pebble would have powerful sensors on board for tracking Soviet missiles that would eliminate the need for expensive satellite sensors such as the Booster Surveillance and Tracking System (BSTS). Powerful computers on-board each Brilliant Pebble (with the computing power of a Cray 1 supercomputer) would direct each Pebble to its target, eliminating the need for expensive communications systems for ground control.

The Brilliant Pebbles concept was endorsed by outgoing SDIO Director Lt-Gen. James Abrahamson,[24] as well as SDIO's new Director Lt-Gen. George Monahan. Vice-President Dan Quayle endorsed Pebbles, saying that 'it could revolutionize much of our thinking about strategic defense if it shows the promise that is expected'.[25] With this high-level support,[26] Brilliant Pebbles quickly became a focus of SDI effort,[27] as it promised to increase the credibility of SDI as a competitor to mobile missiles in reducing the vulnerability of US strategic forces to a Soviet counterforce attack.[28]

All of these claims were soon challenged.[29] The thousands of separately orbiting Brilliant Pebbles would dwarf the number of military satellites

[21] Stroble, W., 'Ex-Head of SDI touts Brilliant Pebbles plan', *Washington Times*, 14 Mar. 1989, p. A4.

[22] Bennet, R., 'Brilliant Pebbles', *Reader's Digest*, Sep. 1989, pp. 128–32 provides a useful although uncritical background.

[23] This description of Brilliant Pebbles is based on Wood, L., 'Brilliant Pebbles missile defense concept advocated by Livermore scientist', *Aviation Week & Space Technology*, 13 June 1988, pp. 151–55; and Wood, L., *Concerning Advanced Architectures for Strategic Defense*, Lawrence Livermore National Laboratory Preprint, UCRL-98424, 13 Mar. 1988.

[24] Abrahamson, J., *End of Tour Report*, letter to the Deputy Secretary of Defense, 9 Feb. 1989.

[25] 'Quayle backs SDI, promotes Brilliant Pebbles', *Aerospace Daily*, 24 Mar. 1989, p. 467.

[26] Barnes, F., 'Pebbles go bam-bam', *New Republic*, 17 Apr. 1989, pp. 12–15.

[27] 'SDIO examines accelerated Brilliant Pebbles testing', *SDI Monitor*, 17 Apr. 1989, pp. 103–104.

[28] 'Too brilliant by half', *New Republic*, 29 May 1989, pp. 7–8.

[29] Bennett, C., 'Brilliant Pebbles? No, loose marbles', *New York Times*, 17 June 1989.

currently in orbit (about five dozen) and would totally overwhelm satellite control facilities.[30] The low cost claimed for each Pebble ($100 000) was considered to be a factor of 10 too low,[31] since it was lower than the cost of a regular air-to-air missile and based in part on the purchase of up to 100 000 Pebbles.[32] The applicability of commercially available hardware to the rigours of the space environment was not generally accepted, nor was the ability of the Pebble's sensors to replace BSTS satellites or the ability to produce the miniature supercomputer.[33] Furthermore, it was feared that the computerized autonomy of each Pebble would lead to a system outside human control.[34]

After a year's study,[35] much of the initial promise of Brilliant Pebbles seemed unlikely to materialize.[36] However, plans were beginning to focus on a system that would include 1500 SBIs deployed on 150 carrier vehicles, as well as 4000 Brilliant Pebbles deployed singly.[37] A final decision on the mix of smart rocks and Brilliant Pebbles was delayed until 1990.[38]

The Ground-Based Interceptor

The next layer of the defence would attack Soviet warheads during the mid-course of their flight, using a Ground Based Interceptor (GBI), which is a smaller and more sophisticated version of the Homing Overlay Experiment that successfully intercepted a warhead in 1984. In 1988 the number of GBIs was significantly increased over the number that was originally planned in 1987. The initial phase of the development of the GBI involves three tests of the Lockheed-built Exo-atmospheric Reentry-vehicle Interception System (ERIS), although the first has been delayed from early 1990 to late 1990.[39] The next phase of the development effort will involve at least four tests of a more capable interceptor, starting in 1992.[40]

The Booster Surveillance and Tracking System

The initial sensor system of an SDI system is a Booster Surveillance and Tracking System, a network of about 5–10 large satellites (probably in near-geosynchronous orbits) that would detect the launch of Soviet missiles and

[30] Davis, B., 'Latest Star Wars strategy to gather momentum would sprinkle Brilliant Pebbles in the heavens', *Wall Street Journal*, 22 May 1989, p. 16.

[31] Smith, J., 'Year of lobbying turned Brilliant Pebbles into top SDI plan', *Washington Post*, 26 Apr. 1989, p. A16.

[32] Broad, W., 'What next for Star Wars? Brilliant Pebbles', *New York Times*, 25 Apr. 1989, pp. C1–C2.

[33] Foley, T., 'Sharp rise in Brilliant Pebbles interceptor funding accompanied by new questions about technical feasibility', *Aviation Week & Space Technology*, 22 May 1989, pp. 20–21.

[34] Jacky, J., 'Throwing stones at Brilliant Pebbles', *Technology Review*, Oct. 1989, pp. 20–21, 76.

[35] 'Brilliant RVs cited as possible Brilliant Pebbles problem', *Defense Daily*, 28 Sep. 1989, pp. 504–505.

[36] Leopold, G., 'Industry group calls Brilliant Pebbles a flop', *Defense News*, 16 Oct. 1989.

[37] 'Mission control', *Military Space*, 4 Dec. 1989, p. 1.

[38] 'Monahan DAB briefing on space-based architecture delayed again', *Defense Daily*, 19 Dec. 1989, p. 427.

[39] 'Exoatmospheric test delay', *Aviation Week & Space Technology*, 15 Jan. 1990, p. 11.

[40] Gilmartin, P., 'Defense Dept. to launch competition for exoatmospheric interceptor design', *Aviation Week & Space Technology*, 6 Nov. 1989, p. 27.

provide initial tracking of their trajectories. BSTS would relay target data to SBI platforms, orbiting a few hundred kilometres above the earth. The competition between Lockheed and Grumman to determine which company will build BSTS has been deferred until February 1991 to provide more time for work on sensors and computers,[41] with the initial flight of the BSTS satellite planned for 1995.

Over the past two years proposals for deployment of the BSTS (one of the sensor elements of the Phase One strategic defence system) to provide improved early warning of missile attack and enhanced intelligence collection and verification capabilities have received increased attention. The BSTS would be much larger and more capable than the current Defense Support Program (DSP). The current DSP requires about 1275 watts of power, while BSTS power requirements range from 4 to 6 kilowatts. The DSP spacecraft sensors have focal plane arrays with about 6700 sensor elements, while the Grumman scanning array has about 80 000 sensor elements, and the Lockheed staring array sensor has up to 8 million sensor elements.[42]

However, the cost of a DSP satellite is about $350 million, while the cost of a BSTS satellite is closer to $1 billion. There are already a large number of DSP spacecraft under contract,[43] leading to doubts about the near-term need to replace this system with BSTS; and the drastic increase in performance capability has led to concerns that BSTS might violate the ABM Treaty.[44]

The Space Surveillance and Tracking System

A combination of sensor systems would be used to identify and track warheads during the mid-course phase of their flight. The Space Surveillance and Tracking System (SSTS), a network of up to 20 satellites orbiting at an altitude of approximately 5000 km, would use cryogenically refrigerated long-wave infra-red sensors for tracking. Little progress has been made in recent years on the SSTS project because of uncertainty about performance requirements for the system; but with the decision in 1989 to add the mid-course sensors of the Ground-based Surveillance and Tracking System (GSTS) and the Ground-Based Radar (GBR), the stage was set for renewed progress on SSTS in 1989. Thus the initial test of SSTS technology will come in the Midcourse Sensor Experiment (MSX), a $400-million 3000-kg spacecraft planned for launch on a modified Titan 2 booster in early 1992.[45]

[41] 'BSTS choice delayed for more work', *Defense Week*, 25 Sep. 1989, p. 5.

[42] *Department of Defense Appropriations for 1990*, US House of Representatives Appropriations Committee, Defense Subcommittee, 101st Congress, 1st Session, part 7, p. 692.

[43] *Department of Defense Authorization for Appropriations for Fiscal Years 1990 and 1991*, US Senate Armed Services Committee, 101st Congress, 1st Session, pp. 197–99.

[44] House of Representatives Appropriations Committee (note 42), p. 685.

[45] Covault, C., 'New SDI surveillance satellite to use upgraded Titan 2 booster', *Aviation Week & Space Technology*, 25 Sep. 1989, p. 31.

In late 1989 TRW and Lockheed were awarded a joint contract to develop a prototype SSTS for launch in late 1995.[46]

The Ground-based Surveillance and Tracking System

A second mid-course sensor is the Ground-based Surveillance and Tracking System, which would use similar sensors that would be lofted into space on ballistic trajectories upon warning of a Soviet attack.[47]

The Ground-Based Radar

A third mid-course sensor is the Ground-Based Radar, which would track Soviet re-entry vehicles during the later part of their trajectory, before they re-enter the atmosphere.[48]

The Phase Two SDI system

Several other systems are also in an advanced state of development and could be included in later versions of the defence system.

The High-altitude Endo-atmospheric Interceptor (HEDI) would be used to intercept Soviet warheads shortly after they begin to re-enter the atmosphere.[49] Technical difficulties delayed the first HEDI test, originally planned for August 1989, into 1990.[50] A total of three tests is planned over a three-year period, although the low priority assigned to this system may stretch the initial testing period out to five years.[51]

The Airborne Optical Adjunct (AOA) is an infra-red sensor system carried on a Boeing 767 that would track warheads in the mid-course and terminal phases of flight. Because it was not chosen as part of the Phase One architecture, AOA has been considered a candidate for eventual cancellation.[52]

After a delay of several years, a contractor and design were finally selected in late 1989 for the Ground-Based Free Electron Laser (GB-FEL) programme, which is the long-term centre-piece of the SDI programme.[53] The $500 million project will use a radio frequency-driven beam generator developed by Boeing and the Los Alamos National Laboratory, which was selected over a linac (induction linear accelerator) developed by TRW and

[46] 'USAF awards SSTS funds to TRW, Lockheed team', *Aviation Week & Space Technology*, 1 Jan. 1990, p. 1.

[47] Gilmartin, T., 'McDonnell Douglas to build surveillance and tracking system for SDI effort', *Defense News*, 12 Sep. 1988, p. 21.

[48] Foley, T., 'Raytheon proposes rail-mobile radar for midcourse SDI sensing', *Aviation Week & Space Technology*, 11 Jan. 1990, p. 22–24.

[49] Adams, P., 'Warhead interceptor will undergo eye checkup in 1990 test', *Defense News*, 28 Nov. 1988, p. 42.

[50] Gilmartin, P., 'Delay of first HEDI test launch caused by flight destruct system replacement', *Aviation Week & Space Technology*, 30 Oct. 1989, p. 21.

[51] Kiernan, V., 'SDIO begins curtailing work to meet budget', *Space News*, 15 Jan. 1990, pp. 1, 37.

[52] Duffy, T., 'SDI's airborne optical adjunct program seen likely to be cancelled', *Electronic Combat Report*, 11 Aug. 1989, p. 1.

[53] Gilmartin, P., 'Boeing Aerospace wins SDI contract for RF-driven free electron laser', *Aviation Week & Space Technology*, 23 Oct. 1989, p. 21.

the Lawrence Livermore National Laboratory. Although the initial FEL will be smaller than previously planned, the details of its capabilities remain sketchy, with some sources suggesting that the laser's power will be in the 20–50 MW class.[54] The initial $500 million version of the FEL will have a 1.5-m beam director mirror, in contrast to the 3.5-m mirror for the originally planned $2 billion facility.[55]

Another major SDI directed-energy project is the Zenith Star space-based chemical laser. This project began in late 1986 as the Laser Integrated Space Experiment, the centre-piece of the effort to implement the Reagan Administration's re-interpretation of the ABM Treaty. Now the space test is intended to demonstrate, prior to a decision to deploy the initial phase of SDI, the possibility of creating a directed-energy weapon that can cope with faster flying Soviet missiles.[56] Although the large amounts of fuel required by this type of laser limit its attractiveness, the technology is relatively well understood, and space-basing avoids the uncertainties of propagating a laser beam through the atmosphere. Ground testing of the 2-MW Alpha chemical laser began in 1989.[57] The space-based 2-MW Zenith Star test, which was initially planned for 1994, is now contemplated to begin in December 1986.[58] A smaller Complementary Space Experiment orbital test of a chemical laser, with a brightness about 1 per cent that of Zenith Star, is now contemplated for 1993.[59]

IV. Anti-satellite weapon systems

After a hiatus of several years, anti-satellite weapons (ASATs) returned to centre stage in 1989. The USA elaborated plans for the deployment of kinetic-energy and directed-energy ASATs by the mid-1990s. The USSR displayed growing openness about its own capabilities in an effort to reduce US perceptions of a Soviet threat. A Soviet suggestion at the Malta summit meeting in December to open discussions on ASATs was rejected by the USA and has not been pursued actively by the USSR.[60] Despite congressional support for negotiated limits on ASAT weapons,[61] the Bush Administration has shown little interest in this subject.

[54] 'Space weapons', *Military Space*, 23 Oct. 1989, p. 7.

[55] 'FEL project wiggles its way to selection', *SDI Monitor*, 27 Oct. 1989, pp. 247–48.

[56] 'Chemical lasers step up with Zenith star', *Military Space*, 19 Dec. 1988, pp. 1, 8.

[57] 'Alpha chemical laser to fire at full power next month', *SDI Monitor*, 10 Nov. 1989, pp. 257–58.

[58] Kiernan, V., 'SDI budget problems slip space testing of Zenith star laser', *Space News*, 9 Oct. 1989, p. 20.

[59] Kiernan, V., 'Scaled-down test of Zenith star concept under DOD review', *Space News*, 11 Dec. 1989.

[60] Oberfdorfer, D., 'SDI given low priority at summit, aides say', *Washington Post*, 6 Dec. 1989, p. A26.

[61] 'House Armed Services lays foundation to build ASAT arms control regime', *Inside the Pentagon*, 14 July 1989, p. 17.

Soviet ASAT developments

The Soviet co-orbital anti-satellite weapon, which has not been tested since 1982, remained in operational status in 1989. A total of 16 SL-11 Cyclone launch vehicles with their associated kill vehicles are on alert at a dedicated two-pad launch complex at the Baikonur cosmodrome.[62] The US Department of Defense (DOD) credits this system with the ability to destroy up to 10 US satellites in low earth orbit in a campaign stretching over two days. Other private estimates suggest that the time to conduct such a campaign could be much longer.[63]

Soviet directed-energy facilities have also been of concern to the USA. General Piotrowski, commander of US Space Command, has testified that 'the Soviets have at least two Megawatt-class lasers at a place called Sary Shagan',[64] and other sources suggest a total of four laser-related facilities at Sary-Shagan.[65] General Piotrowski had stated in the past that the Sary-Shagan lasers could destroy satellites at altitudes of 400–500 km,[66] damage satellite's solar panels in orbits up to an altitude of 1200–1700 km,[67] and cause in-band damage to sensors of satellites at geosynchronous altitude.[68]

However, these concerns were considerably lessened when a US delegation visited Sary-Shagan in July,[69] viewing two Soviet directed-energy facilities that have been of interest to the West for some time.[70] The first facility visited was found to have low-powered lasers suitable for tracking satellites, rather than high-powered lasers for attacking satellites.[71] The capabilities of this laser had been debated within the US intelligence community since the late 1970s.[72] The Central Intelligence Agency correctly concluded that the laser was a low- to moderate-power tracking system. The Defense Intelligence Agency argued that the laser was a high-powered weapon, and although this was proved incorrect, it was accepted by the DOD as a basis for arguing in favour of an expanded US directed-energy programme.[73]

A second laser facility was found to have been dismantled around 1980, or earlier, following what was described as an unsuccessful testing effort in the 1970s.[74] This laser, code-named Tora in the USA,[75] had been given wide

[62] House of Representatives Appropriations Committee (note 42), part 6, p. 212.

[63] Stares, P., *Space and National Security* (Brookings: Washington, DC, 1987), p. 94.

[64] House of Representatives Appropriations Committee (note 42), part 2, p. 480.

[65] 'Laser weapons', *Military Space*, 31 July 1989, p. 8.

[66] 'Sary Shagan visit raises questions', *SDI Monitor*, 24 July 1989, p. 183.

[67] Morrocco, J., 'Soviet ground lasers threaten US geosynchronous satellites', *Aviation Week & Space Technology*, 2 Nov. 1987, p. 27.

[68] Halloran, R., 'General describes Soviet laser threat', *New York Times*, 24 Oct. 1987, p. 62.

[69] 'Soviets display laser facility at Sary Shagan', *Aviation Week & Space Technology*, 17 July 1989, p. 27.

[70] Smith, J., 'Soviet laser said to pose no threat', *Washington Post*, 9 July 1989, p. A19.

[71] 'Sary Shagan and Kyshtym', *Science and Global Security*, vol. 1, no. 1 (fall 1989).

[72] von Hippel, F. and Cochran, T., 'The myth of the Soviet killer laser', *New York Times*, 19 Aug. 1989.

[73] Kaplan, F., 'Feared Soviet laser site is overrated, US team says', *Boston Globe*, 12 July 1989, pp. 1, 8.

[74] Velhikov, Y., 'Science for a nuclear-free world', *International Affairs–Moscow*, Nov. 1988, pp. 48–51.

[75] Zaloga, S., *Soviet Air Defence Missiles* (Jane's Coulsdon, Surrey, 1989), p. 161.

publicity in the West and led to efforts by the Air Force and the Los Alamos National Laboratory to duplicate the Soviet laser to evaluate its military potential.[76]

In August 1989 a US congressional delegation also visited the Kurchatov Institute near Moscow, where they witnessed a 5-second test of a 1-MW carbon dioxide laser built in the late 1970s. One member of the delegation, Dr John Hammond, formerly head of the SDI directed-energy programme, noted that 'militarily, there was not much of significance to this laser. Other components and further size and weight reduction would be necessary to make it a military system'.[77]

Some uncertainty remains about the capabilities of the Soviet facility near Dushanbe, with General Piotrowski noting that, 'While the jury's still out as to whether that's a high power laser, or an imaging laser, it has the potential to be a high-power laser'.[78] US estimates of Soviet space-based laser ASAT capabilities have also been revised. 'In 1983, the Air Force estimated that the Soviet Union would have space-based laser ASAT systems in the early 1990's, with a prototype launched possibly as early as 1986. The latest estimate pushes these dates back around ten years.'[79]

US ASAT developments

Although the rapidly changing international scene has led to a re-evaluation of a broad range of US military commitments, strategic concepts and weapon systems, Administration support for development of an anti-satellite system has not abated. Indeed, the Bush Administration expressed strong support for the Army's new ASAT programme in terms that were hauntingly reminiscent of the initial debate over ASAT weapons in the early 1980s. Defense Secretary Cheney argued that 'the DoD needs an operational ASAT capability to deter and to counter the threat Soviet space systems in low-earth orbit pose to U.S. and Allied space and terrestrial forces'.[80] The Chief of Staff of the US Army in Europe, General Crosbie Saint, stated, 'I see an effective ASAT system as the key to the control of space and also conceivably as the key to victory'.[81]

The Defense Department's strategy is apparently based on the assumed ability, in General Piotrowski's words, to 'build a U.S. ASAT system that is so good that he [the Soviet Union] can't stand you using it so he doesn't use his'.[82] This technological superiority is assumed to invalidate other precedents in the arms race, such as multiple independently targetable re-

[76] 'Soviets build directed energy weapon', *Aviation Week & Space Technology*, 28 July 1980, pp. 47–50.

[77] Gordon, M., 'US visitors see Soviet laser firing', *New York Times*, 17 Aug. 1989, p. 8.

[78] 'Pentagon board names Army to lead revamped ASAT program', *Aviation Week & Space Technology*, 16 Jan. 1989, p. 31.

[79] House of Representatives Appropriations Committee (note 42), part 2, p. 491.

[80] *Congressional Record–Senate*, 28 Sep. 1989, p. S12108.

[81] Saint, C., 'CINCUSAREUR places high priority on ASAT', *Armed Forces Journal International*, Sep. 1989, p. 40.

[82] House of Representatives Appropriations Committee (note 42), part 2, p. 481.

entry vehicles. 'I didn't say they [the Soviet Union] shouldn't build ASAT. I just believe we can build a better one'.[83]

Nevertheless congressional concern about the impact of Soviet ASAT weapons on US space systems continues, typified by the Senate Armed Services, which reported that:

A U.S. ASAT capability alone could be a weak deterrent unless or until the nation substantially improves satellite survivability, jamming resistance, launch responsiveness and the way we approach satellite construction. Yet while the Administration has a program in place for acquiring an ASAT capability, no apparent plan has been submitted to the Congress to develop the other essential ingredients of a sound space control strategy.[84]

Kinetic-energy ASATs

In early 1989 the Defense Department[85] established a tri-service Joint Program Office to formulate an ASAT development plan.[86] The Air Force was responsible for tracking and battle management functions,[87] with the Army and Navy in competition to see which would be the lead service for the programme.[88] By late 1989 the services had developed a comprehensive roadmap for development of a new ASAT capability.[89]

The ASAT interceptor would be similar in concept to the Army's ERIS interceptor. The land-based version would use a new-design 3500-kg two-stage solid-fuelled missile a little more than 9 m long and 0.6 m in diameter. This booster would give a burn-out velocity of 6.8 km per second, providing the ability to attack satellite targets at cross-ranges of up to 7500 km and at altitudes of over 4000 km.[90] The baseline 70-kg kill vehicle, based on ERIS technology, would use both visible and infra-red sensors to home in on Soviet satellites from ranges of several thousand kilometres. Targets would be destroyed by hypervelocity (about 10 km per second) impact, using a 6-m diameter inflatable kill-enhancement device.

An alternative booster considered for deployment at sea on DDG-963 Spruance Class destroyers would weigh 2900 kg, with a diameter of slightly less than 0.6 m and a length of less than 6.8 m, in order to fit within the multi-purpose Mk-41 Vertical Launch System (VLS) tubes on these ships.

[83] House of Representatives Appropriations Committee (note 42), part 2, p. 485.

[84] *Congressional Record–Senate*, 28 Sep. 1989, p. S12079.

[85] Senate Armed Services Committee (note 43), pp. 271–305, constitutes the most readily accessible overview of this topic for 1989.

[86] 'Taft approves kinetic, directed energy ASAT starts', *Aerospace Daily*, 10 Mar. 1989, pp. 385–86.

[87] 'Ground sensors to cue ASAT', *Military Space*, 23 Oct. 1989, pp. 1, 8.

[88] 'Army, Navy prepare for ASAT review', *Military Space*, 4 Dec. 1989, pp. 4–6.

[89] Jellet, M., *Joint KE ASAT Program–Briefing to Industry*, viewgraphs (US Army Strategic Defense Command: Huntsville, Ala., 7 Sep. 1989) is the source for the description below.

[90] Postol, T. (now at MIT), in a letter to Rep. Charles Bennett, US House of Representatives, dated 22 Mar. 1988, describes how a kill vehicle weighing about 70 kg, if mated to a booster consisting of all three stages of a Minuteman III ICBM, could be capable of attacking satellites at altitudes in excess of 40 000 km, including those in geosynchronous orbits, such as communications and early-warning satellites. With an improved third stage, these satellites could be destroyed in little more than two hours after the launch of the interceptor.

Up to 200 ASAT interceptors could be dispersed among the 1342 VLS missile launch tubes on 22 destroyers.[91] An alternative guidance system considered was the ASCOT system proposed by the Defense Advanced Research Projects Agency (DARPA), which would use a ground-based laser to illuminate target satellites, with the ASAT kill vehicle homing on the laser reflection.[92]

A variety of fixed, land-mobile and sea-based deployment schemes were considered.[93] Areas considered for ASAT deployment included the Kwajalein Missile Range and Hawaii in the Pacific, which would provide the opportunity to intercept Soviet satellites within about 30 minutes after launch, as well as Vandenberg Air Force Base in California, Ft Stewart in Georgia and Cape Canaveral in Florida. A system based at one or two of these locations would have the ability to intercept several dozen targets within a period of less than eight hours.

Army proponents argued that the Navy's destroyers were less survivable, since they might be damaged in conventional combat, and that naval arms control agreements in the future might limit the number of VLS tubes available for the ASAT mission.[94] Additional factors included greater performance made possible by a larger booster, as well as a greater potential for growth, since the Navy's system was constrained by the size of the VLS tubes. It was further argued that arms control verification could eventually lead to a requirement to inspect all VLS tubes.[95] In addition, the cost of maintenance and crew training for the Navy system could be higher and maintenance of communication links with the National Command Authority more difficult than with a land-based system.[96]

On 13 December the Defense Acquisition Board accepted the major features of the Army's ASAT plan, rejecting alternative Navy and DARPA concepts.[97] Under this $1.4 billion plan, two initial demonstration/validation tests of the interceptor are planned for 1992, with nine full-scale development tests against targets in space planned for 1994.[98] The total number of missiles operationally deployed by 1996 would be 72 at a single Army base.

Directed-energy ASATs

Initial US anti-satellite testing will use the 2.2-MW Mid-Infrared Advanced Chemical Laser (MIRACL) at the White Sands Missile Range in New Mexico. This plan is in line with the recommendations of a review

[91] Rosenberg, E., 'Navy moving to strip ASAT from Army', *Defense Week*, 10 Oct. 1989, p. 14.
[92] 'Classified DARPA program called ASCOT may compete with HEDI for ASAT mission', *Inside the Pentagon*, 11 Aug. 1989, p. 9.
[93] Gilmartin, P., 'Defense Department to launch design competition for new antisatellite weapon for the 1990s', *Aviation Week & Space Technology*, 24 July 1989, p. 30.
[94] Kiernan, V., 'Army: ground-based ASAT better buy', *Space News*, 11 Dec. 1989, p. 12.
[95] Gilmartin, P., 'Army presses case for ground-based ASAT system over competing sea- and mixed-based alternatives', *Aviation Week & Space Technology*, 4 Dec. 1989, p. 47.
[96] 'ASAT choice', *Aerospace Daily*, 18 Dec. 1989, p. 434.
[97] 'DAB selects ground-based ASAT in kinetic-kill milestone one review', *Aerospace Daily*, 15 Dec. 1989, pp. 425–26.
[98] 'Army studies whether to put new ASAT on military bases or in trucks', *Inside the Army*, 16 Oct. 1989, pp. 1, 6.

committee chaired by Frank Kendall, Assistant Deputy Director for Research and Engineering for Defensive Systems,[99] which suggested that initial testing with MIRACL should be followed by a concentration on the GB-FEL, with a final decision on this plan to be made by 1991.

Funding was provided in the 1989 budget to upgrade MIRACL,[100] including improvements in the ability of the laser's Sky Lite beam director mirror system to follow rapidly moving low-altitude satellites.[101] These improvements will give MIRACL what General Piotrowski terms 'a very modest capability to degrade Soviet satellites in low earth orbit'.[102] Testing is planned for late 1990 or early 1991 against inactive US satellites and space debris.

Although MIRACL may be used for near-term ASAT testing, the leading candidate in the long run for this mission is the Army's multi-megawatt GB-FEL, currently under construction at the White Sands Missile Range in New Mexico. This laser, scheduled for completion in the mid-1990s, will be equipped with a sophisticated atmospheric compensation system that would enable it to destroy satellites at altitudes of thousands of kilometres and potentially to damage spacecraft at higher altitudes. Air Force directed-energy ASAT efforts include work on the ground-based Excimer laser[103] as well as the chemical oxygen–iodine laser (COIL), but these projects are considerably less advanced than MIRACL and the FEL programmes. A single laser ASAT concept is slated for selection in 1991, with the FEL currently the leading candidate.

V. Arms control and military space activities

The ABM Treaty

One of the most significant developments in 1989 was the Soviet announcement of its decision to dismantle the large phased-array radar at Krasnoyarsk, which has long been regarded as a clear violation of the ABM Treaty (see also chapter 11). Initially the Soviet Union sought to link resolution of the Krasnoyarsk issue to US acceptance of the traditional interpretation of the ABM Treaty, but this was rejected by the Bush Administration.[104] At the Jackson Hole, Wyoming, summit meeting Foreign Minister Eduard Shevardnadze announced that the radar would be dismantled, and in a subsequent speech to the Supreme Soviet, he conceded that 'the station had been built on the wrong site . . . All the while, there

---

[99] Gilmartin, T., 'US works to resuscitate antisatellite program', Defense News, 17 Oct. 1988, p. 5.

[100] Strobel, W., 'Anti-satellite laser funds restored', Washington Times, 15 Dec. 1988, p. A2.

[101] Foley, T. M., 'ASAT tests to be conducted with upgraded MIRACL laser', Aviation Week & Space Technology, 19 Dec. 1988, p. 29.

[102] House of Representatives Appropriations Committee (note 42), part 2, p. 480.

[103] Department of Defense Appropriations for 1988, Hearings before the Subcommittee on the Defense Department of the US House of Representatives Appropriations Committee, 100th Congress (US Government Printing Office: Washington, DC, 1987), part 6, p. 716.

[104] Gordon, M., 'Moscow links disputed radar to '72 ABM Treaty', New York Times, 14 May 1989, p. 8.

stood the station, the size of an Egyptian pyramid, representing, to put it bluntly, a violation of the ABM Treaty'.[105]

Questions about the compliance of another Soviet radar system with the ABM Treaty were also resolved in 1989, although this issue has never achieved the significance of Krasnoyarsk. The ABM Treaty permits ABM radars to be located only at ABM test ranges or at the one permitted deployment site. However, in March 1987 the United States noticed that the Soviet Union had moved FLAT TWIN and PAWN SHOP radars, part of the ABM-X-3 rapidly deployable system, to an electronics factory near the city of Gomel. In addition, another PAWN SHOP radar van had been moved to the Vnukovo Airport near Moscow. The USSR maintained that these radars had been dismantled and were no longer ABM-capable, and had been moved to these locations for utilization for 'national economic purposes'.[106] A US team visited these radars on 23–24 March 1989 and concluded that, while the radars were not ABM-capable, they had not been properly dismantled according to agreed procedures.[107] It was subsequently reported that these radars had been satisfactorily dismantled.[108]

The Soviet move on the Krasnoyarsk radar has not had any impact on the issue of the US phased-array radars at Thule and Fylingdales.[109] Although the Soviet Government has repeatedly characterized these radars as violations of the ABM Treaty, there is no indication that the US Government is inclined to respond to these charges.

The future impact of the SDI programme continues to be a concern, and there are several tests planned that would raise questions about compliance with the ABM Treaty. Three of the tests that pose the greatest challenge to the traditional interpretation of the ABM Treaty are the Airborne Optical Adjunct sensor system test in 1990, the Booster Surveillance and Tracking System test in 1995, and the Zenith Star space-based chemical laser test in 1996. All of these tests will raise questions about whether testing of these space-based and air-based devices that in many respects are capable of substituting for ABM radars or interceptors would be consistent with Articles V and VI of the ABM Treaty, which ban such testing.

The Nuclear and Space Talks

Although there were a number of developments in the Defence and Space Talks during 1989 (conducted parallel to the START negotiations under the Nuclear and Space Talks), the USA and the USSR continue to have fundamental disagreements over the future role of strategic defences.

Chief US arms control negotiator Richard Burt notes that the major US objective continues to be a Treaty that 'fully protects our options for

[105] 'The Kremlin apology: excerpts from speech', *New York Times*, 25 Oct. 1989.

[106] 'Radar story seen aimed at US–USSR dialogue', *FBIS-SOV-89-101*, 29 May 1989, p. 3.

[107] Gertz, B., 'Soviet radar site remains treaty violation, US says', *Washington Times*, 13 Apr. 1989, p. A6.

[108] 'Soviets dismantle Gomel radars', *Defense News*, 6 Nov. 1989, p. 2.

[109] 'US radars criticized as ABM violations', *FBIS-SOV-89-190*, 3 Oct. 1989, p. 1.

deploying' SDI.[110] The core of the US negotiating position is that the purpose of the new defence and space agreement (separate from the ABM Treaty and not linked to the START agreement) is to facilitate a co-operative stable transition to increased reliance on strategic defences,[111] including the 'conditions necessary to ensure stability before, during and after deployment'.[112]

Key elements of the defence and space agreement under the US proposal would include a specified non-withdrawal period, during which 'treaty compliant testing to evaluate the feasibility and effectiveness of defenses against strategic ballistic missiles, including testing in space of ABM systems based on other physical principles, will be permitted'.[113] Following the expiration of the non-withdrawal period, 'a new strategic regime will begin in which the parties will have the right, should they so choose and give six months notice' to deploy an anti-missile system beyond that permitted by the ABM Treaty.[114] Termination of the treaty prior to the end of the non-withdrawal period would be permitted with the supreme national interests clause that is standard in arms control agreements. The US proposal would exclude all space-based sensors from limitation under a new defence and space treaty.[115]

During the summer of 1989 the Bush Administration amplified the Reagan Administration 'open laboratory' proposals first made in the autumn of 1988.[116] These 'transparency and predictability' provisions are intended to improve the ability of each country to understand the strategic defence programmes of the other, and would provide for annual exchanges on programme status and test schedules, as well as visits to research facilities and observation of tests. Each country would provide the other with a listing of strategic defence research and development facilities, and visits would be arranged on the basis of reciprocity.

As of early 1989 the Soviet Union has reportedly

agreed to annual exchanges of data on ABM development, testing, deployment, modernization and replacement data through the Nuclear Risk Reduction Centers, followed by experts' meetings to discuss the data and to plan observations of tests during the following year. However, they have not agreed to exchange data on research not observable by national technical means, to visit laboratories, or to exchange briefings.[117]

The unofficial US visits to Sary-Shagan and to the Kurchatov Institute of Atomic Energy in Moscow, which paved the way for a Soviet delegation to

[110] Smith, J., ' Burt says US to protect SDI options in talks', *Washington Post*, 6 May 1989, p. A13.
[111] Cooper, H., 'The Defense and Space Talks—small steps towards agreement', *NATO Review*, Aug. 1989, pp. 11–16, forms the basis for much of the following discussion.
[112] Cooper (note 111), p. 12.
[113] Cooper (note 111), p. 13.
[114] Cooper (note 111), p. 13.
[115] Adams, P., 'US, Soviets edge closer to rewritten ABM Treaty at Defense and Space Talks', *Defense News*, 21 Aug. 1989.
[116] 'US, Soviets study open labs pact', *Military Space*, 28 Aug. 1989, pp. 1, 8.
[117] Cooper (note 111), p. 15.

visit the Alpha laser facility and the Los Alamos National Laboratory,[118] all served as trial runs for such an agreement.

During the course of the Geneva Defence and Space Talks in the summer of 1989 the Soviet Union submitted a new version of its long-standing proposal to agree to a list of specific threshold limits that would distinguish between permitted and prohibited activities under the ABM Treaty.[119] The Soviet proposal reportedly included a call for on-site inspection of all space launches to verify that prohibited devices are not being launched into orbit.[120]

A major development in the Defence and Space Talks occurred at the September summit meeting in Jackson Hole, Wyoming, between Soviet Foreign Minister Eduard Shevardnadze and US Secretary of State James Baker.[121] In a reversal of a long-standing linkage, the Soviet side indicated a willingness to ratify the START agreement even if agreement on the ABM issue had not been reached, as long as the parties continued to observe the ABM Treaty as it was signed in 1972.[122] The Soviet side suggested that under this traditional interpretation of the ABM Treaty it would be permissible to conduct research in space as well as specific tests associated with such research, but that it would be prohibited to test space-based ABM systems, components and their prototypes, and that this was the interpretation of the Treaty currently adhered to by the US Congress.

The Soviet side proposed that discussions on strategic stability should begin as soon as the START agreement was signed and that these negotiations should focus on prevention of an arms race in space. This would lead to a protocol to the ABM Treaty strengthening the agreement on activities which are prohibited and permitted in accordance with the Treaty as well as measures to give assurance that it be observed.

The Soviet side also dropped its proposal concerning non-withdrawal from the ABM Treaty for an agreed-upon 10-year period. However, the USSR proposed that the provisions on the rights of the parties to withdraw from the START agreement in the event of a threat to their 'supreme national interests' would also mean the right to withdraw if one of the parties violated the ABM Treaty. The US side rejected this approach, whereupon the USSR indicated that it would make a Unilateral Statement on this point as part of the signing process.[123]

Despite modification of the Soviet position, there was still concern that Soviet judgement of compliance with the ABM Treaty would hinder ratification of a START agreement. Representative Les Aspin, Chairman of the House Armed Services Committee, concluded that: 'The Soviets offer on SDI isn't a real concession. It's a change in form, not substance. Once inside

[118] Stewart, R., 'Soviet scientists to visit 2 key Star Wars labs', *Los Angeles Times*, 14 Dec. 1989.

[119] Strobel, W., 'US, Soviet arms negotiators edge nearer pact', *Washington Times*, 7 Aug. 1989, p. A8.

[120] Adams, P., 'US, Soviets edge closer to rewritten ABM Treaty at Defense and Space Talks', *Defense News*, 21 Aug. 1989.

[121] 'Excerpts from statement on arms', *New York Times*, 25 Sep. 1989, pp. 1 ff.

[122] Gordon, M., 'An arms obstacle falls', *New York Times*, 24 Sep. 1989, pp. 1, 16.

[123] Smith, J., 'Debate erupts over Soviet arms-control proposal', *Washington Post*, 1 Oct. 1989, pp. A1, A11.

the negotiations, it's going to cause a lot of mischief'. Senator Sam Nunn, Chair of the Senate Armed Services Committee, stated that: 'We need to know where they [the Soviet Union] would draw the line between testing and deployment. We need to know what they are going to do on defensive weapons [or else] the Soviets will constantly be jerking our cord on SDI'.[124] Although continuing to favour clarification of the issue, following the Jackson Hole summit meeting the Chiefs appeared willing to accept the ambiguities of the Soviet offer.[125]

Subsequent events indicated that the two parties continue to be far apart on the space weapon issue. In early December, the USSR tabled a new version of its proposal limiting the types of test that would be permitted under the ABM Treaty, similar to the one first put forward in September 1987.[126] This proposal was summarily rejected by the USA.

A few days after the Soviet proposal was tabled in December 1989, the Bush Administration introduced a new draft treaty on space weapons at the Geneva negotiations.[127] The key elements of the new draft follow those of the proposals initially tabled by the Reagan Administration in January 1988[128] and consistently rejected by the Soviet Union.

The new Bush draft continues the Reagan Administration policy of calling for essentially unlimited testing of space-based anti-missile components, under the so-called broad interpretation of the ABM Treaty. The draft also does not contain any linkage between the continuation of the space weapon agreement and the continued implementation of the START agreement.

The withdrawal provisions in the new Bush proposal are the only significant departure from previous Reagan Administration proposals, which had called for an explicit commitment to deploy strategic defences at the end of a definite period, perhaps as soon as 1994. The Joint Chiefs of Staff had objected to this provision, noting that the USA was unlikely to be able to deploy SDI so soon, although they were concerned that the USSR might be able to do so.[129] The new draft also includes provisions that would permit either party to withdraw from the accord and deploy an anti-missile system following three years of consultation and after giving six months' notice. Unlike the current ABM Treaty, neither party would have to claim that a threat to its 'supreme national interest' was the reason for withdrawing from the Treaty.

[124] Fritz, S., 'Key lawmakers discount Soviet shift on arms', *Los Angeles Times*, 26 Sep. 1989, pp. 1, 10.

[125] Smith, J., 'Joint Chiefs willing to sidestep SDI dispute in arms talks', *Washington Post*, 8 Nov. 1989, p. A3.

[126] Strobel, W., 'US rejects proposed limits on SDI experiments', *Washington Times*, 5 Dec. 1989, p. A7.

[127] Smith, J., 'US rejects space-weapon constraints', *Washington Post*, 9 Dec. 1989, p. A22.

[128] Electronic Industries Association, *Ten Year Forecast of Defense Needs* (EIA: Washington, DC, Oct. 1989), p. 326.

[129] Gordon, M., 'Joint Chiefs urge US restraint on "Star Wars" in strategic talks', *New York Times*, 1 June 1989.

VI. Soviet and US military space developments

New US satellite systems

Despite the international political transformations of 1989, the US military space programme is continuing an unprecedented and largely unrecognized expansion. While the terrestrial military is preoccupied with reductions, space forces continue to grow. Indeed, Martin Faga, the first Assistant Secretary of the Air Force for Space (and Director of the National Reconnaissance Office), asserts that 'even if super power tensions truly decline, an environment of unpredictability and uncertainty will still remain—an environment where space systems can and will play a unique role'.[130] He has also noted that conventional force reductions will not reduce the demand for satellite services such as the Navstar navigation satellite, since 'you need to navigate with Navstar regardless of whether it's 50 airplanes or a hundred'.[131] In this conclusion he is joined by US Space Command Deputy Commander Vice Admiral Diego Hernandez who asserts that 'the need for space products becomes increasingly important since you have fewer forces deployed around the world . . . and you need to avoid being surprised'.[132] This expansion is taking place on three levels.

1. Previously planned satellite systems are finally coming into being. The Lacrosse and KH-12 intelligence satellite systems are now reaching operational status, and over the next several years, the Navstar navigation satellite system will be brought up to full strength, and a fleet of new Milstar satellites will come into service.[133]

2. At least four new intelligence collection systems are under development. These include new imaging radar satellites and laser testing monitoring satellites, both for treaty verification, as well as a new Space-Based Wide Area Surveillance System for global aerial and maritime surveillance and the Booster Surveillance and Tracking System for missile launch warning.

3. Entirely novel satellite programmes are in the works, aimed at developing smaller and less expensive satellites to replace existing systems which may become unacceptably vulnerable to anti-satellite attack in coming years. While these so-called Lightsat or Cheapsat systems may not become operational in this century, prototypes will be flying by 1990, and their development may be a central focus of military interest in the 1990s.[134]

---

[130] Faga, M., Prepared Remarks to the National Space Club, 29 Nov. 1989, p. 2.

[131] Foley, T. *et al.*, 'Newsmaker forum', *Space News*, 11 Dec. 1989, p. 54.

[132] McMillan, S., 'Growing reliance on spy satellites seen by official', *Colorado Springs Gazette-Telegraph*, 27 Nov. 1989, p. 1.

[133] Rawles, J., 'Military satellites: the next generation', *Defense Electronics*, May 1988, pp. 46–63.

[134] 'Tacsat requirements sent to Joint Chiefs of Staff', *Aviation Week & Space Technology*, 13 Nov. 1989, pp. 29–30.

Soviet photographic reconnaissance satellites

Despite the general slow-down in the Soviet space programme, 1989 continued to be a busy year for the GRU Cosmic Intelligence Directorate. The Soviets launched a total of 31 photoreconnaissance satellites in 1989, one less than the 32 lofted in 1988, exceeding again the 25 launched in 1987 and matching the 31 launched in 1986. Although these satellites account for roughly one-third of Soviet launch activity, their proportional cost is undoubtedly less. While US film-return satellites in the 1960s used small recoverable capsules to return film to earth, the USSR uses much larger capsules to return the entire camera system, and each capsule is generally used for three[135] or as many as four[136] flights.

A detailed breakdown of the various types of imaging satellite launched in 1989 indicates the changing priorities of the Soviet space effort. One-third of the imaging satellites launched in 1989 (10 out of 31) were devoted to military mapping or civil remote sensing missions, in contrast to the quarter of the launches in 1988 (8 out of 32) with such missions.

Only two medium-resolution third-generation satellites were launched in 1989, down from the four launched in 1988, further continuing the downward trend in the utilization of this system; and the 10 third-generation high-resolution satellites launched in 1989 did not match the 13 close-look film-return satellites that were launched in 1988. The pace of launch activity over the past two years lies about halfway between the 6 launched in 1986 and in 1987, and the high of 18 launched in 1978.

Over half of the 1989 flights still used the 62.8° inclination orbits initiated in late November 1988. Third-generation satellites had not flown at this inclination since Cosmos 1128 was orbited in September 1979. During 1989 the first four high-resolution third-generation flights of the year (Cosmos 2003, 2017, 2019 and 2025) were at this inclination, as were the later flights of Cosmos 2036 and 2048. Although the rationale for the renewed use of this inclination remains unclear, it has become established as the preferred inclination for the high-resolution third-generation satellites.

Seven fourth-generation satellites, which typically remain in orbit for about eight weeks, were launched in 1989, down from the eight launched in 1988 and the nine that were launched in 1986 and 1987. In a rerun of the 1988 experience with Cosmos 1916, Cosmos 2030 was intentionally destroyed by on-board explosives on 28 July when it failed to respond to ground commands to re-enter. By the end of the year, the sole remaining fourth-generation photoreconnaissance satellite in orbit was Cosmos 2052, launched on 30 November.

Two fourth-generation satellites dedicated to military mapping and remote sensing were also launched in 1989 (Cosmos 2021 and 2031), in contrast to the single launch in 1988. The 1988 launch was the first public indication of the existence of this class of satellite, although they have been

---

[135] 'Soviets end Resurs/Pion link', *Flight International*, 15 Nov. 1989, p. 14.
[136] Clark, P., 'Vostok variants for commercial users', *Space Markets*, May 1989, pp. 308–309.

flying for a number of years.[137] Unfortunately, Cosmos 2031 experienced the control problems that have plagued this series, and like Cosmos 2030, it was intentionally destroyed in orbit on 31 August.[138]

With two launches, 1989 was a fairly good year for the newest, fifth-generation reconnaissance satellites, in contrast to the rather poor display in 1988. These satellites use electronic transmission to return images in near real time while the third- and fourth-generation systems use film returned to earth in re-entry capsules.

US imaging intelligence satellites

Continuing the major expansion of the number of US low-altitude intelligence satellites begun in 1988 with the launch of the first Lacrosse imaging radar satellite,[139] on 8 August 1989 the space-shuttle orbiter Columbia deployed what appears to be the first of a long-awaited new generation of photographic reconnaissance satellites, popularly referred to as the KH-12.[140] By early October amateur astronomers had noted that sunlight reflected from this spacecraft was flashing, as though the spacecraft were tumbling out of control.[141] But by mid-November the satellite was observed to have manoeuvred to a higher orbit,[142] suggesting that the spacecraft was operational.

The USA continued operation of three KH-11 photographic intelligence satellites throughout the year. The sixth KH-11, launched in December 1984, remained in orbit at the end of 1989, surpassing by two years the previously demonstrated orbital life for this class of satellite. In the past, these satellites were de-orbited at the end of their operational lifetime, but the unprecedented longevity implied by over five years in orbit raised questions as to whether this satellite is actually operational. The eighth KH-11, launched in October 1987, can be expected to remain operational at least through the end of 1990. The KH-11 launched on 6 November 1988, almost certainly the last of this series, should remain operational through the end of 1992.

The expansion of treaty verification satellite programmes has largely been the result of the efforts of Oklahoma Democratic Senator David Boren, Chairman of the Senate Intelligence Committee. He led the move for the

[137] Johnson, N., *The Soviet Year in Space 1988* (Teledyne-Brown Engineering: Colorado Springs, 1989), p. 22.

[138] 'Soviet space launches in 1989', *Aerospace Daily*, 22 Jan. 1989, p. 120.

[139] Covault, C., 'Atlantis radar satellite payload opens new reconnaissance era', *Aviation Week & Space Technology*, 12 Dec. 1988, pp. 26–28.

[140] The proper nomenclature for the new satellite remains unclear. It is reliably suggested that the US intelligence community no longer uses the KH designation system, and thus there is properly no such satellite as 'KH-12'. Unfortunately, the Byeman code-name for this new spacecraft has not been publicly compromised (the KH-11 was Kennan, KH-9 was Hexagon, and so forth). Thus, the least inaccurate designation for this satellite is probably 'Advanced KH-11'. But this appellation does not do justice to the significant differences between the new and old spacecraft, and is somewhat the equivalent of terming a B-52 an advanced B-47. Since most published reports over the years have referred to this new satellite as the KH-12, that nomenclature is adhered to.

[141] 'Secret CIA satellite launched by Shuttle Columbia observed "tumbling" by astronomers in 7 countries', *Aviation Week & Space Technology*, 9 Oct. 1989, p. 35.

[142] 'Secret DOD shuttle payload boosted to higher orbit', *Aerospace Daily*, 8 Dec. 1989, p. 393.

six-year, $6 billion plan,[143] saying that if the plan were not approved he was prepared to oppose ratification of the START agreement. The plan included procurement of six additional Lacrosse imaging radar satellites, at over $500 million each, for verification of a START arms reduction agreement.[144] In addition, as much as $5 billion was programmed[145] for a new system of satellites that would be deployed in the mid-1990s,[146] or no later than the 1997–99 timeframe[147] to monitor Soviet laser testing.

These satellites would be in addition to the KH-12 and Lacrosse satellites already planned for procurement. There will probably be three or four of each type of these previously planned systems operational in orbit at any one time by the early 1990s.[148] The additional satellites proposed by Senator Boren would add three or four operational spacecraft, bringing the total to somewhere between 9 and 12 satellites. This is in stark contrast to the historical pattern of the 1970s and early 1980s, during which typically two KH-11s would be in orbit year round, joined by a KH-9 for perhaps six months of the year. The fivefold increase in the number of satellites in orbit probably translates into at least a tenfold increase in the number of images returned daily, since most of the new satellites are Lacrosse imaging-radar spacecraft with an all-weather capability.

Initially the Boren plan did not receive the support of the intelligence community, which was concerned about the formidable task of analysing the mountain of data that the additional satellites would generate.[149] Although initial funding for the plan was approved in 1988, Director of Central Intelligence William Webster remained concerned about the impact of the funding requirements for this new programme on existing intelligence efforts.[150] The new Bush Administration recommended termination of the programme in early 1989,[151] but Senator Boren[152] eventually succeeded in obtaining a commitment by President Bush to fund his programme,[153] although with delays of one to two years.[154]

Soviet electronic intelligence satellites

The Soviet electronic intelligence (ELINT) capability consists of three systems, although no new launches were required in 1989 to support

[143] Rasky, S., 'Senators balking over verification', New York Times, 29 Apr. 1988.

[144] Gertz, B., 'Senate panel asks for radar funds', Washington Times, 5 Apr. 1988, p. A3.

[145] 'A secret laser hunter', Newsweek, 3 Oct. 1988, p. 7.

[146] 'CIA chief warns Congress not to cut recon satellites', Aerospace Daily, 30 Nov. 1989, p. 323.

[147] Foley, T., 'Monitoring Soviet space weapons adds to demand for US intelligence', Aviation Week & Space Technology, 27 Feb. 1989, pp. 22–23.

[148] Broad, W., 'US adds spy satellites despite easing tensions', New York Times, 3 Dec. 1989, p. 8.

[149] Evans, R. and Novak, R., 'The Indigo–Lacrosse satellite gets the nod', Washington Post, 6 Apr. 1988, p. A24.

[150] Engelberg, S., 'CIA chief finds Gorbachev a mixed blessing for Agency', New York Times, 11 Dec. 1988, pp. 1, 42.

[151] Gertz, B., 'Bush plan to slight satellites and Boren', Washington Times, 30 Mar. 1989, p. 3.

[152] Rasky, S., 'Bush is accused of backing away from promise on 1988 arms pack', New York Times, 7 Apr. 1989, pp. 1, A9.

[153] 'Bush OKs proceeding with new surveillance sats', Defense Daily, 19 Apr. 1989, p. 102.

[154] Gertz, B., 'Plan to delay space satellite will be costly, sources say', Washington Times, 17 Apr. 1989, p. A4.

operational constellations. Six low-altitude satellites comprise the third generation of Soviet ELINT satellites. Two of the newer 12-tonne fourth-generation ELINT satellites remained in orbit in 1989. And the new fifth-generation ELINT system in geosynchronous orbit gives the USSR the type of continuous, wide-area coverage that the USA has maintained since the early 1970s with systems such as Rhyolite, Chalet and Magnum. Cosmos 1888 and Cosmos 1894, both launched in 1987, appeared to constitute the active members of this constellation in 1989.

US electronic intelligence satellites

Recovering from the apparent failure of an upper stage carrying a Chalet satellite in 1988, the US National Reconnaissance Office and National Security Agency launched the final Chalet (also known as Vortex) on 10 May 1989, and a second Magnum electronic intelligence satellite using the shuttle on 23 November 1989.

The notional ELINT constellation consists of four satellites. In addition to the 1989 launches this constellation now includes the first Magnum, launched on the shuttle in 1985, as well as one older Chalet which probably remains in service despite having been launched in 1981 and having long surpassed its five-year design life. In addition to these geostationary ELINT satellites, two Jumpseat ELINT satellites,[155] launched in 1985 and 1987, remained in service throughout 1989. These satellites, in highly elliptical Molniya-type orbits, provide specialized coverage of the far northern regions of the Soviet Union.

Soviet ocean surveillance satellites

The Soviet Union operates two classes of satellite for locating and identifying Western naval units. The Electronic Ocean Reconnaissance Satellites (EORSATs) pick up radio and radar transmissions. The nuclear-powered Radar Ocean Reconnaissance Satellites (RORSATs) use a radar with a power of several kilowatts to detect surface ships.

Perhaps in response to the problems with the RORSAT system in previous years, 1989 marked major new developments for the EORSAT system. At the beginning of the year the two spacecraft (Cosmos 1949 and 1979), launched in May and November 1988, maintained the nominal constellation of a pair of operational satellites. They were joined on 24 July by a third satellite, Cosmos 2033. Somewhat surprisingly, on 27 September Cosmos 2046 was launched into an orbit 172° apart from the other satellites. On 25 November Cosmos 2051 joined Cosmos 2046 in this new orbital plane. Despite initial problems with Cosmos 2051, for a brief time a total of five EORSATs were operating simultaneously in two distinct orbital planes, although Cosmos 1979 had ceased functioning by the end of the year.

[155] Richelson, J., *The US Intelligence Community* (Ballinger: Cambridge, Mass., 1985), p. 122.

Following the malfunction of the nuclear-powered Cosmos 1900 RORSAT on 12 April 1988,[156] there were no RORSAT launches in 1989.

US ocean surveillance satellites

The US counterpart to the Soviet EORSAT is the White Cloud Naval Ocean Surveillance System (NOSS).[157] Each White Cloud launch places into low polar orbit a cluster of one primary satellite, as well as three smaller sub-satellites that trail along behind the primary at distances of several hundred kilometres. This widely dispersed array of satellites enables the system to determine the location of radio and radar transmissions, using triangulation, and the identity of naval units can be deduced by analysis of the operating frequencies and transmission patterns of the emitters. Although there does not appear to be a definitely fixed constellation size for White Cloud, at the beginning of 1989 the constellation apparently consisted of four clusters of primary and secondary satellites, launched in 1984, 1986, 1987 and 1988. On 6 September, the second launch of a reconditioned Titan 2 booster placed the tenth White Cloud cluster into orbit.

Over the longer run the White Cloud may be augmented or even replaced by the satellites of the Space Based Wide Area Surveillance System (SB-WASS). This new system, with potential NATO[158] and Canadian[159] participation, would be used to track ships and aircraft on a global basis, although there is intense disagreement over the type of sensor that would be used. The Navy favours passive infra-red sensors that would track the heat emitted by ships and aircraft, while the Air Force favours an active radar system, which it believes would have a superior all-weather capability.[160] These technical preferences mark a reversal from earlier preferences. Navy interest in space-based radar extended from the Albatross studies in the early 1960s through the Clipper Bow effort of the late 1970s.[161] The Air Force and DARPA spent almost $500 million developing the Teal Ruby infra-red system before deciding not to fly it.[162]

The choice is more than one of engineering convenience, since the infra-red system could require as few as four satellites for continental air defence or 8–10 for global coverage,[163] while the radar system could require[164] 8–24 massive spacecraft (weighing over 11 000 kg),[165] costing from $8 billion[166]

[156] 'Soviets confirm Cosmos 1900 difficulties', *Aerospace Daily*, 16 May 1988, p. 252.

[157] Richelson (note 155), pp. 140–43.

[158] 'DOD considering 27 new NATO programs for Nunn funds over two years', *Inside the Pentagon*, 25 Aug. 1989, pp. 13–14.

[159] Lowman, R., 'Canada, US work to hone space-based radar objectives', *Defense News*, 20 Nov. 1989, p. 21.

[160] 'Piotrowski says CINCs prefer space-based radar to navy infrared surveillance', *Electronic Combat Report*, 29 Sep. 1989, p. 1.

[161] Robinson, B., 'Space based radar', *Air Force Industry Briefing*, 1 Mar. 1989.

[162] Smith, B., 'Teal Ruby spacecraft to be put in storage at Norton AFB', *Aviation Week & Space Technology*, 8 Jan. 1990, p. 22–23.

[163] Lynch, D., 'Space surveillance effort in limbo', *Defense Week*, 25 Sep. 1989, p. 13.

[164] US Air Force Scientific Advisory Board, *Summer Study on Space Based Radar*, Sep. 1987.

[165] Lynch (note 163).

[166] *Electronic Combat Report* (note 160).

to \$20 billion.[167] The Navy is interested primarily in a system to assist with fleet air defence, while the Air Force requirements also extend to strategic air defence, support of forward-deployed forces in areas such as the Persian Gulf, as well as drug interdiction.[168] The Navy is seeking a system that will be responsive to tasking by fleet commanders, while the Air Force prefers a system that will be centrally directed by the US Space Command.[169] The Services also differ on how the space-based system would complement terrestrial systems, with the Air Force claiming that the space-based system could replace ground-based and air-based radars (such as AWACS—the airborne warning and control system),[170] and the Navy seeing the space-based system more as a complement to terrestrial systems. However, there are serious questions concerning the ability of the SB-WASS to track 'stealth' targets, as well as concerns about the vulnerability of these low-flying satellites to Soviet ASAT attack,[171] and approval of development of this system has been deferred to 1990, with a first test-flight anticipated around 1995.

Soviet military communications satellites

The Soviet military communications network utilizes satellites in three different orbital regimes: low-altitude orbit, elliptical semi-synchronous Molniya orbit and geostationary orbit.

Three classes of satellite operate in low-altitude orbits. The first generation of the spacecraft are launched eight at a time on the SL-8 booster into random locations in a single orbital plane. The actual number of active satellites that make up this constellation is speculative, but the three most recently launched octuplets may be considered to constitute the nominal constellation. In actuality, some of these are likely to be inoperative while a few older satellites may remain in service. Most of the satellites of the two octuplets launched in June 1987 and March 1988 were probably operational in 1989, and they were supplemented by the launch of an additional octuplet in late March.

The second generation of low-altitude communications satellites is much heavier than the first and launched singly by the SL-8 booster. The entire constellation of three satellites, each in a unique orbital plane separated by 120°, was replenished in 1989.

The third-generation satellites are launched in groups of six on a single SL-14 booster. There were two launches in this series in 1989 maintaining a total of 12 satellites operating in two planes.

The Molniya-1 system is apparently primarily used by the Soviet military. A civilian Molniya-2 system operated 1971–77. The newer Molniya-3 system seems to accommodate both military and civilian users.

[167] Hasley, D., 'JCS bid to define space surveillance mission may resolve USAF, Navy fight', *Inside the Pentagon*, 10 Mar. 1989, pp. 1, 10.
[168] 'Drug wars turning to star wars', *Space News*, 9 Oct. 1989, p. 2.
[169] 'Airborne, space radars top ADI needs', *Military Space*, 22 May 1989, pp. 5–6.
[170] Canan, J., 'The big hole in NORAD', *Air Force Magazine*, Oct. 1989, pp. 54–59.
[171] 'Senate Armed Services Committee report', *Inside the Pentagon*, 27 July 1989, p. 8.

Despite the extensive development of the Molniya-3 and geosynchronous systems in recent years, there is little indication of the declining utilization of the Molniya-1 constellation. With the launch of two replacement satellites in February and September, the full complement of eight satellites remained operational at the end of 1989.

A fourth generation of Soviet military communications satellites operates in geostationary orbit, possibly providing data relay support to the Soviet fifth-generation photographic reconnaissance satellites. It is not easy to clearly differentiate these satellites from the Luch Satellite Data Relay Network (SDRN) system that supports the Mir space station, or from the fifth-generation geostationary ELINT system. The Luch SDRN (Satellite Data Relay Network) satellites used to support the Mir space station are located at E 95° on the geostationary arc. The similar Potok satellites, which may be used to relay data from fifth-generation photoreconnaissance satellites, are located at E 80° and W 14°. These satellites are announced as having 'experimental communications' missions. The launch of Cosmos 2054 in late December apparently supplemented Cosmos 1961 in this role.[172] A third class of satellite, located at W 25°, has no announced missions.

US military communications satellites

In contrast to the brisk pace of Soviet communications launches, there were only two such US flights in 1989. However, a number of US military communications systems continued in service.

The Defence Satellite Communications System (DSCS) is used by all four military services as well as a variety of governmental agencies. With a nominal orbital constellation of five operational and two spare satellites,[173] five or six satellites of the DSCS II series launched in the late 1970s remain in service, and three of the more capable and survivable DSCS III spacecraft launched in the early 1980s are also operational. The planned launch on a Titan 34D of a fourth DSCS III and the last DSCS II was delayed from mid-1988 to 4 September 1989 to accommodate the 10 May launch of a Chalet to compensate for the 1988 Chalet launch which suffered an upper stage failure. Beginning in 1991, DSCS III satellites will be launched singly on upgraded Atlas II boosters procured in 1988 under the Medium Launch Vehicle II (MLV-II) programme, with 10 launches planned through 1997.[174]

The Navy is the single largest user of military communications satellites. So-called Gapfiller transponders on three Marisat satellites launched in 1976 continue to be leased from the COMSAT Corporation, although these are now relegated to a back-up role. The first three Fleet Satellite Communications (FLTSATCOM) satellites, launched in 1978, 1979 and 1980, are also on back-up status, with FLTSATCOM 4 and FLTSATCOM 6, launched in 1980 and 1986 respectively, fully operational. FLTSATCOM 5 was lost in a launch vehicle accident on 26 February 1987, and

---

[172] 'Soviets launch Cosmos 2054', *Aerospace Daily*, 3 Jan. 1990, p. 15.

[173] Senate Armed Services Committee (note 43), part 6, p. 141.

[174] 'General Dynamics wins MLV II competition', *Aerospace Daily*, 4 May 1988, p. 185.

FLTSATCOM 7 (the last of the series) was to be launched on 22 September 1989.[175] The Navy's other major system is the Leased Satellite (LEASAT) system, which consists of three Syncom IV spacecraft leased from Hughes, which is also the satellite manufacturer. The final launch of the LEASAT programme is planned for early 1990 on the space shuttle. The Navy embarked on a major new communications satellite effort in 1988, known as the Ultra-High Frequency (UHF) Follow-On (UFO) Program.[176] Hughes was selected to build 10 of these satellites, based on its commercial HS-601 spacecraft, with launches on commercially procured Atlas boosters beginning in 1992, replacing FLTSATCOM and LEASAT satellites as needed.

The new Milstar satellite system has become increasingly controversial, owing to its high cost and uncertain requirements.[177] The current schedule calls for the first satellite to be launched on a Titan 4 Centaur from the Eastern Test Range in 1991, with one satellite launched each year thereafter,[178] and polar Milstar launches beginning in 1996 from the Western Test Range.[179] The constellation will consist of four active satellites (and one spare) in geosynchronous equatorial orbit, as well as three active satellites (and one spare) in geosynchronous polar orbit, with a tenth spacecraft procured as a ground spare in anticipation of a launch failure.[180] The Ground Test Vehicle (currently not planned for launch),[181] three Block I spacecraft and the first two upgraded Block II spacecraft are being financed with development funds, while subsequent spacecraft will be financed out of the procurement account.[182] The cost of reaching a full operational capability has been estimated to be as high as $22 billion, with each spacecraft costing about $800 million.[183] The Bush Administration requested approximately $1 billion for Milstar in the 1990 budget submission, but the House Appropriations Committee approved only $400 million, calling for cancellation of the programme following completion of the three satellites under contract.[184]

In addition to these systems, which are all for communications between terrestrial forces, satellite systems also support near-real-time communications between low-altitude intelligence satellites and ground control stations. In the past, this data relay function was performed by two satellites of the Satellite Data System (SDS). Operating in highly elliptical semi-

---

[175] 'Last FLTSATCOM satellite planned for launch September 22', *Aerospace Daily*, 15 Sep. 1989, p. 466.

[176] 'Navy satellites approach critical replacement stage', *Aviation Week & Space Technology*, 21 Mar. 1988, pp. 46, 51.

[177] 'Milstar woes come out of closet', *Military Space*, 3 July 1989, pp. 3–4.

[178] Munro, N., 'DOD seeks an additional $200 million for Milstar research work', *Defense News*, 8 May 1989, pp. 4, 34.

[179] 'Launch programs', *Military Space*, 22 May 1989, p. 7.

[180] Rawles, J., 'Milstar soars beyond budget and schedule goals', *Defense Electronics*, Feb. 1989, pp. 66–72.

[181] Schultz, J., 'TRW to deliver Milstar payload as House votes to kill satellite program', *Armed Forces Journal International*, Sep. 1989, pp. 75–78.

[182] Rawles, J., 'Milstar soars beyond budget and schedule goals', *Defense Electronics*, Feb. 1989, pp. 66–72.

[183] Hughes, D., 'Milstar terminal capability demonstrated as Congress debates program budget', *Aviation Week & Space Technology*, 30 Oct. 1989, pp. 49–51.

[184] 'Congress splits on milspace budget', *Military Space*, 25 Sep. 1989, pp. 1–2.

synchronous Molniya-type orbits, optimized for coverage of the north polar region, they relayed real-time imagery data from photographic intelligence satellites flying over the Soviet Union, to processing stations in the USA. At the outset of 1989, SDS F-5 and F-5A, launched in 1983 and 1984 respectively, probably remained in service, but these had probably both been retired by the end of the year. They were replaced by NASA's Tracking and Data Relay Satellite System (TDRSS), which plays a major though generally unappreciated role in supporting near-real-time data transmission from low-altitude reconnaissance satellites such as the Lacrosse and KH-12.[185] Thus with the launch of a third TDRSS satellite by the shuttle on 13 March, the two older SDS satellites were no longer needed.

Soviet early-warning satellites

The Soviet ballistic missile early-warning satellite network consists of a constellation of nine satellites in Molniya-type orbits. Although Soviet efforts in the past to maintain this constellation at full complement have been frustrated by launch vehicle and spacecraft failures, 1989 was a comparatively uneventful year, with only two launches required to maintain the operational constellation.[186]

US early-warning satellites

The US Satellite Early Warning System (SEWS) consists of five DSP spacecraft.[187] Three of these provide frontline operational service, with two additional spacecraft available as backups should problems emerge with the primary satellites. The standard operating procedure is that primary reliance is placed on the three most recently launched satellites, with the two older satellites providing backup.[188] But because of the critical importance of this mission, a replacement satellite will normally be launched around the time that the oldest of the five spacecraft on-orbit nears the end of its operational life. This newly launched satellite will assume frontline duty, the eldest of the three frontline spacecraft will assume backup status, and the oldest satellite will be retired.

At the beginning of 1989 five DSP spacecraft were operational. DSP F-11 and DSP F-13, launched in 1981 and 1982 respectively, were on back-up duty, and DSP F-12 and DSP F-6R, both launched in 1984, as well as DSP F-5R, launched in 1987, were the primary operational spacecraft.[189] As their designation indicates, F-5R and F-6R are both refurbished spacecraft that were originally manufactured in the mid-1970s, but they were placed in

[185] Charles, D., 'Spy satellites: entering a new era', *Science*, 24 Mar. 1989, pp. 1541–43.

[186] *Military Space* (note 184).

[187] Ball, D., *A Base for Debate* (Allen & Unwin: London, 1987) is perhaps the most comprehensive discussion of the DSP system.

[188] Kenden, A., 'Military maneuvers in synchronous orbit', *Journal of the British Interplanetary Society*, vol. 36 (Feb. 1983), pp. 88–91.

[189] 'Advanced missile warning satellite evolved from smaller spacecraft', *Aviation Week & Space Technology*, 20 Jan. 1989, p. 45.

storage because of the unexpectedly long operational life of the DSP series. In the early 1980s these two spacecraft were refurbished under the Sensor Evolutionary Development Program (SEDS), which greatly improved the sensitivity of their sensors.[190]

The launch of the first of the Improved DSP (DSP-I) series, which had been delayed from October 1988 by problems with the Titan 4 launch vehicle, finally occurred on 14 June. These satellites, of which spacecraft 14–25 were on order in early 1989 with options for 26–28 under consideration,[191] will incorporate the upgraded sensors of the SEDS satellites, as well as improved resistance to laser attack.[192]

The DSP-I satellites will also carry a laser communications package that will enable the satellites to relay warning information to each other.[193] This will greatly reduce the vulnerability of this system to attacks on its ground stations, since all the satellites will be able to communicate with any of the system's ground stations. However, DSP-I (F-14), launched in June 1989, did not incorporate this laser communications system, due to technical problems.[194] Instead, DSP F-14 will carry an experimental sensor package for the SDIO to assess the utility of ultraviolet sensors for tracking missiles.

Soviet navigation satellites

The USA and the USSR have remarkably similar navigation satellite systems, with a low-altitude constellation of small satellites of modest capabilities (in the US case the Transit system) as well as a constellation of semi-synchronous satellites providing very high accuracy fixes (the US system is Navstar; the Soviet system is known as GLONASS, although the individual satellites are launched under the Cosmos designation). While the US Transit system is used by both military and civilian operators, the Soviets operate separate military and civilian systems, using similar satellites. The military system consists of a six-satellite constellation, and there were four launches in 1989 to maintain this constellation.

The GLONASS system has experienced major developmental problems since its introduction in 1982, with 1988 proving an exceptionally difficult period.[195] The first GLONASS launch of 1989 on 10 January included GLONASS satellites Cosmos 1987 and 1988, as well as Cosmos 1989, the first Etalon geodetic laser reflector satellite. The launch on 31 May of Cosmos 2022 and 2023 was similarly accompanied by Cosmos 2024, a second Etalon geodetic spacecraft. Along with Cosmos 1946, 1947 and

[190] Cushman, J., 'AF seeks invulnerable warning satellites', *Defense Week*, 16 Jan. 1984, pp. 10–14.

[191] 'Air Force to decide by end of month on DSP acquisition method', *Aerospace Daily*, 5 Oct. 1989, pp. 30–31.

[192] Covault, C., 'New missile warning satellite to be launched on first Titan 4', *Aviation Week & Space Technology*, 20 Jan. 1989, pp. 34–40. (This article is an excellent review of the history and status of this programme.)

[193] Cushman (note 190), p. 12.

[194] Goodman, A., 'Problems plague McDonnell Douglas laser', *St. Louis Post Dispatch*, 13 Aug. 1989, p. 1 (an extremely thorough treatment of this problem).

[195] Daly, P., 'GLONASS status', *Aviation Week & Space Technology*, 14 Sep. 1987, p. 108.

1948, launched in May 1988, and Cosmos 1970, 1971 and 1972, launched in September 1988, the two launches in 1989 left the operational GLONASS complement at 10 satellites, still well short of the 21 spacecraft the USSR has stated to be its ultimate goal.

US navigation satellites

The long-running Transit navigation satellite programme continued in operation in 1989, with a total of 12 operational and operable spare Transit satellites in orbit.[196] Oscar 13, launched in 1967, failed in January 1989 after over 21 years of service in orbit. Most of the military users of Transit, such as the Navy's ballistic missile submarines that were the original impetus for Transit, will soon shift to Navstar. However, the current Transit constellation will remain in service to civilian users at least through 1995. With the launch of five new Navstar satellites in 1989, the Air Force has begun to implement the full complement of 21 active and 3 spare satellites necessary for nearly continuous global coverage.[197] Although the first two satellites launched had been nicknamed Elvis (Presley) and Janis (Joplin), this practice ceased with the third and subsequent launches.[198]

Six Navstar navigation satellites, launched between 1980 and 1985, continued in service in 1989. The total number of GPS (Global Positioning System) satellites was originally planned to be 21 active plus 3 spares. This number was reduced to 18 active and 3 spares as a cost saving measure in the early 1980s,[199] but the number of active satellites was returned to 21 in 1987,[200] with this number planned for implementation by 1993.[201] In an action worth almost $1 billion, the Air Force selected General Electric to build up to 26 new Navstars to replenish the constellation of Rockwell satellites in the mid-1990s.[202] Completing its withdrawal from the shuttle, the Air Force decided to remove the remaining two Navstars from the shuttle manifest, with all Navstars to be launched on the improved version of the proven Delta launch vehicle, known as the Delta 2.[203]

Soviet weather satellites

Unlike the United States, the Soviet Union does not operate a separate low-altitude military weather satellite network. Presumably the Soviet military uses data from Meteor 2 and Meteor 3 satellites, of which several are

[196] Danchik, R. *et al.*, *Navy Navigation System Status*, Royal Institute of Navigation NAV-89 Conference, London, 17–19 Oct. 1989.

[197] Kolcum, E., 'First USAF/McDonnell Douglas Delta 2 launch begins new military space era', *Aviation Week & Space Technology*, 20 Feb. 1989, pp. 18–19.

[198] 'News and comment', *Air Force Magazine*, Oct. 1989, p. 29.

[199] Clarke, C., '. . . and a star to steer by', *Defense Electronics*, June 1989, pp. 57–64.

[200] Klass, P., 'Defense Dept. will seek funds to expand Navstar constellation', *Aviation Week & Space Technology*, 5 Oct. 1987, pp. 30–31.

[201] 'Magnavox prepares for GPS buildup', *Military Space*, 25 Sep. 1989, pp. 3–5.

[202] 'GE astro-space over Rockwell for GPS, *World Aerospace Weekly*, 30 June 1989, pp. 1–2.

[203] Smith, B., 'USAF awards McDonnell Douglas contract to build, operate MLVs', *Aviation Week & Space Technology*, 26 Jan. 1988, pp. 20–21.

usually operational. One of each of these spacecraft was launched in 1989, bringing to five the total number of operational meteorological spacecraft.

US weather satellites

The primary US military weather satellite system is the Air Force constellation of two Defense Meteorological Support Program (DMSP) satellites. Following the launch of the fourth DMSP 5D-2 in February 1988, no launches were required in 1989 to maintain two operational satellites in orbit.

VII. Launch vehicles

The contrast in launch vehicle developments in 1989 further underscores the divergence in the Soviet and US space programmes. The major slowdown in Soviet launch activity was coupled with reduced production plans for the Proton, as well as no launches of the Zenith/Energia/Buran (SL-16/17 and shuttle) family of launch vehicles. In contrast, the continued US comeback in space was marked by an expanding fleet of new and redesigned expendable launch vehicles. However, these US programmes were marred by technical problems, schedule delays and cost overruns. Longer-range projects, such as the Advanced Launch System and the National Aerospace Plane, were significantly slowed during the year.

The US expendable launch vehicle programme

With five successful flights in 1989 in addition to two flights in 1988, the US space shuttle programme has taken another step on the slow road to recovery from the Challenger accident on January 1986. However, major uncertainties remain concerning the shuttle's maximum flight rate[204] and safety. These successes have not altered the US military decision to cease reliance on the shuttle system.[205] Indeed, although previous plans had called for two Defense Department missions on the shuttle each year throughout the 1990s,[206] by early 1989 the Air Force has decided to completely withdraw from the shuttle after 1993, flying only those shuttle missions that had been paid for prior to the Challenger accident.[207]

[204] National Research Council, *Post-Challenger Assessment of Space Shuttle Flight Rates and Utilization*, Washington, DC, Oct. 1986.
[205] 'Military launcher program meeting critical milestones', *Aviation Week & Space Technology*, 1 Feb. 1988, pp. 36–38.
[206] US Congress, House of Representatives Committee on Science, Space and Technology, Subcommittee on Space, Science and Applications, *Report on the Fiscal Year 1990 Authorization Request and Budget Estimates for the National Aeronautics and Space Administration*, 100th Congress, 1st Session, p. 296.
[207] Broad, W., 'The military finds an alternative to the space shuttle', *New York Times*, 18 June 1989, p. 6E.

The military's expendable launch vehicle programme got off to a slow start, with inaugural launches planned for 1988 slipping into 1989.[208] Despite this slow beginning, however, total spending on expendable launch vehicles in 1989–94 is slated to approach $10 billion.[209]

The centre-piece of the military's launch vehicle programme is the Titan 4.[210] Engineering problems delayed the initial launch from October 1988 to June 1989,[211] and the Titan 4 development programme experienced a $208 million cost overrun.[212] Additional difficulties have been encountered with the Solid Rocket Motor Upgrade programme which is intended to increase the payload of the booster.[213] Despite these problems, a new contract for 18 of these boosters brought the total order to 41, at a cost of about $7 billion.[214] Of these boosters, 13 will be used by the Air Force[215] for launching Milstar communications satellites and DSP early-warning satellites, while the remaining 28 will be used to launch KH-12 photoreconnaissance and Lacrosse imaging radar satellites.

The first flight of the Delta 2, carrying a Navstar navigation satellite, was delayed from late 1988 to 14 February 1989, due to a variety of minor problems, and subsequent launches also experienced delays.[216] The initial order for 20 Delta 2s has been marred by a $140 million cost overrun,[217] which was somewhat surprising given the relatively minor changes that the Delta 2 represented compared with prior versions of the Delta.[218] Despite these problems, subsequent orders are anticipated at a rate of four per year in the mid- to late 1990s to maintain the Navstar navigation satellite constellation.[219]

A total of 14 Titan 2s are on order, for launching White Cloud naval surveillance satellites, DMSP military weather satellites, National Oceanic and Atmospheric Administration (NOAA) civilian weather satellites, and the LANDSAT 6 resource-monitoring satellite.[220] The second Titan 2 flight came on 6 September 1989, with the successful launch of a White Cloud naval ocean surveillance payload.

[208] Kolcum, E., 'Air Force cannot meet 1988 launch schedule', *Aviation Week & Space Technology*, 23 Jan. 1989, pp. 21–22.
[209] US Senate Armed Services Committee (note 43), p. 171.
[210] Kolcum, E., 'Air Force, contractors predict long life for heavy-lift vehicle', *Aviation Week & Space Technology*, 17 July 1989, pp. 32–34.
[211] Kolcum, E., 'Titan 4, Delta 2 launches generate confidence in military space operations', *Aviation Week & Space Technology*, 19 June 1989, pp. 40–41.
[212] Lynch, D., 'Air Force officials underestimated cost, difficulty of return to space', *Defense Week*, 5 Sep. 1989, pp. 1, 12.
[213] 'Air Force should continue to buy steel case solid rocket motors', *Inside the Pentagon*, 16 Sep. 1989, p. 21.
[214] Kiernan, V., 'Air Force orders 18 more Titan 4 boosters', *Space News*, 11 Dec. 1989, p. 12.
[215] Senate Armed Services Committee (note 43), p. 194.
[216] 'Parts shortage delays Delta 2 launch of Navstar satellites', *Aviation Week & Space Technology*, 13 June 1989, p. 21.
[217] 'McDonnell Douglas Delta 2 booster suffers $140 million cost overrun', *Satellite News*, 4 Dec. 1989, p. 5.
[218] Smith, B., 'USAF awards McDonnell Douglas contract to build, operate MLVs', *Aviation Week & Space Technology*, 26 Jan. 1988, pp. 20–21.
[219] Senate Armed Services Committee (note 43), p. 195.
[220] 'Martin converts USAF Titan 2 to launch vehicle for placing defense payloads into Polar orbit', *Aviation Week & Space Technology*, 10 Aug. 1987, p. 18.

Other booster developments in 1989 included the final Titan 34D launched on 4 September 1989[221] and continued work on the Atlas 2, which will be used primarily for DSCS III communications satellites.[222]

Advanced US launch systems

In addition to these traditional booster programmes, four new launch systems are also under development. The Pegasus and Taurus rockets are intended to support small military satellite programmes in the near term. The Advanced Launch System (ALS) and the National Aero-Space Plane (NASP) programme, initiated by the Reagan Administration in the mid-1980s, are directed at very ambitious long-term objectives. During 1989, increased emphasis was devoted to Pegasus and Taurus, while ALS and NASP were greatly reduced in scope. Indeed, in this regard, the first year of the Bush Administration witnessed the dismantlement of some of the central elements of the Reagan Administration's launch vehicle programme.

The US military's interest in smaller satellites has been matched by an effort sponsored by DARPA to develop the new small boosters that would be needed to launch such satellites. Most prominent of these is the Pegasus, a two-stage solid-fuel winged booster that would be air-launched, initially from the same B-52 that was used to launch the X-15 experimental aircraft in the 1960s.[223] The initial flights of the Pegasus will carry a variety of experimental scientific and engineering test satellites,[224] with each flight costing about $10 million,[225] comparable to the launch cost of other small launchers such as the Scout. As a result of problems encountered during initial captive carry tests, the first flight, initially planned for July 1989,[226] was delayed to March 1990 at the earliest.[227]

Based on their successful development of Pegasus, Orbital Sciences Corporation and Hercules were awarded a contract to develop a more powerful, ground-launched Standard Small Launch Vehicle (SSLV), with an initial flight anticipated in the second quarter of 1991.[228] This new Taurus booster, which consists of a first stage from the MX Peacekeeper ICBM and a second and third stage based on the two stages of the Pegasus, will be able to place about 450 kg into polar orbit at a cost of $16 million.[229] Later growth versions are projected to have double this capacity, as well as the ability to place over 150 kg in geosynchronous orbit.[230] The anticipated

[221] 'Last Titan 3 rocket lofts a secret military satellite', *Washington Post*, 5 Sep. 1989, p. A2.

[222] 'General Dynamics wins MLV II competition', *Aerospace Daily*, 4 May 1988, p. 185.

[223] Carroll, H. *et al.*, 'Design and development of Pegasus propulsion', AIAA Paper 89-2314, 10 July 1989.

[224] Smith, B., 'Pegasus air-launched test vehicle is rolled out', *Aviation Week & Space Technology*, 14 Aug. 1989, pp. 36–40.

[225] Nichols, R., 'The winged horse', *Ad Astra*, Feb. 1989, pp. 30–36.

[226] Covault, C., 'Pegasus commercial launch project to begin rocket motor test firings', *Aviation Week & Space Technology*, 13 Feb. 1989, p. 91.

[227] 'Third Pegasus test flight to validate fixes, data relay system', *Aerospace Daily*, 17 Jan. 1990, p. 91.

[228] 'Milspace programs', *Military Space*, 31 July 1989, p. 7.

[229] 'Space testing', *Military Space*, 23 Oct. 1989, p. 2.

[230] 'Space data scores again with DARPA', *Space Business News*, 7 Aug. 1989, pp. 1–2.

Taurus launch rate is planned to grow from two flights in 1991, to as many as six or seven per year by 1995.[231]

The ALS emerged in the mid-1980s as the rocket that would be used to deploy the space-based elements of the SDI programme. Because SDI was initially projected to require many thousands of tonnes of payload to low earth orbit, ALS was intended to reduce the cost of space transportation by an order of magnitude, from about $10 000 per kilogram to less than $1000 per kilogram.[232] Thus the Bush Administration inherited a plan for development of the Advanced Launch System that called for the Defense Acquisition Board to approve advanced development of the system in early 1990, leading to a first flight in 1998 and a full operational capability in 2000.[233] This effort would lead to the development of a modular family of launch vehicles with a payload capacity to low earth orbit ranging from 5000 kg to 200 000 kg that would replace existing expendable launch vehicles in the 2000–2005 timeframe.[234]

However, by late 1989 it had become increasingly apparent that the requirements for the ALS programme had largely disappeared.[235] The initial phase of SDI would be deployed using existing Titan 4 and Atlas 2 rockets and the launch requirements for subsequent phases of SDI deployment were too vague to require immediate development of ALS.[236] With total development cost of ALS pegged at $15 billion through its first flight in 1998,[237] the need for ALS seemed increasing doubtful.[238] By the end of 1979 the ALS programme, once the centre-piece of space planning, had been reduced to a $150 million per year propulsion development effort.[239]

The most ambitious of the new US launch vehicle programmes is the NASP project, officially known as the X-30 and unofficially as the Orient Express. Begun in 1985, NASP aimed to develop a new type of supersonic combustion ramjet (scramjet) engine that could propel an aircraft to near-orbital speeds.[240] Potential military missions included air defence or reconnaissance. As a space launch vehicle, NASP was thought to promise aircraft-style safety and convenience with operating costs that would be a fraction of those of conventional rockets or the space shuttle.

[231] Covault, C., 'Pegasus, MX boosters combined for new defense launch vehicle', *Aviation Week & Space Technology*, 18 Dec. 1989, pp. 47–50.

[232] 'ALS contractors concentrate on expendable, reusable designs', *Aerospace Daily*, 20 June 1989, p. 463.

[233] Wolfe, M. G. et al., *The Advanced Launch System*, IAF Paper 89-229, 40th International Astronautical Federation Congress, Malaga, Spain, 8–14 Oct. 1989.

[234] Branscome, D. R., 'United States Space Transportation Survey, Proceedings of the 2nd European Aerospace Conference on Progress in Space Transportation' (European Space Agency, ESA SP-293, Aug. 1989), pp. 39–44.

[235] 'Air Force embraces expendable launchers', *Military Space*, 17 July 1989, pp. 3–4.

[236] Adams, P., 'Congress may consider ALS too costly, sources say', *Defense News*, 27 Mar. 1989, p. 25.

[237] Smith, B., 'USAF cuts vehicle design work on advanced launch system', *Aviation Week & Space Technology*, 18 Dec. 1989, p. 112.

[238] Finnegan, P., 'Report: ALS program lacks mission, should be pared to propulsion study', *Defense News*, 25 Sep. 1989, p. 4.

[239] Finnegan, P., 'US Air Force, NASA restructure advanced launch system program', *Defense News*, 15 Jan. 1990, pp. 1, 15.

[240] Lynn, N., 'Mission to mach 25', *Flight International*, 6 May 1989, pp. 42–44.

However, by early 1989 there were increasing doubts that NASP would find military missions other than space launch,[241] as well as growing concerns about the technical feasibility of the concept.[242] Based on these concerns,[243] the Air Force decided in early 1989 to withdraw its support from the project. Initial planning for the X-30 programme had anticipated total funding of $570 million in 1990 and $620 million in 1991, with most of this money coming from the Air Force.[244] In an effort to save the project, the National Space Council gained congressional support for a revised plan, with $254 million for 1990 and $277 million for 1991, about evenly divided between NASA and the Air Force.[245] This reduction in funding delayed the decision on proceeding with the prototype programme from September 1990 to March 1993,[246] the first flight from 1994 to 1996, and the first orbital flight from 1996 to after 1998.[247]

Soviet launch vehicles

In contrast to that of the USA, Soviet launch activity in 1989 was marked by the new launch vehicles that were not used during the course of the year. The SL-16 Zenith, derived from the strap-on booster of the Energia launcher, had seemed well on its way to a major role in the Soviet space effort, with 10 launches since 1985, including a peak of five in 1987.[248] However, no SL-16 launches occurred in 1989. The SL-17 Energia itself, as well as the Buran shuttle, also remained on the ground during the year.

VIII. Military satellite programmes of other countries

While 1988 was a very active year in space for China, with four launches achieved, 1989 was unusually quiescent, with no launch attempts (for the first year since 1980). Although no military-related launches were conducted in 1989, France continues work leading to a 1991 launch of the Syracuse II military communications satellite system[249] and a 1994 launch of the Helios photoreconnaissance satellite which is being developed with the participation of Italy and Spain.[250] France is also studying development of a

---

[241] Augenstein, B. et al., 'Assessment of NASP: future options', RAND Working Draft WD-4437-AF, June 1989, reprinted in 'The National Aerospace Plane', Joint Hearing of the Science Space and Technology and Armed Services Committees of the House of Representatives, 101st Congress, 1st Session.

[242] Air Force Studies Board, Hypersonic Technology for Military Application (National Research Council: Washington, DC, 1989).

[243] Covault, C., 'White House acts to reverse aero-space plane cancellation', Aviation Week & Space Technology, 24 Apr. 1989, pp. 20–21.

[244] 'NASP', Aerospace Daily, 29 Apr. 1988, p. 166.

[245] 'Space Council slows NASP development', Space Business News, 10 July 1989, pp. 1, 7.

[246] 'Space Council stretches out NASP', Military Space, 17 July 1989, p. 6.

[247] Roesch, K., 'Superfast "space plane" off to a slow start', Congressional Quarterly Weekly, 6 Jan. 1990, pp. 35–37.

[248] 'Soviets confirm ten medium-lift Zenit launches', Flight International, 2 Jan. 1990, p. 13.

[249] 'French milspace', Military Space, 5 Dec. 1988, p. 5.

[250] 'Helios to deliver imagery to 3 nations', Military Space, 21 Nov. 1988, pp. 1–3.

2-m resolution imaging radar system to complement Helios.[251] The UK is studying options for a Phase II for the Skynet 4 military communications system, with new satellites in the series to be launched in 1996 and 1997, once Skynet 4A and 4C are launched in 1990.[252] This growing European interest in military space systems, coupled with increasing European integration generally, has led to calls for close collaboration on future military space systems,[253] but thus far to no official action.

Iraq surprised the world on 5 December 1989 with the launch of a rocket from the Al-Anbar test centre characterized as a space launch vehicle.[254] Conflicting reports suggested that the test of the 25-m long 48-tonne rocket, called al Abed (or al Abid, 'the Worshipper'), either terminated at an altitude of 20 km,[255] or succeeded in briefly placing its third stage in orbit (see also chapter 9).[256] As with the Israeli satellite launched in 1988,[257] the impact of the Iraqi test firing is more political than military.[258]

[251] 'France defines satellite to complement spot series', *Aviation Week & Space Technology*, 23 Oct. 1989, p. 48.

[252] Furniss, T., 'UK studies new military satellite plan', *Flight International*, 7 Oct. 1989, p. 4.

[253] 'Collaborative Western European military satellite system needed', *Satellite Week*, 6 Nov. 1989, p. 2.

[254] Gordon, M., 'Iraqis announce test of a rocket', *New York Times*, 8 Dec. 1989, p. 1.

[255] 'Iraqi space launch more modest than claimed', *Flight International*, 20 Dec. 1989, p. 4.

[256] Gordon, M., 'US confirms Iraq has launched rocket that can carry satellites', *New York Times*, 9 Dec. 1989, p. 7.

[257] Kifner, J., 'Israel launches space program and a satellite', *New York Times*, 20 Sep. 1988, pp. 1, 12.

[258] 'New Iraq booster has limited ability to launch payloads, US says', *Space Commerce Bulletin*, 15 Dec. 1989, pp. 1–2.

Appendix 3A. Military satellites launched in 1989

Imaging intelligence

USSR

THIRD-GENERATION—MEDIUM RESOLUTION

Type/Country/ Spacecraft name	Alternative name (Host spacecraft)	Designation	Launch date	Booster	Facility	Mass (kg)	Perigee (km)	Apogee (km)	Inclin. (deg)	Period (min)	Comments
Cosmos 1991	SU PHOTO 3M-105	1989-003A	18 Jan.	SL-4	TT	6 300	325	410	70.25	90.2	
Cosmos 2006	SU PHOTO 3M-106	1989-022A	16 Mar.	SL-4	PL	6 300	249	402	62.90	92.0	

THIRD-GENERATION—HIGH RESOLUTION

Type/Country/ Spacecraft name	Alternative name (Host spacecraft)	Designation	Launch date	Booster	Facility	Mass (kg)	Perigee (km)	Apogee (km)	Inclin. (deg)	Period (min)	Comments
Cosmos 2003	SU PHOTO 3H-264	1989-015A	17 Feb.	SL-4	PL	6 300	249	271	62.80	91.7	Continuation of 1988 flights at 62.8° inclin.
Cosmos 2017	SU PHOTO 3H-265	1989-029A	6 Apr.	SL-4	PL	6 300	244	288	62.80	89.7	
Cosmos 2019	SU PHOTO 3H-266	1989-034A	5 May	SL-4	PL	6 300	194	350	62.80	89.7	May have covered Jerico test in South Africa
Cosmos 2025	SU PHOTO 3H-267	1989-040A	1 June	SL-4	TT	6 300	252	275	62.80	89.6	May have covered Jerico test in South Africa
Cosmos 2028	SU PHOTO 3H-268	1989-047A	16 June	SL-4	PL	6 300	217	314	70.00	89.5	1st time since 1987 with six in orbit at one time (information from G. Perry)
Cosmos 2032	SU PHOTO 3H-269	1989-057A	20 July	SL-4	TT	6 300	193	275	82.30	88.8	
Cosmos 2035	SU PHOTO 3H-270	1989-060A	2 Aug.	SL-4	PL	6 300	191	268	82.60	89.2	
Cosmos 2036	SU PHOTO 3H-271	1989-065A	22 Aug.	SL-4	TT	6 300	248	273	62.80	89.6	
Cosmos 2045	SU PHOTO 3H-272	1989-076A	22 Sep.	SL-4	PL	6 300	216	322	70.00	89.6	De-orbited after 10 days, rather than the expected 14
Cosmos 2048	SU PHOTO 3H-273	1989-083A	17 Oct.	SL-4	PL	6 300	248	270	62.80	91.7	De-orbited after 9 days, rather than the expected 14

THIRD-GENERATION—MILITARY MAPPING AND CIVIL REMOTE SENSING

Type/Country/ Spacecraft name	Alternative name (Host spacecraft)	Designation	Launch date	Booster	Facility	Mass (kg)	Perigee (km)	Apogee (km)	Inclin. (deg)	Period (min)	Comments
Cosmos 1990	SU PHOTO 3E-43	1989-002A	12 Jan.	SL-4	PL	6 300	192	259	82.60	89.6	Covered Armenian earthquake region
Cosmos 2000	SU PHOTO 3E-44	1989-010A	10 Feb.	SL-4	PL	6 300	191	275	82.30	88.8	Coverage will include Antarctica

Name		Designation	Date	Vehicle	Site	Mass	Perigee	Apogee	Incl.	Period	Comments
Resurs-F 1	..	1989-038A	25 May	SL-4	PL	6 300	188	263	82.30	88.7	1st launched as Resurs-F, 2 Pion subsatellites
Resurs-F 2	..	1989-049A	27 June	SL-4	PL	6 300	182	234	82.60	88.7	Announced as natural resources
Cosmos 2029	SU PHOTO 3E-45	1989-051A	5 July	SL-4	PL	6 300	193	270	82.35	88.8	2 Pion subsatellites
Resurs-F 3	..	1989-055A	18 July	SL-4	PL	6 300	195	253	82.60	88.6	
Resurs-F 4	..	1989-063A	15 Aug.	SL-4	PL	6 300	192	258	82.30	89.0	Carried FRG microgravity experiment
Resurs-F 5	..	1989-073A	6 Sep.	SL-4	PL	6 300	185	260	82.30	89.0	
FOURTH-GENERATION											
Cosmos 1993	SU PHOTO 4.91	1989-007A	28 Jan.	SL-4	PL	6 500	173	360	64.90	89.8	
Cosmos 2005	SU PHOTO 4.92	1989-019A	2 Mar.	SL-4	PL	6 500	197	347	62.80	89.7	
Cosmos 2018	SU PHOTO 4.93	1989-031A	20 Apr.	SL-4	TT	6 500	194	350	62.80	89.7	Replaces Cosmos 1993
Cosmos 2020	SU PHOTO 4.94	1989-036A	17 May	SL-4	PL	6 500	180	365	64.70	89.7	
Cosmos 2030	SU PHOTO 4.95	1989-054A	12 July	SL-4	TT	6 500	177	373	67.00	89.7	Disintegrated on 28 July 1989
Cosmos 2047	SU PHOTO 4.96	1989-082A	3 Oct.	SL-4	PL	6 500	178	357	67.00	89.5	
Cosmos 2052	SU PHOTO 4.97	1989-095A	30 Nov.	SL-4	PL	6 500	175	373	67.20	89.7	
FOURTH-GENERATION—MILITARY MAPPING AND CIVIL REMOTE SENSING											
Cosmos 2021	SU PHOTO 4T	1989-037A	24 May	SL-4	PL	6 500	204	302	70.00	89.3	
Cosmos 2031	SU PHOTO 4T	1989-056A	19 July	SL-4	TT	6 500	200	283	50.50	89.0	Disintegrated on 31 August 1989
FIFTH-GENERATION											
Cosmos 2007	SU PHOTO 5-10	1989-024A	23 Mar.	SL-4	TT	6 800	190	300	64.80	89.1	
Cosmos 2049	SU PHOTO 5-11	1989-088A	17 Nov.	SL-4	TT	6 800	189	242	64.80	89.0	
USA											
KH-12A/1	USA-40	1989-061B	8 Aug.	STS	ETR	14 500	450	450	56.90	93.5	Initial malfunction corrected

Electronic intellligence systems

Name		Designation	Date	Vehicle	Site	Mass	Perigee	Apogee	Incl.	Period	Comments
USA											
Chalet 6 Vortex 6	USA-37	1989-035A	10 May	Titan 34D	ETR	1 850	35 780	35 780	1.00	1 436.0	Orbital elements are estimated
Magnum 2	..	1989-090B	23 Nov.	STS	ETR	2 275	35 780	35 780	0.00	1 436.0	Orbital elements are estimated

Type/Country/ Spacecraft name	Alternative name (Host spacecraft)	Designation	Launch date	Booster	Facility	Mass (kg)	Perigee (km)	Apogee (km)	Inclin. (deg)	Period (min)	Comments
Naval intelligence systems											
USSR											
Cosmos 2033	SU EORSAT 1-29	1989-058A	24 July	SL-11	TT	4 250	410	436	65.00	92.3	
Cosmos 2046	SU EORSAT 1-30	1989-079A	27 Sep.	SL-11	TT	4 250	412	431	65.00	92.8	172 degrees away from others, new plane with C-2051
Cosmos 2051	SU EORSAT 1-31	1989-092A	25 Nov.	SL-11	TT	4 250	305	456	64.90	..	Spacecraft problems resolved, five active at one time
USA											
NOSS 10	USA-45	1989-072A	6 Sep.	Titan 2	WTR	450	1 050	1175	63.40	107.5	Orbital elements are estimated
NOSS-SSU 10-1	White Cloud	1989-072C	6 Sep.	Titan 2	WTR	45	1 050	1175	63.40	107.5	
NOSS-SSU 10-2	White Cloud	1989-072D	6 Sep.	Titan 2	WTR	45	1 050	1175	63.40	107.5	
NOSS-SSU 10-3	White Cloud	1989-072E	6 Sep.	Titan 2	WTR	45	1 050	1175	63.40	107.5	
Military communications											
USSR											
Cosmos 2008	SU COM 1-329	1989-025A	24 Mar.	SL-8	PL	45	1 445	1 510	74.00	115.2	
Cosmos 2009	SU COM 1-330	1989-025B	24 Mar.	SL-8	PL	45	1 445	1 510	74.00	115.2	
Cosmos 2010	SU COM 1-331	1989-025C	24 Mar.	SL-8	PL	45	1 445	1 510	74.00	115.2	
Cosmos 2011	SU COM 1-332	1989-025D	24 Mar.	SL-8	PL	45	1 445	1 510	74.00	115.2	
Cosmos 2012	SU COM 1-333	1989-025E	24 Mar.	SL-8	PL	45	1 445	1 510	74.00	115.2	
Cosmos 2013	SU COM 1-334	1989-025F	24 Mar.	SL-8	PL	45	1 445	1 510	74.00	115.2	
Cosmos 2014	SU COM 1-335	1989-025G	24 Mar.	SL-8	PL	45	1 445	1 510	74.00	115.2	
Cosmos 2015	SU COM 1-336	1989-025H	24 Mar.	SL-8	PL	45	1 445	1 510	74.00	115.2	
Cosmos 1992	SU COM 2-44	1989-005A	26 Jan.	SL-8	PL	750	780	810	74.00	100.6	Three-satellite constellation
Cosmos 1994	SU COM 3-31	1989-009A	10 Feb.	SL-14	PL	400	1 397	1 416	82.60	113.9	
Cosmos 1995	SU COM 3-32	1989-009B	10 Feb.	SL-14	PL	400	1 413	1 418	82.60	114.2	

Cosmos 1996	SU COM 3-33	1989-009C	10 Feb.	SL-14	PL	400	1407	1417	82.60	114.1	
Cosmos 1997	SU COM 3-34	1989-009D	10 Feb.	SL-14	PL	400	1401	1417	82.60	114.0	
Cosmos 1998	SU COM 3-35	1989-009E	10 Feb.	SL-14	PL	400	1391	1417	82.60	113.9	
Cosmos 1999	SU COM 3-36	1989-009F	10 Feb.	SL-14	PL	400	1385	1417	82.60	113.8	
Cosmos 2038	SU COM 3-37	1989-074A	15 Sep.	SL-14	PL	400	1395	1425	82.60	113.8	
Cosmos 2039	SU COM 3-38	1989-074B	15 Sep.	SL-14	PL	400	1395	1425	82.60	113.8	
Cosmos 2040	SU COM 3-39	1989-074C	15 Sep.	SL-14	PL	400	1395	1425	82.60	113.8	
Cosmos 2041	SU COM 3-41	1989-074D	15 Sep.	SL-14	PL	400	1395	1425	82.60	113.8	
Cosmos 2042	SU COM 3-42	1989-074E	15 Sep.	SL-14	PL	400	1395	1425	82.60	113.8	
Cosmos 2043	SU COM 3-43	1989-074F	15 Sep.	SL-14	PL	400	1395	1425	82.60	113.8	
Molniya 1-75	..	1989-014A	15 Feb.	SL-6	PL	1 250	486	38 937	62.50	698.0	
Molniya 1-76	..	1989-078A	27 Sep.	SL-6	PL	1 250	650	38 960	62.80	702.0	
Cosmos 2054	Potok	1989-101A	27 Dec.	SL-12	TT	2 120	36 505	36 374	1.52	1 469.5	Similar to Cosmos 1961
USA											
TDRSS D	..	1989-021A	13 Mar.	STS	ETR	2 225	35 800	35 800	0.00	1 436.0	TDRSS-1 placed in storage W 79
DSCS II-16	DSCS A-16 USA-43	1989-069A	4 Sep.	Titan 34D	ETR	619	35 780	35 780	0.00	1 436.0	Double launch with DSCS III
DSCS III-A 2	DFS-2 USA-44	1989-069B	4 Sep.	Titan 34D	ETR	825	35 780	35 780	0.00	1 436.0	Double launch with DSCS II
FLTSATCOM 8	F-8	1989-077A	25 Sep.	Atlas G	ETR	1 884	35 780	35 780	0.00	1 436.0	EHF Package
AFSATCOM SCT-2	(On DSCS III-A2)	1989-069B	4 Sep.	Titan 34D	ETR	28	35 780	35 780	0.00	1 436.0	
AFSATCOM F-8	(On FLTSATCOM 8)	1989-077A	25 Sep.	Atlas G	ETR	0	35 780	35 780	0.00	1 436.0	
Japan											
(On SCS 1A)	Superbird-X 1A	1989-041A	5 June	Ariane 4	KO	..	35 800	35 800	0.00	1 436.0	Two 40-watt X-band transponders
Ballistic missile early warning											
USSR											
Cosmos 2001	SU BMEWS 1-60	1989-011A	14 Feb.	SL-6	PL	1 500	615	39 720	62.90	708.0	Nine-satellite constellation
Cosmos 2050	SU BMEWS 1-61	1989-091A	24 Nov.	SL-6	PL	1 500	603	39 342	62.80	709.0	
USA											
DSP-I 14 F-14	USA-39	1989-046A	14 June	Titan 402A	ETR	2 370	35 780	35 780	1.00	1 436.0	1st DSP-improved, 1st Titan 4

Type/Country/ Spacecraft name	Alternative name (Host spacecraft)	Designation	Launch date	Booster	Facility	Mass (kg)	Perigee (km)	Apogee (km)	Inclin. (deg)	Period (min)	Comments
Navigation											
USSR											
Nadezhda 1	..	1989-050A	4 July	SL-8	PL	750	979	1 026	83.00	104.9	1st identified as Nadezhda = Hope
Cosmos 2004	SU NAV 3-63	1989-017A	22 Feb.	SL-8	PL	750	933	1 031	83.00	105.1	Six-satellite constellation
Cosmos 2016	SU NAV 3-65	1989-028A	4 Apr.	SL-8	PL	750	973	1 036	82.90	104.9	
Cosmos 2026	SU NAV 3-66	1989-042A	7 June	SL-8	PL	750	969	1 022	82.90	104.9	C-1725 was revived to replace C-1864 in early 1989
Cosmos 2034	SU NAV 3-67	1989-059A	25 July	SL-8	PL	750	988	1 026	82.90	105.0	
Cosmos 1987	GLONASS 40	1989-001A	10 Jan.	SL-12	TT	900	19 100	19 150	64.80	676.0	Same plane as Cosmos 1946-48
Cosmos 1988	GLONASS 41	1989-001B	10 Jan.	SL-12	TT	900	19 100	19 150	64.80	676.0	Same plane as Cosmos 1946-48
Cosmos 2022	GLONASS 42	1989-039A	31 May	SL-12	TT	900	19 100	19 150	64.80	674.4	Total of 10 operaing, C 1946-8, C 1970-2, C 1987-8
Cosmos 2023	GLONASS 43	1989-039B	31 May	SL-12	TT	900	19 100	19 150	64.80	674.4	
USA											
Navstar 2A-12	NDS 13 USA-35	1989-013A	14 Feb.	Delta 6925	ETR	818	20 025	20 350	63.25	718.0	Satellite nicknamed Elvis
Navstar 2A-13	NDS 14 USA-38	1989-044A	9 June	Delta 6925	ETR	818	20 025	20 350	63.25	718.0	Satellite nicknamed Janis
Navstar 2A-14	NDS 16 USA-42	1989-064A	18 Aug.	Delta 6925	ETR	818	20 025	20 350	63.25	718.0	Delayed 4 times by weather, no nickname
Navstar 2A-15	NDS 17	1989-085A	21 Oct.	Delta 6925	ETR	818	20 025	20 350	63.25	718.0	
Navstar 2A-16	NDS 18	1989-097A	11 Dec.	Delta 6925	ETR	818	20 025	20 350	63.25	718.0	
Weather											
USSR											
Meteor 2-18	..	1989-018A	28 Feb.	SL-14	PL	2 750	951	974	82.50	104.1	
Meteor 3-3	..	1989-086A	25 Oct.	SL-14	PL	2 750	1 191	1 228	82.60	109.5	5th operational, also M-3-2 & M-2 16,17,18
USA	*No launches in 1989*										

Nuclear explosion detection

USSR   *The Soviet Union presumably uses sensors on unidentified military satellites.*

USA

Name		Designation	Date	Vehicle	Site		Perigee	Apogee	Incl.	Period	Notes
IONDS 5	(On Navstar 12)	1989-013A	14 Feb.	Delta 6925	ETR	–	20 025	20 350	63.25	718.0	Nuclear Detection System (X-Ray & Optical)
IONDS 6	(On Navstar 13)	1989-044A	9 June	Delta 6925	ETR	–	20 025	20 350	63.25	718.0	Nuclear Detection System (X-Ray & Optical)
IONDS 7	(On Navstar 14)	1989-064A	18 Aug.	Delta 6925	ETR	..	20 025	20 350	63.25	718.0	Nuclear Detection System (X-Ray & Optical)
IONDS 8	(On Navstar 15)	1989-085A	21 Oct.	Delta 6925	ETR	–	20 025	20 350	63.25	718.0	Nuclear Detection System (X-Ray & Optical)
IONDS 9	(On Navstar 16)	1989-097A	11 Dec.	Delta 6925	ETR	–	20 025	20 350	63.25	718.0	Nuclear Detection System (X-Ray & Optical)
ARD-1/2 14	(On DSP-1 F-14)	1989-046A	14 June	Titan 402 A	ETR	..	35 780	35 780	1.00	1 436.0	Advanced Radiation Detector

Other military missions

USSR

RADAR CALIBRATION

Name	Designation	Intl	Date	Vehicle	Site		Perigee	Apogee	Incl.	Period	Notes
Cosmos 2002	SU RADCAL 2-19	1989-012A	14 Feb.	SL-8	PL	950	187	2 315	65.80	110.4	Possible radar calibration, but unusual apogee
Cosmos 2053	SU RADCAL 2-20	1989-100A	27 Dec.	SL-14	PL	1 500	1 495	1 525	73.60	95.2	

GEODETIC

Name	Designation	Intl	Date	Vehicle	Site		Perigee	Apogee	Incl.	Period	Notes
Cosmos 2037	SU GEOD 2-12	1989-068A	28 Aug.	SL-14	PL	1 500	1 503	1 537	73.60	116.1	Laser retroreflector, launched with
Etalon 1		1989-001C	10 Jan.	SL-12	TT	1 415	19 100	19 150	64.80	676.0	GLONASS 40 & 41
Cosmos 2024	Etalon 2	1989-039C	31 May	SL-12	TT	900	19 100	19 150	64.80	674.4	

MINOR MILITARY

Name	Designation	Intl	Date	Vehicle	Site		Perigee	Apogee	Incl.	Period	Notes
Cosmos 2027	SU MINMIL	1989-045A	11 June	SL-8	PL	900	484	522	65.90	94.6	Similar to C-1788

Type/Country/ Spacecraft name	Alternative name (Host spacecraft)	Designation	Launch date	Booster	Facility	Mass (kg)	Perigee (km)	Apogee (km)	Inclin. (deg)	Period (min)	Comments
USA											
BALLISTIC MISSILE DEFENSE											
Delta Star	SDI STM-3	1989-026A	24 Mar.	Delta 3920	ETR	2 720	480	500	47.69	94.4	Delta Star—replay of STM-2
VUE	(on DSP-I 14)	1989-046A	14 June	Titan 402 A	ETR	..	35 780	35 780	1.00	1 436.0	Visible/Ultraviolet Experiment 3rd colour sensor
SPACE TEST PROGRAM											
STP-F AMOS 1	Space Test Program[a]	1989-021A	13 Mar.	STS	ETR	0	300	300	28.50	92.0	AF Maui Optical Site STS imagery signature collection
STP-F AMOS 2	Space Test Program[a]	1989-033A	4 May	STS	ETR	0	300	300	28.50	92.0	AF Maui Optical Site STS imagery signature collection
STP-F AMOS 3	Space Test Program[a]	1989-061A	8 Aug.	STS	ETR	0	300	300	28.50	92.0	AF Maui Optical Site STS imagery signature collection
STP-F											
LAT/LON 1	Space Test Program[a]	1989-061A	8 Aug.	STS	ETR	500	400	400	28.50	94.0	Latitude/Longitude Locator space Sextant
STP-F RDE	Space Test Program[a]	1989-061A	8 Aug.	STS	ETR	..	300	300	28.50	92.0	Radiation Detection Experiment
USA-41		1989-061C	8 Aug.	STS	ETR	100	295	305	56.90	90.5	
STP-F STEX	Space Test Program[a]	1989-084A	18 Oct.	STS	ETR	..	300	300	28.50	92.0	Sensor Technology Experiment (classified)

[a] These Space Test Program experiments were carried on the shuttle orbiter, and were not free-flying satellites.

Launch facility abbreviations
ETR: Eastern Test Range, Cape Canaveral, Fla., USA
WTR: Western Test Range, Vandenberg AFB, Calif., USA
KO: Kourou, French Guinea
TT: Tyuratam (Baikonur), USSR
PL: Plesetsk, USSR

Appendix 3B. Operational military satellites in orbit on 31 December 1989

Country/ Mission	Spacecraft name/ Secondary payload	Alternative name/ (Host spacecraft)	Launch date
China			
Communications	STW-1	China 15	8 Apr. 1984
	STW-2	Tungfanghung 2	1 Feb. 1986
	STW-3	China 22	7 Mar. 1988
	STW-4	China 25	22 Dec. 1988
France			
Military	Syracuse I-A	(On Telecom 1A)	4 Aug. 1984
communications	Syracuse I-C	(On Telecom 1C)	11 Mar. 1988
Japan			
Military communications	Superbird-X 1A	(On SCS 1A)	5 June 1989
UK			
Military	SKYNET 2B	9354	23 Nov. 1974
communications	SKYNET 4-B	..	10 Dec. 1988
USSR			
Photoreconnaissance	Cosmos 2052	SU PHOTO 4-97	30 Nov. 1989
	Cosmos 2049	SU PHOTO 5-11	17 Nov. 1989
Electronic	Cosmos 1805	SU ELINT 3-23	10 Dec. 1986
intelligence	Cosmos 1812	SU ELINT 3-24	14 Jan. 1987
	Cosmos 1842	SU ELINT 3-26	27 Apr. 1987
	Cosmos 1908	SU ELINT 3-29	6 Jan. 1988
	Cosmos 1933	SU ELINT 3-30	15 Mar. 1988
	Cosmos 1953	SU ELINT 3-31	14 June 1988
	Cosmos 1975	SU ELINT 3-32	11 Oct. 1988
	Cosmos 1943	SU ELINT 4-7	15 May 1988
	Cosmos 1980	SU ELINT 4-8	23 Nov. 1988
	Cosmos 1888	SU ELINT 5-1	1 Oct. 1987
	Cosmos 1894	SU ELINT 5-2	28 Oct. 1987
Electronic	Cosmos 1949	SU EORSAT 1-27	28 May 1988
ocean reconnaissance	Cosmos 2033	SU EORSAT 1-29	24 July 1989
	Cosmos 2046	SU EORSAT 1-30	27 Sep. 1989
Radar ocean reconnaissance	*None since Cosmos 1932*		
Military	Cosmos 1852	SU COM 1-313	16 June 1987
communications	Cosmos 1853	SU COM 1-314	16 June 1987
	Cosmos 1854	SU COM 1-315	16 June 1987
	Cosmos 1855	SU COM 1-316	16 June 1987

Country/ Mission	Spacecraft name/ Secondary payload	Alternative name/ (Host spacecraft)	Launch date
	Cosmos 1856	SU COM 1-317	16 June 1987
	Cosmos 1857	SU COM 1-318	16 June 1987
	Cosmos 1858	SU COM 1-319	16 June 1987
	Cosmos 1859	SU COM 1-320	16 June 1987
	Cosmos 1924	SU COM 1-321	11 Mar. 1988
	Cosmos 1925	SU COM 1-322	11 Mar. 1988
	Cosmos 1926	SU COM 1-323	11 Mar. 1988
	Cosmos 1927	SU COM 1-324	11 Mar. 1988
	Cosmos 1928	SU COM 1-325	11 Mar. 1988
	Cosmos 1929	SU COM 1-326	11 Mar. 1988
	Cosmos 1930	SU COM 1-327	11 Mar. 1988
	Cosmos 1931	SU COM 1-328	11 Mar. 1988
	Cosmos 2008	SU COM 1-329	24 Mar. 1989
	Cosmos 2009	SU COM 1-330	24 Mar. 1989
	Cosmos 2010	SU COM 1-331	24 Mar. 1989
	Cosmos 2011	SU COM 1-332	24 Mar. 1989
	Cosmos 2012	SU COM 1-333	24 Mar. 1989
	Cosmos 2013	SU COM 1-334	24 Mar. 1989
	Cosmos 2014	SU COM 1-335	24 Mar. 1989
	Cosmos 2015	SU COM 1-336	24 Mar. 1989
	Cosmos 1937	SU COM 2-42	5 Apr. 1988
	Cosmos 1954	SU COM 2-43	21 June 1988
	Cosmos 1992	SU COM 2-44	26 Jan. 1989
	Cosmos 1994	SU COM 3-31	10 Feb. 1989
	Cosmos 1995	SU COM 3-32	10 Feb. 1989
	Cosmos 1996	SU COM 3-33	10 Feb. 1989
	Cosmos 1997	SU COM 3-34	10 Feb. 1989
	Cosmos 1998	SU COM 3-35	10 Feb. 1989
	Cosmos 1999	SU COM 3-36	10 Feb. 1989
	Cosmos 2038	SU COM 3-37	15 Sep. 1989
	Cosmos 2039	SU COM 3-38	15 Sep. 1989
	Cosmos 2040	SU COM 3-39	15 Sep. 1989
	Cosmos 2041	SU COM 3-41	15 Sep. 1989
	Cosmos 2042	SU COM 3-42	15 Sep. 1989
	Cosmos 2043	SU COM 3-43	15 Sep. 1989
Communications	Molniya 1-68	..	5 Sep. 1989
	Molniya 1-71	..	11 Mar. 1988
	Molniya 1-72	..	17 Mar. 1988
	Molniya 1-70	..	26 Dec. 1986
	Molniya 1-73	..	16 Aug. 1988
	Molniya 1-74	..	28 Dec. 1988
	Molniya 1-75	..	15 Feb. 1989
	Molniya 1-76	..	27 Sep. 1989
	Cosmos 1961	Potok 5	1 Aug. 1988
	Cosmos 2054	Potok 6	27 Dec. 1989
Early warning	Cosmos 1793	SU BMEWS 1-51	20 Nov. 1986
	Cosmos 1849	SU BMEWS 1-53	4 June 1987
	Cosmos 1903	SU BMEWS 1-55	21 Dec. 1987
	Cosmos 1922	SU BMEWS 1-56	26 Feb. 1988

Country/ Mission	Spacecraft name/ Secondary payload	Alternative name/ (Host spacecraft)	Launch date
	Cosmos 1966	SU BMEWS 1-57	30 Aug. 1988
	Cosmos 1974	SU BMEWS 1-58	4 Oct. 1988
	Cosmos 1977	SU BMEWS 1-59	25 Oct. 1988
	Cosmos 2001	SU BMEWS 1-60	14 Feb. 1989
	Cosmos 2050	SU BMEWS 1-61	24 Nov. 1989
Navigation	Cosmos 1904	SU NAV 3-61	23 Dec. 1987
	Cosmos 1959	SU NAV 3-63	18 July 1988
	Cosmos 2004	SU NAV 3-64	22 Feb. 1989
	Cosmos 2016	SU NAV 3-65	4 Apr. 1989
	Cosmos 2026	SU NAV 3-66	7 June 1989
	Cosmos 2034	SU NAV 3-67	25 July 1989
	Cosmos 1946	GLONASS 34	21 May 1988
	Cosmos 1947	GLONASS 35	21 May 1988
	Cosmos 1948	GLONASS 36	21 May 1988
	Cosmos 1970	GLONASS 37	16 Sep. 1988
	Cosmos 1971	GLONASS 38	16 Sep. 1988
	Cosmos 1972	GLONASS 39	16 Sep. 1988
	Cosmos 1987	GLONASS 40	10 Jan. 1989
	Cosmos 1988	GLONASS 41	10 Jan. 1989
	Cosmos 2022	GLONASS 42	31 May 1989
	Cosmos 2023	GLONASS 43	31 May 1989
Geodetic	Cosmos 1950	SU GEOD 2-10	30 May 1988
	Cosmos 2037	SU GEOD 2-12	28 Aug. 1989
	Cosmos 1989	Etalon 1	10 Jan. 1989
	Cosmos 2024	Etalon 2	31 May 1989
Minor military	Cosmos 1578	SU MINMIL 6-1	28 June 1984
	Cosmos 2027	SU MINMIL X-1	11 June 1989
Radar calibration	Cosmos 1960	SU RADCAL 2-18	28 July 1988
	Cosmos 1508	SU RADCAL 3A-6	11 Nov. 1983
	Cosmos 1985	SU RADCAL 4-1	23 Dec. 1988
	Cosmos 2053	SU RADCAL 2-20	27 Dec. 1989
Military mapping	*None active at the end of 1989*		
USA			
Photoreconnaisance	KH-11/6	..	4 Dec. 1984
	KH-11/8	..	26 Oct. 1987
	KH-11/9	..	6 Nov. 1988
	KH-12A/1	USA-40	8 Aug. 1989
Electronic intelligence	Chalet 3	Vortex 3	31 Oct. 1981
	Chalet 6	Vortex 6 USA-37	10 May 1989
	Jumpseat 4	..	8 Feb. 1985
	Jumpseat 5	..	14 Feb. 1987
	Magnum 1	..	24 Jan 1985
	Magnum 2	..	23 Nov. 1989

Country/ Mission	Spacecraft name/ Secondary payload	Alternative name/ (Host spacecraft)	Launch date
Electronic ocean reconnaissance	NOSS 7	White Cloud	9 Feb. 1986
	NOSS-SSU 7-1	..	9 Feb. 1986
	NOSS-SSU 7-2	..	9 Feb. 1986
	NOSS-SSU 7-3	..	9 Feb. 1986
	NOSS 8	White Cloud	15 May 1987
	NOSS-SSU 8-1	..	15 May 1987
	NOSS-SSU 8-2	..	15 May 1987
	NOSS-SSU 8-3	..	15 May 1987
	NOSS 9	White Cloud	5 Sep. 1988
	NOSS-SSU 9-1	..	5 Sep. 1988
	NOSS-SSU 9-2	..	5 Sep. 1988
	NOSS-SSU 9-3	..	5 Sep. 1988
	NOSS 10	USA-45	6 Sep. 1989
	NOSS-SSU 10-1	White Cloud	6 Sep. 1989
	NOSS-SSU 10-2	..	6 Sep. 1989
	NOSS-SSU 10-3	..	6 Sep. 1989
Imaging radar	Lacrosse 1	..	2 Dec. 1988
Military communications	AFSATCOM D-8	(On DMSP 5D-2/3)	19 June 1987
	AFSATCOM D-9	(On DMSP 5D-2/4)	3 Feb. 1988
	AFSATCOM F-2	(On FLTSATCOM 2)	4 May 1979
	AFSATCOM F-3	(On FLTSATCOM 3)	18 Jan. 1980
	AFSATCOM F-4	(On FLTSATCOM 4)	31 Oct. 1980
	AFSATCOM F-6	(On FLTSATCOM 6)	4 Dec. 1986
	AFSATCOM F-8	(On FLTSATCOM 8)	25 Sep. 1989
	AFSATCOM S-5	(On SDS F-5)	31 July 1983
	AFSATCOM S-5A	(On SDS F-5A)	28 Aug. 1984
	AFSATCOM SCT-1	(On DSCS III-A1)	30 Oct. 1982
	AFSATCOM SCT-4	(On DSCS III-B4)	3 Oct. 1985
	AFSATCOM SCT-5	(On DSCS III-B5)	3 Oct. 1985
	AFSATCOM SCT-2	(On DSCS III-A2)	4 Sep. 1989
	SDS F-5	..	31 July 1983
	SDS F-5A	..	28 Aug. 1984
	LES 8	AFSATCOM	15 Mar. 1976
	LES 9	AFSATCOM	15 Mar. 1976
	NATO 3-A	..	22 Apr. 1976
	NATO 3-C	..	19 Nov. 1978
	NATO 3-D	..	14 Nov. 1984
	DSCS II-13	DSCS 9443	21 Nov. 1979
	DSCS II-14	DSCS 9444	21 Nov. 1979
	DSCS II-15	DSCS 9445	30 Oct. 1982
	DSCS II-16	DSCS A-16 USA-43	4 Sep. 1989
	DSCS III-A 1	DSCS A-1	30 Oct. 1982
	DSCS III-B 4	DSCS B-4	3 Oct. 1985
	DSCS III-B 5	DSCS B-5	3 Oct. 1985
	DSCS III-A 2	DFS-2 USA-44	4 Sep. 1989
	FLTSATCOM 2	..	4 May 1979
	FLTSATCOM 3	..	18 Jan. 1980
	FLTSATCOM 4	..	31 Oct. 1980
	FLTSATCOM 6	F-7	4 Dec. 1986

Country/ Mission	Spacecraft name/ Secondary payload	Alternative name/ (Host spacecraft)	Launch date
	FLTSATCOM 8	F-8	25 Sep. 1989
	Leasat 1	Syncom IV F-2	30 Aug. 1984
	Leasat 2	Syncom IV F-1	8 Nov. 1984
	Leasat 3	Syncom IV F-3	12 Apr. 1985
	Gapfiller 1	(On Marisat 1)	19 Feb. 1976
	Gapfiller 2	(On Marisat 2)	10 June 1976
	Gapfiller 3	(On Marisat 3)	14 Oct. 1976
Early warning	DSP 10	F-13	6 Mar. 1982
	DSP 11	F-12	14 Apr. 1984
	DSP SED 12	F-6R	22 Dec. 1984
	DSP SED 13	F-5R	29 Nov. 1987
	DSP-I 14 F-14	USA-39	14 June 1989
Navigation	Transit 19	Oscar 24 SOOS 1	3 Aug. 1985
	Transit 20	Oscar 30 SOOS 1	3 Aug. 1985
	Transit 21	Oscar 27 SOOS 2	16 Sep. 1987
	Transit 22	Oscar 29 SOOS 2	16 Sep. 1987
	Transit 23	SOOS 3	26 Apr. 1988
	Transit 24	SOOS 3	26 Apr. 1988
	Transit 25	Oscar 23 SOOS 4	25 Aug. 1988
	Transit 26	Oscar 32 SOOS 4	25 Aug. 1988
	Transit NOVA 1	..	15 May 1981
	Transit NOVA 2	..	16 June 1988
	Transit NOVA 3	..	12 Oct. 1984
	Transit TIP-4	Oscar 11 TRANSAT	28 Oct. 1977
	Navstar 1A-5	..	9 Feb. 1980
	Navstar 1A-6	..	26 Apr. 1980
	Navstar 1R-9	..	13 June 1984
	Navstar 1A-8	..	14 July 1983
	Navstar 1R-10	..	8 Sep. 1984
	Navstar 1R-11	..	9 Oct. 1985
	Navstar 2A-12	NDS 13 USA-35	14 Feb. 1989
	Navstar 2A-13	NDS 14 USA-38	9 June 1989
	Navstar 2A-14	NDS 16 USA-42	18 Aug. 1989
	Navstar 2A-15	NDS 17	21 Oct. 1989
	Navstar 2A-16	NDS 18	11 Dec. 1989
Weather	DMSP 5D-2/4	S-9	3 Feb. 1988
	DMSP 5D-2/3	S-8	19 June 1987
Nuclear detection	NUDETS DSP-9	(On DSP-9)	16 Mar. 1981
	NUDETS DSP-10	(On DSP-10)	6 Mar. 1982
	NUDETS DSP-11	(On DSP-11)	14 Apr. 1984
	ARD-1/2 14	(On DSP-I F-14)	14 June 1989
	NUDETS DMSP-8	(On DMSP 5D-2/3)	19 June 1987
	NUDETS DMSP-9	(On DMSP 5D-2/4)	3 Feb. 1988
	IONDS 1	(On Navstar 1A-8)	14 July 1983
	IONDS 2	(On Navstar 1R-9)	13 June 1984
	IONDS 3	(On Navstar 1R-10)	8 Sep. 1984
	IONDS 4	(On Navstar 1R-11)	9 Oct. 1985

Country/ Mission	Spacecraft name/ Secondary payload	Alternative name/ (Host spacecraft)	Launch date
	IONDS 5	(On Navstar 12)	14 Feb. 1989
	IONDS 6	(On Navstar 13)	9 June 1989
	IONDS 7	(On Navstar 14)	18 Aug. 1989
	IONDS 8	(On Navstar 15)	21 Oct. 1989
	IONDS 9	(On Navstar 16)	11 Dec. 1989
Geodetic	Geosat	..	13 Mar. 1985
Military science	STP P83-1 Hilat	Oscar 16	27 June 1983
	STP P87-1	Polar Bear	14 Nov. 1986
	SDI-S (?)	USA-41	8 Aug. 1989
Ballistic missile defence	SDI STM-3	Delta Star	24 Mar. 1989
	SDI VUE	(On DSP-I F-14)	14 June 1989

4. Chemical and biological warfare: developments in 1989[*]

S. J. LUNDIN

I. Introduction

Chemical weapons (CW), and to a lesser extent biological weapons (BW), continued to be of considerable international interest in 1989. These weapons figured in world events so often that it is has been necessary to select among these instances so as to provide an overview. The main events which drew attention, not listed in order of priority, were the following:

1. No use of chemical or biological weapons was clearly demonstrated during 1989, although allegations of use were made.

2. As thus far negotiated, the chemical weapons convention (CWC) is intended to prohibit all production of chemical weapons upon its entry into force. During the latter part of 1989, a debate arose about whether or not, and under what circumstances, the USA will continue to produce binary weapons. Uncertainty about the continuation of US binary CW production appeared to be on the increase, owing *inter alia* to the technical difficulties of producing this weapon system.

3. The problem of the spread of chemical weapons was highlighted by efforts in the Federal Republic of Germany, in particular, to regulate the export of chemicals, and related equipment for the production of chemical weapons, to Libya and other countries.

4. The US Congress worked on legislation to regulate exports related to chemical weapons and to institute sanctions against companies which do not comply with US regulations.

5. In the context of the conflict in the Middle East, the Arab countries linked the abolition of chemical weapons to the efforts to abolish nuclear weapons. This political move may jeopardize the future entry into force of a CWC.

6. Difficulties were encountered in both the US and Soviet CW destruction programmes. Environmental concerns have long been voiced in the USA about the destruction of old stockpiles of chemical weapons, and similar concerns are now being expressed in the USSR.

A discussion of developments in the negotiations on chemical weapons, of related events and of other international efforts to support or facilitate a

[*] Dr Thomas Stock, Dr Rabinder Nath and Fredrik Wetterqvist of the SIPRI Chemical and Biological Warfare (CBW) Programme have assisted in preparing references and data for this chapter. The references were gathered from the SIPRI CBW Programme Data Base and were also kindly provided by J. P. Perry Robinson, Science Policy Research Unit, University of Sussex, UK, from the Sussex–Harvard information bank.

CWC is presented in chapter 14. Among those events the following are particularly noteworthy.

During 1989 no definite progress was made in the negotiations on a CWC in the Conference on Disarmament (CD) in Geneva despite progress made in the technical deliberations. However, there was obvious progress in the bilateral discussions between the USA and the USSR as regards, for example, information on chemical weapons and their early destruction. At the December 1989 Malta summit meeting between Presidents George Bush and Mikhail Gorbachev the former suggested that a bilateral agreement on mutual reduction of existing stockpiles of chemical weapons might be ready for signature at the summit meeting scheduled for June 1990.[1]

An international conference to strengthen the 1925 Geneva Protocol prohibition against the use of chemical weapons was held in Paris in January 1989, and Australia arranged the international Government–Industry Conference against Chemical Weapons in Canberra in September. Both conferences enjoyed broad international participation.

II. Chemical weapons

Allegations of use of chemical weapons

Although no use of chemical weapons was confirmed during 1989, a number of allegations of use were presented which were not corroborated by any independent international investigations such as those conducted under the auspices of the United Nations.

Afghanistan

Allegations were made of the use of unspecified chemical weapons against the rebels near Jalalabad. A Soviet military spokesman denied that the USSR had delivered any chemical weapons to the government in Kabul.[2]

Angola

Allegations were repeated in 1989 of the use of various kinds of chemical weapons, including nerve gases, against troops of the National Union for the Total Independence of Angola (UNITA) by Cuban forces and the Liberation Movement of Angola (MPLA).[3] An overview of the alleged occasions of use since 1985, based on UNITA sources, was published in 1989.[4] A US

---

[1] See, for example, 'President Bush's initiatives during the Malta meeting',White House factsheet (810), *Wireless File*, EUR-105, 4 Dec. 1989, p. 19.

[2] See, for example, 'Correspondent on chemical weapons in Jalalabad', LD0504162889, Tehran, IRNA, in English, 1525 GMT, 5 Apr. 1989, FBIS-NES-89-065, 6 Apr. 1989, pp. 45–46; 'Doctor says Kabul regime using chemical weapons', BK0504082589, Islamabad Overseas Service, in English, 0800 GMT, 5 Apr. 1989, FBIS-NES-89-064, 5 Apr. 1989, p. 42; Ottaway, D. B., 'Soviets deny supplying chemical arms to Afghans', *Washington Post*, 6 May 1989.

[3] Baumgartner, J., 'Neue Hinweise auf Giftgaseinsätze in Angola', *Neue Zürcher Zeitung*, 16 Sep. 1989, p. 7.

[4] Hallerbach, R., 'Angola als Versuchslabor für chemische Kampfstoffe?', *Europäische Wehrkunde*, vol. 38, no. 7 (1989), pp. 433–35.

Department of Defense spokesman said, however, that the DOD 'never had any definite evidence' to support the charges.[5] MPLA and Cuban sources denied the allegations.[6] A Soviet spokesman, in a denial of Soviet development of new chemical weapons, claimed that the scientist who had investigated the use of chemical weapons in Angola had withdrawn his claims as groundless.[7] The scientist in question reported on a meeting with Soviet experts about the results of his investigations. It appears that he now considers the weapons used to have been incendiary weapons which, according to him, had been provided by the USSR and which could release hydrogen cyanide as a by-product. However, he quotes Soviet experts as arguing that the weapons were not chemical weapons according to the definition of chemical weapons in the 'rolling text' (the continuously updated version of the text of the future convention) of the CWC.[8]

Somalia

Somalia was reported to have used chemical weapons against rebels in northern Somalia. The weapons were said to have been obtained from Libya.[9] The reports were denied,[10] but according to Western intelligence sources Somalia had obtained nerve gas from Libya but refrained from using it for fear of international protest.[11]

Sudan

Sudanese rebels claimed to have been attacked by government forces using chemical weapons, probably mustard gas, which was said to have been obtained from Libya.[12] No denial of the claims seems to have been issued by Sudan.

The USSR

On 9 April 1989, in the city of Tblisi in Soviet Georgia, gas was used to stop demonstrations.[13] The reported number of casualties which resulted from the

[5] 'No evidence of chemical weapons use in Africa', US Defense Department report, 11 Apr. 1989 (690), *Wireless File*, EUR-209, 4 Apr. 1989.
[6] See, for example, 'Cuban chemical weapons supply to MPLA denied', MB0501125789, Luanda Domestic Service, in Portuguese, 1200GMT, 5 Jan. 1989, FBIS-AFR-89-004, 6 Jan. 1989, p. 13.
[7] 'Soviet chemical weapons claims groundless, general argues', TASS (Moscow), 17 Oct. 1989, Permanent Mission of the Soviet Union (Geneva), *Press Bulletin*, no. 196 (1934), 19 Oct. 1989, pp. 4–5.
[8] Heyndrickx, A., reports of 10 and 19 Oct. 1989 in letter to SIPRI, 20 Oct. 1989.
[9] Klingelschmitt, K.-P., 'Somalis berichten von Giftgaseinsatz', *Tageszeitung*, 18 Jan. 1989, p. 2; see also Dorsey, J. M., 'Somalia refrains from using Libyan-delivered nerve gas', *Washington Times*, 30 Jan. 1989, p. A9.
[10] 'Obtaining of Libyan chemical weapons denied', NC1002170789, Paris, AFP, in English, 1654 GMT, 10 Feb. 1989, FBIS-AFR-89-028, 13 Feb. 1989.
[11] See Dorsey (note 9).
[12] See, for example, 'Berichte über einen Einsatz von Giftgas im Südsudan', *Neue Zürcher Zeitung*, 15 Jan. 1989; see also Pear, R., 'Sudan rebels say they are victims of poison gas', *New York Times*, 10 Jan. 1989, p. 12.
[13] See, for example, Keller, B., 'Izvestia says toxic gas felled Georgians', *International Herald Tribune*, 21 Apr. 1989, p. 2; Reuters, 'Georgian official says troops used poison gas', *International*

use of gas varies. One early Soviet report claimed that 61 hospitalized persons showed signs of gas poisoning.[14] The Georgian Health Minister said at a press conference that 600 people had been treated for poisoning symptoms, 63 had been hospitalized because of poisoning and 2 people had died from poisoning. Information was later given that 5 people had died of poisoning and that, in mid-May, about 50 people were still hospitalized with signs of intoxication.[15] However, new poisoning casualties with severe and recurring symptoms continued to appear in Georgia, which may indicate lingering effects of the gas.[16]

After initial confusion about which gases had been used (there were even rumours of nerve-gas use),[17] it now seems established that the gases were the well-known tear-gases CN (chloroacetophenone) and CS (2-chloro-benzalmalononitrile).[18] Chloropicrin, which was used as a tear-gas during World War I, has also been mentioned.[19] Other sources have noted that a substance called 'cheremukha 6' (bird-cherry gas) was used. This agent reportedly could have been either chloropicrin or phenacyl chloride, the latter actually a synonym for chloroacetophenone.[20] An argument that the agent may have been very old can be made based on the fact that neither CN nor chloropicrin was declared as part of current Soviet chemical weaponry at the 1987 display in Shikhany.[21] However, one source claims that chloropicrin was used as a tear-gas in the USSR until 1981, but was then reclassified as a choking chemical warfare agent.[22] According to an interview with the Deputy Chief Military Prosecutor, the substances used were confirmed to be chloroacetophenone and CS. Chloropicrin had not been used, and there were 30 casualties.[23]

Herald Tribune, 25 Apr. 1989, pp. 1, 6; Zhavoronkov, G., Mikadze, A. and Imedashvili, D., 'The danger of lies', *Moscow News Weekly*, no. 21, p. 13.

[14] 'Toxic substance allegedly used', PM2704090589, Tblisi, *Zarya Vostoka*, in Russian, 19 Apr. 1989, p. 3, FBIS-SOV-89-080, 27 Apr. 1989, pp. 62–63.

[15] 'Der umstrittene Gaseinsatz in Tiflis', *Neue Zürcher Zeitung*, 27 Apr. 1989, p. 3; see also, for example, Ember, L., 'Evidence shows Soviets used toxic gases at Tblisi', *Chemical & Engineering News*, vol. 67, no. 24 (1989), p. 20.

[16] 'Noch 230 Gas-Opfer in Krankenhäusen Georgiens', *Frankfurter Allgemeine Zeitung*, 8 May 1989; see also Bolling, A., 'Hemlightesmakeri kring giftgasoffer' ['Secretiveness surrounding poison gas victims'], *Dagens Nyheter* (Stockholm), 17 July 1989, p. 10 (in Swedish), which reports about lingering effects among the victims of the attack, some of which were treated at a hospital in the FRG.

[17] See Keller (note 13); and Simmons, M., 'Army still silent on gas used against Georgians', *The Guardian*, 16 Apr. 1989.

[18] Maj.-Gen. Yefimov in *Red Star*, 22 Apr. 1989, as quoted in 'Poisonous gas in Georgia poses more problems for Gorbachev', *Defense & Foreign Affairs*, vol. 17, nos 5-6 (1989), p. 34; see also Bohlen, C., 'Military gas used in Soviet Georgia', *New York Times*, 25 May 1989; 'Toxic gas confirmed in attack', *Washington Times*, 24 May 1989.

[19] See Ember (note 15).

[20] Keller, B., 'Soviets report use of toxic gas in putting down strife in Georgia', *New York Times*, 20 Apr. 1989, pp. A1, A13; Ottaway, D. B., 'Expert says Soviets used toxic gas', *Washington Post*, 26 May 1989, p. 38; 'Officials discuss Tbilisi', PM2404080589, Moscow, *Krasnaya Zvezda* , in Russian, 22 Apr. 1989, 1st edn, p. 6, FBIS-SOV-89-77, 24 Apr. 1989, pp. 63–64.

[21] SIPRI, *SIPRI Yearbook 1988: World Armaments and Disarmament* (Oxford University Press: Oxford, 1988), p. 111.

[22] 'Französische Ärzte zum Giftgaseinsatz in Tiflis', *Neue Zürcher Zeitung*, 25 May 1989, p. 2.

[23] Belan, N., *Sovetskaya Rossiya* (Moscow), 13 Dec. 1989, p. 4 as translated in FBIS-SOV-89-246, 26 Dec. 1989, pp. 57–60.

As regards both the making of allegations and the use of chemical weapons, the above reports seem to indicate that a trend may be emerging in many countries to regard chemical weapons as effective and permitted weapons against insurgents and rebels inside one's own borders. The use of chemical weapons against the Kurds in Iraq[24] definitely falls into this category, and in Africa, as mentioned above, several governments have been accused of using chemical weapons against guerrilla fighters.

In the negotiations on a CWC it is clearly understood that the use, development, production and stockpiling of tear-gases for law-enforcement purposes will be allowed under the convention but that some limit will have to be drawn as regards their use in war. However, the problem of defining 'war' is a complex issue[25] (see also chapter 14). As is well known and accepted, the use of tear-gas occurs widely both in ordinary police work and in circumstances where riots are common owing to internal conflicts. Although extensive use of riot-control agents in internal conflicts may be questionable from some points of view, even heavy use may save lives even in cases where it may lead to casualties. The risk exists, however, that indiscriminate and uncontrolled use of tear-gas may lead to more severe intoxications.[26] Another serious risk in this context is that where stockpiles of older, more toxic riot-control agents, and perhaps also lethal chemical weapons, exist and are used, the border between generally accepted law-enforcement use and prohibited use of chemical weapons may be seriously blurred or perceived by the attacked persons to have been so.

Allegations of acquisition and possession of chemical weapons

Again in 1989 official allegations of CW possession or of efforts to acquire chemical weapons, and thereby a chemical warfare capability, were made by the USA.[27] When US spokesmen make such accusations it is usually stated that 15 to 20 nations have a chemical warfare capability. However, the states involved are generally not officially named except for (occasionally) Iran, Iraq, Libya and Syria. The general public can then only speculate about which other countries are meant besides Iraq, the USA and the USSR, which are definitely known to be in possession of chemical weapons.[28] The

---

[24] Cook-Deegan, R. M., Physicians for Human Rights, 'Use of lethal poison gas against civilians in Iraqi Kurdistan', Statement before the Committee on Governmental Affairs, US Senate, 9 Feb. 1989, pp. 1–6; see also *SIPRI Yearbook 1988* (note 21), p. 101.

[25] See, for example, Goldblat, J. (ed.), SIPRI, *Agreements for Arms Control: A Critical Survey* (Taylor & Francis: London, 1982), p. 83.

[26] Hu, H., Fine, J., Epstein, P., Kelsey, K., Reynolds, P. and Walker, B., 'Tear gas: harassing agent or toxic chemical weapon?', *Journal of the American Medical Association*, vol. 262, no. 5 (4 Aug. 1989), pp. 660–63.

[27] See, for example, 'Statement of the Honorable William H. Webster, Director of the Central Intelligence Agency', Committee on Governmental Affairs, Hearings on Global Spread of Chemical and Biological Weapons: Assessing Challenges and Responses, 9 Feb. 1989: 'Currently, we believe that as many as 20 countries may be developing chemical weapons', p. 1; President Bush in his address to the 44th UN General Assembly, 25 Sep. 1989, 'More than 20 nations now possess chemical weapons or the capability to produce them', 'U.S. ready to destroy CW if Soviets, others join in effort', *Wireless Files*, EUR-103, 25 Sep. 1989, p. 12.

[28] The problems with this situation are analysed in a paper by Harris, E. D., 'Stemming the spread of chemical weapons', *Brookings Review* (winter, 1989–90), pp. 39–45. A fully documented version

situation is thus very unclear.[29] SIPRI cannot judge the accuracy of the information, and it should also be compared with the voluntary declarations made by a number of countries which have stated that they do not possess chemical weapons. These countries include some of those about which there has been speculation of CW possession. Such declarations, including new ones, the source of the declaration and its wording (as far as it is known to SIPRI) are given in appendix 4A.[30] The reader is also referred to a comprehensive list of alleged possession and acquisition of chemical weapons which is presented in the *Arms Control Reporter*.[31]

In order to evaluate information about CW possession it is necessary to consider the definition of the term 'chemical weapon' (see also the discussion of the Soviet CW stockpile below). Both allegations of possession and declarations of non-possession may be formally defensible owing to ambiguities which exist regarding definitions and formulations. The statements quoted in appendix 4A demonstrate these ambiguities. For instance, what does it mean if a country says that it does not stockpile chemical weapons but does not state whether chemical weapons of an ally may be stockpiled on its territory? What does it mean if a country says that it opposes the possession, production, stockpiling and use of chemical weapons but does not reveal whether or not it possesses them? If a country has old stockpiles of chemical weapons from the two world wars, which are presumably obsolete and unusable, might they not usefully be declared as such? Ambiguities of the kind implied by these questions could be avoided when a country makes a voluntary declaration. It is possible that greater clarification of the declarations made would serve a confidence-building purpose for the negotiations on a CWC. Clear declarations of CW possession or non-possession would also affect the discussion in the CWC negotiations about the appropriate size of the future inspectorate for the first 10 years after ratification of a CWC, when destruction of all chemical

will be published in *New Threats: Responding to the Proliferation of Nuclear, Chemical and Delivery Capabilities in the Third World* (University Press of America, Aspen Strategy Group: Cambridge, Mass.), forthcoming. See also, for example, Carus, W. S., 'Chemical weapons in the Middle East', *Policy Focus*, Washington Institute for Near East Policy, Research memorandum no. 9 (Dec. 1988); Brodie, I., 'Iran "building up stocks" of gas chemicals', *Daily Telegraph*, 30 Jan. 1989, p. 8; Bermudez Jr, J. S., 'Korean People's Army NBC capabilities' (latest revision 2 May 1989), Statement for the Record, Senate Permanent Subcommittee on Investigations, Committee on Governmental Affairs, 9 Feb. 1989.

[29] See, for example, a statement by US Senator John McCain, 'Proliferation in the 1990s: the implications for American policy and force planning', *Congressional Record*, 101st Congress, 1st session, vol. 135, no. 104, Washington, DC, 28 July 1989; and *Arms Control Reporter*, July 1989, p. 704.E3–5.

[30] See SIPRI, *SIPRI Yearbook 1989: World Armaments and Disarmament* (Oxford University Press: Oxford, 1989), p. 112; and 1988 CD/PV documents in which 22 states made declarations of non-possession of chemical weapons: Argentina (CD/PV.465), Austria (CD/PV.457), Brazil (CD/PV.460), Bulgaria (CD/PV.457), Burma [Myanmar] (CD/PV.452), China (CD/PV.453), Egypt (CD/PV.459), the Federal Republic of Germany (CD/PV.437), Finland (CD/PV.441), the German Democratic Republic (CD/PV.481), Hungary (CD/PV.437), India (CD/PV.459), Indonesia (CD/PV.437), Italy (CD/PV.437), Mongolia (CD/PV.442), New Zealand (CD/PV.445), Norway (CD/PV.479), Peru (CD/PV.472), Poland (CD/PV.457), Romania (CD/PV.440), Sweden (CD/PV.481) and the United Kingdom (CD/PV.474).

[31] 'World CW/munition stockpiles and production facilities', *Arms Control Reporter*, July 1989, p. 704.E.1–5; see also note 29.

weapons is to take place. A larger number of CW stockpiles would obviously require a larger inspectorate. In the following discussion some other sources of allegations of CW possession or acquisition are dealt with as regards specific countries.

Egypt

Allegations were made in 1989 that Egypt is in the process of building a CW production facility with some foreign assistance.[32] President Mubarak and other Egyptian officials denied that such a facility is under construction.[33]

Iran

In early 1989 information circulated that Iran had contracted a company in the Federal Republic of Germany to build a facility for production of phosphorus-based pesticides related to those used to produce chemical weapons.[34] Iran also allegedly tried to improve its CW capability by attempting to illegally import from the USA 120 tonnes of thiodiglycol, a precursor (i.e., a chemical from which another particular chemical can be made) for mustard gas.[35] A Swiss company withdrew from a project for the construction of a chemical production facility owing to fears that the facility could be used for making poison gas.[36] According to press reports in June, efforts were also made to provide Iran with 257 tonnes of thionylchloride, it too a precursor for mustard gas, in a deal arranged by an Iranian company located in the FRG. The shipment, via India, was stopped and the authorities in the FRG immediately began an investigation of the matter.[37]

Thionylchloride can also be used for peaceful purposes, and Iran denied that the substance was intended for mustard gas production.[38] However, further investigation showed that the buyer was the Iranian State Defense

[32] See Carus (note 28); Gordon, M. R. and Engelberg, S., 'Egypt accused of big advance in gas for war', *New York Times*, 10 Mar. 1989, pp. A1, A2; Gordon, M. R. and Engelberg, S., 'Swiss firm said to aid Egypt with poison gas capability', *International Herald Tribune*, 11–12 Mar. 1989, p. 1.

[33] See Gordon and Engelberg (note 32); and Goshko, J. M., 'Egypt acquiring elements of poison gas plant', *Washington Post*, 11 Mar. 1989, p. 20.

[34] George, A., 'Iran's chemical weapons potential', *Defence*, Feb. 1989, p. 90.

[35] See Brodie (note 28), p. 5.

[36] See, for example, 'Swiss company pulls out of Iranian chemical plant', *Financial Times*, 10 May 1989, p. 3.

[37] Hazarika, S., 'India firm sold chemical', *International Herald Tribune*, 3 July 1989, p. 2; Associated Press, 'Bonn finds India link in toxin sale', *International Herald Tribune*, 29 June 1989, p. 2; see, for example, Winter, M., 'Erneut Firma wegen Giftgas in Verdacht, Vermittelten Düsseldorfer Chemikalie an Iran?', *Frankfurter Rundschau*, 28 June 1989, p. 1; McCartney, R. J., 'Germans raid firm over Iranian deal', *Financial Times*, 30 June 1989, p. 2; Gordon, M. R. and Engelberg, S., 'A German concern sold chemicals to Iran, U.S. says', *New York Times*, 27 June 1989, pp. A1, A5.

[38] Reuters, 'Tehran denies buying chemicals for poison gas from German firm', *International Herald Tribune*, 1–2 July 1989, p. 2.

Industries Organization (DIO). Whether a violation of the export regulations of the FRG actually occurred was, however, not clear.[39]

India

India declared that it would not ban the manufacture and trade of thionylchloride in the absence of a CWC and emphasized the peaceful uses of thionylchloride.[40] Discussions were said to be going on between India and the Australia Group about Indian restrictions on sales of chemicals and the technology needed for poison gas production.[41] The Australia Group is comprised of 21 countries which, at the initiative of Australia, meet twice a year to discuss which chemicals ought to be subject to various national regulatory measures and ought, accordingly, to be put on a 'warning list' in order that these chemicals not be used to produce CW agents (see also appendix 4B).

Israel

Increasingly disturbed by the threat that the neighbouring Arab countries see it as their right to acquire chemical weapons, Israel took new measures to strengthen protection for its military forces and civilian population.[42] The Israeli representative at the Paris Conference was reported to have stated that Israel 'was taking the necessary action' to defend itself. This is said to have been interpreted as an admission that Israel possesses chemical weapons. However, an Israeli official has stated that Israel does not possess chemical weapons.[43]

The USA

The US budget requests for the chemical and biological weapon programme for fiscal years 1990 and 1991 are listed in table 4.1. The US Army asked for funds for continued and increased production of binary chemical weapons, including a multiple-launch rocket system (MLRS),[44] and for funds to develop two new types of chemical weapons: one that penetrates gas masks and other protective equipment thereby rendering the protective equipment useless, and a 'knock-out gas' which would be non-lethal and act

---

[39] 'Deutsche Vermittlung von C-Waffen an Iran', *ami*, 8 Aug. 1989, p. 10; Protzman, F., 'Bonn asserts Iran chemical sale might be illegal', *New York Times*, 30 June 1989; see also note 38.

[40] Engelberg, S. and Gordon, M. R., 'India seen as key on chemical arms', *New York Times*, 10 July, 1989, pp. A1, A6; Reuters, 'India rejects ban on arms chemical', *International Herald Tribune*, 12 July 1989.

[41] Tran, M., 'India asked to limit export of poison gas chemicals', *International Herald Tribune*, 14 July 1989, p. 5.

[42] See, for example, Fairhall, D., 'Israeli defences against Arab gas attacks', *Guardian Weekly*, vol. 140, no. 11. (12 Mar. 1989), p. 11; Mortimer, E., 'Israel hints it keeps chemical weapons as defensive measure', *Financial Times*, 10 Jan. 1989, p. 1.

[43] Israeli Deputy Foreign Minister Binyamin Netanyahu said that Israel had 'taken steps to ensure that the region doesn't have CW' but denied that Israel had a CW capability in a television interview in London, *Arms Control Reporter*, Feb. 1989, p. 704.B.860.

[44] See, for example, Walker, M., 'US plans major increase in chemical warfare spending', *The Guardian*, 15 Jan. 1989, p. 8.

very quickly but only for a short time. The defence budget request was $7.2 million for FY 1990 and $27.7 million for FY1991.[45] As regards riot-control agents, it was reported in March that the US Department of Justice expected to award a contract of $500 000 for testing chemicals which could 'subdue' fleeing prisoners, rioters and terrorists within 10 seconds and which would remain in effect for half an hour.[46] No published information about any such substances has yet been found by SIPRI. One might also note that all of the various versions of the rolling text which have existed in the CWC have contained a note dealing with the possibility of covering 'chemicals intended to enhance the use of chemical weapons'. This has appeared in the rolling text since the USA presented its draft version of a CWC to the CD in 1984.[47]

With respect to the future production of binary chemical weapons in the USA, the House of Representatives proposed that the Army's appropriated funds for the production of 155-mm binary chemical munitions should be reduced by $47 million.[48] The Senate proposed no such reduction. In the conference between the House and the Senate it was agreed that $45 million be authorized for binary CW production but only at such time as the Secretary of the Army could certify that the reported production difficulties and backlogs had been overcome. A total of $2 million dollars was released for ensuring procurement of some long-term materials;[49] $15 million were also allocated to the Office of the Secretary of Defense for a programme to develop and demonstrate compliance-monitoring capabilities for a CWC. Varying opinions still exist within the USA as to the extent to which the binary CW programme can proceed as planned. For example, the Department of Defense Office of Testing and Evaluation (OTE) and the US General Accounting Office (GAO) maintain that the Bigeye binary chemical bomb must undergo additional testing before full-scale production can start.[50]

[45] See, for example, Grier, P., 'Deterrence or disarmament? Pentagon researching exotic chemical arms', *Christian Science Monitor*, 6 Feb. 1989, pp. 1–2; Mather, I., 'New US chemical weapons', *The Observer*, 9 Apr. 1989, p. 23.

[46] Bennet, J., 'Chemical weapon sought for police', *Washington Times*, 6 Mar. 1989.

[47] USA, Conference on Disarmament document CD/500, 18 Apr. 1984.

[48] 'Proceedings and debates of the 101st Congress, 1st session', *Congressional Record*, vol. 135, no. 103 (27 July 1989), pp. H4383–93.

[49] 'Proceedings and debates of the 101st Congress, 1st session', *Congressional Record*, vol. 135, no. 154 (6 Nov. 1989), pp. S14905–906; *Authorizing Appropriations for Fiscal Year 1990 for Military Activities of the Department of Defense, for Military Construction, and for Defense Activities of the Department of Energy, to Prescribe Personnel Strengths for such Fiscal Year for the Armed Forces, and for other Purposes* (conference report to accompany H.R. 2461), 101st Congress, 1st session, US House of Representatives, Report 101-33 (US Government Printing Office: Washington, DC, 1989).

[50] See, for example, Ember, L., 'Bigeye binary chemical bomb blasted again', *Chemical & Engineering News*, 1 May 1989, p. 7; 'Conflict over Bigeye progress', *Jane's Defence Weekly*, vol. 1, no. 21 (27 May 1989), p. 981; *Bigeye Bomb: Unresolved Developmental Issues*, report to the Chairman, Committee on Foreign Affairs, House of Representatives, GAO/PEMD-89-27; *Bigeye Bomb: Evaluation of Operational Tests*, report to the Chairman, House Armed Services Committee and the Chairman, Senate Armed Services Committee, GAO/PEMD-89-29; Adams, P., 'Chemical bomb to face tests for reliability', *Defense News*, 21 Aug. 1989, p. 6; Ember, L., 'No new funds for chemical arms production likely this year', *Chemical & Engineering News*, 4 Sep. 1989, p. 14; 'F-111 computer too slow for Bigeye—GAO', *Jane's Defence Weekly*, 23 Sep. 1989, p. 564.

Table 4.1. US CBW budget requests for FYs 1990 and 1991
Figures are in US $m.

	FY 1990	FY 1991
Chemical/biological defence		
RDT&E	312.9	326.0
Procurement	240.4	277.3
Operations & maintenance	166.7	170.0
Military construction	19.4	27.7
ASF war reserve	0.0	25.0
Total	**739.4**	**826.0**
Chemical demilitarization programme		
RDT&E	1.1	0.0
Procurement	136.3	174.7
Operations & maintenance	149.1	139.0
Military construction	0.0	96.9
Total	**286.5**	**410.6**
Retaliatory programme		
RDT&E		
MLRS binary warhead	31.4	6.4
Other RDT&E	13.0	30.5
Procurement		
155-mm round production	47.0	71.4
Bigeye production	6.9	69.9
Total	**98.3**	**178.2**
Total programme	**1 124.2**	**1 414.8**

Source: Based on US Government factsheet covering all four of the armed services. See 'News chronology: 1 February', *Chemical Weapons Convention Bulletin*, no. 4 (May 1989), p. 10.

The USSR

In 1989 an official Soviet statement was made that the Soviet Union does not produce chemical weapons, has none outside its borders and has never transferred them to any other state.[51] In 1989 the Soviet Foreign Ministry again stated that the net weight of the CW agents in Soviet CW stockpiles did not amount to more than 50 000 tonnes.[52] The statements about the size and location of Soviet stockpiles have been objected to by British and US officials, who maintain that the Soviet stockpiles are at least six times larger than declared by the USSR.[53] The Soviet explanation that the size of the

[51] Eduard Shevardnadze's speech, Paris Conference on the Prohibition of Chemical Weapons, 7 Jan. 1989.

[52] Karpov, V., Soviet Deputy Foreign Minister, 'Soviet assurances on toxic weapons', *The Times*, 18 Feb. 1989, p. 11. Also stated in interview with Lt-Gen. S. Petrov, Commander of the Chemical Troops of the USSR, TASS commentator S. Kulik, 4 Apr. 1989, as quoted in 'General refutes reports about Soviet chemical weapons', Permanent Mission of the Soviet Union (Geneva), *Press Bulletin*, no. 60 (1798), 6 Apr. 1989, pp. 5–7.

[53] Fairhall, D., 'Britain rejects Russian chemical weapons count', *The Guardian*, 4 Apr. 1989, p. 8; *Statement on the Defence Estimates 1989*, House of Commons Session 1988–89, Defence Committee, 4th Report, vol. 1 (Her Majesty's Stationery Office: London, May 1989), pp. 9–10; Burns, W., Senate Governmental Affairs Committee Hearing, 'Verifying chemical weapons ban held "formidable challenge"', *Wireless File*, EUR-507, 10 Feb. 1989, pp. 21–23.

stockpiles was based on agent weight and excluded the explosive and metallic elements of the munitions has not been accepted by the British Government, which described the figure as 'an absurd underestimate'. British doubts may have been enhanced by a 1988 exchange of visits by CW experts from the UK and the USSR to Shikhany and Porton Down, respectively. During those visits the Soviet experts were able to view from helicopters the areas and places of their choosing,[54] while during its visit at Shikhany the British team was denied access to one facility which it had specifically requested to visit on the basis of a satellite photograph which had been shown to the Soviet hosts during the visit.[55] The denial disappointed the British delegation,[56] and the UK maintains that the USSR has not ceased CW production or testing.[57] President Gorbachev has indicated that a Soviet invitation will be issued to enable verification of the accuracy of the Soviet information.[58]

In the press British intelligence sources have been cited as claiming that the estimated 300 000 tonnes of the Soviet CW stockpiles 'includes weapons that have already been manufactured, and munition and materials assembled for making weapons'.[59] The definition of chemical weapons in the current rolling text of the CWC encompasses both shells for the agents and other equipment unique to the dissemination of chemical weapons as well as the chemical warfare agent *per se*.[60] If this is the definition which was used by British and other intelligence services, then their high figure might well be accurate. However, the lower figure of the Soviet declaration, which comprised only the amount of chemical agents, might then also be correct. That this was the method of calculation was also clarified in an April article in *Pravda* by a Foreign Office spokesman.[61] By late 1989 the US Central Intelligence Agency had allegedly lowered its estimate of the size of the Soviet stockpiles from 300 000 to 75 000 tonnes.[62]

Chemical weapons as a deterrent to nuclear weapons

The question of the relation between chemical and nuclear weapons in the Middle East is one of long standing. It won new attention in 1989 at the January 1989 Paris Conference when the Arab countries coupled CW

[54] See, for example, the communiqués issued by the Chemical Defence Establishment (CDE), Porton Down, UK, on the Soviet Union visit to the CDE: 'Welcoming statement by Dr Graham S. Pearson, Director CDE', 24 May 1988; and 'Soviet Union visit to CDE: statement by Dr Graham S. Pearson, Director CDE', 26 May 1988.

[55] See *Statement on the Defence Estimates 1989* (note 53), p. 10.

[56] See *Statement on the Defence Estimates 1989* (note 53); see also Lundin, S. J., 'Chemical and biological warfare: developments in 1988', *SIPRI Yearbook 1989* (note 30), p. 112.

[57] See *Statement on the Defence Estimates 1989* (note 53).

[58] See, for example, Plok, H., 'Howe puts case on arms control', *The Guardian*, 7 Apr. 1989, p. 2.

[59] Webster, P., 'UK to accuse Kremlin over chemical arms', *The Times*, 23 Jan. 1989, pp. 1, 20.

[60] Article II, Definitions and Criteria, section 1.1, of the 'rolling text', Conference on Disarmament document CD/952, 18 Aug. 1989, pp. 21–22.

[61] Statement by Soviet Foreign Ministry Spokesman, *Vyennyi Vestnik*, 21 Apr. 1989, VOVP2-890421DR33, pp. 1–2.

[62] Moore, M., 'Pentagon lowers its estimate of the Soviet threat', *International Herald Tribune*, 28 Sep. 1989.

disarmament to the progress of nuclear disarmament efforts.[63] This Arab position may, in reality, have had little to do with chemical weapons but may rather have been a political attempt to rid Israel of its presumed nuclear capability since only a few Arab nations appear to be much concerned about acquiring protection against chemical weapons. Without such protection it would not be possible to wage chemical warfare against another country which possessed chemical weapons. Israel, on the other hand, takes such a threat very seriously. Furthermore, Israel has declared that it would respond if it were attacked by chemical weapons.[64] If an Israeli nuclear response is a possibility, then the perception that chemical weapons are a deterrent against nuclear weapons could turn out to be a disastrous option.

Another aspect of the Arab position is that chemical weapons have been used, and used recently—in contrast to nuclear weapons. Arab acquisition of chemical weapons not only threatens Israel but also implies a security risk to the individual Arab states themselves, since the political problems in the region do not only involve Israel.[65] They might thus have to prepare for the possible use of chemical weapons in any conflict which might arise in the region and particularly so with the Iraqi use of chemical weapons fresh in mind. Furthermore, the actual waging of chemical warfare is far more complex and expensive than is generally assumed. The high cost of CW defence to both NATO and the WTO in terms of both money and training is an example of that. There is thus reason to fear that the Arab position on chemical weapons might again lead to chemical warfare if there were again open conflict among some Arab states, rather than between any one of them and Israel. A deeper discussion of the security implications might instead emphasize that comprehensive adherence to the future CWC by both Israel and its neighbours might better serve the security concerns of all parties even if the other problems in the region were not resolved. (See also chapter 14 regarding the suggestions for a chemical weapon-free zone in the Middle East.)

The spread of missile technology and the accompanying missile threat are other aspects of the CW problem in the Middle East. This was illustrated by an interview with the Egyptian Ambassador to Israel, who, in a discussion of peace efforts in the Middle East, stated that certain Arab states with chemical weapons and ground-to-ground missiles could very well constitute a threat to Israel.[66] Chemical weapons may thus constitute a politically useful although internationally prohibited and morally unacceptable type of weapon. However, it should be remembered that the payload in a single

[63] See, for example, Cody, E., 'Banning toxic arms: without Arabs, no pact', *International Herald Tribune*, 13 Jan. 1989, pp. 1–2; Communiqué on the Paris Conference issued by the Council of the League of Arab States at its extraordinary session of 12 Jan. 1989, p. 2; 'Why Arabs want the option of a last resort', *The Independent*, 9 Jan. 1989, p. 8; 'Arab threat to tie ban on gas to A-weapons', *San Francisco Chronicle*, 9 Jan. 1989, p. A11.

[64] See Mortimer (note 42).

[65] See, for example, 'US concerned by Cairo CW capability', *Defense & Foreign Affairs Weekly*, 10 Apr. 1989, p. 4: 'But US officials insisted that Egypt's CW capability is being done [sic] to deter Libya and is not directed against Israel'.

[66] 'Ägyptische Appelle an das israelische Volk: Werben Mubaraks für Vorteile eines Friedens', *Neue Zürcher Zeitung*, 29 Sep. 1989, p. 4.

missile is not sufficient to cover a large area and that CW missiles probably do not exist in great numbers except in the case of the superpowers. These circumstances (depending also upon some technical considerations) could diminish the value of CW missiles for use in regular military chemical warfare in the region, even if a terrible threat to the civilian population in the cities remains.

Measures against the spread of chemical weapons

With respect to present international measures to curb the spread of chemical weapons beyond those countries which now possess them, the most notable events in 1989 related to the alleged CW production facility in Rabta, Libya. Also of significance were the measures taken by a number of countries and, in particular, the Federal Republic of Germany and the USA to strengthen legislative measures hindering export and to institute sanctions against companies which provide other countries with chemical weapons. The following discussion deals with some of the main events of 1989.

During 1988 it became clear that Libya had built a chemical industry complex at Rabta which gave rise to serious concern that the facility might be utilized for CW production.[67] In early 1989 it became clear that some companies in the FRG, including one state-owned company[68] (albeit together with companies from a number of other countries including Austria, Italy, Japan and Thailand[69]) had played a role in providing different kinds of assistance to the Libyan enterprise. This was clarified only gradually and was the cause of significant political embarrassment between the USA and the FRG. While the FRG initially seemed reluctant to investigate and reveal all of the connections that existed between different authorities and chemical industrial enterprises in the FRG, it soon became public that such links had existed. This led to new efforts by the FRG to legislate measures designed to hinder future attempts to export know-how and chemicals which could be utilized to produce chemical weapons.[70]

---

[67] *SIPRI Yearbook 1989* (note 30), pp. 110–11.

[68] See, for example, Winter, M., 'Libyen-Handel war Bonn lange bekannt, BND-Hinweis auf Verdacht gegen Imhausen', *Frankfurter Rundschau*, 14 Jan. 1989, p. 1; Goodhart, D., 'West German companies raided in Libyan inquiry', *Financial Times*, 26 Jan. 1989.

[69] See, for example, Tourn-ngern, S. 'Libya plant has "tight security, secret facilities"', *Bangkok Post*, 12 Jan. 1989, pp. 1, 3; see also list of companies which allegedly contributed to the Rabta facility, presented with the disclaimer that it had been compiled from newspaper reports and without any assertion of its validity by Senator Helms, in the US Senate upon introduction of the Chemical and Biological Warfare Prevention Act, 25 Jan. 1989, *Congressional Record*, pp. 217–18, 679; Lichfield, J., 'Japanese companies linked to gasplant', *The Independent*, 10 Mar. 1989, p. 9; Ali, M. (Washington) and Joseph, J. (Tokyo), 'Mitsubishi "link to Libyan Plant"', *The Times*, 10 Mar. 1989, p. 12; 'Minister denies Libyan chemical plant links', OW1003072489, Tokyo, KYODO, in English, 0416 GMT, 10 Mar. 89, FBIS-EAS-89-046, 10 Mar. 1989, p. 3; Ottaway, D. B., 'U.S. fails to oust Thais at Libya plant', *Washington Post*, 1 June 1989, p. A10.

[70] 'West Germany cracks down on exports of weapons gas', *Nature*, 23 Feb. 1989, p. 678. It was suggested that the following 8 substances be subject to export restrictions: thiodiglycol, phosphorus oxychloride, dimethyl methyl phosphonate, methyl phosphonyl difluoride, methylphosphonyl dichloride, dimethyl phosphite, phosphorous trichloride and trimethyl phosphite. This list was later expanded to 17 substances to correspond to the list of the Australia Group; in Oct., 25 substances were put on the list, 'Sperrliste für C-Waffen-Material: Verschärfte Exportkontrollen in der Bundesrepublik', *Neue Zürcher Zeitung*, 6 Oct. 1989, p. 2.

However, it seems that the new legislation may cause difficulties for the exchange of chemicals for scientific purposes, which could affect more than 100 countries having development agreements with the FRG that necessitate technology transfer.[71] Several accounts exist of the way in which the affair developed and how it was handled by the authorities in the FRG. Some of these accounts trace the activities back to as early as 1980.[72] This incident, and the Iranian export problem mentioned above, increased the demand for tightening export regulations.[73] The USA raised the number of chemicals subject to export regulations from 8 to 40.[74]

As a direct consequence of the Rabta affair, in 1989 the US Congress worked on national legislation (the Chemical and Biological Warfare Elimination Act) prohibiting export of sensitive chemicals and CW and BW technology and instituting sanctions for violations, which were to be decided upon by the US President.[75] However, the Senate decision was blocked owing to some unresolved legal problems. The matter will thus not be settled until 1990.[76] The European Community recommended export controls on eight substances.[77] *Sweden* is preparing to list 32 chemicals for export restrictions in 1990.[78]

It is necessary to differentiate between national measures to curb the spread of chemical weapons such as those proposed today by specific international political groups like the Australia Group and the global measures which will be agreed upon internationally under the future CWC. The measures which are currently being taken, and those which would be in effect under a convention, must be seen in two different contexts. Currently the acquisition of chemical weapons is not prohibited, whatever political and

[71] Dickman, S., 'Export curbs threaten science', *Nature*, vol. 342, no. 6246 (9 Nov. 1989), p. 106.

[72] See, for example, *Deutscher Bundestag Stenographischer Bericht*, 126 Sitzung, Bonn, 17 Feb. 1989, pp. 9259-304; 'Die Kontrollmöglichleiten reichen für sensitive Exporte nicht aus: Der Bericht der Bundesregierung über die Beteiligung deutscher Firmen am Bau der C-Waffen-Fabrik im libyschen Rabta. Teil I-III', *Frankfurter Rundschau*, 17 Feb. 1989, p. 14–15; 18 Feb. 1989, p. 12; 20 Feb. 1989, p. 8; Wulf, H., *Waffenexport aus Deutschland: Geschäfte mit den fernen Tot* (Rowohlt: Reinbek bei Hamburg, Nov. 1989), pp. 1–172; Brzoska, M., 'Behind the German export scandals', *Bulletin of the Atomic Scientists*, July–Aug. 1989, vol. 45, pp. 32–35.

[73] See, for example, 'Gas inquiry', *The Independent*, 30 June 1989, p. 8.

[74] 'Export of chemicals, bioagents banned', *Chemical & Engineering News*, vol. 67, no. 10 (6 Mar. 1989), p. 23; the US list was expanded from 17 to 23 compounds, including diethyl methyl-phosphonite, ethyl phosphorous difluoride and O-ethyl 2-(diisopropylamino) ethylmethylphosphonite or QL; see, for example, 'U.S. exports: foreign policy controls (820)', 'Chemical/biological weapons precursors controls', USA prohibits export of 40 chemicals to Iran, Iraq, Libya and Syria, *Wireless File*, EUR-411, 6 Apr. 1989, p. 14.

[75] Suggestions by Senators Helms, Pell and Dole in S. 195 Chemical and Biological Weapons Control Act of 1989, 101st Congress, 1st session, US Senate, 25 Jan. 1989; Fascell *et al.* in H.R. 3033, 'Title I: Measures to prevent the proliferation of chemical and biological weapons, Title II: Measures to deter the use of chemical and biological weapons, Title III: Miscellaneous provisions', US House, 27 July 1989. The House approved the Chemical and Biological Warfare Elimination Act which was then sent to the Senate on 13 Nov. 1989, *Congressional Record*, 13 Nov. 1989, pp. H8405–11.

[76] See 'Weekly report: chemical-arms sanctions bill casualty of turf dispute', *Congressional Quarterly*, 2 Dec. 1989, p. 3323.

[77] Wolf, J., 'EC to curb chemical exports in novel defense initiative', *Wall Street Journal*, 17 Feb. 1989; see also 14 Feb. 1989 entry, *Chemical Weapons Convention Bulletin*, 'The point is established that the regulation is to arise not from EC treaties but from informal political agreement among the ministers', no. 4 (May 1989), p. 12.

[78] Porne, L., 'Kemikalier blir krigsmateriel' ['Chemicals become war materials'], *Svenska Dagbladet* (Stockholm), 14 Nov. 1989, p. 8 (in Swedish).

moral objections may be raised. Under international law it is not illegal for any nation to acquire chemical weapons (except for those which have renounced their possession), and in this context one should recall that it is the government of a nation, not its chemical industry, which decides upon such acquisition. Thus in the absence of a global CWC it is much more difficult and more politically intrusive to investigate the possible spread of CW capability by some generally accepted means, even if such suggestions have been put forward.[79] Under the future CWC the situation will be completely different. First, a state party will have given up the option to acquire chemical weapons. Second, it will have taken on the obligation to see to it that its own institutions verify that no violations occur, be it nationally or on behalf of other nations. Third, it will have accepted that international verification on its own territory be conducted by the verification agency of the CWC. These conditions provide for a much more effective system for deterring and detecting clandestine violations of the CWC than current measures, even if today's ability to at least detect hidden production facilities seems to be remarkably effective.

One issue which has been the subject of some confusion was the Libyan offer that foreign experts visit the facility at Rabta to verify that production of CW agents was not being conducted there. The initial Libyan invitations to journalists did, in fact, not induce confidence in the seriousness of the offer.[80] However, in the USA and other countries further arguments were made that it would be easy to remove any signs of CW agent production (allegedly within less than 24 hours), and thus an inspection would be meaningless. This reasoning seems to have been supported by statements that the Libyans were in the process of converting the facility to a pharmaceutical production facility.[81] However, this is an area in which sufficient knowledge does not seem to be available at all levels of the political hierarchy. While it is quite true that it would have been difficult to demonstrate whether there had been any *intent* to produce CW agents, it would have been technically possible to determine whether CW agent production or production of any specific chemical had taken place, if sufficient intrusiveness had been allowed. Modern analytical methods in chemistry make it possible to detect the presence of extremely small amounts of a substance even years after production has ceased.[82]

It is also obvious that ordinary intelligence methods are being used to discover information about the spread of CW capabilities. As mentioned above, in its *Statement on the Defence Estimates 1989* the British Ministry of Defence reported the Soviet refusal to grant the British inspection team's

[79] See, for example, Ember, L., 'Chemical warfare organization debated', *Chemical & Engineering News*, 6 Feb. 1989, p. 21; for further discussion of the suggestion of the International Chemical Warfare Authority see, Utgoff, V. A., *Neutralizing the Value of Chemical Weapons: a Supplement to Chemical Weapons Arms Control*, Occasional Paper, Atlantic Council of the United States, 1989.

[80] See, for example, Walker, T., 'Libya fails to impress its good intentions on the world press', *Financial Times*, 9 Jan. 1989, p. 2.

[81] Engelberg, S., 'U.S. believes Libya is converting plant', *International Herald Tribune*, 3 Mar. 1989.

[82] UK, Conference on Disarmament document CD/15, 29 Apr. 1978, p. 3; see also Finland, Conference on Disarmament document CD/CW/WP.253, 26 June 1989.

request to visit the Soviet CW facility at Shikhany in 1988, a request which was based on a satellite photograph of the site.[83] This constitutes another occasion where satellite pictures actually seem to have been used to question whether facilities might have some connection with chemical weapons. Similar previous allegations concerned Rabta in Libya.[84] It thus seems that the use of satellites could play a role in future verification activities under a CWC or, prior to that, as part of national efforts to follow developments of interest to a nation's security in the absence of a convention. This presupposes that commercial satellites such as Landsat or SPOT are available for the provision of sufficiently detailed pictures for use by those countries which do not themselves possess satellite imaging systems. It thus seems motivated to analyse the specific information provided by these pictures and to ascertain the way in which they served to create or support suspicion. Similar suggestions have been made before, both in the context of the CWC negotiations and in the negotiations on the reduction of conventional arms in Europe.

New chemical weapons

Now and then information appears that possible new CW agents have been found. Usually such assertions do not seriously appraise the actual suitability of such chemicals as CW agents. One might recall, without denying the possibility that new CW agents may have been or will be discovered, that over the years only about 20 or so chemicals seem to have been found which are suitable for use as chemical weapons, and also that the binary weapon technique still does not seem to be satisfactory after 20 years of development.[85] In the 1989–90 edition of *Jane's NBC Protection Equipment*, concern is expressed about the possible use of the substance perfluoroisobutene as a 'choking agent'. The substance, which is clear and odourless, causes death by production of pulmonary oedema (i.e., by filling the lungs with fluid). Perfluoroisobutene is claimed to be capable of penetrating existing CW protective equipment.[86] Its toxicity is about 1000 mg min/m³, and it is accordingly characterized as a super-toxic, lethal compound which would be regulated under the CWC.[87] These types of substance have been known for quite some time and were described in the literature at least as

[83] See *Statement on the Defence Estimates 1989* (note 53).

[84] See, for example, Ottaway, D. B., 'How the CIA tracked chemical plant', *The Guardian*, 15 Jan. 1989, pp. 17–18; Broad, W. J., 'Non-superpowers are developing their own spy satellite systems', *New York Times*, 3 Sep. 1989, pp. 1, 6.

[85] See SIPRI, *The Problems of Chemical and Biological Warfare: CB Weapons Today*, vol. 2 (Almqvist & Wiksell: Stockholm, 1973,) p. 288; see also SIPRI, *Chemical Disarmament: New Weapons for Old* (Almqvist & Wiksell: Stockholm, 1975), pp. 22, 139.

[86] Gander, T. (ed.), 'Foreword', *Jane's NBC Protection Equipment 1989-90*, p. 9; 'Treaties "unlikely to halt secret chemical weapons production"', *The Guardian*, 25 Sep. 1989.

[87] UK, 'Verification of the non-production of chemical weapons: an illustrative example of the problem of novel toxic compounds', Conference on Disarmament document CD/CW/WP.239, 12 Apr. 1989, pp. 1–6; see also Lailey, A. F., Leadbeater, L., Maidment, M. P. and Upshall, D. G., 'The mechanism of chemically-induced pulmonary oedema', *Proceedings, Third International Symposium on Protection Against Chemical Warfare Agents*, Umeå, Sweden, 11–16 June 1989, FOA report C 40266-4.6, 4.7, June 1989, pp. 153–61.

early as 1959.[88] However, as appears from the British CD Working Paper of 12 April 1989, what caused the current interest in this subject is that per-fluoroisobutene can be easily formed from the substances used for producing polytetrafluoroethene (TFE), the inert lining of frying pans, and the like. These substances thus presumably could be placed on the list of substances the production of which might have to be declared and controlled under the future CWC. This would cause considerable difficulties and points to the need for further elaboration of the methods used for deciding which new chemical compounds are to be covered by the CWC.

In his speech to a conference in Umeå, Sweden, on protection against chemical and biological weapons (see below) the Head of the Chemical Defence Establishment, Porton Down, UK, warned of new possibilities of developing CW and BW agents in the 'grey zone' which he considered to exist between current definitions and understanding of what constitutes these two types of weapon. He mentioned bioregulators and toxins as being of particular concern.[89] Although it can be argued that such substances are already covered by the BWC, or will be covered by the CWC, it is obvious that full control of such substances cannot be obtained until the entry into force of the CWC.

Destruction and disposal of old chemical weapons

One of the CW issues which has attracted increased attention is the problem of destruction. This question not only relates to the negotiations on a CWC and its requirement that all chemical weapons be destroyed within 10 years after the entry into force of the convention but is also relevant to the environmental threat constituted by ageing CW stockpiles. Furthermore, some existing chemical weapons are no longer usable since the delivery system for which a particular chemical munition was once constructed no longer exists. Also, even today, World War I chemical munitions continue to be found on the old battlefields and need to be destroyed. The realization that, in general, toxic chemicals have to be disposed of is growing both nationally and internationally. The ability of the environment to contain and gradually destroy toxic compounds is limited, and vast efforts are needed to cope with the whole problem of toxic waste and hazardous emissions of chemicals into the air. This is clearly demonstrated by the international debate and negotiations dealing with the elimination of toxic wastes and the best means of disposing of them.[90]

---

[88] See, for example, Lohs, K., *Synthetische Gifte*, 4th edn (Militärverlag der Deutschen Demokratischen Republik: Berlin, 1974), pp. 192–93.

[89] Pearson, G. S, 'The technical challenge to counter the CBW spectrum', *Proceedings, Third International Symposium on Protection Against Chemical Warfare Agents* (see note 87), p. 375.

[90] During 1989 a number of international meetings took place which dealt with the ecological consequences of the release of toxic or damaging chemicals into the environment of the world. This is not the place for a review of those events but for an example of the type of problem involved see US Environmental Protection Agency, *The Toxic-Release Inventory: a National Perspective, 1987* (US Government Printing Office: Washington, DC, 1989).

Belgium

Belgium is planning to build a facility to destroy old chemical munitions from World War I. Roughly 20 tonnes of ammunition are found every year. The munitions which have been discovered have been stockpiled for the past eight years, but environmental concerns and repeated casualties among the personnel handling these munitions are now forcing a solution for their destruction to be found.[91]

Canada

During 1988 there was debate in Canada about the extent of Canadian involvement, together with the USA and other NATO countries, in the development and testing of chemical weapons and protective equipment against these weapons. Allegations were also made that accidents had occurred during this work. In response to the debate the Canadian Government ordered an investigation to be carried out by the former Canadian Ambassador to the CD, William Barton. The report which resulted from this investigation was released on 25 January 1989.[92] It found the activities of the Canadian Defence Research Establishment Suffield (DRES) in Alberta, to be in accordance with acceptable standards, although it suggested that improvements could nevertheless be made. It also proposed that the old programme to destroy World War II chemicals be revived, which would imply that not only 18 tonnes of mostly mustard gas but also some nerve gases and other CW agents would be destroyed within a three-year-period.[93] The Defence Minister also announced that he had invited Soviet representatives to visit DRES to inspect the destruction and to share information.[94] The visit took place at DRES on 17–19 July 1989. A Soviet invitation for a return visit to the USSR was said to be forthcoming.

Federal Republic of Germany

In 1989 there was further debate in the Federal Republic of Germany about removal of the US CW stockpiles from the FRG. In the Rheinland-Pfalz Parliament demands were made that the stockpiles be transferred out of the country before 1992, the date previously promised by President Reagan,[95] and at the opening of the Vienna Negotiation on Conventional Armed Forces in Europe (CFE), US Secretary of State James Baker stated that the

[91] Lewis, J. A. C., 'Belgian centre to handle First World War CW', *Jane's Defence Weekly*, 28 Jan. 1989, p. 124; du Bois, M., 'Deadly harvest after 70 years: fields of Flanders still yield relics of gas attacks', *Wall Street Journal*, 8 Aug. 1989, pp. 1, 8.

[92] 'News Conference on the Barton report' (speech by Canadian Minister of National Defence, Perrin Beatty), *National Defence Press Release*, 25 Jan. 1989.

[93] See, for example, 'Beatty acts on Barton Report', *Disarmament Bulletin*, vol. 9 (fall-winter 1988), p. 4.

[94] See, for example, Ovenden, N., 'Beatty invites Soviets to check Suffield complex', *Edmonton Journal*, 26 Jan. 1989.

[95] See, for example, 'Mainzer Landtag fordert einstimmig C-Waffen-Abzug', *Frankfurter Rundschau*, 20 Jan. 1989.

USA would investigate that possibility.[96] However, US military spokesmen pointed to the difficulty of rapidly developing safe transportation methods and adequate stockpiling arrangements on Johnston Atoll in the Pacific, where destruction of these weapons will presumably take place.[97] There has been considerable discussion as to whether the stockpiles could safely be transported first through the FRG and then to Johnston Atoll.[98] None the less there are US plans for removal of the chemical weapons before 1992 in spite of the safety concerns expressed by the Army. Furthermore, the US Congress stated that the US Secretary of Defense must certify that, at the time of transportation, the USA would have an adequate stockpile of binary chemical weapons and that the transportation could be carried out with minimal technical and operational risk and maximum safety for the civilian population.[99] According to some US observers, these conditions may jeopardize the possible 1990 removal of the US stockpile.[100] However, in a press release, the Defence Ministry of the FRG declared that the chemical munitions are safe and not leaking, that these munitions will not be replaced by US binary weapons and that removal of the chemical weapons is to begin in 1990 utilizing adequate safety precautions.[101]

The USA

In May 1988 a facility for the destruction of the hallucinogenic agent BZ began operation in Pine Bluff, Arkansas, and by October 1989 the entire US stockpile of this agent was supposed to have been destroyed.[102] The latest effort in the long-standing US programme for CW destruction, the destruction facility at Johnston Atoll, was ready to start test-runs by mid-1989.[103] Full operation and the actual destruction of chemical weapons may, however, not begin until April 1990, seven months behind schedule, or even

---

[96] 'Ziehen USA Giftgas vorzeitig ab?', *Frankfurter Rundschau*, 7 Mar. 1989; 'U.S. urges Soviets to join move against chemical weapons' (text of Baker statement at CFE meeting), *Wireless File*, EUR-104, 7 Mar. 1989, p. 3; see also US Senate, National Defense Authorization Act for fiscal years 1990 and 1991, report to accompany S. 1352, *Authorizing Appropriations for FYs 1990 and 1991 for Military Activities of the Department of Defense, for Military Construction, and for Defense Activities of the Department of Energy, to Prescribe Personnel Strengths for such Fiscal Years for the Armed Forces, and for other Purposes together with Additional Views*, Report 101-81, 19 July 1989, p. 19.

[97] Gordon, M. R., 'Limelight is elusive if arms is the rub', *New York Times*, 10 Apr. 1989, p. B7.

[98] 'Amerikaner ziehen alle C-Waffen ab', *Mainzer Rhein-Zeitung*, 1 Feb. 1989; Grabenströer, M., 'Das Giftgas-Depot von Fischbach soll 1990 geräumt werden', *Frankfurter Rundschau*, 19 May 1989, p. 1.

[99] Smith, J., 'U.S. to speed removal of gas', *International Herald Tribune*, 16 Oct. 1989, pp. 1, 6; see also *Congressional Record* (note 49), p. S14906.

[100] See, for example, Siemens, J., 'Abzug der chemischen Waffen aus der Bundesrepublik ungewiss', *Frankfurter Rundschau*, 14 Nov. 1989, pp. 1, 3.

[101] Der Bundesminister der Verteidigung, Informations- und Pressestab, 'Abtransport der chemischen Waffen aus der Bundesrepublik Deutschland', *Mitteilung an die Presse*, vol. 16, no. 68, (17 Oct. 1989), p. 4.

[102] 'The U.S. chemical weapons demilitarization program (600)', 'Factsheet on U.S. program to destroy CW', *Wireless File*, EUR-408, 14 Sep. 1989, p. 3; see also Program Manager for Chemical Demilitarization, 'Disposal of chemical agents and munitions stored at Tooele Army depot, Tooele, Utah', *Final Environmental Impact Statement*, July 1989.

[103] 'U.S., USSR will have framework to destroy chemical weapons' (text of remarks by US Ambassador Max Friedersdorf at the CD on 4 Apr. 1989), (2910), US Information Service, Press Section, *Wireless File*, Stockholm, 5 Apr. 1989, pp. 5–10.

later.[104] The US destruction operation on Johnston Atoll is also said to include test-runs for a period of 16 months. Concern has been voiced by Greenpeace that incineration techniques used at the Johnston Atoll facility could give rise to the emission of toxic substances into the environment.[105] Information also appeared during 1989 that the entire US destruction programme had been delayed and that a number of leakages of warfare agents had occurred during destruction operations.[106] However, the destruction efforts continued and in July, after release of an Environmental Impact Statement, a decision was taken to establish a new CW destruction facility at the US Army's Tooele base in Utah. The new destruction facility will be adjacent to a previous destruction facility, where destruction methods have been tested, which has been operating since the end of the 1970s. The new facility will cost $138 million, will have a work force of about 400 people and be operational by 1992.[107] In November 1989 President Bush made a statement at the ground-breaking ceremony for the new destruction plant reaffirming the US commitment to halt the spread of chemical weapons and to eliminate these weapons for all time, but mentioning also the 'difficult technical challenge of finding a way to safely, efficiently and quickly demilitarize those stocks'.[108]

When completed in 1997 the US destruction programme, as outlined by the Congress, will have cost much more than $3 billion, not counting the costs incurred prior to enacting the programme.[109] Still higher cost estimates were given as recently as several years ago.[110] Environmental concerns have also been continuously expressed in the USA with regard to the destruction of chemical weapons.[111] The Congress also approved a bill for continued research and development of the chemical demilitarization cryofracture programme.[112]

The USSR

During the Paris Conference on the Prohibition of Chemical Weapons (see also chapter 14), Soviet Foreign Minister Eduard Shevardnadze repeated earlier Soviet statements about the size of the Soviet stockpile and stated again that the USSR does not produce chemical weapons. He declared that

[104] Almond, P, 'Chemical arms cutback to have little impact on military', Washington Times, 26 Sep. 1989, p. 8; Gordon, M. R., 'As oratory fades, obstacles to chemical arms multiply', New York Times, 31 Oct. 1989, p. 13.

[105] Picardie, A., 'Greenpeace review of Johnston Atoll chemical agent disposal system (JACADS)', (Greenpeace International Pacific Campaign: Washington, DC, 2 Aug. 1989).

[106] See, for example, Reed, C., 'Multiple mishaps hit US gas weapons disposal plants', The Guardian, 27 Sep. 1989.

[107] 'Pentagon picks on-site burning to dispose of chemical weapons', New York Times, 20 Sep. 1989, p. 10.

[108] 'Bush underscores U.S. commitment to eliminate chemical arms', Wireless File, EUR-111, 30 Oct. 1989, p. 17.

[109] See 'U.S., USSR will have framework to destroy chemical weapons' (note 103).

[110] Stössel, W. J., Report of the Chemical Warfare Review Commission (US Government Printing Office: Washington, DC, 1985).

[111] See, for example, Atchison, S. D., 'The toxic morass in Denver's backyard', Business Week, 9 Jan. 1989, p. 31.

[112] See Congressional Record (note 49), p. S.14906.

the USSR intends to be an initial signatory member of the CWC. He also announced that the USSR would start destruction of its CW stockpiles later in 1989 and that foreign observers would, again, be invited to see the process.[113] At the same time Soviet scientists announced that they were studying processes by which CW agents might be converted into products capable of being used for peaceful purposes.[114] In February a Soviet news correspondent visited the CW destruction facility situated in the city of Chapayevsk, in the Kuibyshev Region on the right bank of the Volga, and reported on the visit.[115] The installation was intended to carry out destruction 100 days per year and to devote the rest of the time to maintenance and other preparations. The munitions were to be dismantled and decontaminated and then, in a second step, the CW agent would have been destroyed by neutralization. The facility also made preparations to allow international on-site inspection to verify that the destruction would be performed in accordance with the CWC. The end-products which would have resulted were ascertained to be environmentally safe. However, when the purpose of the facility was announced in the city, the citizens and its local administration became concerned about the environmental risks involved and asked for guarantees that the facility would be environmentally safe.[116] (In the USA numerous Environmental Impact Statements concerning the safe construction and operation of CW destruction facilities have been produced over the years, the most recent in 1989.[117]) By the end of 1989 it was clear that the Chapayevsk destruction facility would not open until 1990 and that it would then serve primarily as a training and experimental centre for future Soviet destruction efforts. The USSR is, however, 'working on a special program that calls for building several chemical weapons destruction facilities, whose aggregate capacity would make it possible to meet the deadline set in the Convention for the destruction of all chemical weapons stocks'.[118] In his speech to the UN General Assembly the Soviet CD delegate called for international co-operation in the destruction of chemical weapons.[119] A number of conclusions about developments in the USA and

---

[113] See, for example, 'E. Shevardnadze's speech to Paris Conference', Paris, 8 Jan. 1989, TASS, Permanent Mission of the Soviet Union (Geneva), *Press Bulletin*, no. 4 (1742), 10 Jan. 1989, pp. 3–8.

[114] 'Soviet scientist: peaceful use of chemical weapons', Moscow, Jan. 4, TASS, Permanent Mission of the Soviet Union (Geneva), *Press Bulletin*, no. 2 (1740), 5 Jan. 1989, p. 5; see also Peel, Q., 'Soviet studies start into reprocessing weapons', *Financial Times*, 9 Jan 1989.

[115] See, for example, 'Chemical weapons destruction plant nears completion', Chapayevsk Kuibyshev region, TASS, 13 Feb. 1989, as translated and quoted in Permanent Mission of the Soviet Union (Geneva), *Press Bulletin*, no. 28 (1766), 15 Feb. 1989, pp. 2–5. The article covering the visit was published in *Pravda* and also contained a picture of the facility; see Kulik, C. and Chernychev, V., 'Zavod gde umirajot ov', *Pravda*, 15 Feb. 1989, p. 2.

[116] See note 114; and Flikalo, C., 'District infected with rumors', *Izvestia*, 13 May 1989.

[117] Final Environmental Impact Statement (see note 102); see also, for example, Smith, J., 'Army poison gas stockpile raises worries in Kentucky', *Washington Post*, 22 Jan. 1989, pp. A1, A8, A9.

[118] Smidovich, N., commentator to Workshop I: Concluding the CW Convention: government–industry co-operation, session C: National measures in support of the negotiations, Government–Industry Conference against Chemical Weapons, document GICCW/WSI/8, Canberra, 20 Sep. 1989, p. 6.

[119] Statement by Soviet Representative in the First Committee of the 44th Session of the UN General Assembly, Permanent Mission of the Soviet Union (New York), *Press Release*, 30 Oct. 1989, pp. 1–8.

the USSR regarding the destruction of existing CW stocks during 1989 can be drawn, including the following:

1. Despite long preparations and studies, particularly in the USA, it still seems technically difficult to bring large CW destruction facilities into operation owing largely to the extreme care required in handling the lethal or dangerous toxic payloads. (Such seems not to have been the case for the destruction of missiles under the INF Treaty, which was completed on schedule.)

2. The environmental concerns among the civilian population in Europe, the USA and the USSR are strong and will force rigorous safety arrangements for transportation of chemical weapons and for destruction operations.

3. The costs of destruction will be enormous, and this applies not only to the superpowers with their huge stockpiles but also to other countries which may only have to destroy old World War I chemical munitions on their soil or at sea, as is the case, for example, for Belgium, Denmark and the Federal Republic of Germany.

4. In view of the fact that the destruction of substantial amounts of chemical weapons (from tens to thousands of tonnes) will ultimately take up to 10 years and cost billions of dollars, it might be of interest to those states considering the acquisition of chemical weapons to seriously weigh the economic and environmental costs of these weapons in light of the fact that their destruction will, in the end, be unavoidable.

Protection against chemical weapons

Protection against chemical weapons is an area which is currently attracting increased interest in not only the research aspect but also as relates to development and procurement. A clear indication of this was the Third Symposium on CW Protection, held in Umeå, Sweden, in June 1989. These symposia started in 1983, and attendance at them has increased in terms of the number of countries represented, the individuals participating and the companies presenting the accompanying exhibitions.[120] While it is natural that interest in CW protection should increase in a period when the most extensive use of chemical weapons since World War I has occurred, it may be a negative signal about the expectations for completion of a CWC, particularly within industrial circles. The keynote speaker at the symposium emphasized the need to maintain protective efforts until a CWC has eliminated chemical weapons, and warned that premature abandonment of protection would only make chemical weapons more attractive to those who might find value in their possible use.[121] It should be added that the presentations and exhibitions concerned themselves to a significant extent with

[120] Proceedings, Third International Symposium on Protection Against Chemical Warfare Agents (see note 87).
[121] Ooms, A. J. J., 'Chemical weapons, what to do about them?', Proceedings, Third International Symposium on Protection Against Chemical Warfare Agents (see note 87), p. 11.

protection against chemical (and biological) weapons for the *civilian* population, not least children.[122]

A reference from the medical literature about recent developments in research on pharmacological protection against nerve gases—which argues that humans can largely be protected against the lethal and incapacitating effects of these compounds on a chemical battlefield—illustrates the importance of protection in diminishing the CW threat.[123] It is also appropriate to note that already in 1989 *Jane's* produced a second edition of a 1988 book on protective equipment against nuclear, chemical and biological (NBC) weapons which, besides a thorough description of the existing protection in different countries against NBC weapons, contains short descriptions of these weapons, their effects and a list of acronyms used in this field.[124]

III. Biological weapons

The question of biological weapons was not of as profound political importance in 1989 as was that of chemical weapons. However, allegations about the acquisition and production of biological weapons were made which parallel those made about chemical weapons. The rounds of information exchanges agreed upon at the 1985 Review Conference of the Biological Weapons Convention (BWC) continued with a new round in April 1989 (see chapter 14). Concerns were again expressed about the possible abuse of new genetic techniques for BW purposes.

Allegations of violation of the 1925 Geneva Protocol and the BWC

Although a number of allegations continued to be put forward that at least 10 countries have violated the BWC[125] by being in the process of developing or producing biological weapons, no explicit *evidence* seems to have been presented.[126] These allegations must, however, be closely watched, not least in light of the planned 1991 BWC Review Conference.

US allegations that at least 10 countries, among these the USSR, possessed or were in the process of acquiring biological weapons were

---

[122] Mauritzson-Sandberg, E., and Sandberg, L., 'Psychological problems associated with the wearing of respiratory protective devices: childrens reactions', *Proceedings, Third International Symposium on Protection Against Chemical Warfare Agents* (see note 87), p. 301.

[123] Dunn, M. A. and Sidell, F. R.,'Progress in medical defense against nerve agents', *Journal of the American Medical Association*, no. 262 (1989), pp. 649–52.

[124] Gander, T. J. (ed.), *Jane's NBC Protection Equipment 1989–90*, 2nd edn (Jane's Information Group: Coulsdon, Surrey, UK,1989).

[125] A generally accepted definition of biological weapons (agents) does not exist. However, in the 1969 report of the UN Secretary-General the definition, for the purpose of the report, was given as 'living organisms, whatever their nature, or infective material derived from them, which are intended to cause disease or death in man, animals and plants, and which depend for their effects on their ability to multiply in the person, animal or plant attacked'. The Biological Weapons Convention does not define either biological weapons or toxins, which are also covered by the Convention.

[126] See Webster (note 27): 'at least 10 countries are working to produce both previously known and futuristic biological weapons', p. 3; see also Adams, P., '10 countries now have biological weapons', *Defense News*, vol. 4, no. 8 (20 Feb. 1989), p. 14.

repeated throughout 1989. The claims were not further substantiated but were said to be based on secret intelligence sources.[127] The alleged Soviet storage of anthrax—which was claimed to have caused an epidemic in Sverdlovsk after an accident at the storage site—has still not been clarified to the satisfaction of US authorities,[128] despite private US efforts in co-operation with Soviet officials to clarify the incident.[129] Mutual acceptance by the USA and the USSR of an explanation of this occurrence would decidedly increase confidence in the BWC. Perhaps this stumbling-block can be removed in the present atmosphere of openness in US–Soviet relations.

In the annual US Department of Defense publication *Soviet Military Power*, US allegations that the USSR maintains a BW programme were repeated. None the less, compared with the language in earlier editions the accusations in 1989 were considerably toned down.[130] British newspapers accused the USSR of developing and testing new 'genetic' weapons by application of genetic-engineering techniques. The allegations were refuted by a Soviet expert.[131]

The BWC also covers toxins, and in early 1989 allegations were made that Iraq had possibly acquired mycotoxins in small quantities in 1987 and been assisted by scientists from the FRG in conducting BW work. These allegations were denied by a government spokesman of the FRG.[132]

In 1989 it was also disclosed that an Iranian researcher had attempted to acquire *Fusarium*, a strain of mold related to the strains that give rise to the mycotoxins alleged to be possible chemical toxin warfare agents prohibited by the BWC. Requests had been made to a researcher in Canada and to an institute in the Netherlands, which keeps 'banks' of micro-organisms for peaceful purposes. However, since the reasons for the request were not felt to be well founded, delivery to Iran was stopped. It was not proven that the strain was intended for prohibited purposes.[133] This incident illustrates that awareness of the problem and the ability to take measures within the scientific community may make it possible to prevent misuse of micro-organisms for non-permitted purposes, although it does not imply that a fail-proof verification method could be founded on that basis. The risk of false accusation would also be large. The incident occurred during a debate in the

[127] Holmes, H. A., 'Biological weapons proliferation', statement before the Senate Governmental Affairs Committee on 17 May 1989, *Department of State Bulletin*, July 1989, pp. 43–45; 'Holmes testifies on biological weapons (4.040)' (text of an unofficial transcript of 26 July testimony), *Wireless File*, EUR-511, 28 July 1989, pp. 27–34; see also McCain (note 29).

[128] USIA, 'The U.S. biological defense research program (1200)', *Fact Sheet*, EUR-104, 18 Sep. 1989, p. 4.

[129] *SIPRI Yearbook 1989* (note 30), p. 114.

[130] US Department of Defense, *Soviet Military Power: Prospects for Change 1989* (US Government Printing Office: Washington, DC, 1989), pp. 68, 91, 104.

[131] Adams, J., 'Russia develops a new breed of genetic weapons', *Sunday Times* (London), 1 Oct. 1989; Permanent Mission of the Soviet Union (Geneva), 'Leading Soviet expert on genetic weapons', TASS, 8 Oct. 1989, from *Press Bulletin*, no. 190 (1928), 11 Oct. 1989, pp. 2–4.

[132] See, for example, Schreitter-Schwarzenfeld, H., 'Bonn verneint Parallele zu Libyen-Affäre', *Frankfurther Rundschau*, 27 Jan. 1989, p. 1.

[133] See, for example, Gordon, M. R., 'Iranian quest for toxic fungi was blocked, spy experts say', *International Herald Tribune*, 14 Aug. 1989; 'Wollte Iran Schimmelkulturen für biologische Waffen Kaufen?', *Frankfurter Allgemeine Zeitung*, 16 Aug. 1989, p. 3.

US Congress on a new law to control biological weapons,[134] a measure which thus far had not been taken by the USA in spite of US ratification of the BWC in 1976.

New developments related to biological weapons

In 1989 no allegations occurred of the development of totally new biological weapons in violation of the BWC. Concerns are, however, recurrently expressed over the vaccination programmes which are undertaken by some nations.[135] The possibility of using genetic-engineering techniques for the development of new, militarily more reliable BW agents has also been widely discussed. As mentioned above, such allegations have been made in the Western press against the Soviet Union and have been denied by the USSR.[136]

The question of the misuse of genetic-engineering techniques is by no means a problem related only to apprehensions about biological weapons, and it is a highly complex question. In fact the problems associated with *civilian* use of this technology are at the centre of the debate in many industrialized and developing countries owing to the possible enormous impact of this technology on human beings and nature. National legislation to deal with these concerns has been introduced in many countries, and international industrial co-operation is developing in this field. In this context the existence of the BWC is, despite its shortcomings, a necessary corner-stone upon which to build.

One important scientific achievement during 1989 was the chemical synthesis of palytoxin ($C_{129}H_{223}N_3O_{54}$), a chemically very complicated toxin first isolated from a Hawaiian coral.[137] This achievement showed that even very complicated, highly poisonous toxins can now be chemically synthesized, although in this case as the result of very laborious research efforts over a period of eight years. This is of relevance to the BWC, which also prohibits the development of toxin weapons. The achievement of this chemical synthesis also underlines an often-heard argument that toxins are chemicals which will automatically also be covered by the CWC, when it enters into force.[138]

Of interest in the context of the BWC is a US 'big science' project (an expression usually applied only to the building of the big 'atom smashing'

[134] Pitts, D., 'New law to control biological weapons predicted (560)', *Wireless File*, EUR-209, 8 Aug. 1989, pp. 7–8; and Thatcher, G., 'Bush pushes ban on bio-weapons', *Christian Science Monitor*, 2 Aug. 1989, p. 8.

[135] See, for example, 'Research supported by Pentagon stirs germ warfare accusations', *New York Times*, 19 Mar. 1989, p. 30; see also note 128.

[136] 'Production of bacteriological weapons denied', PM3101132589, Moscow, *Izvestia*, morning edn, in Russian, 28 Jan. 1989, p. 4, FBIS-SOV-89-020, 1 Feb. 1989, pp. 3–4; and 'Effective limits on biological weapons sought', PM1204093189, Moscow, *Pravda*, in Russian, 2nd edn, 11 Apr. 1989, p. 5, FBIS-SOV-89-069, 12 Apr. 1989, pp. 3–4.

[137] See also, for example, Stinson, S. C., 'Total synthesis of huge palytoxin molecule achieved at Harvard', *Chemical & Engineering News*, 18 Sep. 1989, p. 23.

[138] 'Statement by Soviet representative at the First Committee of the 44th session of the UN General Assembly', *Press Release*, Permanent Mission of the Soviet Union (New York), 30 Oct. 1989.

machines in physics or to space programmes) in the biological field. The project is a 15-year, $3 billion project based in the USA, which is conducted in co-operation with scientists throughout the world, to map the human genome (i.e., to identify all human genes and their location).[139]

The BW concern about this research relates to the idea that it might be possible, for example, to develop substances and organisms which could be used against ethnic groups displaying genetic differences making such groups unduly sensitive to certain chemical or biological agents. The concept of 'ethnic weapons' is by no means a new one and is, for example, reflected in the British allegations against the USSR which were mentioned above. The idea was put forward as early as the mid-1970s and was also reflected in the efforts by the socialist bloc in the CD during the 1970s to work out a convention prohibiting the development and production of new types of weapons of mass destruction in the Conference of the Committee on Disarmament (CCD).[140] While possible development of this threat indeed merits close watching, one might hope that, when the future CWC enters into force, its existence and that of a strengthened BWC will leave no loopholes for development of such weapons. However, other problems of a more general nature will certainly have to be discussed when it comes to the possible peaceful application of the results of genetic research. A number of questions will need to be asked. Conversely, the benefit of, for example, finding cures for illnesses and lessening the effects of genetic defects might be extremely valuable.

IV. Conclusions

In 1989 the CW question focused mainly on different international efforts to assist the work on the CWC (see chapter 14). Developments in relation to chemical and biological weapons *per se* and their use, or alleged use, were not dramatic. The widespread use of riot-control agents, the unfortunate use on one occasion of an old and more toxic tear-gas in the USSR and information that new riot-control agents are being sought make it necessary to be on the lookout for new developments and applications in this field. In the absence of a CWC 'the grey area' between the existing BWC and the yet unfinished CWC is a cause for concern.

The USA and the USSR appear to be on the verge of reaching a bilateral agreement on chemical weapons, while simultaneously continuing to pledge their adherence to the ultimate goal of obtaining a comprehensive global CWC. However, the possible option that the USA might continue to produce binary chemical weapons for deterrence purposes during the first eight years of a CWC, or even after that, evokes serious concern. This would be a change from previous US pledges to cease all CW production from the time

[139] Robert, L., 'New game plan for genome mapping', *Science*, vol. 245 (22 Sep. 1989), pp. 1438–40; see also Blakeslee, S. 'Scientists work out USD 3-billion world project to map genes', *International Herald Tribune*, 12 Oct. 1989, p. 9.
[140] SIPRI, *World Armaments and Disarmament: SIPRI Yearbook 1976* (Almqvist & Wiksell: Stockholm, 1976), pp. 311–14.

of entry into force of the CWC. Continued production of binary weapons would constitute a serious threat to the chance to obtain an effective, global CWC. The same view was also earlier held by France which, however, abandoned this position in 1989 (see also chapter 14). However, at the Malta summit meeting with President Gorbachev, President Bush offered, under certain conditions, to reconsider the US decision to continue binary CW production under a CWC.

The issue of the spread of chemical weapons was more apparent in 1989. The complex, secret trading activities related to chemical weapons, which went on in the past and which continued in 1989, were touched upon above, particularly in the discussion of the assistance given Libya in building its chemical production facility in Rabta. Efforts to constrain the trade of chemicals and CW equipment have, however, increased. The USA has worked on new legislation which provides for sanctions against countries which do not follow the existing regulations. In this context the question of the definition of the term 'chemical weapon' has become of increasing importance in connection with declarations of the possession or non-possession of chemical weapons. Without an agreed definition, declarations are difficult to interpret. Many of the declarations which have been given in the past could be further clarified, and it might serve as a confidence-building measure if, for example, the provisional definition in the draft CWC were utilized (see also chapter 14).

The important technical matter of the destruction of existing chemical weapons has become of increasing importance. In both the USA and the USSR the destruction programmes have been delayed owing to technical problems as well as to civilian environmental concerns. Such concerns about normal chemical production and storage have grown, and this must be taken into account as regards the technical aspects of the destruction of chemical weapons.

The increasing effort to develop and produce protection against chemical weapons is not only an ominous sign of how industry and business perceive the chances for completion of a CWC but also reflects activities to make such protection available to civilians. It may thus now be appropriate to look at the efforts to abolish chemical weapons also from a general societal point of view. In the future there will be increased attention given to the major risks constituted by toxic chemicals, the use or release of which has not been adequately regulated, and when accidents occur which involve large chemical stockpiles or large production complexes. Such concerns may ultimately contribute to the efforts to ban chemical weapons.

Appendix 4A. Statements of possession or non-possession of chemical weapons

THOMAS STOCK

State	Source/date of declaration	Wording of the statements
Afghanistan	Paris Conference 1989[a]	'The Republic of Afghanistan while [sic] once again proclaims its adherence to its past commitments and obligations with regard to the non-use and banning of chemical weapons, declares that it shall never use, develop, acquire or stockpile chemical or biological weapons'
Albania	Paris Conference 1989[a]	'Non seulement elle a été et elle est toujours pour la prohibition de l'emploi des armes chimiques, contre la production et le stockage de ces armes'
Argentina	CD/PV.465, 1988[b]	'many countries, among them Argentine Republic, have declared that they do not possess chemical weapons'
Australia	CD/PV.426, 1987[b]	'several countries, including Australia, have indicated that they do not possess such weapons or facilities'
Austria	CD/PV.471, 1988[b]	'Austria does not possess or produce chemical weapons, and has no facilities to produce such weapons'
Bahrain	Paris Conference 1989[a]	'Bahrain does not possess nor intends to possess chemical weapons'
Belgium	CD/PV.424, 1987[b]	'Belgium has no chemical military capability and has no intention of acquiring such a capability'
Brazil	CD/PV.460, 1988[b]	'Brazil does not possess chemical weapons and does not intend to develop, produce or stockpile any'
Bulgaria	CD/PV.409, 1987[b]	'May I recall that my country is not developing chemical weapons, does not manufacture such weapons and has none stationed on its territory'
Burma (Myanmar)	CD/PV.452, 1988[b]	'Burma does not possess, develop, produce, stockpile or use chemical weapons'
Canada	CD/PV.433, 1987[b]	'Canada does not possess any chemical weapons and does not intend to produce or acquire such weapons'
Chile	Paris Conference 1989[a]	'le Chili ne développe pas, ne fabrique pas et ne possède pas d'armes chimiques'
China	CD/PV.453, 1988[b]	'China, a non-chemical-weapon State'
China	Paris Conference 1989[a]	'China neither possesses nor produces chemical weapons'
Cook Islands	Paris Conference 1989[a]	'countries in the insular South Pacific region harbour no chemical weapons to date'

Country	Source	Statement
Colombia	Paris Conference 1989[a]	'La Colombie joint sa voix à celle des autres Etats qui ne possèdent pas de technologie apte à produire des armes de destruction massive'
Cyprus	Paris Conference 1989[a]	'We have no chemical weapons; we condemn their use by any state under any circumstances'
Czechoslovakia	Statement of the Government of the Czechoslovak Socialist Republic[c]	'The Czechoslovak Socialist Republic does not either possess or manufacture of chemical weapons or stockpile on its territory any chemical weapons. No facilities destined for development or manufacture of chemical weapons exist in the Czechoslovak Socialist Republic. Research and laboratory work conducted in the Czechoslovak Socialist Republic serve exclusively purposes of protection against effects of chemical weapons and peaceful objectives.'
Democratic People's Republic of Korea	Statement of the Ministry of Foreign Affairs, 26 January 1989[d]	'the government of the Republic, in the future, too, as in the past, will not test, produce, store and introduce from the outside nuclear and chemical weapons and will never permit the passage ... through our country'
Denmark	A/C.1/43/PV.16[e]	'We do not have any chemical weapons. We do not want any'
Egypt	CD/PV.459, 1988[b]	'Egypt does not produce, develop or stockpile such weapons'
Ethopia	CD/PV.487, 1989[b]	'my country does not produce or stockpile chemical weapons'
Finland	CD/PV.441, 1988[b]	'does not possess chemical weapons and will never acquire such weapons'
France	A/43/PV.10[f]	'The proposals put forward by France, who has no chemical weapons'
German Democratic Republic	CD/PV.481, 1988[b]	'does not possess or produce any chemical weapons'
Federal Republic of Germany	CD/PV.437, 1988[b]	'The Federal Republic of Germany does not possess any chemical weapons and gave a solemn pledge in 1954 not to produce them'
Greece	Paris Conference 1989[a]	'Mon pays qui ne dispose pas d'armes chimiques'
Grenada	Paris Conference 1989[a]	'We do not manufacture any weapons, chemicals or otherwise'
Guinea-Bissau	Paris Conference 1989[a]	'La Guinée-Bissau n'a pas la moindre intention d'acquérir des armes chimiques'
Hungary	CD/PV.437, 1988[b]	'has no stockpile of chemical weapons or industrial establishments manufacturing such weapons'
Iceland	Paris Conference 1989[a]	'Iceland has no chemical weapons and prohibits the storing or stationing of such weapons on its territory'
India	CD/PV.459, 1988[b]	'India does not possess any chemical weapons, nor does it have any intention of producing or acquiring them in the future'
Indonesia	CD/PV.437, 1988[b]	'Indonesia, as a country which has never possessed chemical weapons'
Ireland	Paris Conference 1989[a]	'Ireland does not possess chemical weapons. Nor is Ireland a producer of chemicals generally regarded as central to acquiring a chemical weapons capability'

State	Source/date of declaration	Wording of the statements
Italy	CD/PV.437, 1988[b]	'For many years, Italy has had no chemical weapons, nor does it station them on its territory'
Japan	CD/PV.424, 1987[b]	'Japan possesses no chemical weapons and has no intention to acquire them'
Kenya	Paris Conference 1989[a]	'Kenya has no capacity to manufacture chemical weapons. Kenya does not desire to acquire such capacity and Kenya will neither purchase nor use chemical weapons on human or on any living thing'
Kuwait	Paris Conference 1989[a]	'Kuwait which does not have any chemical weapons'
Lao People's Democratic Republic	Paris Conference 1989[a]	'Pour sa part, la RPD Lao, qui n'a ni les moyens de fabriquer des armes chimiques, ni l'intention de les utiliser contre qui que ce soit'
Madagascar	Paris Conference 1989[a]	'Elle n'a jamais fabriqué, acquis, ni utilisé des armes chimiques'
Malaysia	Canberra Conference 1989[g]	'We do not possess or intend to acquire, develop or produce chemical weapons'
Malta	Paris Conference 1989[a]	'Malta does not produce or possess chemical weapons'
Mexico	Paris Conference 1989[a]	'Mi pais no posee armas quimicas; jamás las ha poseido y no tiene la menor intencion de adquirirlas'
Mongolia	CD/PV.442, 1988[b]	'Mongolia has no chemical weapons and does not intend to develop, produce or acquire any'
Morocco	CD/PV.367, 1986[b]	'The Kingdom of Morocco does not possess chemical weapons and will never seek to acquire them'
Netherlands	CD/PV.446, 1988[b]	'we suggest that all countries who do not have chemical weapons within their territories, and my country is one of them, will just make a statement to that effect'
New Zealand	CD/PV.445, 1988[b]	'does not have, and never had, chemical weapons, and it does not permit chemical weapons to be stationed on its territory'
Nicaragua	Paris Conference 1989[a]	'Nicaragua, que jamás ha poseido ni producido armas de esta naturaleza, ni aspira hacerlo, desea reiterar su firme compropiso, sin reservas con las prohibiciónes contenidas en el protocolo de 1925'
Nigeria	Canberra Conference 1989[g]	'Nigeria has no chemical weapons, and does not intend to produce such ominous weapons'
Norway	CD/PV.479, 1988[b]	'Norway, which has no chemical weapons'
Pakistan	CD/PV.339, 1986[b]	'Pakistan neither possesses chemical weapons nor desires to acquire them'
Panama	Paris Conference 1989[a]	'Panamá … quien no fabrica ni posee armas químicas'
Papua New Guinea	Paris Conference 1989[a]	'Papua New Guinea has no chemical weapons and … we undertake not to allow transit of chemical weapons through our territory'
Peru	CD/PV.472, 1988[b]	'my country does not possess or produce chemical weapons'

Country	Statement	Source
Poland	'Poland, being a country which does not produce, possess or intend to acquire chemical weapons'	CD/PV.419, 1987[b]
Republic of Korea	'the Republic of Korea has never possessed and does not have at its disposal any type of chemical weapons. Nor will we consider developing, producing or stockpiling such weapons on the Korean Peninsula'	Paris Conference 1989[a]
Romania	'that Romania has no chemical weapons and that there are no stocks of such weapons on its territory'	CD/PV.440, 1988[b]
Senegal	'Pour sa part, le Sénégal a réaffirmé . . . qu'il ne possède pas d'armes chimiques, n'entend pas en disposer, ni à en accueillir sur son territoire'	Paris Conference 1989[a]
South Africa	'The South African Government wishes to go on record clearly, as being firmly opposed to the production, stockpiling and use of chemical weapons anywhere on earth or in space'	Paris Conference 1989[a]
Spain	'Spain . . . does not possess such weapons today and does not wish to possess them'	CD/PV.422, 1987[b]
Sweden	'Sweden does not possess chemical weapons'	CD/PV.481, 1988[b]
Switzerland	'Switzerland has not acquired chemical weapons abroad. Thus it does not possess any stockpiles of such weapons'	CD/PV.270, 1984[b]
Tanzania	'Tanzania . . . does not possess or intend to produce chemical weapons under any circumstances'	Paris Conference 1989[a]
Thailand	'Thailand also reaffirms its strong opposition to the production, development, stockpiling and particularly the use of chemical weapons in any circumstances and for whatever reason'	Paris Conference 1989[a]
Togo	'Mon pays, le Togo, s'est déjà déclaré non-possesseur d'armes chimiques, et non désireux de s'engager dans une programme de mise au point, de fabrication et de stockage de telles armes'	Paris Conference 1989[a]
Turkey	'Turkey does not have chemical weapons in stock nor does it aspire to possess any in future'	Paris Conference 1989[a]
Uganda	'Uganda does not produce nor possess chemical weapons'	Paris Conference 1989[a]
UK	'The United Kingdom gave up its chemical weapons capability in the 1950s' 'the United Kingdom does not possess chemical weapons either within its own territory or within the territory of any other State. There are no chemical weapons possessed by any other State within the territory of the United Kingdom'	CD/PV.421, 1987[b] CD/PV.474, 1988[b]
USA	'For many years, until 1969, the United States produced and stockpiled chemical munitions as a deterrent to a possible chemical attack by an adversary'	Report of the US Chemical Warfare Review Commission, 1985
USSR	'while possessing chemical weapons has never, even in our most tragic times, used those weapons . . . is not producing chemical weapons'	Paris Conference 1989[a]
Venezuela	'Venezuela desea declarar categoricamente que no posee armas quimicas ni por cuenta propia, ni por cuenta de terceros, y que no tiene intention de adquirirlas'	Paris Conference 1989[a]
Viet Nam	'Le Vietnam ne produit ni ne stocke aucune arme chimique'	Paris Conference 1989[a]

State	Source/date of declaration	Wording of the statements
Yugoslavia	Canberra Conference 1989[g]	'Yugoslav chemical industry does not produce chemicals listed in Schedule I and II'
Zimbabwe	Canberra Conference 1989[g]	'Zimbabwe does not possess chemical weapons nor does it manufacture them'

[a] The Paris Conference citations are the statements made by a country's representatives at the Conference on the Prohibition of Chemical Weapons in Paris on 7–11 Jan. 1989. The official records of the conference have not yet been published. The statements quoted here are from the 'Compilation of declarations of States concerning the possession/non-possession of chemical weapons' which was prepared and distributed in Apr. by the GDR's Delegation to the CD. This document has also been referred to in *Chemical Weapons Convention Bulletin*, no. 5 (Aug. 1989).

[b] Conference on Disarmament document.

[c] 'Statement of the Government of the Czechoslovak Socialist Republic on issues concerning prohibition and elimination of chemical weapons', made in Prague on 5 Jan. 1989. Reported in Conference on Disarmament document CD/878, 18 Jan. 1989.

[d] See FBIS-EAS-89-016, 26 Jan. 1989, p.9.

[e] United Nations General Assembly (UNGA), 43rd session, First Committee, 20 Sep.–20 Oct. 1988.

[f] UNGA, 43rd session, 20 Sep.–22 Dec. 1988.

[g] Statements made by the representatives of the country at the Canberra Government–Industry Conference against Chemical Weapons, Sep. 1989.

Appendix 4B. Export warning list[1]

Below is the chemical weapons precursor export warning list, as current on 1 September 1989, used by the Australia Group of countries: Australia, Belgium, Canada, Denmark, France, Germany (Federal Republic), Greece, Ireland, Italy, Japan, Luxembourg, Netherlands, New Zealand, Norway, Portugal, Spain, Switzerland, the United Kingdom and the United States, plus the European Community (represented as such, in addition to its member states). The list is circulated by Australia Group governments to their industry with the advice that caution should be exercised in relation to the export of these chemicals, because of their potential dual-purpose use.

The first nine substances on the list currently form the 'core list', for which all Australia Group countries have introduced or are introducing export controls. The controls require that a permit be obtained before exporting a 'core list' chemical. The 'core list' has been gradually expanded. Many Australia Group countries have also introduced controls for other chemicals on the export warning list.

It should be emphasized that export controls simply place certain conditions on exports. They are not export bans. [The CAS number is the US Chemical Abstracts Service registry number.]

	CAS no.
1. Thiodiglycol	(111-48-8)
2. Phosphorus Oxychloride	(10025-87-3)
3. Dimethyl Methyl Phosphonate	(756-79-6)
4. Methyl Phosphonyl Difluoride	(676-99-3)
5. Methyl Phosphonyl Dichloride	(676-97-1)
6. Dimethyl Phosphite	(868-85-9)
7. Phosphorus Trichloride	(7719-12-2)
8. Trimethyl Phosphite	(121-45-9)
9. Thionyl Chloride	(7719-09-7)
10. 3-Hydroxy-1-Methylpiperidine	(3554-74-3)
11. n,n-Diisopropyl-2-Aminoethyl Chloride	(96-79-7)
12. n,n-Diisopropyl-2-Aminoethane Thiol	(5842-07-9)
13. 3-Quinuclidinol	(1619-34-7)
14. Potassium Fluoride	(7789-23-3)
15. 2-Chloroethanol	(107-07-3)
16. Dimethylamine	(124-40-3)
17. Diethyl Ethylphosphonate	(78-38-6)
18. Diethyl-n,n-Dimethylphosphoramidate	(2404-03-7)
19. Diethyl Phosphite	(762-04-9)
20. Dimethylamine Hydrochloride	(506-59-2)
21. Ethyl Phosphinyl Dichloride	(1498-40-4)
22. Ethyl Phosphonyl Dichloride	(1066-50-8)
23. Ethyl Phosphonyl Difluoride	(753-98-0)
24. Hydrogen Fluoride	(7664-39-3)

[1] As quoted from *Trade Union Report on Chemical Weapons*, first published in Sep. 1989 by the International Confederation of Free Trade Unions (ICFTU) and the International Federation of Chemical, Energy and General Workers' Unions (ICEF).

25. Methyl Benzilate   (76-89-1)
26. Methyl Phosphinyl Dichloride   (676-83-5)
27. n,n-Diisopropyl-2-Amino Ethanol   (986-80-0)
28. Pinacolyl Alcohol   (464-07-3)
29. QL (0-Ethyl-2-Diisopropylaminoethyl Methylphosphonite)   (57856-11-8)
30. Triethyl Phosphite   (122-52-1)
31. Arsenic Trichloride   (7784-34-1)
32. Benzilic Acid (2,2-Diphenyl-2-Hydroxyacetic Acid)
    (2,2-Diphenyl-glycollic Acid)   (76-93-7)
33. Diethyl Methylphosphonite   (15715-41-0)
34. Dimethyl Ethylphosphonate   (6163-75-3)
35. Ethyl Phosphinyl Difluoride (Ethyl Phosphorous Difluoride)   (430-78-4)
36. Methyl Phosphinyl Difluoride (Methyl Phosphorous Difluoride) (753-59-3)
37. 3-Quinuclidone   (1619-34-7)
38. Phosphorous Pentachloride   (10026-13-8)
39. Pinacolone (3,3-Dimethyl-2-Butanone)   (75-97-8)
40. Potassium Cyanide   (151-50-8)
41. Ammonium Hydrogen Fluoride (Ammonium Bifluoride)   (1341-49-7)
42. Potassium Hydrogen Fluoride (Potassium Bifluoride)   (7789-29-9)
43. Sodium Bifluoride (Sodium Hydrogen Fluoride)   (1333-83-1)
44. Sodium Fluoride   (7722-88-5)
45. Sodium Cyanide   (143-33-9)
46. Tris-ethanolamine   (102-71-6)
47. Phosphorous Pentasulphide   (1314-80-3)
48. Di-isopropylamine   (108-18-9)
49. Diethylaminoethanol   (100-37-8)
50. Sodium Sulphide   (1313-82-2)

Part II. Military expenditure, the arms trade and armed conflicts

5. World military expenditure

SAADET DEGER*

I. Introduction

In 1989, Europe experienced profound political change. The Third World was more concerned with economic security than with military security. A new President in the United States faced increasing budgetary problems in sorting out defence priorities. The Soviet Union embarked, probably for the first time in 20 years, on a major re-allocation of resources from the military to the civilian sector. Arms control negotiations looked increasingly as if they were close to success. Political factors coalesced with the forces of technological and economic structural disarmament, raising hopes for significant reductions in world military expenditure.

Performance did not match up to promises, however. The actual reduction of world military expenditure (after adjustments for inflation) between 1988 and 1989 was modest, slightly less than 2 per cent according to preliminary SIPRI estimates. For the fourth year in a row the United States presented defence spending figures with a clear downward trend, although the decline remains modest in comparison with the still high levels of expenditure. In an unprecedented demonstration of openness the Soviet Union for the first time published defence spending data on a par with SIPRI estimates. Both the Soviet Union and the United States, discussed in sections II and V, reduced their defence expenditure by about 2 per cent, while that of European NATO countries (section III) remained stable. Large cuts were announced for the non-Soviet members of the Warsaw Treaty Organization (WTO), but remain as yet unverified. With the rapid changes taking place in Eastern Europe, burden-shedding and past burden-sharing of the WTO countries take on new importance. These issues are discussed in section VI. Developments in China and the Third World are discussed in section VII.

In the area of defence spending most governments seemed to be satisfied to follow a policy of 'wait and see'. The rapid increases of the early 1980s have disappeared, but deep cuts in defence spending are still not visible, nor are the rewards, if any, of the current disarmament process. Military expenditure is now in a stable and gentle decline, probably in anticipation of successful and verifiable arms control negotiations. As these emphasize weapon assets, importance is given to procurement policies. This chapter presents the first time-series estimates of purchases of major weapon equipment for all NATO countries and the European Community.

---

* Section V on the Soviet Union was researched jointly with Somnath Sen.

II. The United States

1989 was the first year of President George Bush's Administration. It was a year of both continuity and change. Continuity characterized domestic policy, with the President in conflict and co-operation with Congress regarding the budget deficit and its impact on various categories of government expenditure, including defence. Change marked US foreign policy, with the initially cautious President pressed to keep apace with the swift transitions in Eastern Europe and the promise of success in the arms control process.

In terms of budget outlays, military expenditure fell for the second successive year. According to US budget authority, defence spending has now fallen in four successive years.[1] The trend for US military expenditure is clearly downward, reinforced by technological, economic and political forces for disarmament, the latter in the form of increasing demands for arms control. As of yet, actual reductions are modest when compared with the rapid rise in military expenditure over the first half of the 1980s. Plans and expectations are being cut more savagely than actual forces or equipment. Nevertheless, given the hopes regarding arms control, military expenditure in the United States is expected to fall more rapidly in the future.

The budget

The year began with the traditional bipartisan concord between Congress and the new President. By the summer, however, the consensus seems to have broken down, as a result of Bush's insistence on reducing capital gains tax—a measure disapproved by the Democratic Party since it tends to favour the wealthier sections of society. In October the Gramm–Rudman–Hollings Act ceiling on the budget deficit was invoked,[2] since agreement to hold the budget deficit to $110 billion (as estimated by the Office of Management and Budget, OMB) failed to materialize. However, a late compromise was reached in November, when the President signed the appropriations measures which established the budget law for fiscal year (FY) 1990 (1 October 1989 to 30 September 1990). The result was a mixture of confusion and cuts (some across the board), demonstrating the short-term nature of the annual US budgetary process. Defence spending was also reduced, although by less than what was originally expected. If a compromise had not been reached, the mandatory cuts under the Gramm–Rudman–Hollings Act would have meant a reduction from the original budget authority by $13 billion in US defence spending for FY 1990. This could potentially have been the largest reduction of the 1980s. (Ironically, it would have been the

---

[1] For details see the following: *Budget of the United States Government 1990* (US Government Printing Office: Washington, DC, 1989); *United States Budget in Brief 1990* (US Government Printing Office: Washington, DC, 1989); *Special analyses, Budget of the United States Government 1990* (US Government Printing Office: Washington, DC, 1989); *National Defense Budget Estimates for 1989/1990* (Office of the Assistant Secretary of Defense (Comptroller), US Department of Defense: Washington, DC, 1989).

[2] See Deger, S., 'World military expenditure', SIPRI, *SIPRI Yearbook 1989: World Armaments and Disarmament* (Oxford University Press: Oxford, 1989), p. 135, including note 1.

result not of arms control measures, but of the peculiarities of the US fiscal and legislative processes.) In practice however, the actual reduction from the original budget was much less—of the order of $4 billion.

In addition, long-term prospects of significant arms reductions, emanating from the democratization process in Eastern Europe and positive shifts in Soviet foreign policy, are also putting pressure on the defence budget. There is now need for a formal re-evaluation of US strategic policy, to take account of the combined effect of these short-term and long-term pressures.

The US budgetary process for FY 1990 is more complicated than usual, as the outgoing and the incoming Presidents presented different budgets. Nevertheless, there are similarities in objectives and spending patterns, and the total amount of resources allocated in each budget does not differ greatly. The following discussion concentrates on budget outlays (rather than budget authority), since this corresponds more closely to the amount actually spent.

In January 1989 President Reagan presented his FY 1990 budget, in which $303 billion was allocated to national defence. The estimated outlay for FY 1989 was $298.3 billion. The increase of about $4.7 billion was not enough to cover inflation, however, meaning that even in the last Reagan budget there was a real decline. It should be noted in this regard that the budget authority originally requested by Reagan was a 2 per cent real growth (from $298.8 billion in FY 1989 to $315.2 billion in FY 1990).

President Bush's budget for FY 1990 was presented in February 1989. He opted for 'zero growth' in his budget authority. The estimated value of national defence outlay for FY 1990 presented by Bush amounted to about $300.6 billion. This figure was disputed by the Congressional Budget Office, however, which estimated that the actual programmes of the military would result in an outlay of $304 billion.[3]

In April an initial budget agreement was reached by congressional leaders on a bipartisan level. As mentioned, however, various problems, in particular the controversy about capital gains tax reductions, stopped the agreement from being binding. In October, at the beginning of the budgetary year (FY 1990), the budget had still not been finalized and a sequestration, required by the Gramm–Rudman–Hollings Act, came into effect. The act's ceiling on the aggregate budget deficit in FY 1990 is $100 billion plus 10 per cent discretionary. The aggregate budget deficit must therefore be less than $110 billion. According to estimates made by the OMB in October 1989 (at the beginning of FY 1990), the Bush budget deficit would significantly exceed this ceiling, hence the sequestration order. Various compromises, and some imaginative accounting practices, allowed the final budget bill to be signed two months after the beginning of the fiscal year. To bring the forecasted budget deficit down to the maximum permitted level, the sequestration order will operate until February 1990, but the final effect on the defence budget will be a minimal reduction of about $1.7 billion.

---

[3] *Congressional Quarterly*, vol. 47, no. 7 (25 Nov. 1989).

It is estimated that the outlay for national defence in FY 1990 will be approximately $302.9 billion, which is about $4 billion more than the appropriations for the previous fiscal year. Taking into account the inflation rate, there is a real decline of about 3 per cent between FYs 1989 and 1990, supporting the trend of a modestly falling defence budget. The Department of Defense (DOD) receives $286 billion, and the rest is allocated to defence-related activities, in particular to the nuclear programmes of the Department of Energy (DOE). A new element of the funding structure was the reduction of the Strategic Defense Initiative (SDI) budget from its 1989 allocation, the first such reduction in the six years that the programme has existed. In his budget proposal President Bush had requested $4.9 billion, but he settled for $3.8 billion, a cut in proposed funding of $1.1 billion.[4] Significantly, however, the cut meant a reduction in money terms of only $234 million from President Reagan's 1989 SDI budget. This being said, it should also be noted that in the FY 1991 defence budget, presented in January 1990, the funding requested for SDI will allow it to reach a new high of $4.5 billion.[5]

One of the most startling pronouncements regarding US military expenditure in 1989 was made by Secretary of Defense Richard Cheney, who in November stated that there were plans to reduce the DOD budget by $180 billion over five years. This turned out to be much less dramatic than was first thought. What Cheney did was to conduct a hypothetical budget planning exercise. The services were asked to calculate the effect of an annual 5 per cent real reduction in their budgets for FYs 1991–94, instead of, as in the current defence plan, a 1 per cent real annual growth in FYs 1991–92 and a 2 per cent real annual growth in FYs 1993–94. Each of the armed services was asked to suggest cuts that would allow the DOD to accommodate the new budget plan. The Army proposed to demobilize 90 000–200 000 men (the equivalent of three active divisions) and to cancel the upgrade programme of the M-1 Abrams main battle tank (called M-1A2) or to cut back estimated annual production from 600 to 200 units. The Air Force proposed to reduce production of F-16 fighter aircraft from 150 to 108 per year, to slow down purchase of the B-2 bomber, to close 15 bases and to cut five fighter wings. The Navy proposed to reduce the number of carrier groups from the planned 14 to 12, to cut personnel by 10 per cent (60 000 men) and to scrap 62 ships and settle for a 500-ship Navy.[6]

These plans may be interpreted in two ways. From the military's point of view, the cuts are real. The anticipated levels of forces and assets, from which the reductions are to be made, were based on security needs established by the Government. Lower levels of projected military assets are therefore a significant indication of reduced defence capability. However, from a financial point of view, the new plans are less significant since the cuts are taking place from an unrealistically projected budget baseline. In a 'zero growth scenario' many of these cuts would take place automatically,

[4] *Washington Times*, 30 Nov. 1989, p. 6.

[5] *The Guardian*, 29 Jan. 1990; *The Guardian*, 30 Jan. 1990.

[6] *Defense News*, vol. 4, no. 48 (27 Nov. 1989), p.1; *The Economist*, 25 Nov. 1989, p. 47; *Business Week*, 4 Dec. 1989, p. 32.

Table 5.1. US national defence expenditure outlays, FYs 1980–89

Figures are in US $b., current prices.

	1980	1981	1982	1983	1984	1985	1986	1987	1988	1989
Personnel	40.9	47.9	55.2	60.9	64.2	67.8	71.5	72.0	76.3	78.2
O&M^a	44.8	51.9	59.7	64.9	67.4	72.4	75.3	76.2	84.5	85.4
Procurement	29.0	35.2	43.3	53.6	61.9	70.4	76.5	80.7	77.2	80.7
RDT&E^b	13.1	15.3	17.7	20.6	23.1	27.1	32.3	33.6	34.8	37.0
Energy, defence	2.9	3.4	4.3	5.2	6.1	7.1	7.4	7.5	7.9	7.9
Other	3.3	3.8	5.1	4.7	4.7	7.9	10.4	12	9.7	9.1
Total	**134**	**157.5**	**185.3**	**209.9**	**227.4**	**252.7**	**273.4**	**282.0**	**290.4**	**298.3**

^{a} Operations and maintenance
^{b} Research, development, testing and evaluation.

Source: *United States Budget in Brief* (US Government Printing Office: Washington, DC, 1989).

since the total defence budget allocation would be insufficient. If future arms control agreements require deep cuts, then the spending plans from which the hypothesized cuts have been estimated become even less relevant.

SIPRI estimates show that, with a 4 per cent per annum real reduction in US military expenditure over the five fiscal years 1990–94, the US DOD budget would still be higher (after adjusting for inflation) than in any peace-time period in the history of the United States prior to FY 1983. The impact would in fact be greater than if the Cheney cuts were implemented, since the latter, as discussed above, are based on unrealistically high baselines. In other words, a major and substantial real reduction would still leave US military expenditure at historically unprecedented levels for peacetime operations. SIPRI estimates also show that if US defence spending were to be reduced by 8 per cent annually (after adjusting for inflation) over FYs 1990–94, it would still leave US military expenditure in 1994 at the level inherited by the Reagan Administration.

The past

During the decade of the 1980s the USA spent over $2300 billion on military expenditure. Out of this total, about $635 billion was spent on personnel costs (27.6 per cent), about $609 billion on weapon procurement (26.5 per cent) and $255 billion on research and development (R&D) (11.1 per cent). Table 5.1 gives the detailed allocations.

In the 40 years from FY 1951 to FY 1990, US DOD outlays peaked three times: they reached $260.5 billion in FY 1953, in part due to the Korean War effort; $293.6 billion in FY 1968, the highest in the Viet Nam War period; and $296.4 billion (in constant FY 1989 prices) in FY 1987. As the figures show, the highest annual DOD expenditure over the past four decades was recorded at the end of the Reagan Administration.

This massive expenditure was used to attain the largest peacetime build-up ever of the US military. In addition to the quantitative expansion, there was also a massive investment in qualitative improvements. This includes technological innovations (such as 'stealth' technology), increasing R&D systems enhancement (such as systems for destroying deeply buried or mobile targets) and rapid modernization (two new bomber forces—the B-1B and the B-2—within the same decade). It would be surprising if this amount of funding did not buy much in terms of new technology. However, a cost–benefit analysis should also consider whether this expansion and modernization resulted in substantial improvements in force structure, capabilities and efficiency.[7]

As regards the armed forces, there was little proportional change in active duty military personnel between FY 1980 and FY 1989, with growth of less than 1 per cent per year. Only the Navy increased its personnel figures substantially. The Army added two light divisions, probably suited for low-intensity conflict and rapid deployment.

Modernization continued throughout the decade, but the number of new major weapons could for reasons of cost not match the vast increase in procurement and R&D expenditure. For new weapons, unit costs increase with annual production rates; only after a large cumulative total production (a threshold) do unit costs start declining. For example, the decision to reduce purchases of MX missiles from 100 to 50 will raise unit costs, although total spending on the package will be less than planned. (If the Midgetman Small ICBM is added on to the arsenal to compensate for the reduction in MX missiles—as Congress has done this year by funding both—then total costs will not be less). To take another example, although the B-2 bomber is equipped with exotic 'stealth' technology that, according to its proponents, 'threatens to render Soviet air defences obsolete' and to undermine totally the Soviet Air Defence system,[8] the $70 billion price tag for the whole package (possibly rising to $100 billion—one-third of the annual defence budget—if operations and support costs are included) is clearly too steep to be accepted without challenge. Congress has allowed two planes to be bought in FY 1990 and has begun a searching critique of the system's usefulness. As Senator William Cohen wrote in 1989: 'The B-2 Bomber: Mission Questionable, Cost Impossible'.[9]

Survivability of ICBMs in response to a first strike has been a key indicator of the efficiency of the strategic nuclear triad.[10] The debate continued

[7] Niskanen, W. A., 'More defense spending for smaller forces: what hath the DOD wrought', *Policy Analysis* (CATO Institute), no. 110 (29 July 1988), pp. 1–21.

[8] The quote is taken from Lepingwell, J. W. R., 'Soviet strategic air defense and the Stealth challenge', *International Security*, vol. 14, no. 2 (autumn 1989), p. 64. There are currently 5 air programmes which embody 'stealth' technology: the Advanced Cruise Missile (ACM), the Advanced Technology Bomber (ATB) or B-2, the Air Force's Advanced Tactical Fighter (ATF), the Navy's Advanced Tactical Aircraft and the F-117A. For a general review of 'stealth' technology, see Welch, J., 'Assessing the value of stealthy aircraft and cruise missiles', *International Security*, vol. 14, no. 2 (autumn 1989), pp. 47–63.

[9] Cohen, W. S., 'The B-2 bomber: mission impossible, cost impossible', *Arms Control Today*, vol. 19, no. 8 (Oct. 1988), pp. 3–8.

[10] For a general discussion, see Carnesale, A., 'The enduring problem of ICBM basing', ed. E. H. Arnett, *US Strategic Forces Modernization Under Arms Control and Budget Constraints*, proceedings from a seminar for members of Congress and congressional staff, 1 June 1989 (American Association for the Advancement of Science: Washington, DC, 1989).

Table 5.2. US national defence expenditure authority, FYs 1980–89

Figures are percentages.

	1980	1981	1982	1983	1984	1985	1986	1987	1988	1989
Personnel	33.0	30.1	27.7	26.3	25.5	23.3	23.5	26.0	26.5	26.7
O&M	30.4	29.3	27.9	27.0	27.1	27.1	27.0	28.8	29.2	29.8
Procurement	24.4	27.2	30.6	33.8	33.4	33.8	32.8	28.6	28.1	27.2
RDT&E	9.3	9.3	9.5	9.6	10.4	10.8	12.0	12.8	12.9	13.0
Other	2.9	4.1	4.3	3.3	3.6	5	4.7	3.8	3.3	3.3

Source: SIPRI data base.

during 1989, as it had done over the decade, with few results. According to plans, the MX missiles, currently based in hardened silos, are to be dispersed over seven states and placed on railcars. Congress appropriated $1.1 billion in FY 1990 for the re-deployment. The total cost, including operations and support, will be $12 billion for the 50 in stock, with each armed with 10 multiple independently targetable re-entry vehicles (MIRVs). The argument over vulnerability has gone through so many twists and turns, however, that continued silo basing may be preferred. Congress also authorized $1.1 billion for FY 1990 to make the single-MIRV Midgetman road mobile.[11] The issue of survivability, and hence efficiency, remains debatable, however.

As regards force readiness and sustainability, little seems to have changed. According to the DOD, 'mission capable' equipment was only 'slightly increasing' or may have remained constant during 1980–85.[12] Only in terms of the quality of military personnel can the US military claim unequivocal success during this period. Qualification and experience have increased, as has the ability to handle complex weapon systems, yet personnel expenditure has grown the least in comparison with procurement, operations and maintenance (O&M) and R&D; thus combat efficiency has increased at minimum cost.

The allocation of such massive levels of military expenditure throughout the decade (see table 5.2 for yearly figures) will also have an indirect influence. This can be explained in terms of 'push' and 'pull' factors. The 'push' effect works when budget authority rises faster (or falls more slowly) than budget outlay or actual spending. As the investment component (procurement, construction and R&D) of the US military budget grew rapidly compared to operating costs (personnel and O&M) the 'push' factor became important. In effect, funding is authorized for a single year, but spending takes place over a longer period for weapon research, development, testing, evaluation and purchase. If expenditure has to be reduced for such obligations, inherited from the past, then cancellations (with extra penalty costs) are required. However, cancellations create political problems and the Government is unwilling to upset major defence contractors. Expenditures on such practically automatic obligations now take up 40 per

[11] *New York Times*, 30 Nov. 1989, p.1.
[12] See Niskanen (note 7).

cent of the spending budget.[13] Total pay (and pensions) consume another 40 per cent. Therefore, 80 per cent of annual military spending cannot be touched in the medium term; it is as if 80 per cent of the budget is already committed even before the fiscal year begins.

The 'pull' factor operates when research, development, testing and evaluation (RDT&E) expenditure rises fast, particularly for sophisticated technology, such as that used in the 'stealth' or SDI Phase I programmes (see chapters 1 and 3). When projects are near completion they tend to 'pull up' expenditures. Proponents can claim that it would be 'wasteful' not to continue procurement. For example, it was argued in 1989 that the $23 billion already invested in the B-2 programme (until recently classified information) would be wasted if the programme were to be cancelled at this stage. As RDT&E spending has been the fastest-growing outlay of the US defence budget in the 1980s, as shown in table 5.1, it is clear that this 'pull' factor will remain significant in the decade to come.

The trend of military expenditure in the medium term may change as the military seeks to achieve a balance between essentially political factors (arms control and negotiations) and techno-economic factors (unwarranted technological sophistication and subsequent cost increases). Representative Dennis Hertel, of the House Armed Services Committee, said in 1989: 'If the top chain of command decided a plane must be able to fly faster than the speed of light, travel backwards in time to attack targets throughout history, and complete the mission by landing on the sun, the acquisition system may express greater reservation about the scientific problem than about the cost or necessity of doing any of these things'.[14]

This state of affairs could definitely change in what may be termed a 'scissors crisis', with the two blades of the scissors, one political and the other structural, forcing the relevant cuts.

The future

There are three factors that will shape the future of US military expenditure. First, there is the speed of arms control. Even more than the actual levels negotiated, the very fact that the Conventional Armed Forces in Europe (CFE) Negotiation and the Conference on Security and Co-operation in Europe (CSCE) are taking place puts political pressure on the Administration to reduce defence spending. Second, the improving political climate in Europe and the remarkable domestic transformation in East European countries imply that threat perceptions need to be modified. The spectre of WTO military spending can no longer be used to justify increases in US defence expenditure. Third, technological and economic structural disarmament will cause cancellations and/or postponement of major programmes.

---

[13] Adams, G. and Cain, S. A., 'Defense dilemmas in the 1990s', *International Security*, vol. 13, no. 4 (spring 1989), pp. 5–15.

[14] Rep. Dennis M. Hertel, House Armed Services Committee, in a statement from 16 Aug. 1989, quoted in *Defence Monitor*, vol. 18, no. 7 (1989), p. 2.

The future may therefore see not only an end to military spending growth but, more important, a reduction of US strategic commitments.

The Bush Administration has inherited a costly legacy of military commitments. These include the construction of a space-based 'shield' to protect military targets against a nuclear attack, the ability to deter potential aggressors with strategic nuclear forces as well as substantial conventional forces, to defend Europe and provide stability in a period of rapid change, to protect bases around the globe, to conduct low-intensity warfare anywhere in the Third World, to control the high seas, to provide substantial security assistance to a large number of countries and to project power in defence of US as well as allied interests anywhere.

In 1989 a number of specific concerns surfaced. These include discussions on the modernization of the Lance short-range missile (see chapter 18); the possible withdrawal of some US forces from Europe and the role of the USA within the changing political and military structure of Europe; a congressional amendment to the defence bill asking for greater Japanese burden-sharing; military assistance to Colombia for narcotics control; the use of US air facilities in the Philippines to help Philippine President Corazon Aquino put down a military revolt; and the invasion of Panama.

In this context, it would seem to be important for the President to order a defence review to chart the course of military expenditure for the 1990s.[15] Technology and economics are bound to push for structural disarmament. It is now necessary to utilize the political incentives for arms control to negotiate a substantive deal and then re-order domestic priorities.

III. European NATO

NATO celebrated its 40th anniversary in 1989 with what seemed to be a middle age crisis. The arms control process and the rapid pace of political change in Europe produced different types of challenge. The former requires planning for weapon reductions when NATO's objective for the past four decades has been weapon accumulation. The latter questions the very rationale for NATO and suggests that the predominantly military alliance must now become a more political grouping.

Since the current arms control negotiations will have the maximum impact on procurement spending on *major* weapon acquisition, the analysis of that process assumes greater importance. SIPRI has for the first time estimated comprehensive 10-year time series data for equipment expenditures (for the calendar years 1980–89) for all NATO countries. These are provided in current prices, local currencies (table 5.3) as well as in constant-price 1988 US dollars (table 5.4). The estimates have been based on raw data provided by NATO, using the NATO definition, which differs substantially from what is usually called 'procurement' in national defence budgets.

[15] Kaufman, W. W., 'Restructuring defense', *Brookings Review*, vol. 7, no. 1 (winter 1988–89), pp. 63–67, analyses the conflicting pressures and the hard choices that the President has to face. See also the more general analysis in the context of US foreign policy: Steinbrunner, J. D., *Restructuring American Foreign Policy* (Brookings Institution: Washington, DC, 1989).

Table 5.3. NATO major weapon procurement expenditure, in local currency, 1980–89

Figures are in current prices.

		1980	1981	1982	1983	1984	1985	1986	1987	1988	1989
North America											
Canada	m. dollars	847	1 000	1 332	1 688	1 971	1 941	2 140	2 434	2 486	2 350
USA	m. dollars	28 076	34 487	42 028	50 202	58 328	66 348	72 525	76 362	71 808	75 081
Europe											
Belgium	m. francs	16 669	17 596	17 969	18 853	18 363	18311	19 618	20 360	18 078	14 896
Denmark	m. kronor	1 468	1 803	1 960	2 075	2 048	1 841	1 867	2 182	2 249	2 435
France	m. francs	23 786	29 444	34 637	39 772	42 216	46 492	49 664	55 943	56 564	59 773
FR Germany	m. DM	7 181	9 029	9 437	9 774	9 450	8 680	9 561	9 326	8 938	9 047
Greece	m. drachmas	18 231	29 287	29 966	30 741	41 604	46 687	53 477	67 605	112 141	116 230
Italy	b. lire	1 436	1 707	2 046	2 664	2 843	3 494	3 693	4 900	5 451	5 903
Luxembourg	m. francs	28	31	44	36	36	91	74	106	89	135
Netherlands	m. guilders	1 896	2 135	2 444	2 794	3 012	3 019	2 661	2 359	2 713	2 608
Norway	m. kronor	1 591	1 799	2 147	2 615	2 297	3 846	3 303	3 784	4 018	6 293
Portugal	m. escudos	2 650	3 375	3 318	3 761	4 416	3 675	8 818	16 088	20 356	27 837
Spain	m. pesetas	69 033	70 966	84 291	116 707	170 745	113 380	168 812	210 633	172 918	134 089
Turkey	b. lira	87	29	48	56	105	168	334	553	853	1 233
UK	m. pounds	2 901	3 218	3 545	4 122	4 629	4 907	4 762	4 744	4 904	4 759

Sources: NATO publications; author's calculations. Figures for France are based on national data.

Table 5.4. NATO and EC major weapon procurement expenditure, in US dollars, 1980–89

Figures are in US $m., at constant (1988) prices.

	1980	1981	1982	1983	1984	1985	1986	1987	1988	1989
North America										
Canada	1 114	1 169	1 405	1 683	1 883	1 784	1 887	2 058	2 020	1 860
USA	40 281	44 854	51 493	59 581	66 359	72 917	78 219	79 396	71 808	71 813
Europe										
Belgium	663	650	611	595	545	518	548	560	492	394
Denmark	360	396	390	386	359	308	301	339	334	346
France	6 863	7 490	7 878	8 255	8 151	8 492	8 850	9 648	9 496	9 722
FR Germany	5 003	5 919	5 879	5 892	5 563	5 002	5 520	5 369	5 089	4 998
Greece	534	689	583	497	569	535	498	541	790	733
Italy	2 482	2 469	2 540	2 883	2 778	3 128	3 122	3 954	4 188	4 285
Luxembourg	1.1	1.1	1.5	1.1	1.0	2.5	2.0	2.9	2.4	3.6
Netherlands	1 178	1 243	1 344	1 494	1 560	1 523	1 346	1 202	1 373	1 308
Norway	468	465	499	560	463	734	588	620	617	924
Portugal	70	74	59	54	49	34	73	123	141	174
Spain	1 265	1 135	1 180	1 456	1 914	1 168	1 593	1 895	1 484	1 093
Turkey	88	215	271	241	304	336	496	559	600	548
UK	8 260	8 189	8 307	9 240	9 881	9 878	9 270	8 859	8 736	7 884
European NATO total	**27 235**	**28 293**	**29 543**	**31 554**	**32 137**	**31 659**	**32 207**	**33 672**	**33 342**	**32 413**
NATO total	**68 630**	**74 958**	**82 441**	**92 818**	**100 379**	**106 360**	**112 313**	**115 126**	**107 170**	**106 086**
EC	26 735	28 269	28 820	30 762	31 397	30 612	31 166	32 516	32 170	30 984

Sources: NATO publications; author's calculations. Figures for France are based on national data.

Only in the case of France have estimates been made from national sources,[16] since French forces are not integrated with those of the rest of NATO. The trend for France, however, is consistent and comparable with all other countries.

For the whole of NATO, aggregate cumulative equipment expenditure for major weapons amounted to $860 billion over the 1980s (in constant 1988 prices and exchange-rates). Of this amount, the USA accounted for $635 billion and European NATO for $208 billion. From 1980 to the peak year 1987 expenditures rose continuously in real terms. After 1987 they began to fall. In the 1980–87 period major procurement spending increased by 7.7 per cent per year for NATO, 10.2 per cent per year for the USA and 3.1 per cent per year for the European NATO countries. In comparison, the fall from 1987 to 1989 has been modest. Between 1987 and 1989 major equipment expenditures declined by 4 per cent per year for NATO, 4.5 per cent per year for the USA and 1.7 per cent for the European NATO countries.

Forecasts have also been produced to show how long it would take from 1989 for procurement spending to reach the 1980 level if the rate of reductions over 1987–89 are carried on into the future. European NATO would need until the year 2000 to attain the annual level of equipment spending (in constant prices) it had in 1980. In other words, it would take more than 10 years of continuous reduction at the present rate simply to reach the level of expenditure that was prevalent at the beginning of the decade.

Similar forecasts for the United States show that if the present rates of reductions continue, it will take 12 years, until 2002, before procurement spending on major weapons reaches the level it had at the beginning of the Reagan buildup in 1980. However, past history also shows that rapid procurement buildups in the USA have very quickly been reversed once the process of disarmament speeds up. For example, the Viet Nam War military expansion saw procurement budgets rising from $51 billion to $86 billion (in constant 1989 prices) between FYs 1965 and 1969. Yet, by FY 1973 spending had fallen to $47 billion.

The foregoing estimates indicate that political will is central to the control of weapon acquisition. There is no automatic mechanism by which arms control will guarantee reductions. Since technological sophistication is costly, modernization can continue and costs escalate even with deep cuts in numbers and under low ceilings.

As regards individual countries, over the past three years the trends point modestly downwards for the major European NATO countries, that is, the Federal Republic of Germany, the United Kingdom and (to a lesser extent) France. In addition to overall budgetary constraints and market saturation, recent progress in arms control may have had an impact, particularly for the FRG. However, the downward trend is not firmly established and may change in the absence of political motivation. In addition, procurement cycles could have produced lower expenditures in the latter half of the 1980s after the rapid rise in the first half of the decade. In Italy procurement

---

[16] For French budget data, see French Ministry of Defence, *Projet de loi de Finances pour 1989* (Government Printer: Paris, 1988).

spending on major weapons has been rising steadily throughout the decade and shows no sign of abating.

Another trend worth noting is that for the three major European NATO countries, procurement declines have not been matched by similar changes in R&D expenditures. For the FRG, the budget category of *Forschung und Entwicklung* (R&D) has increased steadily while the value of *Material-beschaffung* (procurement) has fallen rapidly (in real terms) from 1986 to 1989. In the UK, real spending on all categories has declined since around FY 1986. However, the fall in R&D expenditure is much less than that in procurement. For France, the proportion of the total defence budget allocated to *Études* (R&D) has grown during the past three years.[17]

It is possible that the 'pull' factors discussed above with reference to the USA could also apply to these three European NATO countries, which tend to take the lion's share of research activities in the region. As new weapon systems are developed, tested and evaluated, pressure for acquisition will mount in the future. This would point to a future rise in military expenditure, after a lag, unless arms control measures result not only in the destruction of existing assets but also in a slow-down of modernization.

The planning process for reductions in assets in anticipation of a CFE final agreement in 1990 began in earnest in 1989.[18] A number of questions remain to be answered: What are the proportions of older and newer weapons to be scrapped? How can the transfer of modern equipment from countries which will have a surplus to countries which can still utilize them be ensured under the agreed-upon counting rules? How can 'rationalization' be achieved so that conventional assets may be distributed among the Allies more equitably? How will the financing of this expensive redistribution take place? Who will pay for what? The problems are complex. As one NATO official acknowledged: 'Look, we have been working for dozens of years to get everyone to standardize their equipment. Now, within six months we are supposed to get everyone to agree on complex technology transfer. It's asking a lot'.[19]

The political transformation in Eastern Europe, and the demise of the homogeneous political structure of the WTO, means that NATO's military threat assessment needs to be altered. It has been claimed that conventional war is no longer an option in Europe. Clearly, a purely military alliance is difficult to justify under the circumstances. In 1989 repeated calls were made by President Bush and others in the US Administration to transform NATO into a political bloc. It was also suggested that it might even have an economic role,[20] presumably to cushion the economic effects of disarmament which may follow from the deep cuts implicit in a future CFE round.

---

[17] The data for the UK, the FRG and France are from: *Statement of the Defence Estimates, 1989–1990* (Her Majesty's Stationery Office: London, 1989), vol. 2; *IAP Dienst Sicherheitspolitik*, no. 24/23 (23 Nov. 1989), p. 10; *Erläuterungen und Vergleiche zum Regierungsentwurf des Verteidigungshaushalts 1989* (FRG Ministry of Defence: Bonn, 31 Aug. 1989); French Ministry of Defence (note 16).

[18] *Washington Times*, 30 Nov. 1989, pp. 1, 21.

[19] Almond, P., 'NATO acts to cut weaponry', *Washington Times*, 1 Nov. 1989, p. 1.

[20] *The Independent*, 16 Oct. 1989.

It is anticipated that these changes will have an impact on military expenditure. The most direct consequence of arms control could be the reduction of procurement expenditure and the cost of major weapon acquisition, which varies from 15 to 25 per cent of total military spending. The political changes taking place in Eastern Europe will also put pressure on the size and requirements of armed forces in general. It will be difficult to justify large-scale arms programmes that, as now, involve expenditures that add up to 3–4 per cent of the national output, armed forces that make up 2–3 per cent of the labour force and defence spending that amounts to 8–9 per cent of total central government expenditure.

However, the 1989 military expenditure figures for European NATO clearly demonstrate that caution rather than change is the order of the day. According to SIPRI estimates, between 1988 and 1989 there was no decline in military expenditure for the region. Rather there was an overall increase, although it was very modest (on the order of one-half per cent) and could have been a statistical artifact. Nevertheless, there is no discernible downward trend over the past few years. The only change is that the growth of defence spending observable in the first half of the 1980s (following NATO's 3 per cent per annum increase directive) has disappeared. Military expenditure is now at a plateau, and political will is needed to bring it down.

The annual NATO Defence Planning Committee, meeting in June 1989, dutifully called for an annual 3 per cent rise in defence budgets.[21] Since NATO aggregate defence spending has been falling slightly from 1987 in real terms (mainly due to US budgetary cuts), this call is largely symbolic.

IV. The European Community

The European Community (EC) has since its inception been a major player in international economic relations. Its aggregate gross national product (GNP) is catching up with that of the United States, and it has a greater population. Its military expenditure, taken as the sum of member countries' national totals, is about $150 billion, more than five times that of Japan. Total EC defence spending is about half that of the United States which on the other hand has global interests to maintain. With only European commitments, the EC is roughly comparable (see table 5.5). Its aggregate military forces exceed those of the United States. In terms of resources and forces, therefore, it is a major political player. Whether it will take up the initiative to focus on a common foreign and defence policy remains to be seen, but a number of events in 1989 indicated that a greater role for the EC in international political and security affairs is in the making regardless.

1. There was the co-ordination of all Western assistance (including that of the United States) to the newly democratically oriented East European countries. Noting that the political renaissance of Eastern Europe could only

[21] *Jane's Defence Weekly*, vol. 11, no. 24 (17 June 1989), p. 1213.

Table 5.5. Comparative economic and military indicators of the European Community countries, the USA and Japan, 1988

Country	GDP (US $b.)	Population (m.)	Per capita GDP (US $)	Per capita real growth rate 1980–87 (%)	Military expenditure (US $m.)	Military expenditure real growth 1980–88 (%)	Armed forces (thou.)	Weapon procurement expenditure (US $m.)
FRG	1 202.0	61.2	19 641	1.7	35 097	0.5	494.3	5 089
France	949.2	55.9	16 989	1.1	36 105	1.3	466.3	9 496
Italy	828.9	57.4	14 431	1.9	20 429	4.5	390.0	4 188
UK	807.5	57.1	14 147	2.5	34 629	1.4	311.7	8 736
Spain	340.1	39.1	8 709	1.6	7 171	1.8	285.0	1 484
Netherlands	227.5	14.8	15 413	1.0	6 729	0.5	103.6	1 373
Belgium	152.5	9.9	15 373	1.3	4 107	–1.3	92.4	492
Denmark	107.6	5.1	20 975	2.5	2 320	–0.1	31.6	334
Greece	53.6	10.0	5 355	0.9	3 378	0.6	208.5	790
Portugal	41.9	10.4	4 048	1.0	1 347	1.7	75.3	141
Ireland	31.5	3.5	8 898	0.3	462	–0.7	13.0	45
Luxembourg	7.0	0.4	18 919	..	86	3.8	0.8	2
EC total	4 749.3	324.7	14 628[a]	1.7[a]	151 860	1.5[a]	2 472.5	32 170
USA	4 839.4	246.3	19 646	2.1	294 901	5.0	2 124.9	71 808
Japan	2 858.9	122.6	23 317	3.2	28 521	4.7	247.0	7 964

[a] Average figure.

Sources: SIPRI data base; author's calculations.

become meaningful if economic regeneration took place, the Group of Seven countries (Canada, France, the FRG, Italy, Japan, the UK and the USA) in their annual summit meeting in 1989 pledged large sums of foreign assistance (including food aid to Poland). For the first time the EC was entrusted with the task of co-ordinating this effort and acting as a bridge between East and West.[22] Although there was no explicit political mandate, the nature of the task implies an acknowledged foreign policy dimension.

2. The Delors Report (after Jacques Delors, President of the EC Commission) on economic and monetary union was submitted in April 1989.[23] In it some controversial points were raised relating to budgetary policy, with implications for military expenditures in a future West European entity. Also, as a result of the discussions of the Report at the Madrid and Strasbourg EC summit meetings, the question of the status of the 1958 Treaty of Rome was again raised. The Treaty has by many been considered to forever preclude a common stand on foreign policy. The principle has now been accepted that technical impediments such as Treaty revisions cannot stand in the way of political unity, if this is desired by the EC member states themselves.

3. Preparations for the integrated and single European market in 1992 gathered momentum during 1989. In a 1988 report investigating the progress towards the internal market the EC Commission had stated: 'The question of defence procurement will also need to be addressed in the light of both the provisions of the EEC Treaty and the European Cooperation provisions of the Single Act'.[24] To speed up the market integration process, the EC Commission took a more active interest in public procurement, competition policy within the single market and cross-border mergers. The linkages between procurement budgets, policies and purchases will become crucial, specifically for the arms manufacturers. Delors has in an interview claimed that the arms industry 'is the most immobile—because of national vanities, captive markets, the power of the military, we do not cooperate sufficiently and we waste money'.[25] Some of the long-term issues are discussed below in the context of procurement spending. An in-depth review of the links between arms control and industry is to be found in chapter 8.

4. There was the impact of the changes taking place in Eastern Europe. The effect of this process in the West was to open a floodgate of debate on whether there should be 'widening' or 'deepening' of European structures. The requirements of EC membership were debated with an explicit political overtone, with particular emphasis on the question of whether the EC is to wait for the East to catch up or to move forward with rapid economic and structural change.

---

[22] *International Herald Tribune*, 17 July 1989, p. 2.

[23] *Report of the Committee for the Study of Economic and Monetary Union* (European Committee: Luxembourg, Apr. 1989). For a perceptive analysis on the Report by an academic Committee member, see Thygesen, N., 'The Delors Report and European integration', *International Affairs*, vol. 65, no. 4 (autumn 1989), pp. 637–52.

[24] *Completing the Internal Market* (Commission of the European Communities: Brussels, 17 Nov. 1988).

[25] See the interview with Delors in *Financial Times*, 14 Mar. 1989.

All of these events signal changes that may take place in the military expenditure process and budgetary allocation mechanism. A forward-looking analysis needs therefore to consider these implications seriously. Three major factors stand out as important for the EC member states' future total defence spending. All of them are systemic and long-term, but they were also significantly affected by events in 1989.

The first systemic factor relates to a common foreign policy for the EC and consequently a defence policy that will affect military expenditure. The effect of the Single European Act and the integrated market after 1992 means that the EC will have a comprehensive common market for goods, services and labour. In the next stage will come a monetary union with free financial flows (capital movements) across countries and the fixing of exchange-rates. As yet, there is no agreement regarding a common or even 'parallel' currency—one of the proposals advocated by the founders of the European Monetary System, Valéry Giscard d'Estaing and Helmut Schmidt. With a monetary union, however, a common currency would necessarily follow. The next stage envisages an economic union with four components: a single market for all goods and services, a competitive trade policy, common policies for social change and regional development, and co-ordination of national budgets with binding rules for budget deficits.

The second factor arises out of the demands for the co-ordination of fiscal policy. Although the British Government is totally opposed ('a diversion from the main course of European debate'[26]) it makes economic sense to have a common budgetary policy for the whole EC. It is difficult to envisage a union of market, money and economy without one. If such an integration does occur, it would be hard to imagine that military expenditure could be kept out of the ambit of the future EC. The UK, France and the FRG spend around 10–12 per cent of their central government expenditure on defence. This is a sizeable proportion, and it must be affected if aggregate budgets are controlled by the EC.

The third factor relates to EC interests in opening up all public sector procurement to market forces. This relates directly to defence procurement expenditures, whose size and composition would interact with overall public procurement policy.[27] According to SIPRI estimates, the EC countries spent over $32 billion (in 1988 prices) on *major* weapon purchases alone in 1989. Although some weapon imports will inevitably come from the United States, a dominant part of the demand for such arms will be supplied by European firms. (The British Government, for example, spends 80 per cent of its defence procurement budget within the country.) This is potentially a very large market that under competitive conditions could function much more efficiently than it does at present. In addition, there are other types of procurement spending (on food, fuel and construction material) that could

[26] See former Chancellor of the Exchequer Nigel Lawson's speech at the Royal Institute of Economic Affairs, 25 Jan. 1989; Thygesen (note 23); *The Economist*, 22 Apr. 1989, pp. 16, 27.

[27] Walker, W. and Gummett, P., 'Britain and the European armaments market', *International Affairs*, vol. 65, no. 3 (summer 1989), pp. 419–42.

amount to another $42 billion. Public expenditure on buying goods for the defence sector within the EC was worth around $75 billion in 1989.

Three of the four proposals for economic union in the Delors Report would affect the arms industries as well. These relate to the single market, open-bid procurement policies and national budgetary co-ordination (the setting of upper limits to arms purchases).

The primary factors affecting arms industries in the EC can be summarized as 'C⁴I': (arms) control, competition, commercialization, concentration and integration. All of these work through and are closely integrated with the member countries' procurement expenditures, particularly those for major weapon acquisition. Arms control negotiations, if successful in achieving deep cuts, will put pressure on governments to reduce procurement budgets. Lower budgets and higher unit costs (of new-generation equipment) will induce governments to encourage competition in the arms industry. In addition, commercial motives will take precedence over narrow national security interests, and defence ministries will ask for 'value for money' rather than whether there is a viable domestic industry or not. Technology and mergers are already concentrating European defence firms in larger units. If there is lower procurement then the movement towards concentration will continue. At the same time integration, in the civilian economy, will force defence subsidiaries also to consider themselves as 'European' in the broader sense of the term, independent of ownership.

V. The Soviet Union

For the Soviet Union 1989 was an important year, with the coming together of three movements, each marked by both successes and failures: the opening of the political system, a more determined effort towards economic restructuring and the attempts to demilitarize foreign policy. All three relate to the issue of military expenditure. The new openness in the political system made possible the publication of credible Soviet defence spending figures. Economic changes have required the re-allocation of resources from the defence sector. Reduction of military expenditure and force levels have reduced threat perceptions and allowed foreign policy to be less militarized.

In spite of significant foreign policy successes, the crucial constraint of the reforms instituted under President Gorbachev seems to be domestic economic and political problems. There is now a close link between achievements on the home front (particularly the availability of food and consumer goods), the continuation of the present leadership's political programmes and the conduct of foreign policy, specifically in the area of arms control. As Academician Vitali Zhurkin rightly points out: 'The problem of carefully *coordinating foreign policy and domestic goals* and the methods for achieving them become all the more important'.[28]

---

[28] Zhurkin, V., Karagonov, S. and Kortunov, A., 'New and old challenges to security', *Kommunist*, no. 1 (1988), p. 42. For an evaluation, see also Gross, N., 'Glasnost and the Soviet military', *RUSI and Brassey's Defence Yearbook 1989* (Brassey's: London, 1989) pp. 159–73; emphasis added.

In order to evaluate Soviet military capabilities and costs, the details of how much (and under what comparable categories) the USSR spends on defence must first be well understood. In this context, the estimate of Soviet military expenditure may be used in a number of ways.

1. It is an aggregate measure of defence capability that is easy to understand and to use as a means of comparison.

2. Its allocation over time into various component parts gives an indication of force structure and military capability trends.

3. Its growth indicates the preference and perceptions of policy makers.

4. It measures economic costs for a weak economy and shows how vulnerable the country can be from the point of view of non-military threats to security. This may be important in the context of stability.

5. It can be used by Western governments, particularly in the United States, to demonstrate how belligerent or benign the Soviet Union is. Since Soviet foreign policy in the past has been considered essentially militaristic, its defence spending has served as a measure of threat.

6. It can be used by other governments to convince domestic political groups of the necessity to increase military expenditure. In his State of the Union message in 1981, President Reagan claimed that the Soviet Union in the 1970s had spent $300 billion more than the United States on defence. The dubious method used to calculate that figure notwithstanding, the President sought to justify the largest peacetime expansion ever of US military spending using Soviet defence expenditures.

There are numerous aspects of Soviet military expenditure that are currently of interest. The financial figures cannot be properly evaluated, nor their implications understood, unless they are related to a number of wide-ranging factors, both military and economic. The discussion on Soviet military spending is related to budgetary allocations, procurement targets, economic reforms, industrial organization and foreign policy objectives. To impose some order in the discussion, the subsequent analysis is conducted under the headings of *glasnost*, *perestroika* and *konversiya*. Under the rubric of *glasnost*, the implications of all available information are discussed. The section on *perestroika* analyses the nature of re-structuring in the military sector and the possibilities for significant reductions in defence spending. The framework of *konversiya* used here is much broader than the usual concept of industrial conversion; it encompasses resource re-allocation and investigates whether the defence sector can provide the panacea for the problems that the overall Gorbachev reform programme now faces.

Glasnost: what is known?

After many years of presenting an increasingly untenable figure, the Soviet Government, consistent with the spirit of *glasnost* and confidence-building measures, in 1989 presented a figure (in roubles) for military spending that has a semblance of reality. The reason for not revealing the truth earlier was given by General Mikhail Moiseyev, Chief of the General Staff of the Soviet Armed Forces:

Knowledge of the defence budget allows many people to judge . . . a country's defence capability . . . For this reason many countries of the world sought to conceal the part of their budget allocated for defence . . . Taking into consideration the military and political situation in the world and guided by the need to accelerate the solution of the difficult and numerous problems involved in the building of socialism, the Soviet state had to conceal information about its defence expenditures and changes in this process.[29]

On 30 May 1989, President Gorbachev, speaking to the Congress of People's Deputies, announced that the Soviet military expenditure for the current year would be 77.3 billion roubles—a figure almost four times higher than the official defence budget of 20.2 billion roubles. He said:

But in the modern world the possibilities are increasing for security to be safeguarded by political and diplomatic means. This enables military spending to be cut on the basis of giving a new quality to the USSR Armed Forces without any detriment to the country's defence capability. In 1987–1988 military spending was frozen; this made a savings in the budget, in comparison of the 5-year plan, of R10 billion. Here I am announcing to the Congress this real figure for military spending: R77.3 billion. There is a proposal being made to reduce military spending as early as 1990–1991 by another R10 billion, that is by 14 percent . . .[30]

These figures are somewhat lower than the SIPRI estimates produced in December 1988 and published in the *SIPRI Yearbook 1989*, placing Soviet defence spending in the neighbourhood of 80 billion roubles plus 10–20 per cent for unaccountable elements.[31]

In news media presentations of the new official figures, Western intelligence estimates in the range of around 120 billion roubles were also cited.[32] A recent NATO estimate puts the 1987 defence outlay of the USSR at between 130 and 140 billion roubles.[33] Prime Minister Margaret Thatcher is reported to have claimed in Parliament that the stated amount was only half of that which Western experts believe to be the actual Soviet expenditure.[34] The DOD claims, in its publication *Soviet Military Power 1989*, that the Soviet Union spent $150 billion on its military in 1988.[35] A perceptive Soviet economist has cast doubt on the absolute spending figure as well as on the figure for the military burden (military spending as a proportion of GNP). He claims that both figures, and in particular that for the defence

[29] Moiseyev, M. (Gen.), 'Soviet defence budget', *Pravda*, 11 June 1989.

[30] From President Gorbachev's speech to the USSR Congress of the People's Deputies on 30 May 1989, published in *Foreign Broadcast Information Service Daily Report: Soviet Union, Supplement; USSR Congress of the People's Deputies* (FBIS-SOV-89-103S), 31 May 1989.

[31] Deger (note 2), pp. 133–94.

[32] Peel, Q., 'Gorbachev reveals "real" defence bill', *Financial Times*, 31 May 1989, p. 3.

[33] Wilkinson, C., 'Soviet defence expenditure: past trends and prospects', *NATO Review*, no. 2 (Apr. 1989), pp. 16–22.

[34] See *Jane's NATO & Europe Today*, vol. 4, no. 38 (13 June 1989), p. 4.

[35] *Soviet Military Power 1989: Prospects for Change* (US Department of Defense: Washington, DC, 1989).

Table 5.6. Official Soviet military expenditure, 1989–90

Figures are in b. current roubles.

	1989	Percentage share	1990	Percentage share	Percentage change 1989–90[a]	Change needed in 1990–91 to meet targets (%)[a, b]
Personnel, O&M	20.2	26.1	19.3	27.3	– 4.5	– 7.9
Pensions	2.3	3.0	2.4	3.4	+ 4.4	
Procurement	32.6	42.2	31.0	43.7	– 4.9	– 11.5
Construction	4.6	6.0	3.7	5.2	– 19.6	
R&D	15.3	19.8	13.2	18.6	– 13.7	
Others	2.3	3.0	1.3	1.8	– 43.5	
Total[c]	**77.3**	*100*	**71**	*100*	– 8.2	– 6.6
Military space[d]	3.9					

[a] (–) reduction; (+) increase.

[b] SIPRI estimates.

[c] Items may not add up to totals due to rounding.

[d] For allocations under military space, see section V.

Sources: Pravda, 8 June 1989, p. 3; *Foreign Broadcast Information Service Daily Report: Soviet Union, Supplement: USSR Congress of the People's Deputies* (FBIS-SOV-89-109), 8 June; *Izvestia*, 16 Dec. 1989; author's estimates.

burden, are too low relative to what is known about Soviet military capability and assets.[36] It has also been claimed that some Soviet analysts believe informally that the military burden is of the order of 22–30 per cent of GNP rather than, as is officially stated, 9 per cent.[37] The controversy continues.

More significant than this aggregate are the allocations of the total amount to personnel, O&M, pensions, procurement, construction and R&D. Table 5.6 shows the figures for 1989 announced by Prime Minister Nikolai Ryzkhov to the Congress of People's Deputies in June. The previously stated spending of 20.2 billion roubles for 1989 is now known to cover only personnel costs (salaries and payments to conscripts) and O&M (food, clothing, fuel and repairs). This is only a quarter of the total figures. Major weapon acquisition takes over 40 per cent of spending, and R&D accounts for 20 per cent.

The categories under which the aggregate Soviet figures are divided are similar to the ones used by the United States. In a detailed discussion of the 1989 spending figures General Moiseyev has compared the Soviet figures with those of the United States.[38] In addition to explaining why the figures for the USSR are allegedly low, his analysis also clearly demonstrates the similarities of the various budgetary categories. It also allows independent analysts to check on the plausibility of the figures.

In contrast to the Soviet figure, NATO's analysis of the same subject shows a somewhat different picture. Table 5.7 gives the NATO data on the Soviet Union for 1987 (which are not radically different from 1989 data

[36] Izyumov, A., 'Military glasnost lacks openness', *Moscow News*, 17–24 Sep. 1989.

[37] Åslund, A., *Gorbachev's Struggle for Economic Reform, 1985–88* (Pinter: London, 1989).

[38] Moiseyev (note 29).

Table 5.7. NATO estimates of Soviet military expenditure, 1987

Figures are in b. current roubles.

Item	Low estimate	Percentage share	High estimate	Percentage share
Personnel (incl. pensions)	10.4	8	11.2	8
O&M	39.0	30	42.0	30
Procurement	52.0	40	56.0	40
Construction	2.6	2	2.8	2
R&D	26.0	20	28.0	20
Total	**130**	*100*	**140**	*100*

Source: Wilkinson, C., 'Soviet defence expenditure: past trends and prospects', *NATO Review*, no. 2 (Apr. 1989), pp. 16–22.

except for a modest inflationary adjustment). The aggregate figures and those for sectorial allocations are vastly different. What is remarkable, however, is the similarity between NATO and Soviet figures for the cost of procurement (of major weapons) and of R&D as shares of total costs. By all accounts the Soviet Union spends 40 per cent of its total military budget on weapon procurement and 20 per cent on research. Independent of the actual figures, these two shares seem to be exceedingly high. The comparable share for the United States' spending on procurement and research is 27 per cent and 12 per cent (for FY 1989), respectively. The high payments made to volunteer soldiers in the USA tend to make its personnel cost share high and other shares relatively low. But even for the FRG, which has a conscript army, the corresponding proportions are around 21.5 per cent and 6.7 per cent. In a shortage economy, where skills, materials, intermediate inputs, and so on, are insufficient to meet demands, such a large proportionate diversion towards the military simply compounds the already high costs of defence expenditures.[39]

The total military expenditure figures revealed by the Government seem to be of the correct order of magnitude, except for some possible omissions and underestimates. It is not clear, for example, whether the separately announced spending for military space programmes is included in the total budget or not. Expenditure on defence-related space is claimed to be 3.9 billion roubles, out of a total Government outlay on space programmes of 6.9 billion roubles. No separate figures were given for nuclear weapon acquisition by the Soviet strategic forces. In the United States this is funded through the DOE and is not part of the DOD budget, even though it is a component of 'national defence expenditure'. If the Soviet Union follows the same pattern, it is possible that the total of 77.3 billion roubles does not contain spending on this category of weapons. Using the same percentage as in the USA, and making other adjustments, the (possible) exclusion might have reduced the total spending figure by about 10 per cent. There is also no mention of Soviet military aid, which is substantial. Even though the

[39] The FRG figures are from *Erläuterungen und Vergleiche zum Regierungsentwurf des Verteidigungshaushalts 1989* (note17); the US figures are calculated from table 5.1.

military support to the Afghanistan Government is less burdensome since the troop withdrawal, and the direct cost of stationing forces is eliminated, military assistance still continues. Some estimates have put military aid to Afghanistan at $3 billion per year,[40] but this figure seems to be too high. Nevertheless, military assistance to Afghanistan, Angola, Cambodia and Nicaragua must mean a heavy drain on defence-related spending.

Another category of spending that seems to be relatively low is O&M. The Soviet armed forces are spread over a large geographical area, maintain high-cost foreign bases in Eastern Europe, have a substantial commitment in all four force groupings (land, air, naval and strategic forces) and are required to spend heavily in maintaining a numerically massive inventory of assets. Under the circumstances it is difficult to believe that personnel and maintenance could only be 20.2 billion roubles, about a quarter of total spending. Even accounting for the low costs of conscript pay (although other costs such as food, housing and clothing are similar for officers and conscripts), this category of expenditure needs to be supplemented to arrive at a more reasonable figure.

The main difficulty with assessing Soviet defence expenditure is the arbitrary method by which prices are determined. This is particularly true for major weapons, where the aggregate budget for procurement can be heavily distorted if inappropriate prices are used for costing. The entire Soviet economic system is prone to such problems, since most prices are determined not by market forces but by administrative orders. Hence, when demand exceeds supply there may be 'repressed inflation' and prices may not be able to rise to clear the market. This distortion is increased considerably in priority sectors such as the military industries, where the value of weapons may be fixed independently of cost or demand.

General Moiseyev, at a joint press conference with US Admiral William J. Crowe, Jr,[41] claimed that a modern Soviet fighter such as the Su-25 costs 5.8 million roubles. The price of a comparable US F-16 is $28 million. Comparing at an official exchange-rate is meaningless as the Soviet rate is set at artificial levels. Using a purchasing power parity (conversion rate to ensure comparability) of $2.5 to a rouble, the Su-25 would cost $14.5 million, slightly more than half the cost of the F-16. Unless the US production method is terribly inefficient, which is unlikely, there must be an explanation for why in comparable prices its fighter costs twice as much as the Soviet aircraft. One explanation is 'goldplating' (unnecessary expenditure), corruption, cost-plus contracts and high profit rates that are prevalent in the US defence industry. This alone cannot explain the difference, however. An alternative explanation is that the Soviet fighter is underpriced.

It is believed that weapon prices are kept artificially low to accommodate unrealistic budgets. If so, then procurement expenditure on weapon systems is undervalued. In a free market, or even in a planned economy where the

[40] See Krauthammer, C., 'Soviet empire: a paradoxical collapse', *International Herald Tribune*, 14–15 Oct. 1989.
[41] Press conference with General Moiseyev and Admiral Crowe, *Krasnaya Zvezda*, 22 June 1989, p. 3.

military sector is given the same economic priority as the civilian economy, prices and spending on weapons and procurement would be higher than announced. The pricing mechanism of the defence activities has been explained as follows:

Military representatives at each defense plant monitor production and inspect for quality. These representatives also negotiate each year with plant management to reset the established price of the product . . . In the negotiations, the plant manager would argue for keeping the price constant, or more likely, raising it to cover increasing costs. The military representative would counter that the price should be lowered as the plant learns to produce the product more efficiently. The actual price set in a year is determined by the relative bargaining strengths of the two sides . . . Unlike the civilian case, the *price of a military product can be forced down.*[42]

Another controversial problem is how to calculate the share of national product spent on the military. The military burden is difficult to estimate, not only because of the dispute about defence spending but also, more importantly, because of the lack of consensus as to what is the true value of Soviet GNP.[43] There is now a major debate both inside and outside the country regarding the validity of figures on Soviet output and its value. If the GNP is overestimated as claimed, then clearly the military burden will rise even though the estimate of military expenditure remains the same. Official statistics only started giving GNP figures from 1987 onwards; prior to that only net material product (NMP, GNP minus most service income) data were provided. Using official data alone the military share in national output is about 8–9 per cent in 1989. This seems to be unrealistically low, given the rough parity that the USSR has with the USA in military capability. Claims at the other extreme give figures as high as 22–30 per cent for the share of the GNP going to the military.

Preliminary SIPRI estimates indicate that Soviet military spending is higher than what the Soviet Union has itself claimed but that the orders of magnitude are not fundamentally incorrect. The current SIPRI estimate for Soviet military expenditure for 1988 is 90–100 billion roubles. *Using official GNP figures*, the military burden is estimated by SIPRI to be around 12 per cent, or roughly double that of the United States.[44] If the actual GNP

[42] CIA, *A Guide to Monetary Measures of Soviet Defense Activities, A Reference Aid* (US Central Intelligence Agency: Washington, DC, Nov. 1987); emphasis added.
[43] CIA, *Revising Soviet Economic Performance Under Glasnost: Implications for CIA Estimates* (US Central Intelligence Agency: Washington, DC, Sep. 1988).
[44] In 1988 the official Soviet GNP was 866 billion roubles; see *Pravda*, 22 Jan. 1989, p. 3. The NMP was 625 billion roubles, or approximately 72 per cent of GNP; for the NMP figure see *Izvestia*, 21 Jan. 1989, p. 1. In 1987, the first year in which such data were revealed, the official estimate was 825 billion roubles; see *SSSR v tsifrakh v 1987 godu* [USSR in figures 1987] (Finansy i Statistika: Moscow, 1988). The same source also stated that growth of GNP in 1981–87 was 3.9 per cent per year. This is substantially higher than the widely used CIA data for Soviet national accounts. A critique of various statistical measures is to be found in *Revisiting Soviet Economic Performance Under Glasnost: Implications for CIA Estimates* (note 43). The UN Economic Commission for Europe *Economic Survey of Europe in 1988–1989* (United Nations: New York, 1989) also provides an incisive criticism of Soviet statistics, particularly its handling of inflation and growth rates. A major Soviet critic of official claims of high growth rates from the 1960s to the 1980s is Gorbachev's economic adviser, Abel Aganbegîan, who in his book *The Economic Challenge to Perestroika*

is sizeably lower, the estimate of the military burden will rise commensurably. For example, if Soviet national income is one-third less than its postulated official value, the military burden is 18 per cent, according to the SIPRI estimate.

It should be stressed that SIPRI relies on open sources only, above all on a wide range of Western sources, the possible bias of which cannot be discounted. Furthermore, these Western sources are surrounded by varying degrees of secrecy as well, meaning that details on methodology and method are often not revealed. For example, it has been claimed by a distinguished sovietologist that the US Defense Intelligence Agency (DIA) figure for Soviet military spending is derived by simply dividing the total budget by three.[45] Clearly, all independent evaluation is by necessity subjective and subject to margins of error. However, in the absence of more detailed information by either side, there can be no substitute for independent analytical judgements. The usual caveat applies: all statistics in this research area, independent of source, should be treated with extreme care and caution.

Perestroika: what can be changed?

Of more interest, in terms of international security and threat perception, is whether there are significant reductions in military expenditure currently in the Soviet Union. Almost all sources agree that there are positive signs and that in 1989 Soviet defence spending has been reduced. There are a number of indicators which point in this direction; see table 5.8.

1. The unilateral reductions in armed forces and assets (including 500 000 men, of which one-third are officers) announced at the end of 1988 are being carried out,[46] contributing to a sizeable fall in some categories of spending (although pension and welfare costs may rise somewhat).
2. The 1987 US–Soviet Treaty on the Elimination of their Intermediate-range and Shorter-range Missiles (the INF Treaty) called for the destruction of missiles the maintenance, replacement and modernization of which required moderate amounts of spending.

(Indiana University Press: Bloomington, Ind., 1988) claims that the Soviet growth rate was almost zero in 1981–85. According to official figures, the national income had risen by 16.5 per cent during this period. SIPRI estimates, based on Aganbegian's figures, show that the actual Soviet GNP figure could be about 33–40 per cent less than what is officially stated. This has some startling implications. For instance, the figure of 100 billion roubles for military expenditure could imply a defence burden (military expenditure share of national output) of either 12 per cent, using the official GNP figures, or 18–20 per cent, using the alternative estimates of GNP.

[45] Holzman, F. D., 'Politics and guesswork: CIA and DIA estimates of Soviet military spending', *International Security*, vol. 14, no. 2 (autumn 1989), pp. 101–31, is a devastating critique of the whole estimation procedure used by Western intelligence analysts to calculate Soviet defence spending. For earlier analyses by the same author see, 'Are the Russians really outspending the US on defence?', *International Security*, vol. 4, no. 4 (spring 1980), pp. 86–104; and 'Soviet military spending: assessing the numbers game', *International Security*, vol. 6, no. 4 (spring 1982), pp. 78–101.

[46] On 15 Dec. it was announced that 265 000 troops have been discharged as part of the unilateral reductions; in addition 173 000 troops have been released from conscription. Soviet Army total for 1 Jan. 1990 has been set at 3 993 000. *Izvestia*, 16 Dec. 1989, TASS report, 15 Dec. 1989; translation in FBIS-SOV-89-103S (note 30).

Table 5.8. Soviet military expenditure reductions, 1989

Area of reduction	Budget category	Expenditure reduction	Comment
Withdrawal from Afghanistan	Personnel O&M	Max. R 5 b. per annum	Military assistance to Afghanistan continues
INF Treaty cuts	O&M Procurement	R 300–500 m. per annum	Costs of elimination of missile systems
Unilateral force reductions	Personnel O&M	R 2.4 b. per annum	Possible dissatisfaction among demobilized forces
Strategic weapon system reductions	Procurement	..	Reduced deployment of SS-18, SS-24, Typhoon, Blackjack
Increased home-porting of naval forces	O&M	..	Possibly linked to demands for naval arms control
New aircraft-carrier cancelled	Procurement	Planned cost of one carrier	Linked to naval arms control
3 major plants converted to civilian production	Procurement	Profits to defence ministries	Defence ministries do not bear costs of conversion
Space R&D used for civilian purposes	R&D	..	Overall R&D cuts are not significant for 1989

3. The war in Afghanistan was a financial drain and is reputed to have cost the country 45 billion roubles over eight years. Disinvolvement could save 5 billion roubles per year, although continued military assistance to the Najibullah regime will reduce savings.

4. Civilian industrial activities have begun to replace military production. Thus, defence-related spending will fall as the growth of arms procurement and production is reduced.

5. Recent Western intelligence reports indicate that production and deployments of certain categories of advanced weapons have been halted and such changes must contribute to expenditure cuts.

As mentioned above, according to official information total Soviet defence spending will be reduced during the two years 1990–91 by 14.2 per cent, while procurement cuts will amount to 19.5 per cent. Troop reductions of the order of 12 per cent will also be implemented. In 1991 the planned aggregate Soviet military expenditure is to be 67.3 billion roubles, a reduction of 10 billion roubles from the current level. There is some confusion regarding the time period over which the procurement budget is to be reduced. In a report in *Pravda* in June 1989, General Moiseyev seemed to imply that procurement budget reductions are to take place over the three-year period 1989–91, rather than the two-year period envisaged in President

Gorbachev's May announcements.[47] If this is so then reductions in procurement spending are already under way in 1989. That is also consistent with the qualitative information available (see table 5.8). Some reports suggest that in 1989 procurement expenditure was reduced by about 4.5 per cent compared to the 1988 level. It has also been claimed, although in somewhat vague terms, that total reductions from the *planned levels* of military expenditure during the 12th five-year plan 1986–90 are on the order of 30 billion roubles, or 40 per cent of annual defence spending.[48] If this figure is correct it would indeed be a substantial cut. However, as in the case of the Cheney cuts in the US defence budget discussed above, it is difficult to substantiate this figure and to examine its implications.

During November and December 1989, the US news media revealed details of a classified intelligence report (prepared by the DOD, the Central Intelligence Agency (CIA) and the National Security Agency (NSA) and presented to the President in May) which claimed that the Soviet Union had indeed started the process of reducing its defence spending. It stated that 'there is broad agreement within the US intelligence community' that the USSR 'has decided to reverse a 20 year pattern of growth in military spending and force structure in order to boost the civil economy and Soviet foreign policy'.[49] It also stated that the share of military expenditure in GNP could have fallen from the previously claimed range of 15–17 per cent to 14–16 per cent. These changes in information must have taken place very recently; as late as April 1989, in the annual joint CIA/DIA report to Congress, *Allocation of Resources in the Soviet Union and China–1987*, the claim had been made that the postulated defence burden was around 15–17 per cent.[50] Such a change in the share, however, although apparently small (on the order of 1 per cent), implies a dramatic reduction in the level of defence spending. SIPRI estimates, based on such figures, show that military spending itself could have fallen by 6–7 per cent. Supporting these financial figures is information on Soviet procurement and deployment reductions of major strategic weapon systems, such as the Blackjack bomber, the Typhoon Class submarine, and the SS-20 and SS-23 missiles.

It is significant that little qualitative or quantitative information was made available throughout the year on reductions in military R&D activities.

[47] *Pravda*, 11 June 1989.

[48] Deputy Defence Minister of Armaments General Anatoly Shabanov claims that the projected cuts will save 30 billion roubles; *Jane's Defence Weekly*, vol. 12, no. 16 (21 Oct. 1989), p. 870. In his speech to the Congress of People's Deputies on 7 June, Prime Minister Nikolai Ryzkhov is more explicit: 'Including the proposed reduction of expenditure for the forthcoming 2 years, the overall savings of defense expenses in relation to the approved 5-year plan will amount to nearly R30 billion'; published in FBIS-SOV-89-109S, 8 June 1989, pp. 27–28.

[49] Smith, R. J., 'Soviets slow strategic weapons programs', *Washington Post*, 12 Nov. 1989, p. 1; Friedman, T. L., 'Military spending by Soviets slows', *New York Times*, 14 Nov. 1989, p. 14; Smith, R. J. and Tyler, P. E., 'Bush knew in May of Soviet arms shift', *International Herald Tribune*, 12 Dec. 1989, p. 12.

[50] Central Intelligence Agency/Defense Intelligence Agency, 'The Soviet economy in 1988: Gorbachev changes course', Report presented to the Subcommittee on National Security Economics of the Joint Economic Committee of the US Congress, 14 Apr. 1989 (unpublished mimeo). See also *Allocations of Resources in the Soviet Union and China—1987*, Hearings before the Subcommittee on National Security Economics of the Joint Economic Committee of the US Congress, 101st Congress (US Government Printing Office: Washington, DC, 1989).

Marshal Sergey Akhromeyev, in an interview in *Krasnaya Zvezda*, simply stated: 'A general reduction of military expenditure also means reduction of expenditure for military R&D'.[51]

In his speech detailing defence spending for 1989, Prime Minister Ryzkhov was rather defensive about research expenditure for space programmes. About 57 per cent of all space R&D is on the military; if part of the Buran space shuttle system has military uses then the share rises towards 70 per cent. It is claimed that such technology increases the efficiency of the armed forces by a factor of 1.5–2.[52]

In other statements Soviet military experts have expressed concern about US technological progress in military fields such as 'stealth' technology, anti-satellite capability and space research for SDI. Defence Minister Dimitri Yazov said in September 1989 that: 'As long as a military threat exists the principle of reasonable sufficiency should be backed up by further technological modernization of the armed forces on a qualitatively new basis. And this requires appropriate expenditures'.[53]

Hence, in spite of the reductions in total expenditure and assets, technological modernization and further high R&D could not be ruled out. In November 1989 it was believed that aggregate military expenditure reductions were taking place (although by a relatively small amount in 1989), procurement spending was going down more rapidly than the total budget itself and R&D was yet to be substantially affected. In December 1989, Soviet military expenditure allocation estimates were published for 1990.[54] It was possible for the first time ever to compare and contrast two successive years of defence allocations as well as to apply consistency checks for discrepancies between earlier plans and current estimates.

The 1990 budget presents a number of surprises (see table 5.6, column 3). Total expenditure is to be reduced by 8.2 per cent; this is consistent with the postulated 14.2 per cent reduction claimed for the two-year period 1990–91. Pensions increase marginally, since demobilized soldiers presumably need extra funding for job losses. However, both procurement expenditures and personnel costs (including O&M) fall by very small amounts. Given the postulated cut of 19.5 per cent for major weapon systems, the actual planned reduction in 1989–90 is only 4.9 per cent. In similar fashion, personnel costs are cut by only 4.5 per cent even though over half of the unilateral troop reductions (500 000 men or 12 per cent of the total) are claimed to have been completed. The greatest surprise is the massive proportionate

---

[51] Interview with Marshal S. Akhromeyev in *Krasnaya Zvezda*, 10 May 1989.

[52] Ryzkhov (note 48).

[53] The quotaion is from an interview with Yazov in *Izvestia*, 16 Sep. 1989. Soviet worries about technological competition with the United States and its ability to keep up with R&D are well known. In particular, SDI has been a perennial headache. In his testimony to the House Armed Services Committee of the US Congress on 21 July 1989, Marshal Akhromeyev suggested that the United States and the USSR should consider a formal agreement to limit military R&D; see *Defense News*, vol. 4, no. 30 (24 July 1989), p.1. In a rather curt comment in an interview published in *Krasnaya Zvezda* (note 51) he said that a general reduction of military expenditure means a reduction also of expenditure for military R&D; however, he did not give any figures. Little quantitative information on cuts in research spending in the military sector was available prior to the publication of the 1990 Soviet budget in late 1989.

[54] *Pravda*, 16 Dec. 1989.

reductions in R&D expenditures, which are expected to fall by 13.7 per cent. As discussed above, non-financial or qualitative information on technological progress would indicate that research on modernization has not suffered to the same extent as have other parts of the defence sector.

In the absence of more details, only informed forecasts can be made. In 1989, the first tentative steps were taken to slow down weapon acquisition and to reduce inventories. In 1990, the slow-down will continue at the same pace. If the target of 19.5 reduction is to be met, the cut in the procurement budget will have to be very large in 1991—of the order of 11.5 per cent. By comparison, in spite of recent talk of US defence cuts, the US DOD has yet to cut its procurement expenditure by more than 5–6 per cent in any one year starting from the mid-1980s. Unless arms control negotiations are formally completed, and the CFE agreement is ratified, it will be difficult to convince the military of such drastic cuts in procurement in one year. Whether the postulated 19.5 per cent reductions in procurement expenditure are to be achieved by the end of 1991 remains to be seen.

In addition, the implied 12 per cent cut in personnel expenditure (due to 12 per cent troop reductions and the fall in associated costs) will require a 7.9 per cent cut in 1991 alone. This is also a very large reduction. SIPRI has made independent estimates from available information about the probable reductions required in 1991 to reach the various announced targets (see table 5.6, column 6). In addition, to meet the targets for 1991, the reductions in personnel and procurement alone (1.5 and 3.5 billion roubles, respectively) will have to be greater than the aggregate budget reduction (4.7 billion roubles). This may mean that some other categories of expenditure, possibly R&D, will rise again.

Many questions remain about the changes in military expenditure and allocation in the Soviet Union. It would be of great help to analysts to receive details about the military expenditure budget for 1988 (and for earlier years as well) so that a real comparison can be made with the facts presented in the 1989 and 1990 budgets. Furthermore, since Prime Minister Ryzkhov has claimed that military expenditure reductions, implemented and continuing until 1991, will save 30 billion roubles from the original five-year plan (1986–90),[55] it should be possible for the authorities to reveal precisely what those earlier planned figures were.

Konversiya: what resources can be re-allocated?

For many years, the Soviet military sector has absorbed vast quantities of resources. High defence spending is an easily identifiable metric or measure that represents the scale of resource diversion, indicative of a wide complex of heterogeneous resources that are suitable for re-allocation. The need now, as President Gorbachev himself has stated, is to transform the 'economy of armament into an economy of disarmament'. 1989 was the first year in which significant attempts were made to redirect resources from the military

[55] Ryzkhov (note 48).

to the civilian sectors. The question, therefore, is how large and significant this 'disarmament dividend' potentially is.

There are at least 10 ways in which military expenditure reductions and resource re-allocation can help rejuvenate the economy. Even though there are interconnections between them, conceptually they should be kept separate. Furthermore, the cuts will differently affect the various parts of the defence budget—personnel, procurement, construction and R&D.

1. There is the direct impact on the state budget deficit which, in the light of recent revelations, is known to be alarmingly high. In 1989–90 the budget deficit is to be reduced from 120 billion roubles to 60 billion roubles. This is a huge reduction —50 per cent—and it is not very likely that the target will be met. Defence spending cuts are postulated to be about 7 billion roubles. In other words, the military sector will account for just over 11 per cent of the aggregate deficit reduction. Although significant, the contribution is not large.

2. This expenditure could possibly be transferred to other, more useful avenues of social expenditure, such as health or housing. Some expenditure diversion to socio-economic categories has been postulated. For example, it has been suggested that funds (and personnel) from military construction could be used to provide increasingly scarce civilian housing. The largest proportionate cuts in 1989–90 in the military budget have been in construction. The 900 million roubles saved (see table 5.6) could be used to build an estimated 90 000 flats. Government expenditure on health and education must also be a strong priority.[56] It is not surprising that Ryzkhov emphasized health care when he talked about 'the reorientation of the national economy to meet social demands'; in calling for a greater contribution of defence to the national economy he wished that 'above all, this [would apply] to medical equipment'.[57]

3. There is the release of skilled manpower. This is an issue in particular for the Russian and Baltic Republics, faced with demographic changes that will lead to labour shortages. Troop reductions could alleviate such shortages, mainly as regards the need for young and skilled workers. The armed forces constitute 4 per cent of the total labour force, an extremely high figure in a fully employed economy with no additional manpower reserves to draw upon. As a means of comparison, in the United States military personnel as a proportion of the total labour force is around 2.5 per cent; the mainly conscript army of the FRG employs (both civilian and military personnel) about 2.4 per cent of the total labour force. More significantly for the Soviet Union, around 10 per cent of all male Slavs at the university level

[56] Fesbach, M., 'Demographic trends in the Soviet Union: serious implications for the Soviet military', NATO Review, vol. 37, no. 5 (Oct. 1989), pp. 11–15. The author discusses both general problems associated with health care and its relation to demographic changes which may affect the military. In certain areas of the Soviet Union the infant mortality rate is worse than that of the poorest Third World countries; in Turkmenia, for example, the rate is 51%, which is higher than China, Albania or Mongolia.

[57] Ryzkhov (note 48).

are conscripted or diverted to the military officer corps.[58] This deprives the economy of its most talented young personnel.

4. There are anticipated future savings to be made as weapons are destroyed under the framework of arms control and O&M costs (particularly for fuel) are slashed. Fixed ceilings on military assets, as implied by the CFE Negotiation, will also mean less replacement of old equipment and the release of physical resources which would otherwise have remained geared to arms production. The INF Treaty apparently created a saving of around 300 million roubles, used to fund the construction of over 30 000 flats.[59] Deep cuts under the CFE agreement will increase such savings in the long run and could provide welcome respite, particularly in what is termed the 'social sphere'.

5. There is the direct contribution that defence factories can make in the provision of machinery for the consumer goods and processed foodstuffs industries, whose output is in short supply and a major source of discontent. Throughout 1988 and 1989 the defence industry ministries and industries have been exhorted to increase production and supply of machineries for the food-processing sector. As discussed above, supply shortages in food and consumer goods could be the main stumbling-block in the short term of the whole reform process, hence the urgency. Five of the nine defence industry ministries[60]—Aviation, Defence, General Machine-Building, Radio Industry and Shipbuilding—have specifically been asked to provide equipment for a variety of food-processing areas, from fruit and vegetable processing to refrigeration equipment to ovens for bakeries. It is planned that these ministries are to provide almost 50 per cent of all machinery required for food processing during 1988–95; the amount of machines expected to come from the military production industries alone is almost equal to the *total* aggregate value of installed machinery in the food-processing sector during this decade.[61]

6. The heavy industrial components of the defence industrial base can be helpful in retooling civilian industries in general and can form the spring-board of industrial modernization. Except for the ministries of the Communications, Electronics, Civil Aviation and Radio defence industries, the industry ministries attached to defence production are already involved in the supply of machine tools for the civilian economy. Given the ageing structure of Soviet industries and the heavy investment orientation (high capital output ratios), retooling is clearly essential for technological efficiency. The modest success, or possibly failure, of the earlier quality control programme (*gospriyemka*) in civilian industries has forced the leadership to turn to the military for help.

[58] Wilkinson (note 33), p. 20.

[59] Deger (note 2), p. 174, note 46.

[60] There are 9 defence industry ministries: Defence, Aviation, General Machine-Building, Radio, Electronics, Shipbuilding, Communications, Civil Aviation and the State Committee for Computing and Information. For detail, see Cooper, J., 'The defence industry and the new Soviet Government', unpublished mimeo, Centre for Russian and East European Studies (CREES), Birmingham, Aug. 1989. See also the the interview with the Chairman of the Military Industrial Commission, I. S. Belousov, in *Krasnaya Zvezda*, 23 July 1989, p. 2.

[61] See note 50.

The machine-building and metal-working (MBMW) sector has planned 'radical measures' to increase its productivity as the main provider of intermediate inputs into the production of consumer goods. Traditionally, the military base has been a mainstay of this sector and will therefore have to take a leading role in this process. Using CIA data, it can be estimated that military procurement constitutes over 50 per cent of MBMW output.[62] With procurement expenditure reduced, part of this output can now be directed to civilian use.

7. Some of the current output of the defence factories, particularly in transportation (trucks and helicopters), can be transferred immediately to the civilian sectors. There is now a plethora of information available about such transfers.[63]

8. The product mix of factories producing both civilian and military goods can be transformed in favour of the former. In terms of actual output produced directly, the share of civilian output from the arms-producing industries is to rise from its current level of over 40 per cent to 50 per cent in 1991 and 60 per cent by the middle of the next decade. By the end of the 13th five-year plan, therefore, the Soviet defence industrial base, currently the largest in the world, will be more oriented towards non-military production (see chapter 8).

As announced in President Gorbachev's UN speech on 7 December 1988, three small defence plants were *totally* converted to civilian production in 1989. These are the Yoshkarola and Yuruzun plants and the Leninskaya Koznitsa naval shipyard in Kiev.[64] Even the most advanced defence factories are also being utilized to produce consumer goods. For example, the Khrunichev plant near Moscow, in addition to being one of the most sophisticated factories in the world for space technology, is now producing children's bicycles.[65]

More important will be the qualitative orientation. High-tech industrialization, in the form of automation, computerization and the use of microprocessors, is now a priority. Investment-intensive smoke-stack industries must give way to new technology. Four civilian machine-building industries were amalgamated with the Defence Ministry of the Electronics Industry to satisfy the demand for computerized equipment. Factory automation is now top priority, and almost every single new product entering into production contains micro-processors.

9. If military industries have lower priority for major intermediate inputs (electronic components and high-quality materials) then these can be provided to the civilian economy much faster. Endemic shortages and input rationing will then be eased and a major impediment to inefficiency may be removed, making Soviet industry more competitive. One of the main reasons for the chronic shortages at the industrial level for the civilian indus-

[62] Author's estimate for the late 1980s, based on CIA/DIA (note 50).

[63] TASS interview with General A. Shabanov, *Daily Review* (Novosti Press), 27 Sep. 1989.

[64] Vid, L., 'Guns into butter, Soviet style', *Bulletin of the Atomic Scientists*, Jan.–Feb. 1990, pp. 17–19.

[65] Steel, J., 'Glasnost comes to Soviet rocket factory', *The Guardian*, 21 Nov. 1989; Zakharchuk, M., 'The post office box: a view from inside', *Sotsialisticheskaya Industriya*, 23 May 1989, p. 2.

trial sector is the allocation structure. Both sectors compete directly for materials (steel, coal and construction stuff) and vital intermediates (ball-bearings and micro-electronics). When there is an overall shortage and there is no market mechanism or price system to determine which enterprise should get the product first, the military industries have always had priority. Part of the inefficiency of Soviet civilian production is due to this factor. If the proposed transformations succeed, this allocation process will change.

10. The high-quality R&D and the large numbers of scientists and engineers employed in the defence sector can now be channelled to civilian sectors for the benefit of the economy as a whole.[66] By its own reckoning, in 1989 the USSR spent about 1.8 per cent of its GDP on military R&D. Using Western intelligence estimates, the proportion rises to 3.2 per cent. The corresponding figures for the USA are revealing. At the peak of military expenditure under the Reagan Administration, known for its encouragement of scientific innovation in the SDI programme, US military R&D amounted to about 0.8 per cent of the national output. Japan spends 0.01 per cent while the FRG spends 0.11 per cent of their respective national products. With a much smaller economic base, and a higher level of spending on military technology, the Soviet Union simply cannot afford to be so wasteful, particularly as its civilian economy is known to be underdeveloped. Both in terms of the quality of research and the number of scientists and engineers employed, the loss to civil society must be immense. The 13 per cent cut in military R&D in 1989–90 is therefore an important step forward.

What is surprising is that in spite of past claims of the close integration of military and civilian production, and the use of 'dual-use technology', there seems to be very little interconnection between the two and few civilian spin-offs from defence R&D. It seems as if the two industrial sectors have been hermetically sealed off from each other. President Gorbachev's warning about the existence of the Soviet Union's 'internal COCOM' [with reference to NATO's Coordinating Committee on Export Controls], which precludes advanced technology transfer from defence to civil industry, is a clear indication of the pervasiveness of this dichotomy. In his speech on 30 May 1989, in which he revealed Soviet military expenditure, he also said: 'Immense possibilities lie in using in the civilian sector the unique technology developed at the defence ministry enterprises. Conditions have been created today to put an end to the irrational secrecy, finishing up with with the so called internal COCOM'.[67]

Any relaxation of such restrictions is likely to increase productivity and introduce technological progress in the non-military sector similar to the levels attained in defence production.

The optimistic scenario sketched above, where *konversiya*—defined in the broadest sense—will be able to rejuvenate the economy, may not work

[66] The Sukhoi design bureau, known for its the advanced fighters of the Su series, is increasingly moving into civilian aircraft design. It has designed a sports aeroplane, the Su-26M, and has plans (announced at the 1989 Paris air show) for a joint venture with the US firm Gulfstream to design and produce a supersonic business jet. See Cook, N., 'New challenges facing Soviet military industry', *Jane's Defence Weekly*, 16 Sep. 1989, pp. 507–509.

[67] FBIS-SOV-89-103S (note 30).

out as planned. There are formidable structural and systemic weaknesses in the system which may hinder the transformation desired.

1. The amount of financial resources available from military expenditure (assuming that Soviet figures are correct) is rather small, particularly if compared to the astronomical budget deficit and the competing demands for governmental socio-economic spending.

2. There are significant short-term costs of demobilization and reduction or destruction of weapon stocks. Unemployed military officers are already complaining bitterly about the lack of opportunities and of amenities such as housing. The formation in 1989 of *Shchit* (Shield), the first Soviet military trade union,[68] is indicative of the armed forces' concern about their deteriorating position in society. Destruction of weapons, at the initial stages, can also be quite expensive.[69] Figures released during 1989 pertaining to disarmament provisions of the INF Treaty and to unilateral cuts are indicative of these costs.

3. The industrial organization structure required to extract the rewards of conversion may not yet be present in the Soviet Union. The leadership prefers existing arms factories to be converted into partial or full production of civilian goods. The alternative of transferring equipment and personnel to new or existing civilian factories is considered less desirable. Yet, the first option may be more expensive since new types of fixed costs will have to be incurred. It is thought that since military industries are inherently more efficient, converting existing facilities will in some sense carry over this efficiency to the production of new civilian products. This may not be the case. As discussed above, the high productivity of military industries was possible because they were insulated from the systemic weaknesses of the economy. They faced less shortages, had priority to high-quality input, paid lower prices for inputs and were covered by state subsidies if they failed to make adequate profits. Without such assistance their efficiency would be questionable. Changing over to civilian production will not alter these systemic weaknesses.

4. Since 1 January 1989, many military industries are operating under 'self financing' (*khozraschet*). This has been the norm for civilian industry for some time but is new to the defence sector. It, too, will now be compelled to make profits and can no longer count on being bailed out in case of bankruptcy. As military industries begin producing consumer durables, competing on an open market, they may have to increase prices or lower quality to remain solvent and profitable.[70] Quality control is a perennial problem. Utilizing their monopoly, such industries can pass off

[68] See Cornwell, R., 'Soviet soldiers left out in the cold', *The Independent*, 27 Nov. 1989. Criticism as well as spirited defence of the armed forces surfaced during a meeting of the Congress of People's Deputies; *The Guardian*, 31 May 1989. The problems of low-quality housing and housing shortages was voiced in *Moskovskiye Novosti* and reported in *Jane's Defence Weekly*, 8 July 1989, p. 38.

[69] See 'What's the price of blasting a missile?', *Krasnaya Zvezda*, 20 Oct. 1989.

[70] Kireyev, A., 'Restructuring the military-industrial complex', *New Times*, no. 36 (5–11 Sep. 1989), cited in *Strategic Review*, vol. 17, no. 4 (autumn 1989), pp. 83–84.

sub-standard goods to consumers. If sub-standard components cannot be used for a defence product, a factory may use them for its civilian output.

5. The method of allowing military industries to take up civilian production does not tackle the basic problem of 'internal COCOM'. The transfer of technology is still being internalized within the defence industrial ministries. Its effect could be described as that of a martial law for industry, with the efficient military system called in to sort out the difficulties of civilian society.[71] It is not surprising that Colonel Professor Ivan Yudin has recalled the success of self-financing for military industries during the 'Great Patriotic War'.[72]

There can be little doubt that economic conversion from a military to a non-military mode of production will help the economy. The question is how large the beneficial effects will be and how long it will take to acquire the 'disarmament dividend'. Certainly in the long run, once the systemic problems discussed above are corrected, the economic effects of the transformation must be positive. Unfortunately, the leadership needs to show results quickly, particularly in the supply of consumption goods.

In terms of Soviet military expenditure, 1989 was a remarkable year. For the first time in two decades defence spending slowed down and was probably also reduced in real terms. Acquisition of military assets was being cut and procurement expenditure for the year was probably lower than for earlier years. There was also a promise of substantial future reductions in the pace of modernization, brought about by planned cuts in R&D spending. Large-scale conversion has been initiated, although it is still fraught with teething troubles. Uncertainties remain, but hopefully *glasnost* will dispel some of the opaqueness that still characterizes Soviet military expenditure. The Soviet military system is bound to become 'leaner'. Whether it will become 'meaner' is now purely a political question. The answer will depend on the success of the arms control process.

VI. Eastern Europe

Far-reaching economic reforms are now under way in all of Eastern Europe. Central planning is expected to be abandoned, and the command structure of the economy is being replaced by decentralized economic decision making. The most advanced of such market-oriented reforms have taken place in Hungary, which has experimented with a mixed economy for some time. The most rapid transformation is taking place in Poland, where the dismantling of the state economic apparatus is to be completed by 1990.

[71] Kireyev (note 70) states scathingly: 'The defense industry can, of course, fulfill the role of a fire brigade and put out, for a time, the seething discontent with the shortages of goods of prime necessity. But will it help to solve the problem completely? I am afraid it will not. By reducing the defense industry to an average and rather low level and making it produce kneading machines or electric shock guns for cattle slaughter, we are losing our last technological advantage'. See also Kireyev, A., 'What will global peace bring us?', *Pravda*, 14 Sep. 1989.

[72] Yudin, I., 'Defence industry and *khozraschet*', *Soviet Military Review*, no. 1 (Oct. 1989). The economics of military expenditure are discussed in Yudin, I., 'The effectiveness of using defence resources', *Soviet Military Review*, no. 12 (Dec. 1989).

Grave economic crisis threatens most of these countries, and structural adjustments may cause great hardships in the short term. Having faced the problems of communism—shortages, queues, low-quality products, black markets and systemic corruption—they are about to face the problems of capitalism—unemployment, inflation and inequality. There are few easy solutions. As is the case for the Soviet Union, foreign policy is now intricately linked with the domestic economic process. In the interests of European stability, Eastern Europe must succeed in its economic and political reforms. The specific problems of external debt and economic crisis are dealt with in chapter 6.

In the case of the non-Soviet WTO (NSWTO) countries, two issues deserve particular attention: defence burden-shedding and defence burden-sharing. The first relates directly to events in 1989, when large reductions were claimed. The second relates to the past and future role of Soviet forces in the defence of Eastern Europe as a whole. Analysis of burden-sharing also permits an evaluation of whether the withdrawal of Soviet troops, as required by arms control agreements, in economic terms will mainly benefit Eastern Europe or the Soviet Union.

Burden-shedding

Following President Gorbachev's lead and prodded both by economic difficulties and the desire for arms control, almost all the NSWTO countries in early 1989 announced sizeable reductions in defence budgets and armed forces.[73] Bulgaria stated that it has reduced its 1989 military spending by 12 per cent from the level of the previous year. Czechoslovakia claimed a reduction of 15 per cent in 1989–90. The German Democratic Republic announced a cut of 10 per cent in 1989–90 as well. Romania had already claimed that it had made some reductions in 1985–88; no new cuts were announced in 1989.

In the case of Hungary some difficulties remain in the interpretation of the data. New budgetary accounting methods have been introduced, and the time series and the trend may not be comparable with what has previously been published.[74] The Hungarian Parliament refused to ratify the defence budget for 1989, claiming that the proposed cut was insufficient. It is now claimed that total *real* reductions will amount to 17 per cent for 1989 for Hungary. If true, this could be the largest military expenditure reduction in the wave of cuts within the WTO.

In the case of Poland the situation is similar to that of many Latin American countries, in that it is becoming extremely difficult to estimate military expenditure because of high inflation. The original Polish budget for 1989 was almost double that of the level set for 1988. However, inflation in 1988 was more than 50 per cent, and the Government probably expected prices to rise much faster in 1989, probably more than 100 per cent. In other

[73] See the following 1989 issues of *Jane's Defence Weekly*: 7 Jan., p. 6; 14 Jan., p. 43; 21 Jan., p. 82; 11 Feb., p. 250; 25 Feb., p. 305; 24 June, pp. 1314–15; 7 Oct., p. 719; 4 Nov., p. 973.

[74] SIPRI is currently revising Hungarian military expenditure data.

words, there would in any case have been a real reduction. Actual inflation is now claimed to be running at 500 per cent or more, which means that if military expenditure in money terms has not risen fivefold, there has been a cut. Although precise figures for Poland's actual military expenditure in 1989 are not available as yet, it is expected that the real reduction is of the order of 5 per cent.

In addition to cuts in military expenditure, there are reports of force and armament reductions in the WTO countries. For example, in 1989–90 the Polish Army is to reduce the strength of its forces by 40 000 from its current level of over 400 000 men. In addition, 850 tanks, 900 artillery, 700 armoured troop carriers and 80 aircraft are to be removed from the inventory. Similarly, the Hungarian armed forces will be reduced by 9300 men, 250 tanks, 430 artillery and 9 air defence aircraft.

Little is known from domestic sources about NSWTO defence spending and allocations. Detailed information has been considered a state secret. A general picture can be obtained from the single-line entries for defence budgets, and from occasional snippets of information as to whether border guards or internal security personnel are included or not. An elementary functional division, between investment and current military expenditures, is provided in the Polish defence budget only, although the investment element is so small that it cannot include procurement. R&D expenditures are generally not revealed, although it is thought that only Poland and Czechoslovakia (the two major arms-producing countries using indigenous designs) have sizeable military research budgets.

In spite of the paucity of data and the general secrecy surrounding military spending in NSWTO countries, however, there is more confidence in the NSWTO aggregate figure than in the corresponding figure for the Soviet Union. The reason is that, unlike the near-constant Soviet budget, NSWTO military expenditures have risen consistently with their national products. There has been a close connection between military spending trends and general economic trends. Also, known force modernizations have been reflected in the figures for revealed military expenditure. An important study by the DIA using the building-block method, which costs components of the defence sector (military personnel, individual weapons and military R&D) in US prices and dollars, has shown that overall there is little discrepancy between official budget data and the DIA's own estimates.[75] This is in stark contrast to the DIA analysis for the Soviet Union, which implies that even the new figures presented by President Gorbachev could be only half of their own estimates.

Using the building-block method, the DIA has produced cost figures for Czechoslovakia, Hungary, Poland and Romania which are only 15 per cent

[75] See Clements, T. W., 'The costs of defence in the non-Soviet Warsaw Pact: a historical perspective', *East European Economies: Slow Growth in the 1980s, vol. 1: Economic Performance and Policy, Papers submitted to the Joint Economic Committee* (US Government Printing Office: Washington, DC, 1985), pp. 451–74. See also, in the same volume, Alton, T. P., Lazarcik, G., Bass, E. A. and Badach, K., 'East European defense expenditures 1965–1982', pp. 475–501. For an earlier analysis of burden-sharing see Rice, C., 'Defense burden-sharing', eds D. Holloway and J. M. O. Sharp, *The Warsaw Pact: Alliance in Transition?* (Macmillan: London, 1984).

higher than the amounts given in the official military expenditure for these countries. For the GDR, the DIA figures are even *lower* than the official data. Until 1989, Bulgaria was the only country in the WTO which had not published any military expenditure data at all for the previous 10 years.

Burden-sharing

As Soviet troops plan to leave Eastern Europe, and member countries such as Hungary are even considering leaving the WTO, the discussion of burden-sharing seems increasingly academic. It is important, however, to analyse how the WTO countries shared the costs of alliance. If the costs to the NSWTO have been high, economic gains may be made from a future Soviet withdrawal. Alternatively, if the USSR has been shouldering most of the burden, then the cost of ensuring security without a Soviet presence will rise in the long run. As long as Europe is not demilitarized, caution will require that security forces be maintained at relatively high levels. If the NSWTO countries currently are 'free riders', they would have to compensate for future Soviet withdrawals by expanding their own defence commitments and costs.

The main problem with analysing WTO burden-sharing is the lack of reasonable data even at the aggregate level. Military expenditure data in a common currency (generally the US dollar) are difficult to estimate because suitable conversion rates are not easy to find. Official exchange-rates in the past have generally been meaningless since they do not reflect price structures but are officially set. Purchasing power parities are either not available on a time-series basis, or differ substantially between defence and national product, or are unreliable, varying considerably from one analysis to another. Again, the building-block method seems to provide the best estimates. It is widely believed that such estimates are upwardly biased. However, if the bias exists in one direction only, and is relatively uniform, then it should not distort the value of shares and ratios.

Table 5.9 gives military expenditure figures for the WTO countries in two groups (NSWTO and the USSR). It should be emphasized that the data are based on Western intelligence estimates and are not derived by SIPRI. However, SIPRI has made adjustments utilizing its own estimates of real growth rate (to measure volume changes between 1980 and 1988); in addition, the US military price deflator has been used to obtain price changes and current dollar estimates for the two years.

It is clear that the Soviet Union shoulders the lion's share of WTO spending on defence. The NSWTO countries account for about 16 per cent of total WTO expenditure and 25 per cent of the armed forces. Even if its global and strategic commitments are taken into account, the Soviet Union still accounts for the overwhelming share of total expenditures. For example, if it is assumed that only 50 per cent of Soviet military spending is for Europe, then NSWTO spending corresponds to about one-third of total WTO spending. As regards the armed forces, NSWTO troop strengths are

Table 5.9. Burden-sharing in the Warsaw Treaty Organization, 1980 and 1988

	Military expenditure (US $b.)		Armed forces (thousands)	
	1980	1988	1980	1988
Non-Soviet WTO	32	58	1 345	1 451
USSR	174	303	4 100	4 000
WTO total	**206**	**361**	**5 445**	**5 851**
Non-Soviet WTO share of total (%)	*16*	*16*	*25*	*25*

Source: Clements, T. W., 'The costs of defence in the non-Soviet Warsaw Pact: a historical perspective', *East European Economies: Slow Growth in the 1980s, vol. 1: Economic Performance and Policy, Papers submitted to the Joint Economic Committee* (US Government Printing Office: Washington, DC, 1985), pp. 451–74; ACDA, *World Military Expenditure and Arms Transfers 1988* (US Arms Control and Disarmament Agency: Washington, DC, 1988); author's estimates.

about a quarter of the total, that is, the ratio of forces maintained between the USSR and the other members of the WTO is approximately 3:1.

From military expenditure figures it is clear that there has been little burden-sharing within the WTO. Most of the costs of collective security have been borne by the Soviet Union during peacetime, probably on the assumption that some advantages will accrue during a conflict.

For the host countries there could have been indirect costs associated with the Soviet bases, such as for construction, operations and support. The basing agreements for the GDR, Hungary and Poland do not specify who pays for what. The Polish Status of Forces Agreement with the Soviet Union states that the forces will utilize barracks, exercise grounds, artillery ranges, buildings, equipment, means of transport, electric power, and public and commercial services and that the rates of pay will be determined in a separate agreement.[76] Since costing is not stipulated, it is not possible to estimate whether the share paid by host governments is high or not. There is more detail in the Czechoslovak Status of Forces Agreement from 1968. A Rand Corporation study analyses it thus:

It stipulates that the Soviet Union will cover maintenance costs, but Czechoslovakia will provide barracks, housing, service, warehouses, airfields, and other services. Soviet trade establishments are to purchase goods and services from their Czech counterpart for sale to Soviet troops at state retail prices minus the wholesale discount. The Soviets pay in transferable rubles converted into koruna at a ratio determined by the ratio of domestic Czech prices to foreign trade prices.

[76] Text of the *Treaty on the Legal Status of Soviet Troops Temporarily Stationed in Poland, Warsaw, 17 December 1956, Zbiór Dokumentów* [Collection of Documents] 1956, no. 12 (Polish Institute of International Affairs: Warsaw, 1956), pp. 1879–90. Similar treaties were signed with other WTO countries. For Hungary, for instance, see *Treaty on the Legal Status of Soviet Troops Temporarily Stationed in Hungary, Budapest, 27 May 1957, Zbiór Dokumentów* [Collection of Documents] 1957, no. 5 (Polish Institute of International Affairs: Warsaw, 1956), pp. 1273–85.

None of this evidence indicates that the East Europeans cover any of the operational costs of the Soviet troops located in their countries.[77]

The same Rand study also claims that the Soviet Union probably bears most of the variable costs of its troops at the bases: weapons, ammunition, and spares are Soviet, since East European manufacture is not standardized; wages are paid in roubles; and subsistence is also paid for as the above-mentioned Czechoslovak Agreement shows. Major weapons almost certainly belong to the Soviet Union. Thus the only expenditure to the host government is probably for the construction and maintenance of the bases. Whether or not the USSR pays rent as well is not known. However, the host countries have probably paid large sums for hidden costs outside the normal defence budget. These would include expenditures for transportation, water, electricity and waste disposal. In addition, the opportunity costs of rents and taxes forgone on prime land and facilities could be substantial. Nothing is known about such costs to the NSWTO countries.

It has also been claimed that the Soviet Union could have forced the NSWTO countries to increase their military expenditure, even if not warranted by changing threat perceptions or economic growth. This would be strong evidence of coercion as well as of indirect costs that would have to be accounted for as a burden. This seems to have been the case at the WTO Political Consultative Committee meeting in 1978. In response to NATO's call for a 3 per cent growth rate of annual military expenditure, the Soviet Union persuaded the WTO to call for a corresponding increase. With one notable exception, however, the NSWTO countries failed to meet this goal. Throughout the 1980s economic constraints played a far greater role in controlling NSWTO defence spending than any Soviet coercion. Only the GDR showed large increases in defence spending, which may be explained by the fact that its economy is by far the healthiest in Eastern Europe. The GDR is also the one WTO country in which the Soviet Union is in some way reimbursed for its defence commitments.

Overall, the NSWTO countries have contributed less to alliance security than would have been possible if the Soviet Union had not assumed so much of the common burden. The alliance has been of greater political and military significance to the USSR than to the other allies, and it has also shouldered a greater economic burden. Conversely, the NSWTO countries have probably acted as 'free riders' in an economic sense. However, the requirements of security imposed by the Soviet Union on the WTO were undesirable to the East European countries, and the new governments of Czechoslovakia, Hungary and Poland have already informed Moscow that all Soviet troops must leave and the bases be shut down.[78]

[77] Crane, K., *Military Spending in Eastern Europe*, Prepared for the Office of the Under Secretary of Defense (Rand Corp.: Santa Monica, Calif., 1987); emphasis added.
[78] *Financial Times*, 19 Jan. 1990, p. 18.

VII. China and the Third World

Since the mid-1980s Third World military expenditure has been declining in real terms. The trend continued in 1989, although it is not yet possible to give any precise figures. This decline is due to several factors. In particular in the case of Latin America and Africa it is the result of economic difficulties. The end of the Iraq–Iran War, as well as the reduction of inter-state conflicts in certain regions—in particular in southern Africa–have also contributed to the decline.

The decline is also a reflection of the fact that, to Third World countries as well, economic security is becoming a more vital concern than military threat perceptions. In particular, the debt crisis has had an increasingly felt impact on welfare and growth, fuelling insecurity of a different kind. The relationship between debt, defence and development, in the context of military expenditure, is discussed in further detail in chapter 6.

Another contributing factor is that inter-state conflicts seem to be on the decline. A number of events highlighted this trend in 1989: Viet Nam withdrew its forces from Cambodia; the Association of South East Asian Nations (ASEAN) re-evaluated its security interests in the light of Viet Nam's withdrawal and Australia's new proposals for increased formal economic co-operation in the Asia–Pacific region; India speeded up its own withdrawal of the Indian Peace Keeping Forces (IPKF) from Sri Lanka; Namibia gained independence and South Africa promised no interference; and the Arab Co-operation Council (ACC) increased its membership and proposed greater co-ordination among members.

At the same time, however, intra-state conflicts seemed to increase in intensity in many parts of the Third World during 1989 (see also chapter 10). The Palestinian *intifada* on the West Bank and Gaza Strip continued unabated; US military assistance was provided to the Colombian Government in its fight against narcotics dealers; the Peruvian Government faced a challenge to its legitimacy from the 'Shining Path' guerrillas; civil war continued unabated in Afghanistan despite the withdrawal of Soviet troops; and the Philippines faced a significant army revolt and an attempted *coup d'état*.

Even if military expenditure (as defined by SIPRI) declines, 'security spending' in the widest sense of the term will probably have to rise if such trends continue, with adverse effects on national economies. A vicious circle could be set in motion, with development failures exacerbating existing domestic conflicts, in turn triggering new increases in defence and security spending.

Many of these factors played a role in forming developments in China in 1989. President Gorbachev's historic visit to Beijing in May 1989 signalled the beginning of a new phase in Sino-Soviet relations, after three decades of hostility. The three main obstacles to *détente*—boundary disputes, Soviet support for Viet Nam and the Soviet invasion of Afghanistan—were addressed, mainly as a result of Soviet initiatives. At the same time as inter-state disputes were being resolved, however, China suffered an acute domestic political crisis, culminating in the brutal use of military force at Tiananmen Square in June 1989 to suppress a popular movement for democratic reforms and political pluralism. The importance attached to the armed forces in quelling the democratic movement prompted fears that the influence of the military was increasing and that defence spending could rise in the future as a 'payment' for the military's support of the political leadership.[79]

It is not easy to categorize China. In terms of per capita income and levels of development it remains a Third World country; as an actor on the international arena—and in particular in terms of its security policies—it is a major power. China is one of five countries in the world with a strategic nuclear force; it is a permanent member of the United Nations Security Council; it is a major arms exporter, utilizing arms transfers both as a foreign policy tool and as an earner of foreign exchange; it has contributed to the proliferation of ballistic missiles—yet it is the only major power whose military expenditure has consistently declined throughout the decade.

After the publication in 1989 of credible Soviet defence expenditure figures, China is now the only major country in the world which still refuses to allow an inspection of its defence spending. Very little is known from open sources about the absolute level of Chinese military expenditure—the sole source of official information is a single-line entry in the state budget bearing the title 'defence'. There is some evidence that China uses the Soviet method of national accounting,[80] concealing military spending in much the same way as is done in the Soviet budget. The published budget would then include personnel costs and O&M, while procurement and R&D would be left out. The NMP accounts have three broad components: consumption, social consumption and accumulation. Defence spending on food, clothing, fuel, maintenance, and so on, would fall under the first two categories, while expenditure on weapon procurement (including construction) could be listed under the latter. Military R&D may be subsumed under more general research expenditure as part of the science budget.

A recent Western European Union report implied that personnel costs are not included in the defence budget.[81] This runs contrary to what is known of socialist national accounting. Instead, it is highly probable that weapon procurement is hidden in accounts for industry and accumulation of reserves. SIPRI estimates show that actual Chinese military expenditure in 1988 could have exceeded 40 billion yuan, almost double the official figure, amounting to around 4 per cent of national output and 15 per cent of central Government expenditure.

Official defence expenditure for China in 1989 was 24.55 billion yuan, up from 21.8 billion yuan in 1988.[82] In nominal terms this was a rise of 12.6 per

---

[79] 'Tiananmen 1989: a symposium', *Problems of Communism*, Sep.–Oct. 1989.

[80] Crane (note 77).

[81] *Western European Security: Defence Implications of the People's Republic of China's Evolving Geopolitical Situation*, Report of the Assembly of the Western European Union, 6 Nov. 1989 (Western European Union: Paris, 1989).

[82] *Asian Security 1989–1990* (Brassey's: London, 1989).

cent; however, after adjustment for estimated high inflation, military expenditure probably fell by 5–6 per cent. The decline maintains the trend for the whole decade.[83] As a share of total Government expenditure, official defence spending has fallen in relative terms, from 10.4 per cent to 8.4 per cent between 1985 and 1989. The reduction has been made possible by a cut in forces by over one million men, postponing some modernization, slowing down plans for an expansion of the Navy, using revenues from arm sales to finance imports of weapon technology which can be adapted to local use, producing their own food, doing contract work—such as in construction—for civilian sectors and launching a major programme of industrial conversion using spare capacity of the defence industrial base to produce civilian goods which can be sold for profit.[84]

For the Third World as a whole (including China), although military spending has declined in absolute terms, the fall has been relatively modest and its share in government expenditure still remains high. Development failures may have served to reduce military spending, but it is not clear whether national priorities have changed substantially. The President of the World Bank, Barber Conable, mixed hope with caution when he said in 1989:

While there is much variation among developing countries, as a group low-income countries allocate around 20 per cent of central government budgets to defense. In the mid-1980s military spending in developing countries exceeded spending on health and education combined. While many components of national budgets have been cut, the $200 billion which the developing world spends annually on the military has largely been protected. In evaluating their military expenditure, governments should be realistic, but they should also remember the human consequences of these choices.[85]

VIII. Conclusions

After the dizzy heights of the 1980s, global defence spending began to fall in 1989. The decline was modest, however, slightly less than 2 per cent compared to the figure for 1988, and largely the result of systemic factors—technological sophistication, budget constraints and increases in the unit cost of new generation weaponry. Neither the political will to pursue reductions beyond this level nor the reward in the form of a 'disarmament dividend' or 'peace prize' are forthcoming. Only if the major military alliances and powers seize the opportunity presented by the events of 1989 to demilitarize their foreign policies will military expenditure decline significantly.

[83] 'The Chinese economy in 1988 and 1989: reforms on hold, economic problems mount: a report by the CIA presented to the Subcommittee on Technology and National Security of the Joint Economic Committee, July 7, 1989' (unpublished mimeo).

[84] Klintworth, G., *China's Modernization: The Strategic Implications for the Asian–Pacific Region* (Australian Government Publishing Service: Canberra, 1989).

[85] Address by B. Conable on 26 Sep. 1989 at the World Bank meeting in Washington, quoted in *Defense and Economy World Report*, issue 1153 (13 Dec. 1989), p. 6535.

Appendix 5A. Tables of world military expenditure, 1980–89

SAADET DEGER and SOMNATH SEN, assisted by Carl-Gustaf Lagergren, Phitsamone Ljungqvist-Souvannavong and Fredrik Wetterqvist

Sources and methods are explained in appendix 5B.

Table 5A.1. World military expenditure, in current price figures

Figures are in local currency, current prices.

		1980	1981	1982	1983	1984	1985	1986	1987	1988	1989
NATO											
North America											
Canada	m. dollars	5 499	6 289	7 655	8 562	9 519	10 187	10 811	11 529	12 180	12 542
USA	m. dollars	143 981	169 888	196 390	218 084	238 136	263 900	282 868	289 391	294 901	302 294
Europe											
Belgium	m. francs	115 754	125 689	132 127	136 615	139 113	144 183	152 079	155 422	150 647	155 164
Denmark	m. kroner	9 117	10 301	11 669	12 574	13 045	13 343	13 333	14 647	15 620	15 813
France	m. francs	111 672	129 708	148 021	165 029	176 638	186 715	197 080	209 525	215 073	223 868
FR Germany	m. D. marks	48 518	52 193	54 234	56 496	57 274	58 649	60 130	61 354	61 638	63 269
Greece	m. drachmas	96 975	142 865	176 270	193 340	271 922	321 981	338 465	393 052	479 236	521 209
Italy	b. lire	8 203	9 868	12 294	14 400	16 433	18 584	20 071	23 788	26 590	28 653
Luxembourg	m. francs	1 534	1 715	1 893	2 104	2 234	2 265	2 390	2 730	3 163	3 142
Netherlands	m. guilders	10 476	11 296	11 921	12 149	12 762	12 901	13 110	13 254	13 300	13 583
Norway	m. kroner	8 242	9 468	10 956	12 395	12 688	15 446	16 033	18 551	18 865	21 117
Portugal	m. escudos	43 440	51 917	63 817	76 765	92 009	111 375	139 972	159 288	193 864	207 738
Spain	m. pesetas	350 423	400 940	465 695	540 311	594 932	674 883	715 306	852 767	835 353	912 173
Turkey	b. lira	186	313	448	557	803	1 235	1 868	2 477	3 789	6 105
UK	m. pounds	10 923	12 004	14 203	15 605	17 104	18 156	18 581	19 125	19 439	20 803

WTO

Country	Unit										
Bulgaria	m. leva	822	874	989	965	1 093	1 127	1 404	1 547	1 751	1 605
Czechoslovakia	m. korunas	21 269	21 349	22 220	23 332	24 387	25 512	26 435	27 362	28 374	28 193
German DR	m. marks	9 875	10 705	11 315	11 970	12 830	13 041	14 045	15 141	15 654	14 871
Hungary	m. forints	17 700	19 060	20 050	21 900	22 700	37 700	38 800	41 500	49 200	49 200
Poland	b. zlotys	74	85	176	191	251	315	466	576	889	2 154
Romania	m. lei	10 394	10 490	11 340	11 662	11 888	12 113	12 208	11 597	11 552	11 753
USSR	m. roubles	:	:	:	:	:	:	:	:	:	:

Other Europe

Country	Unit										
Albania	m. leks	899	917	912	888	986	1 700	978	1 055	1 080	1 075
Austria	m. schillings	12 423	12 864	14 140	14 845	15 843	17 875	18 768	18 295	17 650	17 905
Finland	m. markkaa	3 612	4 128	5 182	5 656	6 082	6 555	7 245	7 636	8 419	9 192
Ireland	m. pounds	176	203	241	250	263	283	306	298	303	317
Sweden	m. kronor	15 932	17 467	18 500	19 550	21 164	22 762	24 211	25 662	27 215	29 399
Switzerland	m. francs	3 152	3 349	3 727	3 862	4 009	4 576	4 282	4 203	4 458	4 603
Yugoslavia	b. new dinars	76.3	101	118	155	247	465	979	1 985	5 838	14 600

Middle East

Country	Unit										
Bahrain	m. dinars	59.2	80.7	106	62.3	55.6	56.6	60.4	60.3	70.4	70
Cyprus	m. pounds	10.9	17.5	17.9	19.1	19.9	18.5	13.7	16.7	20.4	:
Egypt	m. pounds	:	1 238	1 435	1 801	2 173	2 108	2 493	2 742	2 862	3 462
Iran	b. rials	364	346	341	340	363	455	486	459	505	483
Iraq	m. dinars	990	1 350	2 400	3 200	4 300	4 000	3 600	4 350	4 000	:
Israel	m. new shekels	23.6	53.2	113	309	1 626	4 055	4 936	5 684	6 093	7 373
Jordan	m. dinars	136	160	179	196	197	219	243	253	256	:
Kuwait	m. dinars	257	291	370	416	434	469	430	380	408	438
Lebanon	m. pounds	980	654	1 215	3 554	2 030	2 448	3 740	:	10 640	:
Oman	m. riyals	407	522	581	670	728	745	665	584	519	510
Saudi Arabia	m. riyals	64 076	75 723	87 695	84 311	77 817	71 992	62 418	60 726	55 750	:
Syria	m. pounds	8 884	9 653	10 703	11 309	12 601	13 000	14 440	14 327	16 638	:
United Arab Emirates	m. dirhams	6 330	7 672	7 268	7 042	7 093	7 500	6 900	5 800	5 800	5 376
Yemen Arab Republic	m. rials	1 978	2 016	2 933	3 104	2 585	2 616	2 808	3 124	5 533	:
Yemen PDR	m. dinars	42.6	56.0	57.5	65.8	67.0	65.3	68.8	72	76	:

		1980	1981	1982	1983	1984	1985	1986	1987	1988	1989
South Asia											
Bangladesh	m. taka	2 985	3 210	4 190	5 080	5 325	5 790	7 495	9 080	9 931	11 200
India	m. rupees	38 238	45 371	53 193	61 945	70 834	83 651	105 291	124 965	129 878	131 500
Nepal	m. rupees	242	273	337	430	493	601	866	1 153	1 304	1 565
Pakistan	m. rupees	14 598	17 731	22 637	26 915	30 689	35 110	39 764	43 997	49 991	54 479
Sri Lanka	m. rupees	971	1 051	1 117	1 653	2 194	5 140	7 926	10 103	7 190	7 233
Far East											
Brunei	m. dollars	410	416	480	530	534	617	700	568	: :	: :
Hong Kong	m. dollars	1 353	1 521	1 478	1 537	1 523	1 639	1 530	1 645	1 676	: :
Indonesia	b. new rupiahs	1 708	2 153	2 613	2 858	3 106	2 856	3 089	3 058	3 164	3 378
Japan	b. yen	2 215	2 388	2 532	2 712	2 911	3 118	3 296	3 473	3 655	3 865
Korea, North	m. won	2 750	3 009	3 242	3 530	3 819	3 935	3 976	3 971	3 863	4 060
Korea, South	b. won	2 252	2 831	3 163	3 406	3 573	3 957	4 372	4 915	5 753	6 226
Malaysia	m. ringgits	3 389	4 693	4 975	4 820	4 370	4 320	4 215	6 142	4 160	4 638
Mongolia	m. tugriks	590	630	716	726	764	764	790	837	900	850
Myanmar (Burma)	m. kyats	1 491	1 712	1 643	1 630	1 760	1 973	1 858	1 875	: :	
Philippines	m. pesos	5 829	6 746	7 778	8 530	8 288	7 827	8 662	9 268	10 972	16 447
Singapore	m. dollars	1 259	1 507	1 659	1 640	2 204	2 516	2 403	2 439	2 659	2 920
Taiwan	b. dollars	96.5	117	136	139	138	152	158	164	179	186
Thailand	m. baht	34 625	37 375	41 250	45 875	49 500	52 275	51 825	53 125	54 655	57 176
Oceania											
Australia	m. dollars	3 247	3 767	4 371	4 992	5 601	6 298	6 932	7 305	7 535	7 715
Fiji	m. dollars	4.4	3.6	4.2	4.7	4.5	4.5	4.8	9.1	10.3	11.6
New Zealand	m. dollars	426	549	628	656	724	825	1 017	1 211	1 340	1 404
Africa											
Algeria	m. dinars	3 417	3 481	3 893	4 477	4 631	4 793	5 459	5 805	6 070	6 756
Angola	m. kwanzas	15 060	15 060	15 060	23 295	31 943	34 306	34 572	: :	26 161	23 438
Benin	m. francs	4 700	5 400	7 821	9 500	9 280	10 190	10 610	9 367	11 420	10 405
Botswana	m. pulas	26.9	28.5	25.2	28.2	34.9	41.7	64.5	124	90.1	: :

Country	Unit										
Burkina Faso	m. francs	7 471	9 216	10 800	11 170	11 780	11 810	17 724	15 241	16 003	4 414
Burundi	m. francs	2 500	2 700	3 300	3 200	3 900	4 200	4 780	3 910	3 198	..
Cameroon	m. francs	19 540	21 415	41 015	63 105	73 658	81 920	86 905	83 150	77 889	50 000
Cent. Afric. Rep.	m. francs	2 816	4 029	5 000	6 500	6 500	6 189	5 892	5 610	..	..
Chad	m. francs	..	..	..	15 000	17 496	17 000	16 850	10 307	20 000	23 580
Congo	m. francs	10 050	11 250	16 500	18 600	21 596	25 000	25 625	26 200	20 440	37 193
Côte d'Ivoire	m. francs	26 643	25 000	28 400	29 658	30 706	31 320	33 547	35 336	36 250	37 193
Ethiopia	m. birr	744	760	802	845	897	923	972	1 182	1 407	1 687
Gabon	m. francs	18 600	25 600	29 100	33 000	35 100	42 900	47 100	43 407	40 000	40 680
Ghana	m. cedis	175	488	587	894	1 605	3 432	4 605	6 659	4 603	8 028
Kenya	m. shillings	2 016	2 182	2 662	2 778	2 523	2 395	3 342	3 909	3 945	4 328
Liberia	m. dollars	27.1	51.6	46.9	25.3	25.2	24.4	23.0	25.8	27.4	..
Libya	m. dinars	1 058	1 310	1 330	1 107	1 096	1 096	819	549	582	..
Madagascar	m. francs	19 315	23 500	27 200	29 600	31 730	33 520	39 830	39 200	39 200	..
Malawi	m. kwachas	43.2	36.0	29.0	26.1	26.6	28.6	46.1	47.8	61.6	71.5
Mali	m. francs	8 100	8 600	9 700	10 200	11 100	13 400	13 000	13 300	12 300	23 000
Mauritania	m. ouguiyas	3 700	3 293	2 931	2 639	..	..	..	..	..	..
Mauritius	m. rupees	42.6	47.7	30.8	34.4	36.5	36.1	36.3	38.5	64.9	81.8
Morocco	m. dirhams	4 400	5 047	5 814	4 675	4 960	6 453	6 837	7 190	7 630	..
Mozambique	m. meticais	4 419	5 741	6 900	8 300	10 300	10 300	11 214	29 600	50 400	80 000
Niger	m. francs	3 867	4 286	4 232	4 389	4 775	5 075	5 325	5 175	..	..
Nigeria	m. nairas	1 352	1 319	1 113	1 179	928	976	957	810	1 270	1 034
Rwanda	m. francs	2 027	2 500	2 622	2 693	2 500	2 760	3 050	2 979	2 800	..
Senegal	m. francs	19 870	21 565	23 505	25 110	27 046	28 235	28 490	28 784	29 630	28 476
Sierra Leone	m. leones	14.1	17.5	17.9	18.6	23.3	29.4	64.5	101	125	161
Somalia	m. shillings	601	824	826	1 300	1 786	1 751	2 300	3 800	3 500	..
South Africa	m. rands	2 419	2 615	2 967	3 314	3 922	4 414	5 412	6 717	7 835	9 873
Sudan	m. pounds	132	131	139	212	361	468	562	723	968	1 831
Swaziland	m. emalangeni	10.9	12.0	16.2	16.0	16.1	15.7	15.9	16.8	21.5	24.0
Tanzania	m. shillings	1 688	2 122	2 433	2 651	3 201	4 277	7 073	11 047	16 250	21 574
Togo	m. francs	5 155	6 202	6 138	6 328	7 007	8 632	9 200	13 047	13 047	13 765
Tunisia	m. dinars	78.6	113	284	364	296	357	413	434	460	460
Uganda	m. shillings	29.6	54.1	82.3	144	327	782	1 157	4 805	8 500	..

		1980	1981	1982	1983	1984	1985	1986	1987	1988	1989
Zaire	m. zaires	430	316	873	723	1 928	2 013	2 700	5 000	6 500	14 869
Zambia	m. kwachas	106	154	148	161	148	167	480	637	717	896
Zimbabwe	m. dollars	243	284	296	353	398	436	554	661	720	804
Central America											
Costa Rica	m. colones	265	317	528	928	1 140	1 202	1 426	1 504	1 586	1 660
Cuba	m. pesos	973	1 011	1 109	1 133	1 386	1 335	1 307	1 300	1 350	1 377
Dominican Rep.	m. pesos	99	126	128	129	164	191	202	250	298	346
El Salvador	m. colones	254	322	395	442	534	630	964	885	:	:
Guatemala	m. quetzales	143	161	208	231	270	371	378	495	645	731
Haiti	m. gourdes	100	105	104	102	110	131	138	150	:	:
Honduras	m. lempiras	120	125	160	240	335	445	450	450	:	:
Jamaica	m. dollars	62.0	81.8	98.8	97.8	104	124	125	125	:	:
Mexico	b. pesos	24.7	37.9	47.4	90.3	181	297	470	894	1 470	1 673
Nicaragua	m. cordobas	1	1.3	1.7	3.4	4.9	26.8	91	921	93 827	77 721
Panama	m. balboas	42.2	46.5	55.0	60.0	88.0	92.0	105	105	113	76
Trinidad and Tobago	m. dollars	296	371	563	545	490	465	465	:	:	:
South America											
Argentina	m. australes	1.8	3.9	8.9	31.2	236	1 387	2 727	5 863	28 224	300 000
Bolivia	t. bolivianos	4.8	8.0	19.0	58.0	721	94 677	299 374	327 547	400 300	489 214
Brazil	b. cruzados	0.2	0.3	0.8	1.4	4.7	16	45	131	1 023	7 458
Chile	m. pesos	72 525	94 810	117 831	124 901	182 203	194 877	258 675	277 417	385 145	446 768
Colombia	m. pesos	29 023	35 830	44 661	69 531	91 753	105 092	135 712	176 989	265 484	398 226
Ecuador	m. sucres	5 213	5 848	6 870	8 833	12 086	19 743	25 598	35 442	52 595	83 839
Guyana	m. dollars	98	96	108	142	156	192	276	:	:	:
Paraguay	m. guaranies	7 644	10 581	11 566	11 676	12 826	15 937	20 097	26 885	32 643	57 978
Peru	m. intis	265	515	1 480	2 530	3 875	11 900	23 900	37 000	103 842	800 000
Uruguay	m. new pesos	2 693	4 770	5 168	5 877	7 708	12 831	22 828	36 831	59 962	:
Venezuela	m. bolivares	6 899	8 952	9 905	8 488	9 800	9 457	10 520	15 197	17 585	21 049

Table 5A.2. World military expenditure, in constant price figures

Figures are in US $m., at 1988 prices and exchange-rates.

	1980	1981	1982	1983	1984	1985	1986	1987	1988	1989
NATO										
North America										
Canada	7 230	7 353	8 077	8 534	9 093	9 362	9 535	9 747	9 897	9 928
USA	206 573	220 955	240 616	258 828	270 923	290 026	305 076	300 890	294 901	289 139
Europe										
Belgium	4 614	4 657	4 502	4 323	4 139	4 092	4 261	4 287	4 107	4 116
Denmark	2 235	2 260	2 323	2 342	2 287	2 234	2 153	2 275	2 320	2 245
France	32 222	32 995	33 668	34 252	34 104	34 103	35 118	36 137	36 105	36 410
FR Germany	33 807	34 216	33 786	34 054	33 712	33 796	34 719	35 320	35 097	34 955
Greece	2 841	3 360	3 428	3 128	3 717	3 688	3 152	3 144	3 378	3 286
Italy	14 174	14 269	15 262	15 585	16 057	16 634	16 964	19 199	20 429	20 821
Luxembourg	60	62	63	64	64	63	66	75	86	83
Netherlands	6 510	6 575	6 555	6 497	6 608	6 533	6 633	6 753	6 729	6 811
Norway	2 422	2 447	2 545	2 656	2 558	2 946	2 853	3 037	2 895	3 101
Portugal	1 145	1 142	1 142	1 099	1 021	1 036	1 166	1 213	1 347	1 299
Spain	6 423	6 413	6 518	6 738	6 669	6 952	6 772	7 672	7 171	7 434
Turkey	1 876	2 316	2 528	2 393	2 325	2 467	2 772	2 647	2 664	2 715
UK	31 100	30 549	33 283	34 981	36 511	36 548	36 173	35 713	34 629	34 466
EC	135 656	137 000	141 039	143 541	145 352	146 151	147 669	152 253	151 860	152 388
WTO										
Bulgaria	678	718	810	780	877	800	1 071	1 180	1 337	1 225
Czechoslovakia	3 491	3 473	3 454	3 589	3 716.	3 838	3 962	4 097	4 241	4 207
German DR	4 685	5 068	5 357	5 667	6 075	6 181	6 656	7 176	7 419	7 048

	1980	1981	1982	1983	1984	1985	1986	1987	1988	1989
Hungary	1 551	1 597	1 571	1 599	1 531	2 375	2 321	2 285	2 343	2 006
Poland	4 389	4 117	4 262	3 796	4 332	4 730	5 945	5 863	5 657	5 431
Romania	1 597	1 578	1 458	1 425	1 437	1 470	1 483	1 407	1 402	1 426
USSR	..	..	..	..	..	..	..	..	..	..
Other Europe										
Albania	150	153	152	148	164	283	163	176	180	179
Austria	1 342	1 300	1 355	1 378	1 392	1 521	1 571	1 510	1 429	1 410
Finland	1 467	1 496	1 714	1 726	1 733	1 765	1 895	1 919	2 013	2 054
Ireland	525	502	509	478	463	472	492	465	462	462
Sweden	4 596	4 539	4 380	4 253	4 263	4 268	4 357	4 431	4 442	4 504
Switzerland	2 765	2 761	2 907	2 926	2 949	3 255	3 022	2 926	3 047	3 055
Yugoslavia	2 571	2 431	2 151	2 019	2 080	2 272	2 520	2 314	2 314	..
Middle East										
Bahrain	185	226	273	156	139	145	158	161	187	186
Cyprus	35	50	48	49	48	43	31	37	44	..
Egypt	..	5 392	5 442	5 889	6 070	5 252	5 013	4 607	4 089	4 222
Iran	16 108	12 321	10 230	8 523	8 082	9 705	9 339	7 679	7 353	..
Iraq	12 306	14 007	21 952	28 596	31 590	23 506	16 531	17 073	12 868	..
Israel	6 110	6 887	7 314	8 000	8 420	5 249	4 318	4 134	3 811	3 849
Jordan	490	535	557	581	562	607	673	703	689	..
Kuwait	1 181	1 246	1 470	1 579	1 629	1 733	1 574	1 382	1 463	1 529
Lebanon	102	59	96	262	107	93	97	..	26	..
Oman	691	859	1 016	1 296	1 478	1 517	1 730	1 189	1 350	1 326
Saudi Arabia	16 114	18 557	21 614	20 899	19 513	18 666	16 684	16 384	14 887	..
Syria	3 960	3 635	3 526	3 511	3 582	3 152	2 573	1 601	1 482	..
United Arab Emirates	1 847	2 088	1 955	1 966	2 091	2 211	2 004	1 587	1 580	1 454
Yemen Arab Republic	332	322	456	457	339	323	325	340	566	..
Yemen PDR	197	249	234	241	243	225	224	221	220	..

South Asia										
Bangladesh	219	203	235	261	247	243	283	313	313	311
India	5 547	5 819	6 325	6 582	6 955	7 778	9 006	9 822	9 332	9 030
Nepal	23	23	26	29	33	37	45	54	56	62
Pakistan	1 350	1 466	1 767	1 974	2 122	2 299	2 516	2 658	2 777	2 803
Sri Lanka	71	65	63	82	93	214	306	362	226	205
Far East										
Brunei	263	245	265	290	283	319	356	287	..	..
Hong Kong	313	309	271	256	235	245	223	226	215	..
Indonesia	2 012	2 596	2 505	2 451	2 410	2 116	2 163	1 960	1 877	1 876
Japan	20 099	20 628	21 291	22 400	23 504	24 672	25 924	27 289	28 521	29 350
Korea, North	1 279	1 400	1 508	1 642	1 776	1 830	1 849	1 847	1 797	1 888
Korea, South	4 924	5 103	5 318	5 535	5 675	6 135	6 593	7 195	7 865	8 030
Malaysia	1 689	2 132	2 129	1 990	1 742	1 716	1 664	2 406	1 589	1 725
Mongolia	197	210	239	242	255	255	263	279	300	283
Myanmar (Burma)	461	528	481	452	465	488	421	340	..	..
Philippines	797	815	854	851	550	422	463	478	520	708
Singapore	739	816	866	845	1 107	1 258	1 218	1 230	1 321	1 414
Taiwan	4 460	4 432	5 000	5 043	5 007	5 526	5 704	5 891	6 348	6 346
Thailand	1 886	1 808	1 895	2 031	2 174	2 240	2 182	2 181	2 161	2 160
Oceania										
Australia	4 827	5 070	5 309	5 524	5 934	6 272	5 334	6 166	5 910	5 692
Fiji	5	4	4	4	4	4	4	7	7	8
New Zealand	687	768	756	735	765	754	822	845	879	879
Africa										
Algeria	1 144	1 016	1 066	1 138	1 107	1 036	1 050	1 040	1 026	1 047
Angola	502	502	502	777	1 065	1 144	1 152	..	872	781
Benin	34	29	40	44	41	43	43	35	38	32
Botswana	33	30	24	24	27	30	42	75	50	..
Burkina Faso	36	42	43	41	42	39	60	53	54	..

	1980	1981	1982	1983	1984	1985	1986	1987	1988	1989
Burundi	31	30	34	31	33	34	38	29	23	23
Cameroon	134	133	225	296	311	341	336	303	262	154
Central African Rep.	14	18	20	23	22	19	18	18	..	..
Chad	..	..	..	61	59	54	62	39	67	..
Congo	62	60	78	81	84	91	91	91	69	76
Côte d'Ivoire	135	117	124	122	121	121	121	127	122	123
Ethiopia	488	469	475	496	486	420	490	611	680	780
Gabon	93	117	114	117	118	134	139	129	134	142
Ghana	18	23	23	16	20	39	42	44	23	35
Kenya	251	243	247	231	190	160	214	238	222	222
Liberia	38	67	58	30	30	29	26	28	27	..
Libya	3 596	4 452	4 520	3 762	3 725	3 725	2 784	1 866	1 978	..
Madagascar	53	50	44	40	39	37	39	33	28	..
Malawi	60	44	33	26	22	21	30	25	24	25
Mali	38	39	42	42	44	51	47	47	41	74
Mauritania	95	71	56	50	..	..	..	..	..	..
Mauritius	5.5	5.3	3.1	3.3	3.2	3.0	3.0	3.1	4.8	5.4
Morocco	980	999	1 042	788	744	898	876	896	929	..
Mozambique	59	61	58	55	53	42	36	75	101	126
Niger	17	15	13	14	14	15	16	17	..	..
Nigeria	1 134	914	717	616	347	346	322	248	281	..
Rwanda	38	45	42	40	35	38	43	40	37	..
Senegal	117	120	111	106	103	95	90	95	100	..
Sierra Leone	24	24	19	12	8.9	6.4	7.7	4.3	4.0	4.1
Somalia	64	60	49	57	41	29	28	36	21	..
South Africa	3 206	3 003	2 970	2 956	3 137	3 036	3 139	3 355	3 468	3 802
Sudan	242	194	163	191	242	216	208	239	215	272
Swaziland	14	13	15	13	12	9.7	8.8	8.3	9.5	9.5
Tanzania	143	144	127	109	98	97	121	146	164	170
Togo	25	25	22	21	24	30	31	44	44	46
Tunisia	175	231	509	599	449	502	549	538	536	501

Uganda	72	82	83	116	185	190	104	128	80	..
Zaire	62	34	69	32	57	48	44	46	35	53
Zambia	110	140	120	109	84	69	130	121	87	83
Zimbabwe	374	387	364	353	331	334	371	394	400	393
Central America										
Costa Rica	25	21	19	25	27	25	27	24	21	19
Cuba	1 254	1 303	1 429	1 460	1 786	1 721	1 685	1 676	1 740	1 775
Dominican Republic	62	73	69	66	66	56	54	58	49	..
El Salvador	199	219	241	238	258	249	288	212	..	..
Guatemala	134	135	174	184	208	241	180	209	246	258
Haiti	29	28	26	23	23	25	25	31	..	..
Honduras	94	89	105	145	194	249	241	235	..	..
Jamaica	32	38	43	38	32	30	26	25	..	..
Mexico	1 080	1 296	1 015	959	1 161	1 208	1 027	842	647	615
Nicaragua	265	279	292	445	473	810	352	352	348	..
Panama	50	51	58	62	90	93	106	105	113	76
Trinidad and Tobago	177	194	264	222	176	155	144	..	..	..
South America										
Argentina	5 414	5 711	4 927	3 897	4 056	3 087	3 194	2 966	3 225	3 000
Bolivia	170	243	238	202	182	201	169	162	170	..
Brazil	4 609	3 362	4 532	3 276	3 703	3 857	4 428	3 908	3 899	3 691
Chile	1 276	1 394	1 574	1 313	1 597	1 307	1 451	1 299	1 572	1 568
Colombia	499	484	483	629	715	660	716	758	887	1 053
Ecuador	147	142	143	124	129	165	174	186	174	158
Guyana	47	37	34	40	35	37	50	..	..	..
Paraguay	57	69	71	63	58	57	55	60	59	59
Peru	422	492	785	671	487	568	641	534	806	6 21
Uruguay	223	294	268	205	173	167	169	166	167	..
Venezuela	1 489	1 663	1 678	1 354	1 392	1 207	1 204	1 357	1 213	7 52

Table 5A.3. World military expenditure as a percentage of gross domestic product

	1979	1980	1981	1982	1983	1984	1985	1986	1987	1988
NATO										
North America										
Canada	1.7	1.8	1.8	2.0	2.1	2.1	2.1	2.1	2.1	2.0
USA	5.0	5.4	5.7	6.3	6.5	6.4	6.6	6.7	6.4	6.1
Europe										
Belgium	3.3	3.3	3.4	3.3	3.2	3.1	3.0	3.0	2.9	2.7
Denmark	2.3	2.4	2.5	2.5	2.5	2.3	2.2	2.0	2.1	2.2
France	3.9	4.0	4.1	4.1	4.1	4.0	4.0	3.9	4.0	3.8
FR Germany	3.3	3.3	3.4	3.4	3.4	3.3	3.2	3.1	3.1	2.9
Greece	6.3	5.7	7.0	6.8	6.3	7.1	7.0	6.2	6.3	6.4
Italy	2.4	2.1	2.1	2.3	2.3	2.3	2.3	2.2	2.4	2.5
Luxembourg	0.9	1.0	1.1	1.0	1.1	1.0	0.9	0.9	1.1	1.1
Netherlands	3.2	3.1	3.2	3.2	3.2	3.2	3.1	3.1	3.1	3.0
Norway	3.1	2.9	2.9	3.0	3.1	2.8	3.1	3.1	3.3	3.2
Portugal	3.5	3.5	3.5	3.5	3.3	3.3	3.1	3.2	3.1	3.2
Spain	2.1	2.3	2.4	2.4	2.4	2.4	2.4	2.2	2.4	2.1
Turkey	4.3	4.3	4.9	5.2	4.8	4.4	4.5	4.8	4.2	3.8
UK	4.4	4.7	4.7	5.1	5.1	5.3	5.1	4.9	4.6	4.3
WTO										
Bulgaria	3.1	3.0	3.0	3.3	3.1	3.3	3.4	4.0	4.2	4.4
Czechoslovakia	3.2	3.1	3.1	3.1	3.2	3.3	3.3	3.4	3.4	3.4
German DR	4.1	4.2	4.4	4.5	4.5	4.7	4.6	4.8	5.0	5.0
Hungary	2.4	2.5	2.4	2.4	2.4	2.3	3.6	3.6	3.4	3.5
Poland	2.9	3.0	3.1	3.2	2.8	2.9	3.0	3.6	3.4	3.0
Romania	2.0	1.7	1.6	1.5	1.5	1.4	1.4	1.3	1.2	1.2
USSR	:	:	:	:	:	:	:	:	:	:

Other Europe

Austria	1.3	1.2	1.2	1.2	1.2	1.2	1.3	1.3	1.2	1.1
Finland	1.8	1.9	1.9	2.1	2.1	2.0	1.9	2.0	1.9	1.9
Ireland	1.8	1.9	1.8	1.7	1.6	1.6	1.6	1.6	1.5	1.4
Sweden	3.1	3.0	3.0	2.9	2.8	2.7	2.6	2.6	2.6	2.5
Switzerland	1.9	1.9	1.8	1.9	1.9	1.9	2.0	1.8	1.7	1.7
Yugoslavia	4.7	4.9	4.6	4.0	3.8	3.7	3.9	3.9	3.6	3.6

Middle East

Bahrain	5.3	4.8	5.9	7.5	4.3	3.8	4.2	5.1	5.3	5.0
Cyprus	2.0	1.4	2.0	1.7	1.7	1.5	1.2	0.9	0.9	1.0
Egypt	2.9	:	6.5	6.3	6.7	6.9	5.8	6.1	6.2	:
Iran	6.3	5.4	4.3	3.4	2.6	2.5	3.0	:	:	:
Iraq	6.9	6.3	12.3	19.0	24.4	29.1	27.5	:	:	:
Israel	26.1	25.0	23.5	19.0	20.2	21.4	14.4	11.3	10.2	9.1
Jordan	17.7	13.8	13.7	13.5	13.8	13.1	13.6	14.8	15.0	15.0
Kuwait	3.3	3.5	4.4	6.0	6.8	6.8	7.9	8.6	7.0	7.3
Lebanon	4.1	4.1	2.4	4.3	12.0	:	:	:	:	:
Oman	20.9	19.7	21.0	22.2	24.5	23.9	21.6	23.8	17.6	:
Saudi Arabia	21.1	16.6	14.5	21.1	20.3	20.9	22.0	22.4	22.7	:
Syria	16.0	17.3	14.7	15.6	15.4	16.7	15.6	14.4	11.3	:
United Arab Emirates	5.5	5.8	6.3	6.5	6.8	7.0	7.6	8.7	6.7	6.6
Yemen Arab Republic	20.9	15.0	12.6	14.7	14.2	10.4	8.4	7.3	7.2	:
Yemen PDR	17.5	17.8	19.7	18.7	19.1	17.7	16.7	:	:	:

South Asia

Bangladesh	1.3	1.4	1.3	1.5	1.6	1.4	1.3	1.5	1.6	:
India	3.5	3.0	3.0	3.1	3.1	3.2	3.3	3.7	3.9	3.7
Nepal	1.0	1.0	0.9	1.1	1.2	1.2	1.3	1.6	1.8	2.2
Pakistan	5.6	5.7	5.9	6.6	6.9	6.8	6.8	7.3	7.1	6.9
Sri Lanka	1.5	1.5	1.2	1.1	1.4	1.4	3.2	4.4	5.1	3.2

	1979	1980	1981	1982	1983	1984	1985	1986	1987	1988
Far East										
Brunei	6.1	3.9	4.5	5.3	6.5	6.5	7.7	:	:	:
Hong Kong	0.6	1.0	0.9	0.8	0.7	0.6	0.6	0.5	0.5	0.4
Indonesia	4.1	3.8	3.7	4.2	3.7	3.5	3.0	3.0	2.5	2.3
Japan	0.9	0.9	0.9	0.9	1.0	1.0	1.0	1.0	1.0	1.0
Korea, North	10.4	10.7	11.5	11.8	12.3	12.0	:	:	9.5	8.7
Korea, South	5.1	5.9	6.0	5.8	5.3	4.9	4.9	4.7	4.5	4.6
Malaysia	5.5	6.4	8.1	7.9	6.9	5.5	5.6	5.9	6.1	6.3
Mongolia	:	:	:	:	:	:	11.2	11.0	11.3	11.7
Myanmar (Burma)	3.8	3.9	4.1	3.6	3.3	3.3	3.6	3.2	:	:
Philippines	2.4	2.2	2.2	2.3	2.2	1.5	1.3	1.4	1.3	1.3
Singapore	5.0	5.0	5.1	5.1	4.5	5.5	6.5	6.3	5.8	5.5
Taiwan	6.8	6.6	6.7	7.3	6.8	6.1	6.4	5.9	6.3	6.0
Thailand	5.4	5.1	4.8	4.9	5.0	5.0	5.0	4.7	4.3	4.0
Oceania										
Australia	2.4	2.6	2.6	2.7	2.8	2.8	2.8	2.8	2.6	2.4
Fiji	0.4	0.4	0.3	0.4	0.4	0.4	0.3	0.3	0.6	0.7
New Zealand	1.8	1.9	2.1	2.1	2.0	1.9	1.9	2.0	2.0	2.1
Africa										
Algeria	2.1	2.1	1.8	1.9	1.9	1.8	1.7	1.7	1.7	1.5
Angola	14.0	12.8	13.8	11.9	16.5	22.0	28.4	28.4	:	21.5
Benin	1.9	1.9	1.8	1.9	2.2	2.0	2.0	1.9	:	:
Botswana	3.6	3.7	3.7	2.7	2.4	2.4	2.1	2.7	4.2	2.7
Burkina Faso	2.7	2.7	2.8	3.0	2.9	3.0	2.5	3.5	3.0	:
Burundi	2.6	2.9	3.0	3.5	3.1	3.2	3.0	3.4	2.7	2.2
Cameroon	1.5	1.2	1.1	1.7	2.2	2.1	2.2	2.1	2.1	:
Central African Rep.	2.0	1.7	2.1	2.0	2.6	2.3	2.0	1.8	1.7	:
Chad	:	:	:	:	7.0	7.8	5.7	6.0	3.8	:
Congo	3.7	2.8	2.1	2.3	2.3	2.3	2.6	4.0	:	:
Côte d'Ivoire	1.1	1.2	1.1	1.1	1.1	1.1	1.0	1.0	1.2	:

Ethiopia	8.8	8.5	8.4	8.4	8.4	9.0	8.9	8.9	10.6	10.0
Gabon	1.9	2.1	2.4	2.4	2.6	2.3	2.6	4.0	4.3	3.9
Ghana	0.5	0.4	0.7	0.7	0.5	0.6	1.0	0.9	0.9	0.5
Kenya	4.4	3.8	3.6	3.8	3.6	2.9	2.4	2.9	3.0	2.6
Liberia	1.5	2.8	4.8	4.3	2.3	2.4	2.3	2.2	:	:
Libya	14.2	10.0	14.0	15.0	13.0	14.5	15.2	12.7	:	:
Madagascar	2.9	2.8	3.0	2.7	2.4	2.3	2.2	2.2	1.8	:
Malawi	4.2	4.4	3.3	2.4	1.9	1.6	1.5	1.8	1.6	:
Mali	:	2.3	2.3	2.4	2.4	2.4	2.7	2.3	:	:
Mauritania	10.5	9.7	7.6	6.9	5.7	:	:	:	:	:
Mauritius	0.2	0.5	0.4	0.3	0.3	0.2	0.2	0.2	0.2	0.2
Morocco	5.6	6.3	6.6	6.5	4.9	4.7	5.4	5.1	5.0	5.0
Mozambique	:	5.6	7.0	8.0	10.7	12.1	11.7	10.4	:	:
Niger	0.7	0.7	0.7	0.6	0.7	0.7	0.7	0.8	0.8	:
Nigeria	2.5	2.5	2.3	1.8	1.9	1.3	1.2	1.2	0.7	0.9
Rwanda	1.8	1.9	2.0	2.0	1.9	1.6	1.6	1.9	:	:
Senegal	3.3	3.1	2.8	2.8	2.7	2.7	2.5	2.2	2.0	:
Sierra Leone	0.7	1.0	1.0	0.8	0.7	0.7	0.6	1.1	:	:
Somalia	6.8	4.9	4.3	3.4	3.8	2.7	1.8	1.8	1.8	:
South Africa	4.3	3.9	3.7	3.7	3.7	3.7	3.7	3.7	4.0	3.9
Sudan	2.0	2.3	2.0	1.7	2.1	2.9	2.6	2.1	:	:
Swaziland	2.3	2.1	2.2	2.9	2.6	2.3	1.8	1.7	:	:
Tanzania	7.6	4.0	4.3	4.2	3.9	3.8	3.8	4.7	4.7	:
Togo	2.2	2.2	2.4	2.3	2.2	2.3	2.6	2.5	2.6	:
Tunisia	2.2	2.2	2.7	5.9	6.6	4.7	5.2	5.9	5.5	5.3
Uganda	1.3	2.2	3.8	2.7	3.0	5.0	5.9	3.8	3.5	:
Zaire	3.0	2.5	1.3	2.8	1.2	1.9	1.4	1.3	1.5	1.5
Zambia	4.8	3.5	4.4	4.1	3.9	3.0	2.4	3.7	3.2	3.2
Zimbabwe	6.0	7.1	6.4	5.7	5.7	6.2	5.7	6.2	6.5	5.8
Central America										
Costa Rica	0.6	0.6	0.6	0.5	0.7	0.7	0.6	0.6	0.5	0.4
Cuba	10.5	9.9	8.8	9.1	8.8	10.1	9.6	10.2	10.7	11.3

	1979	1980	1981	1982	1983	1984	1985	1986	1987	1988
Dominican Republic	2.0	1.5	1.7	1.6	1.5	1.6	1.4	1.3	1.3	1.1
El Salvador	1.8	2.8	3.7	4.4	4.4	4.6	4.4	4.9	3.8	:
Guatemala	1.7	1.8	1.9	2.3	2.6	2.9	3.3	2.4	2.8	3.2
Haiti	1.4	1.4	1.4	1.3	1.2	1.1	1.2	1.4	:	:
Honduras	2.2	2.4	2.3	2.8	4.0	5.2	6.4	6.0	5.5	:
Jamaica	0.9	1.3	1.6	1.7	1.4	1.1	1.1	0.9	0.8	:
Mexico	0.6	0.6	0.6	0.5	0.5	0.6	0.7	0.6	0.5	:
Nicaragua	3.1	4.4	5.3	6.0	10.3	10.9	23.2	20.9	34.2	:
Panama	1.5	1.2	1.2	1.3	1.4	1.9	1.9	2.0	2.0	2.5
Trinidad and Tobago	1.9	2.0	2.3	2.9	2.9	2.6	2.6	2.7	:	:
South America										
Argentina	6.3	6.4	7.1	6.0	4.6	4.5	3.5	3.7	3.4	3.0
Bolivia	3.6	4.0	5.3	4.5	3.9	3.4	3.4	2.8	2.9	3.1
Brazil	0.9	1.3	1.3	1.6	1.2	1.2	1.1	1.2	1.1	1.1
Chile	7.0	6.7	7.4	9.5	8.0	9.6	7.6	8.0	6.8	7.8
Colombia	1.7	1.8	1.8	1.8	2.3	2.4	2.1	2.0	2.0	2.3
Ecuador	2.0	1.8	1.7	1.7	1.6	1.5	1.8	1.9	2.0	1.7
Guyana	5.1	6.5	6.0	7.5	9.7	9.2	9.8	12.4	:	:
Paraguay	1.3	1.4	1.5	1.6	1.4	1.2	1.1	1.1	1.1	1.0
Peru	3.9	5.3	6.0	8.5	8.1	5.6	6.4	6.6	5.0	2.5
Uruguay	2.4	2.9	3.9	4.0	3.2	2.6	2.4	2.3	2.1	2.1
Venezuela	2.4	2.7	3.1	3.4	2.9	2.4	2.0	2.1	2.1	1.9

Table 5A.1: Military expenditure figures are given in local currency at current prices. Figures for recent years are budget estimates.
Table 5A.2: This series is based on the data given in the local currency series, deflated to 1988 price levels and converted into dollars at 1988 period-average exchange-rates. Local consumer price indices (CPI) are taken as far as possible from *International Financial Statistics* (IFS) (International Monetary Fund: Washington, DC). For the most recent year, the CPI is an estimate based on the first 6–10 months of the year. For a few countries, where CPI is not available, current prices are used. Period-average exchange-rates are taken as far as possible from the IFS. For WTO countries, purchasing power parities (PPP) are used.
Table 5A.3: The share of gross domestic product (GDP) is calculated in local currency. GDP data are taken as far as possible from the IFS. For some socialist economies, gross national product (GNP) or net material product (NMP) is used.

Appendix 5B. Sources and methods

I. Methods and definitions

Since the publication of the first *SIPRI Yearbook* (1968/69), SIPRI has provided annual 10-year time series data on world military expenditure. The main purpose of the data is to provide an easily identifiable measure, over time, of the scale of resources absorbed by the military in various countries. Expenditure data are only indirectly related to military strength, although their change over time can be utilized to measure the perception of governments towards military capability.

In recent years, the information available on world military expenditure has increased in quantitative terms while there has been a decline in the quality of information provided. Compared to the past there are now many more sources. At the same time, however, the reliability of the available data has gone down. In addition to the primary sources of national budgets and documents published by international organizations, the military expenditure project also studies over 50 specialist journals, annual reference volumes and newspapers.

The NATO definition of military expenditure is utilized as a guide-line. Where possible, the following items are included: all current and capital expenditure on the armed forces, in the running of defence departments and other government agencies engaged in defence projects as well as space projects; the cost of paramilitary forces and police when judged to be trained and equipped for military operations; military R&D, tests and evaluation costs; and costs of retirement pensions of service personnel, including pensions of civilian employees. Military aid is included in the expenditure of the donor countries. Excluded are items on civil defence, interest on war debts and veteran's payments. Calendar year figures are calculated from fiscal year data where necessary, on the assumption that expenditure takes place evenly throughout the year.

Three changes are made in the tables on military expenditure in this *Yearbook*. First, the constant price series is now expressed in 1988 prices and exchange-rates. Second, the system of using brackets, to distinguish between uncertain and other data, has been dropped. Given the contradiction of increase in quantity and decrease in quality of data sources, this distinction can no longer be justified. It must be emphasised that all military expenditure data for recent years are estimates with some degree of uncertainty. This applies in particular to data for Eastern Europe which, in light of recent changes, are currently being completely revised. The present data should be considered provisional.[1] Third, the ratio of military expenditure as a share of GDP for the latest year (here, 1989) is no longer provided. Estimates of very recent GDP data are increasingly unreliable or not available (particularly for high inflationary countries).

It should be stressed that even though SIPRI provides military expenditure in constant prices, it does not encourage close comparison between individual countries. Priority is given to the choice of providing a uniform definition *over time for each country* to show a correct time trend, rather than to adjusting the figures for single years according to the common definition. In addition, the recent phenomenon of violently fluctuating exchange-rates (and their lack of correlation

---

[1] In this context it should be noted that SIPRI is currently producing a detailed research report on the methodology and quality of all its data, which will contain much more information than is possible in the *Yearbook*. This is expected to be a major benefit to researchers who wish to do country

to inflationary differentials) makes common dollar figures more difficult to compare. In the absence of explicit military prices, obeying purchasing power parity, the present system must therefore be kept.[2]

II. Main sources of military expenditure data

Estimates of military expenditure are made on the basis of national sources, including budgets, White Papers and statistical documents published by the government or the central bank of the country concerned. The reference publications listed below are also used. Journals and newspapers are consulted for the most recent figures.

NATO

Financial and Economic Data Relating to NATO Defence, annual press release (NATO: Brussels)

Non-Soviet WTO

Alton, T. P., Lazaricik, G., Bass, E. M. and Badach, K., 'East European defense expenditures, 1965–1982', *East European Economies: Slow Growth in the 1980s,* vol. 2: *Economic Performance and Policy*, selected papers submitted to the Joint Economic Committee, US Congress (US Government Printing Office: Washington, DC, 1985)

Annual reference publications

Government Finance Statistics Yearbook (International Monetary Fund: Washington, DC)
Statistical Yearbook (United Nations: New York)
Statistical Yearbook for Asia and the Pacific (United Nations: Bangkok)
Statistik des Auslandes (Federal Statistical Office: Wiesbaden)
Europa Yearbook (Europa Publications: London)

---

and regional studies based on military expenditure data. The report will be available at the end of 1990, and readers are requested to write to SIPRI to acquire a copy.

[2] For an earlier discussion of methodology, see SIPRI, *SIPRI Yearbook 1984: World Armaments and Disarmament* (Taylor & Francis: London and Philadelphia, 1984), appendix 3B, pp. 132–36.

6. Debt, financial flows and international security

SOMNATH SEN

I. Introduction: the lost decade

As the 1980s drew to a close it became apparent that for many Third World countries, particularly in Africa and Latin America, this was a 'lost decade' in terms of welfare and growth. The post-war period has generally been characterized by sustainable growth of per capita income, disturbed by occasional cyclical fluctuations; even during the oil price rise of the 1970s, Third World countries managed to protect their international economic position, principally through the recycling of petro-dollars. For the first time in

Table 6.1. The Third World external debt, selected regions, 1982–90

Figures are in US $b. (current prices).

Region	1982	1984	1986	1988	1990
Africa	121.4	133.0	171.3	199.8	206.0
Latin America and the Caribbean	331.2	358.2	383.6	402.7	417.5
Total debt	**826.6**	**918.3**	**1 086.7**	**1 197.2**	**1 246.3**
Total debt-service payments	**135.8**	**136.1**	**144.8**	**170.0**	**175.8**

Source: International Monetary Fund, *World Economic Outlook*, Oct. 1989.

around 40 years, however, long-term per capita growth rates have turned negative for many developing countries, implying a rapid decline in the standard of living of the majority of their populations. As a tragic irony, this occurred at a time when most industrialized countries experienced some expansion and some developing economies achieved a relatively high stage of development. A major contributory factor towards this decline has been the debt crisis that has bedevilled the Third World for almost the entire decade of the 1980s (see table 6.1). The security implications of this international debt problem have become increasingly crucial.

In terms of international strategic relations, the end of the decade shows a remarkable and positive transformation. Peaceful solutions are being found to old conflicts, particularly in Europe, and the two superpowers have embarked on the path of *détente*. It is tempting to believe that global security will continue to improve and that conflicting issues increasingly will be resolved by peaceful negotiations. Yet if the socio-economic status of the world's poor continues to deteriorate in the next decade, the prospects for true peace are not good. The non-military dimensions of security will become increasingly important. If food, development and environment needs continue not to be met, a different form of conflict will emerge. If the

Table 6.2. Third World per capita growth of GDP, selected regions, 1981–88

Figures are percentages.[a]

Region	1981–86	1987	1988	Decline (1981–88)
Sub-Saharan Africa	– 2.6	– 4.5	– 0.4	– 16.3
Latin America and the Caribbean	– 0.7	– 0.6	– 0.6	– 4.7
East Asia	+ 6.7	+ 7.0	+ 7.9	+ 59.4
Highly indebted countries	– 1.2	– 0.6	– 0.6	– 7.1

[a] (–) decline in per capita income; (+) increase in per capita income.

Source: The World Bank Annual Report 1989 (World Bank: Washington, DC, 1989); author's calculations.

trends established in this decade are allowed to continue, there is reason to be more cautious when speaking about the future of peace.

The President of the World Bank, Barber Conable, said in 1988: 'The stubborn fact of the Eighties is that growth has been inadequate, poverty is still on the rise and the environment poorly protected. Unchanged, these realities would deny our children a peaceful, decent and livable world'.[1] The facts bear out this gloomy prognosis. Throughout the 1980s the two regions of sub-Saharan Africa as well as Latin America and the Caribbean experienced a negative growth rate in their per capita gross domestic product (GDP). The level of *real* (after adjusting for inflation) income per head in 1988 for sub-Saharan Africa was 17 per cent less than in 1981. The corresponding figure for Latin America (and the Caribbean) was around 5 per cent; and for the highly indebted countries, over 7 per cent. By contrast, in East Asia the income per head rose by around 60 per cent during the same period.[2] The last column of table 6.2 shows the approximate decline of per capita income of various regional groupings of countries.

There are many reasons why the global economic crisis has had such a heavy impact on Third World economies. The most catastrophic element has been the debt crisis, which has affected many developing countries throughout the decade. Table 6.3 presents statistics for long-term debt. Of particular interest here is the negative transfer of resources. Owing to accumulated debt, the Third World countries as a whole are now paying back to the First World in excess of $50 billion more than they receive in new money. To put it bluntly, the poor are subsidizing the rich.

By the late 1970s the international financial system had at its disposal large amounts of surplus funds from the oil-producing countries which it lent at low rates of interest. In 1981 the incoming Reagan Administration decided on the largest peacetime military expenditure programme in the history of the USA. This huge increase in government expenditure was financed by borrowing on the international money market rather than through taxation or money creation. This led to a rapid rise in interest rates

[1] Quoted in United Nations Children's Fund, *The State Of The World's Children 1989* (Oxford University Press: Oxford, 1989).
[2] For details see *The World Bank Annual Report 1989* (World Bank: Washington, DC, 1989).

Table 6.3. Third World long-term debt, financial flows, official development assistance and arms imports, 1984–88[a]

Figures are in US $b.

Year	Total debt	Debt service	Principal	Interest	Net transfer	ODA[b]	Arms imports
1984	686.7	101.8	48.6	53.2	– 10.2	28.7	41.9
1986	893.9	116.4	61.5	54.9	– 28.7	36.7	32.6
1988	993.2	142.4	75.4	67.0	– 50.1	48.1	30.8

[a] Debt-service is expressed in total and as principal and interest. Net transfer is the remainder of new loans minus debt-service.

[b] Official development assistance from Western countries.

Source: The World Bank Annual Report 1989 (World Bank: Washington, DC, 1989); US Arms Control and Disarmament Agency, *World Military Expenditures and Arms Transfers 1988* (US Government Printing Office: Washington, DC, 1989); OECD, *Development Co-operation in the 1990s* (Organization for Economic Co-operation and Development: Paris, 1989); authors' estimates.

and an over-valuation of the dollar. World interest rates rose in response, and the burden of debt-servicing for the Third World increased dramatically.

Since 1982, when Mexico failed to meet its debt-servicing obligation,[3] the debt crisis has passed through three phases. The first phase focused on the possibility that a major debtor country would default or refuse to pay interest or capital. The second phase was associated with the fear that individual banks were vulnerable to non-payment of debt obligations. Both of these risks were averted by schemes which protected the international money system.

The third phase has now begun and will be characterized by very heavy damage to the economy of the debtors. These countries face major social, political and economic difficulties as they struggle to service their debts.[4] The central problem is how to earn enough foreign exchange to pay the interests that have accrued. The cost of interest payment in the 1980s has been *over five times* that of the 1970s.[5] In their scramble to increase exports, debtors have diverted their national output from domestic consumption and investment. Consumer goods and food have been sold abroad, poverty alleviation programmes have been stopped, investment has declined, capital stock is ageing, and growth has fallen.[6]

[3] The origins of the debt crisis are discussed in Nunnenkamp, P., *The International Debt Crisis of the Third World: Causes and Consequences* (Wheatsheaf Books: Brighton, E. Sussex, 1986).

[4] As table 6.3 shows, interest payment is around 50 per cent of total debt-servicing.

[5] See Deger, S., 'World military expenditure', SIPRI, *SIPRI Yearbook 1989: World Armaments and Disarmament* (Oxford University Press: Oxford, 1989), p. 177, note 103. See also Congdon, T., *The Debt Threat* (Basil Blackwell: Oxford, 1988).

[6] The Latin American debt problem and its implications for the domestic economies are discussed in Griffith-Jones, S. and Sunkel, O., *Debt and Development Crises in Latin America: The End of an Illusion* (Clarendon Press: Oxford, 1986). Recent economic problems of nine Latin American countries are discussed in *Economic Panorama of Latin America 1988* (Economic Commission for Latin America and the Caribbean: Santiago de Chile, 1988). The security implications of debt in Latin America are explored in the US Congressional Report, *Economic Development in Latin America and the Debt Problem*, Selected Essays prepared for the Joint Economic Committee, United States Congress (US Government Printing Office: Washington, DC, 1987); see in particular Mayio, A.,

In spite of the economic concepts which are used to describe and solve the debt problem, the essential elements of a solution must lie in political factors. Until and unless the political will is present, whereby the main economic powers accept the need for a permanent solution without destroying the debtors, there will be little chance of resolution of this issue. As Professor Rudiger Dornbusch puts it, 'solving debt problems is mostly politics, not economics'.[7] The first formal recognition of this was offered in 1989 by the US Government. The so-called Brady Plan (after US Treasury Secretary Nicholas Brady) marks the first acceptance of debt forgiveness as an important option for selected Third World countries.[8] The United States has thereby acknowledged that situations exist in which borrowing countries may be unable to complete repayments of massive debts. In addition, the Brady Plan also points to the crucial importance of political and strategic factors. The three countries for which a solution is being sought, with the powerful backing of the US Government, are Costa Rica, Mexico and the Philippines. Media analysis has clearly focused on the security implications of helping these countries: 'All US efforts have been directed at securing an early agreement—not only because Mexico is the second largest debtor but also because of its geographic position on America's southern border. National security considerations have never been far from the surface'; in similar fashion, 'Costa Rica would not normally be a priority for international banks. That it is third in line for the Brady treatment shows in large part the country's importance in terms of foreign policy, as a close political ally to the United States in Central America'.[9] All three countries are of major strategic importance for US defence and foreign policy; hence they need to be helped.

'Economic and political development in South America: the new style military regimes 1964–1985', pp. 275–327; and Vaky, V.P., 'Political change in Latin America: a foreign policy dilemma for the United States', pp. 328–36. There are numerous analyses of the socio-economic crisis in Africa, particularly for sub-Saharan Africa. One of the most perceptive is the report published in 1989 by the UN Economic Commission for Africa, *African Alternative Framework to Structural Adjustment Programmes* (ECA: Addis Abeba, 1989). For a detailed description of the African social and economic problems emanating from external debt, focusing on the role of the World Bank and the IMF, see Onimode, B. (ed.), *The IMF, The World Bank and African Debt*, vol. 1: *The Economic Impact* and vol. 2: *The Social and Political Impact* (Zed Books: London, 1989).

[7] Dornbusch, R., *Dollars, Debts and Deficits* (MIT Press: Cambridge, Mass., 1986).

[8] For details and analysis of the Brady Plan, see *Financial Times*, 11–12 Mar. 1989; 'Approaches to debt reduction', *Finance and Development*, vol. 26, no. 3 (Sep. 1989), p. 16; 'Acid test for Brady plan', *Stuttgarter Zeitung*, 25 July 1989; 'IMF/World Bank meetings: bye, bye, Brady', *The Economist*, 30 Sep. 1989 p. 96; Zawadzky, K, 'Changing course in the debt srategy', *Development and Cooperation*, no. 3 (1989), p. 27.

[9] Details on IMF participation in the Brady Plan for the three countries (as well as initial support for Venezuela) are given in Dooley, M. and Watson, C. M., 'Reinvigorating the debt strategy', *Finance and Development*, Sep. 1989, pp. 8–11. The agreement on Mexico is analysed in *Financial Times*, 25 July 1989, p. 3, from which the quotation is taken. The agreement with Costa Rica within the same framework is discussed in *Financial Times*, 30 Oct. 1989, p. 3.

II. Official development assistance and military expenditure of donor countries

There are three distinct causes of the current debt crisis. First, there are domestic issues in Third World countries themselves; these are discussed in section III. Second, the global economic climate in this decade has produced a number of adverse factors which have seriously affected developing countries. The structurally weak economies have been incapable of handling these external shocks, some of which have been severe. Faced with the adverse political and electoral consequences of high inflation at the beginning of the decade, most Western governments—particularly in Europe—cut down aggregate demand and controlled monetary growth. The fall in demand led to a collapse in commodity prices, the main export earner for many poor countries. At the same time, the price of Third World imports from the industrial countries remained stable. Thus the terms of trade—the price of Third World export relative to the price of imports—have fallen rapidly, leading to high borrowing to finance minimum requirements for imported goods, in particular for indispensable machinery.

However, the single most important factor in exacerbating world debt has been governmental budgetary policy in the USA. The financing of defence spending under the Reagan Administration, through excessive reliance on borrowing, has made the USA the largest debtor country in the world.[10] President Bush's first budget, presented in February 1989, estimated the FY 1989 federal budget deficit to be about $160 billion.[11] The aggregate outstanding debt of the Government now exceeds $2000 billion, of which about $300 billion are owed to foreign lenders. In 1989 probably the first significant turn-around occurred in US Government thinking on the budgetary imbalance. Although increases in taxation still remain taboo (and the President has fought a bruising battle with Congress about reducing capital gains tax), ambitious plans have been put forward to reduce significantly military expenditure in the medium term (FY 1992–95).[12]

However, neither the level of US defence spending nor the US budget deficit in itself constitutes the main problem in this regard. The indirect effect of these factors has been more pernicious in that they have created a huge trade deficit, with imports far exceeding exports. This external imbalance can only be financed by international capital flows to the USA, which in turn has deprived other countries of foreign exchange. In 1981 the USA had a current account (export minus import) surplus of about $6.9 billion; in 1987 the *deficit* was of the order of $144 billion.[13] Although the deficit fell somewhat by 1989, the level is forecasted to peak again in 1990.

---

[10] The foreign debt of the United States, the world's largest debtor country, was $533 billion at the end of 1988; see *International Herald Tribune*, 30 June 1988, p. 11.

[11] *Congressional Quarterly*, 11 Feb. 1989, p. 248.

[12] US Defense Secretary Richard Cheney's plans to reduce US military expenditure through force cuts and procurement reductions are discussed in chapter 5.

[13] *World Economic Outlook, October 1989* (International Monetary Fund: Washington, DC, Oct. 1989).

Table 6.4. Current account balance of selected trading countries, 1986–90

Figures are in US $b.

	1986	1987	1988	1989	1990
Japan	85.8	87.0	79.6	72.0	89.7
FR Germany	39.4	45.2	48.6	53.4	56.8
Asian NICs[a]	23.2	30.3	27.8	26.1	25.0
Total of surplus countries	**148.4**	**165.2**	**156.0**	**151.5**	**171.5**
USA	– 133.3	– 143.7	– 126.5	– 125.1	– 138.7
UK	– 0.2	– 4.8	– 26.0	– 30.6	– 26.7
Total of deficit countries	**– 133.1**	**– 148.4**	**– 152.5**	**– 155.7**	**– 165.4**

[a] Newly industrializing countries: Hong Kong, Singapore, South Korea and Taiwan.

Source: International Monetary Fund, *World Economic Outlook*, Oct. 1989

Traditionally, developed countries have had foreign trade surpluses (exports greater than imports) which have been utilized to finance the deficits (imports greater than exports) of developing nations. At earlier stages of development, countries have imported machineries and other investment goods to foster growth; this leads to external deficits which are financed by foreign borrowing. This trend was reversed in the 1980s with the USA (and to a lesser extent the United Kingdom) soaking up the financial capital surplus produced globally. The major trade surplus countries in 1989 are Japan, the Federal Republic of Germany and the four Asian so-called newly industrializing countries (NICs): Hong Kong, Singapore, South Korea and Taiwan. Table 6.4 shows how the trade surplus of these countries is almost exactly absorbed by the USA and the UK combined, leaving little for the rest of the world. In a sense the Third World is being starved of funds owing to the excessive imports (consumption) of these two major powers.

Many of these issues were forcefully reiterated in the Report of the Independent Commission on Financial Flows (known as the Schmidt Commission after its Chairman, former FRG Chancellor Helmut Schmidt) presented in 1989.[14] One innovative element was the strong emphasis on official development assistance (ODA), potentially a major vehicle of help to the Third World that developed countries in both West and East could provide. In particular, ODA can be increased through the 'disarmament dividend', as a conduit to the Third World for some of the resources released through the reductions in military expenditure that are the result of arms control negotiations.

SIPRI has estimated the increase in the value of ODA that could be provided if modest reductions in military expenditure by the major powers were transferred as aid. A 10 per cent reduction in the annual military expenditure of the European Community (EC), the USA and Japan together would permit a doubling of the total volume of assistance currently provided by the West. By reducing its defence spending by as little as 1 per cent, the USA

---

[14] *Facing One World*, Report by an Independent Group on Financial Flows to Developing Countries (Chairman Helmut Schmidt), 1 June 1989.

Table 6.5. Official development assistance as share of GNP and military expenditure, and military expenditure as share of GDP: major donor countries, 1988

Figures are percentages.

Country	ODA/GNP[a]	Milex/GDP[b]	ODA/Milex[c]
Canada	0.49	2.0	23.7
France	0.72	3.8	19.0
FR Germany	0.39	2.9	13.6
Italy	0.39	2.5	15.6
Japan	0.32	1.0	32.0
UK	0.32	4.3	7.6
USA	0.21	6.1	3.4
USSR	0.30	11.5	29.6

[a] Official development assistance as proportion of GNP; OECD figures.
[b] Military expenditure as proportion of GDP.
[c] Official development assistance as proportion of military expenditure.

Source: OECD, *Development Co-operation in the 1990s* (Organization for Economic Co-operation and Development: Paris, 1989); SIPRI data base; author's calculations.

would release sufficient funds to increase its ODA by 29 per cent. A similar 1 per cent reduction and transfer would allow the USSR to raise its development assistance by 39 per cent.

Total ODA for the Western nations and Japan is around $48 billion per year. The share of ODA as a proportion of national product is still quite low for major donor countries and is generally far below the 0.7 per cent set as a target by the United Nations.[15] The figures for France fall substantially—to around 0.5 per cent—if its overseas territory recipients are excluded. For the USA the share is extremely low, even though it is the largest donor by actual size. Japan is set to become the largest donor country by 1990. The data on the ratio of ODA to military expenditure are also revealing (table 6.5). They demonstrate the extent to which major powers, such as the USA, the USSR and the UK, provide very little foreign aid relative to their massive defence spending. Once again, a slight re-allocation of resources would make a substantial contribution to global economic security.

III. Security, development and democracy

In terms of debt-servicing (payment of principal and interest), the Third World now pays back more to the industrialized nations than it receives. As mentioned above, there is now a net transfer of resources from poor to rich countries. Between 1983 and 1987 Latin America paid back about $90 billion more to developed countries than it received. Such negative transfers are unprecedented in the whole history of financial transactions.

[15] In 1988, the latest year for which figures are available, total ODA by Western nations (Australia, Canada, Japan, New Zealand, the USA and Western Europe) was $48.1 billion, amounting to 0.35 per cent of the combined GNP of these countries. See also Wheeler, J., 'The critical role for Official Development Assistance in the 1990s', *Finance and Development*, Sep. 1989, pp. 39–40.

The worst domestic effect of Third World debt comes from the fact that much of it is concentrated in government hands. Unless there is a government bankruptcy, which is not conceivable, the payments on obligations will be made. Thus government expenditure has to be reduced in other fields if debt-servicing is to be maintained. Spending on health, education, infrastructure, economic development, food subsidies, job creation and poverty alleviation is therefore reduced. Since the state is the major provider in these areas in developing countries, the socio-economic effects of such cuts would be devastating. Former President Julius Nyerere of Tanzania puts it starkly: 'Must we starve our children to pay our debts?'[16]

It is often thought that part of the problems of the Third World is self-inflicted. In particular, it is held that high military expenditures constitute a drain on resources, and that savings can be made here to pay for welfare services. This is partly true—some of the high debt burdens are associated with arms imports and government deficits to finance defence spending. In many of the highly indebted countries, such as Argentina, Brazil and the Philippines, new democratic governments are paying the price of the high defence spending of previous military governments.[17]

A major reason for international indebtedness has also been the import of arms, much of which was financed by borrowing during the 1970s. According to the SIPRI arms trade data base, the volume of major weapons transferred to the Third World (excluding China) more than doubled between 1970 and 1980.[18] Using US price indices, the dollar value of arms transferred at current prices would mean a fourfold increase in weapon imports during this period. With both the USA and the USSR striving to earn foreign exchange during this period, a substantial part of this import by the Third World could have been debt-financed.[19] It is difficult to make estimates of the burden of debt arising out of weapon purchases, but it is thought to be significant. Earlier estimates show that around 20 per cent of Third World debt until around 1980 was due to arms imports alone.[20] In 1989 World Bank President Conable estimated that a full one-third of the debt of some major Third World countries can be attributed to arms imports.[21] The profligacy of military governments, which were the rule rather than the exception during the 1970s, has come to haunt today's democratic leaders.

---

[16] Note 1, p. 30.

[17] For a critical evaluation of military spending in Argentina during the military dictatorships of the 1970s, see the World Bank country study *Argentina: Economic Memorandum* (World Bank: Washington, DC, 1985).

[18] See SIPRI, *SIPRI Yearbook 1989: World Armaments and Disarmament* (Oxford University Press: Oxford, 1989), appendix 6A, pp. 226–29.

[19] For an evaluation of Soviet hard currency earnings from arms sales, see Kanet, R. E., 'Soviet and East European arms transfers to the Third World: strategic, political and economic factors', *External Relations of CMEA Countries: Their Significance and Impact in a Global Perspective, NATO Colloquium 1983* (NATO: Brussels, 1983), pp. 171–94. A more theoretical analysis is conducted in Deger, S., 'The economics of Soviet arms trade', ed. R. Cassen, *Soviet Relations in the Third World* (Royal Institute of International Affairs, Sage: London, 1989), pp. 159–76.

[20] The figure is derived in Brzoska, M., 'The military-related debt of Third World countries' *Journal of Peace Research*, vol. 20, no. 3 (1983), pp. 271–77.

[21] *Defense and Economy World Report*, issue 1152 (13 Dec. 1989), p. 6535.

In recent years many Third World countries have made significant progress towards democratization, with constitutional governments elected in free, multi-party elections. In Asia, Pakistan and the Philippines now enjoy civilian governments after years of military rule. In Africa, Nigeria is expected to have a non-military government in 1992. The most dramatic shift towards democratic ideals, however, is in Latin America, where free elections are being held and where non-military governments are now the rule rather than the exception. In Argentina, Brazil and Chile, three of the region's major powers, constitutional governments have been elected in 1989. However, if democracy also implies political participation to achieve social and economic equity, then these new regimes have none the less failed. As the food riots of Venezuela and the attempted military *coup* in the Philippines showed in 1989, the foundations for a stable democracy are still weak. In his inaugural speech in December 1988, President Carlos Salinas de Gortari warned: 'In economic stagnation, democracy would fade'. The debt crisis has been a major cause of instability for these young democracies, which might yet fail to achieve political maturity.[22]

A positive development is that military expenditure has been falling in the Third World since around 1985. As a result of both the resolution of conflicts and economic constraints, governments have sought to reduce the burden of defence. As 1990 approaches, inter-state conflicts are on the decline—as witnessed by the end of the Iraq–Iran War, the Soviet withdrawal from Afghanistan, relative stability in Southern Africa, and *rapprochement* in the Horn of Africa and the Maghreb.

On the other hand, there is now a corresponding growth of sub-nationalism, with the legitimacy of central government and even of the nation-state as such, increasingly called into question: the Palestinian *intifada* on the West Bank and Gaza Strip, anti-apartheid movements conducted by the church in South Africa, narcotic traffickers in Colombia, guerrilla movements in Peru, army revolts in Argentina, lawlessness among Afghan migrants in Pakistan and ethnic violence in Sri Lanka are just a few examples of intra-state conflicts that have been of major concern in 1989 (see also chapter 10).[23] Many of these instances are traceable to developmental failures and the inability of the 'haves' to buy off the 'have-nots'.

Just as military expenditure is a severe drain on resources in poor countries, imaginatively utilized ODA can be of crucial help to the Third World. The ratio of ODA to military expenditure among Third World countries contains wide variations, reflecting both specific security concerns and the political relationship between donors and recipients (see table 6.6). For some countries, such as Costa Rica, where military spending is very low,

---

[22] For a perceptive analysis of the relationship between debt and democracy, see Graham, C. L., 'The Latin American quagmire: beyond debt and democracy', *Brookings Review*, vol. 7, no. 2 (spring 1989), pp. 42–47. The political economy of debt is also emphasized in 'Need to staunch the haemorrage', *Financial Times*, 2 Feb. 1989, from which the quotation is taken.

[23] The growing concern in the United States about the events in Colombia, and the threat to the legitimacy of the state from narcotics dealers, led to military aid being appropriated to an internal security issue. It has been suggested that funds saved from cutting US military expenditure should be diverted towards such forms of security assistance to combat drug-related terrorism.

Table 6.6. Official development assistance as share of GNP and military expenditure, and military expenditure as share of GDP: selected recipient countries, 1986–87

Figures are percentages.

Country	ODA/GNP[a]	Milex/GDP[b]	ODA/Milex[c]
Argentina	0.3	3.4	3.6
Chile	0.05	6.8	1.7
China	0.5	4.0	12.8
Costa Rica	5.7	0.7	632.9
Egypt	4.7	6.2	35.1
El Salvador	10.2	3.8	241.0
India	1.1	3.8	19.2
Israel	6.2	9.0	25.6
Ivory Coast	2.9	1.2	125.0
Mozambique	16.7	10.5	159.0
Nicaragua	2.3	44.1	5.2
Nigeria	0.3	1.0	32.9
Pakistan	2.6	6.8	33.7
Paraguay	1.5	1.1	167.2
Peru	1.2	8.0	13.2
Zaire	10.7	1.3	1 389
Zimbabwe	5.1	6.5	74.1

[a] 1986–87 average official development assistance as proportion of 1986 GNP; OECD figures.

[b] 1987 military expenditure as proportion of GDP; not strictly comparable with the previous column.

[c] 1987 official development assistance as a proportion of military expenditure.

Source: OECD, *Development Co-operation* (Organzation of Economic Co-operation and Development: Paris, 1988); SIPRI data base; author's calculations.

maximum use can be made of ODA. For countries in unstable regional areas, such as Egypt, defence spending is a major drain on resources which ODA cannot hope to replace. The same is true for large countries such as China and India, which receive low levels of assistance compared to their size, yet maintain large military forces to protect regional security interests.

IV. Debt and arms control in the Third World

It is remarkable that in spite of the progress of arms control negotiations in the East–West framework and the usefulness of such a model for stability and security elsewhere, there is no functioning formal arms control mechanism in any Third World conflict situation. The Non-Proliferation Treaty, in the nuclear sphere, is the only modestly successful implementation of arms control that has a Third World dimension (see chapter 16). Other attempts, such as in the spheres of chemical and biological weapons, ballistic missiles and conventional weapons trade, have generally ended in failure. The much heralded Conventional Arms Transfer Talks (CATT) in 1977–78 between the United States and the Soviet Union ended in failure both for systemic reasons (pressure from the arms industry at a time of low domestic procurement budgets in the USA) and because of the cooling of international relations between the superpowers.[24] In 1988 and 1989 there was increasing concern over ballistic missile acquisition by major countries in the Third World (see chapter 9). However, attempted arms transfer controls have so far failed to deter countries which are determined to acquire such arsenals. Few formal attempts have been made to negotiate, codify and establish confidence- and security-building measures (CSBMs) among Third World countries, either bilaterally or in the context of geographical regional security.

There are many reasons why such formal arms control mechanisms have failed.[25] As the 1980s drew to a close, however, it became increasingly clear that arms control and disarmament can only be hastened in the Third World through systemic and structural change. Domestic economic problems will force countries to cut back on their military expenditure and procurement budgets, which would have an immediate impact on arms transfers. The major powers could then act as catalysts to speed up the process by non-interference, promotion of co-operative actions, emphasis on common security and encouragement of transfer of resources from the military to the civilian sectors.

The process is not fundamentally different from that taking place in the USSR. The Soviet Union has found it increasingly difficult to allocate 10–20 per cent (depending on how the aggregate figures are measured) of its national output to defence. Its attempts at unilateral disarmament and at speeding the arms control negotiation process are indicative of a strong desire to relate domestic re-allocation of scarce resources to a co-operative and peaceful framework for inter-state relations. In the case of the Third World, the socio-economic problems are even more acute and the external threats generally less intimidating. Hence, the desire for arms control may be more intense as the economic crisis tends to take priority over the military security crisis.

The debt burden can therefore be used as a window of opportunity through which in particular Third World countries can reduce military expenditure, concomitant arms procurement and transfer, as well as foster an atmosphere of arms control. The combination of high military spending and debt repayment creates an untenable and explosive situation for Third World governments, as they fail to meet the most basic welfare needs of their citizens. For many Third World governments, military expenditure and public external debt-service take an overwhelming proportion of earned revenue (income). As table 6.7 shows, foreign debt repayments and defence for many countries account for 40–80 per cent of current government revenue. This does not take into account private sector debts (sometimes guaranteed by the government), nor does it account for domestic debts,

---

[24] See Husbands, J. L. and Cahn, A. H., 'The Conventional Arms Transfer Talks: an experiment in mutual arms trade restraint', ed. T. Ohlson, SIPRI, *Arms Transfers Limitations and Third World Security* (Oxford University Press: Oxford, 1988), pp. 110–25.

[25] These issues are discussed in Ohlson (note 24).

Table 6.7. Military expenditure and external public debt-service as shares of current government revenue, selected Third World countries, 1987

Figures are in percentages.

Country	External debt-service	Military expenditure	Debt-service plus military expenditure
Argentina	23.6	15.8	39.4
Colombia	50.7	14.5	65.2
Chile	25.6	22.0	47.6
Egypt	11.8	19.6	31.4
Indonesia	35.5	13.9	49.4
Israel	13.1	30.9	44
Jordan	36.2	48.9	85.1
Morocco	30.9	19.5	50.4
Pakistan	20.4	40.1	60.5
Philippines	48.1	15.5	63.6
Sri Lanka	24.2	30.7	54.9
Zimbabwe	23.5	22.5	46

Sources: *World Development Report* (World Bank: Washington, DC, 1989); SIPRI data base; author's calculations.

which for some countries are also very high. The amount of resources remaining for all other forms of government expenditure—health, education, social security, economic services, infrastructure, food subsidies and salaries—is very limited after these two major spending categories are financed. The result is a domestic crisis which erodes legitimacy and condemns the masses to greater poverty.

The debt crisis may force Third World governments to re-evaluate their priorities and seriously consider whether their military expenditures have crossed the limits of reasonable sufficiency. SIPRI data indicate that real or inflation-adjusted total military expenditure has declined steadily from around 1985. If the Iraq–Iran War is excluded from the aggregate, the decline is quite sharp. The SIPRI arms trade register (see appendix 7B) also indicates that the trend indicator value of arms imports by the Third World (excluding China) has also fallen slightly since the peak of the early 1980s.[26] The debt crisis and inadequate financial flows must account at least in part for these signals of arms control. The major military and economic powers can hasten this process by suitable policies which link foreign assistance with progress in arms control in the Third World. At the same time they must be willing to provide more ODA as military spending is reduced following reductions in East–West tensions. The Schmidt Commission made an interesting suggestion that ODA should be increased to countries which have a ceiling of 2 per cent on the share of defence in GDP.[27] Such measures, together with other initiatives such as setting up a disarmament–

[26] See Deger, S., 'Recent patterns of arms trade and regional conflict', paper presented at the 39th Annual Pugwash Conference, Cambridge, Mass., 23–28 July 1989.

[27] The Schmidt Commission report (note 14) recommends that donor nations should give special consideration to countries which spend less than 2 per cent of their GNP on military expenditure.

development fund as suggested in the United Nations, could help promote the demilitarization of the Third World. However, all will be to no avail if development failures, prompted by the debt crisis, increase conflict.

One major problem from a security point of view is that even though total government spending—including defence expenditure—is falling, the share of the military in the total could be rising. Hence, defence expenditure exhibits 'resilience' in the sense that it seems to be protected to some degree—at the expense of other expenditures, such as on welfare—from the ravages of austerity cuts. It should be noted that in countries where the share of defence spending has fallen, the share of internal security spending may be rising, but limited data make it difficult to establish a trend at this stage.

V. Eastern Europe

Eastern Europe experienced remarkable change in 1989 as movements for democratization and political pluralism spread across the region. However, economic problems were also all-pervasive as countries struggled to adjust to the difficulties of restructuring their economies. The debt burden contributed heavily to their problems. The East European debt problem is qualitatively different from that of the Third World. However, many of the issues discussed above have relevance to at least some countries of the region. In particular for Poland and Hungary there exists a close link between security and debt which merits special attention.

The Soviet Union has a large hard currency debt of the order of $41.7 billion in gross terms.[28] Its net debt position is manageable, however, largely due to its export potential to the West of raw materials, in particular oil and natural gas. It also has large reserves of dollar deposits in Western banks; the net value of debt after taking account of such deposits is quite small in relation to the Soviet GNP (about $27.3 billion). In Romania the Ceausescu regime paid off the foreign debt at the cost of extreme domestic recession and hardship, and for this it has since paid the price. As one of its first measures, the new regime reduced exports to satisfy domestic consumption.

Poland and Hungary both have sizeable foreign debts: the ratio of debt to GNP amounts to around 57 and 62 per cent, respectively, for 1988. Particularly in the case of Poland, the burden of debt-servicing is increasing dramatically and has become a major impediment to domestic economic reforms. The aggregate stock of debt now approaches almost 60 per cent of national output; 12 per cent of exports are utilized to service foreign debt alone leaving a diminished amount to finance essential imports of food and machinery required for welfare and growth.[29]

Poland has requested $1.2 billion from the multilateral institutions, the International Monetary Fund (IMF) and World Bank. In addition, it would

[28] Johnson, R., 'Western lending to the Soviet Union', paper presented at the Workshop on US–USSR Commercial Relations, sponsored by the Congressional Research Service for the Senate Foreign Relations Committee, US Senate, Washington, DC, 17 Apr. 1989.

[29] Managing the Transition: Integrating the Reforming Socialist Countries into the World Economy, first year report (Institute for East–West Security Studies: New York, 1989).

like to receive around $1 billion from the Group of Seven countries[30] to maintain its foreign reserves at an adequate level. The latter amount is particularly crucial since there must be confidence in the financial system to prevent a devaluation on the zloty, which would destroy its convertibility and create a financial crisis. IMF conditionality will require a large reduction in the Government's budget deficit. This will predominantly have to come from eliminating subsidies, particularly on food and coal. A substantial rise in food and fuel costs will exacerbate tensions within the country. The possibility of food riots cannot be ruled out. Earlier attempts at reducing subsidies, leading to high prices, led to urban discontent and rioting. The impact on internal security and the fragile democratic process could be substantial.[31]

The amount of foreign assistance and government-backed credit authorized so far by Western countries is quite small. The total amount pledged by the end of 1989 to Eastern Europe (excluding the USSR) is of the order of $4.3 billion. In addition, with the establishment of the European Development Bank at the 1989 EC summit in Strasbourg, it was in principle agreed that the bank immediately be authorized to lend 10 billion European Currency Units (ECUs) (approximately $8.7 billion). Assuming that about $5 billion will be available in the short term from this new financial institution, the total amount of public foreign capital will still be less than $10 billion. Although it seems a large sum, it is small compared to the debt burden that Eastern Europe currently shoulders. The GDR, Hungary and Poland have an accumulated foreign debt of approximately $78 billion. Although no precise figures are available, preliminary estimates indicate that the debt-service of these three countries could amount to $10 billion per annum. In other words, the total new finance pledged by the West could be eaten up simply by one year's debt repayments.

It is instructive to compare this situation with the period immediately following World War II, when massive amounts of foreign capital were used to rejuvenate the economies of Western Europe and to foster stability and peace. Under the Marshall Plan, the USA provided $12.8 billion to Europe between 1948 and 1952.[32] Most of this money was in the form of grants; the credit element was minimal. The recipients had no earlier burden of debt which needed a reverse transfer of funds. There was little need to restructure markets and try to make them more efficient. None of these favourable conditions is present today in Eastern Europe, yet the financial flows received are insignificant compared to the previous era. In 1989 prices the value of Marshall aid would be $67.5 billion.[33] By contrast, the total amount promised to Eastern Europe at the end of 1989 by Western governments is estimated to be around $10 billion. Much of it is long-term loans and its real value is substantially reduced by the demands of debt-servicing.

[30] Canada, France, the FRG, Italy, Japan, the UK and the USA.
[31] Sachs, J. D., 'Democratic Poland can make it if the West weighs in quickly', *International Herald Tribune*, 31 Oct. 1989.
[32] See Huhne, C., 'East European changes are chance for historic bargains', *The Guardian*, 13 Dec. 1989.
[33] Estimate, based on the increase in the US GNP deflator between 1950 and 1989.

It is also worth noting that in November 1989, President Bush signed the appropriations measures which provide aid authorizations by Congress for financial assistance to Hungary and Poland; in FY 1990 a total of only $532.8 million will be distributed.[34]

There is a close connection between debt and military expenditure in Poland as well. As the total stock of debt has risen, as well as its share in output, military expenditure has declined from the mid-1980s. This is in spite of the perceived threat from NATO's 3 per cent growth rate of defence spending affirmed over the decade. With recent political changes, and the first non-communist government in Eastern Europe, the process of demilitarization is set to continue. Yet, as discussed above, true security and stability will not be possible without economic restructuring. This will require foreign assistance, on relatively easy terms, so that austerity does not destroy the fabric of the society. Ralf Dahrendorf has expressed the general sentiment as follows: 'The new democracies need and deserve help in their painful transitions. . . Marshall plan or not, a massive economic recovery programme for Eastern Europe is the only way to prove that we do not respond to Eastern abuses of power with Western selfishness of prosperity (to quote from a plea by Countess Dönhoff and ex-Chancellor Schmidt in the West German weekly *Die Zeit*)'.[35]

VI. Conclusion

Speaking before a joint session of Congress on 15 November 1989, Lech Walesa, leader of the Polish Solidarity independent trade union, said that aid 'is the best investment in the future and in peace, better than tanks, warships and warplanes, an investment leading to greater security'.[36]

Unless the recent trends of economic crisis are reversed, conflicts will continue. Their underlying causes, however, will increasingly be developmental failures rather than political actions. The catalyst will be the difference between actual growth and expected growth, and the inability of debtor governments to meet the aspirations of major sections of their populations. Unless the security implications of the debt crisis are fully understood, and political solutions take precedence over economic technicalities, the recent dawn of peace may be darkened by new clouds of conflict.

---

[34] *Congressional Quarterly*, 18. Nov. 1989, p. 3172.
[35] Dahrendorf, R., 'A revolution to tumble barricades', *The Observer*, 19 Nov. 1989.
[36] Dahrendorf (note 35).

7. The trade in major conventional weapons

IAN ANTHONY and HERBERT WULF

I. The arms trade in 1989

During the 1980s the value of the trade in major conventional weapons fluctuated between roughly $30 billion in 1980 and almost $39 billion in 1987, an exceptional 'peak' year.[1] These statistics are trend indicators of the deliveries of major conventional weapons and not figures which measure what was actually paid for the arms supplied. In contrast to the 1970s, which were characterized by a high growth rate, the overall trend in the 1980s was a shrinking of the value of the global trade in major conventional weapons since 1982. The value for 1989, expressed in 1985 US dollars, decreased once again, to $31 819 million.

A major change in the international arms market—the growing importance of imports by industrialized countries—was also in evidence in 1989. The share of the industrialized countries in the global trade was approximately 33 per cent in 1987, 42 per cent in 1988 and 50 per cent in 1989. In contrast, the share of imports of major conventional weapons by Third World countries, expressed in US dollar values, fell substantially to $16 427 million in 1989—the lowest level since 1976.

The gradual but constant growth of imports of major conventional weapon systems by industrialized countries during the period 1985–89 reflects the rising importance of Japan and—despite the prospects for conventional arms control in Europe—the NATO countries.

The declining importance of the Third World on the global arms market was associated with a number of political and economic factors. The three most important factors were the following:

1. Less hard currency has been available to a number of leading importers, several of whom are highly indebted and cannot spend as much on arms imports as in the past. Ironically one result of the debt crisis has been a reduction in arms imports, and recovery from debt could cause an upswing in the trade in arms unless agreements to provide assistance with debt servicing are conditional on funds not being used for armaments programmes (see also chapter 6). The members of the Organization of Petroleum Exporting Countries (OPEC) have fewer funds at their disposal as a result of declining oil prices.

---

[1] SIPRI reports actual deliveries of major arms (aircraft, armour and artillery, guidance and radar systems, missiles and warships) in 1985 US dollar values; see appendix 7D on the sources and methods for the explanation of what is recorded in SIPRI's statistics. The high volume in 1987 was to a large extent a result of the Iraq–Iran War, as reported in Anthony, I., 'The trade in major conventional weapons', SIPRI, *SIPRI Yearbook 1989: World Armaments and Disarmament* (Oxford University Press: Oxford, 1989), chapter 6.

2. Several 'hot wars' ended—notably that between Iraq and Iran and between South African and Cuban/Angolan forces in Namibia. As a result arms imports by these countries have dropped considerably. In contrast, fighting escalated in Afghanistan after the final withdrawal of Soviet troops on 15 February 1989. The Afghan armed forces received large quantities of weapons from the Soviet Union in 1989. The transfer of arms to countries at war is discussed in section IV.

Table 7.1. The leading exporters of major weapons, 1985–89

The countries are ranked according to 1985–89 aggregate exports. Figures are in US $m., at constant (1985) prices.

Exporters	1985	1986	1987	1988	1989	1985–89
To the Third World						
1. USSR	8 563	10 327	10 759	8 238	8 515	46 402
2. USA	4 024	4 925	6 270	3 649	2 528	21 397
3. France	3 588	3 355	2 518	1 312	1 527	12 299
4. China	1 017	1 193	1 960	1 781	718	6 669
5. UK	903	1 020	1 530	1 165	993	5 610
6. FR Germany	395	649	252	480	149	1 925
7. Italy	578	398	319	360	30	1 685
8. Netherlands	38	132	263	402	572	1 406
9. Brazil	172	134	491	338	182	1 318
10. Israel	160	242	273	117	216	1 008
11. Czechoslovakia	124	124	198	176	287	908
12. Sweden	35	141	298	240	134	847
13. Spain	139	185	160	206	143	833
14. Egypt	124	159	194	232	62	771
15. North Korea	95	48	98	123	–	364
Others	621	528	587	437	371	2 547
Total	**20 576**	**23 560**	**26 170**	**19 256**	**16 427**	**105 989**
To the industrial world						
1. USA	4 776	5 347	6 259	6 856	8 228	31 465
2. USSR	4 233	4 252	3 960	4 226	3 137	19 807
3. France	382	650	379	888	1 205	3 503
4. FR Germany	631	458	422	952	631	3 094
5. UK	797	409	135	132	628	2 101
6. Czechoslovakia	373	373	373	373	259	1 750
7. Sweden	129	183	191	338	189	1 029
8. Canada	99	433	350	49	8	939
9. Poland	92	92	92	92	92	462
10. Italy	68	58	69	78	119	392
11. Switzerland	13	6	15	19	305	357
12. Netherlands	51	109	2	130	58	350
13. Spain	–	8	–	6	262	276
14. China	71	–	–	62	62	194
15. Norway	36	9	43	16	72	176
Others	176	91	378	145	137	932
Total	**11 927**	**12 478**	**12 668**	**14 362**	**15 392**	**66 827**

Table 7.1 *cont.*

Exporters	1985	1986	1987	1988	1989	1985–89
To all countries						
1. USSR	12 796	14 579	14 718	12 464	11 652	66 209
2. USA	8 800	10 272	12 529	10 505	10 755	52 862
3. France	3 970	4 005	2 896	2 199	2 732	15 802
4. UK	1 699	1 429	1 665	1 297	1 620	7 711
5. China	1 088	1 193	1 960	1 842	779	6 862
6. FR Germany	1 025	1 108	674	1 432	780	5 019
7. Czechoslovakia	497	497	570	548	546	2 658
8. Italy	646	456	388	438	149	2 077
9. Sweden	163	324	489	577	323	1 877
10. Netherlands	88	240	265	532	631	1 756
11. Brazil	188	150	507	356	183	1 385
12. Israel	227	250	346	133	228	1 183
13. Spain	139	193	160	212	404	1 109
14. Canada	132	472	387	75	37	1 103
15. Egypt	124	159	194	232	62	771
Others	922	710	1 089	777	938	4 432
Total	**32 504**	**36 037**	**38 837**	**33 619**	**31 819**	**172 816**

Source: SIPRI data base.

3. The expansion of arms industries in a number of Third World countries has meant that a reduction in arms imports by historically large importers—notably Egypt and Israel—does not imply a reduced armaments dynamic in those countries.[2] Other countries are now seeking to develop arms production facilities—notably Iran and Iraq. The development of arms programmes in the Middle East is discussed in section III.

The Soviet Union and the United States continued to dominate the trade in major conventional weapons in 1989, accounting for 37 and 34 per cent, respectively, of the world total (see table 7.1). The overall situation—with France as third largest exporter, followed by the UK, China and the FRG—has not changed significantly from 1988.

China remains the fifth largest exporter of major conventional arms for the period 1985–89, with a total of nearly $7 billion in sales. The growth in Chinese arms exports in the 1980s was closely linked to supplying Iraq and Iran. In 1989, total exports were reduced to half the value for the previous year, and Pakistan and North Korea emerged as the major importers of Chinese arms. China has returned to its pre-1980 export pattern.

For the first time in 20 years the Middle East was not the leading importing region. South Asia (largely because of deliveries to India and Afghanistan) replaced the Middle East as the region with the highest arms imports (see appendix 7A).

---

[2] Ohlson, T. and Brzoska, M., SIPRI, *Arms Production in the Third World* (Taylor & Francis: London, 1986).

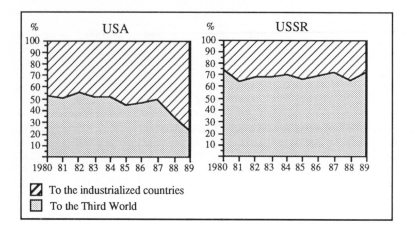

Figure 7.1. Shares of exports of major conventional weapons by the USSR and the USA to the Third World and industrialized countries, 1980–89

II. The major exporters and importers

The major exporters

While the value of total exports of major conventional arms diminished in 1989, several suppliers increased their share of the market—notably France, the United Kingdom and Spain. Soviet exports to the Third World increased (to $8.5 billion), while Soviet exports to industrialized countries fell (to $3.1 billion). For the United States the opposite trend is noticeable, with supplies of major conventional weapons to the Third World falling substantially and the increase in US exports to industrialized countries continuing (see figure 7.1). Several Third World arms exporters that had increased their share of the world arms trade in the 1980s sold fewer weapons for the second consecutive year. In 1989, arms exports of Third World countries were down to one-third of the 1987 sales, amounting to less than 2 per cent of the global trade in arms. This decline was mainly due to reduced deliveries to countries at war, especially to Iraq and Iran.

The Soviet Union

Despite the recent increase in Soviet information on military issues, the assessment of Soviet arms exports remains complicated. Public criticism of arms exports by the Soviet Union did not lead to the abandonment of traditional secrecy surrounding arms exports.[3] SIPRI records are still based almost exclusively on information that becomes public only when arms are delivered.

---

[3] See, for example, the criticism in *Pravda*, 14 Sep. 1989.

According to SIPRI data, the Soviet Union remains the largest exporter of major weapons, despite a small reduction recorded for 1989, supplying $66 billion in 1985–89. In arms exports to Third World countries, the USSR became more dominant in 1989. Although fewer Third World countries imported major conventional weapons from the Soviet Union than from the United States during the period 1985–89 (31 Soviet against 58 US clients), more than half of the value of these weapons is accounted for by the USSR. Traditional Middle Eastern importers of Soviet weapons, especially Iraq and Syria, received only a fraction of their previous Soviet weapon supplies. In other areas, such as North Africa, and in countries such as Angola, Ethiopia and Nicaragua, the Soviet Union also followed a policy of restraint. Three countries—Afghanistan, India and North Korea—accounting for two-thirds of Soviet exports of major conventional arms to the Third World in 1989.

Other Warsaw Treaty Organization countries

Czechoslovakia and Poland, and to a lesser extent Romania and the German Democratic Republic, have been exporters of weapons to the Third World in the past. Information about the export of arms by these countries was normally based on reports from recipients, but this situation is changing.

In Czechoslovakia, the largest non-Soviet WTO exporter, with exports of major conventional arms to the Third World of $908 million from 1985 to 1989, no legal provisions to regulate the arms trade existed during this period. Arms exports were considered a sensitive issue that was not discussed publicly, and decisions were taken in the Council of Defence of the State, an organ which in the previous political system was responsible for operative decisions on military and security affairs.[4]

Polish arms exports to countries outside the WTO have been smaller— major conventional arms exports to the Third World amounted to $135 million in the period 1985–89. Decisions on exports (as well as imports) of weapons and military equipment are taken by a special department of the Ministry of Foreign Economic Relations (CENZIN) and are subject to export licensing.[5] The ministry has served as an agent between the producers of arms in Poland and foreign governments. Arms exports were considered as 'special sales' that also required licences from the Ministry of Foreign Economic Relations.

The Western perception of the German Democratic Republic has never been as a major exporter of arms to the Third World but as a specialized source of technical military assistance. According to official information released in the GDR, arms and technical assistance were in fact supplied

---

[4] Correspondence with the Czechoslovak Ambassador in Sweden, 20 Oct. 1988. For an analysis of the legal regulations of arms exports in the major exporting countries, see Courades Allebeck, A., 'Arms trade regulations', *SIPRI Yearbook 1989* (note 1), chapter 8.

[5] A list of goods and services that require export licences is published in the *Register of Bills of the Polish People's Republic*, no. 21 (7 Apr. 1989), item no. 114. This information is given in Zukrowska, K., 'Organisation of Polish arms trade', manuscript supplied to SIPRI in Oct. 1989. As one of the examples of criticism of Polish exports, see Karkoszka, A., 'Socialist weapons trade', *Polityka* (export–import supplement), no. 26 (Dec. 1989).

mainly to Cuba, Ethiopia, India, Iraq, Kampuchea and Viet Nam as well as to 'certain other countries'.[6] Iraq was supplied with trucks, and radar installations were serviced and repaired by technicians from the GDR. Two major contracts were agreed in 1989 for the supply of refurbished MiG-21 fighters to Iran and 200 T-55 tanks to Ethiopia, of which 152 were delivered when the supply was stopped as a result of the political upheavals in the GDR in November and December 1989.[7] According to the Deputy Minister for Foreign Trade, Hans-Ulrich Metzler, and Major-General Joachim Goldbach, Deputy Minister for National Defence, the Nationale Volksarmee was requested to supply a list of weapons and military equipment that could be withdrawn and refurbished for exports.[8] It is plausible that these weapons were part of the equipment unilaterally withdrawn by the GDR and other WTO countries to promote the disarmament process in Europe. If the transfer of weapons withdrawn from the armed forces in Europe to Third World countries becomes standard practice this would be a high price to pay for disarmament in Europe.

Part of the problem for the non-Soviet WTO countries is economic. The demand for new weapons will shrink in these countries as a result of limits imposed by arms control agreements. If arms could be sold to the Third World, some of the over-capacities created in industrial facilities may be offset (see chapter 8 for a detailed analysis). This is not likely unless the overall decline in the demand for arms is reversed. If deployed weapons which have been withdrawn from the armed forces have to be destroyed or converted for civilian uses, costs will be incurred. One way to reduce this economic burden would be to sell or even give away the arms withdrawn from the armed forces to friendly Third World governments. To prevent this development provisions for the destruction of arms withdrawn should be made in a Conventional Armed Forces in Europe (CFE) agreement.

The United States

The value of US exports of major conventional weapon systems increased slightly from 1988 to 1989. The main importer of US major conventional arms in 1989 was Japan (buying as much as 30 per cent of all US arms exports). Other allies—Australia, FR Germany, Greece, the Netherlands, Spain and Turkey—were also important customers.

The value of US exports to the Third World decreased and although as many as 58 Third World countries were recipients of US major conventional arms between 1985 and 1989 a small group of countries dominate US exports to the Third World. In 1989 five countries—Brazil, South Korea, Pakistan, Taiwan and Thailand—accounted for over 70 per cent of US major conventional arms exports to the Third World. However, deliveries to

---

[6] See interview on 14 Dec. 1989 with the Deputy Minister for Foreign Trade, Hans-Ulrich Metzler, and interview on 22 Dec. 1989 with Major-General Joachim Goldbach, both reprinted in *Horizont*, no. 1 (1990), p. 31.

[7] Earlier Western sources reported the export of 50 tanks; *Frankfurter Allgemeine Zeitung*, 24 June 1989.

[8] Interview in *Horizont* (note 6).

traditional clients—notably Egypt, Israel and Saudi Arabia—were considerably reduced. The reduced exports to countries in the Middle East reflect constraining legislative measures rooted in congressional concern over the security implications for Israel of arms transfers to certain Arab countries.[9]

France

After a period of reduced exports, French arms sales increased in 1989 by almost 25 per cent. These exports—still below the level of 1985 and 1986— occurred in spite of shrinking exports to Iraq. Deliveries of Mirage 2000 fighter aircraft to Greece and the United Arab Emirates took place after protracted disputes concerning costs and payments.[10] It was reported that the French Government vetoed a sale of additional Mirage fighters to Iraq, the most important French Third World customer in the 1980s, because Iraq was not able to pay debts of FFr 25 billion ($3.7 billion) accumulated during the war with Iran. Half of the debt is for military equipment. In September 1989 the two countries agreed on re-scheduling the debt to enable French companies to resume sales.[11] The French Government continued to promote arms sales in order to offset relatively low domestic demand for arms. One parliamentary report emphasized that France depends on exports to lower the price of weapons bought by the French armed forces.[12] The report explained the decrease in French exports partly by noting that French industry receives less government assistance than companies from other countries, especially the United Kingdom. In particular, French companies are not able to assemble 'package deals' for recipients that include offsets, credit guarantees, technology transfers and maintenance agreements. The report requested more government assistance with exports.[13] A more liberal interpretation of French arms export regulations emerged with regard to Libya. The French Government authorized Dassault to return three Mirage fighter aircraft under repair in France in 1986, which had been blocked in 1987 by an Economic Community (EC) Council of Ministers' decision. Libya is also seeking to buy 20 Mirage 2000 fighters.[14]

The United Kingdom

The United Kingdom remained the fourth largest arms exporter in the world in 1989 in spite of efforts by the British Government to boost arms exports. After 1985 the Defence Export Services Organization (DESO) within the Ministry of Defence established a computerized data base using information

[9] Bajusz, W. and Lousher, D., *Arms Sales and the U.S. Economy* (Westview Press: Boulder, Col., 1988), pp. 63–70.

[10] *Jane's Defence Weekly*, 12 Aug. 1989, p. 234; and *Mednews*, 30 Oct. 1989.

[11] See *Jane's Defence Weekly*, 30 Sep. 1989, p. 674; and *Le Monde,* 18 Sep. 1989, p. 13.

[12] Avis présenté au nom de la Commission de la Défense Nationale et des Forces Armées sur le Projet de loi de finances pour 1990, *Assemblée Nationale*, no. 923 (12 Oct. 1989), p. 12. In the report it is pointed out that unemployment in the armaments sector rose by 3.4 per cent in 1987 and 3.6 per cent in 1988, mainly because of reduced exports; see pp. 12–13.

[13] *Assemblée Nationale*, no. 923 (note 12), p. 14.

[14] *Defense & Foreign Affairs Weekly*, 27 Nov.–3 Dec. 1989, pp. 3–4.

from British intelligence sources to compile marketing information for British companies. The finance support division assists customers in raising finance alongside the Export Credit Guarantee Department in the Department of Trade, which provides insurance for British companies against defaults on payments by customers and pays interest rate subsidies to British banks—allowing them to reduce repayment schedules on loans to customers of British companies.[15]

The British Government claims to have had aggregate sales of roughly $50 billion from 1979 to 1988.[16] SIPRI records exports for the same period as roughly $16 billion. Part of the discrepancy is explained by the fact that the SIPRI figure excludes the involvement of British companies as subcontractors on foreign and collaborative programmes. However, it is also the case that the figures used by the DESO are based on the value of contracts signed or even sometimes on the value of Memoranda of Understanding (MOUs), whereas SIPRI figures are based on deliveries.[17] MOUs are not always turned into contracts. When they are, the terms of the contract are not revealed by companies or governments. Even the National Audit Office of the House of Commons was refused access to background information pertaining to contracts involving Jordan, Malaysia and Saudi Arabia.[18] The MOU with Malaysia signed at the end of 1988, said to be worth over $1.5 billion, actually led to contracts worth less than $300 million by the end of 1989.[19] Contracts to sell Tornado fighter aircraft and Hawk jet trainers to Saudi Arabia, signed in 1985 and 1988, involve shipments of 400 000 barrels of oil a day to Shell and British Petroleum. The proceeds of the sale of this oil are then paid to the requisite British companies. However, the declining price of oil has meant that British companies, especially British Aerospace, have received far less money than originally intended.[20] Saudi purchases of helicopters built under licence in the UK by Westland were also included in the 1988 MOU, but no contract was signed by the end of 1989.[21]

While exports to industrialized countries increased in 1989, over 60 per cent of British exports still go to Third World countries, and Saudi Arabia alone received over 20 per cent of British arms exports over the five-year period 1985–89. Arms exports are dominated by sales from British Aerospace, and this company has accounted for 60 per cent of British exports over the same five-year period.

---

[15] For an overview of the structure of British arms exports, see *Ministry of Defence: Support for Defence Exports*, Report by the Comptroller and Auditor General, National Audit Office to the House of Commons, 10 Apr. 1989.

[16] Alan Clark, Minister of State for Defence, answering oral questions in the House of Commons, 28 Nov. 1989, reported in *Defence Industry Digest*, Jan. 1990, p. 19.

[17] *Ministry of Defence: Support for Defence Exports*, Report by the Comptroller and Auditor General, National Audit Office to the House of Commons, 10 Apr. 1989.

[18] *Defence Industry Digest*, Jan. 1990, p. 19.

[19] *Flight International*, 4 Nov. 1989, p. 5; *Defence & Foreign Affairs Weekly*, 4–10 Dec. 1989, p. 2.

[20] *Financial Times*, 27 Nov. 1989, p. 8; Miller, C. and Silverberg, D., 'British loan to help Saudis pay for arms sales', *Defense News*, 4 Dec. 1989, p. 3.

[21] According to Alan Jones, Westland's chief executive, *Financial Times*, 5 Dec. 1989, p. 25.

The Federal Republic of Germany

Three arms deals dominated the debate over the arms exports of the Federal Republic of Germany: the continuing parliamentary investigations into the supply of submarine blueprints to South Africa, the supply of technology to produce chemical weapons in Libya and the involvement of companies in supplying technology for the Condor 2 missile to Argentina, Egypt and Iraq (see also chapters 4 and 9). Especially the transfer of technology to Libya and the inaction of the government to stop these sales—despite numerous warnings by the intelligence services of both the USA and FR Germany—led to heated public debates that finally forced the government to publish a detailed report on these activities.[22] Immediate action was announced that included tighter restrictions and an increase in personnel to control exports.[23] At the end of 1989 the new export regulations were still discussed in parliamentary committees, and the opposition claims that the intended tight restrictions have in the meantime been watered down by alterations suggested by government.[24] The FRG remained the sixth largest exporter of arms for the period 1985–89. However, arms exports declined substantially in 1989 as a result of the financial difficulties of some of the previous major importers, particularly Argentina.

The major importers

A small group of countries—Egypt, India, Iraq, North Korea, Saudi Arabia and Syria in the Third World, and Czechoslovakia, Japan, Poland, Spain and Turkey in the industrialized world—account for the major share of global arms imports (see table 7.2). In 1985–89 the 15 leading Third World importers accounted for 78 per cent of Third World imports and the 15 leading importers in the industrialized world accounted for 83 per cent of industrialized world imports. Argentina is no longer represented in the list of the leading Third World importers, as imports have continued to fall since the mid-1980s; Argentina has been replaced by Thailand—which has imported large quantities of weapons in all categories from China, the FRG, Israel, Italy, the Netherlands, Switzerland, the UK and the USA.

Third World recipients

Almost all the Middle Eastern countries reduced their imports of weapons, and Iraq's imports are only 10 per cent of the figure recorded for 1987. This development is discussed in section III.

---

[22] Deutscher Bundestag, *Plenarprotokoll* 11/126, 17 Feb. 1989, pp. 9259–311.

[23] See Wulf, H., *Waffenexport aus Deutschland* (Rowohlt: Reinbek, 1989).

[24] *Frankfurter Rundschau,* 10 Nov. 1989.

In South Asia, by contrast, overall imports have increased. India is by far the largest importer of major weapons in the world. All branches of the armed forces receive imported equipment in addition to Indian-produced weapons. The primary suppliers are the FRG, Sweden, the UK and the

Table 7.2. The leading importers of major weapons, 1985–89

The countries are ranked according to 1985–89 aggregate imports. Figures are in US $m., at constant (1985) prices.

Importers	1985	1986	1987	1988	1989	1985–89
Third World						
1. India	1 876	3 683	4 585	3 383	3 819	17 345
2. Iraq	2 871	2 447	4 247	2 005	418	11 989
3. Saudi Arabia	1 447	2 395	1 956	1 770	1 196	8 764
4. Syria	1 690	1 508	1 169	1 172	336	5 876
5. Egypt	1 282	1 665	2 347	348	152	5 795
6. North Korea	977	876	487	1 383	1 553	5 275
7. Afghanistan	82	611	687	939	2 289	4 610
8. Angola	694	975	1 135	890	24	3 719
9. Libya	969	1 359	294	65	499	3 186
10. Taiwan	664	866	640	513	263	2 946
11. Iran	710	746	685	538	261	2 940
12. Pakistan	675	616	467	467	694	2 919
13. South Korea	388	267	597	934	607	2 794
14. Israel	193	446	1 629	327	93	2 687
15. Thailand	305	74	644	510	330	1 862
Others	5 753	5 026	4 601	4 012	3 893	23 285
Total	**20 576**	**23 560**	**26 170**	**19 256**	**16 427**	**105 989**
Industrial world						
1. Japan	1 634	1 745	1 771	2 343	3 062	10 554
2. Czechoslovakia	1 332	1 086	967	1 067	828	5 280
3. Spain	270	1 039	1 513	1 580	749	5 152
4. Turkey	604	621	1 153	1 238	1 134	4 751
5. Poland	427	1 057	983	1 063	1 118	4 649
6. Canada	877	828	732	526	444	3 408
7. Greece	192	156	93	860	1 813	3 114
8. GDR	663	482	325	865	625	2 960
9. Australia	352	699	478	579	847	2 955
10. Netherlands	814	702	296	154	761	2 727
11. USSR	497	473	497	483	359	2 310
12. Bulgaria	589	666	598	220	–	2 073
13. Hungary	759	507	592	–	–	1 859
14. FR Germany	199	411	320	301	613	1 844
15. Yugoslavia	103	103	234	748	450	1 639
Others	2 615	1 903	2 116	2 335	2 589	11 552
Total	**11 927**	**12 478**	**12 668**	**14 362**	**15 392**	**66 827**

Table 7.2 *cont.*

Importers	1985	1986	1987	1988	1989	1985–89
All countries						
1. India	1 876	3 683	4 585	3 383	3 819	17 345
2. Iraq	2 871	2 447	4 247	2 005	418	11 989
3. Japan	1 634	1 745	1 771	2 343	3 062	10 554
4. Saudi Arabia	1 447	2 395	1 956	1 770	1 196	8 764
5. Syria	1 690	1 508	1 169	1 172	336	5 876
6. Egypt	1 282	1 665	2 347	348	152	5 795
7. Czechoslovakia	1 332	1 086	967	1 067	828	5 280
8. North Korea	977	876	487	1 383	1 553	5 275
9. Spain	270	1 039	1 513	1 580	749	5 152
10. Turkey	604	621	1 153	1 238	1 134	4 751
11. Poland	427	1 057	983	1 063	1 118	4 649
12. Afghanistan	82	611	687	939	2 289	4 610
13. Angola	694	975	1 135	890	24	3 719
14. Canada	877	828	732	526	444	3 408
15. Libya	969	1 359	294	65	499	3 186
Others	15 472	14 142	14 811	13 847	14 198	72 463
Total	**32 504**	**36 037**	**38 837**	**33 619**	**31 819**	**172 816**

Source: SIPRI data base.

USSR.[25] Hopes for a settlement of the conflict in Afghanistan have not been fulfilled, and fighting escalated during 1989. Massive military support to the Afghan Government came from the Soviet Union. US officials claim that Afghanistan continues to receive military supplies, worth $250–300 million per month, from the USSR. In contrast, US military aid to Afghan rebels is reported as $600 million in 1989.[26] According to the SIPRI major weapons trend indicator, Afghan imports (by both the government and the Mujahideen) more than doubled in 1989.

Recipients of the industrialized world

In contrast to decreasing arms imports by the Third World, the trend of increasing imports by industrialized countries continued. This overall growth is actually due to specific developments in a few countries. While some WTO countries remained leading importers of (mainly Soviet) major conventional arms, the trend of reduced imports by WTO countries continued; in 1989 the recorded value was $2.7 billion, compared to $4 billion in 1985. It is likely but far from certain that this trend will continue because of the political changes in these countries in 1989, unilateral withdrawal of weapons and possible reductions as a result of arms control agreements.

Arms imports by NATO countries, however, have grown over the period 1985–89 from $3.8 billion to $7 billion. Major modernization programmes in Greece, Spain, Turkey and—to a lesser extent—Norway were not

[25] Discussed in more detail in Anthony (note 1).
[26] *Milavnews*, Nov. 1989, p. 1; *The Independent,* 19 Oct. 1989.

affected, at least in the short term, by political changes in the WTO countries or prospects for conventional arms control agreement. (See chapter 8 for a detailed discussion of the changes in procurement and the effects on the arms industry.)

In the Pacific region, Japan and Australia have both increased their arms imports and invested heavily in the expansion of their respective arms industrial bases (see chapter 8).[27] For 1989, Japan is recorded as the second largest importer of the world, with $3.1 billion, surpassed only by India. Australia's position as a leading importer in the Pacific region is likely to be strengthened by the 1989 decision to produce 10 frigates in Australia (two of them for New Zealand) based on the Blohm & Voss Meko-200 Class design. While the Pacific region has not recently been a region of particular importance in terms of arms production or trade, this situation is changing in a period when political developments in Europe promise disarmament.

The arms imports of the neutral and non-aligned countries in Europe have never been decisive in determining the value and the fluctuations of global arms imports. In 1989 these countries imported roughly $900 million; over the period 1985–89 less than 3 per cent of the trade in arms is recorded for this group of countries.

III. The Middle East and changing East–West relations

In the past, the dominant position of Middle Eastern recipients has been a central feature of the overall arms trade.[28] In the Middle East a great deal of importance is still attached to enhancing military capabilities in spite of the reduction in the volume of arms imported by countries of the region.

Political conflicts concerning the Mediterranean are also emerging. There are disagreements both between and within European governments over whether conventional arms reductions in Europe should be linked to arms transfer control. There is a basic conflict between Soviet calls for general-purpose naval forces to be drawn into the arms control process (along with strategic nuclear forces on naval platforms which are already included in the Strategic Arms Reduction Talks) and the increasing naval capabilities of countries on NATO's southern flank.

Military programmes throughout the Middle East have figured in public statements by important decision makers in 1989. In Vienna in March 1989, Soviet Foreign Minister Shevardnadze said:

in close proximity to Europe, powerful weapons arsenals are being created. It is not enough just to mention that 25 000 tanks and 4500 aircraft are deployed and ready for combat in the Middle East and there is a real danger of nuclear and chemical weapons appearing there; missiles have already appeared with an operational range

---

[27] See Anthony (note 1), pp. 215–16.
[28] For a recent discussion, see Neuman, S. G., 'The arms market: who's on top?', *Orbis*, autumn 1989.

of 2500 km . . . The conclusion is obvious: the processes of disarmament in Europe and settlement in the Middle East have to be synchronised.[29]

While it remains an important arms supplier to the region, the Soviet Union has also become a significant participant in political initiatives aimed at conflict resolution in the Middle East.

The Middle East remains a conflict-ridden region. There are conflicts between Israel and Arab countries, in Lebanon, and between Islamic countries—between Turkey and Syria, Iraq and Syria as well as Iraq and Iran. Conflicts also exist within countries in the region and between governments and stateless peoples—notably Kurds and Palestinians. Moreover, the threat perceptions of Middle Eastern governments are affected by unresolved conflicts in Afghanistan, Chad and Sudan.

Drawing a boundary around the region is extremely difficult in the face of overlapping geographical, racial, religious, strategic and political sub-groups which coexist within what is broadly called the Middle East.[30] The Arab world, the Muslim world, the Maghreb, the Levant, Palestine or the Gulf states all describe elements of the Middle East. The Middle East as defined here includes all countries from Algeria to Iran and from Turkey to North and South Yemen, a total of 19 sovereign states.[31] There are wide disparities between these countries, as measured by size, level of development, population, resources or almost any other indicator, and this regional diversity permits the continuous evolution of shifting political alignments. Within most Arab countries, both nationalism and pan-Arabism have political support, the level of which has ebbed and flowed over time; in addition, it is not unprecedented for conflicts to emerge between countries shortly after they have discussed unification into a single political entity.[32]

The changing international environment

The importance of Middle Eastern military programmes has many dimensions:

1. Some Middle Eastern military programmes have been perceived as a potential threat by the Soviet Union, the United States and southern flank NATO countries.

---

[29] Quoted in Sivers, A., *Conventional Arms Control: Considering New Directions*, Faraday Discussion Paper no. 13 (Council for Arms Control: London, 1989), p. 51. One might add that the Soviet Government should have thought of this before agreeing to sell so many of these systems to countries in the region. In recent years the Soviet Union has been the main supplier of arms to Iraq, Libya, both North and South Yemen, and Syria in particular, as well as being an important supplier to Iran, Jordan and Kuwait.

[30] Even the expression 'Middle East' is objected to in Asian countries since the region lies to the west and is not in the middle of anything easily identifiable. However, SIPRI uses this as the traditional regional nomenclature.

[31] Algeria, Bahrein, Egypt, Iran, Iraq, Israel, Jordan, Kuwait, Lebanon, Libya, Oman, Qatar, Saudi Arabia, Syria, Tunisia, Turkey, the United Arab Emirates, North Yemen and South Yemen.

[32] For example, in 1977 Egyptian and Libyan forces clashed along their border although the two countries had discussed union in 1973. By 1989 relations were normalized.

2. These programmes have affected the position of the major powers in talks concerning conventional arms control in Europe.

3. These programmes have conditioned attitudes towards the issue of nuclear proliferation both in potential nuclear weapon states and among those concerned with preventing the addition of new members to the 'nuclear club'.

4. These programmes have complicated progress towards the signature of a chemical weapons convention.[33] (The third and fourth elements of Middle Eastern development are discussed more fully in chapters 4 and 16, respectively, and will only be touched on here.)

Parallel to these developments, the influence of major powers—and in particular the superpowers—has been reduced by changes in the global and regional political environment and changes in the nature of military technology available to countries within the region.

Changes in the global political environment

The most important global political developments have been the changes in policy in the United States, Western Europe and the Soviet Union. Changes in internal conditions within these countries—and the policies required to manage those changes—have had direct repercussions for foreign policy (see table 7.3).

The United States

Arms transfers remained an important aspect of US policy towards Israel and Egypt as a consequence of the Camp David Agreement of 26 March 1979.[34] However, around the Persian Gulf, the importance of US arms transfers has declined during the 1980s.

After the Iranian revolution and the Soviet invasion of Afghanistan in December 1979, US policy in and around the Persian Gulf has emphasized, through demonstrative actions and direct intervention, the local capabilities of US forces. Supporting the military capabilities of regional countries, in particular Saudi Arabia, remained important to the Reagan Administration, but the policy was constrained by the more active role of Congress in arms export decision making. All arms exports worth in excess of $14 million for 'significant military equipment' and $50 million for other weapons must be approved by Congress, and since 1986 Bahrain, Jordan, Kuwait, Oman, Qatar, Saudi Arabia and the United Arab Emirates have all had one or more requests for approval refused by Congress.

---

[33] The issues of arms transfers and exports of chemical agents were raised at the Paris Conference on the Prohibition of Chemical Weapons in Jan. 1989; see chapter 14.

[34] Nachimas, N., *Transfer of Arms, Leverage and Peace in the Middle East* (Greenwood Press: New York, 1988). However, since 1987 both Israel and Egypt have been involved more with indigenous programmes to refurbish equipment in service (often with imported sub-systems) than with the purchase of new major weapons. Israel still has 65 F-16 fighters, corvettes and submarines on order from the USA and the FRG.

Table 7.3. The changing percentage of arms imported from the USA, Western Europe*a* and the USSR, by selected Middle Eastern countries, 1970s–1980s

Country	Percentage of arms imports from the USA		Percentage of arms imports from W. Europe		Percentage of arms imports from the USSR	
	1970s	1980s	1970s	1980s	1970s	1980s
Egypt	3	67	7	22	87	–
Israel	96	99	4	–	–	–
Iran	78	3	20	10	1	–
Iraq	–	5	8	22	90	53
Libya	1	1	18	21	74	72
Saudi Arabia	70	46	26	36	–	–
Syria	–	–	1	–	95	91
Turkey	72	40	28	60	–	–

a Western Europe here includes only members of NATO.

Source: SIPRI data base.

In 1989 congressional attitudes have changed somewhat, and major US transfers to the region, including the sale of 42 F/A-18 Hornet fighter aircraft to Kuwait and 315 M-1 main battle tanks to Saudi Arabia, have been approved. However, attitudes to the prospective sale of up to 110 new fighter aircraft to Saudi Arabia are less easy to determine.[35]

The US Congress has since 1974 supported major programmes aimed at helping Egypt and Israel, including large-scale financial assistance. From fiscal year 1974 until 1984, Egypt and Israel had part of their military loan repayments waived.[36] Since 1985 Egypt and Israel have had all loans forgiven.[37] Since 1985 the value of non-repayable military assistance (effectively grant money) offered through these direct programmes has been over $3 billion per year.[38] Against this, the total value of all US arms exports has been in the region of $9–12.6 billion per year since 1985.[39] Therefore, it is not unreasonable to say that since 1985 the US Government has consistently subsidized arms exports up to 30 per cent of their total value; and it was not uncommon for this subsidy to rise to 40 per cent during the late 1980s. Moreover, this excludes any offset agreements, the impact of which has also been considerable.

[35] Starr, B., 'M1A1 sale to test water for future Saudi deals', *Jane's Defence Weekly*, 30 Sep. 1989, p. 629; Blitzer, W., 'Confrontation unlikely in US arms sale to Saudi', *Jerusalem Post* (intl edn), week ending 14 Oct. 1989, p. 3; Siverberg, D., 'White House seeks Saudi arms sale', *Defense News*, 2 Oct. 1989, p. 1.

[36] The only other country to make partial loan repayments in this period was Sudan.

[37] In 1988 the US Congress authorized partial forgiven loans for Pakistan and Turkey.

[38] All of the data on US security assistance are taken from *Security Assistance: Update of Programs and Related Activities*, General Accounting Office Fact Sheet for the Chairman, Subcommittee on National Security Economics, Joint Economic Committee, Congress of the United States, GAO/NSIAD-89-78FS, Dec. 1988.

[39] ACDA, *World Military Expenditures and Arms Transfers* (US Government Printing Office: Washington, DC, 1988), p. 107. For the same period the SIPRI figure for the United States is slightly lower, reflecting the different methodologies applied.

The Soviet Union

For the Soviet Union the urgent need for domestic change has overshadowed other elements of policy. Linkages to some Third World countries, notably Syria in the Middle East, have been a drain on financial resources and there may be Soviet domestic pressure to cut the cost of these ties. However, relations with Syria have brought other benefits, such as a greater Soviet involvement in regional diplomatic initiatives.

Ties to Kuwait have yielded foreign exchange benefits since Kuwait is in a position to make hard currency payments for arms. The domestic pressure in the Soviet Union might be to strengthen this relationship, which also has important political benefits since Kuwait is a member of the Gulf Cooperation Council (discussed below), other members of which are more closely linked to Western countries.

Whether or not there is an overall economic advantage from Soviet relations with Iran and Iraq is more difficult to ascertain. While both countries are oil producers, the level of oil revenue is small compared with the enormous debts accruing from the Iraq–Iran War. For Iran the position has been improved somewhat by the US agreement to free $567 million of Iranian money frozen in US financial institutions since 1979 as a response to the taking of US hostages during the Iranian revolution. Some of this money may be used to clear debts for past Iranian arms purchases or to make new orders.[40] Under the terms of the agreement of June 1989 between President Gorbachev and Ali Akbar Hashemi Rafsanjani, Speaker of the Iranian Majlis, the Soviet Union would appear to have agreed to give short-term economic assistance to Iran in the expectation of receiving long-term economic benefits.[41]

Unconfirmed reports suggest that Iran requested MiG-29 fighters at the meeting between Gorbachev and Rafsanjani.[42] The development of an infrastructure to assist local trade between the Central Asian republics of the Soviet Union and both Iran and Afghanistan has political as well as economic significance. The economies of Afghanistan and Iran have been ruined by war, but the process closely resembles the pattern of regional development laid down by President Gorbachev in his speech to the 19th All-Union Conference of the Communist Party of the Soviet Union of 28 June–1 July 1988.

One of the central tasks is to create conditions for the greater independence of regions, and to carry forward cooperation whereby each republic should be interested in improving the end results of its economic activity as the basis for its own well being and the common prosperity and power of the Soviet Union.

[40] A further $9.5 billion remains frozen in US banks and financial institutions; *Sunday Times*, 1 Nov. 1989, p. A21.

[41] The USSR will build facilities for the extraction of oil and natural gas in Iran and has offered to construct a railway link from Ashkabad in the USSR to Meshad in Iran. These cities are already linked by road.

[42] Ottaway, D. B., 'US cautions Russia against an Iran arms deal', *International Herald Tribune*, 22 June 1989; *AAS-Milavnews*, July 1989, p. 18.

The internationalization of the economy and all other areas of society is a law governed process. Any gravitation towards national isolationism can only cause economic and cultural impoverishment.

We shall have to legislatively elaborate an essentially new mechanism for forming republican and local budgets, and to substantially enhance their role in the socio-economic development of the various regions . . .[43]

Soviet republics and regional political bodies may be allowed greater latitude in defining relations with neighbouring countries in economic and cultural affairs in an effort to prevent the further growth of separatism based on religious or nationalist identity. In the short term, however, the heavy fighting in the Soviet Central Asian republics at the end of 1989 and the beginning of 1990 makes the short-term pattern of developments unpredictable.

Western Europe

West European countries have become more active arms suppliers throughout the Middle East in the 1980s. As indicated in table 7.3, former US and Soviet clients now look to European suppliers to meet a significant proportion of their equipment needs. However, while this growing regional involvement in the arms trade requires a co-ordinated European response to regional developments no such co-ordination has emerged.

Multinational European initiatives by the Council of Ministers of the EC—such as arms embargoes on Libya and Syria—have been reactive, responding to specific events, rather than representing a coherent West European policy. In 1989 basic disagreements between West European governments have underlined that common policies will not be easy to agree.

The decision by the British Government not to allow British Aerospace to proceed with the supply of Hawk jet trainers to Iraq contrasts with the French role as one of Iraq's most important suppliers.[44]

The regional political environment

The most important recent political development in the Middle East has been the revival of efforts by Arab countries to develop mechanisms for collective political and economic action in order to increase their bargaining power *vis-à-vis* the major powers.

At the October 1988 meeting of the Gulf Cooperation Council (formed in 1981 by Bahrain, Kuwait, Oman, Qatar, Saudi Arabia and the United Arab Emirates) the respective member governments revived a 1984 proposal for the creation of a unified rapid deployment force drawn from the armed forces of the six countries and agreed to increase the number of joint

[43] *19th All Union Conference of the CPSU: Report by Mikhail Gorbachev, General Secretary of the CPSU Central Committee* (Novosti Publishing House: Moscow, 1988), p. 148.
[44] 'BAe Hawk sale blocked, Mirage missile revealed', *AAS Milavnews*, Aug. 1989, p. 14; 'Iraq seeks deal for local built AS-30', *Jane's Defence Weekly*, 4 Nov. 1989, p. 949.

exercises by the armed forces of GCC members. In February 1989 Egypt, Iraq, Jordan and North Yemen formed the Arab Cooperation Council (ACC), and Algeria, Libya, Mauritania, Morocco and Tunisia formed the Union Maghrebine Arab (UMA).[45] Membership of these organizations reflects the national interests of member states—such as the pattern of foreign trade or threat perception—rather than any ideological or political goals such as Muslim or Arab unity.

The military implications of these groupings are less clear than their importance for economic policy. There is still a basic tension between the political imperative to avoid dependence on a single source of supply and the financial imperative to reduce expenditure on defence procurement.

Within the ACC, there is already considerable co-operation between Egypt, Iraq and, to a lesser extent, Jordan through arms transfers. The Egyptian Minister of State for Military Production stated in July 1989: 'When Iraq needed weapons, we provided them with all their requirements. Now we provide them with certain production requirements'.[46] However, in terms of action, the ACC has not gone beyond defining projects in which members are interested and holding meetings of scientists and specialists. This is mainly because of the recognition in Egypt and Iraq that the arms industry draws on a wider industrial base which is poorly developed in both countries.[47]

Within the GCC it is declared policy for members to acquire a smaller range of standard weapon systems to increase the inter-operability among their armed forces, reduce purchase costs and lower maintenance and running costs.[48] There have been steps in this direction with multiple orders for the Hawk family of jet trainer aircraft—in service or on order in four of the six GCC air forces. However, the purchase of front-line fighter aircraft has not been co-ordinated, as illustrated by the different fighter aircraft in service or planned by GCC members (see table 7.4). Here, countries have preferred to remain with traditional suppliers with whose operational and maintenance procedures they are already familiar.

Less formal avenues for co-operation have including increased arms transfers between Arab countries, closely linked to the pattern of armed conflict in the region, and discussed in that context below. There has also been increased attention to the prospects for the creation of an Arab arms industry, which would be an important development. Given the low costs of production, Middle Eastern suppliers may even have competitive advantages as producers and sellers of components and sub-assemblies to the Soviet Union, Western Europe and North America. This process might build on close historic ties such as those between Turkey and FR Germany, Egypt and France, Egypt and the UK, Libya and Italy or Israel and the USA.

[45] 'An opportunity to lower Arab barriers', *South*, Sep. 1989, p. 23; 'Unity on the Maghreb front', *South*, Sep. 1989, p. 83.
[46] *International Defense Intelligence*, 24 July 1989, p. 1.
[47] 'Arab Cooperation Council could become arms forum', *Defense Electronics*, May 1989, p. 14.
[48] Interview with King Fahd of Saudi Arabia, 8 Dec. 1984, and Kuwaiti Defence Minister Sheikh Salim al-Sabah al-Salim, 23 Mar. 1985, in Ramazani, R. K., *The Gulf Cooperation Council: Record and Analysis* (University of Virginia Press: Charlottesville, Va., 1988).

Table 7.4. Selected fighter aircraft in service and on order with GCC countries, 1989

Country	System in service	Seller	System ordered	Seller
Bahrain	F-5	USA	F-16	USA
Kuwait	Mirage F-1	France	F/A-18	USA
Oman	Hunter/Jaguar	UK[a]	Hawk-200	UK
Qatar	Mirage F-1	France	Mirage F-1	France
Saudi Arabia	F-15/Tornado	USA/UK[b]	F-15/Tornado	USA/UK
UAE	Mirage 2000	France	Mirage 2000	France

[a] The Jaguar is produced by an Anglo-French consortium.
[b] The Tornado is produced by a British–FRG–Italian consortium.

Source: SIPRI data base.

Changes in regional military technologies

Some key Middle Eastern countries have been engaged in defence production for a long time—both Egypt and Israel have arms industries dating back to 1948. However, in the second half of the 1980s new kinds of weapon and equipment were developed and produced.

The development of Third World arms industries during the 1970s was largely dependent on the assembly of imported kits, a form of technology transfer in which the opportunities for the development of an indigenous research and manufacturing base in the recipient country are constrained. This pattern remains in most countries, but there are some signs that it is slowly changing. For example, table 7.5 illustrates that there are now growing military electronics industries in some of the larger Middle Eastern countries.

There is a wide range of technological development among regional countries. Israel, for which this represents a very small selection of locally developed electronics equipment, is at a level of technological advancement ahead of many industrialized countries. Egypt, Iran and Turkey have limited capabilities. Elsewhere, notably in Iraq, the electronics industry is at the level of simple modifications to imported equipment.

All of the systems listed in table 7.4 draw on technologies that form the basis of modern industries—integrated circuitry, digital switches and microchips. Moreover, almost all of the systems named have direct civilian applications. Mobile car telephones, air traffic control radars at airports, national telecommunications networks, personal computers and data terminals are part of the fabric of modern societies. These systems are also becoming more important elements of regional military capabilities.[49]

[49] Steinberg, G. M., 'The impact of new technology on the Arab–Israel military balance', eds S. L. Spiegel, M. A. Heller, and J. Goldberg, *The Soviet–American Competition in the Middle East* (D. C. Heath: Lexington, Mass., 1988).

Table 7.5. Recent Middle Eastern military electronics programmes,[a] 1989

Producer country	System name	Description	Producer	Comments
Egypt	AN/TPS-63	Fire control radar	Benha Electronics	Licensed from Westinghouse (USA)
	FMD-4016	Mobile radio	Electrolab	
	FS-155/455	Hand-held radio	Electrolab	
	MT/UT	Hand-held radio	Electrolab	
	PTM-60	VHF transceiver	Electrolab	
	SS-150	Base station radio	Electrolab	
Iran	Goya 630	VHF radio	Iran Electronics Industry	
	MR-600	Receiver	Iran Electronics Industry	
	Payam	Transceiver	Iran Electronics Industry	Exported to Dubai
	SB-22	Switchboard	Iran Electronics Industry	Developed to US specifications
	41D220	Antenna	Iran Electronics Industry	
Israel[b]	AMDR	Missile detection radar	Elta (subsidiary of Israeli Aircraft Industries)	
	El/M-2200 series	Surveillance radars	Elta	Naval, airborne and land mobile versions
	Phalcon	AEW radar	Elta	
	El/M-2035	Airborne fire control radars	Elta Elta	
	El/M-2021	Airborne fire control radars	Elta Elta	
	El/M-2032	Airborne fire control radars	Elta	Including a 'look-down' capability
	SIS	Space tracking system	Elta	
	D-35	Missile detection system	ELOP Industries	
	Tranex-4CH	Elint system	Elbit Computers Tadiran	
	CR-2740	Elint system	Elbit Computers Tadiran	
	Raj-101	Airborne jammer	Rafael	
	Rattler	Airborne jammer	Rafael	
	El/L-8202	Airborne ECM pod	Elta	
	El/L-8231	Airborne ECM pod	Elta	
	NS-9005	Shipborne jammer	Elisra Electronics	
	MCCS-800	Communication system	Elbit Computers	Part of a national C^3 network
	FM-607	Fibre optic telephone	Fibronics	
	TAC	Personal computer	Tadiran	IBM-compatible
	BT-3502	Teleprinter/fax	Koor Systems	

Table 7.5 *cont.*

Producer country	System name	Description	Producer	Comments
Turkey	4500 series	Hand-held radio	ASELSAN	
	PRC/VRC-4600	Radio transmitter	ASELSAN	Assisted by Netherlands company Hollandse Signaal-apparaten
	4800 series	Mobile radio	ASELSAN	Assisted by Harris (USA)
	7221	Portable data terminal	ASELSAN	
	6200	Field telephone	ASELSAN	

[a] For additional information on Middle Eastern military production programmes, see appendix 7C.

[b] This represents a small selection of Israeli military electronics programmes.

Source: Jane's Military Communications 1989 and *Jane's Radar and Electronic Warfare 1989–90* (Jane's: Coulsdon, 1989).

The information in table 7.4 suggests that neither the Arab countries nor Iran have yet reached a significant level of indigenous capability in arms production. The equipment in production is very simple in comparison to that produced by Israel. However, there is no doubt that Egypt, Iran and Iraq in particular intend to further develop their arms producing capabilities.

Egypt

Egyptian capabilities could be summarized as complete autonomy in the production of rockets and ammunition, the ability to repair and maintain all of the aircraft in service in Egypt and an ability to licence-produce both aircraft and short-range missiles. These capabilities are well recognized and long established.[50] Egypt also produces a range of artillery rockets, notably the SAKR 80, an 80-km range rocket in advanced development.[51]

In Egypt, Lt.-General Ibrahim Abd al Ghafur al Urabi, the Chairman of the Arab Organization for Industry, and D. Jamal al din al Sayyid Ibrahim, the Minister of State for Military Production, have described existing Egyptian production capacities and confirmed plans for future expansion in collaboration with ACC partners such as Iraq.[52]

At the end of September 1989, President Mubarak announced that Egypt was withdrawing from the Badr II/Condor programme pursued in conjunction with Argentina. However, both Argentinian and Egyptian officials

[50] SIPRI has reported the licensed production of missiles and aircraft since 1978; SIPRI, *World Armaments and Disarmament: SIPRI Yearbook 1978* (Taylor & Francis: London, 1978), p. 214.

[51] *Jane's Armour and Artillery, 1989–90* (Jane's: Coulsdon, 1989), pp. 682–83.

[52] Quoted in *AAS-Milavnews*, Mar. 1989; and *International Defense Intelligence*, 24 July 1989, respectively.

Table 7.6. Selected independent arms programmes in Iraq and Iran, 1989

Country/ Weapon name	Weapon description	Source	Comment
Iraq			
Assad Babyle	Main battle tank	Displayed at Baghdad exhibition	Modified Soviet T-72
Adnan-1	Airborne early warning system	Iraqi Air Force	Soviet Il-76 Candid
Baghdad	Airborne early warning system	Col. Zboon, Baghdad Project Manager	Soviet transport aircraft with French Tiger radar
Majnoon	155-mm howitzer	Displayed at Baghdad exhibition	Austrian, French, S. African and Yugoslavian assistance have been suggested. Truth not clear.
Al Fao	210-mm howitzer	Displayed at Baghdad exhibition	Franco-Spanish assistance
Iran			
Turboprop	Trainer aircraft trainer	Iranian Republic News Agency	
Zafar	Helicopter	Iranian Revolutionary Guard Committee	
Oghab	Artillery rocket	Displayed at Gabon Army Exhibition	Version of a Chinese rocket system
Shahin-2	Artillery rocket	Displayed at Gabon Army Exhibition	
Nazeat	Artillery rocket	Displayed at Gabon Army Exhibition	

Source: SIPRI data base.

continued to insist that this had been a satellite launch vehicle programme and not a missile programme.[53]

Iran and Iraq

Both Iran and Iraq claim to have established a considerable military industrial capacity. Table 7.6 presents official government information about arms programmes and notes systems which have been put on public display for Western journalists. From these programmes it is clear that both countries intend to further develop their arms industrial base and that few if any of these programmes have been achieved without foreign assistance.

Iraq, while acknowledging that there are a lot of foreign sub-systems used in Iraqi programmes, denies that there is any formal collaboration. Iraq's Minister of Industry and Military Industrialisation, Husayn Kamil, noted that Iraq relied 'on its own efforts to produce and develop a new generation of long-range missiles'.[54] The Iraqi Director General of Information drew

[53] 'US says Cairo drops missile project embroiled in a smuggling scandal', *International Herald Tribune*, 21 Sep. 1989, p. 4; 'Egypt has pulled out of Condor programme', *Jane's Defence Weekly*, 30 Sep. 1989, p. 630; 'Mubarak poses mystery over status of Argentina's Condor II missile', *Latin American Weekly Report*, 5 Oct. 1989, p. 1.

[54] *Jane's Defence Weekly*, 13 May 1989, p. 843.

attention to the fact that dozens of sources exist for sub-systems and components world-wide.[55] In fact, 17 British, 35 French companies and 3 Italian companies (Agusta, Breda and OTO Melara) exhibited at the Baghdad arms exhibition in April 1989.[56]

Iran exhibited arms which were available for export in two foreign locations in 1989: at the SECARM exhibition in Gabon, and at the IDEA 89 exhibition in Turkey. On both occasions the displays were heavily dominated by artillery rockets. Iran apparently manufactures eight different rocket systems with calibres varying from 40 mm to 355 mm.[57]

Looking at the programmes of Egypt, Iran and Iraq it is possible to draw four conclusions.

1. These countries are quite frank about their intentions to develop their arms industries.

2. Although none can currently produce electronic guidance systems, they intend that their arms industries will eventually provide the weapon systems integral to modern armed forces—including missiles and C^3I equipment.

3. These programmes are not yet at a stage in which large-scale production of modern weapons is possible.

4. Efforts to deny these countries the components needed to develop their defence industries failed during the Iraq–Iran War and are unlikely to succeed in peacetime.

Given that there remains time to address the question of expanding arms industries, it is reasonable to look at the arms control process in the light of the Middle Eastern survey.

New arms programmes and the arms control process

Growing concern about military programmes

As noted by Soviet Foreign Minister Shevardnadze (cited above), the issue of Middle Eastern security may have to be drawn into the overall arms control process. To some extent this has happened in the CFE talks, at which two members of the negotiations—the USSR and Turkey—have been divided into European and non-European areas. These countries can deploy equipment in non-European areas over and above the force levels agreed at Vienna in order to defend against potential Middle Eastern threats.

Parallel to European concerns about Middle Eastern programmes, Middle Eastern countries have legitimate concerns about the pattern of European military development, notably the continuing growth of naval air power.

55 'Iraq defends foreign links as vital for arms industry', *Financial Times* 11 Sep. 1989, p. 3.

56 Willis, G., 'Open sesame!', *International Defense Review*, June 1989, pp. 835–41; Donkin, R. and Henderson, S., 'Matrix confirms it exhibited at Baghdad arms fair', *Financial Times*, 13 Sep. 1989.

57 Daly, M., 'Iranian rockets head SECARM display', *Jane's Defence Weekly*, 11 Feb. 1989, p. 219; 'Iran, a very much noticed presence', *Defense & Armament*, Mar. 1989, pp. 66–67.

In February 1989 the Italian Parliament approved a change in the law allowing the Navy to operate fixed-wing aircraft from the light aircraft-carrier, *Giuseppe Garibaldi*. Italian procurement plans include the construction of a second carrier, the *Giuseppe Mazzini*.[58] Aeritalia signed a Memorandum of Understanding with British Aerospace for joint development of a new version of the Sea Harrier, expected to lead to the purchase of 12–18 aircraft and further collaborative projects between the companies.[59]

Current French procurement plans favour the Navy, with programmes including the construction of two nuclear-powered large-deck aircraft-carriers (one of which was laid down in April 1989) together with new destroyers and frigates. Delays in the development of a naval version of the Rafale fighter led the French Government to lease two US F/A-18 aircraft for trials from the aircraft-carrier *Foch*, suggesting that France may buy up to 20 F/A-18s as an interim measure.[60]

As a further reminder of the Middle Eastern dimension of European naval development, these trials, formally announced as measures to test the interoperability of the French and US navies, were postponed after the redeployment of the *Foch* to the eastern Mediterranean off the coast of Lebanon.[61]

If built, the French aircraft-carriers will increase the number of French fixed-wing combat aircraft at sea from 60 to 80. Adding Italian and Spanish aircraft at sea, this number will become a minimum of 110 fixed-wing combat aircraft (excluding armed helicopters) operated by West European navies. Including aircraft with the US Navy's Sixth Fleet, the number becomes over 270.[62]

It currently seems unlikely that existing arms control processes will reflect this parallel concern in Europe and the Middle East about growing military capabilities. Naval forces are explicitly excluded from the CFE process. Meanwhile there remains considerable resistance to the idea of arms transfer control within the governments of important supplier countries.

In most cases governments continue to regard arms transfers as an activity that should not be subject to international control. The British Minister of State for Defence called a suggestion by parliamentary opponents that arms production and exports should be an element of conventional arms control policy 'claptrap', going on to say: 'It seems extraordinary that Opposition MPs, who deplore the decline in our manufacturing capabilities, should single out this successful sector for the application of such doctrinaire and muddled thinking'.[63]

Other European governments have adopted a slightly different approach to arms transfer control. The Minister for Foreign Affairs of FR Germany,

[58] *Jane's Fighting Ships 1989–90* (Jane's: Coulsdon, 1989), pp. 292–94.
[59] *Interavia Air Letter*, 17 Feb. 1989, p. 5; *Interavia Air Letter*, 24 Feb. 1989, p. 2; 'Aerospace pursues global cooperation', *Wall Street Journal*, 26–27 May 1989, p. 15.
[60] *Defence*, Aug. 1989, p. 622.
[61] *AAS Milavnews*, Oct. 1989.
[62] Duke, S., SIPRI, *US Military Installations in Europe* (Oxford University Press: Oxford, 1989), pp. 199–200. The aircraft figure assumes that US carriers would reach their full air wing strength of 20 F-14, 20 F/A-18, 20 A-6E, 6 EA-6B, 5 E-2C and 10 S-3A aircraft.
[63] Alan Clark, Minister of State for Defence, during the House of Commons debate on the defence budget; quoted in *The Independent*, 20 Oct. 1989, p. 6.

Hans-Dietrich Genscher, stated that 'disarmament treaties should be supplemented by a ban on transferring to the Third World any military capacity that has become superfluous'.[64] However, this statement is compatible with continued exports of new equipment.

Translating concern into arms control

Translating concern about the growth of Middle Eastern arms programmes into a meaningful arms control process will be extremely difficult. None of the arms control processes under way elsewhere can easily accommodate the Middle Eastern countries.

There are a series of linkages between some particular military programmes and arms control. Limiting observations to the types of equipment referred to by Soviet Foreign Minister Shevardnadze—armour and artillery, missiles and aircraft—would include delivery systems of greatly varying characteristics in terms of firepower, range and speed. Some are land-based, some sea-based and some airborne. Many of these systems are capable of delivering nuclear or chemical as well as conventional munitions. These characteristics could place them under the rubric of any or several current arms control processes. It is possible to match each of these broad classes of weapon system to different arms control processes in which their performance characteristics will be relevant (see table 7.7).

However, looking at these processes it is not easy to see how Middle Eastern counties can be drawn into any of them. In the area of conventional arms control (the CFE Negotiation) and confidence- and security-building measures (the CSBM Negotiations), current discussions are geographically confined and exclude these actors.

The Missile Technology Control Regime (MTCR) applies to one limited area of military technologies but is unlikely to make any serious impact as currently constructed, for several reasons (see also chapter 9):

1. Since the members of the MTCR are all Organization for Economic Co-operation and Development (OECD) countries, it is likely to be dismissed by developing countries as another example of efforts by the 'rich man's club' to govern the world.

2. Since the members of the MTCR are all part of the Co-ordinating Committee for East–West Trade Policy (COCOM), its composition excludes such important missile suppliers as China and the Soviet Union, which feel politically constrained from joining.[65]

3. The MTCR (whose members are all allies of the United States) is likely to be resisted by Middle Eastern countries close to the Soviet Union and/or hostile to the United States.

---

[64] 'Security for the 1990s: courage to bear common responsibility for the future', speech to the Conference of the Institute for East–West Security Studies, 19 Oct. 1989.
[65] However, the Soviet Union appears to be sympathetic to the goals of the MTCR.

Table 7.7. Weapon categories and the arms control processes that could address them

Weapon characteristics	Arms control processes
Guns up to 120-mm calibre	Conventional arms control, confidence- and security-building and chemical
Guns over 120-mm calibre	Conventional arms control, confidence- and security-building, chemical, nuclear arms control
Rocket artillery under 500-mm calibre	Conventional arms control, confidence- and security-building and chemical
Rocket artillery over 500-mm calibre	Conventional arms control, confidence- and security-building, chemical, nuclear arms control and MTCR
Missiles with warhead weight under 500 kg	Conventional arms control, confidence- and security-building, chemical and MTCR
Missiles with warhead weight over 500 kg	Conventional arms control, confidence- and security-building, chemical, nuclear arms control and MTCR
Bombers and fighter-bombers (multi-role aircraft)	Conventional arms control, confidence- and security-building, chemical and nuclear arms control

Source: SIPRI data base.

4. Although missiles can be air-launched, sea-launched, submarine-launched or land-based, NATO currently refuses to discuss any controls over sea- or submarine-launched missiles even if they can be brought to bear on the geographical zone encompassed by the CFE Negotiation at Vienna.

5. The MTCR does not place any controls on the sale of surface-to-air missiles and by changing the mission of a surface-to-air missile the effectiveness of the MTCR can be undercut.[66]

6. The MTCR does not seek to place any controls on the transfer of technologies related to space launch vehicles or remotely piloted vehicles (RPVs) although these technologies are very closely related to missiles.[67]

In the areas of chemical and nuclear arms control, current efforts do not focus on delivery systems. Moreover, since most countries in the Middle East deny having or intending to develop chemical or nuclear warheads it would be difficult or impossible to raise the issue in the context of ongoing chemical disarmament talks, which focus on chemical warfare agents, or the 1970 Non-Proliferation Treaty (NPT), which focuses on nuclear explosives. Of the Mediterranean littoral countries all but Algeria are already parties to the 1925 Geneva Protocol, and all but Algeria, France and Israel are parties to the NPT.[68]

[66] The US company Martin Marietta is currently developing a version of a surface-to-air missile—the T-16, based on the MIM-104 Patriot—as a surface-to-surface missile. See chapter 8.

[67] Of the existing nuclear weapon powers, China, the USSR and the USA have derived strategic delivery systems from space launch vehicles. Martin Marietta is entering the competition for the AQM-127, a supersonic RPV, to provide a stand-off attack missile to the US Navy.

[68] Elsewhere in the Middle East, the United Arab Emirates is not a party to the 1925 Geneva Protocol, while Kuwait, Qatar and the United Arab Emirates are not parties to the 1970 NPT (see annexe A for the full list of parties).

While there is universal concern that the Middle East be brought into the arms control process, this prospect did not appear likely at the end of 1989.

IV. The pattern of arms transfers to wars

In 1989 the issue of arms transfers to regions of conflict remained close to the centre of international attention. When signing the Declaration on International Guarantees as part of the 14 April 1988 Geneva Accords concerning Afghanistan, both the Soviet Union and the United States undertook to 'refrain from any form of interference and intervention in the internal affairs of the Republic of Afghanistan and the Islamic Republic of Pakistan' and urged all states to act likewise.[69] During 1989 neither side lived up to its commitment. On the Soviet side large quantities of Scud-B missiles were transferred to Afghanistan; it is estimated that from 200 to over 800 missiles were fired during the period December 1988 to July 1989.[70] The Soviet Government has presented this as a transaction between sovereign governments which does not represent interference but according to the United States at least 300 Soviet troops remain in Afghanistan to operate and maintain these missiles.[71] The United States discontinued the supply of Stinger missiles to the Afghan Mujahideen (and tried without success to recover some of those supplied previously), but deliveries of rocket artillery (from Egypt), mine-clearing rockets, 120-mm calibre mortars (from Spain), small arms and runway cratering shells continued. These sales were jointly financed by the United States and Saudi Arabia.[72] Moreover, there were reports that the US Ambassador to Pakistan, Robert Oakley, attended meetings with the Pakistani Inter-Services Intelligence Agency, the Civilian Intelligence Bureau and the Foreign Office to decide policy vis-à-vis Afghanistan.[73]

Other states also export arms to states involved in conflicts. Three broad groups can be distinguished. The first are those which have decided to establish defence industries in spite of a relatively small domestic demand for weapons. This group of countries, which includes Brazil, China, Egypt and Israel, exports arms essentially in order to make domestic defence industries less of a financial drain.[74]

A second group of countries re-export arms that they do not produce themselves in order to support regional foreign policy interests. In 1989 this

[69] Text of the Geneva Agreements, 14 Apr. 1988, reproduced in *Pakistan Horizon*, July 1988, pp. 165–75.

[70] Ahmed Rashid, 'US and Pakistan ready to back Mujahedin offensive', *The Independent*, 5 July 1989; 'One more throw of the dice', *Middle East*, Aug. 1989, p. 22; *AAS Milavnews*, Aug. 1989, p. 1.

[71] 'US report says Soviets are still operating missiles', *Financial Times*, 11 Oct. 1989; Walker, M., 'CIA claims Soviet troops are violating Afghan accord', *The Guardian*, 11 Oct. 1989.

[72] Ahmed Rashid, 'The big push: US equips rebels for a new offensive', *Far Eastern Economic Review*, 13 July 1989, pp. 20–21; 'One more throw of the dice', *Middle East*, Aug. 1989, p. 22; Tisdall, S., 'US changes strategy in fight to topple Najibullah', *The Guardian*, 4 Sep. 1989; Coll, S., 'US and Pakistan shift Afghan tactics', *International Herald Tribune*, 4 Sep. 1989; Ahmed Rashid, 'Gang warfare', *Far Eastern Economic Review*, 14 Sep. 1989, pp. 23–24.

[73] Ahmed Rashid, 'Give peace a chance', *Far Eastern Economic Review*, 31 Aug. 1989, p. 24.

[74] This rationale for arms exports applies to a more limited degree to West European suppliers.

second group included Iran, Iraq, Israel and Syria, which have supported various factions in Lebanon in an effort to frustrate the policies of regional rivals. In South-East Asia, China and Thailand have used arms supplies to Kampuchean resistance groups to weaken Viet Nam. China and Israel belong in both categories since more than one motive underlies their arms export policies.

Finally, there exists a 'black market' for arms, in particular small arms, to which recipients can turn if foreign governments refuse to meet their needs. The size of this market is impossible to ascertain, and so a true measure of its significance is also elusive. However, even in such cases as those of Iran and Lebanon, illegally transferred small arms constitute a minor share of all the arms transferred to those countries. In an environment in which governments continue to see arms transfers as legitimate instruments of foreign policy, this will continue to be the case.

The Iraq–Iran War

The Iraq–Iran War was the dominant feature of the arms trade with the Third World between 1980 and 1988. Iran and Iraq between them accounted for roughly 25 per cent of the major arms imported by Third World countries in this period, receiving over $27 billion worth of major weapons. This figure excludes large deliveries of small arms, ammunition and other military supplies, spare parts, technical assistance and training to Iran and Iraq and all deliveries to other Gulf countries.[75]

While sharing the same goal—preventing either Iran or Iraq from emerging as the dominant regional power—the superpowers have used different means to that end. The USA found itself excluded from influence in the Iraq–Iran War after the collapse of its relationship with Iran and deployed its own armed forces to protect interests in the region. The USSR—which shares long land borders with both Iran and Iraq—has supplied arms to both sides.

Having been Iraq's largest arms supplier during the 1970s, the USSR refused to supply any arms to Iraq for 18 months after the Iraqi invasion of Iran. The USSR and other WTO countries provided arms to Iran, and the USSR permitted re-transfers of Soviet equipment to Iran from countries such as Libya, North Korea and Syria. After 1981 (and on a much larger scale from 1983 onwards), as Iran gained the upper hand, the Soviet Union became Iraq's largest supplier of arms. In 1988 and 1989, as Iraq regained the military initiative, the USSR and East European countries resumed supplies to Iran.

Reports in 1989 suggested that Iran has received or will receive tanks, anti-tank missiles and anti-aircraft missiles together with defence industrial assistance from Czechoslovakia, a lightweight fighter co-produced by Romania and Yugoslavia (incorporating a British engine), tanks, tank trans-

[75] An overview of arms supplies to the Persian Gulf is contained in a SIPRI fact sheet, 'The Iraq–Iran War 1980-88: military costs and arms transfers', available from SIPRI on request.

porters and artillery from Romania, refurbished MiG-21 fighters from the GDR and military industrial assistance from the Soviet Union.[76] The GDR stopped delivery of the final batch of MiG-21 fighters at the end of 1989, and the new government in Czechoslovakia announced that arms exports would be stopped.[77]

Soviet arms exports in general have been linked to conflict areas. In addition to Afghanistan, Angola (along with Cuban forces in Angola), Iran and Iraq, Nicaragua, Syria and Viet Nam have been important recipients of Soviet arms. Whereas the Arab–Israeli conflicts between 1967 and 1982 took place some distance from the Soviet Union, the USSR shares its border with Afghanistan, Iran and Iraq and has a more direct interest in the internal development of these countries. With the failure of direct intervention in Afghanistan and the lack of alternative strategies—such as the use of economic assistance—arms exports to these countries are likely to remain an important element of Soviet regional policy.

With regard to countries elsewhere in the Third World, abandoning commitments to long-term partners such as Angola, Syria or Viet Nam would be to relinquish any aspirations to a global foreign policy.[78] Nevertheless, the supply of military assistance to Third World governments unable to command political authority inside their own countries has been expensive. This expenditure may become increasingly difficult to defend under the scrutiny of the Defence Committee of the Supreme Soviet while shortages of consumer goods in the Soviet Union continue.

Arms suppliers to countries at war

The traditional major powers remain by far the most important actors in the arms trade, but the role of other suppliers is not insignificant. Moreover, the significance of these exporters as suppliers of countries at war is far greater than their overall importance within the global arms market.

Table 7.8 indicates the relative importance of countries at war to a selected group of exporting countries. As can be seen, imports by countries at war are particularly important to smaller suppliers.

The export performance of newer suppliers has been linked very closely to imports by countries at war and it is questionable whether any new market can substitute for that provided by the Iraq–Iran War. For countries such as China and Brazil, exports to Iran and Iraq represented roughly 40 per cent of total exports during the period 1985–89.

---

[76] 'Iranians tell of pact with Moscow', *International Herald Tribune,* 26 June 1989; 'Iran rebuilds armed forces', *The Guardian,* 29 Apr. 1989; 'Iran negotiating for Oraos?', *Defence,* June 1989, pp. 387–88; George, A., 'UK anxiety grows over Iran's plans to buy warplanes', *The Independent,* 20 May 1989; 'Despite pressure, Iran keeps buying East Bloc weapons', *International Herald Tribune,* 22 Mar. 1989.

[77] The future policy of the Romanian Government is not known.

[78] Among other things, these countries all provide the Soviet Navy with facilities of various kinds. Harkavy, R. E., SIPRI, *Bases Abroad: The Global Foreign Military Presence* (Oxford University Press: Oxford, 1989), pp. 53–54.

Table 7.8. Exports by 10 selected suppliers to countries at war as a percentage of total exports of major conventional weapons, 1980–89

Syria	Libya	Egypt	Brazil	China	USSR	France	UK	USA	FRG
99	96	90	47	40	35	23	9	5	2

Source: SIPRI data base.

While companies from the United States and Western Europe remain politically constrained from sales to Iran, China, Libya and Syria may retain their positions as important suppliers to Iran. Brazil and Egypt may benefit from reduced supplies to Iraq by France and the Soviet Union.

The cease-fire in the Iraq–Iran War has been followed by increased Iraqi involvement in Lebanon, where the supply of arms to Christian forces contributed to an escalation in violence in 1989. Between February and June 1989 the supply of arms by Iraq to Lebanon threatened to bring about a crisis in Iraqi–Syrian relations. Reports that Iraq was sending Soviet-supplied Frog-7 surface-to-surface missiles to Lebanese Christian forces led Syria to impose a naval blockade on Lebanese ports, and Syrian and Lebanese Muslim forces threatened to attack ships suspected of bringing Iraqi weapons to Lebanon.[79]

These developments prompted a Soviet diplomatic intervention with both Iraq and Syria in an effort to diffuse the crisis. On 1 July Iraq announced the suspension of all arms shipments.

In addition, President Gorbachev and President Mitterrand of France called for an immediate cease-fire and a halt to all arms deliveries to Lebanon at the end of Gorbachev's state visit to France on 5 July 1989. France later redeployed the aircraft-carrier *Foch* to the eastern Mediterranean in support of its local interests.

The influence of local factors

The future pattern of arms exports to countries in conflict will also be heavily influenced by the location of these conflicts.

In Beirut, a large city, both Syria and Israel have learnt that heavy equipment and airpower are difficult to employ while relatively unsophisticated small arms and man-portable equipment are effective weapons. Under these conditions the range of suppliers able to meet the requirements of local combatants is greatly expanded. The inventory of small arms and ammunition available in the world is vast. To give some indication, US companies manufactured roughly 6 million personal weapons per year during the Viet

---

[79] *Flight International*, 29 July 1989, p. 11; Kaplan, K., 'IDF worried by Iraq's Lebanon involvement', *Jerusalem Post* (intl edn), week ending 29 July 1989, p. 7; 'The economics of war', *Middle East*, Aug. 1989, p. 34; Hirst, D., 'A finger on the trigger of peace', *The Guardian*, 8 Aug. 1989.

Nam War.[80] Assuming that the USSR and China maintained similar outputs for the duration of the war this would have placed around 18 million small arms of the M-16/AK-47 type in circulation every year. Added to these figures, similar European weapons are also produced in large quantities around the world. The FRG Heckler and Koch G3 rifle is licence-produced in 14 countries (and imported by many more), and the Belgian FAL rifle is licence-produced in 11 countries while others (such as Brazil) have developed local copies.[81]

The widespread co-production and licensed production of small arms has made monitoring or controlling their transfer impossible. Even in the USA, with the most sophisticated control apparatus of any country, the bureaucracy is insufficient for direct control of programmes. Agreements are negotiated on the basis that countries will abide by them. In 1989 the General Accounting Office (GAO) reviewed US military co-production agreements world-wide to examine how compliance with agreements is assured. The findings were that the USA relied on foreign governments to report production quantities and on US embassies to verify information received. However, embassy offices were not specifically tasked with this and did not consider themselves responsible for ensuring compliance. The GAO discovered five cases of unauthorized third-country sales (although the identity of the countries and systems concerned was classified). The State Department took action on some, but not all, of these cases and limited its response to a diplomatic protest. No punitive sanctions of any kind were reported.[82] One co-production agreement in which unauthorized sales certainly took place was that of the M-16 carbine produced in South Korea, the subject of an earlier GAO report.[83] There is no reason to believe that the co-production agreements signed by other countries are more effectively monitored. In addition, many countries manufacture weapons such as heavy machine-guns, 20- to 35-mm calibre cannon, rocket artillery and 60- to 80-mm calibre mortars. Not only is the destructive power of these weapons high but the sheer volume of equipment already available and number of suppliers would also make effective monitoring and verification of their distribution difficult to achieve.

[80] Hoagland, J. H. and Clapp, P. A., 'Notes on small arms traffic', Paper C/70-7, Arms Control Project, Massachusetts Institute of Technology, Mar. 1970.

[81] *Jane's Infantry Weapons 1989–90* (Jane's: Coulsdon, 1989).

[82] *Military Coproduction*, Report GAO/NSIAD-89-117 of the National Security and International Affairs Division of the United States General Accounting Office, 22 Mar. 1989.

[83] *US–Korea Coproduction: A Review of the M-16 Rifle Program*, Report GAO/NSIAD-88-117 of the National Security and International Affairs Division of the United States General Accounting Office, 11 Apr. 1988.

Appendix 7A. Aggregate tables of the value of the trade in major weapons with the Third World, 1970–89

Table 7A.1. Values of imports of major weapons by the Third World: by region, 1970–89[a]

Figures are SIPRI trend indicator values, as expressed in US $m., at constant (1985) prices. A = yearly figures, B = five-year moving averages.[b]

Region[c]		1970	1971	1972	1973	1974	1975	1976	1977
South Asia	A	857	1 274	1 800	1 049	936	584	1 066	1 932
	B	1 135	1 181	1 183	1 129	1 087	1 113	1 278	1 376
Far East	A	2 299	3 582	6 962	1 815	1 920	1 595	1 490	1 983
	B	3 697	3 329	3 316	3 175	2 757	1 761	2 154	2 958
Middle East	A	5 242	6 092	5 842	10 472	6 999	7 014	7 076	9 816
	B	4 813	6 179	6 930	7 284	7 481	8 276	7 716	7 560
North Africa	A	185	224	373	340	591	2 343	2 282	2 619
	B	258	293	342	774	1 186	1 635	2 354	3 386
South America	A	285	786	1 093	2 354	1 338	1 600	1 922	2 836
	B	628	1 033	1 171	1 434	1 661	2 010	2 006	2 066
Sub-Saharan Africa	A	389	441	266	466	869	645	1 044	2 562
	B	278	339	486	537	658	1 117	1 528	1 536
Central America	A	185	135	261	309	299	204	234	557
	B	140	191	238	242	261	321	312	312
South Africa	A	275	104	292	459	533	232	371	171
	B	181	240	333	324	378	353	330	244
Total[d]	**A**	**9 717**	**12 639**	**16 890**	**17 263**	**13 486**	**14 217**	**15 485**	**2 477**
	B	**11 130**	**12 784**	**13 999**	**14 899**	**15 468**	**16 586**	**17 679**	**9 436**

[a] The values include licensed production of major weapons in Third World countries (see appendix 7C). For the values for the period 1951–69, see Brzoska, M. and Ohlson, T., SIPRI, *Arms Transfers to the Third World, 1971–85* (Oxford University Press: Oxford, 1987).

[b] Five-year moving averages are calculated as a more stable measure of the trend in arms imports than the often erratic year-to-year figures.

[c] The regions are listed in rank order according to their values in the column for 1989. The following countries are included in each region:

South Asia: Afghanistan, Bangladesh, India, Nepal, Pakistan and Sri Lanka.

Far East: Brunei, Fiji, Indonesia, Kampuchea, North Korea, South Korea, Laos, Malaysia, Mongolia, Myanmar (formerly Burma), Papua New Guinea, Philippines, Samoa, Singapore, Solomon Islands, Taiwan, Thailand, Vanuatu and Viet Nam.

Middle East: Bahrain, Egypt, Iran, Iraq, Israel, Jordan, Kuwait, Lebanon, Oman, Qatar, Saudi Arabia, Syria, United Arab Emirates, North Yemen and South Yemen.

North Africa: Algeria, Libya, Morocco and Tunisia.

1978	1979	1980	1981	1982	1983	1984	1985	1986	1987	1988	1989
1 871	1 425	2 424	2 583	2 688	2 364	2 036	2 727	4 965	5 867	4 847	6 906
1 744	2 047	2 198	2 297	2 419	2 480	2 956	3 592	4 089	5 063	..	..
3 779	5 944	3 085	2 972	1 777	2 564	2 861	3 156	3 266	3 073	4 118	3 279
3 256	3 553	3 511	3 268	2 652	2 666	2 725	2 984	3 295	3 378	..	..
7 675	6 216	8 377	9 402	11 336	11 774	11 008	9 691	10 371	12 812	7 463	3 270
7 832	8 297	8 601	9 421	10 379	10 642	10 836	11 131	10 269	8 721	..	..
3 936	5 749	3 334	2 990	3 050	1 703	1 499	1 113	1 393	538	381	1 185
3 584	3 726	3 812	3 365	2 515	2 071	1 752	1 249	985	922	..	..
2 335	1 635	2 137	3 215	2 509	2 878	2 980	1 219	1 124	1 655	824	963
2 173	2 432	2 367	2 475	2 744	2 560	2 142	1 971	1 560	1 157	..	..
2 520	909	1 535	2 095	1 728	1 406	1 937	2 007	1 667	1 834	1 392	397
1 714	1 924	1 757	1 534	1 740	1 835	1 749	1 770	1 767	1 459	..	..
268	295	187	657	1 092	901	599	659	618	371	203	300
308	393	500	626	687	782	774	630	490	430	..	..
343	102	109	4	4	158	5	4	154	20	28	3
219	146	112	75	56	35	65	68	42	42	..	..
2 728	**22 275**	**21 189**	**23 917**	**24 184**	**23 748**	**22 925**	**20 576**	**23 560**	**26 170**	**19 256**	**16 301**
0 831	**22 517**	**22 858**	**23 063**	**23 193**	**23 070**	**22 999**	**23 396**	**22 497**	**21 173**	**..**	**..**

South America: Argentina, Bolivia, Brazil, Chile, Colombia, Ecuador, Guyana, Paraguay, Peru, Suriname, Uruguay and Venezuela.

Sub-Saharan Africa: Angola, Benin, Botswana, Burkina Faso, Burundi, Cameroon, Cape Verde, Central African Republic, Chad, Comoros, Congo Côte d'Ivoire, Djibouti, Equatorial Guinea, Ethiopia, Gabon, Gambia, Ghana, Guinea, Buinea-Bissau, Kenya, Lesotho, Liberia, Madagascar, Malawi, Mali, Mauritania, Mauritius, Mozambique, Namibia, Niger, Nigeria, Rwanda, Senegal, Seychelles, Sierra Leone, Somalia, Sudan, Swaziland, Tanzania, Togo, Uganda, Zaire, Zambia and Zimbabwe.

Central America: Bahamas, Barbados, Belize, Costa Rica, Cuba, Dominican Republic, Dominica, El Salvador, Guatemala, Haiti, Honduras, Jamaica, Mexico, Nicaragua, Panama, St Vincent and the Grenadines, and Trinidad and Tobago.

[d] Items may not add up to totals due to rounding.

.. Not applicable.

Source: SIPRI data base.

Table 7A.2. Values of exports of major weapons to regions listed in table 7A.1: by supplier, 1970–89[a]

Figures are SIPRI trend indicator values, as expressed in US $m., at constant (1985) prices. A = yearly figures, B = five-year moving averages.[b]

Supplier[c]		1970	1971	1972	1973	1974	1975	1976	1977
USSR	A	4 589	5 991	7 851	7 263	5 314	3 680	4 509	7 589
	B	5 139	5 594	6 202	6 020	5 723	5 671	6 220	7 383
USA	A	3 551	3 787	5 804	6 318	4 352	6 866	7 064	9 525
	B	3 693	4 514	4 762	5 425	6 081	6 825	6 931	6 853
France	A	687	683	796	1 654	1 270	1 168	1 440	2 276
	B	605	820	1 018	1 114	1 266	1 562	1 657	2 010
UK	A	472	1 214	1 195	1 309	1 070	1 193	833	1 652
	B	897	1 055	1 052	1 196	1 120	1 211	1 192	1 132
China	A	134	358	417	229	368	338	233	120
	B	231	245	301	342	317	258	305	315
Israel	A	5	1	34	4	67	127	61	59
	B	10	10	22	47	59	64	157	189
Brazil	A	..	..	..	..	11	25	154	130
	B	0	0	2	7	38	64	88	108
FR Germany	A	3	86	108	..	462	269	166	204
	B	58	51	132	185	201	220	272	212
Spain	A	..	..	10	..	..	5	3	13
	B	5	3	2	3	4	4	10	14
Italy	A	37	95	137	148	273	144	163	288
	B	95	100	138	159	173	203	238	379
Other Third World	A	26	48	134	30	184	146	227	187
	B	50	53	84	108	144	155	168	232
Other industrialized, West[d]	A	68	223	327	254	83	207	506	184
	B	197	223	191	219	276	247	288	331
Other indus.trialized, neutral[e]	A	3	95	5	10	13	24	63	68
	B	24	25	25	29	23	36	41	135
Other industrialized, East[f]	A	143	60	72	44	19	23	63	183
	B	127	91	68	44	44	67	111	144
Total	**A**	**9 717**	**12 639**	**16 890**	**17 263**	**13 486**	**14 217**	**15 485**	**2 477**
	B	**11 130**	**12 784**	**13 999**	**14 899**	**15 468**	**16 586**	**17 679**	**9 436**

[a] The values include licensed production of major weapons in Third World countries (see appendix 7C). For the values for the period 1951–69, see Brzoska, M. and Ohlson, T., SIPRI, *Arms Transfers to the Third World, 1971–85* (Oxford University Press: Oxford 1987).

[b] Five-year moving averages are calculated as a more stable measure of the trend in arms imports than the often erratic year-to-year figures.

[c] The regions are listed in rank order according to their values in the column for 1989.

[d] Other NATO, Australia and Japan.

[e] Austria, New Zealand, Sweden, Switzerland and Yugoslavia.

[f] Other WTO.

– Nil.

.. Not applicable.

Source: SIPRI data base.

1978	1979	1980	1981	1982	1983	1984	1985	1986	1987	1988	1989
10 010	11 126	9 277	8 370	7 565	7 578	7 537	8 563	10 327	10 759	8 238	8 515
8 502	9 274	9 270	8 783	8 065	7 923	8 314	8 953	9 085	9 280	..	..
6 850	3 961	5 637	6 155	6 989	6 205	4 906	4 024	4 925	6 270	3 649	2 528
6 607	6 425	5 918	5 789	5 978	5 656	5 410	5 266	4 755	4 279	..	..
2 131	3 033	2 617	3 511	3 181	3 070	3 212	3 588	3 355	2 518	1 312	1 527
2 299	2 714	2 894	3 082	3 118	3 312	3 281	3 148	2 797	2 460	..	..
1 214	766	725	1 101	1 594	676	1 083	903	1 020	1 530	1 165	993
1 038	1 092	1 080	973	1 036	1 071	1 055	1 042	1 140	1 122	..	..
465	418	625	334	700	890	1 210	1 017	1 193	1 960	1 781	718
372	393	509	593	752	830	1 002	1 254	1 432	1 334	..	..
470	227	209	252	365	370	263	160	242	273	117	216
205	244	305	285	292	282	280	262	211	202	..	..
120	112	268	271	202	298	271	172	134	491	338	182
157	180	195	230	262	243	215	273	281	264	..	..
258	162	283	938	323	1 174	1 830	395	649	252	480	149
215	369	393	576	910	932	874	860	721	385	..	..
30	21	9	97	360	589	475	139	185	160	206	143
15	34	103	215	306	332	349	310	233	167	..	..
323	975	654	1 333	1 350	1 048	831	578	398	319	360	30
481	715	927	1 072	1 043	1 028	841	635	497	337	..	..
95	507	194	485	580	885	631	430	477	604	684	164
242	294	372	530	555	602	601	606	565	472	..	..
457	301	230	282	437	431	141	129	203	447	461	604
336	291	341	336	304	284	268	270	276	369	..	..
36	485	316	360	202	249	207	263	272	385	282	150
193	253	280	322	267	256	239	275	282	271	..	..
268	181	145	426	336	284	329	216	180	202	181	383
168	241	271	275	304	318	269	242	222	232	..	..
22 728	**22 275**	**21 189**	**23 917**	**24 184**	**23 748**	**22 925**	**20 576**	**23 560**	**26 170**	**19 256**	**16 301**
20 831	**22 517**	**22 858**	**23 063**	**23 193**	**23 070**	**22 999**	**23 396**	**22 497**	**21 173**	**..**	**..**

Appendix 7B. Register of the trade in major conventional weapons with industrialized and Third World countries, 1989

This appendix lists major weapons on order or under delivery during 1989. The column 'Year(s) of deliveries' includes aggregates of all deliveries since the beginning of the contract. The sources and methods for the data collection, and the conventions, abbreviations and acronyms used, are explained in appendix 7D. The entries are made alphabetically, by recipient and supplier.

Recipient	Supplier	No. ordered	Weapon designation	Weapon description	Year of order	Year(s) of deliveries	No. delivered	Comments
I. Industrialized countries								
Australia	Canada	15	LAV-25	APC	1989		2 500	Total cost US $33 m
	France	5	Falcon-900	Trpt aircraft	1988	1988–89	(4)	For VIP use
	Italy	(10)	HSS-1	Surveillance radar	1986	1988–89	(4)	Deal worth $20 m
	South Africa	1	Buffel	Armoured car	1989	1989	1	For Australian UN forces in Namibia
	UK	. .	Rapier	Landmob SAM	1975	1978–89	(520)	
		1	Appleleaf Class	Tanker	1989	1989	1	Ex-Fleet auxiliary leased to Australia
	USA	8	SH-60B Seahawk	Helicopter	1985	1989	8	In addition to 8 ordered 1985
		8	SH-60B Seahawk	Helicopter	1986			
		14	UH-60 Blackhawk	Helicopter	1985	1989	14	
		24	UH-60 Blackhawk	Helicopter	1985			In addition to previous orders for 30 Blackhawk/Seahawks
		15	LAV-25	APC	1989	1989	15	Deal worth $18.7 m
		2	RGM-84A Launch	ShShM launcher	1983	1989	1	Arming FFG-7 frigates produced under licence

Recipient/Supplier	No.	Weapon designation	Weapon description	Year order	Year deliveries	No. delivered	Comments
	2	RIM-66A Launcher	ShAM launcher	1985	1989	1	Arming FFG-7 frigates produced under licence
	..	AIM-7F Sparrow	Air-to-air missile	1984	1986–89	(400)	Arming F/A-18 Hornet fighters
	..	AIM-9M	Air-to-air missile	1984	1986–89	(880)	Arming F/A-18 Hornet fighters
	(22)	RGM-84A Harpoon	ShShM	1987			Arming FFG-7 Class frigates and Oberon Class submarines
	(65)	RIM-67C/SM-2	ShAM/ShShM	(1987)	1989	(10)	Deal worth $50 m
Austria							
Sweden	24	J-35 Draken	Fighter	1985	1988–89	24	Offsets worth 130%
	300	RBS-56 Bill	Anti-tank missile	1989	1989		Deal worth $77 m
USA	36	M-109-A2 155mm	SPH	1988	1989	(12)	Deal worth $36 m; brings total ordered to 109
Belgium							
France	(530)	Magic-2	Air-to-air missile	(1985)	1988–89	(212)	Arming Mirage-5 fighters
	714	Mistral	Portable SAM	1988			Deal worth $93 m incl 118 launchers; offsets worth 75%
Italy	46	A-109	Helicopter	1988	1988		28 to be armed with TOW missiles; deal worth $317 m incl TOW missiles, offsets worth 73%
Sweden	28	Helitow	Fire control system	1988	1988		To equip A-109 helicopters
USA	..	AGM-65C	ASM	1989	1989		Arming F-16 fighters
	545	AIM-9M	Air-to-air missile	1988	1988		Arming F-16 fighters
	940	AIM-9M	Air-to-air missile	1989	1989	(180)	Deal worth $80 m
	(224)	BGM-71A TOW	Anti-tank missile	(1989)			Arming 28 A-109A Mk-2 helicopters
Bulgaria							
USSR	..	SA-13 Launcher	AAV(M)	(1984)	1985–88	(16)	
	..	ZSU-23-4 Shilka	AAV	(1984)	1985–88	(48)	
	..	SA-13 Gopher	Landmob SAM	(1984)	1985–88	(768)	
Canada							
France	10 000	Eryx	Anti-tank missile	(1987)			Programme suspended
Italy	..	EH-101	Helicopter	1988			Status uncertain
	10	Skyguard	Air defence radar	1986	1989	(3)	Part of ADATS contract
Sweden	12	Giraffe	Fire control radar	(1985)	1988	2	For City Class destroyers

Recipient	Supplier	No. ordered	Weapon designation	Weapon description	Year of order	Year(s) of deliveries	No. delivered	Comments
	Switzerland	36	ADATS	SAM system	1986	1989	(10)	Deal worth $1 b incl SAMs, AA guns and fire control radars
	UK	(35)	EH-101	Helicopter	(1987)			
		7	S-500	Surveillance radar	1987	1988–89	(6)	For use as a static training centre
		1	Oberon Class	Submarine	1989	1989	1	Attrition replacements
	USA	28	F/A-18 Hornet	Fighter	1989			
		3	P-3C Update-3	Maritime patrol	1989			
		6	Phalanx	CIWS	1986	1988	(2)	Arming City Class frigates
		4	Phalanx	CIWS	1987	1988–89	(3)	Arming Tribal Class frigates
		6	RGM-84A Launcher	ShShM launcher	(1984)	1988–89	(2)	Arming City Class frigates
		6	Seasparrow VLS	ShAM/PDM launcher	1984	1988–89	(2)	Arming City Class frigates; deal worth $75 m incl modifications to missiles
		4	Seasparrow VLS	ShAM/PDM launcher	1986	1988–89	(3)	Arming Tribal Class frigates; for delivery 1988–90
		184	AIM-7M Sparrow	Air-to-air missile	1985	1987–89	(184)	Arming F/A-18 fighters
		96	AIM-7M Sparrow	Air-to-air missile	(1987)			Arming F/A-18 fighters; deal worth $31 m incl 24 Mk 48 torpedoes
		100	AIM-9M	Air-to-air missile	1988	1989	(50)	Deal worth $21 m
		..	RGM-84A Harpoon	ShShM	1984	1988–89	(16)	Arming City Class frigates
		29	RGM-84A Harpoon	ShShM	1988			Deal worth $47 m incl spares, training and support
		74	RIM-66C/SM-2	ShAM/ShShM	1988	1988–89	(45)	Arming Tribal Class frigates; deal worth $48 m
		22	RIM-67C/SM-2	ShAM/ShShM	1987	1988–89	(22)	Arming Tribal Class frigates
		168	Seasparrow	ShAM	1984	1988–89	(56)	Arming City Class frigates; deal worth $75 m
		(128)	Seasparrow	ShAM	1986	1988–89	(96)	Arming 4 Tribal Class frigates

Recipient	Supplier	No.	Weapon designation	Weapon description	Year of order	Years of deliveries	No. delivered	Comments
	USSR	1	Su-7 Fitter	Fighter	1989	1989	1	For air museum
China	Canada	2	Challenger-601	Trpt aircraft	1988	1988–89	2	Follows order for 3
	France	8	SA-342L Gazelle	Helicopter	1987	1988–89	(8)	Deal worth $29.7 m
		(96)	HOT-2	Anti-tank missile	1987	1988–89	(96)	Arming SA-342L Gazelle helicopters
	USA	6	CH-47D Chinook	Helicopter	1989	1988		Deliveries suspended in June 1989
		4	AN/TPQ-37	Tracking radar	(1987)	1988	2	Deliveries suspended in June 1989 with deliveries of avionics, 4 Mk 46 torpedoes and 155-mm howitzer ammunition
Cyprus	France	6	SA-342L Gazelle	Helicopter	1987	1987–89	6	Armed with HOT anti-tank missiles
		36	AMX-30-B2	Main battle tank	1989	1989	12	Deal worth $115 m; in addition to 16 supplied earlier
		36	VAB	APC	1987	1989	(18)	Armed with HOT anti-tank missiles
		..	HOT-2	Anti-tank missile	1987	1987–89	(234)	Arming SA-342 helicopters and VAB APCs; total deal worth $250 m
		..	Mistral	Portable SAM	(1988)	1989	(180)	Arming VAB APCs and infantry version
	Greece	6	Artemis 30mm	Mobile radar	1988			
	Italy	30	Skyguard	Air defence radar	1987	1988–89	12	Fire control for new 35-mm AAGs
	Switzerland	2	PC-9	Trainer	1987	1989	2	
Czechoslovakia	USSR	..	Mi-17 Hip-H	Helicopter	(1985)	1985–88	(48)	Replacing Mi-4s
		(60)	Su-25 Frogfoot	Fighter/grd attack	(1984)	1984–89	(60)	Replacing MiG-17s
		..	2S1 122mm	SPH	(1979)	1980–89	(360)	May be from Poland
		..	2S4 240mm	SPM	(1985)	1986–89	(36)	
		..	2S7 203mm	SPG	(1987)	1988–89	(48)	First WTO country to deploy
		..	BRDM-2 Gaskin	AAV(M)	1979	1980–89	(100)	
		..	D-30 122mm	Towed howitzer	(1980)	1985–89	(400)	
		..	SA-13 Launcher	AAV(M)	(1984)	1984–89	(30)	
		(24)	SA-8 SAMS	Mobile SAM system	(1986)	1987–89	(24)	
		..	AT-4 Spigot	Anti-tank missile	1979	1980–89	(2 400)	
		..	SA-13 Gopher	Landmob SAM	(1984)	1984–89	(395)	
		..	SA-8 Gecko	Landmob SAM	(1986)	1987–89	(96)	

Recipient	Supplier	No. ordered	Weapon designation	Weapon description	Year of order	Year(s) of deliveries	No. delivered	Comments
		..	SA-9 Gaskin	Landmob SAM	1979	1980–89	(1 600)	
Denmark	France	12	AS-350 Ecureuil	Helicopter	1987			Deal worth $67 m incl Helitow sight system and TOW-2 missiles
	Germany, FR	..	RAM	ShAM/PDM	(1985)			Arming 3 Niels Juel Class frigates
	Norway	3	Type-207	Submarine	1985			
	Sweden	12	Helitow	Fire control	1987			
	UK	6	S-723 Martello	3-D radar	(1984)	1985–89	(6)	
	USA	8	F-16A	Fighter	1985	1987–89	(8)	Deal worth $210 m incl spares
		12	F-16A	Fighter	1988			Arming F-16 fighters; deal worth $24 m
		162	AGM-65D	ASM	1989			Arming 12 AS-350 Ecureuil helicopters
		(196)	BGM-71D TOW-2	Anti-tank missile	1987			Deal worth $61 m incl 336 launchers
		840	FIM-92A Stinger	Portable SAM	1988			For delivery from Seasparrow Consortium
		..	Seasparrow	ShAM	1989			
Finland	France	(20)	Crotale SAMS	Mobile SAM system	1988			Deal worth $230 m
		(6)	TRS-2230/15	Air defence radar	1988			Part of Crotale air defence system
		(360)	Mistral	Portable SAM	1989			Arming Helsinki-2 Class FACs
		(240)	R-440 Crotale	Landmob SAM	1988			
	Sweden	(4)	Giraffe	Fire control radar	(1987)			For Helsinki-2 Class FACs
		..	Giraffe	Fire control radar	(1987)	1988	(5)	Mounted in Finnish Sisu APCs
		4	RBS-15 Launcher	ShShM launcher	1987			Arming Helsinki-2 Class FACs
		64	RBS-15	ShAM/ShShM	(1987)			Arming Helsinki-2 Class FACs
	UK	50	Hawk	Jet trainer	1977	1978–89	(50)	
		12	Hawk	Jet trainer	1989			Second order; deliveries to begin 1989
	USSR	4	Watchman	Surveillance radar	1988	1989	(2)	
		20	BMP-2	MICV	1988	1988–89	(20)	Deal reported to be worth $17.6 m incl AT-4 Spigot ATMs

Recipient	Supplier	No.	Weapon designation	Weapon description	Year of order	Year(s) of deliveries	No. delivered	Comments
France		(100)	MT-LB	APC	(1986)	1986-89	(40)	For delivery 1986-90
		(60)	T-72	Main battle tank	(1986)	1986-89	(40)	Part of $400 m 5-year agreement incl T-72 tanks and MT-LB APCs
		..	AT-4 Spigot	Anti-tank missile	(1986)	1986-89	(240)	Arming BMP-2 APCs
		(40)	AT-5 Spandrel	Anti-tank missile	(1988)	1988-89	(40)	
		(90)	SA-16	Portable SAM	(1987)	1987-89	(90)	
	Nigeria	(14)	SA-330 Puma	Helicopter	1989	1989	(4)	
	Spain	5	C-212-300	Trpt aircraft	1987	1988-89	5	Offset by Spanish order for AS-332 helicopters
		2	CN-235	Trpt aircraft	1988			Initial order of 8 with option for 7 scaled down to 2 with option for 4
	USA	4	C-130H-30	Trpt aircraft	1988	1989	4	Follows order for 6 C-130s in 1987
		4	E-3A Sentry	AWACS	1987			130% offsets in aerospace
		2	RIM-67A Launcher	ShAM launcher	1985	1988	1	Arming Cassard Class frigates
		80	RIM-67A/SM-1	ShAM/ShShM	1985	1988	(40)	Arming Cassard Class frigates
German DR	Bulgaria	..	MT-LB	APC	(1982)	1984-89	(150)	Unconfirmed
	USSR	..	MiG-29	Fighter	(1987)	1988-89	(28)	
		..	2S1 122mm	SPH	(1979)	1980-89	(230)	
		..	2S6	AAV(M)	1988			
		..	BMP-2	MICV	(1978)	1982-89	(800)	May be from Czechoslovak production
		..	BRDM-2 Spandrel	TD(M)	1978	1980-89	(450)	
		..	BTR-70	APC	(1982)	1983-89	(1 000)	Also designated SPW-70
		..	SA-13 Launcher	AAV(M)	(1984)	1985-89	(25)	Unconfirmed
		..	T-72	Main battle tank	(1978)	1979-89	(385)	May be from Poland or Czechoslovakia
		..	AT-4 Spigot	Anti-tank missile	1978	1979-89	(4 200)	
		..	AT-5 Spandrel	Anti-tank missile	1978	1980-89	(11 200)	Arming BMP-2 and BRDM-2 APCs
		..	SA-13 Gopher	Landmob SAM	(1984)	1985-89	(300)	Unconfirmed
Germany, FR	France	23	TRS-3050	Surveillance radar	1987	1987-89	7	Improved fire control radar for Type 148 FACs
	Netherlands	5	Smart	Fire control radar	1989			Fire control radar for Type 123 frigates

Recipient	Supplier	No. ordered	Weapon designation	Weapon description	Year of order	Year(s) of deliveries	No. delivered	Comments
	UK	5	Lynx	Helicopter	1986	1988–89	(5)	For Type 122 Bremen Class frigates; offsets worth 30%
	USA	(100)	Sea Skua	Anti-ship missile	1986	1988–89	(100)	Arming Sea King Mk 41 helicopters
		12	P-3G	Maritime patrol	1989			Deliveries planned from 1996
		3	AN/FPS-117	Air defence radar	1988			
		28	Patriot battery	Mobile SAM system	(1983)	1989	3	14 units on loan from USA, 14 purchased through FMS
		2	RGM-84A Launcher	ShShM launcher	(1986)	1988–89	2	Arming Type 122 Bremen Class frigates
		(2)	Seasparrow Launcher	ShAM/PDM launcher	1986	1988–89	2	Arming Type 122 Bremen Class frigates
		100	AGM-65A	ASM	1988	1989	(12)	
		300	AGM-65D	ASM	(1988)	1989	(36)	
		1 200	AGM-65G	ASM	(1988)	1989	(150)	
		1 182	AGM-88 Harm	ARM	1987	1988–89	(368)	Arming Tornado fighters
		804	MIM-104 Patriot	SAM	1984	1989	150	
		(32)	RGM-84A Harpoon	ShShM	(1986)	1988–89	(32)	Arming Type 122 Bremen Class frigates
		48	Seasparrow	ShAM	(1986)	1988–89	(48)	Arming Type 122 Bremen Class frigates
Greece	France	40	Mirage-2000	Fighter	1985	1988–89	36	36 fighters and 4 trainers
		..	Stentor	Surveillance radar	(1987)	1988	(2)	Prior to licensed production
		(240)	Magic-2	Air-to-air missile	(1986)	1988–89	(220)	Arming Mirage-2000 fighters
		4 000	Milan	Anti-tank missile	1987	1988–89	(2 000)	Deal worth $54 m incl 100 launchers
	Germany, FR	75	Leopard-1-A3	Main battle tank	1988	1988–89	(75)	Gift as offset for Greek order of 4 Meko-200 frigates
		4	MPDR	Surveillance radar	1988	1989	(2)	Deal worth $11.7 m; financed by NATO military aid
		(96)	NATO Seasparrow	ShAM/ShShM	(1988)			Arming Meko-200 Class frigates
		1	Meko-200 Type	Frigate	1988			Deal worth $1.2 b incl 3 to be built under licence; offsets worth $250 m

Recipient/supplier	No. ordered	Weapon designation	Weapon description	Year of order	Year(s) of deliveries	No. delivered/produced	Comments
Italy	25	A-109	Helicopter	(1987)			Negotiating
Netherlands	4	Smart	Fire control radar	1989			For Greek Meko-200 Class
USA	40	F-16C	Fighter	1985		(24)	Includes 6 F-16D versions
	50	F-4E Phantom	Fighter	1988	1988–89	(40)	From US stocks
	19	F-4G Wild Weasel	Fighter	1988	1989	(9)	Part of military aid package with 50 F-4E fighters from US stocks
	300	M-48-A5	Main battle tank	1986	1988–89	(200)	Deal worth $103 m; 250 financed by FMS; from US stocks
	60	M-48-A5	Main battle tank	1989			Deal worth $26 m; refurbished; from US stocks
	2	HADR	Air defence radar	1985	1988–89	(2)	Part of NADGE air defence system
	4	Phalanx	CIWS	(1987)			Arming Meko-200 Class frigates
	(4)	RGM-84A Launcher	ShShM launcher	1989			Arming Meko-200 Class frigates
	(4)	Seasparrow VLS	ShAM/PDM launcher	1988			Arming Meko-200 Class frigates
	(152)	AGM-45A Shrike	ARM	1988	1989	(76)	Arming F-4G Wild Weasels
	80	AIM-7F Sparrow	Air-to-air missile	(1987)	1988–89	(60)	Arming 40 F-4E fighters
	80	AIM-9F	Air-to-air missile	(1987)	1988–89	(60)	Arming 40 F-4E fighters
	1 000	FIM-92A Stinger	Portable SAM	1988	1989	(250)	Deal worth $124 m incl 500 launchers
	16	RGM-84A Harpoon	ShShM	1989			Arming first of 4 Meko-200 Class frigates; deal worth $19 m
	(64)	Seasparrow	ShAM	(1988)			Arming Meko-200 Class frigates
Hungary							
USSR	..	Mi-17 Hip-H	Helicopter	1988			
	..	MiG-29	Fighter	(1988)			
Italy							
France	1	Falcon-50	Trpt aircraft	1988	1989	1	In addition to 2 delivered 1986
Germany, FR	..	Kormoran-2	Anti-ship missile	(1986)	1988–89	30	Arming Tornado fighters
Portugal	4	Boeing-707	Trpt aircraft	1988	1989	4	
UK	(12)	Sea Harrier	Fighter	1989			Order number may be up to 18
USA	20	MLRS 227mm	MRL	1985	1989	(4)	
	2	HADR	Air defence radar	1988	1988	(1)	Part of NADGE system
	6 629	BGM-71C I-TOW	Anti-tank missile	1984	1986–89	(6 629)	Deal worth $67 m incl 1239 practice missiles

Recipient	Supplier	No. ordered	Weapon designation	Weapon description	Year of order	Year(s) of deliveries	No. delivered	Comments
		(3 900)	BGM-71D TOW-2	Anti-tank missile	1987	1987–89	(1 800)	Arming A-129 Mangusta helicopters
		(16)	UGM-84A Harpoon	SuShM	(1986)			Arming Sauro Class submarines
Japan	France	2	Falcon-900	Trpt aircraft	1987	1989	2	
	Italy	3	Sparviero Class	Hydrofoil FAC	(1988)			Deal worth $170 m
	UK	3	BAe-125-800	Utility jet	1989			
	USA	3	C-130H Hercules	Trpt aircraft	1987	1988–89	3	
		2	C-130H-30	Trpt aircraft	1988	1989	2	Deal worth $60 m
		5	E-2C Hawkeye	AEW	1988	1989	3	In addition to 8 previously delivered
		3	E-2C Hawkeye	AEW	1989	1989	3	Deal worth $214 m incl spares
		6	Learjet-35A	Maritime patrol	1985	1985–89	(6)	1 target tug; 5 for recce training
		6	MH-53E	Helicopter	(1987)	1989	4	
		1	Patriot battery	Mobile SAM system	1984	1989	1	To be followed by co-production
		(28)	Phalanx	CIWS	1985	1987–89	16	Arming Asagiri Class and second batch of Hatsuyuki Class
		(8)	Phalanx	CIWS	1988			Part of Aegis air defence system arming new class of Japanese destroyer
		..	RGM-84A Launcher	ShShM launcher	(1979)	1980–89	(41)	Arming various Japanese escorts and Yuushio Class submarines
		(4)	RGM-84A Launcher	ShShM launcher	1988			Part of Aegis air defence system arming new class of Japanese destroyer
		..	Seasparrow Launcher	ShAM/PDM launcher	1980	1981–89	(20)	Arming various classes of Japanese escort
		(8)	Seasparrow VLS	ShAM/PDM launcher	1988			Part of Aegis air defence system arming new class of Japanese destroyer
		55	AGM-84A Harpoon	Anti-ship missile	(1987)	1988–89	(36)	Deal worth $80 m; mix of air-, sea- and submarine-launched versions unclear
		..	FIM-92A Stinger	Portable SAM	(1988)			

Recipient	Supplier	No.	Weapon designation	Weapon description	Year of order	Year of delivery	No. delivered	Comments
		20	MIM-104 Patriot	SAM	1984	1989	20	Arming various Japanese destroyers, frigates and submarines
		..	RGM-84A Harpoon	ShShM	(1979)	1980–89	(953)	
		(64)	RGM-84A Harpoon	ShShM	1988	1988	(16)	Part of Aegis air defence system arming new class of Japanese destroyer Deal worth $173 m
		99	RGM-84A Harpoon	ShShM	1989			Part of Aegis air defence system arming new class of Japanese destroyer
		(350)	RIM-66C/SM-2	ShAM/ShShM	1988			
		..	Seasparrow	ShAM	1980	1981–89	(312)	Arming various Japanese-built frigates and destroyers
Netherlands	France	14	Crotale SAMS	Mobile SAM system	1989			Option on further 7; status uncertain
		(168)	R-440 Crotale	Landmob SAM	1989			
	Switzerland	10	PC-7	Trainer	1988	1989	10	
	USA	21	MLRS 227mm	MRL	1986	1989	(10)	Deal worth $192 m incl 2700 rockets
		46	MLRS 227mm	MRL	1987			
		4	AN/TPQ-37	Tracking radar	1986	1988–89	4	
		4	Patriot battery	Mobile SAM system	1984	1989	3	Deal worth $200 m
		4	Patriot battery	Mobile SAM system	(1988)			
		8	RGM-84A Launcher	ShShM launcher	1985	1987–89	(3)	Arming 8 M Class frigates
		(40)	AGM-84A Harpoon	Anti-ship missile	1988			
		900	AIM-9L	Air-to-air missile	1983	1985–89	(900)	Arming F-16 fighters; deal worth $78 m
		290	AIM-9M	Air-to-air missile	1988			Arming F-16 fighters; deal worth $27 m
		5 285	FGM-77 Dragon	Anti-tank missile	1978	1978–89	5 285	Deal incl 437 launchers
		160	MIM-104 Patriot	SAM	1983	1989	(120)	
		256	MIM-104 Patriot	SAM	(1988)			
		(128)	RGM-84A Harpoon	ShShM	1988	1989	(32)	Includes unspecified mix of air-launched Harpoon missiles; arming M-Class frigates
New Zealand	Australia	24	Hamel 105mm	Towed gun	1986	1987–89	24	
		1	ASL-315	Patrol craft	(1985)	1989	1	For Cook Islands under Pacific Patrol Boat Programme

Recipient	Supplier	No. ordered	Weapon designation	Weapon description	Year of order	Year(s) of deliveries	No. delivered	Comments
		2	Meko-200 Class	Frigate	1989			Option on 2 more; to be built in Australia; deal worth $554.7 m without sonars or helicopters
	Italy	16	MB-339K	Fighter/trainer	1989			Deal worth $120 m; option on 2 more
	USA	..	AGM-65B	ASM	1988	1989	(60)	Arming 22 A-4 Skyhawk fighters
		..	AIM-9P	Air-to-air missile	1988	1989	51	Arming 22 A-4 Skyhawk fighters
Norway	Germany, FR	6	Type-210	Submarine	1983	1989	1	For coastal defence
	Sweden	8	Ersta 120mm	Coastal gun	1986	1986–89	(8)	Final assembly in Norway
		..	Giraffe	Fire control radar	1985	1986–89	(40)	
		(9)	Giraffe 50	Surveillance radar	1989	1989	2	Deal worth $90 m
		..	RBS-70	Portable SAM	1985	1987–89	(290)	Deal worth $90 m; fifth order
		(360)	RBS-70	Portable SAM	1989			Deal worth $80 m; offsets worth 45%; sixth order
	UK	1	SH-3D Sea King	Helicopter	1989			Deal worth $18 m including upgrade of Norwegian Sea King fleet
	USA	6	F-16A	Fighter	1983	1989	2	Attrition replacements
		4	F-16A	Fighter	1989			Deal worth $125 m; option on 4 more
		2	F-16B	Fighter/trainer	1986	1988–89	2	
		18	Model 412	Helicopter	1986	1987–89	(18)	
		4	P-3C Orion	Maritime patrol	1986	1988–89	8	
		16	M-113-A2	APC	(1986)	1988–89	(16)	
		36	M-48-A5	Main battle tank	1986	1987–89	(36)	Deal worth $26 m
		44	M-901 TOW	Tank destroyer	(1986)	1988–89	(44)	
		2	HADR	Air defence radar	1989	1989	1	In addition to 3 supplied in 1985–86; deal worth $45 m
		..	AIM-120A AMRAAM	Air-to-air missile	1989			Deal worth $12.5 m; for evaluation as a mobile SAM

Recipient	Supplier	No.	Weapon designation	Weapon description	Year of order	Year(s) of deliveries	No. delivered	Comments
		7 612	BGM-71D TOW-2	Anti-tank missile	1985	1987–89	(2 000)	Deal worth $126 m incl 300 launchers and spares
Poland	USSR	..	MiG-29	Fighter	(1988)	1989	11	7 MiG-29A and 4 B versions
		..	Su-22 Fitter-J	Fighter/grd attack	(1986)	1986–89	(80)	Eventual requirement may reach 2000
		..	BMP-2	MICV	(1988)			Arming 5 Tarantul Class corvettes; status uncertain
		5	SA-N-5 Launcher	ShAM launcher	(1985)			Arming 5 Tarantul Class corvettes; status uncertain
		..	AA-10 Alamo	Air-to-air missile	(1988)	1989	(36)	Arming MiG-29 fighters
		..	AA-11 Archer	Air-to-air missile	(1988)	1989	(36)	Arming MiG-29 fighters
		..	AA-8 Aphid	Air-to-air missile	(1988)	1989	(96)	Arming Mi-24 Hind helicopters
		..	AA-8 Aphid	Air-to-air missile	(1988)	1989	(36)	Arming MiG-29 fighters
		..	AS-7 Kerry	ASM	(1985)	1986–89	(640)	Arming MiG-29 fighters
		(60)	SA-N-5	ShAM	(1985)			Arming 5 Tarantul Class corvettes
		(60)	SSN-2 Styx	ShShM	(1985)			Arming 5 Tarantul Class corvettes
		(4)	Kilo Class	Submarine	(1984)	1986	1	Replacing Whiskey Class submarines
		(5)	Tarantul Class	Corvette	1985			Order number may be up to 8
Portugal	France	2	Falcon-50	Trpt aircraft	1989	1989	(3)	May be for civilian use
		18	TB-30 Epsilon	Trainer	1987	1989		Deal worth $17 m
		(700)	Milan-2	Anti-tank missile	(1988)	1989	(350)	Partial funding from NATO military fund
	Germany, FR	3	Meko-200 Type	Frigate	1986			Deal worth $700 m; 60% funding from NATO military fund
	Italy	24	Aspide	SAM/ShAM	1986	1986		Arming 3 Meko-200 frigates
	UK	2	Watchman	Surveillance radar	1988	1988		Deal worth $9 m incl 2 AN/TPS-44 radars; funded by NATO military assistance
	USA	20	F-16A	Fighter	(1989)	(1989)		Ex-USAF; to be funded with up to $227 m grant assistance
		..	Model 205 UH-1A	Helicopter	1989	1989		In return for US base rights in the Azores; ex-USAF
		..	Model 209 AH-1G	Helicopter	1989	1989		
		5	SH-2F Seasprite	Helicopter	1989	1989		Deal worth $69 m; equipping Meko-200 type frigates

Recipient	Supplier	No. ordered	Weapon designation	Weapon description	Year of order	Year(s) of deliveries	No. delivered	Comments
		..	SH-60B Seahawk	Helicopter	1989			
		(34)	M-163 Vulcan	AAV	(1987)	1987–89	(34)	
		2	AN/TPS-44	Surveillance radar	1988			
		3	HADR	Air defence radar	1985	1988	1	Part of NADGE air defence system; Ex-USAF
		1	Hawk SAMS	Mobile SAM system	1989			
		3	Phalanx	CIWS	1986			Arming 3 Meko-200 Type frigates
		3	RGM-84A Launch	ShShM launcher	1986			Arming 3 Meko-200 Type frigates
		3	Seasparrow VLS	ShAM/PDM launcher	1986			Arming 3 Meko-200 Type frigates
		..	BGM-71D TOW-2	Anti-tank missile	(1988)			
		24	RGM-84A Harpoon	ShShM	1986			Arming 3 Meko-200 Type frigates
		17	Seasparrow	ShAM	1988			Arming 3 Meko-200 Type frigates
Romania	USSR	..	MiG-23MF	Fighter/interceptor	(1980)	1981–88	(46)	
		..	AT-4 Spigot	Anti-tank missile	(1984)	1985–89	(250)	Arming Romanian APCs
Spain	Canada	(8)	CL-215	Amphibian	1989			
	France	18	AMX-30 Roland	AAV(M)	1984	1988–89	(18)	Deal worth $182.4 m incl 414 Roland-2 SAMs; offsets worth 50%
		(2 000)	HOT	Anti-tank missile	1984	1986–89	(1 750)	Incl 150 launchers
		(3 500)	Milan-2	Anti-tank missile	1984	1986–88	(3 000)	Incl 250 launchers
		3 000	Mistral	Portable SAM	1988			
	Italy	6	Skyguard Launcher	Mobile SAM system	1985	1987–89	(6)	28 launch units in 6 btys
		504	Aspide	SAM/ShAM	1985	1987–89	(504)	Deal worth $129 m incl 28 Aspide/Spada launch systems; offsets worth 40%
	Norway	5	P-3B Orion	Maritime patrol	1988	1988–89	5	Refurbished in USA; deal worth 4 m pesetas
	USA	72	F/A-18 Hornet	Fighter	1983	1986–89	(64)	60 F/A-18A fighters and 12 F/A-18B trainers

Recipient	Supplier	No. ordered	Weapon designation	Weapon description	Year of order	Year(s) of deliveries	No. delivered	Comments
		8	RF-4C Phantom	Fighter/recce	(1988)	1989	8	Deal worth $20.3 m; ex-US National Guard
		4	SH-60B Seahawk	Helicopter	(1988)	(1988)		In addition to 6 previously ordered; equipping FFG-7 Class frigates
		2	AN/TPQ-36	Tracking radar	(1987)	1988	(1)	Follow-on order for 3 more expected
		96	M54 Chaparral	Mobile SAM system	1981	1985-89	(96)	Coastal defence version
		4	RGM-84A Launcher	ShShM launcher	1988	1989	1	Arming fourth FFG-7 Class frigate; dual-purpose launcher for Harpoon ShShMs and Seasparrow SAMs
		1	RIM-67A Launcher	ShAM launcher	(1986)			Deal worth $48 m
		250	AGM-65D	ASM	1989			Arming F/A-18 Hornet fighters; mix of F and G versions
		250	AGM-65F	Anti-ship missile	1989			
		(70)	AGM-84A Harpoon	Anti-ship missile	(1987)			Arming F/A-18 fighters
		80	AGM-88 Harm	ARM	1987			Arming F7A-18 fighters
		(400)	BGM-71D TOW-2	Anti-tank missile	1987			Deal worth $22 m incl spares and support
		50	MIM-23B Hawk	Landmob SAM	(1987)			Deal worth $272 m incl 96 M54 Chaparral launchers
		1 760	MIM-72F	SAM/ShAM	1981	1985-89	(1 760)	
		20	RGM-84A Harpoon	ShShM	1987			Arming fourth FFG-7 Class frigate
		16	RGM-84A Harpoon	ShShM	1989			Arming coastal defence bty
		(64)	RIM-67A/SM-1	ShAM/ShShM	(1986)			Arming fourth FFG-7 Class frigate
		(60)	Seasparrow	ShAM	1989			Arming 5 Baleares Class frigates
Sweden	France	12	AS-332	Helicopter	1987	1988-89	(6)	Deal worth $106 m; for Navy
	USA	(1 000)	BGM-71D TOW-2	Anti-tank missile	1984	1988-89	(1 000)	
Switzerland	France	12	AS-332	Helicopter	1989	1989	1	Deal worth $190 m; offsets worth 100%
	UK	1	Hawk	Jet trainer	1987	1987		Delivery of 1 from UK prior to Swiss co-production of 19
	USA	34	F/A-18 Hornet	Fighter	1988			Deal worth $1.9 b incl 26 C and 8 D versions; offsets worth 100%
		108	M-109-A2 155mm	SPH	1989	1989		Swiss designation PZH88
		54	M-548	APC	1989	1989		Swiss designation RT-68

Recipient	Supplier	No. ordered	Weapon designation	Weapon description	Year of order	Year(s) of deliveries	No. delivered	Comments
Turkey	France	..	AIM-120A AMRAAM	Air-to-air missile	1988			Arming F/A-18 Hornet fighters
		204	AIM-7M Sparrow	Air-to-air missile	1988			Arming F/A-18 Hornet fighters
		(272)	AIM-9L	Air-to-air missile	(1988)			Arming F/A-18 Hornet fighters
		12 000	BGM-71D TOW-2	Anti-tank missile	(1985)	1988	(1 000)	Deal worth $209 m incl 400 launchers and night vision sights
		3 500	FIM-92A Stinger	Portable SAM	1988			Licensed production under discussion
		4	SA-330L Puma	Helicopter	(1988)	1989	4	
		5	Stentor	Surveillance radar	1987	1988–89	(2)	Air defence package incl surveillance radars and command posts; designation uncertain
		1	TRS-2230/15	Air defence radar	1987			
	Germany, FR	2	Tiger	Point defence radar	1987	1988–89	(2)	
		150	F-104G	Fighter	1980	1980–89	150	
		8	Leopard	ARV	1988	1988–89	(150)	
		(150)	Leopard-1	Main battle tank	1986			Part of deal worth $346 m
		100	Leopard-1-A4	Main battle tank	(1987)			
		1	Koeln Class	Frigate	1989	1989	1	In addition to 3 transferred in 1983–84
	Italy	4	Seaguard	CIWS	(1985)	1987–89	(4)	Arming 4 Meko-200 Type frigates
		2	Seaguard	CIWS	1989			Arming 2 Meko-200 Type frigates
		(96)	Aspide	SAM/ShAM	(1986)	1987–89	(96)	Arming 4 Meko-200 Type frigates
		(48)	Aspide	SAM/ShAM	(1989)			Arming 2 Meko-200 Type frigates
	Netherlands	46	F-5A	Fighter	1987	1989	26	Additional 24 will probably be sold to Turkey at very reduced cost
	Spain	33	F-4C Phantom	Fighter	1988	1989	33	
		4	RF-4C Phantom	Fighter/recce	1988	1989	4	
	UK	40	Shorland S-55	APC	1988			
	USA	40	F-4E Phantom	Fighter	1987	1987–89	(40)	Ex-USAF

Recipient	Supplier	No. ordered	Weapon designation	Weapon description	Year of order	Year(s) of deliveries	No. delivered	Comments
		15	Model 205 UH-1H	Helicopter	1988			Brings total UH-1H Huey orders to 183 (including 96 from Italy)
		6	UH-60 Blackhawk	Helicopter	1988	1989	6	Deal worth $40 m
		12	MLRS 227mm	MRL	1988	1988–89	12	Part of $1 b deal; 168 more to be co-produced
		6	AN/TPQ-36	Tracking radar	(1986)	1988–89	(2)	
		3	HADR	Air defence radar	1985			Part of NADGE air defence system
		2	RGM-84A Launcher	ShShM launcher	1989			Arming 2 Meko-200 Type frigates
		2	Seasparrow VLS	ShAM/PDM launcher	1989			
		80	AIM-7F Sparrow	Air-to-air missile	1987			Arming 40 F-4E fighters
		(320)	AIM-7M Sparrow	Air-to-air missile	(1983)	1986–88	(225)	
		80	AIM-9F	Air-to-air missile	1987			Arming 40 F-4E fighters
		(48)	RGM-84A Harpoon	ShShM	1983	1987–89	(48)	Arming 4 Meko-200 Type frigates
		2	Brooke Class	Frigate	1989			Leased from US Navy
		2	Garcia Class	Frigate	1989			Leased from US Navy
UK	Netherlands	9	Goalkeeper	CIWS	1985	1987–88	6	Arming Invincible Class aircraft carriers 130% offsets
	USA	6	E-3A Sentry	AWACS	(1987)			
		1	E-3A Sentry	AWACS	1987			Deal worth $120 m with offsets of 130%; option on 8th AWACS declined July 1989
USA		8	S-76 Spirit	Helicopter	1989			Deal worth $54 m; for Hong Kong
		24	Phalanx	CIWS	(1985)	1985–89	(24)	Arming Type-42 destroyers
		(11)	RGM-84A Launcher	ShShM launcher	1984	1985–89	(8)	Arming Type-22 and Type-23 frigates
		(330)	AIM-120A AMRAAM	Air-to-air missile	(1988)			Status uncertain
		(72)	Trident-2 D-5	SLBM	(1983)			Arming 4 Vanguard submarines
	Canada	(154)	LAV-25	APC	(1987)			
		2	LAV-AD	AAV(M)	1988			Air defence versions
	China	(6)	F-4	Fighter	(1988)	1988–89	(6)	For training
		(6)	F-6	Fighter	(1988)	1988–89	(6)	For training
		(12)	F-7	Fighter	(1988)	1988–89	(12)	For training
	France	(1)	Romeo-2	Fire control radar	(1989)	1989	1	For evaluation

Recipient	Supplier	No. ordered	Weapon designation	Weapon description	Year of order	Year(s) of deliveries	No. delivered	Comments
	Germany, FR	7	Wiesel	Scout car	1988	1989	7	For evaluation as robotic armoured vehicles
	Israel	100	Have Nap	AGM	(1988)	1989	6	May involve US production
	Kuwait	(29)	A-4M Skyhawk-2	Fighter/bomber	1988	1989		
	Norway	(212)	Penguin-3	Anti-ship missile	(1986)	1989	6	
	Spain	3	P-3A Orion	Maritime patrol	(1988)	1989	3	
	Switzerland	4	ADATS	SAM system	1987	1989	4	
	UK	1	Airship	AEW	1987	1989	1	Prototype AEW/communications relay
		6	BAe-125-800	Utility jet	1988	1989	(1)	US designation C-29A
		6	Bulldog-125	Trainer	1988	1989	6	Flight inspection aircraft
		10	Sherpa	Trpt aircraft	1988			In addition to 18 previously ordered
		53	L119 105mm gun	Towed gun	1987	1988–89	(53)	Part of deal worth $161 m; to be followed by US co-production of 489
		1	Watchman	Surveillance radar	1988	1989	1	Deal worth $3.1 m
USSR	Czechoslovakia	..	L-39 Albatross	Jet trainer	(1972)	1974–89	(1 120)	
		..	BMP-1	MICV	(1972)	1972–88	(5 100)	70% of Czechoslovak BMP production
	Poland	..	Mi-2 Hoplite	Helicopter	1965	1965–89	(2 250)	Deliveries started 1965 and continue at approx 90 per year
	Romania	..	Yak-52	Trainer	(1980)	1981–89	(1 650)	About 200 per year produced for USSR
Yugoslavia	USA	(3)	C-130H Hercules	Trpt aircraft	(1989)			
	USSR	36	MiG-29	Fighter	(1987)	1988–89	(24)	Arming MiG-29 fighters
		(216)	AA-7 Apex	Air-to-air missile	(1987)	1988–89	(144)	Arming MiG-29 fighters
		(216)	AA-8 Aphid	Air-to-air missile	(1987)	1988–89	(144)	Arming Mi-8 helicopters; armoured
		..	AT-3 Sagger	Anti-tank missile	(1971)	1971–89	(1 900)	vehicles and field launchers

II. Third World countries

Recipient	Supplier	No.	Weapon designation	Weapon description	Year of order	Year(s) of deliveries	No. delivered	Comments
Afghanistan	China	..	Type-63 107mm	MRL	(1982)	1982–89	(350)	For Mujahideen; 122-mm rockets without launchers supplied from Feb. 1988
	Egypt	..	Hong Ying-5	Portable SAM	(1982)	1982–89	(850)	SA-7 copy; for Mujahideen
		..	Sakr-18 122mm	MRL	(1988)	1988–89	(20)	For Mujahideen; with large quantities of artillery rockets
	USA	..	SA-7 Grail	Portable SAM	(1984)	1985–89	(250)	For Mujahideen; unconfirmed
		..	BGM-71A TOW	Anti-tank missile	(1988)	1988–89	(80)	For Mujahideen
		..	FIM-92A Stinger	Portable SAM	1989	1989	(100)	In addition to 900 supplied earlier
	USSR	..	An-12 Cub-A	Trpt aircraft	(1989)	1989	12	
		..	Mi-24 Hind-D	Helicopter	(1984)	1984–89	(51)	
		..	MiG-23	Fighter/interceptor	(1988)	1988–89	(30)	
		..	MiG-29	Fighter	1989	1989		
		..	Su-22 Fitter-J	Fighter/grd attack	(1979)	1979–89	(50)	
		..	Su-25 Frogfoot	Fighter/grd attack	(1986)	1986–89	(50)	
		..	2S5 152mm	SPG	1989	1989	(12)	First export of this system
		..	BM-27 220mm	MRL	1989	1989	(12)	
		..	BMP-1	MICV	(1979)	1979–89	(206)	May include Czechoslovak-built BMPs
		..	BTR-70	APC	(1988)	1988–89	(180)	
		..	D-30 122mm	Towed howitzer	(1978)	1978–89	(408)	
		..	M-1976 152mm	Towed gun	(1987)	1988–89	(72)	May be D-1 152-mm
		..	M-46 130mm	Towed gun	(1979)	1979–89	(136)	
		..	T-62	Main battle tank	(1979)	1979–89	(105)	
		..	Scud-B Launcher	Mobile SSM system	(1988)	1988	(3)	
		..	AA-8 Aphid	Air-to-air missile	(1979)	1979–89	(300)	Arming Su-22 fighters
		..	Scud-B	SSM	(1988)	1988–89	(800)	
Algeria	Czechoslovakia	16	L-39 Albatross	Jet trainer	1987	1988–89	(16)	
	USSR	4	Il-76 Candid	Trpt aircraft	(1988)	1989	4	
Angola	Spain	(3)	Cormoran Class	FAC	1989			

Recipient	Supplier	No. ordered	Weapon designation	Weapon description	Year of order	Year(s) of deliveries	No. delivered	Comments
	USA	..	FIM-92A Stinger	Portable SAM	1989	1989	(10)	For UNITA
	USSR	..	Mi-8 Hip	Helicopter	(1982)	1983–88	(64)	Follow-on and attrition replacements
		..	MiG-23	Fighter/interceptor	(1986)	1986–88	(48)	
		..	BRDM-2	Scout car	(1985)	1986–89	(100)	
		..	D-30 122mm	Towed howitzer	(1985)	1986–89	(160)	D-44 85-mm guns also delivered
		..	M-46 130mm	Towed gun	(1986)	1986–89	(72)	
		..	T-55	Main battle tank	(1987)	1987–88	(200)	Supplier unconfirmed
		..	T-62	Main battle tank	(1987)	1987–88	(100)	
		..	Barlock	Tracking radar	(1985)	1987–88	(7)	
		..	Flat Face	Tracking radar	(1980)	1981–88	(16)	
		..	SA-6 SAMS	Mobile SAM system	(1979)	1980–88	(68)	
		..	SA-8 SAMS	Mobile SAM system	(1983)	1984–88	(48)	
		..	Side Net	Heighfinding radar	(1979)	1980–88	(25)	
		..	Spoon Rest P-13	Early warning radar	(1979)	1980–88	(16)	
		..	SA-14 Gremlin	Portable SAM	(1987)	1987	(300)	Revealed when captured by UNITA
		..	SA-6 Gainful	Landmob SAM	(1979)	1980–88	(735)	
		..	SA-8 Gecko	Landmob SAM	(1983)	1984–88	(768)	
		..	SA-9 Gaskin	Landmob SAM	(1986)	1987–88	(192)	
Argentina	Brazil	10	HB-355M Esquilo	Helicopter	1987	1989	10	Arming 6 Meko-140 frigates
	France	6	MM-40 Launcher	ShShM launcher	1980	1984–89	(6)	Arming 6 Meko-140 frigates
		48	MM-40 Exocet	ShShM/SShM	1980	1984–89	(48)	Arming A-4 Skyhawk fighters
	Israel	(120)	Shafrir-2	Air-to-air missile	(1986)	1988–89	(120)	
	Italy	4	A-109	Helicopter	1987	1989	(4)	Deal worth $7 m
	Spain	3	C-212-300	Trpt aircraft	1988	1989	3	Deal worth $35 m
Bahrain	USA	12	F-16C	Fighter	(1987)			Partly financed by Saudi Arabia; with electronic countermeasures

Recipient	Supplier	No.	Weapon designation	Weapon description	Year of order	Year of delivery	No. delivered	Comments
		4	F-16C	Fighter	1988	1989	(16)	Follows 1987 order for 12
		80	M-113-A2	APC	1989			Deal worth $33 m
		(24)	AGM-65D	ASM	(1987)			Arming F-16 fighters
		(48)	AIM-7M Sparrow	Air-to-air missile	(1987)			Arming F-16 fighters
		(96)	AIM-9L	Air-to-air missile	(1987)			Arming F-16 fighters
Bangladesh	China	16	F-7	Fighter	(1989)	1989		
	Denmark	2	693 Class	Landing craft	1986			
	Pakistan	40	F-6	Fighter	1989			To be phased out by Pakistan
Benin	France	10	VBL-M11	Armoured car	(1986)	1987–89	10	
		2	VLRA	Scout car	(1988)	1989	2	
		3	VLRA	Scout car	1989	1989	3	
Bolivia	USA	6	C-130B Hercules	Trpt aircraft	(1988)	1988	3	
Botswana	Canada	5	Model 412	Helicopter	(1987)	1988–89	5	Part of $4 m MAP
	USA	..	M-167 Vulcan	Mobile radar	1989			Deal worth $8 m incl 20-mm towed anti-aircraft guns
		..	BGM-71C I-TOW	Anti-tank missile	1989			
Brazil	Canada	11	S2F-1	Fighter/ASW	(1987)	1989	(5)	Upgraded with new PT-6 Turboprops and ASW electronics package
	France	15	AS-332	Helicopter	1987	1988–89	(10)	For Navy
		26	AS-365F	Helicopter	1988	1989	10	Part of deal worth $249 m
		..	Magic-2	Air-to-air missile	1988	1989	(36)	Arming refurbished Mirage-3 fighters
	Indonesia	4	CN-212	Trpt aircraft	1989			
	USA	23	F-5E Tiger-2	Fighter	1988	1988–89	(23)	Deal worth $67 m incl 3 F-5F versions
		3	F-5F Tiger-2	Jet trainer	1988			
		2	KC-135	Tanker/trpt aircraft	(1988)	1989	2	
		4	Model 208	Lightplane	(1987)	1987–89	4	

Recipient	Supplier	No. ordered	Weapon designation	Weapon description	Year of order	Year(s) of deliveries	No. delivered	Comments
		8	Phalanx	CIWS	1988	1989	(2)	Arming 4 Niteroi Class frigates and 4 Inhauma Class corvettes; deal worth $63 m
		4	Garcia Class	Frigate	1989	1989	4	Leased from US Navy
Brunei	France	24	VAB	APC	1988	1988–89	(24)	
		3	MM-40 Launcher	ShShM launcher	1989			
		(48)	MM-40 Exocet	ShShM/SShM	1989			Arming Vigilance Class corvettes
	Germany, FR	(96)	AIM-9L	Air-to-air missile	1989			Arming Vigilance Class corvettes
	Indonesia	(3)	CN-235	Trpt aircraft	1989			Arming 16 Hawk-100 fighters
	Italy	4	SF-260TP	Trainer	(1989)			
	UK	16	Hawk-100	Jet trainer	1989			Part of deal worth 400 m incl 3 corvettes
		..	Vigilance Class	Corvette	1989			Armed with MM-40 exocet; 76-mm gun; 2 40-mm guns
Cameroon	Canada	2	Model 206L	Helicopter	1989			
	France	4	Super Magister	Jet trainer	1989	1989	4	
	UK	1	Peacock Class	OPV	1988			
Chile	France	4	AS-365F	Helicopter	1987			To be deployed on County Class frigates; first export of ASW version
		2	Falcon-20G	Maritime patrol	1988			Part of $210 m deal
		(32)	AM-39 Exocet	Anti-ship missile	1987			Arming 4 helicopters for County Class destroyer
		(16)	AM-39 Exocet	Anti-ship missile	(1988)	1988–89	(12)	Arming 4 AS-332 Super Pumas
	Germany, FR	(30)	Bo-105CB	Helicopter	1985	1986–89	7	
	Indonesia	4	AS-332	Helicopter	1988	1988–89	3	Part of deal worth $210 m incl 4 SA-365Fs from France

Recipient	Supplier	No.	Weapon designation	Weapon description	Year of order	Year of delivery	No. delivered	Comments
	Israel	6	CN-235	Trpt aircraft	1988			
		(8)	Barak Launcher	ShAM launcher	1989			For refit to Chilean frigates
		2	Gabriel L	ShShM launcher	1988	1989	2	Arming SAAR-3 FACs
		2	Phalcon	AEW&C radar	(1989)			Mounted in 707 airframes; deal worth $500 m incl 4 B-707s
	USA	(256)	Barak	ShAM/SAM/PDM	1989			
		8	Gabriel-2	ShShM	1988	1989	8	Arming 2 Saar-3 Class FACs
		2	Saar-3 Class	FAC	1988	1989	2	
		15	Model 280FX	Helicopter	(1988)	1988–89	(15)	Armed with Gabriel-11 anti-ship missiles
Colombia	Argentina	2	IA-58B Pucara	COIN	1989			
	Israel	13	Kfir-C7	Fighter/bomber	1988	1989	11	Includes 2 trainers; partial payment in commodities; deal worth $220 m
		..	Barak Launcher	ShAM launcher	1989			Arming F-1500 Type
	Spain	3	C-212-300	Trpt aircraft	1988	1989	1	
	USA	8	A-37A	COIN	1989	1989	8	
		2	C-130H Hercules	Trpt aircraft	1989	1989	2	Delivered along with jeeps, ambulances, grenade launchers, small arms and communications equipment
		3	UH-60 Blackhawk	Helicopter	1988	1989	3	Deal worth $26 m; second order
		5	UH-60 Blackhawk	Helicopter	1989	1989	5	Deal worth $36 m; third order
Côte d'Ivoire	Netherlands	2	F-100	Trpt aircraft	(1988)	1989	2	
Cuba	USSR	..	MiG-29	Fighter	(1989)	1989	(6)	
Djibouti	Iraq	..	Type 59/1 130mm	Towed gun	1989			Captured from Iran and sold to Djibouti along with mortars
Dominican Republic	USA	5	Model 337	Trainer	(1988)	1988–89	5	
Ecuador	Brazil	10	EMB-312 Tucano	Trainer	1988			Deal worth $19 m

Recipient	Supplier	No. ordered	Weapon designation	Weapon description	Year of order	Year(s) of deliveries	No. delivered	Comments
	Spain	2	CN-235	Trpt aircraft	1988	1989	2	CN-235 M version
		..	Piranha Class	Patrol craft	1989			Some to be built in Ecuador
Egypt	Argentina	50	IA-58C Pucara	COIN	(1988)			
	France	20	Mirage-2000	Fighter	1988			May be fitted with SU-84 Harpoon anti-ship missiles and towed array sonars
	UK	1	Oberon Class	Submarine	1989			
	USA	1	Porpoise Class	Submarine	1989			
		6	Commuter-1900	Trpt aircraft	1985	1988–89	6	Deal worth $73 m; incl spares and training
		2	E-2C Hawkeye	AEW	1989			
		40	F-16C	Fighter	(1987)			Third order of 40; incl 4 F-16D version
		1	F-16D	Fighter/trainer	1988			Deal worth $21 m incl spare parts; attrition replacement
		3	KC-135	Tanker/trpt aircraft	1989			For evaluation
		2	UH-60 Blackhawk	Helicopter	1988			Part of $2 b deal incl 540 to be co-produced
		15	M-1 Abrams	Main battle tank	1988			Deal worth $19 m
		69	M-113-A2	APC	1988			Status uncertain
		..	M-60-A3	Main battle tank	(1988)			Status uncertain
		2	RGM-84A Launch	ShShM launcher	(1988)			
		144	AGM-65D	ASM	1988			Arming F-16 fighters; deal worth $27 m incl training missiles, parts and electronic countermeasure pods
		282	AIM-7M Sparrow	Air-to-air missile	(1987)			Arming F-16 fighters; deal worth $42 m
		560	AIM-9L	Air-to-air missile	(1986)	1987–89	(560)	Arming F-16 fighters; deal worth $42 m
		7 511	BGM-71D TOW-2	Anti-tank missile	1988	1989	(200)	Includes 180 launchers and 504 night vision sights as well as spare parts
		(170)	MIM-23B Hawk	Landmob SAM	1988	1989	(150)	Deal worth $51 m

Recipient/Supplier	No.	Weapon designation	Weapon description	Year of order	Year(s) of deliveries	No. delivered	Comments
Ethiopia	(32)	RGM-84A Harpoon	ShShM	(1988)			Unconfirmed; modernizing 2 Chinese frigates
	514	RIM-7M Sparrow	SAM	(1984)	1985–89	(514)	Deal worth $190 m; part of Skyguard air defence system
Czechoslovakia	..	T-55	Main battle tank	(1985)	1985–89	(380)	May be Soviet-supplied
German DR	210	T-55	Main battle tank	1989	1989	152	Ex-Nationale Volksarmee; supplies stopped end-1989
USSR	..	BM-21 122mm	MRL	(1984)	1984–89	(80)	May be North Korean BM-11
	..	BRDM-1	Scout car	(1985)	1985–88	(120)	
	..	BRDM-2	Scout car	1985	1986–89	(80)	
	..	BTR-60P	APC	(1985)	1985–89	(360)	
	..	D-30 122mm	Towed howitzer	1985	1985–89	(180)	
	..	M-46 130mm	Towed gun	1985	1985–89	(80)	
	..	AT-3 Sagger	Anti-tank missile	1985	1985–89	(320)	
	..	AT-5 Spandrel	Anti-tank missile	1985	1986–89		
Fiji							
Australia	(4)	ASI-315	Patrol craft	1985	1987	(2)	Status of programme unclear after military coup
Gabon							
France	1	ATR-42	Trpt aircraft	1989	1989	1	
Guatemala							
Italy	2	G-222L	Trpt aircraft	1989	1989	1	Deal worth $36.3 m
Guinea							
USSR	1	Matka Class	Hydrofoil FAC	(1988)	1989	1	
Honduras							
USA	12	F-5E Tiger-2	Fighter	1987	1987–89	10	From USAF stocks; deal worth $75 m incl 2 F-5F versions
India							
Korea, South	7	Sukanya Class	OPV	(1987)	1989	1	Licensed production of 212 to follow
Netherlands	(40)	Flycatcher	Mobile radar	1987	1989	(40)	Possibly for licensed production; in addition to 8 in service
Poland	4	Polnocny Class	Landing ship	(1985)	1989	1	

Recipient	Supplier	No. ordered	Weapon designation	Weapon description	Year of order	Year(s) of deliveries	No. delivered	Comments
	Sweden	410	FH-77 155mm	Towed howitzer	1986	1986–89	(410)	Deal worth $1300 m
	UK	1	Sea Harrier T-4	Fighter/trainer	1986	1989	1	
		26	Sea King HAS-5	Helicopter	1983	1989	(20)	Deal worth $900 m incl Sea Eagle anti-ship missiles; 20 B versions and 6 C versions
		21	Westland 30	Helicopter	1986	1988–89	(21)	Arming Navy and Coast Guard Do-228 aircraft
		(156)	Sea Skua	Anti-ship missile	(1985)	1987–89	(54)	
	USSR	24	Il-76 Candid	Trpt aircraft	1984	1985–89	(24)	Order increased from 20 to 24 in 1987
		(8)	Ka-27 Helix	Helicopter	(1985)	1985–88	(4)	8–18 ordered; on Kashin Class destroyers
		(100)	Mi-17 Hip-H	Helicopter	(1984)	1984–89	(100)	Replacing Mi-8s
		10	Mi-26 Halo	Helicopter	1988			Second order
		..	Mi-28 Havoc	Helicopter	(1988)			Indian request; Soviet response unknown
		20	Mi-35	Helicopter	1988	1989	20	EW systems derived from Mi-28 Havoc; deal worth $172 m incl spares and support equipment
		(15)	MiG-29	Fighter	1988	1989	15	Order number may be 20
		8	Tu-142 Bear	Reconnaissance plane	1984	1988–89	8	For Navy
		..	SA-11 SAMS	Mobile SAM system	(1984)	1987–88	(40)	
		..	SA-8 SAMS	Mobile SAM system	(1982)	1984–89	(48)	
		6	SA-N-1 Launcher	ShAM launcher	1982	1986–89	(5)	Arming Kashin Class destroyers
		..	SA-N-5 Launcher	ShAM launcher	(1983)	1986–89	(4)	Arming Khukri Class corvettes
		3	SSN-2 Styx L	ShShM launcher	1982	1986–88	(2)	Arming Kashin Class destroyers
		..	SSN-2 Styx L	ShShM launcher	(1983)	1986–89	(4)	Arming Khukri Class corvette
		..	SA-8 Gecko	Landmob SAM	(1982)	1984–89	(768)	Reportedly operational early in 1984
		(72)	SA-N-1	ShAM	1982	1986–87	(48)	Arming Kashin Class destroyers
		..	SA-N-5	ShAM	(1983)	1986–89	(80)	Arming Khukri Class corvette
		(36)	SSN-2 Styx	ShShM	1982	1986–88	(24)	Arming Kashin Class destroyers
		..	SSN-2 Styx	ShShM	(1983)	1986–89	(48)	Arming Khukri Class corvette

Recipient	Supplier	No. ordered	Weapon designation	Weapon description	Year of order	Year of delivery	No. delivered	Comments
		(24)	SSN-2 Styx	ShShM	(1985)	1988		Arming Tarantul Class corvettes
		1	Charlie-1 Class	SSN	(1985)	1988	1	Leased submarine to be replaced because of concerns about radiation leakages
		3	Kashin Class	Destroyer	1982	1986–88	2	In addition to 3 previously delivered
		8	Kilo Class	Submarine	(1984)	1986–89	7	
		6	Natya Class	MSO	1982	1986–89	(6)	In addition to 6 delivered 1978–80
		6	Yevgenia Class	MSC	(1985)	1986–89		In addition to 6 in service
Indonesia	France	(2)	MM-38 Launcher	ShShM launcher	(1978)	1981	(1)	Arming 2 Yugoslavian frigates
		(24)	MM-38 Exocet	ShShM	(1978)	1981	(12)	Arming 2 Yugoslavian frigates
	Netherlands	2	V. Speijk Class	Frigate	1989	1989	2	In addition to 4 supplied 1986–88
	UK	14	AR-325	Surveillance radar	1989			
		(20)	Rapier SAMS	Mobile SAM system	1985			Deal worth $100 m incl missiles
		(10)	Rapier SAMS	Mobile SAM system	1986			Deal worth $60 m
		(240)	Improved Rapier	Landmob SAM	1985			
		(120)	Improved Rapier	Landmob SAM	1986			
	USA	10	C-130H-30	Trpt aircraft	1989			
		8	F-16A	Fighter	(1986)			Deal worth $336 m incl 4 F-16Bs; offsets worth $52 m
		4	F-16B	Fighter/trainer	1986	1989	3	Deal worth $337 m incl 8 F-16A fighters; status uncertain
		(48)	AGM-65D	ASM	1987			Arming F-16 fighters
		(96)	AIM-9P	Air-to-air missile	(1986)			Arming F-16 fighters
Iran	Brazil	(50)	EMB-312 Tucano	Trainer	1988	1989	(15)	Deal worth $15 m
	China	..	T-59	Main battle tank	(1986)	1987–88	(240)	
		..	Type 501	APC	1986	1986–88	(300)	
		..	Type-63 107mm	MRL	(1982)	1983–88	(900)	
		(2)	HQ-2B	SAM system	(1989)			
		..	Hai Ying-2 L	ShShM launcher	(1986)	1987–88	(8)	
		(48)	HQ-2B	SAM	1989			For coastal air defence buys
		..	Hai Ying-2	ShShM/SShM	1989			US allegation; unconfirmed
		..	Hong Jian-73	Anti-tank missile	(1982)	1982–88	(6 500)	
		..	Hong Ying-5	Portable SAM	(1985)	1985–88	(600)	

Recipient	Supplier	No. ordered	Weapon designation	Weapon description	Year of order	Year(s) of deliveries	No. delivered	Comments
	Czechoslovakia	..	BMP-1	MICV	(1986)	1986–89	(400)	Supplier uncertain
		..	BTR-60P	APC	(1986)	1986–89	(160)	Deal incl assistance with anti-tank missile construction
		(90)	T-54	Main battle tank	1989	1989	(90)	
	German DR	..	MiG-21F	Fighter	(1988)	1989	(25)	According to GDR Secretary for Defence
	Hungary	(90)	T-55	Main battle tank	1989	1989	(90)	
		..	SA-7 Grail	Portable SAM	1989			
	Korea, North	..	T-62	Main battle tank	(1983)	1984–88	(150)	Deliveries incl some Soviet M-46s
		..	Type 59/1 130mm	Towed gun	(1983)	1983–88	(480)	
		..	Hai Ying-2 Launcher	ShShM launcher	(1987)	1988	1	May be retransferred from China. Unit cost reported to be $10 m
		..	Hai Ying-2	ShShM/SShM	(1987)	1988	6	
	Romania	..	Orao	Fighter/grd attack	1989			Ordered with an unspecified number of tank transporters
		150	T-55	Main battle tank	1989			
	UK	(200)	TAB-77	APC	1989	1989	(100)	
		6	AR-3D	3-D radar	(1988)			
	USSR	(300)	T-72	Main battle tank	1989			Old deal reopened after cease-fire
Iraq	Brazil	..	Astros-II SS-30	MRL	(1983)	1984–89	(78)	
		..	Astros-II SS-60	MRL	(1985)	1987–88	(20)	
		250	EE-9 Cascavel	Armoured car	1986	1987–89	(250)	Some with 25-mm AA cannon
		..	Astros Guidance	Fire control radar	(1983)	1984–88	(13)	Fire control system for Astros MRl
		..	SS-60	SSM	(1985)	1987–89	(960)	
	China	..	T-59	Main battle tank	(1981)	1982–88	(700)	
		..	T-69	Main battle tank	(1982)	1983–88	(600)	1000–2000 ordered in early 1980s
		..	Type 531	APC	(1981)	1982–88	(650)	
		..	Type 59/1 130mm	Towed gun	(1981)	1982–88	(720)	

Supplier	No.	Weapon designation	Weapon description	Year of order	Year(s) of deliveries	No. delivered	Comments
Czechoslovakia	:	BMP-1	MICV	(1981)	1981–89	(1 000)	Option for 45 more
Egypt	95	EMB-312 Tucano	Trainer	1983	1985–88	(80)	Supplier uncertain
	:	D-30 122mm	Towed howitzer	(1985)	1985–89	(120)	Egyptian version of BM-21 MRS
	:	Sakr-30 122mm	MRL	(1987)	1987–89	(300)	Unspecified number
France	:	Sakr Eye	Portable SAM	(1987)			
	6	AS-332	Helicopter	1988	1988	(3)	To be delivered from 1991
	6	AS-365N	Helicopter	1989	1989		
	(136)	AMX-30 Roland	AAV(M)	1981	1982–88	(105)	Trailer-mounted versions supplied; some modified as airborne early-warning radar
	:	Tiger	Point defence radar	(1987)	1988–89	(10)	
	(36)	AM-39 Exocet	Anti-ship missile	1989	1989	18	Arming AS-332 Super Puma helicopters
	:	Armat	ARM	(1983)	1983–89	(700)	Up to 75% of French Armat production
	(48)	AS-15TT	Anti-ship missile	1989	1989		Arming SA-365 Dauphin helicopters
	586	AS-30L	ASM	(1984)	1986–88	(180)	Arming Mirage F-1s
	:	HOT	Anti-tank missile	(1981)	1981–88	(1 600)	
	:	Milan	Anti-tank missile	(1981)	1981–88	(4 800)	
	:	Roland-2	Landmob SAM	1981	1982–88	(1 050)	
Germany, FR	16	BK-117	Helicopter	1989	1989	(4)	
Italy	(10)	Aspide/Albatros	ShAM/ShShM launcher	(1981)			Arming Lupo Class frigates and Wadi Class corvettes; delivery prevented by war with Iran
	(10)	Otomat-2 Launcher	ShShM launcher	(1981)			Arming Lupo Class frigates and Wadi Class corvettes; delivery prevented by war with Iran
	(224)	Aspide	SAM/ShAM	(1981)			Arming Lupo Class frigates and Wadi Class corvettes; delivery prevented by war with Iran
	(60)	Otomat-2	ShShM	(1981)			Arming Lupo Class frigates and Wadi Class corvettes; delivery prevented by war with Iran
	4	Lupo Class	Frigate	1981			Order incl Wadi Class corvettes and Stromboli Class support ship
	6	Wadi Class	Corvette	1981			

Recipient	Supplier	No. ordered	Weapon designation	Weapon description	Year of order	Year(s) of deliveries	No. delivered	Comments
	USSR	::	2S1 122mm	SPH	(1986)	1987–88	(80)	Part of deal worth $3 b
		::	2S3 152mm	SPG	(1986)	1987–88	(80)	Mix of 152- and 122-mm guns unknown
		::	BM-21 122mm	MRL	(1986)	1986–88	(360)	Part of deal worth $3 b
		::	MT-LB	APC	(1982)	1983–88	(800)	Modified in Iraq to carry Egyptian 120-mm mortar
		::	T-62	Main battle tank	(1982)	1982–89	(1 000)	
		::	T-72	Main battle tank	(1985)	1985–88	(700)	Modified in Iraq; eventual goal full Iraqi production
		::	AS-14 Kedge	ASM	(1988)	1988–89	(40)	
		::	Scud-B	SSM	(1985)	1986–88	(350)	
Israel	Germany, FR	(2)	Dolphin	Submarine	(1988)			Deal worth $570 m; to be paid for with US FMS funding
	USA	16	AH-64 Apache	Helicopter	1989			Status uncertain; first export order for Apache
		5	F-15D Eagle	Jet trainer	1988			Deal worth $265 m
		(60)	F-16C	Fighter	1988			Order may be up to 75
		4	OH-58A Kiowa	Helicopter	1989			Deal worth $39 m
		(20)	SA-365N	Helicopter	1987	1988–89	(20)	To equip Saar-5 Class corvettes
		12	UH-60 Blackhawk	Helicopter	1988	1989	12	Supplied on 'free lease' arrangement
		3	RGM-84A Launch	ShShM launcher	(1988)			Arming Saar-5 Class corvettes
		(192)	AGM-114A	ASM/ATM	1989			Arming 16 AH-64 Apache helicopters
		(48)	RGM-84A Harpoon	ShShM	(1988)			Arming Saar-5 Class corvettes
		3	Saar-5 Class	Corvette	1988			Built in USA to Israeli design; financed with FMS credits worth $300 m
Jordan	France	12	Mirage-2000	Fighter	1988			Deal worth $1 b incl Super 530 and Magic-2 missiles and Durandal bombs

Recipient	Supplier	No.	Weapon designation	Weapon description	Year of order	Year(s) of deliveries	No. delivered	Comments
	Spain	10	AS-30L	ASM	1988			Arming Mirage 2000 fighters
	UK	(192)	Magic-2	Air-to-air missile	1988			Arming Mirage 2000 fighters
	USA	(96)	Super-530	Air-to-air missile	1988			Arming Mirage 2000 fighters
		8	C-101 Aviojet	Jet trainer	1989			In addition to 16 supplied in 1988
		3	Constitucion Class	Patrol craft	1987			
	USSR	(2)	AN/TPQ-37	Tracking radar	(1986)	1989	(1)	
		..	SA-13 Gopher	Landmob SAM	(1986)	1987–89	(240)	
Kampuchea	USSR	(10)	BM-14-17 140mm	MRL	(1989)	1989	(10)	Shipped with several hundred tonnes of small arms and ammunition
		(10)	BM-21 122mm	MRL	1989	1989	(10)	
		(15)	M-1955 100mm	Towed gun	1989	1989	(15)	
	Viet Nam	(15)	M-46 130mm	Towed gun	(1989)	1989	(15)	Together with large quantities of small arms
		100	T-55	Main battle tank	1988	1988	100	
Kenya	France	37	AML-60	Armoured car	1988	1989	37	Part of deal worth $60 m incl 30 AML-90s and spare parts
		30	AML-90	Armoured car	1988	1989	30	Part of deal worth $60 m incl 37 AML 60s and equipment
	UK	12	EMB-312 Tucano	Trainer	1988	1989	1	Negotiating
		12	Hawk-200	Fighter	1989			
Korea, North	China	(100)	F-6	Fighter	(1986)	1988–89	(48)	Locally modified design
	USSR	(150)	MiG-21MF	Fighter	(1988)	1989	(50)	2 regiments
		60	MiG-2	Fighter/interceptor	(1984)	1985–89	(60)	
		25	MiG-29	Fighter	(1987)	1988–89	15	
		(20)	Su-25 Frogfoot	Fighter/grd attack	(1987)	1988–89	12	
		..	BMP-1	MICV	(1984)	1985–89	(82)	
		(24)	SA-5 SAMS	Mobile SAM system	(1984)	1988–89	(24)	
		(12)	SSN-2 Styx L	ShShM launcher	(1979)	1980–89	(12)	Arming Soju Class FACs
		..	AA-7 Apex	Air-to-air missile	(1987)	1988–89	(120)	Arming MiG-29 fighters: may be AA-10 Alamos

Recipient	Supplier	No. ordered	Weapon designation	Weapon description	Year of order	Year(s) of deliveries	No. delivered	Comments
Korea, South	Germany, FR	..	AA-8 Aphid	Air-to-air missile	(1987)	1988–89	(360)	Arming MiG-29 fighters, Su-25 fighters and other Soviet-supplied aircraft
	UK	(351)	SA-5 Gammon	SAM	1984	1987–89	(351)	
		..	SSN-2 Styx	ShShM	(1979)	1980–89	(100)	Arming Soju Class FACs
		1	Type-209/3	Submarine	1987			Deal worth $600 m incl licensed production of 2 vessels in S. Korea
		12	Lynx	Helicopter	1988			Part of deal worth $200 m incl Sea Skua missiles; follow-on order for 20 likely
		1	MBT-3 BL	Bridge layer	1988			For delivery in 1990
		..	ST-1802	Naval fire control radars	1989			Fire control radars for Javelin portable SAMs; part of deal worth $144 m
		(48)	Sea Skua	Anti-ship missile	1988			Arming Lynx helicopters
	USA	(6)	C-130H-30	Trpt aircraft	(1987)	1988–89	6	
		30	F-16C	Fighter	1981	1987–89	(30)	Cost incl 6 F-16Ds: $931 m; plans for total of 156
		4	F-16D	Fighter/trainer	1988	1989	4	Deal worth $102 m; in addition to 36 delivered previously
		24	F-4E Phantom	Fighter	1988	1988–89	24	Deal worth $246 m incl 6 C versions, spare parts and support
		24	F-4E Phantom	Fighter	1989			Prior to licensed production of 72
		48	F/A-18 Hornet	Fighter	1989			Deal worth $115 m incl 60 engines
		50	Model 205 UH-1H	Helicopter	1986	1987–89	(50)	Deal worth $260 m incl TOW missiles
		70	Model 209 AH-1S	Helicopter	1986	1988–89	(40)	
		..	AIM-7E Sparrow	Air-to-air missile	(1987)	1988–89	72	Arming F-4D Phantom fighters
		76	AIM-7F Sparrow	Air-to-air missile	1988	1988–89	(76)	Arming F-4E fighters; deal worth $54 m
		500	AIM-9P	Air-to-air missile	1989			
		(672)	BGM-71D TOW-2	Anti-tank missile	1986	1988–89	(640)	Arming Model-209 helicopters

Recipient	Supplier	No.	Weapon designation	Weapon description	Year of order	Year(s) of deliveries	No. delivered	Comments
Kuwait		704	BGM-71D TOW-2	Anti-tank missile	1987			
		..	RGM-84A Harpoon	ShShM	(1985)	1985–88	(64)	Arming Ulsan Class frigates
		52	RGM-84A Harpoon	ShShM	1988			Filling reserve stocks
	Egypt	100	Fahd	APC	1988	1989	(40)	Part of $50 m deal incl Amoun air defence system
	UK	..	Sakr Eye	Portable SAM	1987	1989	(24)	
		16	EMB-312 Tucano	Trainer	1989			First export order
		2	Valkyr	APC	1988	1989	2	
		42	F/A-18 Hornet	Fighter	1988			Deal worth $1.9 b incl Sidewinder, Harpoon, Sparrow and Maverick missiles
	USA	300	AGM-65G	ASM	1988			Anti-ship version; arming F/A-18 Hornet fighters
		40	AGM-84A Harpoon	Anti-ship missile	1988			Arming F/A-18 Hornet fighters
		200	AIM-7F Sparrow	Air-to-air missile	1988			Arming F/A-18 Hornet fighters
		120	AIM-9L	Air-to-air missile	1988			Arming F/A-18 Hornet fighters
	USSR	245	BMP-2	MICV	1988	1989	(50)	Deal worth $300 m incl anti-tank missiles
		..	T-72	Main battle tank	1989			Deal worth $700 m, paid partly in oil
		..	SA-8 SAMS	Mobile SAM system	1988			Deal incl BMP-2 APCs
		(1 220)	AT-5 Spandrel	Anti-tank missile	1988	1989	(240)	Arming BMP-2 APCs
		..	SA-8 Gecko	Landmob SAM	1988			
		200	M-84 155-mm	Towed howitzer	1989			
	Yugoslavia	230	T-74	Main battle tank	(1989)			200 tanks, 15 command vehicles and 15 recovery vehicles; part of deal worth $800 m incl 200 152-mm howitzers
Laos	Romania	144	SA-7 Grail	Portable SAM	1989	1989	144	
		120	T-55	Main battle tank	1988	1988–89	(120)	Part of shipment incl 5000 rockets, mortars and grenades
Lebanon	Iraq	120	T-55	Main battle tank	1988	1989	(120)	For Christian Forces
		6	FROG Launcher	Mobile SSM system	1989			Shipped from Iraq to Christian militia but never delivered
		..	FROG-7	Landmob SSM	1989			Shipped from Iraq to Christian militia

Recipient	Supplier	No. ordered	Weapon designation	Weapon description	Year of order	Year(s) of deliveries	No. delivered	Comments
Lesotho	Spain	2	C-212A Aviocar	Trpt aircraft	(1988)	1989	2	
	USA	1	Model 182	Lightplane	(1989)	1989	1	but never delivered
Libya	France	2	Mirage F-1A	Fighter/grd attack	1986	1989	1	
		2	Mirage-5	Fighter	1986			
	USSR	1	Il-76 Candid	Trpt aircraft	(1988)	1989	1	
		(15)	Su-24 Fencer	Fighter/bomber	(1988)	1989	(12)	
		..	SA-5 SAMS	Mobile SAM system	1989			
		..	Square Pair	Tracking radar	(1988)			Part of SA-5 air defence system
		..	AS-14 Kedge	ASM	1989			Arming Su-24 Fencers
		..	SA-5 Gammon	SAM	(1988)			
	Yugoslavia	4	Koncar Class	FAC	1985			
Malaysia	France	1	Falcon-900	Trpt aircraft	1988	1989	1	For VIP use
	Italy	4	Skyguard	Air defence radar	(1987)	1988–89	(4)	Fire control for 1 bty of 35-mm anti-aircraft guns from Switzerland
	Netherlands	1	Flycatcher	Mobile radar	1988	1989	1	
	UK	8	Tornado IDS	MRCA	1989			Deal incl artillery, SAMs, radar and 1 submarine subject to final negotiation
		6	Wasp	Helicopter	1988	1989	6	Second order
		30	FH-70 155mm	Towed howitzer	1988	1989	9	
		(24)	L119 105mm gun	Towed gun	1988			
		12	DN-181 Rapier	Mobile SAM system	1988			
		2	S-723 Martello	3-D radar	(1988)			Part of deal worth $1.4 b
		20	Improved Rapier	Landmob SAM	1988			
		40	Javelin	Portable SAM	1988			

Recipient	Supplier	No.	Weapon designation	Weapon description	Year of order	Year(s) of deliveries	No. delivered	Comments
Mali	USA	(1)	Oberon Class	Submarine	(1988)	1986		
		48	A-4E Skyhawk	Fighter/bomber	1986	1986	48	Held in store as a spare parts reservoir
	USSR	(8)	MiG-21UTI	Jet trainer	(1988)	1989	(2)	
Mauritius	France	2	Batral Class	Landing craft	(1986)	1989	2	Delivered Aug. 1989
Mexico	USA	1	AN/TPS-43	3-D radar	1988	1989	1	
		2	AN/TPS-63	Surveillance radar	(1988)	1988–89	2	W-630 version
Morocco	Denmark	2	Osprey-55 Class	OPV	1989	1989		In addition to 2 delivered in 1988
	Egypt	..	Sakr-30 122mm	MRL	(1984)	1984–88	(50)	
	France	108	AMX-10RC	Scout car	1978	1982–88	(80)	Deliveries halted Jan. 1989 for financial reasons
	Spain	7	CN-235	Trpt aircraft	1989	1989		Deal worth $94 m
		6	Lazaga Class	Patrol craft	1985	1988–89	6	Second order; also called Vigilance Class and Type P-200
	USA	2	F-5E Tiger-2	Fighter	1989	1989	2	
		100	M-48-A5	Main battle tank	1987	1988–89	(100)	Deal worth $68 m incl ammunition and communications equipment
Mozambique	Indonesia	..	CN-212	Trpt aircraft	1988	1988		
		..	CN-235	Trpt aircraft	1988	1988		
	USA	1	Gulfstream-2	Trpt aircraft	1989	1989	1	For VIP transport
Nicaragua	USSR	2	An-32 Cline	Trpt aircraft	1988	1989	2	
		(10)	Mi-17 Hip-H	Helicopter	1988	1989	(10)	
		..	Mi-24 Hind-E	Helicopter	(1988)	1989	(3)	Delivered via Cuba
		..	BTR-60P	APC	(1981)	1984–88	(205)	
		..	D-30 122mm	Towed howitzer	(1981)	1981–88	(96)	According to US DOD
Nigeria	France	12	AS-332	Helicopter	1985	1989	2	Remaining 10 cancelled because of lack of funds

Recipient	Supplier	No. ordered	Weapon designation	Weapon description	Year of order	Year(s) of deliveries	No. delivered	Comments
	India	48	HTT-34	Trainer	(1987)			Payment in commodities
Oman	Egypt	..	Fahd	APC	1989			
	France	4	VAB Mephisto	APC/TD	(1988)	1989	4	Armed with HOT anti-tank missiles; deal worth FFr 100 m
		(48)	HOT	Anti-tank missile	(1988)	1989	(48)	Arming 4 VAB APCs
	Switzerland	2	AS-202 Bravo	Trainer	1988	1989	2	
	UK	(19)	Hawk-200	Fighter	1989	1989		
		2	S-723 Martello	3-D radar	1985	1988–89	2	Deal worth $67 m
		..	Javelin	Portable SAM	1989	1989		
		1	Province Class	FAC	1986	1989	1	In addition to 3 in service; armed with MM-40 Exocet missiles, 76-mm and 40-mm guns
Pakistan	China	75	F-7	Fighter	1983	1986–89	60	
		75	F-7	Fighter	1989			
		..	T-59	Main battle tank	(1975)	1978–89	(900)	Arming M-113 APCs
		..	Hong Ying-5	Portable SAM	(1988)	1988–89	(200)	For final assembly in Pakistan
		2	Romeo Class	Submarine	(1988)			
	France	6	Rasit-3190B	Surveillance radar	1988	1989	(2)	Ordered unspecified ground-based military radars of advanced design
	UK	1	SH-3D Sea King	Helicopter	1989	1989	1	Attrition replacement
	USA	11	F-16A	Fighter	1988	1989		Second order; deal worth $256 m; attrition replacements
		60	F-16A	Fighter	1989			Deal incl 10 F-100 engines but no air-to-surface armaments; to be funded by Saudi Arabia

Recipient/Supplier	No.	Weapon designation	Weapon description	Year of order	Year(s) of deliveries	No. delivered	Comments
	3	P-3C Update-2	Maritime patrol	1988			Deal worth $240 m incl spares, training and services; financed with FMS credit
	6	SH-2F Seasprite	Helicopter	1989	1989	3	Incl 3 SH-2F versions and 3 SH-2Gs
	88	M-109-A2 155mm	SPH	(1985)	1986–89	(88)	Deal worth $78 m
	(20)	M-109-A2 155mm	SPH	1988			Deal worth $40 m incl M-198 howitzers and support equipment
	400	M-113-A2	APC	1989			Possible final assembly in Pakistan
	(20)	M-198 155mm	Towed howitzer	1988			Deal worth $40 m incl M-109-A2 howitzers and support equipment
	5	AN/TPQ-36	Tracking radar	1988	1989	5	
	4	AN/TPQ-37	Tracking radar	(1985)	1987–89	(3)	
	4	Phalanx	CIWS	1989			Arming Brooke Class vessels leased from the US Navy
	(4)	RIM-67A Launch	ShAM launcher	1988	1989	4	Arming 4 Brooke class frigates leased from the US Navy; deal worth $40 m incl 64 Mk-46 torpedoes
	200	AIM-7F Sparrow	Air-to-air missile	1988	1989		Arming F-16 fighters
	360	AIM-9L	Air-to-air missile	1988	1989	(60)	Arming F-16 fighters
	2 030	BGM-71C I-TOW	Anti-tank missile	1986	1987–89	(1 200)	Deal worth $20 m
	2 386	BGM-71D TOW-2	Anti-tank missile	1987			First Pakistani TOW-2 order; with 144 launchers
	..	RGM-84A Harpoon	ShShM	1988	1989	(8)	Arming Agosta Class submarines
	64	RIM-67A/SM-1	ShAM/ShShM	1988	1989	64	Arming 4 Brooke Class frigates leased from the US Navy
	4	Brooke Class	Frigate	1988	1989	4	Mix of Brooke and Garcia Class frigates and 1 repair ship to be leased for $6.3 m annually
	4	Garcia Class	Frigate	1988	1989		
Panama							
Chile	6	T-35 Pillan	Trainer	1988	1989	6	In addition to 4 delivered earlier
Spain	1	CN-235	Trpt aircraft	1987	1989	1	
Papua							
Australia	4	Model 205 UH-1D	Helicopter	1989			Part of MAP worth $1.13 m

Recipient	Supplier	No. ordered	Weapon designation	Weapon description	Year of order	Year(s) of deliveries	No. delivered	Comments
New Guinea		4	ASI-315	Patrol craft	1985	1987–89	(4)	
Peru	Germany, FR	2	BK-117	Helicopter	1989			Part of deal worth $25-30 m incl 6 BK-117 helicopters
		6	Bo-105	Helicopter	1989			Deal worth $25-30 m incl 2 Bk-117 helicopters
	USSR	18	Mi-17 Hip-H	Helicopter	1989			
Philippines	Australia	6	N-24A Nomad	Trpt aircraft	1989			Deal worth $4.5 m
	Italy	18	S-211	Trainer	1988	1989	4	
	USA	15	Bromon BR-2000	Trpt aircraft	1988			
		4	F-5A	Fighter	1988	1989	4	
		20	Model 500D	Helicopter	1988	1989	(10)	Funded by $25 m of MAP
		(45)	V-150 Commando	APC	1987	1988–89	45	
Qatar	France	4	Mirage F-1C	Fighter/interceptor	1987	1986–89	(4)	
		6	TRS-2201	Air defence radar	(1986)	1988–89	(128)	Arming Mirage F-1 fighters
		(128)	AS-30L	ASM	(1987)	1988–89	(128)	Arming Mirage F-1 fighters
		(128)	Magic-2	Air-to-air missile	(1987)	1988–89	(128)	Arming Mirage F-1 fighters
		(128)	R-530	Air-to-air missile	(1987)	1988–89	(128)	Arming Mirage F-1 fighters
Saudi Arabia	Austria	50	GHN-45 155mm	Towed howitzer	1989	1988	(10)	Order signed July 1989
	Brazil	..	Astros-II SS-30	MRL	1987	1987–88	(30)	Part of $500 m deal
		..	Astros-II SS-40	MRL	1987	1987–88	(4)	Part of $500 m deal
		..	Astros Guidance	Fire control radar	1987	1987–88		Part of $500 m deal
	France	12	AS-332	Helicopter	1988	1989	12	Armed with Exocet missiles; deal worth $430 m incl 20 speed boats armed with 20-mm cannon

Supplier	No.	Weapon designation	Weapon description	Year of order	Year(s) of deliveries	No. delivered	Comments
	2	Atlantic-2	Maritime patrol	(1987)	1986–89	(42)	Improved version developed with Saudi financial assistance
	(56)	AMX-30 Shahine	AAV(M)	1984	1986–89	(42)	
	48	Shahine-2 Launcher	Mobile SAM system	1984	1986–89	(24)	Arming 6 of 12 Super Pumas
	..	AM-39 Exocet	Anti-ship missile	1988	1989		Order may be for up to 1000
	600	Mistral	Portable SAM	1989		(800)	Total value of 'Al Thakeb' deal: $4.1
	4 000	Shahine-2	Landmob SAM	1984	1986–89		Deal worth $1.2 b incl Mistral anti-aircraft missiles
	(2)	F-2000 Class	Frigate	1989			Arming 4 F-2000 frigates
Italy	(32)	Otomat-2	ShShM	1988			
UK	12	BAe-125-800	Utility jet	1988	1988–89	4	Part of 1988 Tornado deal; for VIP use
	(4)	BAe-146	Trpt aircraft	1988			Part of 1988 Tornado deal
	30	Hawk	Jet trainer	1985	1987–89	(30)	Part of 1985 Tornado deal
	60	Hawk	Jet trainer	1988			Part of 1988 Tornado deal
	20	Hawk-200	Fighter	1988			Part of 1988 Tornado deal
	24	Tornado ADV	MRCA	1985	1989	8	1985 Tornado deal Al Yamamah I; incl 72 Tornadoes, 30 Hawks, 30 PC-9s, missiles, training and facilities; deal worth $7 b
	36	Tornado ADV	MRCA	1988			1988 Tornado deal Al Yamamah II; incl 48 Tornadoes, 60 Hawks, 12 BAe-125s, 4 BAe-146s, minehunters, missiles, training and facilities; deal worth $17 b
	48	Tornado IDS	MRCA	1985	1986–89	(30)	Part of 1985 Tornado deal
	12	Tornado IDS	MRCA	1988			Part of 1988 Tornado deal
	..	WS-70	Helicopter	1988			Part of 1988 Tornado deal
	40	Shorland S-55	APC	1988			For gendarmerie
	(60)	Transac GS	APC	(1988)			Unconfirmed
	(480)	ALARM	ARM	1986			Arming Tornado IDS fighters; status uncertain
	(480)	Sea Eagle	Anti-ship missile	1985			Arming Tornado IDS fighters
	(560)	Sky Flash	Air-to-air missile	(1986)			Arming Tornado ADV fighters
	6	Sandown Class	Minehunter	1988			

Recipient	Supplier	No. ordered	Weapon designation	Weapon description	Year of order	Year(s) of deliveries	No. delivered	Comments
	USA	12	F-15C Eagle	Fighter	1987			Deal worth $1 b; attrition replacements delivered at same rate as aircraft losses
		15	Model 406CS	Helicopter	1989			Deal worth $84 m; armed with TOW missiles
		13	UH-60 Blackhawk	Helicopter	1989			Part of deal worth $400 m; 1 for VIP use
		315	M-1 Abrams	Main battle tank	1989			Deal worth $1.5 b
		200	M-2 Bradley	MICV	1988	1989	2	Deal worth $550 m incl anti-tank missiles and training
		30	M-88-A1	ARV	1989			Part of a total deal worth $3b; incl heavy trucks spares and support
		(4)	AN/TPQ-37	Tracking radar	1985	1988–89	(4)	
		(6)	AN/TPS-43	3-D radar	1985	1987–89	(3)	
		(6)	AN/TPS-70	Air defence radar	1989			
		671	AIM-9P	Air-to-air missile	1986	1989	(200)	
		..	BGM-71A TOW	Anti-tank missile	1988			Arming WS-70 Blackhawk
		2 538	BGM-71C I-TOW	Anti-tank missile	1983	1986–89	(1 800)	Deal worth $26 m
		4 460	BGM-71D TOW-2	Anti-tank missile	1988			
		100	RGM-84A Harpoon	ShShM	1986	1988–89	(40)	
Singapore	USA	5	F-5E Tiger-2	Fighter	1988	1988–89	5	For limited local assembly
		20	Model 406CS	Helicopter	1989			Deal worth $31 m
		3	AN/TPQ-37	Tracking radar	1989			
		6	Phalanx	CIWS	(1986)	1988	1	Arming 6 Type 62-001 corvettes
		6	RGM-84A Launcher	ShShM launcher	(1986)	1988	1	Arming Type 62-001 corvette
		(6)	RGM-84A Launcher	ShShM launcher	(1987)	1988–89	(2)	Arming TNC-45 FACs
		(96)	RGM-84A Harpoon	ShShM	(1986)	1988	(16)	Arming Type 62-001 corvettes
		(48)	RGM-84A Harpoon	ShShM	(1987)	1988–89	(16)	Arming refitted TNC-45 FACs

Recipient	Supplier	No.	Weapon designation	Weapon description	Year of order	Year of deliveries	No. delivered	Comments
South Africa	Spain	3	C-212-200	Trpt aircraft	(1986)	1988-89	3	For Bophuthatswana Air Force
Sri Lanka	China	2	Y-8	Trpt aircraft	(1987)	1989	2	
	Israel	(2)	Dvora Class	FAC	1987			
	UK	9	Strikemaster	Trainer/COIN	1987			Deal worth $11 m; ex-Kuwaiti Air Force
Sudan	Egypt	..	Fahd	APC	1989			
	Ethiopia	..	SA-7 Grail	Portable SAM	(1986)	1987-88	(80)	Used by SPLA rebels
	Iraq	..	Ababil	MRL	(1989)			Package incl undisclosed items captured from Iran
	Libya	..	MiG-23	Fighter/interceptor	(1987)	1987-88		May be Libyan-operated
	USA	9	V-150 Commando	APC	1988		8	In addition to about 80 previously ordered
Syria	USSR	(8)	MiG-25 Foxhound	Fighter	(1989)			
		..	BMP-1	MICV	1977	1977-89	(2 300)	
		..	T-72	Main battle tank	1980	1980-89	(1 300)	May be from Czechoslovakia
		..	SA-8 SAMS	Mobile SAM system	(1982)	1982-88	(42)	May be from Czechoslovakia or Poland
		..	AT-4 Spigot	Anti-tank missile	(1980)	1981-89	(900)	
		..	AT-5 Spandrel	Anti-tank missile	(1984)	1984-87	(400)	
		..	SA-14 Gremlin	Portable SAM	(1985)	1987-89	(210)	Unconfirmed
		..	SA-8 Gecko	Landmob SAM	1982	1982-89	(744)	Replaces SA-7 Grail
		3	Kilo Class	Submarine	(1987)			
		4	Nanuchka Class	Corvette	(1984)			
Taiwan	USA	12	Commuter-1900	Trpt aircraft	1989	1989	10	Deal worth $74 m
		12	SH-60B Seahawk	Helicopter	1989	1989	1	Arming Gearing Class frigates; deal worth $15 m
		6	Phalanx	CIWS	(1989)	1989	(1)	
		14	RIM-67A Launcher	ShAM launcher	1988	1989		Arming FFG-7 Class frigates to be built under licence
		..	AIM-7M Sparrow	Air-to-air missile	1989			Arming upgraded F-104 and Ching Kuo fighter aircraft

Recipient	Supplier	No. ordered	Weapon designation	Weapon description	Year of order	Year(s) of deliveries	No. delivered	Comments
Thailand	China	(360)	RIM-67A/SM-1	ShAM/ShShM	1988			Arming 8 FFG-7 Class frigates to be built under licence
		60	RIM-67A/SM-1	ShAM/ShShM	(1989)	1989	(10)	Arming Gearing Class frigates
		(24)	F-7	Fighter	1988			
		23	T-69	Main battle tank	1988	1989	(23)	Part of deal worth $47 m incl APCs
		30	T-69	Main battle tank	1988	1989	(7)	Second 1988 order; upgraded version with 105-mm gun
		360	Type 531	APC	1988			Part of deal worth $47 m
		800	Type 531	APC	1988			Second 1988 order; supplied at friendship prices
		55	Type-69 Spaag	AAV(G)	1987	1989	(25)	
		4	Type-74 284mm	MRL	1988			
		..	Type-83 130mm	MRL	(1988)	1988–89	(20)	Seen at 1988 Army Day parades
		1	HQ-2B	SAM system	1988			Part of deal worth $47 m
		(12)	HQ-2B	SAM	1988			
		2	Jiangdong Class	Frigate	1988			Deal worth $272 m incl 2 Jianghu Class to be refitted before delivery
		2	Jianghu Class	Frigate	1988			Part of deal worth $272 m
		2	Jianghu Class	Frigate	1989			In addition to 2 ordered 1988
		(3)	Romeo Class	Submarine	(1986)			
	Germany, FR	(4)	M-40 Type	MSC/PC	1986			In addition to 2 ordered 1984; order may be for 6
	Israel	40	Python-3	Air-to-air missile	1989			
	Italy	(1)	RAT-31S	Surveillance radar	(1988)	1989	(1)	Deal worth $10 m incl data-processing and communications equipment
	Netherlands	1	Skyguard	Air defence radar	1986	1989	1	
		(1)	Flycatcher	Mobile radar	1986	1989	(1)	Fire control for Aspide SAM system

Recipient	Supplier	No.	Weapon designation	Weapon description	Year of order	Year of delivery	No. delivered	Comments
	USA	1	Boeing-737-200L	Trpt aircraft	(1987)	1989	1	For VIP use
		(3)	C-130H-30	Trpt aircraft	1988	1988–89	(3)	Second order
		4	CH-47D Chinook	Helicopter	1988	1989	4	
		6	F-16A	Fighter	1987			
		25	Model 205 UH-1A	Helicopter	1989			
		4	Model 209 AH-1G	Helicopter	1988	1989	(2)	To be armed with TOW missiles
		24	Model 300C	Helicopter	1988	1989	24	
		3	P-3B Orion	Maritime patrol	1989			Armed with Harpoon anti-ship missiles
		4	S-70C	Helicopter	1989			
		17	M-109 155mm	SPH	1988			Part of deal worth $63 m
		17	M-113-A2	APC	1988			Part of deal worth $63 m
		40	M-48-A5	Main battle tank	1989			
		11	M-577-A2	CPC	1988			Deal worth $63 m incl 20 M-981s
		20	M-981	Support vehicle	1988			Deal worth $63 m incl M-577-A2s
		108	Stingray	Light tank	1987	1987–89	(58)	2 trial systems delivered 1987; part of $300 m deal incl 6 F-16s and 40 M-48-A5s
		2	AN/FPS-117	Air defence radar	1989			Deal worth $43 m
		(16)	AGM-65D	ASM	(1987)			Arming F-16 fighters
		6	AGM-84A Harpoon	Anti-ship missile	1987	1989	6	Arming 3 F-27 maritime patrol aircraft
		(12)	AGM-84A Harpoon	Anti-ship missile	1989			Arming 3 P-3 Orion aircraft
		(48)	AIM-9P	Air-to-air missile	(1987)			Arming F-16 fighters
		(48)	BGM-71D TOW-2	Anti-tank missile	(1988)	1989	(24)	Arming 4 Model-209 helicopters
Tonga	Australia	3	ASI-315	Patrol craft	1988	1989	1	
Tunisia	USA	4	F-5E Tiger-2	Fighter	1989	1989	4	Deal worth $60 m incl 70 lorries, spares, ammunition and support equipment
		57	M-198 155mm	Towed howitzer	1986	1988–89	(57)	
Uganda	Italy	5	AB-412 Griffon	Helicopter	1982	1985–89	(5)	
		6	SF-260 Warrior	Trainer/COIN	1987	1988	6	

Recipient	Supplier	No. ordered	Weapon designation	Weapon description	Year of order	Year(s) of deliveries	No. delivered	Comments
United Arab Emirates	France	:	AS-365F	Helicopter	1988			For Abu Dhabi; incl 3 recce versions and 3 2-seat trainers
		18	Mirage-2000	Fighter	1983	1989	18	
		18	Mirage-2000	Fighter	1985	1989	18	For Abu Dhabi; 22 E versions, 8 recce versions and 6 trainers
		2	Crotale Naval Launcher	ShAM launcher	1986			Arming 2 FRG-built Type 62-001 corvettes
		2	MM-40 Launcher	ShShM launcher	1986			Arming 2 Type 62-001 corvettes
		(50)	Crotale Naval	ShAM	1986			Arming 2 Type 62-001 corvettes
		(24)	MM-40 Exocet	ShShM/SShM	1986			Arming TNC-45 Class FACs
		(16)	MM-40 Exocet	ShShM/SShM	(1987)	1988	(5)	
		(208)	Magic-2	Air-to-air missile	1988			Arming Mirage-5 fighters
		(120)	Mistral	Portable SAM	1988			Arming 2 Type 62-001 corvettes; deal incl 2 Sadral launchers
		(80)	R-440 Crotale	Landmob SAM	1988			
		(72)	Super-530	Air-to-air missile	(1983)	1989	(72)	Arming Mirage-2000 fighters
		(72)	Super-530	Air-to-air missile	(1985)	1989	(72)	Arming Mirage-2000 fighters
	Germany, FR	2	Type 62-001	Corvette	1986	1989	2	For Abu Dhabi
	Italy	3	AB-412 Griffon	Helicopter	1989			For Dubai
	Netherlands	2	Goalkeeper	CIWS	1986			Arming 2 Type 62-001 corvettes
	Singapore	2	Jananah Class	Landing craft	1989			
	UK	12	Hawk	Jet trainer	1989			For Abu Dhabi
		12	Hawk-100	Jet trainer	1989			For Abu Dhabi; part of deal worth $340 m incl 12 Hawk trainers
	USA	8	AT-105 Saxon	APC	(1988)	1989	8	
		5	I-Hawk SAMS	Mobile SAM system	1989			Deal worth $168 m incl 45 missiles
		40	AGM-65D	ASM	(1987)			For Bahrain
		(108)	AIM-9P	Air-to-air missile	1983			Arming Mirage-2000 fighters

Recipient	Supplier	No.	Weapon designation	Weapon description	Year of order	Year of delivery	No. delivered	Comments
Uruguay	France	(108)	AIM-9P	Air-to-air missile	(1985)	1989		Arming second batch of 18 Mirage-2000 fighters
		(45)	MIM-23B Hawk	Landmob SAM	1989			Contract signed June 1989; together with 5 launcher units deal worth $185 m
Venezuela	France	1	Riviere Class	Frigate	1988	1989	1	Delivered without Exocet missile launcher
	Brazil	6	EMB-312 Tucano	Trainer	1988	1988–89	6	Attrition replacement
	France	100	EE-11 Urutu	APC	1988	1989	(30)	
		8	AS-332	Helicopter	1988	1989	8	Deal worth $85 m
		11	AS-350 Ecureuil	Helicopter	1989	1989	11	Deal incl modernization of existing Mirage fleet
		12	Mirage-50	Fighter/bomber	1988			Deal worth FFr 200 m
		31	AMX-13-90	Light tank	1989			
		(10)	Rassur	Surveillance radar	1988			Arming Mirage-50 aircraft
		(50)	AM-39 Exocet	Anti-ship missile	(1988)			Arming Mirage fighters; deal worth approx $30 m
		(100)	Magic-2	Air-to-air missile	1988	1989	(20)	
	Indonesia	16	Model 412	Helicopter	1988			
	Israel	2	IAI-202 Arava	Trpt aircraft	1987	1989	2	Attrition replacements from Israeli stocks
	Netherlands	..	Flycatcher	Mobile radar	1988			
	Spain	4	Cormoran Class	FAC	1987			
	Sweden	70	RBS-70	Portable SAM	1989			
	UK	84	Scorpion 90	Light tank	1988	1989	(10)	Deal worth $85 m incl support equipment, ammunition and training
	USA	18	RGM-84A Harpoon	ShShM	1989			Deal worth $50 m; arming Constitution Class FACs
Viet Nam	USSR	..	Matka Class	Hydrofoil FAC	1989	1989	2	First known export of this class; armed with 1 76-mm gun and 1 30-mm gun

Recipient	Supplier	No. ordered	Weapon designation	Weapon description	Year of order	Year(s) of deliveries	No. delivered	Comments
Yemen, North	China	..	F-7	Fighter	(1988)	1989	6	
Zaire	Egypt	12	Fahd	APC	1989			
	France	13	AMX-13	Light tank	1989			Incl Creusot-Loire turrets
Zimbabwe	China	..	F-7	Fighter	(1988)	1989	(12)	
	Spain	6	C-212-200	Trpt aircraft	1987	1987–88	(5)	Second order

Appendix 7C. Register of licensed production of major conventional weapons in industrialized and Third World countries, 1989

This appendix lists licensed production of major weapons for which either the licence was bought, production was under way, or production was completed during 1989. The column 'Year(s) of deliveries' includes aggregates of all licensed production since the beginning of the contract. The sources and methods for the data collection, and the conventions, abbreviations and acronyms used, are explained in appendix 7D. The entries are made alphabetically, by recipient and licenser.

Recipient	Licenser	No. ordered	Weapon designation	Weapon description	Year of licence	Year(s) of deliveries	No. produced	Comments
I. Industrialized countries								
Australia	Germany, FR	10	Meko-200 Class	Frigate	1989			8 for Australia, 2 for New Zealand; option for 2 more; incl US weapon system and Swedish electronics
	Sweden	6	Type-471	Submarine	1987			Agreement involves 70% Australian industry involvement; option for 2 more likely to be exercised
	Switzerland	65	PC-9	Trainer	1986	1987–89	22	In addition to 2 delivered direct; 17 for assembly and 48 for production
	UK	105	Hamel 105mm	Towed gun	(1982)	1988–89	(52) Reserve	Deal worth $112 m; 46 for Army
	USA	73	F/A-18 Hornet	Fighter	1981	1985–89	66	Deal worth $4.8 b incl 2 delivered direct and 18 F/A-18B trainers
		2	FFG-7 Class	Frigate	1983	1989	1	
Belgium	Israel	21	EL/M-2310	Battlefield radar	1989			Refitted to M-113 APCs

Recipient	Licenser	No. ordered	Weapon designation	Weapon description	Year of licence	Year(s) of deliveries	No. produced	Comments
	USA	44	F-16A	Fighter	1983	1988–89	(23)	Follows 116 F-16s previously ordered; deal worth $625 m; offsets worth 80%
Bulgaria	USSR	..	MT-LB	APC	(1980)	1982–88	(130)	
Canada	Germany, FR	..	BK-117	Helicopter	(1986)	1987–88	(10)	Civilian and military versions
		..	Bo-105LS	Helicopter	(1981)			
	USA	..	LAV-25	APC	1982	1983–89	(958)	
		..	LAV-AD	AAV(M)	1988	1989	10 production	Air defence version in low-rate production
China	France	50	AS-365N	Helicopter	1980	1984–89	(50)	Local production continues
		11	Super Frelon	Helicopter	(1981)	1986–89	(11)	
Czechoslo-vakia	USSR	..	BMP-1	MICV	1971	1971–89	(9 100)	70% exported back to USSR
		..	BMP-1 Spigot	TD(M)	1979	1980–89	(236)	
		..	BMP-2	MICV	1978	1983–89	(275)	Many exported to USSR and GDR; small quantities in service in Czechoslovakia
		..	T-72	Main battle tank	1978	1981–89	(710)	
France	USA	100	MLRS 227mm	MRL	1985	1989	(10)	
Germany, FR	USA	202	MLRS 227mm	MRL	1985	1989	(20)	Production to begin 1992
		..	AIM-120A AMRAAM	Air-to-air missile	1989			
			AIM-9L	Air-to-air missile	1978	1980–89	(14 965)	For delivery 1981–89
		10 000	FIM-92 Stinger	Portable SAM	1983			
		(10 000)	RAM	ShAM/PDM	1985			Dornier/Diehl (FRG) main contractor

Recipient/Supplier	No. ordered	Weapon designation	Weapon description	Year of order	Year(s) of deliveries	No. delivered	Comments
Greece							
Austria	292	Steyr-4K 7FA	APC	1986	1987–89	(292)	Follows 300 ordered 1981
Austria	324	Steyr-4K 7FA	APC	1987			Third order signed Dec. 1987
Denmark	2	PC-55 Class	Patrol craft	1988			First of projected 10
Germany, FR	3	Meko-200 Type	Frigate	1988			In addition to 1 frigate delivered direct; deal worth $1.2 b; financial aid from FRG and USA
Italy							
France	23 000	Aster	SAM	1988			
	5 000	Milan	Anti-tank missile	1984	1985–89	6 351	
		Mistral	SAM	(1988)			To be built by Italmissile consortium
Switzerland	..	Fledermaus II	Mobile radar	(1970)	1973–89	(170)	
USA	..	AB-206B	Helicopter	1972	1978–89	(600)	Jetranger-3 version available from 1984
	..	AB-212	Helicopter	1970	1971–89	(175)	In production 1971–92
	..	AB-212ASW	Helicopter	1975	1975–89	(150)	
	..	AB-412 Griffon	Helicopter	1980	1982–89	(54)	Military version of Bell Model 412; Italy holds marketing rights
	..	CH-47C Chinook	Helicopter	1968	1972–89	(182)	Helicopter trainers
	50	Model 500E	Helicopter	1987	1987–89	(11)	In production since 1969
	..	SH-3D Sea King	Helicopter	1965	1969–89	(98)	
	20	Patriot battery	Mobile SAM system	1988			Part of $2.9 b deal incl 1280 missiles; USA to buy Italian equipment as offset
	(1 100)	AGM-65D	ASM	1988			Italy probable supplier of Spanish and Turkish AGM-65 requirements
	(1 280)	MIM-104 Patriot	SAM	1988			Arming 20 Patriot btys
Japan							
UK	(375)	FH-70 155mm	Towed howitzer	1984	1989	(33)	Following direct delivery of 197
USA	..	CH-47D Chinook	Helicopter	(1984)	1988–89	14	Follow-on orders expected
	1	EP-3C Orion	Elint	1988			
	14	F-15DJ	Fighter/trainer	1987	1988–89	(14)	MOU signed Dec. 1984
	55	F-15J Eagle	Fighter/interceptor	1985	1988–89	23	US firms guaranteed 42% of work
	(130)	FS-X	Fighter	1988 (1982)			
..		KV-107/2A	Helicopter	1984–89		(23)	In addition to 61 produced earlier
	..	Model 205 UH-1H	Helicopter	1972	1973–89	(124)	

Recipient	Licenser	No. ordered	Weapon designation	Weapon description	Year of licence	Year(s) of deliveries	No. produced	Comments
	USA	(73)	Model 209 AH-1S	Helicopter	1982	1984–89	(47)	
		100	OH-6D	Helicopter	1977	1982–89	(90)	
		50	P-3C Orion	Maritime patrol	1985	1987–89	50	MOU signed Oct. 1985
		83	SH-3B	Helicopter	1979	1981–89	(80)	
		24	SH-60J Seahawk	Helicopter	1988	1989	12	
		40	UH-60J	Helicopter	(1987)	1988–89	8	
		25	Patriot battery	Mobile SAM system	(1984)	1988–89	20	Part of $2800 m deal incl 980 missiles
		..	AIM-9L	Air-to-air missile	(1982)	1983–89	(3 841)	
		..	BGM-71C I-TOW	Anti-tank missile	(1983)	1985–89	2 359	Total requirement: up to 10 000
		980	MIM-104 Patriot	Landmob SAM	1984	1989	89	
		..	MIM-23B Hawk	Landmob SAM	1978	1978–89	(2 793)	
Netherlands	USA	53	F-16A	Fighter	1983	1987–89	(15)	Fourth order
		10	F-16A	Fighter	1989	1989	(14)	Deal worth $116 m incl 10 engines
		14	F-16B	Fighter/trainer	1983			
Poland	USSR	..	An-2	Lightplane	1960	1960–89	(1 500)	In production since 1960; over 11 000 built; most for civilian use
		..	Mi-2 Hoplite	Helicopter	1965	1965–89	(3 000)	In production since 1965; most for export
		..	2S1 122mm	SPH	(1980)	1982–89	(460)	Some built for export
		..	MT-LB	APC	(1980)	1980–89	(185)	
		(1 900)	T-72	Main battle tank	(1978)	1981–89	(735)	
Portugal	Belgium	100	Jet Squalus	Jet trainer	1989			30 for Portuguese Air Force, 15 for civilian use and 55 for export markets
Romania	France	..	SA-316B	Helicopter	1971	1977–89	(230)	

Recipient	Supplier	No.	Weapon designation	Weapon description	Year of order	Year(s) of deliveries	No. delivered/produced	Comments
	USSR	..	SA-330 Puma	Helicopter	1977	1978–89	(145)	
		..	Ka-126	Helicopter	(1989)	1980–88	(650)	
		..	Yak-52	Trainer	(1979)		trainer	Two-seat piston-engined primary
		..	TAB-77	APC	(1975)	1976–89	(1 620)	Romanian version of Soviet BTR-70
		..	A-90	Air-to-air missile	(1975)	1977–89	(820)	Arming MiG-21 fighters
		..	A-91	Air-to-air missile	(1980)	1983–89	(290)	Arming MiG-21 and MiG-23 fighters
		..	A-911	Air-to-air missile	(1980)	1983–89	(140)	Arming MiG-23 fighters
Spain	France	18	AS-332	Helicopter	1986	1988–89	(6)	
	Germany, FR	..	Bo-105CB	Helicopter	(1978)	1981–89	(87)	In addition to 10 purchased direct
	UK	5	Sandown Class	Minehunter	(1988)			
	USA	1	FFG-7 Class	Frigate	1986			
Sweden	USA	700	AGM-114A	ASM/ATM	1987			Coastal defence version
Switzerland	Germany, FR	345	Leopard-2	Main battle tank	1983	1987–89	(146)	Deal worth $1400 m incl 35 delivered direct; final deliveries due 1993
	UK	19	Hawk	Trainer	1987	1989	(2)	Deal worth $150 m incl training and logistics
Turkey	Germany, FR	4	Meko-200 Type	Frigate	1983	1988–89	2	In addition to 2 built in FRG
		2	Type-209/3	Submarine	1987			Option on 4 more
	Spain	72	CN-235	Trpt aircraft	1989			In addition to 20 for civilian use
	USA	152	F-16C	Fighter	1984	1987–89	25	Part of deal worth $4 b incl 24 D versions and 8 delivered direct
		1 698	AIFV	MICV	1988	1988–89	(260)	Total cost $1.076 b; offsets worth $700 m
		168	MLRS 227mm	MRL	1988			Deal worth $600 m for 180 MLRS; 168 co-produced and 12 delivered direct
		..	FIM-92A Stinger	Portable SAM	1989			Manufacture to begin 1991
UK	Brazil	128	EMB-312 Tucano	Trainer	1985	1987–89	(41)	Deal worth $145–150 m; option on 15 more

Recipient	Licenser	No. ordered	Weapon designation	Weapon description	Year of licence	Year(s) of deliveries	No. produced	Comments
	France	..	Milan	Anti-tank missile	1976	1977–89	(5 969)	Licensed production by Euraam (BAe, MBB, AEG and Marconi)
	USA	67	MLRS 227mm	MRL	1985	1989	(10)	
		223	AIM-120A AMRAAM	Air-to-air missile	1988			
		..	BGM-71A TOW	Anti-tank missile	1980	1982–89	(19 318)	
USA	Israel	..	EL/2106	Point defence radar	(1983)	1985–89	(50)	US designation AN/UPS-3; in production but quantities unknown
	Italy	..	Have Nap	ASM	1987			For co-production with Martin Marietta
		17	Lerici Plus	MCM	1986			Enlarged version of Italian Lerici Class; funding incl $197.2 m in FY 1989
	Switzerland	160	ADATS	SAM system	1987	1989	(3)	Eventual requirement may reach 562
	UK	302	T-45 Hawk	Jet trainer	1986	1988	2	
		391	M-119 105mm	Towed gun	1987			
Yugoslavia	USSR	(350)	T-74	Main battle tank	1977	1983–89	(350)	Yugoslavian designation M-84; includes local modifications

II. Third World countries

Recipient	Licenser	No. ordered	Weapon designation	Weapon description	Year of licence	Year(s) of deliveries	No. produced	Comments
Argentina	Brazil	20	CBA-123	Trpt aircraft	1989			Order for 36; 16 for civilian users
	Germany, FR	6	Meko-140 Type	Frigate	1980	1985–88	4	Armed with MM-40 Exocet ShShMs; last 2 will be available for export
	Italy	4	Type TR-1700	Submarine	1977			In addition to 2 delivered direct
		..	A-109 Hirundo	Helicopter	1988			Deal worth $120 m
Brazil	Austria	..	GHN-45 155mm	Towed howitzer	(1985)			Production expected from early 1990s

Recipient	Supplier	No. ordered	Weapon designation	Weapon description	Year of order	Year(s) of deliveries	No. delivered/produced	Comments
	France	16	HB-350M Esquilo	Helicopter	1988	1989	(5)	In addition to 39 previously produced
	France	10	HB-365F	Helicopter	1988			Part of $249 m deal
	Germany, FR	..	SNAC-1	SSN	1989			For future development by IKL of FRG
	Germany, FR	(3)	Type-209/3	Submarine	1982			In addition to 1 delivered direct
Chile	South Africa	(400)	G-5 155 mm	Towed howitzer	1989	1989	(201)	
	Switzerland	..	Piranha	APC	1980	1981–89	1	
	USA	..	Model 206	Helicopter	(1988)	1989		
	USA	..	T-35 Pillan	Trainer	1980	1985–89	(130)	
Egypt	Brazil	125	EMB-312 Tucano	Trainer	1983	1985–89	(125)	In addition to 10 delivered direct; 30 for Egypt, 95 for Iraq; option for 70 more (45 for Iraq)
	France	15	Alpha Jet	Jet trainer	1985			Second order; status uncertain
	France	..	Sinai 23	Mobile SAM system	1988			Integration of Egyptian weapon systems with French fire control system
	UK	..	Swingfire	Anti-tank missile	1977	1979–89	(5 430)	
	USA	540	M-1 Abrams	Main battle tank	1988	1988		Following delivery of 15; deal worth $2 b
	USA	34	AN/TPS-63	Surveillance radar	1986	1988–89	(9)	Deal worth $190 m
India	France	..	SA-316B Chetak	Helicopter	(1962)	1964–89	(200)	Also for civilian use
	France	5	TRS-2230	3-D radar	(1983)	1988–89	(3)	In addition to 4 supplied direct
	France	(42 000)	Milan	Anti-tank missile	1982	1985–89	(22 577)	First missile completed 1985
	Germany, FR	50	Do-228	Trpt aircraft	1983	1987–89	(18)	Part of deal worth $440 m for production of 110 civil and military versions
	Germany, FR	2	Type-1500	Submarine	1981	1989	1	In addition to 2 delivered direct; second due in the mid-1990s
	Netherlands	212	Flycatcher	Mobile radar	(1987)	1988–89	(14)	In addition to direct deliveries
	UK	46	Jaguar	Fighter	1982	1988–89	(16)	
	USSR	(165)	MiG-27	Fighter/grd attack	1983	1987–89	(60)	First flight 1987 after lengthy delays
	USSR	..	BMP-2	APC/ICV	1983	1987–89	(40)	
	USSR	(1 000)	T-72	Main battle tank	(1980)	1987–89	(300)	

Recipient	Licenser	No. ordered	Weapon designation	Weapon description	Year of licence	Year(s) of deliveries	No. produced	Comments
		..	AA-8 Aphid	Air-to-air missile	(1986)			Unconfirmed
Indonesia	France	..	AS-332	Helicopter	1983	1985–89	(12)	Production switched from Puma to Super Puma 1983
	Germany, FR	(100)	Super Etendard	Fighter	(1988)			French offer under consideration
			BK-117	Helicopter	1982	1986–89	(8)	Total production schedule: 100; 2 pre-production aircraft delivered 1984
		(80)	NBo-105	Helicopter	1987	1988–89	(8)	Follow-on licensed production of 80–100 to include export orders
	Netherlands	(2)	Alkmaar Class	Minehunter	(1988)	1978–89	(28)	Up to 10 may eventually be built
	Spain	(80)	CN-212	Trpt aircraft	1976			
	USA	(20)	Model 412	Helicopter	1982	1986–89	(14)	Others for civilian customers
Iran	China	..	Oghab	SSM	1985	1986–89	(700)	
Iraq	USSR	..	Saddam 122mm	Towed howitzer	(1988)	1989	(50)	
Jordan	USA	100	Model 300C	Helicopter	1989			For civilian and military customers
Korea, North	China	..	Hai Ying-2	SSLM	1976	1977–89	(156)	
	USSR	..	T-62	Main battle tank	(1978)	1980–89	(622)	Including production for export
		..	AT-3 Sagger	Anti-tank missile	1975	1976–89	(1 400)	
		..	SA-7 Grail	Portable SAM	(1985)	1986–89	(400)	
		..	Scud-B	SSM	(1977)	1987–89	(136)	Egyptian assistance
Korea, South	Germany, FR	2	Type-209/3	Submarine	1987			In addition to 1 purchased direct from HDW; follow on order for 3 more likely
	Italy	..	Type 6614	APC	1976	1977–89	(355)	

	No.	Weapon designation	Weapon description	Year of order	Year(s) of deliveries	No.	Comments
USA	6	Lerici Class	Minehunter	(1986)	1988	1	Class may ultimately be of 10 ships
	72	F/A-18 Hornet	Fighter	1989			In addition to 48 delivered direct
	(150)	H-76 Eagle	Helicopter	1986			
	..	Model 500MD	Helicopter	1976	1978–89	(167)	
	272	M-109-A2 155mm	SPH	1983	1985–89	(250)	
	242	M-109-A2 155mm	SPH	1989			
Malaysia UK	..	Harimau	Scout car	1988			Version of Ferret scout car
Mexico USA	..	DN-3 Caballo	Scout car	(1985)	1988	17	
Nigeria Austria	(200)	Steyr-4K 7FA	APC	(1981)		problems	Status uncertain due to financial
Nigeria USA	..	Air Beetle	Trainer	1988			Version of US RV-6
Pakistan China	..	T-69	Main battle tank	(1989)			
	..	Red Arrow-8	Anti-tank missile	1989			
Sweden	(180)	Supporter	Trainer	1974	1977–89	(162)	
Philippines Germany, FR	..	Bo-105C	Helicopter	1974	1976–89	(13)	
UK	..	BN-2A Islander	Lightplane	1974	1974–89	(30)	Others built for civilian customers
Singapore Germany, FR	5	Type 62-001	Corvette	1985			
South Africa Israel	(96)	Gabriel-2	ShShM	(1984)	1986–88	(36)	Unclear whether licence-produced, reverse-engineered or imported direct; South African designation Skorpioen
	(12)	Reshef Class	FAC	1974	1978–86	6	In addition to 3 delivered direct
Taiwan Israel	..	Gabriel Launch	ShShM/SShM launcher	(1978)	1980–89	(77)	Taiwanese designation Hsiung Feng
	..	Gabriel-2	ShShM/SShM	(1978)	1980–89	(465)	Armed with Hsiung Feng ShShMs
Singapore	(22)	Suikiang Class	FAC	(1983)	1986–88	(9)	

Recipient	Licenser	No. ordered	Weapon designation	Weapon description	Year of licence	Year(s) of deliveries	No. produced	Comments
	USA	470	M-60-H	Main battle tank	1984	1985–89	(470)	M-60 chassis, M-48 turret, advanced fire control system
		8	FFG-7 Class	Frigate	1988			Order number reduced from 12
Thailand	France	2	PS-700 Class	Landing ship	(1985)	1988	1	In addition to 2 delivered direct
	Germany, FR	45	Fantrainer	Trainer	1983	1986–89	(38)	
	UK	3	Province Class	FAC	1987			To be armed with 30-mm guns and carry a light helicopter
		1	Province Class	FAC	1989			In addition to 3 under construction

Appendix 7D. Sources and methods

I. The SIPRI sources

The sources of the data presented in the registers are of six general types. Five of these are published sources, available to the general public: newspapers; periodicals and journals; books, monographs and annual reference works; official national documents; and documents issued by international and intergovernmental organizations. The total number of sources regularly searched for arms trade data is about 200. It is from these that the overwhelming bulk of the arms trade registers are compiled. The sources listed below represent a selection of the first-priority sources of arms trade and arms production data. Reliance on publicly available information provides superior accuracy, independence and accountability but cannot provide a comprehensive picture of the arms trade.

The arms trade is not fully reported in the open literature. Published reports provide partial information, and substantial disagreement among reports is common. Therefore, the exercise of judgement and the making of estimates are important elements in compiling the SIPRI arms trade data base. Order dates and the delivery dates for arms transactions are continuously revised in the light of new information, but where they are not disclosed the dates are estimated. The exact number of weapons ordered as well as the number of weapons delivered may not always be known and are sometimes estimated, particularly with respect to missiles. It is common for reports of arms deals involving large platforms—ships, aircraft and armoured vehicles—to ignore missile armaments classified as major weapons by SIPRI. Unless there is explicit evidence that platforms were disarmed or altered before delivery, it is assumed that a weapons fit specified in one of the major reference works such as the *Jane's* or *Interavia* series is carried.

II. Selection criteria

The SIPRI arms trade data cover five categories of major weapons: aircraft, armour and artillery, guidance and radar systems, missiles, and warships. The statistics presented refer to the value of the trade in these five categories only. The registers and statistics do not include the trade in small arms, artillery under 100-mm calibre, ammunition, support items, services and components or component technology, except for specific items. In general, publicly available information is not sufficient to track these other categories satisfactorily.

There are two criteria for the selection of major weapon transfers for the registers. The first is that of military application. The aircraft category excludes aerobatic aeroplanes, remotely piloted vehicles, drones and gliders. Transport aircraft and VIP transports are included only if they bear military insignia or are otherwise confirmed as military registered.

The armour and artillery category includes all types of tanks, tank destroyers, armoured cars, armoured personnel carriers, armoured support vehicles, infantry combat vehicles as well as multiple rocket launchers, self-propelled and towed guns and howitzers with a calibre equal to or above 100 mm. Military lorries, jeeps and other unarmoured support vehicles are not included.

The category of guidance and radar systems is a residual category for electronic-tracking, target-acquisition, fire-control, launch and guidance systems that are either (a) deployed independently of a weapon system listed under another weapon category (e.g., certain ground-based SAM launch systems) or (b) shipborne missile-launch or point-defence (CIWS) systems. The values of acquisition, fire-control, launch and guidance systems on aircraft and armoured vehicles are included in the value of the respective aircraft or armoured vehicle. The reason for treating shipborne systems separately is that a given type of ship is often equipped with numerous combinations of different surveillance, acquisition, launch and guidance systems.

The missile category includes only guided missiles. Unguided rockets such as light anti-armour weapons are excluded. Free-fall aerial munitions (such as 'iron bombs') are also excluded. In the naval sphere, anti-submarine rockets and all torpedoes are also excluded.

The ship category excludes some types of ship, such as small patrol craft (with a displacement of less than 100 t, unless they carry cannon, missiles or torpedoes), research vessels, tugs and ice-breakers. Naval combat support vessels such as fleet replenishment ships are included.

The second criterion for selection of items is the identity of the buyer. The items must be destined for export to the armed forces of another country. Transfers to paramilitary forces or police are included if they involve major weapons. Major weapons received by intelligence agencies are included also. Arms supplied to guerrilla forces pose a problem. For example, if weapons are delivered to the Contra rebels they are listed as imports to Nicaragua with a comment in the arms trade register indicating the local recipient. The entry of any arms transfer is made corresponding to the five weapon categories listed above. This means that missiles and their guidance/launch vehicles are often entered separately under their respective category in the arms trade register.

III. The value of the arms trade

The SIPRI system for evaluating the arms trade was designed as a *trend-measuring device*, to enable the measurement of changes in the total flow of major weapons and its geographic pattern. Expressing the evaluation in monetary terms reflects both the quantity and the quality of the weapons transferred. Aggregate values and shares are based only on *actual deliveries* during the year or years covered in the relevant tables and figures.

The SIPRI valuation system is not comparable to official economic statistics such as gross domestic product, public expenditure and export/import figures. The monetary values chosen do not correspond to the actual prices paid, which vary considerably depending on different pricing methods, the length of production runs and the terms involved in individual transactions. For instance, a deal may or may not cover spare parts, training, support equipment, compensation, offset arrangements for the local industries in the buying country, and so on. Furthermore, to use only actual sales prices—even assuming that the information were available for all deals, which it is not—military aid and grants would be excluded, and the total flow of arms would therefore not be measured.

Production under licence is included in the arms trade statistics in such a way that it should reflect the import share embodied in the weapon. In reality, this share is normally high in the beginning, gradually decreasing over time. However, a single estimate of the import share for each weapon produced under licence is made by SIPRI, and therefore the value of arms produced under licence agreements may be slightly overstated.

IV. Priority sources

Journals and periodicals

AAS Milavnews Air Letter (Romford, UK)
AAS Milavnews News Letter (Romford, UK)
Aerospace Daily (Washington, DC)
Africa Confidential (London)
African Business (London)
Afrique Défense/African Defence (Paris)
Air & Cosmos (Paris)
Air Force (Washington, DC)
Air International (Bromley, London)
Allgemeine Schweizerische Militär Zeitschrift (Bern)
Antimilitarismus Information (Berlin)
Armada International (Zurich)
Armed Forces (London)
Armed Forces Journal International (Washington, DC)
Arms Control Today (Washington, DC)
Asian Defence Journal (Kuala Lumpur)
Aviation Week & Space Technology (New York)
Bulletin of the Atomic Scientists (Chicago)
Campaign Against Arms Trade (London)
Congressional Quarterly Service, Weekly Report (Washington, DC)
Current News (Washington, DC)
DMS Intelligence Newsletter (Greenwich, New York)
Defence (Redhill, UK)
Defence & Armament Héraclès (Paris)
Defence Attaché (London)
Defence Daily (Washington, DC)
Defence Electronics (Palo Alto, California)
Defence Industry Digest (London)
Defence Intelligence Bulletin (Gutenswil, Switzerland)
Defence Journal (Karachi)
Defence Monitor (Washington, DC)
Defence Today (Rome)
Defensa (Madrid)
Defense & Economy World Report (Washington, DC)
Defense & Foreign Affairs Daily (Alexandria, Virginia)
Defense & Foreign Affairs Weekly (Alexandria, Virginia)
Defense Economy World Report (Washington, DC)
Défense Nationale (Paris)
Defense News (Springfield, Virginia)
Der Spiegel (Hamburg)

Europa Archiv (Bonn)
Europäische Wehrkunde (Herford, FR Germany)
Far Eastern Economic Review (Hong Kong)
Flight International (Sutton, UK)
Foreign Broadcast Information Service (Washington, DC)
IDSA Journal (Strategic Analysis) (New Delhi)
IDSA Strategic Digest (New Delhi)
Interavia (Geneva)
Interavia Air Letter (Geneva)
International Defense Review (Geneva)
Israeli Defence Force Journal (Tel Aviv)
JP4 (Florence)
Jane's NATO Report (Coulsdon, UK)
Jane's Defence Weekly (Coulsdon, UK)
Japan Monitor (Tokyo)
Journal of Defence & Diplomacy (McLean, Virginia)
L'Express (Paris)
Le Monde Diplomatique (Paris)
Latin America Political Report (London)
Latin American Economic Report (London)
Latin American Regional Report (London)
Latin American Weekly Report (London)
Marine Corps Gazette (Quantico, Virginia)
Marine Rundschau (Stuttgart)
Med News (Maisons-Laffitte)
Military Technology (Bonn)
NATO's Sixteen Nations (Brussels)
National Defense (Washington, DC)
Naval Forces (Farnborough)
Navy International (Haslemere, UK)
Newsweek (New York)
Österreichische Militärische Zeitung (Vienna)
Pacific Defence Reporter (Kunyung, Victoria, Australia)
Panorama Difesa (Florence)
Proceedings (USNI) (Annapolis, Maryland)
Revista Espanola de Defensa (Madrid)
Soldat und Technik (Frankfurt)
Soviet Military Review (Moscow)
Strategic Digest (New Delhi)
Technología Militar (Bonn)
US News &World Report (Washington, D.C.)
The Wednesday Report: Canada's National Defence Bulletin (Ontario)
Wehrtechnik (Bonn)
Wireless File (US Embassy, Stockholm)
World Weapon Review (Newtown, Connecticut)

Newspapers

Dagens Nyheter (Stockholm)
El País (Madrid)

Financial Times (Europe) (Frankfurt)
Frankfurter Allgemeine Zeitung (Frankfurt)
Frankfurter Rundschau (Frankfurt)
The Guardian (London)
The Independent (London)
International Herald Tribune (Paris)
Japan Monitor (Tokyo)
Jerusalem Post Weekly (Jerusalem)
Le Monde (Paris)
Moscow News (Moscow)
Neue Zürcher Zeitung (Zurich)
Selections from the Regional Press (Islamabad)
Süddeutsche Zeitung (Munich)
Sunday Times (London)
Svenska Dagbladet (Stockholm)
The Times (London)
Times of India (New Delhi/Bombay)
Wall Street Journal (New York)

Annual reference publications

'Aerospace Forecast and Inventory', annually in *Aviation Week & Space Technology* (New York)
Asian Recorder (Recorder Press: New Delhi)
Combat Fleets of the World (Naval Institute Press: Annapolis, Maryland)
Defense & Foreign Affairs Handbook (Perth Corporation: Washington, DC)
Trends in Conventional Arms Transfers to the Third World (Congressional Research Service: Washington, DC)
Interavia Air Forces World (Interavia Publishing Group: Geneva)
Interavia Aircraft Armament (Interavia Publishing Group: Geneva)
Interavia Aircraft Production (Interavia Publishing Group: Geneva)
Interavia World Helicopter Systems (Interavia Publishing Group: Geneva)
Jane's All The World's Aircraft (Jane's Publishing Co.: Coulsdon)
Jane's Armour and Artillery (Jane's Publishing Co.: Coulsdon)
Jane's Fighting Ships (Jane's Publishing Co.: Coulsdon)
Jane's Infantry Weapons (Jane's Publishing Co.: Coulsdon)
Jane's Military Vehicles & Support Equipment (Jane's Publishing Co.: Coulsdon)
Jane's Weapon Systems (Jane's Publishing Co.: Coulsdon)
Keesing's Contemporary Archives (Longman Group: Harlow)
The Middle East Military Balance (Westview Press: Boulder, Colorado)
Military Balance (Jane's Publishing Co.: Coulsdon)
'Military Aircraft of the World', and 'Missile Forces of the World', annually in *Flight International* (Sutton, UK)
Soviet Military Power (US Government printing office: Washington, DC)
Weyers Flotten Taschenbuch 1988/89 (Bernard & Graefe Verlag: Koblenz)
World Fighting Vehicles & Ordnance Forecast (Newtown, Connecticut)
World Military Expenditures and Arms Transfers (US Government Printing Office: Washington, DC)
World Missile Forecast (Forecast International: Newtown, Connecticut)

V. Conventions

The following conventions are used in appendices 7B and 7C:

..	Data not available or not applicable
–	Negligible figure (<0.5) or none
( )	Uncertain data or SIPRI estimate

Abbreviations and acronyms

AA	Anti-aircraft
AAG	Anti-aircraft gun
AAM	Air-to-air missile
AAV	Anti-aircraft vehicle
AAV(G)	Anti-aircraft vehicle (gun-armed)
AAV(M)	Anti-aircraft vehicle (missile-armed)
AC	Armoured car
Acc to	According to
ADATS	Air defence and anti-tank system
ADV	Air defence version
Adv	Advanced
AEV	Armoured engineering vehicle
AEW	Airborne early-warning (system)
AEW&C	Airborne early warning and control
AF	Air Force
AFSV	Armoured fire support vehicle
Amph	Amphibious/amphibian
APC	Armoured personnel carrier
Approx	Approximately
ARM	Anti-radar missile
ARV	Armoured recovery vehicle
AShM	Air-to-ship missile
ASM	Air-to-surface missile
ASV	Anti-surface vessel
ASW	Anti-submarine warfare
ATGM	Anti-tank guided missile
ATM	Anti-tank missile
AV	Armoured vehicle
AWACS	Airborne early warning and control system
BL	Bridge-layer
Bty	Battery
CIWS	Close-in weapon system
CG	Coastal gun
COIN	Counter-insurgency
CP	Coastal patrol
CPC	Command post carrier
CS	Coastal surveillance
DOD	Department of Defense (USA)
ECM	Electronic countermeasure

Elint	Electronic intelligence
EW	Early warning
Excl	Excluding/excludes
FAC	Fast attack craft (missile/torpedo-armed)
FMS	Foreign Military Sales (USA)
FY	Fiscal year
Grd	Ground
ICV	Infantry combat vehicle
IDS	Interdictor/strike version
Incl	Including/includes
IRBM	Intermediate-range ballistic missile
Landmob	Land-mobile (missile)
LC	Landing craft (<600t displacement)
LS	Landing ship (>600t displacement)
LT	Light tank
LOA	Letter of Offer and Acceptance (USA)
LoO	Letter of Offer (USA)
MAP	Military Assistance Program (USA)
Mar patrol	Maritime patrol aircraft
MBT	Main battle tank
MCM	Mine countermeasure (ship)
MICV	Mechanized infantry combat vehicle
Mk	Mark
MOU	Memorandum of Understanding
MR	Maritime reconnaissance
MRCA	Multi-role combat aircraft
MRL	Multiple rocket launcher
MRS	Multiple rocket system
MSC	Minesweeper, coastal
MSO	Minesweeper, ocean
MT	Medium tank
OPV	Offshore patrol vessel
PAR	Precision approach radar
PC	Patrol craft (gun-armed/unarmed)
PDM	Point defence missile
Port	Portable
RAAF	Royal Australian Air Force
Recce	Reconnaissance (aircraft/vehicle)
RN	Royal Navy (UK)
SAM	Surface-to-air missile
SAR	Search and rescue
SC	Scout car
ShAM	Ship-to-air missile
ShShM	Ship-to-ship missile
ShSuM	Ship-to-submarine missile
SLBM	Submarine-launched ballistic missile
SPAAG	Self-propelled anti-aircraft gun
SPG	Self-propelled gun
SPH	Self-propelled howitzer
SPM	Self-propelled mortar

SShM	Surface-to-ship missile
SSM	Surface-to-surface missile
SSN	Nuclear-powered submarine
SuShM	Submarine-to-ship missile
SY	Shipyard
TD	Tank destroyer (gun-armed)
TD(M)	Tank destroyer (missile-armed)
TG	Towed gun
TH	Towed howitzer
Trpt	Transport
UNITA	National Union for the Total Independence of Angola

8. Arms production

IAN ANTHONY, AGNÈS COURADES ALLEBECK,
ESPEN GULLIKSTAD, GERD HAGMEYER-GAVERUS and
HERBERT WULF

I. Introduction: causes of structural change in the arms industrial base

The arms industrial base in both NATO and the WTO has recently been affected by a series of factors: the dramatic political changes in Eastern Europe, the improved arms control negotiations, budgetary pressures, institutional changes in Western Europe, the expansion of Third World arms production facilities, and changing military doctrines and military-related technologies. On balance, these trends are likely to lead to a reduction in the size of the world industrial arms base. Difficulties are likely to be encountered by private companies (mainly in the United States and Western Europe) as well as by state-owned factories (mainly in the Soviet Union) that are heavily dependent on arms production.The purpose of this chapter is to describe the trends affecting the arms industrial base and to present data on the size and characteristics of the arms industry in the East and West.

Since 1945 conventional arms control on the one hand and conventional arms procurement, including plans for arms production, on the other have been conducted as separate activities, each with its own dynamic. Arms controllers and those planning the procurement of conventional weapons have not needed to co-ordinate with one another, while arms control concentrated primarily on nuclear weapons. However, this situation has been altered as a result of major political, economic and military changes.

The mandate accepted by the 23 participants at the Vienna Conference on Security and Co-operation in Europe (CSCE) follow-up meeting for the Negotiation on Conventional Armed Forces in Europe (CFE) states that: 'The objectives of the negotiation shall be to strengthen stability and security in Europe through the establishment of a stable and secure balance of conventional armed forces, which include *conventional armaments and equipment, at lower levels* . . . Each and every participant undertakes to contribute to the attainment of these objectives'.[1]

If successful, the CFE will lead not only to reduced levels of deployed forces and weaponry but also to reduced production runs for major conventional weapon systems. As a result a process of verified reduction of future procurement and arms production will have to be started—and consequently arms control negotiations and procurement planning will have to

---

[1] Mandate for the Negotiation on Conventional Armed Forces in Europe, 10 Jan. 1989, paragraph 9, reprinted in SIPRI, *SIPRI Yearbook 1989: World Armaments and Disarmament* (Oxford University Press: Oxford, 1989), pp. 420–22; emphasis added.

be linked. The CFE Negotiation promises drastic reductions on the WTO side and cuts—although smaller ones—by NATO.[2] If the objectives stated in the CFE mandate are taken seriously by governments, questions arise concerning how far industrial interests are to be taken into account in the negotiations and how arms producers are to be prepared for the outcome of successful conventional arms control negotiations.

Arms control discussions are taking place against a background of significant over-capacities in arms production and with new over-capacities on the horizon (notably in Japan). It is possible for companies and corporations to produce more equipment than governments can absorb. The stagnant demand within the global arms transfer market is discussed in chapter 7 of this *Yearbook*.

More important are the political developments in several WTO countries that occurred in 1989. What the WTO might look like in a few years is an open question, but there can be no doubt that if the present trend of dramatic changes in East–West political relations continues, the structure of the armed forces—and therefore their weapon inventories, procurement policies and the arms industrial base—will undergo substantial change and reform. Reductions of procurement budgets in several WTO countries and reforms to reorient parts of the arms industry (discussed in detail in section IV of this chapter) are being implemented. According to the North Atlantic Treaty, NATO is a defensive alliance that would respond to armed attack on any of its parties within the geographical region of the North Atlantic area as defined by the Treaty. Political changes within the WTO must have effects on NATO.

Within NATO a debate has already begun in the context of the CFE Negotiation. In October 1989 both the Supreme Allied Commander in Europe, General John Galvin, and his Deputy, General Eberhard Eimler, made reference to a plan that would redistribute the latest generation of arms between NATO allies in order to avoid 'significant disarmament in zones which currently have state-of-the-art equipment. It would not make sense to destroy modern weapons systems while keeping obsolete equipment in other parts of the alliance'.[3] What is being proposed is a large internal arms transfer programme within NATO to compensate for the removal of equipment under the terms of a CFE agreement with the modernization of older inventories. Under the proposal, countries with more advanced equipment—the USA, the UK and the Federal Republic of Germany (the role of France in this process is not at all clear)—will give or sell equipment to less advanced armed forces—those of Greece, Italy, Portugal, Spain and Turkey—rather than destroy this equipment. The less developed countries would then destroy equipment which is already planned for replacement.[4]

---

[2] Governments of the WTO countries have agreed in principle to asymmetric cuts. See also chapter 13.

[3] Lewis, P., 'CFE: West plans weapons shuffle', *Jane's Defence Weekly*, 7 Oct. 1989, p. 681; Starr, B., 'SACEUR speaks on arms plans', *Jane's Defence Weekly*, 21 Oct. 1989, p. 833; 'Vienna talks trigger Air Force review', *Aviation Week & Space Technology*, 30 Oct. 1989, pp. 34–36.

[4] For example, the air forces of Greece, Portugal, Spain and Turkey still operate aircraft such as the F-5 and F-104, originally introduced in the 1960s. The Greek Air Force in fact still retains several

This transfer of equipment already produced and in service is mainly intended to minimize the impact of a CFE agreement on NATO capabilities. However, if it is completed and implemented, it may affect the volume of future arms production planned but not yet implemented. For example, 160 F-16 fighters and 1700 armoured vehicles are scheduled for production in Turkey in the 1990s under licences from US companies. Will these plans be affected if Turkey receives aircraft and armoured vehicles from other NATO countries?

Factors other than arms control

The budget environment

Economic burdens from investment in the military sector are not a cause of concern exclusively in the WTO countries—although they are of greater concern there than in the NATO countries. Budgetary constraints in many NATO countries have grown as a result of competing domestic economic priorities, particularly in the context of a generally more favourable East–West climate. The possible success of arms control negotiations may already have had political consequences, affecting governments' readiness to allocate funds to the military. The perception of a disappearing threat and the fading of enemy images seem to be giving finance ministries more power to question military budgets. If procurement budgets do not increase (and are therefore cut, once adjusted to account for inflation) and if planned equipment programmes are postponed or given up, as was discussed at the end of 1989, total corporate arms sales will go down. This process is discussed in section III. Arms contractors both in North America and in Western Europe might not remain in business, let alone in profit.

Changing technologies

Technological advances and increases in weapon costs have already had wide-ranging consequences. Weapon systems are seldom replaced from one generation to the next on a one-for-one basis. Lower numbers are ordered not because of reduced demands from the armed forces but because of funding difficulties. This trend is likely to continue, and costs are likely to become more relevant to weapon design in the future, given the continuous rise in costs for advanced technology.

A preference for smaller numbers of high-technology weapon systems may be fuelled by an arms control process that concentrates on the quantities and not the quality of arms. The unfavourable economic situation in the USSR and its technological inferiority to the United States limit the choices available to the Soviet Union after the principal acceptance and partly implemented policy of reduced numbers of weapons (see section IV). Security needs and technological imperatives have produced a kind of

F-84s built during the Korean War. Jackson, P., 'Is it a bird? Is it a plane?', *Armed Forces*, Oct. 1989, p. 443.

double-track strategy among governments in NATO countries. On the one hand conventional arms control negotiations are undertaken more seriously than previously, and negotiated cuts in manpower and equipment are now NATO policy. On the other hand the process of developing new and sophisticated weaponry has not been halted (as indicated in section II). On the contrary, research and development efforts are seen as essential to compensate for potential future reductions.

West European integration

In addition to these changes, the West European arms industry is confronted with contradicting tendencies for greater co-operation and competition at the same time (discussed in detail in section III). There has been a trend towards multinational decision making on procurement as companies in the European Community (EC) are challenged by the implementation of the Single European Act (the implementation of a single market after 1992) and calls by several West European organizations (the Independent European Programme Group within NATO, the EC Commission, the European Parliament and governments in member countries of the EC) for a co-ordinated and streamlined arms industry. However, despite the announced intention in Western Europe to strengthen co-operation within the European arms industry, this development is certainly not inevitable, and co-operation within the EC may be constrained by Article 223 of the 1957 Treaty of Rome that established the European Economic Community.

Changes in military doctrine

Apart from the economic and political considerations noted above, changes in military doctrine in both East and West (addressed in chapter 13) might also have long-term effects on the arms industry. If concepts of non-offensive defence or less threatening postures of the armed forces that restrict them to their home territory are put into practice, different types of equipment will be procured. Some producers are likely to lose part of their business while others might gain. Which parts of the arms industry are affected will depend on the structural reforms to be undertaken. For example, producers of long-range bombers, long-range missiles and naval vessels might gain new orders as a result of doctrines that aim to prevent the possibility of taking and occupying territory. Concepts of non-offensive defence usually stress the importance of anti-tank and anti-aircraft equipment.

The emergence of new arms producers

The growth of new arms producers outside the major alliances adds momentum to the arms trade. Countries of the Third World with an explicit policy of increasing independence in weapon acquisition have tried to build up their own production facilities. This policy has added to the competition in a stagnating arms transfer market.[5]

On balance, these developments either have reduced or will reduce the size of the arms industrial base in the two major alliances; and, unless these trends are reversed, a reorientation to civil production has to take place. It is therefore appropriate to describe the size and structure of the industry that produces the weapons and other equipment of the armed forces and to analyse the problems and possibilities of reductions and reorientation.

While the arms industrial bases in NATO and the WTO are roughly comparable in size, the information available about them is certainly not. Information about the NATO countries (especially in the United States) is readily available. By using the annual fiscal appropriations published by the US Congress, it is possible to discover to the nearest few dollars the unit cost of almost every item procured for the US military as well as labour costs, production costs, the regional distribution of federal spending in the United States, construction costs and the level of financial assistance to foreign countries. This is—to a lesser degree—possible in other NATO countries, but it is not the case in the WTO countries, despite the recent increase in the flow of information. What is lacking, however, in NATO as well as in the neutral and non-aligned and the Third World countries, is detailed information on the size of the actual producers, the corporations which also play an important role in the weapon acquisition process.

Two different methods describe the arms industries of the WTO and the rest of the world. This *Yearbook* introduces a new data base on the 100 largest arms-producing companies in the OECD (Organization for Economic Co-operation and Development) countries and the Third World (see table 8.2), which will also be published in future *Yearbooks*. Not only because of a lack of basic information but also because the arms industry is organized differently in the WTO, other information is presented as a background to describe the WTO industrial base and its possible future (see sections IV and V).[6]

II. New weapon programmes

Although discussions are taking place on reducing the number of arms produced for deployment in Europe, there is no evidence that there will be a slower pace of technological change in the military area.

One element in the evolution of military technology has been the escalating unit costs of weapon systems. The factor of growing cost has outstripped

[5] However, there are regional exceptions to the overall pattern of stagnation in the global market, notably in Japan and South-East Asia. For an analysis, see chapter 7.

[6] Companies from all the OECD countries and the Third World are included. The WTO countries and other communist countries are excluded since the criteria of 'companies' or 'corporations' used here do not apply to the arms production facilities in these countries. For a detailed account of arms production in the Third World, see Brzoska, M. and Ohlson, T. (eds), SIPRI, *Arms Production in the Third World* (Taylor & Francis: London, 1986). Arms production in China has not been studied by SIPRI. For a survey, see Katz, J. E., *The Implication of Third World Military Industrialisation: Sowing the Dragon's Teeth* (Lexington Books: Lexington, Mass., 1986).

the growth in defence budgets in many countries, entailing a well-documented reduction in the number of weapons deployed by the major powers. This decline in unit numbers of equipment has been offset by an increase in unit capability.[7]

Among governments in NATO countries and in contrast to official NATO policy, longer-range planning has assumed for some time that defence budgets would be flat or decrease after allowing for inflation. Therefore, the current proposals outlined in the CFE talks as the basis for an agreement may do little more than codify reductions in the numbers of weapon systems deployed which in any case would have occurred over time.

Reducing numbers without losing military capability

If the CFE talks are successfully concluded, there will be a reduction in the numbers of weapons deployed in Europe. This reduction in numbers is likely to contribute a new element to the continuous debate within governments and the professional military concerning the limits and possibilities offered by technological development and the implications for strategy and doctrine.[8]

For many years Western, and in particular US, thinking about procurement has been shaped by the idea that superior technology is needed to off-set inferior numbers in the context of the European military balance. The CFE process may eliminate the numerical imbalance, but the development of advanced technology is still held to be necessary for two reasons.

First, the military believes that the development of new weapons will allow them to do their jobs more efficiently in the context of reduced force levels. In 1989 this view was stated as follows: 'The trends in accuracy, reduced size and increased destructiveness mean the devolving of true combined arms capability (including air defence) to smaller and smaller units. It is not inconceivable that units comparable to today's battalions will have the capability of today's brigades or divisions in terms of the type and number of targets they will be able to attack.'[9]

The second justification for sustained investment in new and more advanced technology has been the continuous growth of military capabilities in the Third World. Major powers (and the USA and the Soviet Union in particular) continue to define foreign policy interests which require the military option.[10]

---

[7] What Thomas McNaugher calls the 'quality/quantity decision'. See McNaugher, T. L., *New Weapons, Old Politics: America's Military Procurement Muddle* (Brookings Institution Press: Washington, DC, 1989), pp. 4–10.

[8] Moodie, M., *The Dreadful Fury: Advanced Military Technology and the Atlantic Alliance*, Washington Papers no. 136 (CSIS: Washington, DC, 1989).

[9] Fry, M. D., 'Some thoughts on the role of military forces within a European security system', in eds G. Wachter and A. Krohn, 'Stability and arms control in Europe: the role of military forces within a European security system' (SIPRI: 1989), p. 83.

[10] In his 1989 *Report to Congress*, Admiral Carlisle Trost, Chief of Naval Operations, stated that 'the proliferation of advanced weapons illustrates the requirement to respond to Third World contingencies with high-quality forces capable of controlling or countering increasingly sophisticated and high technology violence'.

Table 8.1. Selected new-generation weapon programmes currently in research in the USA, 1989

Programme name	Description	New technologies
AAWS-H	Anti-tank missile	New rocket engine and guidance system could create a hypervelocity missile
ACM	Advanced cruise missile	More powerful and smaller computer along with more efficient engine may increase the range of cruise missiles
Supersonic Cruise Missile	Supersonic cruise missile	More powerful and smaller computer along with more efficient engine may produce a supersonic cruise missile
ATA	Advanced tactical aircraft	New composite materials reduce weight and offer lower radar signature, computerized flight controls offer greater speed and endurance
ATF	Advanced tactical fighter	Computerized flight controls offer chance to fly at very low altitude at very high speed more safely
Heavy Force Modernization	Main battle tank	Electromagnetic rail gun and electronic fire control may offer greater firepower and reduce weight
X-30	Hypersonic aircraft	Combining heat-resistant composite materials and new engine technologies to produce a speed of 10 000 miles (16 000 km) per hour
Milstar	Communications satellite	Part of wider command and control network offering a tenfold increase in the speed of communications and resistance to electronic interference
Revolution at Sea	Engine design	Use of superconductivity to develop engines with increased power and flexibility

Sources: *World Missile Forecast* (Newport, Connecticut, 1989); *Jane's All the World's Aircraft, 1989–90*; *International Defense Review*, June 1989, pp. 813–15; US Naval Institute *Proceedings*, Dec. 1988.

The policy of increasing technical capacity to offset declining numbers is particularly visible in the United States, where a number of programmes involving new generations of equipment are currently moving from research and development into full-scale production (see table 8.1). The B-2 'stealth' bomber, the F-117A 'stealth' fighter and the Arleigh Burke Class warship all approached deployment or were deployed in 1989. In each case these systems incorporate capabilities and technologies that no other country in the world has yet developed—stealth technologies are those most discussed. Other programmes will, if successful, create an even wider gap in capabilities between the armed forces of the United States and those of the rest of the world.

The weapon programmes in table 8.1 are all currently still in the research stage in the United States, and therefore it is reasonable to be sceptical regarding whether all of them will deliver the promised capability within an affordable cost.[11] Some of the propagated possible technology break-throughs might even be based more on over-ambitious company expectations than on scientific and technological facts. Nevertheless, the impression that these programmes are given high priority is confirmed by the fact that between 1979 and 1989 spending on defence research and development (R&D) in the USA increased by 85 per cent in real terms.[12] There is no indication that this trend will reverse in the USA. In other countries (i.e., in the FRG)—although at a much lower expenditure level—R&D has high priority in an overall tighter military expenditure budget.[13] The two trends of intensified conventional arms control and high priority in new weapon programmes—the double-track strategy mentioned above—entail a built-in contradiction that will eventually result in a slowdown of the arms control process, a reduction of investments in new programmes or a combination of both.

Soviet R&D

There is no clear, detailed picture available of Soviet R&D expenditure. However, there is some information which suggests that activity is not on a level comparable with that in the USA. In the Soviet Union fewer new air-craft designs are tested at the experimental flight-test airfield at Ramenskoye, according to the US Department of Defense.[14] Although not finalized, according to Alexander Batkov, Deputy Minister in the Ministry of Aviation Industry, the Politburo has discussed a proposal to cut aerospace R&D in each of the next three years.[15] Batkov specifically noted that US programmes may reverse the decision to reduce expenditure, stating, 'it is my personal opinion that this particular emphasis placed by the USA on stealth projects may trigger a new round in the arms race'.[16] In an interview on Soviet television the chief designer at one Soviet design bureau has also remarked on a slow-down in R&D.[17]

As discussed in more detail below, there is still insufficient information about the structure and future direction of the Soviet defence budget, but it will be interesting to see how the R&D expenditures will develop in the future.

---

[11] A former director of the US strategic defence programme has described how defence company salesmen have consistently offered more than they can deliver, with any certainty, in terms of new technologies. Bowman, R. M., 'Brilliant Pebbles and the new Star Wars debate', *Space and Security News*, Apr. 1989, pp. 3–10.

[12] 'Preparing for Peace', *IEEE Spectrum*, Nov. 1989, p. 67.

[13] According to official FRG budget figures, R&D expenditure of the Ministry of Defence was 1.7 billion DM in 1980 and 3.0 billion DM in 1989.

[14] *Jane's All the World's Aircraft 1989–90* (Jane's: Coulsdon, 1989), p. 25.

[15] Cook, N., 'New challenge facing Soviet military aircraft industry', *Jane's Defence Weekly*, 16 Sep. 1989, pp. 507–509.

[16] See note 15.

[17] Quoted in *Jane's Soviet Intelligence Review*, Nov. 1989, p. 527.

III. The largest arms-producing companies and their future

The 100 largest arms-producing companies[18]

The compilation of the arms sales[19] of the largest arms producers in the OECD (Organization for Economic Cooperation and Development) countries and those in the Third World reveals a number of important facts about the structure of this industry. Corporations of 15 different countries are represented in the list of the 100 largest companies (see table 8.2) This list provides a clear indication of the arms market of the world outside the socialist countries.

The most outstanding characteristic is the high concentration of US companies among the top 100: almost one-half (48) of all the companies are located in the USA. Far below these US corporations, the three major West European countries form the second largest bloc on the list: 12 British, 10 French and 9 companies from the FRG. Far below this group, five Japanese corporations (clearly reflecting Japan's recent efforts to establish an arms industrial base) appear among the 100 largest companies. The remainder of the list is made up of five more companies from NATO countries (3 Italian, 1 Dutch and 1 Spanish company), 5 from the European neutral countries (4 Swedish and 1 Swiss) and 6 corporations from Third World countries (2 Israeli companies and 1 company each from South Korea, South Africa, Brazil and India); see table 8.3. The importance of US companies is even more clearly highlighted by the fact that all but one of the 10 largest corporations are based in the USA. Of the 20 largest companies, 15 are US, and of the first 60, 34 are US companies. Not only by far the largest *number* of companies but also the *biggest* companies are located in the United States. The 48 US companies combined account for nearly two-thirds (64.1 per cent) of the total arms sales of the corporations included in this list. This is an expression of the size of the procurement budget in the USA and a reflection of the fact that the Government mainly 'buys American'. Although it has been subject to major amendments, the 1933 Buy American Act remains in force. Foreign companies are legally allowed to bid for Department of Defense contracts only because of waivers applied to the Act. In 1989 a private group, the National Council for Industrial Defense, planned to challenge the legality of these waivers in a federal court. Council president William Phillips stated: 'If America is to remain competitive, we need to abide by the laws that are designed to protect the American defense industrial base'.[20] While US global arms exports are the second largest in the world, for most companies exports are not significant compared to sales

[18] As mentioned above, except for the countries with planned economies, companies throughout the world have been included in the survey.

[19] The criterion for the rank order is the dollar value of arms sales. See the notes to table 8.2 for the methodology applied.

[20] Struck, M., 'Council challenges Defense Department's Buy American waivers', *Defense News*, 11 Sep. 1989, p. 52.

Table 8.2. The 100 largest arms-producing companies in the OECD and Third World countries, 1988

Figures in columns 5, 6 and 8 are in US $ million.

1	2	3	4	5	6	7	8	9
Rank	Company	Country	Industry	Arms sales	Total sales	5 as % of 6	Profit	Employment
1	McDonnell Douglas Corp.	USA	AC EL MI	8 500	15 072	56	350	121 000
2	Lockheed	USA	AC	8 400	10 590	79	624	86 800
3	General Dynamics Corp.	USA	AC EL MI SH	8 000	9 551	84	379	102 800
4	General Electric	USA	AC ENG	6 250	49 414	13	3 386	298 000
5	General Motors	USA	AC ENG EL MI	6 000	121 088	5	4 856	766 000
6	Raytheon	USA	EL MI	5 500	8 192	67	490	75 000
7	British Aerospace	UK	AC EL MI	5 470	10 044	54	277	131 300
8	Rockwell International	USA	AC EL MI	5 000	11 946	42	812	116 000
9	Boeing	USA	AC EL MI	4 500	16 962	27	614	153 000
10	Northrop	USA	AC	4 500	5 797	78	104	42 000
11	United Technologies	USA	AC EL MI	4 500	18 000	25	659	186 800
S	Hughes Electronics Corp. (General Motors)	USA	AC	4 500	11 244	40	802	75 000
12	Thomson S.A.	France	A EL	4 470	12 566	36	200	104 000
S	Thomson CSF (Thomson S.A.)	France	A EL	4 320	5 626	77	494	41 400
13	Martin Marietta	USA	MI	4 300	5 728	75	359	67 500
14	GEC	UK	ENG EL	3 850	11 004	35	803	157 000
15	Daimler Benz	FRG	AC ENG MV EL	3 420	41 851	8	969	339 000
16	TRW Inc.	USA	MV EL[a]	3 200	6 982	46	261	73 200
17	Mitsubishi Corporation	Japan	AC MV EL MI	3 100	58 395	5	229	..
18	Grumman	USA	AC EL	3 000	3 649	82	87	32 000
19	Litton Industries	USA	EL MI SH	2 920	4 864	60	167	55 000
20	Westinghouse Electric	USA	EL	2 600	12 500	21	823	119 640
21	Unisys	USA	EL	2 500	9 902	25	681	92 000
22	Aérospatiale	France	AC	2 300	4 700	49	15	34 250
23	Kawasaki Heavy Industries	Japan	AC ENG MI SH	2 230	5 985	37	62	16 600
24	Direction des Constructions Navales	France	SH	2 210	2 214	100	..	28 000
25	Texas Instruments	USA	EL OTH[b]	2 150	6 295	34	366	75 700
26	IRI	Italy	AC ENG EL SH	2 100	37 812	6	731	358 213
27	IBM	USA	OTH[c]	2 100	59 681	4	5 806	387 000
28	Dassault-Breguet	France	AC	2 080	2 964	70	65	13 818
S	Mitsubishi Heavy Industries (Mitsubishi Corporation)	Japan	AC MV EL MI	2 060	13 351	15	221	..
29	MBB	FRG	AC EL MI	1 990	4 054	49	56	40 000
30	Honeywell Marine Systems Division	USA	EL SA/O	1 800	7 148	25	–435	79 000
31	LTV	USA	AC MV EL MI[a]	1 800	7 526	24	–3 154	..
32	Tenneco Inc.	USA	SH	1 670	13 234	13	822	94 000
S	Newport News (Tenneco)	USA	SH	1 670	..	..	175	29 000
33	EFIM	Italy	AC MV EL	1 520	3 551	43	–19	37 405
34	Fiat	Italy	ENG A MV EL	1 500	34 041	4	2 492	277 353
35	Philips	Neth.	EL	1 500	28 371	5	1 228	310 300
36	Allied Signal	USA	AC EL[a]	1 500	11 909	13	463	115 000
37	Textron	USA	AC ENG MV	1 500	7 111	21	234	60 000
38	Singer[d]	USA	EL	1 420	1 903	75	..	28 000
39	Rolls Royce	UK	ENG	1 410	3 514	40	258	40 900
40	ITT	USA	EL	1 400	19 355	7	817	117 000
S	AEG (Daimler Benz)	FRG	EL	1 370	7 618	18	15	89 600

1	2	3	4	5	6	7	8	9
Rank	Company	Country	Industry	Arms sales	Total sales	5 as % of 6	Profit	Employment
41	Thorn EMI	UK	EL	1 200	6 002	20	529	65 400
42	E-Systems	USA	AC EL[a]	1 200	1 439	83	75	..
43	Ford Motor	USA	MV EL	1 200	92 446	1	5 300	360 000
44	Ferranti-International Signal	UK	EL	1 170	1 464	80	65	26 980
45	GIAT	France	A MV	1 150	1 151	100	−83	14 740
46	GET	USA	EL	1 100	16 460	7	1 225	159 000
47	Harris	USA	EL	1 000	2 062	48	101	27 000
48	Loral	USA	EL	1 000	1 440	69	74	14 000
49	CASA	Spain	AC	980	1 515	65	..	10 200
S	MTU (Daimler Benz)	FRG	ENG	970	1 867	52	17	17 200
50	FMC	USA	MV SH[a]	950	3 287	29	129	24 000
51	Oerlikon-Bührle	Switz.	AC A EL	930	2 891	32	−23	27 750
S	AVCO Corp. (Textron)	USA	AC	900	..	..	..	..
52	Hercules	USA	AC MI SA/O[a]	890	2 802	32	120	22 700
S	Aeritalia (IRI)	Italy	AC	880	1 374	64	52	14 177
53	Plessey	UK	EL	880	2 947	30	237	26 216
54	Gencorp	USA	AC ENG EL MI[a]	880	1 891	47	148	15 600
55	VSEL Consortium	UK	MV SH	830	830	100	28	10 782
56	Nobel Industrier	Swed.	A EL MI SA/O	810	3 480	23	113	22 101
57	Siemens	FRG	EL	800	33 823	2	791	353 000
58	Israeli Aircraft Industries	Israel	AC EL MI SH	800	1 060	75	−21	16 500
S	Aerojet (Gencorp)	USA	AC ENG EL MI[a]	800	1 056	76	93	1 000
S	Mitsubishi Electric (Mitsubishi Corporation)	Japan	EL	790	18 480	4	173	75 800
59	SNECMA	France	AC	770	1 722	45	−41	13 482
60	Sequa	USA	ENG EL	700	1 948	36	69	..
61	Hawker Siddeley	UK	AC ENG	680	3 327	20	198	42 000
62	Rheinmetall	FRG	A SA/O	650	1 850	35	47	15 460
S	Fiat Aviazone (Fiat)	Italy	AC	650	802	81	−52	4 749
63	Toshiba	Japan	EL	650	27 876	2	473	122 000
64	AT&T	USA	EL	650	57 974	1	−1 669	305 000
65	Krupp	FRG	MV EL	630	8 391	8	−115	63 391
66	Diehl	FRG	MV SA/O	610	1 360	45	..	14 200
67	Thyssen Industrie	FRG	MI SH	600	9 563	6	211	128 700
68	Ishikawajima-Harima	Japan	ENG SH	600	6 175	10	4	16 000
69	Daewoo Corporation	S. Kor.	EL SH	600	13 438	4	36	94 888
70	Motorola	USA	EL	600	8 250	7	445	102 000
71	Teledyne	USA	ENG EL MI	600	4 401	14	392	43 800
72	Thiokol Corporation	USA	ENG MI	580	1 168	50	33	12 600
S	Dornier (Daimler Benz)	FRG	AC EL	570	1 093	52	23	9 800
73	SAAB-SCANIA	Swed.	AC EL MI	570	6 934	8	255	48 500
S	Oto Melara (EFIM)	Italy	MV	530	539	98	13	2 329
74	Electronique Serge Dassault	France	EL	510	678	75	19	4 100
S	CFM International (General Electric & SNECMA)	USA	AC ENG	500	..	..	..	60
S	Collins International SV Co. (Rockwell)	USA	EL	500	..	..	..	..
S	Agusta (EFIM)	Italy	AC	490	678	72	23	4 316
75	FFV	Swed.	EL SA/O OTH	490	983	50	5	10 037
76	Racal Electronics	UK	EL	480	2 831	17	261	33 702
77	Computer Sciences Inc.	USA	EL[b]	480	1 304	37	53	22 500

1	2	3	4	5	6	7	8	9
Rank	Company	Coun-try	Industry	Arms sales	Total sales	5 as % of 6	Profit	Employ-ment
78	Sundstrand	USA	AC	470	1 477	32	−77	..
S	Krupp Atlas Elektronik (Krupp)	FRG	EL	460	569	81	11	4 200
79	Westland	UK	AC	450	637	71	31	9 163
80	Avondale Industries	USA	SH	450	592	76	4	8 000
81	Matra	France	MI	440	3 239	14	172	19 480
82	Armscor	S. Afr.	AC A MV EL SA/O	440	884	50	..	90 000
83	Hunting Associated Ind.	UK	EL SA/O	440	713	62	33	5 596
S	Hollanse Signaalapparaten (Philips)	Neth.	EL	410	455	90	..	5 300
84	Control Data	USA	EL	400	3 628	11	2	33 500
85	Emerson Electric	USA	EL	400	6 651	6	529	..
86	Harsco	USA	OTH	400	1 278	31	46	..
87	Olin	USA	EL	400	2 308	17	98	..
88	Nippon Electric	Japan	EL	390	19626	2	183	102450
89	Ericsson	Swed.	EL	390	5 107	8	214	65 000
90	Vickers	UK	ENG MV SA/O	390	1 382	28	..	16 731
91	Krauss-Maffei	FRG	MV	380	723	53	1	5 100
S	Mercedes Benz (Daimler Benz)	FRG	MV	380	31 260	1	933	182 100
92	Avibras	Brazil	A MI	370	390	95	1	3 500
93	Hindustan Aeronautics	India	AC	360	494	73	..	48 833
94	Koor Industries	Israel	ENG EL	360	2 638	14	151	26 000
95	SAGEM	France	EL	350	1 606	22	30	17 484
96	Dyncorp	USA	AC EL	350	556	63	−15	..
97	Mitre	USA	EL	350	425	82	..	..
98	Westmark Systems	USA	EL	350	702	50	..	..
S	Thyssen (Thyssen Industries)	FRG	MV SH	340	2 790	12	−1	34 969
99	Renault Véhicules Ind.	France	MV	340	5 707	6	167	34 000
100	Standard Elektronik Lorenz	FRG	EL	320	2 286	14	95	23 000
S	Selenia (IRI)	Italy	EL	320	564	57	2	6 716

Key to abbreviations:
Column 1: S = subsidiary companies (see sources and methods).
Column 4: A = artillery, AC = aircraft, EL = electronics, ENG = engines, MI = missiles,
MV = military vehicles, SA/O = small arms/ordnance, SH = ships, OTH = other

.. Data not available.

[a] Components.
[b] Optics.
[c] Computers.
[d] Figures are for 1987.

Sources and methods

Sources of data: The data presented in table 8.2 are based on the following sources: company reports, a questionnaire sent to 300 companies, corporation news published in the business sections of newspapers and military journals (see appendix 7D for a list of the journals and periodicals). In addition, company archives, marketing reports, government publication of prime contracts and country surveys were consulted. In many cases exact figures were not available mainly because companies often do not report on their arms sales

Table 8.2 *cont.*

or lump them together with other activities. Estimates were therefore made.

Arms sales: The criterion for the rank order of companies is their arms sales.

Subsidiaries: Subsidiaries' arms sales are included in the figure in column 5 for the holding company. Subsidiaries are indicated in the first column (Rank) by an *S* and are listed in the position where they would appear if they were independent companies.

Coverage: The data are for 1988, with one exception (see note *d*). The fiscal year for companies is not always the calendar year. No calculations have been made to adjust fiscal to calendar years.

Exchange-rates: Most figures collected were given in local currencies. To convert figures into US dollars, the period-average of market exchange-rates of the International Monetary Fund, *International Financial Statistics,* were used.

Profit: Profit after taxes is shown for the entire company, not for the arms-producing sector alone. For figures taken from journals and periodicals, it was not always clear whether profit was given before or after taxes.

Employment: The figure shown is either a year-end or yearly average number, as published in the sources used.

Note: The authors would like to acknowledge the assistance of Ivo Sarges and David Wiley in the data collection for table 8.2.

---

on the US market. The USA accounted for about 30 per cent of world military expenditure in 1989.

The 12 British corporations represent, with their share of 10 per cent of the arms sales of the 100 largest companies, a comparatively small percentage; the same is true for the 10 French companies (8.5 per cent of total arms sales) and the 9 FRG companies (5.5 per cent). This state of the industry is the background for many politicians in Western Europe to worry about their competitiveness and for the regular calls for closer co-operation among them in the face of the dominant US companies.

Two other factors in the country distribution are of interest. Japan has been known in the past for its limited involvement in arms production. While the share of Japan's military expenditure in its gross domestic product (GDP) still remains around 1 per cent, the booming Japanese economy means a boom for the arms industry as well. The low priority given to arms production in Japan has changed as several big corporations have invested in this sector, thus adding to the problem of global over-capacities and competition.

Only six companies in Third World countries appear in the list. Many Third World governments have actively promoted indigenous production of arms. Compared to companies of the industrialized countries, these companies are small (not in the number of employees but in the value of their arms sales). They account for barely 1.7 per cent of arms sales among the 100 largest companies. Furthermore, some of these companies have experienced difficulties when the arms trade stagnated. As a result the arms sales of many companies in Argentina, Brazil, Egypt, India, Israel, South Korea, Singapore, South Africa and Taiwan were below the level of approximately $300 million of the 100th company in the list.

Table 8.3. Numbers of companies in the list of 100 largest arms-producing companies, grouped by rank and country

Country	Rank: 1–20	21–40	41–60	61–80	81–100	Total no. of companies
USA	15	10	9	7	7	48
UK	2	1	4	3	2	12
France	1	3	2	1	3	10
FRG	1	1	1	4	2	9
Japan	1	1	–	2	1	5
Italy	–	3	–	–	–	3
Netherlands	–	1	–	–	–	1
Sweden	–	–	1	2	1	4
Spain	–	–	1	–	–	1
Switzerland	–	–	1	–	–	1
Israel	–	–	1	–	1	2
South Korea	–	–	–	1	–	1
South Africa	–	–	–	–	1	1
Brazil	–	–	–	–	1	1
India	–	–	–	–	1	1

Source: Table 8.2.

The volume of arms sales is highly concentrated. The first 5 companies account for more than one-fifth of the arms sales of the top 100. More than 36 per cent is produced by the 10 largest companies, and the top 25 companies account for almost two-thirds of the arms sales included in this list (see table 8.4).

Table 8.4. Arms sales as a share of total sales for companies in the list of 100 largest arms-producing companies

Company rank groups	Share of total sales (%)
1	4.9
1–5	21.6
1–10	36.0
1–25	63.2
1–50	84.2

Source: Table 8.2.

An interesting feature is the dependence of these companies on arms production. This is particularly important in a period—as at present—when contractors expect a cut in orders. How will they react when their weapons business is endangered? The less they depend on arms production the more promising is their scope for alternatives. Most companies have other interests outside the arms business. Only three corporations on the list are totally dependent on arms production: two French state-owned corporations and the British VSEL consortium. In addition to these three producers,

Table 8.5. Major arms-producing companies with low shares of arms sales as a percentage of total sales

Rank	Company	Country	Arms sales as share of total sales
5	General Motors	USA	5
15	Daimler Benz	FRG	8
17	Mitsubishi Corp.	Japan	5
26	IRI	Italy	6
27	IBM	USA	4
34	Fiat	Italy	4
35	Philips	Netherlands	5
40	ITT	USA	7
43	Ford Motor Co.	USA	1
46	GET	USA	7

Source: Table 8.2.

13 companies generate three-quarters or more and another 16 half or more of their sales in the arms sector. Many of the largest US companies are highly specialized in arms production: eight of the 15 US corporations that appear among the top 20 producers depend to 50 per cent or more (reaching 84 per cent) on arms production.

The other side of the coin is the engagement of large, diversified concerns that rank among the top 100 producers but with only a small fraction of their sales in the arms sector. Table 8.5 lists the most important examples.

Most prominently represented in the list of largest companies are aerospace, missile and electronics producers. This reflects the fact that the traditional arms manufacturers that produce artillery, tanks and hulls of fighting ships have lost ground to the high-technology producers. This trend is likely to continue.

Looking at the profit and loss situation it should be emphasized that it is not possible to make a breakdown of the profits and losses generated in the military activities of the corporations. The profit figures shown in table 8.2, column 8, represent profits on total company turnover, both civilian and defence; 11 of the 100 major arms producers have incurred losses during the year reported.

The NATO countries: the arms industry as a 'victim of peace'?

The issue of the future of the NATO arms industrial base has been taken up in studies that have revealed two perspectives.

Some studies warn against undermining industrial capacity, arguing that it has been a central pillar of successful deterrence.[21] With a 'decay in deterrence' and the erosion of the arms industrial base, 'the once-mighty arsenal of democracy could become little more than an electronic laboratory,

---

[21] *The Defense Industrial and Technology Base*, Final report of the Defense Science Board to the Office of the Under Secretary of Defense for Acquisition, Washington, DC, Oct. 1988.

perhaps even incapable of manufacturing the matériel required for deterrence or for protecting U.S. national interests around the globe.'[22]

Similarly, the 1988 Independent European Programme Group action plan, discussed below, calls for a more coherent West European arms industrial base, able to compete with its US counterpart.[23] British and French commentators directly address the possible threat from arms control to future arms procurement.

One British commentator advises West European governments to 'tell their public that adequate defence and deterrent capabilities need to be maintained until Soviet capabilities drop markedly and until the benign intentions of the Soviet Union are established for the long term.' He warns against rapid reductions of procurement and advocates investment in 'intelligence, command and control and short-range "smart" systems' (in addition to increased arms exports). Finally, he concludes that:

governments and companies, especially in Europe, need to prepare in a variety of ways for conventional arms control success. The disproportionate weakening of European defence industrial capabilities as a consequence of modest arms control cuts would be a heavy price to pay, yet European governments should not allow themselves to get into a position where they appear to obstruct arms control progress in order to protect defence industrial assets.[24]

A panel of influential British Government advisers and a former adviser to the French Minister of Defence have independently reached the same conclusion—that unilateral Soviet arms reductions require no decrease in Western capabilities since the removal of obsolete weapons would allow the USSR to concentrate logistic and maintenance assets on more modern units and may actually increase the threat.[25]

Those defending the status quo argue that there is currently no viable alternative to the stable structure represented by a balance of power between two adversarial alliances. This was until mid-1989 the dominant and unquestioned view within NATO and as a result, concern about the efficiency of arms production, rather than concrete planning for a reduced arms industrial base, is on the agenda today in many Western capitals.

However, another perspective has recently been gaining ground. This body of opinion suggests that in reality the status quo cannot be maintained in the face of the international changes currently under way. Some advocate efforts to accelerate international changes that they believe to be desirable. Others argue for change because they believe it cannot be resisted. This

[22] *Deterrence in Decay: The Future of the U.S. Defense Industrial Base* (CSIS: Washington, DC, 1989), p. 1.

[23] *Action Plan on a Stepwise Development of a European Armaments Market,* IEPG document NAD/D-22, 23 Sep. 1988; and *Towards a Stronger Europe,* a Report by an Independent Study Team established by Defence Ministers of nations of the Independent European Programme Group to make proposals to improve the competitiveness of European defence equipment industry, Brussels, 1987.

[24] Taylor, T., 'Conventional arms control—a threat to arms procurement?', *World Today,* July 1989.

[25] Delpech, J.-F., 'Gorbachev and the budget crunch', unpublished paper for the Bow Group seminar on the European Defence Industry and 1992, 22 Sep. 1989; and Keegan, J., 'Defence chiefs at Chequers for arms review', *Daily Telegraph,* 30 Sep. 1989, p. 40.

Table 8.6. Procurement budget decisions by selected NATO countries, 1989

Country	Status
USA	Slow-down of the fiscal year 1990 procurement budget growth. Drastic cuts of current production programmes are planned for FYs 1992–94.
Canada	Fiscal pressures led to the revision of the 1987 White Paper, including the abandonment of several major procurement programmes.
France	The original long-term procurement plan was revised in 1989. From 1990 to 1993 the defence equipment budget is expected to be reduced by FFr 20.8 billion.
UK	Projected defence spending for 1990–91 is to be at the same level as for 1989. After adjustment for inflation this represents a cut. Increased spending on manpower will put pressure on procurement.
FRG	The procurement budget is below the 1985 level in real terms and is planned to decrease further in 1990.
Italy	Cuts in the defence budget forces to reconsider the 10-year plan. Delays and cuts in the acquisition of new equipment are probably inevitable.
Netherlands	Cuts in the budget proposed.
Denmark	Military expenditures are frozen at the 1988 level until 1992.
Belgium	Cuts in the budget necessitated plans to restructure the armed forces.

Source: SIPRI arms production data base.

group may even include some within the US Department of Defense. In its 1989 assessment of Soviet military power the Department of Defense notes the need for 'continuing support of our successful alliance strategy and collective security efforts, which are based on a strong military deterrent, *until the Soviets reduce their armed forces to significantly lower levels.'*[26]

The implication of this is that NATO strategy and even collective security should be reviewed once Soviet force reductions become accomplished fact rather than announced policy. The different processes of change described in section I seem already to have stimulated responses from governments as well from some companies with interests in arms production. Especially since the political changes at the end of 1989 in several WTO countries, a discussion has started in the United States evaluating the possibility of a US–Soviet military conflict. The likelihood is described as perhaps as low as it has ever been at any time in the post-World War II era. Drastic cuts in military expenditure (up to $180 billion between 1992 and 1994) have not been excluded by the US Government. Responses by European NATO countries, mainly due to competing domestic economic priorities, have included revised procurement plans on the part of governments (see table 8.6).[27]

The budget squeeze sets the stage for companies, too. While R&D may continue on the current level, companies have to expect reduced

[26] *Soviet Military Power 1989: Prospects for Change* (US Government Printing Office: Washington, DC, 1989), p. 17; emphasis added.
[27] For a detailed discussion, see chapter 5.

procurement orders. Governments might have to face difficult choices between the political aim of arms control and the economic interests of companies, employees and communities that depend on arms production. The difficulties of companies in the West over the past few years (mainly due to budget constraints and stagnating or decreasing export markets) have led to a situation in which arms-producing companies might feel threatened. Corporations have begun to react, especially since production over-capacities already exist, in anticipation of the expected budget crunch of the 1990s. In a recent interview the managing director of the newly formed Deutsche Aerospace (a subsidiary of Daimler Benz in charge of all aerospace activities, following the merger of MBB with Daimler Benz) said: 'It is not lip-service that I wish arms control efforts to be successful. But we cannot rest assured and say that we will close three factories and lay off 5000 people . . . It would be desirable to have a "soft landing", a planned reorientation of arms production to the manufacture of civil goods.' On the question of the European Fighter Aircraft, in which Deutsche Aerospace will be centrally involved, he said, 'the EFA as a modern defensive aircraft is absolutely necessary . . . Therefore we see no alternative and no reason for speculation.'[28]

In these circumstances reactions of arms enterprises might hinder the conventional arms control process. Powerful economic interest groups threatened with the loss of protected domestic markets, workers fearing for their jobs and governments apprehensive about losing their arms production base may burden the political improvement between East and West. During the past three years some 10 000—possibly even 100 000—jobs in the West European arms industry have been lost, and the same number is likely to be lost between 1990 and 1992. A similar trend emerged in 1989 in the United States. Major US companies have announced the following cutbacks in employment in their arms production divisions: Lockheed Aeronautical Systems Corp., 8000; Hughes Aircraft Corp., 7000; General Electric Aerospace, 4000; Rockwell International Corp., 4000; Grumman Corp., 3100; Northrop Corp., 2500–3000; and Textron, 2500.[29] Some of the cut-backs were compensated through transfers of employees within the companies and to other divisions. In a number of cases workers were laid off. The situation in arms-producing companies in the United States and Western Europe would have been worse had there not been a boom in civil aviation and an unexpected upsurge in orders for commercial shipbuilding. Both the aerospace companies and the shipyards depend heavily on arms production, although they have reduced this dependence during the past few years.

Companies reacted—aside from cutbacks in employment—with different strategies: mergers of arms companies both on a national level and across borders in Western Europe; expansion through the acquisition of other companies; the sale of subsidiaries or discontinuing certain kinds of

[28] *Der Spiegel*, issue 39 (1989), p. 143; unofficial translation.
[29] In addition, Boeing Aerospace & Electronics Division, Norden Systems, Harris Corporation, Texas Instruments, LTV, TRW Inc. and Unisys Corp. have laid off over 8000 workers between them.

production; diversification either within the arms sector or to civil production; and the formation of national or international teams to bid on specific contracts. Taking the improved East–West climate into account, a systematic plan for the reorientation of the arms-producing industry towards civil production is probably needed to cope with the problems ahead. Otherwise it is likely that the number of jobs lost will not be in the tens of thousands but in the hundreds of thousands in each of the major arms-producing countries.

The changing West European arms market

As noted above, the West European NATO countries form the second largest group after the United States, with 37 companies represented in the table of the 100 largest companies. This section looks primarily at institutional developments that affect the arms producers in Western Europe.

The arms market in Western Europe has been affected by three observable trends that are a reflection of both existing over-capacities and the dominant position, in global terms, of US companies. The first is the privatization of production. Although there is still significant production in government-owned establishments and a high degree of company dependence on government decision making, a considerable number of arms-producing facilities (especially in the United Kingdom) have been moved into the private sector in recent years. The second is the increasing number of acquisitions and mergers (mainly on a national but also on an international level) of arms-producing companies. The third is the belief in West European governments that greater competition between suppliers of military equipment will reduce the overall costs to government of procurement.

Although these three trends can be observed, they are not necessarily compatible with one another in a national context in Western Europe. The trend towards concentration will lead to fewer producers—and therefore a smaller number of suppliers—while greater competition requires having a number of potential suppliers from which to choose.

In France, the Federal Republic of Germany and the UK there is, for important major systems, particularly in aerospace, only one company capable of offering itself as a prime contractor. In the electronics sector there are typically several suppliers for major systems such as radars. However, considering the demand of the armed forces for different types of radar, usually only one supplier remains. The many existing smaller military electronics companies have either been bought up by major companies or are specialized and depend on systems management of prime contractors. Except for fighting ships, competition in major weapon systems is either non-existent or very limited. In cases of 'duopoly' there is limited competition since there is a second company for the procurement agency to rely on. This is, however, not genuine competition. In a dual-source competition the loser must be awarded a share of production if it is to be viable in future

Table 8.7. International takeovers in the arms production sector, 1988–89[a]

Buyer company	Head office	Purchased company	Head office	Year
Bombardier Inc.	Canada	Short Brothers PLC	UK	1989
CAE-Link Corp.	Canada	Singer Link divisions	USA	1988
Matra	France	Fairchild Space, Fairchild Communications and Electronics, Fairchild Control Systems	USA	1989
SNECMA	France	FN Moteurs	Belgium	1989
Thomson CSF	France	HSA	Netherlands	1989
Thomson CSF	France	Ocean Defence Corp.	USA	1988
Alcatel	France	ACEC Space, Defence and Telecommunications Division	Belgium	1989
Thomson-Brandt Armements	France	Forges de Zeebrugge	Belgium	1988
Siemens	FRG	Plessey Radar and Defense Systems	UK	1989
Diehl	FRG	BGT	USA[b]	1989
Elsag	Italy	Bailey Controls	USA	1989
Nobel Industries	Sweden	Philips Elektronik-industrier	Netherlands	1989
Astra	UK	BMARC	Switzerland[c]	1989
Astra	UK	Poudriere Réunie Belge	Belgium	1988
Plessey	UK	Leigh Instruments	Canada	1988
Dowty	UK	Palmer Chenard Industries	USA	1989
General Motors	USA	Redifussion Simulation	UK	1988
RJO Enterprises Inc.	USA	ASA	UK	1989

[a] The table lists recent international defence and defence-related company takeovers in which the buyer company has acquired a controlling majority of the shares (i.e., greater than 50%) in the selling company. Minority holdings are excluded.

[b] Bodenseewerk Gerätetechnik GmbH (BGT) was owned by the US Perkins Elmer Group.

[c] BMARC was a subsidiary of the Swiss Oerlikon Bührle Group.

Source: SIPRI arms production data base.

competitions. The customer government is then in a more disadvantageous position than in a monopoly since the costs of splitting production to achieve a 'minimum sustaining rate' of production in the loser company cancel the economies of scale that a monopoly supplier can offer.[30] Genuine competition in defence procurement is therefore only possible in a wider European context or with the inclusion of US companies.

The main instrument for greater concentration in arms production, in an industrial system based on the private sector, is the merging of companies or

[30] Boger, D. C., Greer, W. R. and Liao, S. S., 'Competition in defense acquisition: myths and facts', *Defense Analysis*, Sep. 1989, pp. 245–55.

Table 8.8. Multinational mergers of arms-producing companies, 1988–89[a]

Company	Head office	Company	Head office	Name of merged company	Year
Sema-Metra	France	CAP Group	UK	Sema Group	1988
Dense-Pac Microsystems Inc.	USA	Hybrid Memory Products Ltd.	UK	..	1989
Sagem	France	Sepa	Italy	Italiana Sistemi Inerziala S.P.A.	1989

[a] Mergers between the helicopter divisions of MBB of the FRG and Aérospatiale and between the missile divisions of British Aerospace and the French company Thomson CSF were under discussion at the end of 1989.

Source: SIPRI arms production data base.

the acquisition of one company by another. Within countries this has been a feature of the arms industry for many years. For example, in 1968, 18 companies were able to build helicopters in the United States, 2 in France and 5 in the United Kingdom. By 1988, the number of companies building helicopters was 10, 2 and 2, respectively.[31] In 1961 six companies in the FRG produced military aircraft; as a result of mergers, only one company remains in 1989.

Equally, there has been a relatively long experience of cross-border mergers in the civil sector. As an example, the total number of mergers involving at least one company in an EC state increased from 117 per year in 1982 to 303 in 1987.[32] What is new is the phenomenon of multinational mergers in the arms-producing sector (see table 8.7). Previously, manufacturers of weapon systems operated mainly in their national environment or produced weapon systems in international teams (without significant cross-border capital investments), in particular, the most expensive and sophisticated aerospace systems that could not be produced by a single country.[33] There seems to be a changing trend, however: in the past two years there have been several important mergers or takeovers involving large arms-producing companies. There have been more examples of companies establishing significant shareholdings in other firms, perhaps as a first move towards some more formal integration or co-operation. Tables 8.7 and 8.8 indicate that concentration is not taking place exclusively among companies in European Community countries. Companies from North America and European neutral countries are involved as well. In addition, larger companies tend to buy smaller ones, and these larger units may be

[31] In reality only Aérospatiale in France and Westland in the UK would be able to bid on a major contract. Helicop-Jet in France and Wallis in the UK are producers of small, light helicopters. *Jane's All the World's Aircraft, 1968–69* and *1988–89* (Jane's Publishing Group: Coulsdon, 1969 and 1989).

[32] 'Horizontal mergers and competition policy in the European Community, European Economy 40' (Office of the Official Publications of the European Community: Luxembourg, May 1989).

[33] Wulf, H., 'West European cooperation and competition in arms procurement: experiments, problems, prospects', *Arms Control*, no.1 (1987), pp. 190–206.

better equipped to operate in the world market. Representatives of industry believe that the formation of fewer, larger companies in Western Europe is inevitable. According to Sir Raymond Lygo, chief executive of British Aerospace, 'the big dogs will eat the little dogs, spit the bones out and we will have a centralised defence industry'.[34] However, if the number of producers is reduced, competition for military contracts will also be reduced unless procurement takes place in a multinational context.

The role of the European Community

In this area of industrial concentration, the Commission of the European Community has some jurisdiction. Article 37 and Articles 85–94 of the Treaty of Rome lay down rules of competition applicable to undertakings, prohibit agreements between private or public undertakings and prohibit the abuse of a dominant position in so far as it may affect trade between member states. These Articles also stipulate that state aid which restricts normal competition and affects trade between member states is incompatible with the Common Market. The implementation of these Articles is the responsibility of the Commission, subject to the supervision of the Court of Justice of the European Community, along with the national courts of member states.[35]

National bodies—such as the Monopolies and Mergers Commission (MMC) in the UK and the *Bundeskartellamt* (cartels office) and the *Monopolkommission* (monopolies commission) in the FRG—have been important actors in several recent defence company mergers. Of particular interest is the case involving GEC of the UK and Siemens of the Federal Republic of Germany in a joint bid, launched on 16 November 1988, to buy the British military electronics and telecommunications company Plessey. This take-over might be a model for future West European transnationalization activities—in contrast to the Daimler Benz acquisition of MBB in the FRG where the two biggest arms producers of one country were merged into a single company in 1989. In April 1989 the GEC–Siemens bid succeeded after Ministry of Defence requests and after the MMC accepted that it would not create a monopoly in the British defence electronics sector, where GEC was already the largest single supplier—including sales of its subsidiary Marconi—even prior to the acquisition of part of Plessey.[36] However, the MMC imposed considerable conditions on the merger. The MMC stated that GEC should not acquire any interest in or influence over Plessey's radar or

[34] Quoted in Reed, C., '1992: a minefield for the European defence industry', *Defence*, June 1989, p. 411.
[35] *Fact Sheets on the European Parliament and the Activities of the European Community, European Parliament—Directorate General for Research*, Fact sheet EN-III/G (Office of the Official Publications of the European Community: Luxembourg, 1987).
[36] *The General Electric Company plc, Siemens AG and The Plessey Company plc: A report on the proposed mergers*, Report presented to Parliament by the Monopolies and Mergers Commission, Apr. 1989. For an overview of the joint bid, see the section by Harbor, B. and Walker, W., in 'The GEC–Siemens bid for Plessey: the wider European issues', Working Paper no. 2, Centre for Information and Communication Technologies, Science Policy Research Unit, University of Sussex, UK, Jan. 1989.

defence systems businesses. To preserve competition, therefore, the British Government has made a company based in the FRG a major player in the British defence electronics market. One journal referred to this as 'the end of the era of national champions' in defence.[37] However, the MMC also recommended that the Home Office receive undertakings from Siemens that there should be a majority of directors of British nationality in what were formerly Plessey programmes, that the company should have no foreign executive directors and that board meetings must have a majority of British directors present to form a legitimate quorum.[38]

Both GEC (through the joint venture company GEC-Plessey, formed in April 1988) and Siemens are also major players in the European telecommunications sector, and the EC Commission had an interest in the merger from the perspective of West European competition policy in telecommunications. In August 1989 the Commission approved the merger bid since, from a European Community perspective, Plessey was not a major independent actor and therefore its acquisition could not be said to distort competition.[39] As a result of the provisions the merger has led to the formation of a world market-oriented company in the communications sector while in the field of military procurement some British national strings are still attached.

In legislation arising from an EC Council of Ministers decision adopted on 21 December 1989, which will enter into force on 21 September 1990, the EC Commission will be granted exclusive competence to control mergers and acquisitions between companies whose combined turnover exceeds 5 billion ECUs[40] and where at least one company has an EC turnover of 250 million ECUs.[41] Only major transactions will be under the Commission's control. The goal is to bring the threshold down to a total turnover of 2 billion ECUs in a period of four years, for which a decision will be taken by a majority vote in the Council.[42] In addition to these ceilings, there are three important qualifications to the Commission's exclusive competence over European mergers and acquisitions. First, competence is denied over purely national mergers or even transnational mergers when each of the parties gather two-thirds of its turnover in a single member state.[43] Second, the Commission may transfer its competence to national bodies in sensitive cases of legitimate national interest.[44] Third, the legislation will authorize the Commission to rule in cases where the turnover ceilings are not reached, at the request of a member state.[45]

There is no standard Commission approach to approving or rejecting mergers and acquisitions. On the one hand, concentration can be regarded as bad where it harms competition. On the other hand, mergers can, despite

[37] *Defence*, May 1989, p. 311.

[38] See note 36.

[39] 'Brussels set to clear Plessey bid', *Financial Times*, 25 Aug. 1989.

[40] The ceiling is different for the banking and insurance sectors. The exchange-rate for 1 ECU was just below $1.20 at the end of 1989.

[41] *Europe Documents*, no. 1591 (29 Dec. 1989).

[42] *Le Monde*, 29 Dec. 1989, p. 23.

[43] *Europe Documents* (see note 41).

[44] *Europe Documents* (see note 41).

[45] *Le Monde*, 29 Dec. 1989, p. 23.

their restrictive character, contribute to improving production or distribution or promoting technical progress to the benefit of the consumer. Therefore, the Commission does grant permission, on occasion, to mergers. Moreover, the Commission is in favour of mergers in markets where European companies have to be more efficient in order to avoid massive import penetration from non-European producers. The electronics, aerospace and computer and telecommunications industries, which contain the major arms-producing companies, have been identified as areas in which the Commission sees concentration as being in the wider West European interest.[46]

The EC Commission has also claimed for itself competence in the area of public procurement, including dual-use items bought for defence. In July 1988 the Commission stated: 'The position of defence procurement is more complicated and the rules have often not been properly applied to this sector. *Most procurement by defence agencies is, in fact, subject to the rules.* The only defence procurement contracts not covered are those concerning products for specifically military purposes i. e. arms, munitions and war material.'[47]

This would mean that the Commission could collect, for the EC budget, duties on items imported by EC member governments for their defence agencies from non-EC countries.

However, the degree of influence that the Commission can exert is not clear. Article 223 of the Treaty of Rome states:

(a) No member state shall be obliged to supply information the disclosure of which it considers contrary to the essential interests of its security;
(b) Any member state may take such measures as it considers necessary for the protection of the essential interests of its security which are connected with the production of or trade in arms, munitions and war matériel; such measures shall not adversely affect the conditions of competition in the common market regarding products which are not intended for specifically military purposes.

The role of the EC in the weapon acquisition process is further complicated by the Single European Act of 1986, Article 30 of which states:

a) The High Contracting Parties consider that closer cooperation on questions of European security would contribute in an essential way to the development of a European identity in external policy matters. They are ready to coordinate their positions more closely on the political and economic aspects of security.
b) The High Contracting Parties are determined to maintain the technological and industrial conditions necessary for their security. They shall work to that end both at the national level and, where appropriate, within the framework of the competent institutions and bodies.

---

[46] *Horizontal Merges and Competition Policy in the European Community, European Economy 40* (Office of the Official Publications of the European Community: Luxembourg, May 1989), pp. 24–32.
[47] *Public Procurement and Construction—Towards an Integrated Market European Documentation* (Office of the Official Publications of the European Community: Luxembourg, 1989), p. 23; emphasis added.

c) Nothing in this Title shall impede closer cooperation in the field of security between certain of the High Contracting Parties within the framework of the Western European Union or the Atlantic Alliance.[48]

Title III of the Single European Act, containing Article 30.6, registers statements of intent by contracting parties but does not amend the Treaty of Rome, which remains the legal commitment binding on governments.

The role of the Independent European Programme Group

As noted above, economic pressures have created a tendency within companies to consider cross-border acquisitions as part of their economic strategy. However, the future development of the arms industry will depend to an equally large degree on the attitudes of government. As the GEC–Siemens bid for Plessey indicates, governments have considerable opportunity to intervene in specific company decisions. They also have an opportunity to set the broader framework within which companies must operate in multinational organizations such as the EC, the Western European Union (WEU) or the Independent European Programme Group (IEPG) within NATO.

Of these bodies, the EC and the IEPG have emerged as the more important, although the WEU would like to have a greater say in European defence matters. In 1988 the Chairman of the WEU Assembly noted that:

The Western European Union, apart from being a forum for discussion and harmonisation of European security policy, should also play its role in providing enhanced political direction to the IEPG. If it is accepted that the IEPG is to pursue more vigorously the harmonisation of defence collaboration in its widest sense to include defence research, it should be made certain, on behalf of the national electorates of at least the seven countries of the WEU, that individual national governments do it effectively. Only the elected members of the Assembly of the WEU can do this.[49]

The IEPG was established in 1976 as a forum to foster co-operation in armaments planning and production among European NATO members but outside NATO's institutional framework—because France is not part of the integrated military command. The IEPG is composed of all European NATO countries except Iceland, which does not maintain armed forces. Since 1983–84 it has served as a European interlocutor with the USA in NATO-wide arms projects, and since 1985 IEPG meetings have involved defence ministers rather than civil servants or lower-ranking ministers.[50] Within this body, whose members include all NATO countries except the

---

[48] Article 30.6, Title III of the Single European Act, reproduced in *Treaties Establishing the European Communities, Treaties amending these Treaties and Documents concerning the Accession* (Office for Official Publications of the European Communities: Luxembourg, 1987), p. 1049.

[49] Explanatory Memorandum, submitted by Mr Wilkinson, Chairman and rapporteur in *Report submitted on behalf of the Committee on Scientific, Technological and Aerospace Questions*, Chairman and rapporteur, Assembly of Western European Union, Proceedings, 34th ordinary session, June 1988 (Western European Union: Paris, 10 May 1988).

[50] *Defense News*, 3 July 1989, p. 1.

United States, Canada and Iceland, governments attempt to achieve four basic aims. First, they seek access to the most effective equipment available to meet their national security needs. Second, they try to get access to this equipment at an affordable cost within the constraints imposed by their various national defence budgets. Third, they try to achieve access to equipment at an affordable cost without depending on the much greater production capacity of the United States. Fourth, governments want to achieve these aims while promoting the interests of their national industries or, at the very least, without harming those interests.

All of these influences can be seen at work in the formulation and subsequent implementation of the IEPG.[51]

Based on the 1987 European defence industry study 'Towards a Stronger Europe', a European Armaments Market action plan was approved by IEPG defence ministers in November 1988. They decided:

– that efforts towards a stepwise build-up of a European Armaments Market should be made,
– that obstacles restricting border-crossing competition should be removed,
– that contracts should be placed more readily with suppliers in other countries,
– that research activities should provide for the fullest possible exploitation of European resources in talents and funds,
– that LDDI [Less Developed Defence Industry] countries should be included in arms cooperation.[52]

Two major barriers to the implementation of this action plan exist. First, as mentioned above, over-capacities already exist and will be increased by the necessary cuts in equipment as a result of the CFE agreement and budgetary constraints. The IEPG action plan—probably as a concession to industrial interests in countries such as Spain, Portugal and Greece—foresees the installation of additional arms manufacturing capacities in the so-called LDDI countries in Western Europe.

Second, national interests have been in the past and are likely to be in the future a hindrance to rational joint decision making. Promoting the interests of national industries often conflicts with co-operation in joint projects, and calls for intensified West European co-operation have often been unfulfilled. The fight over the radar system of the European Fighter Aircraft (EFA) between two company consortia, one from Britain and one from the FRG/USA—each backed by the Governments of the FRG and Britain—is one of several examples of this trend. The implementation of the action plan so far (to the end of 1989) highlights the extent to which perceptions of national interest dominate participation in the IEPG. In 1989 a small secretariat was established in Lisbon to administer IEPG activities.[53] The IEPG works through three panels, each of which has responsibility for implementing a different part of the action plan. In January 1989 the UK assumed the chairmanship of the IEPG. The British interpretation of the

[51] *Defense News,* 26 June 1989, p. 37.
[52] See note 23, Annex to IEPG/MIN/D-11, p. 1.
[53] *Jane's Nato & Europe Today,* 27 June 1989, p. 1.

European Armaments Market would not exclude US companies; in fact, US companies might be expected to be project leaders in many multinational teams. This reflects the close trans-Atlantic political and industrial interests of the UK.

The removal of national barriers and the creation of an open defence equipment market is the responsibility of Panel III, which is to be chaired by the Federal Republic of Germany. The FRG might reasonably expect its companies to fare best in a free market environment in arms production much as they fare best in the civil economic sector. The full exploitation of West European resources and research activities is the responsibility of Panel II, which is chaired by France. France maintains the most developed of the West European space industries (in launcher and satellite technologies and also in terms of space transport) and has its own independent nuclear deterrent. The French aerospace and electronics sector has also been maintained by keeping France out of West European collaborative programmes such as the Panavia Tornado or the EFA consortium. In June 1989 France was confirmed to be in the chair of the EUCLID (European Cooperative Long-term Initiative on Defence) programme to draw up a European technology plan into which IEPG governments may invest as much as 120 million ECUs.[54]

In several weapon procurement programmes important members have withdrawn their participation because the production share for the national industries seemed to be small, because they no longer perceived an immediate need for the equipment or because production schedules slipped to a point where modernization programmes could not be delayed in expectation of a co-operatively produced item.

The future of other co-operative programmes outside IEPG responsibility was intimately linked to US participation. In 1989 France, Italy and the United Kingdom withdrew from the programme to build a NATO frigate, the NFR 90, leaving Canada, the FRG, the Netherlands and the USA as the only remaining members.[55] The requirements of these countries are very different. The original NFR 90 requirement was for a ship of 3000 tons. However, while this could meet the needs of the navies of the Federal Republic of Germany and the Netherlands, the United States and Canada are currently building vessels of 4500 tons or more. Alternative discussions are under way which may eventually see a Netherlands–FR German consortium build vessels in Europe while the navies of the United States and Canada follow separate paths.

---

[54] The French role in EUCLID was described by British Defence Minister Tom King in his speech, 'Building a stronger European pillar', to the Bow Group, a Conservative Party think tank, 22 Sep. 1989, p. 10.

[55] Elliott, J., 'USA set to take lead in NFR 90', *Jane's Defence Weekly*, 28 Oct. 1989, p. 894; Elliott, J., 'Five poised for NFR 90 go-ahead', *Jane's Defence Weekly*, 21 Oct. 1989, p. 838. For a full description of the programme, see Anthony, I., SIPRI, *The Naval Arms Trade* (Oxford University Press: Oxford, 1990), pp. 70–78.

On 19 September 1989 the USA and the UK withdrew from a programme aimed at the production of an air-launched Modular Stand-Off Weapon (MSOW) for NATO fighter-bombers. France and Canada had withdrawn in 1988, and only FR Germany, Italy and Spain are now left; the programme is unlikely to continue.[56] These programmes—in line with many past experiences—place a question-mark over whether the four goals of the IEPG laid out above are achievable without a more integrated West European political environment. Access to the very highest level of technology in weapon systems within the constraints imposed by national budgets may only be possible by buying directly from the United States if the narrow interpretation of a West European market, supported by the UK as chairman of the IEPG, is applied. This more integrated political environment in Western Europe creates the potential for a future clash of interest between the EC and the IEPG, either of which may see itself as a logical focus for greater co-operative action.

IV. The arms industry in the USSR

Although the flow of information concerning the Soviet military sector has improved considerably in recent years, it remains unsatisfactory. However, in contrast to the NATO countries, the Soviet leadership has declared its intention to restructure the arms industrial base in the Soviet Union. The need for changes has many causes, but the main reason for the Soviet Government to include the arms industry in its programme of reform is the critical economic situation in the Soviet Union. In the longer term the Soviet economy could benefit from both freeing resources currently invested in the arms industry and redirecting the technological skills within this sector.

Domestic economic imperatives are not the only factor affecting arms production and procurement, which will be also be shaped by the internal debate over both military doctrinal and political change. It is impossible to predict precisely how the internal doctrinal debate will develop—whether the Soviet armed forces will in future be equipped and trained only for operations on home territory or whether the capacity for counter-offensive operations on the territory of an enemy will be retained (see also chapter 13). If the declared aim of creating a non-offensive defence structure for the armed forces is put into practice, significant consequences could result for the production of weapons.

Announced unilateral cuts of manpower, equipment and military expenditures are also bound to affect the structure of the military industrial sector. In addition, the current negotiating position of the Soviet Union at the Vienna CFE talks would lead to deep cuts in Soviet conventional forces. Unless a new cold war emerges, it is inevitable that the number of major weapon systems produced and deployed by the Soviet Union will be reduced substantially.

---

[56] 'UK/US pull-out sounds death knell for MSOW', *Jane's Defence Weekly*, 30 Sep. 1989, p. 631.

Present trends are likely to lead to the creation of numerically smaller, perhaps better trained armed forces equipped with more advanced weapons than those already deployed (although not necessarily approaching the level of sophistication of future US equipment). In the existing improved international environment, an important question remains regarding whether it will be possible to control the competition for ever more sophisticated weaponry—the qualitative arms dynamic. As discussed in section II, at present it seems that the USSR is technologically behind in important areas such as electronics, information-processing technology, computer-aided design and manufacturing technologies.[57] Many reasons for this have been put forward in the USSR, including the bureaucratic system, the lack of incentives, excessive secrecy and attitudes towards work. For whatever reason, major and far-reaching reforms of the arms industrial base have been initiated. The outcome of this reorientation is an open question, but it depends to some extent on the reactions of foreign countries.

The organization and size of the arms industrial base

One of the few detailed studies on the Soviet arms industry, published in 1983, is introduced with the statement: 'The Soviet defence industry is one of the largest in the world; according to American estimates, it is the largest of all. But it is impossible to establish just how big the Soviet defence sector is, for the Soviet authorities have shrouded it in secrecy.'[58]

Despite *perestroika* and *glasnost* in the Soviet Union, more openness in arms control negotiations and an increasing flow of Soviet information about their military sector, it is still not possible to present a systematic and detailed picture of the Soviet arms industry based on verifiable fact.[59] Therefore, three different indicators are chosen here to illustrate the size and capability of the Soviet arms sector. These are the institutional structure of arms production, the number of major weapon systems produced, and military expenditures invested in arms development and procurement.

Institutional structure of the arms industry

The arms industry in the Soviet Union has been hierarchically organized as an integral part of the centrally planned economy. The question in the Soviet Union today is whether this is to remain. Economists as well as parts of the military favour the dissolution of the arms industrial complex to integrate it into the reformed economic system. The planning authorities apparently

[57] For a lengthy list of US superiority in military technology, see *Soviet Military Power 1989* (note 26), pp. 134 and 137.

[58] Holloway, D., 'The Soviet Union', eds N. Ball and M. Leitenberg, *The Structure of the Defense Industry* (Croom Helm: London, 1983), pp. 50–80.

[59] Soviet researchers claim that this is not primarily due to the secrecy that has traditionally surrounded the arms industrial complex and military budget but is mainly a result of the pricing system. Arms are more or less arbitrarily priced, and the price apparently does not reflect labour costs incurred or resources absorbed in production. *Report of the Scientific Council of the USA and Canada Institute in Moscow*, reprinted (in German translation) in *Gesellschaftswissenschaftliche Beiträge*, no. 4 (1989), pp. 372–77.

favour the continuation of a relatively closed arms production complex that they can control. There are distinct differences between military and non-military production, the most striking feature of which is the high priority assigned to arms production. Since the end of the New Economic Policy at the end of the 1920s, Soviet leaders have granted the arms industry first priority in resource allocation to shield arms production from the chronic deficits' elsewhere in the economy. It has access to high technology and skilled personnel, and as a result most Western observers have concluded that the technological level of the Soviet arms industry exceeds civilian production by far. A second feature of arms development and production in the USSR is the almost absolute secrecy surrounding it and its separation and insulation from non-military production—referred to by President Gorbachev as the Soviet Union's 'internal COCOM'.[60] A third special feature of the arms industry is the tight control of the armed forces, through the Ministry of Defence, over development and production programmes.[61] In contrast to other sectors of the economy, the armed forces, as the consumers of the weapons produced, have a decisive say in the production process.

The arms industrial sector consisted until mid-1989 of nine ministries that direct enterprises specialized in the production of weapon systems and factories that produce sub-systems, support equipment, components and materials (see table 8.9). This part of the arms sector is presently being restructured, too. The Ministry for Medium Machine-Building has been integrated into the Ministry of Nuclear Energy, and the Ministry of the Communications Equipment Industry has been integrated into the Ministry for Communications.[62] Additional ministries primarily responsible for civil production also carry out work for the armed forces. Arms production is administered by a council of ministers (*Komissija Soveta Ministrov SSSR po voenno-promyslennym voprosam*, commonly abbreviated VPK). The ministries are large enterprises with production facilities at their disposal. As was stated in a study prepared for the United Nations International Labour Office on the basis of open Soviet sources: 'Apparently there are more than 150 major end-product weapon enterprises and shipyards plus a further 150 enterprises producing combat support equipment such as radar and communications systems and trucks.'[63]

A total of over 500 enterprises, 3500 component suppliers, 450 research and development institutions and 50 major design institutions are believed

[60] For a discussion, see Schröder, H.-H., 'Versorgungskrise, Rüstungsabbau und Konversion in der UdSSR', *Berichte des Bundesinstituts für ostwissenschaftliche Studien*, no. 56–58 (1989), part I, pp. 44–50; and Albrecht, U. and Nikutta, R., *Die sowjetische Rüstungsindustrie* (Westdeutscher Verlag: Opladen, 1989), p. 12.
[61] Albrecht and Nikutta (note 60), pp. 312–13.
[62] Schröder (note 60), part III, p. 49.
[63] Cooper, J., *The Soviet Defence Industry and Conversion: The Regional Dimension*, Working Paper no. 10 (ILO Disarmament and Employment Programme: Geneva, 1988).

Table 8.9. Soviet ministries involved in arms production, 1989

Ministry	Defence production	Civil production
Ministry of the Defence Industry	Tanks, armoured vehicles, artillery, small arms, munitions, solid-fuel missiles, optical equipment, laser technology, surface-to-surface missiles	Tractors, cars, motor cycles, railway cartridges, machine tools, steel, cameras, optical instruments
Ministry of the Aviation Industry	Aircraft, helicopters, air-to-air missiles, air-to-surface missiles, spacecraft	Aircraft, helicopters, machine tools, refrigerators, vacuum cleaners, video recorders, medical instruments
Ministry of Machine-Building	Munitions, fuses, solid propellants	Cycles, refrigerators, tape recorders, video recorders, watches
Ministry for Medium Machine-Building	Nuclear warheads, nuclear reactors, high-energy lasers, uranium mining and processing	Uranium mining and and processing
Ministry for General Machine-Building	Ballistic missiles, launchers, cruise missiles, spacecraft, guidance systems	Spacecraft, tractors, railway carriages, machine tools, refrigerators, television sets
Ministry of the Communications Equipment Industry	Computers, communication equipment, components for radars, electronic battlefield equipment	Computers, television sets, tape recorders
Ministry of the Electronics Industry	Electronic components, micro-computers	Television sets, tape recorders, radio receivers, watches, electronic components, computers, telephones
Ministry of the Radio Industry	Radar and communications systems, special computers, guidance and control systems, lasers	Refrigerators, radio sets, television sets, computers, telephones
Ministry of the Shipbuilding Industry	Naval vessels, naval weapon systems, sonars, radar systems	Ships, off-shore oil platforms, machine tools, washing machines, tape recorders, video recorders, steel

Sources: Compiled from Schröder, H.-H., 'Wirtschaft und Rüstung in der Sowjetunion', *Soldat und Technik*, July 1988, pp. 383–87; Cooper, J., *The Soviet Defence Industry and Conversion: The Regional Dimension*, Working Paper no. 10, ILO Disarmament and Employment Programme, Geneva 1988, p. 3; Tedstrom, J., 'Is the contribution of the defense complex to civilian production growing?', Radio Liberty, *Report on the USSR*, no. 24 (1989), p.3; Albrecht, U. and Nikutta, R., *Die sowjetische Rüstungsindustrie*, (Westdeutscher Verlag: Opladen, 1989).

to be affiliated to the ministries of the military sector. These are mainly concentrated in the region around Moscow.[64]

No reliable, detailed and verifiable statistics exist for the number of people employed in the arms industry, their qualifications or educational background. Estimates have been derived from other military activities in the USSR. These range from 5 to 8 million people employed in the arms industry.[65]

Production of major weapon systems

Another indication of the size and capability of the Soviet arms industry is the number of major weapons produced. However, in contrast to the military budget, where some information is gradually being released by the Soviet Government, there is silence on this issue. Although the annual production of thousands of tanks and armoured vehicles, hundreds of helicopters, missiles, fighters and bombers, approximately 150 000 standard tons of naval ships, split between submarines and surface combat ships, obviously requires a large industrial base, analysts have had to rely on US intelligence sources for more specific details.

It has been estimated that about one-fifth of the total industrial output of the USSR in the 1970s was devoted to arms production. Of the machine-building and metal-working sector, one-third was for arms production; for the chemical industry, one-sixth; and for aircraft and shipbuilding, two-thirds each.[66] According to the US Government, the Soviet arms industry is the largest in the world and out-produces the USA in most categories of weapon systems (see table 8.10).

Different interpretations of this contradictory information are possible:

1. The announced slow-down in Soviet military expenditure might not have affected the arms procurement share of the budget at all. Reductions in military expenditure might have been taken from other sectors of the defence budget—personnel costs may have gone down as a result of troop withdrawals; military exercises and the long-distance operations of the Navy have been reduced. Moreover, the unilateral reductions in military hardware undertaken by the USSR and its allies will affect weapon systems already deployed. In fact, the modernization of equipment could be used as partial compensation for quantitative reductions and to pacify critics of the unilateral actions within the Soviet military establishment.

---

[64] For details on the regional distribution of the arms industry see Cooper (note 63); and Albrecht and Nikutta (note 60), p. 311. Other Western observers mention—although without details—the existence of 18 000 arms production units and more than 575 scientific research and design organizations; Cochran, T. B., Arkin, W. M., Norris, R. S. and Sands, J. I., *Nuclear Weapons Databook*, *Volume IV, Soviet Nuclear Weapons* (Harper & Row: New York, 1989), pp. 76–77.

[65] Melman, S., 'Barriers to conversion from military to civilian industry', paper prepared for the United Nations Centre for Disarmament, *ad hoc* Group of Governmental Experts on the Relationship between Disarmament and Development (Columbia University: New York, Apr. 1980), mimeo, p. 5; Holloway, D., 'The Soviet Union', in Cooper (note 63).

[66] Holloway (note 58), p. 58.

Table 8.10. US Government estimates of trends in Soviet major weapon production, 1980–88[a]

	1980	1981	1982	1983	1984	1985	1986	1987	1988
ICBMs	250	200	175	150	75	100	75	125	150
SLBMs	200	175	175	100	50	100	100	100	100
Tanks	3 100	2 000	2 500	3 000	3 200	3 000	3 300	3 500	3 500
Arm. vehicles	6 500	5 200	4 500	5 000	3 800	3 500	4 200	4 450	5 250
Helicopters	700	800	800	550	600	600	500	450	400
Artillery	2 600	2 850	2 850	2 850	2 950	3 100	2 100	1 900	2 100
Strategic bombers	30	30	35	35	50	50	50	45	45
Fighters/ fighter-bombers	1 300	1 350	1 100	950	800	650	650	700	700
Submarines	13	11	8	10	9	8	8	9	9
Major surface warships	11	9	8	10	9	8	9	8	9

[a] The various issues of *Soviet Military Power* present different figures. In this table, the latest figures available have been used.

Sources: *Soviet Military Power 1984–1989* (US Government Printing Office: Washington, DC, 1984–1989).

2. It can be assumed that cuts in the procurement budget would not have immediately visible short-term effects.

3. It has to be emphasized that the numbers compiled in table 8.10 are far from certain. It is not clear whether exports have been included for every year. Furthermore, substantial differences exist not only between the estimates of major weapons produced between the various US intelligence services but also between the estimates given by the same intelligence service at different times.[67] While the 1989 edition of the US Department of Defense annual publication *Soviet Military Power* claims that 3500 tanks were produced in the Soviet Union in 1988, only after a few weeks of the release of this publication the United States officially announced that Soviet tank production in 1989 was only 1700.[68] If all the estimates given at different times by the US intelligence services were included in the table it would show that many revisions have been made. Corrections of 25–50 per cent are not unusual, and occasionally the revisions go beyond 100 per cent. These corrections might be due to improved information gathering, or might be the result of the fact that US estimates have traditionally been compiled to serve a political function within the overall US policy making and budgetary process.

According to these statistics there have been no recent dramatic changes in the number of major weapons produced in the Soviet Union. The US Government claims that the traditional military resource allocation continued under President Gorbachev. According to this US estimate, total

[67] Schröder (note 60), part II, pp. 14–20 compares estimates of the US Defence Intelligence Agency published in 1984, 1987 and 1988 for nine categories of weapon systems.
[68] *Jane's Defence Weekly*, Oct. 1989, p. 849.

military outlays have grown at a rate of about 3 per cent a year in real terms since 1985, and it was especially expenditure in R&D and in weapons procurement that accounted for this growth.[69] Future reductions of military expenditures by 14.2 per cent and the fact that military expenditures were frozen in 1987 and 1988 (announced in 1989), are not reflected in the volume of major weapons estimated by the US Government.[70] More recent US estimates suggest a reduction of arms production in the Soviet Union, reducing the burden on the economy by 1 per cent of the net material product).[71] The Soviet Union has apparently begun to reduce its military expenditure in the face of economic pressures and deteriorating standards of living. Since the primary sources for these US statistics are classified and since the Soviet Union does not publish its own data on its production of major weapon systems, the information available cannot be verified.

Military expenditures and arms procurement

Until 30 May 1989, when President Gorbachev acknowledged that the Soviet Union would spend 77.3 billion roubles on the military in 1989, the Soviet Union released annually a single figure ranging between approximately 17 billion and 20 billion roubles (see also chapter 5). No information on the procurement budget was available earlier. Concealing the true size of the Soviet budget has not only complicated East–West negotiations but also led to speculation in the West about the real figure for military expenditures.[72] A week after the Gorbachev announcement, Prime Minister Nikolai Ryzhkov gave a breakdown of the 1989 military budget.[73] According to this Soviet source, investment in new weapon systems and other military equipment, buildings and R&D was planned in 1989 in the range of 52.3 billion roubles, amounting to two-thirds of the military budget, 15.6 per cent of the Soviet state budget and around 9 per cent of the net material product (NMP). The 1990 budget at that time was planned to be 12 billion roubles less than the 12th Five-Year Plan target, amounting to 70.9 billion roubles.[74] The figures announced at the end of 1989 are in fact 71 billion roubles for 1990. The amount to be spent for procurement, construction and R&D is planned to be cut from 52.5 billion roubles in 1989 to 47.9 billion roubles in 1990—a reduction of almost 9 per cent.[75] Even before the May 1989 Gorbachev announcement, Soviet politicians and military officers

[69] *Soviet Military Power 1989* (note 26), p. 32.

[70] *Izvestia*, 31 May 1989, p. 2, quoted extensively in Schröder (note 60), p. 31.

[71] Friedman, T. L., 'Military spending by Soviets slows', *New York Times*, 14 Nov. 1989.

[72] Deger, S., 'World military expenditure', SIPRI, *SIPRI Yearbook 1989: World Armaments and Disarmament* (Oxford University Press: Oxford, 1989), p. 152; Schröder (note 60), part II, p. 6, points out that differences between the US CIA, DOD and Joint Chiefs of Staff estimates of Soviet military expenditure exist. For a recent critique, see Holzman, F. D., 'Politics and guesswork: CIA and DIA estimates of Soviet military spending', *International Affairs*, vol. 14, no. 2 (autumn 1989), pp. 101–31.

[73] *Izvestia*, 8 June 1989, p. 3.

[74] *Jane's Defence Weekly*, 11 Nov. 1989, p. 1050.

[75] An evaluation of these statistics and further details can be found in chapter 5.

indicated that the previously cited figure of 20.2 billion roubles was not the total military budget.[76]

The publication of the new Soviet figures has not stopped the debate in the West about the real amount of resources allocated for military procurement. According to US and NATO estimates, the Soviet Union actually spends almost 100 per cent more than it announces—around 60 billion roubles on procurement of weapons and military equipment, 50 billion on the maintenance of the armed forces and 20 billion on personnel.[77] Criticism from the West has led to further explanations by Soviet officials about what the newly published figures mean. Former Chief of Staff Marshal Sergey Akhromeyev (now an adviser to President Gorbachev) noted that the new official figures were not underestimates but reflected the artificially low prices of raw materials.[78] On two occasions General Mikhail Moiseyev, the Chief of the General Staff of the Soviet Armed Forces, has compared US and Soviet weapon systems and their prices. At a joint press conference with US Admiral William Crowe he compared aircraft procurement costs, saying that 'the modern Soviet aircraft Su-25 costs 5.8 million [roubles], whereas the [US] F-16 costs 28 million dollars'.[79] In an article in *Pravda* he wrote:

The price of an American Ticonderoga-class nuclear-powered guided missile cruiser is roughly nine times the price of a similar Soviet ship and the price of an American SH-60 helicopter 11 times the price of a similar Soviet helicopter. This difference results from a higher level of wages of American workers and employees in the defence industry and from the differences in the pricing system. In the USSR raw and other materials are a great deal cheaper than in the United States and the rate of profit in the Soviet Union is regulated by the State. The production of arms and military hardware in the United States ensures the military industrial complex extremely high rates of profit. All these factors must be taken into account in comparing expenditures for defence-related research and development: 15,300 million roubles in the Soviet Union and 37,000 million dollars in the United States.[80]

In summary, while the newly published Soviet figures for arms procurement are more credible than previous statements, these figures are still too general to give a detailed picture of the size of annual arms output.

---

[76] Yudin, I., 'Defence spendings and economics of disarmament', *Soviet Military Review*, June 1989, pp. 28–30. In Aug. 1987 Deputy Foreign Minister Petrovskiy announced that this figure represented only Ministry of Defence expenditures for maintaining military personnel, military pensions, logistics, military construction and 'a number of other articles'. *The Soviet Economy in 1988: Gorbachev Changes Course*, Report by the Central Intelligence Agency and the Defense Intelligence Agency, presented to the Subcommittee on National Security Economics of the Joint Economic Committee, 14 Apr. 1989, p. 17.

[77] *Frankfurter Allgemeine Zeitung*, 2 Aug. 1989.

[78] *Frankfurter Allgemeine Zeitung*, 2 Aug. 1989.

[79] *Krasnaya Zvezda*, 22 June, p. 3; Yudin, I., 'Defence spendings and economics of disarmament' *Soviet Military Review*, June 1989, pp. 28–30.

[80] *Krasnaya Zvezda*, 22 June 1989, p. 3; and *Pravda*, 11 June 1989, p. 5. Apparently General Moiseyev used a rouble conversion rate of approximately 1:1, not far from the official non-commercial tourist exchange-rate, but grossly overvalued.

The future of arms production: conversion to non-military production

Among economic reformers in the Soviet Union there is agreement that the high priority given to the arms industry has been a contributing factor to economic difficulties. It seems a natural course that the Soviet Government is expecting the redirection of resources from the arms sector to contribute to economic development. These expected economic benefits from cuts in military production have combined with a desire to enhance stability between the two military blocs to end the unquestioned priority given to the military sector.[81] In his United Nations General Assembly address of 7 December 1988 President Gorbachev said:

For its part, the Soviet Union is prepared:
– in the framework of our economic reform we are ready to draw up and make public our internal plan of conversion;
– in the course of 1989 to draw up, as an experiment, conversion plans for two or three defense plants;
– to make public our experience in providing employment for specialists from military industry and in using its equipment, buildings and structures in civilian production.[82]

There had been some discussion before about how to use skills and resources from the arms industry for economic modernization. The 1987 INF Treaty had intensified plans to convert industrial capacities. A National Commission to Promote Conversion has been appointed, and several research institutes are engaged in conversion research.[83] The announced conversion plan and the experience had not been published by the end of 1989. Prime Minister Ryzhkov, in his planning speech of December 1989, referred to the conversion plan and emphasized that the arms industrial complex should be kept as a unit, and that increased production of consumer goods, promotion of the agro-industrial complex and the modernization of machine-building were primary aims. Conversion is not a new issue in the Soviet Union. Soviet politicians and researchers have claimed for many years that the redirection of priorities would benefit the economy and furthermore that conversion in a centrally planned economy—in contrast to capitalist countries—could easily be accomplished.[84] However, a more serious discussion and the encounter of practical problems to restructure the

---

[81] Izyumov, A. I., 'Soviet economic conversion', *New Economy*, Feb. 1989, p. 1. Izyumov, a Senior Research Fellow at the Institute of the USA and Canada in Moscow, describes 'economic conversion as an essential part of a successful perestroika program' and mentions the 'growing number of Soviet officials and citizens championing economic conversion domestically and in international affairs'.

[82] Speech by Mikhail Gorbachev at the 43rd Session of the United Nations General Assembly, 7 Dec. 1988, in USSR Ministry of Foreign Affairs, *Soviet Diplomacy Today*, 1989.

[83] Most prominent among these is IMEMO (Institute for World Economy and International Relations). The peace institute Mira has been formed within IMEMO.

[84] United Nations Department of Economic and Social Affairs, *Economic and Social Consequences of Disarmament: Replies of Government and Communications from International Organizations* (62.IX.2), New York, 1962. Similar statements have been made until very recently. See the report by a member of the International Department of the Central Committee of Soviet Union, Remisov, A., 'Disarmament treaties and conversion of military production in USSR', *IDOC Internazionale*, no. 5 (1988), pp. 5–6.

industry have changed the word conversion from a propaganda item to a key term in economic reform discussion.[85]

One important problem inhibiting a planned and systematic conversion process in the USSR is, according to Soviet sources, the 'complete lack of a data base'.[86] This is a result of the secrecy surrounding all military affairs that has kept economists from analysing the arms production process and the neglect of this issue in research. Soviet economists are now looking closely at experiences in other countries.

The Soviet Union and its allies face three basic problems of conversion. Some of these may also be faced by West European NATO countries if, as a result of arms control or domestic pressures, they are committed to troop reductions and arms limitations: first, the integration of soldiers into the civil economy; second, the disposal of weapons withdrawn; and third, the reorientation of arms research and production facilities to non-military use.

As noted above, the reduction of personnel costs is a more immediate saving from the defence budget—although not from the state budget—than is altering equipment programmes. Officials in the Soviet Union have emphasized the savings derived from unilateral reductions. Defence Minister General Dmitri Yazov said in an interview: 'It should be emphasised that the course toward cuts in the armed forces and armaments and the reduction of military spending will enable us to economise almost 30,000 million roubles as compared with the endorsed Five-Year Plan.'[87] General Moiseyev mentioned the same amount, adding that this amounts to '40 per cent of the country's yearly defence budget'.[88]

While the savings anticipated might in the long run benefit the economy, in the short term difficulties have to be expected since many soldiers are not qualified to take a job outside the military sector. From the perspective of the arms industrial base, the more important features of conversion relate to weapon systems to be withdrawn or forgone.

Withdrawal of weapons

The physical liquidation (as President Gorbachev called it) of existing weapon systems, including the destruction of intermediate-range nuclear missiles covered in the INF Treaty, is a large task.[89] The 10 000 tanks, 800 combat aircraft and 8500 artillery pieces that the Soviet leadership have promised to withdraw will have to be destroyed or modified for civilian use. These figures are likely to increase substantially as a result of a CFE agree-

---

[85] Izyumov (note 81), pp. 3–5, calls 'reliance on the strength of a planned economy in these circumstances . . . as senseless as reliance on the "strength of the market mechanism," which is a typical position of conversion opponents in the West.' In the report of the Scientific Council of the Institute of the USA and Canada (note 59), p. 377, it is criticized that for a long period the wrong organization, namely the state planning committee, had been entrusted with the planning of conversion.

[86] Kireyev, A., 'Cost accounting for disarmament economics', *New Times*, Apr. 1989, p. 15.

[87] *Pravda*, 20 June 1989.

[88] *Pravda*, 11 June 1989.

[89] See chapter 12 for the technical problems encountered.

ment. Half of the 10 000 tanks will be scrapped or be used as targets in military exercises, while the other half will be converted for civil use.

Asked what will happen to the military hardware, Defence Minister Yazov said in September 1989:

Part of the reduced tank fleet is used as scrap metal, while the rest are converted into auxilliary vehicles for national economy needs (tractors, fire engines, etc.). The artillery systems taken out of the fighting strength are put into conservation at arms depots, while the obsolete systems are written off completely. The reduced aircraft are being scrapped, too, and only a small share of them are converted into targets to be used in the training of military personnel. All the submarines and surface ships excluded from the fighting strength have been turned into scrap. Three surface ships are to be handed over to young sailors' clubs . . .[90]

According to Soviet sources the INF Treaty saved the economy 300 million roubles in 1988.[91] However, no details have been given about how these resources were saved, and this estimate is probably based on the projected costs had missile production continued. Only a small part of withdrawn equipment is to be utilized outside the military sector.

The destruction of weapon systems, and in particular the need to verify destruction to prove compliance with arms control agreements, requires new investment, and the early experiences with the INF Treaty suggest that it will be more expensive than originally anticipated.[92] Leaving aside exotic alternatives (the bodies of two missiles were turned into water reservoirs in agricultural co-operatives, and parts of missiles were used in a sculpture), the destruction and conversion of weapons are of only marginal benefit to the economy. The FR German Liebherr Company and the Odessa Heavy Crane Manufacturing Unit set up a joint venture in the USSR to mount telescopic cranes on to the former SS-20 transporter. The Swedish Ovako Steel company bought 50 Soviet tanks of a total weight of 2000 tons to be melted to scrap metal.[93] The Soviet Union also bartered 17 submarines, a cruiser, a destroyer and a frigate to Pepsi-Co Inc. in the United States, to be sold for scrap iron, as partial payment for beverage production in the 22 Pepsi-Cola factories in the Soviet Union.[94] Trucks have been transferred to planning authorities in the USSR to be used outside the military sector. Tanks will be converted into heavy earth-moving equipment.

While these activities might be beneficial to the economy, especially compared to the decades of armaments competition, the dismantling or conversion of major weapon systems and sawing or hydraulically crushing modern missiles actually represent the destruction of products that had been manufactured at great cost to the economy.

[90] *Izvestia*, 16 Sep. 1989.
[91] Yudin, I., 'Defence spendings and economics of disarmament', *Soviet Military Review*, June 1989, p. 30.
[92] See chapter 12 for details.
[93] *Süddeutsche Zeitung*, 7 July 1989.
[94] Chen, K. T., 'International arms sales sag', *IEEE Spectrum*, Nov. 1989, p. 57. 'The unsinkable exchanged for the undrinkable.'

Reorientation of the arms industry

The greatest potential long-term economic benefit to the Soviet Union would be the reorientation of the arms industry to non-military production. Trading 'guns for butter' is not a new idea in the Soviet Union, but only since *perestroika* has it been on the political agenda and only after the INF Treaty has it received serious attention.

The reorientation of arms production is not conditioned purely by economic arguments—it is part of a wider arms control process as well as a wider economic reform process. However, reduced arms procurement is expected to free investment resources and release R&D centres and skilled personnel from arms production. The hope in the Soviet Union is that the 19.5 per cent cut in arms production might have far-reaching effects. In his statement quoted above, General Moiseyev also said: 'Under the 13th Five-Year Plan conversion of defence enterprises will result in the production of 250–270 billion roubles worth of consumer goods and bring the share of civilian production at defence plants to more than 60 per cent by 1995.'[95]

The emphasis on consumer goods as an alternative to arms production is no surprise. The systematic modernization of the economy is—according to the resolutions of the 27th Party Congress—directed mainly at the production of consumer goods which are in great demand. Increasing economic difficulties in 1988, especially growing popular dissatisfaction with the slow pace of *perestroika* and falling standards of living, have forced economic policy to focus on improving the supply of consumer goods. Increasing the pressure on the arms industry to step up non-military production was logical since it was the most efficient sector of the economy.

Production of civilian goods is not new to the Soviet arms industry. In 1988 the share of civilian production was said by Soviet sources already to approach 40 per cent. The Soviet journal *Vestnik statistiki* revealed the magnitude of civilian production in eight of nine VPK ministries in 1989. In total they produced almost 10 million television sets, 6 million refrigerators, over 4 million washing machines, almost as many vacuum cleaners and nearly 2.5 million bicycles in 1988. The number of civil items produced had increased in 1988 compared to 1987.[96] As shown in figure 8.1, for many consumer goods, the factories under the administration of the defence department (VPK) are the main producers and in some cases the only producers—that is, sewing machines, video recorders, radio receivers and colour television sets.

Conversion on a substantial scale offers long-term opportunities for economic reform, but considerable problems will be encountered. Most unfinished materials used in arms production (such as steel, copper or fibres), semi-finished goods (ball-bearings and microchips) and production equipment (such as machine tools) can be used for civilian production.

---

[95] *Pravda*, 11 June 1989.
[96] Tedstrom, J., 'Is the contribution of the defense complex to civilian production growing?', Radio Liberty, *Report on the USSR*, no. 24 (1989); Schröder (note 61), part III, p. 11–26; Cooper, J., 'Nuclear milking machines and perestroika', *Detente*, no. 14 (1989), pp. 11–13.

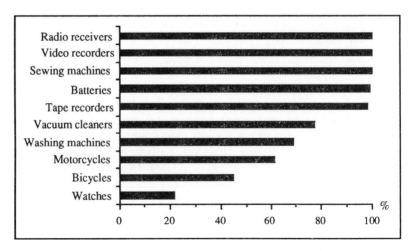

Figure 8.1. Shares of selected civilian production in the Soviet arms industry, 1989

Source: Tedstrom, J., 'Is the contribution of the defense complex to civilian production growing?', Radio Liberty, *Report on the USSR*, no. 24 (1989), p. 5.

Similarly, most of the qualified manpower of the arms industry can make a useful—perhaps the most important—contribution to non-military production. However, bottlenecks and difficulties have already been encountered. Soviet economists openly speak about the *ad hoc* character and ill-planned process of conversion during 1988 and 1989. A number of Soviet authors have—in contrast to the previously heard, widely publicized success stories of 'prams instead of missiles'—pointed to peculiarities of the arms industry that are bound to lead to frictions during the conversion process.

Barriers to conversion

Four basic difficulties could arise: first, the concentration of large sectors of the arms industry on very specific areas of weapon technology; second, the establishment of new producer–customer relations; third, the geographical concentration of factories in specific cities and regions; and fourth, the human element of the response of the workforce to the restructuring of the defence industrial sector.

The quality of consumer products has in the past been poor, and unless economic reform affects factories at the lowest organizational level—the shop floor—it is not likely to increase. Prams produced in tank factories might look more like tanks than prams.[97] The specialization of the defence industry on the production of relatively small numbers of high-quality items might also prevent a smooth transition to the production of fairly unsophisti-

---

[97] Criticism of the quality of the consumer products produced by the arms industry has been raised in Izyumov, A., *Literaturnaja Gazeta*, 7 July 1989, p. 28, quoted in Schröder (note 60), part III, p. 46 and in the above-mentioned report of the Scientific Council of the Institute of the USA and Canada (note 59), pp. 375–76.

cated consumer durables in very large numbers. The expansion of existing consumer product lines may not be the most efficient use of skilled workers and sophisticated machine tools. Rather, a more basic adaptation of military factories to the production of high-technology civilian goods has been seen as 'the best way of using the converted defence enterprises'.[98] The returns from such a reorientation would not be quick but would certainly be most promising over the long term.

In addition to production problems there are difficulties associated with the distribution of consumer goods produced by the arms industry. Marketing strategies are required to sell the consumer products. Whereas in the past the industry had to deal with only one ministry that was in charge of the factories, with the conversion to civil production new means of selling the products have to be developed. Economic problems might arise, too, since civilian products of the arms industry tend to be more expensive than competing products by the non-military sector.

In addition problems are growing out of the geographical concentration of factories in specific cities and regions. These communities are dependent on defence industry for their living. Many social services in the USSR (such as the building of living quarters and child care facilities) are the responsibility of the military–industrial complexes. In areas with a high density of arms factories, conversion is likely to lead to the reduction of the wage fund and thus to a cut in social services. A major bottleneck might be the reaction of the workforce to losing the privileges associated with the high priority enjoyed by the arms production sector.[99] Managers and employees of arms enterprises might resist converting to produce civilian goods if this means a loss of privileges. In a case study of a factory in Votkinsk, where missiles covered by the INF Treaty were produced, the Soviet journal *Soviet Military Review* concludes:

The factory gave birth to the town of Votkinsk and remains the main source of its prosperity . . . 'Secret' shops are staffed with most qualified and hence the highest paid workers. Let us look at the truth openly: is it easy for them to calmly regard the possibility of smaller earnings? Could they, as one newspaper wrote, 'joyfully and with enlightened heart' give up their privileges?

I think it logical that they would draw their average wages for the transitional period. But already there are wage scissors: the wage fund has remained intact but the volume of industrial output has dwindled. In general, the town is tens of millions of roubles behind the planned figures for development, and this figure is growing, revealing the difficulties of the conversion period.[100]

In conclusion the Soviet Union has strong economic incentives for further arms control measures and cuts in military procurement but, in the short term, these might produce higher costs than economic benefits. The long-

---

[98] Kireyev, A., 'Swords into ploughshares: conversion in the USSR', *World Marxist Review*, no. 6 (1989), p. 10. Schröder (note 60), part III, pp. 36–39, quotes several Soviet engineers and economists who raise the issue of technological reorientation difficulties.

[99] Izyumov (note 81), p. 3.

[100] Sabirov, A., 'Prams instead of missiles', *Soviet Military Review*, no. 5 (1989), pp. 30–31.

term prospects are better if parochial interests in the arms industry can be controlled, traditional secrecy is removed and the skills and resources of the military sector are turned in a co-ordinated and systematic fashion towards economic modernization. Exactly how the development and production of arms will be affected is more difficult to predict. Recent reforms have not stopped outside the arms industry and the armed forces.[101] Taking the cuts in the military procurement budget as a measure—with cuts of less than 5 per cent in 1990—the conversion of industry is not a short-term process. In general, centralized decision-making bodies have been partially decentralized, and partial privatization has been tried in the arms industry.[102] Such changes are partly intended to improve attitudes in the workforce and offer a sense of participation as well as being an effort to reduce duplication.

Increasing the efficiency of the military sector—the armed forces as well as arms production—is a goal. Soviet leaders have explicitly emphasized the correlation between intensified economic development and strengthening defence capabilities. The industrial and scientific sectors most prominently promoted in the first two reform years under Gorbachev were those associated with technologies judged to be the most interesting for future weapon development.[103] In the meantime the emphasis has shifted towards the production of consumer durables. Western critics of the Soviet Union maintain that the primary purpose and effect of reform in the arms industry will not fundamentally change Soviet security policy but will simply increase productivity to bring about more efficient production and more modern weapons.[104] Such a statement is difficult to prove or disprove, but a different conclusion can be drawn—that economic difficulties in the Soviet Union have been so dramatic that there was no alternative to tapping the resources of the military sector for economic revival and, in fact, the survival of the system. The budgetary cuts have not yet led to the establishment of a more efficient arms industry but have created great difficulties in those centres unprepared for the reorientation to non-military production.

V. The non-Soviet WTO countries

The structure of the defence industries in the WTO and the amount of reliable data currently available for these countries are insufficient to present a breakdown of defence production similar to that for the Western industrial world. Only general, not very detailed reports on the production of arms in the non-Soviet WTO countries have been published.

---

[101] Gorbachev, quoted in Albrecht and Nikutta (note 60), p. 13. Segbers, K., 'Die sowjetische Umbaupolitik gewinnt Gestalt', Friedensbericht 1988, *Dialog*, no. 1-2 (1988), pp. 28–54, looked at the early reform measures and claimed that the arms industry was protected from *perestroika*.

[102] Rosefielde, S., 'Assessing Soviet reforms in the defense industry', *Global Affairs*, autumn 1989, p. 57–73. Rosefielde claims that, instead of contributing to arms control, this reform is apt to shift resources towards defence production and bolster military industrial productivity.

[103] Schröder, H.-H., 'Gorbachows "Wirtschaftspolitik und die Verteidigung des Vaterlandes". Die sowjetische Rüstungswirtschaft in der Ära der Reformen', *Osteuropa*, no. 8 (1987), pp. 603–19.

[104] Rosefielde (note 102).

This section presents a picture of the size and scale of some elements of defence production in the WTO. In addition, a discussion of the military budgets of members of the Warsaw Treaty Organization is contained in chapter 5 of this *Yearbook*. This section also discusses the possible arms control implications of this defence industrial base both in terms of the conventional arms control negotiations in Europe and in terms of implementing domestic programmes of conversion.

The defence industrial base of the WTO

The quality of information available on defence production in the Soviet Union and the non-Soviet WTO countries is uneven. Of the major producers the information is best for the Soviet Union and Poland and poorest for Czechoslovakia. The Soviet Union produces the full range of military systems, from 7-mm ammunition to intercontinental ballistic missiles. However, other WTO countries produce a much more limited range of systems and have a much less sophisticated arms industrial base than the West European NATO countries. Table 8.11 lists types of equipment in production in Bulgaria, Czechoslovakia, the German Democratic Republic, Hungary, Poland and Romania.

Bulgaria has virtually no defence industry as such but has a significant shipbuilding industry. The GDR, Poland and Romania also have significant shipbuilding capacities.

Throughout the non-Soviet WTO only Romania produces any kind of missiles—these are air-to-air missiles of Soviet design. The extent of Romanian production is very uncertain and may be limited to very minor modifications or final assembly of imported kits. These missiles now appear to be available for export since in 1989 the Romanian producer of missiles, Romtechnica, was represented at the defence exhibition in Baghdad, where copies of Soviet AA-2 and AA-7 missiles were displayed.[105]

The production of electronics and precision small arms is largely confined to Czechoslovakia, the GDR and Poland.[106] There is also limited military electronics production in Hungary. There are relatively sophisticated aircraft industries in Czechoslovakia and Romania and a less sophisticated aircraft industry in Poland. Only Poland and Romania produce helicopters.

In general, however, as suggested by table 8.11, arms production throughout the non-Soviet WTO is dominated by heavy engineering projects producing items with fairly low-level technologies developed in the 1970s.

Other features of the projects noted in the table are first, the extent of dependence on Soviet technology and second, the dependence on the Warsaw Treaty Organization as a market for the arms produced. If one divides the systems produced into the broad categories of aerospace (including missiles), land systems, electronics and small arms, the extent of

[105] *AAS Milavnews*, June 1989, p. 20; *International Defense Review*, June 1989, p. 858.
[106] *Jane's Radar and Electronic Warfare Systems, 1989–90* (Jane's: Coulsdon, 1989).

Table 8.11. Weapon systems currently in production in the non-Soviet WTO countries, 1989

System	Bulgaria	Czechoslovakia	GDR	Hungary	Poland	Romania
Jet trainer aircraft	..	L-39	..	..	PZL I-22 Iryd	IAR-99 Soim
Turboprop trainers	..	Zlin 142 Zlin Z 50L	..	GAK-22 Dino	M-20 Mewa M-26 Iskierka PZL-130	Yak-52
Transport aircraft	..	L-410M L-610	..	..	AN-28	C1-11 Islander
Helicopters	..	..	..	..	Mi-2/2B W-3 Sokol SW-4	IAR-316 IAR-317 IAR-330 KA-126
Tanks	..	T-55 (parts only) T-62 T-72	..	..	T-55 (parts only) T-72	T-55 T-72
APCs	APC-84[a]	OT-62 OT-65 BMP-2	..	OT-65 PSZH-4	OT-62 MTLB	P-224 TAB-77
Other armoured vehicles	..	T-55 ARV BMP-1 ARV	BLG-60 bridgelayer	..	T-55 ARV BTS-2 ARV	..

Trucks and unarmoured vehicles	Madra truck	BAZ SNA Tatra 815 Tatra 148	P3 jeep Robur Lo 1800 L60 PVB	Csepel D-562 Csepel D-566	Star 266 Star 200 Jelcz 315	ARO 240 jeep SR-131 DAC 665 Roman 12135
Tube artillery	..	DANA 152-mm M59 82-mm	..	..	..	122-mm
Rocket artillery	..	RM-70 122-mm	..	..	WP-8 140-mm	122-mm 130-mm[b]
Air-to-air missiles	..	..	..	..	..	AA-1 Alkali AA-2 Atoll AA-7 Apex
Electronics	..	Field telephone switchboard	Radios Digital relays Field telephone switchboard Teleprinter/fax	Radio receivers Microwave radios	Height-finding radar Surveillance radar	..
Hand guns	..	M-50 pistol M-75 M-83 M-85 Skorpion	Pistole M	M-48 PA-63 FEG Model R FEG Model P9	P-64 PM-63	..
Machine-guns	..	Model 59	LMGK	48M	..	Orita

System	Bulgaria	Czechoslovakia	GDR	Hungary	Poland	Romania
Rifles	..	Model 58	Karabiner S MPiK/MS KKMP	AKM-63 AMD-65	AK-47 PMK DGN-60 PMKM	AK-47
Cannon	..	30-mm	..	..	..	..
Light weapons and munitions	..	P-27 RPG-75 Hand grenades	Flamethrower Hand grenades	Flamethrower Hand grenades	Hand grenades	..
Combat ships	Minesweepers Landing craft	..	Corvettes Amphibious support ships Minesweepers	..	Frigates Landing craft Minesweepers	Destroyers Frigates Fast attack craft Minesweepers
Other naval vessels	Tankers Survey vessels	..	Tankers	..	Tankers Survey ships	..

a In 1984 a new APC was seen in Bulgaria, apparently assembled from a Soviet chassis and turret but with a Bulgarian engine and hull.
b Soviet chassis and Czechoslovak rocket tubes assembled in Romania.

Sources: Jane's All the World's Aircraft, 1989–90; Jane's Infantry Weapons, 1989–90; Jane's Fighting Ships, 1989–90; Jane's Radar and EW Systems 1989–90; Jane's Military Communications 1989; Jane's Military Logistics 1988; Jane's Battlefield Air Defence 1988–89; Jane's Armour and Artillery, 1989–90.

the dependence on Soviet designs in different sectors is clearer. In aerospace, Czechoslovakia and Poland have the capacity to design aircraft. Romanian aircraft incorporate a considerable amount of Western design experience as well as sub-systems. The IAR-99 jet trainer is the product of Romanian–Yugoslavian collaboration in which the British company GEC and the French company Thomson-CSF provided most of the avionic equipment.[107] In terms of missile and land systems, all of the non-Soviet WTO countries are completely dependent on the Soviet Union. In terms of electronics (and especially computer software) the GDR and Poland make an important contribution to the overall technology base of the WTO. However, the design and production capabilities are limited compared with those of the Soviet Union.

The lack of information makes it very difficult to assess the implications of recent developments for the arms industries in non-Soviet WTO countries. Of the Soviet allies, only Czechoslovakia has a long tradition of producing armaments: the Skoda Works in Pilsen began producing weapons in the 1880s.[108] The arms industry experienced several cyclical periods between 1945 and 1990. In the late 1950s and early 1960s, more than two-thirds of state investments were reserved for the arms industry. This emphasis was changed. In the 1970s, however, the licensed production of heavy Soviet weapon systems (tanks and fighter aircraft) practically ceased. Production for the armed forces was reoriented and concentrated mainly on heavy, indigenously developed weapon systems in sectors with close links to civilian products (i.e., trucks and light aircraft). At the end of the 1980s a new trend emerged again. Similar to the USSR, the Czechoslovak Government announced in May 1989 unilateral reductions of military personnel, equipment and a cut in arms production of 16 per cent in 1989 and 25 per cent in 1990.[109] Observers in Czechoslovakia point to the fact that the industry has experience in relocating and reorienting production and point to both the period during World War II when production was for strategic reasons moved to the eastern part of the country and to the cold war period when arms production was moved away from the big cities. As a contributing factor to a swift transition to non-military production, it is mentioned that the arms factories are already engaged outside the arms sector: that is, in producing locomotives, equipment for nuclear reactors, office equipment and agricultural machinery. On the other side, it is pointed out at the same time that factories have difficulties since previously ordered equipment has been cancelled and because the conversion decision has been taken *ad hoc* without any advance planning.[110]

According to information in the West and official GDR data, arms production in the GDR seems to be small and will be reduced as a result of cuts in military expenditures that have been announced in conjunction with other

[107] *Jane's All the World's Aircraft 1989–90* (Jane's: Coulsdon, 1989), pp. 143–44.

[108] Tiedtke, St., 'Czechoslovakia', in Ball and Leitenberg (note 59), pp. 181–213.

[109] Matousek, J., 'Aktuelle Probleme der Konversion von Rüstungsproduktion in der Tschechoslowakei', paper presented at the Academy of Sciences of the GDR, Berlin (GDR), 7 Nov. 1989.

[110] Note 109, pp. 3–5.

Table 8.12. Share of arms exports as a percentage of total exports in the non-Soviet WTO countries, 1977–87

Country	1977	1982	1987
Bulgaria	0.2	3.3	2.8
Czechoslovakia	6.7	4.2	4.1
GDR	0.7	0.7	0.7
Poland	3.4	5.9	6.6
Romania	0.6	3.1	2.4[a]

[a] 1986.

Source: US Arms Control and Disarmament Agency, *World Military Expenditures and Arms Transfers 1988* (ACDA: Washington, DC, 1989), table II.

WTO countries. For the first time official figures—that cannot be verified—were given in November 1989: 'Only a few tens of thousands are employed in the defence industry'. Compared to the Federal Republic of Germany, it is said in this information: 'In the GDR the share of defence production is much lower and varies in different industrial branches between 0.2 and 2.0 per cent. These are orders of magnitude that can easily be converted, given good preparation.'[111]

The GDR industry is engaged in small arms production and specializes within the WTO in optics, electronics and components. Whether or not these products are included in the figures mentioned above is not known.

Information released concerning Poland is both very interesting in itself and because it further underlines the need for caution in accepting previous estimates of defence industrial capacities in the WTO. Western estimates of Polish tank production are impossible to confirm and are treated with scepticism within Eastern Europe even by groups which have no interest in shielding the truth. Western estimates put Polish tank production in the 1980s at 700 (1980), 500 (1981), 600 (1982), 550 (1983), 450 (1984) and at 700 per year since 1985.[112] However, in October 1989 the newspaper of Solidarity in Poland noted that 'production capabilities of the Polish defence industry have been and still are overestimated both by Western intelligence and Polish society. The more secrecy concerning production the greater the myths.'[113] When this newspaper article appeared, Solidarity was part of the government in Poland and had access to official data. While production of arms in the WTO is highly concentrated in the USSR, for Poland and Czechoslovakia, arms exports nevertheless play an important role in their foreign trade (see table 8.12). This trade takes place to a large extent

---

[111] Engelhardt, K. and Rechtziegler, E., 'Rüstungskonversion—neue Dimensionen und Herausforderungen', paper presented at Akademie der Wissenschaften, GDR, Berlin (GDR), 7 Nov. 1989, p. 17 and p. 22; translation supplied.

[112] *Soviet Military Power 1985* (US Government Printing Office: Washington, DC, 1985); *Jane's Armour and Artillery 1989–90* (Jane's: Coulsdon, 1989).

[113] 'The vicious circle of arms', *Gazeta Wyborcza*, 10 Oct. 1989; translation supplied.

between the WTO countries, but a substantial portion of arms goes to Third World countries (see chapter 7). According to US information, in some years arms exports made up 6.6 per cent of foreign trade for Poland and 6.7 per cent for Czechoslovakia.

The future of arms production in Poland: 'you can't produce a computer with a hammer'[114]

The principal recent development in Poland has been the acknowledgement that a realistic debate about future alternatives requires a realistic set of data on which to base judgements. No such acknowledgement has been made by other WTO countries, but it is interesting to note information which became available for the first time in 1989.

In Poland the arms industrial base consists of two kinds of enterprise: those acknowledged as having 'special production' and other enterprises. An industrial plant with 'special production' is one in which a minimum of 20 per cent of total sales are to military customers. Apparently 80 of these employ a total of 260 000 people and together supply roughly two-thirds of all Polish military production, the rest being in enterprises with less than 20 per cent of sales to the military.[115] In total, military production represents roughly 3 per cent of total Polish industrial production.[116] In the first six months of 1989, 8.1 per cent of all orders placed by the Polish Ministry of Industry were with factories known to have some military production.

All Polish factories known to have 'special production' also produce some civilian items, but on average, 70 per cent of total production in this sector in 1988 was military production. This had increased from 60 per cent in the previous year but whether this reflects increased military production, decreased civil production or a combination of both is not known.[117]

In 1987 factories known to be involved in defence production also produced 10 500 trucks for civilian customers (in addition to military vehicles); 1350 caravans and trailers; 480 000 televisions, 3.2 million pressurized bottles for butane-type gases; 378 000 radios and cassette recorders; and 15 000 video recorders, in addition to large amounts of kitchen equipment.[118]

The need to increase civilian production and seek external markets is likely to become greater for the defence sector in Poland because of the cuts in the orders for the period 1991–95 placed by the Ministry of Defence. The cuts in orders have been made in response to reductions in the level of man-

[114] Dziadul, J., interview with Zdzislaw Kopczyk, manager at the Bumar Labedy tank plant, in *Polityka*, 14 Oct. 1989.
[115] Bobinski, C., 'Polish arms-makers look for sales in plough-shares market', *Financial Times*, 8 Nov. 1989.
[116] Zukrowska, K., 'The organisation of the Polish arms trade', unpublished paper, Oct. 1989.
[117] Equally, whether the calculation is based on value of sales, value of turnover, cost of production, unit production or some other indicator is not known.
[118] 'The vicious circle of arms', *Gazeta Wyborcza*, 10 Oct. 1989.

power and equipment announced by then Defence Minister Florian Siwicki in January 1989.[119]

In this environment of declining domestic demand the defence sector in Poland is likely to come under increasing economic pressure, some evidence of which is already visible. Plans to reduce the level of output in the WSK Swidnik plant, which manufactures wing assemblies and helicopter assemblies for Soviet aircraft produced under licence in Poland, were among the factors which led to a two-day strike. Another was the decision by the management at the plant not to use more than 30 per cent of capacity in a new joint venture with an Italian company for the production of an Italian-designed tractor. The decision not to retool and convert the entire factory was apparently partly the result of the reluctance of the Ministry of Defence to allow factories to give up the ability to restore military production levels should the international environment change.[120]

There is also a lack of specific information about the nature of past and current conversion initiatives in Poland (as elsewhere in the WTO). As noted above, whether or not an industrial plant is engaged in military production is largely determined in the Polish context by the identity of customers rather than by the nature of the products themselves. Also, as noted above, in all Polish defence companies military and civil production takes place side by side. Therefore, the sale of goods such as trucks, earth movers, helicopters or radars to civilian customers rather than the military is, by one definition, 'conversion'. However, it requires no structural changes in the industrial base and would also meet the Ministry of Defence criterion to retain military production capacities.

Defence industrial managers are apparently sceptical about how much farther the process of conversion can be taken for economic, as well as political, reasons. The senior managers of the Bumar Labedy plant where tanks are produced have stated that they are already making considerable efforts to convert to the production of heavy machinery for the agricultural and construction sector in Poland. This kind of equipment represents the second most important activity after tank production. However, the market for heavy equipment of the kind noted is limited and, in the opinion of the Director General of the plant, Ryszard Jankowski (also a Member of Parliament), simply closing the plant would be less of a drain on the Polish economy than remodelling the factory to produce totally different products.[121]

From the point of view of the factory management, arms exports (especially exports to countries outside the WTO) may be an easier alternative than conversion to civil production. The expected earnings from civil production (which have to compete in the global market) are apparently low

---

[119] In addition to a 4 per cent reduction in the military budget, Poland announced manpower cuts in the 'tens of thousands' to be achieved through retirements and mobilizing smaller numbers of reservists. *Jane's Defence Weekly*, 14 Jan. 1989, p. 43.

[120] Bobinski, C., 'Polish arms-makers look for sales in plough-shares market', *Financial Times*, 8 Nov. 1989; Dziadul, J., interviews with Director General Jankowski in *Polityka*, 14 Oct. 1989.

[121] Dziadul (note 120).

compared to those from arms exports (where the nature of competition is very different). The overall profit from tank exports by Poland greatly exceeds that from civilian automobiles on a 'return per kilo' basis.[122] Arms exports, especially to the Middle East, are preferred to sales to the Ministry of Defence. Whereas some Middle Eastern countries such as Iraq and Libya make payments in a mix of commodities and currency, Bumar Labedy is owed 7 billion zlotys by the Polish Ministry of Defence and is threatening legal action to recover this.[123]

From the economic standpoint, the shipbuilding sector is also in a difficult position when it comes to replacing the Ministry of Defence with other customers. The level of demand for Polish merchant shipping is low, which forces merchant shipbuilders to export in what is already an extremely competitive sector of the international economy.

VI. Conclusions

The Soviet position at the CFE negotiation suggests that the period in which the USSR and its allies tried to compensate with the deployment of large numbers of weapons to offset the technological edge of NATO, and especially the United States, is over. In order to confront domestic economic difficulties, President Gorbachev is prepared to accept lower numbers of weapons in the European military theatre than previously without making any visible technological leap in the quality of Soviet weapons.

This chapter points out that the United States is, in some fields, moving from the development to the deployment of a new generation of military technology. In other areas research efforts are being intensified. Long-range planners in the Soviet Union are having to contemplate a strategic environment in which new actors are beginning to emerge around the periphery of the Soviet Union—in Europe, in Japan and elsewhere in Asia. At the same time the future development of the Warsaw Treaty Organization has become less than certain as allied communist parties, which would formerly have looked to the USSR for support in times of domestic uncertainty, are encouraged to 'do it their way' in the words of Gennadiy Gerasimov's 'Sinatra Doctrine'.

The status of the Soviet Union as a superpower has rested on its military and not its economic power. As the numbers of some categories of conventional weapons will probably be drastically reduced by the Soviet Union, technological development will become even more important than in the past. Unless the Soviet Union can, through the arms control process, change the current trend in military and technological development, it might find itself becoming a secondary military power compared with the United States. This in itself might shape the future military policy of Soviet leaders.

[122] Exports from military production are apparently worth around 320 million zlotys per year, although two-thirds of this goes to WTO countries. 'The vicious circle of arms', *Gazeta Wyborcza*, 10 Oct. 1989; Zukrowska, K., 'The organisation of the Polish arms trade', unpublished paper, Oct. 1989.
[123] Dziadul (note 120).

The USSR may be forced to engage in higher investment in military R&D and programmes aimed at compensation for asymmetric arms control agreements (especially in the naval sphere), even though these are detrimental to economic improvement. At present the contradiction still remains between high investments in new weapon technologies—for weapons that the industry eventually wants to produce—and budgetary constraints that will not allow all of these new programmes to progress from development to production. The question for political leaders in East and West is whether the strong economic and security incentives existing in both the USSR and Western countries to make far-reaching cuts in the military sector, including arms production, represent an opportunity that they can afford to pass over. The arms-producing companies—especially in Western Europe but to some extent in the United States as well—are confronted with a situation in which their business interests might be critically endangered by political improvements. The way in which military equipment has been procured in the past has led to cyclical fluctuations in arms sales of companies with underutilised capacities and layoffs in certain periods and a boom in industry in other periods. The present situation, however, is fundamentally different. Unless a frosty climate or a cold war is introduced again between East and West, the arms industrial base has to be substantially reduced in both major alliances. To what extent this reduction is necessary, of course, depends entirely on the magnitude of cuts in procurement. Since over-capacities already exist—with additional capacities in the stage of installation in Third World countries and Japan—governments in the West should seriously plan for conversion of parts of the arms industry; otherwise corporations may truly consider themselves as 'victims of peace'.

9. Ballistic missile proliferation

AARON KARP

I. Introduction

Concern over the proliferation of ballistic missiles reached a new and unprecedented level of intensity in 1989. This is partially due to the sharp reduction in tension between the superpowers, especially in Europe where the threat of war has receded dramatically: as traditional security fears ease, more attention is devoted to regional conflicts as posing a more immediate danger to international peace and stability. The close relationship between the most serious proliferation threats—ballistic missiles, and the nuclear, chemical or biological warheads they can carry—has created a new fear of arms races among emerging regional powers.

Growing concern is also caused by the accelerated pace of disclosures about regional ballistic missile programmes. Not only is missile proliferation a growing political issue, but much more information is also becoming available about the spread of ballistic missiles and related technologies. Only five years ago, very little was known about domestic missile programmes other than those of the traditional powers, even for countries such as Brazil and India, with long-standing programmes.[1] By the late 1980s, important details had become available on ballistic missile and related projects in 26 countries. While much more is known about some countries than others, the data available are sufficient to make it clear that the problem of ballistic missile proliferation has reached global proportions.

Table 9.1 summarizes the data publicly available on emerging ballistic missile and related programmes, as of 31 December 1989. The table shows the extent of missile proliferation among the countries involved and facilitates comparisons of the programmes themselves. It includes all known long-range missile programmes, including those cancelled before series production or deployment began. Short-range rocket projects are included when they indicate a country's highest level of technical accomplishment, as in the Philippines and Thailand. Civilian sub-orbital sounding rockets and space launch vehicle programmes are also included because of their inherent similarities with military rockets. Cruise missiles are not included owing to difficulties in finding comparable data, although some analysts[2] are convinced that they pose threats similar to those posed by ballistic missiles.

---

[1] For comparison, see Eisenstein, M., 'Third World missiles and nuclear cooperation', *Washington Quarterly* vol. 5, no. 3 (summer 1982), pp. 112–15; and Karp, A., 'Ballistic missile proliferation in the Third World', *International Security*, vol. 9, no. 3 (winter 1984/85), especially pp. 183–84.
[2] For example, W. Seth Carus of the US Naval War College Foundation, and Henry Sokolski and Richard Speier of the US Department of Defense.

II. Table of ballistic misiles

The table covers 116 missiles and missile programmes in 26 countries. The data are arranged in five categories, explained below.

Classifications

Four basic types of rocket are listed: large civilian sounding rockets (SRs) used primarily for atmospheric and rocketry research but convertible for ground-to-ground attack; artillery rockets (ARs), which traditionally are much smaller than ballistic missiles but which increasingly are capable of ranges of 40–120 kilometres—the same as a small ballistic missile—and which can form the basis for later ballistic missile development pro-grammes; ballistic missiles (BMs); and space launch vehicles (SLVs) which can be converted into long-range ballistic missiles.[3]

Stages, weight and range

These parameters offer the simplest guide to the overall capability and sophistication of a particular missile and a country's technical and industrial abilities in rocketry. Multi-stage rockets have only recently been acquired by countries in the Third World and remain confined to the most advanced countries, although many more countries are planning multi-stage ballistic missiles and SLVs in the 1990s. Weights have been rising as well. In the 1980s several countries introduced intermediate-range ballistic missiles (IRBMs) and SLVs weighing over 15 000 kg. Some are planning much larger vehicles with an intercontinental ballistic missile (ICBM) potential. Other countries, however, are developing highly sophisticated missiles with more efficient designs and lower total weight, such as the Israeli Jericho 2 and the multinational Condor 2 missiles.

Year first fired

This refers to the year in which a country first successfully launched the rocket or missile or, in the case of missiles received from abroad, when the system was first delivered. Unsuccessful tests and static (ground) test-firings are not counted.

Current status and number deployed

While general descriptions of emerging ballistic missile programmes can be found, their status and deployments usually remain closely guarded informa-tion and are difficult to estimate. Many programmes are listed in table 9.1 as

---

[3] Balaschak, M., Ruina, J., Steinberg, G. and Yaron, A., *Assessing the Comparability of Dual-Use Technologies for Ballistic Missile Development* (Center for International Studies, Massachusetts Institute of Technology: Cambridge, Mass., June 1981).

under development, but it is often impossible to ascertain how many years away they are from static tests, first flight-test or deployment. Estimates of the number of missiles deployed and the number of launchers—which determine the scale and speed with which a missile attack can be conducted—are even more elusive.

Technology suppliers and technologies supplied

Except for cases where whole missile systems were transferred from a foreign supplier, virtually all emerging ballistic missile and space launch programmes rely extensively on imported components and technical and manufacturing assistance. The entries in table 9.1 list suppliers of technologies known to be important to the programme in question. It is usually not possible to list all suppliers, to rank them in order of importance or to establish whether their assistance was legally licensed or acquired illegally.

Among the most politically significant aspects of any long-range missile programme is its *armament*, especially now that ballistic missile proliferation is inherently related to the proliferation of the nuclear, chemical and biological weapons (CBW) which they may carry. Unfortunately, this question is also among the most poorly understood. While it may be known whether a country is capable of producing nuclear, chemical or biological weapons, there is usually not sufficient data to determine more than whether that country's ballistic missiles are nuclear- or CBW-capable. Information concerning the actual armament is usually not available and remains a subject of speculation.

III. Ballistic missile proliferation in 1989

The 1980s witnessed the transformation of ballistic missile proliferation from a relatively minor international question to an issue at the top of the international agenda.The growing importance of the issue was clearly established when it was placed on the agenda of the 29 May–2 June 1988 US–Soviet Moscow summit meeting. Its salience was reaffirmed at the 22–23 September 1989 Wyoming meeting between US Secretary of State James Baker and Soviet Foreign Minister Eduard Shevardnadze. Their joint statement on arms control noted 'the importance of joint efforts by the United States and the Soviet Union to prevent the proliferation of missiles and missile technology and agreed to activate bilateral consultations on this pressing problem.'[4]

With the emergence of this new and unpredictable threat to international peace and security, Foreign Minister Shevardnadze reminded the delegates at the opening of the Vienna Negotiation on Conventional Armed Forces in Europe (CFE) on 6 March 1989 that, 'In the Middle East and Southwest

---

[4] 'Documents from the foreign ministers' meeting', *Arms Control Today*, Oct. 1989, p. 22.

Asia—that is, in close proximity to Europe—powerful weapons arsenals are being created, that is to say, of precisely the same class that is being eliminated in Europe. . . . The conclusion is obvious: the process of disarmament in Europe and the settlement in the Middle East have to be synchronized.'[5] A few days later, the US Director of Central Intelligence, William Webster, reaffirmed that the new threat was indeed global, telling an audience in Los Angeles that, 'By the year 2000, at least 15 developing countries will be producing their own ballistic missiles.'[6]

Efforts to control ballistic missile proliferation continue to be dominated by US initiatives. President George Bush and Secretary of State Baker have repeatedly spoken of the significance of weapon proliferation—ballistic missiles, and nuclear, chemical and biological weapons—for international security.[7] Baker raised the question of controlling missile technology exports with Shevardnadze when they met in Moscow in May 1989.[8] US officials placed ballistic missile proliferation among a 'fifth basket' of global issues that also includes the environment, illegal drugs and terrorism, issues on which common Soviet–US interests could lead to new forms of bilateral co-operation.[9] Later in the year, speaking in Berlin on the future of Europe and NATO, Baker noted that, 'Regional conflicts, along with the proliferation of missiles and nuclear, chemical and biological weapons, present growing dangers. Intensified Nato consultations on these issues can play an important role in forming common Western approaches to these various threats.'[10] However, specific proposals for better addressing the ballistic missile proliferation threat have not been made.

IV. The future of the MTCR

Control policies continue to centre on the 1987 Missile Technology Control Regime (MTCR).[11] This informal agreement among seven Western nations—Britain, Canada, France, the Federal Republic of Germany, Italy, Japan and the United States—to prohibit exports of ballistic missiles and

[5] Quoted in Friedman, T. L., 'Soviet Mideast diplomacy linked to missile fears', *International Herald Tribune*, 26 Mar. 1989, p. 1.
[6] Speech by William Webster before the Town Hall of Los Angeles, Calif., 30 Mar. 1989, USIS Press Release, 1 Apr. 1989.
[7] For example, see President Bush, 'Security Strategy for the 1990s', Address before the US Coast Guard Academy, 24 May 1989, *Current Policy*, no. 1178, US Department of State; US Secretary of State James Baker, 'The international agenda and FY 1990 Budget Request', *Current Policy*, no. 1147, US Department of State; and US Secretary of State James Baker, 'The challenge of change in US–Soviet relations', address before the Center for Strategic and International Studies, 4 May 1989, *Current Policy*, no. 1170, US Department of State.
[8] Friedman, T. L., 'A new basket of superpower issues', *International Herald Tribune*, 6–7 May 1989, p. 1.
[9] See note 8.
[10] 'Baker outlines blueprint for new era in Europe (Text: Secretary of State's address to Berlin Press Club)', United States Information Service, Press Section, Embassy of the United States of America, Stockholm, WIRE, 12 Dec. 1989, excerpted in 'Baker's new Europe: "A new Atlanticism"', *International Herald Tribune*, 14 Dec. 1989, p. 4.
[11] 'The Missile Technology Control Regime: statement by the Assistant to the President for Press Relations' and 'Fact sheet to accompany public announcement', White House, Santa Barbara, Calif., 16 Apr. 1987.

related technologies has been criticized as inadequate to deal with the problem. In five US congressional hearings held on missile proliferation in 1989, the weaknesses of the MTCR were continually emphasized.[12] It was argued, among other things, that the MTCR includes too few participants, is poorly enforced and does nothing about regional ballistic missile forces already in being.

Yet the MTCR was strengthened in 1989. *Spain* became the eighth nation to join the group. And *Sweden*, while refusing to compromise its non-alignment by joining the MTCR, adopted similar export restrictions.[13] The MTCR was also strengthened by the December decision of participating governments in London to hold regular meetings to discuss MTCR disputes and challenges.[14]

Enforcement of MTCR export restrictions also became more rigorous in several countries. US congressional concern led to the presentation of four bills to strengthen MTCR enforcement. Reacting to disclosures that major European defence contractors were involved in regional ballistic missile programmes and the discovery that US firms sold much of the dual-use manufacturing and testing equipment installed in Iraqi missile facilities, these bills emphasized sanctions against firms violating MTCR provisions. The proposed Missile Technology Control Act of 1989 (HR 963, sponsored by Representative Howard Berman, Democrat, California) sought to forbid the US Government to buy from firms violating the MTCR. This was passed by the House of Representatives in July 1989 by a vote of 417 to 9 as an amendment to the House Defense Authorization Act of 1990. Similar legislation was proposed in the US Senate.[15] The Administration sought to preempt the new legislation by amending the existing Federal Defense Acquisition Regulations with provisions similar to the proposed legislation.[16] The issue is not resolved, and further US legislative action is possible in 1990.

US customs authorities and state and federal courts took a leading role in individual cases. US citizens were found guilty of conspiring to smuggle advanced rocket materials to Egypt and indicted for smuggling guidance technology to South Africa.[17] Federal banking inspectors investigated allegations that the Atlanta branch of the Italian bank BNL provided over $3

[12] US congressional hearings in 1989 concentrating on ballistic missile proliferation were held by the Senate Armed Services Committee, Subcommittee on Defense Industry and Technology, 2 May 1989; Senate Committee on Governmental Affairs, 18 May 1989; Joint Hearings of the House Foreign Affairs Committee, Subcommittee on Arms Control and Trade, 12 July 1989; Separate Hearings before the Senate Foreign Relations Committee and House Foreign Affairs Committee on 31 Oct. 1989; House Foreign Affairs Committee, Subcommittee on the Middle East, 7 Nov. 1989.

[13] Anderson, B. G., ['Weapons technology export controls considered'], *Dagens Nyheter* (Stockholm), 17 Feb. 1989, p. 6 (in Swedish).

[14] Mallet, V., 'Iraq says it tested rocket for space', *Financial Times*, 8 Dec,. 1989, p. 5; and author's discussions with US and British government officials.

[15] Silverberg, D., 'MTCR proposals excepted to ignite friction in Congress, among allies', *Defense News*, 4 Sep. 1989, p. 31.

[16] Starr, B., 'USA debates missile proliferation', *Jane's Defence Weekly*, 11 Nov. 1989, p. 1345; and 'The Pentagon has broadened . . .', *Aviation Week & Space Technology*, 27 Nov. 1989, p. 15.

[17] 'Jail term for a missile crime', *New York Times*, 7 Dec. 1989, p. A12; Weisensee, N., 'Bid to sell US gyroscopes to S. Africa', *Boston Globe*, 17 Nov. 1989, p. 4.

billion in loans for Iraqi military industries, including perhaps $1 billion for ballistic missile projects. Proposed exports of supercomputers to Brazil and Israel, permitted under the MTCR, came under sharp debate since they could be used in ballistic missile development programmes.[18] Several disputes with other governments were addressed bilaterally, as discussed below.

The situation in *the Federal Republic of Germany* continued to be dominated by export policy and enforcement disputes. Largely in reaction to revelations of co-operation by firms from FR Germany in Libya's Rabta chemical weapon plant and the Argentinian–Egyptian–Iraqi Condor 2 IRBM, Chancellor Helmut Kohl presented to the Bundestag a plan for the revision of export regulations and expansion of oversight staff. The issue of civil penalties was raised, but proposed export restrictions have been stalled, while expansion of oversight staff has been slowed by hiring problems.[19] The West German judiciary has been more active, conducting investigations of the alleged involvement of the aerospace giant Messerschmitt-Bölkow-Blohm (MBB) in the Condor 2, and convicting the Munich firm Globe-Sat of aiding ballistic missile work in Libya.[20]

The *British* Government has actively promoted the MTCR by hosting several of its meetings and lobbying both participating and non-participating governments to adhere to its terms. British firms were not implicated in ballistic missile proliferation until the autumn of 1989, when Matrix-Churchill Machine Tools came under investigation for supplying Iraq with suspect equipment, part of the BNL-Atlanta affair.[21]

Italian military export policy remains in flux, subject to a long and unpredictable debate that obscures the future direction of Italian policy on missile technology controls. Nevertheless, in July 1989 charges were brought against former employees of SNIA-BDP, one of Italy's largest defence contractors, after a six-year investigation of involvement in the Condor 2 programme.[22]

Sweden launched an inquiry into alleged co-operation by Bofors in the Condor 2 programme as well.[23] Several reports also point to major roles in

[18] Friedman, A., 'BNL affair underlines West's fears over technology transfer', *Financial Times*, Survey: Italian banking, 22 Nov. 1989, p. III.

[19] Schultze, H., 'West Germany moves to tighten export controls', *Jane's Defence Weekly*, 1 July 1989, p. 1345; March, D., 'MBB chief urges easing of arms control rules', *Financial Times*, 8 Sep. 1989, p. 1; 'Rüstungsexporte beschränkt', *Frankfurter Rundshau*, 15 June 1989, p. 1.

[20] Henderson, S. and Goodhart, D., 'Prosecutor launches inquiry into MBB's Condor missile links', *Financial Times*, 12 Apr. 1989; 'German firm fines for missile parts sale', *Defense News*, 16 Oct. 1989, p. 60.

[21] Garnett, N. and Donkin, R., 'UK company confirms sale of weapons machinery to Iraq', *Financial Times*, 8 Sep. 1989, p. 1; White, D. and Henderson, S., 'Growing concern over Western aid for Third World's missiles', *Financial Times*, 8 Sep. 1989, p. 2.

[22] Silverberg, D., 'Developing nations open new doors to acquire missile technology', *Defense News*, 4 Sep. 1989, p. 30.

[23] Burton, J. and Friedman, A., 'Stockholm investigates Bofors over missile claims', *Financial Times*, 8 Nov. 1989, p. 2.

the Condor 2 programme by Austrian, French and Swiss firms, although no official action appears to have been taken in those countries.[24]

While progress was made towards strengthening the MTCR, the regime continues to come under serious challenges to its comprehensiveness and legitimacy. The most serious challenges come from non-participants, especially the Soviet Union and China. In bilateral discussions, Soviet officials have publicly expressed their sympathy for the MTCR. Soviet territory is facing growing threats from long-range ballistic missiles under development in countries near its borders. However, the Soviet Union objects to the current MTCR approach. Soviet Deputy Foreign Minister Victor Karpov observed in May 1989 that the MTCR 'only includes the suppliers of missiles and missile technology. Moreover, it has no common rigid criteria for the degree of limitations on the supplies of relevant materials, nor for a range of countries on which they may be imposed. Each participant has the right to decide these questions at his own discretion.'[25] Other Soviet officials speak of the need for an approach encouraging co-operation on peaceful uses of outer space. Foreign observers argue that Moscow also may be trying to protect its right to supply Scud ballistic missiles (280-km range) to regional clients and allies.[26] The Soviet Union has shown restraint by refusing to supply clients with larger missiles.[27]

In 1988 Chinese leaders assured Western officials that China's efforts to sell ballistic missiles in the Middle East had ceased. Following the bloody suppression of the Tiananmen Square protests in June 1989 and the strong Western reaction, however, Beijing reversed policy on many issues. US officials have stated that China has apparently resumed negotiations to supply ballistic missiles to Middle Eastern countries.[28] In private meetings, Soviet officials brought up the issue with Chinese leaders but found them unresponsive.[29]

Events in 1989 also revealed substantial disagreements among MTCR participants regarding interpretation of the agreement. The most serious of these arose from a French offer of Ariane Viking rocket engine technology to Brazil. The offer, intended to entice Brazil to buy French communications satellites, drew criticism from the US Government, as a potential violation of the MTCR. This culminated in a formal *démarche* in July. French officials responded that the 1987 agreement explicitly permits transfers of rocket technology for civilian programmes such as the Brazilian space

[24] George, A. and Langsner, H., 'Reigen der Raketen', *Profil* (Vienna), no. 12 (20 Mar. 1989), pp. 36–38; George, A. and Langsner, H., 'Tot durch DOT', *Profil* (Vienna), no. 17 (24 Apr. 1989); 'Alles ganz harmlos', *Der Spiegel*, no. 13 (27 Mar. 1989), pp. 170–73.

[25] See Silverberg, D., 'MTCR more likely to lure Soviet Union than China', *Defense News*, 4 Sep. 1989, p. 31.

[26] See note 25.

[27] 'Syria asks for SS-23', *Flight International*, 16 Sep. 1989, p. 9.

[28] Gordon, M. R., 'US worries that China may again sell missiles', *New York Times*, 9 Nov. 1989, p. A14. Alternatively, Israeli sources state that Syria and other Arab nations may buy Chinese ballistic missiles from North Korea; 'Israel cites signs of missile deals', *International Herald Tribune*, 30 Dec. 1989–1 Jan. 1990, p. 2.

[29] This was reported to SIPRI in a private conversation with Soviet officials after Gorbachev's state visit to China.

launch programme. Arianespace executives added that the US complaint was a commercially motivated attempt to win the Brazilian satellite order for McDonnell Douglas of the USA. The Brazilian Government insisted that the Viking engine technology would not be used for military purposes.[30]

The French offer of Viking rocket engine technology to Brazil exposes one of the most ambiguous aspects of the MTCR: its distinction between proscribed assistance for regional ballistic missile programmes and permissible assistance for civilian space launch projects. Analysts have long argued that there is no clear distinction between military and civilian rocket technology; rather, most rocket technology is inherently dual-purpose. Safeguards to ensure that rocket technology is used exclusively for civilian purposes have not yet been developed. The MTCR exception for civilian rocket exports, originally included to broaden the regime's appeal to France and other export-oriented participants, now threatens to undo the agreement. If the French proposal becomes policy, other would-be missile proliferators could acquire the necessary foreign technology simply by claiming that it is being purchased for civilian applications. British, Canadian and US officials pressed the French at the December MTCR meeting in London to drop the offer to Brazil and preserve the integrity of the MTCR, keeping shut a loophole that could undermine its credibility.[31]

Too little, too late?

While few believe that MTCR-style export restrictions will control the proliferation of ballistic missiles in the long run, the restrictions have slowed the spread of ballistic missiles. Events and disclosures in 1989 revealed that many of the most prominent regional ballistic missile and space launch programmes have encountered serious obstacles owing to lack of foreign technology and assistance. Programmes have also encountered other barriers, especially financial problems and problems resulting from indecisive national decision-making. Although many programmes slowed down in 1989, none stopped altogether. In other countries, missile programmes are making impressive progress.

The clearest example of a slowed regional ballistic missile programme is the Argentinian–Egyptian–Iraqi Condor 2 IRBM (1000-km range). Development work, centred in Argentina, has reportedly been difficult since the flow of Western technology was restrained in 1988. Argentina's inability to manufacture adequate guidance systems and engine casings rules out mass production for the time being. In Egypt, revelations of a high-level conspiracy to smuggle propellant, nose-cone and engine materials from the United States in support of the Condor 2 led to the resignation of Egyptian

---

[30] Davis, B., 'Arianespace offer to Brazil raises US ire', *Wall Street Journal*, European edn, 18 July 1989, p. 2; Silverberg, D., 'French proposal may violate pact on proliferation', *Defense News*, 17 July 1989, p. 4; Gordon, M. R., 'US seeks to stop Brazil's missile-technology deal', *New York Times*, 19 Oct. 1989, p. A6.

[31] Author's discussions with US and British government officials. The London MTCR meeting is noted in Mallet (note 14).

Defence Minister Field Marshal Abdel Halim Abu Ghazala in April 1989. US Assistant Secretary of State John H. Kelly subsequently testified before Congress that Egypt had withdrawn from the Condor 2 programme. The factories that Egypt built for its own production of the missile remain dormant, but Egypt's other ballistic missile programme—manufacturing an improved version of the Soviet-designed Scud—appears to be continuing. The state of Iraqi participation in the Condor 2 is unclear; while President Saddam Hussein has built missile development and production facilities worth over $3 billion, there is no evidence that the Condor 2 is advancing there.[32]

In the mid-1980s, Brazil commissioned several ballistic missile programmes and a large civilian space launcher. The Avibras SS-300 project, thought to be the furthest developed of Brazil's ballistic missile projects, was suspended in 1989 because of lack of funding.[33] Avibras hopes that this and other ballistic missile projects will be revived later. The VLS space launcher has been protracted by a combination of problems. Although the project reached an important milestone with the launching of a one-third sized version of the VLS on 18 May 1989, the first launch of the actual VLS has slipped to 1992 at the earliest.[34] Brazilian officials have stated that the MTCR is largely responsible for their slow progress. The VLS also has encountered domestic opposition from the National Space Research Institute (INPE) which prefers less expensive foreign launch services.[35]

India's ballistic missile and space launch programmes are more advanced and productive, but they have not been immune to technical, financial and political difficulties. In 1989 India unveiled a new artillery rocket programme and continued to develop the Prithvi 240-km missile.[36] On 22 May 1989 India's Defence Research and Development Laboratories launched the Agni, a 2500-km range 'technology demonstrator', proving that India has the ability to manufacture IRBMs. The Agni is based on the civilian SLV-3 space launcher, first launched in 1980 by the Indian Space Research Organization.[37] A recent report establishes that the SLV-3 and the Agni rely on foreign technologies acquired in the 1960s and 1970s, especially design concepts from the United States and engine, nose-cone and guidance technology from FR Germany.[38] As access to foreign technology became

[32] The Condor 2 programme is examined in Friedman, A., 'The flight of the Condor', *Financial Times*, 21 Nov. 1989, p. 10; also see the articles by George and Langsner (note 18). On Egyptian participation, see Cowell, A., 'Cairo aide's ouster tied to effort to get missile parts in US', *New York Times*, 18 Apr. 1989, p. A8; and Ottaway, D. B., 'Egypt drops out of missile project', *Washington Post*, 20 Sep. 1989, p. 32.

[33] Letter to the author from Daniel, Jr. M., Commercial Division, Avibras Indústria Aeroespacial S. A., São José dos Campos, Brazil, 18 Oct. 1989; and Foss, C. F., 'Brazilian programmes being held up by funds shortages', *Jane's Defence Weekly*, 27 May 1989, p. 1009.

[34] Bonalume Neto, R., 'Brazil's two-thirds VLS success', *Nature*, 1 June 1989, p. 329.

[35] Turner, R., 'Brazil says missile technology controls hamper launch industry', *Defense News*, 24 July 1989, p. 18; 'Brazilian space chaos', *Spaceflight*, vol. 31 (June 1989), p. 187.

[36] 'Second successful launch of Prithvi', *Indian Express* (New Delhi), 28 Sep. 1989.

[37] The objectives and accomplishments of the Agni project are described in Nanda, S. P. and Menon, M. C., 'Fire in the sky', *Sunday* (Calcutta), 4 May 1989.

[38] Milholin, G., *Research Report: West German Aid to India's Rocket Program* (Wisconsin Project on Nuclear Arms Control: Washington, DC, 11 Apr. 1989). Indian press reports sought to refute

more restricted in the 1980s, Indian programmes have slowed. Efforts in 1989 to acquire French liquid-fuelled engine technology and US testing equipment were unsuccessful. This and ordinary development problems have compelled India to reduce the number of planned launches and slow the pace of its large rocket programme. The civilian launch programme has also been weakened by the diversion of financial and technical resources to military missiles. India remains firmly committed to its broad rocket and missile programme. Unlike Brazil, India has not suspended work on any of its major missile projects.[39]

Another country encountering difficulties is Saudi Arabia. In March 1988 it was learned that Saudi Arabia had received 50–60 large DF-3 (CSS-2) IRBMs from China. China was heavily criticized for the deal and subsequently promised not to transfer more missiles to the Middle East. Two years after taking possession of the missiles, Saudi Arabia has still not been able to bring them into operation, according to US Assistant Secretary of State Richard A. Clarke. Again, technical difficulties appear to be delaying the programme.[40]

While restrictions on technology transfer slowed some regional ballistic missile programmes in 1989, others accelerated. This was the case in Afghanistan, where ballistic missiles were used on a scale unprecedented since 1945. Kabul Government forces fired over 1000 Soviet-supplied Scud missiles (280-km range) against Mujahideen guerrillas.[41] This was over twice the number of long-range missiles fired by Iran and Iraq during the 'War of the Cities'. In Afghanistan, ballistic missiles effectively replaced the bombing aircraft stymied by US-supplied Stinger anti-aircraft missiles. The impact is difficult to assess. By restoring the Kabul Government's ability to attack Mujahideen camps and bases, the Scuds helped slow the pace of the fighting, but the conventionally armed missiles have not helped to defeat the Mujahideen either. The most significant effect may be further erosion of restraints against the use of ballistic missiles, especially in regional conflicts.

Fighting with Iran ended in August 1988, but Iraq's missile programme continues to expand. Through a massive procurement programme under its Ministry of Industry and Military Industries, the Iraqi Military Production Authority made a major investment in missile factories near Baghdad and a research and development facility near Mosul in the mid-1980s. At least $3 billion was invested in Western technology to equip these facilities, much of it acquired illegally. A Swiss firm, Consen, co-ordinated much of

Milholin's conclusions. For example, see 'Agni developed indigenously', *The Statesman* (Delhi), 14 July 1989; and 'W. Germany refutes report on Agni', *Times of India* (New Delhi), 10 July 1989.

[39] On Indian efforts to acquire French Viking rocket engine technology, see 'To send up a moon', *The Statesman* (Delhi), 12 Mar. 1989. On US technology, see Ottaway, D. B., 'US to bar India's buying missile device', *Washington Post*, 17 July 1989, p. 12. The tensions and conflicts between India's civilian and military rocketry programmes are evaluated by Carus, W. S., 'India's ballistic missile program', unpublished manuscript (US Naval War College Foundation: Newport, R.I., 1 Dec. 1989).

[40] 'Saudi missiles not operational', *Defense News*, 13 Nov. 1989, p. 2.

[41] Pear, R., 'US asserts Soviet advisors are fighting in Afghanistan', *New York Times*, 10 Oct. 1989, p. A1.

this work, involving Austrian and West German construction firms, large quantities of equipment from FR Germany and the United States, financing through Italian and other banks, and extensive support from Egypt.[42]

The first results of the Iraqi ballistic missile programme were seen in the 1988 War of the Cities, in which Iraq fired almost 200 modified Scud missiles, the 650-km range al Hussein. A 900-km version, the al Abbas, was displayed at that time. Other projects were revealed at an arms exhibition in Baghdad in April 1989. These included several types of new artillery rocket with ranges of 8–110 km, ballistic missiles with ranges of 150, 250 and 500 km, and a new transporter-launcher vehicle based on a Swedish truck, the al Waleed.[43] The latter is especially important, since shortages of launchers apparently were the main factor limiting Iraqi missile attacks during the War of the Cities.[44]

Iraq's highly publicized involvement in the Condor 2 programme has not led to actual test-firings. Instead, foreign observers were surprised when Iraq launched the al Abed, a 48-ton, 25-metre high space launch vehicle on 5 December 1989, placing three objects in temporary orbit. Nothing is known about the sources of technology for the al Abed. Iraq also announced the development of a 2000-km range ballistic missile, the Tamuz-1, which may be the local version of the Condor 2.[45]

Israel's ballistic missile programme continued to make progress in 1989. The Soviet Union reported a 1300-km test-firing of the Israeli Jericho 2 missile, the fourth Israeli test since 1986 and the one over the longest distance so far. A declassified version of a US Defense Intelligence Agency report provided the first official indication that Israel's earlier Jericho 1 is capable of delivering nuclear and chemical as well as conventional warheads.[46]

Greater controversy was aroused by a report on 28 October 1989 quoting anonymous US Government sources confirming that South Africa launched an Israeli-supplied Jericho 2 ballistic missile on 5 July. The alleged co-operation would violate the spirit, if not the letter, of a March 1987 decision

[42] George, A., 'Condor-2 missile upsets Israel and the West', *Defense*, May 1989, pp. 305–309; Ottaway, D. B., 'US firms helped Iraq gain ability to make missiles, officials say', *Washington Post*, 3 May 1989, p. 19.

[43] The most comprehensive report of the 28 Apr.–2 May Baghdad International Exhibition for Military Production is 'In the crucible of the war: the Iraqi arms industry', *Mednews* (Maisons-Laffitte, France), 8 May 1989. Also see Willis, G., 'Open sesame! Baghdad show reveals Iraqi military-industrial capabilities', *International Defence Review*, no. 6 (July 1989), pp. 835–38.

[44] Shortages of launchers prevented either Iran or Iraq from launching more than 10 ballistic missiles daily during the 1988 War of the Cities. Four launches daily was more typical, greatly reducing their psychological impact. See Zaloga, S., 'Ballistic missiles in the Third World: Scud and beyond', *International Defense Review*, no. 11 (Nov. 1988), pp. 1423–27.

[45] Gordon, M. R., 'Iraqis announce test of a rocket', *New York Times*, 8 Dec. 1989, p. A9. A later report by George, A., 'Iraq's space rocket test launch "was not powerful enough"', *The Guardian* (Manchester), 18 Dec. 1989, p. 1, confirms that the al Abed (or al Abid) placed several objects in low-earth orbit but maintains that the rocket has limited potential for long-range attack or use as a satellite launcher.

[46] 'Soviets claim Israel has launched ballistic missile', *Jane's Defence Weekly*, 23 Sep. 1989, p. 549. The Defense Intelligence Report is excerpted in 'Pentagon reveals nuclear and chemical warheads for Israeli missile', *News Release* (Natural Resources Defense Council: Washington, DC, 14 Nov. 1989). The report was released through the Freedom of Information Act.

by the Israeli Cabinet not to initiate new military projects with South Africa. Israeli Prime Minister Yitzhak Shamir denounced the report as 'baseless lies ... there is no such thing as any collaboration, cooperation or nuclear co-operation between Israel and South Africa.'[47] US officials would not publicly repeat the charges, but reaffirmed them privately. President George Bush was circumspect, saying that transfers of ballistic missile technology to South Africa would 'complicate' relations with Israel.[48]

Most of the other countries listed in table 9.1 continued to maintain their existing ballistic missile forces. Several continued efforts to develop new ballistic missiles, although these projects—in countries such as Iran, North Korea, Pakistan and Thailand—did not reach major milestones in 1989. Romania, a European country excluded from this list of regional powers, was discovered to be developing long-range ballistic missiles similar to the Condor 2, using many of the same suppliers as the Argentinian–Egyptian–Iraqi project.[49] Other countries pressed ahead with space launch projects, including Indonesia, Pakistan and South Korea. In September 1989 Prime Minister Lee Huan announced that Taiwan had earmarked $400 million to initiate a satellite launch programme for the mid-1990s.[50] If successful, these civilian programmes will create a ready basis for intermediate- or even longer-range ballistic missiles.

V. Conclusion: steps towards long-term control

The 1987 Missile Technology Control Regime remains the only multinational mechanism to restrain the proliferation of ballistic missiles. Recent events demonstrate that the MTCR is an effective tool and that the basic approach of restraining exports of relevant technology is viable in the short run. The MTCR has successfully slowed the availability of foreign technology essential to rapid development of emerging regional ballistic missile forces and slowed their progress. The MTCR will become more effective as more countries establish similar export controls and as participating governments take enforcement responsibilities more seriously.

Export control alone cannot resolve the problem of ballistic missile proliferation. The MTCR can slow the process of proliferation, raise the costs, increase public awareness and encourage further action, but it cannot stop proliferation altogether. It does nothing to address the motives for proliferation. The legitimacy of the basic approach of discriminating against new ballistic missile countries is challenged by developing states and regional

---

[47] The original NBC Nightly News report on Israeli–South African missile co-operation was produced by Robert Windrem and reported by Fred Francis. Quotations from Prime Minister Shamir and President Bush can be found in Curtius, M., 'Israel lashes out at leakers of story on South Africa link', *Boston Globe*, 30 Oct. 1989, p. 2; and 'A case of friendly fallout', *The Economist*, 4 Nov. 1989, pp. 54–56.

[48] See note 47.

[49] 'Dieselbe Fabrik entsteht in Ruminem', *Der Spiegel*, no. 19 (Hamburg), 8 May 1989, pp. 166–69.

[50] McGregor, J., 'Taiwan seeks to build aerospace industry', *Wall Street Journal*, US edn, 6 Nov. 1989, p. B7C.

powers which believe that long-range missiles are essential to their national security. Moreover, export controls do nothing about the thousands of ballistic missiles and the substantial technical endowments already in Latin America, the Middle East, South Asia and East Asia.

In the long run, the spread of ballistic missiles can be brought under control only through measures that address the causes of regional insecurity. Because they are only part of the larger problem of regional arms races—including conventional weapons as well as chemical, biological and nuclear armaments—ballistic missiles probably cannot be controlled independently. Rather, they must be controlled through regional arms control and disarmament measures embracing all long-range weapons and weapons of mass destruction. To be effective, initiatives must emerge from governments within the regions affected by weapon proliferation. Outside powers can offer suggestions, discuss, cajole, threaten and set a valuable example through their own arms control and disarmament agreements, but regional initiatives can succeed only when proliferating nations themselves believe that control is in their national interest.

While regional arms control initiatives remain few and far between, there is growing interest in regional confidence- and security-building measures (CSBMs) that can reduce the dangers of missile proliferation.[51] CSBMs are no substitute for control and reduction, but they can reduce the insecurity and instability that ballistic missiles exacerbate. Measures such as reciprocal visits, military data sharing, notification of exercises and new deployments, and inspection rights increasingly appeal to analysts as feasible and effective interim measures.

Even CSBMs, however, may be too ambitious in regions such as the Middle East and the Korean Peninsula, where countries remain in a state of war, borders are disputed and formal bilateral negotiation is impossible. More appears to be possible elsewhere. In South Asia and South America, limited CSBMs have been established. In 1985, then Prime Minister Rajiv Gandhi of India and President Zia-ul-Haq of Pakistan agreed not to attack each other's nuclear plants. Argentina and Brazil have hosted bilateral consultations and visits to each other's nuclear facilities.[52] Whether such measures can be extended to deal with ballistic missiles has yet to be seen.

Policy makers and analysts are only beginning to develop concrete proposals to stymie the spread of ballistic missiles and weapons of mass destruction. Yet the experiences of 1989 offer grounds for cautious optimism. After drifting quietly for many years, the problem is finally beginning to receive the high-level attention it requires to be managed, controlled and eventually reduced.

---

[51] Proposals for CSBMs to deal with ballistic missile proliferation are advanced in Steinberg, G. M., 'The Middle East in the missile age', *Issues in Science and Technology*, summer 1989, pp. 35–40; and Nolan, J. E., 'Ballistic missiles in the Third World—the limits of nonproliferation', *Arms Control Today*, Nov. 1989, pp. 9–14.

[52] Spector, L. S., *The Undeclared Bomb* (Ballinger: Cambridge, Mass., 1988), chs 3 and 5.

Table 9.1. The proliferation of ballistic missiles and related programmes in 26 countries, 1989

Country/Designation	Type[a]	No. of stages	Weight (kg)	Range (km)	Year first fired	Current status	No. deployed Launchers	No. deployed Missiles	Technology supplier	Technology and assistance supplied
Afghanistan										
Scud B[b]	BM	1	6 370	280	1988	In service	12	>1 000	USSR	Launchers, missiles, training
Algeria										
FROG-4	BM	1	2 000	50	Mid-1970s	Retired	12	32	USSR	Launchers, missiles, training
FROG-7	BM	1	2 500	70	Mid-1970s	In service	12	32	USSR	Launchers, missiles, training
Argentina										
Belier-Centaure	SR	2	490	(50)	1966	Retired	..	..	France	Design, production assistance
Castor	SR	2	1 268	(120)	1972	Retired	..	..	USA	Training
CAM (MAR 350)	AR	1	835	90	1987	Cancelled	..	..	Israel	Design, subsystems
									Egypt	Heat shielding, financing
									France	Inertial guidance
									FRG	Design, integration and simulation, launchers
Condor 1	BM	1	2 500	150	1984	Development	..	..		
Condor 2	BM	2	4 500	1 000	..	Development	..	..	Iraq	launchers
									Italy	Financing
									Sweden	Propulsion
									Switzerland	Warhead fusing Management

Brazil										
Sonda 3	SR	2	1 581	(80)	1976	In service	::	::	FRG / USA	Design, propulsion / Training
Sonda 4	SR	2	7 300	(600)	1984	In service	::	4	FRG	Design, propulsion
SS-60	AR	1	595	60	1983	In service	>12	>100	:	:
X-40	AR	1	654	68	1979	In service	:	>20	:	:
EE-150	BM	1	4 500	150	:	Development	:	:	:	:
SS-300	BM	1	8 000	300	:	Development	:	:	:	:
EE-350	BM	1	(5 500)	350	:	Development	:	:	:	:
EE-600	BM	1	(7 000)	600	:	Planned	:	:	:	:
SS-1000	BM	2	(10 000)	1 000	:	Planned	:	:	:	:
VLS	SLV	4	49 000	(6 000)	:	Development	:	:	:	:
Cuba										
FROG-4	BM	1	2 000	50	1961	In service	10	30	USSR	Launchers, missiles, training
FROG-7	BM	1	2 500	70	mid-1980s	In service	12	36	USSR	Launchers, missiles, training
Egypt[c]										
Sakr 80	AR	1	660	80	1987	In service	>12	>100	France	Design, assistance
FROG-5	BM	1	2 000	50	1968	In service	::	::	USSR	Launchers, missiles
FROG-7	BM	1	2 500	70	1973	In service	12	72	USSR	Launchers, missiles
Scud B	BM	1	6 370	280	1973	In service	12	>100	USSR / N. Korea	Launchers, missiles / Production assistance
al Zafir	BM	1	(4 000)	370	1962	Cancelled	::	::	FRG / USSR	Design, assistance / Missiles
Scud 100	BM	1	(7 000)	(600)	1988	Development	::	::	N. Korea / Iraq	Design, assistance / Financing

Country/ Designation	Type[a]	No. of stages	Weight (kg)	Range (km)	Year first fired	Current status	No. deployed Launchers	No. deployed Missiles	Technology supplier	Technology and assistance supplied
al Kahir	BM	1	(8 000)	600	1962	Cancelled	..	..	FRG	Design, assistance
al Ahred	BM	1	(12 000)	950	..	Cancelled	..	..	FRG	Design, assistance
Condor 2	BM	2	4 500	1 000	..	..	..	..	Argentina	Missiles
									Iraq	Financing
									USA	Equipment
									FRG	Equipment
Greece										
Honest John	BM	1	2 640	37	1959	In service	8	24	USA	Launchers, missiles, training
India										
Centaure	SR	1	530	50	1968	In service	..	..	France	Production licence, assistance
									USA	Training
Rohini	SR	2	1 391	130	1972	In service	..	..	France	Propulsion, assistance
Devil Program	BM	2	(3 000)	140	1972	Cancelled	..	..	USSR	SA-2 (V-750 Dvina) missile
Prithvi	BM	1	4 000	240	1988	Development	..	..	..	Propulsion, guidance
Agni	BM	2	21 000	2 400	1989	Development	..	..	France	Propulsion, guidance
									FRG	Propulsion, guidance, heat shielding

SLV 3	SLV	4	17 300	(1 200)	1980	In service	..	4	France	Propulsion, guidance, assistance
									FRG	Propulsion, guidance, heat shielding, materials
ASLV	SLV	4	39 000	(4 000)	1987	Development	..	2	..	..
PSLV	SLV	4	137 000	(8 000)	1991	Planned	..	..	..	..
GSLV	SLV	..	333 000	(14 000)	..	Planned	..	..	..	..
Indonesia										
RX-250	SR	2	(1 200)	(100)	1987	Development	..	..	France	Training, assistance
SLV	SLV	..	(17 000)	(1 500)	1993	Planned	..	..	..	..
Iran										
Oghab	AR	1	360	45	1987	In service	..	Hundreds	China	Design, production assistance
									N. Korea	Production assistance
Shahin 2	BM	1	580	60	1988	In service	..	..	..	..
Nazeat	BM	1	950	120	1988	In service	..	Hundreds	..	..
..	BM	1	(1 500)	160	..	Development	..	..	..	..
Scud B[d]	BM	1	6 370	280	1985	In service	4	100	Libya	Missiles, launchers
									N. Korea	Missiles
									Syria	Missiles
Iraq[e]										
Ababil 50	AR	1	400	50	1988	Development	..	..	Yugoslavia	Design, assistance
SS-60	AR	1	595	60	1985	In service	30	..	Brazil	Launchers, missiles, training
Sijeel 60	AR	1	588	60	1987	Development	..	..	France	Design, assistance
									Brazil	Training
Ababil 100	AR	1	800	100	1989	Development	..	..	Yugoslavia	Design, assistance

Country/ Designation	Type[a]	No. of stages	Weight (kg)	Range (km)	Year first fired	Current status	No. deployed Launchers	No. deployed Missiles	Technology supplier	Technology and assistance supplied
FROG-7	BM	1	2 500	70	..	In service	30	>90	USSR	Launchers, missiles and training
Laith	BM	1	2 500	90	1988	Development	..	..	..	..
Nissan	BM	1	..	110	..	Development	..	..	..	..
Kassir	BM	1	..	150	..	Development	..	..	..	..
Baraq	BM	1	..	250	..	Development	..	..	..	..
Scud B	BM	1	6 370	280	..	In service	20	>360	USSR	Launchers, missiles and training
Fahd	BM	1	..	500	..	Development	..	..	..	..
al Hussein	BM	1	7 000	650	1987	In service	10	..	USSR Brazil Egypt	Launchers, missiles Training Personnel, assistance
al Abbas	BM	1	8 000	900	1988	Development	..	..	USSR Brazil Egypt	Launchers, missiles Training Personnel, assistance
Condor 2	BM	2	4 500	1 000	..	Development	..	..	Argentina Austria Egypt FRG Sweden USA	Missiles R&D facilities Equipment, assistance Equipment, assistance Launchers Equipment
Tamuz-1	BM	2	(12 000)	2 000	..	..	..	..	..	..
al Abed	SLV	3	48 000	(6 000)	1989	..	..	..	..	..
Israel										
MAR 350	AR	1	835	90	1987	In service	..	..	Argentina	Financing

Lance	BM	1	1 527	120	1976	In service	12	160	USA	Launchers, missiles, training
Flower Project	BM	1	..	200	1977	Cancelled	..	..	Iran	Financing
Jericho 1	BM	1	(3 000)	480	1968	In service	..	(50)	France	Design, production assistance
Pershing 1a	BM	1	4 520	740	..	Refused 1974	..	..	USA	..
Jericho 2	BM	2	(6 500)	750	1980	In service	..	(50)	..	..
Jericho 2B	BM	2	(8 500)	1 450	1987	Development	..	..	..	..
Shavit	SLV	2	(25 000)	(7 500)	1988	In service	..	..	..	..
Korea, North										
FROG-5	BM	1	2 000	50	1969	In service	9	50	USSR	Launchers, missiles, training
FROG-7	BM	1	2 500	70	1970	In service	18	54	USSR	Launchers, missiles, training
Scud B^f	BM	1	6 370	280	1976	In service	12	Hundreds	Egypt	Sample missiles
Scud PIP	BM	1	(7 000)	(600)	1988	Development	..	..	Egypt	Assistance
									Japan	Electronics
Korea, South										
Honest John	BM	1	2 640	37	1959	In service	7	36	USA	Launchers, missiles, training
Nike-Hercules	BM	2	5 200	240	1978	In service	..	100	USA	SAM missiles
Centaur	SLV	1	16 780	(1 500)	..	Cancelled 1980	..	..	USA	Design
SLV	SLV	3	(30 000)	(4 000)	..	Planned	..	..	..	..
Kuwait										
FROG-7	BM	1	2 500	70	1980	In service	4	12	USSR	Launchers, missiles, training

Country/Designation	Type[a]	No. of stages	Weight (kg)	Range (km)	Year first fired	Current status	No. deployed		Technology supplier	Technology and assistance supplied
							Launchers	Missiles		
Libya										
FROG-7	BM	1	2 500	70	Mid-1970s	In service	48	>144	USSR	Launchers, missiles, training
SS-21 Scarab	BM	1	1 500	120	..	Refused 1980s	..	..	USSR	..
EE-150	BM	1	4 500	150	..	Refused 1988	..	..	Brazil	..
Scud B[g]	BM	1	6 370	280	Mid-1970s	In service	80	>240	USSR	Launchers, missiles, training
Otrag	BM	1	..	300	1979	Development	..	..	FRG	Personnel, design, components
M-9	BM	1	6 200	600	..	Uncertain	..	..	China	..
Ittisalt	BM	1	(6 000)	700	..	Development	..	..	FRG	Design, assistance, components
SS-12 Scaleboard	BM	1	9 000	900	..	Refused 1980s	..	..	USSR	..
Pakistan										
Shahpar	SR	2	1 200	(120)	1970s	In service	..	..	France	Missiles, training, assistance
SUPARCO rocket	SR	2	(3 000)	(400)	1980s	In service	..	..	USA	Training
Hatf 1	BM	1	(1 500)	80	1987	In service	..	..	..	..
Hatf 2	BM	1	(3 000)	280	1988	In service	..	..	France	Missiles, training, assistance
..	BM	1	..	600	..	Development	..	..	France	Missiles, training, assistance
SLV	SLV	3	(15 000)	(1 200)	..	Planned	..	..	..	..

Philippines										
Bong bong	AR	1	..	12	1975	Cancelled	..	..	..	..
Saudi Arabia[h]										
SS-60	AR	1	595	60	1985	In service	..	..	Brazil	Launchers, missiles, training
Lance	BM	1	1 527	120	..	Refused 1985	50	..	USA	..
DF-3 (CSS-2)	BM	2	27 000	2 200	1988	In service	60	China	Launchers, missiles, training
South Africa										
Jericho 2B	BM	2	(8 500)	1 450	1989	Development	..	Israel	Missiles, assistance
								France	Subsystems
								FRG	Training
								Israel	Missiles, assistance
SLV	SLV	..	..	..	..	Planned	..	Taiwan	..
Syria										
FROG-7[i]	BM	1	2 500	70	1971	In service	24	96	USSR	Launchers, missiles, training
SS-21 Scarab	BM	1	1 500	120	1983	In service	12	36	USSR	Launchers, missiles, training
Scud B	BM	1	6 370	280	1975	In service	18	54	USSR	Launchers, missiles, training
Otrag	BM	1	..	300	..	Cancelled 1981	..	Libya	..
SS-23 Spider	BM	1	4 690	500	..	Refused 1987	..	USSR	..
M-9	BM	1	6 200	600	..	Negotiations	..	China	..
Taiwan										
Honest John	BM	1	2 640	37	1961	In service	..	USA	Launchers, missiles,

Country/Designation	Type[a]	No. of stages	Weight (kg)	Range (km)	Year first fired	Current status	No. deployed		Technology supplier	Technology and assistance supplied
							Launchers	Missiles		
Ching Feng	..	1	1 500	120	1978	In service	..	..	Israel	training
..	BM	2	(6 000)	1 000	..	Cancelled 1981	..	..	USA	Lance missile design
..	SLV	(3)	..	..	1996	Development	..	..	..	Training
Thailand										
Thanu Fan	AR	1	..	..	..	Development	..	..	..	..
Turkey										
MLRS	AR	1	308	40	1990	In service	..	..	USA	Production assistance, components, training
Honest John	BM	1	2 640	37	1960	Withdrawn	18	54	USA	Launchers, missiles, training
Yemen Arab Republic (North)										
SS-21 Scarab	BM	1	1 500	120	1988	In service	4	12	USSR	Launchers, missiles, training
Yemen, People's Democratic Rep. of (South)										
FROG-7	BM	1	2 500	70	1979	In service	12	36	USSR	Launchers, missiles, training
SS-21 Scarab	BM	1	1 500	120	1988	In service	4	12	USSR	Launchers, missiles, training
Scud B	BM	1	6 370	280	1979	In service	6	18	USSR	Launchers, missiles, training

.. Unknown or not applicable   ( ) Estimates

[a] Acronyms in this column: AR: artillery rocket (military); BM: ballistic missile; SLV: space launch vehicle; SR: sounding rocket.

[b] Since Oct. 1988, the Soviet Union has supplied the Kabul Government with over 1000 Scud B missiles. Most of these were fired soon after delivery against suspected Mujahideen targets.

[c] There are reports that small quantities of al Zafir missiles were fired at Israel during the 1967 war. Several dozen FROG missiles and at least one Scud B were fired during the 1973 war.

[d] Iran received at least 100 Scud B missiles from Libya, North Korea and possibly Syria during its war with Iraq. Most of these were fired before the cease-fire began on 20 Aug. 1988. Iranian Scud B inventories may have been replenished since then, although this cannot be confirmed.

[e] During the 1980–88 war with Iran, Iraq fired approximately 67 FROG-7s, over 100 Scud-Bs and 190 al Hussein Scud versions. The number of Brazilian SS-60 and other large artillery rockets fired was in the thousands. Little is known about the state of Iraq's missile inventories after the 20 Aug. 1988 cease-fire.

[f] In 1985 North Korea agreed to supply 90–100 domestically manufactured Scud B missiles to Iran. Most of these were subsequently fired against Iraq.

[g] Although Libya has not used its ballistic missiles in its fighting with Egypt in 1977 or in Chad from 1978–88, it has sold Scud B missiles to Iran for use against Iraq.

[h] Saudi Arabia may also help finance missile production programmes in Egypt and Iraq.

[i] Syria fired approximately 25 FROG-7 missiles at Israel during the 1973 war. Syrian efforts to purchase longer-range missiles in the 1980s were blocked by Western diplomatic pressure and, in the case of the SS-23, the unwillingness of the USSR to sell a weapon system proscribed under the 1987 INF Treaty.

10. Major armed conflicts in 1989

KARIN LINDGREN, G. KENNETH WILSON,
PETER WALLENSTEEN and KJELL-ÅKE NORDQUIST*

Major armed conflicts were waged in 32 locations in the world during 1989 (see table 10.1, which presents an account of the development of the conflicts up to 31 December 1989, from data available as of 31 January 1990). A major armed conflict is defined as 'a prolonged combat between the military forces of two or more governments or of one government and organized armed opposition forces, involving the use of manufactured weapons and incurring battle-related deaths of at least 1000 persons'.[1] Although 32 conflicts is a very considerable number, it is lower than the numbers recorded for the past three years: 36 conflicts in 1986 and 1987 and 35 in 1988.[2] Thus, the total number of major armed conflicts is on the decline. This pattern was observed in 1988, but in 1989 the full effect of agreements reached is more evident.

Two new conflicts were recorded for 1989: the civil war in Romania and the USA–Panama inter-state conflict. Because some conflicts of long duration reached a phase of no armed action or even resolution, 1989 witnessed an important reduction in conflict frequency. However, experience has shown that such trends have been followed by even higher increases in the number of conflicts.

The total number of ongoing armed conflicts in the world today is staggering. In some locations there are several destructive conflicts going on simultaneously (e.g., Colombia, Ethiopia, India, Lebanon, Myanmar [formerly Burma], Sri Lanka and Uganda). In addition to the major conflicts presented in table 10.1, there are a considerable number of armed conflicts which, by the end of 1989, had not resulted in 1000 battle-related deaths but which were still highly significant for those exposed to them. A rough estimate would suggest that there are more than 75 such conflicts.[3] Among such conflicts are the Basque conflict in Spain, the latest phase of the Tibet conflict (both conflicts approach 1000 battle-related deaths) and the nationality conflicts in the Soviet Union. Other significant disputes which border on the criteria for inclusion in the table are the killing of pro-democracy demonstrators in Tiananmen Square by Chinese armed forces on

---

[1] See the *SIPRI Yearbook 1989*, chapter 9.

[2] Although the *SIPRI Yearbook 1989* listed 33 major armed conflicts for 1988, data subsequently collected showed that two more conflicts met the criteria for inclusion in the table: the Turkey–PKK conflict and the Chittagong Hill Tracts conflict in Bangladesh. These two conflicts are included in the present list, which means that previously reported numbers must be revised accordingly.

[3] A comprehensive presentation and analysis of the major and minor conflicts of 1989 will appear in the forthcoming report *States in Armed Conflict 1989*, by the Department of Peace and Conflict Research of Uppsala University, Uppsala, Sweden.

* Birger Heldt, Ramses Amer, Jean Anderson and Henrik Nyberg have assisted in the data collection and case descriptions.

3–4 June 1989 in Beijing, China, and the dispute in March 1989 involving Mauritanians and Senegalese in Mauritania which, according to a statement by the Mauritanian President in mid-December, resulted in several thousand deaths.

The civil war in Romania was sparked and intensified partly by inflated casualty figures. Deaths in Timisoara, early in the conflict, are estimated at 90 although figures 10–50 times higher were widely circulated. The total number of battle-related deaths for the conflict is estimated at 750–1100.

Some conflicts intensified in certain periods of the year, most notably in Colombia, El Salvador, Ethiopia, Lebanon, Peru, Punjab (India) and Sri Lanka, and all leading to more than 1000 battle-related deaths in 1989 alone. The wars in Afghanistan and Cambodia also remained among those with large numbers of casualties. Another set of conflicts, which had for some time been on a low level of intensity and in which promising peace processes were under way in previous years, escalated during 1989 (Chad, Morocco/Western Sahara and El Salvador). Certain conflicts recorded fewer than 100 deaths during the year, for instance, the conflict over Northern Ireland and the India–Pakistan border conflict.

A process of increasing fragmentation could be observed in several conflicts: actors were split, creating new alliances, and new combat patterns appeared. This has been the case for Lebanon, but similar patterns appeared in Afghanistan, Myanmar and Sri Lanka and were also indicated in conflicts waged on a lower level but with a potential for escalation, notably in the USSR and South Africa (e.g., between the UDF and Inkatha movements).

The reduction in the number of armed conflicts was particularly evident among the inter-state conflicts: cease-fires and the initiation of talks have taken place in several conflicts, sometimes with the involvement of outside third parties but most often without such involvement. Among the major armed conflicts recorded in 1988, no armed battles occurred during 1989 in the China–Viet Nam, Ethiopia–Somalia or the Laos–Thailand conflicts. These conflicts all reverted to a *status quo ante*, or returned to pre-war borders and relationships, and do not appear in the list this year. This was also the case for the Iran–Iraq War where, however, several skirmishes have allegedly taken place between the parties since the August 1988 cease-fire. Although this was not publicly acknowledged by the actors or by independent observers, it did indicate the considerable tension in relations between the parties, also witnessed by the lack of progress in the United Nations-mediated peace process. However, a new inter-state conflict occurred during the year—that between the USA and Panama, leading to the surrender of Panamanian General Manuel Noriega in January 1990. The death figures vary considerably for this conflict.

Conflicts over control of government remained the largest category. In Romania, the new government secured control following a short civil war. In Central American disputes, the peace process made some further gains in August 1989, when an agreement was signed in Nicaragua between the Sandinista Government and the opposition regarding the election process.

Shortly afterwards, the Central American presidents met in Tela, Honduras, to agree on the demobilization of Contra forces, mainly based in Honduras. Peace talks in Mexico between the parties in the El Salvador conflict failed, and the war escalated dramatically in November. In Mozambique, indirect and mediated talks were initiated between the fighting parties. In the war between the Tigrean People's Liberation Front (TPLF, demanding democratic rule for the whole of Ethiopia) and the Ethiopian Government, the TPLF made very substantial military advances in September and October. Talks between the parties opened in November, with the presence of the Italian Government. In December an agreement was signed which ended the war in Malaysia between the Government and the Communist Party. In Lebanon, several serious attempts were made to break deadlocks, resulting in limited cease-fires. At the Saudi Arabia conference, plans for parliamentary reforms were agreed, but fighting in Lebanon continued.

Negotiations over questions of autonomy saw little progress during 1989. Talks were opened in September between the Ethiopian Government and the EPLF, the leading Eritrean military force, and were observed by former US President Jimmy Carter.

UN mediation of conflicts during 1989 did not see any significant breakthroughs.[4] The United Nations did, however, play a role in monitoring the elections in Namibia (in November) and will do so in Nicaragua (elections scheduled for February 1990). In some conflicts, non-governmental organizations and individual governments took on a mediating role (e.g., the Ethiopia–Eritrea and the Ethiopia–TPLF conflicts, and in Mozambique). Publicly acknowledged direct contacts between fighting parties were more common in 1989 than in 1988 (e.g., in Colombia and El Salvador).

In some armed conflicts there was an important change of militarily involved parties during 1989. Most important was the final Soviet withdrawal from Afghanistan under UN auspices, completed on 15 February 1989, which turned the focus of the Afghan war to the conflicts between the Government and different factions. Similarly, Vietnamese troops were withdrawn from Cambodia by the end of September. However, no impartial outside observation of the process was agreed.

In some conflicts, armed combat appeared to diminish in 1989 and be replaced by continuing unarmed or non-violent resistance. This was most obvious in the case of South Africa, where internal opposition has successfully used 'defiance' to pressure the white minority Government. In other cases, military leaders turned against governments to press for political solutions to intractable military situations (Sudan and Ethiopia).

Most of the major armed conflicts listed in table 10.1 were waged in Third World countries. In Europe, the developments in Romania gave rise to the largest armed conflict on the continent since the Soviet invasion of Hungary in 1956.

---

[4] See Urquhart, B., 'Conflict resolution in 1988: the role of the United Nations', in SIPRI, *SIPRI Yearbook 1989: World Armaments and Disarmament* (Oxford University Press: Oxford, 1989), chapter 13.

Table 10.1. Major armed conflicts in the world, 1989

Location	Year formed/ year joined[a]	Warring parties	No. of troops in 1989	Deaths[b] Total (incl. 1989)	Deaths[b] During 1989	Change from 1988[c]
Europe						
Romania	1989/1989	Romania (Ceausescu) Govt/ Securitate	22 000–23 500[d]	1989: 750–1 100[f]	..	n.a.
		vs. National Salvation Front (National Armed Forces)	171 000[e]			
United Kingdom/ Northern Ireland	1969/1969 1986/1986	British Govt vs. IRA and others vs. UVF and others	16 500 200–500 ..	1969–89: >2 700	70	0

Comments: Nicolae Ceausescu succeeded Gheorghe Gheorghiu-Dej as Secretary General of the Romanian Communist Party in 1965. On 14 Dec. 1989 a small-scale protest by the Hungarian minority started in the city of Timisoara against the planned deportation of Laszlo Tökes, an ethnic Hungarian priest and human rights activist, for preaching democracy. Anti-Govt demonstrations jointly by Hungarians and Romanians, consisting of 5000–10 000 people, followed on 17 Dec. Police and military personnel opened fire against demonstrators, leading to 90 deaths, acc. to official (National Salvation Front) figures. Strikes and demonstrations against the Ceausescu Govt continued in Timisoara and occurred in several other cities on 18 Dec. and the following days, partly sparked by exaggerated casualty figures from Timisoara. By 18 Dec. Romania had closed its borders. Following anti-Ceausescu demonstrations in Bucharest on 21 Dec., a state of emergency was declared. On 22 Dec. President Ceausescu fled from Bucharest, the national armed forces turned against the Govt, and the National Salvation Front, consisting of former senior Communist Party officials, intellectuals and dissident artists, seized power. A provisional Govt under the leadership of former Foreign Minister Manescu was formed. The Front had reportedly been in existence (in name) for several months. Fighting erupted in Bucharest and other cities later the same day between security forces (Securitate) loyal to Ceausescu and the armed forces. On 22 Dec. Ceausescu and his wife were arrested. They were both executed on 25 Dec. after being found guilty in a secret trial by a military court. The most intensive fighting occurred during 22–25 Dec. but by 26 Dec. only sporadic resistance from Securitate remained. On 26 Dec. a new Govt was formed with P. Roman as Head of Govt and I. Iliescu as President. The Govt stated that it would serve during an interim period until free elections, to be held in Apr. 1990. On 27 Dec. the situation was reported to be normalized, and on 29 Dec. the armed forces started to pull out of Bucharest.

Comments: The present conflict originates from the division of Ireland in 1922. In 1969 civil rights issues were raised, and since 1970 the Provisional IRA (Irish Republican Army) has constituted the main armed actor on the republican side, demanding reunification under the Republic of Ireland. The British Govt sought to uphold existing ties between Northern Ireland and Great Britain, to protect the interest of the majority of unionist/loyalists. The 1985 agreement between the UK and Ireland, however, increased suspicion among Protestants towards the British Govt. The late 1980s saw the formation of militant Protestant groups, e.g. Ulster Freedom Fighters, Ulster Volunteer Force (UVF) and the Ulster Resistance, responsible for some attacks on IRA-related targets. Arms imports to loyalist militants from S. Africa were reported. Attacks by different sides during 1989 included killing of a Sinn Fein politician (Feb.), bomb attacks on police stations and death of an IRA member (Apr.) and continued attacks on British soldiers in Northern Ireland (e.g. in Feb., Mar., May, Nov., Dec.). Also attacks were made by the IRA outside the area. Most severe was the bombing in Deal, UK, in Sep., when 11 members of an Army band were killed, and a bombing of military barracks in Colchester, UK (Nov.).

Middle East

Iran	1972/1979	Iranian Govt vs. KDPI	305 000^{g,h}	1979–89: >17 000^i	<50	– –
	../1979	vs. Komala	10 500	..		

Comments: Kurds (in particular the Kurdish Democratic Party of Iran, KDPI), seeking greater autonomy or independence in the north-west, became very active militarily following the overthrow of the Shah in 1979. The establishment of 'liberated zones' led to the 1983–84 campaign by Iranian forces to regain control. During the Iran–Iraq War, Kurdish groups were reported to be receiving aid from the Iraqi Govt. In 1989 the KDPI claimed it had taken control of Mahabad in north-western Iran (Sep.), and Komala (or the Kurdish Communist Party of Iran) claimed that it had attacked and destroyed an Iranian Army base in south-western Kurdistan, killing or capturing all personnel (June). Since the revolution, the People's Mujahideen (Khalq) have sought to overthrow the Iranian Govt by force. Both members and sympathizers of the People's Mujahideen have since the cease-fire in the Iran–Iraq War been subject to a spate of summary executions.

Iraq	1961/1980	Iraqi Govt vs. KDP	955 000^{h,j}	1980–89: 5 000–6 000^k	<50 (mil.)	– –
	1975/1980	vs. PUK	5 000–15 000	4 000		

Comments: An attempt at secession by the Kurdish minority in the north-east of Iraq led to general uprising in 1962. In spite of agreement with the Govt in 1970, sporadic clashes continued until 1974 when general hostilities broke out. In 1975 Iran and Iraq concluded an agreement which stopped support from Iran to the Iraqi Kurds, and the resistance declined. During the Iran–Iraq War the Kurdish parties, mainly the Kurdish Democratic Party (KDP) and the Patriotic Union of Kurdistan (PUK), fought the Iraqi Govt with help from Iran. After the cease-fire in the Iran–Iraq War, Iraq moved against the Kurds to drive them out of the country. There were reports of the use of chemical gas by the Iraqi Govt, which Iraq denies. The main resistance apparently ceased, but sporadic actions by Kurdish groups were reported during 1989. In late Sep. 1989 the Iraqi Army launched an offensive, the first in a year, against remaining Kurdish bases near the Iranian border. The Socialist Party of Kurdistan (approx. 1500) also exists, but no clashes were reported between the Govt and SPK in 1989. The Iraqi Govt has proclaimed a 30-km 'security zone' along its borders, moved the Kurdish population to other parts of the country and razed Kurdish villages. The Govt also faces opposition from the Iraqi Communist Party and the Shi'ite organization Supreme Assembly of the Islamic Revolution in Iraq, but no clashes were reported in 1989.

Location	Year formed/ year joined[a]	Warring parties	No. of troops in 1989	Deaths[b] Total (incl. 1989)	During 1989	Change from 1988[c]
Israel/Palestine	1964/1964	Israeli Govt	141 000[k]	1948–89: >10 200	>350	0
		vs. PLO (based in Lebanon)	9 900			
		vs. other Palestinian groups	..			

Comments: Present conflict formed in 1948 with the formation of the Israeli state. Interstate wars in 1948–49, 1956, 1967 and 1973. The 1967 war resulted in the Israeli occupation of the West Bank and Gaza Strip. Israeli invasions of Lebanon in 1978 and 1982, the latter forcing the PLO (Palestine Liberation Organization, founded in 1964) HQ to be moved to Tunisia. PLO-related armed groups are based in Lebanon. Since Dec. 1987 a significant popular uprising, the intifada, has taken place in the occupied territories. During 1989 the two dominant groups in the occupied territories reportedly seem to be the Unified National Leadership of the Uprising (UNLU) and Hamas (or the Islamic Resistance Movement). PLO leader Arafat was elected President of the Palestinian State (proclaimed in Nov. 1988) by the PLO Central Committee in Apr. During 1989 attacks were made by Palestinian groups from Lebanon as well as Jordan and attacks by Israel on Palestinian targets in Lebanon. In the occupied territories the Palestinians continued throughout 1989 to use non-military means in attacks on Israeli soldiers. Israeli counteractions include military actions, arrests, curfews, expulsions and destruction of houses. 640 Palestinians have been killed by Israeli security forces during the intifada (approx. 250 in 1989) as well as over 40 Israelis. In addition, deaths in 1989 include intra-Palestinian killings following accusation of co-operation with Israelis, and killings by Israeli civilians. Several proposals were presented in 1989: by Prime Minister Shamir (Israel, Apr.), President Mubarak (Egypt, Sep.) and Secretary of State Baker (USA, Oct.). The Baker 5-point initiative is aimed at a preparatory dialogue between Israel and Palestinians to be held in Egypt. The initiative was accepted, with reservations by both Israel (Nov.) and Egypt (Dec.).

Lebanon					
	Lebanese Army (Aoun)	1975/1975	15 000–20 000	1975–89: 131 000	>1 150	++
	Lebanese Forces	1975/1975	6 000		
	Druze militia (PSP)	1975/1975	(5 000)		
	Amal	1979/1979	5 000–6 000		
	Hezbollah	1975/1975	3 500		
	LCP	1975/1975	2 000		
	PLO (Fatah)	1964/1964	4 500–5 000		
	PFLP-GC	1968/1968	500		
	SLA	1978/1978	1 200–2 500		
	Syrian Govt	1976/1976	40 000–50 000		
	Israeli Govt	1978/1982	1 000		
	Iranian Govt (Revol. Guards)	1982/1982	2 000		

Comments: Civil war among Christian, Palestinian, Muslim and Druze groups since 1975. Muslims are estimated to form the majority of the population. Christians dominate political and economic life. Syrian troops have been present since 1976. Israeli invasions in 1978 and 1982. Israel keeps soldiers and the Israeli-armed South Lebanese Army (SLA) in the Israeli-proclaimed 'Security Zone'. The UN security force UNIFIL (5850 men in 1989) has been deployed in Lebanon since 1978. Iranian Revolutionary Guards have reportedly been in the Syrian-controlled Bekaa Valley since 1982. Regular Iranian Army troops reportedly entered the Valley in 1989. Two rival Govts, Gen. Aoun (Maronite Christian) and Mr Hoss (Sunni Muslim), headed Lebanon in 1989. The Christian army faction of the national forces, the Lebanese Army, is loyal to Gen. Aoun. Battles in Jan. 1989 between the two Shi'ite Muslim groups Amal (pro-Syrian) and Hezbollah (pro-Iranian), (50 dead). Heavy fighting in the Christian sector of Beirut between the Lebanese Army and the Lebanese Forces (LF, Christian militia) in Feb. After Gen. Aoun's blockade of militia ports and declaration of 'Liberation War' against Syria (aiming to force Syrian out) in early Mar., the worst fighting since 1975 started in Beirut. The LF appear to have joined forces with the Lebanese Army against Syrian troops and Druze militia (probably the Syrian-backed Progressive Socialist Party [PSP]). Approx. 900 killed, mainly civilians during Mar. to late Sep., when a truce took effect. Several Arab League cease-fire attempts and an Arab League peace-keeping force sent to Beirut. On 15 Aug. the UN Secretary-General called an emergency meeting of the Security Council. Over 60 members of the Lebanese Parliament met in Taif (Saudi Arabia) in early Oct. The Parliament met in northern Lebanon in early Nov., despite its dissolution by Gen. Auon, elected a new President, René Muawad, and approved the peace plan (aiming to share power more equally between Christians and Muslims) agreed upon in Oct. The peace plan was rejected by Gen. Aoun because it does not ensure Syrian withdrawal. President Muawad was killed (with 17 other people) on 22 Nov. New President Elias Hrawi (Christian, Syrian-backed) elected on 24 Nov., but was not accepted by Gen. Aoun. From mid-Dec. renewed fighting between Amal and Hezbollah (over 50 killed). During 1989 Israel made 18 air-raids, as well as ground attacks, against forces from Palestinian and Lebanese groups (e.g. the Popular Front for the Liberation of Palestine–General Command, PFLP-GC, Nov.), Hezbollah (Nov.), the Lebanese Communist Party (LCP,

Location	Year formed/ year joined[a]	Warring parties	No. of troops in 1989	Deaths[b] Total (incl. 1989)	During 1989	Change from 1988[c]

Dec.), also north of the 'Security Zone' (over 40 killed). In mid-Dec. PLO forces (mainly from the Fatah faction) attacked Syrian troops in southern Lebanon leaving at least 10 dead, reportedly the first such clash in 2 years.

| Turkey | 1974/1984 | Turkish Govt vs. PKK (Kurdish Workers' Party) | 528 000[h] 300–1 000 | 1984–89: 1 500–3 000 | >150 | + |

Comments: The PKK, established in 1974, seeks independence from Turkey and has since 1984 escalated warfare against the Turkish Govt, mostly in south-eastern Turkey. In 1987 the Govt claimed that PKK had some 1100 armed men operating from within Turkey and approx. 3400 men in the total force. Other sources give lower figures for PKK forces. The Turkish Army has deployed an est. 100 000 soldiers and para-military gendarmerie in the 8 south-eastern provinces. Many PKK members have been arrested and sentenced to death. During 1989 several clashes were reported between PKK members and members of the security force and police. In May PKK intensified its activities, and approx. 80 people were reported to have been killed in May–June. Fighting continued throughout 1989, with no signs of a peace process. Govt also faces opposition from other groups, e.g. the Turkish Workers' and Peasants' Liberation Army, which assumed responsibility for a raid on a gendarmerie post in Aug.

South Asia

| Afghanistan | 1978/1978 | Afghan Govt, USSR vs. Afghan Mujahideen, based in Afghanistan Pakistan (Peshawar) Iran | 55 000[l] – (Feb.)   .. 40 000 .. | 1978–89: 1 000 000[m] | >15 000 | 0 |

Comments: After the Apr. 1978 Govt take-over by PDPA (People's Democratic Party of Afghanistan), a civil war began, with opposition formed along religious lines. In Dec. 1979 the conflict escalated with Soviet intervention. A plan for Soviet withdrawal was established by the 1988 Geneva Accords; UN-supervised withdrawal was completed on 15 Feb. 1989. Acc. to Soviet sources, the total no. of Soviet troops killed 1979–89 was 15 000. Tension between Afghanistan and Pakistan after Soviet-made Afghan missiles repeatedly fell on Pakistani territory in early 1989. Interim Govt formed by Pakistan-based Mujahideen in Feb. 1989, based in Peshawar. Forces of different Govt groups initiated an unsuccessful attack on Jalalabad (Mar.) which developed into continued siege of the city for 3 months. Battles around Jalalabad continued throughout July and were renewed in Nov. Guerrilla shelling of Kabul reported throughout 1989. Struggle around Khost in Aug., Sep., Dec., as well as around Kandahar and Shindand (Aug., Sep.). Continued armed supply for the Afghan Govt by the USSR; to Mujahideen through Pakistan, by several countries incl. the USA and Saudi Arabia. Contacts between the USSR and Mujahideen led to the release of 2 Soviet soldiers (Dec.). In Aug. battle reported between Mujahideen factions in Helmand Province. Heavy fighting was also reported between followers of Hekmatyar (Hezb-i Islami Party) and Massoud (Jamyat-i Islami Party), for instance a massacre in July of Massoud followers and fighting in Aug. On 1 Nov. a UN General Assembly resolution called upon the Secretary-General to facilitate the formation of a broad-based Govt in Afghanistan.

| Bangladesh | 1971/1981 | Bangladesh Govt vs. JSS/SB | 90 000^a 5 000 | 1975–89: >1 000 | <50 | 0 |

Comments: The Parbattya Chattagram Jana Sanghati Samiti (JSS, or the Chittagong Hill Tracts People's Coordination Association) and its military wing, the Shanti Bahini (SB, or Peace Force), were formed in 1971. Guerrilla warfare started in 1974–75 after demands for autonomy for the south-eastern Chittagong Hill Tracts (CHT), previously enjoyed under British rule, met no response from the Govt. Bengali (mainly Muslim) settlers, moving into the area, have been attacked by the SB. Bengali settlers have attacked the tribal people of the CHT (inhabited mainly by the Buddhist Chakma tribe but also by Hindus and Christians), reportedly with the support of the Bangladesh Army on some occasions. Accusations of massacres from both sides; approx. 50 000 in refugee camps in India. SB intensified operations in 1981, and in 1984 the Govt (which seized power in a military coup in 1982) sent the Army into the area. Since 1986 the violence increased, with an est. 100 killed by the SB in 1988. Since Oct. 1985 meetings have been held between the Govt and the JSS/SB but with little progress. In 1989 the Parliament passed four bills designed to provide limited autonomy to the region. JSS/SB reportedly does not think the provisions adequate, and SB stepped up violence in connection with elections (June) to the new district councils.

| India | 1947/1981
1988/1988
1988/1988
1947/1982 | Indian Govt vs. KCF vs. All Bodo Students Union vs. Muslim Liberation Front vs. Jammu and Kashmir Liberation Front | 1 100 000^h >8 000^n .. .. .. | 1983–89: >16 000 | >2 000 | 0 |

Comments: Several Sikh groups, e.g. the Khalistan Commando Force (KCF), the Khalistan Liberation Force, the Council of Khalistan, the Bhindranwale Tiger Force and the Babbar Khalsa, have waged an armed struggle against the central Govt to create an independent Khalistan. In June 1984 the Indian Army stormed the Golden Temple (the main Sikh shrine). Sikhs assassinated Prime Minister Indira Gandhi in Oct. 1984. In 1988 at least 2500 persons died in the Punjab conflict, the death-toll easing off somewhat after the Govt's 'Operation Black Thunder' (May 1988), ending an occupation of the Golden Temple by Sikh groups,

Location	Year formed/ year joined[a]	Warring parties	No. of troops in 1989	Deaths[b] Total (incl. 1989)	During 1989	Change from 1988[c]

many of whom surrendered. In 1989 the Sikh groups continued their struggle for secession. In response to the hanging of 2 of Indira Gandhi's assassins on 6 Jan., sporadic incidents occurred in Amritsar and Delhi. Killings and acts of sabotage occurred in 1989, but according to Rajiv Gandhi, introducing his political reform programme for the Punjab (Mar.), only 1 active Sikh group with religious backing remains. Gandhi proposed measures to end president's (direct) rule and to hold local elections in the Punjab. Political violence in the Punjab remained on a stable high (2000 deaths) in 1989. After the election of pro-separatist candidates from the Punjab in Nov. general elections, the new Prime Minister V. P. Singh in a gesture of reconciliation, prayed at the Golden Temple. On 29 Dec. the Indian Lower House of Parliament voted to repeal the constitutional amendment which in 1987 suspended basic civil rights in Punjab. In Uttar Pradesh a new local authority introduced in early 1989 a law to make Urdu a second official language. This provoked the majority Hindus to rebellion. Cleavages over religious sites have also come to the fore. In 1989 over 600 deaths were recorded in Uttar Pradesh. In Bihar a similar inter-denominational conflict, provoked by election issues, resulted in up to 1000 deaths. Factional fighting between rival Muslim and rival Hindu groups, respectively, took place in Gujarat and Tamil Nadu states, costing 33 lives. General elections (22–26 Nov.) resulted in a further 130 deaths, mainly in Gujarat and Tripura. In Assam, the Bodo people, mainly militia drawn from the All Bodo Students Union (with a few hundred fighters), continued their campaign for a separate state, which started in Mar. 1988. 500 deaths were reported during Jan. to Aug. 1989, when a truce was arranged. In Kashmir, where several groups (mainly the Jammu and Kashmir Liberation Front and the Muslim Liberation Front, with a few hundred men) demand that Kashmir is to become a Pakistani state, the violent struggle continued in 1989.

| India–Pakistan | 1947/1982 | Indian Govt vs. Pakistani Govt | 1 100 000[k] 480 000[k] | 1971: 11 000 1981–89: >500 (mil.) | <50 (mil.) | 0 |

Comments: Since independence in 1947 there have been several military engagements—first over partition (1947), then over Kashmir (1965) and East Pakistan/Bangladesh (1971). An agreement was signed in 1972 to observe the frontier in the Himalayas. Since 1981 renewed sporadic fighting has occurred on Siachen Glacier (Kashmir) over a 72-km-long border determination. Long-standing mistrust between the two countries has been increased by trouble in Punjab Province in India. India claims Pakistan supports Sikh groups. In mid-June 1989 a military experts' meeting of Indians and Pakistanis took place in Islamabad to discuss the situation in the Siachen Glacier area. It was decided to establish a no man's land zone on the glacier. Troops were to be redeployed in non-offensive strategies, force was to be avoided and precise determination of ground positions settled. The details of this latter point are not yet agreed. Routine cross-border exchanges of artillery fire occur in response to army movement of troops along the border (Apr., July, Sep.). In one such exchange of fire in mid-July, 15 soldiers died. Internal pressures on both sides complicate agreement on the crucial issue.

Myanmar (formerly Burma)	1948/1948	Myanmar Govt	182 000–200 000[h]	1948–51: 8 000	.°	n.a.
		vs. BCP (Jan.–Apr.)	10 000–15 000	1950: 5 000		
		vs. BCP (Apr.–Dec.)	200–300	1981–84: 400–600 yearly		
	1989/1989	vs. BNUP (Apr.–)	8 000–12 000	1985–87: >1 000 yearly		
	1989/1989	vs. Noom Suk Ham	..	1988: 500–3 000		
	1989/1989	vs. National Democratic Army	..			
	1948/1949	vs. KNU	4 000–8 000			
	1948/1948	vs. KIA	8 000–10 000			
	1965/1965	vs. SSA	..			

Comments: More than 20 anti-Govt organizations have fought against the central Govt since 1948. The Burma Socialist Programme Party (BSPP) came to power after a military coup in 1962. BSPP changed its name to the National Unity Party (NUP) in Sep. 1988 after pro-democracy demonstrations. These were quelled in Aug.–Sep. 1988 with up to 3000 reported killed (500 acc. to official sources). A military take-over followed. In late May 1989 the country's name was changed to the Union of Myanmar. In 1975 the National Democratic Front (NDF) was formed, consisting of 11 non-communist anti-Govt resistance groups in 1989. On 11 Nov. 1988 the Democratic Alliance of Burma (DAB) was established, comprised of 23 ethnic resistance armies, underground student groups and other anti-Govt organizations. The Burma Communist Party (BCP) staged several campaigns against Govt troops after Sep. 1988, often in co-operation with forces from the Shan State Army (SSA) and Kachin Independence Army (KIA) of the NDF; over 100 soldiers reported killed in Dec. 1988. BCP split in 1989 after a mutiny into at least 4 groups. In mid-Mar. ethnic Kokang Chinese, Wa and Shan troops broke away from BCP and set up the Burma National Democratic Front (BNDF). On 14 Apr., BCP troops, dominated by Wa hill tribesmen, stormed general HQ at Panghsang, and the communist leadership fled to China. Similar mutinies followed in other areas. The new groups, the Burma National United Party (BNUP, and its armed wing, the Burma National United Army; the bulk of the former BCP's 10 000–15 000 troops and primarily Wa hill tribesmen), Nom Suk Ham (the Young Brave Warriors, Shan-dominated), the National Democratic Army (former BCP's Mekong River Division, led by a Chinese volunteer) and the BNDF are organized along ethnic lines. Communist ideology has been discarded. Other BCP troops of Kachin origin joined the KIA, reportedly leaving only a few hundred rebels still regarding themselves as the BCP. A temporary cease-fire was reportedly agreed upon (Apr.) between the Govt and the Kokang group. The Govt also faces opposition from other ethnic groups seeking autonomy, such as the Karen National Union (KNU) which in Sep. 1988 launched an offensive against Govt forces and recaptured a base. Govt made counter-offensives and has seized several important KNU bases along the Thai–Myanmar border. KNU claims to have killed 2000 soldiers; Govt figures are lower. Reports that Govt troops entered Thai territory during its offensives. Thai Govt offer in Apr. to mediate peace talks between Myanmar Govt and ethnic groups (delegates from NDF and DAB met with Thai military representatives and agreed to set up a cease-fire negotiating team) was rejected by Myanmar Govt. Reports of troops shooting and killing 1 person during pro-democracy demonstrations in June 1989 and the imprisonment of thousands of pro-democracy activists since mid-July. Approx. 10 000 additional troops were deployed in Yangon in July. Leaders of the main opposition movement, the National League for Democracy (NLD), were put under house arrest in July for up to a year. Members of NLD were arrested for a bomb attack on an oil refinery (July, killing 3 persons) and, acc. to military officials, admitted responsibility. The Govt set the date for a free and fair election at May 1990.

Location	Year formed/ year joined[a]	Warring parties	No. of troops in 1989	Deaths[b] Total (incl. 1989)	During 1989	Change from 1988[c]
Sri Lanka	1987/1987	Sri Lankan Govt, Indian Govt (IPKF)	40 000 47 000–50 000 (Jan.) 40 000 (Dec.)	1983–89: 14 000–16 000	>5 150	+
	1976/1983	vs. Tamil Tigers (LTTE)	2 000			
	1976/1989	vs. EPRLF/TNA	1 000			
	1969/1987	vs. JVP	1 200			

Comments: Tamil groups, principally the Tamil Tigers (Liberation Tigers of Tamil Eelam, LTTE), demand autonomy or secession for the northern parts of Sri Lanka. An agreement (July 1987) between India and Sri Lanka placed Indian troops (Indian Peace-Keeping Forces, IPKF) on the island. Since Oct. 1987 IPKF have been fighting against forces from Tamil Tigers. Over 1100 IPKF (approx. 600 in 1989) have been killed. Acc. to Tamil sources, they have lost over 650 men in fighting with the IPKF. 5000 civilians have died since 1983 in the Tamil conflict. The Sinhalese People's Liberation Front (JVP), which opposes the partial Tamil autonomy agreement between Sri Lanka and India, became a new party to the conflict in Nov. 1987. In 1989 pressure built up from both JVP and Tamil quarters for Indian troops to be withdrawn. President Premadasas' first 100 days in office (Jan.–Mar.) were marked by some of the worst violence as of that date. Violence increased in connection with general elections held in Feb. A state of emergency was declared in June after several abortive truces in the JVP conflict. Military offensive against JVP after JVP threatened the families of police and security forces. Wholesale killing and arresting of Sinhalese civilians, suspected to be JVP supporters. At the beginning of Sep. a pro-Govt vigilante group 'the Eagles of Central Hills', took revenge on JVP supporters. The leader and vice-leader of the JVP were killed by the Sinhalese Army in Nov. The JVP conflict has cost over 5000 deaths in 2 years, over 4200 in 1989. Fighting continued in 1989 between IPKF and Tamil Tigers, but on a lower level than in 1988. At the end of June, the Tamil Tigers signed an agreement with the Govt which seems to indicate that the (EPRLF) Provincial Council would be dissolved upon Indian withdrawal and demand the prior withdrawal of IPKF before signing a general peace accord. On 18 Sep. India and Sri Lanka signed an agreement that all Indian troops would leave the island by 31 Dec. 1989. India qualified this by making withdrawal conditional upon the guaranteed safety of the Tamil Community. On 19 Sep. the IPKF declared a unilateral cease-fire. The Tamil Tigers, who are still entrenched in Jaffna, the Sri Lankan traditional cultural centre, reciprocated but re-engaged on 29 Sep. At the end of Sep., after internecine fighting between Tamil groups, the Tamil Tigers agreed to political participation conditional upon the evacuation of all Indian troops. Towards the end of the year increased fighting occurred between Tamil Tigers and the Tamil National Army (TNA), the armed wing of EPRLF (Eelam People's Revolutionary Liberation Front) (approx. 350 deaths in Sep.–Dec.), over differences about the conditions of IPKF withdrawal. On 27 Oct. a peace accord was agreed between the Govt, IPKF and EPRLF in which the Tamil Tigers refused to participate. Previously the EPRLF had begun co-operation with the Govt and had taken over some administrative posts in Tamil areas. The IPKF promoted the EPRLF (who were in conflict, in alliance with the Tamil Tigers, with the Govt in 1983–88) as the regional Govt in the Northern and Eastern Provinces, but TNA (armed by India) has subsequently been involved in open conflict also against the Sinhalese Army (Nov.). On 20 Dec. the Tamil Tigers' political wing was reported to have been accepted by the Govt as a legal party for the forthcoming elections. The new Indian Govt announced on 1 Dec. a speeding up of IPKF withdrawal from Sri Lanka, and on 28 Dec. the Indian Foreign Minister announced in Parliament that all Indian troops would be withdrawn from Sri Lanka by 31 Mar. 1990. Approx. 40 000 IPKF remained in Sri Lanka at the end of 1989.

Pacific Asia

Cambodia/ Kampuchea	1977/1977	Cambodian Govt, SRV Govt (Viet Nam)	50 000–70 000 50 000–70 000 (Jan.) – (Oct.)	1979-89: >25 300^p	.^p +
	1975/1979	vs. KR	25 000–40 000		
	1975/1979	vs. KPNLF	10 000–15 000		
	1975/1979	vs. FUNCINPEC/ANS	10 000–20 000		

Comments: Wars, invasion and famines have resulted in 2–3 million deaths since 1970, most during the reign of Pol Pot's Khmer Rouge (1975–78). Border clashes between Kampuchea and Viet Nam during 1977–78 ended with a Vietnamese invasion (Dec. 1978) which ousted the Khmer Rouge (KR) from power (Jan. 1979). Armed opposition is made up of a coalition of KR, Khmer People's National Liberation Front (KPNLF) and Front Uni pour un Cambodge Indépendant, Neutre, Pacifique et Coopératif/Armée Nationale Sihanoukiste (FUNCINPEC/ANS), forming the Coalition Government of Democratic Kampuchea (CGDK) in 1982. In spring 1989 the country's name was changed from the People's Republic of Kampuchea to the State of Cambodia. After a lull in fighting during the first quarter of 1989, the level increased until July. Heavy fighting continued through Aug., in connection with the Cambodia Conference in Paris. Viet Nam began its final withdrawal from Cambodia on 21 Sep. (announced to be completed by 26 Sep.). After the Vietnamese withdrawal heavy fighting was reported from the western and north-western parts of Cambodia between the Govt and the KR as well as the ANS and KPNLF together against the Govt. All 3 groups also stepped up activities deeper inside the country. The Govt acknowledges that there has been an upsurge in the activities of the 3 opposition groups and admits that they have made some territorial gains in the north-west. Shelling by the Govt sometimes affects Thailand. CGDK forces get supplies from Thai territory. Alleged shelling of Cambodian territory by CGDK from the Thai side of the border has also been reported. The Govt accused Thailand of bombing the Cambodian island of Rung Sanlem (Nov.). Diplomatic activities concerning Cambodia were intensive: Cambodian Govt–Thailand (Jan., May, Sep.), Viet Nam–China (Jan., May), the Second Jakarta Informal Meeting (Feb.), Cambodian Govt–FUNCINPEC and KPNLF (May), China–USSR (May), Thai diplomatic initiative (Sep.) and Australian peace proposal (Nov.). In July the Cambodian parties held preparatory talks for the Paris Cambodia Conference in Aug. During the Conference no agreement was reached on the participation of the KR in a future provisional Govt to rule the country during a transition period prior to general elections. Furthermore no international control mechanism to monitor the Vietnamese withdrawal was created.

Location	Year formed/ year joined[a]	Warring parties	No. of troops in 1989	Deaths[b]		
				Total (incl. 1989)	During 1989	Change from 1988[c]
Indonesia/ East Timor	1975/1975	Indonesian Govt vs. Fretilin	14 000	1975–89: 15 000– 16 000 (mil.)	<50	–

Comments: The Revolutionary Front for an Independent East Timor (Fretilin) proclaimed the independent state of the Democratic Republic of East Timor (a former Portuguese colony) in Nov. 1975. Indonesia invaded in Dec., and in July 1977 East Timor became Indonesia's 27th province. By late 1978 most of Fretilin's resistance was quelled. Govt offensives in 1981 and 1983 (after a brief cease-fire). Since the mid-1980s, low-level warfare. Human rights groups report up to 200 000 deaths 1975–89, most caused during the first years after the invasion. During 1989 few clashes reported but Fretilin (approx. 200–400 men) remains in the eastern part of East Timor. Attempts by the church to mediate apparently failed. 14 000 Indonesian troops deployed, acc. to official figures (others put the figure higher) in East Timor. Govt also faces opposition from the Free Papua Movement in Irian Jaya and from Muslim extremist groups on Sumatra.

Location	Year formed/ year joined[a]	Warring parties	No. of troops in 1989	Total (incl. 1989)	During 1989	Change from 1988[c]
Philippines	1968/1986 1981/1984	Philippine Govt vs. NPA vs. RAM	65 000–68 000[d] 23 000–25 000 3 000	1972–89: >37 100	<600	– –

Comments: Main conflict is between Govt and left-wing NPA (New People's Army). In spite of cease-fire and contacts after the formation of the Aquino Govt (Feb. 1986) the conflict has continued. New strategy announced by NPA 'sparrow units' in Mar. 1989, with 'selective' targeting on soldiers and policemen who committed 'serious crimes', following leadership changes. Bombings of US military communications station by opposition, and massacre of civilians by Govt Army unit, were reported in Apr. The same month NPA claimed responsibility for killing US officer Col. James Row. In May assassinations took place in Manila. A massacre by NPA of villages on Mindanao occurred June 1989. Total est. deaths around 500 in NPA–Govt conflict during 1989. Conflicts over regional autonomy have resulted in little violence in 1989. New autonomy laws were passed, providing self-rule for Muslims on Mindanao and for tribal minorities in the Cordillera region. In Apr. and May the largest Muslim armed forces, MNLF (Mindanao National Liberation Front, whose Bangsa Moro Army is est. at 15 000), criticized the laws on Mindanao and indicated possibility of resumption of guerrilla warfare. A truce has been in force between Govt and MNLF since 1986. Occasionally violence has flared up, e.g. in Feb. 1989, although unknown between which parties. MILF (Muslim Islamic Liberation Front, est. 3000 men) has previously also been active in the region. Est. 100 deaths in the region during 1989. Altogether 50 000 people were killed in the Mindanao conflict during 1972–86. Referendum on the autonomy acts on Mindanao in Nov. The 1 Dec. coup attempted by RAM (Reform Movement of the Armed Forces) led to fierce fighting in central Manila with approx. 100 killed, but was eventually repelled by the Aquino Govt.

Africa

Angola	1975/1975	Angolan Govt, Cuban Govt	100 000ʳ 50 000 (Jan.) 25 000 (Dec.) 65 000ˢ	1975–89: >25 600	>600	– –
	1975/1975	vs. UNITA				

Comments: The Govt faces armed opposition by UNITA (National Union for the Total Independence of Angola) which has been supported by S. Africa and the USA. Angola is supported by Cuban troops, the USSR (arms and advisers) and the GDR (advisers). The Aug. 1988 cease-fire between Angola and S. Africa was followed by the signing in Dec. of the Brazzaville Protocol. UNITA started offensive in early Feb. 1989 after rejecting a Govt amnesty (not including UNITA leader Savimbi); however, the offensive was stopped after a request from Côte d'Ivoire Govt. In May the Angolan Govt for the first time announced its willingness to negotiate for peace. Meeting in Gbadolite, Zaire, between President dos Santos (Angola) and Savimbi as well as 18 African leaders resulted in the Gbadolite declaration (22 June), which included agreement on a cease-fire, entered into force on 24 June. However, both sides accused each other of violations, and the cease-fire was ultimately broken on 24 Aug. The fighting, which continued throughout 1989 (over 600 deaths), was reportedly the heaviest since 1988. Govt and UNITA also disagreed over the contents of the declaration. Several attempts, notably the Sep. meeting between 8 African leaders in Kinshasa, Zaire were held with the aim of renewing talks. In late Sep. Savimbi put forward a UNITA peace plan, rejected by the Angolan Govt. After further talks between Mobuto and Savimbi, the latter declared that he was prepared to sign a cease-fire agreement. The Cuban Govt withdrew half of its troops during 1989, acc. to a Cuban military spokesman (under the supervision of UN observer group UNAVEM). By the end of the year the Cuban troops were said (by UNITA) no longer to be involved in fighting. The remainder of Cuban troops are to be progressively withdrawn by mid-1991.

Chad	1982/1987	Chad (UNIR) Govt vs. Islamic Legion	17 000 >2 000	1965–89: 28 000	>800	+ +
	1988/1989	vs. Military opposition	..			

Comments: Different Chadian factions have been fighting each other since 1965 with French and Libyan military interventions. In June 1982 the Forces Armées du Nord led by Hissène Habré seized de facto power, and he became President in Oct. In 1987 the war became a struggle between the combined forces of the Habré Govt and previously Libyan-backed Goukouni Oueddai against Libya, with France giving active support to the Habré Govt. French forces (1700 men) remain in southern parts of Chad. Cease-fire agreed between Chad and Libya in Sep. 1987, and a peace accord was signed in Algeria on 31 Aug. 1989, allowing a 1-year period of negotiations to settle the Aozou Strip dispute. (If negotiations fail, the dispute will be settled by a ruling on the sovereignty issue by the International Court of Justice at the Hague.) The Strip has been occupied by Libya (still with 2000 troops) since 1973 and it has been fought over since 1979. In Feb. 1988, 12 opposition factions joined the ruling UNIR (Union Nationale de l'Indépendence et la Révolution) coalition. In Mar. 1988, 5 GUNT (Govt de l'Unié Nationale Tchadienne) opposition factions met under the chairmanship of Oueddai in Libya to form a new Govt-in-exile in opposition to UNIR. On 3 Mar. 1989, the opposition group Conseil Democratique de la Revolution (CDR, with approx. 1000 troops) joined UNIR. Tribal divisions in the army led to a coup attempt by members of the Habré Govt on 1 Apr. 1989. The leaders of the attempt were from the Bari people living near the border with Sudan, while the President is of the Dazu people in the north. On 16 Oct. 1989, Habré Govt forces launched a pre-emptive attack on a camp on the Sudanese border occupied by the Islamic Legion. In the ensuing 16-day battle over 800 troops were killed, incl. 200 from the Chadian Army. The Islamic Legion consists of Chadian Muslims, members originating in the Middle East (Arabic, probably of Muslim (northern) Chad after their 1987 defeat. The Islamic Legion arose out of the remnants of the anti-Habré forces Druze militia) and some defectors from the Habré Govt (after the coup attempt); it is thought to be led by former officers of the Libyan Army. A French airliner was blown up shortly after leaving the capital city of N'djaména on 17 Sep.; a group calling itself the 'Underground Chadian Movement' was one of several organizations claiming responsibility.

Location	Year formed/year joined[a]	Warring parties	No. of troops in 1989	Deaths[b] Total (incl. 1989)	During 1989	Change from 1988[c]
Ethiopia	1970/1971	Ethiopian Govt vs. EPLF	313 000[h,i]	1962–89: >100 000	10 000	0
	1976/1976	vs. TPLF	30 000			
	1975/1980	vs. EPDM	20 000			
	1977/1977	vs. OLF	..			
	1975/1975	vs. ALF	..			
	1989/1989	vs. Military faction	..			

Comments: War between Ethiopian Govt and Eritreans has gone on since 1961, following the incorporation of Eritrea into the Ethiopian Empire. Main guerrilla movement fighting for Eritrea's independence is today EPLF (Eritrean People's Liberation Front). It has established *de facto* territorial control over some parts of Eritrea. Since 1974 TPLF (Tigray People's Liberation Front) has also waged a military struggle against the Ethiopian Govt. It demands a change of Govt in all of Ethiopia. In the early 1980s EPDM (Ethiopian People's Democratic Movement), with similar demands, also began an armed struggle. In addition OLF (Oromo

Liberation Front) initiated armed struggle demanding the creation of an Oromo state. TPLF and EPLF defeated the Ethiopian Army in Tigray province in early 1989. ALF (Afar Liberation Front) as well as OLF stepped up attacks at this time. The Ethiopian Army abandoned Ma'kale, capital of the province, without a fight in Feb.–Mar. Military faction within Ethiopian armed forces attempted coup against Mengistu Govt (May). 15 generals and 16 officers were killed in Addis Ababa and Asmara, according to official Ethiopian sources. On 5 June Mengistu announced peace initiative. This led to open negotiations with EPLF in Sep. in Atlanta, Ga., USA, with former US President Carter as a 'neutral observer'. Renewed meeting in Nairobi (Nov.) resulting in co-chairmanship by former Tanzanian President Nyerere. A common front, EPRDF, was formed by TPLF and EPDM in May. In Sep. and Oct. TPLF offensive through Wolo province surrounding province capital of Dese. Public discussions initiated between Ethiopian Govt and TPLF in Rome (Nov.) with Italian Govt as participant. Counter-offensive by Govt's newly mobilized forces against TPLF/EPDM in Dec. seemed to have ended in failure. The remaining Cuban troops (in all 2000) left Ethiopia in Sep. 1989.

Location					
Morocco/ Western Sahara	1975/1976	Moroccan Govt vs. Polisario	125 000–150 000 3 500–7 000	1975–89: 10 000– 13 000	400 (mil.) 0

Comments: The former Spanish colony of Western Sahara was divided between Morocco and Mauritania in 1975. Morocco annexed Mauritanian half in 1979, following Mauritanian withdrawal and agreement with the Popular Front for the Liberation of Saguia el Hamra and Rio de Oro (Polisario). Polisario (and its military wing, Sahrawi People's Liberation Army) is fighting for independence for the Saharan Arab Democratic Republic and is based mainly in Algeria. In Apr. 1987 Morocco completed construction of a wall to keep Polisario out. In Aug. 1988 Morocco and Polisario accepted a UN peace plan, including a referendum (to be supervised jointly by the UN and the Organization for African Unity) to decide upon the status of the territory (part of Morocco or independent state). Meeting between King Hassan of Morocco and leaders of Polisario in Jan. 1989 was followed by a truce. Several rounds of talks between UN Secretary-General de Cuellar and political leaders in Algeria, Morocco and Mauritania as well as with Polisario leaders during 1989. However, fighting was renewed in late Sep., with major battles in Oct. and Nov.

| Mozambique | 1975/1976 | Mozambican Govt, Zimbabwe, Nigeria, Malawi vs. MNR | 37 000 3 000–12 000 .. 600 10 000–20 000 | 1985–89: 7 000–9 000 (mil.) 100 000 (civ.) | 300–400 – – |

Comments: The MNR (National Resistance Movement or RENAMO), which has been fighting the Mozambican Govt since 1976, receives e.g. weapons, training and logistics from S. Africa, and its apparent goal is to disrupt and destroy Govt infrastructure. The Mozambican (Frelimo) Govt has received military aid from the UK and France, and economic help from the USA. In addition, military co-operation takes place between

Location	Year formed/ year joined[a]	Warring parties	No. of troops in 1989	Deaths[b]		
				Total (incl. 1989)	During 1989	Change from 1988[c]

Mozambican Govt and Zimbabwe, Nigeria and Malawi. Tanzanian troops sent to help the Govt in 1987 were withdrawn in Jan. 1989. In Sep. 1988 the presidents of Mozambique and S. Africa held talks on the reactivization of the 1984 Nkomati (non-aggression) accord. Sporadic clashes between Govt forces and MNR occurred throughout 1989 but with fewer lives lost than in 1988. The est. total number of war-related deaths in 1976–89 is 600 000–900 000, incl. massacres and famine deaths as well as battle deaths. During the past 3 years, the MNR made 80 raids on an oil pipeline, 270 attacks on the railway from Zimbabwe, as well as repeated raids on power cables. MNR raids into Zimbabwe are reported to have caused 360 Zimbabwean deaths in 2 years. Hundreds of MNR fighters have accepted the Govt's year-old amnesty, extended in Jan. for a further 12-month period. A large-scale Govt offensive against the MNR base in central Mozambique took place at the end of July. At S. Africa's request the US Govt offered to mediate in the conflict (Feb.). The presidents of Zimbabwe and Kenya agreed to try to negotiate a settlement to the conflict (July). Indirect peace talks were opened on 8 Aug. President Chissano has during the year been subjected to pressure from the USSR to negotiate with the MNR. The Mozambican Govt presented a 12-point document through Catholic and Anglican Church leaders, which indicated that Govt policy was now concentrated on national unity rather than ideological considerations. Talks bogged down in early Oct. over recognition of MNR. The Govt insisted that no change of power was possible. The MNR launched an offensive on 8 Oct., mainly directed against Mozambican Army logistical targets. A large quantity of military equipment was captured, and 93 soldiers and police were claimed to have been killed by MNR.

| Somalia | 1981/1981 1989/1989 | Somalia Govt vs. SNM vs. SPM | 61 000 10 000 3 000 | 1988–89: >700 (mil.)[d] | >500 (mil.) | 0 |

Comments: The Somali National Movement (SNM) composed largely of the Isaaq clan in the north of the country, has waged an armed struggle against the Barre Govt since 1981. In 1988 fighting escalated, following the attempt by SNM to establish bases inside Somalia, to replace those previously held on Ethiopian territory. The Govt forces retaliated brutally. SNM claimed in Mar. to hold countryside areas in the north. Attacks were also reported in July in provinces adjoining Djibouti. Defectors from the Army apparently filled the ranks of the SNM. In Dec. SNM attacked Hargesia, the regional capital of northern Somalia. A military mutiny in the south was reported in Mar., and an anti-Govt organization called 'Abris' appeared. The revolt spread to other towns in the south throughout Apr., and in early Aug. opposition still seemed to hold the town of Kisimayu in the south. Opposition now operating under the name of SPM (Somali Patriotic Movement) based on the Ogadeni clan. President Barre comes from the smaller Marehan clan. In late Sep. fighting in the south spilled over into Kenya. In July a massacre took place in Mogadishu. Govt sources put the number of deaths at 24; other sources mentioned 450. In Aug. Govt announced the introduction of a multi-party system and elections in 1990. A total of 50 000 Somalis are estimated to have died from war and famine in May 1988–Dec. 1989.

South Africa	1950/1984	S. African Govt	136 000^v	1984-89: 4 750^w	750^w	0
		vs. ANC	10 000			
South Africa/ Namibia	1966/1967	S. African Govt	21 000 (Jan.)	1967-89: >12 800	>300 (mil.)	– –
			– (Dec.)			
		vs. SWAPO (based in Angola)	9 000 (Jan.)			
			– (Dec.)			

Comments: The conflict over the apartheid politics of the Nationalist Party (NP) forming Govt since 1948 has continued since 1950. Since early 1960s ANC (African National Congress) has been main armed opponent. Armed as well as unarmed struggle has intensified since 1984. In 1989 a shift to non-armed actions was evident. In Jan. ANC announced the closing of military bases in Angola and 1989 was declared 'the year of mass action'. S. African forces still reported stepped up ANC attacks on military targets during the first quarter of 1989, incl. an attack on an air force base near the border with Botswana. In Feb. a bomb attack on a military hospital in Johannesburg occurred as well as a bomb outside an army officers' club in Durban in Mar. Govt renewed emergency in June. At least 30 deaths occurred in election-related protest in Aug.–Sep. against the exclusion of the majority from voting. The Mass Democratic Movement, a new anti-apartheid coalition which appeared in Aug., evidently bringing together ANC, UDF (United Democratic Front, a broad grouping against apartheid) and trade unions, initiated non-violent opposition in Aug.–Sep. In Oct. former ANC Secretary General Walter Sisulu was released from prison together with several other former ANC leaders. In Dec. President F. W. de Klerk held a short meeting with jailed ANC leader Nelson Mandela. Most battle-related deaths in 1989 related to antagonism between UDF and Inkatha, a Zulu-based black organization led by Kwa Zulu leader Chief Buthuelezi. Violence in Natal Province led to approx. 500 deaths Jan.–July. Negotiations between the 2 organizations resulted in some reduced violence. However, 178 deaths were reported for Dec. A bomb attack on the governing NP in May was reportedly carried out by a white right-wing organization. In Nov. it was revealed that S. Africa operated 'hit squads' attacking members of ANC.

Comments: In 1966 the UN renounced S. Africa's mandate over South West Africa and renamed it Namibia. The national anti-colonial movement SWAPO (South West African People's Organization and its military wing, the People's Liberation Army of Namibia, PLAN) has been leading the war for independence. The Brazzaville Protocol, signed in Dec. 1988 by the Govts of Angola, Cuba and S. Africa, facilitates the independence process of Namibia. On 1 Apr. 1989, the day when UN Resolution 435 entered into force, approx. 1500 PLAN troops went into Namibia (Ovamboland) and clashed with the local police force. SWAPO did not admit the intrusion, originally stating that there were no PLAN men in the area and that it was a provocation by S. Africa. However, SWAPO later claimed that PLAN troops had been in the area all along waiting for the UN troops which, acc. to SWAPO, would transport the PLAN troops back to their Angolan bases, and that the PLAN troops were attacked by S. African troops. Following an ultimatum to the UN by S. Africa, which threatened to stop the whole independence process, S. Africa was allowed to use military force against PLAN. 2600–4500 S. African troops and additional troops from SWATF (South West

Location	Year formed/ year joined [a]	Warring parties	No. of troops in 1989	Deaths [b] Total (incl. 1989)	During 1989	Change from 1988 [c]

Africa Territory Forces) were used, causing over 300 deaths (the majority being PLAN troops), in fighting described as the fiercest during the entire conflict. On 9 Apr. an agreement was signed between S. Africa, Angola and Cuba on the withdrawal of PLAN troops. The majority of PLAN forces returned to Angola without help from the UN, although this had been stipulated in the agreement. By May they were all said to be out of Namibia. During a 3.5-month period, starting in early June, 41 000 Namibians returned with the help of the UN, incl. SWAPO leader Sam Nuoma. The election campaign, leading to election on 7–11 Nov. in which SWAPO gained the majority of votes (57%), was calm, although some clashes were reported between SWAPO and DTA (Democratic Turnhalle Alliance) members (reported to have occurred also after the election). By late Nov. all S. African troops were reported to have left Namibia and, acc. to SWAPO's Secretary General, the military command of PLAN had been disbanded. 4650 UN soldiers are deployed in Namibia. The Constituent Assembly is preparing the Constitution, to be implemented on 1 Apr. 1990, when independence is expected to be declared.

| Sudan | 1980/1983 1989/1989 | Sudanese Govt *vs.* SPLA/SPLM *vs.* Military faction | 65 000 30 000 .. | 1983–89: >32 000 (mil.) | .. | 0 |

Comments: Since 1983 SPLA/SPLM (Sudanese People's Liberation Army/Movement) has been fighting the central Govt to increase autonomy of the southern region and to repeal the Islamic Law (Sharia) introduced for the entire country, in contradiction to the peace agreement of 1972, according to SPLA. The coalition Govt in Khartoum was dissolved in Dec. 1988 following disagreements over the peace accord signed in Nov. 1988 between one party, the Democratic Unionist Party (DUP), and SPLA. Violent clashes occurred in Dec. 1988 in Khartoum. In Jan. and Feb. 1989 SPLA made military gains in the south of Sudan. In Feb. 150 senior army officers sent a message to Prime Minister Sadiq al-Mahdi calling for an end to the civil war. In Apr. SPLA conquered the town of Akobo and in early May controlled large areas in the south, including 9 major towns. In Apr. SPLA allowed deliveries of humanitarian aid to famine-stricken areas and announced a unilateral cease-fire. On 30 June the Armed Forces of Sudan took power in a bloodless coup, and a new Govt led by Brig.-Gen. el-Bashir was formed. Talks were initiated between SPLA and the new Govt in Addis Ababa in Aug. Acc. to the Govt (Oct.) 259 000 civilians were estimated to have died from the effects of 6 years of war. More than 32 000 soldiers from both sides were said to have been killed during the war. In Oct. relief operations were suspended as the war intensified. In Nov. the Govt made significant military gains. Talks between the parties in Nairobi, Kenya, chaired by former US President Carter, ended in early Dec. without agreement.

Uganda	1988/1988	Uganda (NRM) Govt	70 000x	1981–89: >6 000 (mil.)	600–800 (mil.)	+ +
	1988/1988	vs. UPDA	<1 000	100 000 (civ.)		
	1987/1989	vs. UPA	..			
		vs. HSM (Kony)	200–800			

Comments: The NRM (National Resistance Movement) Govt, which previously fought guerrilla campaigns starting in 1981, seized power in Jan. 1986. The armed forces of the NRM Govt, who are drawn mainly from southern areas of the country, have been fighting forces in the northern and eastern regions, led by 3 previous leaders of Uganda: Amin (1971–79), Obote (1980–85) and Tito Okello (1985–86). The Govt's amnesty to resistance groups, offered in Aug. 1987, was extended to Apr. 1988. During this period most UPDA (Uganda People's Democratic Army, led by John Angelo Okello) forces surrendered. On 16 Apr. 1988, the UPA (Uganda People's Army, led by associates of Obote) accepted a peace agreement, but a faction under the UPA chairman Otai decided to fight on. On 3 June a further agreement was signed by UPDA, and UPDA members were incorporated in the armed forces of NRM, but a faction of UPDA refused to recognize it. Reduced guerrilla groups remained active throughout 1989. Out of the several spiritualist movements in Uganda, the Holy Spirit Movement (HSM), under the leadership of Joseph Kony (formerly led by priestess Alice Lakwena) was militarily active in 1989. The HSM includes former UDPA troops. A Govt offensive in June 1989, against 2 basically rival groups, the UPA and the HSM (combined fighting force of an est. 1500), resulted in heavy losses on both sides (est. over 600) and the capture of 1000 prisoners by the Govt. Guerrilla use of facilities in Zaire and Kenya continued to create tension in these border areas.

Central and South America

Colombia	1949/1978	Colombian Govt	111 000y	1980–89: >7 500	<2 000y	+ +
	1965/1978	vs. FARC	5 000			
	1968/1977	vs. ELN	2 000			
	..	vs. EPL	800			
		vs. Quintin Lame	..			

Comments: Since the 1970s, bombings, kidnappings and armed attacks have been staged by a number of revolutionary groups. A peace accord in May 1984 between the Govt and 6 main groups gradually deteriorated, and in Oct. 1987, 5 groups, unified under the Simon Bolivar Guerrilla Co-ordinating Committee, offered to renew talks with the Govt. Having released the kidnapped leader of the Conservative Party in July 1988, the M-19 (April 19 Movement), the then most heavily armed group, demanded a national dialogue. M-19 declared a unilateral cease-fire after the Govt announced a peace plan in Sep. 1988. Several rounds of talks in 1989 resulted in an agreement on a 6-month transition period during which M-19 is expected to lay down weapons and enter civil political life. No talks in 1989 resulted in an agreement on a 6-month transition period during which M-19 is expected to lay down weapons and enter civil political life. No military activities were recorded between Govt and M-19 in 1989. The most active group during 1989 was the ELN (National Liberation Army), with repeated attacks on oil pipelines as well as on police stations and army groups. Another group, the EPL (Popular Liberation Army) ceased indirect contacts with the Govt,

Location	Year formed/ year joined[a]	Warring parties	Deaths[b]		Change from 1988[c]
			Total (incl. 1989)	During 1989	
		while the FARC (Revolutionary Armed Forces of Colombia) and the indigenist movement Quintin Lame, despite armed clashes with the Govt during 1989, made preparations for talks with the Govt.			
El Salvador	1976/1979	Salvadorean Govt vs. FMLN	1979–89: >23 250 (mil.) 40 000–47 000 (civ.)	4 750 (mil.)	+ +

No. of troops in 1989: El Salvador — 57 000[f], 7 000[g]

Comments: FMLN (Farabundo Martí Front for National Liberation) is a coalition of 5 armed opposition groups (People's Revolutionary Army, ERP; Popular Liberation Forces, FPL; Armed Forces of National Resistance, FARN; Revolutionary Party of Central American Workers, PRTC; Armed Forces of Liberation, FAL) fighting rightist Salvadorean Govt forces, supported by the USA. The FMLN controls significant portions of the countryside. In the wake of the Esquipulas II Accord some exiled members of the political opposition have returned, creating the Democratic Alliance ('Convergencia'). The right-wing Arena Party's strengthened parliamentary position in Mar. 1988 elections was reinforced by the victory of the party's candidate, Alfredo Cristiani, in the Mar. 1989 presidential elections. On 23 Jan. 1989 the FMLN proposed a 5-month postponement of elections as a requirement for participation. Rejected by the then Christian Democrat President Duarte, the FMLN imposed a ban on highway traffic on election day. The FMLN and the Govt held talks on 13 Sep. in Mexico City. On 11 Nov. the FMLN until-then low-activity warfare changed to a major offensive in San Salvador. On 16 Nov., 6 Jesuit academics at Universidad Centroamericana, San Salvador, were murdered by an army-related group of soldiers, causing debate in the US Congress over military and economic support to the Salvadorean Govt. By the end of 1989 the FMLN offensive, the largest since 1981, gradually waned. In late Dec. President Cristiani removed the chief of the air force, following strong criticism of air force bombings of civilian areas in San Salvador during the FMLN offensive. Acc. to Govt figures, a total of 4750 army and FMLN soldiers were killed during 1989, of whom over 2300 died in the Nov. offensive.

| Guatemala | 1967/1968 1989/1989 | Guatemalan Govt vs. URNG vs. Military opposition | 1967–89: >2 500 (mil.) 43 000 (civ.) | >100 | – |

No. of troops in 1989: Guatemala — 40 000[k], 1 500–2 000, ..

Comments: Armed opposition fighting right-wing military Govts dates back to the 1960s. In 1982 the Guatemalan National Revolutionary Unity (URNG) was formed to co-ordinate the forces of 4 groups (Ejercito Guerrillero de los Pobres, EGP; Partido Guatemalteco del Trabajo, PGT; Fuerzas Armadas Rebeldes, FAR; and Organizacion del Pueblo en Armas, ORPA). In 1982–83 a massive counter-insurgency campaign by Govt forces cut the strength of the armed opposition. The election in late 1985 of the Christian Democrat President Cerezo changed the political situation: political activity by democratic parties was allowed and a reduction of political violence took place, but it rose again in 1988 and throughout 1989. Under the Esquipulas II process the National Commission for Reconciliation, including a Govt representative, met with URNG representatives in Sep. 1988 who proposed a 90-day armistice. The proposal was rejected by a military spokesman. On 1 Mar. 1989 the National Dialogue—another part of the Esquipulas II—was opened, but without participation of the URNG. The Govt requires the URNG to lay down weapons before dialogue. Low-level military and guerrilla activities throughout 1989. The human rights situation deteriorated (from May 1988 after an attempted coup of right-wing military origin) throughout 1989, with approx. 2000 civilians deaths during 1989. A similar, unsuccessful coup attempt was staged on 9 May 1989.

Nicaragua	1981/1981	Nicaraguan Govt	73 500[h, aa]	1981–89: >30 000 (mil.)	– –
		vs. Contras	12 000	600–1 300	

Comments: The largely Honduras-based right-wing Contras (counter-revolutionaries) are trying to overthrow the Sandinista Govt that came into power in 1979. Founded in 1981, the US-supported Contras staged major offensives against Nicaraguan Govt troops in 1983 and 1984. Attacks continued throughout 1985 and 1986 but diminished in 1987. In Nov. 1987 Nicaraguan President Ortega proposed direct talks with the Contras, following the Esquipulas II Agreement of Aug. 1987. In Feb. 1989 the 5 Central American presidents met in La Paz, El Salvador, as part of the Esquipulas process, and agreed that the Contras be disbanded in 90 days. The agreement included international observation of Nicaraguan elections scheduled for 25 Feb. 1990 and the release of some 1600 Somoza National Guardsmen. 1645 were released in Mar. 1989. A summit meeting in Tela, Honduras, on 5–8 Aug. agreed to set up a joint Organization of American States–UN Support and Verification Commission for the disbanding of Contra forces, scheduled for 5 Dec., but not carried out by 31 Dec. Approx. 4000 Contra rebels are estimated to roam Nicaragua's countryside after stepped-up infiltration from Honduras since early Oct. Continued attacks throughout 1989. The Govt's unilateral cease-fire, beginning in Mar. 1988, was ended on 1 Nov., followed by minor clashes.

Panama–USA	1988/1988	Panama (Noriega) Govt	4 400[bb]	1989: 542–1 000[cc]	n.a.
	1989/1989	vs. USA Govt	26 000	..	
		vs. Military faction	..		

Comments: Manuel Noriega has been the de facto leader of Panama since 1983. Relations between the US Govt and Panama deteriorated from the mid-1980s. During 1986 the USA accused Noriega of drug trafficking and money laundering and in Feb. 1988 Noriega was indicted by a US court. The following period saw increased economic, political and diplomatic efforts by the US Govt to make him step down, e.g. economic sanctions and dropped drug charges in exchange for leaving the country. Due to cancellation of election results in the May 1989 presidential elections and the suppression of opposition the US Govt acted by e.g. increasing its military presence in the canal zone and endorsing diplomatic efforts by the OAS. In Sep. the US Govt froze its diplomatic relations in response to the inauguration of F. Rodrigues as Panamanian President. An attempt at a military coup in Oct. (approx. 80 deaths) caused further deterioration in relations

Location	Year formed/ year joined[a]	Warring parties	No. of troops in 1989	Deaths[b]		
				Total (incl. 1989)	During 1989	Change from 1988[c]

between the US Govt and Noriega due to passive US support for the coup attempt. In mid-Dec. the Panamanian Parliament stated that their inter-state relations resembled a state of war, caused by what they considered as US subversive actions. On 16 Dec. a US soldier dressed in civilian clothes was killed by Panamanian soldiers, and a US couple who witnessed the event were harassed, leading to heightened military alert on both sides. On 18 Dec. a police officer was shot and wounded by a US soldier. On 20 Dec. G. Endara (winner of May elections) was sworn in as President and given support by the USA as US troops invaded Panama in operation 'Just Cause', using both troops stationed there (13 000) and additional troops (11 000). Armed attacks where launched against Panama military HQ in Panama City and other targets. The US Govt announced four reasons for the operation, among them, to protect US lives and seize and arrest an indicted drug trafficker. On 21 Dec. US troops controlled key points in Panama City, while the Panamanian troops reportedly still controlled the countryside. On 23 Dec. reinforcements (2000) where sent from the USA. On 24 Dec. Noriega and some of his associates entered the Vatican residency in Panama City and applied for political asylum. Resistance from troops loyal to Noriega decreased successively during the weekend, and on 26 Dec. resistance had almost ceased. Meanwhile, US troops beleaguered the Vatican residency, trying to have Noriega extradited. The Vatican residency rejected this, claiming the absence of an extradition treaty. By 31 Dec. Noriega was still inside the Vatican residency. Estimates of the number of deaths vary considerably.

Peru	1980/1981	Peruvian Govt	80 000[d]	1981–89:	>2 300	0
	1984/1986	vs. Sendero Luminoso	4 000–5 000	3 000–5 000 (mil.)		
	1988/1989	vs. MRTA	500	5 000–10 000 (civ.)		
		vs. Rodrigo Franco	..			

Comments: The Sendero Luminoso (Shining Path) describes itself as 'Maoist', with the goal of putting workers and peasants in power. The increased guerrilla activity in Dec. 1988 (after a period of low-intensity conflict) continued in 1989. The death-toll rose (over 2300 killed in 1989 compared with just under 2000 for 1988), especially in the ranks of Sendero Luminoso and the urban guerrilla group MRTA (Tupac Amaru Revolutionary Movement). In 1989 the Sendero Luminoso further extended its territorial occupation. One-third of the country is now subject to the Govt emergency law. Some evidence of an alliance of Sendero Luminoso with coca producers of Upper Huallaga; crop protection in exchange for sophisticated long-range weapons. Sendero Luminoso organized in Nov. 'armed strike' against (local) elections, objective being to provoke a military take-over, but 'peace march' in Lima demonstrated support for the Govt. On 4 Feb. an MRTA leader was captured by Govt troops. The right-wing death-squad Rodrigo Franco killed a left-wing trade union leader in Feb.

a 'Year formed' is the year in which the two warring parties last formed their conflicting policies or the year in which a new party, state or alliance involved in the conflict came into being. 'Year joined' is the year in which the armed fighting last began or the year(s) in which armed fighting recommenced after a period for which no armed combat was recorded. For conflicts with very sporadic armed combat over a long period, the 'year joined' may also refer to the beginning of a period of sustained and/or exceptionally heavy combat.

b The figures for deaths refer to total battle-related deaths during the conflict. The figures exclude, as far as data allow, civilian deaths owing to famine and disease. *'Mil.'* and *'civ.'* refer to estimates, where available, of *military* and *civilian* deaths; where there is no such indication, the figure refers to total military and civilian battle-related deaths in the period or year given. Information about the conflicts which covers a calendar year is by necessity more tentative for the last months of the year. Experience has also shown that the reliability of figures is improved over time; they are therefore revised each year.

c The 'change from 1988' is measured as the increase or decrease in battle-related deaths in 1989 compared with deaths in 1988. Although based on data that cannot be considered totally reliable, the symbols represent the following changes:

++   increase in battle deaths of more than 100%
+   increase in battle deaths of less than 100%
0   stable rate of battle deaths (+ or – 10%)
–   decrease in battle deaths of less than 50%
– –   decrease in battle deaths of more than 50%.

d The figure includes Securitate (20 000 men), the 'Directorate 5 for the Protection of Dignitaries' (1000–1500 men) and a special anti-terrorist force (1000 men). The Border Guards (17 000) reportedly did not participate in Securitate's fight against the National Salvation Front, supported by the national armed forces. The exact figure for those engaged in actual combat unknown.

e Includes total armed forces. The exact figure in actual combat is unknown. Some civilians joined the military in the fighting.

f Romanian hospitals counted 750–800 dead. The Army's losses are given as 196. Victims in Timisoara were 90, according to official figures. Over 40 soldiers were reportedly executed after refusing to shoot at demonstrators in Timisoara. The number of killed Securitate men is unknown.

g In addition, Iran has 250 000 Revolutionary Guard Corps.

h If nothing else is indicated, the figure shows regular army troops (not total armed forces). Not all these troops are necessarily engaged in actual combat.

i Including the 2000 NLA (Iranian National Liberation Army) deaths (1988) in the Iran–Iraq War.

j Iran has 955 000 men in the Army, including perhaps 480 000 recalled reserves.

k A major part is connected with the reported use of chemical weapons in 1988.

l Total armed forces. In addition, para-military forces reach 200 000 or more.

m The figure is likely to include all deaths in connection with the war, that is, not only battle-related deaths.

n This is a provisional figure, based primarily on total Sikh strength for 1988 but allowing for the loss of an unprecedented 700 deaths of separatists during 1989.

o An estimated death figure for 1989 is >1000. Exact figures are not available.

p Battle-related deaths during 1975–78: total: 43 000. Vietnamese losses, according to Viet Nam, 30 000. Khmer Rouge Govt losses 13 000: number of deaths due to the activities of Vietnamese agents numbered 10 000, and 3000 were killed in connection with the Kampuchean authorities' campaigns against alleged Vietnamese agents. These figures were given by the KR in July 1987. (To these figures can be added over 20 000 people who died from illness and food shortage.) No precise figures regarding KR casualties in the fighting against Viet Nam have been given. Other estimates put the number of deaths above the expected normal death rate for the 1975–78 period at 750 000– 1 000 000. The present Cambodian Govt official figure for the same period is 3 314 768 deaths. Battle-related deaths during 1979–89: the only figure avaiable is from official Vietnamese sources, indicating that 25 300 Vietnamese soldiers died in Cambodia. An estimated figure for the period 1979–89, based on various sources, is >50 000, and for 1989, >1000. Exact figures are not avaliable.

q Total Philippine Armed Forces are 112 000, of which the Army is 68 000. In addition there is a Constabulary of 38 000 and Citizen Armed Force Geographical Units (CAFGU) of 45 000.

r Total armed forces.

s Including 28 000 'regulars' (1–2 years of service) and 37 000 'militia'.

t Including an estimated 150 000 People's Militia.

u Prior to the agreement between Ethiopia and Somalia in Apr. 1988, this conflict was regarded as part of the Ethiopia–Somalia conflict.

v Including Army (77 500) and National Service (58 500). In addition the South African police number 55 000.

w Including killings connected with the struggle between UDF and Inkatha supporters.

x The National Resistance Army (NRA), the total armed forces of the Ugandan (NRM) Govt, numbers 70 000. NRA incorporates surrendered Uganda People's Democratic Army (UDPA and Uganda National Liberation Army (the former armies of Obote and Okello).

y Politically related killings (i.e., excluding killings resulting from fighting between Govt and cocaine cartels).

z One source reports that independent estimates suggest some 15 000 in the Nov. offensive.

aa Including 41 500 active and 32 000 recalled reserves and militia.

bb Includes total armed forces. The exact figure for those engaged in actual combat is unknown.

cc Death figures vary considerably. According to official US figures, 542 persons were killed. *Panorama Catolica* (published by the Catholic Church of Panama) reports 655 deaths, based on figures from Panamanian hospitals and mortuaries. According to the Methodist Church of Panama, 1000 persons were killed. 204 persons are reported missing, according to the Panamanian Red Cross. There are also reports of mass graves. Furthermore, other independent sources give figures, partly based on an inventory of damage, of between 3000 and 5000 killed.

Sources: For additional information on these conflicts, see chapters in previous editions of the *SIPRI Yearbooks*—Lindgren, K., Wilson, G. K. and Wallensteen, P., 'Major armed conflicts in 1988', SIPRI, *SIPRI Yearbook 1989: World Armaments and Disarmament* (Oxford University Press: Oxford, 1989), chapter 9; Wilson, G. K. and Wallensteen, P., 'Major armed conflicts in 1987', SIPRI, *SIPRI Yearbook 1988: World Armaments and Disarmament*

(Oxford University Press: Oxford, 1988), chapter 9; and Goose, S., 'Armed conflicts in 1986, and the Iraq–Iran War', SIPRI, *SIPRI Yearbook 1987: World Armaments and Disarmament* (Oxford University Press: Oxford, 1987), chapter 8.

The following other reference books were used: Brogan, P., *World Conflicts* (Bloomsbury: London, 1989); *Defense and Foreign Affairs Handbook* (Copley: Washington, DC, 1976); Gantzel, K.-J. and Meyer-Stamer, J. (eds), *Die Kriege nach dem Zweiten Weltkrieg bis 1984* (Weltforum: Munich, 1986); International Institute for Strategic Studies, *The Military Balance 1989–1990* (Brassey's: London, 1989); Janke, P., *Guerrilla and Terrorist Organisations: A World Directory and Bibliography* (Harvester Press: Hemel Hempstead, 1983); Jongman, B., *War, Armed Conflict and Political Violence* (Polemological Institute, National University: Groningen, the Netherlands, 1982); Kaye, G. D., Grant, D. A. and Emond, E. J., *Major Armed Conflict, A Compendium of Interstate and Intrastate Conflict 1720 to 1985*, report R95 (Operational Research and Analysis Establishment [ORAE], Canadian Department of National Defence: Ottawa, 1985); Keesing's, *Political Dissent* (Longman: Harlow, Essex, 1983); Laffin, J., *The World in Conflict 1989* (Brassey's: London, 1989); Minority Rights Group, *World Directory of Minorities* (Longman: Harlow, Essex, 1989); Sivard, R., *World Military and Social Expenditures* (World Priorities Inc.: Washington, DC, annual); *The Statesman's Yearbook* (Macmillan: London, annual); Small, M. and Singer, J. D., *Resort to Arms, International and Civil Wars 1816–1980* (Sage: Beverly Hills, Calif., 1982); Wallensteen, P. (ed.) *States in Armed Conflict 1988* (Department of Peace and Conflict Research: Uppsala, Sweden, 1989); research reports on particular conflicts; the SIPRI Arms Trade Project data base; and information available at the Department of Peace and Conflict Research, Uppsala University, in the continuing research project on armed conflicts.

The following journals, newspapers and news agencies were consulted: *Africa Confidential* (London); *African Defense* (Paris); *Armed Forces* (London); *Amnesty Press* (Stockholm); *Asian Defence Journal* (Kuala Lumpur); *Boston Globe* (Boston, Mass.); BBC World Service News (London); *Christian Science Monitor* (Boston, Mass.); *Dagens Nyheter* (Stockholm); *Defense and Foreign Affairs* (Alexandria, Va.); *The Economist* (London); *Far Eastern Economic Review* (Hong Kong); *Financial Times* (London and Frankfurt); *The Guardian* (London); *Jane's Defence Weekly* (Coulsdon, Surrey); *IDSA Journal* (New Delhi); *Indian Express* (New Delhi); *The Independent*(London); *International Herald Tribune* (Paris); *Keesing's Contemporary Archives* (Harlow, Essex); *Latin America Weekly Report* (London); *Mexico and Central America Report* (London); *The Middle East* (London); *Nyheter från Latinamerika* (Stockholm); *New Statesman & Society* (London); *Newsweek* (New York); *New York Times* (New York); *The Times* (London); *Der Spiegel* (Hamburg); *Svenska Dagbladet*(Stockholm); *Time* (New York); *Upsala Nya Tidning* (Uppsala;) *US News & World Report* (Washington, DC); *Washington Post* (Washington, DC); *Washington Times* (Washington, DC); *World Reporter* (Datasolve: London).

Part III. Developments in arms control

11. US–Soviet nuclear arms control

REGINA COWEN KARP

I. Introduction

Although the Strategic Arms Reduction Talks (START) did not produce an agreement on the reduction of strategic nuclear weapons in 1989, the USA and the USSR narrowed their differences on some issues that had previously hampered the negotiations. During the year, it also became apparent that the emerging START treaty will neither impede US and Soviet plans to modernize their strategic forces nor bring about substantial changes in the force structure of either side.

Since the START negotiations resumed under the Nuclear and Space Talks (NST) in 1985, hopes of achieving an agreement have been raised repeatedly, only to be dashed during subsequent rounds of negotiation. In August 1987, Max Kampelman, then head of the US delegation in Geneva, reportedly stated that a treaty could be agreed upon and ratified by the US Senate before the Reagan Administration left office. General Secretary Mikhail Gorbachev also voiced his hope that a START agreement could be achieved during the first half of 1988.[1] However, 1988 passed without an agreement. At the December 1989 US–Soviet summit meeting in Malta, the prospects for an agreement were raised yet again with President George Bush's call to resolve all remaining issues by June 1990, in time for the next scheduled summit meeting. If this goal is met, then a START treaty could be ready for signature by the end of 1990.[2]

In order to assess whether the optimism expressed at the Malta summit meeting is indeed justified, this chapter briefly reviews the more recent record of the START negotiations. Second, it describes some of the major obstacles that have prevented agreement in the past and reviews the areas in which progress was achieved during 1989. Third, the discussion examines the emerging START agreement itself and its probable impact upon the structure of US and Soviet strategic nuclear forces. Finally, observations are offered about the possible consequences of a START treaty for strategic stability specifically and US–Soviet relations generally.

II. Understandings reached

The USA and the USSR have already reached substantive agreement on some basic provisions of a START treaty: a ceiling of 1600 strategic nuclear delivery vehicles, with no more than 6000 accountable warheads, and a sub-limit of 4900 ballistic missile warheads, leaving 1100 warheads (for gravity bombs and short-range attack missiles) to be carried by strategic bombers.

[1] Flournoy, M., 'A rocky START: optimism and obstacles on the road to reductions', *Arms Control Today,* vol. 17, no. 8 (Oct. 1987), p. 7.
[2] US Information Service, SSF–705 (US Embassy, Stockholm), 3 Dec. 1989, p. 16.

At the summit meeting in Washington in December 1987, the USA and the USSR agreed to exclude sea-launched cruise missiles (SLCMs) from the 6000-warhead limit. Thus, 758 US nuclear-armed SLCMs and, according to Central Intelligence Agency (CIA) estimates, some 1500 Soviet nuclear-armed SLCMs are excluded.[3] Agreement was also reached to reduce the number of Soviet 10-warhead SS-18 intercontinental ballistic missiles (ICBMs) by half, or from 308 to 154 missiles.[4] Furthermore, a 50 per cent reduction in the throw-weight of Soviet ballistic missiles was agreed.[5]

The USA and the USSR possess 1907 and 2448 strategic nuclear delivery vehicles, respectively. Thus, a reduction to 1600 delivery vehicles would constitute a 16 per cent cut for the USA and a cut of almost 35 per cent for the USSR. To reduce to the sub-limit of 4900 on ballistic missile warheads, both sides will have to implement even larger cuts. The USA, which currently deploys 7602 warheads on ballistic missiles, will have to reduce this number by about 35 per cent; the USSR, which deploys 10 092 ballistic missile warheads, will have to implement reductions of at least 51 per cent.[6]

Counting rules under START

Under the counting rules of the 1979 SALT II Treaty, the number of warheads carried by a ballistic missile was based on the *maximum* number of warheads that a missile had been *flight-tested* to carry. In order to avoid the problem of over-counting under a START agreement, the USA and the USSR agreed to attribute numbers of warheads to the various types of ballistic missile. Attributing maximum numbers of warheads to missiles can indeed be misleading: actual payloads may be less than indicated by the flight-tests.

Under the START counting rules, cuts in the number of ballistic missile warheads are based upon agreed warhead numbers reflecting actual operational levels. Thus, for example, both sides agreed to count the US Poseidon C-3 SLBM as carrying only 10 warheads (previously 14) and the Soviet SS-N-23 SLBM as carrying 4 warheads (previously 10).[7] The number of warheads for the US Trident D-5 SLBM has been set at 8.[8] While START counting rules more accurately reflect the level of operational forces, they will result in substantial demands on a system of verification: to verify less than the maximum number of warheads on a particular missile is expected to be an exceedingly complex enterprise.

[3] US Arms Control and Disarmament Agency, *Annual Report to Congress 1988* (US Government Printing Office: Washington, DC, Mar. 1989), pp. 12-16.

[4] For a breakdown of Soviet ICBMs, see chapter 1, table 1.3.

[5] US Department of Defense, *Soviet Military Power: Prospects for Change 1989* (Government Printing Office: Washington, DC, 1989), p. 90.

[6] These percentages were calculated by the author using SIPRI figures. See chapter 1, tables 1.1 and 1.3.

[7] START counting rules are explained in International Institute for Strategic Studies, *The Military Balance 1988–1989* (Brassey's: London, 1988), pp. 230–32.

[8] Slocombe, W. B., 'Force posture consequences of the START treaty', *Survival,* vol. 30, no. 5 (Sep./Oct. 1988), p. 403.

Restrictions on the number of warheads that may be carried by strategic bombers appear to be severe under START, with a limit of 1100 warheads for both sides if they reach the 4900 ballistic missile warhead sub-limit. At present, the USA maintains a fleet of 311 strategic bombers with a total of 4500 warheads. The USSR fields 162 strategic bombers, carrying 1228 warheads.[9] To comply with the limit on strategic bombers, substantial cuts in the number of warheads would have to be made, particularly by the USA. However, at the 1986 summit meeting in Reykjavik both sides agreed to count each strategic bomber not carrying air-launched cruise missiles (ALCMs) as carrying one warhead irrespective of the actual payload. As a result, the warhead count for strategic bomber forces is greatly understated. For the USA, 166 non-ALCM-carrying bombers would count as only 166 warheads, although these aircraft could carry as many as 1988 warheads; in the case of the USSR, 120 non-ALCM-carrying bombers would count as 120 warheads, although they could carry 1440 warheads.

Taken together, the understandings reached between the USSR and the USA on how to count strategic nuclear weapons under a START treaty tend to favour US force structure requirements and arms control objectives. To implement the sub-limit of 4900 ballistic missile warheads will demand adjustments both within and between Soviet ICBM and SLBM forces. The reduction of the USSR's SS-18 force by half will significantly reduce the threat posed by these missiles to US silo-based ICBMs. The permissive counting rule for warheads carried by strategic bombers favours the USA because the USSR does not maintain aircraft in sufficient number to exploit the counting rule effectively at present.

Overall, the size of the strategic reductions envisaged in a START treaty does not meet the oft-cited 50 per cent figure.[10] Rather, they reduce or cap the number of certain nuclear weapons and warheads. Reduction estimates vary because of different force mixes under START and the fact that ALCM counting rules still have not been resolved. After the START reductions have been implemented, the USA is likely to have a nuclear force of somewhere between 10 000 and 12 000 warheads, and the USSR would have between 9000 and 10 000 warheads. Yet despite the fact that actual warhead numbers exceed the limit of 6000 accountable warheads, individual cuts and limits are significant.

III. Progress on outstanding issues during 1989

Although much progress was achieved during the second Reagan Administration concerning some of the basic components of a START treaty, several major issues were not resolved. This section reviews the main issues and discusses some of the reasons why a number of these issues may be closer to resolution in 1990 and why others continue to plague the negotiations.

[9] See note 6.
[10] Einhorn, R., 'Strategic arms reduction talks', *Survival*, vol. 30, no. 5 (Sep./Oct. 1988), p. 390.

ALCM counting rules

In 1989, some progress was achieved regarding the agreement of counting rules for ALCMs which, unlike SLCMs, are counted against the 6000-warhead limit. The question, therefore, is how many ALCMs should be attributed to each bomber carrying these missiles. Having already agreed to liberal counting rules for non-ALCM-carrying bombers, the USSR, until July, maintained its position of counting those bombers carrying ALCMs with the maximum number of missiles.[11] In other words, the USSR applied the previous counting rule used under the SALT II Treaty. The USA, on the other hand, prefers to negotiate an agreement on the number of ALCMs for each type of bomber, although individual aircraft may carry a greater number of missiles. The USA has proposed counting each bomber type as carrying 10 ALCMs.[12] In July 1989, the USSR modified its position to the extent that it indicated a willingness to count ALCMs on the basis of actual, rather than maximum, payloads. In response, the USA clarified that it does not want to be locked into a regime that would prescribe specific numbers of ALCMs. In the US view, this would result in decreased flexibility in choosing the number of ALCMs to deploy on specific bombers.[13]

The USSR's hesitancy to accept the US counting rule for ALCMs is understandable. The USA has tested its B-52G and B-52H strategic bombers with 20 ALCMs each.[14] Under the US counting rule, the USA's 173 B-52G/Hs would be listed as carrying only 1730 ALCMs, although the actual number deployed could be twice as many. The USSR's fleet of 80 Bear H bombers has also been tested with 20 ALCMs, but authoritative estimates project the actual payload per aircraft to be 8.[15]

Because air-breathing weapons are slow-flying and must penetrate air defences to reach their targets, the USA maintains that these weapons are not suitable for first-strike missions and, therefore, a START treaty should not unduly constrain such weapon systems.[16] Neither should START count ALCM-carrying bombers more heavily than it counts ICBMs, which are regarded as the most threatening systems. Because strategic bombers have always played a relatively minor retaliatory role in Soviet strategy, the USSR in deed, if not in word, may actually agree with the US position.

Nevertheless, the acceptance of the US counting rules by the USSR would serve to codify a US numerical superiority in ALCMs of more than *double* the Soviet capability. From the point of view of the USSR, it may be reasonable to argue that its position on ALCMs has already shifted towards

---

[11] See note 3, p. 14; Gordon, M., 'US may alter missile stand', *International Herald Tribune*, 17–18 June 1989, p. 4; and 'Nuclear and Space Talks: US and Soviet proposals', *Issues Brief* (Office of Public Affairs, US Arms Control and Disarmament Agency: Washington, DC, 21 Sep. 1989), p. 2.

[12] See note 6. See also Lehman, R., 'Interview on US START position', *Defense News*, 31 July 1989; and US Information Service, EUR–408 (US Embassy, Stockholm), 16 Nov. 1989, p. 9.

[13] Dullforce, W., 'Soviet offer on air-launched missiles', *Financial Times*, 28 Sep. 1989, p. 2; *Arms Control Reporter*, July 1989, p. 611.B.565.

[14] See note 6.

[15] See International Institute for Strategic Studies, *The Military Balance 1989–1990* (Brassey's: London, 1989), p. 212; and note 6.

[16] See note 8, p. 389.

that of the USA and that any further concessions should come from the USA. At the same time, however, because the USSR has already demonstrated a willingness to amend its position, US negotiators might be tempted to hold out for further concessions.

SLCMs: the perennial problem

Another vexing problem for negotiators has been the issue of long-range nuclear-armed SLCMs.[17] The USA and the USSR have been trying to find ways to limit SLCMs ever since they agreed at the Washington summit meeting in December 1987 not to count these weapons under the 6000-warhead limit. With regard to US objectives, two reasons speak against a strict limitation of SLCMs: (a) the US Navy believes that limits on SLCMs are not verifiable; and (b) the Navy is concerned that on-site inspection could allow Soviet inspectors to obtain sensitive information beyond that necessary for their official mission. Given these strong reservations about the limitation and verification of SLCMs, the USA has consistently rejected calls for naval arms control measures.

Instead of strict limitations, the USA would prefer a regime whereby the two sides would periodically exchange information about their deployments of nuclear-armed SLCMs. The US nuclear SLCM programme is relatively small—only 758 out of a total of 3994 missiles.[18] However, although the USA is apparently more interested in the conventional version of the SLCM, it opposes a ban on nuclear-armed SLCMs on the grounds that it would be difficult to verify. Prior to 1989, the USSR had suggested a limit of 400 nuclear-armed and 600 conventionally armed SLCMs for each side.[19] The USA rejected the proposal because it required intrusive verification measures and would facilitate the identification of the type and number of US naval vessels equipped with SLCMs.

The steadfast refusal of the US Administration and Navy to address Soviet concerns about naval arms control, however, may be beginning to change. In an interview in early January 1990, retired former chairman of the Joint Chiefs of Staff Admiral William J. Crowe, Jr called for negotiating a ban on tactical nuclear weapons at sea. Crowe reportedly stated that 'the United States should consider negotiating with the USSR to eliminate tactical nuclear weapons from surface warships and submarines, or to reduce [the USA's] naval forces in exchange for major Soviet concessions on strategic

---

[17] For discussions of the SLCM issue, see Rubin, J. P., 'Limiting SLCMs—a better way to START', Arms Control Today, vol. 19, no. 3 (Apr. 1989), pp. 10–16; Terriff, T., 'Controlling nuclear SLCM', Survival, vol. 31, no. 1 (Jan.–Feb. 1989), pp. 52–69; Brooks, L., 'Nuclear SLCM add to deterrence and security', International Security, vol. 13, no. 3 (winter 1988/89), pp. 169–74; Gottemoeller, R., 'Finding solutions to SLCM arms control problems', International Security, vol. 13, no. 3 (winter 1988/89), pp. 175–83; Mustin, H., 'The sea-launched cruise missile', International Security, vol. 13, no. 3 (winter 1988/89), pp. 184–90; and Postol, T., 'Banning nuclear SLCM', International Security, vol. 13, no. 3 (winter 1988/89), pp. 191–202.

[18] Rubin (note 17), p.12.

[19] 'Nuclear and Space Talks: US and Soviet proposals', Issues Brief (Office of Public Affairs, US Arms Control and Disarmament Agency: Washington, DC, 16 Nov. 1988), p. 2.

arms disputes'.[20] Despite the fact that Admiral Crowe made his comments after having retired from the Navy, his outspokenness on the issue does suggest that the US consensus concerning no naval arms control may not be as solid as officially portrayed.

SLCM verification

The problem of how to deal with the issue of SLCM verification has stimulated great interest within the US arms control community. In a major study in 1988, arms control specialists at Stanford University in California investigated a number of SLCM verification issues and concluded that 'it is extremely difficult to devise a verification scheme which would effectively enforce limits on nuclear-armed, long-range SLCMs'.[21] The study explored the relationship between various limitation options and the resultant verification requirements. Among its most important findings, the study concludes that a combination of deployment limits, missile tagging, perimeter portal monitoring and challenge inspections could indeed provide a high degree of confidence in a SLCM verification regime. Whether or not it would be extensive enough to gain the necessary political support in the USA, however, is another question.

In an attempt to demonstrate the feasibility of SLCM verification, Soviet scientists met with a private group of US scientists in July 1989 on board the Soviet missile cruiser *Slava* in the Black Sea. They used sensors to measure radiation emissions. Soviet authorities had, however, removed all sources of radiation other than the cruise missile to be inspected from the ship and provided instructions on where the sensors should be placed.[22] Presence of the nuclear warhead was detected and the experiment was successful in a narrow technical sense, but its usefulness as part of a SLCM verification regime under operational (rather than ideal) conditions is doubtful.

In a surprise move at a meeting of the US and Soviet Foreign Ministers in Jackson Hole, Wyoming, in September 1989, the USSR proposed to limit SLCMs outside of a START treaty, as part of a broader naval arms control agreement and on the basis of reciprocal obligations.[23] Although the USA is still generally opposed to naval arms control, the shift in the Soviet position does indicate that a START treaty might be concluded without an immediate

[20] See Smith, R. J., 'Crowe urges talks on reducing naval weapons', *International Herald Tribune*, 9 Jan. 1990, pp. 1–2.

[21] Center for International Security and Arms Control, 'Potential verification provisions for long-range, nuclear-armed sea-launched cruise missiles', Workshop Report, Stanford University, July 1988, p. 19.

[22] See US Information Service, EUR–508 (US Embassy, Stockholm), 28 July 1989, pp. 15–16; and *Arms Control Reporter*, July 1989, pp. 661.B.557–58. For an eye-witness account of the joint US–Soviet experiment, see Cochran, T. B., 'Black Sea experiment only a START', *Bulletin of the Atomic Scientists*, Nov. 1989, pp. 13–16. Cochran led the Natural Resources Defense Council delegation to the experiment. For a Soviet view on SLCM verification, see ['Disentangling the knots'], *Pravda*, 17 Aug. 1989, p. 4 (in Russian); and ['Another step'], *Krasnaya Zvezda*, 10 Jan. 1990, p. 3 (in Russian).

[23] US Information Service, SUF–705 (US Embassy, Stockholm), 24 Sep. 1989; 'Joint Statement of the Wyoming Ministerial' (US Arms Control and Disarmament Agency: Washington, DC, 23 Sep. 1989), p. 2. The Joint Statement is also reprinted in *Arms Control Today*, vol. 19, no. 8 (Oct. 1989), p. 22.

solution to the impasse over SLCMs. In late December 1989, the USSR provided a further indication of its desire to make progress on the SLCM issue: Soviet chief arms control negotiator Yuri Nazarkin reportedly stated that the USSR might be willing to de-emphasize shipboard verification of SLCMs.[24] Although his remark is not part of the official Soviet negotiating position in Geneva, it could be taken as a sign that the USSR may now be moving significantly closer to the US proposal for a periodic declaration of the number of deployed SLCMs by both sides and that the subject of SLCMs is apparently becoming a negotiable issue for the USSR.

The issue of mobile ICBMs

The issue of the mobile ICBM is a complicated one for the USA. It involves the US arms control position at Geneva, decisions concerning strategic force modernization and the maintenance of a fragile congressional consensus on funding. The Reagan Administration called for a ban on mobile ICBMs to be negotiated at the Geneva talks ostensibly because of the difficulties in verifying these missiles. This ban had effectively postponed a decision to choose one of two possible mobile ICBM systems. In September 1989, contingent upon congressional funding of both the MX and the Small ICBM (SICBM), the Bush Administration decided to drop the US ban on mobile missiles.[25] The USA has not yet deployed a mobile ICBM. The USSR, on the other hand, has deployed mobile SS-24 and SS-25 missiles since 1987 and 1985,[26] respectively, and has opposed a ban on mobile ICBMs throughout the negotiations.

With respect to strategic stability, the mobile ICBM is believed to redress some of the most severe problems of fixed, silo-based ICBMs. With mobile missiles, policy-makers face less pressure to launch them in times of crisis. Because mobile missiles are more difficult to target, they help dissuade an adversary from believing that it could execute a successful first strike. There is little disagreement in the USA that, if the ICBM force has a future at all, then it lies in a shift from a fixed to a mobile basing mode for a considerable portion of the force.[27] Yet while the principles of mobility are not disputed, the systems that are to provide this capability are being debated.

The Bush Administration's surprising decision to go ahead with both strategic systems probably had more to do with Administration uncertainty as to which system Congress would fund than with the view that both systems are necessary for US security. Because Congress is unlikely to fund both systems, a crucial decision concerning US force structure was

[24] Gordon, M. R., 'Soviets consider compromise in Geneva on cruise missiles', *International Herald Tribune*, 20 Dec. 1989, p. 4.
[25] 'US may switch on arms', *International Herald Tribune*, 21 June 1989, p. 4; US Information Service, EUR–204 (US Embassy, Stockholm), 19 Sep. 1989, p. 8; 'Soviets praise US shift on missiles', *International Herald Tribune*, 21 Sep. 1989, p. 2.
[26] See note 4, p. 89; and Welch, L. (Gen.), 'One on one', *Defense News*, 29 May 1989, p. 30.
[27] Gray, R. C., 'The Bush Administration and mobile missiles', *Survival*, vol. 31, no. 5 (Sep./Oct. 1989), pp. 415–31, provides a thorough review of the rationales behind mobile system deployment and the systems involved.

consigned to the congressional budgetary process for resolution.[28] Indeed, congressional support for the Bush Administration's missile package is uneven: many Republicans favour the sole procurement of the MX, while a majority of Democrats argue in support of the SICBM. Still other Democrats are opposed to the procurement of *any* new ICBM. During deliberations in July 1989 over the US defence budget for the 1990 fiscal year, House Democrats mustered enough votes to slice the Administration's budget request for the MX missile by half. Following that decision, liberal Democrats and conservative Republicans joined forces and successfully eliminated all funds for the SICBM.[29] The joint House–Senate budget conference set aside a funding pool of $1.13 billion for the continued development of the SICBM and of a rail-based basing mode for the MX.[30]

Although the Bush Administration in the end managed to secure funding for both the MX and the SICBM for FY 1990, it is far from certain that Congress will continue with the compromise to support both systems. If either missile can *only* be procured by procuring both, then the strain on an already tight defence budget could force the Administration to make some difficult choices. Indeed, defence budget cuts of a substantial nature are already in the offing. In November 1989, Defense Secretary Richard Cheney announced cuts of $180 billion from the projected five-year defence plan, a step which, if carried out, might delay the modernization of the US ICBM force.[31] The USA may then find itself in a post-START security environment with an increasingly vulnerable silo-based ICBM force.

Unresolved issues concerning force structure and the effect of expected cuts in the US defence budget will likely keep the issue of ICBM modernization on the agenda of both the Administration and Congress for some time. If the Administration persists in its determination to procure two ICBM systems, it must convince Congress that this decision is both strategically and financially sound. Senator Sam Nunn and National Security Adviser Brent Scowcroft advocate a ban on US and Soviet multiple-warhead mobile missiles. Both believe that the Soviet 10-warhead SS-24

[28] Finnegan, P., 'Nunn urges Administration to push for both MX, Midgetman', *Defense News*, 19 June 1989, pp. 3 and 58; Finnegan, P., 'Aspin: Midgetman's fate rests with Administration', *Defense News*, 29 May 1989, pp. 4 and 28.

[29] Finnegan, P., 'House hands the Administration setback on strategic programs', *Defense News*, 31 July 1989, p. 8; Graham, H. E., 'House and Senate conferees battle over strategic programs', *Arms Control Today*, vol. 19, no. 8 (Oct. 1989), p. 31; Halverson, T. E., 'As defense budget battles continue, Cheney blasts Congress on Soviet threat', *Arms Control Today*, vol. 19, no. 7 (Sep. 1989), p. 29; Towell, P. and Fessler, P., 'Senate defense bill portends tough fights with House', *Congressional Quarterly Weekly Report*, 5 Aug. 1989, pp. 2053–2058; Morrow, M. 'FY90–91 budget indicates shifting congressional priorities', *Armed Forces Journal International*, Sep. 1989, pp. 11–12; Towell, P. 'House deals Bush team blows on missiles, weapons cuts', *Congressional Quarterly Weekly Report*, 29 July 1989, pp. 1974–75; 'Hitch in START viewed as no barrier to summit', *International Herald Tribune*, 18 Sep. 1989, p. 2.

[30] Famiglietti, L., 'US Congress agrees $305 billion FY90 budget', *Jane's Defence Weekly*, 11 Nov. 1989.

[31] Gordon, M., 'Military to draft plan for a 6% cut in 1992–1994 spending', *New York Times*, 18 Nov. 1989, pp. 1 and 33; Engelberg, S., 'Air Force offers to close 15 bases and scrap missiles', *New York Times*, 19 Nov. 1989, pp. 1 and 22; Black, L., 'Big guns face Pentagon freeze', *The Independent*, 4 Dec. 1989, p. 25; Pringle, P., 'Pentagon faces extra cuts in next budget', *The Independent*, 9 Dec. 1989, p. 10.

and the US 10-warhead MX mobile missile could tempt either side to strike first in a crisis.[32] The reasoning is that one side or the other would only have to employ a relatively small number of MIRVed missiles to destroy a relatively large number of targets, giving an advantage to the side that strikes first. A single-warhead ICBM, they argue, would not offer either side a first-strike incentive: the Soviet SS-25 and the US SICBM would have to be expended in greater numbers to destroy a comparable number of targets.

If one assesses ICBMs purely on the basis of warhead-to-target ratios, then it is certainly the case that one MX or SS-24 missile could destroy many targets. Such an assessment, however, assumes that one side bases its calculations on the advantages of a first strike solely upon the capability of its multiple-warhead ICBM, while ignoring the other side's bomber and submarine-based retaliatory capabilities. While no one knows exactly how a nuclear war would be fought, it is highly unlikely that such a conflict would proceed in an orderly fashion. Hence, for one side to assume that it would be at a relative advantage after having destroyed more targets with fewer warheads is an extremely risky assumption. Even though the case against the MX is on shaky ground from a strategic standpoint, the argument is politically potent: it appeals both to those who are opposed to major new strategic programmes and to those who would like to see the MX used as a bargaining chip in Geneva to be traded against the Soviet SS-24.

In the US Congress, support for one or the other missile appears to be entrenched, and the Bush Administration will have to demonstrate strong leadership in order to maintain both missile programmes. In 1989, the Administration failed to display the kind of political leadership necessary to deal with a Congress divided in its support for major new strategic systems. With its stance in the START talks predicated upon successful and timely procurement of a new force of mobile ICBMs, the Administration needs to resolve the issue of the composition of the future US ICBM force. Congress is neither organized nor equipped to make decisions of such magnitude for the Administration. At present, the future of neither system is assured.

A START treaty and ballistic missile defences

The question of the future of the 1972 Anti-Ballistic Missile (ABM) Treaty and its relationship to the completion of a START treaty has found a solution of sorts. At the meeting of US and Soviet Foreign Ministers in Wyoming, Soviet Foreign Minister Eduard Shevardnadze announced that the USSR would no longer make an agreement on strategic arms reductions conditional upon the resolution of ballistic missile defence (BMD) issues. In an address to the Soviet Parliament, he further announced that the USSR would unconditionally dismantle the Krasnoyarsk radar facility in Siberia,

[32] See Smith, J. R., 'Bush aide pushing arms cuts', *International Herald Tribune*, 16 Jan. 1990, p. 2. For an earlier critique of START and its impact upon US ICBM forces, see, Nixon, R., 'American foreign policy: the Bush agenda', *Foreign Affairs*, vol. 68, no. 1 (1988/89), pp. 212–14. For a rebuttal, see Kampelman, M., 'Comment and correspondence', *Foreign Affairs*, vol. 68, no. 3 (1988/89), pp. 160–61.

referring to it as an open violation of the ABM Treaty.[33] Western experts had long maintained that the radar's position and direction constituted a violation and, although belated, the rectification of this situation by the USSR is, nevertheless, an important demonstration of Treaty compliance.

Prior to the Soviet decision to de-link BMD issues from a START treaty, the Soviet position had been to withhold its signature on a treaty as long as the USA refused to agree not to withdraw from the ABM Treaty for a period of 10 years and to adhere to its provisions in accordance with the traditional interpretation of the Treaty. The USSR had adopted this position in response to a unilateral US re-interpretation of the ABM Treaty in 1985 in which the USA claimed the right to develop and test space-based defences against ballistic missiles. The ABM Treaty permits only the testing, development and deployment of a limited number of fixed land-based ABM systems and their components.[34] The USSR has consistently advocated a strict adherence to the traditional interpretation of the ABM Treaty and has explicitly rejected a broader interpretation of its provisions.[35]

Although the new Soviet position apparently paves the way for the conclusion of a START treaty outside of an immediate agreement on the future of the ABM Treaty, this position actually constitutes more of a policy revision than a policy reversal. As far as the USSR is concerned, the issue of space-based BMD still needs to be settled, preferably within the confines of the traditional narrow interpretation of the ABM Treaty. The USSR still wishes to append agreed statements to a START treaty which state that either party could withdraw from the treaty upon the violation of or withdrawal from the ABM Treaty by the other party.[36] The USA is opposed to any linkage between a START agreement and the ABM Treaty.

At the Defence and Space Talks, proceeding parallel to the START talks under NST, the USA has tried to reach agreement with the USSR on a co-operative transition to increased reliance on strategic defences. No such agreement had been reached by 31 December 1989 (see chapter 3). The USSR, however, has dropped its demand for a specified non-withdrawal period from the ABM Treaty, and the USA has proposed extending the withdrawal notice period from the Treaty from six months to three and a half years. The USSR has yet to respond to the US proposal.[37]

---

[33] 'Kremlin assails its Afghan role', *International Herald Tribune*, 24 Oct. 1989, p. 1; Gordon, M., 'US lauds Moscow on ABM admission', *International Herald Tribune*, 25 Oct. 1989, p. 1; Steele, J., 'Soviet Army "lied" on radar station', *The Guardian*, 24 Oct. 1989, p. 24. In his statement to the Soviet Parliament, Shevardnadze claimed that the Soviet leadership had not been fully informed of the nature and purpose of the radar facility, but stopped short of criticizing the Soviet military. See ['Interview with E. A. Shevardnadze'], *Izvestia*, 25 Sep. 1989, p. 5 (in Russian); ['Talks in Wyoming'], *Izvestia*, 23 Sep. 1989, p. 4 (in Russian); and ['The knots have to be disentangled'], *Krasnaya Zvezda*, 5 Oct. 1989, p. 3 (in Russian).

[34] See Article V of the ABM Treaty in Stützle, W., Jasani, B. and Cowen, R. (eds), *The ABM Treaty: To Defend or Not to Defend?* (Oxford University Press: Oxford, 1987), pp. 208–209.

[35] See note 34, pp. 62–72. See also ['Doubtful experiments'], *Pravda*, 25 May 1989, p. 4 (in Russian); and ['Washington and Geneva talks'], *Krasnaya Zvezda*, 23 Aug. 1989, p. 3 (in Russian).

[36] US Information Service, EUR–505 (US Embassy, Stockholm), 8 Dec. 1989, p. 7; ['What kind of weather in Geneva'], *Pravda*, 31 Oct. 1989, p. 5 (in Russian).

[37] See note 36.

The USA is aware that the revised Soviet position could become extremely troublesome after a START treaty comes into force. The USSR, for example, could invoke the 'supreme national interest' clause of the START treaty and withdraw, if it decides that the USA's Strategic Defense Initiative (SDI)-related activities threaten the supreme national interest of the USSR.[38] Clearly, a START treaty that is dependent upon the USSR's interpretation of what is and is not allowed under the ABM Treaty would not be in the US interest. Moreover, the renewed relevance of the supreme national interest clause leaves little doubt that the SDI issue needs to be resolved in order to assure long-term confidence in a START regime.

National interests aside, the USSR's revised position does suggest more interest in the completion of a START agreement than in the resolution of outstanding issues concerning the ABM Treaty. The Soviet leadership may have reached this conclusion against a backdrop of controversy over the likely feasibility of US SDI technologies, recent congressional actions in support of the ABM Treaty and a declining SDI budget.[39]

The objectives of the SDI programme have been consistently modified. From being heralded as an astro-dome against incoming Soviet ballistic missiles, the programme's current objectives are far more modest: a complication in Soviet planning for a first strike against the USA or a possible defence against a maverick attack from a third country.[40] This scaling back of expectations is rooted in the enormous technical difficulties a space-based BMD regime encounters. Hence, decisions to deploy first-phase systems of the SDI programme have been postponed and previously designated technologies have been discarded. With the departure of Ronald Reagan from the White House, the SDI programme lost its most ardent supporter, leaving it to drift. For the first time, the US Congress in 1989 cut the SDI budget request for 1990 in real terms (after adjustment for inflation) by $1100 million, from $4890 to $3790 million.[41] Congress this year, as in previous years, passed language that prohibits SDI funds to be used for tests not in accordance with the traditional interpretation of the ABM Treaty.[42] With the US Congress as the 'guardian' of the ABM Treaty, the Bush Administration's hands are tied.

Given the limited progress on space-based BMD and the congressional restriction on SDI expenditure, the USSR no longer has an urgent need to

[38] Adams, P., 'START ratification may snag on SDI tests', Defense News, 13 Nov. 1988, p. 4.

[39] ['The fashion of Star Wars'], Pravda, 5 July 1989, p. 5 (in Russian); ['Brilliant Pebbles'], Pravda, 13 Oct. 1989, p. 6 (in Russian); ['Is winning possible in a Star War?'], Krasnaya Zvezda, 19 Sep. 1989, p. 4 (in Russian).

[40] MacDonald, B. W., 'Lost in space: SDI struggles through its sixth year', Arms Control Today, vol. 19, no. 7 (Sep. 1989), pp. 21–26; Bunn, M., 'Pentagon science advisers' report critical of "Brilliant Pebbles"', Arms Control Today, vol. 19, no. 9 (Nov. 1989), p. 31; Leopold, G., 'Industry group calls Brilliant Pebbles a flop', Defense News, 16 Oct. 1989, p. 81; Adams, P., 'Opponents argue SDI is affordable', Defense News, 12 June 1989, pp. 3 and 43; Hecht, J., 'Congress cuts Star Wars down to size', New Scientist, 7 Oct. 1989, p. 24; Piotrowski, J., (Gen.), 'Missile defense not a fantasy', US Information Service, EUR–105 (US Embassy, Stockholm), 13 Nov. 1989, pp. 7–9, first published in Defense News, 13 Nov. 1989.

[41] US Information Service, EUR–502 (US Embassy, Stockholm), 3 Nov. 1989, p. 22.

[42] Graham, H., 'Defense bill shrinks SDI budget for first time', Arms Control Today, vol. 19, no. 9 (Nov. 1989), p. 30.

hold the START negotiations hostage. Indeed, with congressional support for the ABM Treaty, the issue of invoking the supreme national interest clause of a START treaty becomes moot: the US Government, in effect, cannot break out of the ABM Treaty. Thus, the USSR apparently has sufficient confidence in the prudence of the US Congress to propose the conclusion of a START treaty with the ABM–SDI issue unresolved. If break-out or withdrawal cease to be policy options for the USA, then the key question becomes one of how the two sides can adhere to the ABM Treaty in a mutually acceptable fashion.

IV. A START treaty and US–Soviet force structures

After taking office in January 1989, President George Bush directed a review of US strategic policy. Also under review was the text of a Joint Draft START Treaty inherited from the Reagan Administration. During a lengthy review process, the President's advisers recommended proposing a ban on Soviet SS-18 missiles, a ban on mobile missiles with multiple warheads, a limit on the total number of warheads on MIRVed missiles and an increased emphasis on verification.[43] Apart from verification (see section V), none of these proposals entered the US negotiating position in Geneva. That President Bush did not introduce major changes to US strategic arms control policy did not surprise many observers: as Vice President and as a presidential candidate, Bush fully supported the Reagan Administration's approach to arms control.[44]

Therefore, it may be reasonable to assume that, upon reviewing the Reagan record, the President concluded that the emerging START treaty would force the USSR to implement force cuts and to shift the relative weight of each leg of its strategic triad in such a way that US security interests would not be jeopardized but, in some instances, would even provide significant benefits and advantages. Towards the end of 1989, the US position had improved even further: the USSR agreed to deal with the issue of SLCMs separately and decided to de-link progress on a START treaty from a solution to the issue of space-based BMD.

Impact on Soviet force structure

Most estimates of potential Soviet force configurations are based upon tradeoffs between various force deployment options. Thus, it has been suggested that the 4900 limit on ballistic missile warheads will work in favour of the Soviet ICBM modernization programme: that is, some 1100 warheads on SS-24s and SS-25s, and 1540 warheads on 154 SS-18s.[45]

---

[43] *Arms Control Reporter,* Apr. 1989, p. 611.B.538.

[44] Lugar, R. (Sen.), 'Why George Bush is the best arms control candidate', *Arms Control Today,* vol. 19, no. 8 (Oct. 1988), pp. 3–6.

[45] Flournoy, M., 'START cutting Soviet strategic forces', *Arms Control Today,* vol. 19, no. 5 (June/July 1989), p. 18.

Severe cuts are expected in the Soviet strategic submarine force: 62 submarines will be reduced to between 15 and 30 (mostly Delta IVs and Typhoons) in order to accommodate some 1600 warheads.[46] Of course, the USSR could choose to maintain a larger number of submarines, so as not to concentrate SLBMs on a small number of platforms. Most likely, a combination of an assessment of US anti-submarine warfare capabilities and of the noise level of Soviet submarines will guide the USSR in its decision regarding force size and warhead distribution.

With regard to the USSR's strategic bomber capability, it is generally thought that the USSR will not expand its existing force by a significant number. The USSR is now modernizing its fleet of strategic bombers with the Bear H and the Blackjack gaining increased importance.[47] If the USSR does not opt for an expansion in the number of its bombers (permissible under the START counting rules), then the Soviet decision concerning the number of ALCM-carrying bombers will be crucial. Given the relatively small size of their bomber force, a decision to deploy bombs rather than large numbers of ALCMs could affect overall capability considerably.

For all three weapon categories—ICBMs, SLBMs and strategic bombers—the decisions on the distribution of warheads over the number of launchers and carriers will be crucial in order to assure force survivability and effectiveness under START constraints.

Although the Soviet strategic submarine force and silo-based SS-18 ICBMs would be considerably reduced under the proposed START treaty, the USSR is free to move ahead with its intended programme of force modernization, particularly with regard to the transition from silo-based to mobile ICBMs. This shift greatly enhances the survivability of Soviet ICBMs without significantly increasing the threat these missiles pose to US silo-based ICBMs. The latter conclusion, of course, assumes that the USA will indeed follow through with deployment of mobile ICBMs and leave only a small portion of its total ICBM force in silos. Thus, although the USSR has made major concessions to the USA without obtaining compensatory concessions, START provisions do not diminish Soviet security.

Impact on US force structure

The USA will also be able to carry out its strategic modernization programmes within START constraints. However, a lively debate has developed between defence planners and arms controllers on the choice of strategic systems.[48] The USA's large strategic bomber force permits the exploitation of the permissive counting rule for non-ALCM-carrying

---

[46] See note 45, p. 19.

[47] See note 4, p. 89; note 6; and note 45, pp. 20–21.

[48] Holland, Jr, W. J., (Rear Admiral, USN, retired), 'The end of the triad? Why SSBN advances make a diad possible', *Arms Control Today*, vol. 19, no. 7 (Sep. 1989), pp. 10–14; Cohen, W. S., (Sen.), 'The B-2 bomber: mission questionable, cost impossible', *Arms Control Today*, vol. 19, no. 8 (Oct. 1989), pp. 3–8.

strategic bombers, perhaps even to the extent suggested by the Chairman of the Senate Armed Services Committee, Senator Sam Nunn.

During deliberations over the defence budget in the US Senate in July 1989, Senator Nunn reminded opponents of the B-2 'stealth' bomber of the advantages that its procurement would bring to US total warhead numbers. Scheduled acquisition of 132 B-2s, each carrying 20 bombs, would amount to a total of 2640 bombs, of which only 132 would count against the START limit of 6000 warheads.[49] The difference between 132 and 2640 accountable bombs is indeed staggering and may even serve to generate additional support for the B-2 programme, despite the fact that its projected cost is in the region of $70 billion, its capability is uncertain and its mission as a penetrating bomber is yet to be determined.[50] Even if the B-2 programme should be slowed down and its cost spread over a longer period, the US strategic bomber force is expected to remain at the current number of 311.

With this number of strategic bombers in place, the USA will have to make adjustments in its ICBM and SLBM forces in order to conform to the 1600 limit on the number of strategic nuclear delivery vehicles and the limit of 4900 ballistic missile warheads. If the SICBM programme continues to receive funding, then the Bush Administration intends to deploy 300 SICBMs, in addition to 50 rail-based MXs and an as yet unspecified number of silo-based Minuteman IIIs (of which the USA currently deploys 500).[51]

The size of the ICBM force will have crucial implications for that of the SLBM force which currently accounts for just under half of the total number of US warheads. In order to meet the US Navy's projected goal of 20 Trident II nuclear-powered submarines (SSBNs) as the only carriers of SLBMs, the Minuteman III force would have to be kept at 205 missiles. If the Minuteman III force exceeds this number, then the Navy has essentially three options. First, it could procure fewer Trident II submarines, shedding 24 SLBMs and 192 warheads (eight warheads per SLBM) for each SSBN not procured. Second, instead of reducing the number of submarines, the Navy could cut the number of warheads each SLBM carries. Third, the Navy could reduce the number of SLBM launch tubes on each submarine.[52] The possibilities for tradeoffs between ICBM and SLBM forces will most likely also be determined by budget considerations. What is already certain is that, until the configuration of the ICBM force is worked out, decisions on the number of Trident II SSBNs will remain tentative.

[49] Ropelewski, R., 'Target mobility, arms control challenge SAC modernization', *Armed Forces Journal International,* Sep. 1989, p. 72; Finnegan, P., 'B-2 supporters go on offensive to save bomber from budget knife', *Defense News,* 17 July 1989, p. 24; Amouyal, B. 'Air Force leaders call B-2 essential for arms accord', *Defense News,* 24 July 1989, p. 25.

[50] Towell, P., 'Bush team tries to protect "stealth" bomber program', *Congressional Quarterly Weekly Report,* 22 July 1989, p. 1883; 'B-2 survives votes but cuts are sought', *International Herald Tribune,* 27 July 1989, pp. 1 and 4; Bailey, J., 'B-2 bomber "thinks it is a fighter"', *Flight International,* 14 Oct. 1989, p. 23; 'USAF advances B-2 tests to keep political support', *Flight International,* 7 Oct. 1989, p. 22; Wilson, G., 'Range of B-2 bomber is less than expected, surprising lawmakers', *International Herald Tribune,* 8 Oct. 1989, p. 7. For a Soviet view of the B-2, see ['Does it pay to expect the worst'], *Pravda,* 21 Oct. 1989, p. 4 (in Russian).

[51] See note 6.

[52] See note 8, p. 405; and Ropelewski (note 49), p. 68.

V. START and strategic stability

The negotiating positions and the understandings reached to date strongly suggest that the USA and the USSR favour a START agreement that allows them to pursue their planned strategic modernization programmes. By the mid- to late 1990s, the two sides will field modern strategic delivery vehicles and warheads of increasing accuracy. Many START-prescribed force reductions can be met by phasing out older weapons and platforms. START's combination of an overall limit on the number of strategic nuclear delivery vehicles, a sub-limit on the number of ballistic missile warheads and a ceiling on the number of accountable warheads should serve to reassure each side that the forces of the other are not capable of launching a disabling first strike. Improvements in ICBM mobility, together with continued confidence in the opaqueness of the oceans, should sustain the confidence of each side in the survivability of its forces. Thus, the deterrent effect of US and Soviet nuclear forces can be expected to increase and, thereby, to contribute positively to overall strategic stability.

Nevertheless, the largely positive impact upon strategic stability provided by a START treaty can potentially be offset by military capabilities that remain uncontrolled or outside an agreement, the failure of the USA to shift to a mobile basing mode for a considerable part of its ICBM force (if the land-based leg of the triad is to be maintained at all) and a verification regime that fails to provide effective verification of treaty compliance.

Nuclear-armed SLCMs

Since nuclear-armed SLCMs will escape control in a START treaty, the subsequent control of these missiles also remains problematic. Thus, a post-START security environment could be characterized by the existence of some 2200 nuclear-armed SLCMs without any controls whatsoever.

This situation could raise serious concern, because the USSR enjoys a geographic advantage over the USA with respect to the deployment of its nuclear-armed SLCMs. Although many important strategic facilities along the US eastern seaboard are within reach of a Soviet SLCM force operating in international waters, comparable Soviet assets are located deep within the USSR. Thus, US vessels carrying nuclear-armed SLCMs would be forced to operate closer to Soviet territory in order to present a comparable threat. Clearly, this naval mission is not easily accomplished.[53] With the threat of Soviet SLCMs to the USA greater than that posed by the US missiles to the USSR, it will be interesting to note how long the US Government and the US Navy can continue their abstinence from naval arms control negotiations without the loss of public confidence in a START accord.

---

[53] Terriff (note 17), p. 62.

The verification issue

Although a START agreement can be assessed purely on the basis of the military contribution that it makes to strategic stability, this criterion is only a partial yardstick. Of equal importance to the maintenance of strategic stability is the confidence that each party has in its ability to verify the treaty compliance of the other. A START agreement, with the provisions currently envisaged, calls for an enormously efficient verification regime.[54] Several reasons account for this:

1. START reduces nuclear forces; it does not eliminate certain systems as in the case of the INF Treaty. A total ban can be verified after a baseline inventory has been established and the destruction of the weapon systems has been observed. In contrast, a START verification regime must establish a baseline inventory, verify the cuts and verify compliance with permitted force levels.

2. The verification regime has to verify compliance with agreed counting rules. This applies especially to ballistic missile warheads and to ALCM-carrying strategic bombers. If maximum numbers of warheads were counted (as under SALT II), warhead accounting would be relatively straightforward. But because the intent with the START counting rules is to retain deployment flexibility within agreed sub-limits, warhead counting will become a complex and vital exercise.

3. The verification regime must provide for verification without disclosing militarily sensitive information and jeopardizing the effectiveness of permitted forces. The verification of warhead numbers on missiles could inadvertently provide information on warhead design and, by ascertaining the numbers of mobile ICBMs, the survivability of these missiles might be compromised. Thus, to devise methods and instruments that provide as much information for verification purposes as possible without revealing more than they should will be a delicate task.

4. Verification methods and technologies must be able to safeguard against cheating. This problem is especially difficult with respect to the verification of non-deployed ballistic missiles.

To achieve these verification objectives requires the development of complex and sensitive implementation methods and techniques. Here, the experience with the INF Treaty's verification provisions and the record of its implementation may prove to be helpful (see chapter 12). As in the case of the INF Treaty, a system of verification for a START treaty will likely include on-site inspection of missile production, assembly and storage, and deployment areas, and of the actual destruction of the missiles. The verification system will also include the establishment and inspection of perimeter fencing and electronic portal monitoring, the tagging of missiles

[54] Adams, P., 'Strategic pact faces years of delay due to verification questions', *Defense News*, 10 July 1989, pp. 1 and 27. For an earlier assessment, see, Leggett, J. K. and Lewis, P., 'Verifying a START agreement: impact of INF precedents', *Survival*, vol. 30, no. 5 (Sep./Oct. 1988), p. 409; and Adams, P. 'INF success leading to future verification regimes', *Defense News*, 6 Nov. 1989, p. 27.

and the inspection of tags, and the establishment of organizations to conduct challenge inspections of suspect sites and missiles. Thus, the implementation of a system of verification for a START treaty is expected to be extremely complex and labour-intensive.

Relatively early in the negotiations for a START treaty, the USA and the USSR realized that many of the provisions under consideration would require an intensive and comprehensive approach to verification. Yet it was not until the Washington summit meeting in December 1987 that the two sides were able to agree on a general framework for verification of a START treaty.[55] Further progress was made at the Moscow summit meeting in May–June 1988 at which the specific problems of verifying mobile missiles were addressed. The two sides worked out agreements to limit the deployment areas for mobile missiles and the dispersal of such missiles outside these areas. Furthermore, the two sides agreed to the need for strict verification of permitted and non-permitted dispersals.[56] Much remains to be done in working out the specific details of these general agreements.

The Bush initiative of June 1989

In order to intensify efforts to define and clarify verification provisions even while the negotiations for a START treaty were being conducted, President Bush launched a new verification initiative in June 1989.[57] After initially criticizing the initiative (largely on the basis that it might delay the conclusion of a START treaty), the USSR formally joined the initiative at the Wyoming meeting of foreign ministers in September 1989.[58] The resultant Agreement on Verification and Stability Measures provides for so-called 'pilot trials' that would ascertain whether particular START provisions could be verified to the satisfaction of both sides. Following these pilot trials, more specific verification provisions would be negotiated and included in the text of the START Joint Draft Treaty. In an indirect acknowledgment that a START treaty might be delayed by lengthy verification trials, the Wyoming agreement states that these measures must not slow down work on the START treaty 'in any way whatsoever'.[59] Indeed, both sides have moved swiftly in their joint attempts to implement the Wyoming mandate. On 8 December 1989, at the end of the twelfth round of the START negotiations, the USA and the USSR had reached agreement on such specific verification trial measures as the tagging of

[55] See note 10, p. 391.

[56] See note 10, p. 391.

[57] Smith, J., 'US plans new idea on arms', *International Herald Tribune*, 19 June 1989, pp. 1 and 4; Rubin, J., 'As START resumes, Bush pushes early verification', *Arms Control Today*, vol. 19, no. 6 (Aug. 1989), pp. 24–25.

[58] ['From the old positions'], *Pravda*, 22 June 1989, p. 5 (in Russian); ['START in Geneva, but in what direction?'], *Krasnaya Zvezda*, 25 June 1989, p. 3 (in Russian); ['Washington and the Geneva talks'], *Krasnaya Zvezda*, 23 Aug. 1989, p. 3 (in Russian).

[59] 'The Wyoming papers', *Arms Control Today*, vol. 19, no. 8 (Oct. 1989), p. 25.

ballistic missiles, and the inspection of strategic bombers and ballistic missile warheads.[60]

In late November and early December 1989, the two START delegations, together with technical experts from both the USA and the USSR, met in Geneva to exchange information and to demonstrate techniques for ballistic missile tagging. The USA demonstrated its 'reflective particle tag'. This tag is made of plastic material with reflective crystals of random shapes and sizes which, after it is attached to missiles of a particular type, provides unique identification features. The USSR demonstrated its tagging technique and both sides found that their approaches were rather similar, suggesting that their demands concerning reliability, durability and non-removability of the tags are also similar.[61]

The trial inspections of strategic bombers will focus on each side's ability to distinguish between bombers carrying ALCMs and those that do not. Under the agreement, 10 observers from each side will visit an operational airbase in the other's country. They will then be shown three bombers, two carrying ALCMs and one carrying bombs. On the basis of a list of differentiating features supplied by the exhibiting side, the observing side will determine its ability to identify distinguishing features such as ALCM mountings and weapon bays large enough to carry ALCMs. A period of eight hours has been allotted to each exercise, which includes a tour of the respective base. The base tour is important in that it provides information on where bombers might be located during a genuine inspection. The USSR will host the first trial inspections of strategic bombers. The USA will inspect two versions of the Bear bomber which will be followed by Soviet inspections of two types of the B-1B bomber. The inspections are scheduled to take place in the spring of 1990 on a date to be announced.[62]

The trial inspections of ballistic missile warheads serve the purpose of verifying the declared number of warheads on different types of missile. Each side will demonstrate inspection procedures for two of its strategic missiles. The USA will exhibit an MX ICBM and a Trident II SLBM. The USSR will exhibit an SS-18 ICBM and an SS-N-23 SLBM. The first trial inspection will be of the MX ICBM.[63] The entire concept of verifying the number of warheads inside a missile nose-cone is completely new. Indeed, that the two sides could even agree to conduct trial verification of missile warheads at all is, in itself, remarkable. However, the acceptability of the suggested measures will depend upon how each side judges the reliability of as yet untried sensor technology.

Significant progress in establishing common ground for verifying some of the most crucial provisions of a START agreement has been achieved. The three agreements of December 1989 testify to a willingness on the part of

[60] See note 36, pp. 15–17; Williams, F., 'Start makes little progress on big issues', *The Independent*, 9 Dec. 1989, p. 10; Martin, G., 'Arms control agreement reached', *Daily Telegraph*, 9 Dec. 1989, p. 12; 'Round of US–Soviet arms talks ends on optimistic note', *International Herald Tribune*, 9–10 Dec. 1989, p. 2.

[61] See note 36, p. 17.

[62] See note 36, p. 16.

[63] See note 36, pp. 16–17.

the USA and the USSR to tackle complex and sensitive verification issues in a spirit of co-operation. The extent to which improving relations between the two sides facilitates agreement on verification issues and perhaps even lessens the demands upon a verification system cannot be determined at this time. The success of trial verification and other START verification measures yet to be agreed will tell.

VI. Conclusion

Generally speaking, 1989 witnessed about as much progress in the Strategic Arms Reduction Talks as was likely to be made, given the existing negotiating positions, a change of Administration in the USA, the diversion of political focus to conventional arms control negotiations and the dramatic political changes in Europe and the USSR.

At the end of 1988, the ABM–SDI and SLCM issues were identified as the main obstacles to a START agreement.[64] While these obstacles were not resolved during 1989, they were taken out of the START negotiating framework and thus no longer impede the conclusion of a treaty. The issue of ALCMs, which gained some prominence in 1989, also appears to be solvable. The principal task for 1990, then, appears to be the negotiation of a mutually satisfactory verification system.

With regard to the emerging START treaty itself, it is an ambitious undertaking: it attempts to reduce the level of strategic nuclear forces through the implementation of strategic modernization programmes and to implement a verification regime of such complexity that it will sorely test the ingenuity of its designers and the zeal of its inspectors.

Due to the deferral of the ABM–SDI and SLCM issues, the prospective treaty actually achieves less than was originally envisaged. Although successful conclusion of a START treaty is made more likely, it is at the expense of comprehensiveness.

Any agreement on the reduction of strategic nuclear forces touches upon such politically sensitive issues as military budgets, defence procurement and strategic planning, and raises questions about defence policy choices. Also, a START agreement as currently envisaged is likely to come into effect at a time when threat perceptions on both sides are relatively low. For these reasons, a START treaty does not easily lend itself to broad assessments of 'good' or 'bad'. Rather, the USA and the USSR are likely to judge the value of a START treaty on five counts:

1. To what extent does the treaty provide for the continued modernization of strategic nuclear forces? As of the end of 1989, the emerging START treaty will permit the modernization of strategic forces as intended by each side and will provide an opportunity to retire older systems. In particular, the USA must determine if it can, indeed, procure the strategic systems

[64] See Bertram, C., 'US–Soviet nuclear arms control', SIPRI, *SIPRI Yearbook 1989: World Armaments and Disarmament* (Oxford University Press: Oxford, 1989), pp. 359–67.

currently planned. Should the USA fail to do so, a START treaty could well become hostage to political bargaining within Congress, jeopardizing both the timely procurement of strategic systems and the eventual ratification of the treaty.

2. To what extent does the treaty control each side's forces? In this instance, the USA must estimate the survivability of its own forces in a post-START strategic environment and the potential military significance for US security if the USSR were to violate the treaty. Although the USSR will have to address much the same issues, it also must assess the significance of those US forces and activities it has failed to constrain or to control within the context of the START treaty. In this instance, the USSR will be chiefly concerned with the SLCM problem and the relationship between the SDI programme and the ABM Treaty.

3. To what extent can the treaty be verified? Both parties will have to judge the level of verification that will be acceptable to the US Congress, the Soviet Parliament and the military services of each side.

4. To what extent will the mere fact of a START agreement contribute to an ongoing process of improved relations between the two sides? In other words, what is it worth to either side to conclude a START treaty and to conclude it soon? Each side must judge if the compromises necessary to facilitate conclusion of a START treaty are offset by the greater transparency and predictability of their security relationship which it provides.

5. What kind of strategic nuclear arms control should follow a START treaty? Indeed, what role should strategic arms control play in the relationship between the two powers? If further reductions in nuclear forces are implemented, can the nuclear arsenals of Great Britain, France and China remain outside of the negotiations?

Whether or not a START treaty will be signed in 1990 will ultimately depend on how confident both sides are over the coming months about their ability to make these judgements, their willingness to resolve remaining negotiating questions and how they envisage the future of strategic nuclear arms control. In 1990, Presidents Bush and Gorbachev may have the unprecedented opportunity to sign accords on both strategic nuclear and conventional arms. These agreements can be expected to raise fundamental questions concerning the nature of security relations between the USA and the USSR and the shape of European regional security. This process may result in a reassessment of the role of arms control in the design and maintenance of stable political and military structures.

12. The implementation of the INF Treaty

STEPHEN IWAN GRIFFITHS

I. Introduction

This chapter briefly reviews the record of the implementation of the Treaty between the United States of America and the Union of Soviet Socialist Republics on the elimination of their intermediate-range and shorter-range missiles (the INF Treaty), as of 31 December 1989. The Treaty, which entered into force on 1 June 1988, consists of a preamble and 17 articles, as well as three separate documents signed concurrently—a Memorandum of Understanding on the establishment of the data base, a Protocol on Procedures governing the elimination of the missile systems and a Protocol regarding inspections relating to the Treaty.[1]

The INF Treaty is of unlimited duration (see table 12.1) and applicable globally: in essence, the Treaty is concerned with the elimination of *all* ground-launched ballistic and cruise missiles belonging to the USSR and the USA with a range of 500–1000 km (shorter-range) and 1000–5500 km (intermediate-range). Thus, the USSR would eliminate its SS-20, SS-4 and SS-5 intermediate-range missiles and its SS-12 and SS-23 shorter-range missiles. The USA would eliminate its Pershing II intermediate-range missiles, BGM-109G ground-launched cruise missiles (GLCMs) and the non-deployed Pershing 1A shorter-range missiles. The terms of the Treaty apply to both nuclear and non-nuclear missiles, and give both parties the right to carry out extensive verification procedures to monitor compliance.

II. Inspections and eliminations: June 1988–December 1989

The verification provisions in Articles XI, XII and XIII of the Treaty, as well as those in the attached protocols, are by far the most extensive ever associated with an arms control or disarmament agreement. Apart from the usual allowances for the use of national technical means (NTM) of verification, this is the first time that extensive and intrusive forms of on-site inspection (OSI) have been agreed upon by the major powers since the Treaty of Versailles was signed in 1919.[2]

---

[1] For an account of the negotiations and the text of the INF Treaty, see Dean, J., 'The INF Treaty negotiations', SIPRI, *SIPRI Yearbook 1988: World Armaments and Disarmament* (Oxford University Press: Oxford, 1988), pp. 375–489. See also Carter, A., SIPRI, *Success and Failure in Arms Control Negotiations* (Oxford University Press: Oxford, 1989), especially chapter 7, pp. 172–204, and chapter 8, pp. 205–29.

[2] Graybeal, S. N. and Krepon, M., 'The limitations of on-site inspection', *Bulletin of the Atomic Scientists,* Dec. 1987, pp. 22–26. The comparison of the INF Treaty with the Treaty of Versailles, while valid for the provision of on-site inspection, is of only limited utility if one takes into account the controversial nature of the Treaty of Versailles, especially with regard to the issue of national sovereignty.

Table 12.1. Chronology of INF Treaty implementation, from the entry into force of the Treaty on 1 June 1988 until the end of the elimination period on 1 June 1991

Inspections	Year	Eliminations
	1988	
22 June Inspection personnel accepted or rejected by either side.		*11 June* Between 11 June and 1 December, each side may destroy up to 100 missiles by launching them.
1 July Baseline inspections begin. These inspections must be completed within 60 days, or by 29 August.		*1 July* Conversion of INF bases to other uses begins. Missile eliminations begin.
29 August Short-notice inspections begin.		
1 December Deadline for establishment of portal monitoring facilities.		
	1989	
		1 December All shorter-range missiles were destroyed by this date. The Soviet Union eliminated all of its SS-12 and SS-23 missiles, launchers and support structures. The USA eliminated its 169 Pershing 1As.
	1990	
1 June Monitoring of production plants (Votkinsk, USSR, and Magna, Utah, USA) may cease.		*1 November* By this date, both parties may each possess deployed launchers capable of carrying no more than 171 warheads.
	1991	
		1 June End of the INF elimination period. All missiles, launchers, support structures and equipment must be eliminated by this date.

Sources: Compiled from Dean, J., 'The INF Treaty negotiations', SIPRI, *SIPRI Yearbook 1988: World Armaments and Disarmament* (Oxford University Press: Oxford, 1988), pp. 375–489; and *Arms Control Chronicle,* no. 27 (Aug. 1988), p. 9.

Inspection categories

The INF Treaty provides for several forms of OSI to assist with verification. These are outlined in Article XI of the Treaty and the Protocol regarding inspections.[3] By the end of 1989, the US On-Site Inspection Agency (OSIA) had conducted 303 inspections at INF sites, whereas the USSR had conducted 121 inspections.[4] A breakdown of the type and number of inspections carried out as of 1 June 1989 is presented below.

Baseline

Baseline inspections, which are outlined in Article XI, paragraph 3 of the Treaty, were designed to verify the data on the numbers of INF missiles, launchers, support structures and support equipment at all missile operating bases and missile support facilities that are specified in the Memorandum of Understanding (MOU). The MOU specified that these inspections would be carried out between 30 and 90 days after the Treaty entered into force.

The baseline inspections were carried out within the allotted period between 1 July and 29 August 1988. During that time, the USA inspected 129 facilities at 109 locations in the USSR and Eastern Europe. The USSR inspected 18 facilities at 10 locations in the USA, and 13 facilities in Italy, Belgium, Great Britain, the Netherlands and the FRG.

Close-out

Close-out inspections, outlined in Article XI, paragraph 4 of the Treaty, were scheduled to be carried out within a 60-day period following the notified scheduled date of elimination of INF missile operating bases and missile support facilities (other than missile production facilities). These inspections were designed to help verify that all INF-related activities had ceased at these locations and to ensure that no INF systems remained.

By the end of the first year of implementation, four facilities on US territory were considered to be closed-out. Two test ranges, one each at Dugway Proving Grounds, Utah, and at Complex 16, Cape Canaveral, Florida, were closed out. Also closed out were two launcher production facilities, US Air Force Plant 19 at San Diego, California, and the Martin Marietta facility located in Middle River, Maryland.[5] The USSR did not supply corresponding data on closed-out facilities on their territory.

---

[3] For the text of the Protocol regarding inspections relating to the Treaty, see appendix 13D in Dean (note 1), pp. 472–85.

[4] The information in this section is from SIPRI correspondence with the governments of the following countries: Belgium, Czechoslovakia, the Federal Republic of Germany, the German Democratic Republic, Great Britain, Italy, the Netherlands, the Soviet Union and the United States. This correspondence is deposited in the SIPRI library. See also: '1269 missiles destroyed in first year of INF Treaty', *International Herald Tribune,* 2 June 1989, p. 2; and 'INF: the first year', *Arms Control Today,* vol. 19, no. 6 (Aug. 1989), p. 31.

[5] See note 4.

Table 12.2. INF Treaty short-notice inspections of facilities in NATO countries conducted by the USSR during the first year of implementation, 1 June 1988– 1 June 1989

Date	Facility/location	Type of facility	Country
1988			
29 Sep.	Neckarsulm-Waldheide	Missile operating base	FR Germany
1 Nov.	Molesworth	Missile operating base	Great Britain
16 Nov.	Comiso	Missile operating base	Italy
1989			
20 Jan.	Greenham Common	Missile operating base	Great Britain
14 Feb.	Plant 19, San Diego California	Launcher production facility	USA
2 Mar.	Neu-Ulm	Missile operating base	FR Germany
10 Mar.	Sabca, Gosselies	Missile repair facility	Belgium
17 Mar.	Fort Sill, Oklahoma	Training facility	USA
18 Mar.	Martin Marietta, Middle River, Maryland	Launcher production facility	USA
20 Mar.	Davis-Monthan AFB, Arizona	Training facility	USA
29 Mar.	Wüschheim	Missile operating base	FR Germany
6 Apr.	Neckarsulm-Waldheide	Missile operating base	FR Germany
12 Apr.	Redstone Arsenal, Alabama	Missile storage facility	USA
12 Apr.	Complex 16, Cape Canaveral, Florida	Test range	USA
27 Apr.	Schwäbisch-Gmünd	Missile operating base	FR Germany
4 May	Weilerbach	Missile storage facility	FR Germany
10 May	Comiso	Missile operating base	Italy
13 May	Pueblo Depot, Colorado	Missile storage facility	USA
13 May	Dugway Proving Grounds, Utah	Test range	USA
25 May	Woensdrecht	Missile operating base	Netherlands

Source: Data supplied by the US Embassy in Stockholm. Corresponding data from the Soviet Union were not provided.

Short-notice

For 13 years after the Treaty enters into force, the signatories are entitled to conduct short-notice inspections at declared and former missile facilities (Article XI, paragraph 5). The purpose of these inspections is to help confirm that the number of missiles, launchers, support structures and support equipment located at each base or facility at the time of inspection has not changed and that no activities prohibited by the Treaty are carried out. Each party has the right to conduct short-notice inspections of all missile operating bases and all missile support facilities, with the exception of missile production facilities. Short-notice inspections are distinct from baseline and close-out inspections which may also be conducted on a short-notice basis. Under the Treaty, each side may conduct a maximum of 20 short-notice inspections per calendar year for the first three years, 15 per year for the next five years and 10 per year for the last five years of the inspection regime (see table 12.2).

Elimination

Each party is obliged to conduct on-site elimination inspections to confirm that treaty-limited items (TLI) such as missiles, launchers, support equipment and support structures are eliminated in accordance with agreed procedures (Article XI, paragraph 7). Elimination inspections are not limited to specific time intervals, nor are they conducted on a short-notice basis: they are conducted on-site when the inspecting party has been notified that eliminations are scheduled to take place, and they continue as long as elimination procedures on the applicable TLI are being carried out.

Continuous or portal monitoring

The OSIA began portal monitoring inspections at the Votkinsk Machine-Building Plant on 1 July 1988. The USSR began its portal monitoring operation at Magna, Utah, the following day.

Both parties agreed to the creation of portal monitoring facilities at a specific missile production plant (Article XI, paragraph 6). Portal monitoring was designed to ensure that the USSR could not produce the banned SS-20 missile under the guise of being an SS-25: both are manufactured at the same plant, the Votkinsk Machine-Building Plant in the Udmurt ASSR. Similarly, the USSR was given the right to monitor the Hercules Plant at Magna, Utah, where the Pershing II missile was produced. Each side has the right to conduct continuous monitoring for at least 3 and up to a maximum of 13 years. If no production is detected for 12 consecutive months, portal monitoring will cease.

The USA has the right to measure all vehicles exiting the Votkinsk facility and to inspect the interior of those that are large enough to contain an SS-20 missile.[6] In the first year of continuous monitoring, 79 railcars were declared to contain missiles larger than an SS-20. In accordance with the Treaty, the USA viewed the interior of eight of these missile canisters. In addition, the interior of all vehicles large enough to contain an SS-20 were inspected to confirm that they did not contain SS-20s.

At the facility in Magna, Utah, the USSR enjoys the same inspection rights with respect to the Pershing II. In the first year, four missile stages as large or larger than a Pershing II first stage were examined by Soviet inspectors.

[6] See note 4.

Table 12.3. US and Soviet missile elimination data as of 31 December 1989

Country	Type	Total	Deployed	Non-deployed	Eliminated	To be eliminated
USSR	SS-20	654	405	249	339	315
	SS-23	239	127	112	239	0
	SS-4	149	60	89	116	33
	SS-5	6	0	6	6	0
	SS-12	718	85	633	718	0
	SSC-X-4	80	0	80	80	0
Total		**1 846**	**677**	**1 169**	**1 498**	**348**
USA	Pershing II	234	120	114	62	172
	GLCM	443	322	121	220	223
	Pershing 1A	169	0	169	169	0
Total		**846**	**442**	**404**	**451**	**395**

Sources: SIPRI correspondence with the US Government; *The First Anniversary of the INF Treaty* (Novosti Press Agency Publishing House: Moscow, 1989), pp. 13–14; US Information Service, EUR–413 (US Embassy, Stockholm), 4 Jan. 1990.

Eliminations

According to updated data as of 1 June 1988, the parties were to eliminate a total of 2612 missiles.[7] By 31 December 1989, 70 per cent of these missiles had been eliminated (see table 12.3).[8]

Even before the ratification process in the USA had ended, the USSR had prepared its SS-20s at Waren in the GDR for return to the USSR.[9] From February to March 1988, 54 SS-12s were returned to the USSR from missile operation bases located in the GDR.[10] On 31 May, the USA initiated destruction experiments: after 11 days of weather-related delays, a strapped-down Pershing II rocket motor was finally test-fired at Pueblo, Colorado, to determine whether the motors could be safely destroyed.[11] Table 12.4 provides a listing of known elimination sites.[12]

On 6 July 1989, the USA destroyed the last of its 169 Pershing 1As at the Longhorn Army Ammunition Plant in Marshall, Texas.[13] Thus, the USA was the first to eliminate all of its shorter-range missiles, exceeding the deadline of 30 November 1989 by nearly five months. The final Soviet SS-12 was reported to have been destroyed by the time the last of its SS-23 shorter-range missiles was eliminated on 27 October 1989. Thus, the USSR also met the deadline by a comfortable margin.[14]

---

[7] This figure does not include 80 SSC-X-4s which have also been eliminated.

[8] See *The First Anniversary of the INF Treaty* (Novosti Press Agency Publishing House: Moscow, 1989). See also 'Fact sheet on INF numbers based on updated data', *Issues Brief* (Office of Public Affairs, US Arms Control and Disarmament Agency: Washington, DC, 6 Oct. 1988).

[9] See note 4.

[10] See note 4.

[11] *Arms Control Reporter*, June 1988, p. 403.B.686.

[12] See note 4. See also Foley, T. M., 'INF missile destruction accelerates in US, Europe', *Aviation Week & Space Technology*, vol. 129, no. 17 (24 Oct. 1988), p. 22.

[13] US Information Service, EUR–208 (US Embassy, Stockholm), 11 July 1989.

[14] 'News briefs', *Aviation Week & Space Technology*, vol. 131, no. 6 (7 Aug. 1989), p. 30; ['Shorter-range missiles eliminated'], *Pravda*, 7 Oct. 1989 (in Russian).

Table 12.4. Known elimination sites in the USSR, the USA and the FRG with data on the elimination process

Location	Missiles designated for destruction	Comments
USSR		
Kaputsin Yar	SS-20	
Sarny	SS-20 launchers/ transporters	A four-stage elimination process has been adopted: (1) cutting the launching track in half; (2) removing the instrument panel; (3) cutting the erector-launcher system; and (4) cutting the launcher chassis (at least 78 centimetres at the rear axle).
Kansk and Chita	SS-20	Eliminated by launching during a one-week period each month. This activity ceased on 1 Dec. 1988.
Jelgava	SSC-X-4	
Saryozek	SS-12/SS-23	
Stankovo	SS-12/SS-23 launchers/transporters	
Lesnaya	SS-4/SS-5	
USA		
Pueblo Depot, Colorado	Pershing 1A/II	Operation is carried out by the US Army. Elimination by static firing of individual missile stages: the rocket is restricted in a concrete and steel structure and ignited. The empty motor case is then crushed and buried.
Longhorn Army Ammunition Plant, Marshall, Texas	Pershing 1A/II	Last Pershing 1A eliminated on 6 July. Same elimination process as that adopted at Pueblo.
Davis-Monthan AFB, Arizona	GLCMs	Operation carried out by the US Air Force. Elimination is by longitudinal cutting of missile and canister. Wings and tail section were cut and the front section then crushed.
FR Germany		
Hausen	Pershing II	Empty erector launchers have been eliminated at this equipment maintenance centre.

Sources: SIPRI correspondence with NATO governments; *Aviation Week & Space Technology,* vol. 129, no. 17 (24 Oct. 1988), p. 22; and *Atlantic News,* no. 2044 (2 Sep. 1988), p. 1.

III. The INF 'institutions'

As the elimination and inspection process has evolved, a number of what could be termed INF 'institutions' have come to play a major role in the smooth conduct of the implementation process. Although there appears to be a major difference between US and Soviet thinking on the organization and role of these instrumentalities, this may simply be a question of national style—the formality of the OSIA suggests US planning for disarmament missions beyond INF. The relative informality of Soviet arrangements for inspections suggests more of a short-term, single-mission approach.

On-Site Inspection Agency

On 15 January 1988, the US OSIA was established by a presidential directive to oversee the implementation of the verification measures of the INF Treaty.[15] Established as a field operating agency of the Department of Defense (DOD), the OSIA reports to an Executive Committee composed of the Under Secretary of Defense for Acquisition, the Under Secretary of Defense for Policy and the Chairman of the Joint Chiefs of Staff (JCS). Initially, the OSIA received logistical support from the Defense Nuclear Agency. The OSIA, headed by Brigadier General Roland Lajoie, is located at the Fairchild Building in Herndon, Virginia.[16]

By the time ratification had taken place, the OSIA had established an infrastructure that spread across 19 time zones with field offices at Dulles International Airport in Washington, DC, Travis Air Force Base, California, Rhein-Main Air Base in the FRG and Yokota Air Base in Japan. The OSIA's personnel of over 250 people (full- or part-time) consists mostly of representatives of the military services, as well as other government organizations involved in INF Treaty implementation. For example, General Lajoie has a principal deputy from the Arms Control and Disarmament Agency (ACDA), a deputy from the Department of State, and a deputy responsible for security from the Federal Bureau of Investigation.[17]

In addition to the OSIA activities, the Hughes Technical Services Company was contracted on 23 June 1988 to conduct OSI services at Votkinsk—to install, operate and maintain the portal monitoring facility. The value of the contract, over a five-year period, was $24.1 million.[18]

Prior to ratification of the INF Treaty, funds for operations and maintenance totalling nearly $82.9 million were made available by Congress

[15] 'Statement by Roland Lajoie, Brigadier General, US Army, Director, On-Site Inspection Agency before the House of Representatives Foreign Affairs Subcommittee on Arms Control, International Security and Science' (On-Site Inspection Agency: Washington, DC), 2 Mar. 1989.

[16] See note 15, pp. 1–12; 'Insights of an on-site inspector', *Arms Control Today*, vol. 18, no. 9 (Nov. 1988), pp. 3–10; and 'Fact sheet on the On-Site Inspection Agency' (Public Affairs Office, On-Site Inspection Agency: Washington, DC), undated.

[17] See note 15, pp. 1–12.

[18] See note 15, p. 9. See also the statement by Lieutenant Colonel Joseph Wagovitch, a spokesperson for the On-Site Inspection Agency, cited in *Arms Control Reporter*, July 1988, p. 403.B.691.

through a reprogramming request. However, in FY 1988 the total obligated funds used by the OSIA came to only $19.9 million. This is largely explained by the rather late ratification date. [19]

As General Lajoie has made clear, the portal monitoring effort is one of the OSIA's 'most complex tasks'.[20] The Votkinsk monitoring facility is now the second largest US presence in the Soviet Union (after Moscow), while the Soviet Union's monitoring presence at Magna, Utah, is their third largest in the United States (after Washington, DC and New York City).

The OSIA began its operation with four officers supplemented by a regular 10-person inspection team on rotational duty. Since August 1988, the USA's Votkinsk contingent has been manned with up to 30 inspectors (maximum allowed by the Treaty) working different shifts around the clock.

The establishment of the portal monitoring facilities at Votkinsk, however, has not been entirely without controversy. Perhaps the most notable problem is related to the use of X-ray equipment by the USA at the Votkinsk plant (see section IV). More routine disputes have also arisen concerning the right of Soviet personnel to enter a basement complex used by US inspectors as living quarters—this became a source of minor controversy at one of the meetings of the Special Verification Commission. Furthermore, the climate at Votkinsk has proven very severe, with temperatures ranging from −40 to +40 degrees Celsius. These extreme temperatures have slowed construction in the colder months and necessitated additional preventive maintenance for some of the US monitoring equipment, especially the computer terminals.[21]

In the USSR, the main responsibility for organizing inspections and escort services was assigned to the Ministry of Defence (MOD) and to the Ministry of Foreign Affairs. An 'inspection service', headed by Major-General Vladimir I. Medvedev, was also established under the auspices of the USSR's National Nuclear Risk Reduction Centre.[22]

Special Verification Commission

Article XIII, paragraph 1, of the INF Treaty provided for the establishment of the Special Verification Commission (SVC) which was designed to be convened by either of the signatories in an attempt to resolve problems relating to 'compliance with the obligations assumed' and to implement such measures as may be necessary 'to improve the viability and effectiveness' of the Treaty. The SVC can either meet as a complete group or convene select working groups to consider specific issues.

Almost from the outset, the concept of an SVC was attacked. Serge Sur, in his early assessment of of the INF verification regime, wrote 'all that the Treaty does on this subject is to establish procedures that lead virtually

[19] See note 15, pp. 1–12.
[20] See note 15, p. 8.
[21] See note 4.
[22] 'For confidence sake', *Krasnaya Zvezda*, 3 Aug. 1989, pp. 1–5 (abridged translation no. VOVP2–890801dr60 by Novosti Press Agency).

nowhere, it merely pins a name on ordinary bilateral consultations'.[23] Sur considered that the workings of the SVC would be even more 'disastrous' than that of the Standing Consultative Commission set up by the 1972 ABM Treaty. Furthermore, it was thought that the SVC's lack of organization and power would do little to aid the process of implementation.

Overall, the SVC seems to have worked rather well. Although both sides agreed that information relating to SVC activity would be kept confidential, a broad outline of its operations can be gleaned from its decisions. By the end of 1989, six sessions of the SVC had taken place in Geneva:

Session one (6 June–15 July 1988). According to a joint statement issued after the meeting a great deal of progress had been made on measures to enhance the implementation of the Treaty. These measures primarily related to inspection equipment and methods.

Session two (12 September–26 October 1988). A number of subjects were discussed at this meeting: (*a*) the discovery by satellite of Soviet INF missile components at 30 sites prohibited by the Treaty (after consultations, the parts were removed from the sites); (*b*) the dismantling of SS-20 garages and reconstruction at sites not covered by the Treaty; and (*c*) some technical data issues, such as the difference between fuelled and unfuelled missiles, also arose, but were satisfactorily resolved.

Session three (28 November–21 December 1988). At this session, two agreements were concluded: a Memorandum of Understanding regarding the procedures for the operation of the SVC, and an Agreed Statement on certain inspection procedures at Votkinsk.

Session four (17 April–9 June 1989). This session examined further verification measures. According to a statement, the session included the signature of a US–Soviet Agreed Statement on inspection procedures at the portal monitoring facility at Magna, Utah.

Session five (10 October–9 November 1989). A statement issued by the US delegation said that work had continued 'on measures to enhance the effective implementation' of the INF Treaty.[24]

Session six (4–22 December 1989). On this occasion, the SVC met to 'improve the viability and effectiveness of the INF Treaty, as well as to resolve questions on compliance'.[25]

[23] Sur, S., *Verification Problems of the Washington Treaty on the Elimination of Intermediate-Range Missiles,* Research Paper No. 2, United Nations Institute for Disarmament Research, Geneva (United Nations: New York, Oct. 1988), p. 16.

[24] See note 4. See also 'Press release', US Arms Control and Disarmament Agency, Washington, DC, 15 July 1988; 'SVC, SCC resume work on ABM, INF implementation', US Information Service, EUR–309 (US Embassy, Stockholm), 30 Nov. 1989; 'SVC agrees certain verification procedures', US Information Service, EUR–310 (US Embassy, Stockholm), 21 Dec. 1989; 'US–Soviet Commission that oversees INF Treaty meets', US Information Service, EUR–204 (US Embassy, Stockholm), 18 Apr. 1989; 'Implementation of US–Soviet INF Treaty continues', US Information Service, EUR–508 (US Embassy, Stockholm), 9 June. 1989; and 'US–USSR INF oversight commission ends fifth meeting', US Information Service, EUR–406 (US Embassy, Stockholm), 9 Nov. 1989.

[25] US Information Service, EUR–112 (US Embassy, Stockholm), 4 Dec 1989, p. 37.

Nuclear Risk Reduction Centres

Since the early 1960s, both the USA and the USSR have displayed an inter-mittent willingness to consider measures that would reduce the possibilities for misunderstanding and miscalculations that could increase the risk of nuclear confrontation. The 1963 'Hot Line Agreement', and the subsequent 'improvement' measures in 1971 and 1984, which created the first direct communications link between the heads of government of the two super-powers, has probably been the most successful result of Soviet and US initiatives in this area.[26] Despite the 1963 agreement and its subsequent improvements, there were still no direct communication measures in place that allowed a continuous flow of non-crisis information and messages between institutions of government in the two countries.[27]

In 1980, Senators Henry Jackson, Sam Nunn and John Warner first pro-posed the idea of the 'crisis control center'. In 1983, a Center for Strategic and International Studies Congressional Working Group on Nuclear Risk Reductions, chaired by Senators Nunn and Warner, was formed to investi-gate and then to promote specific proposals to reduce the risk of nuclear war. The recommendations of the Nunn–Warner Working Group included the concept of the Nuclear Risk Reduction Centre (NRRC).[28]

As a result of a US initiative based on this new idea, President Reagan and General Secretary Gorbachev agreed at the Geneva summit meeting in November 1985 to establish an 'experts study group' to determine the feasibility of establishing centres to reduce the risk of nuclear war. The group met in Geneva on 5–6 May and 25 August 1986. As a result of these meetings, Reagan and Gorbachev decided at the Reykjavik summit meeting in October 1986 to begin formal negotiations to establish NRRCs. The negotiations took place in Geneva on 13 January and 3–4 May 1987. As a result of these negotiations, the Agreement between the USA and the USSR on the Establishment of Nuclear Risk Reduction Centers was reached. It was signed in Washington, DC on 15 September 1987.

The agreement, of unlimited duration, committed each party to establish an NRRC in its capital. Each party was free to staff its NRRC according to its own needs. The NRRCs became operational in April 1988, and are located in the State Department in Washington, DC, and in the MOD in Moscow respectively. The US NRRC is headed by H. Allen Holmes, the Assistant Secretary of State for Politico-Military Affairs, and the Soviet

---

[26] For the text of the 1963 and 1971 agreements, see Goldblat, J., SIPRI, *Agreements for Arms Control: A Critical Survey* (Taylor & Francis: London, 1982), pp. 155–56 and 190–92.

[27] Other 'communication' measures, the Agreement between the USA and the USSR on measures to reduce the risk of outbreak of nuclear war of 1971 and the 'Common Understanding' of the 1971 agreement settled upon in 1985 have also been agreed. The most thorough analyses in this area are: Blechman, B. M. (ed.), *Preventing Nuclear War: A Realistic Approach* (Indiana University Press: Bloomington, Ind., 1985); Blechman, B. M. and Krepon, M., *Nuclear Risk Reduction Centres, Significant Issues Series*, vol. 8, no.1 (Center for Strategic and International Studies, Georgetown University: Washington, DC, 1986); and Blechman, B. M., 'A minimal reduction of a major risk', *Bulletin of the Atomic Scientists*, Apr. 1988, p. 44–46.

[28] See Blechman, *Preventing Nuclear War* (note 27).

centre is headed by Major-General Medvedev.[29] The NRRCs are not elaborate: for example, that in the State Department has no more than a dozen assigned staff. The centres communicate by direct satellite links, are equipped with high-speed facsimile capabilities and computer terminals, and can rapidly transmit full texts of messages and graphics.[30]

Originally, the NRRC Agreement called for notifications of ballistic missile launches in accordance with the 1971 Agreement between the USA and the USSR on Measures to Reduce the Risk of Outbreak of Nuclear War and the 1972 Agreement between the USA and the USSR on the Prevention of Incidents on and over the High Seas.[31] It was also specified that 'goodwill' notifications could also be sent at the discretion of either party.[32] However, with the entry into force of the the INF Treaty and the signing of the Agreement between the USA and the USSR on Notifications of Launches of Intercontinental Ballistic Missiles and Submarine-Launched Ballistic Missiles at the Moscow summit meeting in May–June 1988, the work of the NRRCs expanded considerably. The main function of the NRRCs, in relation to the INF Treaty, is to forward notification of changes that have or are about to take place in areas covered by the Treaty.[33]

IV. Problems and disputes over Treaty implementation

Despite the fact that the implementation of the Treaty has, for the most part, gone smoothly, a number of problems and disputes have arisen that are worth outlining. Nevertheless, it should also be said that the *way* in which the disputes have been resolved by the superpowers provides further evidence of the new spirit of *détente* which characterizes the current US–Soviet relationship.

Charges of circumvention

On 5 January 1988, Lieutenant-General Viktor Pavlov of the USSR charged the USA with providing misleading information in the Memorandum of Understanding on Data. The charge concerned the announcement on 14 November 1988 by the DOD that two contracts had been issued to McDonnell-Douglas Astronautics and the Convair Division of General Dynamics for the conversion of GLCMs to sea-launched cruise missiles (SLCMs), a conversion activity not allowed under the INF Treaty. This

[29] *Krasnaya Zvezda* (note 21). See also 'USSR, US continue to destroy missiles', *Trud,* 13 Dec. 1988 (translation no. VOVP2-881213DR31 by Novosti Press Agency).

[30] 'Missile destruction process under INF Treaty running smoothly', *Aerospace Daily,* 30 Aug. 1989, p. 372.

[31] For the text of the 1971 and 1972 agreements, see note 26, pp. 192–93 and 195–97.

[32] 'Statement by Marlin Fitzwater' (The White House, Office of the Press Secretary: Washington, DC, 22 Mar. 1988).

[33] In addition to the provision of data contained in the Memorandum of Understanding and regularly updated by the parties (within 30 days after the expiration of each six-month period), notifications should also take place according to specified criteria. These circumstances are outlined in *The First Anniversary of the INF Treaty* (note 8), pp. 26–27.

dispute, which caused a flurry of diplomatic activity in January, originated with a mistake in the initial contract announcement which should have stated that generic cruise missile parts originally intended for use in the construction of GLCMs would be incorporated into SLCMs. The contracts were intended as money-saving measures for the DOD; the General Accounting Office had estimated that the incorporation of generic components originally slated for use in GLCMs could save the Pentagon $114 million in SLCM procurement costs. The original announcement, however, seemingly indicated that the USA had 145 more GLCMs than were included in the original MOU. But, after the Pentagon outlined the details of the mistaken announcement in a statement on 19 January in which the US commitment to the implementation process was reaffirmed, the matter was cleared up.[34]

On 2 December, in a report to the US Congress, the out-going Reagan Administration charged the USSR with five minor violations of the INF Treaty—the most significant of which related to the illegal movement and storage of missiles.[35] Similarly, in February 1989, the USSR made some further minor charges: the one that seemed to concern them most was the appearance of systems covered by the Treaty at an undeclared site, the MacGregor Range in New Mexico.[36] With the prevailing mood of goodwill, little was made of these charges by either side.

By May 1989, however, the USA had apparently again become concerned by a pattern of Soviet circumvention. On 19 May, a senior White House aide reported that US on-site inspections in the USSR in April had uncovered an instance in which pieces of an SS-23 launch vehicle were re-welded after being cut in half. Furthermore, the USA was also worried about a gap in factory markings for the SSC-X-4 and the removal of serial numbers from all SS-20s, in an apparent attempt to avoid on-site accounting. A charge concerning failure to dismantle SS-20 loading mechanisms on transport vehicles was also made by the USA, according to US sources, with no satisfactory response from the USSR.[37]

The X-ray equipment problem

On 17 October 1988, it was reported that the USSR, fearing that the equipment would reveal internal technical information on the SS-25, was refusing permission for the USA to operate its X-ray equipment at the required level of radiation at the portal monitoring facility at Votkinsk. Soviet officials claimed that the use of special radiation detection equipment to determine the number of warheads on missiles had not been agreed. They based this claim on Article IX, paragraph 6 of the Protocol on inspections which

[34] *Jane's Defence Weekly*, 10 Dec.1988. See also 'INF Treaty disputes', *Jane's NATO Report*, 31 Jan. 1989, p. 5; 'USA denies cruise missile breach of INF Treaty', *Jane's Defence Weekly*, 4 Feb. 1989; and 'Soviets charge US missile conversions may violate INF Treaty', *Arms Control Today*, vol. 19, no. 2 (Mar. 1989), p. 26.

[35] *Arms Control Reporter*, Jan. 1989, pp. 403.B.718–19.

[36] *Arms Control Reporter*, Mar. 1989, p. 403.B.729.

[37] *Arms Control Reporter*, June 1989, p. 403.B.733.

permits only 'non-damaging imaging equipment' at the fixed monitoring site. However, the use of 'radiation detection equipment' for challenge inspections is apparently permitted under Article XII, paragraph 14 of the Treaty. This equipment—the Cargoscan system—developed by the Bechtel Corporation, and American Science and Engineering, provides digitally enhanced low-level X-rays which can penetrate several inches of steel.[38] Despite controversy over the installation of this equipment, neither side opted to make it a major issue. On 3 January 1990, the OSIA's Lieutenant Colonel Joe Wagovich reported that the Cargoscan X-ray scanning device 'will become operational in the Soviet Union in the near future'.[39]

The SNF dispute

On 15 April 1989, Foreign Minister Eduard Shevardnadze, in a statement upon the conclusion of an official visit to Bonn, apparently threatened to halt the destruction of its SS-23s, if NATO took the decision to develop a replacement for the short-range Lance missile. Shevardnadze said that such plans were 'an attempt to circumvent the accord . . . an attempt which may jeopardize this major international agreement. . . . Why should we destroy SS-23 missiles, if the other side is developing and will deploy similar Lance-2 missiles?'[40] However, on 26 May 1989, in an apparent attempt to bring the issue to an end, Shevardnadze, in a further statement said that 'no one in the USSR intends to upset the INF Treaty'.[41]

The concern over the re-use of warheads

Something of a controversy over the role of warheads in negotiations between the superpowers had already arisen during the ratification process in the US Senate. Senator Jesse Helms charged that if treaties allowed the re-use of warheads, then they were of negligible military value. The Reagan Administration had dealt with this issue by citing a shortage of fissile material in the USA for use in missile development: retaining the warheads, the Administration argued, was essential for security reasons. It was also suggested that to destroy the warheads would have created an unacceptable environmental hazard.[42]

[38] *Aviation Week & Space Technology*, vol. 130, no. 21 (22 May 1989), p. 95; *Aviation Week & Space Technology*, vol. 130, no. 22 (29 May 1989), p. 107.

[39] *Aviation Week & Space Technology* (note 38), p. 95. See also US Information Service, EUR–413 (US Embassy, Stockholm), 4 Jan. 1990.

[40] 'Moscow warns NATO on missiles', *Financial Times*, 15 Apr. 1989, p. 2. See also: 'Shevardnadze threat over nuclear forces attacked', *The Guardian*, 16 May 1989, p. 5; and 'Soviets threaten to violate INF Treaty over SNF, but quickly back down', *Arms Control Today*, vol. 19, no. 5 (June/July 1989), p. 23.

[41] 'Threat over INF Treaty is dropped by Moscow', *International Herald Tribune*, 26 May 1989, p. 2.

[42] In early 1990, it does not seem that this issue has resulted in a similar debate in the USSR. For a consideration of the wider issues concerning warheads, see 'Focus on nuclear warheads', *Moscow News*, no. 43 (1987), p. 7; Donnelly, W. H., 'Nuclear arms control: disposal of nuclear warheads', *Congressional Record Service Issue Brief*, Library of Congress (6 Feb. 1989); and Taylor, T. B., 'Verified elimination of nuclear warheads', *Science and Global Security*, vol. 1 (1989), pp. 1–26.

In a recent press report on the activities of the Senate Armed Sevices Committee, it was suggested that the USA should take advantage of the clause in the INF Treaty allowing the re-use of INF warheads on other systems to support the Lance replacement programme. The Armed Sevices Committee even went so far as to suggest that, unless there were overriding technical or financial reasons, the Congress should refuse funding for any Lance replacement that does not re-use these warheads.[43] Although this announcement resulted in little comment and even less analysis, a formal political debate, to match that in the academic community, on the importance of addressing the issue of warhead re-use is necessary to facilitate a sustained and militarily significant disarmament process.

US troop withdrawal legislation

In March 1989, Representative Patricia Schroeder (Democrat, Colorado) and Representative Andy Ireland (Republican, Florida), two chief supporters of US troop withdrawal from Europe, took the debate over withdrawal into a new area by introducing a bill to withdraw those troops associated with INF weapon systems from Europe. It was thought that the proposal would involve 20 000–25 000 troops. The raising of this issue so early in the implementation process did little to increase the confidence of those European countries which had agreed with the original decision to deploy the missiles and had contributed to the debate that had raised the whole spectre of the INF issue in the 1980s. It appeared as if the INF Treaty was in danger of generating new arguments about 'burden-sharing'. Winston Churchill, a Conservative member of the British Parliament, commented: 'The reality is that, if there were to be a 20 000 or 25 000 cut in US ground forces in Europe, there would be 25 000 fewer US troops in place than there were in 1983 before the cruise and Pershings were deployed in Europe, because there wasn't a compensating increase at that particular time'.[44]

Environmental considerations

In the USA, growing concerns over environmental effects related to the implementation of the INF Treaty were already in evidence when elimination sites were being sought prior to ratification. As of April 1988, the USA had still not been able to reveal the location of potential sites because of controversy over the environmental consequences of 'burning'. As a consequence of the Treaty, the US Army had 4.3 million pounds (nearly 2 million kg) of Pershing missile solid propellant to burn, and no state had shown willingness to host its destruction. On 2 February 1988, Governor Norm Bangerter of Utah (the most likely designated state for 'burning') had threatened to block the destruction of Pershing IIs in his state

[43] 'US to recycle INF warheads', *The Guardian,* 31 July 1989.
[44] US Information Service, EUR–210 (US Embassy, Stockholm), 7 Mar. 1989. See also 'Bill planned to withdraw INF crews', *Jane's NATO Report,* 7 Mar. 1989, p. ?.

because of environmental concerns.[45] In August 1989, this problem again came to the fore when environmentalists revealed that the solid fuel used to propel the Pershing 1A and II, when burned, combined with moisture to create hydrochloric acid, which may have a serious impact on the surrounding environment. In response to these concerns, the US Senate appropriated $6 million for research into safer methods of disposal.[46]

V. Conclusion

With the elimination of the final SS-23 missile on 27 October 1989, the first phase of the implementation process was successfully concluded. By meeting the official deadline for the elimination of the shorter-range missiles by substantial margins, both the USA and the USSR have demonstrated an enthusiastic commitment to the implementation of the INF Treaty. This, together with the co-operative nature in which the inspection process has been both organized and implemented among all of the countries affected by the Treaty, provides perhaps the clearest indication that the relationship between East and West began to operate on a different plane during 1989.

Certainly, the INF implementation process has provided an area of activity in which the new spirit of *détente* between the USA and the USSR has been able to quietly flourish.[47] The results of the SVC meetings that are publicly known appear to indicate that informally convened bodies can operate effectively and can actually enhance pre-determined verification procedures. Similarly, the NRRCs have transformed communication links between government bodies in the USSR and the USA. Although the inspection instrumentalities are organized differently in the two countries, overall their efficiency has served the implementation process well. In the USA, the OSIA should probably be considered a model for agencies that will have to deal with future implementation processes. Although there have been problems, their significance should not be over estimated.

Two factors have contributed to the success of the INF Treaty implementation: the new relationship between the USA and the USSR, and the detailed nature of the Treaty. Thus, it might also be said that successful treaties may be the result of a fine balance between a commitment to working out as much detail as possible before signing and the realization that a measure of built-in *in*formality permits flexibility on a day-to-day basis. The success of the INF Treaty implementation process in 1989 should serve to illustrate that the worries arising during ratification debates can be exaggerated and that disarmament treaties can be successfully implemented.

---

[45] Cited in *Arms Control Reporter*, Mar. 1988, p. 403.B.628.

[46] 'Arms and the environment', *Newsweek*, 28 Aug. 1989, p. 24.

[47] For a review of strategic nuclear arms control after the signing of the INF Treaty, see Bertram, C., 'US–Soviet nuclear arms control', SIPRI, *SIPRI Yearbook 1989: World Armaments and Disarmament* (Oxford University Press: Oxford, 1989), pp. 359–67. See also chapter 11 of this *Yearbook*.

13. Conventional arms control in Europe

JANE M. O. SHARP*

I. Introduction

This chapter reviews developments in both unilateral and negotiated arms control in Europe during 1989. It begins with an analysis of the programme of unilateral measures announced by President Mikhail Gorbachev in December 1988 and by other WTO leaders in early 1989. These measures included cuts in defence budgets, manpower and military equipment, as well as in the length of compulsory military service, in the WTO countries. The chapter then reviews progress at the Negotiation on Conventional Armed Forces in Europe (CFE) between the 16 NATO and the 7 WTO states, and outlines developments in the 35-state Negotiations on Confidence- and Security-Building Measures (CSBMs).

II. Unilateral cuts in Soviet and East European forces

Fired in large part by the need to free resources for the domestic economy, President Gorbachev launched a programme of extensive arms control and disarmament early in 1986. To justify these cuts, Gorbachev adopted a more conciliatory view of international relations than his predecessors and reshaped the Soviet defence and foreign policy agenda to de-emphasize national security and independence in favour of international security and interdependence. Confrontational and expansionist policies gave way to re-trenchment and a more regional focus. In particular Gorbachev specifically rejected the Brezhnev doctrine of Soviet military intervention to preserve communist regimes in Eastern Europe.[1]

A recurrent theme in his speeches on arms control was the recognition of asymmetry in forces between East and West and that to reach parity the side that was ahead must reduce. When Gorbachev came to power in 1985 he was manifestly impatient with the kind of traditional arms control exemplified by the Mutual and Balanced Force Reduction (MBFR) talks, geared as they were to a modest reduction of stationed Soviet and US forces in Central Europe. Rather than bring MBFR to a successful conclusion, in April 1986 he proposed more radical cuts in conventional arms that proved both the last nail in the coffin of MBFR and the catalyst for the new CFE Negotiation. Gorbachev was not content, however, to wait for a multilateral agreement to reduce the Soviet military burden, but initiated unilateral cuts even before the CFE Negotiation convened.

[1] Speech by President Gorbachev to the Council of Europe in Strasbourg, 6 July 1989.

* Stephen Gatland provided valuable assistance checking data for this chapter.

In a speech to the United Nations on 7 December 1988, he announced that 500 000 men would be cut from the Soviet armed forces by 1991; 50 000 men and their equipment, including 5000 tanks, would be withdrawn from the GDR, Hungary and Czechoslovakia. These would include 6 tank divisions as well as some independent tank regiments. The Soviet divisions remaining in Eastern Europe would be restructured to make them strictly defensive. Another 5000 tanks were to be removed from the European part of the USSR, and total reductions from this region and the territory of the WTO allies would amount to 10 000 tanks, 8500 artillery pieces and 800 combat aircraft. Soviet forces would also be reduced in the Asian part of the USSR and in Mongolia. In addition to cutting forces and equipment 'the armaments economy' would be converted into a 'disarmament economy', and the USSR would make public this experience in conversion.[2] After the December 1988 announcement, all WTO countries except Romania followed Gorbachev's examples with their own unilateral cuts and, in the following months, Gorbachev and other senior WTO spokesmen clarified which forces and equipment were to be withdrawn from where.

To members of the Trilateral Commission in January 1989 Gorbachev said that the 50 000 men to be withdrawn from Eastern Europe would be part of the 240 000 men to be demobilized in the European part of the USSR.[3] Gorbachev said that 200 000 more troops would be demobilized from the East including 75 per cent of those deployed across the border in Mongolia,[4] and 60 000 from the Southern TVD.[5] He also announced cuts of 14.2 per cent in the defence budget and 19.5 per cent in military procurement over the next two years.[6] These percentages did not mean much until late May when he announced a defence budget for 1989 of 77.3 billion roubles, noting that the military budget had been static for 1987 and 1988 and would be cut by 10 billion roubles for 1990–91.[7] Marshal Victor Kulikov told the Trilateral Commission that four armoured divisions would be withdrawn from the GDR, one from Czechoslovakia and one from Hungary[8] (leaving 15 Soviet divisions in the GDR, 4 in Czechoslovakia and 3 in Hungary). General Nikolai Chervov clarified that of the 10 000 Soviet tanks to be withdrawn from the ATTU zone, 5300 would be of the most modern vintage from Eastern Europe; in addition to the disbanding of 6 tank

---

[2] Speech by Mikhail Gorbachev at the UN General Assembly, 7 Dec. 1988, *Soviet Diplomacy Today* (Soviet Ministry of Foreign Affairs), 1989, pp. 40–47.

[3] In this chapter it is assumed, although Soviet spokesmen do not explicitly say so, that references to the European region of the USSR plus the territory of the WTO allies imply the WTO portion of the Atlantic-to-the-Urals (ATTU) zone as specified in the CFE mandate, i.e., the territories of the 6 East European allies plus the 11 Soviet Military Districts (MDs) west of the Urals.

[4] The Far Eastern TVD includes the Siberian, Transbaykal and Far Eastern MDs, as well as Mongolia.

[5] *New York Times*, 19 Jan. 1989.

[6] Izyumov, A., 'Military Glasnost lacks openness', *Moscow News*, no. 7 (10 Sep. 1989); Steele, J., 'Gorbachev comes clean on Soviet defence bill', *The Guardian*, 31 May 1989; unsigned, 'Soviet budget plans to cut deficit by half', *Financial Times*, 26 Sep. 1989.

[7] Gorbachev speech, *Foreign Broadcast and Information Service–Soviet Union (FBIS-SOV)*, FBIS-SOV-89-1035, 31 May 1989, pp. 47–62 and 47–62; see also Kornilov, Y., 'Facts behind the military budget figures', *Soviet Weekly*, 17 June 1989; Steele (note 6).

[8] *FBIS-SOV-89-013*, 23 Jan. 1989, p. 1.

Table 13.1. WTO unilateral cuts to be implemented in the ATTU zone by
1 January 1991

Country	Troops	Tanks	Artillery	Aircraft[a]
Bulgaria	117 500	2 200	3 990	234
Cut	10 000	200	200	20
Left	107 500	2 000	3 790	214
Czechoslovakia	199 700	4 585	3 445	407
Cut	62 000[b]	3 850	..	51
Left	137 700	755	3 445	356
GDR	173 100	3 140	2 435	283
Cut	10 000	600	..	50
Left	163 100	2 540	2 435	233
Hungary	106 800	1 435	1 750	113
Cut	9 300	251	430	9
Left	97 500	1 184	6 320	104
Poland	347 000	3 350	3 065	480
Cut	55 000	850	900	80
Left	292 000	2 500	2 165	400
Romania	171 000	3 200	6 600	156
Total non-Soviet WTO	1 115 000	17 890	14 685	1 673
Cut	146 300	4 901	630	130
Left	968 700	12 789	14 055	1 543
Soviet forces in				
Eastern Europe	555 000	10 970	35 590	3 682
Cut	50 000	5 300	4 250[c]	400[d]
Left	505 000	5 670	31 740	3 282
Soviet MDs	1 903 000	41 580	50 275	5 355
Cut	190 000	4 700	4 250[c]	400[d]
Left	1 713 000	36 880	46 025	4 955
Total WTO	3 573 000	59 470	71 560	5 355
Cut	386 300	14 901	9 130	930
Left	3 186 700	44 569	62 430	4 425
Comparable NATO forces in the ATTU zone				
WTO data	3 660 000	30 690	57 060	5 450
NATO data	3 200 000	22 224	17 328	6 700

[a] Excludes air defence interceptors and naval aircraft.

[b] 12 000 cut announced by Czechoslovak National Defence Council in Jan. 1989; 50 000 cut
announced by President Havel in Jan. 1990.

[c] 8500 Soviet artillery pieces scheduled to be cut from the entire ATTU zone.

[d] 800 Soviet aircraft scheduled to be cut from the entire ATTU zone.

Sources: 'Statement by the Committee of the Ministers of Defence of the WTO member states, on
the relative strength of the armed forces and armaments of the Warsaw Treaty Organization in Europe
and adjacent water areas', 31 Jan. 1989 (WTO, 1989); North Atlantic Treaty Organization,
Conventional Forces in Europe: the Facts, Brussels, Nov. 1988 (NATO, 1988); Forsberg, R., *et al.*,
*Cutting Conventional Forces: An Analysis of the Official Mandate, Statistics and Proposals in the
NATO–WTO Talks on Reducing Conventional Forces in Europe* (IDDS: Brookline, Mass., July
1989); IISS, *The Military Balance 1989–1990* (IISS: London, 1989); US Congress, Committee on
Armed Services, House of Representatives, 101st Congress, 1st Session, *Status of the Soviet Union's
Unilateral Force Reductions and Restructuring of its Forces* (US Government Printing Office:
Washington, DC, 16 Oct. 1989); Mishin, Y., 'Warsaw Pact forces, budget reduction figures',
Argumenty i Fakty, no. 6 (11–17 Feb. 1989), p. 8, in *FBIS-SOV-89-034*, 22 Feb. 1989, p. 3; 'The
Warsaw Pact vanishing', *The Economist*, 27 Jan. 1990, p. 36.

divisions in Eastern Europe (involving the withdrawal of 2300 tanks) 3000 tanks would also be removed as the remaining divisions were restructured into a more defensive posture.[9]

In February 1989, in an interview in *Izvestia*, Defence Minister Dimitri Yazov emphasized that the six Soviet tank divisions to be withdrawn from Eastern Europe were to be disbanded, not deployed elsewhere, and explained how Soviet divisions remaining in Eastern Europe would be restructured.[10] Tanks in motorized infantry divisions would be cut by 40 per cent (from 270 to *c.* 160)[11] and tank regiments would be removed from the motorized infantry divisions, leaving only motorized infantry regiments. In addition, tanks in tank divisions would be cut by 20 per cent (from 330 to *c.* 265)[12] by removing one tank regiment from each tank division. Yazov noted that the combined cuts announced by the WTO countries in the ATTU zone would involve 296 300 men (240 000 Soviet and 56 300 East European), approximately 12 000 tanks (10 000 Soviet and 1900 East European), 9130 artillery systems (8500 Soviet and 630 East European) and 930 warplanes (800 Soviet and 130 East European). When the eastern and southern parts of the USSR are included the unilateral cuts amount to 556 300 men. Since then, however, Poland announced additional cuts of 40 000 troops and Czechoslovakia announced additional cuts of 50 000 troops, 300 tanks and 300 ATCs. The total unilateral WTO cuts from the ATTU zone during 1989–90 will be approximately 386 300 troops and 14 900 tanks (see table 13.1).

In May 1989, President Gorbachev explained to US Secretary of State James Baker that unilateral withdrawals from Eastern Europe would also include 500 nuclear warheads—166 air-launched bombs, 50 nuclear artillery shells and 284 warheads assigned to short-range missiles.[13] In June, Marshal Sergey Akhromeyev said that in addition to the reduction in Soviet capability inherent in these unilateral cuts, forces were also being restructured to make them less offensive and comply with the WTO's defensive doctrine. Akhromeyev said that WTO doctrine now stipulated that WTO forces would repel an attack by defensive actions only for a period of three to four weeks before adopting counter-offensive tactics. He claimed that NATO doctrine, by contrast, was still highly offensive, especially in calling for the use of nuclear weapons after a period of 7–10 days.[14] (NATO's flexible response doctrine is in fact ambiguous. NATO document MC 14/3 provides for an initial non-nuclear phase in any NATO–WTO conflict. Different Supreme Allied Commanders—SACEURs—of NATO forces in Europe have occasionally speculated as to how long that conventional phase might be. General Bernard Rogers said that under most circumstances he

---

[9] Moscow Radio, *FBIS-SOV-89-013*, 23 Jan. 1989; *Arms Control Reporter (ACR)*, p. 407.B.119.
[10] *Izvestia*, 28 Feb. 1989, *FBIS-SOV-89-038*, pp. 1–4.
[11] General G. Batenin cited in *ACR*, 1989, p. 407.B.14.5.
[12] Note 10.
[13] Schevardnadze press conference, *Pravda*, 14 May 1989.
[14] Interview in *Le Figaro*, 13 June 1989, English translation in *FBIS-SOV-89-114*, 15 June 1989, pp. 70–72.

would have been forced to 'go nuclear' after only 7–10 days of conventional operations.[15] General John Galvin, Roger's successor as SACEUR, said he could only guarantee holding out for two weeks against an all-out Warsaw Pact attack before using nuclear weapons.[16])

Following Gorbachev's UN speech announcing unilateral Soviet cuts, all the non-Soviet WTO countries, except Romania, followed suit with announcements of cuts in their own national forces. During 1989 the Soviet and East European governments issued status reports on the implementation of the announced cuts; at the end of the year, and at the beginning of 1990, some of the new reform governments in Eastern Europe wanted Soviet withdrawals to be accelerated.

The German Democratic Republic

Since 1945 there have been 19 divisions of Soviet troops (approximately 380 000 men) stationed in the GDR. This is by far the largest contingent of Soviet forces based on foreign territory—a measure of the importance of the GDR in Soviet military and political thinking. Formerly known as the Group of Soviet Forces in Germany, they were renamed the Western Group of Forces in 1989. According to Colonel General Bronislav Omelichev, first Deputy Head of the Soviet General Staff, the name change was in response to a request from General Secretary Erich Honecker during his visit to Moscow in late June, to de-emphasize the role of Soviet troops as occupation forces.[17]

Honecker announced in January that Soviet withdrawals from the GDR in 1989 would include the 25th and 32nd tank divisions, two independent training regiments and eight independent battalions. Withdrawals in 1990 would include the 7th and 12th tank divisions, an aerial storm brigade, three training regiments and three independent battalions.[18] Even after the proposed unilateral cut (of approximately 20 000–22 000 men) Soviet troops will outnumber national armies by a substantial margin; GDR regular armed forces (excluding paramilitary and *Stasi* troops) numbered 180 000 before the announced cuts. Soviet troops have not, however, been used against GDR citizens since 1953. Indeed, according to Willy Brandt, stationed Soviet forces played a key role in defusing a potentially explosive situation in Leipzig on 9 October 1989.[19]

In October, Soviet Defence Minister Yazov reported that two tank divisions, two flight squadrons, one training regiment, three airborne bat-

[15] Roos, J. G. and Schemmer, B. F., 'Revolution in NATO's conventional defense looms from "competitive strategies" initiative', *Armed Forces Journal International*, Oct. 1988, p. 114.

[16] van Loon, H., 'An exclusive AFJ interview with John R. Galvin, USA Supreme Allied Commander Europe,' *Armed Forces Journal International*, Mar. 1988, pp. 50–52.

[17] TASS report, 'Troop withdrawal from Eastern Europe on schedule', reprinted in *FBIS-SOV-89-125*, 30 June 1989, p. 1; see also Marsh, D., 'Moscow to rename East German army,' *Financial Times*, 3 July 1989.

[18] Erich Honecker at a dinner for the Swedish Prime Minister, Ingvar Carlsson, 23 Jan. 1989; McCartney, R., *Washington Post*, 24 Jan. 1989; *ACR*, pp. 401.B.121–22.

[19] Willy Brandt interview in *Le Monde*, 14 Dec. 1989.

talions and a number of smaller units had been withdrawn from the GDR. These included 1988 tanks, 169 artillery pieces, 126 aircraft and 11 461 troops.[20] By 1 November 1989, 11 620 troops and 247 artillery pieces had been withdrawn.[21] With respect to national forces, in January 1989 Honecker announced cuts of 10 000 men in the GDR armed forces and a 10 per cent cut in the national defence budget. Cuts would include six tank regiments, 600 tanks and an air force squadron with 50 fighter aircraft. In December 1989 Defence Minister Theodore Hoffman announced that the length of conscription would be cut from 18 to 12 months.[22] The exodus of several hundred thousand GDR citizens during late 1989 and early 1990 also meant that many conscripts were moved into the civilian sector.[23] In early January 1990 Gregor Gysi, leader of the Socialist Unity Party of Germany–Democratic Socialist Party, proposed the removal of all foreign troops from both German states by 1999 (consistent with Soviet policy as announced by Deputy Foreign Minister Vladimir Petrovsky at the UN in December 1989) and cuts of 50 per cent in the armed forces of both Germanies.[24] FRG Defence Minister Gerhard Stoltenberg objected to the symmetry of this proposal saying that the *Bundeswehr* was not deployed solely against the army of the GDR but also against stationed Soviet forces in the GDR, hence the *Bundeswehr* could only be cut in proportion to cuts in stationed Soviet forces.[25] GDR Defence Minister Hoffman expressed misgivings about the Gysi proposal, which did not appear to have wide support in the new coalition government in the GDR, and may have been more an election ploy than a serious disarmament measure.[26]

Poland

Two divisions of Soviet troops (approximately 40 000 men) have been in Poland since 1945. They serve the specific military mission of protecting communication links between Soviet troops in the GDR and the Soviet military command in the USSR. Soviet troops have not been employed to suppress political dissidents in Poland as they have in the GDR (1953), Czechoslovakia (1968) and Hungary (1956), nor were they used to impose martial law in 1981. In that instance the crucial factor was Soviet political control over Polish forces.

Soviet troops in Poland were not among those initially announced for withdrawal in December 1988. In late January 1989, after complaints from Poland, Soviet General Chervov and Polish sources announced that three

[20] TASS report reprinted in *FBIS-SOV-89-192*, 5 Oct. 1989, p. 22.
[21] *Pravda*, 5 Nov. 1989.
[22] ADN, 28 Dec. 1989.
[23] Lofgren, B., 'Reforms in East German Armed forces include softening military's image', *Armed Forces Journal International*, Jan. 1990, p. 36.
[24] Schmemann, S., 'The Gysi proposal', *International Herald Tribune*, 8 Jan. 1990.
[25] Casdorff, S.-A., 'Stoltenberg für weiteren Truppenabbau in Europa', *Süddeutsche Zeitung*, 10 Jan. 1990.
[26] AP, 'DDR–Verteidigungsminister "überrascht" von Gysi-Vorschlag', *Süddeutsche Zeitung*, 10 Jan. 1990.

Soviet regiments would be withdrawn during 1989. These would include a tank training regiment, an anti-aircraft missile regiment and a helicopter regiment. Additional units would be withdrawn in 1990.[27] Polish Defence Minister Florian Siwicki had previously announced cuts of 15 000 men in national forces and a 4 per cent cut in defence spending.[28]

Soviet withdrawals from Poland began in June 1989 with the removal of a truck battalion from Swidnica;[29] in July, a chemical defence battalion was withdrawn as well as a tank training regiment from Strachow;[30] an air force regiment was disbanded in August;[31] and 87 tanks had been withdrawn from Poland by September.[32]

In July, President Bush called for the total withdrawal of troops from Poland.[33] In fact, there has not been much clamour in Poland for the total withdrawal of Soviet forces because membership of the WTO and the presence of Soviet troops serve as a guarantee of the Polish borders as outlined in the 1945 Potsdam Protocols—borders that Chancellor Helmut Kohl has been reluctant to guarantee with respect to a future unified Germany.[34]

In January 1990, however, Lech Walesa said that all Soviet troops should be withdrawn from Poland by the end of 1990.[35] He apparently felt that Poland was falling behind the demands of Hungary and Czechoslovakia with respect to stationed Soviet forces. His remarks proved something of an embarrassment for the government, however, which gave a press conference the next day to deny that it was Polish policy to call for complete withdrawal of Soviet forces.[36]

Cuts in national Polish forces in 1989 included disbandment of the 15th Regiment of the Internal Defence Forces, the Opole Regiment, in September.[37] In November plans were announced to disband 4 of its 13 divisions (approximately 40 000 troops) and place 2 others on reserve status.[38]

Czechoslovakia

After World War II no Soviet troops were deployed in Czechoslovakia until the invasion in August 1968. Five Soviet divisions (70 000–80 000 men)

[27] Interview with Nikolai Chervov in *Kosmosolskaya Pravda*, 18 Jan. 1989, cited by Jerzy Malczyk in the Polish News Agency, *FBIS-SOV-89-014*, 24 Jan. 1989, p. 3.

[28] *Jane's Defence Weekly*, 14 Jan. 1989.

[29] TASS, 16 June 1989.

[30] Polish News Agency in *FBIS-EE* (Eastern Europe), 3 July 1989.

[31] Moscow World Service, 'East Europe conventional force cuts noted', *FBIS-SOV-89-165*, 26 Aug. 1989.

[32] TASS, 'General denies NATO statement on tank withdrawal', *FBIS-SOV-89-183*, 22 Sep. 1989.

[33] Hoffman, D., *Washington Post*, 4 July 1989; *ACR*, p. 407.B.198.

[34] Kohl, H., 'Germany in Europe: overcoming the division', exerpts of speech to the Bundestag, 28 Nov. 1989, *Europäische Zeitung*, Dec. 1989, p. IV; and in response: the Statement of Poland's Foreign Affairs Minister, Krzysztof Skubiszewski, 'On the reunification of the two German states', in the Polish Sejm, 7 Dec. 1989; English translation, Polish Embassy, Stockholm, 14 Dec. 1989.

[35] *Trybuna Luda*, 19 Jan. 1990.

[36] *Trybuna Luda*, 20–21 Jan. 1990.

[37] AP, 29 Sep. 1989, reprinted in *FBIS-EE*, 2 Oct. 1989.

[38] AP, *Baltimore Sun*, 9 Nov. 1989.

remained after the invasion: two armoured divisions and three motorized rifle divisions.

In February 1989, Colonel-General Miroslav Vacek, Chief of the Czechoslovak General Staff and Deputy Defence Minister, announced that in 1989 four independent Soviet formations would be withdrawn, including a shock paratroop battalion and an engineers' battalion. This would involve 1500 men, 197 tanks and 20 combat aircraft. In 1990 one Soviet tank division would be withdrawn, including 3800 men and 516 tanks. Two of the four Soviet divisions remaining in Czechoslovakia would be reorganized to assume a more defensive character.[39]

Soviet units began withdrawing from Czechoslovakia in mid-March 1989 when an airborne assault battalion was withdrawn from Riecky Garrison.[40] In May, an army vehicle battalion withdrew from Olomouc,[41] and 23 T-72 tanks left the Krupka Garrison.[42] By November 1500 Soviet troops, 192 combat aircraft and 20 combat aircraft had left Czechoslovakia.[43]

On 14 December, the new Czechoslovak Foreign Minister, Jiri Dienstbier, said that he was continuing talks with Soviet representatives (begun by his predecessor, Jaromir Johanes) on the complete withdrawal of Soviet troops (estimated at 75 000–80 000 men) from Czechoslovakia. He argued that the arrangements under which Soviet troops remained in Czechoslovakia were invalid because they were made under duress in 1968. However, he said that Czechoslovakia would not withdraw unilaterally from either the WTO or the Council for Mutual Economic Assistance (COMECON).[44] In January 1990, after the election of Vaclav Havel as President and Alexander Dubcek as Speaker of the Parliament, a Foreign Ministry spokesman, Lubos Dobrovsky, called for the complete withdrawal of Soviet troops by the end of 1990.[45] Talks stalled in mid-January because of Moscow's preoccupation with the upheaval in Azerbaijan, but Dobrovsky noted that President Havel would continue the dialogue on troop withdrawals on his scheduled visit to Moscow in February 1990.[46]

In January 1989 the Czechoslovak National Defence Council decided to cut its own combat forces (197 000 men) by 12 000 men, 850 tanks, 650 armoured cars and 51 combat aircraft. Three army divisions would be reorganized, with most of their equipment mothballed, retaining only sufficient active duty personnel for maintenance and guard duty. At the same

---

[39] *FBIS-EE*, 6 Feb. 1989; *ACR*, p. 407.B.124.

[40] Yazov, D., *Izvestia*, 22 Apr. 1989.

[41] TASS report of 20 June 1989, reprinted in *FBIS-EE*, 22 June 1989.

[42] Prague Domestic Service, 23 May 1989, *FBIS-EE*, 24 May 1989.

[43] Sautin, N, 'Force reductions in Europe, Mongolia, outlined', *Pravda*, 5 Nov. 1989; translation in *FBIS-SOV-89-213*, 6 Nov. 1989.

[44] AP–Reuters, 'Soviets may quit Prague: new government opens Kremlin talks on troops', *International Herald Tribune*, 15 Dec. 1989; Reuters, 'Prague to trim its army', *International Herald Tribune*, 16–17 Dec. 1989.

[45] Fitchett, J., 'Prague tells Moscow to withdraw all troops before the end of this year,' *International Herald Tribune*, 10 Jan. 1990.

[46] Whitney, C., 'Prague aide links delay on pullout to internal crisis in Soviet Union', *International Herald Tribune*, 18 Jan. 1990; Barber, L., 'Czechoslovakia presses Moscow for speedy removal of troops', *Financial Times*, 7 Feb. 1990.

time construction troops would be increased by 20 000.[47] The dismantling of the Czechoslovak tank regiments began in August 1989.[48] Before the change of government in late 1989, some Western analysts suggested that the planned increase in Czechoslovak construction units was because of the Soviet intention to withdraw completely from Hungary and to erect physical barriers on the southern Czechoslovak border. At the end of 1989, however, the new coalition government in Prague moved quickly to dismantle old barriers rather than build new ones, beginning with those on the Austrian and FRG borders. Former Defence Minister Milan Vaclavik was replaced by former Chief of Staff Lt. General Miroslav Vacek, who announced on 2 January 1990 that the law would soon be changed to reduce the length of military service, to end Communist Party cadres in the armed forces and to offer alternatives to military service.[49] On 19 January 1990, President Vaclav Havel announced additional cuts of 50 000 troops[50] and on 26 January Vacek noted that in all 60 000 troops, 3000 tanks and 3000 ATCs would be cut from Czechoslovakian national forces.[51]

Hungary

Two divisions of Soviet troops were deployed in Hungary during the 1940s and early 1950s. Two extra divisions were deployed in October 1956 to put down what is now officially recognized as a 'popular uprising'. Four Soviet divisions, the Southern Group of Forces, remained until the late 1980s: two armoured divisions and two motorized rifle divisions. It is hard to see what strategic function Soviet troops serve in Hungary, however. There are no vital communication links to protect as in Poland, and a mission against Yugoslavia seems unlikely. Thus, even before Gorbachev announced his programme of unilateral cuts in December 1988, Hungarian officials were calling for the removal of all Soviet troops, albeit usually in the context of cuts negotiated with the NATO countries.

After the Gorbachev announcement, Hungarian Defence Minister Ferenc Karpati and Soviet Colonel-General Matvei Burlako, Commander of the Southern Group of (Soviet) Forces in Hungary, announced on 31 January that about 25 per cent of the Soviet troops then in Hungary would leave over the next two years: 2400 officers, 8000 soldiers, more than 450 tanks, 200 guns and trench mortars, and 3000 motor vehicles. These would include a tank division stationed in Veszprem, a tank training regiment, an air regiment with 40 aircraft, a battalion of assault landing troops, a chemical weapon battalion and the staff of the Szolnock Officers' Military Academy. Following withdrawal, 11 former Soviet garrisons would be handed over to

[47] Prague Domestic Radio, *FBIS-EE*, 30 Jan. 1989.

[48] Czechoslovak Telegraph Agency CTK, 1 Aug. 1989, reprinted in *FBIS-EE*, 2 Aug. 1989.

[49] Reuters (note 44).

[50] 'The Warsaw Pact vanishing', *The Economist*, 27 Jan. 1990, p. 36; Hoagland, J., 'Havel to press troop cut', *International Herald Tribune*, 22 Jan. 1990.

[51] *Rude Pravo*, 26 Jan. 1990.

the Hungarian authorities. Burlako said that remaining Soviet troops would be pulled back from the border in a more defensive posture.[52]

The Hungarian-born Italian MP, Ilona Staller, was on hand with a pair of white doves to inaugurate Soviet withdrawals from Hungary in April, when the 13th Guards Tank Division left Kiskunhalas.[53] In May an independent tank training regiment began to pull out of Debrecen, the 141st Tank Regiment left Sarbogard, and a motorized rifle regiment (with 600 troops, 15 tanks and 30 armoured personnel carriers—APCs) withdrew from Taborflava.[54]

The Hungarian Government was clearly impatient with the pace of Soviet withdrawal and, in late August 1989, a Hungarian National Assembly member, Zoltan Kiraly, proposed early negotiations to withdraw all foreign forces from European soil.[55] On 2 November, Imre Poszgay, Hungarian Minister of State, called on both the USA and the USSR to remove troops from Europe by the end of the century, although this was not a very radical statement since it was consistent with declared Soviet policy.[56] TASS announced on 21 December that during 1990 the USSR would withdraw 6000 more troops, over 40 jet aircraft, 120 tanks, 180 armoured vehicles and over 400 trucks. Defence Minister Karpati agreed that there was no strategic rationale for Soviet troops in Hungary, but argued that unilateral withdrawals could be destabilizing and should, if possible, be undertaken in the context of the CFE Negotiation.[57] This was not good enough for the rest of the Government, however, and on 18 January 1990, Ferenc Somogyi, Secretary of State in the Hungarian Foreign Ministry, called for complete withdrawal of Soviet troops by the end of 1990, or end of 1991 at the latest.[58] In January 1990, Prime Minister Miklos Nemeth told Parliament that Soviet Prime Minister Nikolai Ryzhkov had agreed that Soviet troops should be withdrawn as soon as possible and certainly by the end of 1990. Bilateral talks on the withdrawal schedule began in February in Budapest between Ferenc Somogyi and Deputy Foreign Minister Ivan Aboimov.[59]

With respect to Hungarian national forces, in January 1989 Nemeth announced cuts of approximately 10 per cent: 9300 troops from a total of 99 000, including a tank brigade and 251 tanks, 30 armoured personnel carriers, 430 artillery pieces, 6 missile launching pads and a squadron of 9 interceptor aircraft.[60] Karpati had announced a 10–17 per cent budget cut in early December 1988.[61] In September 1989 Rezso Nyers, Minister of

[52] Hungarian Wire Service (MTI), 31 Jan. 1989; *FBIS-EE*, 11 Jan. 1989.
[53] Viets, S., 'La Cicciolina's doves give life for Hungary peace', *The Guardian*, 26 Apr. 1989.
[54] Budapest domestic radio, 19 May 1989, reported in *FBIS-EE*, 22 May 1989; TASS, 29 May 1989, in *FBIS-SOV-89-103*, 31 May 1989, p. 5.
[55] Budapest Radio, 31 Aug. 1989, cited in *FBIS-EE*, 6 Sep. 1989; *ACR*, p. 407.B.210.
[56] Petrovsky at the UN, 21 Dec. 1989.
[57] MTI, 'Talks on Soviet troop withdrawal from Hungary,' *FBIS-SOV-89-245*, 22 Dec. 1989, p. 2.
[58] White, D., 'Hungary, Poland call for Soviet pullout', *Financial Times*, 19 Jan. 1990.
[59] Reuters, 'Hungary begins talks with Soviets on troop pullout', *International Herald Tribune*, 2 Feb. 1990.
[60] *Budapest Nepszabadsag*, 31 Jan. 1989, in *FBIS-EE*, 2 Jan. 1989.
[61] *ACR*, p. 407.B.101.

State for Economic Affairs, announced the establishment of a new security zone with its neutral neighbours Austria and Yugoslavia, and asked the USSR to withdraw additional forces, including 14 nuclear-capable missiles and two armoured battalions, from their border areas.[62] Until Nicolae Ceausescu's regime had been toppled the Hungarians were not interested in an open border with Romania, but after the December revolution Hungarian Foreign Minister Gulya Horn was the first foreign visitor to Romania and relations between Budapest and Bucharest improved.

Bulgaria

Bulgaria has only a few Soviet military advisers so Soviet withdrawals are not an issue there. In line with most of the other WTO countries, however, Bulgaria announced cuts in its own national forces (158 000 men) and defence budget. In January 1989 Todor Zhikov proposed cuts of 12 per cent in the defence budget and cuts of 10 000 men, 200 tanks, 200 artillery pieces, 20 aircraft and 5 naval units by 1990.[63]

Romania

Soviet troops remained in Romania after World War II but withdrew in 1958. Unlike its WTO partners, Romania did not announce any military cuts in 1989. Since the Romanian Army was instrumental in the overthrow of Ceausescu, and is still key to the effort to eradicate the last remnants of the *Securitate* forces, the new interim government in Romania is not expected to announce cuts in either defence spending or force levels. On the contrary, it seems more likely that the Romanian armed forces, which for years have been deprived of modern equipment in favour of the *Securitate* forces, will be upgraded in status and their equipment enhanced.

Soviet Military Districts

On 20 December 1989 Vladimir Petrovsky, Deputy Soviet Foreign Minister, announced that after approximately half the 500 000 troops scheduled for demobilization had been cut, 627 500 Soviet troops were still deployed outside Soviet territory, and that the USSR would like to bring them all home before the year 2000, preferably by negotiation.[64]

The Soviet General Staff provided regular bulletins during 1989 about withdrawals of Soviet forces from outside Soviet territory: from the Groups of Forces in Eastern Europe and from Mongolia. At the end of the year, the overall cuts announced by Gorbachev in December 1988 appeared to be on schedule (table 13.2). Approximately 50 per cent of each category destined

[62] 'Budapest presses ahead with its own defence cuts', *The Guardian*, 9 Sep. 1989.

[63] Sofia domestic radio, 27 Jan. 1989, cited in *FBIS-EE*, 30 Jan. 1989.

[64] TASS report 'Soviet troop numbers abroad cited for UN session', *Krasnaya Zvezda*, *FBIS-SOV-89-244*, 21 Dec. 1989, p. 1.

Table 13.2. Reported and scheduled Soviet cuts in the ATTU zone, 1989–91

Zone	Tanks	Artillery	Aircraft	Manpower
Groups of Soviet forces cut in 1989				
Western/GDR	1 988	247	126	11 620
Central/Czechoslovakia	192	22	20	1 500
Southern/Hungary	447	176	76	10 800
Northern/Poland	87	16	88	3 500
Total cuts in 4 East European states	2 714	461	310	27 420
Estimated cuts for 10 Soviet MDs	4 406	2 503	425	54 380[a]
Estimated cuts in entire ATTU zone	**7 120**	**2 964**	**735**	**82 000**
Cuts scheduled for 1990				
4 East European states	2 586	..	..	22 580
10 Soviet MDs	294	..	..	114 420
Total scheduled cuts in ATTU zone	**2 880**	**5 536**	**65**	**137 000**
1991 goals (as announced by Gorbachev 7 December 1988)				
4 East European states	5 300	..	..	50 000
10 Soviet MDs	4 700	..	..	190 000
Total cuts in ATTU zone	**10 000**	**8 500**	**800**	**240 000**

[a] Of which 20 000 from the Leningrad MD.

for withdrawal over two years was cut by early December 1989. Over half the total number of tanks (2714 out of 5300) scheduled to leave Eastern Europe by 1 January 1991 were withdrawn by 1 November 1989. To maintain President Gorbachev's schedule the USSR will have to withdraw 2586 more tanks from their Groups of Forces in Eastern Europe, and 294 tanks from the European part of the USSR in 1990. Over half the troops scheduled to leave Eastern Europe (27 420 out of 50 000) left the GDR, Poland, Czechoslovakia and Hungary. Another 22 580 troops are scheduled to leave these countries in 1990.

Reports from the General Staff of cuts inside the Soviet Union were less detailed than those of cuts in Soviet troops based abroad, and are not easy to interpret accurately. As part of the restructuring that accompanied the unilateral cuts in 1989, several Soviet MDs were consolidated. In the central strategic reserve area the Urals and Volga MDs became the Volga–Ural MD with headquarters in Kuybishev MD.[65] The Central Asian MD, which used to be part of the Far Eastern TVD, was abolished as a separate MD and incorporated into the Turkestan MD in the Southern TVD. This restructuring involved the disbanding of the command structures of one army and two army corps in Turkestan (presumably part of the 100 000 men reportedly cut from the eastern part of the country in 1989).[66] In addition three army groups

[65] Mostovshchikov, S., 'Ural Military District abolished: new Volga–Ural Military District created', *Izvestia*, 5 Sep. 1989, *FBIS-SOV-89-171*, 6 Sep. 1989, pp. 89–90.

[66] *Izvestia*, 'General Staff on Central Asia District abolition', 3 June 1989, *FBIS-SOV-89-114*, 15 June 1989, p. 72.

are scheduled to be disbanded in the Far Eastern TVD, one from the Far Eastern MD and two from the Transbaykal MD.[67]

In early November the General Staff reported that 7120 tanks, 2964 artillery systems and 735 aircraft had been withdrawn from Soviet forces in Eastern Europe.[68] Deducting those accounted for in the four groups of Soviet forces in Poland, the GDR, Czechoslovakia and Hungary, it appears that 4406 tanks, 2503 artillery pieces and 425 aircraft were withdrawn from the 10 Soviet MDs in the ATTU zone.[69] On 15 December General Chervov reported that altogether 265 000 Soviet troops had been demobilized in 1989, just over half the 500 000 that Gorbachev promised would be gone at the end of 1991. Of these, 22 900 were from Mongolia, 27 620 from Eastern Europe, 100 000 from the Far Eastern MD, 60 000 from the Southern TVD (mostly withdrawals from Afghanistan),[70] and 20 000 from the Leningrad MD.[71] Of the 265 000 this leaves 34 580 cuts unaccounted for although some would be demobilized by the consolidation of the Urals and Volga MDs and some by cuts in naval personnel.

Soviet security interests clearly determine where forces are cut. Political unrest during 1989 may have precluded reductions of Soviet forces in the Baltic MD (comprising the Republics of Lithuania, Latvia and Estonia), but if restructuring had been designed with East–West confidence building as a priority, the Soviet General Staff should have cut their second strategic echelon forces stationed in the Carpathian, Byelorussian and Baltic MDs, since these are the forces of most concern to NATO planners. Without a more detailed breakdown of the manpower cuts inside the USSR, however, it must be assumed that cuts were not made in the western MDs in 1989, otherwise the Soviet leadership would surely have seized the opportunity to demonstrate the decreased threat to Western Europe.

Monitoring of unilateral cuts

Since the WTO cuts were announced as unilateral measures, there was no contractual obligation to co-operate with the West in verifying implementation by overflights, on-site inspection or any other means of monitoring. While politically and militarily significant, the cuts were a small percentage of the total WTO force (7 per cent in terms of manpower in the ATTU zone—see table 13.1). Without some Soviet co-operation, Western intelligence (always rough and ready with troops and tanks) would probably have had difficulty tracking implementation, and the public relations aspect of the

---

[67] Chernyshev, V., 'Conventional arms cuts in Far East outlined', TASS, 22 Aug. 1989, *FBIS-SOV-89-162*, 23 Aug. 1989, p. 1.

[68] In this chapter it is assumed that the 'European part of the Soviet Union' corresponds to the Soviet Military Districts in the ATTU zone.

[69] 11 MDs were in the ATTU zone as initially defined for the CFE mandate, but since consolidation of the Urals and Volga MDs there are now 10 MDs in the ATTU zone.

[70] Williams, F., 'Moscow sees threat to arms talks', *The Independent*, 26 Jan. 1989.

[71] Cuts of 20 000 were announced to the Norwegian Defence Committee in Moscow in Mar. 1989; see *ACR*, p. 407.B.142. By 1 Jan. 1991 a total of 40 000 will be cut from the Leningrad MD, see *ACR*, p. 407.B.246.

cuts would have been lost. General Yazov said in late February that the USSR intended 'to invite representatives of the media, foreign media included, to cover the most important measures relating to the withdrawal of our forces and armaments from allied states, with the consent of their leaders. The plan is to invite them to the Soviet Union as well to places where certain formations or units are being disbanded'.[72]

As an exercise in political confidence building and *glasnost* on the domestic front, a Moscow-based group was established for Public Monitoring of the Reduction of Armed Forces and Armaments (GON). It was assigned three tasks: to strengthen ties between the public and the army (ties seriously frayed as a result, *inter alia*, of the loss of life in Afghanistan[73]); to study the socio-economic impact of reductions; and to maintain contact with the public overseas. GON reports to the public and to the commissions of the Supreme Soviet that deal with defence and foreign policy. The chairman of the group is Dr Andrei Kokoshin, Deputy Director of the Institute of the USA and Canada, attached to the Soviet Academy of Sciences, and the membership includes activists, scientists and parliamentarians.[74]

By mid-July, GON had made seven trips to Soviet military units in Mongolia, Hungary, Czechoslovakia, Poland, the GDR and the western MDs of the USSR. Kokoshin reported on 14 July that Soviet withdrawals from Eastern Europe were on schedule but that the military were encountering difficulties of a social nature in disbanding army units and divisions.[75] In early November, *Pravda* reported that GON had also monitored the withdrawal of naval forces.[76]

At least one Western group also monitored the Soviet unilateral withdrawals. In August, the newly created Committee on Defence and State Security of the reconstituted Supreme Soviet invited a US congressional delegation (including military analysts as well as legislators) headed by the Committee Chairman, Representative Les Aspin, to observe withdrawals of Soviet units from the GDR, and demobilization and the dismantling of equipment in the USSR.[77]

After the inspection trip the Americans reported that withdrawals from Eastern Europe were on schedule, but not precisely as advertised by General Yazov in February. There was more substitution of defensive for offensive

[72] Yazov interview in *Izvestia*, in *FBIS-SOV-89-038*, 28 Feb. 1989, p. 4.

[73] Urban, M., 'Backward step in status makes officers see red', *The Independent*, 16 Nov. 1989; Cornwell, R., 'Soviet soldiers left out in the cold', *The Independent* , 27 Nov. 1989.

[74] Markov, V., 'Public control over troop withdrawals', *Moscow News*, 30 Mar. 1989; Rogov interview in *Red Star*, 16 May 1989; Sidorov, S., *Krasnaya Zvezda*, 16 May 1989 in *FBIS-SOV-89-097*, 22 May 1989.

[75] TASS, 'Public monitoring group notes Soviet arms cuts', 14 July 1989, in *FBIS-SOV-89-136*, 18 July 1989, p. 3; see also Moscow Domestic Service, 16 July 1989, 'Tank unit to be withdrawn from Poland,' *FBIS-SOV-89-136,* 18 July, 1989, p. 1.

[76] *Pravda*, 5 Nov. 1989

[77] US House of Representatives, Committee on Armed Services (HASC), 101st Congress, 1st Session, *Status of the Soviet Union's Unilateral Force Reductions and Restructuring of its Forces*, Report of the Committee Delegation to West Berlin, East Germany and the Soviet Union, 6–18 Aug. 1989 (US Government Printing Office: Washington, DC, 16 Oct. 1989); Aspin, L., HASC, 101st Congress, 1st Session, *Congressional Visit to Soviet Military Bases* (US Government Printing Office: Washington, DC, 3 Oct. 1989).

equipment than had been anticipated. Les Aspin was concerned that, by October, there was little evidence of any reductions in the USSR west of the Urals especially in the second strategic echelons based in the three western MDs of the ATTU zone.[78]

Unilateral Soviet withdrawals from Eastern Europe began in April.[79] When the group visited the Soviet command centre at Wünsdorf near Berlin (East) in early August, they found the 69th Motorized Rifle Regiment, which had previously belonged to the 32nd Tank Guards Division, supposedly one of the two tank divisions scheduled to leave the GDR in the first stage of withdrawals.

General Valery Fursin, Chief of Staff of the Western Group of Forces, told the visiting congressmen that not all elements of the six tank divisions scheduled for withdrawal from Eastern Europe were being disbanded. Some units would be reassigned to divisions remaining in Eastern Europe. The 69th Motorized Rifle Regiment, for example, was reassigned to the 35th Division, and another motorized rifle regiment from the 35th Division had been disbanded. General Fursin said the more important point was that nothing was being done to compensate for the removal of modern tanks from Eastern Europe.[80] In addition, while the USSR withdrew 81 Su-24 Fencer combat aircraft, a greater number of MiG-29 Fulcrum interceptor aircraft were introduced so that the total number of aircraft had increased, albeit with a more defensive character. The MiG-29 carries half the payload and has a shorter range than the Su-24 bomber.[81] Sergey Rogov, Deputy Chairmen of GON, made similar observations to those of the HASC.[82]

Despite quibbles over details, and some concern over improved defensive armour, the congressional group appeared satisfied that the Soviet cuts represented a genuine effort to pull back those components of its forward posture which had been identified as most provocative to the West: notably the four tank divisions being withdrawn from the GDR and the one from Czechoslovakia that were identified as highly skilled Operational Manoeuvre Groups (OMGs), long considered 'NATO's worst nightmare'.[83] By the end of the year there was broad consensus among Western politicians and analysts that the WTO could not mount an effective short-warning surprise, standing-start attack.[84] These judgements were significant because fear of surprise attack has driven defence budgeting and force planning in

---

[78] HASC, 16 Oct. 1989 (note 77), p. 6.
[79] *ACR* documents the WTO reductions. For progress as of 1 May 1989 see *ACR*, p. 407.B.156–58; as of 1 June 1989, p. 407.B.183–85, as of 1 Sep., p. 407.B.211–13.
[80] Gordon, M., 'Congress inspects a Soviet pullback', *New York Times*, 9 Aug. 1989.
[81] TASS, 'Fighters replace Soviet bombers in East Europe', *International Herald Tribune*, 17 July 1989, *FBIS-SOV-89-136*, 18 July 1989, p. 1.
[82] Moore, M., 'Soviets shuffle troops in East Europe', *International Herald Tribune*, 9 Aug. 1989.
[83] Karber, P. and Arner, W. G., 'The Gorbachev unilateral reductions and the restructuring of Soviet Warsaw Pact forces', testimony to HASC, 13 Sep. 1989.
[84] See for example comments by the directing staff of the IISS when they launched the *Military Balance 1989–1990*, in Oct. 1989: White, D., 'Soviet plans "rule out attack on NATO"', *Financial Times*, 6 Oct. 1989; see also: Aspin, L., *International Herald Tribune*, 18 Oct. 1989.

NATO for many years, despite the fact that many defence analysts thought the risk minimal given the NATO–WTO balance of forces.[85]

NATO planners have always worried more about the WTO capability for mobilization and sustained offensive military action than about a surprise attack. They see the main threat to NATO in the second strategic echelon, made up of forces in the western MDs.[86] Hence, the Soviet cuts most reassuring to NATO will be in these MDs, where NATO's proposals for zonal sub-limits on Soviet forces are primarily aimed.[87]

Increased pressure for NATO cuts

Finance ministries are under both internal and external pressure to cut their trade and budget deficits. In the USA, for example, the Gramm–Rudman–Hollings act would have dictated cuts in the US defence budget in fiscal year 1991, quite apart from the change in perception of the threat from the WTO.[88] During the Reagan years, tendencies to trim defence spending were effectively countered by conservative estimates of the threat. In late 1989, however, a combination of the implementation of Soviet defence cuts with the emergence of democracy in Eastern Europe brought added pressure to cut defence spending in the West. So, for a number of reasons, in late 1989 the Bush Administration joined other NATO countries with heavy trade and budget deficits, in reassessing the potential political and economic dividends that might accrue from unilateral cuts, as well as the potential costs of not reciprocating unilateral measures by the WTO.

General Vladimir Lobov and Marshal Sergey Akhromeyev both hinted at conservative opposition to Gorbachev in the USSR and warned on several occasions during the year that future Soviet cuts would be conditional on some response from the West.[89] If the USSR was willing to reduce unilaterally in ground forces, in which they were superior, then the NATO countries should be willing to cut unilaterally in categories in which they enjoyed superiority, or specifically, air and naval assets. For their part, NATO spokesmen insisted that the announced unilateral cuts in WTO forces only reduced, and did not eliminate, the still overwhelming WTO ground force superiority; thus no reciprocal cuts were required from the West.

[85] Mearsheimer, J. J., 'Why the Soviets can't win quickly in Central Europe', in eds S. E. Miller, and S. M. Lynn-Jones, *Conventional Forces and American Defence Policy*, 2nd edn (MIT Press: Cambridge, Mass., 1989).

[86] Yurechko, J. J., 'Soviet reinforcement and mobilization issues', ed. J. Simon, *NATO: Warsaw Pact Force Mobilization* (National Defence University Press: Washington, DC, 1988), pp. 57–97.

[87] Interview with British delegate B. Cleghorn in *Izvestia, FBIS-SOV-89-137*, 19 July 1989, *ACR*, p. 407.B.203–204.

[88] The Balanced Budget and Emergency Deficit Control Act (Gramm–Rudman–Hollings Bill) specifies a series of holding limits on budget deficit from FYs 1986–91, by which time the deficit is to be eliminated; see SIPRI, *World Armaments and Disarmament: SIPRI Yearbook 1986* (Oxford University Press: Oxford, 1986), p. 215.

[89] Marshal Akhromeyev cited in *FBIS-SOV-89-213*, 6 Nov. 1989, p. 1, and in *Soviet Weekly*, 14 Oct. 1989; Riding, R., 'NATO chief warns on unilateral disarmament', *International Herald Tribune*, 10 Oct. 1989.

Unlike WTO defence ministries, who were all anxious to shed their alliance defence burden in 1989, NATO officials condemned burden-shedding as irresponsible alliance behaviour. Soviet and East European cuts were welcomed as helpful measures designed to correct quantitative asymmetries between NATO and WTO ground forces, rather than gestures that required reciprocal NATO cuts. Speaking to the International Institute for Strategic Studies (IISS) in London in September, for example, Senator Sam Nunn threatened, rather than promised, that the US Congress would cut its forces in Europe unilaterally if the European NATO allies cut forces outside the context of CFE.[90] The following month Manfred Wörner, NATO Secretary General, warned NATO parliamentarians against the temptation to make unilateral cuts.[91] A week later General John Galvin, SACEUR, chastized the allies for 'silent' cuts of some 10 per cent and wished they would 'hang in there until we get an answer from Vienna and take their reductions as part of the [CFE] negotiations'.[92] NATO's Defence Planning Committee meeting in Brussels in early December issued a communiqué that, in paragraph 4, 'welcome[d] the initiation of unilateral conventional force reductions by the USSR and its allies,' and in paragraph 6 're-affirmed our determination not to make any unilateral reductions that could risk undermining the prospect of reaching a CFE accord'.[93]

Nevertheless, towards the end of 1989, events in Eastern Europe, as well as demographic and economic constraints in the West, were forcing NATO defence and finance ministries to consider cuts in defence outlays.[94] In November, the US Central Intelligence Agency (CIA) leaked a 30-page National Intelligence Estimate (NIE) reassessing the WTO threat.[95] Completed before the changes of government in Eastern Europe, it suggested that NATO would have not two weeks' warning of a Soviet attack, as previously assumed, but between five and six weeks, and perhaps even as much as six months.

To most US legislators, this seemed a dramatic reassessment of the threat, and many were angry that the NIE had not been made available in September in time for the FY 1990 budget deliberations.[96] One possible reason for not releasing the document was to counter tendencies (in Western Europe, as well as in the US Congress) towards unilateral cuts that might undermine the CFE talks. Leaking the NIE in late November suggests that the Administration now wanted defence cuts—either because the President and his advisers genuinely felt the threat had abated, or because they saw a

[90] Nunn, S., 'Challenges to NATO in the 1990s', *Survival*, vol. 32, no. 1 (Jan.–Feb. 1990).

[91] Riding (note 89).

[92] Halloran, R., *New York Times*, 18 Oct. 1989.

[93] US Information Service, EUR-304 (US Embassy: Stockholm), 29 Nov. 1989.

[94] Meacham, M., 'East bloc political changes add to West's budget battles', *Aviation Week & Space Technology*, 20 Nov. 1989; Hughes D. and Casidy, J., 'West plans big cuts in defence', *Sunday Times*, 19 Nov. 1989.

[95] Tyler, P. E., 'US cuts estimate of Soviet threat', *International Herald Tribune*, 30 Nov. 1989; Aspin, L., 'Military spending: peace may have broken out', *International Herald Tribune*, 29 Nov. 1989; Harris, A., 'Perestroika, US–style is difficult too,' *Financial Times*, 13 Nov. 1989.

[96] Schemmer, B. F., 'Warning time', *Armed Forces Journal International*, Jan. 1990, p. 5.

need to help to smooth East–West relations to defuse the opposition to Mikhail Gorbachev in Moscow, or to ease deficit problems in the USA.

In August, US Secretary of Defense Richard Cheney had told Congress that it was a mistake to think that the Soviet threat was abating.[97] By November, he judged the likelihood of US–Soviet conflict to be lower than at any time since 1945.[98] With his downgrading of the threat Cheney asked the armed services for proposals that would allow a cut of $180–195 billion from the projected US Defense Department budget over the period 1992–94.[99] This was not such a dramatic cut as it first appeared since the projected US budget for the period assumed an increase of $200 billion.[100] Nevertheless stocks in US defence industries plummetted on Wall Street in response to Cheney's new threat assessment.[101] Meanwhile, in Congress, Les Aspin and others added amendments to the FY 1990 Defense Authorization Act requiring the Bush Administration to submit in January 1990 a report on potential changes in US defence strategy in the context of military parity in Europe, and a study of the budgetary implications of deeper force cuts in a second round of CFE negotiations.[102] The US Army suggested cutting manpower from 764 000 to 630 000, and cutting air and ground forces in Europe to 150 000 from the current 305 000. Three active divisions would be disbanded and the three remaining divisions would form a single army corps comprising a classic mix of tanks, infantry and artillery. Forces based in the continental USA would be reshaped into three different groups: special forces to conduct counter-terrorist operations, a fast-reaction force based on the XVIIIth Airborne Corps, and a set of traditional armoured and mechanized infantry divisions with which to reinforce Europe or elsewhere if required.[103]

Pentagon officials urged that cuts be made in the context of a CFE agreement and urged the Administration to make bolder proposals in Vienna, for example, cuts of 55 000 US troops rather than the 30 000 currently envisaged for CFE.[104] Senator Sam Nunn suggested that the earlier US proposal for a CFE limit of 275 000 stationed forces had been overtaken by

[97] Halloran, R., 'Cheney criticizes cuts in the military', *New York Times*, 24 Aug. 1989.

[98] AP, 'Cheney puts war threat at new low', *Boston Globe*, 21 Nov. 1989.

[99] Kaplan, F., 'Cheney orders Pentagon cuts: services told to pare budgets by $195 billion', *Boston Globe*, 18 Nov. 1989; Gordon M. and Engelberg, S., 'Military ordered to draft a 5% cut in 1992–94 spending', *New York Times*, 18 Nov. 1989.

[100] See chapter 5; Walker, M., 'Peace dividend was nice just as long as it lasted', *The Guardian*, 27 Dec. 1989.

[101] Rachman, G., 'Glasnost hits US military expenditure', *Sunday Correspondent*, 26 Nov. 1989; Campbell, C. and Gliniecki, A., 'Arms industry faces fight for life' *Sunday Correspondent*, 7 Jan. 1990; 'Apocalypse now', *The Economist*, 25 Nov. 1989; Stevenson, R. W., 'Behind the military stock selloff', *New York Times*, 21 Nov. 1989; Biddle, F. M., 'Thoughts turn to conversion', *Boston Sunday Globe* (Business Section), 19 Nov. 1989; Galbraith, J. K., 'Friendly advice to a shrinking military', *New York Times*, 22 Nov. 1989.

[102] Forsberg, R. and Leavitt, R.,'Congress eyes CFE dividends', *Vienna Fax*, no. 6 (10 Nov. 1989).

[103] Vuono, C. (US Army Chief of Staff), *A Strategic Force for the 1990s and Beyond* (US Department of the Army, Washington, DC, 1989), excerpted in the *New York Times*, 12 Dec. 1989; see also Walker, M., 'US plan to reduce European forces by half', *The Guardian*, 13 Dec. 1989.

[104] Tyler, P. E. and Moore, M., 'Pentagon sees possible 50% troop cut in Europe', *International Herald Tribune*, 18 Dec. 1989; Brasier, M., 'Bush told to halve troops in Europe', *The Guardian*, 18 Dec. 1989.

events. Such a limit would validate a higher level of Soviet troops in Eastern Europe than either President Gorbachev or the East Europeans wanted.[105] National Security Adviser Brent Scowcroft suggested that lower CFE limits were possible 'in consultation with the allies'.[106] In the event, in the annual State of the Union address President Bush (after consultation with President Gorbachev as well as the NATO allies) proposed a new ceiling of 225 000 for Soviet and US troops in Europe.[107] Thus instead of a 30 000-troop cut as envisaged in late May 1989, the Administration now proposed a CFE agreement that would withdraw 80 000 US troops from Europe—a measure of how fast political events moved in six months.[108]

When President Bush presented his FY 1991 budget request to Congress, Democrats complained that the 'peace dividend' offered was too small, but the President proposed closing some 60 military bases in the continental USA as well as several overseas, including nine facilities in Western Europe. These include seven US Air Force bases: three in the UK (Greenham Common, Wethersfield and Fairford), one at Comiso in Italy, one at Zweibrücken in the FRG, one at Erhac in Turkey, and one at Hellenikon in Greece, as well as the Nea Makri naval base in Greece and a munitions storage site at Eskisehir in Turkey.[109] These closures would involve some 10 000 troops and 20 000 support staff.[110] While the base closures would be unilateral decisions the troops and equipment withdrawn could be counted as part of NATO cuts in US forces in a CFE agreement signed in 1990.

Throughout 1989 NATO resisted giving the impression that any cutbacks were reciprocal gestures to unilateral cuts by the WTO. Nevertheless GON tried to portray Western cuts this way. Sergey Rogov, Deputy Chairman of GON, reported a number of Western decisions as 'the first practical response by NATO countries to the USSR's unilateral cuts'. Rogov included US plans to cut 30 000 men in FY 1990–91, cancel the 15th aircraft-carrier *Coral Sea*, withdraw 14 obsolete destroyers, delay plans to buy F-14 and F/A-18 aircraft for the US Navy and defer the B-2 bomber,[111] and cited the cancellation of the Canadian nuclear-powered submarine programme and a decision by the FRG to reduce the *Bundeswehr* by 33 000 men.[112]

Several NATO countries floated plans to reduce unilaterally in January 1990. On 25 January Netherlands Defence Minister Relus Ter Beek suggested that 5500 Dutch troops be withdrawn from the FRG shortly,[113] and

[105] Barber, L., 'Nunn calls for deeper US, Soviet troop cuts in Europe', *Financial Times*, 2 Jan. 1990.

[106] Riddel, P., 'US signals flexibility on troop cuts in Europe', *Financial Times*, 8 Jan. 1990.

[107] Barber, L., 'A presidential punch at the Pact and a pat for the allies', *Financial Times*, 2 Feb. 1990.

[108] Smith, R. J., *Washington Post*, 1 Feb. 1990.

[109] Fitchett, J., 'Experts say closure of bases will not harm US efficiency', *International Herald Tribune*, 30 Jan. 1990.

[110] Duke, S., SIPRI, *United States Military Forces and Installations in Europe* (Oxford University Press: Oxford, 1989).

[111] Rogov cited in *Pravda*, 5 Nov. 1989, *FBIS-SOV-89-213*, 6 Nov. 1989, p. 1.

[112] In early Dec. the FRG Defence Minister proposed cuts of 15% in *Bundeswehr* manpower, i.e., to 420 000; Marsh, D., 'Calls grow in Bonn for deeper troop cuts', *Financial Times*, 5 Dec. 1989.

[113] Hilton, I., 'Dutch upset NATO by troop cuts in Germany', *The Independent*, 27 Jan. 1990.

Belgian Defence Minister Guy Coëme said that because the WTO was collapsing militarily he had asked his Chief of Staff to study the impact in military and socio-economic terms of withdrawing the 28 000 Belgian troops from the FRG.[114] These remarks were tempered the next day by Belgian Prime Minister Wilfried Martens who assured his NATO partners that Belgium was only planning withdrawals in the expectation of CFE cuts.[115] Prime Minister Margaret Thatcher consistently refused to discuss cuts in British forces outside the context of CFE, but in January 1990 a Ministry of Defence (MOD) spokesman told reporters that catastrophic reductions were being discussed that would have been totally unthinkable 12 months previously. MOD studies suggest that withdrawing British troops from the FRG would increase the defence budget for at least four years, but bringing the 67 000 troops home is one of the options being considered in London, along with a £20 million cut in defence spending by the end of the decade, 40 per cent cuts in the equipment budget, cancellation of the fourth Trident submarine, the new tank and the European Fighter Aircraft (EFA), cutting active forces and increasing the Territorial Army.[116] An MOD White Paper estimated that keeping British forces in the FRG costs as much as the combined expense of defending British territory and naval operations in the Eastern Atlantic and the English Channel.[117]

III. Developments at the CFE Negotiation

The CFE mandate

In the framework of the 35-state Conference on Security and Co-operation in Europe (CSCE), the 7 WTO states and the 16 NATO states began the Negotiation on Conventional Armed Forces in Europe (CFE) on 6 March 1989. In a mandate signed on 10 January 1989 the 23 participating states agreed that the objectives of the CFE Negotiation were to establish a stable and secure balance of conventional armed forces, to eliminate disparities prejudicial to stability and security, and to eliminate as a matter of priority the capability to launch surprise attack and to initiate large-scale offensive action. The participants agreed to include conventional armed forces and equipment based on the land territory of the participants in Europe from the Atlantic to the Urals, the ATTU zone. They also agreed that nuclear weapons would not be a subject of CFE but that no conventional armaments or equipment would be excluded because they have 'additional' (read nuclear or chemical) capabilities. The mandate states that naval and chemical weapons will not be addressed.[118]

[114] Buchan, D., 'Belgium considers troop pullout from Germany,' *Financial Times*, 26 Jan 1990.

[115] Reuters, 'Belgium reassures NATO on forces', *International Herald Tribun* 27–28 Jan. 1989.

[116] Adams, J., 'Britain prepares sweeping defence cuts', *Sunday Times*, 28 Jan. 1990.

[117] White, D., 'UK spells out cost of forces in Germany', *Financial Times*, 31 Jan. 1990.

[118] Mandate for Negotiation on Conventional Armed Forces in Europe, Annex III of the Concluding Document of the 1986–89 Vienna Meeting of Representatives of the Participating States of the Conference on Security and Co-operation in Europe; for a discussion of the contentious issues

While the formal mandate is clearly circumscribed, these talks are obviously about much more than achieving a balance of conventional forces in the ATTU zone. They are part of the process that is charting a new security system for Europe. One issue is whether such a system will continue to be based on adversarial alliances or on a common pan-European structure. Thus one of the most difficult questions to resolve at the CFE mandate talks during 1987 and 1988 was that of participation.

Most of the NATO states, supported by Switzerland, argued for an inter-alliance forum, while France, Sweden and some of the other neutral and non-aligned and WTO states argued that it should be widened to include all 35 CSCE states. France consistently refused to participate in the MBFR talks from 1973 until 1989, on the grounds that an inter-alliance forum would serve to perpetuate the division of Europe (and subordinate France to intra-bloc discipline). French delegates made the same argument with respect to CFE but were overruled. By way of compromise, the 35 states agreed to conduct two parallel sets of negotiations in Vienna, both under the auspices of the CSCE: the 23 allied states would negotiate force reductions (CFE), and the 35 states would participate in separate Negotiations on Confidence- and Security-Building Measures (CSBMs).

To meet French concerns the mandate lists the 23 countries in alphabetical order and acknowledges that they are signatories of the treaties of Brussels (1948), Washington (1949) or Warsaw (1955) 'and accordingly are members of the North Atlantic Alliance or parties to the Warsaw Treaty', but does not mention NATO or the WTO *per se*. Moreover, at the formal CFE sessions in Vienna, delegates sit in alphabetical order by state, which makes intra-alliance discussion at the table awkward and encourages a more equal exchange of views among the 23 states as a whole.

President Gorbachev's repeated calls for a common European home suggest that he might have preferred an all-European rather than an inter-alliance forum for the CFE Negotiation.[119] A pan-European security system has after all been a persistent theme of both old and new Soviet thinking. The preamble to the 1955 Warsaw Treaty calls for the establishment of a system of European collective security, based on the participation of all European states irrespective of their social and political systems, and Article 11 states that the Treaty shall become inoperative the day a general treaty of collective security enters into force.[120] In the event, however, the USSR did not oppose the decision to restrict force reduction talks to a 23-state forum. Indeed the various attempts to clarify the concept of a common European home in 1989 suggest that, far from wanting to dissolve NATO and the WTO, the Gorbachev leadership came to accept the current alliances as

at the mandate talks see Sharp, J., 'Conventional arms control in Europe: problems and prospects,' SIPRI, *SIPRI Yearbook 1988: World Armaments and Disarmament* (Oxford University Press: Oxford, 1988), pp. 315–37, and 'Conventional arms control in Europe', *SIPRI Yearbook 1989*, pp. 369–402; the text of the mandate is reproduced in appendix 11B, *SIPRI Yearbook 1989*, pp. 420–22.

[119] Gorbachev, M., *Perestroika* (Collins: London, 1987), pp.190–209.

[120] Warsaw Treaty, 14 May 1955, reprinted in US Congress, *Documents on Germany 1944–1961* (US Government Printing Office: Washington, DC, Dec. 1961), pp. 175–78.

underpinning its foundations. While some senior Soviet officials continued to espouse the need to abolish the blocs, others spoke of the alliances as important stabilizers during a period of turbulent political change; albeit change for which Gorbachev himself was indirectly responsible.[121]

Issues in the CFE Negotiation

Each negotiating round had different priorities, but discussion revolved around five issues: (a) what to limit, covering both choice and precise definition of treaty-limited items (TLIs); (b) how to limit, covering numerical limits for each group of states as well as regional and national sub-ceilings; (c) the disposition of TLIs, whether to withdraw and redeploy, or dismantle and destroy; (d) how to monitor and verify compliance with CFE limits; and (e) what stabilizing measures should complement numerical limits.

Round I: 6–23 March 1989

Whereas the MBFR talks were dominated by inter-alliance disputes about data, both NATO and the WTO provided data for forces in the ATTU zone before the CFE meeting convened: NATO in November 1988 and the WTO in late January 1989.[122] The two data sets were not easily comparable, however, because of substantial differences in definitions and counting rules. In addition the WTO data included forces in 'adjacent waters', reflecting both a desire to include NATO carrier-based aircraft and to make the more general point that, while the WTO enjoyed numerical superiority in land forces, when air and naval assets were included the balance was more even. During 1989, as TLI definitions were refined, both alliances had to amend the data initially offered.

Opening WTO proposal, 6 March

When the CFE talks opened in March 1989, the WTO countries were not ready with a detailed proposal but presented a revised version of Gorbachev's three-stage proposal of April 1986 designed to bring WTO forces down to parity with NATO.[123]

Stage I: 1991–94. Imbalances would be corrected in the most destabilizing arms categories (such as attack combat aircraft of short-range

---

[121] Zamyatin, L., interview with Robert Harvey, 'Rival military blocs may be stabilisers says Soviet envoy', *Daily Telegraph*, 1 Dec. 1989; for a useful survey of contradictory Soviet statements on the common European home, see Malcolm, N., 'The "common European home" and Soviet European policy', *International Affairs*, vol. 65, no. 4 (autumn 1989), pp. 659–76.

[122] NATO, *Conventional Forces in Europe: The Facts*, NATO Press Service, Brussels, Nov. 1988; Ministers of Defence of the Warsaw Treaty Member States, 'On the relative strength of the armed forces and armaments of the Warsaw Treaty Organization and the North Atlantic Treaty Organization in Europe and adjacent water areas', *Pravda*, 30 Jan. 1989.

[123] Shevardnadze, E. A., 'Vienna talks under way' (text of Shevardnadze's 6 Mar. speech), *Pravda*, 7 Mar. 1989, *FBIS-SOV-89-043*, 7 Mar. 1989, pp. 1–4.

tactical aviation, tanks, combat helicopters, combat armoured vehicles, armoured troop carriers (ATCs) and artillery including multiple-launch rocket systems and mortars), and force levels would be reduced to 10–15 per cent below the lowest levels currently possessed by either alliance. Zones would be established in which special sub-limits would be negotiated.

Stage II: 1994–97. Once parity was achieved each side would reduce a further 25 per cent (approximately 500 000 men plus 'organic equipment' for each alliance).

Stage III: 1997–2000. Each side would restructure its remaining forces to defensive postures.

Opening NATO proposal, 6 March

NATO delegates criticized the lack of specific numbers in the WTO opening proposal, and offered a set of rules, geographical zones and sub-ceilings as summarized in table 13.3.

Summary of round I

Choice and definition of TLIs. NATO's opening proposal[124] was clearly designed to test Gorbachev's many statements that the side that is ahead should cut most. As outlined in the CFE mandate the focus was on traditional land armaments and, predictably, WTO delegates complained that proposals had been made to select only those TLIs in which the WTO enjoyed numerical superiority rather than areas of NATO strength, such as air assets. At the end of round I all states agreed that CFE would limit tanks, artillery and ATCs. The major differences were that NATO did not include aircraft, combat helicopters or manpower, whereas the WTO envisaged limits on all these categories. NATO also excluded all equipment in storage whereas the WTO wanted to limit both active and stored items. Soviet analysts also complained that NATO accorded much lower priority than the WTO to limiting tactical nuclear weapons and to proposals to restructure forces on more defensive lines.[125]

Problems associated with zonal sub-limits. As was the case in the CFE mandate talks, for unavoidable reasons of geography dividing NATO and WTO territory into zones for different sub-limits caused resentment on the northern and southern flanks of NATO as well as in the southern WTO states. Norway in the north, and Italy, Greece, Turkey, Spain and Portugal in

---

[124] *Negotiations on Conventional Armed Forces in Europe,* position paper provided by the delegations of Belgium, Canada, Denmark, the FRG, France, Greece, Iceland, Italy, Portugal, Spain, Turkey, the UK and the USA, Vienna, 6 Mar. 1989.

[125] Nazarenko, V., 'An accord in the offing', *New Times* (Moscow), no. 1 (Apr. 1989).

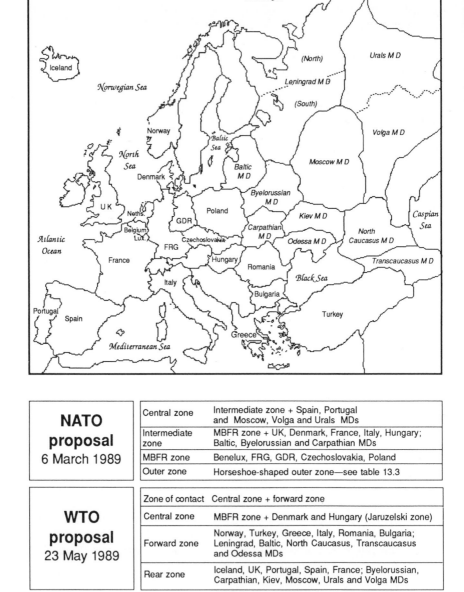

NATO proposal 6 March 1989		
	Central zone	Intermediate zone + Spain, Portugal and Moscow, Volga and Urals MDs
	Intermediate zone	MBFR zone + UK, Denmark, France, Italy, Hungary; Baltic, Byelorussian and Carpathian MDs
	MBFR zone	Benelux, FRG, GDR, Czechoslovakia, Poland
	Outer zone	Horseshoe-shaped outer zone—see table 13.3

WTO proposal 23 May 1989		
	Zone of contact	Central zone + forward zone
	Central zone	MBFR zone + Denmark and Hungary (Jaruzelski zone)
	Forward zone	Norway, Turkey, Greece, Italy, Romania, Bulgaria; Leningrad, Baltic, North Caucasus, Transcaucasus and Odessa MDs
	Rear zone	Iceland, UK, Portugal, Spain, France; Byelorussian, Carpathian, Kiev, Moscow, Urals and Volga MDs

WTO proposal 29 June 1989		
	Central zone	Central zone as of 23 May + UK, France; Baltic, Byelorussian, Carpathian and Kiev MDs
	North zone	Norway and the North Leningrad MD
	South zone	Italy, Greece, Turkey, Bulgaria, Romania; Odessa, North Caucasus and Transcaucasus MDs
	Rear zone	Iceland, Portugal, Spain, South Leningrad, Moscow, Urals and Volga MDs

Figure 13.1. CFE zones in the Atlantic-to-the-Urals region

Table 13.3. NATO proposal for rules, zones and TLI ceilings, 6 March 1989

Rule/Zone	TLI ceiling		
	MBTs[a]	Artillery	ATCs
Rule 1: ATTU zone[b]	40 000	33 000	56 000
Rule 2: Country (30% of zone ceiling)	12 000	10 000	16 800
Rule 3: Stationed forces	3 200	1 700	6 000
Rule 4: Alliance sub-limits			
4.1: ATTU zone	20 000	16 500	28 000[c]
4.2: Central zone	11 300	9 000	20 000
4.3: Intermediate zone	10 300	7 600	18 000
4.4: MBFR zone	8 000	4 500	11 000

[a] Main battle tanks.

[b] As defined in CFE mandate: all European territories of both alliances plus 11 Soviet MDs west of the Urals (see figure 13.1).

[c] No more than 12 000 may be armoured infantry fighting vehicles.

Rule 1: The overall limit—total forces, both alliances, all 23 states of the ATTU zone.
Rule 2: Sufficiency—single-country limit not to exceed 30% of overall limit.
Rule 3: Single-country ceiling for forces stationed outside national borders.
Rule 4: Sub-limits:
4.1: Active plus stored equipment categories for each alliance in the entire ATTU zone.
4.2: Active units only in the central zone.
4.3: Active units only in the intermediate zone.
4.4: Active units only in the MBFR zone.
Note: Implicit in the NATO-designated zones for the centre is a horseshoe-shaped outer zone comprising Iceland, Norway and the Leningrad MD in the north, and Greece, Turkey, Romania, Bulgaria and 4 Soviet MDs (Kiev, Odessa, Transcaucasus and North Caucasus) in the south. NATO does not give ceilings for this outer zone and it is important to emphasize that the sub-ceilings NATO proposes for the inner zones are only for equipment in active units, not stored equipment. Thus each alliance could distribute the balance of forces permitted in the entire zone either in the outer zone or under secure storage in any of the inner zones. This represents a large loophole likely to prove troublesome as the final details of an agreement are resolved. The implied ceilings for NATO's 'horseshoe zone' plus equipment stored ATTU-wide are: MBTs, 8700; artillery, 7500; and ATCs, 8000.

the south all had difficulties in being consigned to an outer zone. Greece objected to the fact that the Turkish port of Mersin was excluded from the ATTU zone, since this was the port from which Turkey launched its attack on Cyprus in 1974.[126] Italy complained that NATO officials in Brussels never took Mediterranean concerns seriously.[127] Spain objected to being placed in a different zone from France with whose military forces it wanted to develop closer relations.[128] In the WTO Bulgaria complained, as did Greece, about the exclusion of south-eastern Turkey from the ATTU zone.[129]

[126] This dispute between Greece and Turkey several times delayed the completion of NATO proposals at the CFE Negotiation. It is well documented in *ACR*, pp. 407.B.113–17.

[127] Haberman, C., *New York Times*, 16 Feb. 1989.

[128] Madrid radio, *ACR*, p. 407.B.139.

[129] Interview with Major General Kamen Petrov by Vladi Vladkov, *Sofia Norodna Armiya*, 7 Mar. 1989, *FBIS-EE*, 10 Mar. 1989; *ACR*, pp. 407.B.139–40.

In the intra-NATO discussions of zones France had said it did not want to recreate the MBFR guidelines, but the core zone in the NATO proposal is identical to the old MBFR zone. The FRG wanted to avoid any national sub-ceilings (a point of contention throughout MBFR), but NATO's sufficiency rule states that no country can host more than 30 per cent of each alliance limit which is a *de facto* ceiling on FRG forces since no other NATO country is likely to approach 30 per cent of the total force.

Disposition of TLIs. In his December 1988 speech at the UN, and in subsequent clarifications, Gorbachev emphasized the need to destroy arms and equipment withdrawn from the ATTU zone. As noted above this was not strictly adhered to in the unilateral Soviet cuts, as the military had to deal with the practical problem of restructuring forces left behind. In NATO's opening proposal the Western position paper refers to the need to establish a system of interlocking sub-limits to prevent redeployment of TLIs withdrawn from one part of the area of application to another.[130] This suggested that all TLIs should be destroyed rather than redeployed, but this was not explicitly stated in the proposal.

Verification. Experts all agreed that a CFE verification regime would be more demanding than that of any previous agreement. One of the NATO arguments against including air assets and manpower in its opening proposal was the difficulty of verifying regional ceilings in these categories.

Whereas at MBFR it was more often Soviet and East European countries that feared intrusive overflights and on-site inspections, at CFE it is often the Western countries, notably major arms producers such as France and the UK, that express concern about the potential threat that intrusive arms control verification regimes pose to arms export revenues.

Round II: 5 May–13 July 1989

The WTO response to NATO, 23 May 1989

In early May 1989, during James Baker's visit to Moscow, Gorbachev fleshed out the earlier WTO proposals with specific numerical limits in six categories of forces; in the case of tank and ATC limits for the entire ATTU zone these were identical to the ceilings already proposed by NATO. This convinced Baker that Gorbachev was serious about an agreement that would radically reduce the WTO military capability in Eastern Europe, although some White House staff were still sceptical.[131]

A new WTO proposal was presented in Vienna on 23 May. The three-stage format was set aside (although not necessarily abandoned) in favour of a framework modelled on NATO's proposal of 6 March. As seen in table 13.4, the WTO offered slightly different ceilings for the three TLIs proposed by NATO and added aircraft, helicopters and manpower.[132]

---

[130] Section 2, para. 2, see *ACR*, p. 407.D.27.

[131] Wilson, G., *Washington Post, 18 May 1989.*

[132] On 23 May the Delegations of Bulgaria, Czechoslovakia, the GDR, Hungary, Poland, Romania and the USSR offered five separate working papers on: (1) levels of conventional armed forces of any

Table 13.4. WTO proposal for ceilings and zones, 23 May 1989

Zone/Category	MBTs	Artillery	ATCs	Aircraft	Helicopters	Manpower
1. Country limit (30%)	14 000	17 000	18 000	1 200	1 200	920 000
2. Stationed forces	4 500	4 000	7 500	350	600	350 000
3. Alliance sub-ceilings (ATTU)	20 000	24 000	28 000	1 500	1 700	1 350 000
4. Zones within ATTU[a]						
4.1. Zone of contact	16 000	16 500	20 500	1 100	1 300	1 000 000
4.2. Central zone	8 700	7 600	14 500	420	800	570 000
4.3. 'Forward zone'	7 300	8 900	6 000	680	500	430 000
4.4. Rear zone	4 000	7 500	7 500	400	400	350 000

[a] The composition of the zones is given in figure 13.1.

Note: The precise definitions for aircraft and helicopter are still at issue.

The Bush initiatives

Once the similarity of the new WTO proposal to the earlier NATO one was clear, the tone of President Bush's remarks about the USSR changed dramatically.[133] He now seemed convinced that the NATO allies wanted more imaginative proposals and developed a four-point plan to present to the NATO summit meeting in Brussels, 29–30 May:[134]

1. Step 1 would lock in WTO acceptance of NATO's proposed ceilings on tanks and ATCs, and seek a similar agreement on artillery once the definitional problems were solved. (In the event, problems of defining tanks and ATCs proved much more difficult than artillery, which was defined first although not until round III in October.)

2. Step 2 would expand the March 1989 NATO proposal to reduce combat aircraft and helicopters to 15 per cent below current NATO levels.

3. Step 3 would set a ceiling of 275 000 on stationed US and Soviet forces in the ATTU zone: a cut of approximately 325 000 for the Soviet Union and 30 000 for the United States. (Bush claimed that 30 000 US troops represented 20 per cent of stationed US combat forces in Europe. This raised

one state (corresponding to NATO's Rule 2 on sufficiency); (2) levels of conventional armed forces of the states of either alliance stationed outside national territories in Europe (corresponding to NATO's Rule 3 on stationed forces); (3) levels of conventional armed forces for either alliance in Europe; (4) ceilings for conventional armed forces of the states belonging to an alliance in the Central European region; and (5) levels of conventional armed forces of the states of either alliance in individual regions of Europe (the latter three corresponding to NATO's Rule 4 on alliance sub-limits).

[133] *Encouraging Political and Economic Reform in Poland*, address by President Bush to the citizens of Hamtrack, Mich., 17 Apr. 1989, *Current Policy* (US State Dept.), no. 1166; *Change in the Soviet Union*, address by President Bush at the Texas Agricultural and Mechanical University Commencement Ceremony, College Station, Tex., 12 May 1989, *Current Policy*, no. 1175; both were rather hard-line speeches when compared with the conciliatory tone of *Security Strategy for the 1990s*, address by President Bush at the Coast Guard Academy Graduation Ceremony, New London, Conn., 24 May 1989, *Current Policy*, no. 1178; and *The Future of Europe*, address by President Bush at Boston University, 21 May 1989, *Current Policy*, no. 1177.

[134] AP, *New York Times*, 30 May 1989. The Bush plan is given as item 17 in the North Atlantic Council Declaration of 30 May 1989, USIS-EUR-205, Stockholm, 30 May 1989.

some eyebrows in Europe as it suggests a 1:1 ratio of support to combat forces; there are currently 305 000 US troops—combat plus support—in the ATTU zone.[135])

4. Step 4 would accelerate the CFE schedule, aiming for an agreement within 6–12 months (i.e., by December 1989 or June 1990) and to accomplish the reductions by 1992 or 1993.

NATO leaders approved all four steps at the summit meeting and charged the High Level Task Force (HLTF) with revising the Western CFE negotiating position accordingly. The Bush initiatives were widely applauded by the general public and by political leaders in Western Europe who felt that President Gorbachev had made all the running so far at the CFE Negotiation, and that NATO was badly in need of some dynamic leadership. But as the Prime Minister of the Netherlands noted: 'As a politician I think it's the right thing to do but the experts may not be so happy about it'.[136] Professionals in the defence and foreign ministries of Western Europe complained that there had been insufficient consultation, that the proposals were too ambitious and risked overloading the arms control system, and that they were domestically motivated rather than in the interests of the alliance.[137] The Bush proposals served several other purposes: they challenged the Soviet Union on manpower cuts while meeting their demands on aircraft and helicopters, they sought to defuse congressional pressures to cut European forces, and they successfully defused what threatened to be a huge row at the NATO summit meeting over whether and how to modernize or limit US short-range nuclear weapons deployed in Europe.

The Soviet response to the Bush initiative

Soviet leaders welcomed the Bush proposals to expand the CFE agenda by the inclusion of aircraft, helicopters and manpower, but objected to some of the details. They wanted to establish limits on all stationed manpower, not just United States and Soviet forces; to exclude air defence interceptor aircraft; and to begin negotiations on shorter-range nuclear forces (SNF) immediately, in parallel with the CFE Negotiation. Despite these reservations, negotiations now began in earnest, and on 29 June WTO delegates in Vienna submitted revisions to the sub-ceilings and geographical zones which they had previously presented in their 23 May proposals.[138]

---

[135] US State Department, ACDA document, cited in *ACR*, p. 407.B.17.

[136] *New York Times*, 30 May 1989.

[137] Pick, H. and Fairhall, D., 'Rocky road ahead for arms talks', *The Guardian*, 1 June 1989.

[138] CSBM/CFE.CS, Statement by the Head of the Czechoslovak Delegation, Ambassador Ladislav Balcar, at the CFE plenary on 29 June 1989. See also *International Herald Tribune*, 30 June 1989.

Revised WTO proposal, 29 June 1989

On 29 June the WTO delegates submitted revisions to the sub-ceilings and geographical zones offered in their 23 May proposals.[139] Instead of the zone of contact, the Jaruzelski zone and the rear zone as outlined on 23 May (see table 13.4), the WTO now proposed a central zone, a northern zone, a southern zone and a rear zone, as shown in figure 13.1.

The Czechoslovak delegate, Ladislav Balcav, who presented the new WTO proposal in Vienna noted that the WTO states had tried to meet NATO concerns about the second strategic echelon by including more Soviet Military Districts in the central zone.[140] (The 29 June proposal brought the Baltic, Byelorussian, Carpathian and Kiev MDs from the rear zone as defined on 23 May into a newly defined central zone.) The WTO states now hoped that NATO would present TLI ceilings for the sub-zones that included not only arms and equipment in active units but also those in storage.

NATO proposal, 13 July 1989

Michael Edes, the British delegate to CFE, offered new Western proposals in Vienna on 13 July based on the Bush proposals.[141] NATO proposed ceilings of 275 000 on Soviet and US stationed manpower in the ATTU zone, specifying that troops withdrawn must be demobilized. For air assets NATO proposed three rules as listed in table 13.5.

Table 13.5. NATO rules for air assets

Rule	Aircraft	Helicopters
Rule A: Overall limit (in the ATTU zone)	11 400	3 800
Rule B: Sufficiency (max. 30% per country)	3 420	1 140
Rule C: Alliance sub-limits[a]	5 700	1 900

[a] Within the area of application delineated under rule 4.1 (see table 13.3).

NATO's proposed alliance ceiling for combat aircraft (5700) was higher than the number of NATO aircraft in the zone according to the data presented in November 1988. Discussion of this anomaly at a press conference on 13 July revealed that new NATO data included training and stored aircraft in the zone, adding 5700 more systems for the WTO and 1300 for NATO.[142] WTO and NATO proposals at the end of round II are summarized in table 13.6.

[139] *International Herald Tribune*, 30 June 1989 and *Neue Zürcher Zeitung*, 1 July 1989.

[140] *Rude Pravo*, 30 June, in *FBIS-EE*, 6 July 1989.

[141] *Negotiations on Conventional Armed Forces in Europe*, Proposal submitted by the Delegations of Belgium, Canada, Denmark, France, the FRG, Greece, Iceland, Italy, Luxembourg, Netherlands, Norway, Portugal, Spain, Turkey, the UK and the USA, Vienna, 13 July 1989.

[142] Forsberg, R. *et al.*, *Cutting Conventional Forces* (IDDS: Brookline, Mass., July 1989.)

Table 13.6. Comparison of the WTO and NATO proposals at the end of round II

	TLI ceilings					
	Tanks	Artillery	ATCs	Aircraft	Helicopters	Manpower
WTO proposal 29 June 1989						
North	200	1 000	150	30	30	20 000
South	5 200	8 500	5 750	290	360	270 000
Rear	1 300	3 000	1 350	60	60	150 000
Central	13 300	11 500	20 750	1 120	1 250	910 000
ATTU						
Alliance	20 000	24 000	28 000	1 500	1 700	1 350 000
Country	14 000	17 000	18 000	1 200	1 350	920 000
Stationed	4 500	4 000	7 500	350	600	350 000
Total	40 000	48 00	56 000	3 000	3 400	2 700 000
NATO proposal 13 July 1989[a]						
ATTU						
Total	40 000	33 000	56 000	11 400	3 800	..
Stationed	3 200	1 700	6 000	..	..	275 000[b]
Country	12 000	10 000	16 80	3 420	1 140	..
Alliance	20 000	16 500	28 000	5 700	1 900	..
NATO zones						
MBFR	8 000	4 500	11 000	..	..	..
Central 2	10 300	7 600	18 000	..	..	..
Central 1	11 300	9 000	20 000	..	..	..

[a] NATO has not proposed any sub-limits within the ATTU zone for air assets, nor any manpower limits other than for US and Soviet forces.

[b] US–Soviet only.

Summary of round II

In early June the CFE delegates formed two working groups. Group A covered definitions, counting rules, information exchange and verification, and group B covered numerical limits and measures of stabilization.

Artillery. NATO wanted to exclude recoilless rifles and larger-calibre anti-tank guns from the artillery limits; the WTO wanted to include them.

ATCs. WTO wanted to include all armoured vehicles; NATO wanted to exclude heavily armoured personnel carriers and combat reconnaissance vehicles.

Tanks. NATO wanted to exclude light tanks from CFE limits. The USSR claims, with some logic and the benefit of history, that excluding a category from limitation usually sets a premium on it as the system of choice, in this case probably leading to a new competition in increasingly armed 'light' tanks.

Aircraft. Aircraft proved difficult to define because most systems serve many different roles and missions. The USSR wanted to exclude its air defence interceptors from CFE limits because they are designed to defend against US strategic bombers and cruise missiles and strictly speaking do not relate to the European theatre. NATO claimed that most interceptors can provide air protection for attacking forces and should be included. There was also a dispute about whether and which training aircraft should be subject to CFE limits.

Britain and France were reluctant to accept limits on their nuclear-capable aircraft. France specifically refused to accept limits on its Mirage IV, but eventually accepted a broad definition of combat aircraft in exchange for assurances that ceilings would be set sufficiently high to avoid a French obligation to reduce them.[143] To support its 13 July proposal on air assets, NATO defined a combat aircraft as a fixed- or swing-wing aircraft permanently land-based, initially constructed or later converted to drop bombs, deliver air-to-air or air-to-surface missiles, fire guns/cannon or employ any other weapon of destruction.[144]

The WTO states did not produce their aircraft definitions until round III.

Combat helicopters. The problem here was to distinguish permitted transport and ambulance helicopters from treaty-limited combat machines. Controlling helicopters threatens to be a troublesome issue as military establishments find combat helicopters increasingly useful, versatile and cost-effective machines for the kind of low-intensity conflict recently practised in interventions in Afghanistan, Grenada and Panama.

In its July proposals on air assets NATO defined a combat helicopter as a permanently land-based, rotary-wing aircraft, constructed or later converted to employ air-to-air or air-to-surface ordnance such as guns, cannon, rockets, bombs, missiles or any other weapon of destruction.[145]

Manpower. Soviet Deputy Foreign Minister Victor Karpov complained that limits on stationed troops should apply not only to US and Soviet but also to non-US NATO forces stationed on foreign territory. He claimed that there were approximately 100 000 such forces in the ATTU zone.[146] In fact there are over 160 000 in the FRG: 69 700 British (3000 in West Berlin); 52 700 French (2700 in Berlin); 26 000 Belgian; 7100 Canadian; and 5700 Netherlands.[147]

Stored versus active equipment. NATO would only apply limits to equipment in active units, not that in storage, so as to accommodate the alliance practice of storing Prepositioned Organizational Material Configured to Unit Sets (POMCUS) in Europe for US forces normally deployed in the continental USA but who are earmarked for, and regularly exercise in, Europe. The USSR does not currently have similar stocks in Eastern Europe. During round II, Polish delegates approached NATO delegates to ask them

[143] 'Arms control: spring hopes eternal', *The Economist*, 14 Oct. 1989, p. 29.

[144] NATO press statement, 13 July 1989.

[145] *Draft Treaty on Conventional Armed Forces in Europe*, proposal submitted by the delegations of Belgium, Canada, Denmark, France, Federal Republic of Germany, Greece, Iceland, Italy, Luxembourg, Netherlands, Norway, Portugal, Spain, Turkey, United Kingdom and United States, 14 Dec. 1989, 13 pp, Article II (j).

[146] Karpov, V. P., 'Moscow's view on the Bush disarmament initiative', *International Herald Tribune*, 13 June 1989.

[147] IISS, *The Military Balance 1989–90* (IISS: London, 1989), p. 65.

to include stored material in CFE ceilings; otherwise, Poland feared, the USSR might insist on storing material in Eastern Europe.[148]

Disposition of TLIs. In presenting his CFE proposals to the NATO summit meeting in late May, President Bush emphasized that equipment withdrawn from the ATTU zone should be destroyed rather than redeployed. The NATO proposal of 13 July states that TLIs that are withdrawn from service to comply with CFE limits 'shall be destroyed in accordance with procedures to be agreed'.[149] It seems clear, however, that only the oldest equipment will be destroyed and that modern equipment will be 'cascaded' down from the wealthy to the poorer states within each alliance group. In early June, Robert Herres, vice-chairman of the US Joint Chiefs of Staff, told the Senate Armed Services Committee that NATO would have to scrap 2224 tanks, 828 artillery pieces, 600 ATCs and 350 combat helicopters and demobilize 325 000 troops. In order to meet the destruction requirement he said, 'we don't intend to destroy new equipment but to redistribute them . . . we have lots of latitude to protect the modernization program that is so important to our posture'. This concept of 'cascading' would withdraw new equipment from the central zones to the periphery and destroy only the older equipment from the periphery. Allies such as Turkey, for example, would receive modern equipment withdrawn from the FRG, permitting the destruction of older and less effective equipment from Turkey. Cascading was not uniformly popular in the alliance when first proposed; France in particular wanted to put withdrawn equipment into secure storage rather than pass it on to less well endowed allies. In Britain, the Treasury might welcome 500 second-hand tanks cascaded from the FRG, but the Vickers company, hoping to build a new tank to replace the ageing British Chieftain, was not enthusiastic.[150]

Round III: 7 September–19 October 1989

Round III kept up the momentum of round II and hopes ran high that a first CFE agreement might yet be signed in 1990. Each group offered very similar proposals in the area of information exchange, stabilization measures and verification. The NATO measures sought to meet the WTO concern about stored versus active equipment and introduced proposals to limit bridging equipment. Both sides agreed on a definition for artillery, but were still unable to agree on tanks, ATCs or air assets. The WTO states approached the NATO position on aircraft by including more categories and raising proposed limits. The WTO reduced its earlier ceiling for stationed manpower, but still insisted on including all stationed forces rather than just US and Soviet.

---

[148] Schmemann, S., *New York Times*, 30 June 1989.
[149] NATO Proposal, 13 July 1989, Press Statement, Rule D: Disposition of Reduced Weapons Systems, reprinted in *ACR*, p. 407.D.31.
[150] *The Economist*, 14 Oct. 1989.

Confidence- and security-building measures at CFE [151]

Differences between Greece and Turkey held up the Western proposal for the opening of round III, but a detailed set of provisions was presented on 21 September.[152] The WTO offered a set of very similar measures on 19 October, but added some provisions on restructuring forward-based forces that might prove difficult for NATO to accept.[153]

Information exchange. Both sides agree to exchange data on TLIs before, during and after implementation of agreed reductions. They differ in only three areas: (*a*) NATO calls for data disaggregated to ground-force battalion and air force squadron level, but the WTO calls for disaggregation to regiment level; (*b*) NATO calls for data on weaponry outside CFE limits, but the WTO deals only with CFE TLIs; and (*c*) NATO calls for data on stationed US and Soviet forces, the WTO calls for detailed data on *all* stationed forces in the ATTU zone.

Verification measures. Both sides call for on-site inspections, unimpeded use of national technical means, special measures for aircraft, and a joint consultative group to resolve any questions or ambiguities about compliance. Again, there are differences in three areas:

1. The WTO wants surveillance at both permanent and temporary entry–exit points such as airfields, railway junctions and seaports; NATO does not, although in intra-alliance discussions before 21 September the USA wanted this kind of surveillance but France and Britain (both with out-of-ATTU security interests) vetoed such measures as too intrusive.[154]

2. The WTO proposes three specific measures to verify aircraft limits; NATO only suggests that co-operative measures to enhance aerial inspection be considered.

3. NATO calls for inspection of military sites not specified in the data exchange; the WTO does not.

Stabilization measures. Both sides agree to constrain exercises, the call-up of reserves and the amount of bridging equipment in active units. There are differences in several areas, however:

1. NATO would set sub-limits on equipment in active units, with the remainder of the TLIs to be placed in monitored storage or 'low strength units'. Removal of TLIs from storage would be limited. The WTO does not distinguish between active and stored equipment and would preserve the freedom to transfer items from storage.

[151] Forsberg, R. and Leavitt, R., 'WTO leaps NATO hurdles, sets own', *Vienna Fax*, no. 5 (26 Oct. 1989), pp. 1–2.
[152] Negotiation on Conventional Armed Forces in Europe, ch. 3: *Measures on Information Exchange, Stabilization, Verification and Non-circumvention,* Proposal submitted by the Delegations of Belgium, Canada, Denmark, France, FRG, Greece, Iceland, Italy, Luxembourg, Netherlands, Norway, Portugal, Spain, Turkey, the UK and the USA, Vienna, 21 Sep. 1989.
[153] WTO Working Paper on Information Exchange and Verification Measures, 19 Oct. 1989, reprinted in *ACR*, p. 407.D.43.44.
[154] Fox, R., *Daily Telegraph* (London), 24 Oct. 1989.

2. NATO proposes a single constraint on exercises: neither alliance may hold more than one exercise annually involving more than 40 000 troops or 800 tanks. The WTO would allow large exercises only every third year and would also impose restrictions on smaller exercises.

3. The WTO calls for more data than NATO on the call-up and movement of reservists.

4. The WTO would limit movement of troops and arms; NATO would only require advance notice of movement.

5. The WTO calls for regular exchange of information on military spending; NATO does not.

6. The WTO calls for the restructuring of residual forces into defensive postures and would prohibit the construction of new, or expansion of existing, foreign military bases in the ATTU zone. These measures are unlikely to be acceptable to NATO unless and until there is a reassessment of NATO's forward defence and Follow On Forces Attack (FOFA) doctrine, a step the WTO would clearly like to encourage.

TLI definitions: one down and five to go

Artillery. As a concession to NATO, the WTO countries agreed to exclude all large-calibre anti-tank artillery. For the purpose of CFE, artillery systems are defined as those with calibre over 100 mm, including guns, howitzers, mortars and multiple-rocket launchers. Each alliance lists more than 40 different kinds of weapon in this category.[155]

Aircraft. NATO states define combat aircraft as any aircraft land-based in the ATTU zone that both flies and shoots; that is, a definition based on capabilities rather than missions. The WTO group, however, tried to differentiate between missions in order to exclude from CFE those aircraft based in the ATTU but designated for training, reconnaisance and defensive (as opposed to offensive) missions. At the opening of round III, Soviet delegate Oleg Grinevsky offered definitions of four categories of aircraft:[156]

1. *Strike aircraft* are designed to support ground forces and attack targets on land with air-to-ground munitions. In the WTO air forces these include: Su-24, Su-17, Su-17MR, Su-22, MiG-27, Su-25, MiG-25BM, MiG-23BN and IAR-93.

2. *Fighter aircraft* are equipped with air-to-air guided weapons and are incapable of using air-to-ground munitions. In the WTO air forces this category includes: Su-27, MiG-23, MiG-29, MiG-21, MiG-21 bis, MiG-15 and MiG-17.

---

[155] Tosunyan, S., 'Grinevskiy cited on progress at CFE talks', *Izvestia*, 21 Oct. 1989; artillery definition is in article no. II (g) of NATO draft treaty (note 145) and article II (7) of *Draft Treaty on Conventional Armed Forces in Europe*, submitted by the delegations of People's Republic of Bulgaria, the Republic of Hungary, the German Democratic Republic, the Polish People's Republic, the Socialist Republic of Romania, the Union of Soviet Socialist Republics and the Czechoslovak Socialist Republic, 14 Dec. 1989, 38 pp.

[156] *ACR*, p. 407.D.33, 8 Sep. 1989.

Table 13.7. Comparison of the WTO and NATO proposals at the end of round III

	TLI ceilings					
	Tanks	Artillery	ATCs	Aircraft	Helicopters	Manpower
WTO						
North	200	1 000	150	30	30	20 000
South	5 200	8 500	5 750	290	360	270 000
Rear	1 300	3 000	1 350	60	60	150 000
Central	13 000	11 500	20 000	1 120	1 250	910 000
ATTU:						
Alliance	20 000	24 000	28 000	4 700[a]	1 900[a]	1 350 000
Country	14 000	17 000	18 000	3 400[a]	1 500[a]	920 000
Stationed	4 500	4 000	7 500	1 200[a]	600	300 000[a]
Total	40 000	48 000	56 000	3 000	3 400	2 700 000
NATO						
ATTU:						
Total	40 000	33 000	56 000	11 400	3 800	..
Stationed	200	1 700	6 000	..	..	275 000
Country	12 000	10 000	16 80	3 420	1 140	..
Alliance	20 000	16 500	28 000	5 700	1 900	..
NATO zones:						
MBFR	8 000	4 500	11 000	..	..	..
Central 2	10 300	7 600	18 000	..	..	..
Central 1	11 300	9 000	20 000	..	..	..

[a] Sub-limits amended in September 1989.

3. *Air defence fighter aircraft* are combat aircraft equipped to employ air-to-air guided weapons, but are incapable of using missiles and bombs on land targets. In the WTO air forces these include: MiG-31, MiG-25P (PDS), Su-27P, Su-15, MiG-23P, MiG-23MF, MiG-23ML, Tu-128 and L-39ZA.

4. *Reconnaissance aircraft* are fitted with specialized equipment and are incapable of firing air-to-surface guided weapons. In the WTO air forces these include: MiG-21R, MiG-25RB, Su-22R, Su-24MR, Yak-28R, Su-24MP, Yak-28PP and Il-28.

Initially the WTO group argued that only strike aircraft should be included in CFE limits, but in mid-September Eduard Shevardnadze told James Baker in Jackson Hole, Wyoming, that the USSR was now willing to accept limits on fighter and reconnaissance aircraft equipped with electronic countermeasures as well as strike aircraft, if not yet on air defence interceptors.[157]

This compromise was incorporated in a working paper offered by GDR delegate Klaus-Dieter Ernst on 28 September.[158] The WTO moved towards the NATO position by including interceptors and training aircraft and by

[157] Gordon, M., *New York Times*, 21 Sep. 1989; 'Baker statement on land-based missiles viewed', *FBIS-SOV-89-182*, 21 Sep. 1989.
[158] Ernst statement reprinted in *ACR*, p. 407.D.42.

closing the gap between the former NATO and WTO proposed ceilings on combat aircraft, raising its former collective ceiling for each alliance from 1500 to 4700, that is, to within 1000 of the proposed NATO ceiling of 5700. For combat helicopters the WTO raised its former alliance ceiling from 1700 to 1900, matching the NATO proposal exactly. For stationed combat aircraft the WTO raised its ceiling from 350 to 1200 and from 1200 to 3400 for a single country, as compared to NATO's proposed single-country ceiling of 3420. The WTO ceiling for stationed combat helicopters remains 600, and for a single country has been raised from 1200 to 1500, as compared to NATO's proposed ceiling of 1140. NATO delegates did not respond to this paper in what remained of round III or in round IV.

Stationed manpower. In October the WTO lowered its initial ceiling of 350 000 for each alliance on all forces stationed outside national boundaries in the entire zone to 300 000. Outgoing US delegate Stephen Ledogar called this a 'step backwards' at the time, but increased congressional and Department of Defense (DOD) interest in cutting defence spending prompted President Bush to propose an even lower ceiling in late January 1990. In terms of reaching an agreed ceiling, one obvious compromise solution would be for NATO to define a ceiling for stationed forces without specifying any national limits. This could allow each alliance freedom to mix within the agreed limit. For the FRG it has been important for deterrence purposes to maintain an international forward-deployed NATO force, so that Soviet military planners would know that they faced all the major NATO powers, not only the FRG, from the start of any engagement. With both alliance structures likely to be in flux over the next few years it is not inconceivable that both NATO and the WTO may want to field multilateral 'peacekeeping' forces in the ATTU zone.

Stored versus active equipment. In an effort to meet WTO concern that US POMCUS stocks in the FRG gave NATO an advantage over the WTO, NATO proposed a category of 'low-strength units' in which the USSR could store equipment over and above the CFE limit for equipment in active units.[159] The WTO states were initially cool to the idea but warmed up to it in round IV. How and whether to count equipment in storage are complicated by the ambiguity about what constitutes stored and active material. NATO has at least six different categories of equipment outside active units: war reserves, POMCUS, equipment in reserve units, equipment in training establishments, equipment in capital repair facilities and a 'fitness repair pool' to replace faulty equipment.

Bridging equipment: a new TLI? No decisions were reached in round IV, but NATO proposed a limit of 700 on armoured vehicle-launched assault bridges. WTO currently has 2500 such vehicles in the ATTU zone compared to 454 for NATO. Bridging equipment has long been identified with offensive actions, and a willingness to drastically reduce in this category

---

[159] This is stabilizing measure 3(D)(i) in the NATO draft package of measures offered on 21 Sep. 1989, reprinted in *ACR*, pp. 407.B.34–40.

would buttress WTO claims to be restructuring for the defensive.[160] Some Soviet bridging equipment was withdrawn from Eastern Europe during 1989 as part of the programme of unilateral cuts initiated by President Gorbachev in December 1988.

Verification of production monitoring. The debate on production monitoring has thus far been more intense within NATO than between NATO and the WTO. The USA proposed almost continual monitoring of weapon production *inside* ATTU. Britain and France wanted minimum interference with production of arms intended for export outside the zone, but wanted the CFE agreement to monitor Soviet arms production *outside* the ATTU zone. The USA opposed this, claiming that such a measure would exceed the CFE mandate and obviously fearing a precedent for monitoring production in the continental USA or for including naval forces in the CFE.[161]

Round IV: 9 November–15 December 1989

Both alliance groups presented draft treaty texts at the end of round IV,[162] but there was no further agreement on defining tanks, aircraft, armoured vehicles or stationed manpower. Positions narrowed, both within and between alliances, on a number of issues but delegates from both NATO and WTO countries agreed that the momentum of rounds II and III had been lost and progress was minimal. WTO delegates also complained that the NATO consultation process appeared excessively slow, and that in round IV more time was spent resolving intra-NATO than East–West issues.[163] At the Malta summit meeting in early December, President Gorbachev and President Bush discussed the possibility of a summit meeting in 1990 to sign a CFE agreement. President Bush emphasized the importance of the CSCE process in charting a new Europe 'whole and free', but he nevertheless proposed a summit meeting for 23 states in 1990. President Gorbachev preferred a summit of the 35 CSCE states. In December 1989 the Austrian Government sought to accommodate both by inviting heads of state attending the signing of the CFE (anticipated in the second half of 1990) to remain in Vienna for a summit of the 35 CSCE states immediately afterwards. As the pace of German unification accelerated in early February 1990, the foreign ministers of the USA, the USSR and the FRG agreed that a 35-state summit meeting in October or November would be the appropriate forum for the two German states to present their proposals on unity to their CSCE partners.[164]

---

[160] Adams, P. and Hitchens, T., 'NATO, Warsaw Pact near agreement on limits for bridging vehicles', *Defense News*, 18 Dec. 1989; *ACR,* interview with Hungarian delegate to CFE cited in *ACR*, p. 407-B-273.

[161] Buchan, D., *Financial Times*, 7 Sep. 189; Smith, J., *Washington Post*, 8 Sep. 1989.

[162] WTO draft treaty (note 155); NATO draft treaty (note 145).

[163] 'NATO attitude slows', Moscow World Service interview with Grinevsky news conference, 28 Dec., reported in *FBIS-SOV*-89-249, 29 Dec. 1989, p. 1.

[164] 'US and Bonn agree reunification timetable', *Financial Times*, 5 Feb. 1990.

TLI definitions

Tanks. NATO overcame resistance by France and Britain to the inclusion of light tanks in CFE limits during round IV, but in the process fudged the categories of tanks and armoured vehicles. The new NATO proposal for defining tanks and armoured combat vehicles (ACVs) was presented to a CFE working group on 12 December.[165] In the MBT category NATO wants to include all those weighing at least 20 tonnes and carrying 75-mm or larger guns (down from 26 tonnes and 90 mm). In addition, NATO would include wheeled vehicles that meet these specifications in the future. This meets the WTO desire to include the Italian wheeled Centauro vehicle in CFE limits. It weighs 24 tons, carries a 105-mm gun and is scheduled for deployment in the early 1990s. NATO's new MBT definition, however, excludes British and French light tanks (approximately 15 tonnes) under development, and leaves the tank ceiling unchanged at 20 000 for each alliance.

Armoured vehicles. NATO's 12 December proposal raised the overall ceiling on ATCs from 28 000 to 30 000 to accommodate a new category of 'heavy armoured combat vehicles' (HACVs). The ACV category would now comprise three sub-categories: ATCs—lightly armed, armoured vehicles 'designed for transportation of combat troops'; AIFVs—armoured infantry fighting vehicles with 'an organic cannon of at least 20 mm, designed to allow troops to fire from inside the vehicle under armoured protection'; and HACVs—lightly armoured, tracked or wheeled vehicles of 7 tonnes or more, carrying an organic mounted direct-fire gun of 75 mm or more, fall outside the definition of MBT, AIFV or ATC.

NATO claimed that the HACV category is designed to capture the light tanks of concern to the WTO, and proposed a new sub-limit of 14 000 on the combined AIFV and HACV category to replace the former limit of 12 000 on AIFVs.[166] NATO's rule 4.1 (see table 13.3) now allows 30 000 ATCs per alliance, of which no more than 14 000 can be a combination of AIFVs and HACVs, in the ATTU zone.

The WTO did not respond to the NATO proposal in round IV, but early indications were that while Poland and Hungary found the proposal constructive, Soviet delegates had reservations, since they had planned to introduce more AIFVs into Eastern Europe to compensate for heavy tank divisions withdrawn under Gorbachev's unilateral reductions.[167]

Aircraft . No further progress was made on aircraft definitions in round IV and WTO delegates complained that there had been no NATO response to

---

[165] NATO proposal on armoured vehicles.
[166] Rule 4.1 for ATCs in NATO's initial proposal (see table 13.3).
[167] Forsberg, R. and Leavitt, R. (eds), 'The new NATO tank-ACV proposal', *Vienna Fax*, no. 9 (21 Dec. 1989), pp. 1–2; FOCUS, Austrian Committee for European Security and Cooperation, no. 16 (Dec. 1989), p. 5; British–American Security Information Council (BASIC), 'West compromises on light tanks', *BASIC Reports from Vienna*, no. 3 (8 Dec. 1989), p. 1.

their 28 September round III proposals, nor to suggestions for informal experts' consultations on aircraft definitions.[168]

Helicopters. The Bush proposal to include combat helicopters in the CFE Negotiation took the NATO allies by surprise and definition proved a problem within the NATO group, largely because the HLTF had under-estimated alliance holdings. November 1988 NATO data listed 2300 combat helicopters.[169] On this basis the HLTF proposed CFE limits of 1900. Later counts based on the 'look-alike count-alike' counting rules revealed 3500 NATO combat helicopters. NATO will thus have to cut 1600 rather than 400 to meet its own limit. The NATO ceiling is also likely to undermine support for the four co-operative helicopter programmes currently under way in Western Europe.[170]

State versus alliance limits

Throughout the CFE process France has emphasized single-state rather than alliance responsibilities. French resistance to alliance ceilings appears to have been overcome in round IV, however, since both NATO and WTO draft treaties define responsibilities for Groups of States, defined as the memberships of the two alliances. Both drafts specify that member states of each alliance bear responsibility for insuring that no member pushes alliance totals above the limit. No one appears to have thought through the obligations of alliances under international law; presumably each state will bear equal responsibility for the group as a whole. Thus if one state exceeds its share of the alliance quota, an alliance partner will have to reduce accordingly. The sufficiency rule, introduced in NATO's initial proposal in March, states that no single state can retain more than 30 per cent of the alliance limit, to prevent any single state dominating either alliance.

Zones: the continuing Greek–Turkish feud

Presentation of the NATO draft treaty text was held up for several weeks because of Greek concern that current definitions of the ATTU zone exclude the Mediterranean port of Mersin. Greece claims that Turkey could use Mersin to mobilize forces—as it did to invade Cyprus in 1974—outside CFE jurisdiction.

Disposition of TLIs; France accepts 'cascading'

Throughout 1989 France resisted participation in NATO plans to redistribute arms and equipment that would be cut under a CFE agreement.

[168] Tosunyan, S., 'Grinevsky cited on situation at Vienna talks', *Izvestia*, 23 Dec. 1989, *FBIS-SOV-89-249*, 29 Dec. 1989.

[169] *NATO, Conventional Forces in Europe: The Facts* (NATO: Brussels, Nov. 1988), p. 18.

[170] Taylor, T., 'The future of European defence industries: problems and prospects', paper presented to BISA conference, University of Kent, Dec. 1989.

In January, however, France agreed to strengthen the HLTF in order to work out the financial and other details of these intra-alliance transfers.[171]

Verification issues

By the end of 1989 it was clear that the 23 CFE states had widely differing capabilities to monitor and verify an agreement. Even the more technically qualified states, like the UK, found the task daunting. The MOD established a Joint Arms Control Implementation Group (JACIG), initially to be staffed by 270, less than half the number planned for a parallel group in the FRG. Plans to create a NATO pool of verification experts which all allies could draw on failed in part because the French insisted that CFE verification is a national not an alliance responsibility, and in part because national intelligence services are unwilling to share their secrets even with allies.[172]

CFE delegates did not make much progress towards the establishment of a multilateral European verification agency during 1989, but a number of analysts and parliamentarians proposed an agency under the auspices of the 35 CSCE states to be based in Berlin.[173]

Round V: 12 January–22 February 1990

CFE made rapid progress during 1989, compared to almost any other arms control forum. But political changes in Eastern Europe, unilateral Soviet withdrawals from the ATTU zone and the prospect of German unification all threatened to overtake even the most rapid progress in Vienna.

Manpower. As round V began, Hungary and Czechoslovakia were negotiating Soviet troop withdrawals in separate bilateral talks with the Soviet leadership. Lech Walesa, speaking for himself rather than the Polish Government, also called for complete withdrawal of Soviet forces. If Soviet forces left Czechoslovakia and Hungary, Soviet stationed forces would have to be accommodated in the GDR and Poland, and both the NATO target of 275 000 and the Soviet proposal of 300 000 for stationed forces looked too high. In late January Soviet CFE delegate Oleg Grinevsky said that all Soviet troops would leave Eastern Europe by 1995 if NATO withdrew stationed forces in Europe.[174] Some suggested that this was an attempt to gain Western concessions for what might otherwise be an ignominious Soviet withdrawal under pressure from the East Europeans.[175]

A few days later, in the annual State of the Union message to Congress, President Bush proposed a new ceiling of 225 000 on stationed Soviet and US forces in Europe, of which only 195 000 may be deployed in Central

[171] White, D., 'France to join NATO plan on arms', *Financial Times*, 11 Jan. 1989.

[172] Fairhall, D., 'Wanted: recruits for Britains's counter attack', *The Guardian*, 12 Jan. 1990.

[173] Voigt, K., Rapporteur, Defence and Security, *North Atlantic Assembly General Report on Alliance Security*, Brussels, Oct. 1989, p. 38.

[174] Smith, R. J., 'A Soviet withdrawal offer', *International Herald Tribune*, 29 Jan. 1990.

[175] White, D., 'Sheathing the long sword', *Financial Times*, 1 Feb. 1990.

Europe, defined as Benelux, Denmark and the FRG for NATO; and Czechoslovakia, the GDR, Hungary and Poland for the WTO (the Jaruzelski zone). The USA could retain 30 000 additional troops elsewhere in Western Europe and the USSR could deploy 30 000 elsewhere in Eastern Europe, although it is clear that Soviet troops are no longer welcome in Bulgaria, Czechoslovakia, Hungary or Romania. The proposal is thus asymmetrical, since it would *de facto* limit the USSR to 195 000 troops in the northern tier of the WTO, while allowing the USA to deploy an additional 30 000 troops in the rest of Western Europe.

The proposal aims in part to compensate for Soviet proximity to the zone of contact between the two alliances by allowing the USA a greater presence in Europe, but messages of reassurance to the WTO states are also implicit in the proposal. Brent Scowcroft implied that 195 000 was a floor for the USA and a ceiling for the USSR.[176] In so far as 195 000 represents a ceiling on Soviet forces, the Bush proposal responds to Hungarian and Czecho-slovak wishes to be free of stationed Soviet troops. In so far as 195 000 can be seen as a long-term floor under a superpower presence in Central Europe, however, it can be interpreted as a message to President Gorbachev that reductions from Europe, and especially from the two German states, will be conducted in an orderly, mutually reassuring way. In the event of a unified Germany, however, the allocation of stationed forces would have to be rethought, since NATO countries are insisting that a unified Germany would have to become a member of NATO, while the GDR and the USSR insist on neutrality for a single German state, the same positions taken by the respective powers in the mid-1950s.[177]

ATCs. At the beginning of round V Hungary tried to resolve East–West differences on armoured vehicles with a proposal that both alliances accept a combined AIFV–HACV sub-ceiling of 17 000–18 000 with an additional sub-ceiling on HACVs of 2000–3000. This would require a large reduction in HACVs from the WTO, but not quite as large as in NATO's December proposal. There would be no reduction of HACVs from NATO but a strict limit on future deployment of light tanks.[178]

Aircraft. NATO moved closer to the WTO position on aircraft in early February, specifically reducing the alliance-wide ceiling for combat aircraft to 4700, the level proposed by the WTO in September (see table 13.7). In another concession NATO proposed a new limit of 500 for air defence inter-ceptor aircraft; air defence interceptors above the 500 limit were to count as part of the 4700 allowed for combat aircraft.[179] NATO spokesmen also suggested that some WTO trainer aircraft would be permitted outside the

[176] Fitchett, J., *International Herald Tribune*, 5 Feb. 1990.

[177] See, for example, 'Note from the Soviet Foreign Ministry to the American Embassy, enclosing Draft for a German Peace Treaty, March 10, 1952' and 'British (Eden) Plan for German Reunification in Freedom, January 29, 1954', *Documents on Germany 1944–1961* (note 120), pp. 116–20 and pp. 146–49 respectively.

[178] Forsberg, R. and Leavitt, R. (eds), 'The emerging tank-ACV agreement', *Vienna Fax*, no. 11 (26 Jan. 1990), pp. 1–5.

[179] 'NATO offers concessions on aircraft and tanks', *International Herald Tribune*, 9 Feb. 1990.

Table 13.8. Comparison of the WTO and NATO proposals at the start of round V

	TLI ceilings					
	Tanks	Artillery	ATCs	Aircraft	Helicopters	Manpower
WTO						
North	200	1 000	150	30	30	20 000
South	5 200	8 500	5 750	290	360	270 000
Rear	1 300	3 000	1 350	60	60	150 000
Central	13 000	11 500	20 000	1 120	1 250	910 000
ATTU:						
Alliance	20 000	24 000	28 000	4 700	1 900	1 350 000
Country	14 000	17 000	18 000	3 400	1 500	920 000
Stationed (all)	4 500	4 000	7 500	1 200	600	300 000
Total	40 000	48 00	56 000	3 000	3 400	2 700 000
NATO						
ATTU:						
Total	40 000	33 000	56 000	11 400	3 800	..
Stationed (US/Soviet)	3 200	1 700	6 000	..	..	225 000[a]
Country	12 000	10 000	16 800	3 420	1 140	..
Alliance	20 000	16 500	30 000[b]	5 200[c]	1 900	..
NATO zones:						
MBFR	8 000	4 500	11 000	..	..	..
Central 2	10 300	7 600	18 000	..	..	..
Central 1	11 300	9 000	20 000	..	..	..

[a] Of which no more than 195 000 in the Jaruzelski zone (the MBFR zone plus Denmark and Hungary).

[b] Of which no more than 14 000 can be AIFVs plus HACVs.

[c] 4700 combat and 500 interceptor aircraft.

CFE limits. Earlier, NATO had insisted that all combat-capable aircraft be counted regardless of assigned mission, but apparently WTO assurances that aircraft would be available for substantial on-site inspection persuaded NATO officials that some aircraft could be designated as trainers or purely defensive aircraft.[180]

Helicopters. NATO redefined combat helicopters as those equipped with anti-tank and air-to-air missiles. Any such helicopters above permitted limits should be destroyed or converted to non-attack capable status.

Prospects for a CFE agreement in 1990

Much remained to be settled: precise definitions of tanks, armoured vehicles, combat aircraft and helicopters; whether only US and Soviet troops would be limited or all foreign-based troops; and many details of a verification and compliance regime. However, NATO concessions offered in February suggested that delegates were taking the Bush schedule seriously and hoping to sign a first CFE agreement in 1990.

[180] Smith, R. J., 'US drafts compromise to speed East–West accord on military planes', *International Herald Tribune*, 1 Feb. 1990.

Table 13.9. Impact of proposed CFE cuts on TLIs in the ATTU zone

	TLI ceilings					
	Tanks	Artillery	ATCs	Aircraft	Helicopters	Manpower
WTO proposals/WTO data						
NATO:						
Now	30 690	57 060	46 900	5 450	5 270	3 660 000
Post-CFE	20 000	24 000	28 000	1 500	1 700	1 350 000
Cuts	10 690	33 060	18 900	3 950	3 570	2 310 000
WTO:						
Now	59 470	71 560	70 330	5 355	2 785	3 570 000
Post-CFE	20 000	24 000	28 000	1 500	1 700	1 350 000
Cuts	39 470	47 560	58 330	3 855	1 085	2 220 000
Unilateral	11 900	9 130	..	930	..	296 300
Left to cut	17 570	3 430	..	2 925	..	1 923 700
NATO proposals/NATO data						
NATO:						
Now	22 224	17 328	47 639	6 700	3 500	2 200 000
Post-CFE	20 000	16 500	30 000	5 200	1 900	..
Cuts	2 224	828	17 639	1 500	1 600	..
WTO:						
Now	51 500	43 400	93 400	9 600	3 700	3 100 000
Post-CFE	20 000	16 500	30 000	5 200	1 900	..
Cuts	31 500	26 900	63 400	4 400	1 800	..
Unilateral	11 900	9 130	..	930	..	296 300
Left to cut	19 600	17 770	63 000	3 470	1 800	..

IV. Negotiations on Confidence- and Security-Building Measures

Separate 35-state CSBM Negotiations have also been under way in Vienna since March 1989. The mandate for this forum, agreed by all 35 states participating in the Third CSCE follow-up meeting in Vienna, 1986–89, is to build upon and expand the 1986 Stockholm Document with the aim of elaborating and adopting a new set of mutually complementary CSBMs designed to reduce the risk of military confrontation in Europe.[181]

To keep the 12 neutral and non-aligned (NNA) participants of the CSCE informed about progress at CFE, the CFE participants are required to 'exchange views and information' with the CSBM forum twice in each negotiating session. By late September it was clear that much of the anticipated agenda at the CSBM forum had been pre-empted by CFE where, in

---

[181] For the mandate for the CSBM Negotiations, see 'Extracts from the Concluding Document of the 1986–89 Vienna Meeting of Representatives of the Participating States of the Conference on Security and Co-operation in Europe', SIPRI, *SIPRI Yearbook 1989: World Armaments and Disarmament* (Oxford University Press: Oxford, 1989), appendix 11B, p. 419.

round III, both NATO and the WTO presented detailed proposals for information exchange, verification and stabilization measures.

Both sets of negotiations in Vienna were preceded by a Conference of Foreign Ministers, 6–9 March 1989. Opening proposals at the CSBM Negotiations were made on 9 March by the group of 16 NATO states and by four WTO states (Czechoslovakia, Hungary, the GDR and Bulgaria),[182] on 22 March by Romania,[183] and on 12 July by the 12 NNA states.[184] Poland and the USSR preferred a flexible position rather than being associated with the opening proposals of their WTO partners.

The Eastern proposal

The proposal is in five parts: (a) six constraining measures seek to limit the scale, number and duration of major military activities in the ATTU zone; (b) a set of CSBMs for air and naval forces; (c) measures to amplify provisions in the Stockholm Document; (d) proposals to establish CSBM zones in Europe in which military forces would be restructured into more defensive postures; and (e) measures to improve the transparency of military activites and postures.[185]

The NATO proposal

At the Conference of Foreign Ministers British Foreign Minister Geoffrey Howe emphasized five goals for the talks: better information exchange, more detailed notification of military exercises, improved arrangements for observing exercises, greater freedom of movement on each other's territory and much stronger provisions for on-site inspection.[186]

The formal NATO proposal offered by Canada proposed 12 CSBMs.[187] The first three related to transparency about military organization: exchange of information on force posture and weapon developments, and ways to establish a random evaluation system. The other nine CSBMs related to transparency about military activities: enhanced information for the annual calendar under the 1986 Stockholm Document and when notifying military

[182] *Negotiations on Confidence- and Security-Building Measures in Europe*, Proposal submitted by the delegations of Belgium, Canada, Denmark, France, the Federal Republic of Germany, Greece, Iceland, Italy, Luxembourg, the Netherlands, Norway, Portugal, Spain, Turkey, the United Kingdom and the United States of America, CSCE/WV.1, Vienna, 9 Mar. 1989; *On a New Generation of Confidence- and Security-Building Measures in Europe*, Proposal submitted by the delegations of Bulgaria, Czechoslovakia, the German Democratic Republic and Hungary, CSCE/WV.2, Vienna, 9 Mar. 1989.

[183] *Confidence- and Security-Building Measures in Europe*, Proposal submitted by the delegation of Romania, CSCE/WV.3, 22 Mar. 1989.

[184] *Proposal submitted by the delegations of Austria, Cyprus, Finland, Liechenstein, Malta, San Marino, Sweden, Switzerland and Yugoslavia*, Vienna, 12 July 1989.

[185] CSCE/WV.2 (note 182).

[186] Foreign Ministers Vienna Meeting 1989 for the Opening of the Negotiations on Confidence- and Security-Building Measures and the Negotiation on Conventional Armed Forces in Europe, *Record of the Opening Statements*, Vienna, 6–8 Mar. 1989, pp. 27–35.

[187] CSCE/WV.1 (note 182).

activities, improved observation modalities, lower observation thresholds, lower thresholds for longer notice of large-scale activities, improved access for observers, improved means of communication, and equal treatment of host and visiting media representatives. As a separate measure the NATO group also proposed a seminar to exchange views on military doctrine.

Seminar on military doctrine

The issue of military doctrine as an item for the CSCE agenda was raised by the WTO countries at the Vienna follow-up meeting as early as 1987, when they adopted an unambiguously defensive political–military doctrine.[188]

NATO countries were initially reluctant to engage in East–West discussions on doctrine not least because of doctrinal differences between France and the other NATO allies. An informal dialogue on doctrine was launched, however, in which serving military officers from NATO and the WTO met in various unofficial East–West forums, organized by SIPRI, Pugwash and the New York Institute for East–West Security Studies. Many official bilateral exchanges also took place during the late 1980s between Admiral William J. Crowe, Jr, Chairman of the US Joint Chiefs of Staff, and Marshal Akhromeyev. SACEUR General John Galvin has visited Pyotr Lushev, Chief of Staff of the WTO, and the Netherlands and Hungary have exchanged information on tactics and forces bilaterally.

At the March 1989 Conference of Foreign Ministers FRG Foreign Minister Hans-Dietrich Genscher and Polish Foreign Minister Tadeusz Olechowski invited CSCE participants to a June conference on doctrines, strategies and military concepts at the Stiftung Wissenschaft Politik in Ebenhausen.[189] This took place on 16 June, and was the forerunner to the seminar on military doctrine that opened in Vienna on 16 January 1990.[190]

Meanwhile in Vienna at the end of round I of the CSBM Negotiations, the US delegate proposed a working group to establish the agenda for such a seminar. This *ad hoc* group was established on 5 May and began work on 16 June.[191] Poland, Spain and Sweden submitted working papers to the group and at the end of round III the CSBM plenary scheduled the seminar for 16 January 1990.[192] This was the only concrete decision in three rounds of talks.

---

[188] Supplement to the WTO Communiqué, *On Military Doctrine of Warsaw Treaty Member States*, Vienna, 29 May 1987.

[189] Note 186, Genscher speech, pp. 91–99 and Olechowski speech, pp. 101–107.

[190] Hamm, M. R., Pohlman, H. and Prystrom J., *Military Doctrines, Strategies and Conventional Arms Control: Introduction Papers to the German–Polish Seminar in Ebenhausen, 21–24 June 1989.*

[191] CSCE/WV.4 (note 182).

[192] *Seminar on Military Doctrines: Illustrative Model*, Spain, 20 June 1989; Proposal submitted by the delegation of Poland on convening a seminar on military doctrine, Working paper, 20 June 1989; CSCE/CSBM, *Seminar on Military Doctrines*, Sweden, 27 June 1989.

Prospects for naval CSBMs

Soviet delegates acknowledged that they had made a concession to Western interests by leaving naval CSBMs out of the 1986 Stockholm Document CSBMs, but warned that they could not be expected to do so indefinitely. At the CSBM Negotiations, WTO countries offered detailed proposals to constrain naval and air activities.[193] There was little response from the Western states and in various forums during 1989 senior Soviet military officials suggested that the USSR might not be willing to implement provisions of a CFE agreement until a decision had been made to discuss naval CSBMs.[194] The NATO countries were divided on the need for naval CSBMs. The USA, France, Britain and Italy were reluctant to accept any restrictions on their naval activities.[195] Vieri Taxler, an Italian delegate at the CSBM talks, emphasized that the Italian Navy must be free to undertake peace-keeping missions outside the ATTU zone and to defend itself against Mediterranean powers not subject to CSCE provisions.[196] Norway stressed that it did not want CSBMs that might constrain the access of NATO allies to northern waters in which the Soviet fleet roamed at all times.[197] On the other hand Norway joined several NATO allies to urge the USA to drop its opposition to a dialogue on naval issues.[198] Delegates from Norway, Iceland, Denmark and Canada urged NATO to begin preparing for an East–West dialogue on naval arms control, even before formal negotiations have been agreed to.[199] Former Norwegian Defence Minister Johan Jørgen Holst has proposed the establishment of a Conference on Security at Sea (either in parallel with or following the CFE talks) to consider the principles that should govern naval CSBMs. Once these principles are established, regional conferences should study the particular problems of the North and South Atlantic, Pacific and Indian oceans, as well as the Baltic and Mediterranean seas.[200]

At the Malta summit meeting President Gorbachev proposed a ban on tactical nuclear weapons on surface ships, an idea first launched by Ambassador Paul Nitze who served several previous US Administrations in bilateral talks with the USSR. President Bush, while positive about other arms control issues under negotiation, opposed naval arms control claiming

---

[193] CSCE/WV/WGB.2, Proposal submitted by the delegations of Bulgaria, the GDR and the USSR on prior notification of military activities of naval and amphibious forces, Vienna, 5 July 1989.

[194] Akhromeyev to US congressional hearing, 21 July 1989, Voigt (see note 173), p. 53; *ACR*, p. 407.B.205.

[195] Vice Admiral Charles Larson before House Armed Services Committee in late Apr. 1989, reported in *Defense News*, 1 May 1989, p. 8; on the British position, see White, D., 'Take lead in talks on naval forces, NATO urged' , *Financial Times*, 24 May 1989.

[196] *ACR*, p. 402.B.227.

[197] *ACR*, p. 402.B.225.

[198] White (note 195).

[199] Prokesch, S., 'Pressure from NATO', *International Herald Tribune*, 7 Dec. 1989.

[200] Holst, J. J., 'Naval arms control prospects', Outline of Remarks to the Swedish Institute of International Affairs, Conference on Naval Arms Control, 11–12 Dec. 1989.

that it did not enhance US security.[201] Nevertheless, there were also signs of a more positive approach in some sectors of the US Navy. Many naval experts and serving officers, for example, are far from enthusiastic about nuclear weapons at sea. During 1988 and 1989, the USA unilaterally withdrew from service hundreds of nuclear-armed depth charges intended for anti-submarine warfare and nuclear-armed surface-to-air missiles deployed on surface vessels. As with other unilateral cutbacks of NATO land forces, however, there was no attempt to score diplomatic points by claiming these measures as reciprocal to WTO cuts. In January 1990, after his retirement as Chairman of the US Joint Chiefs of Staff, Admiral William Crowe spoke out in favour of naval arms control, claiming that now was the time to take advantage of Soviet interest in cutting defence costs to curb nuclear weapons.[202]

V. Conclusion

In the 40 years after World War II, arms control negotiations maintained a civilized East–West dialogue during the worst periods of the cold war, but agreements rarely did more than codify the status quo, usually setting the seal on some aspect of the military balance achieved by unilateral measures. Arms control diplomacy has traditionally reflected rather than affected the state of East–West relations, but in 1989 neither unilateral nor negotiated arms control could keep pace with political change in Europe. Of the three strands of conventional arms control under way during the year, the most dynamic was the programme of unilateral measures to cut WTO forces. Despite implementing their announced cuts on schedule, however, Soviet planners found it difficult and time-consuming to dismantle equipment and reabsorb military personnel and industry into the civilian economy. Moreover, the emerging democracies in Eastern Europe grew increasingly unwilling to tolerate the presence of Soviet forces and demanded greater cuts and speedier withdrawals.

In the NATO countries, finance ministers facing budget deficits invoked new assessments of a reduced WTO threat to justify cuts in defence spending that had previously been resisted by defence ministries. In late 1989, this resistance began to collapse in the face of overwhelming public perception that the threat from the WTO had almost vanished—judgements based more on changed intentions rather than on reduced capabilities. As democracy emerged in one East European country after another it became clear that communism as a factor uniting the WTO countries was now dead, and that there was no longer any intention to attack NATO. The WTO might still be militarily effective in defence of territory but it was clear that the USSR could no longer count on allied assistance for an offensive against the West,

---

[201] Smith, R. J., 'Gorbachev proposed a naval nuclear arms ban', *International Herald Tribune*, 7 Dec. 1989.
[202] Barber, L., 'Crowe in favour of deal over naval nuclear arms control', *Financial Times*, 9 Jan. 1990.

even though the Soviet Union still retains enormously powerful offensive forces.

Unilateral measures to cut national defence budgets would probably save more money than the negotiated cuts at the CFE Negotiation. The US Congressional Budget Office (CBO) estimated that a CFE agreement based on NATO's 13 July proposals could save up to $3 billion annually—some 3 per cent of the combined Army and Tactical Air Force budget for 1990, or less than 1 per cent of the entire DOD budget for that year.[203] These savings would be partially offset by the costs of verification. The CBO notes that verification of the INF Treaty costs the USA about $150 million annually and estimates that CFE verification will be much more expensive, with thousands rather than hundreds of sites to be inspected and monitored regularly.

If unilateral measures save more money, negotiated measures could nevertheless produce a more stable reduction process. Two priority goals were outlined in the CFE mandate: to eliminate both the capability for launching a surprise attack and that for initiating large-scale offensive action. The programme of WTO unilateral measures for 1989–90, plus a CFE agreement based on current proposals, will achieve the first of these; indeed most analysts argue that unilateral cuts implemented by January 1990 have already eliminated a WTO surprise-attack capability.

There is little evidence to suggest, however, that either unilateral cuts or currently envisaged CFE limits are close to achieving the second goal. In particular, there is no evidence yet of cuts in the western Military Districts where the Soviet second strategic echelon forces are based. These forces are an obvious target of NATO proposals at the CFE talks, as are the AIFVs with which the USSR is replacing heavy tanks withdrawn from the first strategic echelon: the Groups of Soviet Forces in Eastern Europe. East European governments may insist on complete withdrawal of Soviet forces outside the context of a CFE agreement, but many Western experts would prefer to see Soviet forces withdraw as part of a treaty obligation and subject to a co-operative multilateral verification regime.

This appears to be the Soviet preference too, and while the current military leadership has tolerated Gorbachev's programme of unilateral measures, it clearly wants the CFE process to generate more ambitious reductions of NATO forces. As Marshal Akhromeyev and others have argued, if the arms control process stops with a first CFE agreement, the USSR risks being left in a militarily inferior position.[204] The WTO will have reduced its numerical superiority in ground forces, but NATO will still retain global advantages in air and naval assets. Hence the repeated calls by Soviet spokesmen to include nuclear and naval forces in follow-up talks.

[203] US Congress, Congressional Budget Office, *Budget and Military Effects of a Treaty Limiting Conventional Forces in Europe* (CBO: Washington, DC, Jan. 1990), pp. 20–23.

[204] Akhromeyev, S., 'The USSR favours dialogue and co-operation. But what about the United States?', *Pravda*, 30 Oct. 1989, *FBIS-SOV-89-209*, 31 Oct. 1989, pp. 1–3; Dobrov, M., 'US stand on naval arms criticized', Moscow World Service, 21 Oct. 1989, *FBIS-SOV-89-204*, 24 Oct. 1989, pp. 6–7.

Events in Eastern Europe make it virtually unthinkable that NATO will now introduce new land-based nuclear weapons in Europe in the name of modernization. Nevertheless, President Bush's FY 1991 budget request calls for $112 million for research and development of a nuclear Follow-on to Lance missile (see also chapter 18).[205] Continued US interest in SNF modernization will reinforce Soviet anxiety to begin formal talks to reduce existing SNF forces and persuade NATO to adopt a no-first-use nuclear doctrine.

As noted above the texts of the NATO and WTO draft CFE treaties offered in December 1989 reflect different degrees of interest in follow-on negotiations; the WTO countries are enthusiastic, the NATO countries are divided but generally more cautious. As 1990 began, radicals on both sides of the political spectrum and in both halves of Europe were calling for an end to traditional arms control to allow the flow of political change to dictate the pace of disarmament. Centrists and conservatives, however, saw the inter-alliance CFE forum as a stabilizer to prevent the pace of change from getting out of control, and as a way of maintaining alliance cohesion. With the exception of Romania, the East European revolutions in 1989 were surprisingly calm and peaceful but instabilities could explode in the Soviet Republics, and in Eastern Europe too, if economic, social and political conditions do not improve fast enough. Maintaining the current alliance structure and controlling the pace of disarmament could provide the safety net that allows political and economic reform to evolve rather than explode. In particular CFE can provide a figleaf to maintain Soviet and US forces in the two German states during what promises to be a difficult period of transition for the GDR.

At the same time, CFE can also provide the building-blocks for a pan-European system of security. The co-operative East–West verification regime that will be necessary to monitor compliance with a CFE agreement will help to further break down the barriers between NATO and the WTO to create genuine pan-European structures and security networks.

To the extent the European powers focus on pan-European solutions, the CSBM forum will also come back into the picture. In 1989, however, the role of the 35-state forum was diminished because the CFE made such headway with stabilization and verification measures.

---

[205] Smith, R. J., *Washington Post*, 1 Feb. 1990.

Appendix 13A. Implementation of the Stockholm Document and calendar of planned notifiable military activities in 1990 and forecast for 1991

AXEL KROHN

The confidence- and security-building measures (CSBMs) established by the 1986 Stockholm Document expanded on the Helsinki confidence-building measures (CBMs) of 1975 and made them mandatory.[1] The Stockholm Document requires the participating states to exchange annual calendars of military activities, to notify exercises above a certain threshold, to invite all 35 states participating in the Conference on Security and Co-operation in Europe (CSCE) to observe exercises above a certain threshold, and to allow on-site challenge inspections of military exercises as a means of verification.

By 15 November each year, participating states must prepare and exchange a calendar of notifiable military activities planned for the following year (paragraph 55). Each state must also provide information on military activities involving more than 40 000 troops planned for the second subsequent year (paragraph 59). The annual calendar for 1990 and the advance forecast for 1991 are presented in table 13A.1. The information included in the table is in accordance with the requirements specified in the Stockholm Document (paragraph 56). Most of the information from the calendars is included in the table.

The table is a compilation (based on official information supplied to SIPRI) of the information from the CSCE states' calendars, and gives an overall picture of all their planned notifiable military activities. The countries are required to report such activities occurring on their territory or in which their participation reaches the notifiable level (paragraph 31). Each military activity is listed as one event, regardless of the number of states notifying or participating, or the number of exercises occurring simultaneously. The activities appear in the table in chronological order. For all activities at or above the threshold for observation, observers must be invited (paragraph 38). The countries are required to give the planned duration and to state the 14-day period ('start window') within which the military activity is planned to start. If states provide the actual exercise dates, these are given in the table.

Implementation

The Stockholm Document entered into force on 1 January 1987. As the information provided to SIPRI by the governments of the CSCE countries was insufficient

---

[1] The Stockholm Document is reprinted in SIPRI, *SIPRI Yearbook 1987: World Armaments and Disarmament* (Oxford University Press: Oxford, 1987), appendix 10A, pp. 353–69. The Document covers all of Europe, has lower thresholds for notifications of manoeuvres and longer periods of prior notification than the Helsinki Final Act and includes verification provisions. See for a comparison Chebali, V.-Y., 'Confidence-building measures within the CSCE process: paragraph-by-paragraph analysis of the Helsinki and Stockholm régimes', United Nations Institute for Disarmament Research (UNIDIR), Research Paper No. 3, Geneva, Mar. 1989.

Table 13A.1. Calendar of planned notifiable military activities in 1990 and forecast for 1991, as required by the Stockholm Document

States/Location	Dates/Start window	Type/Name of activity[a]	Area	Level of command	No. of troops	Type of forces or equipment	No. and type of divisions[a]	Comments
1. USA and FRG in FRG	29 days, 2–30 Jan.	FTX 'Centurion Shield' ('Reforger 90')	Koblenz–Limburg–Giessen–Würzburg–Ansbach–Neumarkt (Opf)–Regensburg–Straubing–Egenfelden–Erding–Dachau–Landsberg/Lech–Ravensburg–Geisingen–Karlsruhe–Pirmasens–Idar–Oberstein–Koblenz	Army group	88 750 (80 000 USA) (8 750 FRG)	Ground and air forces	4 tank divs (–) 3 tank brigs (–) 3 mot. inf. divs (–) 1 mech. inf. brig. (–) 1 mt. div. (–) 2 armoured rec. rgts (–) 1 territorial command (–)	Approx. 17 400 US soldiers from 'Reforger' to take part; observers to be invited
2. USSR and GDR in GDR	5–6 days, 1–14 Feb.	FTX	Haldensleben–Lindau–Dobritz–Brandenburg–Wesenberg–Sewekow	Army of the Western Group of Soviet Forces	13 500 (13 000 USSR) (500 GDR)	Ground and air forces	1 mot. inf. div. (–) 1 tank div. (–)	..
3. USSR	6–7 days, 1–14 Mar.	FTX	Kiev MD–Belaya-Tserkov–Korsoun–Shevchenkovskiy–Grebenka–Schyors–Loyev–Wyschgorod	Army	17 000	Ground forces	3 tank divs (–)	Observers to be invited

States/Location	Dates/Start window	Type/Name of activity[a]	Area	Level of command	No. of troops	Type of forces or equipment	No. and type of divisions[a]	Comments
4. Netherlands and UK in Norway	1–2 days, 10–24 Mar.	Amphibious landing 'Cold Winter 90'	Dyrøy–Tranøy–Laksfjord–Øyfjord–Skarøyvatnet–Ryøya–Nordfjord–Målselv–Veidfjell	Nor. regional command, in conjunction with commander, 3rd Commando Brig. Royal Marines	4 050 (850 Neth.) (3 200 UK)	Amphibious forces	1 brig.	Landing craft and support helicopters
5. USA, UK, Spain, Netherlands, Greece and Italy in Italy	8–13 May	Amphibious exercise 'Dragon Hammer 90'	South-west Sardinia	Regional Command	3 970	Amphibious and air forces	..	..
6. USSR and GDR in GDR	6–7 days, 1–14 Aug.	FTX	Jessen–Vetschau–Guben–Wellmitz–Storkow–Beelitz	Western Group of Soviet Forces	15 700 (15 000 USSR) (700 GDR)	Ground and air forces	1 mot. inf. div. (–) 1 tank div. (–)	..
7. GDR, USSR, and Poland in GDR	7–8 days, 17–30 Aug.	FTX 'Drushba 90'	Gardelegen–Haldensleben–Wittenberg–Potsdam–Nauen–Oranienburg–Havelberg	Deputy minister and commander of ground forces of National People's Army	17 800 (13 800 GDR) (2 000 USSR) (2 000 Poland)	Ground and air forces	1 mot. inf. div (–) and support units (GDR) 1 mot. inf. div. (–) (USSR) 1 mech. div. (–) (Poland)	Observers to be invited
8. USSR	5–6 days, 1–14 Sep.	FTX	Molodechno–Uzda–Slutsk–Bobruysk–Beshenkovichi–Ushachi	Military District	13 000	Ground forces	1 mot. inf. div. (–) 1 tank div. (–)	..

9. UK, USA and FRG in FRG	FTX 'Keystone'	15 days, 2–15 Sep.	Berne–Syke–Wagenfeld–Aerzen–Fürstenau–Erwitte–Dorsten	Division	25 650 (22 000 UK) (3 000 USA) (650 FRG)	Ground forces incl. airborne troops	1 inf. div. 1 tank div. (–) 1 tank bn.	Observers to be invited
10. FRG, USA, France and Belgium in FRG	FTX 'Hessenschild'	12 days, 8–21 Sep.	Eschershausen–Einbeck–Northeim–Friedland along inner German border to Eschwege–Grossenlüder–Karben–Camberg–Neustadt (Wied)–Siegen–Willingen–Eschershausen	Corps	25 000 (20 650 FRG) (500 USA) (3 200 France) (650 Belgium)	Ground and air forces	2 tank divs 2 tank divs (–) 1 mot. inf. div. 1 mot. inf. div. (–)	Observers to be invited
11. Netherlands, Norway, UK and USA in Norway	FTX 'Team Work 90'	5 days, 15–30 Sep.	Kaura–Steinkjer–Snåsa–Hanan–Salen	Norwegian regional command	18 250 (750 Neth.) (7 000 Nor.) (3 200 UK) (7 300 USA)	Ground and air forces	1 light inf. div.	Observers to be invited
12. Netherlands, Norway, UK and USA in Norway	Amphibious landing 'Team-Work 90'	1–2 days, 15–30 Sep.	Kaura–Namdalseid–Ranem–Vemundvik	Norwegian regional command in conjunction with commanders, CG 4th Marine Expeditory Brig. and 3rd Commando Brig. Royal Marines	10 450 (750 Neth.) (3 200 UK) (6 500 USA)	Amphibious forces	2 brigs	Landing craft and support helicopters; observers to be invited

States/Location	Dates/Start window	Type/Name of activity[a]	Area	Level of command	No. of troops	Type of forces or equipment	No. and type of divisions[a]	Comments
13. Hungary, Czechoslovakia and USSR in Hungary	5–6 days, 16–30 Sep.	CPX 'Shield 90'	Tüskevár–Tapolca–Sárszentmihály–Fehérvárcsurgó–Dabas–Kunszentmiklós–Kerekegyháza–Lajosmizse	MOD of Hungary and Commander-in-Chief of joint WTO armed forces	8 000	Ground and air forces	Operative groups, Hqs from Hungarian, Czechoslovak and Soviet Armies and assigned combat units	Below notification threshold
14. Denmark, FRG, Netherlands, UK and USA in Denmark and FRG	26 days, 17 Sep.–1 Oct.	FTX 'Bold Guard 90'	In Denmark: Jutland–Zealand–Lolland-Falster; in FRG: Fehmarn–Travemünde along inner German border to Lauenburg–Ahrensburg–Schenefeld–Brunsbüttel–St. Peter–Klanxbuell	Army group	54 000 (12 000 Den.) (20 000 FRG) (8 000 USA) (13 700 UK) (300 Neth.) (incl. 10 500 UK Marines and 3 200 UK/Neth. amphibious forces)	Ground, air and amphibious forces	2 mot. inf. divs 1 inf. div. (–) 2 amph. brigs 1 inf. brig.	Exercise will take place on territory of Denmark with approx. 23 600 soldiers; observers to be invited
15. Denmark, FRG, Netherlands, UK and USA in Denmark	5 Days, 17 Sep.–1 Oct.	Amphibious landing 'Bold Guard 90'	Jutland (exact location to be decided)	MEB	6 600 (6 600 US) (others to be decided)	Amphibious forces	1 MEB and sub-units	Activity is element of FTX 'Bold Guard 90'; observers to be invited

							Ground forces	Observers to be invited
16. UK and USA in FRG	23 days, 28 Sep.–11 Oct.	FTX 'Quarter Final'	Along inner German border between Soltendiek–Duderstadt and Kreiensen–Helmarshausen–Damme–Delmenhorst–Welle	Division	26 880 (26 800 UK) (80 US)	Ground forces	1 tank div. 1 helicopter sqn (–)	Observers to be invited
17. Switzerland	12 days, 30 Sep.–11 Oct.	FTX 'Exalibur'	Zürich–Zug–Nidwalden–Obwalden–Uri–Schwyz–Glarus	Commander, Mt. Div. 9	15 000	Ground and air forces	1 mt. div. (–) 1 brig.	..
18. Finland	5 days, 8–22 Oct.	FTX 'Harjoitus–90'	Lahti–Joutsa–Mikkeli–Luumäki	Army group	15 000	Ground and air forces	2 brigs	..
19. USSR	5–6 days, 20 Oct.–5 Nov.	FTX	Odessa MD: Kotowka–Rybakowa–Balawnoje–Kowaljowka–Marinowka	Military District	17 000	Ground and air forces	1 mot. inf. div. 1 abn. rgt. 1 mar. inf. rgt.	Observers to be invited
20. Austria	12–17 Nov.	FTX 'RVÜ 90'	Kollerschlag–Reichenthal–Gallneukirchen–Kremsmünster–Stadl Paura	Division	15 000	Ground and air forces	2 mech. brigs	..
21. Switzerland	5 days, 26–30 Nov.	FTX 'Rodeo'	Western parts up to Bern–Basel line	Commander, Field Army Corps 1	15 000	Ground forces	1 mech. div. (–) reinforced during exercise	..
Advance forecast for 1991								
1. USA, FRG and others in FRG	38 days, 25 Feb.–10 Mar.	FTX 'Caravan Guard 91'	Central and southern FRG	Corps	41 000	Ground and air forces	..	Observers to be invited

States/Location	Dates/Start window	Type/Name of activity[a]	Area	Level of command	No. of troops	Type of forces or equipment	No. and type of divisions[a]	Comments
4. FRG, Belgium, Netherlands, UK and USA in FRG	30 days, 25 Aug. –7 Sep.	FTX 'Certain Shield'	Central and northern FRG	Corps	65 000	Ground and air forces	..	In conjunction with 'Reforger 91'; observers to be invited

[a] See the list of abbreviations below. (–) means that the division is below full strength or not comprised of all its component units; (+) means that the division (according to standard organization) is reinforced with other units.

Abbreviations used in the table:

abn.	airborne	mot.	motorized
bn	battalion	mt.	mountain
brig.	brigade	rec.	reconnaissance
CPX	command post exercise	rgt	regiment
div.	division	sqn	squadron
FTX	field training exercise		
inf.	infantry		
mar.	marine		
MEB	Marine Expeditionary Brigade		
mech.	mechanized		

States participating in notified military activities in 1990, by activity number:

Austria: 20
Belgium: 10
Czechoslovakia: 13
Denmark: 14, 15
France: 10
Finland: 18
FRG: 1, 9, 10, 14, 15, 16
GDR: 2, 6, 7
Greece: 5
Hungary: 13
Italy: 5
Netherlands: 4, 5, 11, 12, 14, 15
Norway: 4, 11, 12
Poland: 7
Spain: 5
Switzerland: 17, 21
UK: 4, 5, 9, 11, 12, 14, 15, 16
USA: 1, 5, 9, 10, 11, 12, 14, 15, 16
USSR: 2, 3, 6, 7, 8, 13, 19

States planning no notifiable military activities in 1990: *Belgium*, Bulgaria, Cyprus, *Czechoslovakia*, Denmark, Finland, *France*, *Greece*, the Holy See, Iceland, Ireland, Liechtenstein, Luxembourg, Malta, Monaco, *the Netherlands*, *Poland*, Romania, San Marino, *Spain*, Turkey and Yugoslavia. (States participating in notifiable activities but not responsible for notification are given in italics.)

in the beginning, it was somewhat difficult for SIPRI to establish a comprehensive picture of the planned notifiable military activities and the other important aspects of implementation, such as inspections. The information received by SIPRI has become more comprehensive over the years.[2]

As of January 1990, all 35 participating states have complied with the terms of the Stockholm Document concerning the exchange of annual calendars and forecasts, notifications and observations as well as on-site inspections, and no nation has indicated dissatisfaction with the implementation process. The calendars are still the best single source of publicly available information on the implementation of the Stockholm Document and military activities for the coming year. Although many of the CSCE countries are not willing to provide further official material, it is promising that more and more governments are willing to provide additional documents such as composite calendars and inspection reports.[3] For the central idea of confidence building—openness and transparency—this is an encouraging trend.

Table 13A.2. Military activities at or above the notification/observation threshold which were scaled back in 1989[a]

State(s)/Location	No. of troops reduced from—to	Exercise no. in *SIPRI Yearbook 1989*
Bulgaria	13 000—9 000	18
USSR and GDR in GDR	25 600—13 000 (–)	19
USA, FRG and Netherlands in FRG	83 300—called off, merged with 'Centurion Shield 90'	20
USSR	3 500—1 500	24
Czechoslovakia and USSR in Czechoslovakia	17 000—13 350 (12 980 USSR) (370 Czech.)	27
Turkey	34 000—18 000	28
USSR and Hungary in Hungary	13 500—11 500 (11 000 USSR) (500 Hungary)	30

[a] Information from the corrected compository calendar of the FRG for 1989 and notifications from the respective states. A 14 July note from the GDR states that exercise no. 19 was called off.

Since the exchanged calendars list planned activities, changes might occur, for example, in the number and type of personnel which are supposed to participate in the manoeuvre. This was the case for seven exercises in 1989. These changes are communicated to the other participating states within the framework of the formal notifications for each activity.[4] Table 13A.2 shows the corrections which must be made with regard to military exercises in 1989, according to information received by SIPRI.

[2] By mid-Feb. 1990 SIPRI had not received any information on planned notifiable military activities from Cyprus, France, Ireland, Liechtenstein, Monaco, Romania, San Marino or the UK.

[3] Composite calendars for 1990 and corrections for 1989 were received from the FRG and Sweden. Inspection reports about the 1989 on-site inspections listed in table 13A.4 were received from Czechoslovakia, the FRG, Poland, the USA and the USSR.

[4] As regards the reductions in the size of Soviet exercises, this is in accordance with the Soviet Government decision to reduce and restructure the Soviet armed forces and to withdraw them from the GDR and Hungary. See *Pravda*, 23 July 1989 (TASS, 24 July, VOVP2-890724-DR36).

Calendars

For 1990, 21 military activities have been notified: 7 by WTO countries,[5] 10 by NATO countries and 4 by neutral and non-aligned (NNA) countries; 22 countries will not hold a military activity in 1990 at or above the notification threshold, even though some are participating in such activities. The forecast comprises 2 NATO exercises to be held in 1991. For 1987, 47 military activities were notified in the calendars; this figure decreased to 38 for 1988 and 31 for 1989. The figure for 1990, 21 notified military activities, clearly shows a continuing decline, resulting from the two-thirds reduction of notified military exercises by the WTO (7 in 1990 compared to 17 in 1989). Table 13A.3 shows the numbers of NATO, WTO and NNA exercises notified in the calendars since 1987.

For the period from the implementation of the Stockholm Document in 1987 until December 1990 a total of 137 military activities have been listed in the SIPRI calendars. Until 1987 NATO always conducted fewer military activities than the WTO, though involving higher numbers of troops. The USSR has only forecast one exercise involving more than 40 000 troops,[6] but the WTO has conducted more military activities on a somewhat smaller scale. For 1990 this picture has changed—for the first time WTO countries will conduct fewer military activities at or above the notification threshold than NATO.

Table 13A.3. Annual number of military exercises notified in the annual calendars by NATO, WTO and NNA countries

Bloc	1987	1988	1989	1990	Total
NATO	17	13	11	10	51
WTO	25	22	17	7	71
NNA	5	3	3	4	15

Source: Compiled from *SIPRI Yearbooks 1987/88/89*—1987: appendix 10B; 1988: appendix 11A; 1989: appendix 11A, and the forecast of notifiable military activities for 1990.

NATO has reduced its notifiable military exercises to about 60 per cent of the total for 1987. Although the NATO figure is decreasing less dramatically than that for the WTO, the general trend is towards fewer and smaller exercises.[7] The West is searching for new manoeuvre concepts which are cost effective and less disturbing to the civilian population, indicating a future mixture of command post and field training exercises. The role of computer simulation of combat activities will therefore increase.[8] A general reduction of the number of military exercises and troops involved is already under discussion at the Vienna CSBM Negotiations.[9]

[5] Exercise 'Shield 90', no. 13 in table 13A.1, is below the notification threshold, as only a total of 8000 troops are involved. Such voluntary notifications show an understanding of the need to improve openness, transparency and confidence building within the participating states.

[6] See SIPRI (note 1), appendix 10B, p. 380, activity number 8. In fact, the exercise was carried out with a total of 21 000 troops.

[7] E.g., the West conducted 16 national and multinational manoeuvres in autumn 1989. A total of 205 000 men were involved in these exercises, a reduction of 50 000 troops compared to the same period in the previous year. *Österreichische Militärische Zeitschrift*, vol. 6 (1989), p. 517.

[8] With three manoeuvres (Offenes Visier, White Rhino, Caravan Guard) the Western countries tried this new concept of 'train smart' during 1989. Brüsselbach, M., 'Train smart–maneuver smart/Neue Übungskonzepte auf dem Prüfstand,' *Europäische Wehrkunde Wehrwissenschaftliche Rundschau/European Defence Review*, no. 11 (Nov. 1989), pp. 676–77.

[9] See the Eastern proposal for the CSBM negotiations which states that 'it is necessary to limit the scale, number and duration of military exercises.' The constraints are specified under topic I,

Notifications

The Stockholm Document requires that participating states give notification in writing, through diplomatic channels in an agreed form of content, to all other participating states 42 days or more in advance of the start of notifiable military activities (paragraph 29). Notifications are the final information sent to all CSCE countries concerning the forthcoming military activity. The information given is more detailed than that in the calendars. As far as can be seen from the information provided to SIPRI, all 35 CSCE countries have fulfilled their obligations in providing notification of their military activities.

Observation

There are two important means for verifying compliance with the requirements of the Stockholm Document. First there is the mandatory invitation of observers to notifiable military activities at or above a certain threshold—17 000 regular troops or 5000 amphibious or airborne troops (paragraph 38.4). These observations are compulsory and available to all CSCE states. The observation programme is determined by the host country even though the obligations are laid down in the Document. Observation requirements have been met, but criticism has sometimes been voiced by the West that the WTO programmes have tended to be much more limited than those hosted by NATO and the NNAs.[10] For 1990, 11 military activities will be above the observation level. NATO countries will conduct 8 military activities and the WTO will hold 3.

Inspections

The second important means of verification is the right to conduct on-site challenge inspections with no right of denial (paragraphs 65–66), a useful precedent which might pave the way for further arrangements needed for a CFE regime. During 1989, 16 on-site inspections were conducted (see table 13A.4), compared to 13 in 1988 and 5 in 1987.[11] This means not only a total increase over the whole period but also a relative increase, as the total number of notifiable military activities since 1987 has decreased.

The ratio of inspections conducted was nearly even in 1988 (seven by NATO and six by the WTO). In 1989 the Western countries conducted nine inspections, and the Eastern countries held seven; the USSR held most—with a total of five inspections it was far ahead of the other participating countries. The FRG, the GDR, Italy and the USA each conducted two and Canada, France and the UK each conducted one inspection. Inspections on the territory of the WTO countries have been held in Bulgaria, Czechoslovakia, the GDR and the Soviet Union. Inspections on NATO territory took place in Belgium, Denmark, the FRG, France, Italy and Turkey. This was the first time that Canada, France and Italy made use of the provisions of the Stockholm Document to conduct on-site inspections.

Constraining Measures, point 1–15, in: *On A New Generation of Confidence- and Security-Building Measures in Europe*, Proposal submitted by the Delegations of Bulgaria, Czechoslovakia, the GDR and Hungary, CSCE/WV.2, Vienna, 9 Mar. 1989, p. 2.

[10] Brown, S. (US representative to the CSBM Working Group which produced the Western CSBM proposals), 'CSBM—the other negotiations', *NATO's Sixteen Nations*, Aug. 1989, p. 60.

[11] For lists of inspections for 1987 and 1988 see SIPRI, *SIPRI Yearbook 1989: World Armaments and Disarmament* (Oxford University Press: Oxford, 1989), table 11A.2, p. 411.

Table 13A.4. On-site inspections of military activities conducted in 1989, as permitted by the Stockholm Document

Date	Inspecting state	Host state	Exercise name/area
4–14 Apr.	FRG	GDR	'Zyklus 89'
16–18 Apr.	Italy	USSR	Moscow Military District
28–30 May	USSR	Italy	'Dragon Hammer 89'
19-21 May	USA	GDR	. .
14–16 June	Canada	CSSR	Cheb–Jáchimov–Marianké Lázne
21–23 June	USSR	Denmark	'Avenue Express' 'Bikini 89'
11–13 Aug.	USA	USSR	Dubravka–Vishtitis–Vieshvile
19–21 Aug.	France	USSR	Dubrovo–Shatsk–Berezino–Ulla
13–15 Aug.	Italy	Bulgaria	'Mariza 89'
8–10 Sep.	GDR	FRG	'Caravan Guard 89'
4–6 Sep.	UK	GDR	Gardelegen–Magdeburg–Brandenburg
11–13 Sep.	USSR	FRG	'Offenes Visier'
17–19 Sep.	GDR	Belgium	'Plain Sailing 89'
23–25 Sep.	USSR	France	'Extel 1 Champagne 89'
30 Sep.–2 Oct.	FRG	CSSR	Cheb–Jáchymov–Marianské Lázné
18–20 Oct.	USSR	Turkey	'Mehmetcik 89'

Note: The first inspection in 1990 was made on 6–8 Jan. by the USSR in Belgium ('Reforger').

Available information suggests that all inspections went well and that all host countries met the terms and conditions of the Stockholm Document in that: (*a*) the requesting note was answered promptly; (*b*) initial requests for point of entry were granted; (*c*) overflight clearance formalities were simple; (*d*) visa formalities on arrival were managed with dispatch; (*e*) rations and quarters were suitable; (*f*) helicopter and ground vehicle transportation was available as necessary; and (*g*) vehicle-to-vehicle communication was servicable in those modes used by the inspection team.[12]

The inspection reports seen by SIPRI are basically positive but show that there is still some room for improvement, particularly as regards willingness to provide further information than that mandated by the Stockholm Document, and in connection with denial of access to 'restricted areas' (paragraphs 73–74)[13]—the definition of which requires greater clarity.

[12] See Report of the Canadian Inspection of a Military Activity in the Czechoslovak Socialist Republic, 14 to 16 June 1989, pp. 2–3.

[13] 'The participating State which requests an inspection will be permitted to designate for inspection on the territory of another State within the zone of application for CSBMs, a specific area. Such an area will be referred to as the 'specific area'. The specific area will comprise terrain where notifiable military activities are conducted or where another participating State believes a notifiable military activity is taking place. The specified area will be defined and limited by the scope and scale of notifiable military activities but will not exceed that required for an army-level military activity. (paragraph 73). In the specified area the representatives of the inspecting State accompanied by the representatives of the receiving State will be permitted access, entry and unobstructed survey, except for areas or sensitive points to which access is normally denied or restricted, military and other defence installations, as well as naval vessels, military vehicles and aircraft. The number and extent of the restricted areas should be as limited as possible. Areas where notifiable military activities can take place will not be declared restricted areas, except for certain permanent or temporary military

Even though the latitude given to inspectors is distinctly greater than that granted to the observers of notifiable military activities, who are 'guided' by the host state and expected to follow its 'instructions' (paragraph 53.5),[14] it is obvious that the degree of transparency largely depends on the amount of information provided by the host country. The amount of information given voluntarily by host countries varies. In an exercise held in the GDR and inspected by the FRG, the host country provided information additional to that supplied in the notification; the inspection team reported that its work was aided by the provision of more comprehensive information than required by the Stockholm Document.[15] An exercise held by Soviet and Czechoslovak troops in Czechoslavakia and inspected by the FRG between 30 September and 2 October 1989 gave a somewhat different picture: no additional information was provided at the start of the exercise.[16]

The West has always claimed that it would be helpful if inspectors were told the real designations of the units involved as well as their peacetime location. So far the WTO countries have refused to give this information, and instead give the units special exercise designations. During the military exercise in Czechoslovakia the commander confirmed the Soviet intention to continue this practice until further notice, while Czechoslovakia announced a decision to reveal the designations of the units involved and their peacetime locations openly in future.[17]

Compliance

Even though in some cases there were minor uncertainties about numbers and the participation of certain sub-units,[18] or minor difficulties in communication during the exercises,[19] the inspection reports received by SIPRI show that all host countries were co-operative and that the requirements of the Stockholm Document were met in every inspection. No inspection indicates failure to meet its provisions in terms of notification of numbers of personnel and equipment involved in an activity. Clearly challenge inspections are a success and their value can be seen by the fact that more countries have made use of them. Every inspecting country remarked with appreciation on the co-operative approach of the host nation and expressed the conviction that such inspections are an important component of the confidence-building process in Europe. No questions of compliance arose in 1989.

Assessment and outlook

Assessing the period since the Stockholm Document was implemented in 1987, it can be said that the adoption of its CSBMs 'has made a substantial contribution to increasing the exchange of information, introducing predictability and openness of

installations which, in territorial terms, should be as small as possible, and consequently those areas will not be used to prevent inspection of notifiable military activities. Restricted areas will not be employed in a way inconsistent with the agreed provisions on inspection. (paragraph 74).'

[14] See Chebali (note 1), pp. 69–71.

[15] Inspection Report of the FRG on the inspection held 9–11 Apr. 89 for the military activity conducted by Nationale Volksarmee of the GDR Bundeskanzleramt 221-301 06-Mi 5, p. 2.

[16] Inspection Report of the FRG on the inspection held 30 Sep.–2 Oct. 1989 for the military activity conducted by Soviet and Czechoslovak forces in the CSSR. Verbal note 13, Nov. 89, Auswärtiges Amt 221-373.32/3, p. 2.

[17] Note 16, p. 3.

[18] Note 16, pp. 4–5; and Report of the Canadian Inspection (note 12), p. 3.

[19] Inspection Report of the USSR's inspection of military activities on the territory of France, 23–25 Sep. 1989; and Inspection Report of the USSR's inspection of military activities on the territory of Turkey, 18–20 Oct. 1989.

military activities'.[20] The East is going through a process of increasing openness. More information is given today in the course of observation as well as inspection (even though more information could sometimes be provided), the use of tape recorders and cameras is allowed and the programme even includes helicopter overflights. However, this is still an ongoing process in NATO as well as in the WTO and NNA countries. The results of the past three years are encouraging and the level of implementation is beginning to exceed the written obligations of the Stockholm Document. All participants in the CSCE process are seeking further confidence and security building, based on mutual respect and co-operation between the participating countries in East and West. This is clear from the sets of NATO, WTO and NNA proposals made at the current CSBM Negotiations in Vienna. The proposals show a considerable amount of overlap especially in the fields of enhanced information exchange on military organization and activities, that is, enhanced information on notification, lowering of thresholds for observation, limitation of the scale of notifiable military activities[21] as well as the establishment of a Random Evaluation System with the right to conduct a number of pre-announced visits of limited duration to normal peacetime locations.[22] An interesting proposal for the establishment of a 'centre for the reduction of the risk of war and prevention of surprise attack' has been made by the East.[23] An agreement was reached to convene—in the CSCE framework—a seminar on different aspects of military doctrine which could prove to be a valuable means for achieving the goal of more defensiveness in intention.[24] In addition the Eastern proposal seeks the inclusion of naval activities in the negotiations,[25] a topic so far rejected by the West.

The outcome of the CSBM Negotiations cannot yet be predicted. Nevertheless, the regime established by the Stockholm Document has achieved more openness and transparency in the military field. The results of the ongoing CSBM Negotiations will further enhance the present confidence-building regime of the 35 CSCE countries by improving information exchange, increasing openness and enabling more accurate verification of compliance. If the Vienna Negotiation on Conventional Armed Forces in Europe (CFE), obviously more complex and difficult in this respect, shows corresponding progress the two military alliances as well as the CSCE will see a new set of CBMs. Nevertheless it is doubtful whether they will be sufficiently far-reaching to reflect the exceptional changes in Europe, triggered by the political developments in the East. The rapidly changing political and military environment in Europe might require a qualitatively new generation of confidence- and security-building measures.

[20] Maresca, J. J., Chairman, US Delegation to the Negotiations on Confidence- and Security-Building Measures, *Optimism, Realism, Prudence to guide CSBM Approach* (Excerpt: State Department on CSBM negotiations), *USIS EUR*, 103 05/08/89, p. 1.
[21] *See Negotiations on Confidence- and Security-Building Measures in Europe,* Proposal submitted by the Delegations of Belgium, Canada, Denmark, France, FRG, Greece, Iceland, Italy, Luxembourg, the Netherlands, Norway, Portugal, Spain, Turkey, UK, USA, (CSCE/WV.1), Vienna, 9 Mar. 1989; and CSCE/WV.2 (note 9); as well as the proposal tabled by the NNA delegations as an informal paper (12 July 1989).
[22] See CSCE/WV.2 (note 9).
[23] Point 7 under Topic V 'Measures to improve openness and predictability of military activities, exchange of information and consultation; verification and control measures' in WV.2 (note 21), p. 7.
[24] The seminar took place in Vienna 16 Jan.–5 Feb. 1990 (see chapter 13).
[25] See: Points 1–11, Topic II CSBMs covering naval and air activities, WV.2 (note 21), pp. 3–4.

14. Multilateral and bilateral talks on chemical and biological weapons*

S. J. LUNDIN

I. Introduction

This chapter deals with the developments in 1989 which are related to the problems of the negotiations on the chemical weapons convention (CWC). The status of the Biological Weapons Convention (BWC) is also discussed. After the end of the Iraq–Iran War in 1988 the international community, in 1989, seemed more prepared to take measures against chemical weapons. A number of government-sponsored and private conferences and meetings were held, as were multilateral and bilateral meetings. The developments in 1989 related to chemical and biological weapons are also dealt with in chapter 4, to which the reader is referred for a discussion of the international activities to hinder the spread of chemical weapons. The following are the main events of 1989 which are discussed in this chapter:

1. The negotiations on a comprehensive, global prohibition of chemical weapons continued. Some political and technical progress was achieved, but the CWC was not finalized.

2. The January Paris Conference on the Prohibition of Chemical Weapons was perceived to have strengthened the 1925 Geneva Protocol, which prohibits the use of chemical and bacteriological weapons, and the extensive participation at the conference was seen to provide strong support and commitment for the negotiations on a CWC. However, the pace of the negotiations did not accelerate. Furthermore, the connection between nuclear and CW disarmament, which was made by some nations, caused concern.

3. The September Government–Industry Conference against Chemical Weapons in Canberra, Australia, mustered international support from the chemical industry for the negotiations on the CWC.

4. The bilateral US–Soviet CW talks proceeded well in 1989, and resulted *inter alia* in a Memorandum of Understanding on the exchange and verification of information about chemical weapons. This development is welcome if it serves to speed up the multilateral negotiating process.

Since 1968 deliberations and negotiations on chemical weapons (CW) have been conducted in Geneva by the *Ad Hoc* Committee on Chemical Weapons of the CD with the aim of obtaining a comprehensive, global

* Dr Thomas Stock, Dr Rabinder Nath and Fredrik Wetterqvist of the SIPRI CBW Programme have assisted in preparing references and data for this chapter. The references were gathered from the SIPRI CBW Programme Data Base and were also kindly provided by J. P. Perry Robinson, Science Policy Research Unit, University of Sussex, UK, from the Sussex–Harvard information bank.

convention prohibiting the development, production and stockpiling of chemical weapons and providing for the destruction within 10 years of all CW stockpiles. Together with the BWC, which entered into force in 1975, a chemical weapons convention (CWC) would complement the prohibition on the use, in practice only *first use*, of chemical and biological weapons which is contained in the 1925 Geneva Protocol, so that neither use nor possession of chemical and biological weapons would be possible in the future.

It was relatively easy to agree on the BWC at a time when biological weapons were not considered militarily useful and when intrusive verification of compliance with the provisions—a controversial matter at that time—was accordingly not considered necessary. However, chemical weapons have always been considered to have some military value. They have been stockpiled and ready for use since World War I, and in fact rare use has been made of them during that time. The negotiating 'background' of the negotiations on a CWC has thus been quite different from that of the BWC. In view of the intensification of efforts to obtain a CWC, particularly during 1989, it may be appropriate to provide a brief history of the CWC negotiations and a description of the envisaged convention.

The progress which has been made on a CWC is reported at regular intervals by the CD in the 'rolling text', which contains the text thus far agreed upon by the negotiators, who represent 40 nations. Where common understanding has not yet been achieved, alternative formulations are given within brackets or in notes. The rolling text will not be binding until a draft convention is signed and ratified. The 1989 report comprised 227 pages with Appendix I, the rolling text and its annexes, accounting for 117 pages. Appendix II, documents containing suggestions for areas where common understanding has not yet been reached, made up the remaining 110 pages.[1]

The provisions of the convention deal with sets of important areas of concern. The *definition* of 'chemical weapons' and of 'production facilities for chemical weapons' is one such area, and a crucial distinction needs to be made between chemicals which are used for chemical weapon agents and those which also have peaceful uses. The provisions for *destruction* of chemical weapons outline the order in which different types of stockpiled chemical weapons should be declared and destroyed during the 10-year destruction period, so that undiminished security can be maintained for the parties to the convention. Another major set of provisions deals with the *verification* of compliance in the form of declarations, destruction *per se* and non-production of chemical weapons; also included are provisions for mandatory on-site challenge inspections. Intimately connected to these provisions are those which deal with decision-making, organization and the resources required to implement the verification measures. The states parties are also obliged to adopt national measures to implement the provisions of the CWC. Finally there are provisions pertaining to *co-operation* in the field of chemistry and to the rendering of *assistance* to parties against which CW attacks have been made. Although a number of major political problems

---

[1] Conference on Disarmament document CD/952, 18 Aug. 1989.

regarding the provisions of the CWC have been dealt with, there are still some unresolved issues which relate to the provisions of the convention.

The question of the definition of various terms relates *inter alia* to the political goal that the CWC be a comprehensive treaty. If the convention were to cover only some chemical weapons, for example the nerve gases, it would be unverifiable and the door would be opened to the development, production and stockpiling of other chemical weapons. The 1925 Geneva Protocol, which prohibits the use of all chemical weapons, would also be weakened if the convention were not comprehensive. Other areas of definition which continue to present difficulties include the regulation of tear-gases, herbicides and CW precursors (i.e., a chemical from which another particular chemical can be made).

Another complex of problems in many of the provisions relates to the so-called 'purpose criterion' of the CWC which implies that all CW activities are prohibited unless they are undertaken for scientific, protective or other peaceful purposes. However, activities which were initially undertaken for peaceful reasons might ultimately result in the discovery of information which could potentially be utilized for CW production. This is of particular concern to the chemical industry, since it will be necessary in the future to verify that the chemical industry is not producing chemical weapons. The problems related to such verification, although real, seem to have been considerably exaggerated, in part because they *are* technically difficult to solve and may, to some extent, serve as a political smoke-screen to make the CWC appear impossible to achieve. The details of the composition of the three schedules of chemicals which are to be subject to different verification regimes also need to be worked out. There is a need to devote substantial technical effort to finalizing these provisions, but if the political will is present the problem should be possible to solve. It should also be noted that the chemical industry has expressed its willingness to contribute to this work. It is likely that the chemical industry genuinely wishes to avoid the stigma of being perceived as the intentional producer of chemical weapons. It is after all governments—not the chemical industry—which decide to acquire, produce and use chemical weapons.

Agreement has not yet been reached on the order of the destruction of existing chemical weapons. A serious difficulty in this area arose during 1989 in relation to the possible intention of the USA to continue to produce binary chemical weapons even during the first eight years of the existence of the CWC (see chapter 4). If maintained, this position may destabilize both the work on the CWC and attempts to contain the further spread of chemical weapons prior to the entry into force of the CWC. (In contrast to the nuclear Non-Proliferation Treaty (NPT) the CWC would mean that *all* nations would be obliged to forgo their chemical weapons.) On the other hand, agreement has been achieved on the main political issue of intrusive verification. In 1986 the USSR accepted the principle of on-site verification and particularly the US requirement that it should be possible to undertake on-site inspection anywhere, any time, within 24–48 hours. General understanding exists between the superpowers and their alliances, but many countries outside the WTO and NATO have not yet declared their position on the provision. The remaining problems concern the practical details of how such inspections are to be initiated and carried out. Also agreed upon in principle is the institution of an international authority for the international implementation of the provisions of the CWC. There is intended to be a Conference of the States Parties to the CWC and, under it, an Executive Council and a Technical Secretariat with an International Inspectorate.

One aspect of the CWC which has thus far attracted relatively little attention is the provision on national implementation measures, which will have to be instituted by the parties to the CWC.[2] The provisions on co-operation in the field of chemistry and assistance to states parties attacked with chemical weapons have also not yet been finalized.

A Preparatory Commission is to be instituted immediately after the signing of the CWC. This organ is then to prepare for the entry into force in a number of ways which are elaborated upon in CD document CD/952. The Preparatory Commission will have to deal with those details, mainly of a technical nature, which cannot currently be clearly foreseen in the negoti-ations. It will, for example, help parties to organize their declarations, prepare for the first Conference of the States Parties to the CWC and assist in the establishment of the Executive Council and the Technical Secretariat by *inter alia* arranging for the training of inspectors.

This brief discussion of the many technical and political problems related to a CWC, as well as the problems not mentioned here, may explain why each time a major political agreement has been reached which seems to remove the remaining obstacles to the CWC, some observers predict that another two to three years will be needed to complete the CWC. Such pre-dictions do not take into account the additional two or three years required by the ratification process and the agreed 10 years it will take after the entry into force of the CWC until all chemical weapons have been destroyed.

II. Negotiations in the Conference on Disarmament

Political developments in the negotiations were not conducive to conclusion of the CWC in 1989 despite the many international efforts outside the CD to facilitate its work. However, much technical work was done. Some of the important areas in which contributions were made are addressed below.

The negotiating mandate of the CD has not yet allowed the working out of a final draft convention, and in fact the text will not be final until it has been signed and ratified. Furthermore, one must realize that the final text of the convention will need to be scrutinized so that it is legally correct before the document is presented for signing.

---

[2] A study which addresses these problems will be published by SIPRI in 1990. See Stock, T. and Sutherland, R. (eds), *National Implementation of the Future Chemical Weapons Convention*, SIPRI Chemical & Biological Warfare Studies, no. 11 (Oxford University Press: Oxford, 1990), forthcoming.

It might be useful to mention one aspect of CW disarmament of which few may be aware. As in the case of the BWC, the CWC will not cover such matters as how chemical weapons may be safely handled. There will be no descriptions of how chemical weapons are to be destroyed, and the emissions which will be allowed from the destruction operations will not be specified. (States parties will, however, be prohibited from accomplishing destruction by burying or dumping the weapons.) No safety regulations for transporting these weapons will be worked out, and the conditions for storing them will not be described. Such regulations will have to be adopted on a national basis by the parties to the CWC. Transporting weapons over national borders may, on the one hand, not be allowed since the convention prohibits the 'transfer' of weapons. On the other hand, existing international regulations for safe transport at sea and on land for the purpose of destruction may deal with this difficulty. These problems are currently illustrated by the removal of the US CW stockpiles from the Federal Republic of Germany (see chapter 4). These matters may have to be given consideration before the CWC is concluded.

The 1988 session of the Committee on Chemical Weapons, under the Chairmanship of Ambassador Bogumil Sujka of Poland, formally ended with the 17 January–3 February 1989 session, and the results of its work were reported in CD document CD/881.[3] Despite the then available results of the Paris Conference and the declarations from particularly the USA and the USSR during 1988, the report did not contain any significant, new contributions although laborious work, on the verification and organizational issues in particular, had been conducted in the three working groups which deal with different aspects of the CWC. Appendix I of the 1988 report, the 'rolling text', comprised 100 pages, and Appendix II, documents to serve as a basis for further deliberations, comprised another 52 pages.

Ambassador Pierre Morel of France was appointed as Chairman of the *Ad Hoc* Committee on Chemical Weapons for the 1989 session as recommended by the CD in 1988. Work started on 16 February 1989, and the CD adopted a decision on the mandate for the *Ad Hoc* Committee on Chemical Weapons on 16 February. Again, despite general support of the negotiations which had been given at the Paris Conference, it was not possible to expand the mandate of the CD to include work on a final draft. Five working groups were instituted by the chairman to work on verification, legal and political questions, and institutional, technical and transitional issues, and the Committee also decided to establish a technical group on instrumentation, which later met three times. Besides the 40 negotiating nations of the CD, the number of observer nations increased from 12 to 26, probably as a result of the Paris Conference and other international efforts during the year.[4] It

---

[3] Conference on Disarmament document CD/881, 3 Feb. 1989. For SIPRI's report on the previous session see also SIPRI, *SIPRI Yearbook 1989: World Armaments and Disarmament* (Oxford University Press: Oxford, 1989), pp. 427–36.

[4] Austria, Bangladesh, Chile, Denmark, Democratic People's Republic of Korea, Ghana, Greece, Finland, Ireland, Iraq, Jordan, Libyan Arab Jamahiriya, New Zealand, Norway, Oman, Portugal, Qatar, Republic of Korea, Senegal, Spain, Syrian Arab Republic, Switzerland, Tunisia, Turkey, Viet Nam and Zimbabwe, see CD/952 (note 1), p. 2.

was decided that an inter-sessional, open-ended consultation would be held on 28 November–14 December and a session of the *Ad Hoc* Committee on 16 January–1 February 1990. It was recommended that the *Ad Hoc* Committee appoint Ambassador Carl-Magnus Hyltenius of Sweden as Chairman for the 1990 session. The work of the session was reported at the end of the 1989 summer session.[5]

As mentioned above no major political breakthrough occurred in 1989. In part this may have been because of the political review process going on in the USA under the new president. Only later in 1989 did the USA and the USSR issue their Memorandum of Mutual Understanding and meet in Malta.[6] However, in the absence of political progress, intensive work was done on clarifying and promoting a number of issues mostly of a technical character. Some of the more important results are reported below.

Much criticism was directed against the USA for not contributing in a decisive manner to the work of the *Ad Hoc* Committee. However, in a statement during the spring session of the CD the US representative responded that much work remained to be done for which the US delegation had a clear mandate. He referred particularly to the question of verification by challenge on which a number of delegations had neither given their views nor contributed to the work on shaping the necessary procedures and measures to implement verification on challenge.[7]

In 1988 it was decided that *national* trial inspections (NTIs) should be conducted with the aim of providing the negotiating and observer states with practical illustrations of the problems which may arise when on-site inspections are to be performed under a future CWC. The NTIs, most of which were conducted during 1989, involved the active participation of national chemical industrial facilities and were usually carried out according to the modalities decided upon during the previous session, as outlined in a CD working paper.[8] During 1989 NTIs were performed in 18 countries and reported upon in preparation for further national and, possibly, international trial inspections.[9] The reports were analysed and consulted in the Committee, and the experiences were reported in a CD working paper,[10] on the basis of which further consultations were undertaken in order to prepare for future *international* trial inspections. These were reported in a another

[5] See note 1.

[6] 'U.S. ready to destroy CW if Soviets, others join in effort' (text of Bush address to UN General Assembly), *Wireless File*, EUR-103 (United States Information Service, Press Section: Stockholm, 25 Sep. 1989), p. 13; Porth, J. S., 'December 7, weekly review of arms control: Bush makes concession on binary CW production', *News Backgrounder*, EUR-411, 7 Dec. 1989 (United States Information Service: Stockholm, 8 Dec. 1989), p. 2; see also 'The summit at sea: the key points', *International Herald Tribune*, 4 Dec. 1989, p. 1.

[7] Conference on Disarmament document CD/PV. 504, 18 Apr. 1989, p. 8.

[8] Conference on Disarmament document CD/CW/WP. 213, 19 Sep. 1988.

[9] In Conference on Disarmament documents the following countries were reported to have undertaken NTIs: Australia (CD/CW/WP.234), Austria (CD/CW/WP.260), Belgium (CD/CW/WP.243), Brazil (CD/CW/WP.226/Rev.1), Czechoslovakia (CD/CW/WP.229), the FRG (CD/CW/WP.235), Finland (CD/CW/WP.233), France (CD/CW/WP.240), the GDR (CD/CW/WP.227), Hungary (CD/CW/WP.223), Italy (CD/CW/WP.224), Japan (CD/CW/WP.228), the Netherlands (CD/CW/WP.251), Sweden (CD/CW/WP.216), Switzerland (CD/CW/WP.247), the UK (CD/CW/WP.249), the USA (CD/CW/WP.250) and the USSR (CD/CW/WP.225).

[10] Conference on Disarmament document CD/CW/WP.248/Rev.1, 23 Aug. 1989.

CD working paper.[11] At the end of 1989 several nations were still in the process of undertaking new or additional NTIs. Some of the preliminary results of the evaluations are listed below:

1. There is a need for guide-lines which address both the inspection activities that may be undertaken and the manner in which the so-called facility attachment, the basis for later inspections, should be negotiated.

2. There is a need for a definition of the term 'production facility'.[12]

3. Additional experience of auditing production processes and checking them by the use of internal or external test sampling and analyses is needed.

4. There is a need for further development of analytical equipment for easy and selective analysis of Schedule 1 chemicals.

5. The question of confidentiality needs to be dealt with further.

This summary illustrates the problems encountered and the experience gained. However, the reports on the trial inspections contain a wealth of details which are not easily summarized, and it would probably be worthwhile to undertake a more extensive study of the reports to get a better overview of the knowledge acquired. The results of such an analysis could then be presented to the CD, the chemical industry and national legislators. The inspections also served as a learning process and disseminated information about the CWC.

In a 1988 CD working paper the USSR suggested that CD member states might provide data relevant to the CWC; during 1989 data were provided by Australia, Austria, Czechoslovakia, Italy, Norway and the USSR.[13]

At the end of the spring session France followed up an earlier suggestion that a Scientific Advisory Council be instituted under the CWC[14] which would provide independent advice to the Executive Council and the Technical Secretariat of the CWC about technical and scientific developments of importance for the convention. While no definite decision was taken in the CD on the French proposal, some concern seems to exist about how such a body might best be included in the organization of the convention, particularly since the formal rights of the Council have not yet been fully clarified. The current basis for further deliberations is presented in Appendix II of the 1989 CD report, where emphasis is placed on the role of the Director General of the Technical Secretariat to appoint members of a Scientific Advisory Board (formerly the Scientific Advisory Council), which would primarily advise the Director General.[15]

The British delegation pointed to an important aspect of the CWC, the challenge inspections of military facilities, which is not often discussed in

[11] Conference on Disarmament document CD/CW/WP.257, 14 Aug. 1989.

[12] See note 11.

[13] The suggestion was made in the Soviet Working Paper, Conference on Disarmament document CD/828, 12 Apr. 1988. In 1989 responses appeared in the following documents: CD/907, 23 Mar. 1989; CD/CW/WP.238, 10 Apr. 1989; CD/949, 15 Aug. 1989; CD/CW/WP.220, 3 Feb. 1989; CD/CW/WP.221, 9 Feb. 1989; CD/CW/WP.264, 21 Nov. 1989.

[14] A Scientific Advisory Authority was first suggested by France in Conference on Disarmament document CD/747, 23 Mar. 1987; and a Scientific Advisory Council in Conference on Disarmament documents CD/CW/WP.242, and CD/916, 17 Apr. 1989.

[15] See CD/952 (note 1), Appendix II, p. 189.

the negotiations or in the general debate about the convention, presented in two working papers, one of which dealt with a suggestion about so-called *ad hoc* inspections.[16] The test object for the practice *ad hoc* inspection was an ammunition storage facility. A number of the objects to be verified under a CWC might actually be military facilities which may or may not relate to the military activities covered by the CWC. This poses the questions of how to identify whether stockpiled weapons are, or are not, chemical weapons, and how to inspect a storage facility which may contain both equipment which should be inspected under the convention as well as equipment which is exempted from inspection requirements. It is important in this context that *ad hoc* inspections not be misused in order to obtain information about military matters which are unrelated to the convention. Interesting questions in this context are whether military personnel can be used for the inspection of military facilities, to what extent and with what equipment.

One of the issues which has been raised intermittently during the negotiations on the CWC, but without evoking serious work on the problem, concerns the size and the cost of the entire International Organization for the CWC, and particularly the future Technical Secretariat. The reasons for this lack of effort are obvious. The negotiations have not yet led to a sufficiently clear picture of what such an organization will need to do. There is, for example, no clear indication yet as to how many industrial facilities, CW stockpiles or destruction facilities there are which will need to be monitored and how often. Above all there has been no serious discussion of the extent of the cost of the activities of the International Organization. The need to prepare some estimates of the size of the organization and of possible costs for it, particularly with regard to the verification question, is apparent, and several efforts have been made to address the problem. In the past the delegations of Canada, the Netherlands and the UK, in particular, have presented views on the matter,[17] and the Chairman of the *Ad Hoc* Committee made an attempt to allow a few experts to present their personal views at an informal gathering in order to provide input for further discussions.[18] While the time may not yet be ripe for a detailed discussion of the matter, it seems clear that there exist a number of practical approaches to the problem, which may ultimately result in a Technical Secretariat of a manageable size. One of the crucial questions here may be whether technical surveillance methods will be adequate to monitor stockpiles and moth-balled production facilities or whether large manpower resources will be required. While much work

[16] See Conference on Disarmament documents CD/909, 30 Mar. 1989 and CD/921, 14 June 1989.

[17] See, for example, Conference on Disarmament documents: Canada (CD/823, 31 Mar. 1989), the UK (CD/589, 11 Apr. 1985 and CD/769, 10 July 1987) and the Netherlands (CD/445, 7 Mar. 1984); 'Systems study of an international verification organization on chemical weapons', Canadian Government's work under contract by the University of Saskatchewan, Oct. 1987; Beck, H., 'Verifying the projected chemical weapons convention: a cost analysis', *AFES-Press Report*, no. 13, 1989; Sims, N. A. (ed.), *International Organization for Chemical Disarmament*, SIPRI Chemical & Biological Warfare Studies, no. 8 (Oxford University Press: Oxford, 1987). A comprehensive analysis of the matter of international verification seen from the industry's point of view is presented in Olson, K. B., 'The U.S. chemical industry can live with a chemical weapons convention', *Arms Control Today*, Nov. 1989, pp. 21–25.

[18] Conference on Disarmament document CD/CW/WP.244, 13 June 1989.

remains to be done in this area, these first attempts may serve as an impetus for further work on the problem and may help to combat the view that the International Organization could become far too cumbersome to function well. This hope is also supported by a Finnish working paper which presents the general outline of a verification laboratory.[19] Finland also indicated, at both the Paris Conference and the CD, that it intends to start a training course in verification techniques for Third World trainees. Individuals with such training will be indispensable once the CWC is ratified.[20] In this context it may be of interest to look at the implementation of the INF Treaty, which although bilateral rather than multilateral has instituted a verification organization (see chapter 12). The extent to which this organization and its experiences will be of value to the CWC remains to be seen.

One of the important problems of the CWC is how to guarantee to industry that no confidential information, technical know-how or commercial secrets will inadvertently be disclosed during verification activities or data reporting under the CWC. One of the working groups of the CD CW Committee devoted its efforts to this problem, and the delegations of France and the GDR presented working papers on the matter.[21] Work proceeded on the question of confidentiality, but complete agreement on the issue was not achieved with respect either to whether the material presented would suffice for the working out of regulations or to whether it would be sufficient to have only general references to the need for confidentiality in the relevant articles of the convention (articles VII and VIII), and allow the future International Organization to work out detailed guide-lines as part of its rules and regulations. Other organizations, such as the Organization for Economic Co-operation and Development, have worked out rules for confidentiality,[22] but these are not totally relevant since they relate to groups of nations and could be inadequate for the CWC, which might need to impose much stronger rules in order not to hamper the interests of individual parties to the Convention. It should be noted that the industrial representatives at the Canberra Conference supported the efforts undertaken in the negotiations, as is readily apparent in the industry declaration from the conference which is presented in appendix 14A.

For the third time an informal meeting of CD negotiators and representatives of the chemical industry was held in Geneva.[23] The Canberra Conference made it obvious that the chemical industry ought to take a much more active part in the negotiations. One way to do this might be to strengthen the national delegations to the CD by the addition of industrial experts. The fact that chemical industry has an international character makes it interesting to observe how this may affect the work on the CWC.

[19] Conference on Disarmament document CD/CW/WP.253, 26 June 1989

[20] Conference on Disarmament documents CD/PV.516, 11 July 1989 and CD/932, 12 July 1989.

[21] Conference on Disarmament documents CD/CW/WP. 215, 8 Dec. 1988 (GDR), and CD/901, 16 Mar. 1989 (France).

[22] 'Final report of the expert goup on model forms of agreement for the exchange of confidential data on chemicals', *OECD Environment Monographs*, no. 14 (Mar. 1988).

[23] 'News chronology', *Chemical Weapons Bulletin*, no. 6 (Nov. 1989), p. 4.

As mentioned above, some technical issues were dealt with by the *Ad Hoc* Committee's establishment of a technical group on instrumentation which held three meetings during 1989. The group investigated the need for particular instruments for different tasks and determined what exists and what will have to be developed before the CWC enters into force. It reported on its work in January 1990.[24]

A Canadian working paper tackled the problem of determining criteria for the different types of chemicals to be covered by the CWC and how they might be listed in the different schedules which will provide the basis for verification measures.[25] The working paper proposed three lists of chemicals which are more closely related to the risk chemicals pose to the CWC rather than, as now, three lists of chemicals grouped according to their toxicity. With respect to definitions, the head of the Soviet delegation stated at the UN that the USSR has now abandoned its reservations against toxins also being included in the CWC.[26] Also deserving of mention are the contributions by Finland and Norway on chemical analytical methods which can be used to investigate the presence or absence of chemical substances, precursors or CW agents, either in production facilities or at sites of alleged CW use.[27] The Finnish technical contributions to the CD over the years, the so-called 'blue books', now constitute a wealth of information which the Preparatory Commission, the subsequent International Organization and national authorities will be able to rely upon for the planning and performance of their tasks. A number of technical contributions were presented by other delegations during 1989, which reflected both the volume of technical issues that needs to be considered and also, perhaps, the fact that there was time to produce them in the absence of more substantial political progress. These contributions covered subjects such as the identification of chemical substances, definitions, schedules and toxic chemicals, verification of non-production related to new toxic compounds, toxin epidemiology, analytical techniques and one of the precursors for the nerve agent VX, pinacolyl alcohol.[28]

One of the substantial results on the technical side of the work in the CD in 1989 was achieved in Working Group 4 (Technical Working Group) of the *Ad Hoc* Committee on Chemical Weapons. In a new approach, all of the technical aspects of relevant chemicals were lifted out of the convention text

[24] 'Report of the Technical Group on Instrumentation', Conference on Disarmament document CD/CW/WP.272, 22 January 1990.

[25] Conference on Disarmament document CD/CW/WP. 231, 17 Mar. 1989.

[26] 'Statement by Soviet representative at the First Committee of the 44th session of the UN General Assembly', *Press Release*, Permanent Mission of the Soviet Union (New York), 30 Oct. 1989.

[27] Finland, 'Standard operation procedures for the verification of chemical disarmament, D.2 second proposal for procedures supporting the reference data base', CD/932, 12 July 1989; Finland, 'Verification laboratory: general features and instrumentation', CD/CW/WP. 253, 26 June 1989; Norway, 'Verification of alleged use of chemical weapons: a new approach for verification procedures', CD/936, 21 July 1989; Norway, 'Verification of a chemical weapons convention: headspace gas chromatography: a new technique in verification of alleged use of chemical warfare agents', CD/940, 31 July 1989.

[28] Conference on Disarmament documents CD/CW/WP. 214, 2 Dec. 1989; CD/CW/WP. 231, 17 Mar. 1989; CD/CW/WP. 239 11 Apr. 1989; CD/CW/WP. 254, 3 Aug. 1989; CD/CW/WP. 255, 9 Aug. 1989; CD/CW/WP. 259, 14 Aug. 1989.

per se and placed in an 'Annex on Chemicals'.[29] This annex now compiles some of the definitions, schedules of chemicals, guide-lines for schedules on chemicals, modalities for revision of schedules and guide-lines, and toxicity determinations. It was also suggested that Schedule 2 should consist of two parts. Part A would, as previously, list key precursors to actual or potential CW agents listed in Schedule 1, while Part B would list other chemicals which might pose a risk to the CWC. However, as mentioned above concern was expressed at the Canberra Conference about the lists of chemicals by noting that it would not be possible for the chemical industry to deal with families of chemicals. The purely technical aspects of the chemicals to be covered by the CWC have thereby become more apparent, and the content of the convention proper became more clear-cut by placing the following as annexes: the provisions for confidential information; declarations of chemical weapons and their verification; international verification of destruction; declarations and verification of CW production facilities; the regimes for verification of the chemicals on the schedules; the Preparatory Commission; and guide-lines on the International Inspectorate. The decision to work out the separate Annex on Chemicals seems to offer the possibility of obtaining, in the relatively near future, a convention text which is in a form that could be presented for signature by the negotiating parties. Further work on the applications contained in the annexes could then proceed against the background of this document and might perhaps be turned over in part to the Preparatory Commission which could be instituted as soon as the CWC had been signed. It is conceivable that such a procedure could facilitate the ratification process of the parties to the CWC by allowing more gradual access to the details of the convention. The experiences gained from the INF Treaty might be noted in this context. In this treaty, a basic agreement was worked out and the details, particularly those pertaining to verification methods, were settled after the treaty entered into force (see chapter 12). Thus it is interesting to note the approach of the INF Treaty to verification which included the realization that many unforeseen problems might appear during the verification process thus making it disadvantageous to decide in too great detail about methods and routines.

III. US–Soviet bilateral talks

Bilateral CW talks between the USA and the USSR took place at various levels of government, between Soviet Foreign Minister Eduard Shevardnadze and US Secretary of State James Baker and in December between Presidents George Bush and Mikhail Gorbachev. The progress achieved during these contacts was manifested in a Memorandum of Understanding issued after the September summit meeting in Wyoming, USA, regarding a bilateral verification experiment and data exchange, which will be conducted in two phases. Phase one will involve the exchange of general data on Soviet and US CW capabilities and a series of visits to

[29] See CD/952 (note 1), Appendix 1, pp. 49–64.

relevant military and civil facilities on their respective territories. In phase two the USA and the USSR will exchange data and permit on-site inspections to verify the accuracy of the data.[30]

The relations between the two superpowers on the issue of chemical weapons developed further with the speeches made by President Bush and Foreign Minister Shevardnadze at the opening session of the UN General Assembly (UNGA) in September. President Bush, confirming his commitment to a global, comprehensive ban on chemical weapons, proposed a number of actions which could be undertaken by the two superpowers in order to support the conclusion of a global comprehensive CWC. He proposed to: (a) destroy, before and within the first eight years of a CWC, 98 per cent of the US stockpiles if the USSR were to join the convention; (b) destroy, within 10 years, all US chemical weapons once all nations capable of building chemical weapons 'sign that total ban treaty'; and (c) destroy, even while working on a treaty, 80 per cent of the US stockpiles if the USSR were to join the USA in cutting chemical weapons to an equal level and on verification that stockpiles were destroyed.[31] The President also believed that it would be possible to achieve a level of verification that would provide the confidence required to go ahead with the ban.

Foreign Minister Shevardnadze welcomed the US proposals on the following day and stated that the USSR was ready to: (a) assume mutual obligations with the USA prior to the conclusion of a CWC; (b) cease production of chemical weapons, as already done, including binary chemical weapons; (c) bilaterally, radically reduce or completely destroy chemical weapons as a step towards global destruction of chemical weapons; (d) renounce the use of chemical weapons; and (e) institute rigorous verification of cessation of production of chemical weapons.[32]

Since both declarations endorsed a global, comprehensive CWC, they met with positive responses. However, it was soon pointed out that the proposed undertakings did not really go much beyond those previously made by the two countries.[33] The USA, for instance, was already committed by law to destroy all 'unitary' chemical weapons by 1997,[34] which in practice could mean that under a CWC only the binary chemical weapons which had been produced prior to entry into force of the CWC would remain to be destroyed. Also, a US spokesman soon objected that it would not be possible to cease production of binary weapons.[35] Furthermore, a newspaper report claiming that the US Administration had in fact decided to continue

[30] See, for example, 'The Wyoming papers: documents from the foreign ministers' meeting', *Arms Control Today*, Oct. 1989, pp. 22–25.

[31] See 'U.S. ready to destroy CW if Soviets, others join in effort' (note 6).

[32] 'Statement by Soviet Foreign Minister Shevardnadze at the 44th session of the UN General Assembly', *Press Release*, Permanent Mission of the Soviet Union (New York), 26 Sep. 1989, p. 6.

[33] See, for example, Harris, E. D., 'US proposal on chemical weapons: not much', *New York Times*, 26 Sep. 1989; Smith, R. J., 'Experts differ on chemical arms plan', *Washington Post*, 26 Sep. 1989, p. A10.

[34] See, for example, *SIPRI Yearbook 1989* (note 3), pp. 104–105.

[35] Fairhall, D., 'Bush rejects proposal to eliminate gas weapons', *The Guardian*, 28 Sep. 1989.

binary CW production even after the entry into force of the CWC[36] evoked serious concern about US intentions with respect to the CWC.[37] The information immediately elicited a Soviet response which stated that if it were true that the USA planned to continue binary production, this approach would be a set-back for the CW negotiations and would encourage CW proliferation. The USSR reiterated that it had stopped production of chemical weapons in February 1987.[38] The ambiguous character of the information about US CW binary production was also apparent in an October statement by the Director of the US Arms Control and Disarmament Agency (ACDA), which repeated what President Bush said to the UNGA but which did not make clear whether the USA wishes to retain the option to produce chemical weapons under the CWC.[39]

At the thirteenth bilateral meeting between the delegations of the USA and the USSR in New York on 30 October–3 November it was agreed that work should be continued on the implementation of the Memorandum of Understanding which had resulted from the Wyoming meeting, that arrangements should begin to be made for the exchange of information about the Soviet and US CW stockpiles and that methods to verify the information should be prepared.[40] At the Malta summit meeting between Presidents Bush and Gorbachev—which was not intended to result in concrete disarmament proposals—the implication was nevertheless made that some bilateral disarmament agreements might be ready to be signed by the summit meeting in June 1990, including the START and CW agreements.[41]

The possibility that the USA might intend to continue binary CW production even under a CWC was not a total surprise since the USA had made guarded comments on earlier French proposals in the CD which would have allowed a state party to retain so-called security stocks and even keep a production capability for CW modernization during the 10-year destruction period. The USA has also long advocated the need to retain a CW retaliatory capability during the destruction period. The reaction to the US position was strong among both the negotiators and other commentators. It was pointed out that, above all, this approach would induce nations which did not already have chemical weapons to acquire them prior to the entry into force of the CWC. This would in turn lead to CW proliferation rather than to the

[36] Smith, J. R., 'U.S. to keep producing poison gas', *Washington Post*, 9 Oct. 1989, pp. A1, A8; see also Gordon, M. R., 'As oratory fades, obstacles to chemical arms pact multiply', *New York Times*, 31 Oct. 1989, p. 13.

[37] 'Washington Post: USA setzen Produktion von C-Waffen in jedem Fall fort,' *Neues Deutschland*, 10 Oct. 1989, p. 5; Pringle, P. 'Treaty ban will not stop America from making nerve gas', *The Independent*, 10 Oct. 1989, p. 14.

[38] 'Soviet spokesman on US plans to keep producing poison gas', Moscow, 10 Oct. 1989, TASS, *Press Bulletin*, no. 191(1929), 12 Oct 1989, isssued by Permanent Mission of the Soviet Union (Geneva), pp. 4–5.

[39] Interview with Lehman, R. F., Director of the U.S. Arms Control and Disarmament Agency, on 12 Oct. 1989, Mendelsohn, J. and Guldin, R., 'Arms control in Lehman's terms: director of ACDA surveys an active agenda', *Arms Control Today*, Nov. 1989, pp. 6–7.

[40] '30 Oct.–3 Nov. 1989, The US and USSR held the 13th round of bilateral talks in New York', *Arms Control Reporter*, Nov. 1989, pp. 704.B.384.43–44.

[41] 'Bush makes concession on binary CW production', *News Backgrounder*, EUR-411, 7 Dec. 1989 (United States Information Service: Stockholm, 8 Dec. 1989), p. 2; see also Adams, P., 'Malta quickens pace of arms control talks', *Defense News*, 11 Dec. 1989, p. 4.

phasing out of possession.[42] To an outside observer the question arises: Which security interests would benefit by this development? Would the efforts to hinder the spread of chemical weapons gain from such a move, or would the advantage instead be given to those who perceive a need to be able to retaliate with chemical weapons when these weapons have been introduced into a regional conflict?

The political situation appears similar to that of the NPT, which allows the five members of the Security Council to retain their nuclear weapons but means that the other parties to the treaty have forsworn the right to acquire nuclear weapons. As a consequence of this the so-called threshold states have not acceded to the treaty, and the risk is that a similar situation may arise with the CWC, which might even lead to the failure to achieve a CWC. At the end of 1989 it seemed, however, that the Malta meeting had led to a US offer to halt binary CW production, upon entry into force of a multilateral CWC, on the condition that the USSR accepted the US proposals made by President Bush in his September speech to the UNGA. At the Malta meeting President Bush also proposed that the USA and the USSR sign an agreement at the June 1990 summit meeting to reduce the CW stockpiles of both countries to 20 per cent of the current US level.[43] According to the press briefing at the conclusion of the Malta meeting, the USSR prioritizes a total ban on chemical weapons.[44]

IV. Paris Conference on the Prohibition of Chemical Weapons

The year essentially began with the highly publicized Paris Conference on the Prohibition of Chemical Weapons on 7–11 January 1989. The aims of the Conference, which was hosted by France as the depositary for the 1925 Geneva Protocol, were to: (a) reaffirm the 1925 Geneva Protocol which prohibits the use of chemical weapons; (b) support the Geneva negotiations on a CWC; (c) strengthen the role of the UN Secretary-General in investigating the alleged use of chemical weapons; and (d) contribute to restrictions on export of technology and chemicals for chemical weapons.[45] The communiqué from the conference and a report on the events leading up to the conference were published in the *SIPRI Yearbook 1989*.[46] The following are the main results of the conference:

1. A total of 149 countries participated, and 12 previous non-signatories announced that they would adhere to the 1925 Geneva Protocol.

[42] See, for example, *SIPRI Yearbook 1989* (note 3), p. 107.
[43] See Porth (note 6); see also 'The summit at sea: the key points', *International Herald Tribune*, 4 Dec. 1989, p. 1.
[44] See Porth (note 6), p. 1.
[45] Morel, P. 'The Paris Conference on the Prohibition of Chemical Weapons', *Disarmament*, vol. 12, no. 2, pp. 127–44; see also Herby, P., 'The Paris Conference on Chemical Weapons', *Chemical Weapons Convention Bulletin*, no. 3 (Feb. 1989), p. 12.
[46] See *SIPRI Yearbook 1989* (note 3).

2. A number of the participating nations declared that they did not possess chemical weapons (see also appendix 4A).

3. A unanimously agreed-upon communiqué was issued which called for 'redoubled' efforts to conclude the CWC and which confirmed the importance of the 1925 Geneva Protocol.

The Paris Conference was thus successful in the sense that no country opposed its conclusions, and wide, clear political support for the CWC was thereby given. It was also of importance that so many nations participated, including those which had just fought a war in which chemical weapons had been used. A number of important statements were made which represented new policy commitments on, for example, the destruction of chemical weapons, the non-possession of chemical weapons, the instituting of export restrictions, and so on (see also chapter 4.)

A dissenting note was, however, expressed during the Paris Conference even if it was not clearly reflected in the communiqué. A number of Arab countries including Algeria, Egypt, Iraq, Libya, Morocco, Saudi Arabia, Syria and Tunisia linked chemical and nuclear weapons in statements to the effect that they regarded the acquisition of chemical weapons as a possible option for them as long as no attempts were made to keep the Middle East free of nuclear as well as chemical weapons (i.e., as long as Israel failed to join the NPT).[47] Some of the Arab states accused Israel of possessing chemical weapons, while Israel maintained that Iraq, Libya and Syria possess these weapons. After the conference the Arab League, representing 22 Arab countries, underscored the connection between chemical and nuclear weapons and made reference to the final document of the 1978 First Special Session of the United Nations General Assembly which gave first priority to nuclear disarmament.[48] One of the arguments which has been made for the Arab acquisition of chemical weapons was that chemical weapons were perceived as serving as a deterrent to the use of nuclear weapons, which are claimed to be present in the region.[49]

As time went on it became clear that the Paris Conference had not, during 1989, provided the expected impetus to hasten the pace of the CD negotiations, which was one of the results desired from the Conference.

V. Canberra Government–Industry Conference against Chemical Weapons

After consultations with the USA and other states, Australia took the initiative of arranging a conference to facilitate the conclusion of the CWC. The plan to hold the conference was announced by Australian Foreign Minister Gareth Evans in a press release on 2 March 1989, and by US

---

[47] See Morel and Herby (note 45); Tréan, C., 'Paris Conference outlaws use of chemical weapons', *Guardian Weekly*, 22 Jan. 1989, p. 13.

[48] Communiqué on the Paris Conference issued by the Council of the League of Arab States at its extraordinary session of 12 Jan. 1989.

[49] See, for example, Ezz, E. A., 'The Chemical Weapons Convention: particular concerns of developing countries', *UNIDIR Newsletter*, vol. 2, no. 1 (Mar. 1989), p. 7.

Secretary of State Baker in his address to the Negotiation on Conventional Armed Forces in Europe (CFE) on 6 March 1989.[50] The Government–Industry Conference against Chemical Weapons took place in Canberra on 18–22 September 1989. The aim of the Canberra Conference was to promote understanding and co-operation between governments and industry on the practical issues to be covered by the CWC and the implementation of the CWC. In response to concerns which had been expressed in different contexts, it was particularly stressed that the meeting was in no way to be seen as a substitute for the negotiations in Geneva but rather as a complement to them.[51] In a CD working paper the so-called 'group of 21' (i.e., the 21 neutral and non-aligned member states among the 40 members of the CD) stressed that the Canberra Conference should neither undermine the negotiations on a CWC nor support non-proliferation measures which could hamper international co-operation for peaceful purposes.[52]

Delegations from 66 countries, governments, the UN, the Commission of the European Communities (EC), the European Chemical Industry Federation (CEFIC) and the International Federation of Chemical Energy and General Workers Union (ICEF) participated. Two independent researchers were also invited to present their views about the remaining problems in the negotiations and the implementation of the future CWC. Two workshops were conducted at the conference: Concluding the Chemical Weapons Convention: Government–Industry Co-operation and Implementing the Convention. An industry forum was also held at the conference, at which representatives from the chemical industries of a number of countries presented their views and adopted a statement regarding industry support of the CWC (see appendix 14A).[53] The conference concluded with presentations of the views of the heads of the participating delegations and their industrial representatives.

The governments presented their views on the CWC in a constructive way, but concerns were voiced by a number of representatives about the need for peaceful co-operation and support in the field of chemistry and about non-discriminatory measures against countries which lack defence against chemical weapons and which need to develop their chemical industries. Views were also expressed on the necessity of maintaining security and a military balance in areas where nuclear and chemical

[50] See Conference on Disarmament document CD/897, 8 Mar. 1989 (containing the text of a press release issued by the Australian Minister for Foreign Affairs and Trade, Senator G. Evans on 7 Mar. 1989), p. 2; see also 'U.S urges Soviets to join move against chemical weapons', Baker statement at CFE meeting (3430), *Wireless File*, EUR-104, 6 Mar. 1989, pp. 3–9. For a more comprehensive report of the conference, see Robinson, J. P., 'Review: the Canberra Conference', *Chemical Weapons Convention Bulletin*, no. 8 (Nov. 1989), p. 16.

[51] Australian Minister for Foreign Affairs and Trade, Senator Gareth Evans, 'Banning chemical weapons through government–industry co-operation', opening address at the Government–Industry Conference against Chemical Weapons, document GICCW/P/2, Canberra, 18–22 Sep. 1989.

[52] Conference on Disarmament document CD/951, 17 Aug. 1989.

[53] Report of the Chairman Tom Reynolds, Industry Forum, Government–Industry Conference against Chemical Weapons, document GICCW/P/6, Canberra, 18–22 Sep. 1989.

weapons might be used.[54] A number of countries made statements that they did not have and did not intend to acquire chemical weapons (see also appendix 4A). However, clear concerns were presented with respect to some of the details of the CWC, for example, the composition of the schedules in the context of which the view was expressed that it would be preferable to list single, identifiable substances rather than families of chemicals in order to make verification manageable.[55] The importance to the chemical industry of confidentiality under the CWC, long recognized in the CD negotiations, was also strongly advocated.[56]

A number of national initiatives to support the negotiations on a CWC were also made. At the opening of the conference Australian Foreign Minister Evans announced the intention of his country to create the nucleus of a national authority for the implementation of a CWC, an Australian national CWC secretariat,[57] and several other countries stated that they had already undertaken similar measures or intended to do so. The USA disclosed its intention to suggest the institution of a 'technical experts group' to be of service to the Committee on Chemical Weapons of the CD.[58] The group would provide technical advice and identify research necessary for verification and for problems related to the destruction of stockpiles. The representative of the USSR suggested that special 'assistance groups' made up of industry experts and researchers should be established to facilitate the solution of concrete technical problems in the negotiations.[59]

In summary the conference seems to have met the expectations of the organizers. The industry representatives received an informed presentation of the CWC, and a representative gathering of chemical industry organizations supported the finalization of a CWC. The chemical industry announced its intention to participate more actively in the CD negotiations in order to assist in working out technical problems. The formation of an informal industry forum was suggested in order to follow the negotiations and to meet more often than the current annual meeting of industry experts in Geneva.[60] A number of countries, including those not represented at the CD, expressed support for the CWC, and representatives of countries in Asia and the Pacific got a clearer picture of the work of the CD. Some of the earlier concerns that the Canberra Conference might attempt to adopt specific measures against the spread of chemical weapons or serve as an alternative

[54] See, for example, Canberra Conference statements by Egypt (document GICCW/P/50; p. 265); Israel (document GICCW/P/66, p. 368); Iraq (document GICCW/P/51, p. 349) and Iran (document GICCW/P/32, p. 321).

[55] Statement by the Chemical Industry Union of France, Government-Industry Conference against Chemical Weapons, document GICCW/P/61, Canberra, 18–22 Sep. 1989, p. 275.

[56] See, for example, Reynolds (note 53).

[57] See Evans (note 50), p. 10.

[58] Clarke, R. A, 'Discussant's paper', Workshop 1, Concluding the Chemical Weapons Convention: government–industry cooperation; and Session B, Outstanding questions: What needs to be done by government and by industry?, Government–Industry Conference against Chemical Weapons, Final Record, document GICCW/WSI/2, Canberra, 18–22 Sep. 1989, p. 59.

[59] Soviet Delegation, Government–Industry Conference against Chemical Weapons, document GICCW/WSI/8, Canberra, 18–22 Sep. 1989, p. 105.

[60] See Reynolds (note 52).

to the CD did not materialize. The effort put into arranging the conference thus seems to have been well worthwhile.

VI. Other international CW meetings

During 1989 Australia also took other initiatives to enhance the efforts to abolish chemical weapons, one of which was to arrange a Chemical Weapons Regional Seminar in Canberra on 2–4 August at which 23 nations from South-East Asia and the South Pacific participated. At the conference statements were made that the countries in the region do not possess chemical weapons and that this situation ought to remain unchanged. Support for the CWC was also given, but concern was expressed that small countries which do not have chemical weapons would have neither the incentive nor the resources to join the convention, in spite of its political value. Representatives of the chemical industries of the region expressed their support for the CWC.[61]

The General Assembly of the Federation of Asian Chemical Societies met in Brisbane on 29 August and supported the destruction of chemical weapons, a world-wide ban on production and measures to guard against future production. The members—professional chemical societies from 21 countries from Jordan to Japan and Fiji—also strongly supported the BWC and international efforts to eliminate nuclear weapons.[62]

Other national and international meetings and conferences which dealt with chemical and biological weapons were held in 1989. The American Association for the Advancement of Science, for example, arranged a discussion of CW developments in early 1989.[63] In May the International Commission of Health Professionals held its International Conference on Combatting the Use of Chemical and Biological Weapons in Geneva,[64] which presented views as to how the cause of the CWC might best be advanced. The treatment of individuals wounded by chemical weapons in Iran and other incidents of poisoning by CW agents were presented.

VII. Chemical weapon-free zones

Several countries expressed interest in chemical weapon-free zones (CWFZs) in 1989. Discussion continued on the Australian initiative to institute a CWFZ in South-East Asia.[65] Further efforts to obtain a CWFZ in Europe have not occurred, but in the CD Czechoslovakia praised the value

---

[61] Chemical Weapons Regional Seminar, *Report*, Canberra, 2–4 Aug. 1989.

[62] AAP, 'Asian chemists commit support for international ban on chemical weapons', *Press Release*, 12 Sep. 1989.

[63] American Association for the Advancement of Science, Program on Science, Arms Control and National Security, *Implementing a Global Chemical Weapons Convention*, Proceedings from a 1989 Annual Meeting Symposium, San Francisco, 16 Jan. 1989.

[64] International Commission of Health Professionals, *Preliminary Report on International Conference on Combatting the Use of Chemical and Biological Weapons*, Geneva, 24–27 May 1989.

[65] See, for example, information that Australia and Papua New Guinea talked about prohibiting chemical weapons in the Asia-Pacific region, 'Australia and PNG in CW talks', *Jane's Defence Weekly*, 25 Feb. 1989; see also *SIPRI Yearbook 1989* (note 3), p. 113.

of previous initiatives taken by members of the WTO and the Social Democratic Party of the FRG to institute such a zone in Central Europe.[66] Romania tabled a working paper at the CD which contained the text of the meeting of the Political Consultative Committee of the WTO on the topic of a Europe free from nuclear and chemical weapons.[67] Mention of a CWFZ in the Balkans was also made during 1989.[68] In the CD Viet Nam supported CWFZ efforts for Europe and the Balkans and the Australian initiative to hinder the spread of chemical weapons in South-East Asia and the Pacific.[69] At both the Paris Conference and the Canberra Conference, Israel repeated its 1988 call for a CWFZ to be instituted in the Middle East as a confidence-building measure (CBM) in order to make it possible for the countries in the region to accede to a CWC.[70] At the Paris Conference South Africa invited African nations to a regional conference which aimed to establish a zone free of chemical and biological weapons.[71] At a meeting in Dublin, Ireland, a group of Arab and European parliamentarians called for the establishment of a CWFZ in the Middle East, asked Israel to sign the NPT and urged all countries in the region to refrain from producing, stockpiling or using nuclear, chemical or bacteriological weapons.[72] At the Canberra Conference North Korea suggested the adoption of 'a joint declaration with South Korea on the establishment of a zone free from chemical as well as nuclear weapons throughout the Korean peninsula as one of the measures in support of the negotiations on the CW Convention'.[73] As reported in the *SIPRI Yearbook 1988*, discussions of CWFZs served in some instances as an entry into further deliberations about more general regional political problems.[74] A similar thought was actually expressed by the Israeli delegate at the Canberra Conference.[75]

VIII. UN investigation of alleged use of chemical weapons

On behalf of the UN Secretary-General the UN Group of Experts recommended procedures and measures to enable the Secretary-General to investigate allegations of the use of chemical, bacteriological (biological)

---

[66] Statement made by the Government of Czechoslovakia on 5 Jan. 1989, Conference on Disarmament document CD/878, 18 Jan. 1989, pp. 1–3.

[67] Conference on Disarmament document CD/934, 18 July 1989.

[68] Hentges, V., 'Konkrete Schritte für Balkan ohne Kern- und Chemiewaffen', *Neues Deutschland*, 26 Apr. 1989, p. 6.

[69] Conference on Disarmament document CD/PV.498, 28 Mar. 1989, pp. 9–11.

[70] See Canberra statements (note 53); Mortimer, E., 'Israel hints it keeps chemical weapons as defensive measure', *Financial Times*, 10 Jan. 1989, p. 1.

[71] Urges African chemical, hunger talks', MB1001163089, *The Citizen* (Johannesburg), 10 Jan. 89, p. 2, in FBIS-AFR-89-008, 12 Jan. 1989, pp. 6–7.

[72] Parliamentary Association for Euro-Arab Co-operation and Arab Interparliamentary Union, 'Euro-Arab Parliamentary Dialogue, Final Communiqué', Dublin, 11–14 Sep. 1989. It can be noted that an Egyptian resolution, 'Establishment of a nuclear-weapon-free zone in the region of the Middle East,' A/44/108, 15 Dec. 1989, was adopted by the UN General Assembly by consensus (i.e., Israel did not oppose the resolution).

[73] Statement by the Democratic People's Republic of Korea, Government–Industry Conference against Chemical Weapons, document GICCW/P/49, Canberra, 18–22 Sep. 1989, p. 313.

[74] See, for example, SIPRI, *SIPRI Yearbook 1988: World Armaments and Disarmament* (Oxford University Press: Oxford, 1988), p. 115.

[75] See statement by Israel (note 54).

and toxin weapons.[76] The group was chaired by General Esmat Ezz of Egypt and had as members experts from Bulgaria, France, Sweden, the USA and the USSR. The report presents a thorough description of how such an investigation may be carried out. Nine appendices of detailed suggestions are given. The report also proposes that upon entry into force of the CWC the Secretary-General will co-operate with the organs of the convention in carrying out investigations. Strong support for strengthening the role of the Secretary-General in undertaking such investigations was given during the Paris Conference and mentioned in the communiqué of the conference. The report of the UN Expert Group could presumably serve an important function in working out the CWC verification measures on alleged CW use.

IX. Biological Weapons Convention

A number of allegations of acquisition of biological weapons or of the capability to acquire them were made during 1989. Even if US allegations that the USSR had violated the BWC were toned down, the 10-year-old allegation of production of anthrax in Sverdlovsk for biological warfare purposes is still unresolved. An increased and potentially dangerous mistrust of the ability to rely on the BWC as an obstacle to new development and production of biological weapons seems thus to be developing. This implies a continued need of efforts to strengthen the BWC.

As reported in previous *SIPRI Yearbooks,* for confidence-building purposes the 1986 Review Conference of the BWC decided to institute an exchange of information on activities undertaken by the parties to the BWC which were related to the convention.[77] Such an exchange is to take place on 15 April each year and, in the first year, also on 15 October. Information is to be sent to the UN Department for Disarmament Affairs for further dissemination to the states parties. The following areas are particularly subject to the information exchange: (*a*) the existence and location of high-risk level containment facilities, (*b*) activities related to the BWC, (*c*) publication of research results and the like relating to the BWC, and (*d*) announcement of meetings and conferences dealing with subjects related to the BWC. Three information exchanges have been conducted, and efforts have been made or are under way to evaluate the results of these exchanges.[78] SIPRI will publish a study in 1990 on the subject.[79] Some of the results of the information-exchange efforts are briefly mentioned here.

Only 26 of the 85 states parties to the BWC have provided the requested information, and not all of them have done so at all times. Among those

---

[76] Informal Joint Working Paper of the Group of Qualified Experts Established in Pursuance of General Assembly Resolution 42/37C, documents GEXP/CRP.14/Rev. 2, 17 Feb. 1989, pp. 1–31, and GEXP/1989/1/Rev. 1, 10 Aug. 1989, pp. 1–6; 'Chemical and bacteriological (biological) weapons', report of the Secretary-General, UN General Assembly A/44/561, 4 Oct. 1989, Add. 1 and 2.

[77] See, for example, *SIPRI Yearbook 1988* (note 74), p. 112.

[78] Roffey, R., [*Analysis of the Information Exchange for the BW Convention: Third Reporting Occasion*], Swedish National Defence Research Institute, FOA D 40208-4.4. Sep. 1989 (in Swedish).

[79] Geissler, E., (ed.), *Strengthening the Biological Weapons Convention by Confidence-Building Measures,* SIPRI Chemical & Biological Warfare Studies, no. 10 (Oxford University Press: Oxford, 1990).

which have provided information are the five permanent members of the UN Security Council and a number of industrialized countries. However, only two countries from Asia, one from Africa and none from South America have delivered the requested information. There is perhaps cause for concern that none of the other 85 parties to the BWC has delivered any information. There may be several reasons for this, especially if the request for information was not perceived as binding on those parties which in fact do not have information to provide. It is nevertheless useful that the absence of information, as well as more comprehensive information, be reported and, at least from time to time, repeated in order to induce the fullest possible confidence in the information which has been declared by the parties.

There are also large differences in the extent to which different items are covered by the information exchange. Again, there may be various reasons for this. Larger countries with many activities in the fields related to the convention may, for example, simply miss some available information about activities which did not receive extensive national publicity. Judgements may also have been made about the relevance of the information to the convention. As a matter of fact no definition of what was to be considered as 'relevant to the Convention' was provided either during the 1986 Review Conference or by the Technical Expert Group which worked out the modalities for the reporting of information. This may be an issue for the 1991 Review Conference.

In view of the increased mistrust of the BWC it may be appropriate to discuss possible verification measures for the BWC which could either be included in the current information exchange process or which might serve as the basis for suggestions to be discussed at the 1991 Review Conference. It is often argued that such a discussion should be delayed until the negotiations on the CWC are finalized. While the results of the CWC negotiations will certainly be of relevance, there are differences between the two types of weapon which imply some differences, for example, in the case of technical verification methods, and those could at least be discussed and planned for. It can be argued that a continued, more intrusive and formalized system for exchange of verifiable information about activities 'related to the Convention' should be instituted under the BWC. There may be an increased need to observe the general development and application of genetic engineering and other biological techniques even for civilian purposes, to look at the structure of industry which is based on biological techniques, and to pay attention to the rapid internationalization of these techniques. A CBM that might significantly contribute to the establishment of future verification measures under the BWC would be the resolution of the Sverdlovsk problem between the USA and the USSR (see chapter 4).

X. Conclusions

In 1989 the efforts to promote the work on a comprehensive global CWC were profound and much publicized, with the Paris Conference to strengthen the Geneva Protocol and the Canberra Government–Industry Conference against Chemical Weapons being the most visible of the multilateral efforts. The bilateral discussions between the USA and the USSR were unusually productive. At the Malta meeting between Presidents Bush and Gorbachev in December, President Bush suggested that a bilateral agreement on chemical weapons be signed at the next summit meeting in June 1990.

The two international conferences resulted in a wider participation by states which had not previously been directly involved in the CW negotiations. However, the Paris Conference pledge that the CD negotiation efforts be redoubled was not realized, at least not on the political level—despite express support given by President Bush in reaffirming his commitment to abolish chemical weapons. The Canberra Conference created an increased awareness of the role of the chemical industry and seems to have secured its more active participation in the negotiations. Most important, a representative group of industrialists agreed upon a statement in support of the work on the CWC. Much useful work was done in the CD on a technical level, but it was obvious—particularly after the Canberra Conference—that some technical approaches which have thus far been given preference may need continued careful consideration, in particular the different schedules of chemicals. Several other problems also remain unsolved.

The need for decisive political decisions on the CWC and the amount of (mainly) technical details that remain to be worked out make it imprudent to forecast the date on which the CWC will be open for signature. It is possible that this could take place within one to three years, but this assumes that there is strong political support for working out a basic convention while leaving some technical details to be worked out by the Preparatory Commission. It could, however, take many years if a detailed, completely 'watertight' CWC has to be worked out, as argued by some. None the less the speed with which the bilateral INF Treaty materialized and was implemented gives some hope that the even more complicated, multilateral CWC will be finalized in the not too distant future. (Other factors which influence the work on the CWC are described in chapter 4.)

If the USA maintains the position that it needs to be able to produce binary chemical weapons even during the first eight years of the CWC, work on the CWC may well slow down while other means are sought to stabilize the situation, such as more measures to halt the spread of chemical weapons. Another problem would arise if it became technically difficult for the USA and the USSR to live up to their commitment to destroy all of their chemical weapons within 10 years after the entry into force of the CWC. Other prospective parties to the CWC, whether or not they themselves possess chemical weapons, will most certainly need to be assured that destruction is indeed possible and has taken place. This difficulty may in itself serve as a reminder to those other states which may currently possess chemical weapons or which are contemplating acquiring them. A time will come when these weapons will also have to be destroyed in a lengthy process at costs far surpassing those of obtaining them. These stockpiles will constitute constant hazards to the population and environment although the degree of danger may vary widely from country to country depending on the geographical location of the stockpiles. The argument that binary weapons might meet the above concerns is valid only if these weapons prove to be dependable. In view of the long-standing technical difficulties with the functioning of these sophisticated weapons, they may ultimately turn out to be less effective chemical weapons than has been supposed.

Another source of concern for the finalization of the CWC is the possible bilateral CW agreement between the USA and the USSR which would make it possible for them to eliminate their mutual threat, but which would also imply retaining a retaliatory capability. The preliminary reaction from the meeting between Presidents Bush and Gorbachev indicates that at least the USA may want a bilateral agreement. Although current bilateral efforts are said to explicitly support and facilitate the finalization of a global comprehensive CWC, work on the CWC which is too protracted could lead to a situation in which Soviet and US CW stocks were reduced but not abolished and in which chemical weapons continued to spread in the rest of the world. In any case no decisive breakthrough seems to have occurred during 1989 that would make the conclusion of the CWC more easily predictable.

Yet another factor of importance for the work on the CWC is the future of the BWC. The fact that the information exchange is far from fully developed and does not engage all of the parties to the BWC probably indicates that very few parties have any activities which they perceive as relevant to the BWC and about which they should exchange information. It seems improbable that the majority of these parties are intentionally neglecting their responsibilities under the BWC or hiding information on activities which would imply a violation of the convention. It would, however, remove any ambiguity if all the parties took part in the information exchange and reported even the absence of such activities in order to enhance confidence in the convention. The long-standing issue of US allegations of Soviet production of anthrax at Sverdlovsk for biological weapon purposes, in violation of the BWC, has not been clarified. This may be a matter which is ripe for clarification in the present atmosphere of easing tensions. After the Soviet admission of the function of the Krasnoyarsk radar facility (as a violation of the Anti-Ballistic Missile Treaty), there is now a precedent for admission of a violation, and this might in fact increase confidence about the intentions of a party to a treaty (see also chapter 11). Also if no violation actually occurred at Sverdlovsk, the current intrusive inspections and information exchanges between the USA and the USSR seem to make it possible—by means of explanations and visits—to clarify the matter. If the work on the CWC were to collapse, this would most certainly destroy all confidence in the BWC; likewise if confidence in the BWC cannot be improved, it is likely that this would negatively affect the work on the CWC.

Appendix 14A. Industry declaration from the Canberra Government–Industry Conference against Chemical Weapons

The world's chemical industries, as represented by industry representatives present at the Government–Industry Conference Against Chemical Weapons, held in Canberra from 18 to 22 September 1989:

(i) welcome the Government-Industry Conference Against Chemical Weapons and the constructive dialogue which has taken place between governments and representatives of the world's chemical industries, and between industrial representatives of different countries,

(ii) express their unequivocal abhorrence of chemical warfare,

(iii) express their willingness to work actively with governments to achieve a global ban on chemical weapons, and their willingness to contribute additional momentum to the Geneva negotiating process,

(iv) affirm their desire to foster international cooperation for the legitimate civil uses of chemical products; their opposition to the diversion of industry's products for the manufacture of chemical weapons,

(v) declare their support for efforts to conclude and implement the Chemical Weapons Convention at the earliest date. Industry believes that the only solution to the problem of chemical weapons is a global, comprehensive and effectively verifiable Chemical Weapons Convention which requires the destruction of all existing stockpiles of, and production facilities for, chemical weapons and which implements measures to assure that their future production does not take place,

(vi) express the strong hope that negotiating parties in the Conference on Disarmament in Geneva will resolve urgently the outstanding issues and conclude a Chemical Weapons Convention at the earliest date,

(vii) state their willingness to continue their dialogue with governments to prepare for the entry into force of an effective Chemical Weapons Convention which protects the free and non-discriminatory exchange of chemicals and transfer of technology for economic development and the welfare of all people. The chemical industry indicates its willingness to participate in national measures designed to facilitate early implementation of the Convention following its conclusion.

Source: 'Industry statement', *Final Report*, Government–Industry Conference against Chemical Weapons, Canberra, Australia, 20 Sep. 1989, pp. 218–19.

15. Multilateral and bilateral efforts towards nuclear test limitation

RAGNHILD FERM

I. Introduction

Both bilateral and multilateral forums dealt with the nuclear test limitation issue in 1989. Resumption of the US–Soviet testing negotiations led to agreement on complementing verification provisions for the 1974 Threshold Test Ban Treaty (TTBT) and the 1976 Peaceful Nuclear Explosions Treaty (PNET). More than one-third of the states parties to the 1963 Partial Test Ban Treaty (PTBT) formally submitted to the depositary governments a request for a conference to consider an amendment that would make the Treaty a comprehensive test ban treaty (CTBT). The Conference on Disarmament (CD) again failed to agree on a mandate for the *Ad hoc* Committee on nuclear testing. The CD *Ad hoc* Group of Scientific Experts presented its proposal for a global seismic data exchange system which will be tested in 1990.

II. The US–Soviet test negotiations

In 1986 and 1987 the USA and the USSR held a number of meetings on nuclear testing issues. These talks were formalized in September 1987 when the US Secretary of State and the Soviet Foreign Minister agreed on a mandate for US–Soviet testing negotiations: as a first step, the two sides should agree on verification measures in order to enable ratification of the TTBT and the PNET, and then they should proceed to the negotiation of further limitations on nuclear testing as part of an effective disarmament process. The USA has declared that a CTBT is not in its interests as long as its security depends on nuclear weapons. The Soviet goal remains a total test ban.

The TTBT and the PNET limit the yield of nuclear explosions to 150 kt. The treaties have never been ratified: the USA has refused ratification, claiming that verification methods are not sufficient. In August and September 1988 the USA and the USSR conducted Joint Verification Experiments (JVEs) at each other's test sites to test verification techniques in order to find mutually agreeable technology that would enable both parties to monitor compliance with the two treaties. At the JVE tests the CORRTEX (Continuous Reflectometry for Radius versus Time Experiments) hydrodynamic method was used.[1] The USA maintains that CORRTEX is more accurate than seismic methods; the USSR prefers seismic verification,

---

[1] CORRTEX is an intrusive on-site system which requires placing a cable in or next to the shaft containing the nuclear device. By measuring the speed at which the cable is crushed the size of the test can be measured. The Joint Verification Experiments are described in Ferm, R., 'Nuclear explosions', *SIPRI Yearbook 1989: World Armaments and Disarmament* (Oxford University Press: Oxford, 1989), pp. 52–53, and the text of the US–Soviet JVE Agreement is given in appendix 2B.

arguing that it is more reliable. Both parties agreed that the JVEs were successful and that the two tests should be analysed to provide a basis for further talks. The negotiators started drafting verification protocols to the treaties in autumn 1988, but no final agreement had been reached on verification methods when the negotiations closed in December 1988.

When President Bush took office in January 1989 the new Administration started to review its strategic policy, causing a break in negotiations. In May US–Soviet officials agreed to resume negotiations. This was announced as opponents of US nuclear testing released a letter, signed by 165 members of the US Congress, urging the Administration to seek a mutual verified phase-out of nuclear weapon tests leading to a CTBT in 1995.[2]

The verification protocol for the PNET did not seem to pose great problems and was agreed to by the negotiators at an early stage. (It should be noted that the USA has not conducted peaceful nuclear explosions—PNEs—since 1972 and the USSR seems to be winding down its PNE programme. In 1988 only two Soviet PNEs were conducted and in 1989 none.[3]) It appeared more complicated to reach an agreement on verification methods for the TTBT. Three verification methods were discussed: the CORRTEX method, seismic monitoring and on-site inspections. CORRTEX equipment has to be placed immediately adjacent to the nuclear explosion and is incapable of measuring tests at distances of more than a few dozen metres. Seismic systems are able to register explosions from a great distance and most experts regard them the best means for verifying low-yield explosions. Some US officials have opposed seismic measurement, however, and are believed to have done so for fear that acceptance of seismic verification could lead to a demand for further limitation on the yields of the tests.[4]

At the meeting between the US Secretary of State and the Soviet Foreign Minister in Wyoming, USA, 22–23 September 1989, it was announced that the PNET protocol had already been agreed *ad referendum* by the negotiators and that agreement was reached on the basic provisions for the TTBT protocol. According to news reports a combination of seismic, hydrodynamic (CORRTEX) and on-site verification procedures was proposed. Each side guarantees the other side the right to make hydrodynamic yield measurements of at least two tests per year during the first five years following ratification of the treaty. After five years, each side shall guarantee one such hydrodynamic measurement each year thereafter, unless otherwise agreed by the two sides.[5] For all tests above 35 kt, on-site inspection is permitted, and for tests above 50 kt, the inspecting party can choose between hydrodynamic or seismic measurements with on-site inspections. Even if no test above 50 kt is conducted, the above rights still apply.[6] No official document on the agreement was issued. At the December US–Soviet summit meeting at Malta the Presidents confirmed that the two

[2] *Washington Post*, 12 May 1989.
[3] See also chapter 2.
[4] *Washington Post*, 14 Sep. 1989.
[5] *USIS SUF*, 706, 24 Sep. 1989.
[6] *Arms Control Today*, Oct. 1989.

protocols were close to completion and should be signed by the summit meeting, planned to take place in June 1990.

While the Soviet chief negotiator has stated that the USSR wants to continue the negotiations in accordance with the mandate agreed by both parties in order to reach further limitations without waiting for the ratification of the treaties,[7] the US side argues that it is important to observe the effectiveness of the new protocols before deciding on negotiations on further steps towards test limitations.[8] The fundamental US policy has not changed: a comprehensive test ban is, for the time being, not in the US interest.

III. The PTBT amendment conference

According to Article II of the 1963 PTBT (prohibiting nuclear explosions in the atmosphere, in outer space and under water) any party may propose amendments to the Treaty. If requested by at least one-third of the parties the depositary governments (the USA, the USSR and the UK) shall convene a conference to consider the amendments. The UN General Assembly has urged parties to take advantage of the provisions in the interests of converting the PTBT into a CTBT.[9] In August 1988 six states (Indonesia, Mexico, Peru, Sri Lanka, Venezuela and Yugoslavia) formally submitted to the depositary governments a proposal for an amendment conference.[10] It was stated that such an amendment conference is intended to convert the Treaty into a CTBT. By 1 April 1989, 40 non-nuclear weapon states had joined the request—more than the required one-third of the parties. (As of 1 January 1990 the total number of PTBT parties is 119.) Later 17 more parties became co-sponsors. The three depositary governments informed the PTBT parties that they had consulted among themselves with a view to preparing for convening the conference.[11]

However, the USA and the UK have expressed very clearly, on several occasions, that a CTBT remains only a long-term objective. Accordingly, these two states are opposed to any amendments which would strengthen and widen the scope of the PTBT. Nevertheless both states have affirmed their willingness to fulfil their duty as depositary states to the PTBT to convene an amendment conference.[12] The USSR has reiterated its wish to reach an agreement on a CTBT as soon as possible. It has pledged to stop conducting nuclear explosions if the USA does the same, and it is also ready to co-operate with the other two depositaries in the work for a conference. According to the text of the Treaty a majority of the signatories of the PTBT must approve an amendment to the Treaty in order for it to enter into force and the three depositaries must be included in that majority. The USA has made known that it intends to exercise that right and prevent the amendment from being approved.

[7] *FBIS-SU*, 241, 18 Dec. 1989.
[8] *USIS EUR*, 301, 24 Jan. 1990.
[9] UN General Assembly Resolution 42/26 B, 30 Nov. 1987.
[10] UN document A/44/211, 5 Apr. 1989.
[11] *USIS EUR*, 412, 9 Nov. 1989.
[12] Conference on Disarmament document CD/956, 4 Sep. 1989, pp. 20–21.

Most PTBT parties have not supported the proposal, among them Australia, Canada and Sweden, which have a record of being proponents of a CTBT. They regard the CD as the proper forum for CTBT negotiations and play an active role in the work of the CD *Ad hoc* Group of Scientific Experts for a CTBT verification system. They express scepticism about the outcome of the conference because of the right of the depositary states to block any amendment proposals.[13]

It is argued that a CTBT would be the best way to strengthen the non-proliferation regime; it has even been claimed that the NPT cannot survive without a CTBT as it would be impossible to stop the spread of new and more sophisticated nuclear weapons without a CTBT. There were different views among the parties as to whether the amendment conference should be convened before or after the Fourth NPT Review Conference, to be held in August 1990,[14] and on the impact an amendment conference would have on the NPT Review. The signatories of the proposal had envisioned an amendment conference before the NPT Review Conference. At the three previous NPT review conferences (1975, 1980 and 1985) the non-nuclear weapon states gave priority to a CTBT. The declaration issued at the meeting of the Heads of State of the Non-Aligned Movement in September 1989 states that for the credibility of the NPT regime 'the depositary states should fulfil their obligations by agreeing to negotiate a CTBT which is absolutely essential for the preservation of the NPT regime embodied in the NPT'. Consequently the Non-Aligned Movement states supported an amendment conference as soon as possible in 1990.[15] Others argued that failure (perhaps inevitable) of the amendment conference would create a difficult climate for NPT efforts.

The three depositary states announced in November 1989 that they had agreed to convene the requested amendment conference in January 1991, for a period of two weeks, arguing that an amendment conference prior to the NPT Review would not be constructive.[16] A UN General Assembly resolution adopted in December 1989[17] is a compromise: it recommends a two-part PTBT amendment conference: one part before the NPT Review (May–June 1990) and another after (January 1991). The costs should be shared among the parties on the basis of the UN scale of assessments. The USA and the UK voted against the resolution. There was also opposition to the way of funding: a US official expressed the view that since the PTBT is not a UN treaty the UN funding system should not be applied.[18] After consultations held between the depositary states and the six states which initially proposed the conference, agreement was reached to hold the amendment conference

[13] Conference on Disarmament document CD/PV.492, 7 Mar. 1989; 'NPT, CTB and PTBT: an interview with Maj-Britt Theorin', *Disarmament Newsletter*, Aug. 1989.

[14] Prospects for the fourth NPT Review Conference are examined in chapter 16.

[15] Heads of State or Government of Non-Aligned Countries: Statement on International Security or Disarmament, at their Ninth Conference, Belgrade, 4–7 Sep. 1989, reprinted in *Review of International Affairs*, 20 Sep. 1989.

[16] *Disarmament Times*, vol. 12, no. 5 (Nov. 1989).

[17] UN General Assembly document A/RES/44/106, 12 Jan. 1990.

[18] *Disarmament Times*, vol. 12, no. 6 (Dec. 1989).

in New York on 7–18 January 1991. A preparatory meeting will be held on 29 May–8 June 1990.

Irrespective of its outcome a PTBT amendment conference could be seen as a political exercise, designed to draw attention to the CTBT issue, provoke discussion and perhaps convince the USA to accept a mandate for negotiations in the CD. A conference would give all parties to the PTBT an opportunity to participate in negotiations on strengthening the Treaty.

IV. Conference on Disarmament

The 1985 NPT Review Conference called on all nuclear weapon states to participate in CD negotiations for a CTBT. Such talks have been blocked since 1982 because of lack of consensus on the mandate. The Conference again failed to reach an agreement on a mandate for the *Ad hoc* Committee on nuclear testing. The USA opposes any mandate that sets a CTBT as the goal of the work of the *Ad hoc* Committee. The UK has the same view and France has all along refused to participate in any talks on nuclear testing. China has stated that if and when agreement is reached on the mandate it would participate in the work of the Committee.[19] (France and China have refused to join the PTBT.) Two major proposals for a CTBT have been presented at the CD: one by Sweden in 1983[20] and one by the Group of Socialist Countries in 1987.[21]

The question of adequate verification has been one of the major problems in the efforts to reach a CTBT. Adequate means to deter any clandestine testing under an agreement could be provided by a global seismic monitoring system. The CD *Ad hoc* Group of Scientific Experts was set up in 1976 to 'consider international co-operative measures to detect and identify seismic events'. The Group is open to all CD member states as well as to other UN member states upon invitation of the CD. The Group of Scientific Experts has worked on elements of an international seismic data exchange system to assist states in their national monitoring of compliance with a CTBT. Most of its efforts in the 1989 session were devoted to further planning of a Global System for International Seismic Data Exchange. The system is based on four international data centres (situated in Canberra, Moscow, Stockholm and Washington) and a global network of nationally operated seismic stations using modern communication methods, including satellite links. The first phase of an international experiment for testing the global system for exchanging seismic data was conducted in January–March 1990. It included 43 seismic stations from 20 countries and also transmitted so-called Level II data (original data recorded by seismometers).

[19] Conference on Disarmament document CD/956, 4 Sep. 1989, p. 21.
[20] Committee on Disarmament document CD/381*, 14 June 1983.
[21] Conference on Disarmament document CD/756, 17 June 1987.

Part IV. Special features

16. Prospects for the fourth review of the Non-Proliferation Treaty

HARALD MÜLLER

I. Introduction

The Treaty on the Non-Proliferation of Nuclear Weapons (NPT) is the most widely adhered to arms control agreement to date. It was concluded in 1968 with a view to preventing the addition of new nuclear weapon powers to the five then in existence and since its entry into force in 1970 has continued to attract new members. On the eve of the third Review Conference in 1985 there were 130 parties to the Treaty; at the beginning of 1990 the Treaty had 141 parties (for the list of parties see annexe A). Three nuclear weapon states, the USA, the USSR and the UK, act as depositary governments while the other two, France and China, abstain from membership but conduct, in their own words, a policy in accordance with non-proliferation goals (China) or act 'as if' party to the Treaty (France). Among new members since 1985 the most important are North Korea, Saudi Arabia and Spain. Saudi Arabia is an important voice within the developing world. Its accession strengthened the group of NPT countries in the Third World and was quickly followed by those of Bahrain and Qatar and ratification by Kuwait.

The fourth Review Conference of the NPT, to be held in Geneva in 1990, will set the pace for the 1995 extension conference which, in accordance with Article X, must decide whether to extend the Treaty indefinitely or for a specified period. It is therefore more important than its predecessors and a decisive event for the survival of the Treaty into the next millenium.

So far, review conferences present a fairly mixed record.[1] Although the 1975 Review Conference was close to failure, it adopted a declaration reaffirming the provisions of the Treaty. The second Review Conference, in 1980, failed to reach consensus, particularly over the issue of nuclear disarmament, but a Final Document was adopted recommending a third review. In 1985 the third Review Conference produced a very long, substantial document—to the surprise of many who had expected that the total lack of disarmament and arms control successes would lead the conference to

---

[1] Previous NPT review conferences are well documented in *SIPRI Yearbooks*. For 1975 see 'The implementation of agreements related to disarmament', SIPRI, *World Armaments and Disarmament: SIPRI Yearbook 1976* (Taylor & Francis: London, 1976), pp. 363–92, and 'Final Declaration of the Review Conference of the parties to the Treaty on the Non-Proliferation of Nuclear Weapons, 30 May 1975', appendix 9A, pp. 403–13; for 1980 see 'The Second NPT Review Conference', SIPRI, *World Armaments and Disarmament: SIPRI Yearbook 1981* (Taylor & Francis: London, 1981), chapter 10, pp. 297–338, and 'Final Document of the Second Review Conference of the parties to the Treaty on the Non-Proliferation of Nuclear Weapons', appendix 10A, pp. 339–62; for 1985 see Goldblat, J., 'The third review of the Non-Proliferation Treaty', SIPRI, *World Armaments and Disarmament: SIPRI Yearbook 1986* (Oxford University Press: Oxford, 1986), pp. 469–80, and 'Final Declaration of the third Review Conference', appendix 20A, pp. 481–94.

certain failure. The consensus was a result of minute preparation, based on a precarious balance of mutual compromises, and was uncertain until the very final minutes of the meeting.[2] A repetition of this success in 1990, while by no means excluded, is far from assured. It will depend very much on how the NPT has developed over the past five years and how this development is perceived in the world, particularly in the developing countries.

The institutional and operational mainstay of the non-proliferation regime is the International Atomic Energy Agency (IAEA). Under Article III the NPT assigns to the IAEA the role of verifying that every non-nuclear weapon state party to the NPT meets its obligations not to divert nuclear energy from peaceful uses to nuclear weapons or other nuclear explosive devices. IAEA safeguards agreements cover all the nuclear activities of the non-nuclear weapon states parties to the NPT and are based on a model agreement drawn up by the IAEA in 1970.[3]

The Agency enhanced its standing considerably by its professional handling of the situation after the 1986 Chernobyl nuclear reactor accident. It lent technical help to the Soviet Union, created quickly and effectively an enlarged programme for nuclear safety, and presented the framework for the negotiation and conclusion of two conventions (for early notification of nuclear accidents and mutual assistance in case of such accidents) in summer 1986. It also installed a working group together with the Organization for Economic Co-operation and Development (OECD) to work out a joint protocol for the Vienna and Paris Conventions on nuclear liability.[4] These achievements notwithstanding, the member states have continued to hold the IAEA budget at zero growth for the seventh year in succession.[5] The Agency is also plagued by political problems emerging mainly from regional conflicts. Efforts by the safeguards department to economize on current resources are now pushing against the limits of feasibility. If the safeguards system must be replaced by one of diminished rigour, criticism of the credibility of the Agency's assessments cannot but

---

[2] See Fischer, D. and Müller, H., 'Nonproliferation beyond the 1985 review', *CEPS Papers*, no. 26, Centre for European Policy Studies, Brussels, 1985; Shaker, M. I., 'The legacy of the 1985 Non-Proliferation Treaty Review Conference: the President's reflections', ed. J. Simpson, *Nuclear Non-Proliferation: An Agenda for the 1990s* (Cambridge University Press: Cambridge, 1987); Sanders, B., 'The Third Review Conference of the Non-Proliferation Treaty', ed. J. Kaufmann, *Conference Diplomacy*, vol. 2 (Martinus Nijhoff: Dordrecht, 1989), pp. 255–65.

[3] IAEA document INFCIRC/153 (corrected) (IAEA: Vienna, 1983). IAEA safeguards employ three essential methods of verification: *materials accountancy*, to determine the amount of material unaccounted for over a specific period; *containment*, to restrict access to and prevent or hamper clandestine movement of the material; and *surveillance*, to detect any unreported movement or tampering with safeguarded items; Fischer, D. and Szasz, P., *Safeguarding the Atom: A Critical Appraisal* , ed. J. Goldblat, SIPRI (Taylor & Francis: London, 1985), pp. 26–27.

[4] *IAEA Newsbrief*, vol. 1, no. 1 (Oct. 1986), pp. 1–2; no. 2 (Oct. 1986), pp. 1–2; vol. 2, no. 15 (Nov. 1987), p. 4.

[5] The IAEA operates safeguards in 920 nuclear installations in 57 states with over 200 inspectors. This task is to be implemented from a safeguards budget of $54.2 million (1990), about one-third of the Agency's total funds of $162.6 million: *IAEA Newsbrief*, vol. 4, no. 5 (June 1989), p. 1.

rise. The non-proliferation regime would suffer severely from a weakening of the Agency, whether as a result of economic or political problems.[6]

On the eve of the fourth NPT Review Conference, the Treaty and the non-proliferation regime at large are in a state of precarious stability. The regime has not been shattered profoundly in the past five years, nor have drastic proliferation events upset the fabric of international relations. As was to be expected, however, countries approaching the threshold of a theoretical or actual nuclear capability in 1985 have since enhanced their capabilities. In South Asia *India* and *Pakistan* have continued to work on uranium enrichment and there are indications that both countries have an interest in tritium production;[7] India is thought to have produced some 200–300 kg of plutonium outside international safeguards. Both India and Pakistan have advanced missile programmes.[8] Proposals for simultaneous ratification of the NPT, for the creation of a nuclear weapon-free zone (NWFZ) and even for bilateral inspections have fallen on deaf ears in India. In the Middle East the progress of the *Israeli* nuclear weapon and delivery system programmes has been met by a chemical arms buildup by the Arab states.

In *South Africa* the withdrawal of Cuban troops has removed the last strategic pretence for the need for nuclear weapons. Despite continued operation of two unsafeguarded enrichment facilities the readiness of South Africa to enter serious negotiations on accession to the NPT is less in doubt nowadays. Without NPT membership South Africa is in increasing danger of losing its last natural uranium customers and of forgoing any chance to buy a power reactor in the second half of the 1990s. In South America political developments in *Argentina* and *Brazil* make it less likely than ever that a technical–economic rivalry will degenerate into a military–nuclear rivalry. While the abstention by both countries from stronger non-proliferation commitments remains a source of some discomfort—their accession to the NPT is as unlikely as their full and unconditional membership of the Tlatelolco Treaty—confidence building in their nuclear sectors has improved and deserves support from abroad.[9]

Whether the NPT can weather another five years hinges largely on the degree of consensus its members can achieve on its merits for serving their own national interests. This consensus must be maintained against active attempts of non-parties to undermine the Treaty's stability. Resistance at the UN Third Special Session on Disarmament (UNSSD III) to the inclusion of a positive assessment of the Treaty in the draft resolution was a further clear sign that 'holdouts' do not necessarily plan to behave neutrally.[10]

[6] See Scheinman, *The International Atomic Energy Agency and World Order* (Resources for the Future: Washington, DC, 1987), pp. 211–18; *PPNN Newsbrief*, no. 1 (Mar. 1988), p. 2.

[7] *Congressional Record*, vol. 135, no. 161 (16 Nov. 1989); *Nuclear Fuel*, 6 Apr. 1989, p. 11.

[8] Ballistic missile proliferation is discussed in chapter 9 of this *Yearbook*.

[9] Spector, L., *The Undeclared Bomb* (Ballinger: Cambridge, Mass., 1988), pp. 229–80; *PPNN Newsbrief*, no. 3 (Nov. 1988), p. 2; *Nucleonics Week*, vol. 29, no. 13 (4 Apr. 1988) and vol. 30, no. 41 (12 Oct. 1989), pp. 11–12; Redick, J., *Nuclear Restraint in Latin America: Argentina and Brazil*, PPNN Occasional Paper 1, Southampton University, Southampton, 1988.

[10] *Arms Control Reporter,* July 1988, p. 602.B.148; Akashi, Y., 'Is there still life after SSOD III?', *Disarmament*, vol. 11, no. 3 (autumn 1988), p. 20.

With the main body of the Treaty basically intact, preparations started in 1989 for the 1990 Review Conference. The first two sessions of the Preparatory Committee in 1989 went smoothly, and matters of organization and protocol have been resolved without difficulty. The status of implementation, problems and potential controversies facing the coming Review Conference are discussed below.

II. Status of implementation of the NPT

Article I

Article I obliges nuclear weapon states parties not to assist non-nuclear weapon states to acquire nuclear arms. By implication this obligation also applies to non-nuclear weapon states (curiously this is not part of the language of the Treaty). Have parties lived up to their obligations?

In the case of the superpowers there are indications that geostrategic and alliance interests counteract non-proliferation commitments. While direct assistance was probably absent, indirect assistance to third countries' nuclear weapon programmes is undeniable. It could also be stipulated that Article I implies not only abstaining from direct assistance but also active efforts to prevent proliferation and to persuade potential proliferators to stop undesired activities. Measured by that standard, both superpowers have failed badly.

Whereas no direct Soviet assistance to non-peaceful Indian nuclear activities has been registered, three factors in this co-operation are worrisome enough to deserve mention:

1. While the lease of a Soviet nuclear-powered attack submarine in 1988 to the Indian Navy did not imply delivery of nuclear weapons, it is well known that such submarines can serve as platforms for nuclear arms. They may even use highly enriched, weapon-grade uranium as fuel. This raises the question of whether it is appropriate for a depositary government of the NPT to deliver to a non-NPT country, even on a lease basis, a device which may have a place in a nuclear weapon programme and which uses fuel not subject to international safeguards. Of course, the USSR was not obliged to require safeguards on the fuel: Article 14 of the NPT model safeguards agreement[11] permits the lifting of safeguards on nuclear material to be used for non-explosive military purposes, and in relationships with non-NPT parties the matter is unregulated. But it leads to questions on the commitment of the depositary government if such items are offered to a country which violently opposes the Treaty. While the letter of the NPT was not hurt, its spirit suffered from Soviet forbearance to Indian interests.[12] Ap-

[11] See note 3.
[12] Sanders, B. and Simpson, J., *Nuclear Submarines and Non-Proliferation: Cause for Concern*, PPNN Occasional Papers (Southampton University: Southampton, 1988).

parently this was recognized in Moscow: it has been aired that initial plans to follow up with leasing another three ships have been scrapped.

2. The sale of two nuclear power plants to India, recently concluded under safeguards, breaks the taboo on entering major new contracts with countries conducting unsafeguarded nuclear activities.

3. More disturbing is the repeated supply of Soviet heavy water to India, without safeguards, through an FRG intermediary. Unsafeguarded heavy water helped India considerably in stockpiling plutonium without international controls, materials which can be used for whatever purpose the Indian Government decides. In this wilful neglect, Moscow came very close to a breach of its Article I obligation.[13]

The US Government has continued to support Pakistan militarily despite growing evidence of a Pakistani nuclear weapon programme. In June 1989, President George Bush informed Congress that the breach of the previous Pakistani assurance not to enrich uranium beyond the 5 per cent level was not seen as a sufficient reason to cancel military aid and would not play a role in the further US–Pakistani relationship. Washington has restricted its non-proliferation policy to regular, but mild, admonitions and has otherwise conducted business as usual.

The USA keeps virtually silent on the most advanced nuclear weapon programme in a purportedly non-nuclear weapon state. While it was clearly within US power to pressure Israel towards at least a freeze on the further growth of its nuclear arsenal, even the Vanunu revelations have not stopped Washington looking the other way. Via economic assistance and Foreign Military Sales the US taxpayer indirectly subsidizes Israeli expenditures for the Dimona complex. Worse still, strategic co-operation between the two states was extended to the Strategic Defense Initiative (SDI) in 1985; this includes technologies applicable to improving nuclear weapon delivery.

A new and more worrisome suspicion is raised by recent news that US–French collaboration in the military nuclear sector included information exchanges on nuclear warhead design.[14] Although such collaboration does not negate US obligations under the NPT—assistance to other nuclear weapon states is permitted under Article I—it raises a critical question: If it was possible for the USA to keep this collaboration secret for so long, can it be excluded that similar co-operation was going on with Israel? While the answer is clearly open to speculation, this new issue burdens the already complicated US–Arab relationship in the context of NPT obligations.

There is persistent Third World criticism of Western nuclear collaboration with South Africa. Minor nuclear technology supplies still reach South Africa, which has also been able to secure unlicensed supplies, such as a fuel fabrication measurement device illegally provided by an FRG company. However, most Western countries have visibly severed their nuclear ties to South Africa. All but the FRG and France have suspended natural uranium

[13] Milhollin, G., 'Dateline New Delhi: India's nuclear cover-up', *Foreign Policy*, no. 64 (fall 1986).
[14] Ullman, R. H., 'The covert French connection', *Foreign Policy*, no. 75 (summer 1989), pp. 3–33.

purchases and in 1986 the European Community (EC) Council resolved not to enter any new nuclear supply contracts with South Africa.

Policies of neglect must be added to the above politically motivated short-comings. The USA discovered that its Department of Energy had, through lax security standards, given information on detonators, explosives and firing sites with possible nuclear applications to citizens of Argentina, India, Iran, Israel, Pakistan, South Africa, South Korea and Taiwan. While not a conscious breach of Article I, this must be seen as failure by neglect to live up to the obligations of this article.[15] Other activities which may have contributed to third countries' nuclear programmes fall more clearly under Article III and are discussed in greater depth below.

It can be expected that disputes over the implementation of Article I will very much resemble those in 1985. Israel and South Africa, and their real or alleged ties to the West, will be high on the agenda, while few Third World countries will summon the courage to ask questions about India or Pakistan. Black African states will most likely be highly critical of what they view as continuation of critical Western collaboration with South Africa and may push again for including language in the final document asking NPT parties to cut nuclear ties with South Africa.

The revolutionary changes in East–West relations provide the greatest hopes that Article I can be approached in a fresh way. With the global US–Soviet contest for power subsiding, there is less reason to condone all disputable behaviour by strategic allies. Concomitantly, the risks of pro-liferation will rank higher on the national security agenda of major states once the central threat of a superpower nuclear war loses all probability. It is to be hoped that a reordering of priorities will persuade the governments in Moscow and Washington to put more pressure on their regional allies to freeze their latent or open nuclear weapon programmes. Other Article I problems can be dealt with by a stricter and more consequential application of export controls (see also under Article III).

Article II

Article II of the NPT obliges non-nuclear weapon states parties to the Treaty to refrain from acquiring nuclear weapons. On the surface, this article has been perfectly implemented during the past five years and no NPT party is known to have acquired nuclear weapon status. Some non-nuclear weapon states parties have conducted doubtful activities, however, which give rise to concern; there has been no clear violation of Article II, but several ambiguous cases and one very disturbing development.

The nuclear programmes of Iran and Iraq suffered from the 1980–88 war. Iraq's nuclear venture at Tamuz was destroyed by an Israeli attack on the large Osiraq research reactor in 1981 and repeated Iraqi air strikes damaged the core of Iran's once highly ambitious civilian nuclear programme, the power plant at Busheer. Iraq tried to acquire a substitute for the damaged

[15] *Arms Control Reporter*, Sep. 1989, p. 602.B.167.

reactor from France, but would not agree to the French condition that a modified reactor type be supplied that did not use highly enriched uranium (HEU). Suspicions that Iraq is actively seeking to acquire centrifuge technology for enrichment have been revised after recent reports of criminal investigations of H & H Metallform, the FRG company accused of non-licensed exports of machinery for the production of ultra-centrifuges, but they have not been officially confirmed.[16] Iran has acquired 80 kg of medium-enriched fuel (19.7 per cent) for restarting its Tehran research reactor under safeguards and has made unsuccessful attempts to persuade the FRG to agree to Siemens/KWU rebuilding the Busheer reactors. The FRG makes the resumption of supply contingent upon an Iran–Iraq peace treaty.[17] Although present Iranian capabilities give no cause for real concern, past experience of the incalculable nature of the present regime, its highly compromised position towards international law and some highly critical comments on the NPT lead many observers to view the country with circumspection. Stabilization with a moderate government would presumably remove much of this concern.

Despite Libya's status as a state party to the NPT, statements by Colonel Muammar Qadhafi indicate continued Libyan interest in nuclear weapons.[18] Yet there have been no obvious attempts to acquire the needed technology after Libya was denied advice and technological assistance by Belgium and once ambitious plans for the purchase of Soviet power reactors were scrapped after the Chernobyl accident. Public statements contrary to existing Treaty obligations, made by the leader of a state party, must nevertheless be a cause for concern with regard to compliance with Article II.

Because it is regarded as a 'political entity' rather than a state, Taiwan is not always counted as a party although it has signed and ratified the Treaty and continues to adhere to its rules. There was thus reason to worry when it became clear that the country had embarked on a reprocessing programme. Current and prospective uranium prices make reprocessing uneconomical— it makes little sense for a country with a small nuclear power programme— and the clandestine style of constructing the facility did not augur well for the peaceful purposes behind it. US intervention dissuaded continuation and in 1988 Taiwan agreed to dismantle the plant and to shut down a 40-MW (th)—million (thermal) watts—research reactor that could have become the source of spent fuel for reprocessing.[19]

The failure of one of the Treaty's most recent accessions, North Korea, to conclude the required safeguards agreement with the IAEA is a matter of highest concern since North Korea is said to run indigenously built facilities with clear military possibilities, namely, a research reactor and a reprocessing unit.[20] If the situation does not change before the 1990 Review

[16] *Der Spiegel*, no. 51 (1989), pp. 93–94.
[17] *Nucleonics Week*, vol. 30, no. 45 (9 Nov. 1989), p. 7.
[18] Spector (note 9), pp. 196–206.
[19] *Washington Post*, 24 Mar. 1988; *New York Times*, 23 Mar. 1988.
[20] *Arms Control Reporter*, Nov. 1989, pp. 602.B.20–23.

Conference North Korea will certainly be accused of being the first non-nuclear weapon state poised to breach its obligations under Article II. Given the considerable civilian nuclear and general technological potential of South Korea, the situation on the Korean Peninsula begins to resemble the unfortunate constellation in South Asia.

For Article II, consensus at the Review Conference is threatened by hostility between two pairs of countries. The Iran–Iraq dispute almost wrecked the 1985 Review Conference at the last minute, and mutual recriminations about alleged illegal activities could once more prove a stumbling-block. The Korean situation could be more serious. It would be difficult for the Conference not to support South Korea in a motion to condemn the North Korean failure to comply with its obligation, yet it is likely that some of North Korea's friends and potential arms customers would hurry to lend support. A division of the Conference over this issue would be a serious blow to the NPT and could well wreck any attempt to shape a consensus.

Article III

This is the most important NPT article in operational terms. Article III.1 establishes IAEA safeguards on all peaceful nuclear activities as the verification system to which all non-nuclear weapon states must subject themselves. Article III.2 obliges all nuclear exporters to require safeguards on nuclear materials, equipment and technology sold abroad.

Safeguards on peaceful nuclear activities

With the exception of North Korea all states parties to the NPT which have nuclear activities have accepted full-scope safeguards. This does not mean that the safeguards system has seen five quiet years. Anti-nuclear critics have maintained that safeguards are virtually unreliable and have questioned the ability of the IAEA to certify with a sufficient degree of certainty the absence of nuclear material diversion.[21] In heavily safeguarded industrial countries tolerance for safeguards is limited. Governments tend to support the nuclear industry and the utilities in resisting demands by the IAEA safeguards department for more extensive rights of access or for redundant use of containment and surveillance instruments. It has also been difficult to agree on the use of new equipment not mentioned in the initial facility attachments, the documents which delineate the points of access, frequency of inspection and methods for safeguarding a particular plant. In some cases it has long been impossible to conclude facility attachments for a large proportion of facilities in the country. Countries such as Belgium have a tradition of complaining about the cost of safeguards to its nuclear industry and ensuring that the IAEA confines itself to a minimum approach.

---

[21] The IAEA has pointed to the high standards against which it evaluates its own achievements and is satisfied it could discover significant diversion of weapon-grade material. See *IAEA Press Releases*, 2 June 1988, 10 June 1988 and 3 Aug. 1988.

This attitude contains severe dangers because the budgetary freeze will increasingly force the IAEA to compromise on safeguards. There are growing demands from the industrialized countries to concentrate safeguards 'where it really matters'. A regional concentration on 'suspected countries' would discriminate against certain countries by applying more intrusive safeguards schemes there than elsewhere. Alternatively, focusing safeguards on more sensitive facilities, such as reprocessing, enrichment or MOX (mixed oxides of plutonium and uranium) fuel fabrication, makes economic sense but would be a dangerous move in a political environment in which safeguards efficiency is already questioned. Any apparent relaxation of present standards would be interpreted as a capitulation of the IAEA to the demands of the 'nuclear lobby' and as a serious erosion of the credibility of the system. Risking such a public reaction while the NPT is entering its most decisive five years would not seem wise.

This is all the more true as the capability of the IAEA to implement its self-defined objectives is strained to its limits after seven years of zero budgetary growth. Expanding safeguards tasks, in the long run, requires expanded resources. Not only are more complex facilities coming on stream but, in the context of increasingly sophisticated verification schemes for recent and future arms control agreements, the impression must be avoided that IAEA safeguards are becoming old-fashioned and outdated. This requires keeping safeguards technologies up-to-date by introducing new equipment as and when available. For real as well as perceptual reasons, the zero budgetary growth policy, imposed on the Agency by the Western group and accepted by most members, is increasingly dangerous for the objectives of the NPT, even if no breach of the Treaty has occurred.

New challenges to the safeguards regime emerge from new technologies entering civilian use and from new safeguarding problems on the horizon.[22]

1. Developments in laser enrichment technology are under way in a large number of industrialized states and several threshold states. There is no agreed list of equipment items to be monitored for the purpose of export controls, and no safeguarding system exists for these facilities.[23]

2. Large bulk-handling facilities containing weapon-usable material, such as enrichment facilities, reprocessing plants or MOX fuel fabrication units, pose generic safeguarding problems. Material is not readily accessible in the processing stage and its radioactivity necessitates shielded handling in some cases. Real-time accounting is difficult and surveillance, containment and permanent inspectors are needed. No satisfactory approach has been worked out for safeguarding large commercial reprocessing facilities.[24]

[22] For this discussion see von Baeckmann, A., *Modern Nuclear Fuel Cycle Technologies: Challenges to IAEA Safeguards,* PPNN Occasional Paper 4 (Southampton University: Southampton, 1989), pp. 7–14; the author is also grateful for information from Martin Kalinowski.

[23] The implications of laser isotope separation technologies are discussed in chapter 17 of this *Yearbook.*

[24] *IAEA Newsbrief,* vol. 4, no. 6 (July/Aug. 1988), p. 2; Walker, W. and Berkhout, F. , 'Safeguards and the expansion of civil reprocessing and plutonium use', paper presented to the PPNN Core Group Meeting, Baden, Austria, 18–19 Nov. 1989.

3. Direct end-storage, whether the material is stored recoverably or irrecoverably, presents considerable difficulties for the present safeguards approach. Accounting of highly radioactive materials is not yet possible but permanent safeguards are essential because over time fission products break down to stable end-stages and radioactivity ceases to provide a natural shield against diversion.

4. Apart from fissionable materials subject to safeguards under the IAEA statute, auxiliary materials such as heavy water and materials directly used in nuclear weapons, such as beryllium and tritium, are highly critical items in international nuclear trade. Heavy water is safeguarded on an *ad hoc* basis, following the determination of the London Suppliers' Club to monitor the peaceful use of this material.[25] However, no safeguards exist for beryllium, used as a neutron reflector in nuclear warheads; tritium, a heavy hydrogen isotope used to enhance the yield of fissionable material in boosted nuclear weapons, needed for neutron enhanced weapons and for warheads with selectable yields; or lithium 6, used as lithium-deuteride in thermonuclear weapons to breed tritium during the explosion. The first two are widespread in civilian uses, and no stage in the production chain poses difficulties to clandestine operation or would facilitate verification. The civilian demand for tritium is comparatively small and could be met by other isotopes; it does not occur naturally in exploitable amounts and must be produced in nuclear reactors or other high neutron flux sources. Tritium presents special accountancy problems because it is a gas and there are no multilateral agreements for its control. A decision to introduce international safeguards on tritium would add a new burden to IAEA safeguards.[26]

5. Acquisition of nuclear submarines raises the issue of permitted withdrawal from safeguards of fissionable material for non-explosive military purposes. Before cancelling its planned acquisition of nuclear submarines for budgetary reasons the Canadian Government pondered the idea of a completely unsafeguarded fuel cycle, from enrichment to reprocessing and storage, under the official rationale that it was for non-explosive military purposes. This daring interpretation would obviate 20 years of faithful support of the non-proliferation regime. The precedent was set, however, and while Canada considered the purchase the nuclear submarine folly reached Argentina, Brazil and India. Without the Canadian reversal, the Review Conference could have witnessed a confrontation between Ottawa and its previous fellows of the 'white angel' group of particularly non-proliferation-minded countries like Australia, Ireland, New Zealand and Sweden. It is to be hoped that the nuclear submarine Pandora's box remains closed among NPT parties for a long while.[27]

---

[25] Heavy water and heavy water production plants were added by the London Suppliers' Club to a list of items that should trigger safeguards in a set of *Guidelines for Nuclear Transfers,* INFCIRC/254, 1977.

[26] This paragraph owes much to the advice of and various papers on tritium control by Martin Kalinowski.

[27] Sanders and Simpson (note 12).

6. The IAEA may confront new safeguarding requirements in the coming decade as a result of current nuclear armament negotiations. One possibility would be to follow the 1985 Swedish proposal[28] to extend the application of IAEA safeguards in nuclear weapon states from a few facilities picked from a 'voluntary offer' list to the full civilian fuel cycle. Since China signed a safeguards agreement on 20 September 1988[29] the IAEA may apply selective safeguards in all five nuclear weapon states parties.

What at first glance appears a waste of money and, at best, the perfection of the 'equality of misery' principle (subjecting nuclear weapon states to the same burdens as non-nuclear weapon states) can be seen as a well-considered precurser to a meaningful disarmament measure, namely, the cut-off of the production of fissile material for military purposes. To guarantee such a cut-off would, of course, require verification at military nuclear sites. Such verification would, however, only make sense if the verifying party could be sure that no circumvention of agreements could take place by using allegedly civilian nuclear facilities for military purposes. This, logically, would make mandatory control of all nuclear facilities, civilian as well as military, in nuclear weapon states. The Swedish argument is that, rather than starting such a verification scheme from scratch, it is better to extend safeguards coverage incrementally in order to spread the inevitable cost rise over an extended period. In this way, the extension of safeguards to the military fuel cycle would only add marginally to an already sizeable safeguards burden, and opposition to such a marginal extension would not be supported by cost considerations.

Cost concerns, however, have been the greatest obstacle so far to pursuing the Swedish proposal further. Depending on the calculation, the cost increase to the safeguards burden accruing from extending Agency activities to the British, US and Soviet civil nuclear industry, ranks from 200 to 400 per cent over the present budget. This opens the question of burden-sharing: cost-minded countries such as Belgium plead for nuclear weapon states to carry the full burden (indeed Belgium has argued that those privileged by the regime should pay for the whole safeguards bill in all countries). The USA and the USSR on the other hand have indicated that they would expect non-nuclear weapon states to pick up the bill if they moved towards ending their own privilege, a step they are not obliged to take under the provisions of the NPT. For these reasons it is to be feared that there is no quick solution in sight to the cut-off idea. The USSR has unilaterally declared the shut-down of several military plutonium reactors and an end to weapon-grade enrichment, but continues to produce plutonium and maintains 14 dual-purpose reactors. The USA has not followed this example even in its

---

[28] NPT-Conf.3-SR.2, 2 Sep. 1985, p. 24; NPT-Conf.3-47, 10 Sep. 1985; NPT-Conf.3-54, 12 Sep. 1985.

[29] *Arms Control Reporter*, Dec. 1988, p. 602.B.153; the 'Swedish Proposal' was repeated by the Nordic Countries Group at UNSSD III in a working paper: *Arms Control Reporter*, June 1988, p. 602.B.146; see also von Baeckmann, A., 'IAEA safeguards in nuclear weapons states: a review of objectives, purposes and achievements', *IAEA Bulletin*, vol. 30, no. 1. (1988), pp. 22–25.

declaratory policy; it is closer to a shut-down in practice, however, because safety mismanagement at US military nuclear facilities forced a clean-up costing at least $110 billion.[30] Moreover, Congress is increasingly reluctant to grant funds for the construction of new weapon-grade material production plant in a period of diminishing military and rising budgetary threats. Maybe (even if at present there is no willingness to act) all parties could be interested in an in-depth study.[31]

One serious possibility compromising the utility of IAEA safeguards is the trend in US policy to abandon the time-honoured strict distinction between civilian and military nuclear fuel cycles. Attempts to blur this distinction started in the mid-1980s when the Reagan Administration, for reasons of cost and convenience, considered the upgrading of civilian-produced plutonium for weapon use. The 1983 Hart–Simpson–Mitchell amendment to the Atomic Energy Act closed this route. However, a presidential order signed by President Ronald Reagan in November 1988 opens the way for seizing a civilian reactor, in case of 'national techno-logical emergency' for either plutonium or tritium production. In 1989, the Department of Energy (DOE) continued not to rule out the employment of LWRs for the production of scarce tritium.[32] This would be a most serious blow to the present regime.

Another possible task for the IAEA is custody and civilian recycling of fissile material extracted from nuclear warheads as a consequence of disarmament. Under the INF Treaty, destruction concerns only launchers and carriers, not the nuclear material contained in the warheads. Different solutions can be envisaged for future disarmament agreements. Under its statute, the IAEA cannot be involved in warhead dismantling and destruction, which fall clearly within the military realm. However, once the material is extracted from nuclear warheads, the IAEA could take it into custody and assure the parties that it is not used for military purposes. Depending on the nature of the material, the language of the agreements concerned and the prevailing fuel cycle policies, the material could be either stored under IAEA control or recycled for civilian power generation. Both alternatives would serve useful symbolic political purposes: the first would set a precedent for international plutonium storage, an old thoroughly studied proposal never realized because of national sovereignty concerns but one whose time may have come again.[33]

Plutonium recycling will be but a fraction of that envisaged 10 or 15 years ago for the last decade of the century. The bad economics of recycling pose the question of how to deal with the plutonium already separated but which the countries concerned may prefer not to transform into MOX fuel. Given

[30] See SIPRI, *SIPRI Yearbook 1989: World Armaments and Disarmament* (Oxford University Press: Oxford, 1989), chapter 1, pp. 10–11.

[31] *New York Times*, 14 July 1988; *PPNN Newsbrief*, no. 4 (Jan. 1989), p. 6; *PPNN Newsbrief*, no. 5 (Apr. 1989), p. 2; *Nucleonics Week*, 1 June 1989.

[32] *Nucleonics Week*, vol. 30, no. 29 (20 July 1989), p. 10; *PPNN Newsbrief*, no. 4 (Jan. 1989), p. 6.

[33] See Van Doren, C. N., *Toward an Effective International Plutonium Storage System*, Report 81-255 (Congressional Research Service: Washington, DC, 1981).

the strong objections voiced in many countries to all kinds of nuclear storage, not least plutonium, internationally owned and controlled storage systems may lend some legitimacy to such badly needed facilities. Such systems would greatly enhance the non-proliferation regime.

The second alternative would revitalize President Dwight D. Eisenhower's time-honoured 'atoms-for-peace' idea: the transfer of nuclear material from military to civilian purposes. Even the partial transfer of plutonium or HEU from destroyed warheads to the IAEA could counter criticism by non-nuclear weapon states that superpower disarmament was not serious because the material was recycled militarily. This would have a healthy effect with regard to the divisive nature of Article VI issues.

Safeguards on exports

Article III.2 requires states parties to request safeguards on all relevant exports and, by implication, to create the necessary legal and administrative conditions needed to live up to this obligation.

The past five years have seen some breath-taking events in this context. Nuclear equipment, material and technology were transferred without safeguards by FRG companies to India (beryllium and heavy water), Pakistan (enrichment technology, maraging steel, enrichment equipment, uranium hexafluoride containers, tritium, tritium extraction and purification technology) and South Africa (fuel fabrication measurement devices). Switzerland sometimes played the role of transit stage for subsidiaries of FRG firms. Norway was the innocent supplier of heavy water to India—the Norwegian supplier was told the destination would be the FRG.[34]

Parliamentary investigations revealed serious weaknesses in the export control system. The responsible agencies were understaffed and under-funded and the ministries charged with their supervision held a policy of export first, control second. The law left wide gaps: transit trade and activities abroad were not punishable at all. Penalties were ridiculous in comparison to the profits to be gained from perpetrations, and serious investigations were rarely launched lest companies suffer undue competitive disadvantages. While the FRG kept to the letter of the Treaty, implementation was less than sufficient and the spirit of the NPT was violated. There is some suspicion that many other industrial countries would not fare better in this regard. Without adequate precautions, the creation of a unified EC market after 1992 may mean that nuclear-related goods drift freely towards those member countries with the weakest controls on trade with the outer world. While the FRG has hastened since early 1989 to close loopholes and regain lost reputation, such gaps may remain in other countries and may well be abused in the future. In some cases, NPT parties may even use such exports to collect hard currency. Romania, for example, is reported to have illegally transhipped Norwegian heavy water to Israel. Norwegian

---

[34] Müller, H., *After the Scandals: West German Nonproliferation Policy*, PRIF Report (Peace Research Institute: Frankfurt, 1990).

inquiries to clear the matter have not been answered by Romanian authorities.[35]

Loopholes in the control systems for international trade are:

1. There is no register of 'small quantity' trade with fissionable material.

2. There are no controls on materials below given specifications. This applies to materials such as beryllium or maraging steel, defined as nuclear-usable only above a certain purity.

3. Transit-trade transactions—when merchandise does not touch ground in the home country of the trading company—mean that a company will not be prosecuted if such trade is not regulated by law in the home country.

4. Shipper–receiver communications are imperfect in nuclear materials not supervised by the IAEA, such as heavy water, which is usually safe-guarded only on specific request by the seller in non-NPT countries. (Norway has stopped all exports of heavy water, but other suppliers stay in the market.)

5. Shipper–receiver responsibility to inform the IAEA about transactions of non-fissionable material triggering safeguards is also a source of concern. Such imports to NPT countries must be reported but in good time before material is brought into such facilities. In trade between NPT shippers and non-NPT receivers, both sides are often in default on their reporting require-ments. Recent investigations of the German–Brazilian nuclear deal have shown that FRG companies left it to the government to inform the IAEA, while the government was waiting for the companies to do the reporting.

6. Dual-capable technologies and items remain a 'grey area', with considerable scope for abuse.

7. New technologies which are clearly nuclear relevant but not yet inter-nationally defined or regulated often lack control at national levels, too.

8. There is no rule for controlling trade in tritium and lithium deuteride, two critical materials for second- and third-generation nuclear weapons.

9. Specific weapon-usable items not needed for civilian nuclear purposes but which may have civilian applications outside the nuclear sector are not listed or controlled.

It is clear that as the sophistication of third country (or even sub-national) purchasing agencies grows, there is considerable room for improving existing international co-operation among suppliers. Such co-operation has been slow and piecemeal, one reason being that some governments were shy of offending developing countries. This fear raises one of the trickiest problems in the export-safeguards context: how to deal with those non-NPT countries which are advanced in nuclear technology and which may be able to enter (or stay in) the nuclear export business themselves. Foremost among these, Argentina has exported research reactors to Peru and Algeria and is on the verge of exporting further research reactors to Albania, Turkey and perhaps Egypt. Argentina has an ambitious programme for offering small—

---

[35] *New York Times*, 25 May 1988.

25 MW(e) [million (electric) watts]—and medium-sized—380 MW(e)—reactors to developing countries and provides fuel services to Algeria, Brazil, Iran and Peru. Its new government is reportedly interested in opening a sales and co-operation campaign in the Middle East.[36]

Despite financial difficulties, Argentina is a potent exporter. In principle the other 'threshold' states possess the same possibilities. It is feared that those new suppliers would not act with the same degree of caution and responsibility as traditional suppliers are supposed to (but do not always) apply. So far, however, new suppliers have, by and large, behaved responsibly. South Africa has said it will apply London Guidelines standards on all exports (although recent rumours of an exchange of uranium for Israeli missile technology raise some questions).[37] Argentina has declared it will demand safeguards on its nuclear trade and has so far stuck to this unilateral commitment; its sale of a research reactor to Algeria, however, does not require safeguards on eventual replications of that facility, a weaker safeguards policy than proposed by the London Guidelines. Brazil has forced China to accept, for the first time, the obligation to tolerate safeguards on possible nuclear items from Brazil, a stipulation which industrialized countries have not been able to extricate from China. The other countries have no known exports, and India is reported to have denied Colonel Qadhafi a nuclear explosive in exchange for oil exports.

In the past the one troublesome exception was China, which started in the 1960s as a strong (verbal) supporter of nuclear multipolarity. However in practice China presumably exported uranium and heavy water to Argentina and, possibly, South Africa, without safeguards. There are some indications that China—or Chinese scientists—may have helped Pakistan with weapon technology, although this has never been fully substantiated. After a long and conflict-filled negotiation with the USA on nuclear co-operation, the Chinese Prime Minister made public statements that China would not foster proliferation and would require those importing its nuclear merchandise to accept IAEA safeguards. Its recent supply contract for a 300-MW(e) power reactor to Pakistan appears to contain such a safeguards clause.[38]

The fact that the threshold countries/emerging suppliers are both targets of non-proliferation policy and players one would like to integrate presents philosophical and practical problems for a consistent export approach. Attempts to draw them closer to the regime are difficult because they feel—with some justification—that it is inappropriate for them to accept, for example, the London Guidelines as an export approach since it was designed to contain their own unsafeguarded nuclear developments in the first place. To abolish all export restraints towards these countries, on the other hand, opens the route to possible abuse. The transfer of knowledge and

[36] *IAEA Newsbrief*, vol. 4, no. 4 (May 1989); *IAEA Bulletin*, vol. 31, no. 1 (1989), p. 57; *Nucleonics Week*, vol. 30, no. 14 (6 Apr. 1989), p. 8, and vol. 30, no. 18 (4 May 1989), p. 13.

[37] *Arms Control Reporter*, Nov. 1989, pp. 706.B.20–21.

[38] *Nucleonics Week*, vol. 30, no. 47 (23 Nov. 1989), p. 1.

personnel from imported/safeguarded to autonomous/unsafeguarded activities is frequent, and very embarrassing to the exporter.

Aside from the manifest economic interest of nuclear exporters such as Belgium, the FRG or Switzerland, these difficulties have fuelled the hot debates on full-scope as opposed to exported-item safeguards in the past. This controversy has dominated the discussion on export policy and the meaning of Article III since the beginning of the NPT and produced the most heated dispute among the industrialized countries at the 1985 Review Conference. Under the leadership of the FRG the 'liberal exporters' compromised on language obliging parties to strive to achieve full-scope safeguards on exports—which left open a small escape (i.e., to renounce full-scope safeguards if such efforts were unsuccessful with the trading partner).[39] Since then, the only countries to enter new major export contracts with non-nuclear weapon states have been non-party China (with Pakistan) and depositary USSR (with India); the Soviet sale of two 1000-MW units for soft currency, countertrade and a preferential 2.5 per cent interest loan is particularly remarkable.[40]

Other government-approved exports concerned the implementation of past contracts and minor supplies such as spare parts and safety control equipment, but no massive sales. Under the pressure of the illegal export scandals, the FRG Government declared its intention to live up to the language of the third Review Conference Final Document and not to enter any major new contracts with countries where nuclear material was circulating free of safeguards. The past strategy of entangling non-NPT parties into the regime by co-operation was seen to be a double-edged sword. Reorganization of the Brazilian nuclear establishment has deprived the FRG of residual control over sensitive activities and raised the spectre of German technology ending up in unsafeguarded facilities.

Under present circumstances and with a sharpened awareness of the risks of proliferation to its own reputation if not national security, it is unlikely that the FRG will again take the lead of those opposed to full-scope safeguards. It is interesting to note that Switzerland has also tightened up its export legislation and regulations considerably since 1985.[41]

Summary

The implementation of Article III by North Korea is in open doubt, which will probably lead to a very tough debate at the Conference should the matter not be resolved by that time. Other countries which have failed to conclude their safeguards agreements with the Agency are in formal default with their obligations, but their lack of nuclear activities makes this less urgent. The recent conclusion of a safeguards agreement by Nigeria, coming on the heels of a strange statement by the country's foreign minister on the

[39] Fischer and Müller (note 2), pp. 18–22.
[40] *Nucleonics Week*, vol. 29, no. 47 (24 Nov. 1988), pp. 3–4.
[41] *Nucleonics Week*, vol. 30, no. 30 (27 July 1989), pp. 4–6; *Arms Control Reporter*, July 1988, p. 602.B.149; *Nuclear Fuel*, vol. 4, no. 2 (17 Jan. 1986), p. 14.

need for a Black African bomb, was a welcome event;[42] it demonstrated serious commitment to the NPT by the largest Black African state.

The negligence of some exporters, notably the FRG, in revamping their own export control policies and systems promptly after the discovery of the very first weaknesses raises serious doubts about whether Article III.2 obligations have been properly met. Urgent changes of export policy, law and administration are needed to demonstrate that there is serious willingness to live up to the Treaty commitment. The FRG will have to present an impressive and convincing record of changes in its export control system to silence critical voices.

International co-ordination of export policy has been a controversial matter because of its exclusivity among industrialized countries. For technical reasons, it is unlikely that this constellation will change. Maybe it would help to mitigate controversy if the Conference could decide to allow exporters to conduct further co-ordination and to report to the 1995 Conference. The exporters could then point to this mandate in legitimizing their further proceedings, and the non-exporters could satisfy themselves that export control co-ordination was mandated by an international body and that they would maintain a kind of '*droit de regard*' over the outcome.

Article IV

Article IV requires parties to co-operate as fully as possible in the field of peaceful nuclear applications, including technology transfer, with particular attention to the needs of the developing countries. This article has been seriously affected by the Chernobyl accident and its consequences for world nuclear industry: in the industrial world the use or expansion of nuclear energy stopped abruptly in Belgium, the FRG, Finland, Italy, the Netherlands, Spain and Switzerland. Sweden decided to accelerate the phase-out of its current nuclear power plants (although there appear to be second thoughts on the matter). Expansion plans were scaled down in many other countries, and developing countries now think twice before considering nuclear energy programmes.

The present state of affairs should not negate the importance of civilian nuclear power in the world energy picture. At present, 434 power reactors with a combined capacity of 316 GW(e) [thousand (electric) megawatts] operate in 27 countries; 100 units are under construction, including units in five countries not yet users of nuclear electricity. Nuclear power supplies about 17 per cent of the world's electricity; in 11 countries—all industrial ones—the share is above 30 per cent, but at present, interest in the Third World is confined to a handful of buyers: Indonesia, South Korea, maybe in the distant future Bangladesh among NPT parties, India and Pakistan among non-parties.[43] It is open to debate whether this decline in interest is good or

[42] *PPNN Newsbrief*, no. 2 (July 1988), p. 2.
[43] *New York Times*, 7 Mar. 1989; *Nucleonics Week*, vol. 30, no. 17 (27 Apr. 1989), p. 11; *PPNN Newsbrief*, no. 4 (Jan. 1989), p. 4; *Nucleonics Week*, vol. 28, no. 12 (19 Mar. 1987), pp. 3–5.

bad for non-proliferation. The deceleration of nuclear expansion can be seen as good for non-proliferation, yet at the same time it weakens an important incentive to appreciate the NPT commitment. If the NPT is a bargain between the haves and the have-nots, the depreciation of nuclear technology must devalue the importance of the Treaty to those with no great interest in nuclear matters. This group is already a majority among the developing countries. If it is enlarged by those major parties which, so far, have been interested in the Treaty because of the prospects for civilian nuclear energy use, the consequences for NPT stability are not necessarily beneficial.

Prospects for reviving interest in nuclear energy in developing countries, however, are by and large dim. An IAEA study concluded that only a handful of countries would provide a market for small-scale reactors; a recent survey showed that even developing countries have not followed up the proposals of the small and medium power reactor project.[44] Interest in small power reactors has been awakened in industrial countries, in the context of research on 'inherent safety', replacement needs in the 1990s and preference for smaller, incremental additions rather than large-scale units.[45] So far no visible market exists in the Third World.

An IAEA study on nuclear financing enumerated several obstacles to nuclear power development such as lack of infrastructure, of adequate legislation on radiation protection, of appropriate overall energy requirement studies and of development plans. Rather than concrete steps towards financial assistance better grounds for risk assessment were recommended. There is little chance of improving the prospects for nuclear expansion from this angle. The recent finding of the World Bank that the Angra III nuclear power plant in Brazil is not eligible for financing because of unviability only verifies the difficulties explained in the experts' study.[46]

Loss of interest by the Third World may help explain the muted negative response to two failures to achieve global consensus on the conditions for peaceful co-operation on nuclear energy—the UN Conference on the Promotion of International Cooperation for the Peaceful Uses of Nuclear Energy (PUNE) and the IAEA Committee on the Assurances of Supply (CAS). PUNE was first created to counter perceived nuclear suppliers' collaboration against technology 'have-nots'. While PUNE provoked many interesting technical papers it failed on the issue of conditions for peaceful co-operation. The Group of Seventy-Seven (G-77) countries, led by India, Argentina and Brazil, would have preferred a document obliging suppliers to unconditional collaboration.[47] The industrial countries, in contrast, insisted on a clear link between the degree of non-proliferation commitment

---

[44] IAEA, *Small and Medium Power Reactors: Project Initiation Study, Phase I*, IAEA-Tecdoc-347 (IAEA: Vienna, 1985); IAEA, *Promotion and Financing of Nuclear Power Programmes in Developing Countries* (IAEA: Vienna, 1987), pp. 30–32.

[45] For new research into new, inherently safe reactors compare *IAEA Bulletin*, vol. 31, no. 3 (1989), pp. 5–55.

[46] IAEA, *Promotion and Financing of Nuclear Power Programmes in Developing Countries* (note 44); *Nucleonics Week*, vol. 30, no. 9 (2 Mar. 1989), p. 9.

[47] 'The Group of Seventy-Seven' is a term used to denote the developing countries acting as a bloc. The group originally consisted of 77 countries; it now contains many more.

and the entitlement for unimpeded access to technology. This controversy, which prevented PUNE from reaching a final consensus, was also preeminent in CAS, another attempt to shape such a consensus during the course of seven years. CAS agreed on some promising proposals but failed on the non-proliferation commitment which would entitle recipients to enjoy the advantages of these agreements.[48] Both forums clearly showed one of the basic weaknesses of the NPT: leadership within the developing world is exerted by countries which are non-parties to the Treaty, if not its outright enemies. The domination of this group over faithful NPT adherents hinders all NPT parties from shaping consensus on these issues by themselves without the interference of outsiders.

Nuclear co-operation on non-energy applications concerns geology, medicine, agriculture, material testing, irradiation of food, and basic research. On a bilateral basis, the expansion of research reactors must be noted. Bangladesh and Indonesia have acquired research reactors under safeguards. Saudi Arabia contracted for the supply of two research reactors with an FRG firm. While nuclear energy is stagnating, the development of nuclear research goes on. A total of 325 research reactors are in operation throughout the world, including 41 units in 22 developing countries.

Under IAEA auspices, the technical assistance and co-operation budget has reached $45.5 million, a remarkable growth from the $35.9 million in 1984. In 1988 the IAEA supported 1009 projects, including 88 regional and interregional training programmes. It assigned 2023 experts and processed 3386 equipment purchases.[49] The 'gentlemen's agreement' that expenditures on safeguards and technological co-operation should be comparable produces a permanent difficulty for the balance between the IAEA's budget and expenditures. Co-operation projects have to be financed by extra-budgetary voluntary contributions. Beyond that, developed countries sometimes pick up projects which the IAEA cannot afford to fund. These 'footnote a' projects are the best way to give privilege to NPT parties.[50]

Whereas Article IV can be said to be implemented, parties derive too little satisfaction from this fact. Objective difficulties in making Article IV benefits an effective incentive for parties to regard the Treaty as beneficial, and the subjective problem of reaching agreement between developed and developing countries in forums where the G-77 is led by non-parties, prevent its true success. Budgetary restraint policy limits the remaining possibilities.

Article IV is not expected to cause as much trouble for the Review Conference as in the past. Complaints over trade restrictions and oligopoly abounded in 1980, but were muted by 1985. It is unlikely that the develop-

[48] *Arms Control Reporter,* July 1987, p. 602.B.127; *Nucleonics Week,* vol. 28, no. 12 (19 Mar. 1987), pp. 11–12.

[49] *IAEA News Features,* no. 4 (Sep. 1988); *IAEA Newsbrief,* vol. 4, no. 5 (June 1989), p. 1 and vol. 4, no. 6 (July/Aug. 1989), p. 1; *IAEA Bulletin,* vol. 31, no. 2 (1989), p. 48; compare also the articles in *IAEA Bulletin,* vol. 29, no. 1 (1987), pp. 5–25 and no. 2 (1987), pp. 5–32.

[50] Projects deemed worthwhile by the Agency but for which no sufficient funds are available are listed in footnote a of the IAEA *Technical Co-operation Budget Document.*

ing countries as a group will put great energy into such complaints. Several individual countries may well do so, however. Iran was denied research reactor fuel by the USA and had to turn to non-NPT Argentina for supplies. Since 1984 the FRG Government has refused to grant licences for 7000 tonnes of Trigger List[51] equipment needed to complete the Busheer power plants and has dissuaded Siemens from resuming work as long as no peace treaty is signed with Iraq. Iran strongly criticized this attitude at the 1989 IAEA General Conference and can be expected to repeat this in 1990.[52]

Iraq may complain about its failed attempt to contract for a replacement for the Osiraq reactor, but since its partner, France, was a non-party this is outside the NPT context. Libya was the victim of Soviet foot-dragging over the supply of two reactors but, in the aftermath of the Chernobyl accident, decided it was no time to start a nuclear power programme. Otherwise there were no cases of denial; on the contrary, some important NPT parties acquired research reactors for the first time. The issue of technology denial should not loom large on the agenda. This also applies to the US pressure on Taiwan to refrain from reprocessing, but Taiwan will not be represented at the Conference. The problem of restricting reprocessing as far as possible ceased to be a North–South issue with the FRG decision not to proceed with the Wackersdorf commercial reprocessing plant and the reduction if not renouncement of plutonium recycling plans in Western countries. The London Guidelines stipulation to exert 'restraint' in the export of sensitive technology stands on firmer and more defensible ground.

While substantial issues are less controversial than in the past, the complaint of insufficient technology assistance may arise. The Egyptian project of a nuclear energy fund, discussed at the 1985 Review Conference, was not supported by the IAEA expert group study. The risk of losing the benefit side of the NPT bargain will certainly be expressed, and with some reason. It is time to consider additional incentives for Third World countries to regard this Treaty as beneficial to their interests.

There is little other possibility than to expand budgetary and voluntary contributions. A second area where help should and could be expanded— and which should receive special attention in 1990—is nuclear safety. As the appalling case of a radioactive source found in a waste-disposal site in Brazil signals, even in developing countries with an advanced nuclear industry there are inherent problems of safety assessment and administration. As more countries enter research and non-energy application programmes, increasing assistance will be needed in this field.[53]

Finally, the Conference should concern itself with regional co-operation including non-parties, which holds a potential to mitigate nuclear rivalries and mutual fear and to build some confidence even in the absence of NPT

---

[51] The Trigger List is a list of items the export of which to a non-nuclear weapon state requires the application of safeguards on the plant in which it is used or on the material or processes used. It is only relevant to export to non-NPT states in this category. The original list was agreed in 1974; it has been expanded and forms part of the 1977 London (Suppliers') Guidelines (note 25).

[52] *Nucleonics Week*, vol. 30, no. 45 (9 Nov. 1989), p. 7; vol. 27, no. 44 (30 Oct. 1986), pp. 4–5.

[53] Compare *IAEA Press Release*, 87/32, 15 Oct. 1987 and 87/40, 1 Dec. 1987.

membership. The present IAEA plan to expand regional and interregional projects from 15 to more than 25 per cent of the technical assistance programme is commendable in this respect.[54]

Article V

Article V provides for peaceful nuclear explosion (PNE) services by the nuclear weapon states to non-nuclear weapon states under international supervision. It was the outgrowth of nuclear euphoria towards the end of the 1960s which included the purported benefits of PNEs for mining, large construction projects such as channels, secondary oil and gas production, and expanding sub-surface caverns for the storage of natural gas. The prospects for these activities faded quickly. Only the USSR has conducted a few PNEs each year. Whereas in 1988 the Soviet delegate to the annual meeting of OPANAL (Agency for the Prohibition of Nuclear Weapons in Latin America) praised the merits of the PNE programme, the USSR has repeatedly declared its willingness to cease PNEs in the context of a comprehensive test ban treaty (CTBT). Although the present status of the Soviet PNE programme is unclear, given the growing protests within the USSR against the use of nuclear power and against testing,[55] it is not too risky to predict the end of Soviet PNEs in the near future, even in the absence of a CTBT. The main arguments against PNEs are cost and radiological safety concerns. If these apply in an industrial country like the USA, they weigh all the heavier in developing countries without an adequate safety infrastructure.[56]

Many have proposed that Article V be abolished. It has been used by non-parties as an argument that PNEs are a serious option and legitimizes their refusal to renounce this option. Rather than removing Article V, which would open the door for further amendments, a frank discussion about the questionable value of PNEs would be preferable. A Soviet statement announcing the end of the PNE programme in the USSR would be a great help. If the Conference could resolve to declare that no benefit is to be derived from PNEs in the foreseeable future and that unwillingness to renounce PNEs is a matter of political concern, such a consensus would be more realistic and certainly more helpful politically in discussions with non-members than futile attempts to amend the Treaty.

Article VI

In Article VI all parties, nuclear as well as non-nuclear weapon states, commit themselves to faithful negotiations towards nuclear and complete and comprehensive disarmament. No issue, besides regional conflicts, has

---

[54] *IAEA Newsbrief*, vol. 3, no. 10 (Dec. 1988).

[55] See also chapter 2 of this *Yearbook*.

[56] Findlay, T., 'Peaceful nuclear explosions and the NPT: letting a dead letter lie', Paper presented to the PPNN Core Group Meeting, 18–19 Nov. 1989, Baden, Austria.

such a potential for causing controversy at the 1990 Review Conference. Lack of implementation of Article VI by the superpowers made it hard to reach consensus in 1975, wrecked the final document in 1980 and necessitated the most inventive diplomatic language—permitting parties to disagree on one point in the framework of a consensus—in 1985.[57]

Non-nuclear weapon states, notably developing countries, view Article VI as the only major concession by the nuclear weapon states to compensate for the renouncement of the most powerful weapons by the non-nuclear weapon states. Article VI is part of a basic bargain: failure to realize its promise thus opens the question for many countries of whether the bargain is worth maintaining. For many Third World countries, the substance of Article VI is identical to a ban on nuclear weapon tests—an erroneous but powerful interpretation.

A comprehensive analysis of the preamble and Article VI show that an assessment of implementation must examine a number of aspects. How have the different aspects of disarmament been fulfilled since 1985?[58]

1. *Measures to improve crisis stability and prevent nuclear escalation.* In 1987 the USA and the USSR agreed to install nuclear risk reduction centres to permit quick and undisturbed communication, the exchange of information and assessment, and independent evaluation of the other side's position.[59] Since 1988 a new agreement obliges each superpower to notify the other of ballistic missile test plans, including range and direction of tested devices.[60] An agreement to avoid incidents emerging from operations on land, including brief border operations, was added in the same year,[61] comparable to the highly successful 1972 US–Soviet Incidents at Sea Agreement.[62] In 1989 the exchange of information on bomber alerts and exercises was also agreed.[63] Together with measures already in place, these new steps virtually eliminate the possibility of local incidents escalating to a world-wide nuclear war.

---

[57] Fischer and Müller (note 2), pp. 23–29.

[58] Progress on disarmament is documented in more detail in other chapters in this *Yearbook*: for progress towards a START treaty see chapter 11; for the implementation of the INF Treaty up to 31 December 1989 see chapter 12; for the progress of the CFE Negotiation see chapter 13; for negotiations on a chemical weapons convention see chapter 14; and for details on nuclear test talks and progress towards PNET and TTBT ratification, see chapter 15.

[59] Agreement between the United States of America and the Union of Soviet Socialist Republics on the Establishment of Nuclear Risk Reduction Centers. The agreement is reproduced in SIPRI, *SIPRI Yearbook 1988: World Armaments and Disarmament* (Oxford University Press: Oxford, 1988), appendix 13E, pp. 486–89.

[60] Agreement between the United States of America and the Union of Soviet Socialist Republics on Notifications of Launches of Intercontinental Ballistic Missiles and Submarine-Launched Ballistic Missiles, reproduced as appendix 1A in *SIPRI Yearbook 1989* (note 30), pp. 46–47.

[61] *International Herald Tribune*, 8 June 1989, pp. 1 and 8.

[62] Agreement between the USA and the USSR concerning the Prevention of Incidents on and over the High Seas, reproduced in Fieldhouse, R. (ed.), SIPRI, *Security at Sea: Naval Forces and Arms Control* (Oxford University Press: Oxford, 1990), appendix B, pp. 256–58.

[63] Agreement between the Government of the United States of America and the Government of the Union of Soviet Socialist Republics on Reciprocal Advance Notification of Major Strategic Exercises; see *Department of State Bulletin*, Nov. 1989, pp. 20–21.

2. *Measures to create confidence among the parties.* Confidence building is naturally served by the above measures. The main measure to achieve this goal was, however, the 1986 Stockholm Document, creating a precise advance calendar for major exercises and providing for observation and *ad hoc* inspection.[64] The heavily militarized region of Central Europe, with the greatest density of deployed nuclear weapons, has become that much more transparent through these measures, with the welcome corollary that the risks of nuclear escalation are reduced.

3. *Measures to remove the potential causes of armed conflict.* Hand-in-hand with these developments went the removal of possible reasons for the superpowers to go to war against each other. Mutual consultation on regional issues has been accelerated and intensified. The results are visible in the termination or scaling down of some armed conflicts in the world and the prospects of negotiated solutions in some other cases (Southern Africa, the Gulf War, South-East Asia, Afghanistan).[65] In Europe the thought of a violent clash between the blocs has become all but unthinkable after the reforms in Eastern Europe and the extreme tolerance of the USSR towards these changes.

4. *Measures to reduce nuclear arsenals.* For the first time in history, a category of nuclear weapons, intermediate-range nuclear forces, is being completely eliminated as a consequence of the 1987 INF Treaty. The physical destruction of missiles and launchers is on schedule and the stipulations of the agreements are duly observed by each side. The only shortcoming of the agreement is that the fissile material contained in the warheads, as well as guidance electronics, are free for military reuse. This inconsequence, however, should not detract from the merits of the agreement in Article VI terms; it is the first visible sign that the direction of the nuclear arms race may be reversible.

Negotiations on a START treaty have been progressing well and have been accelerated since the 1989 Malta summit. A treaty would be a major step towards fulfilling Article VI commitments. There are also plans to begin talks on short-range nuclear forces (SNF) after the conclusion of a CFE agreement. Some categories of SNF platform are already indirectly included in the CFE talks.

5. *Measures to move towards complete and comprehensive disarmament.* The CFE Negotiation in Vienna is making rapid progress and the conclusion of a treaty is likely in 1990. A second phase, including further reductions and a restructuring towards more defensive structures, is in principle agreed upon. Negotiations on a chemical weapons convention (CWC) are making slow but steady progress; the main obstacle may not be the superpowers in this case, but some Third World states.

6. *Measures to stop nuclear testing.* The protocols to the 1974 Threshold Test Ban Treaty (TTBT) and the 1976 Peaceful Nuclear Explosions Treaty

---

[64] The Stockholm Document is reproduced in SIPRI, *SIPRI Yearbook 1987: World Armaments and Disarmament* (Oxford University Press: Oxford, 1987), appendix 10A, pp. 355–69.

[65] For a report on ongoing armed conflicts in 1989, see chapter 10 of this *Yearbook*.

(PNET) are now being finalized and prepared for ratification. Perhaps more important were the unprecedented mutual observation and measurement activities which took place at the US and Soviet test sites in 1988.[66]

Clearly the nuclear weapon states can present an unprecedented record on Article VI. Not even in 1975, at the height of the first *détente* period, was such an impressive array of arms control and disarmament achievements at hand. To compound this success there are prospects for further progress once the present negotiations are concluded. While the prospects for complete nuclear disarmament are not bright for the immediate future, the perspective of considerable reductions is bright. More important, the probability of a nuclear war is the lowest since 1945. Given the fact that the first and foremost purpose of the NPT is to contribute to the prevention of nuclear war and that all articles must be seen in this light, the progress made under Article VI is certainly the most important and significant change between 1985 and 1990. This record not only concerns the two superpowers. It involves most of their allies, which participated directly (the FRG by renouncing possession of the Pershing 1A nuclear-capable missile[67]) or indirectly in the INF negotiations and are direct participants in the CFE and CSBM negotiations. Article VI obliges not only nuclear weapon states but all states parties to engage faithfully in negotiations, not only towards nuclear but also towards comprehensive and general disarmament.

Despite this good record the lack of serious progress towards a CTBT is a bone of contention. The CTBT was at the centre of non-nuclear weapon states' criticism of the superpowers in 1985 and remains the disarmament measure on which many minds in developing countries remain focused. There is particular embitterment because it is the only nuclear arms control measure discussed in a multilateral forum, the Geneva Conference on Disarmament (CD). The impression of disinterest by the major Western powers in multilateral disarmament has been greatly strengthened by the neglectful conduct of the USA during UNSSD III in 1988; failure to reach consensus on a final document was widely ascribed to needless US intransigence.[68] However, while the connection of a CTBT to the NPT is a special one—it is the only arms control measure mentioned explicitly in the Treaty—its impact on the course of disarmament as such is limited. While it would prevent the development of new and improved nuclear weapons, it would neither lead directly to disarmament nor reduce the number of weapons in place. While it is legitimate to criticize the failure to even negotiate on the matter and to press forcefully for a CTBT, it makes little sense to hinge the fate of the NPT on this single disarmament measure

---

[66] The US–Soviet Joint Verification Experiment is covered by Ferm, R., 'Nuclear explosions', SIPRI, *SIPRI Yearbook 1989: World Armaments and Disarmament* (Oxford University Press: Oxford, 1989), chapter 2, pp. 52–55, and the text of the agreement is given in appendix 2B of the same volume.

[67] Risse-Kappen, T., *The Zero Option: INF, West Germany and Arms Control* (Westview Press: Boulder, Colo., 1988).

[68] *PPNN Newsbrief*, no. 2 (July 1988), p. 2.

which is of some but not of overwhelming importance to the course of disarmament.[69] The argument cuts both ways, however. The US refusal to enter further talks on testing limitation is unjustified. If the report is correct that a high-ranking US official has indicated that the USA would cease to support the extension of the NPT after 1995 if a link were established between this extension and an end to testing,[70] this would also set wrong priorities, given the marginal contribution of further testing to US security.

Because of this evaluation of the CTBT, Article VI contains an explosive potential for the 1990 Review Conference, compounded by the initiative of the Parliamentarians for Global Action to persuade PTBT parties to ask for an amendment conference.[71] Since two of the three powers with a veto right are opposed, the prospects for its success are nil.

Another matter for concern is the lack of attention devoted to disarmament progress in the Third World. It seems that the INF Treaty, greeted with so much relief in Europe, was almost ignored or depreciated as unimportant in the Third World. The series of measures for the prevention of nuclear war were hardly noticed. The connection of confidence building and conventional arms control to the NPT, though clearly defined in the text of the Treaty, are not widely realized. It is an astonishing political reality that bilateral or bloc-to-bloc negotiations in Europe largely escape attention, let alone a correct and thorough evaluation, in other parts of the world.

Thus there is a considerable danger that there will be a clash along the North–South axis on the issue of disarmament for the single reason of the lack of a CTBT. The USSR is unlikely to side with the Third World; it will rather try to take a mediating position. Yet on the question of whether the nuclear weapon states have to present a good Article VI record, in all probability the 'Northern' world will stick together this time.

There is even some possibility of a counter-attack. US officials have grown increasingly angry at what they perceive to be hypocritical criticism of a strongly improved record and are likely to ask Third Word countries what they have done to live up to their Article VI obligations. They can point to the spread of ballistic missiles, to reluctance to agree to a CWC and to buildup of conventional arms even under conditions of a serious debt crisis in the South. There is some truth in this analysis but it would certainly not steer the Review Conference towards an agreement if the Article VI discussion were to end in a dispute over who has fared worse, North or South, on disarmament.

The conference would be greatly helped if a START treaty were already signed and if the superpowers had agreed on a framework mandate for follow-up talks on strategic arms reduction. It would also make sense, after the unforeseen changes in Eastern Europe in late 1989, to start negotiations

---

[69] For the background to the CTBT debate see Goldblat, J. and Cox, D. (eds), SIPRI, *Nuclear Weapon Tests: Prohibition or Limitation?* (Oxford University Press: Oxford, 1988).

[70] *Arms Control Reporter*, Nov. 1989, p. 706.B.19.

[71] Dhanapala, J., 'Article VI and the PTBT amendment proposal', Paper presented to the PPNN Core Group meeting, 18–19 Nov. 1989, Baden, Austria.

on short-range nuclear forces immediately after the CFE.[72] Also, a carefully circumscribed mandate for studying the framework of a CTBT, and for starting with the construction of a verification system, would be a compromise offer which many in the developing world would justifiably welcome. It would be particularly unhelpful if the USA continues to vote against even studying interim verification measures and the setting up of an international seismic monitoring network.[73]

Such modest steps would not remove criticism of the stubborn objections to a test ban. This criticism will understandably and justifiably not cease unless a test ban comes into force, but the compromise would signal willingness on the part of the Western powers to listen to the disarmament wishes of non-nuclear weapon states and to meet them half-way. Those parties might in turn accept the good record on disarmament. It would also be great progress for the 1995 conference, if the Review Conference could open the way to a better understanding of priorities in nuclear disarmament and the (albeit limited) role a CTBT can play in this framework.

Article VII

Article VII confirms the right of parties to set up nuclear weapon-free zones in their regions. In the past NWFZ issues have been confined to a propaganda struggle between the East (pushing its various NWFZ proposals for Europe against the requirements of NATO's flexible response strategy) and the West (struggling to reject WTO proposals so as not to endanger alliance unity).[74] However, the issue is increasingly likely to open more substantial conflicts along the North–South fault line, with the Western nuclear weapon states as the main targets for criticism.

The Tlatelolco Treaty and the Rarotonga Treaty establish NWFZs in Latin America and the South Pacific, respectively.[75] There have been serious talks on the creation of a NWFZ in the ASEAN region. The USA has made it clear that this would be contrary to its national interest and that pursuing the idea further would jeopardize US protection for the states concerned. In the Middle East and South Asia, the NWFZ concept has become an instrument in the ongoing propaganda war, and in Africa it has so far failed to attract South African attention. In Europe proposals for NWFZs in the northern region, in the Baltic, along the Central Front and in the Balkans have so far failed because of the different alliance strategies.

Two very fundamental questions must be answered:

1. What happens when the national interests of small regional states clash with the strategic interests of states with global commitments?[76] The USA

---

[72] See also chapter 18 of this *Yearbook*.
[73] *Arms Control Reporter*, Feb. 1988, p. 608.B.151.
[74] Fischer and Müller (note 2), pp. 23–24, 27.
[75] For the status of implementation, see annexe A.
[76] See Krohn, A., *Nuklearwaffenfreie Zone: Regionales Disengagement unter der Rahmenbedingung globaler Großmachtinteressen* (Nomos: Baden-Baden, 1989).

and to a lesser degree the UK have maintained alliances far from their own borders and have thus been obliged to be prepared to rally to their allies' assistance over great distances. Freedom of the high seas and the unimpeded movement of armed forces have been essential for the protection of allies. Protecting the innocent, of course, is a good excuse which overrules the quietist desire of regional states to be left alone as far as nuclear weapons are concerned. When the main threat disappears, however, the ethical justification for this kind of intrusive movement is devalued and the legitimate interests of countries in 'transit regions' deserve a second hearing.

2. Is the operational principle of some Western navies compatible with Article VII? Denuclearization of regional zones runs contrary to the principle of nuclear-armed navies of neither confirming nor denying the presence of nuclear weapons aboard their ships and contradicts the principles of freedom of passage and transit through territorial waters which are established by international law.[77] This clash became visible with New Zealand's objections to port visits by nuclear-armed ships. Rather than break with tradition and disclose which ships were not armed with nuclear weapons, the USA abandoned its defence relationship with New Zealand. The NWFZ issue puts this conflict in a broader context. By establishing NWFZs, regional powers pursue several objectives: to support the non-proliferation principle by adding a regional layer to the system, to reduce the danger of becoming a nuclear target, in some cases to diminish superpower presence, and finally to assert national sovereignty through an action of collective solidarity. These interests are as legitimate as those of a nuclear weapon state and they gain legitimacy by being applied to territory close to home. If the operational principle of Western navies makes it impossible even to consider recognition of those interests, then it must be asked whether this principle is compatible with a non-proliferation regime that contains Article VII of the NPT. Is it not this principle that must be changed rather than the legal rights of the countries negated? The insistence on narrow military perspectives in a world in which the main rationale for such perspectives has dramatically changed is a definite danger to the non-proliferation regime. The discriminatory character of the regime is tenable only if it remains at a minimum. Direct objections raised against the very principle of the NWFZ by the US Government[78] leave countries in such zones—or in prospective zones—with the feeling that nuclear weapon states are not willing to sacrifice some minor privileges even where relatively small costs are involved. This connection of the NWFZ issue with the very character of the regime and the NPT will give it greater weight in 1990, and presumably in 1995, than it has possessed in the past. Finally, the direct implications of the NPT for regional interests are remote for many countries. NWFZs are a way to make the NPT more directly relevant to national

<hr>

[77] Byers, R. B., 'Sea power, nuclear weapons and arms control', and Dunn, D. J., 'NATO navies and arms control', both in ed. R. B. Byers, *The Denuclearization of the Ocean* (Croom Helm: London, 1986), pp. 167–68 and 187–296, respectively.

[78] *Arms Control Reporter*, Sep. 1988, p. 456.B.78.

security interests and thereby to create stronger support for the survival of the regime. If this attempt fails because of intransigence by the nuclear weapon states the support may be replaced by cynicism. The Western nuclear weapon states would be well advised to take the misgivings over Article VII very seriously, even though most of the countries voicing them will be among the smaller members of the family of nations.[79]

The key to mitigating conflict over the issue is for the USA to revoke its principle objections against the zone approach and to underline the right of nations to engage in the establishment of NWFZs, depending on the merits of the approach in the respective region. Given the present plans for a retrenchment in the Pacific, based on the possibility that the US bases in the Philippines will be closed, this should be easier than in the past. Second, the USA and the UK should review their past decision not to sign the Rarotonga Treaty; this would put France in a spot, but for the time being France does not have the same obligations towards the NPT as the other two Western nuclear weapon states. In the long run it is likely that a policy of testing nuclear weapons far from one's own territory will not be tenable anyway. Third, the neither-confirm-nor-deny principle should be re-evaluated. Fourth, the nuclear weapon states should agree to discuss constraints on naval movements to the degree needed to respect the NWFZ.

Such decisions would be greeted with apprehension by non-nuclear weapon states pretending to keep their territory nuclear weapon-free while enjoying the nuclear umbrella provided by their alliances, but the right of countries to enact Article VII must take precedence over the luxury of conducting two contradictory policies simultaneously for the sole purpose of silencing domestic anti-nuclear opposition. As a positive side-effect, naval arms control would become much easier and the non-proliferation regime would in turn profit .

Article VIII

Article VIII of the NPT contains the rules for changing the Treaty. A purely procedural stipulation, Article VIII is of growing importance as the crucial year 1995 is approached. It is thus appropriate to take a closer look at its substance.

Each party has the right to forward any proposed amendment to the depositaries who are obliged to circulate it to all parties. If so requested by at least one-third of the parties to the Treaty, the depositaries must convene an amendment conference at which the amendment must be approved by a majority of the parties to the Treaty (to include all nuclear weapon states parties and all non-nuclear weapon states parties which, at the time of circulation of the amendment, are members of the IAEA Board of Governors). The same quorum is required for ratification. In other words, the Treaty is

[79] For a critical account see Fujita, E., *The Prevention of Geographical Proliferation of Nuclear Weapons: Nuclear Weapon Free Zones and Zones of Peace in the Southern Hemisphere* (UNIDIR: Geneva, Apr. 1989).

virtually unamendable and it could be suspected that this was exactly the intention of its drafters.

If an amendment process were started by some parties, however, it would undeniably be both cumbersome and divisive. Article VIII contains no time limits for the various procedures, so it could be an enormously protracted act. The precarious balance between the various interests which the Treaty represents makes it unlikely that a consensus could easily be formed on any change. Disputing amendments would inevitably weaken loyalty to the Treaty as it stands and lead to a dangerous erosion of Treaty support.

The basic complaints to have emerged over the past 20 years all concern implementation rather than substance. If relationships with threshold countries were unambiguous, if nuclear and other energy co-operation yield-ed tangible benefits to developing countries, if disarmament were going on in a steady fashion and if NWFZs were respected, there would be reason to believe that no basic changes to the Treaty would be proposed—except by non-parties for whom alleged shortcomings in the Treaty provide the excuse not to join.

If the main supporters of the Treaty want to avoid amendment debates, then they should see to it that the NPT is implemented well. Since com-plaints are usually voiced against the depositary powers themselves, their policy is the key to the future stability of the Treaty. This reasoning gains weight in view of 1995: there is a distinct danger that this critical date will tempt some parties to try to change the NPT.

Nigeria has already aired the idea of a protocol on negative security assurances. Such considerations will be based on quite legitimate concerns that the Treaty has not worked too well in this regard. The already difficult task of the 1995 extension conference will become unmanageable if it must also serve as an amendment conference. The 1990 Review Conference is thus an appropriate occasion for a double strategy: to address straight-forwardly the dissatisfaction of some parties by taking them seriously and promising remedy; and by initiating a campaign against changes in the Treaty.[80]

Article IX

The accession and membership issue may become a difficult one because of two regional conflicts. The first problem is connected to South Africa. South African accession to the NPT appears far more possible today than it did a few years ago. When former President P. W. Botha announced negotiations on NPT membership in 1987, this was widely perceived as a ploy to avoid expulsion from the IAEA. Under the de Klerk Government, however, the hardliners in the military have lost ground. The depositary powers are

[80] Compare Fischer, D., 'The 1995 Nuclear Non-Proliferation Treaty Extension Conference: issues and prospects' and Müller, H., 'Smoothing the path to 1995: amending the Nuclear Non-Proliferation Treaty and enhancing the regime', in ed. J. Simpson, *Nuclear Non-Proliferation: An Agenda for the 1990s* (Cambridge University Press: Cambridge, 1987), pp. 155–64 and 123–36, respectively.

encouraged that Pretoria is seriously exploring the possibility of accession. In this case, however, South Africa would wish to be granted some advantages, such as a guarantee against suspension of IAEA membership rights and the promise of new nuclear supplies—in other words, to be treated as a normal state in the field of civilian nuclear energy. By implication, this would mean the right to take a seat at the NPT Review Conference, should Pretoria deposit its instruments of ratification before that event.

The objections of Black African countries to the apartheid regime, however, mean that they cannot be expected to welcome South Africa at the conference. A heavy fight over credentials can be expected, if domestic reform does not accompany accession—not an impossible, but an unlikely prospect. Denying a member the right to sit in the conference is illegal; Western countries—perhaps also the USSR—would therefore be likely to argue for South African credentials. This would be a divisive development which could exacerbate more germane debates during the conference.

A second problem is the status of the Palestine Liberation Organization (PLO). With the support of Arab states, the PLO has applied for full membership of different international organizations as the state of Palestine. It is quite possible that the PLO will seek admission as observer under the label of Palestine. The USA would fight vehemently against such a decision. The situation would be compounded if the PLO decided to deposit its instruments of ratification with the Soviet Union. The USSR would be trapped between its good relationship with the Arab countries and its responsibility to steer the NPT through smooth waters. If it accepted PLO ratification, the Review Conference could well arrive at a stalemate over a purely procedural issue, since the USA would never accept Palestine as a party; under present legislation, the US delegation would be forced to walk out of the conference. If Moscow refuses acceptance, this would be the painful precedent of a prospective party being refused accession and could seriously alienate part of the Arab world. Hence, one can only hope that the situation is avoided by Arab prudence and wisdom.

The Vanunu revelations and the fact that Israel may have breached a peaceful-use commitment in a heavy-water supply contract with Norway are events which affect the non-proliferation regime directly and will be used by the Arab countries in turn to argue against observer status for Israel.

There are possible solutions for both problems. For South Africa, the best situation would be to announce accession immediately before the Conference and to deposit the instruments of ratification immediately afterwards, that is, before the IAEA General Conference meets in Vienna. There would then be five years to work on reforms within South Africa that would meet Black African demands for changing the apartheid regime. Without progress towards domestic justice, however, South African accession will pose serious troubles for 1995: maybe more troubles than benefits would be derived from a threshold state becoming a party. The PLO problem could then perhaps be removed by a compromise recently reached during the

IAEA General Conference (the PLO was admitted as Palestine, but still filed as an international organization, not as a state).

Article X

Article X contains two important stipulations. First, it permits parties to withdraw on three months' advance notice if superior national interests related to the substance matter of the Treaty force them to. This article has drawn criticism, mainly from people unfamiliar with international law which permits under the principle of *rebus sic stantibus* the revocation of contractual commitments under extreme circumstances. Article X is rather restrictive compared with this wider principle, in that it prescribes a specific time limit and a specific connection to the Treaty's substance, as well as a specific procedure—parties must explain to other parties and the UN Security Council the factors that have precipitated the decision to withdraw.

No party has thus far used this clause to leave the Treaty and there is no immediate sign that this would occur. Yet there have been some rumours that the unfettered development of the Israeli nuclear weapon capability has compelled several Arab leaders to look very carefully at the meaning of Article X. There is no immediate prospect of withdrawal, but the mere possibility would recommend stronger efforts by the depositaries to at least think hard about concepts and actions to remedy the situation in the Middle East. It is unlikely that five more years of passivity will prepare the ground well for Arab support for an extension of the Treaty, or continued membership, after 1995.

The extension conference is the second stipulation of Article X. Contrary to popular interpretations, the Treaty does not terminate in 1995. The extension conference has a mandate to decide on the length of extension, not on termination. Of course, a short enough extension would be the equivalent of termination. If the Conference does not reach consensus, the prevailing view among lawyers is that the Treaty would continue to be valid; but there are few who would like to see its survival dependent on non-consensus. Rather, there is general agreement that a substantial extension—another 25 years if not an indefinite extension—based on unanimity rather than on a majority vote, would be the desired outcome.

The 1990 conference would do well to set the framework for review and extension in 1995.[81] It is not clear whether there should be (*a*) two conferences, one on a five-year review and one on extension; (*b*) one conference, devoting half of its time to each issue; or (*c*) a pure extension conference, which would take up the review procedure within its own proceedings. It is hardly conceivable to waive a review of 1990–95 when the previous four five-year periods were subjected to careful scrutiny; neither is it desirable, if it is assumed that the next five years will witness considerable progress in

---

[81] Compare Fischer, D., 'Article X and the nature of the 1995 Extension Conference', Paper presented to the PPNN Core Group Meeting, 18–19 Nov. 1989, Baden, Austria.

arms control, disarmament, and conflict management and solution, all of which would bear rather positively on a successful extension conference. One realistic solution could be to start with a two-week review, but without the purpose of producing a final document, to continue with a debate on the general merits and experiences of the Treaty (that is, a general review of the 25 years of its existence) and then to proceed towards producing an extension resolution.

Three issues are likely to shape the prospects for extension and the debate in 1995: universalism, nuclear co-operation and disarmament. The Treaty is meant to cover the whole world, yet it has failed to attract a handful of important states. It cannot be ruled out that some of them may accede before 1995; even the two abstaining nuclear weapon states may reconsider their traditional position if the fate of the NPT is at stake. China is surrounded by potential threshold states; France may appreciate the high value of the NPT for the balance of power in Europe. A South African accession would enable the Black African front-line states to reverse their present position. A new, democratically elected government in Chile may see reason to break with its predecessor's refusal to accede. Still, while such accessions would certainly strengthen the Treaty, important holdouts would still remain.

Some may be tempted to argue for changing and amending the NPT. Such thoughts have been aired by scholars and officials from developing countries and India has presented the Gandhi plan,[82] which prescribes a detailed timetable until complete disarmament is reached in 2010, as an alternative to the NPT.

If one agrees, however, that the problems in the two most difficult proliferation regions—South Asia and the Middle East—are related more to regional security issues than to questions of universal equality and justice, then the prospects of attracting these bystanders by changes in the Treaty's language are dim indeed. It is thus more reasonable to try to keep the Treaty intact and to deal with those regional issues on their own merits and in their own context, without losing sight of the positive effects a solution of these problems would have on the NPT.

By implication, this means that the Gandhi proposal should not be treated as an alternative to the NPT. This does not mean, however, that it should not be discussed. Besides outrageous features—such as asking for a safeguarded end to fissionable material production in nuclear weapon states while keeping silent on such materials in non-nuclear weapon states (i.e., India)—it contains some ideas worth considering; among these is the suggestion to create procedures and institutions for regional conflict solution without recourse to force. To set up a forum in which these proposals—and others contained in the Brandt or Palme Commission Reports—can be discussed is particularly appropriate now that the sources of conflict in Europe appear to be diminishing. It is extremely desirable for the survival of a universal treaty such as the NPT that the world not be divided into two different cultures of

---

[82] *PPNN Newsbrief*, 2 July 1988, p. 2.

conflict solution—one managed by consensus and international institutions and one in which the sword and the gun still reign. To have such a forum ready before 1995 would presumably make it easier for many Third World countries to agree to an extension, because it would be a considerable sign of goodwill by the North to consider proposals from the South. At the same time, it would be made clear that the NPT is not dispensable.

Third World enthusiasm for a continuation of the Treaty will, to a certain degree, depend on the benefits expected from its further existence (see the above discussion of Article IV). It is unlikely that nuclear technical assistance alone will offer the same prospects as it did in 1968. Disillusionment about the reality of rapid nuclear growth in the world at large, and in the developing countries in particular, is too great. It is for this reason that the industrialized world would be well advised to carefully consider the resources likely to be free for future aid and their distribution between the needs of the reforming countries in Eastern Europe and the traditional recipients in the Third World. It must be assumed that greater efforts and sacrifices will be necessary and appropriate in the rich countries to meet the needs of either alternative. From this pool of resources, a considerable share must be devoted to energy and environmental projects. If the developed countries use the period between now and 1995 to design a package of energy/environmental aid programmes, if possible in co-operation with the respective UN agencies, and present this package under the auspices of Article IV in 1995, this would certainly improve the atmosphere of the 1995 conference.

It is stated above that prospects appear bright for unprecedented progress in disarmament in the next five years, a reversal of the Soviet situation excluded. Under these circumstances, a second START agreement is likely with further reduction of strategic nuclear arms and, perhaps, a binding commitment of the smaller nuclear weapon states not to expand their arsenals beyond a fixed number of warheads, an agreement curtailing nuclear weapons in Europe down to a few hundred, and some additional limitations on nuclear testing. Under these circumstances, it is not impossible that the total number of nuclear weapons in the world would be less in 1995 (or at least under the treaties concluded by that date) than when the NPT entered into force in 1970. While this would still not satisfy all parties, it would presumably be adequate to reach agreement on extension.

The 1990 conference would be well advised to deal with the procedural issues foreseen for 1995. Agreement on how to proceed would relieve the preparations for 1995 from unneeded tensions on these issues. The parties should also try in 1990 to exchange views on the standards against which the issue of extension will be evaluated in 1995. Some clarity about expectations will help diplomatic preparations.

III. Conclusions

As the article-by-article review shows, there are many details which, despite the generally favourable political climate, make it likely that the 1990 Review Conference will be a difficult one for international diplomacy. Perhaps it would be easier if the shadow of the 1995 extension conference did not already hang over the conferees.

In the final instance, the NPT is an unfit battleground for the unresolved problems of regional conflict. It presents too precarious a balance to withstand these antagonistic interests. Success of the 1990 Review Conference and survival of the Treaty beyond 1995 hinge either on the exclusion of regional issues and their diplomatic reverberations from the proceedings of the conference, or on the solution of the very conflicts which disturb the non-proliferation regime in the first place. Success in 1990 appears to depend on the following factors:

1. Sober assessment by non-nuclear weapon states, particularly developing countries, of the objective merits of the NPT as a measure of world security from which they, directly or indirectly, profit.

2. A major reconsideration of US priorities: the NPT appears to be accorded less importance than previously and the obvious disdain for multilateralism displayed by the US Government is a major annoyance for the Third World, maybe without Washington fully realizing its impact. Preoccupation with rather narrowly defined, supposed military or geostrategic interests hinders the USA from recognizing the dangers in this attitude for the future of a Treaty so essential for maintaining world order.

3. Willingness by the North, including the WTO states, to incur the material sacrifices necessary to keep the South interested in the Treaty.

4. The capability of the Third World to recognize the tremendous progress in arms control with regard to Article VI of the Treaty.

5. The ability of all actors to keep regional issues in proper perspective and not to let such issues be confused with the main body of the Treaty.

If one or more of these five factors lead to dissension, or a series of divisive motions to take majority votes (it came close to that in 1985), the consequences for 1995 would be dire. If they are all adequately dealt with, a tough but successful conference can be expected.

17. Laser isotope separation: technological developments and political implications

RICHARD KOKOSKI

I. Introduction

All plutonium for weapons has thus far been produced via nuclear reactors, and weapon-grade uranium has been enriched mainly by two costly and somewhat inefficient methods. In this regard, a major issue throughout 1989 concerned the planned construction in the USA of the first large-scale plant using laser techniques to purify plutonium for weapon purposes. It is clear that present stockpiles and recycling of plutonium from old warheads are sufficient to meet current needs and, should anticipated nuclear reductions occur, a definite surplus would exist. The conflict between oversupply and the perceived need for substantially adding to the plutonium production capability, especially in the present East–West climate with its renewed arms control possibilities, was a cause of mounting concern throughout most of the year. In early 1990 this concern, coupled with fiscal constraints, finally resulted in cancellation of the plant construction, raising expectations for negotiated constraints on fissile material production.

The other major and ongoing concern with respect to laser enrichment techniques which is dealt with here is the possibility of their use for weapon-grade uranium production in small, difficult-to-detect facilities. This is becoming increasingly important as the technology is now in advanced stages of development in many countries throughout the world, several of which are not party to the 1970 Non-Proliferation Treaty. The chapter looks at these issues in detail and includes a discussion of the technology itself to bring the current situation into focus and enable the reader better to assess the possible impact of future technological developments.

II. The major issues

Plutonium isotope separation

The implementation of the 1987 INF Treaty is proceeding as scheduled, and an agreement on strategic arms reductions (START) is very likely to be concluded in 1990.[1] Possible START follow-on talks under discussion may allow for even more substantial cuts in the nuclear arsenals of the two superpowers. Given these and other very positive developments in East–West relations, the need for fissile materials for nuclear weapons would seem to be on the decline. With the exception of tritium (with a half-life of about 12 years) the important elements of nuclear weapons—plutonium-239

---

[1] See chapter 11 of this *Yearbook*.

and uranium-235—decay extremely slowly and thus, unless a very unlikely buildup in nuclear forces takes place, can be recycled from existing or retired weapons in order to construct more modern ones if need be.

Such recycling has become common practice. Although the USA wishes to keep the warheads being withdrawn under the INF Treaty intact,[2] the Department of Energy (DOE) has stated that reprocessed plutonium from warheads aboard newly retired Poseidon submarines will satisfy their near-term defence requirements.[3] A START treaty would make substantially more plutonium available; according to the DOE itself, a backlog in plutonium would result.[4] At the same time, however, the DOE has continued to press for the creation of a new plutonium source 'technologically diverse from production reactors',[5] and the various issues associated with them, in order to provide 'flexibility in *rapid increases* in plutonium production capacity'.[6] For this purpose, a Special Isotope Separation (SIS) facility was planned for completion in 1995, to employ a sophisticated laser technique to remove the unwanted isotopes from Defense Department plutonium, upgrading it to weapon-grade material.

Much concern arose over the inherent conflict in a policy which would authorize several billion dollars to construct and operate a laser facility to produce material not currently needed, and which is likely to be in over-abundant supply in the not-too-distant future (if not already). In a December 1989 report, the National Academy of Sciences affirmed the adequacy of currently available plutonium to maintain a nuclear stockpile similar to the one which now exists.[7]

Further implications involved the long-standing US tenet on non-proliferation: to keep the military and civil uses of nuclear energy separate. Although the use of commercial spent fuel for weapon purposes is forbidden by the Hart–Simpson–Mitchell amendment[8] to the Atomic Energy Act, the DOE has admitted that, while the design life of the plant is 30 years, given its planned capacity there is only enough Defense Department feed to keep it occupied for about 9 years. There had been concern that, once a plant was built and running, pressure would have been brought to bear on Congress to allow commercial spent fuel to be used.[9]

[2] Hearings on National Defense Authorization Act for Fiscal Year 1989—H.R. 4264 and *Oversight of Previously Authorized Programs, DOE National Security Programs*, before the Procurement and Military Nuclear Systems Subcommittee of the Committee on Armed Services, House of Representatives, 100th Congress, 2nd Session (US Government Printing Office: Washington, DC, 1988), p. 257 (hereafter DOE-NSP/89).

[3] *Energy and Water Development Appropriations for 1989*, Hearings before a Subcommittee of the Committee on Appropriations, House of Representatives, 100th Congress, 2nd Session (US Government Printing Office: Washington, DC, 1988), Part 6, p. 773 (hereafter EWDA/89).

[4] EWDA/89 (note 3), p. 1118.

[5] DOE-NSP/89 (note 2), p. 490.

[6] EWDA/89 (note 3), p. 1145; emphasis added.

[7] *New York Times*, 21 Dec. 1989.

[8] Cochran, T. B., *et al.*, *Nuclear Weapons Databook, Vol. II, U.S. Nuclear Warhead Production*, (Ballinger: Cambridge, Mass., 1987), p. 96; Palmer, G. and Bolef, D. I., 'Laser isotope separation: the plutonium connection', *Bulletin of the Atomic Scientists*, Mar. 1984, p. 30.

[9] See also a 26 May 1989 letter from Paul Leventhal, President of the Nuclear Control Institute (NCI), to Sam Nunn, Chairman of the Senate Armed Services Committee. Co-signed by 28 leading arms control experts it recommended against SIS construction, stating that this could 'severely

The purification of plutonium by the USA and perhaps other nuclear weapon states could complicate current investigations of methods of nuclear warhead verification as well.[10] These rely on neutron emission from the plutonium-240 (^{240}Pu) which makes up about 6 per cent of current weapon-grade plutonium. For example, the presence of ^{240}Pu in a warhead has been shown to be of potential use in verification of sea-launched cruise missiles (SLCMs).[11]

The DOE had planned to begin construction of the SIS facility in 1989,[12] and have it fully operational by 1995.[13] The Energy Secretary, strongly backing the project earlier in 1989, began questioning its necessity by the end of the year.[14] Finally, citing both the availability of plutonium from other sources and funding priorities the DOE decided in early 1990 to cancel SIS construction. Research and development will reportedly continue, however.[15]

Safety concerns have temporarily halted plutonium production for weapons in the USA, and the USSR closed down three plutonium production reactors in 1989 (although it continues to produce substantial quantities in its 11 remaining dedicated reactors).[16] Growing interest is now being expressed in the elimination not only of nuclear delivery vehicles, but also of nuclear warheads and fissile materials. In 1989, Soviet proposals for verifiable cut-offs in fissile material production for nuclear weapons were put forward by President Mikhail Gorbachev in May and Foreign Minister Eduard Shevardnadze in September.[17] In July the US Congress passed an amendment calling on the Administration to look into the implications of a bilateral cut-off of all nuclear weapon material production.[18] These are promising signs and the halt in SIS construction is expected to encourage further advances in this area.[19]

compromise U.S. non-proliferation objectives'. Concern is also expressed that SIS operation 'would set a precedent for the use of such plutonium purification technology in the nuclear programs of other nations, including non-nuclear weapons states'. Regarding the technologies to be employed in the plant (see below) the authors point to 'unprecedented challenges to containing the nuclear programs of emerging and advanced industrial nations to exclusively peaceful purposes' and fear the precedent-setting nature of AVLIS demonstration in increasing the risks of diversion and terrorism. (Copy courtesy Deborah Holland, NCI)

[10] Letter from NCI to Sam Nunn (note 9).

[11] Cochran, T. B., 'Black Sea experiment: only a start', *Bulletin of the Atomic Scientists*, Nov. 1989, pp. 13–16.

[12] EWDA/89 (note 3), p. 923.

[13] DOE-NSP/89 (note 2), pp. 235, 263; EWDA/89 (note 3), p. 1110.

[14] *Washington Post*, 28 Nov. 1989, p. A6; 28 Jan. 1990, p. A4.

[15] Adams, P., 'DoE drops funds for Idaho plutonium plant', *Defense News*, vol. 5, no. 6 (5 Feb. 1990), p. 40.

[16] von Hippel, F., testimony before the House Committee on Foreign Affars, Subcommittee on Arms Control, International Security and Science, 20 June 1989, mimeo, p. 3; Lanouette, W., 'Plutonium—no supply, no demand?', *Bulletin of the Atomic Scientists*, Dec. 1989, p. 45.

[17] Hibbs, M. and MacLachlan, A., 'Soviet official pessimistic about IAEA role in verifying Pu production cutoff', *Nuclear Fuel*, vol. 14, no. 21 (16 Oct. 1989), p. 2; Lanouette (note 16), p. 45.

[18] *Congressional Record*, vol. 135, no. 103 (27 July 1989), H4361.

[19] *New York Times*, 27 Jan. 1990, p. 13.

Uranium enrichment

The two most prevalent methods for uranium enrichment employed world-wide at the present time are gaseous diffusion and the gas centrifuge process, representing roughly 90 per cent and 10 per cent of the world enrichment market respectively.[20] Although no known facility produces substantial amounts of enriched uranium using laser techniques today, proliferation concerns have been raised regarding the use of these techniques for the production of highly enriched uranium (HEU) since the processes themselves were understood in the early 1970s. One of the major worries in this context is that the nature of the technology could allow for smaller and more readily concealed clandestine enrichment facilities than other methods. Also, while the USA has not produced enriched uranium for weapon purposes since 1964[21] and the USSR announced in April 1989 that it had also halted its production,[22] the potential small size of laser facilities for HEU production would also be important in assessing the verifiability of fissile material cut-off proposals.

In addition, as shown below, despite current uranium enrichment over-capacity,[23] the spread of laser enrichment technology has proceeded rapidly in the past decade, with many countries—including many not party to the NPT—investing substantial amounts of time and effort in research and development. These developments may be hastened as nuclear power is re-examined in the light of growing evidence for a greenhouse effect. New and supposedly safer reactors[24] may use uranium more highly enriched than that prevalent today, heightening proliferation concerns. Laser processes, now forecast to be capable of more economical uranium enrichment, will doubtless become the focus of much greater attention should such trends materialize.

The choice of enrichment technology depends on the relative importance of several aspects of the processes concerned. These technical and economic factors are of course weighted differently when a decision is made to employ a given method. Depending on whether, for example, a relatively small amount of HEU is required for a few nuclear weapons or large amounts of inexpensively produced fuel for a light water reactor (LWR), very dissimilar approaches may be chosen. In order to understand how such trade-offs are made and gain insight into the level of scientific expertise necessary for the various methods, a cursory look at diffusion and centrifuge techniques,[25] with subsequent explication of the technology involved in the laser methods, is first provided.

[20] Erkens, J. W., 'CRISLA aims to reduce costs', *Nuclear Engineering International*, vol. 34, no. 419 (June 1989), p. 48.

[21] EWDA/89 (note 3), pp. 1034–35.

[22] *Arms Control Today*, May 1989, p. 25.

[23] Clark, R. G. and Addington-Lee, F., 'Overcapacity leaves buyers in the driving seat', *Nuclear Engineering International*, vol. 34, no. 419 (June 1989), p. 42.

[24] Broad, W. H, 'Now, a meltdown-proof reactor', *International Herald Tribune*, 17 Nov. 1988.

[25] An earlier and very thorough examination of enrichment techniques can be found in Krass *et al.*, SIPRI, *Uranium Enrichment and Nuclear Weapon Proliferation* (Taylor & Francis: London, 1983), which also examines the relationship with non-proliferation issues. For a good earlier overview of the

III. The technology

Uranium enrichment

Natural uranium (containing only 0.7 per cent ^{235}U, with ^{238}U making up the rest) can be used in heavy water reactors, but ^{235}U must be enriched to 2–4 per cent to fuel the more prevalent light water reactors. Uranium must be enriched to more than 90 per cent ^{235}U for weapon purposes and to about 93–97 per cent for many nuclear submarine and research reactors. In all the techniques described below for enriching uranium the process involves the separation of the input or 'feed' stream of material into two streams: a 'product' stream in which the ^{235}U is enriched and a 'tails' stream in which ^{235}U is depleted.[26]

The most prevalent means of enriching uranium today is via *gaseous diffusion*. This method involves separating molecules of uranium hexa-fluoride (UF_6) containing ^{235}U from those containing ^{238}U. The diffusion method depends on the fact that lighter molecules in a gas will move with a greater average velocity. In a gaseous diffusion unit UF_6 under high pressure is allowed to diffuse through a porous barrier, the higher speed of the molecules containing ^{235}U allowing for more collisions with the barrier and hence more of a chance for them to escape through one of the holes (typically 10 millionths of a millimetre in diameter.)[27] The emerging gas is thus slightly enriched in UF_6 molecules containing the desired ^{235}U atom.

A more advanced technique which allows higher separation factors[28] than gaseous diffusion while still providing a reasonable (though smaller) throughput[29] is the *gas centrifuge* process which uses centrifugal accelera-tion created in a cylinder rotating at very high speed. UF_6 gas is fed into the rotating cylinder and acceleration of rotation increases the concentration of UF_6 molecules containing ^{235}U closer to the centre of the cylinder for collec-tion.[30] The high rate of rotation necessary to obtain useful enrichment factors is more effectively achieved using high-strength lightweight materials in cylinder construction and by operation in a vacuum container.[31]

Principles of laser enrichment

The laser's ability to produce collimated light of a very precise frequency allows it to be used to deposit exact amounts of energy to given atoms or

more technical aspects see Villani, S. (ed.), *Topics in Applied Physics, Vol. 35, Uranium Enrichment* (Springer-Verlag: West Berlin, 1979).

[26] See, e.g., *Advanced Uranium Enrichment Technologies*, Hearing before the Subcommittee on Energy Research and Production of the Committee on Science and Technology, US House of Representatives, 96th Congress, 1st Session (US Government Printing Office: Washington, DC, 1979), p. 86 (hereafter HR-AUET).

[27] *Nuclear Weapons Databook Vol. II* (note 8), p. 129.

[28] The separation factor is defined as the percentage of ^{235}U in the product stream divided by the percentage in the tails stream.

[29] *Nuclear Weapons Databook Vol. II* (note 8), p. 130.

[30] Soubbaramayer, 'Centrifugation', in Villani (note 25), p. 186.

[31] Krass (note 25), pp. 130–32.

molecules—a fact which can be exploited in the isotopic separation of both uranium and plutonium. Laser isotope separation has been discussed widely since the late 1960s,[32] and the fact that lasers are useful for many other applications[33] ensures their continued development and increasing availability. Since some laser methods also use UF_6 as feed material, this has implications for the ease with which they might be introduced into the enrichment processes now in use.

Atomic Vapor Laser Isotope Separation

To illustrate the technology involved, the particular process in which the United States has invested most of its efforts is described. The Atomic Vapor Laser Isotope Separation (AVLIS) process is being developed at the Lawrence Livermore National Laboratory (LLNL) with support from the Oak Ridge National Laboratory[34] and is similar to processes being developed in several other countries. In the AVLIS process, the feed material is uranium metal, heated by bombarding it with a beam from an electron gun to produce a stream of uranium vapour.[35] This vapour contains both ^{235}U and ^{238}U atoms. The difference in size of the two respective nuclei (and to a lesser extent the difference in mass and other characteristics)[36] affects the specific wavelengths of light which produce allowable transitions between electron energy levels. These differences are very small, but with finely tuned lasers it is possible selectively to produce transitions leading to ionization in the ^{235}U atoms alone. Once positively charged, the ^{235}U atoms are selectively extracted from the vapour stream by attraction to negatively charged plates, leaving the uncharged ^{238}U atoms to continue on their path relatively unimpeded.

In the laser system itself copper-vapour lasers[37] 'pump' (provide excitation energy for) dye lasers[38] that are tuned to the particular red-orange wavelengths that ^{235}U absorbs.[39] Four different laser frequencies are used: three to excite the ^{235}U atoms and a fourth to allow ionization. This complex procedure uses the part of the spectrum where the dye lasers are more efficient[40] and enhances the selection of ^{235}U since each frequency takes advantage of a separate electron energy level difference.[41]

[32] 'Uranium enrichment: rumors of Israeli progress with lasers', News and Comment, *Science*, vol. 183 (22 Mar. 1974), p. 1174.

[33] For example, atomic spectroscopy, chemical reaction research—see Casper, B. M., 'Laser enrichment: a new path to proliferation?', *Bulletin of the Atomic Scientists*, Jan. 1977, p. 41.

[34] 'DOE extends Martin Marietta contracts', *Nuclear Fuel*, vol. 13, no. 26 (26 Dec. 1988), p. 11.

[35] HR-AUET (note 26), p. 72; *Nuclear Weapons Databook Vol. II* (note 8), p. 132.

[36] Krass, A. S., 'Laser enrichment of uranium: the proliferation connection', *Science*, vol. 196, no. 4291 (13 May 1977), p. 723.

[37] See, e.g., Svelto, O., *Principles of Lasers,* 2nd edn (Plenum: New York, 1982), p. 210.

[38] See, e.g., Svelto (note 37), p. 239.

[39] Thurston, C., 'AVLIS program to gear up to full-scale 1-million SWU/yr module test by 1988', *Nuclear Fuel*, vol. 10, no. 15 (29 July 1985), p. 4.

[40] 'Laser enrichment process called proliferation resistant', *Physics Today*, July 1979, p. 18.

[41] *Nuclear Weapons Databook Vol. II* (note 8), p. 132.

Molecular Laser Isotope Separation (MLIS)

The chemical properties of molecules formed from different isotopes of the same element (UF_6 composed of six fluorine atoms and either one ^{235}U or one ^{238}U atom, for example) are basically identical. Chemical separation of the molecules is correspondingly difficult. Lasers can be used, however, to impart energy to molecules containing only one of the isotopic forms, enabling the chemical changes needed for subsequent chemical separation. These changes are principally of two types—photodissociation and photo-reaction.[42] Both have been investigated in some detail and an example of each is discussed below.

1. *Photodissociative separation.* In a general photodissociative process the laser energy is used to *break chemical bonds* selectively—that is, in molecules made from one particular isotope. This process uses a laser to remove a fluorine atom from only those UF_6 molecules containing ^{235}U. The most advanced research in this method has been carried out in the FRG by a consortium led by Uranit (Uran-Isotopentrennungs-Gesellschaft mbH).[43] In the process, gas containing UF_6 is first cooled by expansion through a nozzle. Light from an infra-red laser is then used to excite molecular vibrations in the UF_6 molecules containing ^{235}U, leaving those containing ^{238}U unaffected. Subsequently further irradiation by either an infra-red or ultraviolet laser then dissociates only the excited molecules into uranium pentafluoride (UF_5) and a fluorine atom. The desired UF_5 quickly condenses into a powdered form ('laser snow') which can be easily collected.[44]

2. *Photoreactive separation.* The US-based firm Isotopes Technologies (IT, headed by a former DOE Deputy Assistant Secretary for Uranium Enrichment) believes it can have a laser enrichment plant operating in 1994 at a cost of under $50 million using a specific type of photoreactive laser separation.[45] Employing 'off-the-shelf' modular technology,[46] the process has been called CRISLA (Chemical Reaction by Isotope Selective Laser Activation). As in photodissociative separation, UF_6 molecules containing ^{235}U are first preferentially excited by a laser (carbon monoxide in this case). The process then makes use of the fact that when a mixture of UF_6 and a proprietary reagent (called RX) is irradiated by the laser, the rate of reaction of the excited UF_6 molecules with RX is over 10 000 times[47] that of the unexcited molecules. The product of the reaction (called URX) is therefore enriched in ^{235}U and, being chemically and physically distinct from UF_6, is easily separated by standard techniques. The power of the lasers in this

[42] Robinson, C. P. and Jensen, R. J., 'Laser methods of uranium isotope separation', in Villani (note 25), p. 280.

[43] Hibbs, M., 'Laser team of West Germany's Uranit "fights for survival" of MLIS R&D', *Nuclear Fuel*, vol. 13, no. 19 (19 Sep. 1988), p. 4.

[44] Krass (note 25), p. 170.

[45] 'Longenecker to head Isotope Technologies', *Nuclear Fuel*, vol. 14, no. 13 (26 June 1989), pp. 1–2.

[46] Lindeman, E., 'Isotope technologies marketing SWU on small scale to U.S. utilities', *Nuclear Fuel*, vol. 14, no. 4 (20 Feb. 1989), p. 4.

[47] Erkens (note 20), p. 48.

process is potentially lower than in the other methods described since the laser is used only for excitation and not for ionization or dissociation. Such techniques are sometimes referred to as 'laser-assisted' processes, and their number is continually growing.[48]

Enrichment technologies compared

In addition to scientific feasibility the important features of any enrichment technology include: (a) the separation factor, (b) the throughput, (c) inventory requirements, (d) energy requirements, (e) the capital cost and (f) operating cost elements (including reliability).[49]

An advantage of diffusion and to some extent the gas centrifuge is that they involve to varying degrees tried and true technology. However, since the separation factor is so small for each stage, diffusion requires a 1200-stage 'cascade' (each stage enriching the uranium slightly more) in order to produce 3 per cent ^{235}U reactor-grade uranium from natural uranium.[50] Weapon-grade uranium requires about 4000 stages. In the case of the gas centrifuge only about 10 stages are required for reactor-grade and about 35 for weapon-grade material. On the other hand the capacity of a given gas-centrifuge cascade is very small, and many thousands of individual centrifuges are required to produce substantial quantities of enriched product.[51] With lasers, however, the AVLIS process is expected to be able to enrich natural uranium to 3–5 per cent in a single stage[52] and 'possibly could be developed to produce HEU'.[53]

In addition, laser isotope separation of uranium can remove most of the ^{235}U from the uranium ore, whereas gaseous diffusion can leave more than a quarter of the ^{235}U. Lasers could also be used to remove the remaining ^{235}U from wastes of other types of separation.[54] Laser techniques can be more selective in their enrichment capability than either gaseous diffusion or centrifuges. Unwanted and potentially dangerous ^{232}U, ^{234}U and ^{236}U are not enriched by laser processes.[55] On the other hand, laser facilities are expected to require more frequent replacement of worn parts than gaseous diffusion equipment.[56] Comparing the advanced gas centrifuge to the AVLIS process for uranium enrichment, the DOE's then Deputy Assistant Secretary for Uranium Enrichment stated in 1986: 'The AVLIS technology is less capital intensive, requires significantly less investment prior to a decision to deploy, has a lower estimated (operating) cost, has greater potential for cost

---

[48] Krass (note 25), pp. 171–72.
[49] HR-AUET (note 26), pp. 69, 87.
[50] HR-AUET (note 26), p. 10.
[51] Casper (note 33), p. 30.
[52] Lindeman, E., 'Less feed, fewer SWU, lower assay needed to enrich REPU with AVLIS, DOE says', *Nuclear Fuel*, vol. 12, no. 12 (15 June 1987), p. 9.
[53] *Fiscal Year 1989 Arms Control Impact Statements* (US Government Printing Office: Washington, DC, 1988), p. 145.
[54] Palmer and Bolef (note 8), p. 26.
[55] *Nuclear Fuel*, vol. 14, no. 6 (21 Mar. 1989), p. 4.
[56] MacLachlan, A., 'Sales increase for Franc's Pechiney', *Nuclear Fuel*, vol. 13, no. 11 (30 May 1988), p. 13.

reductions through technology improvements, and is more adaptable to deployment in increments that can match the evolving needs of the enrichment marketplace'.[57]

Further insight into the relative merits of laser enrichment in general and the different specific laser technologies can be gained by looking at the vigour of current research, the planned facilities and the choices made by individual countries or companies and (where possible) the reasons for making them. These are discussed below.

Plutonium isotope separation

The ^{239}Pu used in nuclear weapon construction does not occur in nature, but can be produced from ^{238}U atoms in nuclear reactors. Depending on how the reactor is configured and run, other isotopes of plutonium are produced to varying degrees. US nuclear weapons, for example, are designed to operate with 'weapon-grade' plutonium composed of 6 per cent ^{240}Pu or less, the rest composed of ^{239}Pu (with very small amounts of the other isotopes).[58] It is possible to produce such plutonium in reactors, although this results in less than optimal power output. Commercial reactors discharge plutonium which is still mainly ^{239}Pu but also contains typically about 25 per cent ^{240}Pu and significant amounts of the other isotopes.[59] Chemical methods are then used to extract the plutonium and uranium separately.

In 1986 the USA selected the AVLIS process to convert fuel-grade ^{240}Pu (7–19 per cent)[60] owned by the Defense Department to weapon-grade plutonium.[61] Technologically there is considerable overlap in the uranium and plutonium AVLIS processes. In the LLNL facility most of this overlap is in the laser systems. Copper vapour and dye lasers will be used for both, although tuned to slightly different frequencies.[62] In fact the laser hardware in LLNL's Laser Demonstration Facility is used to supply laser light for both the plutonium and uranium separation programmes.[63] The interdependence is not only technological: a DOE official warned that funding cuts to SIS would affect the AVLIS uranium enrichment programme.[64] There are differences in the operation and design of the production processes, however, primarily in the separator technology and with materials

[57] *Fiscal Year 1987 Department of Energy Authorization,* Hearings before the Subcommittee on Energy Research and Production of the Committee on Science and Technology, House of Representatives, 99th Congress, 2nd Session (US Government Printing Office: Washington, DC, 1986), Vol. 1, pp. 26–27 (hereafter DOE-CST/87).

[58] EWDA/89 (note 3), pp. 1117, 1144.

[59] Lovins, A.B., 'Nuclear weapons and power-reactor plutonium', *Nature,* vol. 283 (28 Feb. 1980), p. 818.

[60] DOE-NSP/89 (note 2), p. 314.

[61] 'DOE selects AVLIS for Pu production also', *Nuclear Fuel,* vol. 11, no. 9 (5 May 1986), p. 13; EWDA/89 (note 3), p. 733; 'Laser technology', *Energy and Technology Review,* July/Aug. 1989, p. 20.

[62] DOE-CST/87 (note 57), p. 71.

[63] 'Special isotope separation program', *Energy and Technology Review,* July/Aug. 1989, p. 24.

[64] Jordan, B., 'Congress asked to reconsider SIS based on nonproliferation concerns', *Nuclear Fuel,* vol. 14, no. 11 (29 May 1989), p. 14.

handling.[65] Although not as much is known (other than regarding the US programme) about the state of development of plutonium laser separation methods world-wide, the similarity in US AVLIS approaches to separating plutonium and uranium indicates the possibilities available for countries developing similar techniques for uranium.

IV. Current developments in laser isotope separation

Of the NPT signatories, the USA in 1982 selected the AVLIS process in preference to two other advanced uranium enrichment techniques for further development. In 1985 the AVLIS process was again selected for future US enrichment needs, this time in preference to the advanced gas centrifuge.[66] The stated reasons for using AVLIS for uranium enrichment in the USA are to remain competitive in the future and to 'assure the country has the military security that it requires for its Naval Propulsion Program and other programs'.[67] Congress appropriated over $500 million towards the development of AVLIS from 1973 to 1987.[68] Funding for fiscal year 1990 has been set at $134 million with the House–Senate Conference directing the DOE to accelerate completion of the AVLIS technology and ensure the development has an industrial perspective.[69] In its annual report for 1987, the DOE announced the successful demonstration of laser enrichment technology at one-half plant scale.[70] The DOE is committed to complete a production demonstration by the end of 1991,[71] and the DOE's contractors are known to favour having an AVLIS plant in operation by 1996.[72] Current plans are for deployment in the late 1990s.[73]

Although information is rather sparse, research into uranium laser isotope separation has been carried out in the USSR at the Institute of Spectroscopy and the Kurchatov Institute.[74] The head of the development of laser uranium enrichment in the USSR reportedly stated in 1985 that the process had already been 'turned . . . over to industry' and they are thought to have made

[65] DOE selects AVLIS for Pu production also', *Nuclear Fuel*, vol. 11, no. 9 (5 May 1986), p. 13.

[66] *DOE Uranium Enrichment Program*, Hearing before the Subcommittee on Energy Conservation and Power of the Committee on Energy and Commerce, US House of Representatives, 99th Congress, 2nd Session (US Government Printing Office: Washington, DC, 1986), p. 18 (Hereafter DOE-UEP); *Nuclear Weapons Databook Vol. II* (note 8), p. 132.

[67] DOE-CST/87 (note 57), pp. 8, 36.

[68] 'Senate would require DOE to study putting AVLIS at idle enrichment plant', *Nuclear Fuel*, vol. 12, no. 25 (14 Dec. 1987), p. 3.

[69] 'Funding bill would allow DOE to buy uranium from West German stockpile', *Nuclear Fuel*, vol. 14, no. 19 (18 Sep. 1989), p. 9.

[70] 'DOE reports '87 net loss of $385-million; SWU sales total nearly 1.13-billion', *Nuclear Fuel*, vol. 13, no. 12 (13 June 1988), p. 4.

[71] 'Enrichment budget sent to Congress', *Nuclear Fuel*, vol. 14, no. 2 (23 Jan. 1989), p. 12.

[72] 'DOE's contractors pushing strategy for early AVLIS plant construction', *Nuclear Fuel*, vol. 14, no. 5 (6 Mar. 1989), p. 9.

[73] Note 53, p. 161.

[74] Central Intelligence Agency, *USSR Energy Atlas* (US Government Printing Office: Washington, DC, 1985), p. 43, cited in *Nuclear Weapons Data Book, Vol. IV, Soviet Nuclear Weapons* (Ballinger: Cambridge, Mass., 1989), p. 94; Robinson, C. P. and Jensen, R. J., 'Laser methods of uranium isotope separation', in Villani (note 25), p. 272.

a great deal of progress.[75] However, recent reports suggest that the USSR does not have plans to build additional enrichment capacity.[76]

In *Japan*, the Japan Atomic Energy Research Institute (JAERI) has been researching the AVLIS process since 1976. The Laser Atomic Separation Engineering Research Association (LASER) of Japan was formed in 1987.[77] Annual spending on AVLIS has risen from \$5 million a year to about \$65 million a year.[78] It was expected that LASER would conduct a small-scale test by 1990 and, given good results, become commercial early in the 21st century.[79] The MLIS process is being developed by the Institute of Physical & Chemical Research (IPCR) which in 1988 reported achieving a separation factor of 4.7 (a separation factor of about 4.3 is required to enrich natural uranium to 3 per cent reactor-grade ^{235}U).[80] Further, the Industrial Research Institute (IRI) is reportedly evaluating the CRISLA process.[81]

The *Federal Republic of Germany*, now thought to have developed the most advanced MLIS technology, has chosen to concentrate on this method, believing it to be superior to the atomic laser process at least in part since it uses UF_6—not requiring high temperature or 'highly aggressive' uranium vapour.[82] The leader of MLIS research in the FRG is Uranit,[83] and funding for 1988 was approximately DM 13 million (\$6.8 million). A separation factor of 15 has recently been achieved on a laboratory scale, putting this effort well ahead of the Japanese MLIS (and of the US, British and French efforts, all of which abandoned MLIS after only achieving a separation factor of approximately 2.5). Current Uranit planning involves a 1/100-scale pilot plant costing about DM 120 million (\$63 million), which it is hoped will be operational by 1996, and a 1/10-scale follow-up pilot to be completed sometime in the next century.[84]

In the *UK*, the United Kingdom Atomic Energy Authority (UKAEA), having originally concentrated on molecular laser separation, in 1984 decided in favour of the atomic separation process. British Nuclear Fuels plc (BNFL) initiated a laser isotope separation programme in 1982 and by 1986 felt it would be in a position to consider plant installation in the late 1990s.[85] Development work in conjunction with the UKAEA is proceeding, and a

---

[75] DOE-CST/87 (note 57), p. 44.

[76] 'European enrichers say they are hurt by Soviet/Chinese aggressiveness' *Nuclear Fuel*, vol. 14, no. 1 (9 Jan. 1989), p. 7.

[77] Usui, N., 'Japanese set up AVLIS research group', *Nuclear Fuel*, vol. 12, no. 3 (9 Feb. 1987), p. 12.

[78] Hiruo, E., 'U.S. share of enrichment market said to hinge on AVLIS operation date', *Nuclear Fuel*, vol. 13, no. 6 (21 Mar. 1988), p. 5.

[79] MacLachlan, A. and Usui, N., 'Urenco using REPU enrichment as lure for Japanese business', *Nuclear Fuel*, vol. 12, no. 11 (1 June 1987), p. 7.

[80] Usui, N., 'Japan's IPCR reports breakthrough using MLIS enrichment process', *Nuclear Fuel*, vol. 13, no. 8 (18 Apr. 1988), p. 7.

[81] Ushio, S., 'Japanese move forward with AVLIS plans', *Nuclear Fuel*, vol. 11, no. 12 (16 June 1986), p. 8.

[82] Hibbs, M., 'Laser team of West Germany's Uranit "fights for survival" of MLIS R&D', *Nuclear Fuel*, vol. 13, no. 19 (19 Sep. 1988), pp. 4–5.

[83] Hibbs, M., 'Late funding effort may save German laser enrichment project', *Nuclear Fuel*, vol. 13, no. 21 (17 Oct. 1988), p. 3.

[84] Note 82, p. 5.

[85] 'Enrichers discuss prospects for laser SWU', *Nuclear Fuel*, vol. 11, no. 18 (8 Sep. 1986), p. 5.

small-scale demonstration is planned for the mid-1990s. In the UK it is believed that centrifuge technology will be viable for some time in the future and that by 1992 it should be clear whether laser separation will be competitive with advanced centrifuge technology.[86]

Aspects of both MLIS and AVLIS are being investigated in *the Netherlands*. In *Canada,* Atomic Energy Canada Ltd (AECL) has recently expanded its activities in laser separation research, and research has reportedly also been conducted in *Australia*.[87]

Of the non-signatories to the NPT, work on laser enrichment of uranium is under way in *Brazil* at the Institute for Energy and Nuclear Research (IPEN) as well as at the Air Force's Aerospace Technology Center (CTA). However, it has been judged highly unlikely that the technique is close to being mastered[88] and, as far as the CTA effort is concerned, it has recently been reported that it is now de-emphasized.[89]

As early as 1974 a physicist with the Ministry of Defence of *Israel* stated that Israel had demonstrated the feasibility of laser enrichment.[90] In 1986 Mordechai Vanunu told of the existence of an Israeli laser separation facility at the Dimona Centre which can be used to enrich uranium and purify plutonium.[91] According to Vanunu, in 1981 Israeli scientists began actually to use lasers to separate uranium isotopes, expanding the unit to production scale when he left Dimona in 1985.[92] An LLNL source reports that Israel has been investigating the AVLIS process.[93]

In *France*, laser enrichment technology development is being pursued by the CEA (Commissiariat à l'Energie Atomique). Although believed to be behind the USA in laser enrichment development,[94] the French are also pursuing AVLIS ('SILVA' in French) and evaluated and abandoned centrifuge technology even before a similar decision was taken by the USA.[95] At the CEA's Saclay centre a pre-industrial SILVA process plant began operating several years ago; full results are expected in 1990, when plans call for beginning construction of a pilot plant with the target date for full industrial-scale plant operation set at around 2000.[96]

[86] Marshall, P., 'BNFL says operating profit is up while export earnings drop 12%', *Nuclear Fuel*, vol. 13, no. 23 (14 Nov. 1988), p. 5; *Atom*, no. 389 (Mar. 1989), p. 46.

[87] Silver, R., 'Canadian officials looking at advances for fuel cycle, including enrichment', *Nuclear Fuel*, vol. 13, no.13 (27 June 1988) p. 6; Casper (note 33), p. 40; Krass (note 25), p. 235.

[88] Spector, L. S., *The Undeclared Bomb* (Ballinger: Cambridge, Mass., 1988), pp. 259–60.

[89] Hibbs, M., 'Bonn: there is "no military background" to Brazil's unsafeguarded program', *Nuclear Fuel*, vol. 14, no. 16 (7 Aug. 1989), p. 13.

[90] Quoted in *Science*, vol. 183 (note 32), p. 1172.

[91] Barnaby, F., *The Invisible Bomb: The Nuclear Arms Race in the Middle East* (I.B. Tauris: London, 1989), pp. 25–26.

[92] Barnaby (note 91), p. 40.

[93] Thurston, C., 'AVLIS program to gear up to full-scale 1-million SWU/yr module test by 1988', *Nuclear Fuel*, vol. 10, no. 15 (29 July 1985), pp. 3–5.

[94] Thurston (note 93), p. 5.

[95] DOE-CST/87 (note 57), p. 44.

[96] MacLachlan, A., 'French find chemical enrichment is a pleasant economic surprise', *Nuclear Fuel*, vol. 12, no. 2 (26 Jan. 1987), p. 2; Capron, J-P., 'Nuclear electricity, the answer to energy challenges', *Atom*, no. 388 (Feb. 1989), p. 34; MacLachlan, A., 'Cogema will not deploy AVLIS for reprocessed U until after 2000', *Nuclear Fuel*, vol. 13, no. 10 (16 May 1988), p. 4.

Begun in the early 1970s, research in *China* into laser isotope separation has involved both the molecular and atomic processes, but since 1985 concentration has focused on the atomic process. A pilot plant may be installed in the early 1990s.[97] Gas centrifuge technology is also being investigated, and China hopes to decide on an enrichment priority by the turn of the century.[98] At Fudan University a replica of CRISLA developed by the US-based Isotope Technologies firm has been constructed (though not yet duplicating the IT results) using published data.[99]

India is also reportedly conducting research into laser enrichment techniques at the Bhabha Atomic Research Center.[100]

Co-operative efforts involve Eurodif, a multinational uranium enrichment company, which is reported to be actively pursuing an AVLIS capability. It is planning plant demonstrations of the process in the early 1990s.[101] In a recent joint statement[102] the UK and the FRG have expressed their receptivity to the proposal that laser enrichment technology be included in their co-operation in Urenco. In its 1988 annual report Urenco stated that it was unlikely that significant, commercial-scale laser technology would be introduced before the next century.[103] It has also recently been stated that any future collaboration on enrichment between France and the FRG will involve laser methods.[104]

V. Proliferation and uranium laser enrichment

Unlike weapon-grade plutonium which can be produced in a small nuclear reactor, the production of substantial quantities of HEU has, until now, required a large dedicated effort. It has been said that 'one of the hardest things on earth to hide is a gaseous diffusion plant; its mere presence on the landscape, easily detected by satellites, is a dead give-away of a nation's intentions'.[105] It is believed that the fewer stages necessary and the subsequent smaller size of gas-centrifuge uranium enrichment plants means that their appearance is not as distinctive as diffusion plants but that the effort required for their construction would still permit identification. Laser enrichment plants need less uranium for processing and can be smaller still, which would contribute to the difficulty in detecting and monitoring them.[106] Given the data in section IV on the number of states *known* to be involved in

[97] 'China has been selling enriched uranium commercially since 1981, official says', *Nuclear Fuel*, vol. 13, no. 20 (3 Oct. 1988), p. 12.

[98] Lindeman, E., MacLachlan, A. and Hibbs, M., 'Nuclear fuel survey: views differ on market impact of Soviet, Chinese U/SWU', *Nuclear Fuel*, vol. 14, no. 1 (9 Jan. 1989), p. 7.

[99] Knapik, M., 'Looking ahead to the enrichment marketplace of the 1990s', *Nuclear Fuel*, vol. 14, no. 13 (26 June 1989), p. 2.

[100] Spector, L. S., *The New Nuclear Nations* (Vintage: New York, 1985), p. 101.

[101] Hiruo (note 78), p. 5.

[102] Joint Declaration Between the UK and West Germany on the Peaceful Use of Nuclear Energy, signed in Bonn, 25 July 1989, reprinted in *Nuclear Fuel*, vol. 14, no. 16 (7 Aug. 1989), p. 5.

[103] 1988 Urenco Annual Report quoted in *Nuclear Fuel*, vol. 14, no. 7 (3 Apr. 1989), p. 5.

[104] MacLachlan, A., 'Potential French–German enrichment cooperation will be in lasers', *Nuclear Fuel*, vol. 14, no. 13 (26 June 1989), p. 4.

[105] *Science*, vol. 183 (note 32), pp. 1172–73.

[106] EWDA/89 (note 3), p. 1196; DOE-UEP (note 66), p. 192.

research and active planning of deployment of laser enrichment facilities, a primary and increasing concern regarding the proliferation of nuclear weapon capabilities is the possible construction of clandestine laser enrichment facilities.

In this context, one prominent cause for concern, should its developers' claims be borne out, is the CRISLA process. The apparatus size, about 7 m in length, and the fact that it reportedly employs simpler technology than AVLIS[107] carry obvious proliferation concerns. Also, although almost two decades of US research on AVLIS have not yet resulted in plant construction, it must be noted that the stated purpose of the LLNL uranium enrichment programme is 'to prove, by *large-scale* technology demonstrations, the *economic viability* of uranium enrichment for commercial reactor fuel'[108]—considerations which may not be very important for other potential developers, in particular countries planning to produce a few nuclear weapons.

It has been predicted that AVLIS, because of its projected lower cost, will possibly force world enrichment prices down in the future. In addition, developers of the process are predicting that, because the feed and product material is quite different from the UF_6 gas used in most of today's separation, AVLIS will change the nuclear fuel cycle.[109] Thus there are potential economic and logistical incentives likely to further the spread of laser enrichment technology to other nations interested in a share of the world uranium market. A danger from the proliferation standpoint then arises that laser technology could lead to the production of HEU and its subsequent mixing with depleted tails or natural uranium for LWR fuel, creating the danger of diversion to weapon production. (Of course, if this HEU were being produced for reactors utilizing HEU, there is a diversion potential independent of the materials source.)[110] The DOE does, in fact, acknowledge proliferation to be a primary concern in connection with laser enrichment and has stated a desire to focus much attention on this, as they have tried to do with diffusion and the gas centrifuge.[111]

Safeguards

Employing AVLIS for uranium enrichment will require the development of new safeguards methods and devices, and this has been acknowledged by the USA.[112] A former divisional director in the IAEA Department of Safeguards sees no difficulty in developing safeguards for uranium enrichment plants using laser methods and expects them to progress as the technology

[107] Note 46, p. 4.

[108] 'Laser technology', *Energy and Technology Review*, July/Aug. 1989, p. 20; emphasis added.

[109] Hiruo, E., '10-year enrichment services pacts may be outdated, ex-DOE official says', *Nuclear Fuel*, vol. 13, no. 10 (16 May 1988), p. 11.

[110] Greenwood, T., Rathjens, G. W. and Ruina, J., 'Nuclear power and weapons proliferation', *Adelphi Paper*, no. 130 (IISS: London, 1977), p. 28.

[111] DOE-CST/87 (note 57), p. 36

[112] EWDA/89 (note 3), p. 1229

itself matures.[113] The inventory at any one time would be relatively small and the sensitive enrichment technology is confined to one step. The major safeguards problem is believed to be the above-mentioned construction of small clandestine HEU production facilities.[114] On the other hand, a senior Western safeguards official believes that the laser upgrading of plutonium, by blurring the civilian–military distinction in relation to nuclear energy, 'will pose a major challenge to the international safeguards regime'.[115] Facilities like the proposed SIS plant would require substantial new efforts on the part of the IAEA, as safeguards would be needed for the large amounts of ^{240}Pu and ^{241}Pu which would be produced in addition to the ^{239}Pu.[116] The question of the development of export controls for critical elements of laser isotope separation is also important. A recent US Government report has stated that while 'equipment for economic production of LEU or HEU is readily distinguishable from that needed for most other applications . . . it could be difficult to detect and hence control the export of equipment suitable for AVLIS smaller scale experimentation'.[117] Clearly this issue merits further investigation.

VI. Outlook

The 1990s will undoubtedly see many important developments in laser enrichment technology. The cancellation of SIS construction must be seen as a positive development, opening new possibilities for bilateral fissile material cut-off proposals. However, regarding uranium laser enrichment, the developments of the past two decades have shown the technology to be advanced to the point at which some countries are on the verge of making decisions on full-scale laser enrichment plant construction and many others are considering deployment of demonstration or prototype facilities. The precedent-setting nature of developments in more technologically advanced nations, coupled with new potentially more accessible methods of laser isotope separation is a combination which gives particular cause for concern with regard to nuclear weapon proliferation.

---

[113] Seneviratne, G., 'Former IAEA official warns of problems ahead for IAEA safeguards regime', *Nuclear Fuel*, vol. 12, no. 2 (26 Jan. 1987), p. 10.

[114] von Baeckmann, A., 'Modern fuel cycle technologies: challenges to IAEA safeguards?' in *New Technology, the NPT and the IAEA Safeguards System, Programme for Promoting Nuclear Non-Proliferation*, Occasional Paper 4 (Centre for International Policy Studies: Southampton, Oct. 1989), p. 9.

[115] Hibbs, M. and MacLachlan, A., 'Soviet Union postpones completion of Siberian reprocessing plant', *Nuclear Fuel*, vol. 14, no. 21 (16 Oct. 1989), p. 2.

[116] Letter of NCI to Sam Nunn (note 9), p. 2.

[117] Note 53, p. 165.

18. The debate over the modernization of NATO's short-range nuclear missiles

CATHERINE M. KELLEHER*

I. Introduction

One of the major arms control disputes in 1989 was the internal NATO debate on the modernization of short-range nuclear forces (SNF). Rooted in NATO's dual-track decision of December 1979 to deploy 572 Pershing II and ground-launched cruise missiles (GLCMs) in Western Europe, the debate over whether or not to modernize short-range nuclear systems surfaced in the aftermath of the 1987 US–Soviet Treaty on the Elimination of their Intermediate-range and Shorter-range Missiles (the INF Treaty) but escalated into a full-fledged alliance crisis by early 1989. It reached its peak in April and May 1989, only to be dealt an official *coup de grâce* by the Federal Republic of Germany in November 1989.[1] Few issues look less lively now than if, when or how to modernize NATO's short-range nuclear missiles; yet there are still compelling reasons to examine carefully this latest in a series of NATO tactical nuclear weapon modernization crises.

One reason is simply the uncertainty of the future and the fact that NATO modernization planning continues apace with new political developments. More important is the fact that the modernization crisis of 1989 was really three crises nested together. Only one—disagreements about the value of a Lance follow-on missile, a land-based short-range missile with a new range of over 450 kilometres (known as Follow-on to Lance, FOTL)—turned in familiar ways on questions of nuclear weapons and doctrine, and on the dictates of forward defence and flexible response in the post-INF Treaty era. The other two crises were highly politicized and newly complex: (*a*) an alliance crisis concerning the limits of US leadership and the new requirements for consensus-building; and (*b*) a 'German' crisis involving both external charges of a national FRG agenda-setting and an internal debate about ill-considered Bonn subservience to alliance pressures. Both crises were deeply influenced by the emerging changes in the USSR and Eastern Europe. Both were vibrantly coloured by what different actors perceived to be the lessons and fears of the experience with the INF Treaty (see chapter 12).

Given the complexity of the SNF debate, this chapter first analyses the events and then investigates each of the crises in turn, recognizing from the outset that they were inextricably intertwined and interdependent.

---

[1] Oberdorfer, D., 'West Germans rule out modernizing missiles', *Washington Post*, 22 Nov. 1989, p. A18.

* Grateful acknowledgement is made of the excellent research assistance of Alice Ackermann in the preparation of this chapter.

Table 18.1. Chronology of the NATO debate on SNF modernization, 1979–89

12 Dec. 1979	NATO dual-track decision is taken
27 Oct. 1983	Montebello decision is taken
27 Mar. 1985	Presentation of NATO Nuclear Weapons Requirement Study report mandating nuclear modernization
8 Dec. 1987	The US–Soviet INF Treaty is signed
3 Mar. 1988	FRG Chancellor Helmut Kohl pledges no 'third zero' but calls for negotiations to equal SNF ceilings after Conventional Armed Forces in Europe (CFE) Negotiation and chemical talks
28 Apr. 1988	NATO Nuclear Planning Group (NPG) endorses step-by-step modernization
2 Dec. 1988	Chancellor Kohl tells UK Prime Minister Margaret Thatcher that he seeks decision on SNF modernization by 1989
7 Dec. 1988	In a UN speech Soviet President Mikhail Gorbachev announces unilateral Soviet force cuts and restructuring in the USSR/Eastern Europe
13 Feb. 1989	Chancellor Kohl tells US Secretary of State James Baker that the FRG will not yet make commitment to Lance modernization; Belgium, Denmark and Greece support FRG position
13 Apr. 1989	FRG Cabinet shift: Gerhard Stoltenberg replaces Rupert Scholz as Defence Minister
20 Apr. 1989	At NPG meeting, NATO defence ministers agree on a common position of no early SNF modernization/no early negotiation
21 Apr. 1989	FRG says no Lance modernization decision until 1992, early SNF negotiations within *Gesamtkonzept*
25 Apr. 1989	FRG Foreign Minister Hans-Dietrich Genscher and Defence Minister Stoltenberg in Washington
11 May 1989	President Gorbachev proposes withdrawal of 500 SNF missiles
30 May 1989	NATO summit meeting; SNF compromise
9 Nov. 1989	Berlin Wall opened
21 Nov. 1989	Foreign Minister Genscher in Washington; no Lance follow-on, given changes in Europe
15 Dec. 1989	NATO foreign ministers assert that division of Europe can be overcome but US nuclear forces must remain in Europe

II. Background to the crises

All three SNF crises were, in essence, the legacy of the INF debates, deployments and withdrawals that preoccupied the NATO alliance and its publics from 1979 until 1987 (see table 18.1). SNF nuclear forces had existed in Europe since the mid-1950s, as air- and ground-based tactical nuclear weapons; the NATO 1954 decision on nuclear first-use became the West's reply to overwhelming Soviet superiority in conventional weapons.[2] The Lance missile, a dual-capable system with a range of 125 km and a nuclear yield of 100 kt, was first deployed in 1972, and by 1988 numbered some 100 launchers and 692 missiles/warheads on European territory.[3]

The INF negotiations gave new prominence to SNF forces and their eventual modernization in several separate ways. The INF forces, the Pershing IIs and the GLCMs, were only one of the categories of nuclear forces which NATO decided to restructure and modernize in the face of growing Soviet deployment of SS-20s, begun in 1977.[4] In the public furore in Europe over the INF deployments, especially in 1981–82, questions emerged about the future of all ground-based nuclear forces in Europe, and calls for a 'denuclearized Europe' became commonplace for the first time in 20 years.[5] The INF Treaty included the total elimination not only of the Pershings, GLCMs and Soviet SS-20s (with ranges of 1000–5500 km), referred to as the 'first zero', but also a 'second zero', the elimination of shorter-range missiles with a range of 500–1000 km—the Soviet SS-12 and SS-23 and the FRG's 72 Pershing 1As.[6] To opposition parties and mobilized publics alike, the attainment of a 'third zero'—the negotiated elimination of SNF forces, i.e., the remaining missiles below 500 km in range and the often-questioned battlefield artillery—seemed only a question of time or political will. The 1979 dual-track decision had already arranged for the unilateral withdrawal of 1000 US warheads, largely from the SNF forces.[7]

Another impact of the INF deliberations on SNF issues stemmed from the decisions NATO had reached at the Nuclear Planning Group (NPG) meeting at Montebello, Canada, on 27–28 October 1983 regarding future nuclear force structures. Given what then seemed assured INF deployments, NATO committed itself to the maintenance of a minimum nuclear stockpile and the rapid implementation of a 'decision as to the precise composition of the

---

[2] See Kelleher, C. M., *Germany and the Politics of Nuclear Weapons* (Columbia University Press: New York, 1975) for background.

[3] SIPRI, *SIPRI Yearbook 1989: World Armaments and Disarmament* (Oxford University Press: Oxford, 1989), pp. 13–14; ACA, 'Fact Sheet: nuclear missiles deployed in Europe after INF' (Arms Control Association: Washington, DC, May 1989).

[4] See NATO, *Texts of Final Communiqués 1975–1980* (NATO Information Service: Brussels, 1981), pp. 121–23.

[5] See, for instance, Kelleher, C. M., 'Alliance issues', Committee on International Security and Arms Control, National Academy of Scientists, *Reykjavik and Beyond* (National Academy Press: Washington, DC, 1988), pp. 34–45.

[6] See Risse-Kappen. T., *The Zero Option: INF, West Germany and Arms Control* (Westview Press: Boulder, Colo., 1988).

[7] The completed unilateral reduction of 1000 warheads was spelled out in the Montebello decision, 27 Oct. 1983; see NATO, *Texts of Final Communiqués 1981–1985* (NATO Information Service: Brussels, 1986), p. 106.

stockpile'.[8] It agreed at the very least to reduce unilaterally a further 1400 warheads by the mid-1990s, in light of the continuing problems of obsolescence and the new advantages stemming from greater accuracies and survivability that continuing modernization would bring.[9]

The Lance missile became almost the exclusive focus of public attention on modernization even before the signing of the INF Treaty in 1987. The replacement of the Lance with a more accurate, efficient and longer-range system, the FOTL, had been planned since the early 1980s and was to begin by the mid-l990s.[10] The Lance had never enjoyed great confidence, not the least because of its four-hour reload time, deficient accuracy (a circular error probable (CEP) optimistically calculated at 400 metres), and outdated fuel and electronics systems.[11] It had, however, been at hand to replace several obsolescent systems (the Sergeant and Honest John missiles), and the NATO leadership had in 1986 implemented the Lance Service Life Extension Program (SLEP) to update guidance and warhead components.[12] This, it was argued, would keep Lance in the inventory for at least another decade.[13]

US and SHAPE (Supreme Headquarters Allied Powers Europe) military planners insisted, however, that it was crucial to extend the FOTL's range to at least 220–250 km; some argued later to as far as 450 km or more.[14] The reason was in part the long-felt need among some in the US Army for 'a corps-support weapon', one that would allow coverage up to 250 km. Others, with former Supreme Allied Commander Europe (SACEUR) General Bernard Rogers, wanted broader theatre coverage, to counter Soviet Scud assets (later SS-21s) and to close a gap in NATO capabilities.[15]

A further reason stemmed from the doctrinal arguments of the 1970s and 1980s: the requirement under the NATO doctrine of Follow-On Forces Attack (FOFA) to hold East European airfields and fixed installations at risk from the outset of a conflict. Increasingly accurate Soviet air defences, it was argued, made the use of aircraft less likely at a time when NATO airfields were also becoming more vulnerable to attack in the first hours of a conflict. Moreover, NATO air assets were organized in separate commands and were less responsive to the direct needs of the ground commander.[16]

From the outset, the leading FOTL candidate was the US Army Tactical

---

[8] NATO (note 7).

[9] NATO (note 7).

[10] NATO (note 7).

[11] Binnendijk, H., 'NATO's nuclear modernization dilemma', *Survival*, vol. 31, no. 2 (Mar.–Apr. 1989), p. 140.

[12] James, J., 'Tactical nuclear modernization: the NATO decision that won't go away', *Arms Control Today*, vol. 18, no. 10 (Dec. 1988), p. 21.

[13] Sloan, S., 'NATO nuclear modernization and arms control', Congressional Research Service, Issue Brief (US Library of Congress: Washington, DC, 29 Sep. 1989), p. 4.

[14] See, for example, statement by Lt. General Donald Phil, Army Research, Development and Acquisition, in *Department of Defense Appropriations for 1989*, Hearings before the Subcommittee of the Committee on Appropriations, US House of Representatives, 100th Congress (US Government Printing Office: Washington, DC, 1988), Part 7, p. 37; see also *NATO Defense and the INF Treaty*, Hearings before the Committee on Armed Services, 100th Congress (US Government Printing Office: Washington, DC, 1988); Sommer, T., 'Raketen—wider deutschen Willen', *Die Zeit*, 5 May 1989; Head, S., 'The battle inside NATO', *New York Review of Books*, 18 May 1989, pp. 41–46.

[15] Interview with defence expert by A. Ackermann, Nov. 1989.

[16] Wilson, G., 'Short-range missiles called vital', *Washington Post*, 11 June 1989, p. A24.

Missile System (ATACMS), originally planned as a conventional weapon system with a range of over 200 km and scheduled for deployment in the early 1990s.[17] It was to be launched from the MLRS (Multiple Launcher Rocket System), co-developed with the European allies and to be deployed in many hundreds in NATO forces in the 1990s. All that was needed for FOTL was the design of a new nuclear warhead and associated modifications to make the missile and the launcher dual-capable.[18]

It was at this point that the third legacy of the INF debate affected SNF modernization. In the early 1980s, largely because of the controversy over the INF forces, the US Congress had taken an increasingly critical stance towards funding the development of new theatre nuclear forces (TNF). Beginning in 1985, Congress barred development of a nuclear ATACMS, arguing that development of weapons which were not politically acceptable to the allies for deployment in Europe was unnecessary and probably counter-productive.[19] There were also questions about developing a new dual-capable weapon, given the need for arms control purposes of functionally-related observable differences (FRODs) between conventional and nuclear weapons.[20] Moreover, there were echoes of the neutron bomb controversy between Bonn and Washington in the late 1970s, but the clearest referent was to the political upheavals during the deployment of Pershing IIs and GLCMs in 1983.

The position of the FRG did little to allay congressional fears. During the last stages of the INF negotiations, FRG Chancellor Helmut Kohl had argued intensely against the second INF zero (500–1000 km) without the fullest consideration being given to the resulting conventional and nuclear balance in Europe. He had agreed to the final INF bargain only under great pressure from the USA and especially from the UK and after the failure of France to support his position on the need for immediate negotiations on SNF and conventional reductions. Particularly painful was the anomalous position of the Pershing 1As, the only NATO system in Europe in the 500–1000 km range, and the only 'third party' system affected by the INF Treaty.[21]

In the fiscal year (FY) 1989 military budget submission, the Reagan Administration gave up the nuclear ATACMS fight and proposed development funds for a new missile to be launched from the MLRS, one with an extended range which came quite close to the INF Treaty lower limit of 500 km.[22] However, Congress declined to undertake even a major research and development (R&D) commitment without a positive political decision for

[17] See *Department of Defense Appropriations for 1989*, Part 1 (note 14).

[18] *Department of Defense Appropriations for 1989* (note 14); see also Binnendijk (note 11); Gordon, M., 'U.S. moves ahead on replacement for Lance missile', *International Herald Tribune*, 18–19 Feb. 1989, p. 3.

[19] See Sloan (note 13), p. 6; de Andreis, M., *U.S. Policymaking on the Modernization of NATO Theater Nuclear Weapons* (School of Public Affairs, University of Maryland: College Park, Md., 1989), pp. 15–16.

[20] *National Defense Authorization Act for Fiscal Years 1990–1991*, Report of the Committee on Armed Services, US House of Representatives, 101st Congress (US Government Printing Office: Washington, DC, 1989), p. 146.

[21] See, for instance, Phil (note 14) and de Andreis (note 19).

[22] See *Department of Defense Appropriations for 1989* (note 14); de Andreis (note 19), pp. 15–16.

later deployment by the NATO allies.[23]

Another candidate to take over the Lance's mission was a tactical air-to surface missile (TASM) on NATO's tactical nuclear-capable aircraft, which were also undergoing modernization. The choice raised inter-service hackles as well as questions about the possible pre-emptive effect of using strike aircraft in this role.[24] However, the US Department of Defense (DOD) had already decided to develop a TASM (designated in 1989 to be the 250-km range Short Range Attack Missile-Tactical, SRAM-T) with a stand-off range of 400 km, that was supposed to be operational by the early 1990s. These could then be deployed on the additional 50 F-/FB-111 aircraft which the USA in the post-INF era had decided to deploy forward to the UK.[25] The UK had also pledged new air assets to compensate for INF withdrawals.[26]

There the question of Lance modernization stood, in both US and NATO consideration, in the beginning of 1988 when the publicly visible debate over the FOTL began. The principal forums throughout 1988 were the regularly scheduled NATO meetings—the NATO Council, the Defence Planning Committee, the defence ministers' meeting and the sessions of the NPG— and the numerous visits and bilateral talks, especially those between the USA, the FRG and the UK. What was sought was a satisfactory formula that would allow for ongoing nuclear modernization, especially the FOTL, and (a) minimize the adverse impacts on future arms control, and (b) meet FRG insistence on early negotiations grounded in a new comprehensive concept.[27]

Throughout 1988 the outward tone of the generally conservative governments in Britain, the FRG and the USA was deliberately low-key and vague. Government downplaying was in part due to what was variously perceived as public exhaustion or unwarranted tendencies towards euphoria after the signing of the INF Treaty. Of at least equal concern was electoral vulnerability, especially for the weakening Bonn coalition that faced a decline in Chancellor Kohl's popularity, growing restiveness among Foreign Minister Hans-Dietrich Genscher's Free Democrat Party (FDP) colleagues on economic issues and the growing prospect of a Social Democratic Party of Germany (SPD)/Green Party coalition.[28]

However, there was a sharp division within the alliance from the outset; with the US and British governments pressing with increasing force for a firm modernization commitment to secure not only congressional FOTL authorization but also the post-INF Treaty initiative. There were to be no further negotiations with the USSR on tactical nuclear weapon issues until the more pressing questions of Soviet conventional weapon superiority and

[23] Fitchett, J., 'NATO's missile compromise', *International Herald Tribune*, 2 Mar. 1989, p. 1.

[24] Interview by the author, Oct. 1989.

[25] Dembinsky, M. *et al.*, *No End to Modernization?*, PRIF Report no. 6–7 (Peace Research Institute Frankfurt: Frankfurt/M., May 1989), p. 4.

[26] Bulloch, J. and Urban, M., 'Britain offers to take new nuclear arms', *The Independent*, 20 Apr. 1989, p. 1.

[27] Mauthner, R., 'In search of a concept for NATO', *Financial Times*, 20 Dec. 1988, p. 19; Fitchett (note 23); 'Über Modernisierung einig?', *Frankfurter Allgemeine Zeitung*, 25 Mar. 1989, p. 1; 'NATO nuclear weapons; well, later, maybe', *The Economist*, 27 May 1989, p. 28.

[28] Discussed in Dembinsky (note 25).

its buildup of chemical stockpiles had been satisfactorily resolved.[29] The Reagan Administration took a conciliatory tone towards FRG political worries; Prime Minister Margaret Thatcher stood adamant.

The FRG as well as increasingly Belgium, Denmark, Italy and Greece suggested rather that there were pressing political and military needs for further discussion and deliberation and for exploration of future arms control options. Negotiations need not be tied to modernization; Lance would last until at least the mid-1990s, and the improvements in nuclear artillery and aircraft were at least on track. What mattered far more to the ultimate security of Europe was to exploit opportunities to test Soviet intentions and to lower arsenals on both sides.[30]

The hard times came in the first half of 1989, with the peak of all three SNF crises in April and May 1989. Perhaps the opening shot was a newspaper interview given by Chancellor Kohl just before the first visit of the new US Secretary of State, James Baker, to Bonn in February 1989. The Chancellor, beset by coalition difficulties with the FDP and facing a substantial decline in Christian Democratic Union (CDU) electoral fortunes, asserted that: (a) the FRG would not be pressured into a decision on modernization; (b) a decision on the FOTL must be deferred until 1991–92 (a date after the next federal elections in 1990); and (c) the FRG was not an 'unreliable partner in NATO'.[31] Much in the statement was not new but the intensity and timing was such, as interviewer David Marsh reported, that '[Kohl's] underlying message for the West is that the rest of NATO and the European Community will have to accept a stronger and more assertive Federal Republic that will no longer allow itself to suffer a subtle form of international discrimination because of the Nazi past'.[32] Kohl reportedly then told Baker that the FRG was still against a 'third zero' and for early negotiations to bring SNF to equal East–West ceilings but that Bonn was not prepared to make an early commitment to FOTL.[33] Baker learned in subsequent visits that virtually all the continental allies—with the possible exception of the Netherlands—endorsed the FRG position. Only Britain, Canada and the USA were clearly in favour of early Lance modernization.[34]

---

[29] 'NATO could cut nuke warheads once arsenal modernized', USIS Wireless File, 25 Apr. 1989, pp. 43–54; Galvin, J. R., 'Modernization of theatre nuclear forces', NATO's Sixteen Nations, vol. 34, no. 1 (special edition, Apr. 1989), pp. 25–28.

[30] A series of press accounts between 1988 and 1989 attest to these positions; see, for instance, Palmer, J., 'UK "isolated" over nuclear renewal', Guardian Weekly, 28 Apr. 1988, p. 12; 'Genscher will Abrüstung auch bei den Kurzstreckenraketen', Frankfurter Rundschau, 22 Aug. 1988, p. 4; 'Belgium opposes NATO arms move', International Herald Tribune, 22–23 Oct. 1988; 'USA setzen Europäer stark unter Druck', Frankfurter Rundschau, 27 Apr. 1989, pp. 1–2; 'NATO deeply divided on talks with Warsaw Pact', Guardian Weekly, 28 Apr. 1989, p. 5; Sheridan, M., 'Rome backs Bonn on nuclear missiles', The Independent, 1 May 1989, p. 8.

[31] Marsh, D., 'A chancellor for all seasons: David Marsh talks to West Germany's Helmut Kohl', Financial Times, 10 Feb. 1989, p. 16.

[32] Marsh (note 31).

[33] Fitchett, J. 'Bonn seeks to tie an updated Lance to East–West talks', International Herald Tribune, 13 Feb. 1989, p. 5; 'Bonn denkt bei den Kurzstreckenraketen wieder an einen Doppel-Beschluss', Frankfurter Allgemeine Zeitung, 14 Feb. 1989, p. 1.

[34] See, for instance, the following press comments: Friedman, T., 'Baker confronts the "Gorbachev factor"', International Herald Tribune, 15 Feb. 1989; 'Athen gegen Modernisierung', Süddeutsche Zeitung, 17 Feb. 1989, p. 7; 'Auch Brüssel gegen US-Wünsche', Frankfurter Rundschau, 17 Feb. 1989, p. 2; 'US said to be planning Lance replacement', Jane's NATO Report, 21 Feb. 1989, p. 3.

The next seven weeks saw intense intra-NATO negotiations, signalling, compromises and continuing disagreement. Finally, the NATO defence ministers' meeting in April came up with a new compromise statement, arguing in essence that there would be neither early modernization nor early East–West negotiation on SNF reductions. NATO would adhere to modernization, at least in principle, but would give priority to a conventional arms agreement.[35] This created the appearance of a consensus among NATO allies.[36] Moreover, a week prior to the NATO meeting came news of a cabinet reshuffle in Bonn, including the hasty replacement of pro-modernization Defence Minister Rupert Scholz by CDU Vice-Chairman and former Finance Minister Gerhard Stoltenberg, and the intensification of FDP calls for early arms control negotiations on SNF whatever the fate of modernization.[37]

The new Coalition Agreement of 21 April and Kohl's official statement to the *Bundestag* on 27 April completed the circle.[38] There were five critical points: (*a*) the FRG saw no alternative to deterrence; (*b*) the development of Lance was a US national, not an alliance, decision; (*c*) the decision on FOTL within NATO should come first in 1992; (*d*) there must be early negotiations on SNF within a Comprehensive Concept (*Gesamtkonzept*); and (*e*) the goal must be not a 'third zero' but a reduction of missiles and nuclear artillery to equal ceilings.[39]

Five weeks followed of public and private recriminations and attacks, numerous visits and personal and telephone consultations that resulted in stalemate, frozen silences in NATO forums and intense back-channel negotiation and bargaining.[40] The public disarray was all the more acute given the planned May celebration of NATO's 40th anniversary to be staged in Brussels and to include all heads of government. The accusations of bad faith and the heated debate about intentions and options in Bonn, Washington, London and even an officially silent Paris reached the heights of the most intense INF negotiation sessions—which only reinforced and exaggerated tendencies to draw parallels and fears from the 1981–83 period.

[35] See, for example, US Defense Secretary Richard Cheney's statement, 'Cheney: conventional forces agreement of greater concern', *USIS Wireless File*, 20 Apr. 1989, pp. 3–9; see also 'Nuklearplanungstreffen der NATO in Brüssel', *Neue Zürcher Zeitung*, 21 Apr. 1989, p. 1.
[36] See 'Cheney satisfied with NATO nuclear consensus', *The Independent*, 21 Apr. 1989, p. 10; 'Konsenssuche der NATO im Abrüstungsdialog', *Neue Zürcher Zeitung*, 22 Apr. 1989, p. 1.
[37] McCartney, R., 'Kohl replaces 8 ministers in major shift to counter rise of West German right', *International Herald Tribune*, 14 Apr. 1989, p. 1.
[38] Eisenhammer, J., 'Bonn seeks to heal NATO missile rift', *The Independent*, 22 Apr. 1989, p. 12; Presse- und Informationsamt der Bundesregierung, 'Regierungserklärung des Bundeskanzlers vor dem Deutschen Bundestag', *Bulletin*, no. 40 (28 Apr. 1989), p. 361.
[39] 'Im Wortlaut: Bonn's Raketen Position. Für "baldige Verhandlungen"', *Frankfurter Rundschau*, 24 Apr. 1989, p. 2.
[40] For the Bush–Thatcher consultation following the coalition compromise, see 'U.S. will oppose Bonn on missile talks', *International Herald Tribune*, 24 Apr. 1989, p. 1; for Genscher's and Stoltenberg's visit to the USA, see Pringle, P., Eisenhammer, J. and Hughes, C., 'Bonn's nuclear shift hits stiff US opposition', *The Independent*, 25 Apr. 1989; for Thatcher's visit to the FRG, see Eisenhammer, J., 'Thatcher and Kohl fail to end NATO row', *The Independent*, 2 May 1989, p. 1; for consultations with Italy and France, see 'Kohl und Genscher versichern sich in Rom und Paris der Unterstützung im Streit über Kurzstreckenraketen', *Süddeutsche Zeitung*, 3–4 May 1989, p. 1; for Stoltenberg's visit to Washington, see 'Stoltenberg rechnet mit Einigung im Raketen-Streit', *Süddeutsche Zeitung*, 20–21 May 1989.

Ten days before the Brussels meeting, the Bush Administration accepted SNF negotiations in principle, but they were only to begin once a CFE (Conventional Armed Forces in Europe) agreement was reached (see chapter 13). Also, any SNF reductions were to be to less than total and only implemented after a CFE agreement was carried through, perhaps after five years.[41] NATO disarray subsided but continued.

Finally, in a last-minute dramatic development, Bush announced a new compromise formula, one which promised both time and concessions in the terms set by the Kohl Government, particularly the Comprehensive Concept for which Kohl had pushed for so long. The instrument was a new proposal for the CFE Negotiation, now to include both aircraft and personnel as the East had pushed for, and to involve an agreement in 6–12 months and reductions by 1992–93.[42] All was also to be embedded in the new NATO 'Comprehensive Concept of Arms Control and Disarmament' made public in the final communiqué.[43] Subsumed were both a decision on FOTL deployment in 1992 with a 'national decision' on its R&D funding and the pledge of US preparedness 'to enter into negotiations to achieve a partial reduction of US and Soviet land-based nuclear missile forces of shorter range to equal and verifiable levels'.[44] Short-range nuclear forces, as reliance on nuclear deterrence, would be needed in Europe 'as far as can be foreseen' but clearly the numbers of SNF and their characteristics were neither fixed nor determinate.[45]

This way out of the modernization impasse began to lose value within days of the NATO summit meeting. Press reports referred to quibbling over academic exercises, and the possibility of a *de facto* 'third zero' through delay, congressional inaction and technological obsolescence. In early June addresses to the Bundestag, both Kohl and Genscher suggested that some restrictive provisions of the Comprehensive Concept regarding SNF would change with time and circumstance.[46] Genscher, in particular, argued that while the concept suggested that a FOTL decision would be taken 'in light of the overall security developments,' the FRG would work 'to shape developments so that there will be no compulsion for a follow-on system'.[47]

[41] Ross, J., 'Bush cites progress in missile dispute', *International Herald Tribune*, 22 May 1989, pp. 1–2; Smith, R. J., 'U.S. stance on arms opens conflict with Britain', *International Herald Tribune*, 22 May 1989; McCartney, R., 'Bonn turns down 3 U.S. conditions in missile dispute', *International Herald Tribune*, 23 May 1989, p. 2.

[42] NATO, *Declaration of the Heads of State and Government Participating in the Meeting of the North Atlantic Council, 29–30 May 1989* (NATO Information Service: Brussels, May 1989), p. 6–7; Mauthner, R. and White, D., 'NATO compromise opens way for fresh arms talks', *Financial Times*, 31 May 1989; 'NATO summit: SNF debate resolved, Bush CFE plan', *Jane's NATO and Europe Today*, 31 May 1989, pp. 1–2; 'Good sense from NATO', *Financial Times*, 31 May 1989, p. 18.

[43] NATO, *A Comprehensive Concept of Arms Control and Disarmament* (NATO Information Service: Brussels, May 1989).

[44] NATO (note 43), p. 11.

[45] NATO (note 43), p. 10.

[46] Presse- und Informationsamt der Bundesregierung, 'Erklärung der Bundesregierung zur NATO-Gipfelkonferenz in Brüssel und zum Besuch des Präsidenten der Vereinigten Staaten', Abgegeben von Bundeskanzler Dr. Helmut Kohl vor dem Deutschen Bundestag, *Bulletin*, no. 55 (2 June 1989), pp. 489–94; for Genscher's statement, see Deutscher Bundestag, 'Abgabe einer Erklärung der Bundesregierung zum NATO-Gipfel am 29/30. Mai 1989 in Bruessel', Abgegeben von Bundesminister Genscher, *Stenographischer Bericht*, Bonn, 1 June 1989.

[47] 'Worten müssen auch bei uns Taten folgen', Spiegel Gespräch mit Aussenminister Hans-Dietrich

However, the compromise still provided sufficient cover to defuse the modernization crises and to permit the restoration of outwardly harmonious discussions in NATO and elsewhere. After an appeal by SACEUR John Galvin, Congress restored funding for R&D for the FOTL.[48] NATO and US sources began listing five more or less realistic FOTL alternatives: a Lance upgrade, a nuclear ATACMS, SRAM II, a British (or perhaps British–French) TASM and SLCMs.[49] In its October 1989 meeting, the NPG ordered a 'concept study' by the NATO High Level Group on the role of all nuclear weapons in NATO.[50]

However, under the impact of the political transformations occurring at a dizzying pace in Eastern Europe throughout the autumn, all discussions of nuclear modernization assumed an air of increasing unreality. Perhaps the final blow was struck during Genscher's Washington visit on 21 November 1989 after the momentous changes in the German Democratic Republic and the intimation of more to come in Czechoslovakia and Bulgaria.[51] Officials travelling with Genscher pointed out that there were now no possible grounds on which to re-open the FOTL issue or to continue with NATO nuclear modernization in general. The reasons cited were recent developments in Eastern Europe, and the fact that modernization 'would have given a pretext to the [anti-NATO] hard-liners in many countries'.[52]

III. The nuclear crisis

As the latest in a long line of NATO crises over TNF, the SNF modernization case proved significant but not particularly new. The arguments had all been heard before; few of the major actors, military or political, revealed any new concepts or strategies. What was novel, however, was the re-interpretation of these arguments to meet the realities of the post-INF era. The removal of the Pershings and GLCMs had removed two rungs of the escalatory ladder. What was then the continuing justification for the other rungs— the applicability of continued advocacy of the flexible response doctrine?

The SNF debate focused on these questions in two quite different contexts. The first addressed SNF modernization as compensation for INF withdrawals; the second involved a debate over end-goals that emerged as 'deterrence versus a third zero'. In neither was there a satisfactory resolution; indeed, much of the debate seemed a dialogue of the deaf.

The 'compensation' issue

Detractors of SNF and its modernization put their case simply; the importance which NATO military authorities and the Reagan Administration

Genscher über das Ost–West Verhältnis und die Deutschen, *Der Spiegel*, 12 June 1989, pp. 20–23.

[48] Towell, P., 'With House floor debate near, Cheney argues for "stealth"', *Congressional Quarterly Weekly Report*, 15 July 1989, p. 1805.

[49] Interviews by the author, Dec. 1989; Sloan (note 13).

[50] Healy, M., 'NATO sets study of changed need for battlefield A-arms', *Washington Post*, 26 Oct. 1989, p. A43.

[51] Oberdorfer (note 1).

[52] Oberdorfer (note 1).

attached to an extended-range FOTL proved that it was intended to compensate for the deep-strike capabilities of INF and thus to circumvent the intention, if not the literal provisions, of the INF Treaty. This was the position of many on the political Left. Katrin Fuchs of the German SPD, for example, forced the issue in Bundestag questioning as early as April 1988.[53] The SPD and the Greens confronted the Government on NATO's 'compensatory actions' again in December 1988.[54] Wilfried Martens, Prime Minister of the Belgian Left–Centre coalition, raised the question of SNF modernization 'violations' as late as early April 1989.[55]

Compensation became an increasingly frequent charge as the SNF debate escalated. Efforts by NATO military authorities, especially SACEUR Galvin, to explain the FOTL mission and to downplay the range factor only fuelled suspicions.[56] Those who suspected the motives for FTOL were even more convinced when Galvin in October 1988 attempted to win support for the FOTL by suggesting that he personally would give up all of NATO's remaining nuclear artillery for a modernized longer-range missile.[57]

The increasingly active Soviet campaign for SNF negotiations tied to or parallel with the CFE Negotiation emphasized the issue of compensation as well.[58] Perhaps the low point was a charge made by Soviet Foreign Minister Eduard Shevardnadze during a May 1989 visit to Bonn.[59] Why, he mused in a prepared statement, should the USSR continue to destroy its SS-23 missiles with a range just at or over 500 km when the West was preparing to develop a FOTL just under the 500-km threshold?[60] An avalanche of negative responses from both critics and proponents of SNF modernization soon brought a hasty retreat.[61]

Objectively viewed, the FOTL was clearly not going to replace the INF capability, being phased out in number, range or mission. Modernized SNF, even extended to 450–480 km, would not be able to reach targets on Soviet territory in the early phases of battle, as specified under the General Political Guidelines (GPG) adopted in 1986 to govern NATO nuclear use. Those roles were to be assigned to additional aircraft deployed forward to Britain (the F- and FB-111, modernized F-15 and perhaps B-52 as well), equipped with new stand-off missiles (the SRAM II-T with perhaps a 250-km range),

[53] Fuchs, K., 'Wie lange will die Bundesregierung noch die Wahrheit verbergen?', *Die SPD im Deutschen Bundestag*, Bonn, 21 Apr. 1988.

[54] Deutscher Bundestag, 'Aktuelle Stunde: Haltung der Bundesregierung zur Modernisierung nuklearer Kurzstreckenwaffen', *Stenographischer Bericht*, Bonn, 7 Dec. 1988.

[55] Cited in *Arms Control Reporter*, Apr. 1989, p. 408.B.28.

[56] Galvin, J. R. 'The alliance in a period of transition', *European Security Towards the Year 2000*, FHSF seminar report, no. 1 (Alumni Association of the Norwegian Defence College: Oslo, Nov. 1988).

[57] Fairhall, D., 'NATO nuclear protest is smothered', *Guardian Weekly*, 29 Oct. 1988, p. 5.

[58] For a series of statements, see 'Chervov on NATO arms "compensation" for INF', *FBIS-SOV*, 12 Jan. 1988, pp. 1–2; 'Press conference by Soviet Defence Minister, Berne, 17 March 1988', *Pravda*, 18 Mar. 1988, reprinted in *Daily Review*, 18 Mar. 1988, pp. 1–8; Mauthner, R., 'Pact offers new nuclear arms talks', *Financial Times*, 13 Apr. 1989, p. 2; WTO concerns over compensation were also expressed in the following: 'Communiqué by the Warsaw Treaty Organisation's Political Consultative Committee', *Pravda*, 17 July 1988, reprinted in *Daily Review*, 18 July 1988, pp. 1–13; and 'Kommunique, Appell für eine Welt ohne Krieg', *Neues Deutschland*, 13 Apr. 1989.

[59] For Shevardnadze's text, see *Arms Control Reporter*, May 1989, p. 408.B.47.

[60] Shevardnadze (note 59).

[61] For a sampling, see *Arms Control Reporter*, May 1989, p. 408.B.48.

and to sea-based systems, including submarine-launched cruise missiles (SLCMs).[62] Moreover, while the total number of MLRS eventually deployed might equal 1000, the number of nuclear ATACMS was never discussed as equalling even the 572 INF missiles of the original dual-track decision. There was no special class of targets that these weapons would be able to cover uniquely—as indeed had also been the case with the INF forces.

However, the FOTL proponents failed to make the rationale for the extended range either clear or compelling; publicly, it was not even clear that NATO had formally agreed to the extension from 250 km to over 450 km. Galvin spoke of the logic of the FOFA mission, itself still a matter of controversy within some European governing coalitions and always disputed by the parties of the political left. Others stressed the simple availability of the technology for range-extension and the cost-effectiveness of using this technology to multiply the value of the MLRS.[63] To the horror of European and congressional proponents of arms control, still others stressed that the USSR would not be able to distinguish between conventional and nuclear MLRS launchers, thereby increasing their value for deterrence and perhaps avoiding a truly verifiable agreement on a 'third zero'.[64]

Whatever their motives, the NATO defence establishments took great care to avoid a public debate on range. Throughout most of 1988, official statements were rather vague on the precise numbers and on the 'common' desire for extension. Press reports generally emphasized that no final decision had been reached and that all that was being talked about was the necessary R&D to secure options for choice.[65]

More precise statements surfaced following the submission of Galvin's 1988 Nuclear Weapons Requirement Study (NWRS) to the NATO High Level Group.[66] The NWRS reportedly recommended a 25 per cent further reduction in the quite unpopular nuclear artillery in return for the modernization of forces able to reach second-echelon forces. Galvin emphasized that the range of a follow-on model would not only go 'directly out to the front but . . . to the flanks' as well.[67]

However optimistic the talk, the fact nevertheless remained that a range of over 450 km still covered only targets in the western parts of Eastern

---

[62] Cited in *Arms Control Reporter*, Mar. 1989, p. 408.408.B.21.

[63] *Department of Defense Appropriations for 1989* (note 14), p. 37. There are opposing views on whether or not compensation for INF systems was sought. In an interview conducted in Oct. 1989, a defence expert expressed the view that the DOD did not seek a deliberate compensation but was primarily motivated by the availability of technology.

[64] See Pihl statement in *Department of Defense Appropriations for 1989* (note 14), p. 70, contrasting 'military' and 'arms control' perspectives, and the views of Binnendijk (note 11).

[65] For a sampling see Evans, M., 'NATO nearer to nuclear accord', *The Times*, 23 Apr. 1988, p. 7; White, D., 'NATO moves towards arms modernisation', *Financial Times*, 29 Apr. 1988, p. 2; Reifenberg, J., 'Die NATO fordert die Modernisierung der nuklearen Kurzstreckenwaffen', *Frankfurter Allgemeine Zeitung*, 22 Oct. 1988.

[66] Fouquet, D., and Cook, N., 'NATO forced to rethink nuclear battlefield', *Jane's Defence Weekly*, 4 Feb. 1989, p. 178; see also Hoffmann, H., 'Gründe für die Modernisierung der NATO Kernwaffen in Europa', *Neue Zürcher Zeitung*, 17 Feb. 1989; 'NATO's Commander urges Lance upgrade', *Defense News*, 20 Feb. 1989, p. 33.

[67] 'Galvin interview with William Tuohy', *ACE Output*, Mar. 1989, pp. 2–3. The NWRS was introduced to the NPG meeting on 18–19 Apr. 1989. The final communiqué stressed that the NWRS provisions would 'allow a shift in emphasis towards relatively longer ranges across the entire spectrum including both ground-launched and air-delivered capabilities'; see 'NATO Nuclear

Europe, most probably the GDR, Poland and Czechoslovakia, not the USSR. In the view of many in European political élites and in European militaries, all that was being enhanced was the possibility of nuclear use limited to Europe at lower levels of conflict. For liberals and socialists, opposition to this outcome was an item of political faith. Along with Alfred Dregger of Bavaria's Christian Socialist Union (CSU) and the CDU's Volker Rühe, conservatives who might have been expected to favour SNF asked what was then the value of SNF modernization. For Dregger, the real issue was elimination of nuclear artillery; for Rühe, it was the need to reinforce deterrence by the threat of retaliation against Soviet targets and to reduce the number of systems whose only effect would be to kill more Germans from German soil.[68] Compensation in this form was therefore neither sufficient nor desirable. In Kohl's words of 27 April 1989 this was not consistent with the FRG's special obligations growing out of World War II to the people of Czechoslovakia and Poland, as well as those to 'the other part of our fatherland'.[69]

Deterrence versus the 'third zero'

It was over the issue of the 'third zero' that a few new arguments over the role of nuclear weapons were joined. Proponents of a 'third zero' usually proceeded simply from an ideological position; nuclear weapons should be limited and then eliminated, regardless of location, size or planned use. Those who advanced military arguments limited themselves to emphasizing the benefits of reducing the far larger numbers of Soviet SNF first to low, equal numbers, then quickly or eventually to zero. Moreover, the West had other air- and sea-based systems to fit SNF missions, and the elimination of ground-based systems would resolve the long-discussed incentives for hasty or unauthorized battlefield use (the 'use 'em or lose 'em' dilemma).

Towards the end of the SNF debate, a number of 'third zero' supporters began to hedge towards a position closer to the classical minimum deterrence argument.[70] A small number of SNF—perhaps 500 warheads for specially designated and identifiable launchers—might actually serve the interests of East–West stability, particularly in the foreseeable future. These would not be integrated into standing forces, as at present, but rather maintained in special locations with special provisions for both verification transparency and survivability.[71]

Proponents of FOTL argued for many different kinds of forces—ranging from much lower levels equal to those of the USSR to as many and as long-ranged SNF as the INF Treaty did not specifically forbid. They were united, however, in their emphasis on the importance of SNF for the continuation of

[68] Dregger had made his opposition to nuclear artillery dramatically clear throughout 1988 and into 1989. See, for example, his views at the 1989 *Wehrkunde* meeting quoted in the *Arms Control Reporter*, 28–29 Jan. 1989. For statements by Rühe emphasizing the need to reduce SNF to minimum levels, see *Arms Control Reporter*, 15 Mar. 1988, pp. 403.B.666–67 and 21 Feb. 1989, p. 408.B.15.

[69] Cited in *Arms Control Reporter*, 27 Apr. 1989, p. 408.B.40.

[70] Interviews by author, Sep. and Oct. 1989.

[71] Interviews by author (note 70).

extended deterrence.[72] The USSR still had an overwhelming conventional advantage in Europe that could be used without risk of escalation if SNF were eliminated or even significantly reduced. Moreover, the Soviet nuclear threat would remain even if all Soviet SNF were withdrawn, given the longer-range Soviet missiles stationed even east of the Urals and targeted (or quickly targetable) against Europe. Without SNF there were only highly mobile air and sea forces, which could be deployed away from Europe, and nuclear artillery, never conceived as a free-standing force and the object of continuing opposition in some European and US military quarters.[73]

What was intriguing in the SNF debate were the new accents SNF proponents added to the arguments so often heard during the INF debate and before. Perhaps the most striking was the argument that the SNF's value was not dependent on its role as a counter to the Soviet conventional weapon capability—a reversal of arguments used as early as 1954 to justify integration of TNF into NATO forces and the alliance policy of first-nuclear-use against a successful Soviet conventional offensive. The argument used was not even the deterrence argument of the 1970s—e.g., the Pershing and GLCM as a response to the SS-20, that is, deterrence through the maintenance of balanced (not necessarily equal) capabilities. SNF and indeed all TNF were increasingly portrayed as having a deterrent effect in and of themselves, as being an existential deterrent or trip-wire almost regardless of their number, dislocation and survivability.[74] Some of this may have been circumstantial, reflecting fears of an inevitable popular rush to a denuclearized Europe under the impact of SNF cuts or an abandonment of FOTL and the attraction of the continuing stream of Soviet arms control proposals. Some of it seemed to reflect long-buried intra-alliance military debates stemming from the Kennedy–McNamara period and pressed by some in both the British and FRG (and of course French) military. However, it was a clear departure from the previous line of official NATO argument.

A second, more usual deviation was insistence that deterrent value lay in continuing uncertainty. Dual-capable weapons were to be prized not only because they—as with MLRS—lowered costs or resulted in operational efficiency and organic unit relationships. Deterrence thus lay in the opponent's uncertainty that he could prevail, that he could target and destroy all the relevant capability, not in the fear of swift, assured retaliation.[75] A third, considerably less serious addition to deterrence arguments came in April 1989, at the peak of British outrage over resistance to FOTL. Obsolete weapons, Prime Minister Thatcher declared in a press interview, do not deter; only the most modern ones do.[76]

[72] Sommer (note 14).

[73] Galvin, J. R., 'Nuclear modernization: points for the discussion', *International Herald Tribune*, 18 Apr. 1989; see also Wilson (note 16).

[74] See General Galvin's testimony on 11 June 1989 and the British statements of 30 May, quoted in the *Arms Control Reporter*, 11 June 1989, p. 408.B.62 and 10 May 1989, p 408.B.59, respectively. See also Wilson (note 16).

[75] *Department of Defense Appropriations for 1989* (note 14).

[76] *Arms Control Reporter*, 6 Apr. 1989, p. 408.B.27.

IV. The NATO crisis

The NATO crisis engendered by SNF modernization was perhaps never as important as that surrounding the INF deployment of 1982–83. There was, however, both a level of acrimony and a type of division rarely seen in NATO's history, even in the series of TNF crises.[77] As during the INF debate, the cleavages activated all cut in the same political direction—the divisions between the nuclear and the non-nuclear allies, the perceived demands of domestic politics, and the questions raised about the role the USA played in stimulating and maintaining the crisis.

The nuclear versus the non-nuclear NATO states

Perhaps the most painful wound opened by the SNF modernization debate within NATO was the old division between the nuclear and non-nuclear allies. The experience particularly of the last stages of the INF negotiations had re-emphasized the dilemma of the non-nuclear nations, especially the FRG. During the INF negotiations Britain and France had both insisted that none of their nuclear-capable forces would be subject to reduction or elimination, and neither the USA nor the USSR had seriously pressured either state to participate or to include their forces in reductions at a future time.

The Kohl Government, which had argued against the 'second INF zero', felt particularly angry at the way in which the elimination of the Pershing 1As had been virtually imposed on the FRG as a by-product of the Soviet–US agreement. The anger was directed first and foremost at the USA and the presentation by Secretary of State George Shultz of the 'second zero' as a final *fait accompli* after his Moscow trip in May 1987.[78] Kohl, who had earlier found himself pilloried at home for his support of the US 'go-slow' position on negotiations, now found himself facing a negotiated outcome over which he had little say and for which he could count on little political compensation.

Bonn's hostility was perhaps even deeper towards the governments of Margaret Thatcher and François Mitterrand. Both had at first supported the FRG demand that all missiles in Europe, including those in the 0–500 km (SNF) range, be included in the INF negotiation, but had then reversed course.[79] The SNF modernization debate only exacerbated these differences and suspicions between the FRG and Britain; France remained largely distant throughout the SNF debate.[80] Beginning with the post-INF summit meeting in March 1988, Prime Minister Thatcher placed herself at the front of the pro-modernization, no-negotiation forces and pursued this line relent-

---

[77] For an overview of these crises, see Kelleher (note 2) and Schwartz, D., *NATO's Nuclear Dilemmas* (Brookings Institution: Washington, DC, 1983).

[78] Interviews by A. Ackermann, Nov. 1989; interviews by the author, Sep. 1989.

[79] Ackermann (note 78).

[80] For conflicting French statements see Webster, P., 'Chirac falls into line with Mitterrand on nuclear weapons build-up', *Guardian Weekly*, 2 Mar. 1988, p. 7; Chinelli, R., 'Mitterrand bei Kurzstreckenraketen für Rücksicht auf Bonn', *Süddeutsche Zeitung*, 1 Mar. 1989; White, D., 'Britain and France fear for their nuclear arsenals', *Financial Times*, 26 Apr. 1989, p. 2; Fitchett, J., 'Mitterrand rejects early short-range arms talks', *International Herald Tribune*, 19 May 1989, pp. 1, 5.

lessly for the next 18 months. One of her arguments was that the FRG was not to be allowed to dictate the future of the NATO nuclear force structure.[81] Moreover, modernization had been agreed to by all the NATO partners at Montebello in 1983 and after, including the March 1988 summit meeting.[82] Failure to modernize meant a drift towards a 'third zero' and the effect of a denuclearization of Europe.[83]

Thatcher's public insistence on this position was in part to demonstrate the renewed special relationship with the USA, in part to cap what she saw as her total victory over the Labour Party and the other anti-nuclear forces in the INF case. But there also was more than a fair amount of increasingly strident German-bashing, never a losing theme in post-war British politics.[84]

Despite frequent visits and exchanges, the Bonn–London relationship grew colder and colder. The culmination was perhaps the Thatcher threats that (a) British forces might not stay in the FRG if Bonn did not agree to the maintenance of modernized nuclear weapons,[85] and (b) Britain would boycott any SNF negotiations even if the other 15 NATO allies agreed.[86]

The FRG's relations with the USA were similarly cool but somewhat less emotional, at least at the outset of the FOTL debate. There were FRG claims that the SNF modernization was being used as a 'litmus test',[87] and later comments that the hard-liners in the Pentagon had made SNF modernization the only test of Bonn's loyalty.[88] Both Bonn and Washington seemed to take advantage in the enforced hiatus in discussions during the last months of the Reagan Administration and the first somewhat inactive month of the Bush Administration. Even the clear opposition shown by Bonn during Baker's initial visit in February 1989 was met primarily by increased concern for Kohl's domestic political difficulties and the unattractiveness of any conceivable alternative or a more left-wing oriented government.[89]

There was, however, a dramatic deterioration in FRG–US relations, following Bonn's sudden rejection of a FOTL commitment in April 1989. The new Bush team, flush from what it thought had been a successful NPG compromise only 24 hours before, felt betrayed that Bonn had reneged on its part of the NPG bargain.[90] The arrival of Genscher and Stoltenberg with a

[81] 'Genscher begins push for SNF talks', *Jane's NATO Report*, vol. 4, no. 25 (Mar. 1989), p. 3.

[82] It was argued that there was an ambiguity in the German translation of the term 'modernization'. The German text of the Mar. summit meeting communiqué referred to modernization as 'changes to keep weapons up to date where necessary'. Prime Minister Thatcher asserted that this was irrelevant given that the NATO communiqué was negotiated in English; see Naughtie, J., 'PM defends NATO deal', *Guardian Weekly*, 5 Mar. 1988, p. 1. The English version of the March summit meeting text reads as follows: 'This is a strategy of deterrence based upon an appropriated mix of adequate and effective nuclear and conventional forces which will continue to be kept up to date where necessary'; see NATO, *NATO Communiqués 1988* (NATO Information Service: Brussels, 1988), p. 18.

[83] Owen, R. and Evans, M., 'Thatcher urges nuclear update', *The Times*, 3 Mar. 1988, p. 1.

[84] Smith (note 41); Johnstone, D., 'No nukes is good nukes in NATO, if not Washington', *These Times*, 17–23 May 1989, pp. 9–10.

[85] Eisenhammer, J., Bevins, A. and Pringle, P., 'Thatcher joins fray on Kohl's defence shift', *The Independent*, 26 May 1989.

[86] Report in *London Sunday Telegraph*, 7 May 1989, cited in *Arms Control Reporter*, 7 May 1989, p. 408.B.44.

[87] Kohl interview with D. Marsh (note 31).

[88] Pond, E., 'Sie gehören alle geprügelt', *Die Zeit*, 19 May 1989, p. 6.

[89] Aeppel, T., 'West Germany's new assertiveness', *Christian Science Monitor*, 4 May 1989, p. 3.

[90] Eisenhammer, J., 'Bonn seeks to heal NATO missile rift', *The Independent*, 22 Apr. 1989, p. 12;

fully negotiated coalition agreement only a few days later fuelled the dispute.[91] Genscher's stock , never high with the Reagan Administration, fell even lower as he was perceived as the architect of the FOTL defeat.[92]

Bonn carried its share of the blame for alliance hostility as well. The FRG position underwent several twists and turns at decisive points in 1988 and early 1989, the result of Kohl's search for a pragmatic middle way and the increasing difficulties of coalition management with the FDP. Despite all the exchanges and the mutual acrimony, however, the nuclear and the non-nuclear weapon powers seemed to be engaged in a dialogue of the deaf. Once the crucial elections were over, the FRG and the other non-nuclear states were expected to fall into line behind the FOTL policy already set in motion by the USA with the support of Britain.

The role of US alliance leadership

Much of the SNF debate really turned on what might be called a competition over which domestic political constraints were to be given precedence in alliance deliberations over weapon choices. The principal invoker of domestic public opinions was the Kohl Government. The least constrained, but most adamant about its domestic constraints, was the USA. Both the Reagan and the Bush Administrations consistently cited congressional concerns as the reasons why the FOTL issue had to be pushed through to Alliance commitment. Without evidence of allied acquiescence, it was said endlessly, Congress would not approve the funds needed for the R&D that would ensure timely procurement before Lance was phased out. But neither the Reagan nor the Bush team had mounted full pressure on the FOTL issue and there never seemed any intention to do so. Indeed, after the May 1989 NATO summit meeting, Congress restored the cut FOTL funds solely on the appeal of SACEUR Galvin.[93]

In hindsight the SNF modernization crises and their costs to all concerned need probably not have happened. If there is a single causal factor, it was the decision of the Reagan and then the Bush leadership to push hard for the FOTL commitments. As was clear almost from the outset, the Reagan–Bush rationale was that the setting of another loyalty test would strengthen NATO coupling, while preventing President Mikhail Gorbachev from attracting more supporters within NATO itself, or from achieving the long-desired Soviet goal of a denuclearized Europe.

This logic showed an uncanny resemblance to US policies towards INF deployment—and reflected what at least one group thought it had learned from the experience. The instruments the USA used to sell its message once formulated were also virtually the same employed during the INF debate—

Pringle, P., Eisenhammer, J. and Hughes, C., 'Bonn's nuclear shift hits stiff US opposition', *The Independent*, 25 Apr. 1989; Hughes, C., Lichfield, J. and Eisenhammer, J., 'Kohl prompts fear of NATO split', *The Independent*, 24 Apr. 1989, p. 1.

[91] Interview by the author, Oct. 1989.

[92] Marsh, D., 'Stoltenberg the counterweight faces his allies', *Financial Times*, 26 May 1989; 'Genscher faces U.S.–British resolve on missiles', *International Herald Tribune*, 25 Apr. 1989, p. 1.

[93] Towell (note 48).

high-level bilateral talks, visiting high-level spokesmen, ever-new intelligence data on the state and modernization of comparable Soviet assets and the large volume of personal telephone calls from the White House to recalcitrant capitals. Reliance on the NATO Secretariat machinery continued, although it was soon clear that the new Secretary-General, Manfred Wörner, was at a substantial disadvantage compared to Lord Carrington, given the nature of the issue and his lack of allied constituencies, even in the FRG.

Most important of all, the USA in the form of the Bush Administration found it difficult to deal with new European opposition. The style of the US SNF modernization drive was more in line with what the USA had done in the period of its unquestioned alliance superiority than with the style to be anticipated from a 'first among equals' burdened with a budget deficit and domestic social problems. SNF questions were not even included in the broad Bush strategic foreign policy review, but were left to Baker and his team as questions almost of right. It was therefore not surprising that the depth of allied and especially FRG antipathy came as a shock, and an Administration that thought it was being sensitive to the FRG's concerns felt itself betrayed.[94]

V. The crisis over the future role of the FRG

In some respects, the crisis over the future foreign policy role of the FRG had the least to do with the particular details of SNF modernization. The dynamics were largely the result of domestic political calculations, and the SNF modernization debate was just the proximate spark.

Yet it was not surprising that the SNF issue did prove to be such a strong catalyst. Throughout its 35-year membership in NATO, the FRG had repeatedly found nuclear weapon questions the most neuralgic framework for foreign policy choices and testing. Nuclear-capable armament in 1956, the Multi-Lateral Force in the mid-1960s, the question of INF deployment in the 1980s—all involved a definition of the FRG's national interests that somehow integrated efforts to secure the US security guarantee, to take account of common European concerns and to preserve freedom of manoeuvre *vis-à-vis* the GDR, the USSR and the other states of Eastern Europe. In each of the earlier cases, the FRG's foreign policy élite—often both Government and opposition—had given precedence to securing the US commitment and had adapted, however reluctantly or enthusiastically, to US policy preferences.[95]

The clear and successful challenge that the Kohl–Genscher Government mounted to US SNF policy thus represented a significant breaking-point in post-war FRG foreign policy. Although it is too simple to portray this crisis—as was sometimes done in Washington—as a struggle between the views of Kohl and Genscher, it is true that Genscher occupied a crucial position in its outcome. In the SNF crisis Genscher followed a narrow pro-negotiation line, refusing to be drawn on the question of supporting a 'third

[94] Ackermann (note 78).
[95] Kelleher (note 2).

zero' and stressing only the need to test Gorbachev's words and intentions. Modernization was wrong if it impeded efforts to find a new European balance in a waning East–West conflict.[96]

To Genscher more than to Kohl, negotiations over SNF and other issues were steps in a broader strategy. Simply phrased, the goal was, within the changing East–West environment, to bring the FRG's political influence and room for diplomatic manoeuvre fully up to the level suggested by its economic and technical strength. The US lifeline was still fundamental but less than in the past, given the potential for change in the East and, secondarily, the growing self-absorption of a United States seeing itself in decline. More importantly, the strategy would recognize the FRG's potential as an 'ordinary' country, one no longer suspect or bound by the legacy of the horrible past except at its own choosing.[97]

Perhaps the best indicator of the scope and depth of the change in élite thinking in the FRG catalysed by the SNF debate are the words of Richard von Weizsäcker, the articulate and highly respected FRG President. Von Weizsäcker took rare public positions during the SNF modernization debate, arguing against an unconsidered commitment to modernization at any cost and emphasizing the new opportunities for negotiating a new European security regime. In his official speech on the 40th anniversary of the founding of the FRG he called for the definition of a new FRG foreign policy role: 'We are not a great power. But we are also not a playing ball for others. It is to our benefit to have friends and partners. But for their part, the Alliance, Western Europe, and the whole [European] continent are decisively dependent on our contribution. Our political weight derives from our central location, the special situation of Berlin, the size of our population, our productivity, and our stability'.[98]

What grew out of the cabinet debate and tactical party-political manoeuvres over SNF was a forceful agreement not to accept an imposed NATO nuclear modernization which threatened the potential for the future or imposed unacceptable costs on the FRG for little foreseeable benefit.

VI. Military and political implications of the SNF crises

The question of the future of short-range nuclear forces must be discussed primarily in the context of an implemented CFE agreement. Given the limits it would impose on WTO personnel and equipment and the resulting balance in conventional forces and reduction in WTO targets, a CFE treaty would significantly reduce the need for a substantial integrated nuclear force structure. A reduced conventional force structure could also mean fewer personnel (now perhaps 15 000–20 000 in number) for the operation of nuclear forces. Moreover, remaining nuclear forces would surely be the focus of new arms control negotiations almost immediately.

[96] 'Taking Gorbachev at his word', speech by FRG Foreign Minister Hans-Dietrich Genscher at the World Economic Forum, Davos, Switzerland, 1 Feb. 1987, reprinted in *Statements and Speeches*, vol. 10, no. 3 (6 Feb. 1987).

[97] Discussed in Kohl's interview with D. Marsh (note 31).

[98] See Schmemann, S., *New York Times*, 25 May 1989.

Yet the implementation of a CFE treaty probably will not mean the withdrawal of nuclear weapons from European territory. Neither current US and NATO nor present Soviet policy statements envisage a nuclear weapon-free Europe. Although the deterrence rationale is cited as the most compelling argument for the maintenance of nuclear forces on European territory, the dramatic changes and upheavals in the USSR and Eastern Europe may equally be used to support the position that nuclear weapons are essential in times of political uncertainty.[99] French and British forces will certainly remain for the foreseeable future.

However, the political conditions both in East and West now make nuclear modernization plans politically unacceptable. In light of the revolutionary political, military, economic and social changes in the USSR and particularly in Eastern Europe, SNF modernization would cause tremendous popular dissent in Western Europe. Pressures on the USA for SNF arms control will thus continue even prior to the planned 1992 FOTL decision.[100]

The political role nuclear weapons have played in reassuring West European publics has essentially vanished following the changes in Eastern Europe. What assures European publics now are assertive economic and political responses to East European and Soviet initiatives seeking to transform to pluralist political systems and free-market economic structures.

Furthermore, risk-sharing between the USA and Western Europe as well as the goal of NATO cohesion—both traditional political functions of nuclear weapons—are now secondary to the future of the alliance itself. Although the external threat to NATO has been shattered, both NATO and the WTO are needed as stabilizing elements in the transformation of the European political order. A restructuring of the two security regimes for tasks beyond those of organizing the political transition and guaranteeing arms reductions seems imminent.

Last, deep commitment to democratic values and principles on the part of West European governments and their respective publics has significantly changed the domestic political cultures of most West European nations. One effect is that democratic norms have permeated the issue areas of foreign and security policies since the late 1970s causing both a crisis of legitimacy about nuclear deterrence and flexible response, and a democratization of security policies.[101] In this respect the events of 1989 prove that the latter has become a permanent feature of Western political life and that the future of nuclear weapons will remain highly controversial. The debate over SNF modernization was, in retrospect, only a first step in a significant transformation within NATO as well as throughout Europe.

[99] See for instance, Sloan, S. (ed.), *NATO in the 1990s* (Pergamon-Brassey's: Washington, DC, 1989). Similar notions were expressed by defence experts at the AAAS Science and Security Colloquium, 'Science and security: technology advances and the arms control agenda', Washington, DC, 16–17 Nov. 1989.

[100] The DOD budget for FY 1991 called for $112 million for tactical nuclear modernization R&D.

[101] Discussed by Risse-Kappen, T., *Die Krise in der Sicherheitspolitik* (Grünewald & Kaiser: Mainz and Munich, 1988); see also Heisler, M., 'Trapped governments in alliance: security dependence and constraints on the autonomy of the modern democratic state', Paper presented at the annual meeting of the American Political Science Association, Washington, DC, Sep. 1986.

19. The SIPRI 1989 Olof Palme Memorial Lecture: 'The responsibility of scientists in the nuclear age'

In October 1986, SIPRI's Governing Board decided to arrange an annual public lecture, named after the late Swedish Prime Minister Olof Palme. The lecture is to be delivered in Stockholm by a political leader of international stature or an eminent scholar in order to highlight the need for, and problems of, peace and security, in particular of arms control and disarmament. The lecture is also intended to draw attention to SIPRI's commitment to a future with fewer arms and more freedom. On 18 September 1987, Willy Brandt, former Chancellor of the Federal Republic of Germany, delivered the first annual Olof Palme Memorial Lecture. On 29 September 1988, Sergey F. Akhromeyev, Chief of General Staff, First Deputy Minister of Defence and Marshal of the Soviet Union, delivered the second lecture. On 26 September 1989, Victor F. Weisskopf, Professor Emeritus, Massachusetts Institute of Technology, USA, delivered the third lecture.

VICTOR F. WEISSKOPF

I would like to express my deep gratitude to SIPRI for bestowing upon me the great honour of delivering the third Olof Palme Memorial Lecture. I knew Olof Palme personally and always had the greatest admiration for him as a person and for his activities. Let me reserve some time at the end of my lecture to say more about this remarkable man.

The responsibility of scientists is a wide subject, with many ramifications, and my talk will cover only some of its aspects. I would like to start with a personal event in my life. In 1929 I was a student of Max Born studying quantum mechanics in Göttingen. This was and is a rather difficult and esoteric subject, and at that time I wanted to change to medicine. I felt that medicine had more relation to human beings compared to the abstract and esoteric study of theoretical physics. Max Born said to me, 'No, you should stay in physics. You will see how deeply the new physics will be involved in human affairs.' How right he was in many respects, both positive and negative. We should not forget the positive effects: new technology and the deeper understanding of atomic structure have helped humankind in many ways. The negative effects, of course, have been rather terrible: the new weapons of war, the nuclear bomb and other terrible things of this kind.

I. Scientists and the bomb

The problem that Max Born predicted came earlier than expected. The first serious encounter of scientists, physicists at least, with the problem of responsibility for their actions came during World War II when we were asked to participate in the construction of the nuclear bomb. Clearly, nuclear weapons are an abuse of science for mass destruction—this feeling was only offset by the fear that Hitler could have an atomic bomb before the West did. After all, fission was discovered in Germany, and Germany had very good physicists and engineers. In 1942, as a recent immigrant to the United States, I decided to join the programme because of the overriding fear of Hitler and to help a host country that had received me with so much grace. We did not know that Hitler had not developed the bomb. It is an important question, and one which I cannot answer, whether the CIA or the British secret services knew this. They did not tell us. I do not want to accuse them, but it may be that they did not want to tell us because they wanted the bomb to be constructed. However, I have no proof of this.

A very interesting moment as regards the feeling of responsibility actually came in May 1945 at the time of Hitler's defeat, when it was clear that he did not have the bomb. Now, should we continue? Should we go on working on this weapon of mass destruction? We all, or almost all, continued; we were three months from the completion of the weapon and unfortunately, I say this with a certain feeling of shame, we did not think, at least I did not think, of stopping at that moment. The rationalizations were that the war with Japan was killing many, many people—there were 40 000 victims of the fire bombing each day—and an invasion would cost a million deaths on each side. These were rationalizations; in any event we went on. Perhaps unfortunately, one of the reasons was the attraction of the problem. Since we had worked almost day and night for three years, and were just three months from the fulfilment of this work, it was almost unthinkable not to continue. Robert Oppenheimer coined a term which I do not like very much, namely, 'technically sweet'. There is a lesson here, a dangerous lesson. Today we have similar 'technically sweet' problems in America, for example, for those people who work on the Strategic Defense Initiative (SDI) programme. Some of these people know that SDI—Star Wars—would really do more damage than good if they were ever to succeed—a question in itself—but because the programme presents interesting, technically sweet problems some scientists are attracted to work on them.

When we knew the war would soon be over, ethical questions arose. What was this weapon? What would it mean for mankind? At that time, Niels Bohr joined the group in Los Alamos. He always taught us that we are responsible for our work. At that time, of course, we did not have much influence on what the government would do with the bomb. There were four possibilities.

The first possibility was not to use the bomb at all. The second was to demonstrate its use over an uninhabited area. The third was to demonstrate the bomb over a military target, for example, a harbour where a large concentration of the Navy was assembled. The fourth possibility was to throw it over an inhabited city. Nobody took the first option seriously. It was unthinkable that the military would desist from using its most potent weapon in a war. A number of physicists, in particular under the influence of James Frank, wrote a memorandum to the government, supporting the second option, but the government was unimpressed, afraid that the bomb might fizzle out and amount to nothing. Unfortunately, the third option was not considered either, and the fourth was the solution chosen as the one that would make the biggest impression on the world. The destruction of

Hiroshima was bad enough but, looked at today, the decision to destroy a second city after three days was certainly a crime.

After this, the war ended and we were considered heroes. We were seen as the ones who brought back all the young people who were in Japan. Relieved of the pressure of the work, we were inspired by Niels Bohr to think about our work. We felt, some of us very strongly, a responsibility to make use of this fateful weapon for peace. It was Niels Bohr's idea, in particular, that the only way that this weapon could lead to a peaceful world would be an internationalization of all nuclear matters—bombs and energy production. We considered it our task to acquaint the public with the disastrous consequences of nuclear war. We wrote articles, gave talks and founded organizations: the Federation of American Scientists, the *Bulletin of the Atomic Scientists*, an emergency committee of scientists headed by Einstein, the Pugwash Movement, and later, the Union of Concerned Scientists. We wanted to teach the horrible consequences of a nuclear war and to investigate the question, 'how can we avoid a catastrophe?'

Bohr, unfortunately, was right when he said that 'Either there is an internationalization or we will have an arms race'. We got the arms race. Internationalization was impossible because neither side was ready for it. Stalin on the Russian side, of course, was not at all willing to have international negotiations about this. People in the West thought that the bomb made them powerful and that it would be 20 years before the Russians could really construct a bomb. Of course the only real secret was that the bomb was *possible*; this was obviously shown and the Soviet Union had it after little more than three years, as most of the scientists predicted. Then bigger and better bombs were constructed, and missiles that could deliver them within a few hours. The hydrogen bomb was invented by both sides at roughly the same time, and nuclear weapons became a symbol of power. The USA, the USSR and then Great Britain, France and China obtained the bomb, and so it went on. Probably India, Israel, Pakistan and South Africa have it too; we do not know. Actually one should be surprised that there are not more nuclear powers.

Then followed a shameful period, the period of the cold war and the arms race. And it is not yet over. I called this period 'a case of collective mental disease', with 50 000 warheads, almost 100 times as many as necessary to destroy the whole world. If that does not suggest a mental disease, I would not know what does!

The attitude can be expressed by a metaphor: 'The tighter we draw the bow the safer we become'—silly, but that is what they said. More responsible scientists tried to educate the public. Unfortunately responsible scientists are always in a minority. Most scientists just work in their profession, but there is a group among them that does feel responsibility for their actions. The responsible scientists demonstrated the craziness of the situation but did not get very far. The cold war psychology was dominant, insisting that we must be stronger, we must protect ourselves from aggression, we must deter the other side, as if a suicide threat could act as deterrence. Any application of these weapons would mean destruction on both sides.

Among those who fought that psychology, of course, Olof Palme was one of the most active personalities. We had a few successes. First, through the 1963 Partial Test Ban Treaty it was decided that bomb tests should be conducted underground. Linus Pauling should get the credit for this. It was not very effective, however, because tests can be carried out just as well underground as on the surface of the earth, and so the treaty did not prevent the further development of bombs. Only a comprehensive test ban would do that. Second, the 1972 Anti-Ballistic Missile (ABM) Treaty, part of the SALT I accords, was an interesting political case. It was decided to construct anti-ballistic missiles, defences against bombs, only on a very small scale, on the rationale that both sides would make more bombs to overcome such measures. It was very difficult to convince the Soviet Union at that time. The Pugwash Movement helped a great deal. I remember how we discussed these questions with the Soviet representatives who were then all really representatives of their government. (Today it is better, and the Soviet participants are a little more independent.) But we did convince them—it took some time. They always said 'defence cannot be dangerous, defence is all right'. They had to be convinced that this kind of defence would only accelerate the arms race. Paradoxically, the situation is now reversed. It is the Soviet Union that tries to convince the US Government that SDI is counter-productive for the same reason. The roles have changed.

On the whole, I must say that the scientists' effort was not very successful—perhaps because a few influential scientists had opposite views. The nuclear arms race went on and on, both qualitatively and quantitatively. Of course we studied arms control methods, how to check violations, and so on. But this was almost a purely theoretical activity because neither government was ready to do anything. Only in the past decade have people begun to think seriously about these issues, but this was not the result of scientists' efforts. Other organizations, such as the International Physicians for the Prevention of Nuclear War, have had a great influence; seemingly doctors have more influence than scientists. It is interesting that the pastoral letter of the US National Conference of Catholic Bishops was quite effective in pointing out the immorality of that kind of deterrence. And, of course, last but not least, Mikhail Gorbachev has changed the whole atmosphere of East and West for the better—an interesting example of how important personalities are in history. People are beginning to see that war is impossible. Nuclear missiles are not weapons of war; their use would lead to mutual annihilation. Co-operation is needed instead of confrontation. We have already seen some signs in that direction, for example, the INF Treaty abolishing intermediate-range and shorter-range missiles in Europe, and the Vienna negotiations on the reduction of conventional forces in Europe. So the struggle of the responsible scientists was not quite in vain, but far from a real success. Things are improving, however. The wind is already blowing from another direction, but still much too feebly. I remember that Richard von

Weizsäcker, the President of the German Federal Republic, made two statements that impressed me very much. In a talk at Harvard University in 1986 he said: 'We must find currencies other than military power for dealing with one another and we begin now to do that'. His second important remark was: 'Disarmament is important, but history teaches us that it is usually not disarmament which leads to peace but peaceful co-operation to disarmament.' He is probably right.

II. Science and technology

So much about the development of the atomic bomb as an example of scientific responsibility. Let me now make a few more remarks about the roots of this responsibility. This, of course, has to do with the relation between science and technology; the two are not the same. Science, basic science as opposed to applied science at least, is concerned with gaining more insights into the workings of nature, to find out how things work. Technology and applied science deal with making use of nature for practical purposes, good or bad. Technology actually predates science. In the old days, even in classical times, there were agricultural technology, building and construction technology, bridge and highway construction, and metallurgy, but they were not much connected with science. It is only since the beginning of the nineteenth century that science has had a direct influence on practical applications. The most important examples were Faraday's, Ampère's and Weber's discoveries of the connection between electricity and magnetism in the 1830s, which only 30 years later led Werner von Siemens and others to invent the dynamo and the electric motor. In these cases we have science first and technology afterwards. It must be recognized that the effect of this science-based technology on human society has been enormous. Whereas at that time 80 per cent of the people were working in agriculture, the corresponding figure in the developed countries today is only 4 per cent. It is now technically possible to feed and house everybody who lives on earth—possible, but this has not been realized. If you compare the carriage in which the Emperor Hadrian travelled from Rome to Vienna in the early days of our era with that in which Mozart made the same journey, you will find that they look alike. Since then, the coming of railroads and jet engines has revolutionized transport.

Developments in medicine have led to what I would call 'death control'. We now have a kind of death control with the eradication of most epidemics, a doubled life expectancy and the introduction of hygiene. Strenuous labour can be avoided in the construction of buildings, bridges, and so on: it can be carried out by machines, although this is not always the case. It is interesting that all these achievements are double negatives: the abolition of hard work, of hunger, of stress and trouble. I will return to this later.

The human and social effects of these developments are enormous, and it is the responsibility of the scientist to be aware of them. Some of these effects were very positive. It was possible to humanize industrialization: we have the eight-hour working day, we have abolished child labour, we have medical care for the workers, social services and security for old age. All these things represent great progress. Western Europe is ahead of America in this respect and, of course, both are ahead of some of the Eastern nations and the Third World, but still, this progress should not be forgotten. However, there are also negative effects.

I would like to subsume all negative effects under the term 'pollution'— material pollution and spiritual pollution. Material pollution is well known: the effects of the expansion of technology on the environment are no longer negligible. This is an old story; the Romans, for example, destroyed the east coast of the Adriatic by cutting down all the forest in order to build warships. There are still not many forests there. Today the problem has acquired a global scale. Humankind became aware of this rather late, perhaps too late, only two or three decades ago. It could have been predicted earlier and indeed it was, but nobody listened. Now we are facing these grave problems. The greenhouse effect caused by the increase of carbon dioxide and methane in the atmosphere, the reduction of the ozone layer and the decay of the forests, intentional and unintentional (intentional in the rain forests that are cut down; unintentional in Europe and other places as a result of exhaust fumes). I believe that these terrible things can *probably* be solved by technical means. We do not need to have so many polluting energy sources. We can use solar energy. I also propose nuclear energy, because it can be made safer than it is. We can clean our industries and reduce the emission of harmful gases into the atmosphere. We can stop wasting energy, and of course we can stop the intentional destruction of the forests.

This returns us to the responsibilities of scientists and engineers. New developments and new inventions are needed. Technical creativity should be directed not towards new gadgets and new ways to increase our comfort, but towards protection of our environment. Much can be done, but it will be expensive and lead to a reduction of products considered necessary for our comfort. There will be political resistance to reduced industrial production and profits, and resistance from the developing countries. They do not want to be hindered in their industrial development, arguing that it was not they but the developed countries which polluted the atmosphere; but of course their development would add to the pollution. We are facing tremendous political and financial problems. Their solution is the responsibility not only of natural scientists and engineers but also of social scientists. Science will play an essential role. Many people propose a science moratorium, but that is self-defeating, because science is needed to understand these badly understood processes. I believe that solutions are possible—but only if sacrifices are faced. We must sacrifice many comforts and we must have stable conditions. We must have birth control to counteract the death control of medical science, and we must have steady and peaceful developments in the Third World. This is far from what we see today when, for example, the Third World pays more for weapons than it receives in financial support from the developed countries.

Since I have to restrict myself to sketches and cannot go into details, let me move on to spiritual pollution. Technology has freed humanity of burdens, at least in the developed parts of this world. The question arises, 'freed for what?' What does one do if one's life is no longer a fight for survival? The individual is thrown back on his- or herself. What is the meaning of life when work is mostly secondary and there is no personal achievement, no pride and little influence on what goes on at the workplace? Where is human dignity? Whereas religion formerly gave meaning and sense to life, it now plays a much smaller role. Indeed religion can also be dangerous as we see in some of the autocratic fundamentalist governments still to be found all over the world. In this respect fundamentalism can often be seen as a form of spiritual pollution.

I would like to define religion in a very general way, in a wider sense, as a feeling of deep commitment to a great cause beyond one's personal interest, a cause whose value is never put into question. In this sense, there are many religious people, among them the social workers who devote their lives to the improvement of society; medical people, conducting research or caring for the sick; and scientists, for whom the greatness of scientific insight is a source of inspiration.

For most people, however, when the most important needs are met, what remains generally amounts to a desire for passive entertainment: watching television, driving a car or, at worst, sexual excesses and drugs. Indeed, drug abuse is perhaps the most dangerous immediate threat of spiritual pollution that humanity faces today. However, despite improvements in the past few years, restrictions of human rights are equally threatening. Torture and the persecution of political opposition are still rampant in too many places.

It is the responsibility of the social scientists to find a way to what I call the 'second humanization' of the industrial age. The present forms of industrial organization are anti-democratic. They are based upon centrally controlled authoritarian leadership in the industries. A more popular form of control is needed, with workers' participation and smaller units of production, as pioneered in Sweden. 'Small is beautiful' but, let us not forget, it is more expensive and less efficient, and here we need inventiveness, not only technical inventiveness, but also inventiveness in social management.

There is another point which, as a scientist, I am very interested in. Non-scientists are mostly unaware of, and rarely inspired by, the great scientific insights of this century—perhaps the greatest intellectual achievements of the twentieth century. It has contributed less in art and other fields of endeavour, but in science it has certainly contributed enormously. These insights should be more widely known and they should contribute to the pride of being alive at the present day. More effort should be made to convey the greatness and the wonders of science to the lay public in an understandable way. It is possible, but often more difficult than doing research, and it has been neglected. This is a responsibility which I believe scientists have not borne well. Not enough is done. If you compare, for example, music, you will see that the performer is often much more celebrated than the composer. At least they usually get more money. Unfortunately, this is not so in science.

The following six points somehow summarize in a very superficial way my view of the responsibility of scientists of all kinds, not only natural scientists, but also social scientists, engineers and statesmen—in other words, everybody.

1. To prevent war.
2. To prevent environmental catastrophe.
3. To provide a creative, purposeful life for the majority.
4. To provide assistance and education for the Third World.
5. To insist on freedom of thought and the value of doubt.
6. To create an awareness of complementary attitudes.

These points are not listed in order of importance; they are all equally important. First, we must help to prevent wars. We must show how terrible war is; this is already slowly penetrating into people's minds. It makes little difference whether we speak of nuclear or conventional war. Even conventional war is terrible, and if the powers have nuclear weapons then the losing side will certainly use them. The public must be made aware of how destructive modern weapons are. We must help arms reduction by proposing new methods of verification. Second, we must help to prevent environmental catastrophe. I am not sure myself whether this is not even the greater problem. To prevent a nuclear war is simple: do not use nuclear weapons. We do not even know exactly what causes environmental catastrophes and, as I said before, we face enormous political and social difficulties. Scientists must explain the processes leading to the catastrophes, expose technical abuses and redirect technical and societal creativity towards solutions. Third, we must provide a creative, purposeful life for the majority of the population, a very difficult but necessary task. Fourth, we must help to solve Third World problems by assistance and education. This is always a very difficult problem since it is very easy to feel superior because we are advanced. We are not superior, we are just further ahead—both in use and in abuse—but we still have to help them in many ways. Fifth, it is our responsibility as scientists to proclaim freedom of thought—to teach how doubt and discussions of different opinions are important. We have to demand the freedom for discussion and doubt to be recognized in all communities, and we know very well that the fight is far from won.

Finally, and here I speak as a Bohr disciple, we must create a sense of complementary attitudes. What do I mean by this? There are several, indeed many, approaches to human problems apart from science: ethical, artistic and religious. They are not contradictory but complementary to science. Science can never decide what is good or what is bad, what is beautiful or what is ugly, or what is or is not great art. Education should not only be in science; it should attach equal importance to all these approaches so as to teach tolerance and even enthusiasm for the variety of human endeavours. Whenever one way of dealing with the human situation is dominant, abuses come about. In medieval times, when the religious view was the dominant one, there were crusades, the Inquisition and the religious wars; today, in some ways, the scientific–technical 'religion' is dominant. The abuses are only too well known. What we need is a sense of complementarity. This is not relativism. It is not a denial of values to say that everything has values. Ethical principles and a value system must be derived from many sources, not just one, in order to foster openness and understanding for the different complementary approaches to the realities of life. I think that these are the pre-conditions for the survival of our civilization. In spite of its troubles, problems and abuses, our civilization is a great civilization. It can provide us with much that is good, beautiful and uplifting, but not yet for the majority of humankind. Once I said that what made my life worth living in the terrible days of Nazism which I lived through were Mozart and quantum mechanics. What I really meant was art and science, the great everlasting creations of the human mind.

This brings me to the end of my statements. Let me say a few words about Olof Palme. His achievements are well known to the audience. Palme understood better and earlier than many people the dangers to humankind of the nuclear threat, the arms race and the neglect of the Third World. He was aware of the tragic mistakes of the superpowers in working against each other. He always emphasized that they can only survive together or perish together. When he died, the peace movements were at a low point. But he was always an optimist. He once said: 'Wisdom will grow with every generation, even if there are temporary setbacks.' The findings of the Palme Commission seemed at the time of publication to be too visionary and unrealistic. I wish he could see today that the world is moving, albeit slowly, in the direction which he pointed out. It is one of the great tragedies of humanity that a second's irresponsibility can destroy an edifice of goodwill, of good action and good influence built through a lifetime. His loss was a tragic event for the world.

Let me end with a quotation from John Donne's *Devotions upon Emergent Occasions:*

No man is an island entire of itself,
Every man is a piece of a continent,
A part of the main,
If a clod be washed away by the sea
Europe is the less,
As well if a promontory were,
As well if a manor of thy friends
Or of thy own were.
Any man's death diminishes me
Because I am involved in mankind. . .

Olof Palme's death diminished us more than we are aware today. Not a clod, not a promontory, but a basic rock of Europe has been washed away by the sea.

Annexes

Annexe A. Major multilateral arms control agreements

Annexe B. Chronology 1989

Annexe A. Major multilateral arms control agreements

RAGNHILD FERM

For the full texts of the arms control agreements, see Goldblat, J., SIPRI, *Agreements for Arms Control: A Critical Survey* (Taylor & Francis: London, 1982).

I. Summaries of the agreements

Protocol for the prohibition of the use in war of asphyxiating, poisonous or other gases, and of bacteriological methods of warfare (Geneva Protocol)

Signed at Geneva on 17 June 1925; entered into force on 8 February 1928.

Declares that the parties agree to be bound by the above prohibition, which should be universally accepted as part of international law, binding alike the conscience and the practice of nations.

Antarctic Treaty

Signed at Washington on 1 December 1959; entered into force on 23 June 1961.

Declares the Antarctic an area to be used exclusively for peaceful purposes. Prohibits any measure of a military nature in the Antarctic, such as the establishment of military bases and fortifications, and the carrying out of military manoeuvres or the testing of any type of weapon. Bans any nuclear explosion as well as the disposal of radioactive waste material in Antarctica, subject to possible future international agreements on these subjects. An international convention on the regulation of Antarctic mineral resource activities was signed in Wellington, New Zealand, in 1988. It has not yet entered into force.

At regular intervals consultative meetings are convened to exchange information and hold consultations on matters pertaining to Antarctica, as well as to recommend to the governments measures in furtherance of the principles and objectives of the Treaty.

Treaty banning nuclear weapon tests in the atmosphere, in outer space and under water (Partial Test Ban Treaty—PTBT)

Signed at Moscow on 5 August 1963; entered into force on 10 October 1963.

Prohibits the carrying out of any nuclear weapon test explosion or any other nuclear explosion: (*a*) in the atmosphere, beyond its limits, including other space, or under water, including territorial waters or high seas; (*b*) in any other environment if such explosion causes radioactive debris to be present outside the territorial limits of the state under whose jurisdiction or control the explosion is conducted.

Treaty on principles governing the activities of states in the exploration and use of outer space, including the moon and other celestial bodies (Outer Space Treaty)

Signed at London, Moscow and Washington on 27 January 1967; entered into force on 10 October 1967.

Prohibits the placing into orbit around the earth of any objects carrying nuclear weapons or any other kinds of weapons of mass destruction, the installation of such weapons on celestial bodies, or the stationing of them in outer space in any other manner. The establishment of military bases, installations and fortifications, the testing of any type of weapons and the conduct of military manoeuvres on celestial bodies are also forbidden.

Treaty for the prohibition of nuclear weapons in Latin America (Treaty of Tlatelolco)

Signed at Mexico City on 14 February 1967; entered into force on 22 April 1968.

Prohibits the testing, use, manufacture, production or acquisition by any means, as well as the receipt, storage, installation, deployment and any form of possession of any nuclear weapons by Latin American countries.

The parties should conclude agreements with the IAEA for the application of safeguards to their nuclear activities.

Under *Additional Protocol I* the extra-continental or continental states which, *de jure* or *de facto*, are internationally responsible for territories lying within the limits of the geographical zone established by the Treaty (France, the Netherlands, the UK and the USA) undertake to apply the statute of military denuclearization, as defined in the Treaty, to such territories.

Under *Additional Protocol II* the nuclear weapon states undertake to respect the statute of military denuclearization of Latin America, as defined and delimited in the Treaty, and not to contribute to acts involving a violation of the Treaty, nor to use or threaten to use nuclear weapons against the parties to the Treaty.

Treaty on the non-proliferation of nuclear weapons (NPT)

Signed at London, Moscow and Washington on 1 July 1968; entered into force on 5 March 1970.

Prohibits the transfer by nuclear weapon states, to any recipient whatsoever, of nuclear weapons or other nuclear explosive devices or of control over them, as well as the assistance, encouragement or inducement of any non-nuclear weapon state to manufacture or otherwise acquire such weapons or devices. Prohibits the receipt by non-nuclear weapon states from any transferor whatsoever, as well as the manufacture or other acquisition by those states of nuclear weapons or other nuclear explosive devices.

Non-nuclear weapon states undertake to conclude safeguard agreements with the International Atomic Energy Agency (IAEA) with a view to preventing diversion of nuclear energy from peaceful uses to nuclear weapons or other nuclear explosive devices.

The parties undertake to facilitate the exchange of equipment, materials and scientific and technological information for the peaceful uses of nuclear energy and to ensure that potential benefits from peaceful applications of nuclear explosions will be made available to non-nuclear weapon parties to the Treaty. They also undertake to pursue negotiations in good faith on effective measures relating to cessation of the nuclear arms race at an early date and to nuclear disarmament, and on a treaty on general and complete disarmament.

Twenty-five years after the entry into force of the Treaty (1995), a conference shall be convened to decide whether the Treaty shall continue in force indefinitely or shall be extended for an additional fixed period or periods.

Treaty on the prohibition of the emplacement of nuclear weapons and other weapons of mass destruction on the sea-bed and the ocean floor and in the subsoil thereof (Sea-Bed Treaty)

Signed at London, Moscow and Washington on 11 February 1971; entered into force on 18 May 1972.

Prohibits emplanting or emplacing on the sea-bed and the ocean floor and in the subsoil thereof beyond the outer limit of a 12-mile sea-bed zone any nuclear weapons or any other types of weapons of mass destruction as well as structures, launching installations or any other facilities specifically designed for storing, testing or using such weapons.

Convention on the prohibition of the development, production and stockpiling of bacteriological (biological) and toxin weapons and on their destruction (BW Convention)

Signed at London, Moscow and Washington on 10 April 1972; entered into force on 26 March 1975.

Prohibits the development, production, stockpiling or acquisition by other means or retention of microbial or other biological agents, or toxins whatever their origin or method of production, of types and in quantities that have no justification of pro-phylactic, protective or other peaceful purposes, as well as weapons, equipment or means of delivery designed to use such agents or toxins for hostile purposes or in armed conflict. The destruction of the agents, toxins, weapons, equipment and means of delivery in the possession of the parties, or their diversion to peaceful purposes, should be effected not later than nine months after the entry into force of the Convention.

Convention on the prohibition of military or any other hostile use of environmental modification techniques (Enmod Convention)

Signed at Geneva on 18 May 1977; entered into force on 5 October 1978.

Prohibits military or any other hostile use of environmental modification tech-niques having widespread, long-lasting or severe effects as the means of destruc-tion, damage or injury to states party to the Convention. The term 'environmental modification techniques' refers to any technique for changing—through the deliberate manipulation of natural processes—the dynamics, composition or structure of the Earth, including its biota, lithosphere, hydrosphere and atmosphere, or of outer space. The understandings reached during the negotiations, but not written into the Convention, define the terms 'widespread', 'long-lasting' and 'severe'.

Convention on the prohibitions or restrictions on the use of certain conventional weapons which may be deemed to be excessively injurious or to have indiscriminate effects ('Inhumane Weapons' Convention)

Signed at New York on 10 April 1981; entered into force on 2 December 1983.

The Convention is an 'umbrella treaty', under which specific agreements can be concluded in the form of protocols.

Protocol I prohibits the use of weapons intended to injure by fragments which are not detectable in the human body by X-rays.

Protocol II prohibits or restricts the use of mines, booby-traps and similar devices.

Protocol III prohibits or restricts the use of incendiary weapons.

South Pacific Nuclear Free Zone Treaty (Treaty of Rarotonga)

Signed at Rarotonga, Cook Islands, on 6 August 1985; entered into force on 11 December 1986.

Prohibits the manufacture or acquisition by other means of any nuclear explosive device, as well as possession or control over such device by the parties anywhere inside or outside the zone area described in an annex. The parties also undertake not to supply nuclear material or equipment unless subject to IAEA safeguards; and to prevent in their territories the stationing as well as the testing of any nuclear explosive device. Each party remains free to allow visits, as well as transit, by foreign ships and aircraft.

Under Protocol 1, France, the UK and the USA would undertake to apply the treaty prohibitions relating to the manufacture, stationing and testing of nuclear explosive devices in the territories situated within the zone, for which they are internationally responsible.

Under Protocol 2, China, France, the UK, the USA and the USSR would undertake not to use or threaten to use a nuclear explosive device against the parties to the treaty or against any territory within the zone for which a party to Protocol 1 is internationally responsible.

Under Protocol 3, China, France, the UK, the USA and the USSR would undertake not to test any nuclear explosive device anywhere within the zone.

II. Status of the implementation of the major multilateral arms control agreements, as of 1 January 1990

Number of parties

1925 Geneva Protocol	125
Antarctic Treaty	39
Partial Test Ban Treaty	119
Outer Space Treaty	93
Treaty of Tlatelolco	23
Additional Protocol I	3
Additional Protocol II	5
Non-Proliferation Treaty	141
NPT safeguards agreements (non-nuclear weapon states)	82
Sea-Bed Treaty	83
BW Convention	112

Enmod Convention	55
'Inhumane Weapons' Convention	32
Treaty of Rarotonga	11
Protocol 1	0
Protocol 2	2
Protocol 3	2

Notes

1. The table records year of ratification, accession or succession.

2. The Partial Test Ban Treaty, the Outer Space Treaty, the Non-Proliferation Treaty, the Sea-Bed Treaty and the Biological Weapons Convention provide for three depositaries—the governments of the UK, the USA and the USSR. The dates given for these agreements are the earliest date on which countries deposited their instruments of ratification, accession or succession—whether in London, Washington or Moscow. The dates given for the other agreements, for which there is only one depositary, are the dates of the deposit of the instruments of ratification, accession or succession with the depositary in question, except in the case of the 1925 Geneva Protocol, where the dates refer to the date of notification by the depositary.

3. The 1925 Geneva Protocol, the Partial Test Ban Treaty, the Outer Space Treaty, the Non-Proliferation Treaty, the Sea-Bed Treaty, the BW Convention, the Enmod Convention and the 'Inhumane Weapons' Convention are open for all states for signature.

The Antarctic Treaty is subject to ratification by the signatories and is open for accession by UN members or by other states invited to accede with the consent of all the contracting parties whose representatives are entitled to participate in the consultative meetings provided for in Article IX.

The Treaty of Tlatelolco is open for signature by all the Latin American republics; all other sovereign states situated in their entirety south of latitude 35° north in the western hemisphere; and (except for a political entity the territory of which is the subject of an international dispute) all such states which become sovereign, when they have been admitted by the General Conference; Additional Protocol I—by 'all extra-continental or continental states having *de jure* or *de facto* international responsibility for territories situated in the zone of application of the Treaty'; Additional Protocol II—by 'all powers possessing nuclear weapons', that is, the USA, the USSR, the UK, France and China.

The Treaty of Rarotonga is open for signature by members of the South Pacific Forum; Protocol 1—by France, the UK and the USA; Protocol 2—by France, China, the USSR, the UK and the USA; Protocol 3—by France, China, the USSR, the UK and the USA.

4. Key to abbreviations used in the table:
S: Signature without further action
PI, PII: Additional Protocols to the Treaty of Tlatelolco
P1, P2, P3: Protocols to the Treaty of Rarotonga
CP: Party entitled to participate in the consultative meetings provided for in Article IX of the Antarctic Treaty
SA: Nuclear safeguards agreement in force with the International Atomic Energy Agency as required by the Non-Proliferation Treaty or the Treaty of Tlatelolco, or concluded by a nuclear weapon state on a voluntary basis.

5. The footnotes are listed at the end of the table and are grouped separately under the heading for each agreement. The texts of the statements contained in the footnotes have been abridged, but the wording is close to the original version.

6. A complete list of UN member states and year of membership appears in section III.

State	Geneva Protocol	Antarctic Treaty	Partial Test Ban Treaty	Outer Space Treaty	Treaty of Tlatelolco	Non-Proliferation Treaty	Sea-Bed Treaty	BW Convention	Enmod Convention	'Inhumane Weapons' Convention	Treaty of Rarotonga
Afghanistan	1986		1964	1988		1970 SA	1971	1975	1985	S	
Albania	1989										
Algeria			S								
Antigua and Barbuda	1989[2]		1988[1]	1988[1]	1983[2]	1985[1]	1988[13]		1988[8]		
Argentina	1969	1961 CP	1986	1969	S[1]		1983[1]	1979	1987[1]	S	
Australia	1930[1]	1961 CP	1963	1967		1973 SA	1973	1977	1984	1983	1986
Austria	1928	1987	1964	1968		1969 SA	1972	1973[1]		1983	
Bahamas			1976[1]	1976[1]	1977[2]	1976[1]	1989	1986			
Bahrain	1988,[3]					1988[2]		1988[2]			
Bangladesh	1989[1]		1985	1986		1979 SA		1985	1979		

Country										
Barbados	1976²					1980		1973	1982	
Belgium	1928¹	1960 CP	1966	1973		1975 SA	1972	1979	S	S
Belize						1985¹		1986		
Benin	1986		1964	1986		1972	1986	1975	1986	1989¹
Bhutan	1979		1978			1985 SA		1978		
Bolivia	1985		1965	S	1969²	1970	S	1975	S	
Botswana			1968¹	S		1969	1972	S		
Brazil	1970	1975 CP	1964	1969²	1968³		1988²	1973	1984	
Brunei Darussalam						1985 SA				
Bulgaria	1934¹		1963	1967		1969 SA	1971	1972	1978	1982
Burkina Faso	1971		S	1968		1970				
Burma see: Myanmar										

State	Geneva Protocol	Antarctic Treaty	Partial Test Ban Treaty	Outer Space Treaty	Treaty of Tlatelolco	Non-Proliferation Treaty	Sea-Bed Treaty	BW Convention	Enmod Convention	'Inhumane Weapons' Convention	Treaty of Rarotonga
Burundi			S	S		1971	S	S			
Byelorussia	1970[4]		1963[2]	1967[3]			1971	1975	1978	1982	
Cameroon	1989		S	S		1969	S				
Canada	1930[1]	1988	1964	1967		1969 SA	1972[3]	1972	1981	S	
Cape Verde			1979			1979	1979	1977	1979		
Central African Republic	1970		1964	S		1970	1981	S			
Chad			1965			1971					
Chile	1935[1]	1961 CP	1965	1981	1974[4]			1980			
China	1952[5]	1983 CP		1983	PII: 1974[5]			1984[3]		1982[2]	P2: 1989[1] P3: 1989[1]
Colombia		1989	1985	S	1972[2] SA	1986	S	1983			
Congo						1978	1978	1978			

Country										
Cook Islands										1985
Costa Rica			1967		1969[2] SA[16]	1970 SA	S	1973		
Côte d'Ivoire	1970		1965			1973 SA	1972	S		
Cuba	1966	1984		1977[4]			1977[4]	1976	1978	1987
Cyprus	1966[2]		1965	1972		1970 SA	1971	1973	1978	1988[3]
Czechoslovakia	1938[6]	1962	1963	1967		1969 SA	1972	1973	1978	1982
Denmark	1930	1965	1964	1967		1969 SA	1971	1973	1978	1982
Dominica					S	1984[1]				
Dominican Republic	1970		1964	1968	1968[2] SA[16]	1971 SA	1972	1973		
Ecuador	1970	1987	1964	1969	1969[2] SA[16]	1969 SA		1975		1982
Egypt	1928		1964	1967		1981[3] SA	1982	S	1982	S

State	Geneva Protocol	Antarctic Treaty	Partial Test Ban Treaty	Outer Space Treaty	Treaty of Tlatelolco	Non-Proliferation Treaty	Sea-Bed Treaty	BW Convention	Enmod Convention	'Inhumane Weapons' Convention	Treaty of Rarotonga
El Salvador	S		1964	1969	1968[2] SA[16]	1972 SA		S			
Equatorial Guinea	1989		1989	1989		1984	S	1989			
Ethiopia	1935		S	S		1970 SA	1977	1975	S		
Fiji	1973[1,2]		1972[1]	1972[1]		1972[1] SA		1973			1985
Finland	1929	1984 CP	1964	1967		1969 SA	1971	1974	1978	1982	
France	1926[1]	1960 CP		1970	PI: S[6] PII: 1974[7]	[4]		1984		1988[4]	
Gabon			1964			1974		S			
Gambia	1966[2]		1965[1]	S		1975 SA	S	S			
German Democratic Republic	1959	1974[1] CP	1963	1967		1969 SA	1971	1972	1978	1982	

FR Germany	1929	1979² CP	1964⁴	1971⁵		1975⁵ SA	1975⁵	1983⁴	1983²	S
Ghana	1967		1963	S		1970 SA	1972	1975	1978	
Greece	1931	1987	1963	1971		1970 SA	1985	1975	1983	S
Grenada	1989²				1975²	1975¹		1986		
Guatemala	1983		1964³		1970² SA¹⁶	1970 SA	S	1973	1988³	1983
Guinea						1985	S			
Guinea-Bissau	1989		1976	1976		1976	1976	1976		
Guyana				S				S		
Haiti			S	S	1969²	1970		S		
Holy See (Vatican City)	1966			S		1971⁶ SA			S	
Honduras			1964	S	1968² SA¹⁶	1973 SA	S	1979		

State	Geneva Protocol	Antarctic Treaty	Partial Test Ban Treaty	Outer Space Treaty	Treaty of Tlatelolco	Non-Proliferation Treaty	Sea-Bed Treaty	BW Convention	Enmod Convention	'Inhumane Weapons' Convention	Treaty of Rarotonga
Hungary	1952	1984	1963	1967		1969 SA	1971	1972	1978	1982	
Iceland	1967		1964	1968		1969 SA	1972	1973	S	S	
India	1930[1]	1983 CP	1963	1982			1973[6]	1974[5]	1978	1984	
Indonesia	1971[2]		1964	S		1979[7] SA		S			
Iran	1929		1964	S		1970 SA	1971	1973	S		
Iraq	1931[1]		1964	1968		1969 SA	1972[4]	S	S		
Ireland	1930[7]		1963	1968		1968 SA	1971	1972[6]	1982	S	
Israel	1969[8]		1964	1977							
Italy	1928	1981 CP	1964	1972		1975[8] SA	1974[7]	1975	1981	S[5]	

Jamaica	1970[2]		S	1970	1969[2] SA[16]	1970 SA	1986	1975			
Japan	1970	1960 CP	1964	1967		1976[9] SA	1971	1982	1982	1982	
Jordan	1977[9]		1964	S		1970 SA	1971	1975			
Kampuchea (Cambodia)	1983[10]					1972	S	1983			
Kenya	1970		1965	1984		1970		1976			
Kiribati						1985[1]					1986
Korea, Dem. People's Rep. of (North)	1988[4,11]	1987				1985		1987	1984		
Korea, Republic of (South)	1988[1]	1986 CP	1964[3]	1967[4]		1975[10,11] SA	1987	1987[7]	1986[4]		
Kuwait	1971[12]		1965[5]	1972[6]		1989[12]		1972[8]	1980[5]		
Lao People's Dem. Republic	1989		1965	1972		1970	1971	1973	1978	1983	

State	Geneva Protocol	Antarctic Treaty	Partial Test Ban Treaty	Outer Space Treaty	Treaty of Tlatelolco	Non-Proliferation Treaty	Sea-Bed Treaty	BW Convention	Enmod Convention	'Inhumane Weapons' Convention	Treaty of Rarotonga
Lebanon	1969		1965	1969		1970 SA	S	1975	S		
Lesotho	1972[2]			S		1970 SA	1973	1977			
Liberia	1927		1964			1970	S	S	S		
Libya	1971[13]		1968	1968		1975 SA		1982			
Liechtenstein						1978[13] SA				1989	
Luxembourg	1936		1965	S		1975 SA	1982	1976	S	S	
Madagascar	1967		1965	1968[7]		1970 SA	S	S			
Malawi	1970		1964[1]			1986		S	1978		
Malaysia	1970		1964	S		1970 SA	1972	S			
Maldives	1966[2]					1970 SA					

Mali		S	1968		1970	S	S			
Malta	1964²	1964¹			1970	1971	1975			
Mauritania		1964								
Mauritius	1961²	1969¹	1969¹		1969 SA	1971	1972			
Mexico	1932	1963	1968	1967²,⁸ SA	1969¹⁴ SA	1984⁸	1974⁹		1982	
Monaco	1967									
Mongolia	1968¹⁴	1963	1967		1969 SA	1971	1972	1978	1982	
Morocco	1970	1966	1967		1970 SA	1971	S	S	S	
Myanmar (formerly Burma)		1963	1970			S	S			
Nauru					1982 SA					1987
Nepal	1969	1964	1967		1970 SA	1971	S			

State	Geneva Protocol	Antarctic Treaty	Partial Test Ban Treaty	Outer Space Treaty	Treaty of Tlatelolco	Non-Proliferation Treaty	Sea-Bed Treaty	BW Convention	Enmod Convention	'Inhumane Weapons' Convention	Treaty of Rarotonga
Netherlands	1930[15]	1967	1964	1969	PI: 1971[9] SA[17]	1975 SA	1976	1981	1983[6]	1987[6]	
New Zealand	1930[1]	1960 CP	1963	1968		1969 SA	1972	1972	1984[7]	S	1986
Nicaragua	S		1965	S	1968[2,10] SA[16]	1973 SA	1973	1975	S	S	
Niger	1967[2]		1964	1967			1971	1972			
Nigeria	1968[1]		1967	1967		1968 SA		1973		S	
Niue											1986
Norway	1932	1960 CP	1963	1969		1969 SA	1971	1973	1979	1983	
Pakistan	1960[2]		1988	1968				1974	1986	1985	
Panama	1970		1966	S	1971[2] SA	1977	1974	1974			
Papua New Guinea	1981[1,2]	1981	1980[1]	1980[1]		1982 SA		1980	1980		1989

Paraguay	1933[16]		S		1969[2] SA[16]	1970 SA	S	1976		S	
Peru	1985	1981 CP	1964	1979	1969[2] SA[16]	1970 SA		1985			
Philippines	1973	1965[3]	S	S		1972 SA	1971	1973	1978	S	
Poland	1929	1961 CP	1963	1968		1969 SA	1975	1973	S	1983	
Portugal	1930[1]		S			1977 SA	1975	1975	S	S	
Qatar	1976					1989	1974	1975			
Romania	1929[1]	1971[3]	1963	1968		1970 SA	1972	1979	1983	S[7]	
Rwanda	1964[2]		1963	S		1975	1975	1975			
Saint Christopher and Nevis	1989[2]										
Saint Lucia	1988					1979[1]		1986[10]			
Saint Vincent and the Grenadines						1984[1]					

State	Geneva Protocol	Antarctic Treaty	Partial Test Ban Treaty	Outer Space Treaty	Treaty of Tlatelolco	Non-Proliferation Treaty	Sea-Bed Treaty	BW Convention	Enmod Convention	'Inhumane Weapons' Convention	Treaty of Rarotonga
Samoa, Western			1965			1975 SA					1986
San Marino			1964	1968		1970[10]		1975			
Sao Tome and Principe						1983	1979	1979	1979		
Saudi Arabia	1971			1976		1988	1972	1972			
Senegal	1977		1964			1970 SA	S	1975			
Seychelles			1985	1978		1985	1985	1979			
Sierra Leone	1967		1964	1967		1975	S	1976	S	S	
Singapore			1968[1]	1976		1976 SA	1976	1975			
Solomon Islands	1981[2]					1981[1]	1981[13]	1981[10]	1981[8]		1989
Somalia			S	S		1970		S			
South Africa	1930[1]	1960 CP	1963	1968			1973	1975			

Spain	1929[17]	1982 CP	1964	1968		1987 SA	1987	1979	1978	S
Sri Lanka	1954		1964	1986		1979 SA		1986	1978	
Sudan	1980		1966			1973 SA	S			S
Suriname					1977[2] SA[16]	1976[1] SA				
Swaziland			1969			1969 SA	1971			
Sweden	1930	1984 CP	1963	1967		1970 SA	1972	1976	1984	1982
Switzerland	1932		1964	1969		1977[13] SA	1976	1976[11]	1988[9]	1982
Syria	1968[18]		1964	1968[8]		1969[10]		S	S	
Taiwan	1929[19]		1964	1970[9]		1970	1972[9]	1973[12]		
Tanzania	1963		1964				S	S		
Thailand	1931		1963	1968		1972 SA		1975		

State	Geneva Protocol	Antarctic Treaty	Partial Test Ban Treaty	Outer Space Treaty	Treaty of Tlatelolco	Non-Proliferation Treaty	Sea-Bed Treaty	BW Convention	Enmod Convention	'Inhumane Weapons' Convention	Treaty of Rarotonga
Togo	1971		1964			1970	1971	1976		S	
Tonga	1971[2]		1971[1]	1971[1]		1971[1]		1976			
Trinidad and Tobago	1962[2]		1964	S	1970[2]	1986					
Tunisia	1967		1965	1968		1970	1971	1973	1978	1987	
Turkey	1929		1965	1968		1980[15] SA	1972	1974	S[10]	S	
Tuvalu						1979[1]					1986
Uganda	1965		1964	1968		1982			S		
UK	1930[1]	1960 CP	1963[6]	1967	PI: 1969[11] PII: 1969[11]	1968[16] SA[17]	1972[10]	1975[13]	1978	S	
Ukraine			1963[2]	1967[3]			1971	1975	1978	1982	
United Arab Emirates								S			
Uruguay	1977	1980[4] CP	1969	1970	1968[2] SA[16]	1970 SA	S	1981			

USA	1975[20]	1960 CP	1963	1967	PI: 1981[12] PII: 1971[13] SA[17]	1970 SA[18]	1972	1975	1980	S[3]	
USSR	1928[21]	1960 CP	1963	1967	PII: 1979[14]	1970 SA[19]	1972	1975	1978	1982	P2: 1988[2] P3: 1988[2]
Venezuela	1928		1965	1970	1970[2,15] SA[16]	1975 SA		1978			
Viet Nam	1980[1]			1980		1982	1980[11]	1980	1980	S	
Yemen Arab Republic	1971		S			1986	S	S	1977		
Yemen, People's Dem. Rep. of	1986[22]		1979	1979		1979	1979	1979	1979		
Yugoslavia	1929[23]		1964	S		1970[20] SA	1973[12]	1973		1983	
Zaire			1965	S		1970 SA		1977	S		
Zambia			1965[1]	1973			1972				

The 1925 Geneva Protocol

[1] The Protocol is binding on this state only as regards states which have signed and ratified or acceded to it. The Protocol will cease to be binding on this state in regard to any enemy state whose armed forces or whose allies fail to respect the prohibitions laid down in it.
Australia withdrew its reservation in 1986, New Zealand in 1989.

[2] Notification of succession. (In notifying its succession to the obligations contracted in 1930 by the UK, Barbados stated that as far as it was concerned the reservation made by the UK was to be considered as withdrawn.)

[3] The accession of Bahrain to the Protocol shall in no way constitute recognition of Israel or be a cause for the establishment of any relations with it.

[4] In a note of 2 Mar. 1970, submitted at the UN, Byelorussia stated that 'it recognizes itself to be a party' to the Protocol.

[5] On 13 July 1952 the People's Republic of China issued a statement recognizing as binding upon it the 1929 accession to the Protocol in the name of China. China considers itself bound by the Protocol on condition of reciprocity on the part of all the other contracting and acceding powers.

[6] Czechoslovakia shall cease to be bound by this Protocol towards any state whose armed forces, or the armed forces of whose allies, fail to respect the prohibitions laid down in the Protocol.

[7] Ireland does not intend to assume, by this accession, any obligation except towards the states having signed and ratified this Protocol or which shall have finally acceded thereto, and should the armed forces or the allies of an enemy state fail to respect the Protocol, the government of Ireland would cease to be bound by the said Protocol in regard to such state. In Feb. 1972, Ireland declared that it had decided to withdraw the above reservations made at the time of accession to the Protocol.

[8] The Protocol is binding on Israel only as regards states which have signed and ratified or acceded to it. The Protocol shall cease to be binding on Israel as regards any enemy state whose armed forces, or the armed forces of whose allies, or the regular or irregular forces, or groups or individuals operating from its territory, fail to respect the prohibitions which are the object of the Protocol.

[9] The accession by Jordan to the Protocol does not in any way imply recognition of Israel. Jordan undertakes to respect the obligations contained in the Protocol with regard to states which have undertaken similar commitments. It is not bound by the Protocol as regards states whose armed forces, regular or irregular, do not respect the provisions of the Protocol.

[10] The accession was made on behalf of the coalition government of Democratic Kampuchea (the government in exile), with a statement that the Protocol will cease to be binding on it in regard to any enemy state whose armed forces or whose allies fail to respect the prohibitions laid down in the Protocol. France declared that as a party to the Geneva Protocol (but not as the depositary) it considers this accession to have no effect. A similar statement was made by Austria, Bulgaria, Cuba, Czechoslovakia, GDR, Hungary, Mauritius, Netherlands, Poland, Romania, USSR and Viet Nam, which do not recognize the coalition government of Kampuchea.

[11] The Dem. People's Rep. of Korea states that it will not exclude the right to exercise its sovereignty *vis-à-vis* the other contracting party which violates the Protocol in its implementation.

[12] The accession of Kuwait to the Protocol does not in any way imply recognition of Israel or the establishment of relations with the latter on the basis of the present Protocol. In case of breach of the prohibition laid down in this Protocol by any of the parties, Kuwait will not be bound, with regard to the party committing the breach, to apply the provisions of this Protocol.

[13] The accession to the Protocol does not imply recognition of Israel. The Protocol is binding on Libya only as regards states which are effectively bound by it and will cease to be binding on Libya as regards states whose armed forces, or the armed forces of whose allies, fail to respect the prohibitions which are the object of this Protocol.

[14] In the case of violation of this prohibition by any state in relation to Mongolia or its allies, Mongolia shall not consider itself bound by the obligations of the Protocol towards that state.

[15] As regards the use in war of asphyxiating, poisonous or other gases and of all analogous liquids, materials or devices, this Protocol shall cease to be binding on the Netherlands with regard to any enemy state whose armed forces or whose allies fail to respect the prohibitions laid down in the Protocol.

[16] This is the date of receipt of Paraguay's instrument of accession. The date of the notification by the depositary government 'for the purpose of regularization' is 1969.

[17] Spain declared the Protocol as binding *ipso facto*, without special agreement with respect to any other member or state accepting and observing the same obligation, that is, on condition of reciprocity.

[18] The accession by Syria to the Protocol does not in any case imply recognition of Israel or lead to the establishment of relations with the latter concerning the provisions laid down in the Protocol.

[19] The Protocol, signed in 1929 in the name of China, is taken to be valid for Taiwan (the Republic of China, which is part of the People's Republic of China.) However, unlike the People's Republic of China, Taiwan has not reconfirmed its accession to the Protocol.

[20] The Protocol shall cease to be binding on the USA with respect to use in war of asphyxiating, poisonous or other gases, and of all analogous liquids, materials, or devices, in regard to an enemy state if such state or any of its allies fail to respect the prohibitions laid down in the Protocol.

[21] The Protocol only binds the USSR in relation to the states which have signed and ratified or which have definitely acceded to the Protocol. The Protocol shall cease to be binding on the USSR in regard to any enemy state whose armed forces or whose allies *de jure* or in fact do not respect the prohibitions which are the object of this Protocol.

[22] In case any party fails to observe the prohibition under the Protocol, the People's Democratic Republic of Yemen will consider itself free of its obligation.

[23] The Protocol shall cease to be binding on Yugoslavia in regard to any enemy state whose armed forces or whose allies fail to respect the prohibitions which are the object of the Protocol.

The Antarctic Treaty

[1] The GDR stated that in its view Article XIII, paragraph 1 of the Treaty was inconsistent with the principle that all states whose policies are guided by the purposes and principles of the UN Charter have a right to become parties to treaties which affect the interests of all states.

[2] FR Germany stated that the Treaty applies also to Berlin (West).

[3] Romania stated that the provisions of Article XIII, paragraph 1 of the Treaty were not in accordance with the principle according to which multilateral treaties whose object and purposes concern the international community, as a whole, should be open for universal participation.

[4] In acceding to the Treaty, Uruguay proposed the establishment of a general and definitive statute on Antarctica in which the interests of all states involved and of the international community as a whole would be considered equitably. It also declared that it reserved its rights in Antarctica in accordance with international law.

The Partial Test Ban Treaty

[1] Notification of succession.

[2] The USA considers that Byelorussia and Ukraine are already covered by the signature and ratification by the USSR.

[3] With a statement that this does not imply the recognition of any territory or regime not recognized by this state.

[4] FR Germany stated that the Treaty applies also to Berlin (West).

[5] Kuwait stated that its signature and ratification of the Treaty do not in any way imply its recognition of Israel nor oblige it to apply the provisions of the Treaty in respect of the said country.

[6] The UK stated its view that if a regime is not recognized as the government of a state, neither signature nor the deposit of any instrument by it, nor notification of any of those acts, will bring about recognition of that regime by any other state.

The Outer Space Treaty

[1] Notification of succession.

[2] Brazil interprets Article X of the Treaty as a specific recognition that the granting of tracking facilities by the parties to the Treaty shall be subject to agreement between the states concerned.

[3] The USA considers that Byelorussia and Ukraine are already covered by the signature and ratification by the USSR.

[4] With a statement that this does not imply the recognition of any territory or regime not recognized by this state.

[5] FR Germany stated that the Treaty applies also to Berlin (West).

[6] Kuwait acceded to the Treaty with the understanding that this does not in any way imply its recognition of Israel and does not oblige it to apply the provisions of the Treaty in respect of the said country.

[7] Madagascar acceded to the Treaty with the understanding that under Article X of the Treaty the state shall retain its freedom of decision with respect to the possible installation of foreign observation bases in its territory and shall continue to possess the right to fix, in each case, the conditions for such installation.

[8] Syria acceded to the Treaty with the understanding that this should not mean in any way the recognition of Israel, nor should it lead to any relationship with Israel that could arise from the Treaty.

[9] China declared as illegal and null and void the signature and ratification of the Outer Space Treaty by the Taiwan authorities.

The Treaty of Tlatelolco

[1] On signing the Treaty, Argentina stated that it understands Article 18 as recognizing the rights of parties to carry out, by their own means or in association with third parties, explosions of nuclear

devices for peaceful purposes, including explosions which involve devices similar to those used in nuclear weapons.

[2] The Treaty is in force for this country due to a declaration, annexed to the instrument of ratification in accordance with Article 28, paragraph 2, which waived the requirements for the entry into force of the Treaty, specified in paragraph 1 of that Article: namely, that all states in the region deposit the instruments of ratification; that Protocol I and Protocol II be signed and ratified by those states to which they apply; and that agreements on safeguards be concluded with the IAEA. (Colombia made this declaration subsequent to the deposit of ratification, as did Nicaragua and Trinidad and Tobago.)

[3] On signing the Treaty, Brazil stated that, according to its interpretation, Article 18 of the Treaty gives the signatories the right to carry out, by their own means or in association with third parties, nuclear explosions for peaceful purposes, including explosions which involve devices similar to those used in nuclear weapons. This statement was reiterated at the ratification. Brazil also stated that it did not waive the requirements for the entry into force of the Treaty laid down in Article 28. *The Treaty is therefore not yet in force for Brazil.*

[4] Chile has not waived the requirements for the entry into force of the Treaty laid down in Article 28. *The Treaty is therefore not yet in force for Chile.*

[5] On signing Protocol II, China stated, *inter alia*: China will never use or threaten to use nuclear weapons against non-nuclear Latin American countries and the Latin American nuclear weapon-free zone; nor will China test, manufacture, produce, stockpile, install or deploy nuclear weapons in these countries or in this zone, or send its means of transportation and delivery carrying nuclear weapons to cross the territory, territorial sea or airspace of Latin American countries. The signing of the Protocol does not imply any change whatsoever in China's stand on the disarmament and nuclear weapons issue and, in particular, does not affect its stand against the Non-Proliferation Treaty and the Partial Test Ban Treaty.

China holds that, in order that Latin America may truly become a nuclear weapon-free zone, all nuclear countries, and particularly the superpowers, must undertake not to use or threaten to use nuclear weapons against the Latin American countries and the Latin American nuclear weapon-free zone, and implement the following undertakings: (1) dismantle all foreign military bases in Latin America and refrain from establishing new bases there, and (2) prohibit the passage of any means of transportation and delivery carrying nuclear weapons through Latin American territory, territorial sea or airspace.

[6] On signing Protocol I, France made the following reservations and interpretative statements: The Protocol, as well as the provisions of the Treaty to which it refers, will not affect the right of self-defence under Article 51 of the UN Charter; the application of the legislation referred to in Article 3 of the Treaty relates to legislation which is consistent with international law; the obligations under the Protocol shall not apply to transit across the territories of the French Republic situated in the zone of the Treaty, and destined to other territories of the French Republic; the Protocol shall not limit, in any way, the participation of the populations of the French territories in the activities mentioned in Article 1 of the Treaty, and in efforts connected with the national defence of France; the provisions of Articles 1 and 2 of the Protocol apply to the text of the Treaty as it stands at the time when the Protocol is signed by France, and consequently no amendment to the Treaty that might come into force under Article 29 thereof would be binding on the government of France without the latter's express consent.

[7] On signing Protocol II, France stated that it interprets the undertaking contained in Article 3 of the Protocol to mean that it presents no obstacle to the full exercise of the right of self-defence enshrined in Article 51 of the UN Charter; it takes note of the interpretation of the Treaty given by the Preparatory Commission for the Denuclearization of Latin America and reproduced in the Final Act, according to which the Treaty does not apply to transit, the granting or denying of which lies within the exclusive competence of each state party in accordance with the pertinent principles and rules of international law; it considers that the application of the legislation referred to in Article 3 of the Treaty relates to legislation which is consistent with international law. The provisions of Articles 1 and 2 of the Protocol apply to the text of the Treaty as it stands at the time when the Protocol is signed by France. Consequently, no amendment to the Treaty that might come into force under the provision of Article 29 would be binding on the government of France without the latter's express consent. If this declaration of interpretation is contested in part or in whole by one or more contracting parties to the Treaty or to Protocol II, these instruments would be null and void as far as relations between France and the contesting state or states are concerned. On depositing its instrument of ratification of Protocol II, France stated that it did so subject to the statement made on signing the Protocol. On 15 Apr. 1974, France made a supplementary statement to the effect that it was prepared to consider its obligations under Protocol II as applying not only to the signatories of the Treaty, but also to the territories for which the statute of denuclearization was in force in conformity with Article 1 of Protocol I.

[8] On signing the Treaty, Mexico said that if technological progress makes it possible to differentiate between nuclear weapons and nuclear devices for peaceful purposes, it will be necessary to amend the relevant provisions of the Treaty, according to the procedures established therein.

[9] The Netherlands stated that Protocol I shall not be interpreted as prejudicing the position of the Netherlands as regards its recognition or non-recognition of the rights or of claims to sovereignty of the parties to the Treaty, or of the grounds on which such claims are made.

[10] Nicaragua stated that it reserved the right to use nuclear energy for peaceful purposes such as the removal of earth for the construction of canals, irrigation works, power plants, and so on, as well as to allow the transit of atomic material through its territory.

[11] When signing and ratifying Protocol I and Protocol II, the UK made the following declarations of understanding: In connection with Article 3 of the Treaty, defining the term 'territory' as including the territorial sea, airspace and any other space over which the state exercises sovereignty in accordance with 'its own legislation', the UK does not regard its signing or ratification of the Protocols as implying recognition of any legislation which does not, in its view, comply with the relevant rules of international law.

The Treaty does not permit the parties to carry out explosions of nuclear devices for peaceful purposes unless and until advances in technology have made possible the development of devices for such explosions which are not capable of being used for weapon purposes.

The signing and ratification by the UK could not be regarded as affecting in any way the legal status of any territory for the international relations of which the UK is responsible, lying within the limits of the geographical zone established by the Treaty.

Should any party to the Treaty carry out any act of aggression with the support of a nuclear weapon state, the UK would be free to reconsider the extent to which it could be regarded as committed by the provisions of Protocol II.

In addition, the UK declared that its undertaking under Article 3 of Protocol II not to use or threaten to use nuclear weapons against the parties to the Treaty extends also to territories in respect of which the undertaking under Article I of Protocol I becomes effective.

[12] The USA ratified Protocol I with the following understandings: The provisions of the Treaty made applicable by this Protocol do not affect the exclusive power and legal competence under international law of a state adhering to this Protocol to grant or deny transit and transport privileges to its own or any other vessels or aircraft irrespective of cargo or armaments; the provisions of the Treaty made applicable by this Protocol do not affect rights under international law of a state adhering to this Protocol regarding the exercise of the freedom of the seas, or regarding passage through or over waters subject to the sovereignty of a state, and the declarations attached by the United States to its ratification of Protocol II apply also to its ratification of Protocol I.

[13] The USA signed and ratified Protocol II with the following declarations and understandings: In connection with Article 3 of the Treaty, defining the term 'territory' as including the territorial sea, airspace and any other space over which the state exercises sovereignty in accordance with 'its own legislation', the ratification of the Protocol could not be regarded as implying recognition of any legislation which does not, in the view of the USA, comply with the relevant rules of international law.

Each of the parties retains exclusive power and legal competence, unaffected by the terms of the Treaty, to grant or deny non-parties transit and transport privileges.

As regards the undertaking not to use or threaten to use nuclear weapons against the parties, the USA would consider that an armed attack by a party, in which it was assisted by a nuclear weapon state, would be incompatible with the party's obligations under Article 1 of the Treaty.

The definition contained in Article 5 of the Treaty is understood as encompassing all nuclear explosive devices; Articles 1 and 5 of the Treaty restrict accordingly the activities of the parties under paragraph 1 of Article 18.

Article 18, paragraph 4 permits, and US adherence to Protocol II will not prevent, collaboration by the USA with the parties to the Treaty for the purpose of carrying out explosions of nuclear devices for peaceful purposes in a manner consistent with a policy of not contributing to the proliferation of nuclear weapon capabilities.

The USA will act with respect to such territories of Protocol I adherents, as are within the geographical area defined in Article 4, paragraph 2 of the Treaty, in the same manner as Protocol II requires it to act with respect to the territories of the Parties.

[14] The USSR signed and ratified Protocol II with the following statement:

The USSR proceeds from the assumption that the effect of Article 1 of the Treaty extends, as specified in Article 5 of the Treaty, to any nuclear explosive device and that, accordingly, the carrying out by any party to the Treaty of explosions of nuclear devices for peaceful purposes would be a violation of its obligations under Article 1 and would be incompatible with its non-nuclear status. For states parties to the Treaty, a solution to the problem of peaceful nuclear explosions can be found in accordance with the provisions of Article V of the Non-Proliferation Treaty and within the framework of the international procedures of the IAEA. The signing of the Protocol by the USSR does not in any way signify recognition of the possibility of the force of the Treaty being extended beyond the territories of the states parties to the Treaty, including airspace and territorial waters as defined in accordance with international law. With regard to the reference in Article 3 of the Treaty to 'its own legislation' in connection with the territorial waters, airspace and any other space over which the states parties to the Treaty exercise sovereignty, the signing of the Protocol by the USSR does not signify recognition of their claims to the exercise of sovereignty which are contrary to generally accepted standards of international law. The USSR takes note of the interpretation of the Treaty given in the Final Act of the Preparatory Commission for the Denuclearization of Latin America to the effect that the transport of nuclear weapons by the parties to the Treaty is covered by the prohibitions in Article 1 of the Treaty. The USSR reaffirms its position that authorizing the transit of nuclear weapons in any form would be contrary to the objectives of the Treaty, according to which, as specially mentioned in the preamble, Latin America must be completely free from nuclear weapons, and that it would be incompatible with the non-nuclear status of the states parties to the Treaty and with their obligations as laid down in Article 1 thereof.

Any actions undertaken by a state or states parties to the Treaty which are not compatible with their non-nuclear status, and also the commission by one or more states parties to the Treaty of an act of aggression with the support of a state which is in possession of nuclear weapons or together with such a state, will be regarded by the USSR as incompatible with the obligations of those countries under the Treaty. In such cases the USSR reserves the right to reconsider its obligations under Protocol II. It further reserves the right to reconsider its attitude to this Protocol in the event of any actions on the part of other states possessing nuclear weapons which are incompatible with their obligations under the said Protocol. The provisions of the articles of Protocol II are applicable to the text of the Treaty of Tlatelolco in the wording of the Treaty at the time of the signing of the Protocol by the Soviet Union, due account being taken of the position of the USSR as set out in the present statement. Any amendment to the Treaty entering into force in accordance with the provisions of Articles 29 and 6 of the Treaty without the clearly expressed approval of the USSR shall have no force as far as the USSR is concerned.

In addition, the USSR proceeds from the assumption that the obligations under Protocol II also apply to the territories for which the status of the denuclearized zone is in force in conformity with Protocol I of the Treaty.

[15] Venezuela stated that in view of the existing controversy between Venezuela on the one hand and the UK and Guyana on the other, Article 25, paragraph 2 of the Treaty should apply to Guyana. This paragraph provides that no political entity should be admitted, part or all of whose territory is the subject of a dispute or claim between an extra-continental country and one or more Latin American states, so long as the dispute has not been settled by peaceful means.

[16] Safeguards agreements under the Non-Proliferation Treaty cover the Treaty of Tlatelolco.

[17] Safeguards agreements under Protocol I.

The Non-Proliferation Treaty

[1] Notification of succession.

[2] Bahrain declared that its accession to the Treaty shall in no way constitute recognition of Israel or be a cause of establishment of any relations of any kind therewith.

[3] On the occasion of the deposit of the instrument of ratification, Egypt stated that since it was embarking on the construction of nuclear power reactors, it expected assistance and support from industrialized nations with a developed nuclear industry. It called upon nuclear weapon states to promote research and development of peaceful applications of nuclear explosions in order to overcome all the difficulties at present involved therein. Egypt also appealed to these states to exert their efforts to conclude an agreement prohibiting the use or threat of use of nuclear weapons against any state, and expressed the view that the Middle East should remain completely free of nuclear weapons.

[4] France, not party to the Treaty, declared that it would behave like a state adhering to the Treaty and that it would follow a policy of strengthening appropriate safeguards relating to nuclear equipment, material and technology. On 12 Sep. 1981 an agreement between France, the European Atomic Energy Community (Euratom) and the IAEA for the application of safeguards in France entered into force. The agreement covers nuclear material and facilities notified to the IAEA by France.

[5] On depositing the instrument of ratification, FR Germany reiterated the declaration made at the time of signing: it reaffirmed its expectation that the nuclear weapon states would intensify their efforts in accordance with the undertakings under Article VI of the Treaty, as well as its understanding that the security of FR Germany continued to be ensured by NATO; it stated that no provision of the Treaty may be interpreted in such a way as to hamper further development of European unification; that research, development and use of nuclear energy for peaceful purposes, as well as international and multinational co-operation in this field, must not be prejudiced by the Treaty; that the application of the Treaty, including the implementation of safeguards, must not lead to discrimination of the nuclear industry of FR Germany in international competition; and that it attached vital importance to the undertaking given by the USA and the UK concerning the application

of safeguards to their peaceful nuclear facilities, hoping that other nuclear weapon states would assume similar obligations.

In a separate note, FR Germany declared that the Treaty will also apply to Berlin (West) without affecting Allied rights and responsibilities, including those relating to demilitarization. In notes of 24 July, 19 Aug. and 25 Nov. 1975, respectively, addressed to the US Department of State, Czechoslovakia, the USSR and the GDR stated that this declaration by FR Germany had no legal effect.

[6] On acceding to the Treaty, the Holy See stated, *inter alia*, that the Treaty will attain in full the objectives of security and peace and justify the limitations to which the states party to the Treaty submit, only if it is fully executed in every clause and with all its implications. This concerns not only the obligations to be applied immediately but also those which envisage a process of ulterior commitments. Among the latter, the Holy See considers it suitable to point out the following: (*a*) The adoption of appropriate measures to ensure, on a basis of equality, that all non-nuclear weapon states party to the Treaty will have available to them the benefits deriving from peaceful applications of nuclear technology. (*b*) The pursuit of negotiations in good faith of effective measures relating to cessation of the nuclear arms race at an early date and to nuclear disarmament, and on a treaty on general and complete disarmament under strict and effective control.

[7] On signing the Treaty, Indonesia stated, *inter alia*, that it attaches great importance to the declarations of the USA, the UK and the USSR affirming their intention to provide immediate assistance to any non-nuclear weapon state party to the Treaty that is a victim of an act of aggression in which nuclear weapons are used. Of utmost importance, however, is not the action *after* a nuclear attack has been committed but the guarantees to prevent such an attack. Indonesia trusts that the nuclear weapon states will study further this question of effective measures to ensure the security of the non-nuclear weapon states. On depositing the instrument of ratification, Indonesia expressed the hope that the nuclear countries would be prepared to co-operate with non-nuclear countries in the use of nuclear energy for peaceful purposes and implement the provisions of Article IV of the Treaty without discrimination. It also stated the view that the nuclear weapon states would observe the provisions of Article VI of the Treaty relating to the cessation of the nuclear arms race.

[8] Italy stated that in its belief nothing in the Treaty was an obstacle to the unification of the countries of Western Europe; it noted full compatibility of the Treaty with the existing security agreements; it noted further that when technological progress would allow the development of peaceful explosive devices different from nuclear weapons, the prohibition relating to their manufacture and use shall no longer apply; it interpreted the provisions of Article IX, paragraph 3 of the Treaty, concerning the definition of a nuclear weapon state, in the sense that it referred exclusively to the five countries which had manufactured and exploded a nuclear weapon or other nuclear explosive device prior to 1 Jan. 1967, and stressed that under no circumstance would a claim of pertaining to such category be recognized by Italy for any other state.

[9] On depositing the instrument of ratification, Japan expressed the hope that France and China would accede to the Treaty; it urged a reduction of nuclear armaments and a comprehensive ban on nuclear testing; appealed to all states to refrain from the threat or use of force involving either nuclear or non-nuclear weapons; expressed the view that peaceful nuclear activities in non-nuclear weapon states party to the Treaty should not be hampered and that Japan should not be discriminated against in favour of other parties in any aspect of such activities. It also urged all nuclear weapon states to accept IAEA safeguards on their peaceful nuclear activities.

[10] A statement was made containing a disclaimer regarding the recognition of states party to the Treaty.

[11] On depositing the instrument of ratification, the Republic of Korea took note of the fact that the depositary governments of the three nuclear weapon states had made declarations in June 1968 to take immediate and effective measures to safeguard any non-nuclear weapon state which is a victim of an act or an object of a threat of aggression in which nuclear weapons are used. It recalled that the UN Security Council adopted a resolution to the same effect on 19 June 1968.

[12] On depositing the instruments of ratification, Kuwait declared that the ratification of the Treaty does not mean in any way a recognition of Israel. No treaty relation will arise between Kuwait and Israel.

[13] On depositing the instruments of accession and ratification, Liechtenstein and Switzerland stated that activities not prohibited under Articles I and II of the Treaty include, in particular, the whole field of energy production and related operations, research and technology concerning future generations of nuclear reactors based on fission or fusion, as well as production of isotopes. Liechtenstein and Switzerland define the term 'source or special fissionable material' in Article III of the Treaty as being in accordance with Article XX of the IAEA Statute, and a modification of this interpretation requires their formal consent; they will accept only such interpretations and definitions of the terms 'equipment or material especially designed or prepared for the processing, use or production of special fissionable material', as mentioned in Article III of the Treaty, that they will expressly approve; and they understand that the application of the Treaty, especially of the control measures, will not lead to discrimination of their industry in international competition.

[14] On signing the Treaty, Mexico stated, *inter alia*, that none of the provisions of the Treaty shall be interpreted as affecting in any way whatsoever the rights and obligations of Mexico as a state party to the Treaty of Tlatelolco.

It is the understanding of Mexico that at the present time any nuclear explosive device is capable of being used as a nuclear weapon and that there is no indication that in the near future it will be possible to manufacture nuclear explosive devices that are not potentially nuclear weapons. However, if technological advances modify this situation, it will be necessary to amend the relevant provisions of the Treaty in accordance with the procedure established therein.

[15] The ratification was accompanied by a statement in which Turkey underlined the non-proliferation obligations of the nuclear weapon states, adding that measures must be taken to meet adequately the security requirements of non-nuclear weapon states. Turkey also stated that measures developed or to be developed at national and international levels to ensure the non-proliferation of nuclear weapons should in no case restrict the non-nuclear weapon states in their option for the application of nuclear energy for peaceful purposes.

[16] The UK recalled its view that if a regime is not recognized as the government of a state, neither signature nor the deposit of any instrument by it, nor notification of any of those acts, will bring about recognition of that regime by any other state.

[17] This agreement, signed by the UK, Euratom and the IAEA, provides for the submission of British non-military nuclear installations to safeguards under IAEA supervision.

[18] This agreement provides for safeguards on fissionable material in all facilities within the USA, excluding those associated with activities of direct national security significance.

[19] The agreement provides for the application of IAEA safeguards in Soviet peaceful nuclear facilities designated by the USSR.

[20] In connection with the ratification of the Treaty, Yugoslavia stated, *inter alia*, that it considered a ban on the development, manufacture and use of nuclear weapons and the destruction of all stockpiles of these weapons to be indispensable for the maintenance of a stable peace and international security; it held the view that the chief responsibility for progress in this direction rested with the nuclear weapon powers, and expected these powers to undertake not to use nuclear weapons against the countries which have renounced them as well as against non-nuclear weapon states in general, and to refrain from the threat to use them. It also emphasized the significance it attached to the universality of the efforts relating to the realization of the Non-Proliferation Treaty.

The Sea-Bed Treaty

[1] On signing and ratifying the Treaty, Argentina stated that it interprets the references to the freedom of the high seas as in no way implying a pronouncement of judgement on the different positions relating to questions connected with international maritime law. It understands that the reference to the rights of exploration and exploitation by coastal states over their continental shelves was included solely because those could be the rights most frequently affected by verification procedures. Argentina precludes any possibility of strengthening, through this Treaty, certain positions concerning continental shelves to the detriment of others based on different criteria.

[2] On signing the Treaty, Brazil stated that nothing in the Treaty shall be interpreted as prejudicing in any way the sovereign rights of Brazil in the area of the sea, the sea-bed and the subsoil thereof adjacent to its coasts. It is the understanding of Brazil that the word 'observation', as it appears in paragraph 1 of Article III of the Treaty, refers only to observation that is incidental to the normal course of navigation in accordance with international law. This statement was repeated at the time of ratification. The USA declared, in 1989, that under customary international law and Article III of the Treaty, these observations may be undertaken whether or not they are incidental to a so-called 'normal course of navigation,' and that such activity is not subject to unilateral coastal state restriction. The USSR and the FRG also stated that they did not agree with Brazil's interpretation of the term 'observation'.

[3] In depositing the instrument of ratification, Canada declared: Article I, paragraph 1, cannot be interpreted as indicating that any state has a right to implant or emplace any weapons not prohibited under Article I, paragraph 1, on the sea-bed and ocean floor, and in the subsoil thereof, beyond the limits of national jurisdiction, or as constituting any limitation on the principle that this area of the sea-bed and ocean floor and the subsoil thereof shall be reserved for exclusively peaceful purposes. Articles I, II and III cannot be interpreted as indicating that any state but the coastal state has any right to implant or emplace any weapon not prohibited under Article I, paragraph 1 on the continental shelf, or the subsoil thereof, appertaining to that coastal state, beyond the outer limit of the sea-bed zone referred to in Article I and defined in Article II. Article III cannot be interpreted as indicating any restrictions or limitation upon the rights of the coastal state, consistent with its exclusive sovereign rights with respect to the continental shelf, to verify, inspect or effect the removal of any weapon, structure, installation, facility or device implanted or emplaced on the continental shelf, or the subsoil thereof, appertaining to that coastal state, beyond the outer limit of the sea-bed zone referred to in Article I and defined in Article II. On 12 Apr. 1976, FR Germany stated that the declaration by Canada is not of a nature to confer on the government of this country more far-reaching rights than

those to which it is entitled under current international law, and that all rights existing under current international law which are not covered by the prohibitions are left intact by the Treaty.

[4] A statement was made containing a disclaimer regarding recognition of states party to the Treaty.

[5] On ratifying the Treaty, FR Germany declared that the Treaty will apply to Berlin (West).

[6] On the occasion of its accession to the Treaty, the government of India stated that as a coastal state, India has, and always has had, full and exclusive rights over the continental shelf adjoining its territory and beyond its territorial waters and the subsoil thereof. It is the considered view of India that other countries cannot use its continental shelf for military purposes. There cannot, therefore, be any restriction on, or limitation of, the sovereign right of India as a coastal state to verify, inspect, remove or destroy any weapon, device, structure, installation or facility, which might be implanted or emplaced on or beneath its continental shelf by any other country, or to take such other steps as may be considered necessary to safeguard its security. The accession by the government of India to the Treaty is based on this position. In response to the Indian statement, the USA expressed the view that, under existing international law, the rights of coastal states over their continental shelves are exclusive only for the purposes of exploration and exploitation of natural resources, and are otherwise limited by the 1958 Convention on the Continental Shelf and other principles of international law. On 12 Apr. 1976, FR Germany stated that the declaration by India is not of a nature to confer on the government of this country more far-reaching rights than those to which it is entitled under current international law, and that all rights existing under current law which are not covered by the prohibitions are left intact by the Treaty.

[7] On signing the Treaty, Italy stated, *inter alia*, that in the case of agreements on further measures in the field of disarmament to prevent an arms race on the sea-bed and ocean floor and in their subsoil, the question of the delimitation of the area within which these measures would find application shall have to be examined and solved in each instance in accordance with the nature of the measures to be adopted. The statement was repeated at the time of ratification.

[8] Mexico declared that in its view no provision of the Treaty can be interpreted to mean that a state has the right to emplace nuclear weapons or other weapons of mass destruction, or arms or military equipment of any type, on the continental shelf of Mexico. It reserves the right to verify, inspect, remove or destroy any weapon, structure, installation, device or equipment placed on its continental shelf, including nuclear weapons or other weapons of mass destruction.

[9] Ratification of the Treaty by Taiwan is considered by Romania as null and void.

[10] The UK recalled its view that if a regime is not recognized as the government of a state neither signature nor the deposit of any instrument by it, nor notification of any of those acts, will bring about recognition of that regime by any other state.

[11] Viet Nam stated that no provision of the Treaty should be interpreted in a way that would contradict the rights of the coastal states with regard to their continental shelf, including the right to take measures to ensure their security.

[12] On 25 Feb. 1974, the Ambassador of Yugoslavia transmitted to the US Secretary of State a note stating that in the view of the Yugoslav Government, Article III, paragraph 1, of the Treaty should be interpreted in such a way that a state exercising its right under this Article shall be obliged to notify in advance the coastal state, in so far as its observations are to be carried out 'within the stretch of the sea extending above the continental shelf of the said state'. On 16 Jan. 1975 the US Secretary of State presented the view of the USA concerning the Yugoslav note, as follows: In so far as the note is intended to be interpretative of the Treaty, the USA cannot accept it as a valid interpretation. In addition, the USA does not consider that it can have any effect on the existing law of the sea. In so far as the note was intended to be a reservation to the Treaty, the USA placed on record its formal objection to it on the grounds that it was incompatible with the object and purpose of the Treaty. The USA also drew attention to the fact that the note was submitted too late to be legally effective as a reservation. A similar exchange of notes took place between Yugoslavia and the UK on 12 Apr. 1976. FR Germany stated that the declaration by Yugoslavia is not of a nature to confer on the government of this country more far-reaching rights than those to which it is entitled under current international law, and that all rights existing under current international law which are not covered by the prohibitions are left intact by the Treaty.

[13] Notification of succession.

The BW Convention

[1] Considering the obligations resulting from its status as a permanently neutral state, Austria declares a reservation to the effect that its co-operation within the framework of this Convention cannot exceed the limits determined by the status of permanent neutrality and membership of the UN.

[2] Bahrain declared that its accession to the Convention shall in no way constitute recognition of Israel or be a cause of establishment of any relations of any kind with it.

[3] China stated that the BW Convention has the following defects: it fails explicitly to prohibit the use of biological weapons; it does not provide for 'concrete and effective' measures of supervision and verification; and it lacks measures of sanctions in case of violation of the Convention. China hopes that these defects will be corrected at an appropriate time, and also that a convention for

complete prohibition of chemical weapons will soon be concluded. The signature and ratification of the Convention by the Taiwan authorities in the name of China are considered illegal and null and void.

[4] On depositing its instrument of ratification, FR Germany stated that a major shortcoming of the BW Convention is that it does not contain any provisions for verifying compliance with its essential obligations. The Federal Government considers the right to lodge a complaint with the UN Security Council to be an inadequate arrangement. It would welcome the establishment of an independent international committee of experts able to carry out impartial investigations when doubts arise as to whether the Convention is being complied with.

[5] In a statement made on the occasion of the signature of the Convention, India reiterated its understanding that the objective of the Convention is to eliminate biological and toxin weapons, thereby excluding completely the possibility of their use, and that the exemption with regard to biological agents or toxins, which would be permitted for prophylactic, protective or other peaceful purposes, would not in any way create a loophole in regard to the production or retention of biological and toxin weapons. Also any assistance which might be furnished under the terms of the Convention would be of a medical or humanitarian nature and in conformity with the UN Charter. The statement was repeated at the time of the deposit of the instrument of ratification.

[6] Ireland considers that the Convention could be undermined if the reservations made by the parties to the 1925 Geneva Protocol were allowed to stand, as the prohibition of possession is incompatible with the right to retaliate, and that there should be an absolute and universal prohibition of the use of the weapons in question. Ireland notified the depositary government for the Geneva Protocol of the withdrawal of its reservations to the Protocol, made at the time of accession in 1930. The withdrawal applies to chemical as well as to bacteriological (biological) and toxin agents of warfare.

[7] The Republic of Korea stated that the signing and ratification of the Convention does not in any way mean or imply the recognition of any territory or regime which has not been recognized by the Republic of Korea as a state or government.

[8] In the understanding of Kuwait, its ratification of the Convention does not in any way imply its recognition of Israel, nor does it oblige it to apply the provisions of the Convention in respect of the said country.

[9] Mexico considers that the Convention is only a first step towards an agreement prohibiting also the development, production and stockpiling of all chemical weapons, and notes the fact that the Convention contains an express commitment to continue negotiations in good faith with the aim of arriving at such an agreement.

[10] Notification of succession.

[11] The ratification by Switzerland contains the following reservations:

1. Owing to the fact that the Convention also applies to weapons, equipment or means of delivery designed to use biological agents or toxins, the delimitation of its scope of application can cause difficulties since there are scarcely any weapons, equipment or means of delivery peculiar to such use; therefore, Switzerland reserves the right to decide for itself what auxiliary means fall within that definition.

2. By reason of the obligations resulting from its status as a perpetually neutral state, Switzerland is bound to make the general reservation that its collaboration within the framework of this Convention cannot go beyond the terms prescribed by that status. This reservation refers especially to Article VII of the Convention as well as to any similar clause that could replace or supplement that provision of the Convention.

In a note of 18 Aug. 1976, addressed to the Swiss Ambassador, the US Secretary of State stated the following view of the USA with regard to the first reservation: The prohibition would apply only to (a) weapons, equipment and means of delivery, the design of which indicated that they could have no other use than that specified, and (b) weapons, equipment and means of delivery, the design of which indicated that they were specifically intended to be capable of the use specified. The USA shares the view of Switzerland that there are few weapons, equipment or means of delivery peculiar to the uses referred to. It does not, however, believe that it would be appropriate, on this ground alone, for states to reserve unilaterally the right to decide which weapons, equipment or means of delivery fell within the definition. Therefore, while acknowledging the entry into force of the Convention between itself and Switzerland, the USA enters its objection to this reservation.

[12] The deposit of the instrument of ratification by Taiwan is considered by the Soviet Union as an illegal act because the government of the People's Republic of China is regarded by the USSR as the sole representative of China.

[13] The UK recalled its view that if a regime is not recognized as the government of a state, neither signature nor the deposit of any instrument by it nor notification of any of those acts will bring about recognition of that regime by any other state.

The Enmod Convention

[1] Argentina interprets the terms 'widespread, long-lasting or severe effects' in Article I, paragraph 1, of the Convention in accordance with the definition agreed upon in the understanding on that article. It likewise interprets Articles II, III and VIII in accordance with the relevant understandings.

[2] The FRG declared that the Convention applies also to Berlin (West). The USSR and the GDR stated that the West German declaration was 'illegal', while France, the UK and the USA confirmed its validity.

[3] Guatemala accepts the text of Article III on condition that the use of environmental techniques for peaceful purposes does not adversely affect its territory or the use of its natural resources.

[4] It is the understanding of the Republic of Korea that any technique for deliberately changing the natural state of rivers falls within the meaning of the term 'environmental modification techniques' as defined in Article II of the Convention. It is further understood that military or any other hostile use of such techniques, which could cause flooding, inundation, reduction in the water-level, drying up, destruction of hydrotechnical installations or other harmful consequences, comes within the scope of the Convention, provided it meets the criteria set out in Article I thereof.

[5] Kuwait made the following reservations and understanding: This Convention binds Kuwait only towards states parties thereto; its obligatory character shall *ipso facto* terminate with respect to any hostile state which does not abide by the prohibition contained therein. It is understood that accession to this Convention does not mean in any way recognition of Israel by Kuwait; furthermore, no treaty relation will arise between Kuwait and Israel.

On 23 June 1980, the UN Secretary-General, the depositary of the Convention, received from the government of Israel a communication stating that Israel would adopt towards Kuwait an attitude of complete reciprocity.

[6] The Netherlands accepts the obligation laid down in Article I of the Enmod Convention as extending to states which are not party to the Convention and which act in conformity with Article I of this Convention.

[7] New Zealand declared that, in its interpretation, nothing in the Convention detracts from or limits the obligations of states to refrain from military or any other hostile use of environmental modification techniques which are contrary to international law.

[8] Notification of succession.

[9] Because of its obligation incumbent upon it by virtue of its status of perpetual neutrality, Switzerland made a general reservation specifying that its co-operation in the framework of this Convention cannot go beyond the limits imposed by this status. This reservation refers, in particular, to article V, paragraph 5, of the Convention, and to any similar clause which may replace or supplement this provision in the Convention (or in any other arrangement).

[10] On signing the Convention, Turkey declared that the terms 'widespread', 'long-lasting' and 'severe effects' contained in the Convention need to be more clearly defined, and that so long as this clarification was not made, Turkey would be compelled to interpret for itself the terms in question and, consequently, reserved the right to do so as and when required. Turkey also stated its belief that the difference between 'military or any other hostile purposes' and 'peaceful purposes' should be more clearly defined so as to prevent subjective evaluations.

The 'Inhumane Weapons' Convention

[1] The accession of Benin refers only to Protocols I and III of the Convention.

[2] Upon signature, China stated that the Convention fails to provide for supervision or verification of any violation of its clauses, thus weakening its binding force. The Protocol on mines, booby traps and other devices fails to lay down strict restrictions on the use of such weapons by the aggressor on the territory of the victim and to provide adequately for the right of a state victim of an aggression to defend itself by all necessary means. The Protocol on incendiary weapons does not stipulate restrictions on the use of such weapons against combat personnel.

[3] Cyprus declared that the provisions of Article 7, paragraph 3b, and Article 8 of Protocol II of the Convention will be interpreted in such a way that neither the status of peace-keeping forces or missions of the UN in Cyprus will be affected nor will additional rights be, *ipso jure*, granted to them.

[4] France ratified only Protocols I and II. On signing the Convention France stated that it regretted that it had not been possible to reach agreement on the provisions concerning the verification of facts which might be alleged and which might constitute violations of the undertakings subscribed to. It therefore reserved the right to submit, possibly in association with other states, proposals aimed at filling that gap at the first conference to be held pursuant to Article 8 of the Convention and to utilize, as appropriate, procedures that would make it possible to bring before the international community facts and information which, if verified, could constitute violations of the provisions of the Convention and the Protocols annexed thereto. Reservation: Not being bound by the 1977 Additional Protocol I to the Geneva Conventions of 1949, France considers that the fourth paragraph of the preamble to the Convention on prohibitions or restrictions on the use of certain conventional

weapons, which reproduces the provisions of Article 35, paragraph 3, of Additional Protocol I, applies only to states parties to that Protocol. France will apply the provisions of the Convention and its three Protocols to all the armed conflicts referred to in Articles 2 and 3 common to the Geneva Conventions of 1949.

[5] Italy stated its regret that no agreement had been reached on provisions that would ensure respect for the obligations under the Convention. Italy intends to undertake efforts to ensure that the problem of the establishment of a mechanism that would make it possible to fill this gap in the Convention is taken up again at the earliest opportunity in every competent forum.

[6] The Netherlands made the following statements of understanding: A specific area of land may also be a military objective if, because of its location or other reasons specified in Article 2, paragraph 4, of Protocol II and in Article I, paragraph 3, of Protocol III, its total or partial destruction, capture, or neutralization in the prevailing circumstances offers a definitive military advantage; military advantage mentioned in Article 3, paragraph 3 under c, or Protocol II, refers to the advantage anticipated from the attack considered as a whole and not only from isolated or particular parts of the attack; in Article 8, paragraph 1, of Protocol II, the words 'as far as it is able' mean 'as far as it is technically able'.

[7] Romania stated that the provisions of the Convention and its Protocols have a restricted character and do not ensure adequate protection either to the civilian population or to the combatants as the fundamental principles of international humanitarian law require.

[8] The USA stated that it had strongly supported proposals by other countries to include special procedures for dealing with compliance matters, and reserved the right to propose at a later date additional procedures and remedies, should this prove necessary, to deal with such problems.

The Treaty of Rarotonga

[1] In signing Protocols 2 and 3 China declared that it respected the status of the South Pacific nuclear-free zone and would neither use nor threaten to use nuclear weapons against the zone nor test nuclear weapons in the region. However, China reserved its right to reconsider its obligations under the Protocols if other nuclear weapon states or the contracting Parties to the Treaty took any action in 'gross' violation of the Treaty and the Protocols, thus changing the status of the zone and endangering the security interests of China.

[2] In signing Protocols 2 and 3 the USSR stated the view that admission of transit of nuclear weapons or other nuclear explosive devices by any means, as well as of visits by foreign military ships and aircraft with nuclear explosive devices on board, to the ports and airfields within the nuclear-free zone would contradict the aims of the Treaty of Rarotonga and would be inconsistent with the status of the zone. It also warned that in case of action taken by a party or parties violating their major commitments connected with the nuclear-free status of the zone, as well as in case of aggression committed by one or several parties to the Treaty, supported by a nuclear-weapon state, or together with it, with the use by such a state of the territory, airspace, territorial sea or archipelagic waters of the parties for visits by nuclear weapon-carrying ships and aircraft or for transit of nuclear weapons, the USSR will have the right to consider itself free of its non-use commitments assumed under Protocol 2.

The Soviet Union ratified Protocols 2 and 3 to the Treaty without reference to the conditions included in its statement made at the time of signature. It expressed the hope that all states members of the South Pacific Forum would join the Treaty, and called upon the nuclear powers, which had not done so, to sign and ratify the relevant Protocols.

III. UN member states and year of membership

In the following list of names of the 159 UN member states, the countries marked with an asterisk are also members of the Geneva-based Conference on Disarmament (CD).

Afghanistan, 1946
Albania, 1955
*Algeria, 1962
Angola, 1976
Antigua and Barbuda, 1981
*Argentina, 1945
*Australia, 1945
Austria, 1955
Bahamas, 1973
Bahrain, 1971
Bangladesh, 1974
Barbados, 1966
*Belgium, 1945
Belize, 1981
Benin, 1960
Bhutan, 1971
Bolivia, 1945
Botswana, 1966
*Brazil, 1945
Brunei Darussalam, 1984
*Bulgaria, 1955
Burkina Faso, 1960
Burma (see Myanmar)
Burundi, 1962
Byelorussia, 1945
Cameroon, 1960
*Canada, 1945
Cape Verde, 1975
Central African Republic, 1960
Chad, 1960
Chile, 1945
*China, 1945
Colombia, 1945
Comoros, 1975
Congo, 1960
Costa Rica, 1945
Côte d'Ivoire, 1960
*Cuba, 1945
Cyprus, 1960
*Czechoslovakia, 1945
Denmark, 1945
Djibouti, 1977
Dominica, 1978
Dominican Republic, 1945
Ecuador, 1945
*Egypt, 1945
El Salvador, 1945
Equatorial Guinea, 1968
*Ethiopia, 1945
Fiji, 1970
Finland, 1955
*France, 1945
Gabon, 1960
Gambia, 1965
*German Democratic Republic, 1973
*FR Germany, 1973

Ghana, 1957
Greece, 1945
Grenada, 1974
Guatemala, 1945
Guinea, 1958
Guinea-Bissau, 1974
Guyana, 1966
Haiti, 1945
Honduras, 1945
*Hungary, 1955
Iceland, 1946
*India, 1945
*Indonesia, 1950
*Iran, 1945
Iraq, 1945
Ireland, 1955
Israel, 1949
*Italy, 1955
Ivory Coast (see Côte d'Ivoire)
Jamaica, 1962
*Japan, 1956
Jordan, 1955
Kampuchea (Cambodia), 1955
*Kenya, 1963
Kuwait, 1963
Lao People's Democratic Republic, 1955
Lebanon, 1945
Lesotho, 1966
Liberia, 1945
Libya, 1955
Luxembourg, 1945
Madagascar, 1960
Malawi, 1964
Malaysia, 1957
Maldives, 1965
Mali, 1960
Malta, 1964
Mauritania, 1961
Mauritius, 1968
*Mexico, 1945
*Mongolia, 1961
*Morocco, 1956
Mozambique, 1975
*Myanmar (formerly Burma), 1948
Nepal, 1955
*Netherlands, 1945
New Zealand, 1945
Nicaragua, 1945
Niger, 1960
*Nigeria, 1960
Norway, 1945
Oman, 1971
*Pakistan, 1947

Panama, 1945
Papua New Guinea, 1975
Paraguay, 1945
*Peru, 1945
Philippines, 1945
*Poland, 1945
Portugal, 1955
Qatar, 1971
*Romania, 1955
Rwanda, 1962
Saint Christopher and Nevis, 1983
Saint Lucia, 1979
Saint Vincent and the Grenadines, 1980
Samoa, Western, 1976
Sao Tome and Principe, 1975
Saudi Arabia, 1945
Senegal, 1960
Seychelles, 1976
Sierra Leone, 1961
Singapore, 1965
Solomon Islands, 1978
Somalia, 1960
South Africa, 1945
Spain, 1955
*Sri Lanka, 1955
Sudan, 1956
Suriname, 1975
Swaziland, 1968
*Sweden, 1946
Syria, 1945
Tanzania, 1961
Thailand, 1946
Togo, 1960
Trinidad and Tobago, 1962
Tunisia, 1956
Turkey, 1945
Uganda, 1962
*UK, 1945
Ukraine, 1945
United Arab Emirates, 1971
Uruguay, 1945
*USA, 1945
*USSR, 1945
Vanuatu, 1981
*Venezuela, 1945
Viet Nam, 1977
Yemen Arab Republic, 1947
Yemen, People's Democratic Republic of, 1967
*Yugoslavia, 1945
*Zaire, 1960
Zambia, 1964
Zimbabwe, 1980

Annexe B. Chronology 1989

RAGNHILD FERM

For the convenience of the reader, key words are indicated in the right-hand column, opposite each entry. They refer to the subject-areas covered in the entry. The wording in the entries is as close as possible to the original statements or documents. Definitions of the acronyms can be found on page xv.

30 Dec. 1988– *1 Jan. 1989*	At the Indian–Pakistani summit meeting in Islamabad (30 Dec. 1988–1 Jan. 1989) the two Prime Ministers sign an agreement prohibiting attack on each other's nuclear installations.	Regional conflicts: India/Pakistan
4 Jan.	Two US F-14 fighters shoot down two Libyan MiG-23 fighters some 110 km off the Libyan coast.	Regional conflicts: Middle East; USA/Libya
4 Jan.	China deposits the instruments of ratification for Protocols 2 and 3 to the 1985 South Pacific Nuclear Free Zone Treaty (Treaty of Rarotonga).	NWFZ: South Pacific; Nuclear tests
7–11 Jan.	An international Conference on the Prohibition of Chemical Weapons is held in Paris (the Paris Conference).	CW
8 Jan.	At the Paris Conference on chemical weapons the Soviet Foreign Minister declares that the USSR intends to be among the initial signatories of a convention prohibiting chemical weapons. He suggests that, without waiting for the signing of the convention, an international experiment be staged to try out procedures for verifying the non-production of chemical weapons. He further states that the USSR has no chemical weapon stockpiles outside Soviet territory and that in 1989 it will start the elimination of its chemical weapons at a plant specially built for this purpose.	CW; USSR
11 Jan.	In the final declaration adopted by the Paris Conference on chemical weapons, the participating states call for 'redoubled' efforts to conclude a CW convention and confirm the importance of the 1925 Geneva Protocol.	CW; Geneva Protocol
15 Jan.	The concluding document of the third CSCE follow-up meeting is adopted in Vienna. It includes a provision for negotiation between the 23 member states of NATO and the WTO on Conventional Armed Forces in Europe (CFE). The objectives of the negotiation are to strengthen stability and security in Europe through a stable and secure balance of conventional armed forces, which include conventional armaments at lower levels; the elimination of disparities prejudicial to stability and security; and the elimination of the capability for launch-	CSCE; CFE; CSBM

ing surprise attack and for initiating large-scale offensive action. It is stated that the participating states will hold regular meetings with the rest of the CSCE states in order to exchange views and information concerning the course of the negotiation.

The concluding document also contains a provision for negotiations among all 35 CSCE states on confidence- and security-building measures (CSBMs) in Europe to build upon and expand the results achieved at the Stockholm Conference.

15 Jan.	In an interview with *Pravda* the Soviet Deputy Foreign Minister says that the official Soviet military spending of 20 billion roubles, which is presented as the military budget, represents only a part of Soviet defence spending.	Military spending; USSR
18 Jan.	At a meeting in Moscow with eminent politicians and business people from the USA, Western Europe and Japan, President Gorbachev announces that the Soviet defence budget will be reduced by 14.2% and the production of armaments and military hardware by 19.5%.	Military spending; USSR
19 Jan.	Addressing the closing session of the CSCE the Soviet Foreign Minister announces that the USSR will withdraw units with all their armaments, including tactical nuclear systems, from Central Europe as part of its previously announced (7 Dec. 1988) withdrawal of military units from Central Europe.	CSCE; SNF; USSR; Withdrawals
23–27 Jan.	The leaders of the GDR, Czechoslovakia, Bulgaria, Poland and Hungary announce future unilateral reductions in their countries' conventional forces and military budgets.	Force reductions; Military spending
30 Jan.	The WTO issues for the first time detailed data on its conventional force strength, as well as its estimate of NATO conventional forces. In a statement by the WTO defence ministers it is expressed that 'all the components of the military balance in Europe may be characterized as a rough parity which denies either side any hope of achieving a decisive military superiority'.	Conventional forces; NATO/WTO
1 Feb.	The USA announces that it has cancelled its annual 1989 'Reforger' military manoeuvre. It will merge with the 1990 'Reforger' exercise to take place Jan.–Mar. 1990.	CBM; USA
2 Feb.	The final meeting of the 1973–89 Mutual (and Balanced) Force Reduction [M(B)FR] Talks is concluded in Vienna.	M(B)FR
9 Feb.	In an article in *Pravda* the Soviet Defence Minister says that the Soviet armed forces in Europe and the armed forces of the other WTO countries will be reduced by altogether 296 300 men, almost 12 000 tanks and 930 aircraft by 1991.	Force reductions; WTO

13 Feb.	In a meeting with the US Secretary of State, the Chancellor of FR Germany reaffirms his position that NATO should delay until 1991 or 1992 a decision on whether to modernize NATO's short-range Lance missile.	SNF; FRG
14 Feb.	The Presidents of Costa Rica, El Salvador, Guatemala, Honduras and Nicaragua, meeting in San Salvador, declare that they have agreed to draw up a plan within 90 days to dismantle Contra bases in Honduras and to relocate the approximately 11 000 Contras to other countries. In exchange Nicaragua pledges to hold general elections no later than 25 Feb. 1990.	Regional conflicts: Central America
15 Feb.	In accordance with the Geneva Accords (14 Apr. 1988) the USSR completes its troop withdrawal from Afghanistan. It reiterates its proposal for an immediate cease-fire and a simultaneous end to arms shipments to Afghanistan by all countries.	Regional conflicts: Afghanistan; Withdrawals
20 Feb.	The European Community (EC) member states approve export controls on 8 key chemicals that can be used for the production of chemical weapons.	CW; EC
3 Mar.	It is reported by TASS that Mongolia has decided to reduce its armed forces by 13 000 men in 1989–90. 1000 trucks, 90 caterpillars and armoured vehicles will be phased out to be adapted for civilian use.	Force reductions; Mongolia
6 Mar.	The foreign ministers of the CSCE states hold the opening sessions of the CSBM Negotiations (35 CSCE states) and the CFE Negotiation (23 NATO and WTO states) in Vienna. See *15 Jan.*	CSCE; CSBM; CFE
6 Mar.	In his opening speech at the CFE Negotiation, the Soviet Foreign Minister presents a proposal for reductions in troops and conventional weapons with the goal of making both NATO and the WTO 'strictly defensive' by the year 2000. He also proposes separate NATO–WTO negotiations on short-range nuclear forces, as soon as possible.	CFE; USSR; SNF
6 Mar.	The NATO proposal is presented by the UK at the CFE Negotiation. It includes measures that would lead to a reduction of around 50% in tanks and artillery, and cuts in the number of armoured personnel carriers.	CFE; NATO
9 Mar.	At the UN headquarters it is announced that, according to a letter from the Soviet Foreign Minister, the USSR has accepted the jurisdiction of the International Court of Justice to settle disputes in questions concerning human rights.	UN; USSR; ICJ
9 Mar.	The first working sessions of the CSBM Negotiations and the CFE Negotiation, both within the CSCE framework, are held in Vienna.	CSCE; CFE; CSBM

9 Mar.	At the CSBM Negotiations the NATO states present their proposal, which builds upon and expands the 1986 Stockholm Document. It includes directions for notice of major conventional weapon systems introduced in the zone as well as evaluation of peacetime locations (inspections to ensure that supplied data are accurate). A seminar on military doctrines in relation to conventional forces in the zone is also suggested.	CSBM; NATO; Military doctrines
9 Mar.	At the CSBM Negotiations Bulgaria, Czechoslovakia, the GDR and Hungary present their proposal: 'On a new generation of Confidence- and Security-Building Measures in Europe'. It includes restrictions on the size, number and duration of military exercises and the extension of CSBMs to air force and naval activities as well as a proposal for periodic discussions on military doctrines.	CSBM; WTO
13–16 Mar.	The Eighteenth Islamic Conference of Foreign Ministers is held in Riyadh, Saudi Arabia. It calls upon all states, particularly the states of the region concerned, to respond positively to the proposals for the establishment of nuclear weapon-free zones in Africa, the Middle East and South Asia. It reaffirms the determination of member states to prevent nuclear proliferation on a non-discriminatory and universal basis.	NWFZ: Africa; NWFZ: Middle East; NWFZ: South Asia; NPT
14 Mar.	The European Parliament adopts a resolution calling on the EC Commission to examine arms exports from member states and consider a special industrial reconversion programme. Member states are requested to authorize customs officials to check the validity of end-use certificates in order to stop illegal trade and the EC is urged to develop a common arms sales policy through European Political Co-operation. The Council, Commission and member states of the EC are called to embargo the sales of the technology and raw materials for the production of chemical and biological weapons (CBW) to those countries currently using or producing them.	Arms trade; Conversion; CBW; EC
17 Mar.	In a letter to the UN, the USSR and Mongolia transmit the text of their agreement concerning the withdrawal in 1989–90 of Soviet military units from Mongolia. The units will include 3 full divisions—including 2 tank divisions—2 aviation divisions and a number of individual units.	Withdrawals; USSR/ Mongolia; UN
21 Mar.	The Supreme Soviet Presidium issues a decree to reduce in 1989–90 the Soviet armed forces by 500 000 troops while substantially cutting the volume of conventional weapons and military expenditure according to the Soviet state budget. The Council of Ministers is instructed to take measures to implement the decree.	Force reductions; Military spending; USSR

31 Mar.	The Foreign Ministers of Costa Rica, El Salvador, Guatemala, Honduras and Nicaragua request the UN Secretary-General to set in motion the verification mechanism of a UN Observer Group in Central America.	Regional conflicts: Central America; UN
3 Apr.	Israel agrees to re-open negotiations with Norway over inspection rights of its nuclear facilities. (Background: Norway's wish to investigate whether heavy water sold to Israel 20 years ago was used to make nuclear weapons.)	NPT; Norway/Israel
5 Apr.	Viet Nam, Laos and Cambodia (Kampuchea) issue a joint statement announcing that all Vietnamese troops would be withdrawn from Cambodia by 30 Sep. The statement calls for the cessation of foreign interference in Cambodia's internal affairs, and for the ending of all foreign military aid to the various factions by the same date.	Regional conflicts: Viet Nam/ Cambodia
6 Apr.	The Prime Minister of Israel, meeting President Bush, outlines a 4-point Middle East peace plan. It includes proposals for elections in the West Bank and Gaza Strip. The plan is approved by the Israeli Cabinet on 14 May.	Regional conflicts: Israel/ Palestinians
7 Apr.	A Soviet Mike Class nuclear-powered submarine catches fire and sinks off the Norwegian coast; most of the crew is killed. The International Atomic Energy Agency (IAEA) is notified of the accident on the following day. It is informed that Soviet experts conclude that there is no danger of a nuclear explosion or radioactive contamination.	NPT; USSR; IAEA
7 Apr.	In a speech held in the Guildhall, London, President Gorbachev announces that the USSR has decided to cease production of enriched weapon-grade uranium in 1989. In addition to the industrial reactor for the production of weapon-grade plutonium shut down in 1987, 2 more such reactors will be closed in 1989–90 without being replaced. In the same speech he also gives figures for the numerical strength of the Soviet armed forces.	NPT; USSR
12 Apr.	In a statement issued at the end of the WTO Foreign Ministers' Meeting in Berlin a formal proposal is made to the NATO states to start in the near future separate talks on short-range nuclear forces in Europe, including the nuclear components of dual-purpose systems.	SNF; WTO
13 Apr.	In an article published in *Krasnaya Zvezda* the Soviet Defence Minister outlines a restructuring for the Soviet armed forces and says that they will be reduced from 4 258 000 to 3 760 000 by the end of 1990.	Force reductions; USSR

20 Apr.	At a press conference held before the NATO Nuclear Planning Group Meeting in Brussels, the US Secretary of Defense states that there is consensus within the Alliance that eliminating all short-range nuclear forces from Europe should be avoided.	SNF; NATO
20 Apr.	In the final communiqué of the NATO Nuclear Planning Group Meeting, held in Brussels, it is stated that NATO must be assured diversified, survivable and operationally flexible nuclear forces across the entire spectrum. These forces should be kept up-to-date where necessary.	Nuclear forces; NATO
4 May	The US Administration announces that it will accept in principle legislation to impose sanctions against countries using CW and companies providing such technology to Third World nations.	CW; USA
6 May	Bolivia, Brazil, Colombia, Ecuador, Guyana, Peru, Suriname and Venezuela (parties to the 1978 Treaty for Amazonian Co-operation) issue a declaration on the development and protection of the rich heritage of the Amazon territories. They commit themselves to use nuclear energy exclusively for peaceful purposes and urge the nuclear weapon states to cease nuclear testing and promote progressive elimination of their nuclear arsenals.	NPT; Nuclear tests; South America
10–11 May	The US Foreign Secretary meets with the Soviet Foreign Minister in Moscow. It is agreed that the Strategic Arms Reduction Talks (START) will be resumed in June as well as the work of the Standing Consultative Commission; talks on nuclear testing will be resumed on 26 June; and new emphasis will be put on the problem of chemical weapons and missile proliferation. The Soviet Foreign Minister announces that the USSR is prepared to totally dismantle the Krasnoyarsk radar, if the USA agrees to adhere to the strict interpretation of the ABM Treaty.	START; Nuclear tests; CW; Missile proliferation; Space: ABM Treaty
11 May	Receiving the US Secretary of State in Moscow President Gorbachev offers to unilaterally reduce Soviet short-range nuclear weapons by 500 warheads before the end of the year. In addition he proposes that the CFE Negotiation should aim at an agreement within two years setting equal levels of troops and armaments for NATO and the WTO: 1 350 000 troops, 1500 tactical aircraft, 1700 helicopters, 20 000 tanks, 24 000 artillery pieces and 28 000 armoured vehicles.	Force reductions; SNF; USSR

12 May	In a speech at the Texas Agricultural and Mechanical University, President Bush suggests that the plan proposed by President Eisenhower in 1955, called 'Open Skies', should be revived. It would allow unarmed aircraft from the USA and the USSR to fly over the territory of the other country. Such surveillance flights, complementing satellites, would provide regular scrutiny for both sides.	Open Skies; CBM
15–18 May	President Gorbachev pays an official visit to China. (This is the first Sino-Soviet summit meeting in 30 years.) The two leaders agree to intensify the consideration of those parts of the Sino-Soviet border on which agreement has not yet been reached and work out solutions simultaneously for the eastern and western parts of the border. The Soviet leader announces the reduction in 1989–90 of 200 000 troops in Soviet Asia, including 12 ground force divisions, 11 air force regiments and 16 warships from the Pacific Fleet, as well as the reduction of 75% of Soviet forces in Mongolia, including 3 ground divisions and all air units.	USSR/China; USSR/ Mongolia; Force reductions
22 May	India conducts a test of a surface-to-surface ballistic missile with a range of 2400 km.	Missile proliferation; India
22 May	India and Pakistan agree to pull back troops from the Siachen glacier, on the northern edge of Kashmir, to positions from which they can no longer shoot at each other.	Regional conflicts: India/Pakistan; Withdrawals
23 May	A formal Soviet proposal (based on a Soviet proposal outlined at the visit of the US Secretary of State to Moscow on 10–11 May) is presented at the CFE Negotiation. It imposes limits on military forces in the Atlantic-to-the-Urals (ATTU) region as regards (a) single country ceilings, (b) foreign deployment ceilings and (c) alliance-wide ceilings. The limits would require the removal of 40 000 tanks, 47 000 artillery pieces and 42 000 armoured vehicles from the WTO force structure.	Force reductions; CFE; WTO
23–24 May	Representatives from Albania, Bulgaria, Greece, Romania, Turkey and Yugoslavia meet in Bucharest to discuss measures for strengthening confidence- and security-building measures in the region.	Balkans; CSBM
29 May	At a press conference held before the NATO summit meeting in Brussels, President Bush announces a 4-step arms control initiative: (a) WTO acceptance of the proposed NATO ceiling on tanks and armoured troops in Europe, (b) a 15% reduction for each side below current NATO levels in helicopters and land-based combat aircraft, (c) a ceiling of 275 000 on stationed US and Soviet	Force reductions; CFE; NATO

forces in the ATTU zone: a cut of approximately 325 000 for the USSR and 30 000 for the USA, and (*d*) acceleration of the CFE timetable to reach an agreement along the above-mentioned lines, and to complete the force reductions by 1992.

30 May	The heads of government of NATO states, meeting in Brussels, endorse President Bush's conventional force reduction plan (see *29 May*). It is agreed that negotiations on reducing short-range nuclear weapons will take place only when implementation of negotiated conventional force reduction is under way. Future US–Soviet negotiations should not accept the complete elimination of short-range nuclear forces from Europe. Modernization or replacement of the US Lance missile will be delayed until 1992. The meeting adopts a report, prepared by the NATO Council: 'A Comprehensive Concept of Arms Control and Disarmament'.	NATO; SNF; CFE
30 May	In a speech to the Soviet Congress of People's Deputies, President Gorbachev announces that the USSR will spend 77.3 billion roubles on military expenditures in the current fiscal year, which is four times the official defence budget. (This is the first such public Soviet statement on Soviet military spending.)	Military spending; USSR
30 May	At the CFE Negotiation the WTO states offer to cut by half their troops and conventional arms stationed in Central Europe.	CFE; WTO
4 June	Soldiers of the Chinese People's Liberation Army take control of Central Beijing by force, causing many casualties. Demonstrators protesting against the Government's policy had occupied Tiananmen Square since late April. The USA, the UK and France place an arms embargo on China following the event.	China
8–9 June	NATO Defence Ministers, meeting in Brussels, stress that there is no alternative to the strategy of deterrence based upon an appropriate mix of adequate and effective nuclear and conventional forces which will continue to be kept up-to-date where necessary. There remains a continuing need to increase resources devoted to defence. Continuing real increases in defence expenditure of the order of 3% appear both necessary and affordable.	NATO; SNF
9 June	At the CSBM Negotiations the Netherlands, on behalf of the NATO countries, presents a proposal for the expanding of the Stockholm Document to include more detailed briefings from on-site inspections of military manoeuvres; increasing the size of inspection teams from 4 to 6; lowering the threshold for exercises which would be subject to observation; and increasing the number of permitted annual on-site inspections from 3 to 5.	CSBM; NATO

12 June	The USA and the USSR sign, in Moscow, an Agreement on the Prevention of Dangerous Military Activities. The agreement is designed to prevent accidental armed conflicts between the two parties. It enters into force on 1 Jan. 1990.	CBM; USA/USSR
13 June	In a joint statement, issued in Bonn, President Gorbachev and the Chancellor of FR Germany pledge to strive for disarmament and overcoming the division of Europe. The right of states to determine their destiny and build their relations with one another in a sovereign manner on the basis of international law must be guaranteed. An agreement is reached between the two leaders on establishing a 'hot line' between their offices.	CBM; USSR/FRG
19 June	The US–Soviet Strategic Arms Reduction Talks (START) under the Nuclear and Space Talks (NST) are resumed after a recess of more than seven months.	START
21 June	At the US–Soviet START negotiations the USA presents its proposal for measures to improve verification under a START treaty: elaborate exchange of nuclear weapon data, trial monitoring of mobile-missile factories, direct inspection of missile warheads or re-entry vehicles, a ban on encoding telemetry from missile flight-tests, a demonstration of weapon tags, and exploration of a ban on 'short time-of-flight' missile flight-tests that could lead to surprise attack.	START; USA
27 June	At the CSBM Negotiations Sweden presents a proposal for convening a seminar on military doctrines in relation to the posture, structure and activities of conventional forces in the zone. (The proposal is a compromise between two separate proposals put forward by Poland and Spain on 20 June.)	CSBM; Military doctrines; Sweden
29 June	The WTO countries present a proposal to the CFE Negotiation. It is a revised version of the 23 May proposal and includes suggestions for the regional division of the ATTU zone and for corresponding sub-ceilings.	CFE; WTO
4 July	The USSR and France sign, in Moscow, an Agreement on the Prevention of Incidents on and over the High Seas.	USSR/France; CBM
5 July	South Africa conducts a test of a surface-to-surface ballistic missile with a maximum range of c. 1450 km.	Missile proliferation; South Africa

6 July	In an address to the Council of Europe in Strasbourg, President Gorbachev outlines his vision of a concept of a 'common European home' which rules out the possibility of the use or threat of force within as well as between the alliances. A second Helsinki-type conference is needed. A doctrine of restraint should replace the doctrine of deterrence. He offers to make further unilateral cuts in Soviet short-range missiles in Europe, provided NATO agrees to join negotiations on the reduction of such weapons. He also announces that the USSR intends to reduce by 33.4–50% the share of defence allocations in the national income by the year 1995. A proposal for a joint working group within the framework of the UN Economic Commission of Europe to study the problems of conversion is also presented in his address.	Europe; CSCE; SNF; Military spending; Conversion; UN
6 July	The last of the US shorter-range missiles (Pershing 1A) and their launchers are eliminated under the INF Treaty.	INF; USA
7–8 July	The annual meeting of the WTO Political Consultative Committee is held in Bucharest. The final communiqué stresses the growing interconnection of domestic and foreign policies in the member countries. It is stated that universal socialist models do not exist; building a new society is a creative process which develops in each of the countries in accordance with its conditions, traditions and requirements. At the meeting a statement is adopted, entitled 'For a Stable and Safe Europe Free From Nuclear and Chemical Weapons, for a Substantial Reduction of the Armed Forces, Armaments and Military Spending'.	WTO; Europe
10 July	The Soviet Deputy Foreign Minister says that the USSR is willing to accept the US START proposal for trial inspection (see *21 June*) if it affects both countries equally and covers several types of arms beyond those mentioned in the US proposal.	START; USSR
12 July	The neutral and non-aligned (NNA) states submit their proposal to the CSBM Negotiations. It calls for improved information on military matters such as the annual calendar, communications and consultations, verification, observers, etc. Limits on the number of troops carrying out military activities are also proposed.	CSBM; NNA states
13 July	At the CFE Negotiation the NATO states formally present the proposal which was outlined by President Bush on 29 May. The proposal provides specific ceilings for aircraft, helicopters and troops.	CFE; NATO

21 July	Marshal Akhromeyev, adviser to President Gorbachev, speaking before the US House Armed Services Committee, presents the actual Soviet national security policy as well as figures on the current Soviet strategic forces and military spending. He criticizes the reluctance of the US Administration to open negotiations with the USSR on bilateral reductions of naval forces.	USA/USSR; Military spending; Strategic forces; Naval forces
27 July	The UN Security Council unanimously adopts a resolution endorsing the efforts of Central American countries for a peace settlement in the region expressed in the Guatemala Agreement of 7 Aug. 1987. It appeals to governments in the region and beyond, which supply aid to 'irregular forces or insurrectional movements in the area', immediately to halt such aid, except for humanitarian aid.	Regional conflicts: Central America; UN
30 July– *30 Aug.*	An international Conference on Cambodia (Kampuchea) is held in Paris. The conference fails to formulate a common agreement.	Regional conflicts: Cambodia
2 Aug.	In an appeal to the US Congress the Supreme Soviet states that the USSR is prepared to announce, on the basis of reciprocity, a moratorium on all nuclear explosions, leading to a verifiable agreement on a CTB.	Nuclear tests; USSR
7 Aug.	The Presidents of Costa Rica, El Salvador, Guatemala, Honduras and Nicaragua, meeting in Tela, Honduras, agree on a plan to disband the Nicaraguan Contras by 5 Dec. 1989. In return, Nicaragua is obliged to hold free elections no later than 25 Feb. 1990. The Presidents also call for a cease-fire and negotiations in El Salvador between the Salvadorean rebels and the government. (See also *14 Feb.*)	Regional conflicts: Central America
15 Aug.	The UN Security Council, convened in emergency session, unanimously appeals for a total and immediate cease-fire by all parties to the conflict in Lebanon.	Regional conflicts: Middle East; UN
4–7 Sep.	The Ninth Conference of Heads of State or Governments of Non-Aligned Countries is held in Belgrade, Yugoslavia. In a political document adopted at the Conference, the three depositary parties to the Non-Proliferation Treaty (UK, USA and USSR) are urged to fulfil their obligations by agreeing to negotiate a comprehensive test ban treaty.	Non-aligned movement; Peaceful settlement of disputes; Nuclear tests
11 Sep.	Addressing the National Assembly the President of South Korea outlines a detailed proposal for the achievement of unification with North Korea.	South Korea/ North Korea
12 Sep.	The UN Secretary-General proposes a more vigorous role for the Security Council, including periodic private meetings at foreign ministerial level to avert crisis.	UN

15 Sep.	The President of Egypt presents a 10-point Middle East peace plan, calling for elections in the occupied territories. The plan extends an election proposal put forward by the Israeli Prime Minister (see also *6 Apr. 1989*). The PLO is in favour of the initiative as is the Israeli Labour Party. Radical Palestinian groups and the Likud Party reject the plan.	Regional conflicts: Israel/ Palestinians; Egypt
18 Sep.	India and Sri Lanka sign an agreement on the withdrawal of 40 000 Indian troops from Sri Lanka by 31 Dec. 1989.	Regional conflicts: Sri Lanka; Withdrawals
18–22 Sep.	An international Government–Industry Conference against Chemical Weapons is held in Canberra, Australia. The participants issue a declaration urging speedy resolution of a convention banning CW.	CW
19–28 Sep.	The Third Review Conference of the Parties to the Sea-Bed Treaty is held in Geneva. In the final declaration issued at the end of the Conference, the states parties reaffirm their common interest in avoiding an arms race on the sea-bed and confirm that they have not placed any nuclear weapons or other weapons of mass destruction on or under the sea-bed outside a 12-mile limit from the coastline.	Sea-Bed Treaty
21 Sep.	At the CFE Negotiation the NATO states present proposals for information exchange, stabilizing measures, verification and non-circumvention.	CFE; NATO
22–23 Sep.	The Soviet Foreign Minister, meeting with the US Secretary of State in Jackson Hole, Wyoming, USA, announces that the USSR is prepared to conclude a START treaty even if an agreement on weapons in space is not complete. Nevertheless, the two sides must continue to observe the ABM Treaty as signed in 1972. Violation of the ABM Treaty by either side would be a reason for the other party to abrogate any strategic arms reduction treaty. However, some experiments and tests in space could be permitted. The Krasnoyarsk radar station will be completely dismantled. The USA promises to consider Soviet concerns about the US radar stations in Greenland and the UK. A group of Soviet experts is invited to visit US SDI laboratories. The USA withdraws its proposal that a START treaty ban mobile ICBMs. At the meeting bilateral agreements are reached on: advance notification of strategic exercises which include heavy bomber aircraft; verification and stability measures in the strategic arms area; travelling across the Bering Straits and resolving disputes concerning these straits; interpretation of law concerning innocent passage; enhancing the role of the International Court of Justice in the resolution of international disputes; and a verification	USA/USSR; Space: ABM Treaty, SDI; START; Law of the sea; ICJ; Nuclear tests; CW

regime for the 1974 Threshold Test Ban Treaty and the 1976 Peaceful Nuclear Explosions Treaty. A Memorandum of Understanding is reached regarding a bilateral verification experiment and data exchange related to the prohibition of CW. In addition, the two sides agree to hold a summit meeting in the late spring or early summer of 1990.

25 Sep.	Speaking before the UN General Assembly, President Bush announces that in the first 8 years of a CW convention the USA is ready to destroy 98% of its CW, provided the USSR joins such a convention. All US CW will be eliminated within 10 years, once all states capable of manufacturing CW have signed the convention. In the period during which a convention is worked out and completed the USA is ready to destroy more than 80% of its CW if the USSR joins in cutting its CW to an equal level and in verification inspections to verify that stockpiles are destroyed are agreed on.	CW; USA; UN
26 Sep.	Speaking before the UN General Assembly, the Soviet Foreign Minister says that the USSR will join the USA and radically reduce or completely destroy its CW and stop the production of CW, including binary weapons, as well as renounce the use of CW under any circumstances. He says that the USSR has revised the number and yield of explosions in its nuclear testing programme and reiterates the Soviet proposal for a US–Soviet moratorium on nuclear explosions, and suggests that the USSR and the USA stop producing weapon-grade plutonium. He reaffirms the Soviet goal not to have a single Soviet soldier outside the country. He welcomes President Bush's Open Skies proposal (see *12 May*) and calls for opening up lands, waters and outer space. Naval forces should also be discussed at a multilateral forum attended by all states concerned.	CW; Nuclear tests; NPT; Withdrawals; Open Skies; Naval forces; UN; USSR
26 Sep.	The last 26 000 Vietnamese troops are reported to have left Cambodia (Kampuchea).	Regional conflicts: Viet Nam/ Cambodia; Withdrawals
28 Sep.	At the CFE Negotiation the USSR formally proposes a summit meeting of the 23 states in the second half of 1990 to sign a treaty on radical cuts in conventional forces. Compromise proposals for aircraft and helicopter ceilings under a treaty are also set out.	CFE; USSR
1–6 Oct.	The Soviet Defence Minister pays a visit to the USA (the first by a Soviet Defence Minister). Information is exchanged on details of US–Soviet military strategies, doctrines, force structures and defence spending plans.	USA/USSR; Military spending

2 Oct.	At its annual conference the British Labour Party decides to renounce its 8-year support for unilateral nuclear disarmament.	Nuclear disarmament; UK
4 Oct.	At a press conference at the UN headquarters the Soviet Deputy Foreign Minister announces that the USSR has outlined a set of proposals that are intended to give the UN a greater role in preventing conflicts. It includes the establishment of war risk reduction centres around the world.	UN; USSR
10 Oct.	In an article in *Pravda* President Gorbachev's adviser, Marshal Akhromeyev, says that the USSR will unilaterally reduce its troops by 500 000 men in 1989–90.	Force reductions; USSR
10 Oct.	It is reported by TASS that the withdrawal of 50 320 troops, 3118 tanks, 768 artillery pieces and 351 combat aircraft from Mongolia and other countries, planned for 1989, has been concluded ahead of schedule.	Withdrawals; USSR/ Mongolia
10 Oct.	The US Secretary of State puts forward an initiative proposing an Israeli–Palestinian meeting to discuss the holding of elections in the occupied territories. On 5 Nov. the Israeli Cabinet endorses the plan, on the assumption that the USA will provide certain guarantees, mainly that Israel will not negotiate with the PLO.	Regional conflicts: Israel/ Palestinians; USA
11 Oct.	A US State Department spokesman says that the USA will ensure that during the 10-year period of phased destruction of CW it still has safe and secure weapons. For that reason, binary weapons will be brought in to replace its ageing, unstable unitary weapons.	CW; USA
19 Oct.	At the CFE Negotiation the WTO states offer to allow continuous inspections at dozens of military airfields, naval ports and railway junctions in exchange for similar rights in Western Europe.	CFE; WTO
23 Oct.	Addressing the Supreme Soviet, the Soviet Foreign Minister publicly condemns the construction of the Krasnoyarsk radar station, acknowledging that it is a violation of the 1972 ABM Treaty. He claims that details about the purpose of the radar have not previously become known to the Soviet leadership and says that the station will be dismantled.	Space: ABM; USSR
24–25 Oct.	The NATO Nuclear Planning Group, meeting in Almansil, Portugal, orders NATO's High Level Group of nuclear experts to carry out a study on the strategic role of the nuclear weapons in Western Europe once Soviet conventional arms are reduced in WTO countries.	NATO

26 Oct.	President Gorbachev, visiting Finland, announces that the USSR will eliminate its remaining nuclear-missile submarines in the Baltic Sea by the end of 1990. He states that Soviet short-range weapons are now stationed in such a way that they do not reach the Nordic countries, and says that the USSR unconditionally recognizes Finland's neutral status and will continue to observe it in full measure. He also proposes that a CSCE summit meeting be held in 1992.	USSR/ Finland; Withdrawals; SNF; CSCE
27 Oct.	The last of the Soviet shorter-range missiles (SS-23) and their launchers are eliminated under the INF Treaty.	INF; USSR
1 Nov.	Citing continued guerrilla attacks the Nicaraguan President ends his government's 19-month cease-fire with the Contras and threatens to cancel elections, scheduled for Feb. 1990.	Regional conflicts: Central America
5 Nov.	*Pravda* announces that the Soviet military forces have been decreased by 235 000 troops. More than 7000 tanks and 700 aircraft have been withdrawn from Europe.	Force reductions; Europe/USSR
9 Nov.	The Berlin Wall which has since 1961 divided the two German states is allowed to be crossed freely.	FRG/GDR
16 Nov.	The UN General Assembly adopts a resolution on peace, security and international co-operation, jointly sponsored by the USA and the USSR, by consensus and without a debate. The resolution reaffirms support for the UN Charter and urges all states to abide by it.	UN; USA/USSR
20 Nov.	The USSR and Canada sign, in Moscow, an Agreement on the Prevention of Incidents on and over the High Seas.	USSR/Canada; CBM
26 Nov.	A referendum is held in Switzerland on the 'People's initiative for a Switzerland without an army and for a comprehensive politics of peace'. 68.6% of those entitled to vote participate: of these, 35.6% vote in favour of the initiative, 64.4% against it.	General disarmament; Switzerland
27 Nov.	A resolution on environmental questions is adopted by the Supreme Soviet. It includes a recommendation to consider ceasing nuclear testing at the Semipalatinsk test site and urges the Council of Ministers to investigate the effects of the tests at the test site on Novaya Zemlya.	Nuclear testing; USSR
28 Nov.	The Chancellor of FRG presents to the Bundestag a 10-point programme to overcome the division of the two German states and Europe. Under the plan the two German states could build federal structures based on joint committees and a permanent consultation council.	FRG/GDR

30 Nov.	President Gorbachev, visiting Italy, suggests a 1990 summit meeting of the leaders of the CSCE states. The purpose would be to agree on a new framework for the development of a 'new Europe'. The Soviet and Italian Foreign Ministers sign a joint Declaration on Co-operation in Converting Military Production to Civilian Use.	CSCE; USSR; USSR/Italy; Conversion
2–3 Dec.	At the US–Soviet summit meeting held in Malta, President Gorbachev proposes that the two powers agree to ban all short-range nuclear weapons from surface war-ships and reiterates the Soviet call for limitations on SLCMs. At the meeting it is implied that bilateral disarmament agreements, including START, CW, and Protocols to the TTBT and the PNET, might be ready to be signed at the next summit meeting, to be held in June 1990.	USA/USSR; Naval forces; START; CW
4 Dec.	At a press conference in Brussels, President Bush states that a possible unification of the two German states should occur in the context of a continued commitment to NATO and an increasingly integrated European Community.	FRG/GDR; NATO; EC; USA
5 Dec.	At the NST Defence and Space Talks, the USA presents a draft space weapon treaty. It calls for essentially unlimited testing of space-based anti-missile components under the 'broad' interpretation of the ABM Treaty and includes provisions that would permit either party to withdraw from the Treaty and deploy anti-missile systems following three years of consultation and after giving six months' notice.	NST; Space: ABM
6 Dec.	The FRG Government announces that it intends to cut its military forces by one-fifth by the mid-1990s.	Force reductions; FRG
7 Dec.	The GDR Communist Party states that it supports the idea of working towards a confederation of the two German states. See *28 Nov.*	FRG/GDR
12 Dec.	In a speech held in Berlin, the US Secretary of State outlines new 'missions' for a future NATO: (*a*) a NATO Arms Control and Verification Staff to assist member governments in monitoring compliance with arms ocntrol and CBM agreements, (*b*) NATO consultations on regional conflicts and proliferation of missiles, nuclear weapons and CBW, (*c*) initiatives through the CSCE process to create economic and political ties with Eastern Europe, and (*d*) demonstration of a different approach to security to offer East European states a new model for international relations.	NATO; CBM; Regional conflicts, Missile proliferation; CBW; CSCE
14 Dec.	At the CFE Negotiation the NATO states present their draft treaty on conventional armed forces in Europe.	CFE; NATO

14 Dec.	At the CFE Negotiation the WTO states present their draft treaty on conventional armed forces in Europe.	CFE; WTO
14–19 Dec.	A team of Soviet scientific experts visit 2 US SDI research laboratories. (The invitation was made at the US–Soviet Foreign Ministers' meeting; see *22–23 Sep.*)	USA/USSR; Space: SDI
15 Dec.	At a news conference at the UN headquarters the Soviet Deputy Foreign Minister says that there are currently 627 500 Soviet troops outside the USSR. The goal is to have no troops at all abroad. (This is the first public Soviet statement on the number of troops abroad.)	USSR; Withdrawals
15 Dec.	The North Atlantic Council, meeting in Brussels, asserts that even if the division of Europe is overcome the presence of US forces in Europe remains vital. The Council adopts a document on the basic elements of an 'Open Skies' regime. (A conference on the issue will be held in Ottawa in Feb. 1990.)	Europe; NATO; Open Skies
15 Dec.	At the CSBM Negotiations the USSR presents a proposal on the transition to a universal method of notification of military activities. It involves ground, air and naval forces when any of the components include more than 13 000 troops, or 250 combat tanks, or 130 aircraft.	CSBM; USSR
15 Dec.	At the CSBM Negotiations France and Hungary present a joint proposal on 'Developing Military Contacts between States Participating in the CSCE Process'.	CSBM; France; Hungary
15 Dec.	The UN General Assembly adopts a resolution recommending a conference to amend the 1963 Partial Test Ban Treaty. A preparatory committee should meet in May/June 1990 and two conference sessions be held in June 1990 and January 1991. The USA and the UK vote against the resolution.	Nuclear tests; UN
16 Dec.	The Soviet Defence Ministry announces that Soviet defence expenditure will be 8.2% less in 1990 than in 1989. Allocations as regards items of expenditure are also announced.	Military spending; USSR
17 Dec.	Romanian troops and police forces attack protesters in Timisoara, Romania, causing many casualties. The violence spreads to other parts of Romania, including Bucharest.	Romania
19 Dec.	The Government of Austria invites the leaders of the CSCE states to a summit meeting, to be held in Vienna before the end of 1990.	CSCE; Austria
20 Dec.	US troops invade Panama to attack the forces of Panama's leader General Noriega. (He surrenders to US authorities on 3 Jan. 1990.)	USA/Panama

30 Dec.	The USSR and Italy sign an Agreement on the Prevention of Incidents on and over the High Seas.	USSR/Italy; CBM
31 Dec.	In his new-year speech the French President says that he foresees a European confederation in the 1990s which unites all states on the continent in a common and permanent interchange for peace and security.	Europe; France

About the contributors

Dr Ian Anthony (United Kingdom) is a Researcher on the SIPRI arms transfers and arms production project. He is the author of the SIPRI monograph *The Naval Arms Trade* (1990) and a contribution in E. Arnett (ed.), *New Technologies for Security and Arms Control* (1989). He is the author of chapters in the *SIPRI Yearbooks 1988* and *1989*.

William M. Arkin (United States) is Director of the Nuclear Information Unit of Greenpeace USA. In 1981–89 he was Director of the National Security Program of the Institute for Policy Studies, Washington, DC. He is co-editor of the *Nuclear Weapons Databook* series, and co-author of *Volume IV, Soviet Nuclear Weapons* (1989) and chapters in the *SIPRI Yearbooks* since 1985. He is a member of the editorial board of the *Bulletin of the Atomic Scientists* and the author of the forthcoming book *Encyclopedia of the US Military*.

Andrew S. Burrows (United Kingdom) is a Research Associate with the *Nuclear Weapons Databook* Project of the Natural Resources Defense Council, Washington, DC. He is co-author of the forthcoming NRDC publication *Nuclear Weapons Databook, Volume V, British, French, Chinese Nuclear Weapons and Nuclear Weapon Proliferation* and of chapters in the *SIPRI Yearbooks* since 1985.

Dr Thomas B. Cochran (United States) is Senior Staff Scientist and Co-director of the Nuclear Program and the *Nuclear Weapons Databook* project of the Natural Resources Defense Council, Washington, DC. He has initiated a series of nuclear weapon verification projects with the Soviet Academy of Sciences. He is a co-author of several NRDC volumes of the *Nuclear Weapons Databook*, and of chapters in the *SIPRI Yearbooks* since 1985. His publications include articles on nuclear weapon research and production, arms control, nuclear weapon proliferation, safeguards, seismic verification, national energy R&D policy and radiation exposure standards.

Dr Regina Cowen Karp (Federal Republic of Germany) is a Researcher and Leader of the SIPRI project on 'Security Without Nuclear Weapons?'. She is a co-editor of the SIPRI volume *The ABM Treaty: To Defend or Not to Defend?* (1987), and author of a contribution in G. M. Dillon (ed.), *Defence Policy Making, A Comparative Analysis* (1988) and a chapter in the *SIPRI Yearbook 1988*. She is the editor of a forthcoming SIPRI volume, *Security with Nuclear Weapons? Different Perspectives on National Security*.

Agnès Courades Allebeck (France) is a Research Assistant on the SIPRI arms transfers and arms production project. She was formerly a Research Assistant at the European Parliament, Luxembourg (1985), has done research on the external relations of the European Community, and is the author of a chapter in the *SIPRI Yearbook 1989*.

Dr Saadet Deger (Turkey) is Senior Researcher and Leader of the SIPRI world military expenditure project. She was formerly a Research Fellow at Birkbeck College, University of London (1977–87) and a member of the UN Working

Group of Experts for the UN Regional Centre for Peace and Disarmament in Africa (1989). She is a member of the Board of *Defence Economics: An International Journal.* She is the author of *Military Expenditure in Third World Countries: The Economic Effects* (1986) and co-editor of *Defence, Security and Development* (1987). She has published articles for international journals on disarmament and development, the economics of security in the Third World and the arms trade, and is the author of chapters in the *SIPRI Yearbooks 1988* and *1989.*

Ragnhild Ferm (Sweden) is Researcher on the SIPRI arms control and disarmament project. She has published chapters on nuclear explosions, a comprehensive test ban, arms control agreements and the chronologies of arms control events in the *SIPRI Yearbooks* since 1982. She is the author of the annual SIPRI publication *Rustning eller Nedrustning?* (in Swedish) [*Armaments or Disarmament?*].

Richard W. Fieldhouse (United States) is Senior Research Associate at the Natural Resources Defense Council, Washington, DC, and co-author of the forthcoming NRDC publication *Nuclear Weapons Databook, Volume V, British, French, Chinese Nuclear Weapons and Nuclear Weapon Proliferation.* In 1985–89 he was a Researcher at SIPRI and leader of the project on naval forces and arms control. He is the editor of the SIPRI volume *Security at Sea: Naval Forces and Arms Control* (1990) and co-author of its companion volume *Superpowers at Sea: An Assessment of the Naval Arms Race* (1989).

Stephen Iwan Griffiths (United Kingdom) is Research Assistant on the SIPRI project on 'Security without Nuclear Weapons?'. He was formerly a Teaching Assistant at the Department of Politics, University of Aberdeen.

Espen Gullikstad (Norway) is a Research Assistant on the SIPRI arms transfers and arms production project. His previous research is in the field of the administrative aspects of the European Community. He is a contributor to a chapter in the *SIPRI Yearbook 1989.*

Gerd Hagmeyer-Gaverus (Federal Republic of Germany) is Researcher on the SIPRI arms transfers and arms production project. He was formerly a Researcher at the Centre for Social Science Research at the Free University, Berlin, where he co-authored several research reports, and is the co-author of chapters on world military expenditure in the *SIPRI Yearbooks 1985, 1987* and *1988.*

Aaron Karp (United States) is Olin Fellow in Economics and Security, Harvard University. In 1987–89 he was the Leader of the SIPRI arms trade project, where he authored chapters in the *SIPRI Yearbooks 1988* and *1989.*

Dr Catherine M. Kelleher (United States) is Director of the Center for International Security Studies at Maryland (CISSM) and a Professor in the School of Public Affairs at the University of Maryland. She served on the National Security Council staff during the Carter Administration and has had a wide range of academic involvement in international security studies. She has published extensively on issues of arms control, alliance relations, East–West relations and European security. Her recent publications include contributions in S. Sloan (ed.) *NATO in the 1990s* (1989), in S. Szabo (ed.) *The Bundeswehr* (forthcoming), and in S. Biddle and P. Feaver (eds.) *Battlefield Nuclear Weapons: Issues and Options* (forthcoming).

Dr Richard Kokoski (Canada) is a Researcher on the SIPRI military technology and arms control project. He was formerly Research Associate at the Department of Physics, University of Toronto, where he did research on nuclear test ban verification for the Arms Control and Disarmament Division, Department of External Affairs, Canada. He has published articles in the field of elementary particle physics and verification seismology and is co-editor of a forthcoming SIPRI publication on conventional arms control verification.

Dr Axel Krohn (Federal Republic of Germany) is a Researcher on the SIPRI project on the security system in Europe. He is the author of *Nuklearwaffenfreie Zone: Regionales Disengagement unter der Rahmenbedingung globaler Großmachtinteressen, Das Fallbeispiel Nordeuropa* (1989). He is the co-editor of a SIPRI Research Report, *Stability and Arms Control in Europe: The Role of Military Forces within a European Security System* (1989), and co-author of an appendix in the *SIPRI Yearbook 1989*.

Karin Lindgren (Sweden) is Leader of the armed conflicts data project at the Department of Peace and Conflict Research, Uppsala University, Sweden, and Information Secretary of NORDSAM (Nordic Co-operation Committee for International Politics), Stockholm. She is the author of *Participation of Women in Decision-making for Peace, Case Study on Sweden* (1989) and co-author of a contribution in P. Wallensteen (ed.), *States in Armed Conflict 1988* (1989) and chapters in the *SIPRI Yearbooks 1988* and *1989*.

Dr S. J. Lundin (Sweden) is Senior Researcher and Head of the SIPRI chemical and biological warfare programme. He is on leave of absence as Director of Research at the Swedish Defence Research Institute (FOA), and was formerly Scientific Adviser to the Swedish Disarmament Delegation (1969–85) and to the Swedish Supreme Commander (1985–87). He is the author of chapters in the *SIPRI Yearbooks 1988* and *1989* and has written extensively in the field of chemical and biological weapons.

Dr Harald Müller (Federal Republic of Gemany) is Senior Researcher and Director of International Programs at the Peace Research Institute Frankfurt (PRIF). Among his most recent publications, he is the author of *A Survey of European Nuclear Policy, 1985–87* (1989) and the editor of *Deciding on the Atom: How Western European Nuclear Policy is Made* (1990).

Kjell-Åke Nordquist (Sweden) is Research Associate and Director of Studies at the Department of Peace and Conflict Research, Uppsala University, Sweden. He is the author of *Conflicting Peace Proposals: Four Peace Proposals in the Palestine Conflict Appraised* (1985) and of a contribution in C. Alger and M. Stohl (eds), *A Just Peace Through Transformation* (1988).

Dr Robert S. Norris (United States) is Senior Staff Analyst at the Natural Resources Defense Council, Washington, DC. He was formerly Senior Research Analyst for the Center for Defense Information, Washington, DC. He is a co-editor of the 1987 and 1989 volumes of the *Nuclear Weapons Databook,* and a co-author of chapters in the *SIPRI Yearbooks* since 1985. He is a co-author of a column for the *Bulletin of the Atomic Scientists* in his field of nuclear weapon research and production, arms control and nuclear weapon testing.

John Pike (United States) is the Associate Director for Space Policy at the Federation of American Scientists, Washington, DC. He is a co-author of *The Impact of US and Soviet Ballistic Missile Defense Programs on the ABM Treaty* 1985) and the author of a chapter in the *SIPRI Yearbook 1989.*

Dr Somnath Sen (India) is a Researcher on the SIPRI world military expenditure project. He was a lecturer at the Universities of Calcutta and Birmingham as well as a Visiting Fellow at the Delhi School of Economics. He is currently on leave from a Senior Lecturership at the University of Birmingham. His publications include *Protectionism, Exchange Rates and the Macroeconomy* (1985) and several articles on disarmament and development and macroeconomics.

Jane M. O. Sharp (United Kingdom) is a Researcher and Leader of the SIPRI project on 'Europe after American Withdrawal: Myth and Reality'. She was previously a researcher at Harvard University and Cornell University, and National Director of the Council for a Livable World, Washington, DC. She is a co-editor of *The Warsaw Pact: Alliance in Transition?* (1985), and the editor of *Opportunities for Disarmament* (1978) and of the forthcoming SIPRI publication *Europe After an American Withdrawal: Economic and Military Issues.* She is the author of chapters in the *SIPRI Yearbooks 1988* and *1989* and several articles or chapters on East–West security and alliance politics.

Dr Thomas Stock (German Democratic Republic) is a Researcher on the SIPRI chemical and biological warfare programme. He was formerly a Researcher at the Researcher Unit for Chemical Toxicology of the Academy of Sciences of the GDR. He is co-author of an article in the SIPRI volume *Non-Production by Industry of Chemical-Warfare Agents: Technical Verification under a Chemical Weapons Convention* (1988) and is the co-editor of a forthcoming SIPRI publication, *National Implementation of the Future Chemical Weapons Convention.*

Dr Walther Stützle (Federal Republic of Germany) is the Director of SIPRI. In 1983–86 he was International Security and Defence Correspondent for the *Stuttgarter Zeitung,* and in 1976–82 Head of the Planning Staff and Under-Secretary for Defence Planning and Policy of the FRG Ministry of Defence. He is the author of *Adenauer und Kennedy in der Berlin Krise 1961/62* (1973) and *Politik und Kräfteverhältnis* (1983), and a co-editor of *Europe's Futures— Europe's Choices* (1966) and of the SIPRI volume *The ABM Treaty: To Defend or Not to Defend?* (1987). He is the author of introductory chapters in the *SIPRI Yearbooks 1987, 1988* and *1989,* and of numerous articles on international security.

Professor Peter Wallensteen (Sweden) holds the Dag Hammarskjöld Chair in Peace and Conflict Research and is the Head of the Department of Peace and Conflict Research, Uppsala University, Sweden. He is the author of *Structure and War* (1973), *Dilemmas of Economic Coercion* (1983), *Global Militarization*

(1985), *Peace Research: Achievements and Challenges* (1988) and *States in Armed Conflict* (1988). He is a co-author of chapters in the *SIPRI Yearbooks 1988* and *1989*.

Professor Victor Weisskopf (Austria) is Professor Emeritus at the Massachusetts Institute of Technology and President of the American Physical Society. He was formerly Group Leader at the Los Alamos Scientific Laboratory, General Director of the European Organization for Nuclear Research (CERN) and President of the American Academy of Arts and Sciences. His most recent books are *Physics in the Twentieth Century* (1972) and *The Privilege of Being a Scientist* (1989).

G. Kenneth Wilson (United Kingdom) is a Research Associate at the Department of Peace and Conflict Research, Uppsala University, Sweden. He is the author of *A Global Peace Study Guide* (1982) and a co-author of chapters in the *SIPRI Yearbooks 1988* and *1989*.

Dr Herbert Wulf (Federal Republic of Germany) is a Researcher and Leader of the SIPRI project on arms transfers and arms production. He is on a leave of absence from the Hamburg University Institute for Peace Research and Security Policy. Prior to his work in peace research, he was Director of the German Volunteer Service in India. He is a co-author of *Alternative Produktion statt Rüstung* (1987) and the author of *Rüstungsexport aus Deutschland* (1989). He has published numerous articles on arms production, arms transfers, conversion, and disarmament and development.

SIPRI Yearbook 1990: World Armaments and Disarmament
Oxford University Press, Oxford, 1990, 714 pp.
(Stockholm International Peace Research Institute)
ISBN 0-19-827862-4

ABSTRACTS

ARKIN, W. M., BURROWS, A. S., COCHRAN, T. B., FIELDHOUSE, R. W. and NORRIS, R. S., 'Nuclear weapons', in *SIPRI Yearbook 1990*, pp. 3–50.

For the first time since World War II, East–West political developments may permit fundamental change to the nuclear postures and practices of the five acknowledged nuclear weapon states (the USA, the USSR, the UK, France and China). Historic political changes, widespread economic constraints and impending arms control agreements may all serve to reduce the role and number of nuclear weapons world-wide. Nonetheless, all 5 nations continued with their nuclear weapon modernization plans during 1989, albeit more slowly than originally anticipated. All the shorter-range US and Soviet INF missiles were eliminated during the year, and there were several noteworthy unilateral reductions or slow-downs. The nuclear weapon developments of these 5 states are documented and major trends are analysed.

FERM, R., 'Nuclear explosions', in *SIPRI Yearbook 1990*, pp. 51–57.

27 nuclear explosions were conducted in 1989, fewer than the yearly average for the past 28 years. This was because the USA and the USSR carried out fewer tests than in previous years. For the first time in many years no so-called peaceful nuclear explosion was conducted. Protests against nuclear testing—for environmental as well as for disarmament reasons—increased. Demonstrations at the Soviet test site at Semipalatinsk were reported by Soviet mass media. The Kazakhstan government requested the authorities to close the test site and stop the testing programme.

PIKE, J., 'Military use of outer space', in *SIPRI Yearbook 1990*, pp. 59–106.

Military space activities are an increasingly anomalous exception to the general relaxation of the East–West military confrontation. The US military space budget continues to grow, with ongoing work on the Strategic Defense Initiative, a renewed anti-satellite weapon programme and significant expansion of networks of military satellite systems. Although the USSR recently completed deployment of its Moscow anti-missile system, declining budgets have forced cutbacks in other elements of the Soviet space programme. The prospects for arms control negotiations on space weapons remain uncertain.

LUNDIN, S. J., 'Chemical and biological warfare: developments in 1989', in *SIPRI Yearbook 1990*, pp. 107–40.

In 1989 no confirmed use of chemical and biological weapons in violation of the 1925 Geneva Protocol occurred. Concern about proliferation and alleged possession of chemical and biological weapons led to work on national legislation and export sanctions. The long-standing issue of a link between chemical and nuclear weapons drew attendtion, particularly in the Middle East. Future US production of binary chemical weapons and US and Soviet CW destruction programmes were debated. Interest in protection against chemical weapons increased. Concerns that new genetic techniques might endanger the Biological Weapons Convention were expressed.

DEGER, S., 'World military expenditure', in *SIPRI Yearbook 1990*, pp. 143–202.

The profound political changes affecting Eastern Europe and the possibility of successful arms control negotiations had a modest but measurable impact on world military expenditure in 1989. The USA and the USSR reduced their military spending by about 2%. Third World military expenditure went down as well, while the spending level of the European NATO allies remained stable. A 10-year time series on NATO major weapon acquisitions shows that procurement spending has acquired greater importance in recent years. Economic and military data on the European Community shows that the EC is an increasingly important actor. In its annual presentation of military expenditure, the USSR for the first time presented figures at credible levels. The impact of Soviet defence cuts (in personnel, procurement, research and development) on the whole economic structure is crucial to the success of *perestroika*.

SEN, S., 'Debt, financial flows and international security', in *SIPRI Yearbook 1990*, pp. 203–17.

The debt crisis has bedevilled large sections of the Third World throughout the 1980s, contributing to a decline in per capita income and to negative growth rates, particularly in Africa and Latin America. The international security implications of this debt problem are crucial. At the same time as peaceful solutions are being found to old conflicts in Europe and among the superpowers, the non-military threats to security in the Third World become more important. Eastern Europe is also affected by this phenomenon. Official development assistance is still small, and the new democracies are threatened by instability. On the level of the individual debtor country, however, the crisis can also be used as a lever to achieve systemic arms control, through reduction of weapon imports, cuts in military expenditure and increases in ODA.

ANTHONY, I. and WULF, H., 'The trade in major conventional weapons', in *SIPRI Yearbook 1990*, pp. 219–316.

The value of the global trade in major conventional weapons, $31 819 million in 1989, continued to decrease. The USSR and the USA accounted for 37% and 32%, respectively, of the total. France remains the third largest exporter, followed by the UK, the FRG and China. Within this global total the importance of arms imports by industrialized countries continued to grow. Imports of major conventional weapons by Third World countries fell to $16 427 million, the lowest level since 1976. For the first time in 20 years, the Middle East was not the leading importing region. South Asia, with heavy imports by India and Afghanistan, replaced the Middle East as the region with the highest arms imports. The countries of the Far East also collectively imported a greater value of arms than Middle Eastern countries. The pattern of arms exports to countries at war indicates that smaller suppliers depend to a large extent on ongoing wars.

ANTHONY, I., COURADES ALLEBECK, A., GULLIKSTAD, E., HAGMEYER-GAVERUS, G. and WULF, H., 'Arms production', in *SIPRI Yearbook 1990*, pp. 317–68.

The arms industrial base in NATO and the WTO has been affected by political changes in Eastern Europe, improved arms control negotiations and budgetary pressures. A description of the size and structure of the arms industrial base includes a list of the largest 100 arms-producing companies of the world and a discussion of arms production in the WTO. This is the background for a discussion of the problems and prospects for reorienting arms industry to non-military production. Currently, the contradiction remains between high investments in programmes for new weapon technologies and progress in conventional arms control and budgetary constraints. Unless a frosty East–West climate or a cold war is introduced again, the arms industrial base must be substantially reduced in both major alliances.

KARP, A., 'Ballistic missile proliferation', in *SIPRI Yearbook 1990*, pp. 369–91.

Concern over ballistic missile proliferation reached a new and unprecedented level of intensity in 1989, due in part to declining tensions between the superpowers and to a flurry of disclosures about new and expanding middle programmes elsewhere. Missile proliferation remained high on the international agenda, discussed at US–Soviet summit meetings in Moscow and Wyoming, and pressed upon delegations to the Negotiation on Conventional Armed Forces in Europe. Little actual progress was made controlling missile proliferation, although enforcement efforts and bilateral diplomacy have helped slow several very visible regional programmes. An attempt by France to sell rocket engines to Brazil threatened to undermine the foundation of existing control efforts. 116 programmes of 26 countries are described.

LINDGREN, K., WILSON, G. K., WALLENSTEEN, P. and NORDQUIST, K.-Å., 'Major armed conflicts in 1989', in *SIPRI Yearbook 1990*, pp. 393–419.

In 1989, 32 major armed conflicts were waged in the world. This was a lower number than recorded at any time since SIPRI began publishing such data in 1986. Most of the conflicts have continued for a considerable period of time and were on a rather low level of intensity in 1989. One-third of the conflicts resulted in more than 1000 battle-related deaths during the year (e.g. Sri Lanka, Ethiopia and Afghanistan). Two conflicts were initiated and terminated during the year: the revolution in Romania and the USA–Panama war. A considerable number of peace initiatives were taken, leading to direct or indirect contacts between warring parties. The old Communist revolt in Malaysia was terminated through a formal agreement. A significant development was the withdrawal of Soviet troops from Afghanistan and Vietnamese troops from Cambodia.

COWEN KARP, R., 'US–Soviet nuclear arms control' in *SIPRI Yearbook 1990*, pp. 423–42.

In 1989 the Soviet Union discontinued linking the conclusion of a START treaty to a resolution of the ballistic missile defence issue and offered to deal separately with the issue of strategic sea-launched cruise missiles. The USA dropped its ban on mobile ICBMs and these systems are now subject to the negotiations. The two sides did not find a way to agree on how to count air-launched cruise missiles. Both the USA and the USSR agreed on trial verification measures for inspection of bombers and ballistic missile warheads. The emerging START treaty is ambitious, but less comprehensive than originally envisaged: the problems of space-based defences and SLCMs are not covered. In a post-START security environment, both sides will have highly capable nuclear forces with older systems retired to meet the prescribed reductions. Verification of a START treaty may well be the most challenging issue in 1990 and much detailed work remains to be done in order to finalize a treaty.

GRIFFITHS, S. I., 'The implementation of the INF Treaty', in *SIPRI Yearbook 1990*, pp. 443–58.

In 1989 the INF implementation process illustrated the new spirit of *détente* between the USA and the USSR. On 6 July the USA destroyed the last of its Pershing 1As, and by 27 October the USSR had destroyed the last of its SS-23s and SS-12s, comfortably meeting the deadline of 30 November. The inspection process has also gone smoothly, with both sides fulfilling their obligations. Despite a number of disputes and problems, the 'INF institutions'—the Special Verification Commission, the Nuclear Risk Reduction Centres and the On-Site Inspection Agency—have fulfilled their missions and demonstrated their worth as models for future arms control and disarmament measures. The success of the INF Treaty implementation process in 1989 should serve to illustrate that disarmament treaties can be successfully implemented.

SHARP, J. M. O., 'Conventional arms control in Europe', in *SIPRI Yearbook 1990*, pp. 459–520.

During 1989 unilateral cuts in WTO forces proceeded in parallel with the Negotiations on Conventional Armed Forces in Europe and on Confidence- and Security-Building Measures, both under the auspices of the Conference on Security and Co-operation in Europe. CFE was complicated by a series of revolutions in Eastern Europe, but made rapid progress at the first three rounds, with congruence on stabilization and verification measures and agreement to focus on 6 categories of treaty-limited items. President Bush set 1990 as the target for an agreement, but momentum was lost in the late-1989 struggle to define TLIs more precisely. At the CSBM forum, the only concrete decision was to hold a seminar on military doctrine in January–February 1990. There was little sign of a new generation of CSBMs appropriate to the new political situation in Europe, and the WTO states made little headway with their campaign to institute naval CSBMs.

LUNDIN, S. J., 'Multilateral and bilateral talks on chemical and biological weapons', in *SIPRI Yearbook 1990*, pp. 521–44.

In the wake of the Iraq–Iran War the international community tried to take measures against the use of chemical weapons. The Paris Conference on the Prohibition of Chemical Weapons, the Canberra Government–Industry Conference against Chemical Weapons, and bilateral US–Soviet meetings were held in 1989. The pledge from the Paris Conference that the negotiation efforts in the Conference on Disarmament be redoubled was not realized on the political level. The Canberra Conference created an increased awareness of the role of the chemical industry; a group of industrialists agreed on a statement in support of the chemical weapons convention. Much useful work was done at the CD, but technical and other problems remained unsolved. Efforts to strengthen confidence in the Biological Weapons Convention, particularly in the information exchange by the states parties, continue.

FERM, R., 'Multilateral and bilateral efforts towards nuclear test limitation', in *SIPRI Yearbook 1990*, pp. 545–49.

US–Soviet testing negotiations were resumed and led to agreement on basic verification provisions for the 1974 Threshold Test Ban Treaty and the 1976 Peaceful Nuclear Explosions Treaty. More than one-third of the states parties to the 1963 Partial Test Ban Treaty formally submitted a request for an amendment conference to expand the Treaty into a comprehensive test ban. The Conference on Disarmament again failed to reach agreement on a mandate for the *Ad hoc* Committee on nuclear testing. The CD *Ad hoc* Group of Scientific Experts, however, outlined the design for an international data-exchange system for verification of nuclear testing restrictions. The initial phase of a large-scale experiment is now under way.

MÜLLER, H., 'Prospects for the fourth review of the Non-Proliferation Treaty', in *SIPRI Yearbook 1990*, pp. 553–86.

With the fourth Review Conference, in 1990, the Non-Proliferation Treaty enters a critical phase before it is up for extension in 1995. While the Treaty has 141 parties, some important countries remain outside and are increasing their unsafeguarded nuclear materials. Superpower collaboration with those countries compromises their commitment to the NPT, and other industrialized countries have damaged the non-proliferation regime by neglectful export policies. There are four main threats to consensus at the Review Conference: Third World dissatisfaction over the insufficient advantages to be drawn from NPT membership; complaints by neutral and non-aligned states over the lack of implementation of the disarmament obligation, particularly failure to conclude a comprehensive test ban treaty; unwillingness of Western nuclear weapon states to establish nuclear weapon-free zones; and regional conflicts. Extension after 1995, however, depends on better implementation of the NPT and recognition of Third World demands.

KOKOSKI, R., 'Laser isotope separation: technological developments and political implications', in *SIPRI Yearbook 1990*, pp. 587–601.

A renewed interest in a verifiable halt to fissile material production, prospects for a START agreement in 1990 and continued recycling of fissile material from retired warheads all tend to obviate the further production of weapon-grade nuclear materials. At odds with these facts are present US proposals to construct a facility for the purification of plutonium to weapon-grade using a highly efficient laser technique. Variants of this laser isotope separation technology are also currently being developed to enrich uranium in a large number of countries throughout the world, several not party to the Non-Proliferation Treaty. These developments and their implications are explored, with particular reference to nuclear proliferation concerns.

KELLEHER, C. M., 'The debate over the modernization of NATO's short-range nuclear missiles', in *SIPRI Yearbook 1990*, pp. 603–22.

Unlike other NATO controversies, the 1989 debate on the modernization of short-range nuclear forces entailed two politicized dimensions: the role of US leadership in an alliance experiencing a transforming Soviet Union/Eastern Europe, and a 'German crisis' with both internal and external challenges. The SNF debate turned on the post-INF Treaty legacy of missile modernization, both in range and mission, and on the virtues of deterrence versus a negotiated elimination of remaining nuclear systems below 500-km range. The crisis highlighted a US (and British) leadership style of unquestioned NATO authority among an array of non-nuclear weapon powers eager to seize momentum on arms control and disarmament. In the debate on the role of the FRG, the SNF issue led to a significant turning-point in the foreign policy of the FRG *vis-à-vis* the USA in NATO. What grew out of incongruent SNF policies was a continuing political burden as NATO searched for a new role.

WEISSKOPF, V. M., 'The SIPRI 1989 Olof Palme Memorial Lecture: "The responsibility of scientists in the nuclear age"', in *SIPRI Yearbook 1990*, pp. 623–31.

The first serious encounter of scientists with the problem of responsibility for their actions came during the construction of the atomic bomb; during the arms race it became clear that nuclear missiles are not weapons of war but instruments of mutual annihilation. Some progress in the path from confrontation to co-operation is illustrated by the 1963 Partial Test Ban Treaty, the 1972 ABM Treaty and the 1987 INF Treaty. Technological developments have not only improved living conditions for many but also created material and spiritual pollution. Scientists must strive to prevent war and environmental catastrophe, to help provide a purposeful life for the majority, and assistance and education for the Third world, to foster freedom of thought and an awareness of complementary attitudes.

Errata

SIPRI Yearbook 1989: World Armaments and Disarmament

Page 480, Status of the implementation of the major multilateral arms control agreements, as of 1 January 1989:

Owing to a printer's error, several countries on this page are listed as parties to the wrong agreements. Please see Annexe A of this edition for the correct list of parties.

Pages 109 and 120:

'The Australian Group' should read 'The Australia Group'.

Page 112, sub-section 'Bilateral visits':

The wording might lead to misunderstanding about which British facilities were visited. The visited facilities were: the Chemical Defence Establishment (CDE), Porton Down, including CDE facilities for the storage, disposal and destruction of agents and additional locations chosen by the Soviet delegation; the Defence Nuclear, Biological and Chemical Centre at Winterbourne Gunner; and the DHSS Public Health Laboratory Service, Centre for Applied Microbiology and Research. (*Source*: 'Soviet Union visit to CDE: statement by Dr Graham S. Pearson, Director CDE', communiqué issued by CDE, Porton Down, UK, 26 May 1988.)

INDEX